A
TREASURY OF THE WORLD'S
Great Speeches

EACH SPEECH PREFACED WITH

ITS DRAMATIC AND BIOGRAPHICAL SETTING

AND PLACED

IN ITS FULL HISTORICAL PERSPECTIVE

Selected and edited by

HOUSTON PETERSON

REVISED AND ENLARGED EDITION

Grolier
INCORPORATED
New York

LIBRARY OF CONGRESS CATALOG CARD NUMBER: 53–9693

MANUFACTURED IN THE UNITED STATES OF AMERICA

To
Judge Daniel E. Fitzpatrick of New York
and
in Memory of
The Late Judge Thomas C. Gould of California

In Praise of Eloquence

If truth were self-evident, eloquence would not be necessary.
—CICERO

Surely whoever speaks to me in the right voice, him or her I shall follow.　　　　—WALT WHITMAN

Eloquence may set fire to reason.　—OLIVER WENDELL HOLMES, JR.

To disparage eloquence is to depreciate mankind.　—JOHN MORLEY

I do not know of any kind of history, except the event of a battle, to which people listen with more interest than to any anecdote of eloquence; and the wise think it better than a battle.
—RALPH WALDO EMERSON

It is the peculiarity of some schools of eloquence that they embody and utter, not merely the individual genius and character of the speaker, but a national consciousness—a national era, a mood, a hope, a dread, a despair—in which you listen to the spoken history of the time.　　　　—RUFUS CHOATE

Speeches are veritable transactions in the human commonwealth; in fact, very gravely influential transactions.　—G. W. F. HEGEL

Every investigation that can be made as regards those duties for which an orator should be held responsible, I bid you make. And what are those duties? To discern events in their beginnings, to foresee what is coming, and to forewarn others.　—DEMOSTHENES

The breastplate and the sword are not a stronger defense on the battlefield than eloquence is to a man amid the perils of prosecution.   —TACITUS

The power of eloquence—so very effective in convincing us of either wrong or right—lies open to all. Why, then, do not the good zealously procure it that it may serve the truth, if the wicked, in order to gain unjustifiable and groundless cases, apply it to the advantages of injustice and error?   —ST. AUGUSTINE

Rhetoric, or the art of conveying our thoughts to others by speech with advantages of clearness, force, and elegancy, so as to instruct, to persuade, to delight the auditors: of how great benefit is it, if it be well used! How much may it conduce to the service of God and edification of men!   —ISAAC BARROW

Oratory, phrases, the evocative power of verbal symbols must not be despised, for these are and have been one of the chief means of uniting the United States and keeping it united.   —D. W. BROGAN

Our statesmen have been compelled, by the very exigencies of their position, to be "masters of the word"; and however much men may decry the word, in this age of the brutal act, the fact remains that the word—the word which expresses creative thought—is the ultimate master of the act.   —ERNEST BARKER

The written word has never, in times of tension and doom, the strength of warm and living speech, the vocal call to arms.
                                                    —STEFAN ZWEIG

TABLE OF CONTENTS

Epilogue

PART II: The Christian Triumph

PART III: Renaissance and Reformation

PART IV: Toward Freedom—American, English, Irish

PART V: India and the Trial of Warren Hastings

PART VI: The Federal Constitution

PART VII: The African Slave Trade

PART VIII: The French Revolution

PART IX: Napoleon Over Europe

PART X: Fire Bells in the Night

PART XI: Agitation, Reform, and Revolt

PART XII: A House Divided

PART XIII: Blood and Iron

PART XIV: Triumphant Democracy

PART XV: Race and Empire

PART XVI: Party Politics and Class Struggle

PART XVII: The First World War

PART XVIII: A Sick World

PART XIX: The Second World War

PART XX: The Sinews of Peace

ACKNOWLEDGMENTS

DURING MORE than six years of reading speeches and writing about them, I have incurred obligations to many generous friends. The first acknowledgment goes to the infectious Max Schuster, who persuaded me to do this book at the very moment I was trying to inoculate him with the idea of another. Then there were Henry W. Simon, an editor wonderfully keen and gentle, but disarmingly firm, and Wallace Brockway, brittlely brisk and well-nigh omniscient. Paul Kuntz, Julius Bloom, Mason W. Gross, Joseph Neyer, Miriam and Eli Shorr also contributed much more than they suspected.

In a large project of this sort there almost inevitably comes a moment of exhaustion and discouragement, and that moment came after I had been immersed in eloquence more or less continually for nearly three years. It was then my old friend V. J. McGill reappeared and saw me dashingly, dauntlessly, through the long middle lap of the journey. There remained eighteen months of further rearranging, abridging, correcting, polishing. Of course, it was my wife, Mitzi, who, with gaiety, candor and energy, oversaw the entire project.

HOUSTON PETERSON

INTRODUCTION

RALPH WALDO EMERSON, master of the lecture and a life-long student of public speaking, began one of his later essays with these words: "I do not know any kind of history, except the event of a battle, to which people listen with more interest than to any anecdote of eloquence; and the wise think it better than a battle. It is a triumph of pure power, and it has a beautiful and prodigious surprise in it." This book is a record of such triumphs and near-triumphs, with scores of anecdotes throwing light and color on scores of speeches, from the ancient Hebrews, Greeks and Romans, to MacArthur, Stevenson and Eisenhower.

In a broader sense this book depicts the crises and cruxes of history as seen from the platform and interpreted to a deathless audience. For "it is the peculiarity of some schools of eloquence," said Rufus Choate, "that they embody and utter, not merely the individual genius and character of the speaker, but a national consciousness—a national era, a mood, a hope, a dread, a despair—in which you listen to the spoken history of the time."

Only yesterday, fifty years ago, thirty years ago, the immediate demise of oratory was confidently predicted—the rostrum crushed by the printing press, the speaker stifled by newspapers. Yet it has turned out that in no period of history have public speakers swayed such masses of people and held such positions of power. Consider Theodore Roosevelt, Sun Yat-sen, Georges Clemenceau, Lloyd George, Woodrow Wilson, Lenin, Trotsky, Hitler, Mussolini, Gandhi, Nehru, Franklin D. Roosevelt, Sir Winston Churchill. Far from declining in favor of the press, the voice has been immensely strengthened by the loud-speaker, the radio, and television. Only in our time could a General MacArthur have stirred the country in speaking before a joint session of Congress or a Governor Stevenson have won a nationwide audience overnight.

These facts are no solace to those who would abolish the whole art of eloquence as a magical art, a black art, which has always misled mankind. Why is it not possible to get along with simple, clear, truthful statements, without elaboration or ornament? Cicero gives the quick, obvious answer: "If truth were self-evident, eloquence would not be necessary." But as truth is not ordinarily self-evident and a human being is a complicated mixture of reason, feeling and impulse, with stores of knowledge and stores of ignorance, all wonderfully related, speakers who would move audiences must play on many strings, must appeal to hope and fear, anger, mercy, pity, as well as to pure truth and the laws of logic. While some speakers have been too loftily logical, many more have been viciously irrational. But emotions are not necessarily opposed to reason. Anger and indigation may be righteous, disgust may be justifiable, fear may be rational, and mercy and pity the greatest wisdom. As long as human nature is what it is, eloquence will remain a double-edged sword, to be used for noble and ignoble purposes—but used inevitably.

Of course, I do not mean to suggest that every speaker captures his audience, changes the vote or sets in motion a new train of events. All too many speeches have been weak in substance, all too many have been badly delivered. Some have fallen on deaf ears, only to weave a spell on later generations. In going through a collection of speeches, the reader to some degree joins the audience. But what kind? There are apathetic, sleeping audiences that must be awakened; there are hostile audiences that must be defied and conquered; there are alienated or sullen audiences that must be won back; there are frightened audiences that must be calmed. There are loyal, affectionate audiences that must be further inspired. There are cool, skeptical audiences that must be coolly convinced. There are heterogenous audiences that must be moulded into some kind of unity.

In line with Webster's dictum that true eloquence exists not merely in the speech but "in the man, the subject, and in the occasion," each selection in this book is preceded by a foreword giving, when possible, some idea of the speaker, his problem and the setting, including, of course, the audience. And each speech is followed by an afterword, showing, when possible, the immediate effect of the speech and its reverberations in history. Of Churchill's unforgettable speech on the evacuation of Dunkirk, Somerset Maugham said, "It reads as well as I am sure it sounded." And our ideal here is to include selections that read as well as they probably sounded. Sir Winston's war speeches still tingle in our ears. But even when the speaker lived long before our time, we can recapture him and his moment in history, and share some of the emotions of his original hearers.

Here then, side by side, are prophets, warriors, preachers, lawyers, authors, scientists and agitators. Here are ruthless demagogues and unworldly saints. Here is the tense courtroom and the buoyant banquet hall, the battlefield and the burial ground, the mass meeting and the street crowd. Here are subtle and purple passages, the conversational and the vehement styles. Here are even a few instances of near gibberish proclaimed with magnetism, eternal truths uttered with disarming humility. Here are audiences hostile and friendly, sleeping and skeptical, alienated and alert. Here are the ears of humanity open to mighty voices.

HOUSTON PETERSON

New York City
December 11, 1953

INTRODUCTION TO REVISED AND
ENLARGED EDITION

O F COURSE I am delighted that the original edition of *A Treasury of the World's Great Speeches* passed through several printings, and that I can now add some historic utterances of the past decade.

As for the matter of selecting new material, an editor can only hope that his taste is good and that through wide hearing, wide reading and perhaps wide speaking, he has acquired some sound criteria for inclusion and exclusion. No one can be infallible in such judgments, but at least I would point out that you do not have to admire a speaker or agree with him in order to appreciate his oratorical power. Granting that Hitler was hateful, General MacArthur somewhat grandiose, and General de Gaulle at times too godlike, there were reasons for including them in the first edition and retaining them in this one. As for the late additions, whatever one's political or ethnic views, Nikita Khrushchev, John F. Kennedy and Martin Luther King, Jr. have been outstanding voices of the past ten turbulent years.

If one were forced to put the history of public address into a preposterous nutshell, one might say that it began with some kind of leader charming, calming or exciting a responsive audience with his spontaneous verbal magic. In the classic Greco-Roman centuries distinguished orators wrote out their speeches, memorized them, delivered them with great éclat—and revised them for posterity. With the emergence of newspapers, the prominent speaker could hope that some, if not all, of his speech would appear in print the next day or the next week. With journalism triumphant the captive audience often became merely the excuse for giving a speech that would inevitably appear in the newspapers. And now comes the reversal: television rivals and begins to supplant the influence of newspapers in the realm of speechmaking. It is suspected that the Nixon-Kennedy debates in the fall of 1960 ultimately determined the result of that election. The bitter quarrels about whether or not TV debates should be held in the political campaigns of the fall of 1964 indicated the influence of the medium. There will be losses and gains if the balance of power shifts from journalism to television. Some splendid personalities will not "project" impressively; some dubious personalities will suffer from too much "exposure."

If I were asked to select the most readable of all speeches, fit for a long, quiet, reflective evening, I would propose Edmund Burke's speech on conciliation with the American colonies, delivered in the House of Commons on March 22, 1775, less than a month before the battles of Concord and Lexington. In the whole history of eloquence Burke probably had the finest mind and, on most occasions, the worst delivery—and this was one of the occasions. But in reading the speech we can assume a superb presentation and appreciate to the fullest his principles and precepts, his timeless warnings on liberty, conciliation and peace.

HOUSTON PETERSON
New York City
October 19, 1964

PART ONE

THE ANCIENT WORLD

Hebrews - Greeks - Romans

THE ORIGINS of eloquent speech are lost in the mists of antiquity. But we can be sure that tens of thousands of years ago there were individuals who cast spells over their fellows with the magic of words. At first it was not words so much as the rhythm, the sounds, the incantation that was a part of ritual. Chiefs, priests, medicine men, millenniums before the heroes of Homer, must have risen to power through skill in speech as well as skill in arms. They must have addressed themselves, in hope or in terror, to the mysterious forces of nature and to the spirits of dead relatives. Then as now stirring words helped to hurry men to the hunt or to battle, and afterward the defeat or the victory would be relived with those who had remained behind. Perhaps the first formal orations were delivered at the graves of heroes.

The so-called primitive or nonliterate peoples who still survive give us some hint of the earliest stages of eloquence. We may open our book with a noble sample of this eloquence, taken from our own American history. After the Yellow Creek Massacre of 1774 in which members of his family were slaughtered, the Indian leader known as Logan was invited to attend a peace conference by Governor Dunmore of Virginia, through his messenger, John Gibson. Logan's reply to Gibson was brought back and read at the conference.

"I appeal to any white man to say if ever he entered Logan's cabin hungry, and he gave him not meat, if ever he came cold and naked, and he clothed him not. During the course of the last long and bloody war Logan remained idle in his cabin, an advocate for peace. Such was my love for the whites that my countrymen pointed at me as they passed, and said: 'Logan is the friend of white men.'

"I had even thought to have lived with you, but for the injuries of one man. Colonel Cresap, the last spring, in cold blood and unprovoked, murdered all the relations of Logan, not sparing even my women and children. There runs not a drop of my blood in the veins of any living creature.

"This called on me for revenge. I have sought it. I have killed many. I have glutted my vengeance. For my country, I rejoice at the beams of peace. But do not think that mine is the joy of fear. Logan never felt fear. Logan will not turn on his heel to save his life. Who is there to mourn for Logan? Not one!"

There is doubt as to how accurately this speech, or any such speech, could have been reported, but Thomas Jefferson went so far as to say that it was equal to any passage in ancient or modern oratory.

With this bow to the primitive, let us turn to the main sources of western civilization, to the ancient Hebrews and the ancient Greeks.

MOSES PROCLAIMS THE TEN COMMANDMENTS

[c. 1250 B.C.]

In reading the Bible by chapter and verse (an editorial arrangement derived from the Renaissance) we hardly realize that the Old Testament is largely made up of speeches, orations, and sermons, that are still unsurpassed models of eloquence. "The Hebrews were so fond of oratory," writes Edgar J. Goodspeed, "that they cast their entire law in the form of speeches, uttered by God to Moses, or by Moses to the people, the priests or the elders. . . . Hebrew eloquence breaks like a flood in The Book of Deuteronomy. The great feature of it is the address of Moses to the people as they stand at last, after forty years of wandering, on the borders of the Promised Land. . . . The poet-orators of Judaism, that long line of prophets from Amos, Hosea, Micah, and Isaiah in the eighth century before Christ, on to Malachi, Obadiah, and Joel in the fifth, . . . were beyond doubt the great contribution of the ancient Hebrew genius to the thought of mankind." (How to Read the Bible, 24–7)

Moses, the mighty law-giver, who probably lived in the thirteenth century, B.C., was not portrayed in writing until hundreds of years later, in Exodus, Leviticus, Numbers and Deuteronomy. But his towering personality repels historic doubt and confronts us visibly in the statue by Michelangelo. According to the second chapter of Exodus, "Moses said unto the Lord, O my Lord, I am not eloquent, neither heretofore, nor since thou has spoken unto thy servant: but I am slow of speech, and of a slow tongue. And the Lord said unto him, Who hath made man's mouth? or who maketh the dumb, or deaf, or the seeing, or the blind? have not I the Lord? Now therefore go, and I will be with thy mouth, and teach thee what thou wilt say."

As his life drew to an end, within sight of the Promised Land, Moses called all Israel together, and said:

> "... *out of the midst of the fire, of the cloud,*
> *and of the thick darkness.*"

HEAR, O ISRAEL, the statutes and judgments which I speak in your ears this day, that ye may learn them, and keep and do them.

The Lord our God made a covenant with us in Horeb.

The Lord made not this covenant with our fathers, but with us, even us, who are all of us here alive this day.

The Lord talked with you face to face in the mount out of the midst of the fire, (I stood between the Lord and you at that time, to shew you the word of the Lord: for ye were afraid by reason of the fire, and went not up into the mount) saying,

I am the Lord thy God, which brought thee out of the land of Egypt, from the house of bondage.

Thou shalt have none other gods before me.

Thou shalt not make thee any graven image, or any likeness of anything that is in heaven above, or that is in the earth beneath, or that is in the waters beneath the earth:

Thou shalt not bow down thyself unto them, nor serve them: for I the Lord thy God am a jealous God, visiting the iniquity of the fathers upon the children unto the third and fourth generation of them that hate me,

And shewing mercy unto thousands of them that love me and keep my commandments.

Thou shalt not take the name of the Lord thy God in vain: for the Lord will not hold him guiltless that taketh his name in vain.

Keep the sabbath day to sanctify it, as the Lord thy God hath commanded thee.

Six days thou shalt labour, and do all thy work:

But the seventh day is the sabbath of the Lord thy God: in it thou shalt not do any work, thou, nor thy son, nor thy daughter, nor thy manservant, nor thy maidservant, nor thine ox, nor thine ass, nor any of thy cattle, nor thy stranger that is within thy gates; that thy manservant and thy maidservant may rest as well as thou.

And remember that thou wast a servant in the land of Egypt, and that the Lord thy God brought thee out thence through a mighty hand and by a stretched out arm: therefore the Lord thy God commanded thee to keep the sabbath day.

Honour thy father and thy mother, as the Lord thy God hath commanded thee: that thy days may be prolonged, and that it may go well with thee, in the land which the Lord thy God giveth thee.

Thou shalt not kill.

Neither shalt thou commit adultery.

Neither shalt thou steal.

Neither shalt thou bear false witness against thy neighbor.

Neither shalt thou desire thy neighbor's wife, neither shalt thou covet thy neighbor's house, his field, or his manservant, or his maidservant, his ox, or his ass, or anything that is thy neighbor's.

These words the Lord spake unto all your assembly in the mount out of the midst of the fire, of the cloud, and of the thick darkness, with a great voice: and he added no more. And he wrote them in two tables of stone, and delivered them unto me.

And it came to pass, when ye heard the voice out of the midst of the darkness, (for the mountain did burn with fire,) that ye came near unto me, even all the heads of your scribes, and your elders;

And ye said, Behold, the Lord our God hath shewed us his glory and his greatness, and we have heard his voice out of the midst of the fire: we have seen this day that God doth talk with man, and he liveth.

Now therefore why should we die? for this great fire will consume us: if we hear the voice of the Lord our God any more, then we shall die.

For who is there of all flesh, that hath heard the voice of the living God speaking out of the midst of the fire, as we have, and lived?

Go thou near, and hear all that the Lord our God shall say: and speak thou unto us all that the Lord our God shall speak unto thee; and we will hear it, and do it.

And the Lord heard the voice of your words, when ye spake unto me; and the Lord said unto me, I have heard the voice of the words of this people, which they have spoken unto thee: they have well said all that they have spoken.

O that there were such an heart in them, that they would fear me, and keep all my commandments always, that it might be well with them, and with their children for ever!

Go say to them, Get you into your tents again.

But as for thee, stand thou here by me, and I will speak unto thee all the commandments, and the statutes, and the judgments, which thou shalt teach them, that they may do them in the land which I give them to possess it.

Ye shall observe to do therefore as the Lord your God hath commanded you: ye shall not turn aside to the right hand or to the left.

Ye shall walk in all the ways which the Lord your God hath commanded you, that ye may live, and that it may be well with you, and that ye may prolong your days in the land which ye shall possess.

DEUTERONOMY, CH. 5
Authorized Version

Through twenty-one more "chapters" Moses went on to set forth the law and its reorganization on a higher level. "The great main oration [of The Book of Deuteronomy] reflects the progress of Hebrew legislation toward the close of the seventh century," concludes Dr. Goodspeed, "for it is almost certainly the Book of the Law found in the course of repairing the Temple in the time of Josiah, 621 B.C., and immediately adopted as the law of the land, as so vividly related in II Kings, chs. 22 and 23."

ISAIAH CRIES OUT
FOR SOCIAL JUSTICE

[c. 720 B.C.]

The aristocratic Isaiah, generally conceded to be the greatest of the prophets, was one of the most influential personages in Judah during the reign of King Hezekiah. He was sagacious enough to suggest an alliance with Assyria rather than with the declining power of Egypt, but unfortunately his counsels were disregarded. When the inevitable war with Assyria came, he strengthened Hezekiah's resolution, and the invaders were repelled—miraculously, it seems. Under King Manasseh, who reintroduced the worship of the baalim, the inflexibly monotheistic Isaiah fell into disfavor. The tradition is that he was executed by being sawed asunder.

Ewald, the noted Biblical scholar, called the first chapter of the Book of Isaiah the "Great Arraignment." In it Judah and Jerusalem are summoned before God's tribunal and denounced for disloyalty and social injustice. The accused plead that they have costly offerings to Jehovah. But the plea is con-

temptuously thrust aside: sacrifice and prayer from hearts not truly contrite betoken superstition, not worship.

"Learn to do well; seek judgment, relieve the oppressed, judge the fatherless, plead for the widow."

HEAR, O HEAVENS, and give ear, O earth: for the Lord hath spoken, I have nourished and brought up children, and they have rebelled against me. The ox knoweth his owner, and the ass his master's crib: but Israel doth not know, my people doth not consider. Ah sinful nation, a people laden with iniquity, a seed of evildoers, children that are corrupters: they have forsaken the Lord, they have provoked the Holy One of Israel unto anger, they are gone away backward.

Why should ye be stricken any more? ye will revolt more and more: the whole head is sick, and the whole heart faint. From the sole of the foot even unto the head there is no soundness in it; but wounds, and bruises, and putrefying sores: they have not been closed, neither bound up, neither mollified with ointment. Your country is desolate, your cities are burned with fire: your land, strangers devour it in your presence, and it is desolate, as overthrown by strangers. And the daughter of Zion is left as a cottage in a vineyard, as a lodge in a garden of cucumbers, as a besieged city. Except the Lord of hosts had left unto us a very small remnant, we should have been as Sodom, and we should have been like unto Gomorrah.

Hear the word of the Lord, ye rulers of Sodom; give ear unto the law of our God, ye people of Gomorrah. To what purpose is the multitude of your sacrifices unto me? saith the Lord: I am full of the burnt offerings of rams, and the fat of fed beasts; and I delight not in the blood of bullocks, or of lambs, or of he goats. When ye come to appear before me, who hath required this at your hand, to tread my courts? Bring no more vain oblations; incense is an abomination unto me; the new moons and sabbaths, the calling of assemblies, I cannot away with; it is iniquity, even the solemn meeting. Your new moons and your appointed feasts my soul hateth: they are a trouble unto me; I am weary to bear them. And when ye spread forth your hands, I will hide mine eyes from you: yea, when ye make many prayers, I will not hear: your hands are full of blood.

Wash you, make you clean; put away the evil of your doings from before mine eyes; cease to do evil. Learn to do well; seek judgment, relieve the oppressed, judge the fatherless, plead for the widow. Come now, and let us reason together, saith the Lord: though your sins be as scarlet, they shall be as white as snow; though they be red like crimson, they shall be as wool. If ye be willing and obedient, ye shall eat the good of the land. But if ye refuse and rebel, ye shall be devoured with the sword: for the mouth of the Lord hath spoken it.

How is the faithful city become an harlot! it was full of judgment; righteousness lodged in it; but now murderers. Thy silver is become dross, thy wine mixed with water. Thy princes are rebellious, and companions of thieves; every one loveth gifts, and followeth after rewards; they judge not the fatherless, neither doth the cause of the widow come unto them. Therefore saith the Lord, the Lord of hosts, the mighty One of Israel, Ah, I will ease me of mine adversaries, and avenge me of mine enemies: and I will turn my hand upon thee, and purely purge away thy dross, and take away all thy tin: and I will restore thy judges as at the first, and thy counsellors as at the beginning: afterward thou shalt be called, The city of righteousness, the faithful city. Zion shall be redeemed with judgment, and her converts with righteousness. And the destruction of the transgressors and of the sinners shall be together, and they that forsake the Lord shall be consumed. For they shall be ashamed of the oaks which ye have desired, and ye shall be confounded for the gardens that ye have chosen. For ye shall be as an oak whose leaf fadeth, and as a garden that hath no water. And the strong shall be as tow, and the maker of it as a spark, and they shall both burn together, and none shall quench them.

Great moral force though he was, Isaiah could not do the impossible and morally regenerate a whole nation. He had to content himself with the idea of the survival of a small number of the elect—the "Saving Remnant"—and indeed was largely responsible for its ability to survive.

PERICLES, IN A DEATHLESS FUNERAL ORATION, SUMS UP THE GLORY THAT WAS ATHENS

[430 B.C.]

Although accepted as human poetry and not divine revelation, the Iliad and the Odyssey together served the ancient Greeks much as the Old Testament served the ancient Hebrews—two different guides to life depicted in immortal lan-

guage. Epic poetry seems to signify violence and bloodshed, the clash of arms
and the shouts of fighting men, but the Homeric epics are filled with speeches
and debates, in councils and assemblies, for the Greek heroes had to be skilled
in both word and deed. "Your aged father sent me out to teach you how to be
a fine speaker and a man of action," said old Phoinix to his former pupil, the
sulking Achilles, on the plains of Troy. And Odysseus, in returning from Troy,
said to a boor: "I do not like your way of speaking. We know the gods do not
grant all the graces to any man, handsome looks and good sense and eloquence
together."

It was the power and the prestige of the Homeric poems that prepared the
way for the great flowering of oratory in the fifth century B.C., after the united
Greeks turned back two invasions of mighty Persia, and Athens celebrated in
the age of Pericles, 461–29 B.C.

Athens, the polis, the city-state, was a city in our sense of the word, but it
was also a beloved country, a magnificent dream. The resident citizen population of adult males numbered probably between thirty and forty thousand. All
these citizens were members of the Assembly, the sole legislative body, which
met once a month, but perhaps five or six thousand regularly attended. "Any
citizen could speak—if he could get the Assembly to listen; anybody could propose anything, within certain strict constitutional safeguards. But so large a
body needed a committee to prepare its business, and to deal with matters of
urgency. This committee was the Council of Five Hundred, not elected but
chosen by ballot, fifty from each tribe. . . . The jury was virtually a section
of the Assembly, varying in size from one hundred and one to one thousand and
one, according to the importance of the case. There was no judge, only a purely
formal chairman, like our 'foreman.' There were no pleaders: the parties conducted their own case, though in fact a plaintiff or defendant might get a professional 'speech-writer' to make up his speech: but then he learned it and gave
it himself." (H. D. F. Kitto: The Greeks)

These bare facts indicate the enormous importance of oratory for the ancient
Athenians. Life, liberty, property, prestige, power, all depended on it to a degree
we cannot imagine. Is it surprising that the Sophists, professional teachers of
rhetoric, the art of public speaking, met with such success in the fifth century?
The famous Sophist Gorgias (in Plato's dialogue of the same name) was probably speaking in character when he boasted that he taught "the greatest good
of man, that which gives to men freedom in their own persons, and to individuals the power of ruling over others in their several states. What is there
greater than the word that persuades the judges in their courts, or the senators
in the councils, or the citizens in the assembly, or at any other political
meeting?"

There seems little doubt that Pericles (c.500–429) became "the most fin-

ished of them all in the art of eloquence" and largely through that art maintained his virtual control over the Assembly for thirty years. He urged the
adornment of Athens, the cultivation of colonies, the wise treatment of the
poor. It was probably he who was responsible for the building of the Long
Walls in 458–56, for he foresaw that the imperial growth of Athens would
arouse the hostility of Sparta. When the "irrepressible conflict" approached
with warnings and counterwarnings, with the gathering of allies on each side,
Pericles advised his city to accept the inevitable.

Three of his speeches come down to us in Thucydides' incomparable History
of the Peloponnesian War. This is not the place to praise that work, but only
to point out that much of its strength lies in its forty-one speeches, nearly a
fourth of the whole work. Of course, it is tempting to include many of these
speeches here, if only because Demosthenes, the greatest of Greek orators, is
said to have copied the History eight times. But the supreme speech of Pericles
must suffice, along with Thucydides' own disarming explanation of his method:
"With reference to the speeches in this history, some were delivered before the
war began, others while it was going on; some I heard myself, others I got from
various quarters; it was in all cases difficult to carry them word for word in one's
memory, so my habit has been to make my speakers say what was in my opinion
demanded of them by the various occasions, of course adhering as closely as
possible to what they really said."

Thucydides knew Pericles well and he was probably present when Pericles
delivered the funeral oration for those who were killed in the first year of the
war. To what extent the speech was a description of what Athens actually was
and a vision of what Athens might be, we shall never know. Like Lincoln's
Gettysburg Address, it was a commemoration, a celebration, meant to inspire
a shaken, sorrowing people.

"As a city we are the school of Hellas."

MOST of my predecessors in this place have commended him who
made this speech part of the law, telling us that it is well that it
should be delivered at the burial of those who fall in battle. For myself, I
should have thought that the worth which had displayed itself in deeds
would be sufficiently rewarded by honors also shown by deeds; such as
you now see in this funeral prepared at the people's cost. And I could
have wished that the reputations of many brave men were not to be imperiled in the mouth of a single individual, to stand or fall according as
he spoke well or ill. For it is hard to speak properly upon a subject where

it is even difficult to convince your hearers that you are speaking the truth. On the one hand, the friend who is familiar with every fact of the story may think that some point has not been set forth with that fullness which he wishes and knows it to deserve; on the other, he who is a stranger to the matter may be led by envy to suspect exaggeration if he hears anything above his own nature. For men can endure to hear others praised only so long as they can severally persuade themselves of their own ability to equal the actions recounted: when this point is passed, envy comes in and with it incredulity. However, since our ancestors have stamped this custom with their approval, it becomes my duty to obey the law and to try to satisfy your several wishes and opinions as best I may.

I shall begin with our ancestors: it is both just and proper that they should have the honor of the first mention on an occasion like the present. They dwelt in the country without break in the succession from generation to generation, and handed it down free to the present time by their valor. And if our more remote ancestors deserve praise, much more do our own fathers, who added to their inheritance the empire which we now possess, and spared no pains to be able to leave their acquisitions to us of the present generation. Lastly, there are few parts of our dominions that have not been augmented by those of us here, who are still more or less in the vigor of life; while the mother country has been furnished by us with everything that can enable her to depend on her own resources whether for war or for peace. That part of our history which tells of the military achievements which gave us our several possessions, or of the ready valor with which either we or our fathers stemmed the tide of Hellenic or foreign aggression, is a theme too familiar to my hearers for me to dilate on, and I shall therefore pass it by. But what was the road by which we reached our position, what the form of government under which our greatness grew, what the national habits out of which it sprang; these are questions which I may try to solve before I proceed to my panegyric upon these men, since I think this to be a subject upon which on the present occasion a speaker may properly dwell, and to which the whole assemblage, whether citizens or foreigners, may listen with advantage.

Our constitution does not copy the laws of neighboring states; we are rather a pattern to others than imitators ourselves. Its administration favors the many instead of the few; this is why it is called a democracy. If we look to the laws, they afford equal justice to all in their private differences; if to social standing, advancement in public life falls to reputation for capacity, class considerations not being allowed to interfere with merit; nor again does poverty bar the way, if a man is able to serve the state, he is not hindered by the obscurity of his condition. The freedom which we enjoy in our government extends also to our ordinary life. There, far from exercising a jealous surveillance over each other, we do not feel called upon to be angry with our neighbor for doing what he likes, or even to indulge in those injurious looks which cannot fail to be offensive, although they inflict no positive penalty. But all this ease in our private relations does not make us lawless as citizens. Against this fear is our chief safeguard, teaching us to obey the magistrates and the laws, particularly such as regard the protection of the injured, whether they are actually on the statute book or belong to that code which, although unwritten, yet cannot be broken without acknowledged disgrace.

Further, we provide plenty of means for the mind to refresh itself from business. We celebrate games and sacrifices all the year round, and the elegance of our private establishments forms a daily source of pleasure and helps to banish the spleen; while the magnitude of our city draws the produce of the world into our harbor, so that to the Athenian the fruits of other countries are as familiar a luxury as those of his own.

If we turn to our military policy, there also we differ from our antagonists. We throw open our city to the world, and never by alien acts exclude foreigners from any opportunity of learning or observing, although the eyes of an enemy may occasionally profit by our liberality; trusting less in system and policy than to the native spirit of our citizens; while in education, where our rivals from their very cradles by a painful discipline seek after manliness, at Athens we live exactly as we please, and yet are just as ready to encounter every legitimate danger. In proof of this it may be noticed that the Lacedaemonians do not invade our country alone, but bring with them all their confederates, while we Athenians advance unsupported into the territory of a neighbor and, fighting upon a foreign soil, usually vanquish with ease men who are defending their homes. Our united force was never yet encountered by any enemy, because we have at once to attend to our marine and to dispatch our citizens by land upon a hundred different services; so that, wherever they engage with some such fraction of our strength, a success against a detachment is magnified into a victory over the nation, and a defeat into a reverse suffered at the hands of our entire people. And yet if with habits not of labor but of ease, and courage not of art but of nature, we are still willing to encounter danger, we have the double advantage of escaping the experience of hardships in anticipation and of facing them in the hour of need as fearlessly as those who are never free from them.

Nor are these the only points in which our city is worthy of admiration. We cultivate refinement without extravagance and knowledge without effeminacy; wealth we employ more for use than for show, and place the real disgrace of poverty not in owning to the fact but in declining the struggle against it. Our public men have, besides politics, their private affairs to attend to, and our ordinary citizens, though occupied with the pursuits of industry, are still fair judges of public matters; for, unlike any other nation, regarding him who takes no part in these duties not as unambitious but as useless, we Athenians are able to judge at all events if we cannot originate, and instead of looking on discussion as a stumbling-block in the way of action, we think it an indispensable preliminary to any wise action at all. Again, in our enterprises we present the singular spectacle of daring and deliberation, each carried to its highest point, and both united in the same persons; although usually decision is the fruit of ignorance; hesitation, of reflection. But the palm of courage will surely be adjudged most justly to those who best know the difference between hardship and pleasure and yet are never tempted to shrink from danger. In generosity we are equally singular, acquiring our friends by conferring not by receiving favors. Yet, of course, the doer of the favor is the firmer friend of the two, in order by continued kindness to keep the recipient in his debt; while the debtor feels less keenly from the very consciousness that the return he makes will be a payment, not a free gift. And it is only the Athenians who, fearless of consequences, confer their benefits not from calculations of expediency, but in the confidence of liberality.

In short, I say that as a city we are the school of Hellas; while I doubt if the world can produce a man who, where he has only himself to depend upon, is equal to so many emergencies and graced by so happy a versatility as the Athenian. And that this is no mere boast thrown out for the occasion, but plain matter of fact, the power of the state acquired by these habits proves. For Athens alone of her contemporaries is found when tested to be greater than her reputation, and alone gives no occasion to her assailants to blush at the antagonist by whom they have been worsted, or to her subjects to question her title by merit to rule. Rather, the admiration of the present and succeeding ages will be ours, since we have not left our power without witness, but have shown it by mighty proofs; and far from needing a Homer for our panegyrist, or other of his craft whose verses might charm for the moment only for the impression which they gave to melt at the touch of fact, we have forced every sea and land to be the highway of our daring, and everywhere, whether for evil or for good, have left imperishable monuments behind us. Such is the Athens for which these men, in the assertion of their resolve not to lose her, nobly fought and died; and well may every one of their survivors be ready to suffer in her cause.

Indeed, if I have dwelt at some length upon the character of our country, it has been to show that our stake in the struggle is not the same as theirs who have no such blessings to lose, and also that the panegyric of the men over whom I am now speaking might be by definite proofs established. That panegyric is now in a great measure complete; for the Athens that I have celebrated is only what the heroism of these and their like have made her, men whose fame, unlike that of most Hellenes, will be found to be only commensurate with their deserts. And if a test of worth be wanted, it is to be found in their closing scene, and this not only in the cases in which it set the final seal upon their merit, but also in those in which it gave the first intimation of their having any. For there is justice in the claim that steadfastness in his country's battles should be as a cloak to cover a man's other imperfections; since the good action has blotted out the bad, and his merit as a citizen more than outweighed his demerits as an individual. But none of these allowed either wealth, with its prospect of future enjoyment, to unnerve his spirit or poverty, with its hope of a day of freedom and riches, to tempt him to shrink from danger. No, holding that vengeance upon their enemies was more to be desired than any personal blessings, and reckoning this to be the most glorious of hazards, they joyfully determined to accept the risk, to make sure of their vengeance and to let their wishes wait; and while committing to hope the uncertainty of final success, in the business before them they thought fit to act boldly and trust in themselves. Thus choosing to die resisting rather than to live submitting, they fled only from dishonor, but met danger face to face, and after one brief moment, while at the summit of their fortune, escaped, not from their fear, but from their glory.

So died these men as became Athenians. You, their survivors, must determine to have as unaltering a resolution in the field, though you may pray that it may have a happier issue. And not contented with ideas derived only from words of the advantages which are bound up with the defense of your country, though these would furnish a valuable text to a speaker even before an audience so alive to them as the present, you must yourselves realize the power of Athens, and feed your eyes upon her from day to day, till love of her fills your hearts; and then when all her greatness shall break upon you, you must reflect that it was by courage, sense of duty, and a keen feeling of honor in action that men were enabled to win all this, and that no personal failure in an enterprise could make them consent to deprive their country of their valor, but they laid it at her feet as the most glorious contribution that they could offer. For this offering of their lives made in common by them all they each of them individually received that renown which never grows old, and for a sepulcher, not so much that in which their bones have been deposited, but that noblest of shrines wherein their glory is laid up to be eternally remem-

bered upon every occasion on which deed or story shall fall for its commemoration. For heroes have the whole earth for their tomb; and in lands
far from their own, where the column with its epitaph declares it, there
is enshrined in every breast a record unwritten with no tablet to preserve
it, except that of the heart. These take as your model, and judging happiness to be the fruit of freedom and freedom of valor, never decline the
dangers of war. For it is not the miserable that would most justly be un-
sparing of their lives; these have nothing to hope for: it is rather they to
whom continued life may bring reverses as yet unknown, and to whom a
fall, if it came, would be most tremendous in its consequences. And
surely, to a man of spirit, the degradation of cowardice must be immeasurably more grievous than the unfelt death which strikes him in the midst
of his strength and patriotism!

Comfort, therefore, not condolence, is what I have to offer to the parents of the dead who may be here. Numberless are the chances to which,
as they know, the life of man is subject; but fortunate indeed are they
who draw for their lot a death so glorious as that which has caused your
mourning, and to whom life has been so exactly measured as to terminate
in the happiness in which it has been passed. Still I know that this is a
hard saying, especially when those are in question of whom you will constantly be reminded by seeing in the homes of others blessings of which
once you also boasted: for grief is felt not so much for the want of what
we have never known as for the loss of that to which we have been long
accustomed. Yet you who are still of an age to beget children must bear
up in the hope of having others in their stead; not only will they help you
to forget those whom you have lost, but will be to the state at once a reinforcement and a security; for never can a fair or just policy be expected
of the citizen who does not, like his fellows, bring to the decision the interests and apprehensions of a father. While those of you who have
passed your prime must congratulate yourselves with the thought that
the best part of your life was fortunate, and that the brief span that remains will be cheered by the fame of the departed. For it is only the love
of honor that never grows old; and honor it is, not gain, as some would
have it, that rejoices the heart of age and helplessness.

Turning to the sons or brothers of the dead, I see an arduous struggle
before you. When a man is gone, all are wont to praise him, and should
your merit be ever so transcendent, you will still find it difficult not
merely to overtake, but even to approach their renown. The living have
envy to contend with, while those who are no longer in our path are honored with a good will into which rivalry does not enter. On the other
hand, if I must say anything on the subject of female excellence to those

of you who will now be in widowhood, it will be all comprised in this brief exhortation. Great will be your glory in not falling short of your natural character; and greatest will be hers who is least talked of among the men whether for good or for bad.

My task is now finished. I have performed it to the best of my ability, and in words, at least, the requirements of the law are now satisfied. If deeds be in question, those who are here interred have received part of their honors already, and for the rest, their children will be brought up till manhood at the public expense: the state thus offers a valuable prize, as the garland of victory in this race of valor, for the reward both of those who have fallen and their survivors. And where the rewards for merit are greatest, there are found the best citizens.

And now that you have brought to a close your lamentations for your relatives, you may depart.

(TRANSLATED BY RICHARD CRAWLEY)

Pericles was not only a statesman, he was a great strategist as well. But it was his misfortune that he was almost alone in realizing that his long-term strategy would work. The Athenians were demoralized when plague struck the city in 430 B.C. and carried off a fourth of the population. Accused of carrying on the war for his own selfish interests, Pericles defended himself and reminded his hearers that they could not have the prizes of empire without sharing its burdens.

Great speech though it was, Pericles had made too many enemies during the years he had administered Athens to escape scot free. He was tried for embezzlement, fined, and—elected general again. But he, too, caught the plague and died in 429.

The Spartans sued for peace a few years later. When the war was renewed the Athenians fatally weakened themselves by a mad, impossible expedition against Sicily.

DEMOSTHENES DENOUNCES THE
IMPERIALISTIC AMBITIONS
OF PHILIP OF MACEDON

[341 B.C.]

Isocrates (436–338 B.C.) is often referred to as a "great Greek orator," but it is quite likely that he never delivered a speech—he was too timid, and his voice was too weak. However, he was vastly influential for almost three-quarters of a century (he lived to ninety-eight), being a serious rival of Plato in educational philosophy and of Demosthenes in political strategy. His lifelong concern—his lifelong obsession, one might say—was that of preventing fratricidal wars among the Greek city-states, Athens and Sparta being the worst offenders. He sought to unify these jealous elements in a war against Persia. To that end he is said to have spent ten years in preparing his famous Panegyricus (festival oration) for the Olympic games of 380 B.C. This he did not certainly deliver.

When Athens and Sparta failed to respond to the grand strategy of the Panegyricus, Isocrates spent many more years in seeking out some powerful personage who could unite the city-states. He successively approached Dionysius I of Syracuse, Archidamus III of Sparta, and finally Philip II of Macedon. In this third choice he aligned himself with the pro-Macedonian party, whose program was Panhellenism under Macedonian leadership.

Demosthenes (384–322 B.C.), an Athenian lawyer with a large practice, saw the naïveté of Isocrates' plan. He noted that Macedonian nationalism had emerged after Philip had crushed the ambitions of the tribes of barbarians that made up his kingdom. Wasteful and horrible were the continual wars between the Greek city-states, but were they worse than subjection to the ruthless, efficient parvenus of the north? Would appeasement of Philip bring anything more than dishonor and slavery to the Greeks? Demosthenes thought not, and he said so in his famous four Philippics. The third of these is his finest deliberative speech, showing him at his loftiest as a political thinker.

> "There must be some cause, some good reason, why the
> Greeks were so eager for liberty then, and now are
> eager for servitude."

MANY SPEECHES, men of Athens, are made in almost every assembly about the hostilities of Philip, hostilities which ever since the treaty of peace he has been committing as well against you as against the rest of the Greeks; and all (I am sure) are ready to avow, though they forbear to do so, that our counsels and our measures should be directed to his humiliation and chastisement: nevertheless, so low have our affairs been brought by inattention and negligence, I fear it is a harsh truth to say, that if all the orators had sought to suggest, and you to pass resolutions for the utter ruining of the commonwealth, we could not methinks be worse off than we are. A variety of circumstances may have brought as to this state; our affairs have not declined from one or two causes only:

but, if you rightly examine, you will find it chiefly owing to the orators, who study to please you rather than advise for the best. Some of whom, Athenians, seeking to maintain the basis of their own power and repute, have no forethought for the future, and therefore think you also ought to have none; others, accusing and calumniating practical statesmen, labor only to make Athens punish Athens, and in such occupation to engage her, that Philip may have liberty to say and do what he pleases. Politics of this kind are common here, but are the causes of your failures and embarrassment. I beg, Athenians, that you will not resent my plain speaking of the truth. Only consider. You hold liberty of speech in other matters to be the general right of all residents in Athens, insomuch that you allow a measure of it even to foreigners and slaves, and many servants may be seen among you speaking their thoughts more freely than citizens in some other states; and yet you have altogether banished it from your councils. The result has been that in the assembly you give yourselves airs and are flattered at hearing nothing but compliments, in your measures and proceedings you are brought to the utmost peril. If such be your disposition now, I must be silent: if you will listen to good advice without flattery, I am ready to speak. For though our affairs are in a deplorable condition, though many sacrifices have been made, still, if you will choose to perform your duty, it is possible to repair it all. A paradox, and yet a truth, am I about to state. That which is the most lamentable in the past is best for the future. How is this? Because you performed no part of your duty, great or small, and therefore you fared ill: had you done all that became you, and your situation were the same, there would be no hope of amendment. Philip has indeed prevailed over your sloth and negligence, but not over the country: you have not been worsted; you have not even bestirred yourselves.

If now we were all agreed that Philip is at war with Athens and infringing the peace, nothing would a speaker need to urge or advise but the safest and easiest way of resisting him. But since, at the very time when Philip is capturing cities and retaining divers of our dominions and assailing all people, there are men so unreasonable as to listen to repeated declarations in the assembly that some of us are kindling war, one must be cautious and set this matter right: for whoever moves or advises a measure of defense is in danger of being accused afterward as author of the war.

I will first then examine and determine this point, whether it be in our power to deliberate on peace or war. If the country may be at peace, if it depends on us (to begin with this), I say we ought to maintain peace, and I call upon the affirmant to move a resolution, to take some measure, and not to palter with us. But if another, having arms in his hand and a large force around him, amuses you with the name of peace while he carries on the operations of war, what is left but to defend yourselves? You may profess to be at peace, if you like, as he does; I quarrel not with that. But if any man supposes this to be a peace, which will enable Philip to master all else and attack you last, he is a madman, or he talks of a peace observed toward him by you, not toward you by him. This it is that Philip purchases by all his expenditure, the privilege of assailing you without being assailed in turn.

If we really wait until he avows that he is at war with us, we are the simplest of mortals: for he would not declare that, though he marched even against Attica and Piraeus, at least if we may judge from his conduct to others. For example, to the Olynthians he declared, when he was forty furlongs from their city, that there was no alternative, but either they must quit Olynthus or he Macedonia; though before that time, whenever he was accused of such an intent, he took it ill and sent ambassadors to justify himself. Again, he marched toward the Phocians as if they were allies, and there were Phocian envoys who accompanied his march, and many among you contended that his advance would not benefit the Thebans. And he came into Thessaly of late as a friend and ally, yet he has taken possession of Pherae: and lastly he told these wretched people of Oreus, that he had sent his soldiers out of good will to visit them, as he heard they were in trouble and dissension, and it was the part of allies and true friends to lend assistance on such occasions.

People who would never have harmed him, though they might have adopted measures of defense, he chose to deceive rather than warn them of his attack; and think ye he would declare war against you before he began it, and that while you are willing to be deceived? Impossible. He would be the silliest of mankind, if, whilst you the injured parties make no complaint against him, but are accusing your own countrymen, he should terminate your intestine strife and jealousies, warn you to turn against him, and remove the pretexts of his hirelings for asserting, to amuse you, that he makes no war upon Athens. O heavens! would any rational being judge by words rather than by actions who is at peace with him and who at war? Surely none. Well, then; Philip immediately after the peace, before Diopithes was in command or the settlers in the Chersonesus had been sent out, took Serrium and Doriscus, and expelled from Serrium and the Sacred Mount the troops whom your general had stationed there. What do you call such conduct? He had sworn the peace. Don't say—what does it signify? how is the state concerned?—Whether it be a trifling matter, or of no concernment to you, is a different question: religion and justice have the same obligation, be the subject of the offense great or small. Tell me now; when he sends mercenaries into Chersonesus, which the king and all the Greeks have acknowledged to be yours, when he avows himself an auxiliary and writes us word so, what are such proceedings? He says he is not at war; I cannot, however, admit such conduct to be an observance of the peace; far otherwise: I say, by his attempt on Megara, by his setting up despotism in Euboea, by his present advance into Thrace, by his intrigues in Peloponnesus, by the whole course of operations with his army, he has been breaking the peace and making war upon you; unless, indeed, you will say that those who establish batteries are not at war until they apply them to the walls. But that you will not say: for whoever contrives and prepares the means for my conquest is at war with me before he darts or draws the bow. What, if anything should happen, is the risk you run? The alienation of the Hellespont, the subjection of Megara and Euboea to your enemy, the siding of the Peloponnesians with him. Then can I allow that one who sets such an engine at work against Athens is at peace with her? Quite the contrary. From the day that he destroyed the Phocians I date his commencement of hostilities.

Defend yourselves instantly, and I say you will be wise: delay it, and you may wish in vain to do so hereafter. So much do I dissent from your other counselors, men of Athens, that I deem any discussion about Chersonesus or Byzantium out of place. Succor them—I advise that—watch that no harm befalls them, send all necessary supplies to your troops in that quarter; but let your deliberations be for the safety of all Greece, as being in the utmost peril. I must tell you why I am so alarmed at the state of our affairs: that, if my reasonings are correct, you may share them, and make some provision at least for yourselves, however disinclined to do so for others: but if, in your judgment, I talk nonsense and absurdity, you may treat me as crazed, and not listen to me, either now or in future.

That Philip from a mean and humble origin has grown mighty, that the Greeks are jealous and quarreling among themselves, that it was far more wonderful for him to rise from that insignificance than it would now be, after so many acquisitions, to conquer what is left; these and similar matters, which I might dwell upon, I pass over. But I observe that all people, beginning with you, have conceded to him a right which in former times has been the subject of contest in every Grecian war. And what is this? The right of doing what he pleases, openly fleecing and pillaging the Greeks, one after another, attacking and enslaving their cities. You were at the head of the Greeks for seventy-three years, the Lacedaemonians for twenty-nine; and the Thebans had some power in these latter

times after the battle of Leuctra. Yet neither you, my countrymen, nor
Thebans nor Lacedaemonians were ever licensed by the Greeks to act as
you pleased; far otherwise. When you, or rather the Athenians of that
time, appeared to be dealing harshly with certain people, all the rest,
even such as had no complaint against Athens, thought proper to side
with the injured parties in a war against her. So, when the Lacedaemonians became masters and succeeded to your empire, on their attempting
to encroach and make oppressive innovations, a general war was declared
against them, even by such as had no cause of complaint. But wherefore
mention other people? We ourselves and the Lacedaemonians, although
at the outset we could not allege any mutual injuries, thought proper to
make war for the injustice that we saw done to our neighbors.

Yet all the faults committed by the Spartans in those thirty years, and
by our ancestors in the seventy, are less, men of Athens, than the wrongs
which, in thirteen incomplete years that Philip has been uppermost, he
has inflicted on the Greeks: nay, they are scarcely a fraction of these, as
may easily be shown in a few words. Olynthus and Methone and Apollonia, and thirty-two cities on the borders of Thrace, I pass over; all which
he has so cruelly destroyed that a visitor could hardly tell if they were
ever inhabited: and of the Phocians, so considerable a people extermi-
nated, I say nothing. But what is the condition of Thessaly? Has he
not taken away her constitutions and her cities, and established tetrarch-
ies, to parcel her out, not only by cities, but also by provinces, for subjection? Are not the Euboean states governed now by despots, and that
in an island near to Thebes and Athens? Does he not expressly write in
his epistles, "I am at peace with those who are willing to obey me"? Nor
does he write so and not act accordingly. He is gone to the Hellespont;
he marched formerly against Ambracia; Elis, such an important city in
Peloponnesus, he possesses; he plotted lately to get Megara: neither Hellenic nor barbaric land contains the man's ambition. And we the Greek
community, seeing and hearing this, instead of sending embassies to one
another about it and expressing indignation, are in such a miserable state,
so intrenched in our separate towns, that to this day we can attempt nothing that interest or necessity requires; we cannot combine, or form any
association for succor and alliance; we look unconcernedly on the man's
growing power, each resolving (methinks) to enjoy the interval that another is destroyed in, not caring or striving for the salvation of Greece:
for none can be ignorant that Philip, like some course or attack of fever
or other disease, is coming even on those that yet seem very far removed.
And you must be sensible that whatever wrong the Greeks sustained from
Lacedaemonians or from us was at least inflicted by genuine people of

Greece; and it might be felt in the same manner as if a lawful son, born to a large fortune, committed some fault or error in the management of it; on that ground one would consider him open to censure and reproach, yet it could not be said that he was an alien, and not heir to the property which he so dealt with. But if a slave or a spurious child wasted and spoiled what he had no interest in—heavens! how much more heinous and hateful would all have pronounced it! And yet in regard to Philip and his conduct they feel not this, although he is not only no Greek and noway akin to Greeks, but not even a barbarian of a place honorable to mention; in fact, a vile fellow of Macedon, from which a respectable slave could not be purchased formerly.

What is wanting to make his insolence complete? Besides his destruction of Grecian cities, does he not hold the Pythian games, the common festival of Greece, and, if he comes not himself, send his vassals to preside? Is he not master of Thermopylae and the passes into Greece, and holds he not those places by garrisons and mercenaries? Has he not thrust aside Thessalians, ourselves, Dorians, the whole Amphictyonic body, and got preaudience of the oracle, to which even the Greeks do not all pretend? Does he not write to the Thessalians, what form of government to adopt? send mercenaries to Porthmus, to expel the Eretrian commonalty; others to Oreus, to set up Philistides as ruler? Yet the Greeks endure to see all this; methinks they view it as they would a hailstorm, each praying that it may not fall on himself, none trying to prevent it. And not only are the outrages which he does to Greece submitted to, but even the private wrongs of every people: nothing can go beyond this! Has he not wronged the Corinthians by attacking Ambracia and Leucas? the Achaians, by swearing to give Naupactus to the Aetolians? from the Thebans taken Echinus? Is he not marching against the Byzantines his allies? From us— I omit the rest—but keeps he not Cardia, the greatest city of the Chersonesus? Still under these indignities we are all slack and disheartened, and look toward our neighbors, distrusting one another instead of the common enemy. And how think ye a man who behaves so insolently to all, how will he act when he gets each separately under his control?

But what has caused the mischief? There must be some cause, some good reason, why the Greeks were so eager for liberty then, and now are eager for servitude. There was something, men of Athens, something in the hearts of the multitude then, which there is not now, which overcame the wealth of Persia and maintained the freedom of Greece, and quailed not under any battle by land or sea; the loss whereof has ruined all, and thrown the affairs of Greece into confusion. What was this? Nothing subtle or clever: simply that whoever took money from the aspirants for

power or the corruptors of Greece were universally detested: it was
dreadful to be convicted of bribery; the severest punishment was inflicted
on the guilty, and there was no intercession or pardon. The favorable
moments for enterprise, which fortune frequently offers to the careless
against the vigilant, to them that will do nothing against those that discharge all their duty, could not be bought from orators or generals; no
more could mutual concord, nor distrust of tyrants and barbarians, nor
anything of the kind. But now all such principles have been sold as in
open market, and those imported in exchange by which Greece is ruined
and diseased. What are they? Envy where a man gets a bribe; laughter if
he confesses it; mercy to the convicted; hatred of those that denounce the
crime: all the usual attendants upon corruption. For as to ships and men
and revenues and abundance of other materials, all that may be reckoned
as constituting national strength—assuredly the Greeks of our day are
more fully and perfectly supplied with such advantages than Greeks of
the olden time. But they are all rendered useless, unavailable, unprofitable, by the agency of these traffickers.

That such is the present state of things, you must see, without requiring my testimony: that it was different in former times, I will demonstrate, not by speaking my own words, but by showing an inscription of
your ancestors, which they graved on a brazen column and deposited in
the citadel, not for their own benefit (they were right-minded enough
without such records), but for a memorial and example to instruct you
how seriously such conduct should be taken up. What says the inscription, then? It says: "Let Arthmius, son of Pythonax the Zelite, be declared
an outlaw, and an enemy of the Athenian people and their allies, him and
his family." Then the cause is written why this was done: because he
brought the Median gold into Peloponnesus. That is the inscription. By
the gods! only consider and reflect among yourselves what must have
been the spirit, what the dignity, of those Athenians who acted so. One
Arthmius a Zelite, subject of the king (for Zelea is in Asia), because in
his master's service he brought gold into Peloponnesus, not to Athens,
they proclaimed an enemy of the Athenians and their allies, him and his
family, and outlawed. That is, not the outlawry commonly spoken of: for
what would a Zelite care, to be excluded from Athenian franchises? It
means not that; but in the statutes of homicide it is written, in cases
where a prosecution for murder is not allowed, but killing is sanctioned,
"and let him die an outlaw," says the legislator: by which he means that
whoever kills such a person shall be unpolluted. Therefore they considered that the preservation of all Greece was their own concern (but for
such opinion, they would not have cared, whether people in Peloponne-

sus were bought and corrupted), and whomsoever they discovered taking bribes, they chastised and punished so severely as to record their names in brass. The natural result was that Greece was formidable to the barbarian, not the barbarian to Greece. 'Tis not so now: since neither in this nor in other respects are your sentiments the same. But what are they? You know yourselves: why am I to upbraid you with everything? The Greeks in general are alike and no better than you. Therefore I say our present affairs demand earnest attention and wholesome counsel. Shall I say what? Do you bid me, and won't you be angry?

[Here is read the public document which Demosthenes produces, after which he resumes his address.]

There is a foolish saying of persons who wish to make us easy that Philip is not yet as powerful as the Lacedaemonians were formerly, who ruled everywhere by land and sea, and had the king for their ally, and nothing withstood them; yet Athens resisted even that nation, and was not destroyed. I myself believe that, while everything has received great improvement, and the present bears no resemblance to the past, nothing has been so changed and improved as the practice of war. For anciently, as I am informed, the Lacedaemonians and all Grecian people would for four or five months, during the season only, invade and ravage the land of their enemies with heavy-armed and national troops, and return home again: and their ideas were so old-fashioned, or rather national, they never purchased an advantage from any; theirs was a legitimate and open warfare. But now you doubtless perceive that the majority of disasters have been effected by treason; nothing is done in fair field or combat. You hear of Philip marching where he pleases, not because he commands troops of the line, but because he has attached to him a host of skirmishers, cavalry, archers, mercenaries, and the like. When with these he falls upon a people in civil dissension, and none (for mistrust) will march out to defend the country, he applies engines and besieges them. I need not mention that he makes no difference between winter and summer, that he has no stated season of repose. You, knowing these things, reflecting on them, must not let the war approach your territories, nor get your necks broken, relying on the simplicity of the old war with the Lacedaemonians, but take the longest time beforehand for defensive measures and preparations, see that he stirs not from home, avoid any decisive engagement. For a war, if we choose, men of Athens, to pursue a right course, we have many natural advantages; such as the position of his kingdom, which we may extensively plunder and ravage, and a thousand more; but for a battle he is better trained than we are.

Nor is it enough to adopt these resolutions and oppose him by warlike measures: you must on calculation and on principle abhor his advocates here, remembering that it is impossible to overcome your enemies abroad until you have chastised those who are his ministers within the city. Which, by Zeus and all the gods, you cannot and will not do! You have arrived at such a pitch of folly or madness or—I know not what to call it: I am tempted often to think that some evil genius is driving you to ruin— for the sake of scandal or envy or jest or any other cause, you command hirelings to speak (some of whom would not deny themselves to be hirelings), and laugh when they abuse people. And this, bad as it is, is not the worst: you have allowed these persons more liberty for their political conduct than your faithful counselors: and see what evils are caused by listening to such men with indulgence. I will mention facts that you will all remember.

In Olynthus some of the statesmen were in Philip's interest, doing everything for him; some were on the honest side, aiming to preserve their fellow citizens from slavery. Which party now destroyed their country? or which betrayed the cavalry, by whose betrayal Olynthus fell? The creatures of Philip; they that, while the city stood, slandered and calumniated the honest counselors so effectually that the Olynthian people were induced to banish Apollonides.

Nor is it there only, and nowhere else, that such practice has been ruinous. In Eretria, when, after riddance of Plutarch and his mercenaries, the people got possession of their city and of Porthmus, some were for bringing the government over to you, others to Philip. His partisans were generally, rather exclusively, attended to by the wretched and unfortunate Eretrians, who at length were persuaded to expel their faithful advisers. Philip, their ally and friend, sent Hipponicus and a thousand mercenaries, demolished the walls of Porthmus, and established three rulers, Hipparchus, Automedon, Clitarchus. Since that he has driven them out of the country, twice attempting their deliverance: once he sent the troops with Eurylochus, afterward those of Parmenio.

What need of many words? In Oreus Philip's agents were Philistides, Menippus, Socrates, Thoas, and Agapaeus, who now hold the government: that was quite notorious: one Euphraeus, a man that formerly dwelt here among you, was laboring for freedom and independence. How this man was in other respects insulted and trampled on by the people of Oreus were long to tell: but a year before the capture, discovering what Philistides and his accomplices were about, he laid an information against them for treason. A multitude then combining, having Philip for their paymaster, and acting under his direction, take Euphraeus off to prison as a disturber of the public peace. Seeing which, the people of Oreus, instead of assisting the one and beating the others to death, with them were not angry, but said his punishment was just, and rejoiced at it. So the conspirators, having full liberty of action, laid their schemes and took their measures for the surrender of the city; if any of the people observed it, they were silent and intimidated, remembering the treatment of Euphraeus; and so wretched was their condition that on the approach of such a calamity none dared to utter a word until the enemy drew up before the walls: then some were for defense, others for betrayal. Since the city was thus basely and wickedly taken, the traitors have held despotic rule; people who formerly rescued them, and were ready for any maltreatment of Euphraeus, they have either banished or put to death; Euphraeus killed himself, proving by deed that he had resisted Philip honestly and purely for the good of his countrymen.

What can be the reason—perhaps you wonder—why the Olynthians and Eretrians and Orites were more indulgent to Philip's advocates than to their own? The same which operates with you. They who advise for the best cannot always gratify their audience, though they would; for the safety of the state must be attended to: their opponents by the very counsel which is agreeable advance Philip's interest. One party required contribution; the other said there was no necessity: one were for war and mistrust; the other for peace, until they were ensnared. And so on for everything else (not to dwell on particulars); the one made speeches to please for the moment, and gave no annoyance; the other offered salutary counsel that was offensive. Many rights did the people surrender at last not from any such motive of indulgence or ignorance, but submitting in the belief that all was lost. Which, by Jupiter and Apollo, I fear will be your case when on calculation you see that nothing can be done. I pray, men of Athens, it may never come to this! Better die a thousand deaths than render homage to Philip, or sacrifice any of your faithful counselors. A fine recompense have the people of Oreus got for trusting themselves to Philip's friends and spurning Euphraeus! Finely are the Eretrian commons rewarded for having driven away your ambassadors and yielded to Clitarchus! Yes; they are slaves, exposed to the lash and the torture. Finely he spared the Olynthians, who appointed Lasthenes to command their horse, and expelled Apollonides! It is folly and cowardice to cherish such hopes, and, while you take evil counsel and shirk every duty, and even listen to those who plead for your enemies, to think you inhabit a city of such magnitude that you cannot suffer any serious misfortune. Yea, and it is disgraceful to exclaim on any occurrence, when it is too late, "Who would have expected it? However—this or that should have been done, the other left undone." Many things could the Olynthians mention now which, if foreseen at the time, would have prevented their destruction. Many could the Orites mention, many the Phocians, and each of the ruined states. But what would it avail them? As long as the vessel is safe, whether it be great or small, the mariner, the pilot, every man in turn should exert himself, and prevent its being overturned either by accident or design: but when the sea hath rolled over it, their efforts are vain. And we, likewise, O Athenians, whilst we are safe, with a magnificent city, plentiful resources, lofty reputation—what must we do? Many of you, I dare say, have been longing to ask. Well, then, I will tell you; I will move a resolution: pass it, if you please.

First, let us prepare for our own defense; provide ourselves, I mean, with ships, money, and troops—for surely, though all other people consented to be slaves, we at least ought to struggle for freedom. When we have completed our own preparations and made them apparent to the Greeks, then let us invite the rest, and send our ambassadors everywhere with the intelligence, to Peloponnesus, to Rhodes, to Chios, to the king, I say (for it concerns his interests, not to let Philip make universal conquest); that, if you prevail, you may have partners of your dangers and expenses, in case of necessity, or at all events that you may delay the operations. For, since the war is against an individual, not against the collected power of a state, even this may be useful; as were the embassies last year to Peloponnesus, and the remonstrances with which I and Polyeuctus, that excellent man, and Hegesippus, and Clitomachus, and Lycurgus, and the other envoys went round, and arrested Philip's progress, so that he neither attacked Ambracia nor started for Peloponnesus. I say not, however, that you should invite the rest without adopting measures to protect yourselves: it would be folly, while you sacrifice your own interest, to profess a regard for that of strangers, or to alarm others about the future, whilst for the present you are unconcerned. I advise not this: I bid you send supplies to the troops in Chersonesus, and do what else they require; prepare yourselves and make every effort first, then summon, gather, instruct the rest of the Greeks. That is the duty of a state possessing a dignity such as yours. If you imagine that Chalcidians or Megarians will save Greece while you run away from the contest, you imagine wrong. Well for any of those people, if they are safe themselves. This work belongs to you: this privilege your ancestors bequeathed to you, the prize of many perilous exertions. But if everyone will sit seeking his pleasure, and studying to be idle himself, never will he find others to do his work, and, more than this, I fear we shall be under the necessity of doing all that we like not at one time. Were proxies to be had, our inactivity would have found them long ago; but they are not.

Such are the measures which I advise, which I propose: adopt them, and even yet, I believe, our prosperity may be re-established. If any man has better advice to offer, let him communicate it openly. Whatever you determine, I pray to all the gods for a happy result.

(TRANSLATED BY CHARLES RANN KENNEDY)

This great speech, considered by many the artistic peak of Greek oratory, almost achieved its end. It did succeed in enspiriting Athens, in bringing the Greek city-states together. But their tardy reconciliation was not sufficient to meet the crushing force of Macedon. Philip's victory over Athens and Thebes at Chaeronea in 338 B.C. marked the end of Greek independence.

THE CONSPIRACY OF CATILINE
CICERO POURS ON THE VITRIOL

[63 B.C.]

While the power of Macedon declined after the death of Alexander the Great, the power of Rome increased steadily until it dominated the Mediterranean basin and most of Europe by the middle of the first century B.C. But doubly conquered little Greece became the school of mighty Rome as Athens had been the school of Greece.

Cicero, in an imaginary dialogue, *Brutus*, traced briefly the course of Greek oratory and then more fully sketched the great Roman orators, down to himself. He included, among many others, Cato the Censor, the brothers Gracchi, Marcus Antonius, grandfather of the triumvir, Crassus, Calvus with his severe "Attic" style, and Hortensius with his "Asiatic" luxuriance. The story does end fittingly with Cicero, for he was undoubtedly one of the greatest orators that ever lived, although he was also a vain, garrulous, boastful man, a social climber, and a trimmer, who was sometimes absurdly timid and at other times incredibly bold.

Born fairly low in the social scale, Marcus Tullius Cicero (106–43 B.C.) soon determined to rise high in the legal profession and in public affairs, through the art of speaking. He met with early success in the law but went abroad for his health and studied philosophy and rhetoric for two years at Athens and Rhodes. He tells us in the *Brutus* that Molo, the celebrated teacher at Rhodes, "toiled zealously at the task of chastening me—prolix and exuberant and overflowing my banks with a sort of juvenile impunity and license—and strove, so to speak, to confine my style in its proper channel. . . . I returned home not only more adequately equipped for my life's work, but almost a new man." He goes on to pillory the indolence, the ignorance, the comparative illiteracy of his rivals at the bar. "None understood the value of a momentary digression for amusement's sake; none could move the judge to profound indignation or to pity or to any other emotions which the situation might demand—the one paramount talent of the orator."

He tried many interesting, if not important, cases, but his big opportunity came in 70 B.C. when the Sicilians retained him to prosecute the rapacious governor, Verres. By his furious attack Cicero not only secured a conviction and drove Verres into exile but also clearly eclipsed the recognized leader of the Roman bar, the flamboyant Hortensius. And so, pursuing a legal, a literary, and a political career, side by side, he managed to win a consulship at forty-three.

In this memorable year, 63 B.C., Lucius Sergius Catiline, a Roman noble who aspired to the consulate but was unable to stand because of charges of his misgovernment, organized a plot against the senatorial clique that governed Rome. What was this famous conspiracy? A reckless and ruthless plan to take over Rome, a "revolutionary movement fanned by the discontent of temperamental or embittered subversives and the desperation of ruined men"? Or was it "a debtors' protest," an imprudent but understandable movement of people caught up in economic dissolution—an ancient version of the bonus march on Washington during the Hoover regime? Whatever the danger, it seems to have been enormously exaggerated by Cicero—and the case for the other side has come down to us only as written by Catiline's enemies.

One thing seems reasonably certain—Catiline had planned to kill Cicero, then consul, and his hired assassins had been repulsed from Cicero's doors. Two days later the veteran orator delivered the first of four pitiless exposures of his enemy's schemes.

*"Nature has formed you, desire has trained you, fortune
has preserved you for this insanity."*

WHEN, O CATILINE, do you mean to cease abusing our patience? How long is that madness of yours still to mock us? When is there to be an end of that unbridled audacity of yours, swaggering about as it does now? Do not the nightly guards placed on the Palatine Hill—do not the watches posted throughout the city—does not the alarm of the people, and the union of all good men—does not the precaution taken of assembling the Senate in this most defensible place—do not the

looks and countenances of this venerable body here present have any effect upon you? Do you not feel that your plans are detected? Do you not
see that your conspiracy is already arrested and rendered powerless by
the knowledge which everyone here possesses of it? What is there that
you did last night, what the night before—where is it that you were—
who was there that you summoned to meet you—what design was there
which was adopted by you, with which you think that any one of us is
unacquainted?

Shame on the age and on its principles! The Senate is aware of these
things; the consul sees them; and yet this man lives. Lives! aye, he comes
even into the Senate. He takes a part in the public deliberations; he is
watching and marking down and checking off for slaughter every individual among us. And we, gallant men that we are, think that we are doing our duty to the Republic if we keep out of the way of his frenzied
attacks.

You ought, O Catiline, long ago to have been led to execution by command of the consul. That destruction which you have been long plotting
against us ought to have already fallen on your own head.

What? Did not that most illustrious man, Publius Scipio, the Pontifex
Maximus, in his capacity of a private citizen, put to death Tiberius Gracchus, though but slightly undermining the Constitution? And shall we,
who are the consuls, tolerate Catiline, openly desirous to destroy the
whole world with fire and slaughter? For I pass over older instances,
such as how Gaius Servilius Ahala with his own hand slew Spurius Mae-
lius when plotting a revolution in the state. There was—there was once
such virtue in this republic that brave men would repress mischievous
citizens with severer chastisement than the most bitter enemy. For we
have a resolution of the Senate, a formidable and authoritative decree
against you, O Catiline; the wisdom of the Republic is not at fault, nor
the dignity of this senatorial body. We, we alone—I say it openly—we,
the consuls, are wanting in our duty.

The Senate once passed a decree that Lucius Opimius, the consul,
should take care that the Republic suffered no injury. Not one night
elapsed. There was put to death, on some mere suspicion of disaffection,
Gaius Gracchus, a man whose family had borne the most unblemished
reputation for many generations. There were slain Marcus Fulvius, a man
of consular rank, and all his children. By a like decree of the Senate the
safety of the Republic was intrusted to Gaius Marius and Lucius Valerius,
the consuls. Did not the vengeance of the Republic, did not execution,
overtake Lucius Saturninus, a tribune of the people, and Gaius Servilius,
the praetor, without the delay of one single day? But we, for these twenty

days, have been allowing the edge of the Senate's authority to grow
blunt, as it were. For we are in possession of a similar decree of the Senate, but we keep it locked up in its parchment—buried, I may say, in the
sheath; and according to this decree you ought, O Catiline, to be put to
death this instant. You live—and you live, not to lay aside, but to persist
in your audacity.

I wish, O conscript fathers, to be merciful; I wish not to appear negli-
gent amid such danger to the state; but I do now accuse myself of remissness and culpable inactivity. A camp is pitched in Italy, at the entrance
of Etruria, in hostility to the Republic; the number of the enemy in-
creases every day; and yet the general of that camp, the leader of those
enemies, we see within the walls—aye, and even in the Senate—planning
every day some internal injury to the Republic. If, O Catiline, I should
now order you to be arrested, to be put to death, I should, I suppose,
have to fear lest all good men should say that I had acted tardily rather
than that anyone should affirm that I acted cruelly. But yet this, which
ought to have been done long since, I have good reason for not doing as
yet; I will put you to death then, when there shall be not one person possible to be found so wicked, so abandoned, so like yourself, as not to allow that it has been rightly done. As long as one person exists who can
dare to defend you, you shall live; but you shall live as you do now, surrounded by my many and trusty guards, so that you shall not be able to
stir one finger against the Republic; many eyes and ears shall still observe
and watch you, as they have hitherto done, though you shall not perceive
them.

For what is there, O Catiline, that you can still expect, if night is not
able to veil your nefarious meetings in darkness, and if private houses
cannot conceal the voice of your conspiracy within their walls—if everything is seen and displayed? Change your mind; trust me; forget the
slaughter and conflagration you are meditating. You are hemmed in on
all sides; all your plans are clearer than the day to us; let me remind you
of them. Do you recollect that on the twenty-first of October I said in the
Senate that on a certain day, which was to be the twenty-seventh of October, C. Manlius, the satellite and servant of your audacity, would be in
arms? Was I mistaken, Catiline, not only in so important, so atrocious, so
incredible a fact, but, what is much more remarkable, in the very day? I
said also in the Senate that you had fixed the massacre of the nobles for
the twenty-eighth of October, when many chief men of the Senate had
left Rome, not so much for the sake of saving themselves as of checking
your designs. Can you deny that on that very day you were so hemmed in
by my guards and my vigilance that you were unable to stir one finger

against the Republic; when you said that you would be content with the flight of the rest and the slaughter of us who remained? What? when you made sure that you would be able to seize Praeneste on the first of November by a nocturnal attack, did you not find that that colony was fortified by my order, by my garrison, by my watchfulness and care? You do nothing, you plan nothing, you think of nothing which I not only do not hear, but which I do not see and know every particular of.

Listen while I speak of the night before. You shall now see that I watch far more actively for the safety than you do for the destruction of the Republic. I say that you came the night before (I will say nothing obscurely) into the Scythedealer's street, to the house of Marcus Laeca; that many of your accomplices in the same insanity and wickedness came there, too. Do you dare to deny it? Why are you silent? I will prove it if you do deny it; for I see here in the Senate some men who were there with you.

O ye immortal gods, where on earth are we? in what city are we living? what constitution is ours? There are here—here in our body, O conscript fathers, in this the most holy and dignified assembly of the whole world—men who meditate my death, and the death of all of us, and the destruction of this city, and of the whole world. I, the consul, see them; I ask them their opinion about the Republic, and I do not yet attack, even by words, those who ought to be put to death by the sword. You were, then, O Catiline, at Lecca's that night; you divided Italy into sections; you settled where everyone was to go; you fixed whom you were to leave at Rome, whom you were to take with you; you portioned out the divisions of the city for conflagration; you undertook that you yourself would at once leave the city, and said that there was then only this to delay you, that I was still alive. Two Roman knights were found to deliver you from this anxiety, and to promise that very night, before daybreak, to slay me in my bed. All this I knew almost before your meeting had broken up. I strengthened and fortified my house with a stronger guard; I refused admittance, when they came, to those whom you sent in the morning to salute me, and of whom I had foretold to many eminent men that they would come to me at that time.

As, then, this is the case, O Catiline, continue as you have begun. Leave the city at last; the gates are open; depart. That Manlian camp of yours has been waiting too long for you as its general. And lead forth with you all your friends, or at least as many as you can; purge the city of your presence; you will deliver me from a great fear when there is a wall between me and you. Among us you can dwell no longer—I will not bear it, I will not permit it, I will not tolerate it. Great thanks are due to the immortal gods, and to this very Jupiter Stator in whose temple we are, the most ancient protector of this city, that we have already so often escaped so foul, so horrible, and so deadly an enemy to the Republic. But the safety of the commonwealth must not be too often allowed to be risked on one man. As long as you, O Catiline, plotted against me while I was the consul-elect, I defended myself not with a public guard, but by my own private diligence. When, in the next consular comitia, you wished to slay me when I was actually consul, and your competitors also, in the Campus Martius, I checked your nefarious attempt by the assistance and resources of my own friends, without exciting any disturbance publicly. In short, as often as you attacked me, I by myself opposed you, and that, too, though I saw that my ruin was connected with great disaster to the Republic. But now you are openly attacking the entire Republic.

You are summoning to destruction and devastation the temples of the immortal gods, the houses of the city, the lives of all the citizens; in short, all Italy. Wherefore, since I do not yet venture to do that which is the best thing, and which belongs to my office and to the discipline of our ancestors, I will do that which is more merciful if we regard its rigor, and more expedient for the state. For if I order you to be put to death, the rest of the conspirators will still remain in the Republic; if, as I have long been exhorting you, you depart, your companions, those worthless dregs of the Republic, will be drawn off from the city, too. What is the matter, Catiline? Do you hesitate to do that when I order you, which you were already doing of your own accord? The consul orders an enemy to depart from the city. Do you ask me, are you to go into banishment? I do not order it; but, if you consult me, I advise it.

For what is there, O Catiline, that can now afford you any pleasure in this city? for there is no one in it, except that band of profligate conspirators of yours, who does not fear you—no one who does not hate you. What brand of domestic baseness is not stamped upon your life? What disgraceful circumstance is wanting to your infamy in your private affairs? From what licentiousness have your eyes, from what atrocity have your hands, from what iniquity has your whole body ever abstained? Is there one youth, when you have once entangled him in the temptations of your corruption, to whom you have not held out a sword for audacious crime, or a torch for licentious wickedness?

What? when lately by the death of your former wife you had made your house empty and ready for a new bridal, did you not even add another incredible wickedness to this wickedness? But I pass that over, and willingly allow it to be buried in silence, that so horrible a crime may not be seen to have existed in this city, and not to have been chastised. I pass over the ruin of your fortune, which you know is hanging over you against the ides of the very next month; I come to those things which relate not to the infamy of your private vices, not to your domestic difficulties and baseness, but to the welfare of the Republic and to the lives and safety of us all.

Can the light of this life, O Catiline, can the breath of this atmosphere be pleasant to you, when you know that there is not one man of those here present who is ignorant that you, on the last day of the year, when Lepidus and Tullus were consuls, stood in the assembly armed; that you had prepared your hand for the slaughter of the consuls and chief men of the state, and that no reason or fear of yours hindered your crime and madness but the fortune of the Republic? And I say no more of these things, for they are not unknown to everyone. How often have you endeavored to slay me, both as consul-elect and as actual consul? how many shots of yours, so aimed that they seemed impossible to be escaped, have I avoided by some slight stooping aside, and some dodging, as it were, of my body? You attempt nothing, you execute nothing, you devise nothing that can be kept hid from me at the proper time; and yet you do not cease to attempt and to contrive. How often already has that dagger of yours been wrested from your hands? how often has it slipped through them by some chance, and dropped down? and yet you cannot any longer do without it; and to what sacred mysteries it is consecrated and devoted by you I know not, that you think it necessary to plunge it in the body of the consul.

But now, what is that life of yours that you are leading? For I will speak to you not so as to seem influenced by the hatred I ought to feel, but by pity, nothing of which is due to you. You came a little while ago into the Senate: in so numerous an assembly, who of so many friends and connections of yours saluted you? If this in the memory of man never happened to anyone else, are you waiting for insults by word of mouth, when you are overwhelmed by the most irresistible condemnation of silence? Is it nothing that at your arrival all those seats were vacated? that all the men of consular rank, who had often been marked out by you for slaughter, the very moment you sat down left that part of the benches bare and vacant? With what feelings do you think you ought to bear this? On my honor, if my slaves feared me as all your fellow citizens fear you, I should think I must leave my house. Do not you think you should leave the city? If I saw that I was even undeservedly so suspected and hated by my fellow citizens, I would rather flee from their sight than be gazed at by the hostile eyes of everyone. And do you, who, from the consciousness of your wickedness, know that the hatred of all men is just and has been long due to you, hesitate to avoid the sight and presence of those men whose minds and senses you offend? If your parents feared and hated you, and if you could by no means pacify them, you would, I think, depart somewhere out of their sight. Now, your country, which is the common parent of all of us, hates and fears you, and has no other opinion of you than that you are meditating parricide in her case; and will you neither feel awe of her authority, nor deference for her judgment, nor fear of her power?

And she, O Catiline, thus pleads with you, and after a manner silently speaks to you: there has now for many years been no crime committed but by you; no atrocity has taken place without you; you alone unpunished and unquestioned have murdered the citizens, have harassed and plundered the allies; you alone have had power not only to neglect all laws and investigations, but to overthrow and break through them. Your former actions, though they ought not to have been borne, yet I did bear as well as I could; but now that I should be wholly occupied with fear of you alone, that at every sound I should dread Catiline, that no design should seem possible to be entertained against me which does not proceed from your wickedness, this is no longer endurable. Depart, then, and deliver me from this fear; that, if it be a just one, I may not be destroyed; if an imaginary one, that at least I may at last cease to fear.

If, as I have said, your country were thus to address you, ought she not to obtain her request, even if she were not able to enforce it? What shall I say of your having given yourself into custody? what of your having said, for the sake of avoiding suspicion, that you were willing to dwell in the house of Manius Lepidus? And when you were not received by him, you dared even to come to me, and begged me to keep you in my house; and when you had received answer from me that I could not possibly be safe in the same house with you, when I considered myself in great danger as long as we were in the same city, you came to Quintus Metellus, the praetor, and, being rejected by him, you passed on to your associate, that most excellent man, Marcus Marcellus, who would be, I suppose you thought, most diligent in guarding you, most sagacious in suspecting you, and most bold in punishing you; but how far can we think that man ought to be from bonds and imprisonment who has already judged himself deserving of being given into custody?

Since, then, this is the case, do you hesitate, O Catiline, if you cannot remain here with tranquillity, to depart to some distant land, and to trust your life, saved from just and deserved punishment, to flight and solitude? Make a motion, say you, to the Senate (for that is what you demand), and if this body votes that you ought to go into banishment, you say that you will obey. I will not make such a motion, it is contrary to my principles, and yet I will let you see what these men think of you. Be gone from the city, O Catiline, deliver the Republic from fear; depart into banishment, if that is the word you are waiting for. What now, O Catiline? Do you not perceive, do you not see the silence of these men; they permit it, they say nothing; why wait you for the authority of their words when you see their wishes in their silence?

But had I said the same to this excellent young man, Publius Sextius, or to that brave man, Marcus Metellus, before this time the Senate would deservedly have laid violent hands on me, consul though I be, in this very temple. But as to you, Catiline, while they are quiet they approve, while they permit me to speak they vote, while they are silent they are loud and eloquent. And not they alone, whose authority forsooth is dear to you, though their lives are unimportant, but the Roman knights too, those most honorable and excellent men, and the other virtuous citizens who are now surrounding the Senate, whose numbers you could see, whose desires you could know, and whose voices you a few minutes ago could hear—aye, whose very hands and weapons I have for some time been scarcely able to keep off from you; but those, too, I will easily bring to attend you to the gates if you leave these places you have been long desiring to lay waste.

And yet, why am I speaking? that anything may change your purpose? that you may ever amend your life? that you may meditate flight or think of voluntary banishment? I wish the gods may give you such a mind; though I see, if alarmed at my words you bring your mind to go into banishment, what a storm of unpopularity hangs over me, if not at present, while the memory of your wickedness is fresh, at all events hereafter. But it is worth while to incur that, as long as that is but a private misfortune of my own, and is unconnected with the dangers of the Republic. But we cannot expect that you should be concerned at your own vices, that you should fear the penalties of the laws, or that you should yield to the necessities of the Republic, for you are not, O Catiline, one whom either shame can recall from infamy, or fear from danger, or reason from madness.

Wherefore, as I have said before, go forth, and if you wish to make me, your enemy as you call me, unpopular, go straight into banishment. I shall scarcely be able to endure all that will be said if you do so; I shall scarcely be able to support my load of unpopularity if you do go into banishment at the command of the consul; but if you wish to serve my credit and reputation, go forth with your ill-omened band of profligates; betake yourself to Manlius, rouse up the abandoned citizens, separate yourself from the good ones, wage war against your country, exult in your impious banditti, so that you may not seem to have been driven out by me and gone to strangers, but to have gone invited to your own friends.

Though why should I invite you, by whom I know men have been already sent on to wait in arms for you at Forum Aurelium; who I know has fixed and agreed with Manlius upon a settled day; by whom I know that that silver eagle, which I trust will be ruinous and fatal to you and to all your friends, and to which there was set up in your house a shrine, as it were, of your crimes, has been already sent forward. Need I fear that you can long do without that which you used to worship when going out to murder, and from whose altars you have often transferred your impious hand to the slaughter of citizens?

You will go at last where your unbridled and mad desire has been long hurrying you. And this causes you no grief, but an incredible pleasure. Nature has formed you, desire has trained you, fortune has preserved you for this insanity. Not only did you never desire quiet, but you never even desired any war but a criminal one; you have collected a band of profligates and worthless men, abandoned not only by all fortune but even by hope.

Then what happiness will you enjoy, with what delight will you exult, in what pleasure will you revel, when in so numerous a body of friends you neither hear nor see one good man! All the toils you have gone through have always pointed to this sort of life; your lying on the ground not merely to lie in wait to gratify your unclean desires, but even to accomplish crimes; your vigilance, not only when plotting against the sleep of husbands, but also against the goods of your murdered victims, have all been preparations for this. Now you have an opportunity of displaying your splendid endurance of hunger, of cold, of want of everything; by which in a short time you will find yourself worn out. All this I effected when I procured your rejection from the consulship, that you should be reduced to make attempts on your country as an exile, instead of being able to distress it as consul, and that that which had been wickedly undertaken by you should be called piracy rather than war.

Now that I may remove and avert, O conscript fathers, any in the least reasonable complaint from myself, listen, I beseech you, carefully to what I say, and lay it up in your inmost hearts and minds. In truth, if my country, which is far dearer to me than my life—if all Italy—if the whole Republic were to address me, "Marcus Tullius, what are you doing? will you permit that man to depart whom you have ascertained to be an enemy? whom you see ready to become the general of the war? whom you know to be expected in the camp of the enemy as their chief, the author of all this wickedness, the head of the conspiracy, the instigator of the slaves and abandoned citizens, so that he shall seem not driven out of the city by you, but let loose by you against the city? Will you not order him to be thrown into prison, to be hurried off to execution, to be put to death with the most prompt severity? What hinders you? is it the customs of our ancestors? But even private men have often in this republic slain mischievous citizens. Is it the laws which have been passed about the punishment of Roman citizens? But in this city those who have rebelled against the Republic have never had the rights of citizens. Do you fear odium with posterity? You are showing fine gratitude to the Roman people who have raised you, a man known only by your own actions, of no ancestral renown, through all the degrees of honor at so early an age to the very highest office, if from fear of unpopularity or of any danger you neglect the safety of your fellow citizens. But if you have a fear of unpopularity, is that arising from the imputation of vigor and boldness, or that arising from that of inactivity and indecision most to be feared? When Italy is laid waste by war, when cities are attacked and houses in flames, do you not think that you will be then consumed by a perfect conflagration of hatred?"

To this holy address of the Republic, and to the feelings of those men who entertain the same opinion, I will make this short answer: if, O conscript fathers, I thought it best that Catiline should be punished with death, I would not have given the space of one hour to this gladiator to live in. If, forsooth, those excellent men and most illustrious cities not only did not pollute themselves, but even glorified themselves by the blood of Saturninus, and the Gracchi, and Flaccus, and many others of old time, surely I had no cause to fear lest by slaying this parricidal murderer of the citizens any unpopularity should accrue to me with posterity. And if it did threaten me to ever so great a degree, yet I have always been of the disposition to think unpopularity earned by virtue and glory, not unpopularity.

Though there are some men in this body who either do not see what threatens or dissemble what they do see; who have fed the hope of Catiline by mild sentiments, and have strengthened the rising conspiracy by not believing it; influenced by whose authority many, and they not wicked, but only ignorant, if I punished him would say that I had acted cruelly and tyrannically. But I know that if he arrive at the camp of Manlius to which he is going, there will be no one so stupid as not to see that there has been a conspiracy, no one so hardened as not to confess it. But if this man alone were put to death, I know that this disease of the Republic would be only checked for a while, not eradicated forever. But if he banish himself, and take with him all his friends, and collect at one point all the ruined men from every quarter, then not only will this full-grown plague of the Republic be extinguished and eradicated, but also the root and seed of all future evils.

We have now for a long time, O conscript fathers, lived among these dangers and machinations of conspiracy; but somehow or other, the ripe-ness of all wickedness, and of this long-standing madness and audacity, has come to a head at the time of my consulship. But if this man alone is removed from this piratical crew, we may appear, perhaps, for a short time relieved from fear and anxiety, but the danger will settle down and lie hidden in the veins and bowels of the Republic. As it often happens that men afflicted with a severe disease, when they are tortured with heat and fever, seem at first to be relieved if they drink cold water, but after-ward suffer more and more severely, so this disease which is in the Re-public, if relieved by the punishment of this man, will only get worse and worse, as the rest will be still alive.

Wherefore, O conscript fathers, let the worthless begone—let them separate themselves from the good—let them collect in one place—let them, as I have often said before, be separated from us by a wall; let them cease to plot against the consul in his own house—to surround the tribunal of the city praetor—to besiege the Senate House with swords—to prepare brands and torches to burn the city; let it, in short, be written on the brow of every citizen what are his sentiments about the Republic. I promise you this, O conscript fathers, that there shall be so much dili-gence in us the consuls, so much authority in you, so much virtue in the Roman knights, so much unanimity in all good men, that you shall see everything made plain and manifest by the departure of Catiline—every-thing checked and punished.

With these omens, O Catiline, begone to your impious and nefarious war, to the great safety of the Republic, to your own misfortune and in-jury, and to the destruction of those who have joined themselves to you in every wickedness and atrocity. Then do you, O Jupiter, who were con-secrated by Romulus with the same auspices as this city, whom we rightly call the stay of this city and empire, repel this man and his com-panions from your altars and from the other temples—from the houses and walls of the city—from the lives and fortunes of all the citizens; and overwhelm all the enemies of good men, the foes of the Republic, the robbers of Italy, men bound together by a treaty and infamous alliance of crimes, dead and alive, with eternal punishments.

(TRANSLATED BY WILLIAM ROSE)

JULIUS CAESAR OBJECTS TO ILLEGAL EXECUTION OF THE CAPTURED CONSPIRATORS

[63 B.C.]

Catiline tried vainly to reply: his words were drowned in cries of execration. He fled from Rome, which action was naturally taken as evidence of guilt. Meanwhile, the nervous senators gave full support to Cicero's emergency measures. These included the punishment (without trial) of five of Catiline's fellow conspirators. The first voices demanded death, but Gaius Julius Caesar, not yet forty, though already a man of destiny to those who could read the omens, took a moderate legal stand. A delicate yet bold politician, he was by no means deaf to the justice of some Catilinarian proposals.

Before following Caesar into the Senate chamber, and listening to his gently reasonable voice, let us turn momentarily to Quintilian's Institutes of Oratory, a vast guidebook to eloquence written more than a century after Caesar's death, but nevertheless filled with echoes and anecdotes of his oratorical power. Quintilian reminds us that the conqueror and statesman, the superman, could have been quite as supreme in the courts if he had so willed. He writes: "As for Gaius Caesar, if he had had leisure to devote himself to the courts, he would have been the one orator who could have been considered a serious rival to Cicero. Such are his force, his penetration, and his energy that we realize that he was as vigorous in his speech as in his conduct of war. And yet all these qualities are enhanced by a marvelous elegance of language, of which he was an exceptionally zealous student."

"Take care . . . how your present decrees may affect posterity."

IT IS THE DUTY of all men, conscript fathers, in their deliberations on subjects of difficult determination, to divest themselves of hatred and affection, of revenge and pity. The mind when clouded with such passions cannot easily discern the truth, nor has any man ever gratified his own headstrong inclination and at the same time answered any worthy purpose. When we exercise our judgment only, it has sufficient force, but when passion possesses us, it bears sovereign sway and reason is of no avail. I could produce a great many instances of kings and states pursuing wrong measures when influenced by resentment or compassion. But I had rather set before you the example of our forefathers, and show how they acted in opposition to the impulses of passion, but agreeably to wisdom and sound policy. In the war which we carried on with Perses, King of Macedonia, Rhodes, a mighty and flourishing city, which owed all its grandeur, too, to the Roman aid, proved faithless, and became our enemy: but when the war was ended, and the conduct of the Rhodians came to be taken into consideration, our ancestors pardoned them, that none might say the war had been undertaken more on account of their riches than of injuries. In all the Punic wars, too, though the Carthaginians, both in time of peace and even during a truce, had often insulted us in the most outrageous manner, yet our ancestors never improved any opportunity of retaliating; considering more what was worthy of themselves than what might in justice be done against them.

In like manner, conscript fathers, ought you to take care that the wickedness of Lentulus and the rest of the conspirators weigh not more with you than a regard to your own honor; and that, while you gratify your resentment, you do not forfeit your reputation. If a punishment, indeed, can be invented adequate to their crimes, I approve the extraordinary proposal made; but if the enormity of their guilt is such that human invention cannot find out a chastisement proportioned to it, my opinion is that we ought to be contented with such as the law has provided.

Most of those who have spoken before me have in a pompous and affecting manner lamented the situation of the State; they have enumerated all the calamities of war, and the many distresses of the conquered; virgins and youths violated; children torn from the embraces of their parents; matrons forced to bear the brutal insults of victorious soldiers; temples and private houses plundered; all places filled with flames and slaughter; finally, nothing but arms, carcasses, blood, and lamentations to be seen.

But, for the sake of the immortal gods, to what purpose were such affecting strains? Was it to raise in your minds an abhorrence of the conspiracy, as if he whom so daring and threatening a danger cannot move could be inflamed by the breath of eloquence? No; this is not the way: nor do injuries appear light to anyone that suffers them; many stretch them beyond their due size. But, conscript fathers, different allowances are made to different persons: when such as live in obscurity are transported by passion to the commission of any offenses, there are few who know it, their reputation and fortune being on a level: but those who are invested with great power are placed on an eminence, and their actions viewed by all; and thus the least allowance is made to the highest dignity. There must be no partiality, no hatred, far less any resentment or animosity, in such a station. What goes by the name of passion only in others when seen in men of power is called pride and cruelty.

As for me, conscript fathers, I look on all tortures as far short of what these criminals deserve. But most men remember best what happened last; and, forgetting the guilt of wicked men, talk only of their punishment, if more severe than ordinary. I am convinced that what Decius Silanus, brave and worthy man, said was from his zeal to the state, and that he was biased by neither partiality nor enmity; such is his integrity and moderation, as I well know. But his proposal appears to me not, indeed, cruel (for against such men what can be cruel?), but contrary to the genius of our government. Surely, Silanus, you were urged by fear, or the enormity of the treason, to propose a punishment quite new. How groundless such fear is it is needless to show; especially when, by the diligence of so able a consul, such powerful forces are provided for our security; and, as to the punishment, we may say, what indeed is the truth, that, to those who live in sorrow and misery, death is but a release from trouble; that it is death which puts an end to all the calamities of men, beyond which there is no room for care and joy. But why, in the name of the gods, did not you add to your proposal that they should be punished with stripes? Was it because the Porcian law forbids it? But there are other laws, too, which forbid the putting to death a condemned Roman, and allow him the privilege of banishment. Or was it because whipping is a more severe punishment than death? Can anything be reckoned too cruel or severe against men convicted of such treason? But if stripes are a lighter punishment, how is it consistent to observe the law in a matter of small concern, and disregard it in one that is of greater?

But you will say, "Who will find fault with any punishment decreed against traitors to the state?" I answer, time may, so may sudden conjectures; and fortune, too, that governs the world at pleasure. Whatever punishment is inflicted on these parricides will be justly inflicted. But take care, conscript fathers, how your present decrees may affect posterity. All bad precedents spring from good beginnings, but when the administration is in the hands of wicked or ignorant men, these precedents, at first just, are transferred from proper and deserving objects to such as are not so.

The Lacedaemonians, when they had conquered the Athenians, placed thirty governors over them; who began their power by putting to death, without any trial, such as were remarkably wicked and universally hated. The people were highly pleased at this, and applauded the justice of such executions. But when they had by degrees established their law-less authority, they wantonly butchered both good and bad without dis-tinction; and thus kept the state in awe. Such was the severe punishment which the people, oppressed with slavery, suffered for their foolish joy.

In our own times, when Sulla, after his success, ordered Damasippus, and others of the like character, who raised themselves on the misfor-tunes of the state, to be put to death, who did not commend him for it? All agreed that such wicked and factious instruments, who were con-stantly embroiling the commonwealth, were justly put to death. Yet this was an introduction to a bloody massacre: for whoever coveted his fellow citizen's house, either in town or country, nay, even any curious vase or fine raiment, took care to have the possessor of it put on the list of the proscribed.

Thus they who had rejoiced at the punishment of Damasippus were soon after dragged to death themselves; nor was an end put to this butch-ery till Sulla had glutted all his followers with riches. I do not, indeed, apprehend any such proceedings from M. Cicero, nor from these times. But in so great a city as ours there are various characters and disposi-tions. At another time, and under another consul, who may have an army too at his command, any falsehood may pass for fact; and when, on this precedent, the consul shall, by a decree of the Senate, draw the sword, who is to set bounds to it? who to moderate its fury?

Our ancestors, conscript fathers, never wanted conduct nor courage; nor did they think it unworthy of them to imitate the customs of other nations, if they were useful and praiseworthy. From the Samnites they learned the exercise of arms, and borrowed from them their weapons of war; and most of their ensigns of magistracy from the Tuscans; in a word, they were very careful to practice whatever appeared useful to them, whether among their allies or their enemies; choosing rather to imitate than envy what was excellent.

Now, in those days, in imitation of the custom of Greece, they in-flicted stripes on guilty citizens, and capital punishment on such as were condemned: but when the commonwealth became great and powerful, and the vast number of citizens gave rise to factions; when the innocent began to be circumvented, and other such inconveniences to take place; then the Porcian and other laws were made, which provided no higher punishment than banishment for the greatest crimes. These considera-tions, conscript fathers, appear to me of the greatest weight against our pursuing any new resolution on this occasion: for surely their share of vir-tue and wisdom, who from so small beginnings raised so mighty an em-pire, far exceeds ours, who are scarce able to preserve what they acquired so gloriously.—"What! shall we discharge the conspirators," you will say, "to reinforce Catiline's army?" By no means; but my opinion is this: that their estates should be confiscated; their persons closely confined in the most powerful cities of Italy; and that no one move the Senate or the people for any favor toward them, under the penalty of being declared by the Senate an enemy to the state and the welfare of its members.

(TRANSLATED BY WILLIAM ROSE)

CATO DEMANDS THE IMMEDIATE EXECUTION OF THE CONSPIRATORS

[63 B.C.]

Caesar's cool clarity seemed to convince the majority of the Senate, including Cicero, but then the thirty-three-year-old tribune-elect, Marcus Porcius Cato, harsh, inflexible, and a model "old Roman," took the floor.

"Our liberties, our lives, are in danger."

I AM very differently affected, conscript fathers, when I view our present situation and the danger we are in, and then consider the proposals made by some senators who have spoken before me. They appear to me to have reasoned only about the punishment of those who have entered into a combination to make war on their country, on their parents, on religion, and private property; whereas, our present circumstances warn us rather to guard against them than to consider in what manner we shall punish them. You may take vengeance for other crimes after they are committed; but if you do not prevent the commission of this, when it is once accomplished, in vain will you have recourse to the tribunals. When the city is once taken, no resource remains to the conquered citizens.

Now, I conjure you, by the immortal gods! you who have always valued your splendid palaces, your pictures, your statues, more than the welfare of the state; if you are desirous to preserve these things which, whatever their real value be, you are so fond of; if you would have leisure for pursuing your pleasures; rouse for once out of your lethargy, and take on you the defense of the state. The debate is not about the public revenues, nor the oppression of our allies; no, our liberties, our lives, are in danger.

Often, conscript fathers, have I spoken in this assembly; often have I complained of the luxury and avarice of our fellow citizens; on which account I bear the enmity of many: I, who never indulged myself in any vice, nor even cherished the thought of any, could not easily pardon the crimes of others. And though you little regarded my remonstrances, yet the commonwealth remained firm; her native strength supported her even under the negligence of her governors. But the present debate is not about the goodness or depravity of our morals, nor about the greatness or prosperity of the Roman Empire: no; it is whether this empire, such as it is, continue our own, or, together with ourselves, fall a prey to the enemy.

And, in such a case, will anyone talk of gentleness or mercy? We have long since lost the true names of things. To give away what belongs to others is called generosity; to attempt what is criminal, fortitude; and thence the state is reduced to the brink of ruin. Let them, since such is the fashion of the times, be generous from the spoils of our allies; merciful to the plunderers of the treasury; but let them not be prodigal of our blood, and, by sparing a few bad citizens, destroy all the good.

Gaius Caesar has just now spoken, with great strength and accuracy, concerning life and death; taking for fictions, I doubt not, the vulgar notions of an infernal world, where the bad, separated from the good, are confined to dark, frightful, and melancholy abodes. Accordingly, his proposal is that their estates be confiscated and their persons confined in the corporate towns; from an apprehension, I imagine, that if they were kept at Rome they might be rescued by force, either by their fellow conspirators or a mercenary mob; as if wicked and profligate persons were only to be found in this city, and not all over Italy; or as if there were not more encouragement to the attempts of the desperate where there is least strength to resist them.

This, then, is an empty proposal, if he fears any danger from them; but if, amid this so great and universal consternation, he alone is void of fear, so much the more does it concern me to be afraid, both for myself and you.

Hence, in determining the fate of Lentulus and the other prisoners, be assured that you likewise determine that of Catiline's army and all the conspirators. The more vigor and resolution you exert, so much the less spirit and courage will they have; but if they observe the least remissness in your proceedings, they will presently fall on you with fury.

Do not think it was by arms our ancestors raised the state from so small beginnings to such grandeur: if so, we should have it in its highest luster; as having a greater number of allies and citizens, of arms and horses, than they had. But there were other things from which they de-

rived their greatness, such as we are entirely without. They were industrious at home, and exercised an equitable government abroad; their
minds were free in council, swayed by neither crimes nor passion. Instead
of these virtues, we have luxury and avarice; poverty in the state, and
great wealth in the members of it: we admire riches, and abandon ourselves to idleness; we make no distinction between the virtuous and the
wicked; and all the rewards of virtue are possessed by ambition. Nor is it
at all strange, while each of you pursues his separate interest; while you
abandon yourselves to pleasure at home, and here in the Senate are slaves
to money or favor, that attacks are made on the state when thus forsaken.
But no more of this.

Romans of the highest quality have conspired to destroy their country,
and are endeavoring to engage the Gauls, the sworn enemies of the Roman name, to join them. The commander of the enemy is hovering over
us with an army, and yet at this very juncture you delay and hesitate how
to proceed against such of the conspirators as are seized within your
walls. Would you extend your compassion toward them? Be it so; they
are young men only, and have offended through ambition: send them
away armed, too; what would be the consequence of this gentleness and
mercy? Why, this: when they got arms in their hands, it would prove
your utter ruin.

Our situation is indeed dangerous; but you are not afraid: yes, you
are very much; only from effeminacy and want of spirit, you are in suspense, everyone waiting the motions of another; trusting, perhaps, to the
immortal gods, who have often saved this commonwealth in the greatest
dangers. But assistance is not obtained from the gods by idle vows and
supplications, like those of women; it is by vigilance, activity, and wise
counsels that all undertakings succeed. If you resign yourselves to sloth
and idleness, it will be in vain to implore the assistance of the gods; you
will only provoke them to anger, and they will make you feel your un-
worthiness.

In the days of our ancestors, T. Manlius Torquatus, in a war with the
Gauls, ordered his son to be put to death for having engaged the enemy
without orders; and thus a young man of great hopes was punished for
too much bravery. And do you demur about the doom of the most barbarous parricides?

Their present offense, perhaps, is unsuitable to their former character:
show a tender regard then for the dignity of Lentulus, if you find that he
himself ever showed any for his own chastity, for his honor, for gods or
men; pardon Cethegus, in consideration of his youth, if this is not the second time of his making war on his country: for what need I mention

Gabinius, Statilius, Coeparius? who, if they had possessed the least degree of reflection, would never have embarked in such wicked designs against the state.

Finally, conscript fathers, were there any room for a wrong step on this occasion, I should suffer you to be corrected by the consequences, since you disregard my reasonings. But we are surrounded on all sides: Catiline is hovering over our heads with an army; we have enemies within the walls, and in the very heart of the city. No preparations can be made, no measures taken, without their knowledge: hence the greater reason for dispatch.

My opinion, then, is this: that since by a detestable combination of profligate citizens the state is brought into the greatest danger; since they are convicted, by the evidence of Volturcius, and the deputies of the Allobroges, and their own confession, to have entered into a conspiracy for destroying their fellow citizens and native country, by slaughter, conflagration, and other unheard-of cruelties; they be put to death, according to the ancient usage, as being condemned by their own mouths.

(TRANSLATED BY WILLIAM ROSE)

Although himself a Stoic of the sternest caste, Cato—by appealing to them as embattled property holders—had cleverly voiced the fears of most of the senators. Also, without saying so, he had suggested that Caesar was merely a politician with a foot in the other camp. Again the Senate called for the immediate execution of five of the Catilinarian ringleaders, which summary and unconstitutional act was carried out by Cicero as consul. Momentarily he was hailed as pater patriae (an unusual honor in republican Rome), but he was bitterly to repent of having put Roman citizens to death without trial. This ill-advised deed, which his enemies were to use against him for years, left a permanent stain on his reputation.

CATILINE RALLIES HIS SMALL,
DESPERATE ARMY ON THE
EVE OF BATTLE

[62 B.C.]

Catiline, with a tiny, ill-equipped army, tried to make a dash for Gaul, but was forced to offer battle to a much larger force sent out to crush him. The struggle took place at Pistoria (modern Pistoia), rather more than two hundred miles from Rome. Before the fighting began Catiline sent his horses behind the lines so that no one would be tempted to flee. The historian Mommsen, who detested Catiline, admitted that at this critical moment he showed that "nature had destined him for no ordinary things . . . he knew at once how to command as a general and how to fight as a soldier." And Sallust, whose vivid history of the plot is somewhat vitiated by his anxiety to prove that his hero Caesar had no connection with it, puts this noble before-the-battle speech into the mouth of Catiline. Perhaps these are his words—more likely they merely preserve the tenor of his words.

The speech is a fine example of the military harangue with which officers have inspired their troops, and Napoleon, at his peak, gave the final momentum to invincible armies.

"Your spirit, your age, your valor, give me confidence—to say nothing of necessity, which makes even cowards brave."

I AM WELL AWARE, soldiers, that words cannot inspire courage; and that a spiritless army cannot be rendered active, or a timid army valiant, by the speech of its commander. Whatever courage is in the heart of a man, whether from nature or from habit, so much will be shown by him in the field; and on him whom neither glory nor danger can move, exhortation is bestowed in vain; for the terror in his breast stops his ears.

I have called you together, however, to give you a few instructions, and to explain to you, at the same time, my reasons for the course which I have adopted. You all know, soldiers, how severe a penalty the inactivity and cowardice of Lentulus has brought upon himself and us; and how, while waiting for reinforcements from the city, I was unable to march into Gaul. In what situation our affairs now are, you all understand as well as myself. Two armies of the enemy, one on the side of Rome, and the other on that of Gaul, oppose our progress; while the want of corn, and of other necessaries, prevents us from remaining, however strongly we may desire to remain, in our present position. Whithersoever we would go, we must open a passage with our swords. I conjure you, therefore, to maintain a brave and resolute spirit; and to remember, when you advance to battle, that on your own right hands depend riches, honor, and glory, with the enjoyment of your liberty and of your country. If we conquer, all will be safe; we shall have provisions in abundance, and the colonies and corporate towns will open their gates to us. But if we lose the victory through want of courage, those same places will turn against us; for neither place nor friend will protect him whom his arms have not protected. Besides, soldiers, the same exigency does not press upon our adversaries, as presses upon us; we fight for our country, for our liberty, for our life; they contend for what but little concerns them, the power of a small party. Attack them, therefore, with so much the greater confidence, and call to mind your achievements of old.

We might, with the utmost ignominy, have passed the rest of our days in exile. Some of you, after losing your property, might have waited at Rome for assistance from others. But because such a life, to men of spirit, was disgusting and unendurable, you resolved upon your present course. If you wish to quit it, you must exert all your resolution, for none but conquerors have exchanged war for peace. To hope for safety in flight, when you have turned away from the enemy the arms by which the body is defended, is indeed madness. In battle, those who are most afraid are always in most danger; but courage is equivalent to a rampart.

When I contemplate you, soldiers, and when I consider your past exploits, a strong hope of victory animates me. Your spirit, your age, your valor, give me confidence—to say nothing of necessity, which makes even cowards brave. To prevent the numbers of the enemy from surrounding us, our confined situation is sufficient. But should fortune be unjust to your valor, take care not to lose your lives unavenged; take care not to be taken and butchered like cattle, rather than fighting like men, to leave to your enemies a bloody and mournful victory.

(TRANSLATED BY JOHN S. WATSON)

Catiline, fighting bravely, was killed in the brief battle, which resulted in a decisive victory for the senatorial forces. Opportunist or not, Catiline had endeared himself to the Roman poor, who for years, it is said, strewed flowers on his grave.

EPILOGUE

As the stakes in Roman politics became higher, life for a moderate like Cicero, however subtle his trimming, became increasingly difficult. Amazingly, a playful note appears fitfully in his letters to his old friend Atticus, almost to the very end. As an upholder of the Roman constitution (almost as vague an entity as the British constitution), he must have been quite as vexed with his friends as with his enemies, though he was inclined to forgive a few personages almost anything. He accepted Caesar but deplored his sweep toward despotism. Thus, while not participating in the assassination, he privately applauded it. But, after his cautious, safety-first life, he now made an irretrievable mistake. He refused to co-operate with Mark Antony, "Caesar's pinchbeck imitator." Cicero went, as the saying is, into opposition, either delivering in the Senate or in the Forum or otherwise making public fourteen Philippics against Antony—echoes, of course, of Demosthenes' speeches against Philip of Macedon.

During the republican reaction, which culminated in Antony's defeat at Mutina, it looked as if Cicero's attempt to stave off the shift to despotism might work. But suddenly whole armies deserted to Antony, and young Octavian, Caesar's heir, who had temporarily co-operated with Cicero, now joined Antony and Lepidus to form the Second Triumvirate. This meant that Cicero was doomed: Antony's price for his adherence to the coalition was Cicero's head —in fact, his name stood first on the list of two hundred finally proscribed. When the triumvirs' assassins came upon him in the grounds of his Formian villa, he met death stoically. His head and hands were fastened up above the rostrum at Rome.

Besides speeches, delightful letters, and urbane philosophical writings, Cicero left an unsurpassed series of works, De Oratore, Brutus and Orator, on the character and training of the orator, on the history of oratory, and on the ideal orator. No one else has been able to combine theory with an immense amount of experience in such lively profusion. The unknown Greek, miscalled Longinus, who probably wrote the celebrated treatise On the Sublime (or better, Of the Height of Eloquence) in the first century B.C., compared Demosthenes and Cicero in these words: "Our orator [Demosthenes], owing to the fact that in his vehemence—aye, and in his speed, power, and intensity—he can as it were consume by fire and carry away all before him, may be compared to a thunderbolt or flash of lightning. Cicero, on the other hand, it seems to me, after the manner of a widespread conflagration, rolls on with all-devouring flames, having within him an ample and abiding store of fire, distributed now at this point now at that, and fed by an unceasing succession."

Whatever the differences, each was supreme in his own language, and each was brought to a violent end by the exercise of his art.

PART TWO

THE CHRISTIAN TRIUMPH

IN THE ROME of the early Empire—in the Rome, that is, of the Julio-Claudian and Flavian emperors (none of whom was much interested in free speech except for himself), there was no apparent need of, and little opportunity for, oratory. It was toward the end of the first century A.D. that the historian Tacitus, in a mood of irony and nostalgia, wrote a dialogue on the decline of Roman oratory, the closing sections of which have a perennial application:

"Great eloquence, like fire, grows with its material; it becomes fiercer with movement, and brighter as it burns. On this same principle was developed in our state, too, the eloquence of antiquity. Although even the modern orator has attained all that the circumstances of a settled, quiet, and prosperous community allow, still in the disorder and license of the past more seemed to be within the reach of the speaker, when, amid a universal confusion that needed one guiding hand, he exactly adapted his wisdom to the bewildered people's capacity of conviction. . . .

"There is, indeed, a wide difference between having to speak on a theft, a technical point, a judicial decision, and on bribery at elections, the plundering of the allies, and the massacre of citizens. Though it is better that these evils should not befall us, and the best condition of the state is that in which we are spared such sufferings, still when they did occur they supplied a grand material for the orator. His mental powers rise with the dignity of his subject, and no one can produce a noble and brilliant speech unless he has got an adequate case. Demosthenes, I take it, does not owe his fame to his speeches against his guardians, and it is not his defense of Publius Quintius or of Licinius Archias that makes Cicero a great orator; it is his Catiline, his Milo, his Verres, and Antonius that have shed over him this luster.

"Not, indeed, that it was worth the state's while to endure bad citizens that orators might have plenty of matter for their speeches, but, as I now and then remind you, we must remember the point, and understand that we are speaking of an art that arose more easily in stormy and unquiet times. Who knows not that it is better and more profitable to enjoy peace than to be harassed by war? Yet war produces more good soldiers than peace. Eloquence is on the same footing. The oftener she has stood, so to say, in the battlefield, the more wounds she has inflicted and received, the mightier her antagonist, the sharper the conflicts she has freely chosen, the higher and more splendid has been her rise, and ennobled by these contests she lives in the praises of mankind. . . .

"Could a community be found in which no one did wrong, an orator would be as superfluous among its innocent people as a physician among the healthy. As the healing art is of very little use and makes very little progress in nations that enjoy particularly robust constitutions and vigorous frames, so the orator gets an inferior and less splendid renown where a sound morality and willing obedience to authority prevail. What need there of long speeches in the Senate when the best men are soon of one mind, or of endless harangues to the people when political questions are decided not by an ignorant multitude, but by one man of pre-eminent wisdom? What need of voluntary prosecutions when crimes are so rare and slight, or of defenses full of spiteful insinuation and exceeding proper bounds when the clemency of the judge offers itself to the accused in his peril?"

Certainly Roman oratory had degenerated into legal quibbling, pedantic display, obsequious panegyrics. Imperial peace and order did not encourage eloquence in the Senate or in the Forum—and it never does.

But in a remote, insignificant corner of the Empire there had arisen, unnoticed, a new art of oratory. The way of speaking may not have been new, for pedants could say that others had spoken in parables (both prophets and rabbis had done that), but the message was unquestionably new.

JESUS OF NAZARETH DELIVERS THE SERMON ON THE MOUNT

[*c.* A.D. 33]

The Gospel according to St. Matthew relates that Jesus "went up into a mountain: and when he was set, his disciples came unto him. And he opened his mouth, and taught them."

Thus, very simply, is the stage set for the most famous of all speeches, whose predominant theme is the supremacy of the law of love.

"For where your treasure is, there will your heart be also."

B LESSED are the poor in spirit:
For theirs is the kingdom of heaven.

Blessed are they that mourn:
For they shall be comforted.

Blessed are the meek:
For they shall inherit the earth.

Blessed are they which do hunger and thirst after righteousness:
For they shall be filled.

Blessed are the merciful:
For they shall obtain mercy.

Blessed are the pure in heart:
For they shall see God.

Blessed are the peacemakers:
For they shall be called the children of God.

Blessed are they which are persecuted for righteousness' sake:
For theirs is the kingdom of heaven.

Blessed are ye, when men shall revile you, and persecute you, and shall
say all manner of evil against you falsely, for my sake.
Rejoice, and be exceeding glad: for great is your reward in heaven: for
so persecuted they the prophets which were before you.

Ye are the salt of the earth: but if the salt have lost his savour, wherewith shall it be salted? it is thenceforth good for nothing, but to be cast
out, and to be trodden under foot of men.
Ye are the light of the world. A city that is set on a hill cannot be hid.

Neither do men light a candle, and put it under a bushel, but on a candle-stick; and it giveth light unto all that are in the house. Let your light so shine before men, that they may see your good works, and glorify your Father which is in heaven.

Think not that I am come to destroy the law, or the prophets: I am not come to destroy, but to fulfil. For verily I say unto you, "Till heaven and earth pass, one jot or one tittle shall in no wise pass from the law, till all be fulfilled." Whosoever therefore shall break one of these least com-mandments, and shall teach men so, he shall be called the least in the kingdom of heaven: but whosoever shall do and teach them, the same shall be called great in the kingdom of heaven. For I say unto you, "Ex-cept your righteousness shall exceed the righteousness of the scribes and Pharisees, ye shall in no case enter into the kingdom of heaven."

Ye have heard that it was said by them of old time, "Thou shalt not kill"; and whosoever shall kill shall be in danger of the judgment. But I say unto you, "Whosoever is angry with his brother without a cause shall be in danger of the judgment: and whosoever shall say to his brother, 'Raca,' shall be in danger of the council: but whosoever shall say, 'Thou fool,' shall be in danger of hell fire." Therefore if thou bring thy gift to the altar, and there rememberest that thy brother hath ought against thee; leave there thy gift before the altar, and go thy way; first be reconciled to thy brother, and then come and offer thy gift. Agree with thine adversary quickly, while thou art in the way with him; lest at any time the adversary deliver thee to the judge, and the judge deliver thee to the officer, and thou be cast into prison. Verily I say unto thee, "Thou shalt by no means come out thence, till thou has paid the uttermost farthing."

Ye have heard that it was said by them of old time, "Thou shalt not commit adultery." But I say unto you, "Whosoever looketh on a woman to lust after her hath committed adultery with her already in his heart. And if thy right eye offend thee, pluck it out, and cast it from thee: for it is profitable for thee that one of thy members should perish, and not that thy whole body should be cast into hell. And if thy right hand offend thee, cut it off, and cast it from thee: for it is profitable for thee that one of thy members should perish, and not that thy whole body should be cast into hell." It hath been said, "Whosoever shall put away his wife, let him give her a writing of divorcement." But I say unto you, "Whosoever shall put away his wife, saving for the cause of fornication, causeth her to commit adultery: and whosoever shall marry her that is divorced com-mitteth adultery."

Again, ye have heard that it hath been said by them of old time, "Thou shalt not forswear thyself, but shalt perform unto the Lord thine oaths."

But I say unto you, "Swear not at all; neither by heaven; for it is God's throne: nor by the earth; for it is his footstool: neither by Jerusalem; for it is the city of the great King. Neither shalt thou swear by thy head, because thou canst not make one hair white or black. But let your communication be, 'Yea, yea'; 'Nay, nay': for whatsoever is more than these cometh of evil."

Ye have heard that it hath been said, "An eye for an eye, and a tooth for a tooth." But I say unto you, "Resist not evil: but whosoever shall smite thee on thy right cheek, turn to him the other also. And if any man will sue thee at the law, and take away thy coat, let him have thy cloak also. And whosoever shall compel thee to go a mile, go with him twain. Give to him that asketh thee, and from him that would borrow of thee turn not thou away."

Ye have heard that it hath been said, "Thou shalt love thy neighbour, and hate thine enemy." But I say unto you, "Love your enemies, bless them that curse you, do good to them that hate you, and pray for them which despitefully use you, and persecute you; that ye may be the children of your Father which is in heaven: for he maketh his sun to rise on the evil and on the good, and sendeth rain on the just and on the unjust." For if ye love them which love you, what reward have ye? do not even the publicans the same? And if ye salute your brethren only, what do ye more than others? do not even the publicans so? Be ye therefore perfect, even as your Father which is in heaven is perfect.

Take heed that ye do not your alms before men, to be seen of them: otherwise ye have no reward of your Father which is in heaven. Therefore when thou doest thine alms, do not sound a trumpet before thee, as the hypocrites do in the synagogues and in the streets, that they may have glory of men. Verily I say unto you, "They have their reward." But when thou doest alms, let not thy left hand know what thy right hand doeth: that thine alms may be in secret: and thy Father which seeth in secret himself shall reward thee openly.

And when thou prayest, thou shalt not be as the hypocrites are: for they love to pray standing in the synagogues and in the corners of the streets, that they may be seen of men. Verily I say unto you, "They have their reward." But thou, when thou prayest, enter into thy closet, and when thou has shut thy door, pray to thy Father which is in secret; and thy Father which seeth in secret shall reward thee openly. But when ye pray, use not vain repetitions, as the heathen do: for they think that they shall be heard for their much speaking. Be not ye therefore like unto them: for your Father knoweth what things ye have need of, before ye ask him. After this manner therefore pray ye:

Our Father which art in heaven,
Hallowed be thy name.
Thy kingdom come.
Thy will be done
In earth, as it is in heaven.

Give us this day
Our daily bread.
And forgive us our debts,
As we forgive our debtors.
And lead us not into temptation,
But deliver us from evil:

For thine is the kingdom,
And the power,
And the glory,
For ever. Amen.

For if ye forgive men their trespasses, your heavenly Father will also forgive you: but if ye forgive not men their trespasses, neither will your Father forgive your trespasses.

Moreover when ye fast, be not, as the hypocrites, of a sad countenance: for they disfigure their faces, that they may appear unto men to fast. Verily I say unto you, "They have their reward." But thou, when thou fastest, anoint thine head, and wash thy face; that thou appear not unto men to fast, but unto thy Father which is in secret: and thy Father, which seeth in secret shall reward thee openly.

Lay not up for yourselves treasures upon earth,
Where moth and rust doth corrupt,
And where thieves break through and steal:

But lay up for yourselves treasures in heaven,
Where neither moth nor rust doth corrupt,
And where thieves do not break through nor steal.

For where your treasure is, there will your heart be also.

The light of the body is the eye: if therefore thine eye be single, thy whole body shall be full of light. But if thine eye be evil, thy whole body shall be full of darkness. If therefore the light that is in thee be darkness, how great is that darkness!

No man can serve two masters: for either he will hate the one, and love the other; or else he will hold to the one, and despise the other. Ye cannot serve God and Mammon.

Therefore I say unto you, "Take no thought for your life, what ye shall eat, or what ye shall drink; nor yet for your body, what ye shall put on." Is not the life more than meat, and the body than raiment? Behold the fowls of the air: for they sow not, neither do they reap, nor gather into barns; yet your heavenly Father feedeth them. Are ye not much better than they? Which of you by taking thought can add one cubit unto his stature? And why take ye thought for raiment? Consider the lilies of the field, how they grow; they toil not, neither do they spin: and yet I say unto you that even Solomon in all his glory was not arrayed like one of these.

Wherefore, if God so clothe the grass of the field, which today is, and to-morrow is cast into the oven, shall he not much more clothe you, O ye of little faith? Therefore take no thought, saying, "What shall we eat?" or, "What shall we drink?" or, "Wherewithal shall we be clothed?" (For after all these things do the Gentiles seek): for your heavenly Father knoweth that ye have need of all these things. But seek ye first the kingdom of God, and his righteousness; and all these things shall be added unto you. Take therefore no thought for the morrow: for the morrow shall take thought for the things of itself. Sufficient unto the day is the evil thereof.

Judge not, that ye be not judged. For with what judgment ye judge, ye shall be judged: and with what measure ye mete, it shall be measured to you again. And why beholdest thou the mote that is in thy brother's eye, but considerest not the beam that is in thine own eye? Or how wilt thou say to thy brother, "Let me pull out the mote out of thine eye"; and, behold, a beam is in thine own eye? Thou hypocrite, first cast out the beam out of thine own eye; and then shalt thou see clearly to cast out the mote out of thy brother's eye.

Give not that which is holy unto the dogs,
Neither cast ye your pearls before swine,
Lest they trample them under their feet,
And turn again and rend you.

Ask, and it shall be given you;
Seek, and ye shall find;
Knock, and it shall be opened unto you:

> For every one that asketh receiveth;
> And he that seeketh findeth;
> And to him that knocketh it shall be opened.

Or what man is there of you, whom if his son ask bread, will he give him a stone? Or if he ask a fish, will he give him a serpent? If ye then, being evil, know how to give good gifts unto your children, how much more shall your Father which is in heaven give good things to them that ask him? Therefore all things whatsoever ye would that men should do to you, do ye even so to them: for this is the law and the prophets.

Enter ye in at the strait gate: for wide is the gate, and broad is the way, that leadeth to destruction, and many there be which go in thereat: because strait is the gate, and narrow is the way, which leadeth unto life, and few there be that find it.

Beware of false prophets, which come to you in sheep's clothing, but inwardly they are ravening wolves. Ye shall know them by their fruits. Do men gather grapes of thorns, or figs of thistles? Even so every good tree bringeth forth good fruit; but a corrupt tree bringeth forth evil fruit. A good tree cannot bring forth evil fruit, neither can a corrupt tree bring forth good fruit. Every tree that bringeth not forth good fruit is hewn down, and cast into the fire. Wherefore by their fruits ye shall know them.

Not every one that saith unto me, "Lord, Lord," shall enter into the kingdom of heaven; but he that doeth the will of my Father which is in heaven. Many will say to me in that day, "Lord, Lord, have we not prophesied in thy name? and in thy name have cast out devils? and in thy name done many wonderful works?" And then will I profess unto them, "I never knew you: depart from me, ye that work iniquity."

Therefore whosoever heareth these sayings of mine, and doeth them, I will liken him unto a wise man, which built his house upon a rock; and the rain descended, and the floods came and the winds blew, and beat upon that house; and it fell not: for it was founded upon a rock. And every one that heareth these sayings of mine, and doeth them not, shall be likened unto a foolish man, which built his house upon the sand: and the rain descended, and the floods came, and the winds blew, and beat upon that house; and it fell: and great was the fall of it.

(AUTHORIZED VERSION)

It would be an impertinence to try to assess briefly the historical importance of the Sermon on the Mount. Rather than attempt the impossible, let us quote from T. R. Glover's fascinating book, The Conflict of Religions in the Early Roman Empire—nothing more apt has been written about Jesus as a speaker.

"What stamps the language of Jesus invariably is its delicate ease, implying a sensibility to every real aspect of the matter in hand—a sense of mastery and peace. Men marveled at the charm of his words. . . . The homely parable may be in other hands coarse enough, but the parables of Jesus have a quality about them after all these years that leaves one certain that he smiled as he spoke them. There is something of the same kind to be felt in Cowper's letters, but in the stronger nature the gift is of more significance. At the cost of a little study of human character, and close reading of the Synoptists, and some careful imagination, it is possible to see him as he spoke—the flash of the eye, the smile on the lip, the gesture of the hand, all the natural expression of himself and his thought that a man unconsciously gives in speaking, when he has forgotten himself in his matter and his hearer—his physiognomy, in fact. We realize very soon his complete mastery of the various aspects of what he says. That he realizes every implication of his words is less likely, for there is a spontaneity about them —they are 'out of the abundance of his heart'; the form is not studied; they are for the man and the moment. But they imply the speaker and his whole relation to God and man—they cannot help implying this, and that is their charm. Living words, flashed out on the spur of the moment from the depths of him, they are the man. It was not idly that the early Church used to say, 'Remember the words of the Lord Jesus.' On any showing, it is of importance to learn the mind of one whose speech is so full of life, and it is happily possible to do this from even the small collection we possess of his recorded sayings."

CHRYSOSTOM PREACHES ON THE FALL
OF EUTROPIUS, MINISTER OF STATE

[A.D. 398]

After the fabulous missionary travels of St. Paul, Christianity spread steadily throughout the Roman Empire in the face of persecution and innumerable martyrdoms. An illegal sect appealing at first mainly to the poor, the weak, the miserable, had little need for learning and conscious eloquence. It was sufficient to pass on the glad tidings of the New Testament simply, directly, fearlessly. The forms as well as the substance of pagan culture were suspect and continually denounced. But inevitably the two currents mingled more and more as the new faith began to crystallize into doctrine while in fierce conflict with other religions.

In 303 the Emperor Diocletian began the last full-scale persecution of Christianity and failed in his purpose. Nine years later Constantine took the cross as his symbol in the victorious battle against Maxentius, and in 323 he made Christianity the official religion of the Roman Empire. In 325 the first general council of the Church was held at Nicaea, where after long, bitter argument the Arian doctrine that Christ was not of the same nature but of like nature with God was rejected for the Athanasian doctrine that Christ was of the same nature with God the Father. At last, after two hundred and fifty years, the springs of Christian learning, argument, eloquence, could pour forth comparatively unobstructed.

We turn to the great preacher who is always remembered by the name he won for himself, Chrysostom, "the golden-mouthed" (c. 346–407). Born into a noble family in the rich city of Antioch and christened John, he became the favorite pupil of the famous pagan teacher of rhetoric, Libanius, and would no doubt have succeeded his master had not his devout mother drawn him into religion. Completely dedicated, he went into the desert for nearly a decade of study and self-discipline. Illness rather than ambition brought him back to Antioch, where he was ordained deacon and later presbyter, or elder, under the city's bishop.

It was while presbyter, in 387, that he gave his memorable series of sermons, "On the Statues," to allay the terrors of the people of Antioch. In an hour of rage against extra taxes they had torn down and dragged through the streets statues of the Emperor Theodosius and his deceased wife, and then in agony they awaited the imperial punishment. Chrysostom succeeded in calming them with his homilies on the Christian scorn of death and perhaps saved them from the brutal retribution that was visited on some cities at the time. In this case the baths were closed and Antioch deprived of its civil dignity for a period.

In 398 Chrysostom was suddenly called to the archbishopric of Constantinople by the Emperor Arcadius, and was, in fact, spirited away secretly by the Emperor's agents lest his devout parishioners prevent him from going. In Constantinople his piety, his charity, and his eloquence at once won him a vast following, but his denunciation of corruption in the clergy and in the court made him enemies in high places.

When the cruel and avaricious minister, Eutropius, fell from the Emperor's favor, he fled to Santa Sophia for sanctuary, although while in office he had tried to abolish ecclesiastical asylum. Chrysostom saved the wretch from a mob and then preached one of his most dramatic sermons while Eutropius clung to a column of the Holy Table, in full view of the congregation.

"For who was more exalted than this man?"

"VANITY OF VANITIES, all is vanity"—it is always seasonable to utter this, but more especially at the present time. Where are now the brilliant surroundings of thy consulship? where are the gleaming torches? Where is the dancing, and the noise of dancers' feet, and the banquets and the festivals, where are the garlands and the curtains of the theater, where is the applause that greeted thee in the city, where the acclamation in the hippodrome and the flatteries of spectators? They are gone—all gone: a wind has blown upon the tree, shattering down all its leaves, and showing it to us quite bare, and shaken from its very root; for so great has been the violence of the blast that it has given a shock to all these fibers of the tree and threatens to tear it up from the roots. Where now are your feigned friends, where are your drinking parties, and your suppers, where is the swarm of parasites, and the wine that used to be poured forth all day long, and the manifold dainties invented by your cooks, where are they who courted your power and did and said everything to win your favor? They were all mere visions of the night, and dreams that have vanished with the dawn of day: they were spring flowers, and when the spring was over they all withered: they were a shadow that has passed away—they were a smoke that has dispersed, bubbles that have burst, cobwebs that have been rent in pieces. Therefore we chant continually this spiritual song—"Vanity of vanities, all is vanity." For this saying ought to be continually written on our walls and garments, in the market place and in the house, on the streets and on the doors and entrances, and above all on the conscience of each one, and to be a perpetual theme for meditation. And inasmuch as deceitful things and maskings and pretense seem to many to be realities it behooves each one every day both at supper and at breakfast, and in social assemblies, to say to his neighbor and to hear his neighbor say in return, "Vanity of vanities, all is vanity."

Was I not continually telling thee that wealth was a runaway? But you would not heed me. Did I not tell thee that it was an unthankful servant? But you would not be persuaded. Behold, actual experience has now proved that it is not only a runaway and ungrateful servant, but also a murderous one, for it is this which has caused thee now to fear and tremble. Did I not say to thee when you continually rebuked me for speaking the truth, "I love thee better than they do who flatter thee?" "I who reprove thee care more for thee than they who pay thee court?"

Did I not add to these words by saying that the wounds of friends were more to be relied upon than the voluntary kisses of enemies. If you had submitted to my wounds, their kisses would not have wrought thee this destruction: for my wounds work health, but their kisses have produced an incurable disease. Where are now thy cupbearers, where are they who cleared the way for thee in the market place and sounded thy praises endlessly in the ears of all? They have fled, they have disowned thy friendship, they are providing for their own safety by means of thy distress. But I do not act thus—nay, in thy misfortune I do not abandon thee, and now when thou art fallen I protect and tend thee. And the Church, which you treated as an enemy, has opened her bosom and received thee into it; whereas the theaters, which you courted and about which you were oftentimes indignant with me, have betrayed and ruined thee. And yet I never ceased saying to thee, "Why doest thou these things?" "Thou art exasperating the Church, and casting thyself down headlong." Yet thou didst hurry away from all my warnings. And now the hippodromes, having exhausted thy wealth, have whetted the sword against thee, but the Church, which experienced thy untimely wrath, is hurrying in every direction in her desire to pluck thee out of the net.

And I say these things now not as trampling upon one who is prostrate, but from a desire to make those who are still standing more secure; not by way of irritating the sores of one who has been wounded, but rather to preserve those who have not yet been wounded in sound health; not by way of sinking one who is tossed by the waves, but as instructing those who are sailing with a favorable breeze, so that they may not become overwhelmed. And how may this be effected? By observing the vicissitudes of human affairs. For even this man, had he stood in fear of vicissitude, would not have experienced it; but whereas neither his own conscience nor the counsels of others wrought any improvement in him, do ye at least who plume yourselves on your riches profit by his calamity: for nothing is weaker than human affairs. Whatever term, therefore, one may employ to express their insignificance, it will fall short of the reality: whether he calls them smoke, or grass, or a dream, or spring flowers, or by any other name; so perishable are they, and more naught than nonentities; but that together with their nothingness they have also a very perilous element we have a proof before us. For who was more exalted than this man? Did he not surpass the whole world in wealth? had he not climbed to the very pinnacle of distinction? did not all tremble and fear before him? Yet, lo! he has become more wretched than the prisoner, more pitiable than the menial slave, more indigent than the beggar wasting away with hunger, having every day a vision of sharpened swords

and of the criminal's grave, and the public executioner leading him out to
his death; and he does not even know if he once enjoyed past pleasure,
nor is he sensible even of the sun's ray, but at midday his sight is dimmed
as if he were encompassed by the densest gloom. But even let me try my
best I shall not be able to present to you in language the suffering he must
naturally undergo, in the hourly expectation of death. But indeed what
need is there of any words from me, when he himself has clearly depicted
this for us as in a visible image? For yesterday, when they came to him
from the royal court, intending to drag him away by force, and he ran
for refuge to the holy furniture, his face was then, as it is now, no better
than the countenance of one dead: and the chattering of his teeth, and
the quaking and quivering of his whole body, and his faltering voice,
and stammering tongue, and in fact his whole general appearance were
suggestive of one whose soul was petrified.

Now I say these things not by way of reproaching him, or insulting his
misfortune, but from a desire to soften your minds toward him, and to
induce you to compassion, and to persuade you to be contented with the
punishment that has already been inflicted. For since there are many inhuman persons amongst us who are inclined, perhaps, to find fault with
me for having admitted him to the sanctuary, I parade his sufferings
from a desire to soften their hardheartedness by my narrative.

For tell me, beloved brother, wherefore art thou indignant with me?
You say it is because he who continually made war upon the Church has
taken refuge within it. Yet surely we ought in the highest degree to glorify
God, for permitting him to be placed in such a great strait as to experience both the power and the loving-kindness of the Church—her power in
that he has suffered this great vicissitude in consequence of the attacks
he made upon her; her loving-kindness in that she whom he attacked now
casts her shield in front of him and has received him under her wings
and placed him in all security, not resenting any of her former injuries,
but most lovingly opening her bosom to him. For this is more glorious
than any kind of trophy, this is a brilliant victory, this puts both Gentiles
and Jews to shame, this displays the bright aspect of the Church: in that
having received her enemy as a captive, she spares him, and when all
have despised him in his desolation, she alone, like an affectionate mother,
has concealed him under her cloak, opposing both the wrath of the king
and the rage of the people and their overwhelming hatred. This is an ornament for the altar. A strange kind of ornament, you say, when the
accused sinner, the extortioner, the robber is permitted to lay hold of the
altar. Nay! say not so: for even the harlot took hold of the feet of Jesus,
she who was stained with the most accursed and unclean sin: yet her

deed was no reproach to Jesus, but rather redounded to His admiration and praise: for the impure woman did no injury to Him who was pure, but rather was the vile harlot rendered pure by the touch of Him who was the pure and spotless one. Grudge not then, O man. We are the servants of the crucified one who said, "Forgive them, for they know not what they do."

But, you say, he cut off the right of refuge here by his ordinances and divers kinds of laws. Yes! yet now he has learned by experience what it was he did, and he himself by his own deeds has been the first to break the law, and has become a spectacle to the whole world, and silent though he is, he utters from thence a warning voice to all, saying, "Do not such things as I have done, that ye suffer not such things as I suffer." He appears as a teacher by means of his calamity, and the altar emits great luster, inspiring now the greatest awe from the fact that it holds the lion in bondage; for any figure of royalty might be very much set off if the king were not only to be seen seated on his throne arrayed in purple and wearing his crown, but if also prostrate at the feet of the king barbarians with their hands bound behind their backs were bending low their heads. And that no persuasive arguments have been used, ye yourselves are witnesses of the enthusiasm and the concourse of the people. For brilliant indeed is the scene before us today, and magnificent the assembly, and I see as large a gathering here today as at the Holy Paschal Feast. Thus the man has summoned you here without speaking and yet uttering a voice through his actions clearer than the sound of a trumpet: and ye have all thronged hither today, maidens deserting their boudoirs, and matrons the women's chambers, and men the market place, that ye may see human nature convicted, and the instability of worldly affairs exposed, and the harlot face that a few days ago was radiant (such is the prosperity derived from extortion) looking uglier than any wrinkled old woman, this face I say you may see denuded of its enamel and pigments by the action of adversity as by a sponge.

Such is the force of this calamity: it has made one who was illustrious and conspicuous appear the most insignificant of men. And if a rich man should enter the assembly he derives much profit from the sight: for when he beholds the man who was shaking the whole world now dragged down from so high a pinnacle of power, cowering with fright, more terrified than a hare or a frog, nailed fast to yonder pillar, without bonds, his fear serving instead of a chain, panic-stricken and trembling, he abates his haughtiness, he puts down his pride, and, having acquired the kind of wisdom concerning human affairs that it concerns him to have, he departs instructed by example in the lesson that Holy Scripture teaches by precept: "All flesh is grass and all the glory of man as the flower of grass: the grass withereth and the flower faileth," or "They shall wither away quickly as the grass, and as the green herb shall they quickly fail," or "Like smoke are his days," and all passages of that kind.

Again, the poor man, when he has entered and gazed at this spectacle, does not think meanly of himself, nor bewail himself on account of his poverty, but feels grateful to his poverty, because it is a place of refuge to him, and a calm haven and secure bulwark; and when he sees these things he would many times rather remain where he is than enjoy the possession of all men for a little time and afterward be in jeopardy of his own life. Seest thou how the rich and poor, high and low, bond and free, have derived no small profit from this man's taking refuge here? Seest thou how each man will depart hence with a remedy, being cured merely by this sight? Well! have I softened your passion, and expelled your wrath? have I extinguished your cruelty? have I induced you to be piti- ful? Indeed I think I have; and your countenances and the streams of tears you shed are proofs of it.

Since, then, your hard rock has turned into deep and fertile soil, let us hasten to produce some fruit of mercy and to display a luxuriant crop of pity by falling down before the Emperor, or rather by imploring the merciful God so to soften the rage of the Emperor, and make his heart tender, that he may grant the whole of the favor we ask. For indeed al- ready since that day when this man fled here for refuge no slight change has taken place; for as soon as the Emperor knew that he had hurried to this asylum, although the army was present, and incensed on account of his misdeeds, and demanded him to be given up for execution, the Em- peror made a long speech endeavoring to allay the rage of the soldiers, maintaining that not only his offenses, but any good deed he might have done, ought to be taken into account, declaring that he felt gratitude for the latter, and was prepared to forgive him as a fellow creature for deeds that were otherwise. And when they again urged him to avenge the in- sult done to the imperial majesty, shouting, leaping, and brandishing their spears, he shed streams of tears from his gentle eyes, and having reminded them of the Holy Table to which the man had fled for refuge, he suc- ceeded at last in appeasing their wrath.

Moreover, let me add some arguments that concern ourselves. For what pardon could you deserve, if the Emperor bears no resentment when he has been insulted, but ye who have experienced nothing of this kind display so much wrath? and how after this assembly has been dissolved will ye handle the holy mysteries, and repeat that prayer by which we are commanded to say "forgive us as we also forgive our debtors," when ye are demanding vengeance upon your debtor? Has he inflicted great wrongs and insults on you? I will not deny it. Yet this is the season not for judgment, but for mercy; not for requiring an account, but for showing loving-kindness; not for investigating claims, but for conceding them; not for verdicts and vengeance, but for mercy and favor. Let no one, then, be irritated or vexed, but let us rather beseech the merciful God to grant him a respite from death, and to rescue him from this impending destruction, so that he may put off his transgression, and let us unite to approach the merciful Emperor, beseeching him for the sake of the Church, for the sake of the altar, to concede the life of one man as an offering to the Holy Table. If we do this, the Emperor himself will accept us, and even before his praise we shall have the approval of God, who will bestow a large recompense upon us for our mercy. For as He rejects and hates the cruel and inhuman, so does He welcome and love the merciful and humane man; and if such a man be righteous, all the more glorious is the crown that is wreathed for him; and if he be a sinner, He passes over his sins, granting this as the reward of compassion shown to his fellow servant. "For," He saith, "I will have mercy and not sacrifice," and throughout the Scriptures you find Him always inquiring after this, and declaring it to be the means of release from sin. Thus, then, we shall dispose Him to be propitious to us, thus we shall release ourselves from our sins, thus we shall adorn the Church, thus also our merciful Emperor, as I have already said, will commend us, and all the people will applaud us, and the ends of the earth will admire the humanity and gentleness of our city, and all who hear of these deeds throughout the world will extol us. That we then may enjoy these good things, let us fall down in prayer and supplication, let us rescue the captive, the fugitive, the suppliant, from danger that we ourselves may obtain the future blessings by the favor and mercy of our Lord Jesus Christ, to whom be glory and power, now and forever, world without end. Amen.

(TRANSLATED BY W. R. W. STEPHENS, IN *A Select Library of the Nicene and Post-Nicene Fathers*, EDITED BY PHILIP SCHAFF)

Soon after Chrysostom had held his vast audience spellbound by this sermon, the wretched Eutropius escaped from the Church, probably under the hope or promise of exile rather than execution. But he was imprisoned, tried, and beheaded, at the instigation of the Empress Eudoxia.

Chrysostom's continued attacks on the clergy and the court and his pointed references to the vicious Eudoxia herself aroused her fury. She managed to have him deposed and banished, but he was recalled in response to the violent demands of the people. He had not learned his lesson. He resumed his moral diatribes, was again banished, and died under guard on his way to one of the most inaccessible regions of the Caucasus.

Down through the centuries St. John Chrysostom has met with uninterrupted praise. Even Edward Gibbon speaks of the "genuine merits" of the Archbishop of Constantinople. In the seventeenth century, famous for its pulpit orators, Barrow in England, Bourdaloue in France, and Segneri in Italy turned back to John of Antioch for materials and inspiration. In the nineteenth century John Henry Newman painted some notable pictures of the Fathers of the Church and especially of Chrysostom: "He spoke, because his heart, his head, were brimful of things to speak about. His elocution corresponded to that strength and flexibility of limb, that quickness of eye, hand and foot, by which a man excels in manly games of mechanical skill. It would be a great mistake, in speaking of it, to ask whether it was Attic or Asiatic, terse or flowing, when its distinctive praise was that it was natural. His unrivaled charm, as that of every really eloquent man, lies in his singleness of purpose, his fixed grasp of his aim, his noble earnestness."

POPE URBAN II CALLS FOR THE FIRST CRUSADE

[1095]

In the eyes of recent historians, the Crusades loom as a movement much larger than a militant religious pilgrimage of vast proportions. They had repercussions in other fields—political, economic, intellectual, and aesthetic—and released creative energies that might have otherwise been bottled up for years. They initiated new patterns of thought and behavior that affect our life even today.

For ages it was held as a pious belief that the First Crusade was instigated by Peter the Hermit, an itinerant monk whose picturesque aspect helped to popularize the legend among those who prefer a colorful fantasy to the drab truth. Yet the truth was, in this case, far from drab. Pope Urban II, in France for the Council of Clermont (ostensibly met to discuss such perennial troubles as lay investiture, simony, and clerical marriage), announced an open-air meeting on November 27, 1095. When the multitudes were gathered, Urban called on Western Christendom to come to the rescue of Eastern Christendom.

Urban's speech is given in five separate versions, three of the chroniclers writing as if they had been present. A fourth got his version at second hand, while William of Malmesbury, whom we follow, wrote his plausible version thirty years afterward. "But," as Steven Runciman, the latest historian of the

Crusades, writes, "it is clear that each author wrote the speech that he thought the Pope ought to have made and added his own favorite rhetorical tricks."

"A station of perpetual safety will be awarded you, for the exertion of a trifling labor against the Turks."

YOU RECOLLECT, my dearest brethren, many things that have been decreed for you at this time: some matters in our council have been commanded, others inhibited. A rude and confused chaos of crimes required the deliberation of many days; an inveterate malady demanded a sharp remedy. For while we give unbounded scope to our clemency, our papal office finds numberless matters to proscribe, none to spare. But it has hitherto arisen from human frailty that you have erred, and that, deceived by the speciousness of vice, you have exasperated the long suffering of God, by too lightly regarding His forbearance. It has arisen, too, from human wantonness that, disregarding lawful wedlock, you have not duly considered the heinousness of adultery. From too great covetousness, also, it has arisen that, as opportunity offered, by making captive your brethren, who were bought by the same great price, you have outrageously extorted from them their wealth.

To you, however, now suffering this perilous shipwreck of sin, a secure haven of rest is offered, unless you neglect it. A station of perpetual safety will be awarded you, for the exertion of a trifling labor against the Turks. Compare now the labors you underwent in the practice of wickedness and those you will encounter in the undertaking I advise. The intention of committing adultery or murder begets many fears, for, as Solomon says, "There is nothing more timid than guilt"; many labors, for what is more toilsome than wickedness? But "He who walks uprightly walks securely." Of these labors, of these fears, the end was sin; the wages of sin is death; the death of sinners is most dreadful. Now the same labors and apprehensions are required from you for a better consideration. The cause of these labors will be charity, if, thus warned by the command of God, you lay down your lives for the brethren; the wages of charity will be the grace of God; the grace of God is followed by eternal life.

Go then prosperously; go then with confidence to attack the enemies of God. For they long since, O sad reproach to Christians! have seized Syria, Armenia, and, lastly, all Asia Minor, the provinces of which are Bithynia, Phrygia, Galatia, Lydia, Caria, Pamphylia, Isauria, Lycia, Cilicia; and now they insolently domineer over Illyricum and all the hither countries, even to the sea that is called the Straits of St. George. Nay, they usurp even the sepulcher of our Lord, that singular assurance of our faith, and sell to our pilgrims admission to that city, which ought, if Christians had a trace of their ancient courage left, to be open to Christians only. This alone might be enough to cloud our brows; but now who, except the most abandoned or the most hostile to the reputation of Christians, can endure that we do not divide the world equally with them?

They inhabit Asia, the third portion of the world, as their native soil, which was justly esteemed by our ancestors equal, by the extent of its tracts and greatness of its provinces, to the two remaining parts. There, formerly, sprang up the first germs of our faith; there, all the Apostles, except two, glorified God by their deaths; there, at the present day, the Christians, if any survive, sustain life by a wretched kind of agriculture, and pay these miscreants tribute. Even with stifled sighs, they long for participation in your liberty, since they have lost their own. They hold Africa also, another portion of the world, already possessed by their arms for more than two hundred years; which I declare to be derogatory to Christian honor, because that country was anciently the nurse of celebrated geniuses, who by their divine writings will mock the rust of antiquity as long as there shall be a person who can relish Roman literature: the learned know the truth of what I say. Europe, the third portion of the world, remains; of which how small a part do we Christians inhabit! for who can call all those barbarians who dwell in remote islands of the frozen ocean Christians, since they live after a savage manner? Even this small portion of the world belonging to us is oppressed by the Turks and Saracens. Thus, for three hundred years, Spain and the Balearic Isles have been subjugated by them, and the possession of the remainder is eagerly anticipated by feeble men, who, not having courage to engage in close encounter, love a flying mode of warfare. The Turk never ventures upon close fight; but, when driven from his station, he bends his bow at a distance, and trusts the winds to cause the wound he intends. As he has poisoned arrows, venom, and not valor, inflicts death on the man he strikes. Whatever he effects, then, I attribute to fortune, not to courage, because he wars by flight and by poison. It is apparent, too, that every race born in that region, being scorched with the intense heat of the sun, abounds more in reflection than in blood; and, therefore, they avoid coming to close quarters, because they are aware how little blood they possess. Whereas the people who are born amid the polar frosts, and distant from the sun's heat, are less cautious indeed, but, animated by their copious and rich flow of blood, they fight with the greatest alacrity. You are a nation born in the more temperate regions of the world, who may be both prodigal of blood in defiance of death and wounds; and you are not deficient in prudence. For you equally preserve good conduct in camp and are considerate in battle. Thus endued with skill and with valor, you undertake a memorable expedition.

You will be extolled throughout all ages if you rescue your brethren from danger. To those present, in God's name, I command this; to the absent I enjoin it. Let such as are going to fight for Christianity put the form of the cross upon their garments, that they may outwardly demonstrate the love arising from their inward faith. Let them enjoy, by the gift of God and the privilege of St. Peter, absolution from all their crimes. Let this in the meantime soothe the labor of their journey; satisfied that they shall obtain, after death, the advantages of a blessed martyrdom. Put an end, then, to your crimes, that Christians may at least live peaceably in these countries. Go, and employ in noble warfare that valor and that sagacity which you used to waste in civil broils. Go, soldiers, everywhere renowned in fame, go, and subdue these dastardly nations. Let the noted valor of the French advance, which, accompanied by its adjoining nations, shall affright the whole world by the single terror of its name.

But why do I delay you longer by detracting from the courage of the Gentiles? Rather bring to your recollection the saying of God: "Narrow is the way that leadeth to life." Be it so then; the track to be followed is narrow, replete with death, and terrible with dangers; still this path will lead to your lost country. No doubt you must "by much tribulation enter into the kingdom of God." Place, then, before your imagination, if you shall be made captive, torments and chains; nay, every possible suffering that can be inflicted. Expect, for the firmness of your faith, even horrible punishments; that so, if it be necessary, you may redeem your souls at the expense of your bodies. Do you fear death, you men of exemplary courage and intrepidity? Surely human wickedness can devise nothing against you worthy to be put in competition with heavenly glory; for "the sufferings of the present time are not worthy to be compared to the glory which shall be revealed in us." Know ye not "that for men to live is wretchedness, and to die is happiness"? This doctrine, if you remember, you imbibed with your mother's milk, through the preaching of the clergy; and this doctrine your ancestors, the martyrs, held out by example. Death sets free from its earthy prison the human soul, which then takes flight for the mansions fitted to its virtues. Death brings near their country to the good; death cuts short the wickedness of the ungodly. By means of death, then, the soul, made free, is either soothed with joyful hope or is punished without further apprehension of worse. So long as it is fettered to the body, it derives from it earthly contagion; or, to say more truly, is dead. For earthly with heavenly, and divine with mortal, ill agree. The soul, indeed, even now, in its state of union with the body, is capable of great efforts; it gives life to its instrument, secretly moving and animating it to exertions almost beyond mortal nature. But when freed from the clog that drags it to the earth, it regains its proper station, it partakes of a blessed and perfect energy, communicating after some fashion with the invisibility of the divine nature. Discharging a double office, therefore, it ministers life to the body when it is present, and is the cause of its change when it departs. You must observe how pleasantly the soul wakes in the sleeping body, and apart from the senses sees many future events, from the principle of its relationship to the Deity. Why, then, do ye fear death, who love the repose of sleep, which resembles death? Surely it must be madness, through lust of a transitory life, to deny yourselves that which is eternal. Rather, my dearest brethren, should it so happen, lay down your lives for the brotherhood.

Rid God's sanctuary of the wicked; expel the robbers; bring in the pious. Let no love of relations detain you; for man's chiefest love is toward God. Let no attachment to your native soil be an impediment; because all the world is exile to the Christian, but from another point of view all the world is his country. Thus exile is his country, and his country exile. Let none be restrained from going by the largeness of his patrimony, for a still larger patrimony is promised him: not of such things as soothe the miserable with vain expectation, or flatter the indolent disposition with the mean advantages of wealth, but of such as are shown by perpetual example and approved by daily experience. Yet these too are pleasant, but vain, and, to such as despise them, produce reward a hundredfold.

These things I publish, these I command: and for their execution I fix the end of the ensuing spring. God will be gracious to those who undertake this expedition, that they may have a favorable year, both in abundance of produce and in serenity of season. Those who may die will enter the mansions of heaven; while the living shall behold the sepulcher of the Lord. And what can be greater happiness than for a man, in his lifetime, to see those places where the Lord of heaven lived as a man? Blessed are they who, called to these occupations, shall inherit such a recompense; fortunate are those who are led to such a conflict, that they may partake of such rewards.

Before the Pope had finished, the crowd cried out again and again, "God wills it! God wills it!" And thousands took the cross at once.

Henry Adams, in that beautiful book on the Middle Ages, Mont-Saint-Michel and Chartes, said: "The first crusade was altogether the most interesting event in European history. Never has the Western world shown anything like the energy and unity with which she then flung herself on the East, and for the moment made the East recoil. Barring her family quarrels, Europe was a unity then, in thought, will, and object. Christianity was the unit. Mont-Saint-Michel and Byzantium were near each other. The Emperor Constantine and the Emperor Charlemagne were figured as allies and friends in the popular legend. The East was the common enemy, always superior in wealth and numbers, frequently in energy, and sometimes in thought and art. The outburst of the first crusade was splendid even in a military sense, but it was great beyond comparison in its reflection in architecture, ornament, poetry, colour, religion, and philosophy. Its men were astonishing, and its women were worth all the rest."

BERNARD OF CLAIRVAUX SHOWS THAT THE NAME OF JESUS IS A SALUTARY MEDICINE

[1136]

It was in 1112 that a young man of noble family, born near Lyons, led a band of his relatives and friends into the Cistercian monastery at Cîteaux. Three years later, for fuller seclusion, he founded a new monastery at Clairvaux, where he remained abbot for the rest of his life. But never did such seclusion have such repercussions. "Through the prodigious power of his personality," wrote Henry Osborn Taylor, in The Medieval Mind, "St. Bernard gave new life to monasticism, promoted the reform of the secular clergy and the suppression of heresy, ended a papal schism, set on foot the Second Crusade, and for a quarter of a century swayed Christendom as never holy man before or after him. An adequate account of his career would embrace the entire history of the first half of the twelfth century."

Ruthless in his pursuit of the heresies of Abélard and Arnold of Brescia, skillful in supporting the claims of Innocent II to the papacy and in persuading the Lombards to accept Emperor Lothair II, Bernard was above all a preacher of sermons and a writer of letters that gave a new vitality, a new color, to the emotional life of Europe. It was he who developed the cult of the Virgin Mary and depicted with irresistible vividness the human sufferings of Jesus. It was

Bernard as the symbol of contemplation who guided Dante through the last three cantos of The Divine Comedy to the ultimate vision of "the love that moves the sun and all the other stars."

Among the hundreds of Bernard's sermons that have come down to us, there is the series of eighty-six on the Song of Songs that he delivered to his brothers at Clairvaux, beginning in Advent, 1135. Although they must have been carefully thought out in advance, they contain afterthoughts, comments on the behavior of the audience, one long interpolation on his mourning for his brother, indicating that some at least were written out after delivery. The fifteenth of the sermons on the Song of Songs shows "In what manner the name of Jesus is a salutary medicine to faithful Christians in all adversities."

"Approach, ye nations; your salvation is at hand."

WHERE, NOW is that Voice of thunder which made itself heard so frequently and so terribly by the people of old time: *I am the Lord! I am the Lord!* In its place there is dictated to me a prayer, which commences with the sweet name of *Father*, and thus affords good ground for confidence that the petitions that follow will be granted. Those who were servants are now called friends; and the Resurrection of Jesus is announced, not even to disciples only, but to those who are named brethren. And I do not wonder that this pouring forth of the Holy Name was made when the fullness of time came; for God thus fulfilled what He had promised by Joel, and poured out His Spirit upon all flesh; and I read that something similar had taken place among the Hebrews in ancient times. Your minds, I dare say, outstrip my words, and you already know what I am about to mention. For of what nature was the answer, I would ask, that was given to Moses when he inquired at first who was speaking to him? I AM THAT I AM? and I AM *hath sent me unto you?* I know not whether Moses himself would have understood it thus if the Name had not been already poured forth. But that was done, and it was understood, not only poured but poured forth; for the inpouring was already achieved. Already the heavens possessed it; already it had been made known to the angels. But it is [now] sent forth abroad; and the Name, which had been so infused into the angels that it was become even familiar to them, was sent forth among men also, so that thenceforth the cry of joy would be with justice raised from earth, *Thy Name is as oil poured forth,* if the odious obstinacy of an ungrateful people had not hindered. For He says: *I am the God of Abraham, the God of Isaac, and the God of Jacob.*

Approach, ye nations; your salvation is at hand. That Name is poured forth which whosoever calls upon shall be saved. The God of angels names Himself the God of men also. He has shed forth oil upon Jacob and it has fallen upon Israel. Say, then, to your brethren, *Give us of your oil.* But if they will not, pray ye the Lord for oil, that He may send it unto you also. Say ye unto Him, *Take away our reproach.* Permit not, I entreat, an evil tongue to insult Thy beloved, whom Thou hast been pleased to call from the ends of the earth, and that with so much the greater bounty as he was less worthy [of Thy goodness]. Is it fitting, I beseech Thee, that a wicked servant should shut out those whom their kind Father has invited? *I am,* Thou sayest, *the God of Abraham, the God of Isaac, and the God of Jacob.* And are there no more [than these]? Pour forth, pour forth; open still wider Thy Hand, and fill with blessing every living thing. Let them come from the east and from the west, and sit down with Abraham, Isaac, and Jacob in the kingdom of heaven. Let the tribes, the tribes of the Lord come, let them come; unto the testimony of Israel, to give thanks unto the Name of the Lord. Let them come, and take the seats of guests; let them feast in gladness of great joy; let there everywhere be heard but one great chorus of thanksgivings and praises, one song of them that feast: *Thy Name is as oil poured forth.* Of one thing I am sure, that if we have Philip and Andrew for porters at the gate of heaven, whosoever among us seeks for this celestial oil, whosoever of us desires to see Jesus, will encounter no repulse. At once Philip cometh and telleth Andrew, and again Andrew and Philip tell Jesus. But what will Jesus say? Without doubt what He has already said: *Except a corn of wheat fall into the ground and die, it abideth alone: but if it die it bringeth forth much fruit.* Let the grain, then, die, and let there rise from it the harvest of the Gentiles. It is needful that Christ should suffer, that He should rise from the dead, and that repentance and remission of sins should be preached in His Name, not only in Judea, but among all nations; insomuch that from one Name, which is Christ, thousands of thousands of believers shall be called Christian, and shall say: *Thy Name is as oil poured forth.*

I recognize that Name also in that which I have read in Isaiah: *The Lord God shall call His servants by another Name, in which he that is blessed in the earth shall be blessed in God. Amen.* O Blessed Name! O oil everywhere poured forth! How far does it penetrate? It spreads from heaven to Judea, and thence over the whole earth; and from every part of the earth rises the adoring cry of the Church: *Thy Name is as oil poured forth.* Behold the Christ, behold Jesus, whether infused into angels, or effused upon men—yea, upon men who had defiled themselves as beasts upon their dunghill, saving both men and beasts, in like manner as God has multiplied His mercy. How dear is that Name, but how common [vile]!—common, but precious in its power to heal! If it were not common it would not have been poured out upon a sinner such as I; and if it had no power of healing it would have profited me nothing. I am a sharer in that Name—a sharer, too, in its heavenly inheritance. I am a Christian; I am even the brother of Christ; and if I be truly that which I am thus called, I am an heir of God, and a joint heir with Christ. What wonder is it if the Name of the Bridegroom be thus poured forth, when He Himself is poured forth likewise? For when He emptied Himself did He not take upon Him the form of a servant? Therefore He says: I am poured out like water. The plenitude of His Divinity was poured forth when He dwelt in bodily form upon the earth; so that we all who bear about a mortal body should participate in that plenitude, and, being filled with an odor of life, should say: *Thy Name is as oil poured forth.* I go on to say, *What* is that Name which is poured forth, in what manner, and in what degree?

First, why is it called *oil?*—for this I have not as yet explained. I had begun to do so in a former sermon, but another subject suddenly presented itself that seemed to me to require to be treated of. But I have deferred to speak of this longer than I supposed, for which I see no other reason than this, that Wisdom is as the virtuous woman in the Book of Proverbs, who layeth her hands to the spindle, and her hands hold the distaff, for she knows how out of a little wool or flax to draw out the thread and to broaden the web with the shuttle, and so to clothe all her servants in garments both of linen and of wool. There is no doubt that oil has its points of resemblance to the Name of the Bridegroom, and that not without reason has the Holy Spirit compared the one to the other. Perhaps you may discern better than I the reasons for this; but, as far as I am able to judge, the reasons are three: that it gives light, it gives nourishment, and it anoints. It maintains flame, it nourishes the flesh, it relieves pain; it is light, it is food, and it is medicine. Notice now that the same thing can be said of the Name of the Bridegroom: for when preached it enlightens the mind, when it is meditated upon it is food to the mind, and when invoked it softens and alleviates the wounds of mind and soul. Let us examine each of these qualities separately.

Whence do you suppose so bright and so sudden a light of faith has been kindled in the whole world, except by the preaching of the Name of Jesus? Is it not by the light of this sacred Name that God has called us into His marvelous light, so that when we had been enlightened by it, and in that light we had seen light, St. Paul was enabled to say to us: *Ye were sometimes darkness, but now are ye light in the Lord.* This Name, in conclusion, it was that the same Apostle was bidden to bear before the Gentiles, and Kings, and the children of Israel; this Name he bore as a lamp to enlighten his country and his people, crying everywhere: *The night is far spent, the day is at hand: let us, therefore, cast off the works of darkness, and put upon us the armor of light: let us walk honestly, as in the day.* To all he displayed a lamp shining upon its pillar, when in every place he preached Jesus Christ, and Him crucified. How resplendent was that Light; how it dazzled the eyes of all beholders, when, coming forth as a lightning flash from the mouth of Peter, it set the lame man upon sound and strong limbs; when it restored to sight many who were spiritually blind! Did it not shoot forth a light of fire, when he said, *In the Name of Jesus Christ of Nazareth rise up and walk?* But the Name of Jesus is not only light; it is also nourishment. Do you not feel spiritually strengthened as often as you meditate upon it? What enriches the mind of the thinker as does the Name of Jesus? What so restores exhausted powers, strengthens the soul in all virtues, animates it to good and honorable conduct, fosters in it pure and pious dispositions? Dry and tasteless is every kind of spiritual food, if this sweet oil be not poured into it; and insipid, if it be not seasoned with salt. A book or writing has no single point of goodness for me if I do not read therein the Name of Jesus; nor has a conference any interest for me, unless the Name of Jesus be heard in it. As honey to the mouth, as melody in the ear, as a song of gladness to the heart, is the Name of Jesus. But it is also a medicine. Is any of you sad? Let Jesus come into your heart; let His Name leap thence to your lips, and behold, when that blessed Name arises [as a sun], its light disperses the clouds of sadness, and brings back serenity and peace. Is any falling into crime, or even, in his despair, rushing upon death? Let him call upon that life-giving Name; does he not speedily begin to breathe again and revive? In the presence of that saving Name, who has ever remained fast bound (as is the case with some of us) by hardness of heart, ignoble sloth, rancor of mind, or cold indifference? Who has not known the fountain of his tears, which seemed dried up, to burst forth anew, and with added abundance and sweetness, at the calling upon the Name of Jesus? Who, when in fear and trembling in the midst of dangers, has called upon that Name of power, and has not found a calm assurance of safety, and his apprehensions at once driven away? Where is the man who, when laboring under doubt and uncertainty, has not had the clear shining of faith restored to him by the influence of the Name of Jesus?

Or who has not found new vigor and resolution given to him at the sound of that Name full of help, when he was discouraged by adversities, and almost ready to give way to them? Those are the diseases and ailments of the soul, and for them this is the remedy. And what I say is proved by these words: *Call upon Me in the day of trouble; I will deliver thee, and thou shalt glorify Me.* Nothing is so powerful as the Name of Jesus to restrain the impulse of anger, to repress the swelling of pride, to cure the wound of envy, to bridle the impulse of luxury, and extinguish the flame of fleshly desire; to temper avarice, and put to flight ignoble and impure thoughts. For, when I utter the Name of Jesus, I set before my mind, not only a Man meek and humble in heart, moderate, pure, benign, merciful, and, in short, conspicuous for every honorable and saintly quality, but also in the same individual the Almighty God, who both restores me to spiritual health by His example and renders me strong by His assistance. All these things are said to me when the Name of Jesus is pronounced. From Him, inasmuch as He is Man, I derive an example; inasmuch as He is the Mighty One, I obtain assistance. Of His example I make, as it were, medicinal and salutary herbs, and His help is an instrument to prepare them; thus I obtain a remedy of power, such as none among physicians is able to compound. . . .

(TRANSLATED BY SAMUEL J. EALES)

If such sermons, delivered in the quiet of Clairvaux, were more characteristic of Bernard, his recruiting speeches for the Second Crusade are more famous— although only by hearsay. After the Turks captured Edessa in 1144 and began to threaten Jerusalem, Pope Eugenius III induced Bernard to preach another great war against the infidel. On March 31, 1146, at Vézelay, in Burgundy, Bernard inflamed a vast throng in the presence of the French king and queen and then went on a triumphant campaign through France and into Germany, where masses of people were persuaded to take the cross even when they could not understand the preacher's language. At the cathedral of Speyer, Bernard converted the King of Germany, Conrad III, to the cause and so completed his main task.

None of these speeches has come down to us, but the indefatigable Bernard also wrote many letters to peoples and rulers beyond the range of his voice, and at least two of these have been preserved. A letter to the Bavarians, who were engaged in a civil war, contains this passage, which is often mistaken for a speech: "Contemplate, O ye sinners, this abyss of the divine mercy and take heart. It is not your death he desires, but rather that you be converted and live. He seeks an occasion of benefiting, not of destroying you. Tell me, does it not appear a wonderful thing, a great mystery of divine love, that the Lord

God Omnipotent deigns to accept service from murderers, robbers, adulterers, perjurers, and men abandoned to every vice? Have confidence, therefore, ye transgressors, for the Lord is merciful. Did He purpose to punish you, so far from claiming your service, He would even refuse it if offered.

"Again, I say, consider the riches of the Divine Goodness, the design of His tender compassion—how He pretends or condescends to need your help, in His loving desire to help you in your necessities. He longs to be made your debtor, so that you may be entitled to demand from Him, in compensation for service rendered, the pardon for your sins and glory everlasting. Happy, therefore, do I call this generation which has obtained a life of such liberal indulgence, which has been favored with this holy year of jubilee and pardon. The benediction is common to the whole world, and everywhere men are eagerly flocking to the standard adorned with the sign of life.

". . . Now gallant knight, now brave warrior, you have an enemy with whom you may contend without danger to your souls; you have a combat in which it is glorious to conquer and gainful to die. If you be wise merchants, ardent seekers after the wealth of this world, lose not the profitable bargains now proposed to you. Accept the cross, and with it the full pardon of all your sins, provided you confess them with sorrow. Looking to the material, this badge of the crusader is in truth very little; nevertheless, it will be worth for you the kingdom of heaven if worn over a faithful and devoted heart."

(TRANSLATED IN A. J. LUDDY, *Life and Teaching of St. Bernard.*)

History records that the Second Crusade ended in horrible disaster and that the broken armies of Louis VII and Conrad III straggled back to Europe in despair. Bernard was bitterly denounced and lost much of his popularity for the time being, but he retained his composure, with the assurance that salvation is won through suffering and that the ways of God are mysterious.

PART THREE

RENAISSANCE AND REFORMATION

THE DIVISION of history into sharp, neat periods is unscholarly and misleading. The appearance of Augustine, "the first modern man," in the fourth century, and of Abélard and Héloïse in the twelfth, and of Marco Polo as a contemporary of Dante in the thirteenth is embarrassing to those who see a vast gulf between the Middle Ages and modern times, or imagine that the Renaissance started suddenly with the fall of Constantinople in 1453. Yet some rough, flexible division of history into periods is unavoidable, and it is not merely arbitrary to say with Henry Adams that "the century 1150–1250, expressed in Amiens Cathedral and the Works of Thomas Aquinas," is "the point of history when man held the highest idea of himself as a unit in a unified universe," or to say with Edward P. Cheyney, in The Dawn of a New Era, that "by the middle of the thirteenth century the real Middle Ages were over."

The causes for the vast change lay far in the past. It was in the growth of cities and the formation of the middle class in the eleventh century that Henri Pirenne found the beginnings of the new Europe. With the revival of commerce and the development of navigation the capitalist spirit proceeded to undermine the feudal, agrarian economy. And with wide-ranging commerce heresy began to trouble Christendom for the first time since the fourth century.

The enthusiasm for the First Crusade (1096–99) and the subsequent contact with the Moslem world released dormant energies that could never again be harnessed. Motion became characteristic of a continent. National differences were sharpened within the united front against the infidel. The Italian cities that were to profit most from the crusades grew warlike as well as wealthy.

Yet these divergent forces coalesced briefly in the glories of the thirteenth century, at Mont-Saint-Michel and Chartres, in the philosophy of St. Thomas Aquinas, in the unchallenged prestige of the papacy.

Then suddenly that prestige declined when Pope Boniface VIII vainly attempted to dictate on temporal matters to the kings of France and England. In the spirit of the growing nationalism they rejected his proposals without suffering excommunication. Equally disastrous was the decision of Clement V to abandon the historic setting of imperial Rome and remove the papal court to Avignon, where his successors remained until 1378. Finally, there was the

Great Schism at the end of the fourteenth century during which two Popes for a time claimed the throne of St. Peter. Such vicissitudes of the once omnipotent and united Church weakened her authority over the emerging nations of Europe and indeed over the submerged masses who were to break out from time to time in desperate but futile revolt.

There was another disillusioning event of this period, a ghastly prolonged event, the Black Death, which spread across Europe between 1347 and 1350, and wiped away one fifth, perhaps two or three fifths, of the population. It colored the emotions and shook the faith of Western man for generations to come. It decimated the high and the low, the strong and the weak, and leveled off social distinctions. It inspired in writers and painters the inescapable theme of the Dance of Death. It inspired a more violent Dance of Life. The storytellers in Boccaccio's Decameron went into the country to escape the plague in Florence but indulged in neither penitence nor prayer.

It was at this time also, between 1342 and 1353, that Petrarch wrote a strange little book, Secretum or De contemptu mundi, which prefigures much of the Renaissance to come. In an imaginary dialogue with the forbidding St. Augustine, Petrarch exults in his knowledge of the ancients, in his fame, his style, and even in his Platonic love of Laura. "My principle is that, as concerning glory, which we may hope for here below, it is right for us to seek here below." Thus speaks the Renaissance humanist of the next century, who was even less troubled with the sense of sin and even more thirsty for knowledge of this world.

A great revival of classical learning, a new sense of the potentialities of the individual, a vindication of human love, were on the horizon. Voyages of discovery extended the narrow frontiers of medieval maps, while astronomical speculation opened up infinite space, with an infinity of worlds. In such figures as Leonardo and Rabelais science and humanism joined hands. While Francis Bacon was far less interested in the revival of ancient learning than in the future applications of science, the once worldly John Donne ended preaching on the medieval themes of sin, death, and God.

SAVONAROLA EXHORTS THE PEOPLE OF FLORENCE TO REPENT

[May 12, 1496]

A young Italian nobleman, Pico della Mirandola (1463–94), typified in many ways the expanding forces of the Renaissance. It would be ideal to present here Pico's famous "Oration on the Dignity of Man," which he composed at the

age of twenty-three as an introduction to a public debate at Rome on his nine
hundred theses of doubtful orthodoxy. He exulted in the unique plasticity, the
unique freedom of Man, which enabled Man to share the properties of all other
beings, to descend as low as the animals but to ascend as high as the angels.
But the Pope prohibited the little book which contained Pico's nine hundred
theses, the public disputation was never held, and the "Oration on the Dignity
of Man" was never delivered. After 1486 Pico receded to a more austere, devout, mystical position and became a supporter of Savonarola.

Girolamo Savonarola (1452–98), who was born at Ferrara, despaired of the
world and joined the Dominican order in his early twenties. "Worn to a
shadow" by his studies and his austerities, he made little stir with his preaching
when he first went to Florence in 1482, and he was soon repelled by the gaiety
and the gaudiness of the city of the lilies. But after he had become famous for
his fiery, prophetic sermons in St. Gimignano and Brescia he was recalled to
Florence, perhaps at the suggestion of Pico, by Lorenzo the Magnificent, that
lavish patron of the arts and uncrowned king of the golden city of the Italian
Renaissance. The results were not what Lorenzo could have anticipated. This
gaunt, uncouth prophet was no Renaissance figure, no advocate of "the dignity
of man" and "the unity of truth." His themes were doom, pestilence, and
divine wrath—the corruption of the papacy and the wickedness of Italy. Over
and over again he preached that the Church would be scourged, the Church
would be renewed, and the time was at hand. Over and over again he denounced everything that the Medici stood for.

When Lorenzo was dying in the spring of 1492, he called for Savonarola
to shrive his soul, but when he refused to restore the liberties of Florence, the
monk refused, and Lorenzo died unshriven. For the last four years, until his
own death in 1498, Savonarola was the virtual ruler of Florence.

At the peak of his power and of his fiery, awkward eloquence, Savonarola
preached in the crowded Duomo on the Feast of the Ascension, May 12, 1496.

"The ass alone saw the angel, the others did not; so open

your eyes."

IN EVERYTHING am I oppressed; even the spiritual power is
against me with Peter's mighty key. Narrow is my path and full of
trouble; like Balaam's ass, I must throw myself on the ground and cry:
"See, here I am; I am ready to die for the truth." But when Balaam beat
his fallen beast, it said to him: "What have I done to thee?" So I say to

you: "Come here and tell me: what have I done to you? Why do you beat me? I have spoken the truth to you; I have warned you to choose a virtuous life; I have led many souls to Christ." But you answer: "Thou hast spoken evil of us, therefore thou shouldst suffer the stripes thou deservest." But I named no one, I only blamed your vices in general. If you have sinned, be angry with yourselves, not with me. I name none of you, but if the sins I have mentioned are without question yours, then they and not I make you known. As the smitten beast asked Balaam, so I ask you: "Tell me, am I not your ass? And do you not know that I have been obedient to you up to this very moment, that I have even done what my superiors have commanded, and have always behaved myself peaceably?" You know this, and because I am now so entirely different, you may well believe that a great cause drives me to it. Many knew me as I was at first; if I remained so I could have had as much honor as I wanted. I lived six years among you, and now I speak otherwise, nevertheless I announce to you the truth that is well known. You see in what sorrows and what opposition I must now live, and I can say with Jeremiah: "O, my mother, that thou hast borne me a man of strife and contention to the whole earth!" But where is a father or a mother that can say I have led their son into sin; one that can say I have ruined her husband or his wife? Everybody knows my manner of life, therefore it is right for you to believe that I speak the truth which everybody knows. You think that it is impossible for a man to do what the faith I have preached tells him to do: with God it would be easy for you.

The ass alone saw the angel, the others did not; so open your eyes. Thank God, many have them open. You have seen many learned men whom you thought wise, and they have withstood our cause: now they believe; many noted masters who were hard and proud against us: now humility casts them down. You have also seen many women turn from their vanity to simplicity; vicious youths who are now improved and conduct themselves in a new way. Many, indeed, have received this doctrine with humility. That doctrine has stood firm, no matter how attacked with the intention of showing that it was a doctrine opposed to Christ. God does that to manifest His wisdom, to show how it finally overcomes all other wisdom. And He is willing that His servants be spoken against that they may show their patience and humility, and for the sake of His love not be afraid of martyrdom.

O ye men and women, I bid you to this truth; let those who are in captivity contradict you as much as they will, God will come and oppose their pride. Ye proud, however, if you do not turn about and become better, then will the sword and the pestilence fall upon you; with famine

and war will Italy be turned upside down. I foretell you this because I
am sure of it: if I were not, I would not mention it. Open your eyes as
Balaam opened his eyes when the angel said to him: "Had it not been for
thine ass, I would have slain thee." So I say to you, ye captives: "Had it
not been for the good and their preaching, it would have been woe unto
you." Balaam said: "If this way is not good, I will return." You say likewise, you would turn back to God, if your way is not good. And to the
angel you say as Balaam said: "What wilt thou that we should do?" The
angel answers thee as he answered Balaam: "Thou shalt not curse this
people, but shalt say what I put in thy mouth." But in thy mouth he puts
the warning that thou shouldst do good, convince one another of the
divine truth, and bear evil manfully. For it is the life of a Christian to do
good and to bear wrong and to continue steadfast unto death, and this is
the Gospel, which we, according to the text of the Gospel for today, shall
preach in all the world.

"What wilt thou have of us, brother?" you ask. I desire that you serve
Christ with zeal and not with sloth and indifference. I desire that you do
not mourn, but in thankfulness raise your hands to Heaven, whenever
your brother or your son enters the service of Christ. The time is come
when Christ will work not only in you but through you and in others;
whoever hears, let him say: "Come, brother." Let one draw the other.
Turn about, thou who thinkest that thou art of a superior mind and
therefore canst not accept the faith. If I could only explain this whole
Gospel to thee word for word, I would then scourge thy forehead and
prove to thee that the faith could not be false and that Christ is thy God
who is enthroned in heaven, and waits for thee. Or dost thou believe?
Where are thy works? Why dost thou delay about them?

Hear this: There was once a monk who spoke to a distinguished man
about the faith and got him to answer why he did not believe. He answered thus: "You yourself do not believe, for if you believed you would
show other works." Therefore, to you also I say: If you believe, where are
your works? Your faith is something everyone knows, for everyone knows
that Christ was put to death by the Jews, and that everywhere men pray
to Him. The whole world knows that His glory has not been spread by
force and weapons, but by poor fishermen. O wise man, do you think the
poor fishermen were not clever enough for this? Where they worked,
there they made hearts better; where they could not work, there men remained bad; and therefore was the faith true and from God. The signs
which the Lord had promised followed their teaching: in His name they
drove out the devil; they spoke in new tongues; if they drank any deadly
drink, they received therefrom no harm. Even if these wonders had not

occurred, there would have been the wonder of wonders, that poor fishermen without any miracle could accomplish so great a work as the faith.
It came from God, and so is Christ true and Christ is thy God, who is in
heaven and awaits thee.

You say you believe the Gospel, but you do not believe me. But the
purer anything is, so much the nearer it stands to its end and purpose.
The Christian life purifies the heart and places it very near to the truth.
To the Christian life will I lead you, if you would have the knowledge of
the truth. If I had wished to deceive you, why should I have given you as
the chief of my gifts the means of discovering my fraud? I would be
verily a fool to try to impose upon you with a falsehood which you would
soon detect; only because I offered you the truth, did I call you. Come
here, I fear you not; the closer you examine, the clearer the truth will
become to you.

There are some, however, who are ashamed of the cross of Jesus
Christ, and say: "If we should believe that, we should be despised everywhere, especially by the wisest." But if you would know the truth, look
only on the lives of those who would have to cry woe on their unbelief if
they should be measured by deeds. If you are ashamed of the cross, the
Lord was not ashamed to bear that cross for you, and to die on that cross
for you. Be not ashamed of His service and of the defense of the truth.
Look at the servants of the devil who are not ashamed in the open places,
in the palaces, and everywhere to speak evil and to revile us. Bear then a
little shame only for your Lord; for whoever follows Him will, according
to our gospel, in His name drive out the devil; that is, he will drive out his
sins and lead a virtuous life; he will drive out serpents; he will throw out
the lazy who come into the houses, and say evil things under the pretense
of righteousness, and so are like poisonous serpents. You will see how
children can withstand them with the truth of God and drive them away.
If a believer drinks anything deadly it will not hurt him: this deadly drink
is the false doctrines of the lazy, from whom, as you contend with them,
a little comes also to you. But he who stands unharmed in the faith, cries
to you: "See that you do good; seek God's glory, not your own." He that
does that is of the truth, and remains unharmed. The Lord says further
of the faithful: "They shall lay their hands on the sick and shall heal
them." The hands are the works, and the good lay such hands on the
weak that they may support them when they totter. Do I not teach you
according to the Gospel? Why do you hesitate and go not into the service
of the Lord? Do you ask me still what you ought to do? I will, in conclusion, tell you.

Look to Christ and you will find that all He says concerns faith. Ask

the Apostle; he speaks of nothing else than of faith. If you have the
ground of all, if you have faith, you will always do what is good. Without faith man always falls into sin. You must seek faith in order to be
good, or else your faith will become false. Christ commanded His disciples to preach the Gospel to all the world, and your wise men call a man
a little world, a microcosm. So then, preach to yourself, O man, woman,
and child. Three parts the world has in you also. Preach first of all to your
knowledge, and say to it: "If you draw near this truth, you will have
much faith; wherefore do you hesitate to use it?" To your will, say: "Thou
seest that everything passes away; therefore love not the world, love
Christ." Thereupon turn to the second part of your world, and say to it:
"Be thankful, O my memory, for the mercies God has shown thee, that
thou thinkest not of the things of this world but of the mercy of thy creation, and thy redemption through the blood of the Son of God." Then go
to the third part, to thy imagination, and proclaim to it: "Set nothing before my eyes but my death, bring nothing before me but the Crucified,
embrace Him, fly to Him." Then go through all the cities of thy world,
and preach to them. First say to thine eyes: "Look not on vanity." To thy
ears say: "Listen not to the words of the lazy, but only to the words of
Jesus." To thy tongue say: "Speak no more evil." For thy tongue is as a
great rock that rolls from the summit of a mountain, and at first falls
slowly, then ever faster and more furiously. It begins with gentle murmuring, then it utters small sins, and then greater, until it finally breaks
forth in open blasphemy. To thy palate say: "It is necessary that we do a
little penance." In all thy senses be clean, and turn to the Lord, for He it
is who will give you correction and purity. To thy hands say: "Do good
and give alms"; and let thy feet go in the good way. Our reformation has
begun in the Spirit of God, if you take it to heart that each one has to
preach to himself. Then will we in the name of Jesus drive out the devils
of temptation. Yes, call upon Jesus as often as temptation approaches:
call upon Him a hundred times and believe firmly, and the temptation
will depart. Then will we speak with new tongues; we will speak with
God. We shall drive away serpents; the enticement of the senses are these
serpents. If we drink anything deadly it will not hurt us; if anger and lust
arise in us, at the name of Jesus they will have to give way. We shall lay
our hands upon the sick and heal them; with good deeds shall we
strengthen the weak soul. If thou feelest thy weakness, flee to God, and
He will strengthen; therefore He is thy only refuge. He is thy Savior and
thy Lord, who went into the heavens to prepare a place for thee, and to
wait thee there. What do you intend to do? Go and follow Jesus, who is
praised from everlasting to everlasting. Amen.

(TRANSLATED BY JOSEPH CULLEN AYER)

The effect of Savonarola's eloquence was almost unparalleled. His faithful followers threw their "vanities" into the religious bonfires, and in short space the pagan indulgence of the city gave way to a pious austerity foreshadowing the ardor and conformity of Calvin's Geneva. A zealous preacher, poor in art, had captured the greatest city of the Renaissance. He remained its master for several years until the enmity of the Pope and the revulsion of the people turned the tide. He was consigned to the stake in 1498.

In his well-known work on The Civilization of the Renaissance in Italy Jacob Burckhardt sums up the genius of Savonarola: "The instrument by means of which he transformed and ruled the city of Florence (1494–98) was his eloquence. Of this the meager reports that are left to us, which were taken down mostly on the spot, give us evidently a very imperfect notion. It was not that he possessed any striking outward advantages, for voice, accent, and rhetorical skill constituted precisely his weakest side; and those who required the preacher to be a stylist, went to his rival Fra Mariano da Genazzano. The eloquence of Savonarola was the expression of a lofty and commanding personality, the like of which was not seen again till the time of Luther. He himself held his own influence to be the result of a divine illumination and could therefore, without presumption, assign a very high place to the office of the preacher, who, in the great hierarchy of spirits, occupies, according to him, the next place below the angels."

LUTHER DEFENDS HIMSELF AT THE DIET OF WORMS

[April 18, 1521]

The son of a small landholder and mine worker in Saxony, Martin Luther (1483–1546) appeared to be happy in his law studies in Erfurt. But in the summer of 1505, when twenty-one, he was caught in a terrifying thunderstorm, and seeing in it a divine warning for him to forsake the "world," vowed to St. Anne to become a monk. Two weeks later he entered the Augustinian monastery at Erfurt. Eventually he was ordained a priest and then went on to teach, first at Erfurt and afterward at the newly founded university at Wittenberg. But for a decade he suffered from a sense of sin and inevitable damnation. He agonized, studied, and pondered until 1515, when he began to prepare his lectures on Paul's Epistle to the Romans, with its momentous sentence, "The just shall live by faith." To Luther that soon came to mean, "The just shall live by faith alone," with the consequence that sacraments, "good works," and all the immense apparatus of the Church receded into the background. He now began to denounce the indiscriminate sale of indulgences, by which the temporal punishment still due to sin after it had been forgiven was remitted—and by which popularly, though improperly, guilt itself was removed.

It was on October 31, 1517, that Luther nailed up on the door of the Castle Church at Wittenberg his ninety-five theses, points for debate regarding the use and abuse of indulgences. Fierce debate did follow, warnings came from Rome, pamphlets came from Luther's pen: "The Address to the German Nobility," "The Babylonian Captivity," and "The Freedom of the Christian Man." A papal bull condemning forty-one of his sayings was burned by Luther at Wittenberg, and consequently he was excommunicated as a heretic.

At this juncture he was ordered to appear before the Diet of Worms, an assembly of nobles presided over by young Charles V, newly elected Emperor of the Holy Roman Empire and already King of Spain. There was tension between the Spanish and the German members of the Diet. "Had there been as many devils there as tiles on the roofs, I would have sprung into their midst gladly." But when confronted with so much power and dignity and asked suddenly if a certain number of books were his and if he would recant the heresies they contained, Luther asked for time to consider and he was given until the next day.

"Here I stand; I cannot do otherwise, so help me God!"

Most Serene Emperor, Illustrious Princes, Gracious Lords:

IN OBEDIENCE to your commands given me yesterday, I stand here, beseeching you, as God is merciful, so to deign mercifully to listen to this cause, which is, as I believe, the cause of justice and of truth. And if through inexperience I should fail to apply to any his proper title, or offend in any way against the manners of courts, I entreat you to pardon me as one not conversant with courts, but rather with the cells of monks, and claiming no other merit than that of having spoken and written with that simplicity of mind which regards nothing but the glory of God and the pure instruction of the people of Christ.

Two questions have been proposed to me: whether I acknowledge the books that are published in my name, and whether I am determined to defend or disposed to recall them. To the first of these I have given a direct answer, in which I shall ever persist that those books are mine and published by me, except so far as they may have been altered or interpolated by the craft or officiousness of rivals. To the other I am now about to reply; and I must first entreat your Majesty and your Highnesses to deign to consider that my books are not all of the same description. For there are some in which I have treated the piety of faith and morals

with simplicity so evangelical that my very adversaries confess them to
be profitable and harmless and deserving the perusal of a Christian. Even
the Pope's bull, fierce and cruel as it is, admits some of my books to be
innocent, though even these, with a monstrous perversity of judgment, it
includes in the same sentence. If, then, I should think of retracting these,
should I not stand alone in my condemnation of that truth which is acknowledged by the unanimous confession of all, whether friends or foes?

The second species of my publications is that in which I have inveighed against the papacy and the doctrine of the papists, as of men
who by their iniquitous tenets and examples have desolated the Christian
world, both with spiritual and temporal calamities. No man can deny or
dissemble this. The sufferings and complaints of all mankind are my witnesses that, through the laws of the Pope and the doctrines of men, the
consciences of the faithful have been ensnared, tortured, and torn in
pieces, while, at the same time, their property and substance have been
devoured by an incredible tyranny, and are still devoured without end
and by degrading means, and that too, most of all, in this noble nation
of Germany. Yet it is with them a perpetual statute that the laws and
doctrines of the Pope be held erroneous and reprobate when they are
contrary to the Gospel and the opinions of the Fathers.

If, then, I shall retract these books, I shall do no other than add
strength to tyranny and throw open doors to this great impiety, which
will then stride forth more widely and licentiously than it has dared
hitherto; so that the reign of iniquity will proceed with entire impunity,
and, notwithstanding its intolerable oppression upon the suffering vulgar,
be still further fortified and established; especially when it shall be proclaimed that I have been driven to this act by the authority of your serene
Majesty and the whole Roman Empire. What a cloak, blessed Lord,
should I then become for wickedness and despotism!

In a third description of my writings are those which I have published against individuals, against the defenders of the Roman tyranny
and the subverters of the piety taught by men. Against these I do freely
confess that I have written with more bitterness than was becoming either my religion or my profession; for, indeed, I lay no claim to any espe-
cial sanctity, and argue not respecting my own life, but respecting the
doctrine of Christ. Yet even these writings it is impossible for me to retract, seeing that through such retraction despotism and impiety would
reign under my patronage, and rage with more than their former ferocity
against the people of God.

Yet since I am but man and not God, it would not become me to go
further in defense of my tracts than my Lord Jesus went in defense of

His doctrine; who, when He was interrogated before Annas, and received a blow from one of the officers, answered: "If I have spoken evil, bear witness of the evil; but if well, why smitest thou me?" If then the Lord Himself, who knew His own infallibility, did not disdain to require arguments against His doctrine even from a person of low condition, how much rather ought I, who am the dregs of the earth and the very slave of error, to inquire and search if there be any to bear witness against my doctrine! Wherefore, I entreat you, by the mercies of God, that if there be anyone of any condition who has that ability, let him overpower me by the sacred writings, prophetical and evangelical. And for my own part, as soon as I shall be better instructed I will retract my errors and be the first to cast my books into the flames.

It must now, I think, be manifest that I have sufficiently examined and weighed, not only the dangers, but the parties and dissensions excited in the world by means of my doctrine, of which I was yesterday so gravely admonished. But I must avow that to me it is of all others the most delightful spectacle to see parties and dissensions growing up on account of the word of God, for such is the progress of God's word, such its ends and object. "Think not I am come to send peace on earth; I came not to send peace, but a sword. For I am come to set a man at variance against his father, and the daughter against her mother, and the daughter-in-law against her mother-in-law; and a man's foes shall be those of his own household."

Moreover, we should reflect that our God is wonderful and terrible in His counsels; so that His work, which is now the object of so much solicitude, if we should found it in the condemnation of the word of God, may be turned by His providence into a deluge of intolerable calamity; and the reign of this young and excellent prince (in whom is our hope after God), not only should begin, but should continue and close under the most glowing auspices.

I could show more abundantly by reference to scriptural examples—to those of Pharaoh, the king of Babylon, the kings of Israel—that they have brought about their own destruction by those very counsels of worldly wisdom which seemed to promise them peace and stability. For it is He who taketh the wise in their craftiness and removeth the mountains, and they know not, and overturneth them in His anger. So that it is the work of God to fear God. Yet I say not these things as if the great personages here present stood at all in need of my admonitions, but only because it was a service that I owed to my native Germany, and it was my duty to discharge it. And thus I commend myself to your serene Majesty

and all the princes, humbly beseeching you not to allow the malice of my
enemies to render me odious to you without a cause. I have done.

*When Luther had finished this speech, he was required to answer the simple
question: would he recant?*

Since your most serene Majesty and the princes require a simple
answer, I will give it thus: Unless I shall be convinced by proofs from
Scripture or by evident reason—for I believe neither in popes nor councils, since they have frequently both erred and contradicted themselves
—I cannot choose but adhere to the word of God, which has possession
of my conscience; nor can I possibly, nor will I ever make any recanta-
tion, since it is neither safe nor honest to act contrary to conscience! Here
I stand; I cannot do otherwise, so help me God! Amen.

*Luther was asked to repeat in Latin. He did so, and then, surrounded by a
protecting circle of the German members of the Diet, he withdrew to the outraged hisses of the Spaniards. The Protestant Reformation, or Rebellion, or
Schism, was now in full motion, and Luther survived for twenty-five years to
witness the results.*

*"Luther at Worms is the most pregnant and momentous fact in our history,"
said Lord Acton. Whether he was the great restorer of true Christianity or the
arch-destroyer of Christian unity remains a subject of hot debate. There is little
debate about his elemental personality, utterly fearless and furiously sincere.*

QUEEN ELIZABETH RALLIES HER ARMY
DURING THE ARMADA PERIL

[July 29, 1588]

*It is easy to imagine the horror and fascination that affected Englishmen in
1588, when they learned that the vast Spanish Armada was on its way, a mighty
empire moving relentlessly in tall ships toward the shores of England. Queen
Elizabeth, whose parsimony had hampered defense preparations so far, though
she certainly paid her troops better than other sovereigns of the time, now put
aside all thoughts of peace and, at the head of an enthusiastic people, faced the
enemy with spirit and determination. In spite of the danger involved she resolved to visit her troops in Tilbury, and an army was accordingly formed to*

protect her in case the enemy landed. For although the Armada had been defeated by this time, even Drake did not realize the plight of Parma, who was
poised on the other side of the Channel, and an invasion was expected momentarily. As she swept along the ranks at Tilbury with many a "God bless you,"
her soldiers kneeled. The speech that she then gave is believed to have been
dependably reported.

"I have the heart of a king."

MY LOVING PEOPLE, we have been persuaded by some, that are
careful of our safety, to take heed how we commit ourselves to
armed multitudes, for fear of treachery; but I assure you, I do not desire
to live to distrust my faithful and loving people. Let tyrants fear; I have
always so behaved myself that, under God, I have placed my chiefest
strength and safeguard in the loyal hearts and good will of my subjects.
And therefore I am come amongst you at this time, not as for my recrea-
tion or sport, but being resolved, in the midst and heat of the battle, to
live or die amongst you all; to lay down, for my God, and for my kingdom, and for my people, my honor and my blood, even the dust. I know
I have but the body of a weak and feeble woman; but I have the heart
of a king, and of a king of England, too; and think foul scorn that Parma
or Spain, or any prince of Europe, should dare to invade the borders of
my realms: to which, rather than any dishonor should grow by me, I
myself will take up arms; I myself will be your general, judge, and re-
warder of every one of your virtues in the field. I know already, by your
forwardness, and that you have deserved rewards and crowns; and we
do assure you, on the word of a prince, they shall be duly paid you. In the
mean my lieutenant general shall be in my stead, than whom never
prince commanded a more noble and worthy subject; not doubting by
your obedience to my general, by your concord in the camp, and by your
valor in the field, we shall shortly have a famous victory over the enemies
of my God, of my kingdom, and of my people.

The defeat of the Spanish Armada was the glorious climax of Elizabeth's reign.
Thirteen years later her prestige had reached its lowest point with the execution
of her former favorite, the brilliant and popular Earl of Essex, but within a few
months she had regained much of the old devotion with a few words to her
last turbulent Parliament.

Parliament at this time was willing to make extraordinary grants for defense, for a Spanish army had landed in Ireland, but could no longer stomach the greed of the royal monopolies. When the storm broke, the Queen replied graciously, promising an immediate remedy of the abuse, and welcomed a deputation of one hundred and forty members to hear her "golden" words. "Mr. Speaker," she said, "you give me thanks, but I am more to thank you, and I charge you, thank them of the lower house from me; for, had I not knowledge from you, I might have fallen into the lapse of an error, only for want of true information. . . . That my grants shall be made grievances to my people, and oppressions be privileged under the color of our patents, our princely dignity shall not suffer. When I heard it, I could give no rest to my thoughts until I had reformed it. . . . It is not my desire to live or reign longer than my life and reign shall be for your good. And though you have had, and may have, many mightier and wiser princes sitting in this seat, yet you have never had, nor shall have, any that will love you better."

JOHN DONNE, DEAN OF ST. PAUL'S, DELIVERS HIS OWN FUNERAL SERMON

[First Friday in Lent, 1631]

"Any man's death diminishes me because I am involved in mankind, and therefore never send to know for whom the bell tolls; it tolls for thee." These few lines, which repetition does not seem to dull, come not from a poem or a sermon by John Donne, but from a curious spiritual diary that the great preacher kept while he was recovering from a serious illness in 1623. It was published under the title of Devotions upon Emergent Occasions.

Born a Catholic, Donne ultimately reached the position that "there was truth in each form of the Christian religion; and that it is wisest and best for each man to accept the faith of his own country." After entering the Church of England, he waited for years for some kind of secular preferment, but when that was not forthcoming, he took holy orders and within a few years was rewarded with the rich deanery of St. Paul's, where he delivered some of the most impressive sermons in English history.

In January, 1630, he was living in the country, disabled by a painful illness —and now let his dear friend, Izaak Walton, take up the story:

"Before that month ended, he was appointed to preach upon his old constant day, the first Friday in Lent: he had notice of it, and had in his sickness so prepared for that employment that as he had long thirsted for it, so he resolved his weakness should not hinder his journey; he came therefore to London some few days before his appointed day of preaching. At his coming thither, many of his friends—who with sorrow saw his sickness had left him but so much flesh as did only cover his bones—doubted his strength to perform that task, and did therefore dissuade him from undertaking it, assuring him, however, it was like to shorten his life: but he passionately denied their requests, saying 'he would not doubt that that God, who in so many weaknesses had assisted him with an unexpected strength, would now withdraw it in his last employment; professing an holy ambition to perform that sacred work.' And when, to the amazement of some beholders, he appeared in the pulpit, many of them thought he presented himself not to preach mortification by a living voice, but mortality by a decayed body and a dying face. And doubtless many did secretly ask that question in Ezekiel (37:3): 'Do these bones live?' or, 'Can that soul organize that tongue, to speak so long time as the sand in that glass will move toward its center and measure out an hour of this dying man's unspent life?' Doubtless it cannot. And yet, after some faint pauses in his zealous prayer, his strong desires enabled his weak body to discharge his memory of his preconceived meditations, which were of dying; the text being, 'To God the Lord belong the issues from death.' Many that then saw his tears, and heard his faint and hollow voice, professing they thought the text prophetically chosen, and that Dr. Donne had preached his own Funeral Sermon."

"When my mouth shall be filled with dust . . ."

IT WAS a prerogative peculiar to Christ, not to die this death, not to see corruption. What gave Him this privilege? Not Joseph's great proportion of gums and spices, that might have preserved His body from corruption and incineration longer than He needed it, longer than three days, but it would not have done it forever. What preserved Him, then? Did His exemption and freedom from original sin preserve Him from this corruption and incineration? It is true that original sin hath induced this corruption and incineration upon us; if we had not sinned in Adam, *mortality had not put on immortality* (as the Apostle speaks), nor *corruption had not put on incorruption,* but we had had our transmigration from this to the other world without any mortality, any corruption at all. But yet since Christ took sin upon Him, so far as made Him mortal,

He had it so far too as might have made Him see this corruption in incineration, though He had no original sin in Himself; what preserved Him, then? Did the hypostatical union of both natures, God and man, preserve Him from this corruption and incineration? It is true that this was a most powerful embalming, to be embalmed with the Divine Nature itself, to be embalmed with eternity, was able to preserve Him from corruption and incineration forever. And He was embalmed so, embalmed with the Divine Nature itself, even in His body as well as in His soul; for the Godhead, the Divine Nature, did not depart, but remained still united to His dead body in the grave; but yet for all this powerful embalming, His hypostatical union of both natures, we see Christ did die; and for all His union which made him God and man, He became no man (for the union of the body and soul makes the man, and he whose soul and body are separated by death as long as that state lasts is properly no man). And therefore as in Him the dissolution of body and soul was no dissolution of the hypostatical union, so there is nothing that constrains us to say that, though the flesh of Christ had seen corruption and incineration in the grave, this had not been any dissolution of the hypostatical union, for the Divine Nature, the Godhead, might have remained with all the elements and principles of Christ's body, as well as it did with the two constitutive parts of His person, His body, and His soul. This incorruption, then, was not in Joseph's gums and spices, nor was it in Christ's innocency and exemption from original sin, nor was it (that is, it is not necessary to say it was) in the hypostatical union. But this incorruptibleness of His flesh is most conveniently placed in that: *Non dabis, thou wilt not suffer thy Holy One to see corruption;* we look no further for causes or reasons in the mysteries of religion, but to the will and pleasure of God; Christ Himself limited His inquisition in that *ita est, even so, Father, for so it seemeth good in thy sight.* Christ's body did not see corruption, therefore, because God had decreed it should not.

The humble soul (and only the humble soul is the religious soul) rests himself upon God's purposes and the decrees of God which He hath declared and manifested, not such as are conceived and imagined in ourselves, though upon some probability, some verisimilitude; so in our present case Peter proceeds in his sermon at Jerusalem, and so Paul in his at Antioch. They preached Christ to have been risen without seeing corruption, not only because God had decreed it, but because He had manifested that decree in His prophet, therefore doth St. Paul cite by special number the Second Psalm for that decree, and therefore both St. Peter and St. Paul cite for it that place in the Sixteenth Psalm; for when God declares His decree and purpose in the express words of His prophet, or when He declares it in the real execution of the decree, then He makes it ours, then He manifests it to us. And therefore, as the mysteries of our religion are not the objects of our reason, but by faith we rest on God's decree and purpose (it is so, O God, because it is Thy will it should be so), so God's decrees are ever to be considered in the manifestation thereof. All manifestation is either in the word of God or in the execution of the decree; and when these two concur and meet it is the strongest demonstration that can be: when therefore I find those marks of adoption and spiritual filiation which are delivered in the word of God to be upon me; when I find that real execution of His good purpose upon me, as that actually I do live under the obedience and under the conditions which are evidences of adoption and spiritual filiation; then, so long as I see these marks and live so, I may safely comfort myself in a holy certitude and a modest infallibility of my adoption. Christ determines Himself in that, the purpose of God was manifest to Him; St. Peter and St. Paul determine themselves in those two ways of knowing the purpose of God, the word of God before the execution of the decree in the fullness of time. It was prophesied before, said they, and it is performed now, Christ is risen without seeing corruption.

Now this which is so singularly peculiar to Him, that His flesh should not see corruption, at His second coming, His coming to judgment, shall extend to all that are then alive; their flesh shall not see corruption, because, as the Apostle says, and says as a secret, as a mystery, *Behold I shew you a mystery, we shall not all sleep* (that is, not continue in the state of the dead in the grave), *but we shall all be changed in an instant,* we shall have a dissolution, and in the same instant a redintegration, a recompacting of body and soul, and that shall be truly a death and truly a resurrection, but no sleeping in corruption; but for us that die now and sleep in the state of the dead, we must all pass this posthume death, this death after death, nay, this death after burial, this dissolution after dissolution, this death of corruption and putrefaction, of vermiculation and incineration, of dissolution and dispersion in and from the grave, when these bodies that have been the children of royal parents, and the parents of royal children, must say to Job, *To corruption, thou art my father, and to the worm, thou art my mother and my sister.* Miserable riddle, when the same worm must be my mother, and my sister, and myself! Miserable incest, when I must be married to my mother and my sister, and be both father and mother to my own mother and sister, beget and bear that worm which is all that miserable penury; when my mouth shall be filled with dust, and the *worm shall feed, and feed sweetly* upon me; when the ambitious man shall have no satisfaction, if the poorest alive tread upon him, nor the poorest receive any contentment in being made equal to princes, for they shall be equal but in dust. *One dieth at his full strength, being wholly at ease and in quiet; and another dies in the bitterness of his soul, and never eats with pleasure;* but *they lie down alike in the dust, and the worm covers them.* In Job and in Isaiah, it covers them and is spread under them, *the worm is spread under thee, and the worm covers thee.* There are the mats and the carpets that lie under, and there are the state and the canopy that hang over the greatest of the sons of men. Even those bodies that were *the temples of the Holy Ghost* come to this dilapidation, to ruin, to rubbish, to dust; even the Israel of the Lord, and Jacob himself, hath no other specification, no other denomination, but that *vermis Jacob,* thou worm of Jacob.

Truly the consideration of this posthume death, this death after burial, that after God (with whom are the issues of death) hath delivered me from the death of the womb, by bringing me into the world, and from the manifold deaths of the world, by laying me in the grave, I must die again in an incineration of this flesh, and in a dispersion of that dust. That that monarch, who spread over many nations alive, must in his dust lie in a corner of that sheet of lead, and there but so long as that lead will last; and that private and retired man, that thought himself his own forever, and never came forth, must in his dust of the grave be published, and (such are the revolutions of the grave) be mingled with the dust of every highway and of every dunghill, and swallowed in every puddle and pond. This is the most inglorious and contemptible vilification, the most deadly and peremptory nullification of man, that we can consider. . . .

"Being full of joy that God had enabled him to perform this desired duty, he hastened to his house; out of which he never moved, till, like St. Stephen, 'he was carried by devout men to his grave.' "—Izaak Walton, The Life of Dr. Donne

THOMAS HARRISON, REGICIDE, SPEAKS FROM THE SCAFFOLD

[October 13, 1660]

There was a growing tension between Elizabeth and her Parliament which subsided somewhat at the beginning of the reign of James I and then steadily increased. Charles I ascended the English throne in 1625 and lost his head in

1649. From 1649 until 1660, England was a militant Puritan Commonwealth, with Cromwell as Lord Protector from 1653 until his death in 1658.

Richard Cromwell succeeded his father as Lord Protector but, spurned by the army and openly ridiculed in the House of Commons, he resigned after eight months. Again the country was in confusion. It was now that General George Monk, the soldier-diplomat, who had switched from Charles I to Cromwell ten years before, marched down from Scotland with his army, took over London, dissolved the fragmentary Parliament, called into being a larger Parliament which favored the restoration, and brought back Charles II, "and all this without one bloody nose," as Richard Baxter put it.

Clever and colorful, licentious and treacherous in the extreme, the second Charles received a more than royal welcome on entering London May 29, 1660. In a conciliatory gesture he had proclaimed a general amnesty, but this did not include those who had been responsible for the execution of his father. Twenty-seven regicides were quickly rounded up, tried in five days, found guilty, and sentenced to be hanged, drawn, and quartered. The most conspicuous of these, and the first to be put to death as an example, was Thomas Harrison (1606–60). He had fought valiantly during the two civil wars, "as if he had been in a rapture," was one of the most zealous advocates of the King's execution, and aided Cromwell in expelling the Rump of the Long Parliament in 1653. A radical in religion and politics, he was disappointed when Cromwell assumed the Protectorate, and fell into disfavor. At the restoration he made no attempt to escape, and when denied counsel at the trial, he bluntly defended his actions. And now he speaks from the scaffold.

"By my God I will go through this death,
and He will make it easy to me."

Gentlemen:

I DID NOT EXPECT to have spoken a word to you at this time; but seeing there is a silence commanded, I will speak something of the work God had in hand in our days. Many of you have been witnesses of the finger of God, that hath been seen amongst us of late years, in the deliverance of His people from their oppressors, and in bringing to judgment those that were guilty of the precious blood of the dear servants of the Lord. And how God did witness thereto by many wonderful and evident testimonies, as it were immediately from Heaven, insomuch that many of our enemies—who were persons of no mean quality—were forced to confess that God was with us; and if God did but stand neuter, they should not value us; and, therefore, seeing the finger of God hath been pleading this cause, I shall not need to speak much to it; in which work I, with others, was engaged; for the which I do from my soul bless the name of God, who out of the exceeding riches of his grace accounted me worthy to be instrumental in so glorious a work. And though I am wrongfully charged with murder and bloodshed, yet I must tell you I have kept a good conscience both toward God and toward man. I never had malice against any man, neither did I act maliciously toward any person, but as I judged them to be enemies to God and His people; and the Lord is my witness that I have done what I did out of the sincerity of my heart to the Lord. I bless God I have no guilt upon my conscience but the spirit of God beareth witness that my actions are acceptable to the Lord, through Jesus Christ; though I have been compassed about with manifold infirmities, failings, and imperfections in my holiest duties, but in this I have comfort and consolation, that I have peace with God, and do see all my sins washed away in the blood of my dear Savior. And I do declare as before the Lord that I should not be guilty wittingly, nor willingly, of the blood of the meanest man—no, not for ten thousand worlds, much less of the blood of such as I am charged with.

I have again and again besought the Lord with tears to make known His will and mind unto me concerning it, and to this day He hath rather confirmed me in the justice of it, and, therefore, I leave it to Him, and to Him I commit my ways; but some that were eminent in the work did wickedly turn aside themselves, and to set up their nests on high, which caused great dishonor to the name of God and the profession they had made. And the Lord knows I could have suffered more than this, rather than have fallen in with them in that iniquity, though I was offered what I would if I would have joined with them; my aim in all my proceedings was the glory of God, and the good of his people, and the welfare of the whole Commonwealth.

Gentlemen, by reason of some scoffing that I do hear, I judge that some do think I am afraid to die, by the shaking I have in my hands and knees; I tell you no, but it is by reason of much blood I have lost in the wars, and many wounds I have received in my body, which caused this shaking and weakness in my nerves; I have had it this twelve years; I speak this to the praise and glory of God; He hath carried me above the fear of death; and I value not my life, because I go to my Father, and am assured I shall take it up again.

Gentlemen, take notice that for being instrumental in that cause and interest of the Son of God, which hath been pleaded amongst us, and which God hath witnessed to my appeals and wonderful victories, I am brought to this place to suffer death this day; and if I had ten thousand lives, I could freely and cheerfully lay them down all, to witness to this matter.

Oh, what am I, poor worm, that I should be accounted worthy to suffer anything for the sake of my Lord and Savior Jesus Christ! I have gone joyfully and willingly, many a time, to lay down my life upon the account of Christ, but never with so much joy and freedom as at this time; I do not lay down my life by constraint, but willingly, for if I had been minded to have run away, I might have had many opportunities; but being so clear in the thing, I durst not turn my back, nor step a foot out of the way, by reason I had been engaged in the service of so glorious and great a God. However men presume to call it by hard names, yet I believe, ere it be long, the Lord will make it known from heaven that there was more of God in it than men are now aware of.

I do desire as from my own soul that they and everyone may fear the Lord, that they may consider their latter end, and so it may be well with them; and even for the worst of those that have been most malicious against me, from my soul, I would forgive them all so far as anything concerns me; and so far as it concerns the cause and glory of God, I leave it for Him to plead; and as for the cause of God, I am willing to justify it by my sufferings, according to the good pleasure of His will. I have been this morning, before I came hither, so hurried up and down stairs (the meaning whereof I knew not) that my spirits are almost spent; therefore, you may not expect much from me.

Oh, the greatness of the love of God to such a poor, vile, and nothing creature as I am! What am I, that Jesus Christ should shed His heart's blood for me, that I might be happy to all eternity, that I might be made a son of God, and an heir of heaven! Oh, that Christ should undergo so great sufferings and reproaches for me! And should not I be willing to lay down my life, and suffer reproaches for Him that hath so loved me; blessed be the name of God that I have a life to lose upon so glorious and so honorable an account.

I have one word more to the Lord's people that desire to serve Him with an upright heart; let them not think hardly of any of the good ways of God for all this; for I have been near this seven years a suffering person, and have found the way of God to be a perfect way, His word a tried word, a buckler to them that trust in Him, and will make known His glorious arm in the sight of all nations. And though we may suffer hard things, yet He hath a gracious end, and will make a good end for His own glory, and the good of His people; therefore be cheerful in the Lord your God, hold fast that which you have and be not afraid of suffering, for

God will make hard and bitter things sweet and easy to all that trust in Him; keep close to the good confession you have made of Jesus Christ, and look to the recompense of reward; be not discouraged by reason of the cloud that now is upon you, for the sun will shine, and God will give a testimony unto what He hath been doing, in a short time.

And now I desire to commit my concernments into the hands of my Lord and Savior Jesus Christ, He that hath delivered Himself for the chief of sinners; He that came into the world, was made flesh, and was crucified; that hath loved me and washed me from my sins in His own blood, and is risen again, sitting at the right hand of God, making intercession for me.

And as for me, Oh! who am I, poor, base, vile worm, that God should deal thus by me? For this will make me come the sooner into His glory, and to inherit the kingdom and that crown prepared for me. Oh, I have served a good Lord and Master, which hath helped me from my beginning to this day, and hath carried me through many difficulties, trials, straits, and temptations, and hath always been a very present help in time of trouble; He hath covered my head many times in the day of battle; by God I have leaped over a wall, by God I have run through a troop, and by my God I will go through this death, and He will make it easy to me. Now into Thy hands, O Lord Jesus, I commit my spirit!

"The sentence was then executed to the letter. He was flung off, hanged a moment or two, but cut down still alive, for the opening of his body. As the hangman was at this savagery, nerve and muscle worked strongly in the half-dead man, and he struck the hangman a blow in the face. The head and heart were shown to the people, and there were great shouts of joy." (David Masson)

PART FOUR

TOWARD FREEDOM—AMERICAN,

ENGLISH, IRISH

WE TURN NOW to some fifty years of impassioned reason, from the courtroom masterpiece of a Philadelphia lawyer to the greatest triumph of Ireland's classic orator and to the public confession of faith of England's noblest political thinker.

Charles II, after a reign of a quarter of a century, died in 1685, to be succeeded by his even more vindictive, treacherous brother, James II, who was deposed in the bloodless "Glorious Revolution" of 1688. That revolution was given firm middle-class justification by the philosopher John Locke, who took a fairly sanguine view of human nature and argued for man's natural right to life, liberty, and property. William and Mary brought comparative calm to the English people after a century of violence or violent extremes. Queen Anne continued on that moderate course, and not even George I or George II became a grave center of disturbance. English armies kept the balance of power straight on the continent; the aristocratic Tories quarrelled with the aristocratic Whigs regarding the royal prerogative; and the middle class moved invincibly forward. Ireland writhed in poverty and impotence, and in memory of Cromwell's depredations.

Meanwhile the thirteen colonies in America were growing toward maturity and often growing restless under royal governors. They had been settled by people who had come for religious, political, and economic reasons, by people who had been "dissenters" in some form or another. Some of those settlers had fought in the English Civil War against the armies of Charles I, and indeed some of them had a hand in the execution of the King. The colonists of 1730 were familiar with the facts of the "Glorious Revolution" and with John Locke's justification of it. They were no doubt familiar with a ringing remark of Richard Rumbold, pronounced from the scaffold: "None comes into the world with a saddle on his back, neither any booted and spurred to ride him." Just because the colonists were so well off on the whole, they were peculiarly sensitive to the hand of oppression—more so than if they had been utterly oppressed.

ANDREW HAMILTON, "THE DAY STAR OF THE AMERICAN REVOLUTION," DEFENDS THE FREEDOM OF THE PRESS

[August 4, 1735]

Collections of American speeches almost invariably begin with James Otis speaking against the infamous writs of assistance in 1761. But the speech we are about to read was delivered in a New York courtroom twenty-six years earlier, and forty years before Concord and Lexington. The defendant in the case was a printer, John Peter Zenger (1697–1746), charged with libel. His attorney was Andrew Hamilton (1676–1741), whose name is too often forgotten while Zenger's alone is remembered. The key to the case lay in the law that permitted the jury only to decide on the fact of publication of the so-called "libel," while the judge alone was to decide on criminality. It was Hamilton's problem to speak over the head of the judge to the jury and persuade them to decide on both law and fact.

George William Curtis, the famous orator and publicist, told the story well in an address before the New York State Press Association in 1881:

"In 1725, the famous printer, William Bradford, issued the first newspaper in New York, the New York Gazette. Favored by the government, it supported the governor. But the people grew weary of the endless rapacity of the royal favorites who were sent over to rule them, and in 1732, when Governor Cosby, to advance a suit of his own, removed the chief justice of the province, sneering that the people were tainted with 'Boston principles,' and that he had great political interest in England to protect him in anything he chose to do, a storm of popular indignation broke upon him in lampoons and ballads and scorching denunciation. The storm did not blow over. In the next year, 1733, John Peter Zenger, who had been Bradford's apprentice and partner, issued a new paper, the New York Weekly Journal, as the advocate of the popular opposition. It opened an incessant battery of argument and wit and raillery and satire against the government—a cannonade of hot shot which was music to the public ear, but warning thunder to the governor and council. After copies of the paper had been publicly but vainly burned by their order, Zenger was arrested and imprisoned on a charge of seditious libel. In jail, where he lay for nine months, he still edited his paper. The grand jury refused to find an indictment, but the attorney general filed an information for malicious and seditious libel, and when Zenger's counsel excepted to the commissions of two of the judges as illegal, the court struck the names of the counsel from the list of

attorneys. The only other able lawyer in New York had been retained by the governor, and Zenger was left virtually without counsel.

"But Andrew Hamilton, the most eloquent advocate in Pennsylvania, and famous through all the colonies, heard the cry from New York. He was eighty years old [sic], but age had not withered him, and, born during the great struggle of the English commonwealth, its principles had been his natal air, and his heart beat high for liberty. He came from Philadelphia to New York and appeared before the amazed court to plead for Zenger. With impassioned eloquence, Hamilton, who doubtless knew by heart Milton's immortal plea for Unlicensed Printing, made his own great argument. He admitted the publication of the articles. 'Then the verdict must be for the King,' cried the attorney general. 'Not so,' answered Hamilton, 'the jury are judges of the law and the fact, and if it be truth it is not a libel.' With infinite skill and sparkling humor he followed with remorseless logic the attorney general's plea, searching his sophistry, confounding him at every point, and then, with a proud and lofty pathetic appeal, Hamilton declared that it was not the cause of a poor printer, nor of New York alone, but of America and of liberty, that was committed to the jury, and to their just and incorrupt verdict he looked with confidence for the defense of the liberty to which nature and the law entitled their fellow citizen; 'the liberty of both exposing and opposing arbitrary power, in these parts of the world at least, by speaking and writing truth.' "

*"The loss of liberty to a generous
mind is worse than death."*

MAY IT PLEASE your honors, I agree with Mr. Attorney [Richard Bradley] that government is a sacred thing, but I differ very widely from him when he would insinuate that the just complaints of a number of men, who suffer under a bad administration, is libeling that administration. Had I believed that to be law, I should not have given the court the trouble of hearing anything that I could say in this cause. I own when I read the information, I had not the art to find out (without the help of Mr. Attorney's innuendoes) that the Governor was the person meant in every period of that newspaper; and I was inclined to believe that they were written by some who, from an extraordinary zeal for liberty, had misconstrued the conduct of some persons in authority into crimes; and that Mr. Attorney, out of his too great zeal for power, had exhibited this information to correct the indiscretion of my client, and at the same time to show his superiors the great concern he had, lest they should be treated with any undue freedom. But from what Mr. Attorney had just now said, to wit, that this prosecution was directed by the Governor and council, and from the extraordinary appearance of people of all conditions which I observe in court upon this occasion, I have reason to think that those in the administration have by this prosecution something more in view, and that the people believe they have a good deal more at stake than I apprehended; and therefore, as it is become my duty to be both plain and particular in this cause, I beg leave to bespeak the patience of the court.

I was in hopes as that terrible court where those dreadful judgments were given and that law established, which Mr. Attorney has produced for authorities to support this cause, was long ago laid aside as the most dangerous court to the liberties of the people of England that ever was known in that kingdom, that Mr. Attorney, knowing this, would not have attempted to set up a Star Chamber here, nor to make their judgments a precedent to us; for it is well known that what would have been judged treason in those days for a man to speak, I think, has since not only been practiced as lawful, but the contrary doctrine has been held to be law.

There is heresy in law as well as in religion, and both have changed very much; and we well know that it is not two centuries ago that a man would have been burned as a heretic for owning such opinions in matters of religion as are publicly written and printed at this day. They were fallible men, it seems, and we take the liberty, not only to differ from them in religious opinion, but to condemn them and their opinions too; and I must presume that in taking these freedoms in thinking and speaking about matters of faith or religion, we are in the right; for, though it is said there are very great liberties of this kind taken in New York, yet I have heard of no information preferred by Mr. Attorney for any offenses of this sort. From which I think it is pretty clear that in New York a man may make very free with his God, but he must take special care what he says of his Governor. It is agreed upon by all men that this is a reign of liberty, and while men keep within the bounds of truth, I hope they may with safety both speak and write their sentiments of the conduct of men of power; I mean of that part of their conduct only which affects the liberty or property of the people under their administration; were this to be denied, then the next step may make them slaves. For what notions can be entertained of slavery beyond that of suffering the greatest injuries and oppressions without the liberty of complaining; or if they do, to be destroyed, body and estate, for so doing?

It is said, and insisted upon by Mr. Attorney, that government is a sacred thing; that it is to be supported and reverenced; it is government that protects our persons and estates; that prevents treasons, murders, robberies, riots, and all the train of evils that overturn kingdoms and states and ruin particular persons; and if those in the administration, especially the supreme magistrates, must have all their conduct censured by private men, government cannot subsist. This is called a licentiousness not to be tolerated. It is said that it brings the rulers of the people into contempt so that their authority is not regarded, and so that in the end the laws cannot be put in execution. These, I say, and such as these, are the general topics insisted upon by men in power and their advocates. But I wish it might be considered at the same time how often it has happened that the abuse of power has been the primary cause of these evils, and that it was the injustice and oppression of these great men which has commonly brought them into contempt with the people. The craft and art of such men are great, and who that is the least acquainted with history or with law can be ignorant of the specious pretenses which have often been made use of by men in power to introduce arbitrary rule and destroy the liberties of a free people. . . .

This is the second information for libeling of a governor that I have known in America. And the first, though it may look like a romance, yet, as it is true, I will beg leave to mention it. Governor Nicholson, who happened to be offended with one of his clergy, met him one day upon the road; and, as it was usual with him (under the protection of his commission), used the poor parson with the worst of language, threatened to cut off his ears, slit his nose, and, at last, to shoot him through the head. The parson, being a reverend man, continued all this time uncovered in the heat of the sun until he found an opportunity to fly for it; and coming to a neighbor's house felt himself very ill of a fever, and immediately wrote for a doctor; and that his physician might be the better judge of his distemper, he acquainted him with the usage he had received, concluding that the Governor was certainly mad, for that no man in his senses would have behaved in that manner. The doctor, unhappily, showed the parson's letter; the Governor came to hear of it, and so an information was preferred against the poor man for saying he believed the Governor was mad; and it was laid in the information to be false, scandalous, and wicked, and written with intent to move sedition among the people and bring his Excellency into contempt. But, by an order from the late Queen Anne, there was a stop put to the prosecution, with sundry others set on foot by the same Governor against gentlemen of the greatest worth and honor in that government.

And may not I be allowed, after all this, to say that, by a little countenance, almost anything which a man writes may, with the help of that useful term of art called an innuendo, be construed to be a libel, according to Mr. Attorney's definition of it; that whether the words are spoken of a person of a public character or of a private man, whether dead or living, good or bad, true or false, all make a libel; for, according to Mr. Attorney, after a man hears a writing read, or reads and repeats it, or laughs at it, they are all punishable. It is true, Mr. Attorney is so good as to allow, after the party knows it to be a libel; but he is not so kind as to take the man's word for it.

If a libel is understood in the large and unlimited sense urged by Mr. Attorney, there is scarce a writing I know that may not be called a libel, or scarce any person safe from being called to account as a libeler, for Moses, meek as he was, libeled Cain; and who is it that has not libeled the devil? For, according to Mr. Attorney, it is no justification to say one has a bad name. Eachard has libeled our good King William; Burnet has libeled, among many others, King Charles and King James; and Rapin has libeled them all. How must a man speak or write, or what must he hear, read, or sing? Or when must he laugh, so as to be secure from being taken up as a libeler? I sincerely believe that were some persons to go through the streets of New York nowadays and read a part of the Bible, if it were not known to be such, Mr. Attorney, with the help of his innuendoes, would easily turn it into a libel. As for instance: Isaiah 11:16: "The leaders of the people cause them to err, and they that are led by them are destroyed." But should Mr. Attorney go about to make this a libel, he would read it thus: "The leaders of the people" (*innuendo*, the Governor and council of New York) "cause them" (*innuendo*, the people of this province) "to err, and they" (the Governor and council meaning) "are destroyed" (*innuendo*, are deceived into the loss of their liberty), "which is the worst kind of destruction." Or if some person should publicly repeat, in a manner not pleasing to his betters, the tenth and the eleventh verses of the fifty-sixth chapter of the same book, there Mr. Attorney would have a large field to display his skill in the artful application of his innuendoes. The words are: "His watchmen are blind, they are ignorant," etc. "Yea, they are greedy dogs, they can never have enough." But to make them a libel, there is, according to Mr. Attorney's doctrine, no more wanting but the aid of his skill in the right adapting his innuendoes. As, for instance, "His watchmen" (*innuendo*, the Governor's council and assembly) "are blind, they are ignorant" (*innuendo*, will not see the dangerous designs of his Excellency). "Yea, they" (the Governor and council, meaning) "are greedy dogs, which can never have enough" (*innuendo*, enough of riches and power). Such an instance as this seems only fit to be laughed at, but I may appeal to Mr. Attorney himself whether these are not at least equally proper to be applied to his Excellency and his ministers as some of the inferences and innuendoes in his information against my client. Then, if Mr. Attorney be at liberty to come into court and file an information in the King's name without leave, who is secure whom he is pleased to prosecute as a libeler? And as the crown law is contended for in bad times, there is no remedy for the greatest oppression of this sort, even though the party prosecuted be acquitted with honor. And give me leave to say, as great men as any in Britain have boldly asserted that the mode of prosecuting by information (when a grand jury will not find *billa vera*) is a national grievance and greatly inconsistent with that freedom which the subjects of England enjoy in most other cases. But if we are so unhappy as not to be able to ward off this stroke of power directly, let us take care not to be cheated out of our liberties by forms and appearances; let us always be sure that the charge in the information is made out clearly, even beyond a doubt; for, though matters in the information may be called form upon trial, yet they may be, and often have been found to be, matters of substance upon giving judgment.

Gentlemen, the danger is great in proportion to the mischief that may happen through our too-great credulity. A proper confidence in a court is commendable, but as the verdict (whatever it is) will be yours, you ought to refer no part of your duty to the discretion of other persons. If you should be of opinion that there is no falsehood in Mr. Zenger's papers, you will, nay (pardon me for the expression), you ought to say so; because you do not know whether others (I mean the court) may be of that opinion. It is your right to do so, and there is much depending upon your resolution, as well as upon your integrity.

The loss of liberty to a generous mind is worse than death; and yet we know there have been those in all ages who, for the sake of preferment or some imaginary honor, have freely lent a helping hand to oppress, nay, to destroy, their country. This brings to my mind that saying of the immortal Brutus, when he looked upon the creatures of Caesar, who were very great men, but by no means good men: "You Romans," said Brutus, "if yet I may call you so, consider what you are doing; remember that you are assisting Caesar to forge those very chains which one day he will make yourselves wear." This is what every man that values freedom ought to consider; he should act by judgment and not by affection or self-interest;

for where those prevail, no ties of either country or kindred are regarded; as, upon the other hand, the man who loves his country prefers its liberty to all other considerations, well knowing that without liberty life is a misery. . . .

Power may justly be compared to a great river; while kept within its bounds, it is both beautiful and useful, but when it overflows its banks, it is then too impetuous to be stemmed; it bears down all before it, and brings destruction and desolation wherever it comes. If, then, this be the nature of power, let us at least do our duty, and, like wise men who value freedom, use our utmost care to support liberty, the only bulwark against lawless power, which, in all ages, has sacrificed to its wild lust and boundless ambition the blood of the best men that ever lived.

I hope to be pardoned, sir, for my zeal upon this occasion. It is an old and wise caution that "when our neighbor's house is on fire, we ought to take care of our own." For though, blessed be God, I live in a government where liberty is well understood and freely enjoyed, yet experience has shown us all (I am sure it has to me) that a bad precedent in one government is soon set up for an authority in another; and therefore I cannot but think it mine and every honest man's duty that, while we pay all due obedience to men in authority, we ought, at the same time, to be upon our guard against power wherever we apprehend that it may affect ourselves or our fellow subjects.

I am truly very unequal to such an undertaking, on many accounts. And you see I labor under the weight of many years and am borne down with great infirmities of body; yet old and weak as I am, I should think it my duty, if required, to go to the utmost part of the land, where my service could be of any use in assisting to quench the flame of prosecutions upon informations, set on foot by the government to deprive a people of the right of remonstrating, and complaining too, of the arbitrary attempts of men in power. Men who injure and oppress the people under their administration provoke them to cry out and complain, and then make that very complaint the foundation for new oppressions and prosecutions. I wish I could say there were no instances of this kind. But, to conclude, the question before the court, and you, gentlemen of the jury, is not of small nor private concern; it is not the cause of a poor printer, nor of New York alone, which you are now trying. No! It may, in its consequence, affect every free man that lives under a British government on the main continent of America. It is the best cause; it is the cause of liberty; and I make no doubt but your upright conduct, this day, will not only entitle you to the love and esteem of your fellow citizen, but every man who prefers freedom to a life of slavery will bless and honor you as men who have baffled the attempt of tyranny, and, by an impartial and uncorrupt verdict, have laid a noble foundation for securing to ourselves, our posterity, and our neighbors that to which nature and the laws of our country have given us a right—the liberty of both exposing and opposing arbitrary power (in these parts of the world at least) by speaking and writing truth.

"When Sir Henry Vane was carried to the scaffold, it was said that justice was seen sitting by his side; and when the Zenger jury cried 'Not Guilty,' and Andrew Hamilton left the courtroom, like an aureole around his reverend head shone the freedom of the American press. The thunder of the cannon, the music of the bells, the joyous feasting, and the fervidly grateful address of the city, saluted not the orator only, but American liberty which had caught a fresh breath of life from his burning lips." (Curtis)

Hamilton's speech has been called the "greatest oratorical triumph won in the colonies prior to the speech of James Otis against the writs of assistance." (H. L. Osgood) We may go further and say that it was a more powerful speech and bolder by twenty-six years. It pointed straight toward the American Bill of Rights and Charles James Fox's new libel law of 1792.

JOHN WESLEY DENOUNCES THE DOCTRINE OF PREDESTINATION

[April 29, 1739]

In complete contrast to the classic court preacher, Bossuet, with his orthodox doctrine, his carefully prepared sermons, and his small, aristocratic congregation, was John Wesley, who preached thousands of times to audiences of thousands.

One of nineteen children born to Samuel Wesley, a clergyman of the Church of England, and his indomitable wife Susanna, young John went to Oxford, where he was a leader of religious ascetics even then ridiculed as "methodists." Later he went as missionary to the Indians of Georgia and was himself deeply touched by the grave piety of the Moravians. But it was not until 1738, when he was thirty-five, that he experienced the conversion that became a turning point in modern religious history. The oft-quoted passage from the famous Journal reads: "In the evening I went very unwillingly to a society in Aldersgate Street where one was reading Luther's preface to the Epistle to the Romans. About a quarter before nine, while he was describing the change which God works in the heart through faith in Christ, I felt my heart strangely warmed. I felt I did trust in Christ, Christ alone, for salvation, and an assurance was given me that he had given away my sins, even mine, and saved me from the law of sin and death."

Instantly almost, Methodism became a great movement. The English masses, unwarmed by the cool formality of the Church of England, turned with enthusiasm to Wesley, George Whitefield, and the rest of the new evangelists. Such numbers and such excitement were unwelcome in most of the Anglican churches. Whitefield took to field preaching, and Wesley followed his example at Bristol in April, 1739. "I could scarce reconcile myself," he wrote in the Journal, "at first to this strange way, having been all my life, till very lately, so tenacious of every point relating to decency and order that I should have thought the saving of souls almost a sin, if it had not been done in a church." But he added that the Sermon on the Mount was "one pretty remarkable precedent of field preaching" and "I suppose there were churches at that time also." After the first trial was made, he wrote: "I submitted to be more vile, and proclaimed in the highways the glad tidings of salvation, speaking from a little eminence in a ground adjoining the city to about three thousand people."

It was on that field near Bristol, on April 29, 1739, that Wesley preached the sermon on "Free Grace," which may well have been the greatest of all his efforts.

"You represent God as worse than the devil; more false, more cruel, more unjust."

H E, THAT SPARED not His own Son, but delivered Him up for us all, how shall He not with Him also freely give us all things?" Romans 8:32.

How freely does God love the world! While we were yet sinners, "Christ died for the ungodly." While we were "dead in sin," God "spared not His own Son, but delivered Him up for us all." And how freely with Him does He "give us all things!" Verily, *free grace* is all in all!

The grace or love of God, whence cometh our salvation, is *free in all*, and *free for all*.

First: it is free *in all* to whom it is given. It does not depend on any power or merit in man; no, not in any degree, neither in whole, not in part. It does not in any wise depend either on the good works or righteousness of the receiver; not on anything he has done or anything he is. It does not depend on his endeavors. It does not depend on his good tempers, or good desires, or good purposes and intentions; for all these flow from the free grace of God; they are the streams only, not the fountain. They are the fruits of free grace, and not the root. They are not the cause, but the effects of it. Whatsoever good is in man, or is done by man, God is the author and doer of it. Thus is His grace free in all; that is, no way depending on any power or merit in man, but on God alone, who freely gave us His own Son, and "with him freely giveth us all things."

But is it free *for all* as well as *in all?* To this some have answered, "No: it is free only for those whom God hath ordained to life; and they are but a little flock. The greater part of mankind God hath ordained to death; and it is not free for them. Them God hateth; and therefore, before they were born, decreed they should die eternally. And this He absolutely decreed; because so was His good pleasure; because it was His sovereign will. Accordingly, they are born for this, to be destroyed body and soul in hell. And they grow up under the irrevocable curse of God, without any possibility of redemption; for what grace God gives He gives only for this, to increase, not prevent, their damnation.". . .

But if this be so, then is all preaching vain. It is needless to them that are elected; for they, whether with preaching or without, will infallibly be saved. Therefore, the end of preaching, to save souls, is void with regard to them. And it is useless to them that are not elected, for they cannot possibly be saved. They, whether with preaching or without, will infallibly be damned. The end of preaching is therefore void with regard to them likewise; so that in either case our preaching is vain, as your hearing is also vain.

This, then, is a plain proof that the doctrine of predestination is not a doctrine of God, because it makes void the ordinance of God: and God is not divided against Himself. A second is that it directly tends to destroy that holiness which is the end of all the ordinances of God. I do not say, none who hold it are holy (for God is of tender mercy to those who are unavoidably entangled in errors of any kind); but that the doctrine itself —that every man is either elected or not elected from eternity, and that the one must inevitably be saved and the other inevitably damned—has a manifest tendency to destroy holiness in general. For it wholly takes away those first motives to follow after it, so frequently proposed in Scripture, the hope of future reward and fear of punishment, the hope of heaven and fear of hell. That these shall go away into everlasting punishment, and those into life eternal, is no motive to him to struggle for life who believes his lot is cast already: it is not reasonable for him so to do, if he thinks he is unalterably adjudged either to life or death. You will say, "But he knows not whether it is life or death." What then?—this helps not the matter: for if a sick man knows that he must unavoidably die or un-avoidably recover, though he knows not which, it is unreasonable for him to take any physic at all. He might justly say (and so I have heard some speak, both in bodily sickness and in spiritual), "If I am ordained to life, I shall live; if to death, I shall die: so I need not trouble myself about it." So directly does this doctrine tend to shut the very gate of holiness in general, to hinder unholy men from ever approaching thereto or striving to enter in thereat.

As directly does this doctrine tend to destroy several particular branches of holiness. Such as meekness and love: love, I mean, of our enemies; of the evil and unthankful. I say not that none who hold it have meekness and love (for as is the power of God, so is His mercy); but that it naturally tends to inspire, or increase, a sharpness or eagerness of temper which is quite contrary to the meekness of Christ; as then espe-cially appears when they are opposed on this head. And it as naturally inspires contempt or coldness towards those whom we suppose outcasts from God. "Oh, but," you say, "I suppose no particular man a reprobate." You mean, you would not if you could help it. But you cannot help some-times applying your general doctrine to particular persons: the enemy of souls will apply it for you. You know how often he has done so. But you rejected the thought with abhorrence. True: as soon as you could: but how did it sour and sharpen your spirit in the meantime? You well know it was not the spirit of love which you then felt towards that poor sinner whom you supposed or suspected, whether you would or no, to have been hated of God from eternity.

Thirdly, this doctrine tends to destroy the comfort of religion, the happiness of Christianity. This is evident as to all those who believe themselves to be reprobated, or who only suspect or fear it. All the great and precious promises are lost to them; they afford them no ray of comfort: for they are not the elect of God: therefore, they have neither lot nor portion in them. This is an effectual bar to their finding any com-fort or happiness, even in that religion whose ways are designed to be "ways of pleasantness, and all her paths peace.". . .

Again: how uncomfortable a thought is this, that thousands and mil-lions of men, without any preceding offense or fault of theirs, were un-changeably doomed to everlasting burnings! How peculiarly uncomfort-able must it be to those who have put on Christ! To those who, being filled with bowels of mercy, tenderness, and compassion, could even "wish themselves accursed for their brethren's sake"!

Fourthly: this uncomfortable doctrine directly tends to destroy our zeal for good works. And this it does, first, as it naturally tends (according to what was observed before) to destroy our love to the greater part of mankind, namely, the evil and unthankful. For whatever lessens our love must so far lessen our desire to do them good. This it does, secondly, as it cuts off one of the strongest motives to all acts of bodily mercy, such as feeding the hungry, clothing the naked, and the like; *viz.*, the hope of saving their souls from death. For what avails it to relieve their temporal wants who are just dropping into eternal fire? "Well: but run and snatch them as brands out of the fire." Nay, this you suppose impossible. They were appointed thereunto, you say, from eternity, before they had done either good or evil. You believe it is the will of God they should die. And "who hath resisted His will?" But you say, you do not know whether these are elected or not. What then? If you know they are the one or the other, that they are either elected or not elected, all your labor is void and vain. . . .

But, fifthly, this doctrine not only tends to destroy Christian holiness, happiness, and good works, but hath also a direct and manifest tendency to overthrow the whole Christian revelation. The point which the wisest of the modern unbelievers most industriously labor to prove is that the Christian revelation is not necessary. They well know, could they once show this, the conclusion would be too plain to be denied, "If it be not necessary, it is not true." Now this fundamental point you give up. For supposing that eternal, unchangeable decree, one part of mankind must be saved, though the Christian revelation were not in being, and the other part of mankind must be damned, notwithstanding that revelation. And what would an infidel desire more? You allow him all he asks. In making the Gospel thus unnecessary to all sorts of men, you give up the whole Christian cause. "Oh, tell it not in Gath! Publish it not in the streets of Askelon! lest the daughters of the uncircumcised rejoice"; lest the sons of unbelief triumph!

And as this doctrine manifestly and directly tends to overthrow the whole Christian revelation, so it does the same thing, by plain consequence, in making that revelation contradict itself. For it is grounded on such an interpretation of some texts (more or fewer it matters not) as flatly contradicts all the other texts, and indeed the whole scope and tenor of Scripture. . . .

Thus manifestly does this doctrine tend to overthrow the whole Christian revelation, by making it contradict itself; by giving such an interpretation of some texts as flatly contradicts all the other texts, and indeed the whole scope and tenor of Scripture—an abundant proof that it is not of God. But neither is this all: for, seventhly, it is a doctrine full of blasphemy; of such blasphemy as I should dread to mention, but that the honor of our gracious God, and the cause of His truth, will not suffer me to be silent. In the cause of God, then, and from a sincere concern for the glory of His great name, I will mention a few of the horrible blasphemies contained in this horrible doctrine. But, first, I must warn every one of you that hears, as ye will answer it at the great day, not to charge me (as some have done) with blaspheming because I mention the blasphemy of others. And the more you are grieved with them that do thus blaspheme, see that ye "confirm your love towards them" the more, and that your hearts' desire, and continual prayer to God, be, "Father, forgive them, for they know not what they do."

This premised, let it be observed that this doctrine represents our blessed Lord, "Jesus Christ, the righteous," "the only begotten Son of the Father, full of grace and truth," as a hypocrite, a deceiver of the people, a man void of common sincerity. For it cannot be denied that He everywhere speaks as if He was willing that all men should be saved. Therefore, to say He was not willing that all men should be saved is to represent Him as a mere hypocrite and dissembler. It cannot be denied that the gracious words which came out of His mouth are full of invitations to all sinners. To say, then, He did not intend to save all sinners is to represent Him as a gross deceiver of the people. You cannot deny that He says, "Come unto me, all ye that are weary and heavy laden." If, then, you say He calls those that cannot come; those whom He knows to be unable to come; those whom He can make able to come, but will not; how is it possible to describe greater insincerity? You represent Him as mocking His helpless creatures by offering what He never intends to give. You describe Him as saying one thing, and meaning another; as pretending the love which He had not. Him, in "whose mouth was no guile," you make full of deceit, void of common sincerity—then especially, when, drawing nigh the city, He wept over it and said, "O Jerusalem, Jerusalem, thou that killest the prophets, and stonest them that are sent unto thee, how oft *would I* have gathered thy children together—and *ye would not.*" Now, if you say, *they would,* but *He would not,* you represent Him (which who could hear?) as weeping crocodile tears: weeping over the prey which Himself had doomed to destruction! . . .

This is the blasphemy clearly contained in *the horrible decree* of predestination! And here I fix my foot. On this I join issue with every assertor of it. You represent God as worse than the devil; more false, more cruel, more unjust. . . .

Oh, hear ye this, ye that forget God! Ye cannot charge your death upon Him! "Have I any pleasure at all that the wicked should die? saith the Lord God?" Ezekiel 18:23, etc. "Repent, and turn yourselves from all your transgressions; so iniquity shall not be your ruin. Cast away from you all your transgressions, whereby ye have transgressed . . . for why will ye die, O house of Israel? For I have no pleasure in the death of him that dieth, saith the Lord God: wherefore turn yourselves, and live ye." "As I live, saith the Lord God, I have no pleasure in the death of the wicked. . . . Turn ye, turn ye from your evil ways; for why will ye die, O house of Israel?"

The reaction to such sermons was always intense, fervent, and, on the part of many, violent and hysterical. Wesley alone was to preach over forty thousand such sermons, an average of fifteen a week during a period of fifty-three years, while he traveled on horseback some 220,000 miles! The result was immense for both religion and politics. The neglected masses of England were saved for heaven and saved from the revolution that overwhelmed France at the end of the century.

It may be added that Wesley's sermon on "Free Grace," in which he denounced predestinationism, alienated him from Whitefield for some years. We include no example of Whitefield's eloquence, for although he had an unrivaled power over huge congregations, and won the admiration of such diverse observers as David Hume, Lord Chesterfield, William Pitt the elder, and Benjamin Franklin, the printed page belies his reputation more completely perhaps than any other speaker's in history.

JAMES OTIS ARGUES AGAINST ILLEGAL
SEARCH AND SEIZURE

[February 24, 1761]

James Otis (1725–83), politician, publicist, and classical scholar, began his career as a barrister in Boston in 1750. He was outstanding in his courage, integrity, and the advanced character of his ideas. As a pleader, he scorned technicalities and argued his cases on their "broad and substantial foundations." He was a fearless advocate of political equality, "regardless of race, color, or previous condition of servitude," and favored the immediate abolition of slavery.

The colonies at this time, nearly fifteen years before the American Revolution, had need of such a man. In 1760 the British government ordered strict enforcement of the trade laws with the colonies, and writs of assistance were issued to the royal customs collectors. Empowered by these writs, the officers could search the house of any merchant, at any time of day or night, to look for smuggled goods. Since Otis held the post of King's advocate general of the vice-admiralty court at that time, he was expected to uphold the writs. Instead, he resigned this remunerative position to argue the case against them. Otis' speech, which lasted five hours, has not been preserved, save for the exordium, or beginning, which is printed below.

"A man's house is his castle; and whilst he is quiet, he is as well guarded as a prince in his castle."

MAY IT PLEASE your honors, I was desired by one of the court to look into the books, and consider the question now before them concerning writs of assistance. I have, accordingly, considered it, and now appear not only in obedience to your order, but likewise in behalf of the inhabitants of this town, who have presented another petition, and out of regard to the liberties of the subject. And I take this opportunity to declare that, whether under a fee or not (for in such a cause as this I despise a fee), I will to my dying day oppose with all the powers and faculties God has given me all such instruments of slavery, on the one hand, and villainy, on the other, as this writ of assistance is.

It appears to me the worst instrument of arbitrary power, the most destructive of English liberty and the fundamental principles of law, that ever was found in an English lawbook. I must, therefore, beg your honors' patience and attention to the whole range of an argument, that may, perhaps, appear uncommon in many things, as well as to points of learning that are more remote and unusual: that the whole tendency of my design may the more easily be perceived, the conclusions better descend, and the force of them be better felt. I shall not think much of my pains in this cause, as I engaged in it from principle. I was solicited to argue this cause as Advocate General; and because I would not, I have been charged with desertion from my office. To this charge I can give a very sufficient answer. I renounced that office, and I argue this cause from the same principle; and I argue it with the greater pleasure, as it is in favor of British liberty, at a time when we hear the greatest monarch upon earth declaring from his throne that he glories in the name of Briton, and that the privileges of his people are dearer to him than the most valuable prerogatives of his crown; and as it is in opposition to a kind of power the exercise of which, in former periods of history, cost one king of England his head and another his throne. I have taken more pains in this cause than I ever will take again, although my engaging in this and another popular cause has raised much resentment. But I think I can sincerely declare that I cheerfully submit myself to every odious name for conscience' sake; and from my soul I despise all those whose guilt, malice, or folly has made them my foes. Let the consequences be what they will, I am determined to proceed. The only principles of public conduct that are worthy of a gentleman or a man are to sacrifice estate, ease, health, and applause, and even life, to the sacred calls of his country.

These manly sentiments, in private life, make the good citizen; in public life, the patriot and the hero. I do not say that when brought to the test I shall be invincible. I pray God I may never be brought to the melancholy trial; but if ever I should, it will be then known how far I can reduce to practice principles which I know to be founded in truth. In the meantime I will proceed to the subject of this writ.

Your honors will find in the old books concerning the office of a justice of the peace precedents of general warrants to search suspected houses. But in more modern books you will find only special warrants to search such and such houses, specially named, in which the complainant has before sworn that he suspects his goods are concealed; and will find it adjudged that special warrants only are legal. In the same manner I rely on it that the writ prayed for in this petition, being general, is illegal. It is a power that places the liberty of every man in the hands of every petty officer. I say I admit that special writs of assistance, to search special places, may be granted to certain persons on oath; but I deny that the writ now prayed for can be granted, for I beg leave to make some observations on the writ itself, before I proceed to other acts of Parliament. In the first place, the writ is universal, being directed "to all and singular justices, sheriffs, constables, and all other officers and subjects"; so that, in short, it is directed to every subject in the king's dominions. Everyone with this writ may be a tyrant; if this commission be legal, a tyrant in a legal manner, also, may control, imprison, or murder anyone within the realm. In the next place, it is perpetual; there is no return. A man is accountable to no person for his doings. Every man may reign secure in his petty tyranny, and spread terror and desolation around him, until the trump of the archangel shall excite different emotions in his soul. In the third place, a person with this writ, in the daytime, may enter all houses, shops, etc., at will, and command all to assist him. Fourthly, by this writ, not only deputies, etc., but even their menial servants, are allowed to lord it over us. What is this but to have the curse of Canaan with a witness on us; to be the servant of servants, the most despicable of God's creation? Now, one of the most essential branches of English liberty is the freedom of one's house. A man's house is his castle; and whilst he is quiet, he is as well guarded as a prince in his castle. This writ, if it should be declared legal, would totally annihilate this privilege. Customhouse officers may enter our houses when they please; we are commanded to permit their entry. Their menial servants may enter, may break locks, bars, and everything in their way; and whether they break through malice or revenge, no man, no court, can inquire. Bare suspicion without oath is sufficient. This wanton exercise of this power is not a chimerical suggestion of a heated brain. I will mention some facts. Mr. Pew had one of these writs, and when Mr. Ware succeeded him, he indorsed this writ over to Mr. Ware; so that these writs are negotiable from one officer to another; and so your honors have no opportunity of judging the persons to whom this vast power is delegated. Another instance is this: Mr. Justice Walley had called this same Mr. Ware before him, by a constable, to answer for a breach of the Sabbath Day acts, or that of profane swearing. As soon as he had finished, Mr. Ware asked him if he had done. He replied: "Yes." "Well, then," said Mr. Ware, "I will show you a little of my power. I command you to permit me to search your house for uncustomed goods"; and went on to search the house from the garret to the cellar, and then served the constable in the same manner! But to show another absurdity in this writ, if it should be established, I insist upon it that every person, by the 14th of Charles II, has this power as well as the customhouse officers. The words are: "It shall be lawful for any person or persons authorized," etc. What a scene does this open! Every man prompted by revenge, ill humor, or wantonness to inspect the inside of his neighbor's house may get a writ of assistance. Others will ask it from self-defense; one arbitrary exertion will provoke another, until society be involved in tumult and in blood. . . .

John Adams, attending the court as a young man of twenty-five, was captivated by the power of Otis' argument. He later reported that "Otis' oration against the writs of assistance breathed into this nation the breath of life. . . . Otis was a flame of fire! . . . He hurried away everything before him. American independence was there and then born; the seeds of patriots and heroes were then and there sown." And further: "Every man of a crowded audience . . . appeared ready to take up arms against the writs of assistance. Then and there was the first scene of the first act of opposition to the arbitrary claims of Great Britain."

Although Otis lost the case, his speech in its wider effect was victorious. In 1766 Attorney General de Grey upheld Otis' position, ruling that the writs of assistance had not really been authorized. Ten years before the American

Revolution, the British thus backed down on an important issue involving a cherished freedom: that a man's home was his castle. Otis' argument, which invoked natural law as superior to acts of Parliament, was an incendiary force in the revolutionary era that was dawning.

WILLIAM PITT OBJECTS TO TAXATION WITHOUT REPRESENTATION

[January 14, 1766]

The elder William Pitt (1708–78), created Earl of Chatham in 1766, was known as a fiery orator from his early twenties, and also as a relentlessly honest paymaster of the army. But it was not until he was forty-eight, in 1756, that he became the virtual head of the government. Dismissed by George II, who hated him, he was back again after eleven weeks. As England's greatest war minister, during the important phases of the Seven Years' War, he directed the defeat of France in Canada and India as well as on the Continent, and so consolidated the British Empire. Before the conclusion of the war, however, the ambitious young George III came to the throne (1760) and forced the proud Pitt out of office (1761). Pitt's later years and his noblest oratorical efforts aimed to encourage generous policies that would hold the American colonies within the Empire. If his insistent warnings, seconded by Burke and Fox in the next decade, had been heeded, history would have been very different.

In 1766, after a long period of illness and bitterness, he returned to London to find himself in the midst of the violent debate over the Stamp Act, a measure peculiarly obnoxious to the Americans in that it imposed new, crushing taxes on British citizens not represented in Parliament. Focusing his criticism of the government on the principle that taxation was "no part of the governing or legislative power," Pitt rose in the House of Commons, on January 14, 1766, to deliver one of his greatest speeches.

"I rejoice that America has resisted."

Mr. Speaker:

I CAME TO TOWN but today. I was a stranger to the tenor of his Majesty's speech and the proposed address till I heard them read in this House. Unconnected and unconsulted, I have not the means of information. I am fearful of offending through mistake, and therefore beg to be indulged with a second reading of the proposed address. [The address being read, Mr. Pitt went on:] I commend the King's speech, and approve of the address in answer, as it decides nothing, every gentleman being left at perfect liberty to take such a part concerning America as he may afterward see fit. One word only I cannot approve of—an "early" is a word that does not belong to the notice the ministry have given to Parliament of the troubles in America. In a matter of such importance the communication ought to have been immediate.

I speak not now with respect to parties. I stand up in this place single and independent. As to the late ministry, every capital measure they have taken has been entirely wrong! As to the present gentlemen, to those at least whom I have in my eye [looking at the bench where General Conway sat with the lords of the treasury], I have no objection. I have never been made a sacrifice by any of them. Their characters are fair, and I am always glad when men of fair character engage in his Majesty's service. Some of them did me the honor to ask my opinion before they would engage. These will now do me the justice to own I advised them to do it; but, notwithstanding (for I love to be explicit), I cannot give them my confidence. Pardon me, gentlemen [bowing to the ministry], confidence is a plant of slow growth in an aged bosom. Youth is the season of credulity. By comparing events with each other, reasoning from effects to causes, methinks I plainly discover the traces of an overruling influence.

There is a clause in the Act of Settlement obliging every minister to sign his name to the advice which he gives to his sovereign. Would it were observed! I have had the honor to serve the crown, and if I could have submitted to influence, I might have still continued to serve; but I would not be responsible for others. I have no local attachments. It is indifferent to me whether a man was rocked in his cradle on this side or that side of the Tweed. I sought for merit wherever it was to be found. It is my boast that I was the first minister who looked for it, and found it, in the mountains of the north. I called it forth, and drew into your service a hardy and intrepid race of men—men who, when left by your jealousy, became a prey to the artifices of your enemies, and had gone nigh to have overturned the state in the war before the last. These men, in the last war, were brought to combat on your side. They served with fidelity, as they fought with valor, and conquered for you in every part of the world. Detested be the national reflections against them! They are unjust, groundless, illiberal, unmanly! When I ceased to serve his Majesty as a minister, it was not the country of the man by which I was moved—but the man of that country wanted wisdom, and held principles incompatible with freedom.

It is a long time, Mr. Speaker, since I have attended in Parliament. When the resolution was taken in this House to tax America, I was ill in bed. If I could have endured to be carried in my bed—so great was the agitation of my mind for the consequences—I would have solicited some kind hand to have laid me down on this floor, to have borne my testimony against it! It is now an act that has passed. I would speak with decency of every act of this House; but I must beg the indulgence of the House to speak of it with freedom.

I hope a day may soon be appointed to consider the state of the nation with respect to America. I hope gentlemen will come to this debate with all the temper and impartiality that his Majesty recommends and the importance of the subject requires; a subject of greater importance than ever engaged the attention of this House, that subject only excepted when, near a century ago, it was the question whether you yourselves were to be bond or free. In the meantime, as I cannot depend upon my health for any future day (such is the nature of my infirmities), I will beg to say a few words at present, leaving the justice, the equity, the policy, the expediency of the act to another time.

I will only speak to one point—a point which seems not to have been generally understood, I mean to the *right*. Some gentlemen seem to have considered it as a point of honor. If gentlemen consider it in that light, they leave all measures of right and wrong, to follow a delusion that may lead to destruction. It is my opinion that this kingdom has no right to lay a tax upon the colonies. At the same time, I assert the authority of this kingdom over the colonies to be sovereign and supreme, in every circumstance of government and legislation whatsoever. They are the subjects of this kingdom, equally entitled with yourselves to all the natural rights of mankind and the peculiar privileges of Englishmen; equally bound by its laws and equally participating in the Constitution of this free country. The Americans are the sons, not the bastards, of England! Taxation is no part of the governing or legislative power. The taxes are a voluntary *gift* and *grant* of the Commons alone. In legislation the three estates of the realm are alike concerned; but the concurrence of the peers and the Crown to a tax is only necessary to clothe it with the form of a law. The gift and grant is of the Commons alone.

In ancient days, the Crown, the barons, and the clergy possessed the lands. In those days, the barons and the clergy gave and granted to the Crown. They gave and granted what was their own! At present, since the discovery of America, and other circumstances permitting, the Commons are become the proprietors of the land. The Church (God bless it!) has but a pittance. The property of the Lords, compared with that of the

Commons, is as a drop of water in the ocean; and this House represents those Commons, the proprietors of the lands; and those proprietors virtually represent the rest of the inhabitants. When, therefore, in this House we give and grant, we give and grant what is our own. But in an American tax, what do we do? "We, your Majesty's Commons for Great Britain, give and grant to your Majesty"—what? Our own property! No! "We give and grant to your Majesty" the property of your Majesty's Commons of America! It is an absurdity in terms.

The distinction between legislation and taxation is essentially necessary to liberty. The Crown and the peers are equally legislative powers with the Commons. If taxation be a part of simple legislation, the Crown and the peers have rights in taxation as well as yourselves; rights which they will claim, which they will exercise, whenever the principle can be supported by power.

There is an idea in some that the colonies are *virtually* represented in the House. I would fain know by whom an American is represented here. Is he represented by any knight of the shire, in any county in this kingdom? Would to God that respectable representation was augmented to a greater number! Or will you tell him that he is represented by any representative of a borough?—a borough which, perhaps, its own representatives never saw! This is what is called the rotten part of the Constitution. It cannot continue a century. If it does not drop, it must be amputated. The idea of a virtual representation of America in this House is the most contemptible idea that ever entered into the head of a man. It does not deserve a serious refutation.

The Commons of America, represented in their several assemblies, have ever been in possession of the exercise of this their constitutional right of giving and granting their own money. They would have been slaves if they had not enjoyed it! At the same time, this kingdom, as the supreme governing and legislative power, has always bound the colonies by her laws, by her regulations, and restrictions in trade, in navigation, in manufactures, in everything, except that of taking their money out of their pockets without their consent.

[Pitt sat down, and George Grenville rose to defend the government policy, explaining that he saw no difference between internal and external taxes. Saying that the colonies were protected, and therefore justly taxed, he implied that Pitt was inciting them to sedition.]

I do not apprehend [said Pitt, replying immediately to Grenville] I am speaking twice. I did expressly reserve a part of my subject in order to save the time of this House; but I am compelled to proceed in it. I do not speak twice; I only finish what I designedly left imperfect. But if the

House is of a different opinion, far be it from me to indulge a wish of transgression against order. I am content, if it be your pleasure, to be silent. [Here the House shouted: "Go on! go on!"]

Gentlemen, sir, have been charged with giving birth to *sedition* in America. They have spoken their sentiments with freedom against this unhappy act, and that freedom has become their crime. Sorry I am to hear the liberty of speech in this House imputed as a crime. But the imputation shall not discourage me. It is a liberty I mean to exercise. No gentleman ought to be afraid to exercise it. It is a liberty by which the gentleman who calumniates it might have profited. He ought to have desisted from his project. The gentleman tells us America is obstinate; America is almost in open rebellion. I rejoice that America has resisted. Three millions of people, so dead to all the feelings of liberty as voluntarily to submit to be slaves, would have been fit instruments to make slaves of the rest. I come not here armed at all points, with law cases and acts of Parliament, with the statute book doubled down in dog's ears, to defend the cause of liberty. If I had, I myself would have cited the two cases of Chester and Durham. I would have cited them to show that, even under former arbitrary reigns, Parliaments were ashamed of taxing a people without their consent, and allowed them representatives. Why did the gentleman confine himself to Chester and Durham? He might have taken a higher example in Wales—Wales, that never was taxed by Parliament till it was incorporated. I would not debate a particular point of law with the gentleman. I know his abilities. I have been obliged to his diligent researches. But, for the defense of liberty, upon a general principle, upon a constitutional principle, it is a ground on which I stand firm—on which I dare meet any man. The gentleman tells us of many who are taxed and are not represented—the India Company, merchants, stockholders, manufacturers. Surely many of these are represented in other capacities, as owners of land or as freemen of boroughs. It is a misfortune that more are not equally represented. But they are all inhabitants and, as such, are they not virtually represented? Many have it in their option to be actually represented. They have connections with those that elect, and they have influence over them. The gentleman mentioned the stockholders. I hope he does not reckon the debts of the nation as a part of the national estate.

Since the accession of King William, many ministers, some of great, others of more moderate abilities, have taken the lead of government. None of these thought, or even dreamed, of robbing the colonies of their constitutional rights. That was reserved to mark the era of the late administration. Not that there were wanting some, when I had the honor to serve his Majesty, to propose to me to burn my fingers with an American stamp act. With the enemy at their back, with our bayonets at their breasts, in the day of their distress, perhaps the Americans would have submitted to the imposition; but it would have been taking an ungenerous, an unjust advantage. The gentleman boasts of his bounties to America! Are not these bounties intended finally for the benefit of this kingdom? If not, he has misapplied the national treasures!

I am no courtier of America. I stand up for this kingdom. I maintain that the Parliament has a right to bind, to restrain America. Our legislative power over the colonies is sovereign and supreme. When it ceases to be sovereign and supreme, I would advise every gentleman to sell his lands, if he can, and embark for that country. When two countries are connected together like England and her colonies, without being incorporated, the one must necessarily govern. The greater must rule the less. But she must so rule it as *not to contradict the fundamental principles that are common to both.*

If the gentleman does not understand the difference between external and internal taxes, I cannot help it. There is a plain distinction between taxes levied for the purposes of raising a revenue and duties imposed for the regulation of trade, for the accommodation of the subject; although, in the consequences, some revenue may incidentally arise from the latter.

The gentleman asks, when were the colonies emancipated? I desire to know, when were they made slaves? But I dwell not upon words. When I had the honor of serving his Majesty, I availed myself of the means of information which I derived from my office. I speak, therefore, from knowledge. My materials were good. I was at pains to collect, to digest, to consider them; and I will be bold to affirm that the profits to Great Britain from the trade of the colonies, through all its branches, is two millions a year. This is the fund that carried you triumphantly through the last war. The estates that were rented at two thousand pounds a year, threescore years ago, are at three thousand at present. Those estates sold then from fifteen to eighteen years' purchase; the same may now be sold for thirty. You owe this to America. This is the price America pays you for her protection. And shall a miserable financier come with a boast that he can bring "a peppercorn" into the exchequer by the loss of millions to the nation? I dare not say how much higher these profits may be augmented. Omitting the immense increase of people, by natural population, in the northern colonies, and the emigration from every part of Europe, I am convinced on other grounds that the commercial system of America may be altered to advantage. You have prohibited where you ought to have encouraged. You have encouraged where you ought to have prohibited. Improper restraints have been laid on the continent in favor of the islands. You have but two nations to trade with in America. Would you had twenty! Let acts of Parliament in consequence of treaties remain; but let not an English minister become a customhouse officer for Spain or for any foreign power. Much is wrong! Much may be amended for the general good of the whole!

Does the gentleman complain he has been misrepresented in the public prints? It is a common misfortune. In the Spanish affair of the last war, I was abused in all the newspapers for having advised his Majesty to violate the laws of nations with regard to Spain. The abuse was industriously circulated even in handbills. If administration did not propagate the abuse, administration never contradicted it. I will not say what advice I did give the King. My advice is in writing, signed by myself, in the possession of the Crown. But I will say what advice I did not give to the King. I did *not* advise him to violate any of the laws of nations.

The gentleman must not wonder he was not contradicted when, as minister, he asserted the right of Parliament to tax America. I know not how it is, but there is a modesty in this House which does not choose to contradict a minister. Even your chair, sir, looks too often toward St. James'. I wish gentlemen would get the better of this modesty. If they do not, perhaps the collective body may begin to abate of its respect for the representative. Lord Bacon has told me that a great question would not fail of being agitated at one time or another. I was willing to agitate such a question at the proper season, *viz.*, that of the German war—*my* German war, they called it! Every session I called out: has anybody any objection to the German war? Nobody would object to it, one gentleman only excepted, since removed to the Upper House by succession to an ancient barony. He told me he did not like a German war. I honored the man for it, and was sorry when he was turned out of his post.

A great deal has been said without doors of the power, of the strength, of America. It is a topic that ought to be cautiously meddled with. In a good cause, on a sound bottom, the force of this country can crush America to atoms. I know the valor of your troops. I know the skill of your officers. There is not a company of foot that has served in America out of which you may not pick a man of sufficient knowledge and experience to make a governor of a colony there. But on this ground, on the Stamp Act, which so many here will think a crying injustice, I am one who will lift up my hands against it.

In such a cause, your success would be hazardous. America, if she fell, would fall like the strong man; she would embrace the pillars of the state, and pull down the Constitution along with her. Is this your boasted peace

—not to sheathe the sword in its scabbard, but to sheathe it in the bowels of your countrymen? Will you quarrel with yourselves, now the whole house of Bourbon is united against you; while France disturbs your fisheries in Newfoundland, embarrasses your slave trade to Africa, and withholds from your subjects in Canada their property stipulated by treaty; while the ransom for the Manilas is denied by Spain, and its gallant conqueror basely traduced into a mean plunderer—a gentleman whose noble and generous spirit would do honor to the proudest grandee of the country?

The Americans have not acted in all things with prudence and temper: they have been wronged: they have been driven to madness by injustice. Will you punish them for the madness you have occasioned? Rather let prudence and temper come first from this side. I will undertake for America that she will follow the example. There are two lines in a ballad of Prior's, of a man's behavior to his wife, so applicable to you and your colonies, that I cannot help repeating them:

> Be to her faults a little blind;
> Be to her virtues very kind.

Upon the whole, I will beg leave to tell the House what is my opinion. It is that the Stamp Act be repealed absolutely, totally, and immediately. That the reason for the repeal be assigned—*viz.*, because it was founded on an erroneous principle. At the same time, let the sovereign authority of this country over the colonies be asserted in as strong terms as can be devised, and be made to extend to every point of legislation whatsoever; that we may bind their trade, confine their manufactures, and exercise every power whatsoever, except that of taking money from their pockets without consent.

The decision in this controversy came quickly. The English merchant-manufacturers and the bold resistance of the Americans won the day. The Stamp Act was repealed, and there was great rejoicing in the colonies, where toasts were drunk to King George. Pitt, very pleased with his victory, wrote to his wife in a jubilant mood. His speech, as it turned out, was an inspiration to the colonies; it gave them their battle cry, "No taxation without representation," and it taught them that the best way of countering the usurpations of the crown was firm and dogged resistance to its exactions. Pitt hoped that more equitable British policies would bind the loyalty of the colonies, but probably no speech by any American ever did half so much to rouse the colonies to fight consistently for their rights.

The rejoicing in the colonies was premature. A Declaratory Act was passed in the same year, asserting the absolute right of Parliament to tax the colonies, and in 1767 came the Townshend Acts, imposing new taxes and new tax collectors on American ports, provocations that were to light the flame of revolution. The Townshend Acts, strange to tell, were passed during the government of Lord Chatham (July 30, 1766–October 14, 1768). Yet not so strange, for from early 1767 Chatham was "absolutely incapacitated from all attention to business": he was, in short, mad, and so remained until late 1768.

JOHN WILKES DENIES THE RIGHT OF THE HOUSE OF COMMONS TO REJECT DULY ELECTED MEMBERS

[February 22, 1775]

John Wilkes (1727–97), politician, journalist, and reformer, won fame as an opponent of the Tory policies of Bute and King George III and as a defender of English—and American—liberties. "The Americans," he said in 1775, "will triumph." He excited the fury of the Tories but was warmly defended by the Whigs and was loved by the people as a patriot. Even in America his reputation spread, and the city of Wilkes-Barre, in Pennsylvania, was named after him and his colleague in opposition to rampant Toryism, Colonel Isaac Barré.

Entering Parliament in 1757, in 1762 he founded The North Britain, chiefly to criticize the government. At that time the battle for the freedom of the press had not yet been won. In 1763 an article appeared that so incensed the Tories that the House of Commons ordered the issue burned. Pursued then by ruffians, and forced into a duel, Wilkes was obliged to flee to France. In the year following, he was expelled from the House for seditious libel. He was later tried for this offense in his absence, convicted, and outlawed. This persecution, however, had an unintended effect. It made Wilkes a hero and a patriot throughout England. Four years later, in 1768, he returned to England, and though a convict and an outlaw, he was almost unanimously elected to Parliament from Middlesex. There the slogan of the workingmen was "Number 45, Wilkes, and Liberty," 45 being the number of The North Britain that had been burned.

Wilkes' victory was short-lived. Although the outlawry against him was lifted, he was sentenced to two years in prison on the old charge of seditious libel, and the House voted that his seat was vacant. When a new election was held in Middlesex, however, Wilkes was re-elected. But it was not until he had been elected five times that he was permitted to take his seat in Parliament without opposition. He continued to represent Middlesex until the end of his Parliamentary career in 1790. While his seating was disallowed, the people of London had shown their loyalty to him and his cause by naming him an alderman, and then lord mayor of London.

In the following speech, Wilkes tells his own story to the House of Commons in concise but moving terms.

> *"But, sir, if you can expel whom you please, and reject those disagreeable to you, the House will be self-created and self-existing."*

THE MOTION which I shall have the honor of submitting to the House affects, in my opinion, the very vitals of this Constitution, the great primary sources of the power of the people, whom we represent, and by whose authority only, delegated to us for a time, we are a part of the legislative body of this kingdom. The proceedings of the last Parliament in the business of the Middlesex elections gave a just alarm to almost every elector in the nation. The fatal precedents then attempted to be established were considered as a direct attack on the inalienable rights of the people. The most respectable bodies in this kingdom expressed their abhorrence of the measure: they proceeded so far as to petition the Crown for the dissolution of that Parliament, as having been guilty of a flagrant abuse of their trust. Above sixty thousand of our fellow subjects carried their complaints to the foot of the throne; a number surely deserving the highest regard from a minister, if his whole attention had not been engrossed by the small number of the six thousand who return the majority of members to this House. The people, sir, were in a ferment, which has not yet subsided. They made my cause their own, for they saw the powers of government exerted against the Constitution, which was wounded through my sides; and the envenomed shafts of a wicked administration pointed at our laws and liberties, no less at a hated individual. The plan was carried on for some years with a spirit of malevolence and rancor which would have disgraced the very worst, but with a perseverance which would have done honor to the best cause. I do not mean, sir, to go through the variety of persecutions and injuries which that person suffered, I hope, with a becoming fortitude. I have forgiven them. All the great powers of the state at one time appeared combined to pour their vengeance on me. Even imperial Jove pointed his thunderbolts, red with uncommon wrath, at my devoted head. I was scorched, but not consumed. The broad shield of the law protected me. A generous public, and my noble friends, the freeholders of Middlesex, the ever-steady friends of liberty and their country, poured balm into my wounds; they are healed. Scarcely a scar remains: but I feel, I deeply feel, the wounds given to the Constitution; they are still bleeding; this House only can heal them: they only can restore the Constitution to its former state of purity, health, and vigor. May I be permitted to point out the mode of the cure, and the salutary methods I think you ought to apply before I proceed to the remedy, I shall beg the indulgence of the House to state the case; and I hope they will forgive a dry but candid narrative of facts, because I mean to argue from them; I will give them as briefly as possible, and with all the impartiality of a bystander.

Mr. Wilkes was first elected for the county of Middlesex on the twenty-eighth of March, 1768. He was expelled the third of February, 1769, and the second time chosen, without opposition, the sixteenth day of the same month. On the day following, the election was vacated, and he was declared by a majority of the house incapable of being elected into that Parliament. Notwithstanding this resolution of the House, he was a third time, on the sixteenth of March, elected without opposition; for I suppose the ridiculous attempt of a Mr. Dingley, who had not a single freeholder to propose or vote for him, can hardly be called an opposition. That election, however, was declared void the next day. On the thirteenth of April, Mr. Wilkes was a fourth time elected, by a majority of 1143 votes, against Mr. Luttrell, who had only 296. The same day, the House voted, "That Mr. Luttrell ought to have been returned." On the twenty-ninth of April, a petition was presented to the House, from the freeholders of Middlesex, by a worthy baronet (Sir George Savile), who is not only an honor to this House, but to human nature; notwithstanding which, the House, on the eighth of May, resolved, "That Henry Lawes Luttrell, Esq., is duly elected a knight of the shire, to serve in this present Parliament, for the county of Middlesex."

These are the leading facts. I will not trouble the clerk, sir, to read all the resolutions to which I have alluded; they are most of them fresh in the memories of gentlemen; I only call for that of February 17, 1769, respecting incapacity as the certain consequence of expulsion.

[The clerk read the resolution.]

Now, sir, I think it fair to state to the House the whole of what I intend to move in consequence of the facts I have stated and the resolution just read. The first motion I intend is that the resolution of this house of the seventeenth of February, 1769, "That John Wilkes, Esq., having been, in this session of Parliament, expelled this House, was and is incapable of being elected a member to serve in this present Parliament," be expunged from the journals of this House, as being subversive of the rights of the whole body of electors in this kingdom. This I hold of necessity to restore the Constitution, which that resolution tears up by the roots; I shall then, if I succeed, if justice and reverence for the Constitution prevail in this Parliament, proceed to the other motion, "That all the declarations, orders, and resolutions of this House respecting the election of John Wilkes, Esq., for the county of Middlesex as a void election; the due and legal election of Henry Lawes Luttrell, Esq., into the last Parliament, for the county of Middlesex; and the incapacity of John Wilkes, Esq., to be elected a member to serve in the said Parliament, be expunged from the journals of this House, as being subversive of the rights of the whole body of electors of this kingdom."

The words of the resolution of the seventeenth of February, 1769, which I mean particularly, are, "*was* and *is* incapable," and the explanation of them the same day in the order for a new writ, "in the room of John Wilkes, Esq., who is adjudged incapable of being elected a member to serve in this present Parliament." In the first formation of this government, in the original settlement of our Constitution, the people expressly reserved to themselves a very considerable part of the legislative power, which they consented to share jointly with a king and house of lords. From the great population of our island, this power could not be exercised personally, and therefore the many were compelled to delegate that power to a few; who thus became their deputies and agents only, or their representatives. It follows directly, from the very idea of choice, that such choice must be free and uncontrolled, admitting of no restrictions but the law of the land, to which king and lords are equally subject, and what must arise from the nature of the trust. A peer of Parliament, for instance, cannot be elected a member of the House of Commons, because he already forms part of another branch of the same legislative body. A lunatic has a natural incapacity. Other instances might be mentioned, but those two are sufficient. The freedom of election is, then, the common right of the people, their fair and just share of power; and I hold it to be the most glorious inheritance of every subject of this realm, the noblest and, I trust, the most solid part of that beautiful fabric, the English Constitution. . . .

But, sir, if you can expel whom you please, and reject those disagreeable to you, the House will be self-created and self-existing. The original idea of your representing the people will be lost. The consequences of such a principle are to the highest degree alarming. A more forcible en-

gine of despotism cannot be put into the hands of any minister. I wish
gentlemen would attend to the plain consequences of such proceedings,
and consider how they may be brought home to themselves. A member
hated or dreaded by the minister is accused of any crime; for instance, of
having written a pretended libel. I mention this instance as the crime
least likely to be committed by most of the members of this House. No
proof whatever is given on oath before you, because you cannot administer an oath. The minister invades immediately the rights of juries. Before any trial, he gets the paper voted a libel, and the member he wishes
expelled to be the author—which fact you are not competent to try.
Expulsion means, as is pretended, incapacity. The member is adjudged
incapable; he cannot be re-elected, and thus is he excluded from Parliament. A minister by such maneuvers may garble a House of Commons
till not a single enemy of his own, or friend of his country, is left here,
and the representation of the people is in a great degree lost. Corruption
had not lent despotism wings to fly so high in the time of Charles I, or
the minister of that day would have been contented with expelling Hampden and the four other heroes, because they had immediately been adjudged incapable, and he would thereby have incapacitated them from
thwarting in Parliament the arbitrary measures of a wicked court. Upon
all these considerations, in order to quiet the minds of the people, to
restore our violated Constitution to its original purity, to vindicate the
injured rights of this country in particular, and of all the electors of this
kingdom, and that not the least trace of the violence and injustice of the
last Parliament may disgrace our records, I humbly move, "That the
resolution of this House of the seventeenth of February, 1769, 'That
John Wilkes, Esq., having been in this session of Parliament expelled this
House, *was* and *is* incapable of sitting in the present Parliament,' be expunged from the journals of this House, as being subversive of the rights
of the whole body of electors of this kingdom."

*This speech did not win the battle for the freedom of the press, but it fore-
shadowed momentous victories ahead. Seven years later, in 1782, the resolution
denying him a seat in the House was struck from the records as "subversive of
the rights of the whole body of electors of this kingdom," and Wilkes lived to
see the government that had persecuted him completely discredited by its
policies. This lovable rogue and libertine, who is said to have consumed his
wife's fortune in election bribery, had waged a courageous fight that, for many
years to come, was to kindle enthusiasm for free elections and other principles
of liberty, and thus, by example, to weaken the periodic waves of reaction. The
Wilkes case, said Burke, rocked England for twenty years. The mysterious*

"Junius," the unidentified critic of the government, devoted himself to a defense of the principles involved; so did Chatham, while Burke returned to the subject several times.

EDMUND BURKE MAKES A LAST DESPERATE PLEA FOR CONCILIATION WITH THE AMERICAN COLONIES

[March 22, 1775]

In the entire history of eloquence, the mind of Edmund Burke stands out supreme. "To do him justice," said William Hazlitt, "it would be necessary to quote all his work; the only specimen of Burke is all that he wrote." Between 1766, when he entered Parliament, and 1794, when he withdrew, three years before his death, he dealt with such burning issues as the American colonies, Ireland, India, Catholic emancipation, and the African slave trade, with the extravagance of English royalty and the misery of English debtors, and, finally, with the earthquake of the French Revolution.

An Irish Protestant, Burke (1729–97) came to London in his twenties, apparently drawn toward the law by prudence and toward literature by temperament, but his political career was not fairly started until he became private secretary to the Whig leader, Lord Rockingham, through whose influence he entered Parliament from the pocket borough of Wendover.

As Pitt closed his career in the House of Commons with his superb denunciation of the Stamp Act, Burke opened his parliamentary career with two attacks on the same bill, "which were publicly commended by Mr. Pitt, and have filled the town with wonder," according to Dr. Johnson, writing at the time. "It was, indeed," as Macaulay said, "a splendid sunset and a splendid dawn."

While the King's personal government moved steadily toward disaster, Burke brought out in 1770 his masterly warning, Thoughts on the Present Discontents, which was only further confirmed by the twelve-year-old ministry (1770–82) of Lord North. The miniscule tax on tea was retained on principle by Lord North to exemplify the right of Parliament to tax the colonies, and it was opposed on principle by the colonists, who denied that right. The matter came to a head in the Boston Tea Party of December, 1773, followed by British retaliatory measures a few months later. It was at this point in Anglo-American affairs that Burke first displayed the full scale of his gorgeous wrath.

It showed great courage on the part of Burke, a new member, to undertake the cause of the colonists, who, temporarily at least, had lost favor even with most of their friends in Great Britain. To destroy £18,000 of tea had been, to say the least, tactless—though it is not by tact that liberties are won and retained. Burke, as much the friend of liberty as he was later to be the enemy of equality, tried to stay the passage of bills closing the port of Boston and annulling the Massachusetts charter. In vain, for his great speech of April 19, 1774, "On American Taxation," must be counted a glorious failure. The odious bills passed, and the colonists, in reaction, moved many steps nearer to separation from the mother country.

It was some nine months later, on January 20, 1775, that the aged Chatham, recovered from his mental malady but physically most ill, rose in the House of Lords and with much of his old power urged the removal from Boston of the British troops, who were a source of increasing friction. In a passage that must stir every American, Chatham said: "When your lordships look at the papers transmitted us from America, when you consider their decency, firmness, and wisdom, you cannot but respect their cause, and wish to make it your own. For myself, I must declare and avow that in all my reading and observation—and it has been my favorite study: I have read Thucydides, and have studied and admired the master states of the world—that for solidity of reasoning, force of sagacity, and wisdom of conclusion, under such a complication of difficult circumstances, no nation or body of men can stand in preference to the General Congress at Philadelphia. I trust it is obvious to your lordships that all attempts to impose servitude upon such men, to establish despotism over such a mighty continental nation, must be vain, must be fatal."

Present on this occasion was a not-uninterested agent from Pennsylvania, one Benjamin Franklin, who wrote to Lord Stanhope: "Dr. Franklin presents his best respects to Lord Stanhope, with many thanks to his lordship and Lord Chatham for the communication of so authentic a copy of the motion. Dr. Franklin is filled with admiration of that truly great man. He has seen in the course of his life sometimes eloquence without wisdom, and often wisdom without eloquence; in the present instance he sees both united, and both, as he thinks, in the highest degree possible."

However, Chatham's eloquence, as we know, did not secure the removal of General Gage's British troops from Boston, and by March Burke realized that the moment had come for one last desperate effort on his part. Speaking for more than three hours, and rather in sorrow than in anger, he brought forward thirteen resolutions for conciliation, which, if adopted, might have—even at that bitter stage of the quarrel between the colonies and the mother country—postponed the final break for many a year.

"The superior power may offer peace
with honor and with safety."

THE PROPOSITION is peace. Not peace through the medium of war; not peace to be hunted through the labyrinth of intricate and endless negotiations; not peace to arise out of universal discord, fomented, from principle, in all parts of the Empire; not peace to depend on the juridical determination of perplexing questions, or the precise marking the shadowy boundaries of a complex government. It is simple peace; sought in its natural course and in its ordinary haunts. It is peace sought in the spirit of peace, and laid in principles purely pacific. I propose, by removing the ground of the difference, and by restoring the former unsuspecting confidence of the colonies in the mother country, to give permanent satisfaction to your people; and (far from a scheme of ruling by discord) to reconcile them to each other in the same act, and by the bond of the very same interest which reconciles them to British government.

My idea is nothing more. Refined policy ever has been the parent of confusion, and ever will be so, as long as the world endures. Plain good intention, which is as easily discovered at the first view as fraud is surely detected at the last, is, let me say, of no mean force in the government of mankind. Genuine simplicity of heart is a healing and cementing principle. My plan, therefore, being formed upon the most simple grounds imaginable, may disappoint some people when they hear it. It has nothing to recommend it to the prurience of curious ears. There is nothing at all new and captivating in it. It has nothing of the splendor of the project which has been lately laid upon your table by the noble lord in the blue ribbon. It does not propose to fill your lobby with squabbling colony agents, who will require the interposition of your mace at every instant to keep the peace amongst them. It does not institute a magnificent auction of finance, where captivated provinces come to general ransom by bidding against each other until you knock down the hammer, and determine a proportion of payments beyond all the powers of algebra to equalize and settle.

The plan which I shall presume to suggest derives, however, one great advantage from the proposition and registry of that noble lord's project. The idea of conciliation is admissible. First, the House, in accepting the resolution moved by the noble lord, has admitted, notwithstanding the menacing front of our Address, notwithstanding our heavy

Bill of Pains and Penalties, that we do not think ourselves precluded from all ideas of free grace and bounty.

The House has gone further: it has declared conciliation admissible, previous to any submission on the part of America. It has even shot a good deal beyond that mark, and has admitted that the complaints of our former mode of exerting the right of taxation were not wholly unfounded. That right thus exerted is allowed to have something reprehensible in it, something unwise, or something grievous, since, in the midst of our heat and resentment, we, of ourselves, have proposed a capital alteration; and, in order to get rid of what seemed so very exceptionable, have instituted a mode that is altogether new; one that is, indeed, wholly alien from all the ancient methods and forms of Parliament.

The principle of this proceeding is large enough for my purpose. The means proposed by the noble lord for carrying his ideas into execution, I think, indeed are very indifferently suited to the end; and this I shall endeavor to show you before I sit down. But, for the present, I take my ground on the admitted principle. I mean to give peace. Peace implies reconciliation; and, where there has been a material dispute, reconciliation does in a manner always imply concession on the one part or on the other. In this state of things I make no difficulty in affirming that the proposal ought to originate from us. Great and acknowledged force is not impaired, either in effect or in opinion, by an unwillingness to exert itself. The superior power may offer peace with honor and with safety. Such an offer from such a power will be attributed to magnanimity. But the concessions of the weak are the concessions of fear. When such a one is disarmed, he is wholly at the mercy of his superior; and he loses forever that time and those chances which, as they happen to all men, are the strength and resources of all inferior power.

The capital leading questions on which you must this day decide are these two: first, whether you ought to concede; and secondly, what your concession ought to be. On the first of these questions we have gained (as I have just taken the liberty of observing to you) some ground. But I am sensible that a good deal more is still to be done. Indeed, sir, to enable us to determine both on the one and the other of these great questions with a firm and precise judgment, I think it may be necessary to consider distinctly the true nature and the peculiar circumstances of the object which we have before us. Because after all our struggle, whether we will or not, we must govern America according to that nature and to those circumstances, and not according to our own imaginations, nor according to abstract ideas of right; by no means according to mere general theories of government, the resort to which appears to me, in our present situation, no better than arrant trifling. I shall therefore endeavor, with your leave, to lay before you some of the most material of these circumstances in as full and as clear a manner as I am able to state them. . . .

As to the wealth which the colonies have drawn from the sea by their fisheries, you had all that matter fully opened at your bar. You surely thought those acquisitions of value, for they seemed even to excite your envy; and yet the spirit by which that enterprising employment has been exercised ought rather, in my opinion, to have raised your esteem and admiration. And pray, sir, what in the world is equal to it? Pass by the other parts, and look at the manner in which the people of New England have of late carried on the whale fishery. Whilst we follow them among the tumbling mountains of ice, and behold them penetrating into the deepest frozen recesses of Hudson's Bay and Davis Straits; whilst we are looking for them beneath the Arctic Circle, we hear that they have pierced into the opposite region of polar cold, that they are at the Antipodes, and engaged under the frozen Serpent of the south. Falkland Island, which seemed too remote and romantic an object for the grasp of national ambition, is but a stage and resting place in the progress of their victorious industry. Nor is the equinoctial heat more discouraging to them than the accumulated winter of both the Poles. We know that whilst some of them draw the line and strike the harpoon on the coast of Africa, others run the longitude, and pursue their gigantic game along the coast of Brazil. No sea but what is vexed by their fisheries. No climate that is not witness to their toils. Neither the perseverance of Holland, nor the activity of France, nor the dexterous and firm sagacity of English enterprise ever carried this most perilous mode of hardy industry to the extent to which it has been pushed by this recent people; a people who are still, as it were, but in the gristle, and not yet hardened into the bone of manhood. When I contemplate these things; when I know that the colonies in general owe little or nothing to any care of ours, and that they are not squeezed into this happy form by the constraints of watchful and suspicious government, but that, through a wise and salutary neglect, a generous nature has been suffered to take her own way to perfection; when I reflect upon these effects, when I see how profitable they have been to us, I feel all the pride of power sink, and all presumption in the wisdom of human contrivances melt and die away within me. My rigor relents. I pardon something to the spirit of liberty. . . .

Permit me, sir, to add another circumstance in our colonies, which contributes no mean part towards the growth and effect of this untractable spirit. I mean their education. In no country perhaps in the world is the law so general a study. The profession itself is numerous and powerful; and in most provinces it takes the lead. The greater number of the deputies sent to the Congress were lawyers. But all who read (and most do read) endeavor to obtain some smattering in that science. I have been told by an eminent bookseller that in no branch of his business, after tracts of popular devotion, were so many books as those on the law exported to the plantations. The colonists have now fallen into the way of printing them for their own use. I hear that they have sold nearly as many of Blackstone's *Commentaries* in America as in England. General Gage marks out this disposition very particularly in a letter on your table. He states that all the people in his government are lawyers, or smatterers in law; and that in Boston they have been enabled, by successful chicane, wholly to evade many parts of one of your capital penal constitutions. The smartness of debate will say that this knowledge ought to teach them more clearly the rights of legislature, their obligations to obedience, and the penalties of rebellion. All this is mighty well. But my honorable and learned friend on the floor, who condescends to mark what I say for animadversion, will disdain that ground. He has heard, as well as I, that when great honors and great emoluments do not win over this knowledge to the service of the state, it is a formidable adversary to government. If the spirit be not tamed and broken by these happy methods, it is stubborn and litigious. *Abeunt studia in mores.* This study renders men acute, inquisitive, dexterous, prompt in attack, ready in defense, full of resources. In other countries, the people, more simple, and of a less mercurial cast, judge of an ill principle in government only by an actual grievance; here they anticipate the evil, and judge of the pressure of the grievance by the badness of the principle. They augur misgovernment at a distance; and snuff the approach of tyranny in every tainted breeze.

The last cause of this disobedient spirit in the colonies is hardly less powerful than the rest, as it is not merely moral, but laid deep in the natural constitution of things. Three thousand miles of ocean lie between you and them. No contrivance can prevent the effect of this distance in weakening government. Seas roll, and months pass, between the order and the execution; and the want of a speedy explanation of a single point is enough to defeat a whole system. You have, indeed, "winged ministers of vengeance," who carry your bolts in their pounces to the remotest verge of the sea. But there a power steps in, that limits the arrogance of raging passions and furious elements, and says, "So far shalt thou go, and no farther." Who are you, that you should fret and rage, and bite the chains of nature?—nothing worse happens to you than does to all nations who have extensive empire; and it happens in all the forms into which empire can be thrown. In large bodies, the circulation of power must be less vigorous at the extremities. Nature has said it. The Turk cannot govern Egypt, and Arabia, and Kurdistan, as he governs Thrace; nor has he the same dominion in Crimea and Algiers which he has at Brusa and Smyrna. Despotism itself is obliged to truck and huckster. The Sultan gets such obedience as he can. He governs with a loose rein, that he may govern at all; and the whole of the force and vigor of his authority in his center is derived from a prudent relaxation in all his borders. Spain, in her provinces, is perhaps not so well obeyed as you are in yours. She complies too; she submits; she watches times. This is the immutable condition, the eternal law, of extensive and detached empire.

Then, sir, from these six capital sources: of descent; of form of government; of religion in the northern provinces; of manners in the southern; of education; of the remoteness of situation from the first mover of government; from all these causes a fierce spirit of liberty has grown up. It has grown with the growth of the people in your colonies, and increased with the increase of their wealth; a spirit, that unhappily meeting with an exercise of power in England, which, however lawful, is not reconcilable to any ideas of liberty, much less with theirs, has kindled this flame that is ready to consume us. . . .

I do not know that the colonies have, in any general way, or in any cool hour, gone much beyond the demand of immunity in relation to taxes. It is not fair to judge of the temper or dispositions of any man, or any set of men, when they are composed and at rest, from their conduct, or their expressions, in a state of disturbance and irritation. It is, besides, a very great mistake to imagine that mankind follow up practically any speculative principle, either of government or of freedom, as far as it will go in argument and logical illation. We Englishmen stop very short of the principles upon which we support any given part of our Constitution; or even the whole of it together. I could easily, if I had not already tired you, give you very striking and convincing instances of it. This is nothing but what is natural and proper. All government, indeed every human benefit and enjoyment, every virtue, and every prudent act, is founded on compromise and barter. We balance inconveniences; we give and take; we remit some rights, that we may enjoy others; and we choose rather to be happy citizens than subtle disputants. As we must give away some natural liberty, to enjoy civil advantages; so we must sacrifice some civil liberties, for the advantages to be derived from the communion and fellowship of a great empire. But, in all fair dealings, the thing bought must bear some proportion to the purchase paid. None will barter away the immediate jewel of his soul. Though a great house is apt to make slaves haughty, yet it is purchasing a part of the artificial importance of a great empire too dear, to pay for it all essential rights, and all the intrinsic dignity of human nature. None of us who would not risk his life rather than fall under a government purely arbitrary. But although there are some amongst us who think our Constitution wants many improvements, to make it a complete system of liberty; perhaps none who are of that opinion would think it right to aim at such improvement by disturbing his country and risking everything that is dear to him. In every arduous enterprise, we consider what we are to lose as well as what we are to gain; and the more and better stake of liberty every people possess, the less they will hazard in a vain attempt to make it more. These are the cords of man. Man acts from adequate motives relative to his interest; and not on metaphysical speculations. Aristotle, the great master of reasoning, cautions us, and with great weight and propriety, against this species of delusive geometrical accuracy in moral arguments, as the most fallacious of all sophistry. . . .

All this, I know well enough, will sound wild and chimerical to the profane herd of those vulgar and mechanical politicians who have no place among us; a sort of people who think that nothing exists but what is gross and material; and who, therefore, far from being qualified to be directors of the great movement of empire, are not fit to turn a wheel in the machine. But to men truly initiated and rightly taught, these ruling and master principles, which in the opinion of such men as I have mentioned have no substantial existence, are in truth everything and all in all. Magnanimity in politics is not seldom the truest wisdom; and a great empire and little minds go ill together. If we are conscious of our station, and glow with zeal to fill our places as becomes our situation and ourselves, we ought to auspicate all our public proceedings on America with the old warning of the Church, *Sursum corda!* We ought to elevate our minds to the greatness of that trust to which the order of Providence has called us. By adverting to the dignity of this high calling, our ancestors have turned a savage wilderness into a glorious empire; and have made the most extensive and the only honorable conquests, not by destroying, but by promoting the wealth, the number, the happiness of the human race. Let us get an American revenue as we have got an American empire. English privileges have made it all that it is; English privileges alone will make it all it can be.

In full confidence of this unalterable truth, I now (*quod felix faustumque sit*) lay the first stone of the Temple of Peace; and I move you—

"That the colonies and plantations of Great Britain in North America, consisting of fourteen separate governments, and containing two millions and upwards of free inhabitants, have not had the liberty and privilege of electing and sending any knights and burgesses or others to represent them in the high court of Parliament."

By the time Burke had finished, he had lost most of his audience, for he had talked too loftily and too long. Even young Thomas Erskine, who was to become the most eloquent speaker in the history of the British bar, slipped away, exhausted, although he read the speech with delight and could hardly think of anything else!

The vote against Burke's first resolution for conciliation with the colonies was 270–78.

PATRICK HENRY PREPARES VIRGINIA FOR WAR AGAINST THE MOTHER COUNTRY

[March 23, 1775]

At the very moment Edmund Burke was making his great plea in the House of Commons for conciliation with the American colonies, the Virginia convention of delegates to the Continental Congress was meeting for the third anxious day in the Old Church in Richmond. On the following morning, Patrick Henry brought the confusion to a head with three bold resolutions:

RESOLVED:
1. *That a well regulated militia, composed of gentlemen and yeomen, is the natural strength and only security of a free government. . . .*
2. *That such a militia is at this time especially necessary to protect our rights and liberties, which have been rendered insecure by the remissness of government in calling our Legislature together.*
3. *That this Colony be immediately put into a posture of defense.*

Patrick Henry, the rough, ill-educated upcountry lawyer, was now forty and at the height of his reputation as a jury spellbinder and fearless Virginia patriot. As a young man with wife and children, he had failed as a farmer and as a crossroads storekeeper. More or less by chance, he decided to try the law, and after some six or eight weeks of intensive reading he received a license. Within three years he was said to have won almost twelve hundred cases, including the famous Parsons case, in which he defended the planters against the churchmen.

He electrified the House of Burgesses, as every American schoolboy used to know, when, in the course of the bitter discussion of the Stamp Act in 1765, he cried out, "Caesar had his Brutus—Charles I his Cromwell—and George III [he continued, while cries of "Treason!" came from all parts of the hall] may profit by their example. If this be treason, make the most of it."

Now, ten years later, when the revolutionary fervor of the colonists was at fever pitch, the experienced, confident Henry could plunge into the defense of his resolutions with much more assurance.

"Shall we gather strength by irresolution and inaction?"
Mr. President:

NO MAN thinks more highly than I do of the patriotism, as well as abilities, of the very worthy gentlemen who have just addressed the House. But different men often see the same subject in different lights; and, therefore, I hope it will not be thought disrespectful to those gentlemen if, entertaining as I do opinions of a character very opposite to theirs, I shall speak forth my sentiments freely and without reserve. This is no time for ceremony. The question before the House is one of awful moment to this country. For my own part, I consider it as nothing less than a question of freedom or slavery; and in proportion to the magnitude of the subject ought to be the freedom of the debate. It is only in this way that we can hope to arrive at truth, and fulfill the great responsibility which we hold to God and our country. Should I keep back my opinions at such a time, through fear of giving offense, I should consider myself as guilty of treason towards my country, and of an act of disloyalty toward the Majesty of Heaven, which I revere above all earthly kings.

Mr. President, it is natural to man to indulge in the illusions of hope. We are apt to shut our eyes against a painful truth, and listen to the song of that siren till she transforms us into beasts. Is this the part of wise men, engaged in a great and arduous struggle for liberty? Are we disposed to be of the number of those who, having eyes, see not, and, having ears, hear not, the things which so nearly concern their temporal salvation? For my part, whatever anguish of spirit it may cost, I am willing to know the whole truth; to know the worst, and to provide for it.

I have but one lamp by which my feet are guided, and that is the lamp of experience. I know of no way of judging of the future but by the past. And judging by the past, I wish to know what there has been in the conduct of the British ministry for the last ten years to justify those hopes with which gentlemen have been pleased to solace themselves and the House. Is it that insidious smile with which our petition has been lately received? Trust it not, sir; it will prove a snare to your feet. Suffer not yourselves to be betrayed with a kiss. Ask yourselves how this gracious reception of our petition comports with those warlike preparations which cover our waters and darken our land. Are fleets and armies necessary to a work of love and reconciliation? Have we shown ourselves so unwilling to be reconciled that force must be called in to win back our love? Let us not deceive ourselves, sir. These are the implements of war and subjugation; the last arguments to which kings resort. I ask gentlemen, sir, what means this martial array, if its purpose be not to force us to submission? Can gentlemen assign any other possible motive for it? Has Great Britain any enemy, in this quarter of the world, to call for all this accumulation of navies and armies? No, sir, she has none. They are meant for us: they can be meant for no other. They are sent over to bind and rivet upon us those chains which the British ministry have been so long forging. And what have we to oppose to them? Shall we try argument? Sir, we have been trying that for the last ten years. Have we anything new to offer upon the subject? Nothing. We have held the subject up in every light of which it is capable; but it has been all in vain. Shall we resort to entreaty and humble supplication? What terms shall we find which have not been already exhausted? Let us not, I beseech you, sir, deceive ourselves longer. Sir, we have done everything that could be done to avert the storm which is now coming on. We have petitioned; we have remonstrated; we have supplicated; we have prostrated ourselves before the throne, and have implored its interposition to arrest the tyrannical hands of the ministry and Parliament. Our petitions have been slighted; our remonstrances have produced additional violence and insult; our supplications have been disregarded; and we have been spurned, with contempt, from the foot of the throne! In vain, after these things, may we indulge the fond hope of peace and reconciliation. There is no longer any room for hope. If we wish to be free—if we mean to preserve inviolate those inestimable privileges for which we have been so long contending—if we mean not basely to abandon the noble struggle in which we have been so long engaged, and which we have pledged ourselves never to abandon until the glorious object of our contest shall be obtained —we must fight! I repeat it, sir, we must fight! An appeal to arms and to the God of Hosts is all that is left us!

They tell us, sir, that we are weak; unable to cope with so formidable an adversary. But when shall we be stronger? Will it be the next week, or the next year? Will it be when we are totally disarmed, and when a British guard shall be stationed in every house? Shall we gather strength by irresolution and inaction? Shall we acquire the means of effectual resistance by lying supinely on our backs and hugging the delusive phantom of hope, until our enemies shall have bound us hand and foot? Sir, we are not weak if we make a proper use of those means which the God of nature hath placed in our power. Three millions of people, armed in the holy cause of liberty, and in such a country as that which we possess, are invincible by any force which our enemy can send against us. Besides, sir, we shall not fight our battles alone. There is a just God who presides over the destinies of nations, and who will raise up friends to fight our battles for us. The battle, sir, is not to the strong alone; it is to the vigilant, the active, the brave. Besides, sir, we have no election. If we were base enough to desire it, it is now too late to retire from the contest. There is no retreat but in submission and slavery! Our chains are forged! Their clanking may be heard on the plains of Boston! The war is inevitable—and let it come! I repeat it, sir, let it come.

It is in vain, sir, to extenuate the matter. Gentlemen may cry, Peace, Peace—but there is no peace. The war is actually begun! The next gale that sweeps from the north will bring to our ears the clash of resounding arms! Our brethren are already in the field! Why stand we here idle? What is it that gentlemen wish? What would they have? Is life so dear, or peace so sweet, as to be purchased at the price of chains and slavery? Forbid it, Almighty God! I know not what course others may take; but as for me, give me liberty or give me death!

He took his seat. No murmur of applause was heard. The effect was too deep. After the trance of a moment, several members started from their seats. The cry, "To arms!" seemed to quiver on every lip and gleam from every eye. Richard H. Lee arose and supported Mr. Henry, with his usual spirit and elegance. But his melody was lost amid the agitations of that ocean which the master spirit of the storm had lifted up on high. That supernatural voice still sounded in their ears, and shivered along their arteries. They heard, in every pause, the cry of liberty or death. They became impatient of speech—their souls were on fire for action.

The resolutions were adopted; and Patrick Henry, Richard H. Lee, Robert C. Nicholas, Benjamin Harrison, Lemuel Riddick, George Washington, Adam Stevens, Andrew Lewis, William Christian, Edmund Pendleton, Thomas Jefferson, and Isaac Zane, esquires, were appointed a committee to prepare the plan called for by the last resolution.

Thus William Wirt described the aftermath of one of the most crucial speeches in American history, in his pioneering biography (1817) of Patrick

Henry. He had never seen Henry, but he consulted many friends of Henry's, and eyewitnesses of that occasion, including Thomas Jefferson.

LORD CHATHAM, FORMERLY WILLIAM PITT, WOULD STOP THE WAR WITH THE COLONIES

[November 20, 1777]

In March, 1775, a few weeks after his unsuccessful effort to secure the removal of the British troops in Boston, Lord Chatham broke down again and was out of action for two crucial years. When he returned to the House of Lords in the spring of 1777 he still tried to persuade his stubborn colleagues to save the American colonies for the British Empire. At one point he cried: "You may ravage, you cannot conquer. It is impossible. You cannot conquer the Americans." And then the weak, crippled old man made an expressive gesture. "I might as well talk of driving them before me with this crutch."

From a series of five powerful speeches, made later the same year, we turn to a fragment of the second, which was delivered before the news of Burgoyne's disastrous surrender at Saratoga (October, 1777) had reached London.

"You cannot conquer America."

I RISE, my lords, to declare my sentiments on this most solemn and serious subject. It has imposed a load upon my mind which, I fear, nothing can remove; but which impels me to endeavor its alleviation by a free and unreserved communication of my sentiments.

In the first part of the address I have the honor of heartily concurring with the noble earl who moved it. No man feels sincerer joy than I do; none can offer more genuine congratulation on every accession of strength to the Protestant succession; I therefore join in every congratulation on the birth of another princess, and the happy recovery of her Majesty. But I must stop here; my courtly complaisance will carry me no further: I will not join in congratulation on misfortune and disgrace; I cannot concur in a blind and servile address, which approves, and endeavors to sanctify, the monstrous measures that have heaped disgrace and misfortune upon us—that have brought ruin to our doors. This, my lords, is a perilous and tremendous moment! It is not a time for adulation. The smoothness of flattery cannot now avail—cannot save us in this rugged and awful crisis. It is now necessary to instruct the throne in the language of truth. We must dispel the delusion and the darkness which envelop it; and display, in its full danger and true colors, the ruin that is brought to our doors.

This, my lords, is our duty; it is the proper function of this noble assembly, sitting, as we do, upon our honors in this house, the hereditary council of the Crown. And *who* is the minister—*where* is the minister— that has dared to suggest to the throne the contrary, unconstitutional language, this day delivered from it? The accustomed language from the throne has been application to Parliament for advice, and a reliance on its constitutional advice and assistance; as it is the right of Parliament to give, so it is the duty of the Crown to ask it. But on this day, and in this extreme momentous exigency, no reliance is reposed on our constitutional counsels! no advice is asked from the sober and enlightened care of Parliament! but the Crown, from itself, and by itself, declares an unalterable determination to pursue measures—and what measures, my lords?—the measures that have produced the imminent perils that threaten us; the measures that have brought ruin to our doors.

Can the minister of the day now presume to expect a continuance of support in this ruinous infatuation? Can Parliament be so dead to its dignity and its duty as to be thus deluded into the loss of the one and the violation of the other? to give an unlimited credit and support for the *steady* perseverance in measures—that is the word and the conduct proposed for our parliamentary advice, but dictated and forced upon us—in measures, I say, my lords, which have reduced this late flourishing Empire to ruin and contempt? "But yesterday, and England might have stood against the world: now, none so poor to do her reverence." I use the words of a poet; but though it be poetry, it is no fiction. It is a shameful truth that not only the power and strength of this country are wasting away and expiring, but her well-earned glories, her true honor, and substantial dignity are sacrificed. France, my lords, has insulted you; she has encouraged and sustained America; and whether America be wrong or right, the dignity of this country ought to spurn at the officious insult of French interference. The ministers and ambassadors of those who are called rebels and enemies are in Paris; in Paris they transact the reciprocal interests of America and France. Can there be a more mortifying insult? Can even our ministers sustain a more humiliating disgrace? Do they dare to resent it? Do they presume even to hint a vindication of their honor, and the dignity of the state, by requiring the dismissal of the plenipotentiaries of America? Such is the degradation to which they have reduced the glories of England! The people whom they affect to call contemptible rebels, but whose growing power has at last obtained the name of enemies; the people with whom they have engaged this country in war, and against whom they now command our implicit support in every measure of desperate hostility: this people, despised as rebels or acknowledged as enemies, are abetted against you, supplied with every military store, their interests consulted, and their ambassadors entertained, by your inveterate enemy; and our ministers dare not interpose with dignity or effect! Is this the honor of a great kingdom? Is this the indignant spirit of England, who, "but yesterday," gave law to the house of Bourbon? My lords, the dignity of nations demands a decisive conduct in a situation like this. Even when the greatest prince that perhaps this country ever saw filled our throne, the requisition of a Spanish general, on a similar subject, was attended to and complied with; for on the spirited remonstrance of the Duke of Alva, Elizabeth found herself obliged to deny the Flemish exiles all countenance, support, or even entrance into her dominions; and the Count le Marque, with his few desperate followers, was expelled the kingdom. Happening to arrive at the Brille, and finding it weak in defense, they made themselves masters of the place: and this was the foundation of the United Provinces.

My lords, this ruinous and ignominious situation, where we cannot act with success, nor suffer with honor, calls upon us to remonstrate in the strongest and loudest language of truth, to rescue the ear of Majesty from the delusions which surround it. The desperate state of our arms abroad is in part known; no man thinks more highly of them than I do: I love and honor the English troops: I know their virtues and their valor: I know they can achieve anything except impossibilities; and I know that the conquest of English America *is an impossibility*. You cannot, I venture to say it—YOU CANNOT conquer America. Your armies last war effected everything that could be effected; and what was it? It cost a numerous army, under the command of a most able general, now a noble lord in this house, a long and laborious campaign to expel five thousand Frenchmen from French America. My lords, you cannot conquer America. What is your present situation there? We do not know the worst; but we know that in three campaigns we have done nothing and suffered much. Besides the sufferings, perhaps total loss, of the northern force, the best appointed army that ever took the field, commanded by Sir William Howe, has retired from the American lines; he was obliged to relinquish his attempt, and, with great delay and danger, to adopt a new and distant plan of operations. We shall soon know, and in any event have reason to lament, what may have happened since. As to conquest, therefore, my lords, I repeat, it is impossible. You may swell every expense and every effort still more extravagantly; pile and accumulate every assistance you can buy or borrow; traffic and barter with every little pitiful German prince that sells and sends his subjects to the shambles of a foreign prince: your efforts are forever vain and impotent—doubly so from this mercenary aid on which you rely; for it irritates, to an incurable resentment, the minds of your enemies—to overrun them with the mercenary sons of rapine and plunder; devoting them and their possessions to the rapacity of hireling cruelty! If I were an American, as I am an Englishman, while a foreign troop was landed in my country, I never would lay down my arms—never —never—never. . . .

[Chatham continued at some length along these lines, then denounced furiously the employment of Indian troops against the colonists, and finally proposed an amendment to the address to the King offering congratulations on the birth of a princess: "to recommend an immediate cessation of hostilities, and the commencement of a treaty to restore peace and liberty to America, strength and happiness to England, security and permanent prosperity to both countries."]

My lords, I am old and weak, and at present unable to say more; but my feelings and indignation were too strong to have said less. I could not have slept this night in my bed, nor reposed my head on my pillow, without giving this vent to my eternal abhorrence of such preposterous and enormous principles.

The old lion still had the fear and respect of the drowsy House of Lords, but his amendment was lost by a vote of 97 to 24, and his three succeeding pleas were equally futile.

Sinking rapidly under age and illness, he could not understand that the breach between the colonies and the mother country was irreparable, and when he heard that the government was planning to recognize their independence he had himself carried into the House of Lords for his swan song. "He was dressed in a rich suit of black velvet, and covered up to the knees in flannel," wrote an eyewitness. "Within his large wig, little more of his countenance was seen than his aquiline nose and his penetrating eye, which retained all his native fire. He looked like a dying man, yet never was seen a figure of more dignity."

I thank God that I have been enabled to come here today to perform my duty, and speak on a subject which is so deeply impressed on my mind. I am old and infirm. I have one foot—more than one foot—in the grave. I have risen from my bed to stand up in the cause of my country—perhaps never again to speak in this house.

My lords, I rejoice that the grave has not closed upon me; that I am still alive, to lift up my voice against the dismemberment of this ancient and most noble monarchy! Pressed down as I am by the hand of infirmity, I am little able to assist my country in this most perilous conjuncture; but, my lords, while I have sense and memory, I will never consent to deprive the offspring of the royal house of Brunswick, the heirs of the Princess Sophia, of their fairest inheritance. Shall we tarnish the luster of this nation by an ignominious surrender of its rights and fairest possessions? Shall this great nation, that has survived, whole and entire, the Danish depredations, the Scottish inroads, the Norman Conquest—that has stood the threatened invasion of the Spanish Armada, now fall prostrate before the house of Bourbon? Surely, my lords, this nation is no longer what it was! Shall a people that seventeen years ago were the terror of the world now stoop so low as to tell their ancient inveterate enemy, Take all we have, only give us peace? It is impossible.

In God's name, if it is absolutely necessary to declare either for peace or war, and the former cannot be preserved with honor, why is not the latter commenced without delay? I am not, I confess, well informed as to the resources of this kingdom, but I trust it has still sufficient to maintain its just rights, though I know them not. But, my lords, any state is better than despair. Let us at least make one effort, and, if we must fall, let us fall like men!

Obviously, Chatham's mind was clouded, and he was thinking more of his ancient enemy, Bourbon France, than of his admired Americans. A little later he tried again to speak, but fell down in convulsions. He was carried out in the presence of a hushed House and died a few weeks later—England's nearest prototype of that later guardian of empire, Sir Winston Churchill.

HENRY GRATTAN DEMANDS AN INDEPENDENT PARLIAMENT FOR IRELAND

[April 19, 1780]

It is no accident that the subtitle of The Irish Orators *(1916), by Claude G. Bowers, is "A History of Ireland's Fight for Freedom." For one hundred and fifty years, from Henry Flood and Henry Grattan, at the time of the American*

Revolution, down to the final struggle after the First World War, there was not a decade without its brilliant, tragic voice.

The bitter trouble started with the so-called "Poynings' Act" (1494), by which, in the reign of Henry VII, it was enacted that all existing laws should be in force in Ireland, and that no Parliament should be held in Ireland without consent of the King and council, who were empowered to disallow statutes passed by the Irish Houses. Resentment, now muffled, now violent, became the story of Irish-English relations. All classes and almost all interests were touched by it, particularly among the Roman Catholics, who were pointedly discriminated against. Finally, in the eighteenth century, Irish nationalism was aroused by Jonathan Swift and other writers; it was encouraged by the successful revolt of the American colonists; it was inflamed by Henry Flood and the rise of the volunteers. In the English House of Commons, the Anglo-Irishman Burke pleaded for emancipation of the Irish Catholics and helped to alleviate restrictions upon Irish commerce. And it was then that the young Irish Protestant lawyer, Henry Grattan, who had studied law in London, entered the Irish Parliament.

Grattan was thirty-four when he spoke to his motion "that the King's most excellent Majesty and the Lords and Commons of Ireland are the only power competent to make laws to bind Ireland."

"I have no ambition, unless it be the ambition to break your chain and contemplate your glory."

SIR, I have entreated an attendance on this day that you might, in the most public manner, deny the claim of the British Parliament to make law for Ireland, and with one voice lift up your hands against it.

If I had lived when the 9th of William took away the woolen manufacture, or when the 6th of George I declared this country to be dependent and subject to laws to be enacted by the Parliament of England, I should have made a covenant with my own conscience to seize the first moment of rescuing my country from the ignominy of such acts of power; or, if I had a son, I should have administered to him an oath that he would consider himself a person separate and set apart for the discharge of so important a duty; upon the same principle I am now come to move a Declaration of Right, the first moment occurring, since my time, in which such a declaration could be made with any chance of success, and without aggravation of oppression.

Sir, it must appear to every person that, notwithstanding the import of sugar and export of woolens, the people of this country are not satisfied—something remains; the greater work is behind; the public heart is not well at ease. To promulgate our satisfaction; to stop the throats of millions with the votes of Parliament; to preach homilies to the volunteers; to utter invectives against the people, under pretense of affectionate advice, is an attempt, weak, suspicious, and inflammatory.

You cannot dictate to those whose sense you are entrusted to represent; your ancestors, who sat within these walls, lost to Ireland trade and liberty; you, by the assistance of the people, have recovered trade; you still owe the kingdom liberty; she calls upon you to restore it.

The ground of public discontent seems to be: "We have gotten commerce, but not freedom": the same power which took away the export of woolens and the export of glass may take them away again; the repeal is partial, and the ground of repeal is upon a principle of expediency.

Sir, "expedient" is a word of appropriated and tyrannical import; "expedient" is an ill-omened word, selected to express the reservation of authority, while the exercise is mitigated; "expedient" is the ill-omened expression of the Repeal of the American Stamp Act. England thought it "expedient" to repeal that law; happy had it been for mankind if, when she withdrew the exercise, she had not reserved the right! To that reservation she owes the loss of her American empire, at the expense of millions, and America the seeking of liberty through a sea of bloodshed. The repeal of the Woolen Act, similarly circumstanced, pointed against the principle of our liberty—a present relaxation, but tyranny in reserve—may be a subject for illumination to a populace, or a pretense for apostasy to a courtier, but cannot be the subject of settled satisfaction to a freeborn, intelligent, and injured community. It is therefore they consider the free trade as a trade *de facto*, not *de jure;* as a license to trade under the Parliament of England, not a free trade under the charters of Ireland —as a tribute to her strength to maintain which she must continue in a state of armed preparation, dreading the approach of a general peace, and attributing all she holds dear to the calamitous condition of the British interest in every quarter of the globe. This dissatisfaction, founded upon a consideration of the liberty we have lost, is increased when they consider the opportunity they are losing; for if this nation, after the death wound given to her freedom, had fallen on her knees in anguish, and besought the Almighty to frame an occasion in which a weak and injured people might recover their rights, prayer could not have asked, nor God have furnished, a moment more opportune for the restoration of liberty than this, in which I have the honor to address you.

England now smarts under the lesson of the American War; the doctrine of imperial legislature she feels to be pernicious; the revenues and monopolies annexed to it she has found to be untenable; she lost the power to enforce it; her enemies are a host, pouring upon her from all quarters of the earth; her armies are dispersed; the sea is not hers; she has no minister, no ally, no admiral, none in whom she long confides, and no general whom she has not disgraced; the balance of her fate is in the hands of Ireland; you are not only her last connection, you are the only nation in Europe that is not her enemy. Besides, there does, of late, a certain damp and spurious supineness overcast her arms and councils, miraculous as that vigor which has lately inspirited yours—for with you everything is the reverse; never was there a Parliament in Ireland so possessed of the confidence of the people; you are the greatest political assembly now sitting in the world; you are at the head of an immense army; nor do we only possess an unconquerable force, but a certain unquenchable public fire, which has touched all ranks of men like a visitation.

Turn to the growth and spring of your country, and behold and admire it; where do you find a nation who, upon whatever concerns the rights of mankind, expresses herself with more truth or force, perspicuity or justice? not the set phrase of scholastic men, not the tame unreality of court addresses, not the vulgar raving of a rabble, but the genuine speech of liberty, and the unsophisticated oratory of a free nation.

See her military ardor, expressed, not only in forty thousand men, conducted by instinct as they were raised by inspiration, but manifested in the zeal and promptitude of every young member of the growing community. Let corruption tremble; let the enemy, foreign or domestic, tremble; but let the friends of liberty rejoice at these means of safety and this hour of redemption. Yes; there does exist an enlightened sense of rights, a young appetite for freedom, a solid strength, and a rapid fire, which not only put a declaration of right within your power, but put it out of your power to decline one. Eighteen counties are at your bar; they stand there with the compact of Henry, with the charter of John, and with all the passions of the people. "Our lives are at your service, but our liberties—we received them from God; we will not resign them to man." Speaking to you thus, if you repulse these petitioners, you abdicate the privileges of Parliament, forfeit the rights of the kingdom, repudiate the instruction of your constituents, bilge the sense of your country, palsy the enthusiasm of the people, and reject that good which not a minister, not a Lord North, not a Lord Buckinghamshire, not a Lord Hillsborough, but a certain providential conjuncture, or, rather, the hand of God, seems to extend to you. Nor are we only prompted to this when we consider our strength; we are challenged to it when we look to Great Britain. The people of that country are now waiting to hear the Parliament of Ireland speak on the subject of their liberty; it begins to be made a question in England whether the principal persons wish to be free; it was the delicacy of former Parliaments to be silent on the subject of commercial restrictions, lest they should show a knowledge of the fact, and not a sense of the violation; you have spoken out, you have shown a knowledge of the fact, and not a sense of the violation. On the contrary, you have returned thanks for a partial repeal made on a principle of power; you have returned thanks as for a favor, and your exultation has brought your charters, as well as your spirit, into question, and tends to shake to her foundation your title to liberty; thus you do not leave your rights where you found them. You have done too much not to do more; you have gone too far not to go on; you have brought yourselves into that situation in which you must silently abdicate the rights of your country, or publicly restore them. It is very true you may feed your manufacturers, and landed gentlemen may get their rents, and you may export woolen, and may load a vessel with baize, serges, and kerseys, and you may bring back again directly from the plantations sugar, indigo, specklewood, beetle root, and panelas. But liberty, the foundation of trade, the charters of the land, the independency of Parliament, the securing, crowning, and the consummation of everything are yet to come. Without them the work is imperfect, the foundation is wanting, the capital is wanting, trade is not free, Ireland is a colony without the benefit of a charter, and you are a provincial synod without the privileges of a Parliament.

I read Lord North's proposition; I wish to be satisfied, but I am controlled by a paper—I will not call it a law—it is the 6th of George I. [The paper was read.] I will ask the gentlemen of the long robe: is this the law? I ask them whether it is not practice. I appeal to the judges of the land whether they are not in a course of declaring that the Parliament of Great Britain, naming Ireland, binds her. I appeal to the magistrates of justice whether they do not, from time to time, execute certain acts of the British Parliament. I appeal to the officers of the army whether they do not fine, confine, and execute their fellow subjects by virtue of the Mutiny Act, an act of the British Parliament; and I appeal to this House whether a country so circumstanced is free. Where is the freedom of trade? Where is the security of property? Where is the liberty of the people? I here, in this Declaratory Act, see my country proclaimed a slave! I see every man in this House enrolled a slave! I see the judges of the realm, the oracles of the law, borne down by an unauthorized foreign power, by the authority of the British Parliament against the law! I see the magistrates prostrate, and I see Parliament witness of these infringements, and silent—silent or employed to preach moderation to the people, whose liberties it will not restore! I therefore say, with the voice of three million people, that, notwithstanding the import of sugar, beetlewood, and panelas, and the export of woolens and kerseys, nothing is safe, satisfactory, or honorable, nothing except a declaration of right. What! are you, with three million men at your back, with charters in one hand and arms in the other, afraid to say you are a free people? Are you, the greatest House of Commons that ever sat in Ireland, that want but this one act to equal that English House of Commons that passed the Petition of Right, or that other that passed the Declaration of Right—are you afraid to tell that British Parliament you are a free people? Are the cities and the instructing counties, who have breathed a spirit that would have done honor to old Rome when Rome did honor to mankind—are they to be free by connivance? Are the military associations, those bodies whose origin, progress, and deportment have transcended, or equaled at least, anything in modern or ancient story—is the vast line of the northern army—are they to be free by connivance? What man will settle among you? Where is the use of the Naturalization Bill? What man will settle among you? who will leave a land of liberty and a settled government for a kingdom controlled by the Parliament of another country, whose liberty is a thing by stealth, whose trade a thing by permission, whose judges deny her charters, whose Parliament leaves everything at random; where the chance of freedom depends upon the hope that the jury shall despise the judge stating a British act, or a rabble stop the magistrate executing it, rescue your abdicated privileges, and save the Constitution by trampling on the government—by anarchy and confusion!

But I shall be told that these are groundless jealousies, and that the people of the principal cities, and more than one half of the counties of the Kingdom, are misguided men, raising those groundless jealousies. Sir, let me become, on this occasion, the people's advocate and your historian; the people of this country were possessed of a code of liberty similar to that of Great Britain, but lost it through the weakness of the Kingdom and the pusillanimity of its leaders. Having lost our liberty by the usurpation of the British Parliament, no wonder we became a prey to her ministers; and they did plunder us with all the hands of all the harpies, for a series of years, in every shape of power, terrifying our people with the thunder of Great Britain, and bribing our leaders with the rapine of Ireland. The Kingdom became a plantation; her Parliament, deprived of its privileges, fell into contempt; and, with the legislature, the law, the spirit of liberty, with her forms vanished. If a war broke out, as in 1778, and an occasion occurred to restore liberty and restrain rapine, Parliament declined the opportunity; but, with an active servility and trembling loyalty, gave and granted, without regard to the treasure we had left or the rights we had lost. If a partial reparation was made upon a principle of expediency, Parliament did not receive it with the tranquil dignity of an august assembly, but with the alacrity of slaves.

The principal individuals, possessed of great property but no independency, corrupted by their extravagance, or enslaved by their following a species of English factor against an Irish people, more afraid of the people of Ireland than the tyranny of England, proceeded to that excess that they opposed every proposition to lessen profusion, extend trade, or promote liberty; they did more, they supported a measure which, at one blow, put an end to all trade; they did more, they brought you to a condition which they themselves did unanimously acknowledge a state of impending ruin; they did this, talking as they are now talking, arguing against trade as they now argue against liberty, threatening the people of Ireland with the power of the British nation, and imploring them to rest satisfied with the ruins of their trade, as they now implore them to remain satisfied with the wreck of their Constitution. . . .

Sir, we may hope to dazzle with illumination, and we may sicken with addresses, but the public imagination will never rest, nor will her heart be well at ease—never! so long as the Parliament of England exercises or claims a legislation over this country: so long as this shall be the case, that very free trade, otherwise a perpetual attachment, will be the cause of new discontent; it will create a pride to feel the indignity of bondage; it will furnish a strength to bite your chain, and the liberty withheld will poison the good communicated.

The British minister mistakes the Irish character: had he intended to make Ireland a slave, he should have kept her a beggar; there is no middle policy; win her heart by the restoration of her right, or cut off the nation's right hand; greatly emancipate, or fundamentally destroy. We may talk plausibly to England, but so long as she exercises a power to bind this country, so long are the nations in a state of war; the claims of the one go against the liberty of the other, and the sentiments of the latter go to oppose those claims to the last drop of her blood. The English opposition, therefore, are right; mere trade will not satisfy Ireland—they judge of us by other great nations, by the nation whose political life has been a struggle for liberty; they judge of us with a true knowledge of, and just deference for, our character—that a country enlightened as Ireland, chartered as Ireland, armed as Ireland, and injured as Ireland, will be satisfied with nothing less than liberty.

I admire that public-spirited merchant [Alderman Horan], who spread consternation at the Customhouse, and, despising the example which great men afforded, determined to try the question, and tendered for entry what the British Parliament prohibits the subject to export, some articles of silk, and sought at his private risk the liberty of his country; with him I am convinced it is necessary to agitate the question of right. In vain will you endeavor to keep it back; the passion is too natural, the sentiment is too irresistible; the question comes on of its own vitality! You must reinstate the laws!

There is no objection to this resolution except fears; I have examined your fears; I pronounce them to be frivolous. I might deny that the British nation was attached to the idea of binding Ireland; I might deny that England was a tyrant at heart; and I might call to witness the odium of North and the popularity of Chatham, her support of Holland, her contributions to Corsica, and the charters communicated to Ireland; but ministers have traduced England to debase Ireland; and politicians, like priests, represent the power they serve as diabolical, to possess with superstitious fears the victim whom they design to plunder. If England is a tyrant, it is you have made her so; it is the slave that makes the tyrant, and then murmurs at the master whom he himself has constituted. I do allow, on the subject of commerce, England was jealous in the extreme, and I do say it was commercial jealousy, it was the spirit of monopoly (the woolen trade and the Act of Navigation had made her tenacious of a comprehensive legislative authority), and having now ceded that monopoly, there is nothing in the way of your liberty except your own corruption and pusillanimity; and nothing can prevent your being free except yourselves. It is not in the disposition of England; it is not in the interest of England; it is not in her arms. What! can 8,000,000 of Englishmen opposed to 20,000,000 of French, to 7,000,000 of Spanish, to 3,000,-000 of Americans, reject the alliance of 3,000,000 in Ireland? Can 8,000,-000 of British men, thus outnumbered by foes, take upon their shoulders the expense of an expedition to enslave you? Will Great Britain, a wise and magnanimous country, thus tutored by experience and wasted by war, the French Navy riding her Channel, send an army to Ireland, to levy no tax, to enforce no law, to answer no end whatsoever, except to spoliate the charters of Ireland and enforce a barren oppression? What! has England lost thirteen provinces? has she reconciled herself to this loss, and will she not be reconciled to the liberty of Ireland? Take notice that the very constitution which I move you to declare, Great Britain herself offered to America; it is a very instructive proceeding in the British history. In 1778 a commission went out, with powers to cede to the thirteen provinces of America, totally and radically, the legislative authority claimed over her by the British Parliament, and the commissioners, pursuant to their powers, did offer to all or any of the American states the total surrender of the legislative authority of the British Parliament. I will read you their letter to the Congress.

[Here the letter was read.]

What! has England offered this to the resistance of America, and will she refuse it to the loyalty of Ireland? Your fears, then, are nothing but a habitual subjugation of mind; that subjugation of mind which made you, at first, tremble at every great measure of safety; which made the principal men amongst us conceive the commercial association would be a war; that fear which made them imagine the military association had a tendency to treason; which made them think a short money bill would be a public convulsion; and yet these measures have not only proved to be useful, but are held to be moderate, and the Parliament that adopted them is praised, not for its unanimity only, but for its temper also. You now wonder that you submitted for so many years to the loss of the woolen trade and the deprivation of the glass trade; raised above your former abject state in commerce, you are ashamed at your past pusillanimity; so when you have summoned a boldness which shall assert the liberties of your country—raised by the act, and reinvested, as you will be, in the glory of your ancient rights and privileges, you will be surprised at yourselves, who have so long submitted to their violation. Moderation is but a relative term; for nations, like men, are only safe in proportion to the spirit they put forth and the proud contemplation with which they survey themselves. Conceive yourselves a plantation, ridden by an oppressive government, and everything you have done is but a fortunate frenzy; conceive yourselves to be what you are, a great, a growing, and a proud nation, and a declaration of right is no more than the safe exercise of your indubitable authority. . . .

I shall hear of ingratitude; I name the argument to despise it and the men who make use of it; I know the men who use it are not grateful, they are insatiate; they are public extortioners, who would stop the tide of public prosperity and turn it to the channel of their own emolument; I know of no species of gratitude which should prevent my country from being free, no gratitude which should oblige Ireland to be the slave of England. In cases of robbery and usurpation, nothing is an object of gratitude except the thing stolen, the charter spoliated. A nation's liberty cannot, like her treasures, be meted and parceled out in gratitude; no man can be grateful or liberal of his conscience, nor woman of her honor, nor nation of her liberty; there are certain unimpartable, inherent, invaluable properties not to be alienated from the person, whether body politic or body natural. With the same contempt do I treat that charge which says that Ireland is insatiable; saying that Ireland asks nothing but that which Great Britain has robbed her of, her rights and privileges; to say that Ireland will not be satisfied with liberty, because she is not satisfied with slavery, is folly. I laugh at that man who supposes that Ireland will not be content with a free trade and a free constitution; and would any man advise her to be content with less?

I shall be told that we hazard the modification of the Law of Poynings and the Judges' Bill, and the Habeas Corpus Bill, and the Nullum Tempus Bill; but I ask you, have you been for years begging for these little things, and have not you yet been able to obtain them? And have you been contending against a little body of eighty men in Privy Council assembled, convocating themselves into the image of a parliament, and ministering your high office? And have you been contending against one man, an humble individual, to you a Leviathan—the English Attorney General—who advises in the case of Irish bills, and exercises legislation in his own person, and makes your parliamentary deliberations a blank by altering your bills or suppressing them? And have you not yet been able to conquer this little monster? Do you wish to know the reason? I will tell you: because you have not been a parliament, nor your country a people! Do you wish to know the remedy?—be a parliament, become a nation, and these things will follow in the train of your consequence! I shall be told that titles are shaken, being vested by force of English acts; but in answer to that, I observe, time may be a title, acquiescence a title, forfeiture a title, but an English act of Parliament certainly cannot; it is an authority, which, if a judge would charge, no jury would find, and which all the electors in Ireland have already disclaimed unequivocally, cordially, and universally. Sir, this is a good argument for an act of title, but no argument against a declaration of right. My friend who sits above me [Mr. Yelverton] has a Bill of Confirmation; we do not come unprepared to Parliament. I am not come to shake property, but to confirm property and restore freedom. The nation begins to form; we are molding into a people; freedom asserted, property secured, and the army (a mercenary band) likely to be restrained by law. Never was such a revolution accomplished in so short a time, and with such public tranquillity. In what situation would those men who call themselves friends of constitution and of government have left you? They would have left you without a title, as they state it, to your estates—without an assertion of your Constitution, or a law for your army; and this state of unexampled private and public insecurity, this anarchy raging in the Kingdom for eighteen months, these mock moderators would have had the presumption to call "peace."

I shall be told that the judges will not be swayed by the resolution of this House. Sir, that the judges will not be borne down by the resolutions of Parliament, not founded in law, I am willing to believe; but the resolutions of this House, founded in law, they will respect most exceedingly. . . .

The same laws, the same charters, communicate to both kingdoms, Great Britain and Ireland, the same rights and privileges; and one privilege above them all is that communicated by Magna Charta, by the 25th of Edward III, and by a multitude of other statutes, "not to be bound by any act except made with the archbishops, bishops, earls, barons, and freemen of the commonalty," namely, of the Parliament of the realm. On this right of exclusive legislation are founded the Petition of Right, Bill of Right, Revolution, and Act of Settlement. The King has no other title to his crown than that which you have to your liberty; both are founded, the throne and your freedom, upon the right vested in the subject to resist by arms, notwithstanding the oaths of allegiance, any authority attempting to impose acts of power as laws, whether that authority be one man or a host, the second James, or the British Parliament!

Every argument for the house of Hanover is equally an argument for the liberties of Ireland; the Act of Settlement is an act of rebellion, or the declaratory statute of the 6th of George I an act of usurpation; for both cannot be law. . . .

And as anything less than liberty is inadequate to Ireland, so is it dangerous to Great Britain. We are too near the British nation, we are too conversant with her history, we are too much fired by her example, to be anything less than her equal; anything less, we should be her bitterest enemies—an enemy to that power which smote us with her mace, and to that Constitution from whose blessings we were excluded: to be ground as we have been by the British nation, bound by her Parliament, plundered by her Crown, threatened by her enemies, insulted with her protection, while we return thanks for her condescension, is a system of meanness and misery which has expired in our determination, as I hope it has in her magnanimity.

There is no policy left for Great Britain but to cherish the remains of her Empire, and do justice to a country who is determined to do justice to herself, certain that she gives nothing equal to what she received from us when we gave her Ireland.

With regard to this country, England must resort to the free principles of government, and must forgo that legislative power which she has exercised to do mischief to herself; she must go back to freedom, which, as it is the foundation of her Constitution, so it is the main pillar of her Empire; it is not merely the connection of the Crown, it is a constitutional annexation, an alliance of liberty, which is the true meaning and mystery of the sisterhood, and will make both countries one arm and one soul, replenishing from time to time, in their immortal connection, the vital spirit of law and liberty from the lamp of each other's light. Thus combined by the ties of common interest, equal trade, and equal liberty, the constitution of both countries may become immortal, a new and milder Empire may arise from the errors of the old, and the British nation assume once more her natural station—the head of mankind.

That there are precedents against us I allow—acts of power I would call them, not precedent; and I answer the English pleading such precedents, as they answered their kings when they urged precedents against the liberty of England: such things are the weakness of the times; the tyranny of one side, the feebleness of the other, the law of neither; we will not be bound by them; or rather, in the words of the Declaration of Right: "No doing judgment, proceeding, or anywise to the contrary, shall be brought into precedent or example." Do not then tolerate a power—the power of the British Parliament over this land, which has no foundation in utility or necessity, or empire, or the laws of England, or the laws of Ireland, or the laws of nature, or the laws of God—do not suffer it to have a duration in your mind.

Do not tolerate that power which blasted you for a century, that power which shattered your loom, banished your manufacturers, dishonored your peerage, and stopped the growth of your people; do not, I say, be bribed by an export of woolen, or an import of sugar, and permit that power which has thus withered the land to remain in your country and have existence in your pusillanimity.

Do not suffer the arrogance of England to imagine a surviving hope in the fears of Ireland; do not send the people to their own resolves for liberty, passing by the tribunals of justice and the high court of Parliament; neither imagine that, by any formation of apology, you can palliate such a commission to your hearts, still less to your children, who will sting you with their curses in your grave for having interposed between them and their Maker, robbing them of an immense occasion, and losing an opportunity which you did not create and can never restore.

Hereafter, when these things shall be history, your age of thralldom and poverty, your sudden resurrection, commercial redress, and miraculous armament, shall the historian stop at liberty, and observe—that here the principal men among us fell into mimic trances of gratitude—they were awed by a weak ministry, and bribed by an empty treasury—and when liberty was within their grasp, and the temple opened her folding doors, and the arms of the people clanged, and the zeal of the nation urged and encouraged them on, that they fell down, and were prostituted at the threshold?

I might, as a constituent, come to your bar, and demand my liberty. I do call upon you, by the laws of the land and their violation, by the instruction of eighteen counties, by the arms, inspiration, and providence of the present moment, tell us the rule by which we shall go—assert the law of Ireland—declare the liberty of the land.

I will not be answered by a public lie in the shape of an amendment; neither, speaking for the subject's freedom, am I to hear of faction. I wish for nothing but to breathe, in this our island, in common with my fellow subjects, the air of liberty. I have no ambition, unless it be the ambition to break your chain and contemplate your glory. I never will be satisfied so long as the meanest cottager in Ireland has a link of the British chain clanking to his rags; he may be naked, he shall not be in iron; and I do see the time is at hand, the spirit is gone forth, the declaration is planted; and though great men shall apostatize, yet the cause will live; and though the public speaker should die, yet the immortal fire shall outlast the organ which conveyed it, and the breath of liberty, like the word of the holy man, will not die with the prophet, but survive him.

I shall move you, "That the King's most excellent Majesty, and the Lords and Commons of Ireland, are the only power competent to make laws to bind Ireland."

No orator was ever more master of his audience than Grattan. The response to his speech of April 19, 1780, was overwhelming. "The language of Milton or Shakespeare can alone describe its effects": so writes an eyewitness. His hearers voted almost unanimously for his motion, and all Ireland was soon vibrating to the repercussions caused by his magnificent effort. Grattan had started a course of events that culminated, two years later, when the British Parliament repealed "Poynings' Act." The Whig ministry, with some of Grattan's personal admirers, such as Fox and Burke, carried forward legislation that gave Ireland an independent Parliament—"Grattan's Parliament," as it has been called ever since. It was a Parliament composed largely of representatives of the Protestant landowning aristocracy, the Roman Catholics—the masses of the people—being unrepresented. Still, it was a step forward. By popular subscription Grattan was offered £100,000 for his labors, but he accepted only half the sum.

However, the story does not have a happy ending. "Grattan's Parliament" lasted less than twenty years. The machinations of the younger Pitt, doubtless driven on by fears of a French invasion of Ireland, brought about the Act of Union in 1800, and then the long, tragic struggle for home rule started all over again.

BURKE ATTEMPTS TO VINDICATE HIMSELF BEFORE HIS ESTRANGED CONSTITUENTS

[September 6, 1780]

Edmund Burke entered Parliament, it may be recalled, from the pocket borough of Wendover in 1766, and continued that representation until the fall of 1774, when the King dissolved Parliament. He was then technically elected from the inconsequential borough of Malton, when he received news that he was being presented as a candidate at commercially important Bristol, then the second largest city in England. He dashed to Bristol, a sleepless, fourteen-and-a-half-hour stagecoach ride of 270 miles, and went at once to the Guildhall, where he gave a grave little speech before a few hundred electors. "I am not fond," he said, "of attempting to raise public expectations by great promises."

After a turbulent month of electioneering and voting, Burke found himself successful, and now addressed his constituents, first thanking them for their support and then cautioning them on the delicate issue of instructions given to a representative: "Certainly, gentlemen, it ought to be the happiness and glory of a representative to live in the strictest union, the closest correspondence, and the most unreserved communication with his constituents. Their wishes ought to have great weight with him; their opinion high respect; their business unremitted attention. It is his duty to sacrifice his repose, his pleasures, his satisfactions, to theirs; and, above all, ever, and in all cases, to prefer their interest to his own. But his unbiased opinion, his mature judgment, his enlightened conscience, he ought not to sacrifice to you; to any man, or to any set of men living. These he does not derive from your pleasure; no, nor from the law and the Constitution. They are a trust from Providence, for the abuse of which he is deeply answerable. Your representative owes you, not his industry only, but his judgment; and he betrays, instead of serving you, if he sacrifices it to your opinion."

In such aloofness we may anticipate difficulties between Burke and his Bristol constituents, but aside from brief visits in 1774 and 1775 he did not see them again until time for re-election six years later. Meanwhile he brought glory to Bristol and himself by such masterpieces as his speech on conciliation with the colonies, the famous Letter to the Sheriffs of Bristol, and the brilliantly rollicking argument for economic reform of the royal establishment, which had privileges and powers of appointment that were not only absurdly expensive but undermined the independence of Parliament.

It is also in this period that we can catch our best glimpse of Burke at Dr. Johnson's Literary Club. When the elder Sheridan commented on Burke's taking so much pains with his speeches, "knowing with certainty that it would produce no effect, that not one vote would be gained by it" the orator replied: "I shall say in general that it is very well worth while for a man to take pains to speak well in Parliament. A man who has vanity speaks to display his talents; and if a man speaks well, he gradually establishes a certain reputation and consequence in the general opinion, which sooner or later will have its political reward. Besides, though not one vote is gained, a good speech has its effect. Though an act which has been ably opposed passes into a law, yet in its progress it is modeled, it is softened, in such a manner that we see plainly the Minister has been told that the members attached to him are so sensible of its injustice or absurdity from what they have heard that it must be altered."

After an interjection by Dr. Johnson, Burke continued: "The House of Commons is a mixed body. (I except the Minority, which I hold to be pure, but I take the whole House.) It is a mass by no means pure; but neither is it wholly corrupt, though there is a large proportion of corruption in it. There are many members who generally go with the Minister who will not go all lengths. There are many honest, well-meaning country gentlemen who are in Parliament only to keep up the consequence of their families. Upon most of these a good speech will have influence."

However, it was not that familiar, divided audience which Burke faced on September 6, 1780, when he appeared once more in the Bristol Guildhall. It was an audience of sullen constituents, justifiably offended by his long neglect and resentful of his outspoken position on three of the most controversial issues of the day. His speech in self-defense has no parallel in the history of electioneering, and it was considered by Sir Samuel Romilly, the reformer of the penal code, "the finest piece of oratory in our language."

"I will call to mind this accusation; and be comforted."

Mr. Mayor, and Gentlemen:

I AM EXTREMELY PLEASED at the appearance of this large and respectable meeting. The steps I may be obliged to take will want the sanction of a considerable authority; and in explaining anything which may appear doubtful in my public conduct, I must naturally desire a very full audience.

I have been backward to begin my canvass. The dissolution of the Parliament was uncertain; and it did not become me, by an unseasonable importunity, to appear diffident of the fact of my six years' endeavor to please you. I had served the city of Bristol honorably, and the city of Bristol had no reason to think that the means of honorable service to the public were become indifferent to me.

I found, on my arrival here, that three gentlemen had been long in eager pursuit of an object which but two of us can obtain. I found that they had all met with encouragement. A contested election in such a city as this is no light thing. I paused on the brink of the precipice. These three gentlemen, by various merits, and on various titles, I made no doubt were worthy of your favor. I shall never attempt to raise myself by depreciating the merits of my competitors. In the complexity and confusion of these cross-pursuits, I wished to take the authentic public sense of my friends upon a business of so much delicacy. I wished to take your opinion along with me, that, if I should give up the contest at the very beginning, my surrender of my post may not seem the effect of inconstancy, or timidity, or anger, or disgust, or indolence, or any other temper unbecoming a man who has engaged in the public service. If, on the contrary, I should undertake the election, and fail of success, I was full as anxious that it should be manifest to the whole world that the peace of the city had not been broken by my rashness, presumption, or fond conceit of my own merit.

I am not come, by a false and counterfeit show of deference to your judgment, to seduce it in my favor. I ask it seriously and unaffectedly. If you wish that I should retire, I shall not consider that advice as a censure upon my conduct, or an alteration in your sentiments, but as a rational submission to the circumstances of affairs. If, on the contrary, you should think it proper for me to proceed on my canvass, if you will risk the trouble on your part, I will risk it on mine. My pretensions are such as you cannot be ashamed of, whether they succeed or fail.

If you call upon me, I shall solicit the favor of the city upon manly ground. I come before you with the plain confidence of an honest servant in the equity of a candid and discerning master. I come to claim your approbation, not to amuse you with vain apologies, or with professions still more vain and senseless. I have lived too long to be served by apologies, or to stand in need of them. The part I have acted has been in open day; and to hold out to a conduct which stands in that clear and steady light for all its good and all its evil—to hold out to that conduct the paltry winking tapers of excuses and promises—I never will do it. They may obscure it with their smoke, but they never can illumine sunshine by such a flame as theirs.

I am sensible that no endeavors have been left untried to injure me in your opinion. But the use of character is to be a shield against calumny. I could wish undoubtedly (if idle wishes were not the most idle of all things) to make every part of my conduct agreeable to every one of my constituents. But in so great a city, and so greatly divided as this is, it is weak to expect it.

In such a discordancy of sentiments it is better to look to the nature of things than to the humors of men. The very attempt towards pleasing everybody discovers a temper always flashy, and often false and insincere. Therefore, as I have proceeded straight onward in my conduct, so I will proceed in my account of those parts of it which have been most excepted to. But I must first beg leave just to hint to you that we may suffer very great detriment by being open to every talker. It is not to be imagined how much of service is lost from spirits full of activity and full of energy, who are pressing, who are rushing forward, to great and capital objects, when you oblige them to be continually looking back. Whilst they are defending one service, they defraud you of a hundred. Applaud us when we run; console us when we fall; cheer us when we recover: but let us pass on—for God's sake, let us pass on!

Do you think, gentlemen, that every public act in the six years since I stood in this place before you—that all the arduous things which have been done in this eventful period, which has crowded into a few years' space the revolutions of an age—can be opened to you on their fair grounds in half an hour's conversation.

But it is no reason because there is a bad mode of inquiry that there should be no examination at all. Most certainly it is our duty to examine; it is our interest too: but it must be with discretion; with an attention to all the circumstances, and to all the motives; like sound judges, and not like caviling pettifoggers and quibbling pleaders, prying into flaws and hunting for exceptions. Look, gentlemen, to the *whole tenor* of your member's conduct. Try whether his ambition or his avarice have justled him out of the straight line of duty; or whether that grand foe of the offices of active life, that master vice in men of business—a degenerate and inglorious sloth—has made him flag and languish in his course. This is the object of our inquiry. If our member's conduct can bear this touch, mark it for sterling. He may have fallen into errors: he must have faults; but our error is greater, and our fault is radically ruinous to ourselves, if we do not bear, if we do not even applaud, the whole compound and mixed mass of such a character. Not to act thus is folly: I had almost said it is impiety. He censures God who quarrels with the imperfections of man.

Gentlemen, we must not be peevish with those who serve the people; for none will serve us, whilst there is a court to serve, but those who are of a nice and jealous honor. They who think everything, in comparison of that honor, to be dust and ashes will not bear to have it soiled and impaired by those for whose sake they make a thousand sacrifices to preserve it immaculate and whole. We shall either drive such men from the public stage or we shall send them to the court for protection; where, if they must sacrifice their reputation, they will at least secure their interest. Depend upon it that the lovers of freedom will be free. None will violate their conscience to please us, in order afterwards to discharge that conscience, which they have violated, by doing us faithful and affectionate service. If we degrade and deprave their minds by servility, it will be absurd to expect that they who are creeping and abject towards us will ever be bold and incorruptible assertors of our freedom against the most seducing and the most formidable of all powers. No! human nature is not so formed; nor shall we improve the faculties or better the morals of public men by our possession of the most infallible receipt in the world for making cheats and hypocrites.

Let me say, with plainness, I who am no longer in a public character, that if by a fair, by an indulgent, by a gentlemanly behavior to our representatives we do not give confidence to their minds and a liberal scope to their understandings; if we do not permit our members to act upon a *very* enlarged view of things, we shall at length infallibly degrade our national representation into a confused and scuffling bustle of local agency. When the popular member is narrowed in his ideas, and rendered timid in his proceedings, the service of the Crown will be the sole nursery of statesmen. Among the frolics of the court it may at length take that of attending to its business. Then the monopoly of mental power will be added to the power of all other kinds it possesses. On the side of the people there will be nothing but impotence; for ignorance is impotence; narrowness of mind is impotence; timidity is itself impotence, and makes all other qualities that go along with it impotent and useless.

At present it is the plan of the court to make its servants insignificant. If the people should fall into the same humor, and should choose their servants on the same principles of mere obsequiousness and flexibility, and total vacancy or indifference of opinion in all public matters, then no part of the state will be sound; and it will be in vain to think of saving it.

I thought it very expedient at this time to give you this candid counsel; and with this counsel I would willingly close, if the matters which at various times have been objected to me in this city concerned only myself and my own election. These charges, I think, are four in number—my neglect of a due attention to my constituents, the not paying more frequent visits here; my conduct on the affairs of the first Irish trade acts; my opinion and mode of proceeding on Lord Beauchamp's debtors' bills; and my votes on the late affairs of the Roman Catholics. All of these (except perhaps the first) relate to matters of very considerable public concern; and it is not lest you should censure me improperly, but lest you should form improper ópinions on matters of some moment to you, that I trouble you at all upon the subject. My conduct is of small importance.

With regard to the first charge, my friends have spoken to me of it in the style of amicable expostulation; not so much blaming the thing as lamenting the effects. Others, less partial to me, were less kind in assigning the motives. I admit there is a decorum and propriety in a Member of Parliament's paying a respectful court to his constituents. If I were conscious to myself that pleasure or dissipation, or low unworthy occupations, had detained me from personal attendance on you, I would readily admit my fault and quietly submit to the penalty. But, gentlemen, I live at an hundred miles' distance from Bristol; and at the end of a session I come to my own house, fatigued in body and in mind, to a little repose, and to a very little attention to my family and my private concerns. A visit to Bristol is always a sort of canvass; else it will do more harm than good. To pass from the toils of a session to the toils of a canvass is the furthest thing in the world from repose. I could hardly serve you *as I have done*, and court you too. Most of you have heard that I do not very remarkably spare myself in *public* business; and in the *private* business of my constituents I have done very nearly as much as those who have nothing else to do. My canvass of you was not on the 'Change, nor in the county meetings, nor in the clubs of this city: it was in the House of Commons; it was at the Customhouse; it was at the Council; it was at the Treasury; it was at the Admiralty. I canvassed you through your affairs, and not your persons. I was not only your representative as a body; I was the agent, the solicitor of individuals; I ran about wherever your affairs could call me; and in acting for you, I often appeared rather as a ship broker than as a Member of Parliament. There was nothing too laborious or too low for me to undertake. The meanness of the business was raised by the dignity of the object. If some lesser matters have slipped through my fingers, it was because I filled my hands too full; and, in my eagerness to serve you, took in more than any hands could grasp. Several gentlemen stand round me who are my willing witnesses; and there are others who, if they were here, would be still better; because they would be unwilling witnesses to the same truth. It was in the middle of a summer residence in London, and in the middle of a negotiation at the Admiralty for your trade, that I was called to Bristol; and this late visit, at this late day, has been possibly in prejudice to your affairs.

Since I have touched upon this matter, let me say, gentlemen, that if I had a disposition, or a right to complain, I have some cause of complaint on my side. With a petition of this city in my hand, passed through the corporation without a dissenting voice, a petition in unison with almost the whole voice of the kingdom (with whose formal thanks I was covered over), while I labored on no less than five bills for a public reform, and fought against the opposition of great abilities, and of the greatest power, every clause, and every word of the largest of those bills, almost to the very last day of a very long session; all this time a canvass in Bristol was as calmly carried on as if I were dead. I was considered as a man wholly out of the question. Whilst I watched, and fasted, and sweated in the House of Commons—by the most easy and ordinary arts of elections, by dinners and visits, by "How do you do's," and "My worthy friends," I was to be quietly moved out of my seat—and promises were made, and engagements entered into, without any exception or reserve, as if my laborious zeal in my duty had been a regular abdication of my trust.

To open my whole heart to you on this subject, I do confess, however, that there were other times besides the two years in which I did visit you when I was not wholly without leisure for repeating that mark of my respect. But I could not bring my mind to see you. You remember that in the beginning of this American war (that era of calamity, disgrace, and downfall, an era which no feeling mind will ever mention without a tear for England) you were greatly divided; and a very strong body, if not the strongest, opposed itself to the madness which every art and every power were employed to render popular, in order that the errors of the rulers might be lost in the general blindness of the nation. This opposition continued until after our great but most unfortunate victory at Long Island. Then all the mounds and banks of our constancy were borne down at once; and the frenzy of the American war broke in upon us like a deluge. This victory, which seemed to put an immediate end to all difficulties, perfected us in that spirit of domination which our unparalleled prosperity had but too long nurtured. We had been so very powerful, and so very prosperous, that even the humblest of us were degraded into the vices and follies of kings. We lost all measure between means and ends; and our headlong desires became our politics and our morals. All men who wished for peace, or retained any sentiments of moderation, were over-borne or silenced; and this city was led by every artifice (and probably with the more management, because I was one of your members) to dis-tinguish itself by its zeal for that fatal cause. In this temper of your and of my mind, I should have sooner fled to the extremities of the earth than have shown myself here. I, who saw in every American victory (for you have had a long series of these misfortunes) the germ and seed of the naval power of France and Spain, which all our heat and warmth against America was only hatching into life—I should not have been a welcome visitor with the brow and the language of such feelings. When, after-wards, the other face of your calamity was turned upon you, and showed itself in defeat and distress, I shunned you full as much. I felt sorely this variety in our wretchedness; and I did not wish to have the least appear-ance of insulting you with that show of superiority which, though it may not be assumed, is generally suspected in a time of calamity from those whose previous warnings have been despised. I could not bear to show you a representative whose face did not reflect that of his constituents; a face that could not joy in your joys and sorrow in your sorrows. But time at length has made us all of one opinion; and we have all opened our eyes on the true nature of the American war, to the true nature of all its suc-cesses and all its failures.

In that public storm, too, I had my private feelings. I had seen blown down and prostrate on the ground several of those houses to whom I was chiefly indebted for the honor this city has done me. I confess that, whilst the wounds of those I loved were yet green, I could not bear to show my-self in pride and triumph in that place into which their partiality had brought me, and to appear at feasts and rejoicings, in the midst of the grief and calamity of my warm friends, my zealous supporters, my gen-erous benefactors. This is a true, unvarnished, undisguised state of the affair. You will judge of it.

This is the only one of the charges in which I am personally con-cerned. As to the other matters objected against me, which in their turn I shall mention to you, remember once more I do not mean to extenuate or excuse. Why should I, when the things charged are among those upon which I found all my reputation? What would be left to me if I myself was the man who softened, and blended, and diluted, and weakened all the distinguishing colors of my life, so as to leave nothing distinct and de-terminate in my whole conduct?

[Burke then went on to defend in full detail his support of the first Irish trade acts which lightened the economic burdens of the Irish; Beauchamp's debtors' *bills which lightened the burdens of the poor; and various measures instituting civil liberties for Roman Catholics.*]

"But if I profess all this impolitic stubbornness, I may chance never to be elected into Parliament." It is certainly not pleasing to be put out of the public service. But I wish to be a Member of Parliament, to have my share of doing good and resisting evil. It would therefore be absurd to renounce my objects in order to obtain my seat. I deceive myself indeed most grossly if I had not much rather pass the remainder of my life hidden in the recesses of the deepest obscurity, feeding my mind even with the visions and imaginations of such things, than to be placed on the most splendid throne of the universe, tantalized with a denial of the practice of all which can make the greatest situation any other than the greatest curse. Gentlemen, I have had my day. I can never sufficiently express my gratitude to you for having set me in a place wherein I could lend the slightest help to great and laudable designs. If I have had my share in any measure giving quiet to private property and private conscience; if by my vote I have aided in securing to families the best possession, peace; if I have joined in reconciling kings to their subjects, and subjects to their prince; if I have assisted to loosen the foreign holdings of the citizen, and taught him to look for his protection to the laws of his country, and for his comfort to the good will of his countrymen—if I have thus taken my part with the best of men in the best of their actions, I can shut the book —I might wish to read a page or two more—but this is enough for my measure.—I have not lived in vain.

And now, gentlemen, on this serious day, when I come, as it were, to make up my account with you, let me take to myself some degree of honest pride on the nature of the charges that are against me. I do not here stand before you accused of venality or of neglect of duty. It is not said that, in the long period of my service, I have, in a single instance, sacrificed the slightest of your interests to my ambition or to my fortune. It is not alleged that to gratify any anger or revenge of my own, or of my party, I have had a share in wronging or oppressing any description of men or any one man in any description. No! the charges against me are all of one kind, that I have pushed the principles of general justice and benevolence too far; further than a cautious policy would warrant; and further than the opinions of many would go along with me.—In every accident which may happen through life, in pain, in sorrow, in depression, and distress—I will call to mind this accusation; and be comforted.

Gentlemen, I submit the whole to your judgment. Mr. Mayor, I thank you for the trouble you have taken on this occasion: in your state of health, it is particularly obliging. If this company should think it advisable for me to withdraw, I shall repectfully retire; if you think otherwise, I shall go directly to the Council House and to the 'Change, and, without a moment's delay, begin my canvass.

Masterpiece though it was in the long view of history, this speech did not win back Burke's alienated constituents. After two days of canvassing, he decided that his chances were hopeless and withdrew, "declined the poll," in a dramatic farewell.

Gentlemen:

I decline the election.—It has ever been my rule through life to observe a proportion between my efforts and my objects. I have never been remarkable for a bold, active, and sanguine pursuit of advantages that are personal to myself.

I have not canvassed the whole of this city in form. But I have taken such a view of it as satisfies my own mind that your choice will not ultimately fall upon me. Your city, gentlemen, is in a state of miserable distraction; and I am resolved to withdraw whatever share my pretensions may have had in its unhappy divisions. I have not been in haste; I have tried all prudent means; I have waited for the effect of all contingencies. If I were fond of a contest, by the partiality of my numerous friends (whom you know to be among the most weighty and respectable people of the city), I have the means of a sharp one in my hands. But I thought it far better with my strength unspent, and my reputation unimpaired, to do, early and from foresight, that which I might be obliged to do from necessity at last.

I am not in the least surprised nor in the least angry at this view of things. I have read the book of life for a long time, and I have read other books a little. Nothing has happened to me but what has happened to men much better than me, and in times and in nations full as good as the age and the country that we live in. To say that I am no way concerned would be neither decent nor true. The representation of *Bristol* was an object on many accounts dear to me; and I certainly should very far prefer it to any other in the Kingdom. My habits are made to it; and it is in general more unpleasant to be rejected after long trial than not to be chosen at all.

But, gentlemen, I will see nothing except your former kindness, and I will give way to no other sentiments than those of gratitude. From the bottom of my heart I thank you for what you have done for me. You have given me a long term, which is now expired. I have performed the conditions and enjoyed all the profits to the full; and I now surrender your estate into your hands, without being in a single tile or a single stone impaired or wasted by my use. I have served the public for fifteen years. I have served you in particular for six. What is passed is well stored. It is safe, and out of the power of fortune. What is to come is in wiser hands than ours: and He in whose hands it is best knows whether it is best for you and me that I should be in Parliament, or even in the world.

Gentlemen, the melancholy event of yesterday reads to us an awful lesson against being too much troubled about any of the objects of ordinary ambition. The worthy gentleman [Mr. Coombe] who has been snatched from us at the moment of the election, and in the middle of the contest, whilst his desires were as warm and his hopes as eager as ours, has feelingly told us what shadows we are and what shadows we pursue.

It has been usual for a candidate who declines, to take his leave by a letter to the sheriffs; but I received your trust in the face of day: and in the face of day I accept your dismission. I am not—I am not at all ashamed to look upon you; nor can my presence discompose the order of business here. I humbly and respectfully take my leave of the sheriffs, the candidates, and the electors, wishing heartily that the choice may be for the best, at a time which calls, if ever time did call, for service that is not nominal. It is no plaything you are about. I tremble when I consider the trust I have presumed to ask. I confided perhaps too much in my intentions. They were really fair and upright; and I am bold to say that I ask no ill thing for you when on parting from this place I pray that whomever you choose to succeed me, he may resemble me exactly in all things, except in my abilities to serve and my fortune to please you.

PART FIVE

INDIA AND THE TRIAL

OF WARREN HASTINGS

THE STORY of the East India Company, chartered late in the reign of
Elizabeth, is a fabulous record of conquest and exploitation, by a private company of traders, of what was to become by far the richest and most populous
colony in the world. It was the Company, almost singlehanded, that defeated
the French, subjugated native rulers, and, especially under the leadership of
Clive and Hastings, laid the foundations for a century and a half of British rule.
The methods of these buccaneers were get-rich-quick and ruthless, although
both Clive and Hastings introduced reforms and sought to cure the avarice and
corruption that had become a settled habit of Company officials. The net results were deplorable. If British wars, intrigues, and oppressions netted many
easy and handsome fortunes, they left one province of India after another
impoverished, distraught, bleeding, shorn of rights and sovereignty. Was there
no remedy for the rapacity of the Company? By 1783 its despotism and mismanagement were well established. The vast territory with its teeming population that had been secured by Hastings could not be left to the mercies of a
mere company of traders. Charles James Fox therefore brought forward a bill
proposing that authority in India be transferred from the Company to seven
commissioners to be appointed first by Parliament, later by the Crown.

CHARLES JAMES FOX INTRODUCES HIS
BILL TO ABOLISH THE TYRANNY
OF THE EAST INDIA COMPANY

[December 1, 1783]

Charles James Fox (1749–1806), possibly England's most liberal and lovable
statesman, and almost certainly her most brilliant debater, started life under
heavy handicaps. The son of the first Lord Holland, who, as a corrupt paymaster

of the army, had made himself the most unpopular man in England, young Fox was surrounded by luxury and dissipation and his education for public life was, to say the least, inauspicious. Entering Parliament in 1768 at the age of nineteen, he devoted himself for five years to supporting George III's government, to supercilious though brilliant ridicule of all generous causes. Suddenly he shook off his stultifying background, joined with Chatham and Burke in defense of the American colonists, and for the rest of his life—thirty-two years— felt the flattering hatred of the King. For a few months in 1783 he shared a questionable coalition government with the genial but stubborn Lord North, whose support of the King's government was largely responsible for the loss of the American colonies. Fox, as Secretary of State for Foreign Affairs, brought before the House of Commons the India Reform Bill, which was largely inspired by the wide-ranging Burke.

"It matters not whether dominion arise from conquest or from compact."

SIR, the necessity of my saying something upon the present occasion is so obvious that no apology will, I hope, be expected from me for troubling the House, even at so late an hour [two o'clock in the morning]. I shall not enter much into a detailed or minute defense of the particulars of the bill before you, because few particular objections have been made, the opposition to it consisting only of general reasonings, some of little application and others totally distinct from the point in question.

This bill has been combated through its past stages upon various principles; but to this moment the House has not heard it canvassed upon its own intrinsic merits. The debate this night has turned chiefly upon two points—violation of charter and increase of influence; and upon both these points I shall say a few words.

The honorable gentleman who opened the debate [Mr. Powys] first demands my attention, not indeed for the wisdom of the observations which fell from him this night (acute and judicious as he is upon most occasions), but from the natural weight of all such characters in this country, the aggregate of whom should, in my opinion, always decide upon public measures; but his ingenuity was never, in my opinion, exerted more ineffectually, upon more mistaken principles, and more inconsistently with the common tenor of his conduct than in this debate.

The honorable gentleman charges me with abandoning that cause which, he says, in terms of flattery, I had once so successfully asserted. I tell him in reply that if he were to search the history of my life, he would find that the period of it in which I struggled most for the real, substantial cause of liberty is this very moment that I am addressing you. Freedom, according to my conception of it, consists in the safe and sacred possession of a man's property, governed by laws defined and certain; with many personal privileges, natural, civil, and religious, which he cannot surrender without ruin to himself; and of which to be deprived by any other power is despotism. This bill, instead of subverting, is destined to give stability to these principles; instead of narrowing the basis of freedom, it tends to enlarge it; instead of suppressing, its object is to infuse and circulate the spirit of liberty.

What is the most odious species of tyranny? Precisely that which this bill is meant to annihilate. That a handful of men, free themselves, should execute the most base and abominable despotism over millions of their fellow creatures; that innocence should be the victim of oppression; that industry should toil for rapine; that the harmless laborer should sweat, not for his own benefit, but for the luxury and rapacity of tyrannic depredation; in a word, that thirty millions of men, gifted by Providence with the ordinary endowments of humanity, should groan under a system of despotism unmatched in all the histories of the world.

What is the end of all government? Certainly the happiness of the governed. Others may hold other opinions, but this is mine, and I proclaim it. What are we to think of a government whose good fortune is supposed to spring from the calamities of its subjects, whose aggrandizement grows out of the miseries of mankind? This is the kind of government exercised under the East India Company upon the natives of Hindustan; and the subversion of that infamous government is the main object of the bill in question. But in the progress of accomplishing this end, it is objected that the charter of the company should not be violated; and upon this point, sir, I shall deliver my opinion without disguise. A charter is a trust to one or more persons for some given benefit. If this trust be abused, if the benefit be not obtained, and its failure arise from palpable guilt, or (what in this case is full as bad) from palpable ignorance or mismanagement, will any man gravely say that that trust should not be resumed and delivered to other hands, more especially in the case of the East India Company, whose manner of executing this trust, whose laxity and languor, have produced, and tend to produce, consequences diametrically opposite to the ends of confiding that trust, and of the institution for which it was granted? I beg of gentlemen to be aware of the lengths to which their arguments upon the intangibility of this charter may be carried. Every syllable virtually impeaches the establishment by which we sit in this House, in the enjoyment of this freedom, and of every other blessing of our government. These kinds of arguments are batteries against the main pillar of the British Constitution. Some men are consistent with their own private opinions, and discover the inheritance of family maxims, when they question the principles of the Revolution; but I have no scruple in subscribing to the articles of that creed which produced it. Sovereigns are sacred, and reverence is due to every king; yet, with all my attachments to the person of a first magistrate, had I lived in the reign of James II, I should most certainly have contributed my efforts and borne part in those illustrious struggles which vindicated an empire from hereditary servitude, and recorded this valuable doctrine, "that trust abused is revocable."

No man, sir, will tell me that a trust to a company of merchants stands upon the solemn and sanctified ground by which a trust is committed to a monarch; and I am at a loss to reconcile the conduct of men who approve that resumption of violated trust, which rescued and re-established our unparalleled and admirable Constitution with a thousand valuable improvements and advantages at the Revolution, and who, at this moment, rise up the champions of the East India Company's charter, although the incapacity and incompetency of that company to a due and adequate discharge of the trust deposited in them by that charter are themes of ridicule and contempt to the world; and although, in consequence of their mismanagement, connivance, and imbecility, combined with the wickedness of their servants, the very name of an Englishman is detested, even to a proverb, through all Asia, and the national character is become degraded and dishonored. To rescue that name from odium and redeem this character from disgrace are some of the objects of the present bill; and, gentlemen should, indeed, gravely weigh their opposition to a measure which, with a thousand other points not less valuable, aims at the attainment of these objects.

Those who condemn the present bill as a violation of the chartered rights of the East India Company condemn, on the same ground, I say again, the Revolution as a violation of the chartered rights of King James II. He, with as much reason, might have claimed the property of dominion; but what was the language of the people? "No; you have no property in dominion; dominion was vested in you, as it is in every chief magistrate, for the benefit of the community to be governed; it was a sacred trust delegated by compact; you have abused that trust; you have exercised dominion for the purposes of vexation and tyranny—not of comfort, protection, and good order; and we, therefore, resume the power which was originally ours; we recur to the first principles of all government—the will of the many, and it is our will that you shall no longer abuse your dominion." The case is the same with the East India Company's government over a territory, as it has been said by my honorable friend [Mr. Burke], of two hundred and eighty thousand square miles in extent, nearly equal to all Christian Europe, and containing thirty millions of the human race. It matters not whether dominion arise from conquest or from compact. Conquest gives no right to the conqueror to be a tyrant; and it is no violation of right to abolish the authority which is misused. . . .

BURKE SUPPORTS FOX'S BILL AND LAUDS ITS AUTHOR

[December 1, 1783]

Fox was supported in the debate by Burke with one of the speeches that, according to Morley, "rank only below his greatest." We include here the famous passage in which he describes the parade of young officials sent out to India, and the magnificent eulogy on Fox which makes the formal panegyrics of antiquity seem cold indeed.

> *"He has put to hazard his ease, his security, his interest, his power, even his darling popularity, for the benefit of a people whom he has never seen."*

THE NATIVES scarcely know what it is to see the gray head of an Englishman. Young men (boys almost) govern there, without society, and without sympathy with the natives. They have no more social habits with the people than if they still resided in England; nor, indeed, any species of intercourse but that which is necessary to making a sudden fortune, with a view to a remote settlement. Animated with all the avarice of age, and all the impetuosity of youth, they roll in one after another; wave after wave; and there is nothing before the eyes of the natives but an endless, hopeless prospect of new flights of birds of prey and passage, with appetites continually renewing for a food that is continually wasting. . . .

Now, sir, I have finished all I proposed to say as my reasons for giving my vote to this bill. If I am wrong, it is not for want of pains to know what is right. This pledge, at least, of my rectitude I have given to my country.

And now, having done my duty to the bill, let me say a word to the author. I should leave him to his own noble sentiments if the unworthy and illiberal language with which he has been treated, beyond all example of parliamentary liberty, did not make a few words necessary; not so much in justice to him as to my own feelings. I must say, then, that it will be a distinction honorable to the age that the rescue of the greatest number of the human race that ever were so grievously oppressed, from the greatest tyranny that was ever exercised, has fallen to the lot of abilities and dispositions equal to the task; that it has fallen to one who has the enlargement to comprehend, the spirit to undertake, and the eloquence to support, so great a measure of hazardous benevolence. His spirit is not owing to his ignorance of the state of men and things; he well knows what snares are spread about his path, from personal animosity, from court intrigues, and possibly from popular delusion. But he has put to hazard his ease, his security, his interest, his power, even his darling popularity, for the benefit of a people whom he has never seen. This is the road that all heroes have trod before him. He is traduced and abused for his supposed motives. He will remember that obloquy is a necessary ingredient in the composition of all true glory: he will remember that it was not only in the Roman customs, but it is in the nature and constitution of things, that calumny and abuse are essential parts of triumph. These thoughts will support a mind which only exists for honor, under the burden of temporary reproach. He is doing indeed a great good; such as rarely falls to the lot, and almost as rarely coincides with the desires, of any man. Let him use his time. Let him give the whole length of the reins to his benevolence. He is now on a great eminence, where the eyes of mankind are turned to him. He may live long, he may do much. But here is the summit. He never can exceed what he does this day.

He has faults; but they are faults that, though they may in a small degree tarnish the luster, and sometimes impede the march of his abilities, have nothing in them to extinguish the fire of so great virtues. In those faults there is no mixture of deceit, of hypocrisy, of pride, of ferocity, of complexional despotism, or want of feeling for the distresses of mankind. His are faults which might exist in a descendant of Henry IV of France, as they did exist in that father of his country. Henry IV wished that he might live to see a fowl in the pot of every peasant in his kingdom.

That sentiment of homely benevolence was worth all the splendid sayings that are recorded of kings. But he wished perhaps for more than could be obtained, and the goodness of the man exceeded the power of the king. But this gentleman, a subject, may this day say this at least, with truth, that he secures the rice in his pot to every man in India. . . .

. . . There is not a tongue, a nation, or religion in India which will not bless the presiding care and manly beneficence of this House and of him who proposes to you this great work. Your names will never be separated before the throne of the Divine Goodness in whatever language, or with whatever rites, pardon is asked for sin, and reward for those who imitate the Godhead in His universal bounty to His creatures. These honors you deserve, and they will surely be paid, when all the jargon of influence, and party, and patronage are swept into oblivion.

I have spoken what I think, and what I feel, of the mover of this bill. An honorable friend of mine, speaking of his merits, was charged with having made a studied panegyric; I don't know what his was. Mine, I am sure, is a studied panegyric; the fruit of much meditation; the result of the observation of near twenty years. For my own part, I am happy that I have lived to see this day; I feel myself overpaid for the labors of eighteen years when, at this late period, I am able to take my share, by one humble vote, in destroying a tyranny that exists to the disgrace of this nation, and the destruction of so large a part of the human species.

Against the East India Bill were arrayed the vast influence of the Company, strong opposition from the merchant class, but also the opinion of those who did not want to see more power conferred upon a Parliament that had shown itself venal and unprincipled, and doubted whether anything would be gained by putting the affairs of India and the Company into the hands of commissioners who could be expected to know little of the remote and complicated issues that they would be called upon to decide. In spite of this opposition, the bill was carried in the House of Commons by a majority of two to one. In the House of Lords, however, pressure by George III as the result of "secret influence" was successful in destroying the measure, and the King took this occasion to dismiss the Fox-North coalition government on midnight of December 18, 1783. The path to power was thus prepared for William Pitt the younger. Not a year passed before the twenty-four-year-old Prime Minister brought forward his own East India bill. Although similar to the Fox bill, it did not encounter the same opposition, and the dual system of government it set up remained in force until 1858.

BURKE CITES THE CHARGES
AGAINST WARREN HASTINGS

[February 19, 1788]

If Clive won an empire in India, it was Warren Hastings, first Governor General of British India, from 1773 to 1785, who, faced with almost insuperable difficulties, consolidated and preserved it. Against Indian princes and nations, the French, and the hostility of the British Council to which he was subject, he prevailed in the end by his courage and resourcefulness and by his effective strategy of never accepting defeat. The coalition of native powers was broken by intrigue, concession, or military might. Haidar Ali was destroyed, the Marathas were outmaneuvered, and the French, bidding for empire, were turned back, simultaneously. By 1784 British prestige, though it had suffered everywhere else, was never so high as in India.

Hastings' methods, however, had not been above reproach. Though scrupulous in many matters, he had been careless in others, and like other empire builders preferred success to unchallengeable virtue. In India he had made powerful enemies and rivals, such as Philip Francis. In England he had aroused the strong indignation of Burke, Fox, and Sheridan, long-standing enemies of the Company and its policies. The time was approaching when, instead of praising his amazing victories, as he felt he had every right to expect, many of his countrymen would turn the coin to the other side and see there nothing but the crimes of a self-seeking adventurer. Had he not accepted bribes to the amount of £40,000? And what of the spoliation of the princesses of Oudh and the extortion of money from Chait Singh? Bribes, extortion, wars, cruelty, devastation, and perfidy were charged.

Hastings returned to England in 1785 as a hero, was feted by the Company, befriended by George III, and recognized for his high services by Pitt and the Tories. But the storm was gathering. A week after Hastings' return, Burke gave warning of the impending attack, and in February of the following year, 1786, he rose in Parliament to accuse Hastings of supplying the Nawab of Oudh with troops to extirpate the nation of the Rohillas. But this was rejected on the highly technical ground that the accused was not at that time Governor General of Bengal. The second article of the indictment could not be disposed of in this way. It read that Hastings had goaded Chait Singh, the ruler of Benares, into rebellion by exorbitant financial demands and had then given his kingdom to his nephew in return for double the tribute that had been paid before, a gain of £200,000 a year for the Company. Hastings could argue in reply that the crisis in India justified new demands, but it was hard to explain the enormous fine that he had imposed on Chait Singh at one point. Pitt suddenly, and to the surprise of even his close followers, shifted ground and spoke against Hastings. The second article of the impeachment was thus easily carried, the honors going to Fox and Burke, but also to Hastings' vindictive enemy, Francis, and his supposed friend, Pitt.

The next article of the indictment, relating to Hastings' robbery of the princesses of Oudh, was not raised in the House until the following year, February 7, 1787. It was decided that the playwright-politician Sheridan should argue this particular charge, and the choice, as it turned out, could not have been more auspicious. For five and a half hours his voice rang irresistibly in the House. The admiration at the end approached consternation, and the excitement was so great that the House agreed to adjourn the session until the members had recovered from the sway of Sheridan's words. Fox declared it the greatest speech ever delivered in the House, and even Pitt admitted its merit. Sheridan was soon offered £1,000 for his speech if he would only correct it, but this he unfortunately failed to do, and we know it only by report.

Sheridan's speech was a triumph politically, too. When Parliament reconvened, his motion relating to Hastings' treatment of the princesses of Oudh was carried, and the other articles of the indictment as well. The scene was thus laid for the greatest political trial in the history of England. On April 3, 1787, it was voted to impeach Hastings, and on May 21 the accused listened to the long recital of his crimes as set forth in the formal articles of impeachment.

The opening day of the trial presented the impressive scene so vividly described by Macaulay in his memorable essay. Burke, as head of the committee of managers conducting this great affair, behaved with affecting solemnity, his brow "knit with deep laboring thought," as Fanny Burney wrote in her diary. On the fifteenth he began the speech that, in effect, introduced the entire body of charges, and spoke during four sessions. He closed with these words:

"I impeach Warren Hastings, Esquire, of high crimes and misdemeanors.

"I impeach him in the name of the Commons of Great Britain in Parliament assembled, whose parliamentary trust he has betrayed.

"I impeach him in the name of all the Commons of Great Britain, whose national character he has dishonored.

"I impeach him in the name of the people of India, whose laws, rights, and liberties he has subverted; whose properties he has destroyed; whose country he has laid waste and desolate.

"I impeach him in the name, and by virtue, of those eternal laws of justice which he has violated.

"I impeach him in the name of human nature itself, which he has cruelly outraged, injured, and oppressed in both sexes, in every age, rank, situation, and condition of life."

As the great orator described the origin and development of Britain's Asiatic empire and denounced Hastings' rapacious misgovernment, investing his argument with power of image and comparison unsurpassed, even the most unwilling seemed to be convinced. Hastings himself said that for the moment he could not resist the conviction that he was a great criminal, such was Burke's persuasiveness. In the crowded galleries, women were much affected. Sobs and screams were sometimes heard, and Mrs. Sheridan is said to have fainted. Fanny Burney, Hastings' partisan, said that Burke "at last overpowered me; I felt my cause lost. . . . My eyes dreaded a single glance toward a man so accused as Mr. Hastings. I had no hope he could clear himself; not another wish in his favor remained."

RICHARD BRINSLEY SHERIDAN BRINGS THE HASTINGS TRIAL TO A CLIMAX

[June 13, 1788]

Richard Brinsley Sheridan (1751–1816), born in Dublin and educated at Harrow, won the highest distinction both as dramatist and statesman. Admired as the author of The Rivals, The School for Scandal, and other successful plays, he also became one of the most brilliant speakers of a golden age of oratory, employing his dramatic skill in repartee and epigram for serious political purposes. Entering Parliament in 1780, he soon associated himself with Burke and Fox and with the liberal causes they championed. His long career as a member did not end until 1812. Lacking the learning of Burke and the political generalship of Pitt and Fox, he nevertheless exerted an unrivaled fascination on men's minds. Thus the poet Moore could say that, as orator, dramatist, and minstrel, he "ruled like a wizard the world of the heart and could call up its sunshine or bring down its showers." Whereas the House often ignored or interrupted the most magnificent word pictures of Burke, and became irked by the formalism and testiness of Pitt, they listened to Sheridan. He had learned in the theater to arouse men's sympathies and hold their interest.

Although, like Erskine, Sheridan was bewitched by the cold decorum and power of Pitt, he had the courage to stand up against him. On one of the few occasions in which Pitt lost his composure in public, he remarked sarcastically that in the future Sheridan had better save his epigrams for the theater. This gave the playwright the opportunity for one of the most famous jests of the period. "Flattered and encouraged by the right honorable gentleman's panegyric of my talent," Sheridan retorted, he would, if he ever returned to playwriting, improve upon the character of the Angry Boy in Ben Jonson's The Alchemist. The thrust at the young Prime Minister was deft, and the designation—the Angry Boy—was to stick to him for years to come.

Sheridan's most famous speech, on the charges relating to the begums of Oudh, was delivered during the early stages of the Hastings proceedings (February 7, 1788). It remains by reputation the most brilliant speech in the history of English eloquence, though it is almost wholly lost. Happily, the speech he gave as manager of the impeachment has been substantially preserved, despite its having been delivered on four separated sittings: June 3, 6, 10, and 13. We quote from the peroration on the fourth day.

> *"The council erred in nothing so much*
> *as in a reprehensible credulity."*

THE INQUIRY, which now only remains, my lords, is whether Mr. Hastings is to be answerable for the crimes committed by his agents. It has been fully proved that Mr. Middleton signed the treaty with the superior begum in October, 1778. He also acknowledged signing some others of a different date, but could not recollect the authority by which he did it! These treaties were recognized by Mr. Hastings, as appears by the evidence of Mr. Purling, in the year 1780. In that of October, 1778, the jagir was secured, which was allotted for the support of the women of the Khord Mahal. But still the prisoner pleads that he is not accountable for the cruelties which were exercised. His is the plea which tyranny, aided by its prime minister, treachery, is always sure to set up. Mr. Middleton has attempted to strengthen this ground by endeavoring to claim the whole infamy in those transactions and to monopolize the guilt. He dared even to aver that he had been condemned by Mr. Hastings for the ignominious part he had acted. He dared to avow this because Mr. Hastings was on his trial, and he thought he never would be arraigned; but in the face of this court, and before he left the bar, he was compelled to confess that it was for the lenience and not the severity of his proceedings that he had been reproved by the prisoner.

It will not, my lords, I trust, be concluded that because Mr. Hastings has not marked every passing shade of guilt, and because he has only given the bold outline of cruelty, he is therefore to be acquitted. It is laid down by the law of England, that law which is the perfection of reason, that a person ordering an act to be done by his agent is answerable for that act with all its consequences, *quod facit per alium, facit per se*. Middleton was appointed in 1777 the confidential agent, the second self of Mr. Hastings. The Governor General ordered the measure. Even if he never saw nor heard afterward of its consequences, he was therefore answerable for every pang that was inflicted and for all the blood that was shed. But he did hear, and that instantly, of the whole. He wrote to accuse Middleton of forbearance and of neglect. He commanded him to work upon the hopes and fears of the princesses, and to leave no means untried, until, to speak his own language, which was better suited to the banditti of a cavern, "he obtained possession of the secret hoards of the old ladies." He would not allow even of a delay of two days to smooth the compelled approaches of a son to his mother on this occasion! His orders were peremptory. After this, my lords, can it be said that the prisoner was ignorant of the acts or not culpable of the consequences? It is true he did not direct the guards, the famine, and bludgeons; he did not weigh the fetters, nor number the lashes to be inflicted on his victims; but yet he is just as guilty as if he had borne an active and personal share in each transaction. It is as if he had commanded that the heart should be torn from the bosom, and enjoined that no blood should follow. He is in the same degree accountable to the law, to his country, to his conscience, and to his God!

The prisoner has endeavored also to get rid of a part of his guilt by observing that he was but one of the supreme council, and that all the rest had sanctioned those transactions with their approbation. Even if it were true that others did participate in the guilt, it cannot tend to diminish his criminality. But the fact is that the council erred in nothing so much as in a reprehensible credulity given to the declarations of the Governor General. They knew not a word of those transactions until they were finally concluded. It was not until the January following that they saw the mass of falsehood which had been published under the title of "Mr. Hastings' Narrative." They were, then, unaccountably duped to permit a letter to pass, dated the twenty-ninth of November, intended to seduce the directors into a belief that they had received intelligence at that time, which was not the fact. These observations, my lords, are not meant to cast any obloquy on the council; they, undoubtedly, were deceived; and the deceit practiced on them is a decided proof of his consciousness of guilt. When tired of corporal infliction, Mr. Hastings was gratified by insulting the understanding. The coolness and reflection with which this act was managed and concerted raises its enormity and blackens its turpitude. It proves the prisoner to be that monster in nature, a deliberate and reasoning tyrant! Other tyrants of whom we read, such as a Nero or a Caligula, were urged to their crimes by the impetuosity of passion. High rank disqualified them from advice, and, perhaps, equally prevented reflection. But in the prisoner we have a man born in a state of mediocrity; bred to mercantile life; used to system; and accustomed to regularity; who was accountable to his masters, and therefore was compelled to think and to deliberate on every part of his conduct. It is this cool deliberation, I say, which renders his crimes more horrible and his character more atrocious.

When, my lords, the board of directors received the advices which Mr. Hastings thought proper to transmit, though unfurnished with any other materials to form their judgment, they expressed very strongly their doubts, and properly ordered an inquiry into the circumstances of the alleged disaffection of the begums, declaring it, at the same time, to be a debt which was due to the honor and justice of the British nation. This inquiry, however, Mr. Hastings thought it absolutely necessary to elude. He stated to the council, in answer, "that it would revive those animosities that subsisted between the begums and the nabob [Asoph Dowlah], which had then subsided. If the former were inclined to appeal to a foreign jurisdiction, they were the best judges of their own feeling, and should be left to make their own complaint." All this, however, my lords, is nothing to the magnificent paragraph which concludes this communication. "Besides," says he, "I hope it will not be a departure from official language to say that the Majesty of Justice ought not to be approached without solicitation. She ought not to descend to inflame or provoke, but to withhold her judgment until she is called on to determine." What is still more astonishing is that Sir John Macpherson, who, though a man of sense and honor, is rather Oriental in his imagination, and not taught in the sublime and beautiful by the immortal leader of this prosecution, was caught by this bold, bombastic quibble, and joined in the same words, "that the Majesty of Justice ought not to be approached without solicitation." But, my lords, do you, the judges of this land, and the expounders of its rightful laws, do you approve of this mockery, and call it the character of justice, which takes the form of right to excite wrong? No, my lords, justice is not this halt and miserable object; it is not the ineffective bauble of an Indian pagod; it is not the portentous phantom of despair; it is not like any fabled monster, formed in the eclipse of reason, and found in some unhallowed grove of superstitious darkness and political dismay! No, my lords. In the happy reverse of all this, I turn from the disgusting caricature to the real image! Justice I have now before me, august and pure! The abstract idea of all that would be perfect in the spirits and the aspirations of men!—where the mind rises; where the heart expands; where the countenance is ever placid and benign; where her favorite attitude is to stoop to the unfortunate; to hear their cry and to help them; to rescue and relieve, to succor and save; majestic, from its mercy; venerable, from its utility; uplifted, without pride; firm, without obduracy; beneficent in each preference; lovely, though in her frown!

On that Justice I rely; deliberate and sure, abstracted from all party purpose and political speculation; not on words, but on facts. You, my lords, who hear me, I conjure, by those rights which it is your best privilege to preserve; by that fame which it is your best pleasure to inherit; by all those feelings which refer to the first term in the series of existence, the original compact of our nature, our controlling rank in the creation. This is the call on all to administer to truth and equity, as they would satisfy the laws and satisfy themselves with the most exalted bliss possible or conceivable for our nature; the self-approving consciousness of virtue, when the condemnation we look for will be one of the most ample mercies accomplished for mankind since the creation of the world! My lords, I have done.

As Sheridan finished he sank back, apparently exhausted, into the arms of Burke, and the audience knew that it had witnessed one of the most dazzling oratorical displays in English history. This speech, just because it was so carefully contrived, so loudly publicized in advance, lacked the spontaneity and power of his six-hour speech on the same subject before the House of Commons in the previous year. But for the moment it made Sheridan the most conspicuous, sought-after man in England. It was the high point in the trial of Warren Hastings.

THOMAS ERSKINE POINTS OUT THE INEVITABLE CONSEQUENCES OF EMPIRE

[December 9, 1789]

While the trial of Warren Hastings was lumbering through its second year, its conclusion was foreshadowed and indeed influenced by another trial, far less conspicuous, at the Court of King's Bench. One John Stockdale, a London bookseller and printer, was charged with libeling the House of Commons for publishing A Review of the Principal Charges against Warren Hastings, Esq., Late Governor of Bengal, by the Reverend John Logan, an obscure Scotch preacher. Logan took the position that the violent and extravagant charges against Hastings, published before the trial began, unfairly influenced the High Court and the public in advance, and he made a reasoned defense of Hastings, which was a severe criticism of the managers of the trial, Burke, Fox, and Sheridan, passionate, able men who were not lawyers. Indignantly they demanded the prosecution under the seditious libel law of the publisher, John Stockdale, for in the interval the Reverend John Logan, author of the "seditious" pamphlet, had died. Stockdale was fortunate in having as his defender Thomas Erskine, probably England's greatest courtroom lawyer and most eloquent defender of freedom of speech and press, at a time when such freedoms most needed defending.

Thomas Erskine (1750–1823) was the youngest son of an impoverished Scotch lord. Unable to go to a university, he spent a few years in the navy and then in the army, without finding hope or scope for his energies. A chance meeting with the famous judge, Lord Mansfield, inspired him to study law, and soon after admission to the bar he won both reputation and wealth. In a long series of forensic contests he defended and advanced English liberties with consummate skill and vigor, combining an incisive logic, which never lost sight of the case to be won, with poetry and moral and religious fervor. Possessing at all times a mastery of the immediate facts of a case, he had the power to relate them intimately to broad principles which were commonly accepted, and thus he not only won battles for freedom of the press and trial by jury, and struck blows against the seditious libel law and arbitrary search, seizure, and arrest, in his own time, but also built ramparts of defense of present-day liberties, still none too secure. In 1781 he successfully defended Lord George Gordon who, charged with treason for allegedly leading the anti-Catholic riots of the preceding year, was brought to trial in an atmosphere of hysteria and repression. In 1783–84 he made a dazzling defense of William Shipley, the Dean of Asaph, indicted on the charge of seditious libel for writing a tract on the principles of government. In this case the victorious Erskine not only gave strong support to the principle of trial by jury in general, but in particular, established a momentous precedent: that it was the right of the jury, not the judge, to decide whether a publication is libelous (the contention of the American, Andrew Hamilton, in 1735). This decision paved the way for the passage of Fox's new libel bill in 1792, which was to take the place of the old seditious libel law, a law which had produced prosecutions under the Georges almost as tyrannous as the treason trials under the Charleses.

We hear Erskine now in defense of John Stockdale.

"It is mad and preposterous to bring to the standard of justice
and humanity the exercise of a dominion founded
upon violence and terror."

Gentlemen:

I WISH that my strength would enable me to convince you of the author's singleness of intention, and of the merit and ability of his work, by reading the whole that remains of it. But my voice is already nearly exhausted, I am sorry my client should be a sufferer by my infirmity. One passage, however, is too striking and important to be passed over; the rest I must trust to your private examination. The author, having discussed all the charges, article by article, sums them all up with this striking appeal to his readers:

> The authentic statement of facts which has been given, and the arguments which have been employed, are, I think, sufficient to vindicate the character and conduct of Mr. Hastings, even on the maxims of European policy. When he was appointed Governor General of Bengal, he was invested with a discretionary power to promote the interests of the India Company and of the British Empire in that quarter of the globe. The general instructions sent to him from his constituents were: "That in all your deliberations and resolutions, you make the safety and prosperity of Bengal your principal object, and fix your attention on the security of the possessions and revenues of the Company." His superior genius sometimes acted in the spirit rather than complied with the letter of the law, but he discharged the trust, and preserved the empire committed to his care, in the same way, and with greater splendor and success than any of his predecessors in office; his departure from India was marked with the lamentations of the natives, and the gratitude of his countrymen, and, on his return to England, he received the cordial congratulations of that numerous and respectable society whose interests he had promoted, and whose dominions he had protected and extended.

Gentlemen of the jury, if this be a willfully false account of the instructions given to Mr. Hastings for his government, and of his conduct under them, the author and publisher of this defense deserve the severest punishment, for a mercenary imposition on the public. But if it be true that he was directed to make the safety and prosperity of Bengal the first object of his attention, and that, under his administration, it has been safe and prosperous; if it be true that the security and preservation of our possessions and revenues in Asia were marked out to him as the great leading principle of his government, and that those possessions and revenues, amidst unexampled dangers, have been secured and preserved; then a question may be unaccountably mixed with your consideration, much beyond the consequence of the present prosecution, involving, perhaps, the merit of the impeachment itself which gave it birth—a question which the Commons, as prosecutors of Mr. Hastings, should, in common prudence, have avoided; unless, regretting the unwieldy length of their proceedings against him, they wish to afford him the opportunity of this strange anomalous defense. For, although I am neither his counsel, nor desire to have anything to do with his guilt or innocence, yet, in the collateral defense of my client, I am driven to state matter which may be considered by many as hostile to the impeachment. For if our dependencies have been secured, and their interests promoted, I am driven in the defense of my client to remark that it is mad and preposterous to bring to the standard of justice and humanity the exercise of a dominion founded upon violence and terror. It may and must be true that Mr. Hastings has repeatedly offended against the rights and privileges of Asiatic government, if he was the faithful deputy of a power which could not maintain itself for an hour without trampling upon both. He may and must have offended against the laws of God and nature if he was the faithful viceroy of an empire wrested in blood from the people to whom God and nature had given it; he may and must have preserved that unjust dominion over timorous and abject nations by a terrifying, overbearing, insulting superiority, if he was the faithful administrator of your government, which, having no root in consent or affection—no foundation in similarity of interests—nor support from any one principle which cements men together in society, could only be upheld by alternate stratagem and force. The unhappy people of India, feeble and effeminate as they are from the softness of their climate, and subdued and broken as they have been by the knavery and strength of civilization, still occasionally start up in all the vigor and intelligence of insulted nature. To be governed at all, they must be governed with a rod of iron; and our empire in the Eastern world long since must have been lost to Great Britain, if civil skill and military prowess had not united their efforts to support an authority which heaven never gave, by means which it never can sanction.

Gentlemen, I think I can observe that you are touched with this way of considering the subject, and I can account for it. I have not been considering it through the cold medium of books, but have been speaking of man and his nature, and of human dominion, from what I have seen of them myself amongst reluctant nations submitting to our authority. I know what they feel, and how such feelings can alone be repressed. I have heard them in my youth from a naked savage, in the indignant character of a prince surrounded by his subjects, addressing the governor of a British colony, holding a bundle of sticks in his hand, as the notes of his unlettered eloquence. "Who is it?" said the jealous ruler over the desert, encroached upon by the restless foot of English adventure; "who is it that causes this river to rise in the high mountains and to empty itself into the ocean? Who is it that causes to blow the loud winds of winter, and that calms them again in the summer? Who is it that rears up the shade of those lofty forests, and blasts them with the quick lightning at his pleasure?" "The same Being who gave to you a country on the other side of the waters, and gave ours to us; and by this title we will defend it," said the warrior, throwing down his tomahawk upon the ground, and raising the war sound of his nation. These are the feelings of subjugated man all round the globe; and depend upon it, nothing but fear will control where it is vain to look for affection.

These reflections are the only antidotes to those anathemas of superhuman eloquence which have lately shaken these walls that surround us, but which it unaccountably falls to my province, whether I will or no, a little to stem the torrent of, by reminding you that you have a mighty sway in Asia which cannot be maintained by the finer sympathies of life or the practice of its charities and affections; what will they do for you when surrounded by two hundred thousand men with artillery, cavalry, and elephants, calling upon you for their dominions which you have robbed them of? Justice may, no doubt, in such case, forbid the levying of a fine to pay a revolting soldiery; a treaty may stand in the way of increasing a tribute to keep up the very existence of the government; and delicacy for women may forbid all entrance into a zenana for money, whatever may be the necessity for taking it. All these things must ever be occurring. But under the pressure of such constant difficulties, so dangerous to national honor, it might be better, perhaps, to think of effectually securing it altogether, by recalling our troops and our merchants, and abandoning our Oriental empire. Until this be done, neither religion nor philosophy can be pressed very far into the aid of reformation and punishment. If England, from a lust of ambition and dominion, will insist on maintaining despotic rule over distant and hostile nations, beyond all comparison more numerous and extended than herself, and gives commission to her viceroys to govern them with no other instructions than to preserve them, and to secure permanently their revenues, with what color of consistency or reason can she place herself in the moral chair, and affect to be shocked at the execution of her own orders; adverting to the exact measure of wickedness and injustice necessary to their execution, and complaining only of the excess as the immorality, considering her authority as a dispensation for breaking the commands of God, and the breach of them as only punishable when contrary to the ordinances of man?

Such a proceeding, gentlemen, begets serious reflection. It would be better, perhaps, for the masters and the servants of all such governments to join in supplication that the great Author of violated humanity may not confound them together in one common judgment.

Gentlemen, I find, as I said before, I have not sufficient strength to go on with the remaining parts of the book. I hope, however, that, notwithstanding my omissions, you are now completely satisfied that whatever errors or misconceptions may have misled the writer of these pages, the justification of a person whom he believed to be innocent, and whose accusers had themselves appealed to the public, was the single object of his contemplation. If I have succeeded in that object, every purpose which I had in addressing you has been answered.

It now only remains to remind you that another consideration has been strongly pressed upon by you, and, no doubt, will be insisted on in reply. You will be told that the matters which I have been justifying as legal, and even meritorious, have therefore not been made the subject of complaint; and that whatever intrinsic merit parts of the book may be supposed or even admitted to possess, such merit can afford no justification to the selected passages, some of which, even with the context, carry the meaning charged by the information, and which are indecent animadversions on authority. To this I would answer (still protesting as I do against the application of any one of the innuendoes) that if you are firmly persuaded of the singleness and purity of the author's intentions, you are not bound to subject him to infamy because, in the zealous career of a just and animated composition, he happens to have tripped with his pen into an intemperate expression in one or two instances of a long work. If this severe duty were binding on your consciences, the liberty of the press would be an empty sound, and no man could venture to write on any subject however pure his purpose, without an attorney at one elbow and a counsel at the other.

From minds thus subdued by the terrors of punishment, there could issue no works of genius to expand the empire of human reason, nor any masterly compositions on the general nature of government, by the help of which the great commonwealths of mankind have founded their establishments; much less any of those useful applications of them to critical conjunctures by which, from time to time, our own Constitution, by the exertion of patriot citizens, has been brought back to its standard. Under such terrors all the great lights of science and civilization must be extinguished, for men cannot communicate their free thoughts to one another with a lash held over their heads. It is the nature of everything that is great and useful, both in the animate and inanimate world, to be wild and irregular, and we must be contented to take them with the alloys which belong to them, or live without them. Genius breaks from the fetters of criticism, but its wanderings are sanctioned by its majesty and wisdom when it advances in its path; subject it to the critic, and you tame it into dullness. Mighty rivers break down their banks in the winter, sweeping away to death the flocks which are fattened on the soil that they fertilize in the summer; the few may be saved by embankments from drowning, but the flock must perish for hunger. Tempests occasionally shake our dwellings and dissipate our commerce; but they scourge before them the lazy elements, which, without them, would stagnate into pestilence. In like manner, liberty herself, the last and best gift of God to his creatures, must be taken just as she is; you might pare her down into bashful regularity, and shape her into a perfect model of severe, scrupulous law, but she would then be liberty no longer; and you must be content to die under the lash of this inexorable justice which you have exchanged for the banners of freedom.

If it be asked where the line to this indulgence and impunity is to be drawn, the answer is easy. The liberty of the press on general subjects comprehends and implies as much strict observance of positive law as is consistent with perfect purity of intention, and equal and useful society; and what that latitude is cannot be promulgated in the abstract, but must be judged of in the particular instance, and consequently, upon this occasion, must be judged of by you, without forming any possible precedent for any other case; and where can the judgment be possibly so safe as with the members of that society which alone can suffer, if the writing is calculated to do mischief to the public? You must, therefore, try the book by that criterion, and say whether the publication was premature and offensive or, in other words, whether the publisher is bound to have suppressed it until the public ear was anticipated and abused and every avenue to the human heart or understanding secured and blocked up. I see around me those by whom, by and by, Mr. Hastings will be most ably and eloquently defended; but I am sorry to remind my friends that but for the right of suspending the public judgment concerning him till their season of exertion comes round, the tongues of angels would be insufficient for the task.

Gentlemen, I hope I have now performed my duty to my client; I sincerely hope that I have; for certainly, if ever there was a man pulled the other way by his interests and affections—if ever there was a man who should have trembled at the situation in which I have been placed on this occasion—it is myself, who not only love, honor, and respect, but whose future hopes and preferments are linked, from free choice, with those who, from the mistakes of the author, are treated with great severity and injustice. These are strong retardments; but I have been urged on to activity by considerations which can never be inconsistent with honorable attachments, either in the political or social world—the love of justice and of liberty, and a zeal for the Constitution of my country, which is the inheritance of our posterity, of the public, and of the world. These are the motives which have animated me in defense of this person, who is an entire stranger to me, whose shop I never go to, and the author of whose publication, as well as Mr. Hastings, who is the object of it, I never spoke to in my life.

One word more, gentlemen, and I have done. Every human tribunal ought to take care to administer justice as we look, hereafter, to have justice administered to ourselves. Upon the principle on which the Attorney General prays sentence upon my client—God have mercy upon us!—instead of standing before him in judgment with the hopes and consolations of Christians, we must call upon the mountains to cover us; for which of us can present, for Omniscient examination, a pure, unspotted, and faultless course? But I humbly expect that the benevolent Author of our being will judge us as I have been pointing out for your example. Holding up the great volume of our lives in His hands, and regarding the general scope of them, if He discover benevolence, charity, and good will to man beating in the heart, where He alone can look; if He find that our conduct, though often forced out of the path by our infirmities, has been in general well directed, His all-searching eye will assuredly never pursue us into those little corners of our lives, much less will His justice select them for punishment, without the general context of our existence, by which faults may be sometimes found to have grown out of virtues, and very many of our heaviest offenses to have been grafted by human imperfection upon the best and kindest of our affections. No, gentlemen, believe me, this is not the course of Divine justice, or there is no truth in the Gospels of heaven. If the general tenor of a man's conduct be such as I have represented it, he may walk through the shadow of death, with all his faults about him, with as much cheerfulness as in the common paths of life, because he knows that, instead of a stern accuser to expose before the Author of his nature those frail passages which, like the scored matter in the book before you, checker the volume of the brightest and best-spent life, his mercy will obscure them from the eye of his purity, and our repentance blot them out forever.

All this would, I admit, be perfectly foreign and irrelevant if you were sitting here in a case of property between man and man, where a strict rule of law must operate, or there would be an end of civil life and society. It would be equally foreign and still more irrelevant if applied to those shameful attacks upon private reputation which are the bane and disgrace of the press, by which whole families have been rendered unhappy during life, by aspersions cruel, scandalous, and unjust. Let such libelers remember that no one of my principles of defense can, at any time or upon any occasion, ever apply to shield them from punishment, because such conduct is not only an infringement of the rights of men, as they are defined by strict law, but is absolutely incompatible with honor, honesty, or mistaken good intention. On such men let the Attorney General bring forth all the artillery of his office, and the thanks and blessings of the whole public will follow him. But this is a totally different case. Whatever private calumny may mark this work, it has not been made the subject of complaint, and we have, therefore, nothing to do with that, nor any right to consider it. We are trying whether the public could have been considered as offended and endangered, if Mr. Hastings himself, in whose place the author and publisher have a right to put themselves, had, under all the circumstances which have been considered, composed and published the volume under examination. That question cannot, in common sense, be anything resembling a question of law, but is a pure question of fact, to be decided on the principles which I have humbly recommended. I therefore ask of the court that the book itself may now be delivered to you. Read it with attention and, as you shall find it, pronounce your verdict.

When Erskine had finished speaking there was a flutter of intense excitement in the crowded courtroom. The council for the Crown spoke for an hour, seeking to repair the prosecution's case, which Erskine had shattered, and to dispel the magic of his words. Then the jury filed out, returning in two hours with the verdict of "not guilty." Erskine had scored another great victory, a victory for the freedom of speech and the press.

In that same momentous speech Erskine made the logical and most effective defense of Hastings. The crux of his argument was that the "crimes" of Hastings were the inevitable consequence of a vast imperial venture, involving high stakes in national honor and welfare. But the trial of Hastings, which began in 1788, was to drag on for seven years before he was finally acquitted.

It now seems that Hastings was far more efficient, honest and humane than the monster painted by Burke, Fox and Sheridan (and years later by Macaulay, in a famous essay), and had been carrying out many of the reforms that Burke and his colleagues demanded, that his impeachment under the circumstances was uncalled for, and that the crimes and corruptions of the East India Company were well known for years before the trial of Warren Hastings began. According to a recent biographer of Hastings, Pendrel Moon, who has apparently gone through the entire record of the East India Company, "The iniquities of the Company's servants were not brought to public notice by the speeches at the Hastings' trial—they had been notorious and the constant theme of parliamentary discussion throughout the preceding twenty years, and all the essential measures which brought about a reform were taken before and not after the impeachment. The most important of these were the passing of Pitt's India Act in 1784 and the appointment of Lord Cornwallis as Governor General in 1785."

"Thus the impeachment synchronized with a real change for the better; but it was not its cause. It served no useful purpose at the time; but it has acquired a symbolic value in the eyes of posterity."

PART SIX

THE FEDERAL CONSTITUTION

BENJAMIN FRANKLIN, AS THE CONSTITU-TIONAL CONVENTION CLOSES, HAS THE LAST WISE WORD TO SAY

[September 17, 1787]

I N CONTRAST to the public pomp and flamboyant oratory of the Hastings trial, which began so brilliantly and then dragged on for years, was the American Constitutional Convention held in closed sessions in Independence Hall, Philadelphia, during the hot summer of 1787. Fifty-five men, representing all of the thirteen original colonies but Rhode Island, came together to revise the loose Articles of Confederation. They welded themselves into one of the most remarkable deliberative bodies in history. Thirty-nine of them had served in the Continental Congress; twenty-one had fought in the Revolution; eight had signed the Declaration of Independence. According to Charles Warren, "ten men stood out as chiefly responsible for the form which the Constitution finally took—Madison, Randolph, Franklin, Wilson, Gouverneur Morris, King, Rutledge, Charles Pinckney, and Sherman." On the whole, they shared the same fear of "mob rule," of popular democracy; they recognized what seemed to be the natural superiority of the landed aristocracy of the South and the wealthy commercial interests of the North. It remained for the eighty-one-year-old Franklin, who had risen from poverty, to say that "we should not depress the virtue and public spirit of our common people." Of others who had a similar faith, Jefferson was in France as our minister, and Patrick Henry had refused to come to the Convention.

In spite of this general agreement, there were struggles between the representatives of the North and the South, between the large states and the small states, and between those who differed as to the strength of the proposed central government. Tempers flared, but the commanding dignity of Washington, as president of the Convention, and the healing presence of Franklin kept vehemence within bounds.

James Madison, insignificant in appearance and frail in health, was not only the great constructive thinker of the Convention but also its indefatigable recorder. His day-by-day reports of those epoch-making debates were not published until after his death, fifty years later, and they remain too little read even now. For where else can one find so many intense men at one time locked in such thoughtful controversy—with no gallery present? It must suffice here to point out that the wealthy young Philadelphia merchant, Gouverneur Morris, was the most frequent and vigorous speaker; that the handsome governor of Virginia, Edmund Randolph, also in his early thirties, was probably the most finished; and that little Madison, superbly informed in history and political theory, thanks partly to the books that Jefferson had been sending him from France, was ultimately the most effective. Alexander Hamilton spoke brilliantly but without effect, because his conception of a strong central government was too strong even for that group. On the other hand, Maryland's Luther Martin, the chief opponent of the Constitution, was a dull, long-winded speaker who left the Convention before it was over.

The many-sided Franklin was never an orator in any sense of the word, and at eighty-one he was too frail to take much part in the debates, but he attended the meetings regularly for three and a half months and on the last day made his characteristic mark. On September, 17, 1787, after an engrossed copy of the Constitution had been read, the beloved sage of two continents rose and passed his written speech to James Wilson, of the Pennsylvania delegation, who read it to the Convention.

"I cannot help expressing a wish that every member . . .
doubt a little of his own infallibility."

Mr. President:

I CONFESS that there are several parts of this Constitution which I do not at present approve, but I am not sure I shall never approve them: for having lived long, I have experienced many instances of being obliged by better information, or fuller consideration, to change opinions even on important subjects, which I once thought right, but found to be otherwise. It is therefore that the older I grow, the more apt I am to doubt my own judgment, and to pay more respect to the judgment of others. Most men indeed, as well as most sects in religion, think themselves in possession of all truth, and that wherever others differ from them it is so far error. Steele, a Protestant, in a dedication, tells the Pope that the only difference between our Churches in their opinions of the certainty of their doctrines is the Church of Rome is infallible and the Church of England is never in the wrong. But though many private persons think almost as highly of their own infallibility as of that of their sect, few express it so naturally as a certain French lady who, in a dispute with her sister, said, "I don't know how it happens, sister, but I meet with nobody but myself that's always in the right—*Il n'y a que moi qui a toujours raison.*"

In these sentiments, sir, I agree to this Constitution with all its faults, if they are such; because I think a general government necessary for us, and there is no form of government but what may be a blessing to the people if well administered, and believe further that this is likely to be well administered for a course of years, and can only end in despotism, as other forms have done before it, when the people shall become so corrupted as to need despotic government, being incapable of any other. I doubt too whether any other Convention we can obtain may be able to make a better Constitution. For when you assemble a number of men to have the advantage of their joint wisdom, you inevitably assemble with those men all their prejudices, their passions, their errors of opinion, their local interests, and their selfish views. From such an assembly can a perfect production be expected? It therefore astonishes me, sir, to find this system approaching so near to perfection as it does; and I think it will astonish our enemies, who are waiting with confidence to hear that our councils are confounded like those of the builders of Babel; and that our states are on the point of separation, only to meet hereafter for the purpose of cutting one another's throats. Thus I consent, sir, to this Constitution because I expect no better, and because I am not sure that it is not the best. The opinions I have had of its errors, I sacrifice to the public good. I have never whispered a syllable of them abroad. Within these walls they were born, and here they shall die. If every one of us in returning to our constituents were to report the objections he has had to it, and endeavor to gain partisans in support of them, we might prevent its being generally received, and thereby lose all the salutary effects and great advantages resulting naturally in our favor among foreign nations as well as among ourselves from our real or apparent unanimity. Much of the strength and efficiency of any government in procuring and securing happiness to the people depends on opinion, on the general opinion of the goodness of the government, as well as of the wisdom and integrity of its governors. I hope therefore that for our own sakes as a part of the people, and for the sake of posterity, we shall act heartily and unanimously in recommending this Constitution (if approved by Congress and confirmed by the Conventions) wherever our influence may extend, and turn our future thoughts and endeavors to the means of having it well administered.

On the whole, sir, I cannot help expressing a wish that every member of the Convention who may still have objections to it would with me, on this occasion, doubt a little of his own infallibility and, to make manifest our unanimity, put his name to this instrument.

Franklin then moved that the Constitution be signed by the delegates, of which thirty-nine remained of the original fifty-five. In the genial atmosphere thus prepared, a small change in the Constitution was voted unanimously, various members expressed briefly their hopes and fears, and Washington gave his dignified blessing to the proceedings.

While the last members were affixing their signatures (only three abstained), Madison noted that "Doctor Franklin, looking toward the President's chair, at the back of which a rising sun happened to be painted, observed to a few members near him that painters had found it difficult to distinguish in their art a rising from a setting sun. 'I have,' said he, 'often and often in the course of the session, and vicissitudes of my hopes and fears as to its issue, looked at that behind the President without being able to tell whether it was rising or setting: but now at length I have the happiness to know that it is a rising and not a setting sun.'"

PATRICK HENRY FEARS THE STRENGTH OF THE PROPOSED CONSTITUTION

[June 25, 1788]

The assent of nine states was necessary for the ratification of the Federal Constitution, and by June 21, 1788, conventions held in Massachusetts (including Maine), Connecticut, New Hampshire, Delaware, Pennsylvania, New Jersey, Maryland, Georgia, and South Carolina had voted to put the new government of the United States of America into operation. Formally, this was enough, but North Carolina, and Virginia and New York, the two most powerful states of all, still held out. It was at Richmond, Virginia, and at Poughkeepsie, New York, that the most dramatic and searching debates were held.

In Richmond the Constitution was supported by a well-organized group headed by James Madison, with Patrick Henry, ill and prematurely old at fifty-two, leading the opposition. For twenty-three days of tense discussion, Henry sometimes spoke five times a day, nearly a fifth of the entire debate. He who

*had been so fearless in leading the Revolution against the British was fearful
that new chains had been forged at Philadelphia. Perhaps liberty was implicit
in the Constitution; he wanted it made more explicit, and proposed amendment after amendment.*

*On the final day, as the Federalists were calling for the vote, Henry, mag-
nificent as ever, had his last word.*

"As we have the right of desiring amendments, why not exercise it?"

Mr. Chairman:

WHEN we were told of the difficulty of obtaining previous amendments, I contended that they might be as easily obtained as subsequent amendments. We are told that nine states have adopted it. If so,
when the government gets in motion, have they not a right to consider
our amendments as well as if we adopted first? If we remonstrate, may
they not consider and admit our amendments? But now, sir, when we
have been favored with a view of their subsequent amendments, I am
confirmed in what I apprehended; and that is, subsequent amendments
will make our condition worse; for they are placed in such a point of
view as will make this Convention ridiculous. I speak in plain, direct language. It is extorted from me. If this Convention will say that the very
right by which amendments are desired is not secured, then I say our
rights are not secured. As we have the right of desiring amendments, why
not exercise it? But gentlemen deny this right. It follows, of course, that,
if this right be not secured, our other rights are not. The proposition of
subsequent amendments is only to lull our apprehensions. We speak the
language of contradiction and inconsistency to say that rights are secured
and then say that they are not. Is not this placing this Convention in a
contemptible light? Will not this produce contempt of us in Congress and
every other part of the world? Will gentlemen tell me that they are in
earnest about these amendments?

I am convinced they mean nothing serious. What are the rights which
they do not propose to secure—which they reject?—for I contend there
are many essential and vital rights which are omitted. One is the power
of direct taxation. Gentlemen will not even give this invaluable right a
place among their subsequent amendments. And do gentlemen mean seriously that they will oppose us on this ground on the floor of Congress?
If Virginia thinks it one of her dearest rights, she need not expect to have

it amended. No, sir; it will be opposed. Taxes and excises are to be laid on us. The people are to be oppressed and the state legislature prostrated. Very material amendments are omitted. With respect to your militia, we only request that, if Congress should refuse to find arms for them, this country may lay out their own money to purchase them. But what do the gentlemen on the other side say? As much as that they will oppose you in this point also; for, if my recollection has not failed me, they have discarded this also. And shall we be deprived of this privilege? We propose to have it, in case there shall be a necessity to claim it. And is this claim incompatible with the safety of this country—with the grandeur and strength of the United States? If gentlemen find peace and rest on their minds, when the relinquishment of our rights is declared to be necessary for the aggrandizement of the government, they are more contented than I am.

Another thing which they have not mentioned is the power of *treaties.* Two thirds of the Senators present can make treaties; and they are, when made, to be the supreme law of the land, and are to be paramount to the state constitutions. We wish to guard against the temporary suspension of our great national rights. We wish some qualification of this dangerous power. We wish to modify it. One amendment which has been wished for, in this respect, is that no treaty should be made without the consent of a considerable majority of both houses. I might go on and enumerate many other great rights entirely neglected by their subsequent amendments; but I shall pass over them in silence. I am astonished at what my worthy friend [Mr. Innes] said—that we have no right of proposing previous amendments. That honorable gentleman is endowed with great eloquence—eloquence splendid, magnificent, and sufficient to shake the human mind! He has brought the whole force of America against this state. He has also strongly represented our comparative weakness with respect to the powers of Europe. But when I review the actual state of things, I see that dangers from thence are merely ideal. His reasoning has no effect on me. He cannot shake my political faith. He admits our power over subsequent amendments, though not over previous amendments. Where is the distinction between them? If we have a right to depart from the letter of our commission in one instance, we have in the other; for subsequent amendments have no higher authority than previous. We shall be absolutely certain of escaping danger in the one case, but not in the other. I think the apprehension expressed by another honorable gentleman has no good foundation. He apprehended civil discord if we did not adopt. I am willing to concede that he loves his country. I will, for the sake of argument, allow that I am one of the meanest of those who love their country. But what does this amount to? The great and direct end of government is liberty. Secure our liberty and privileges, and the end of government is answered. If this be not effectually done, government is an evil. What amendments does he propose which secure our liberty? I ask pardon if I make a mistake, but it seems to me that his proposed subsequent amendments do not secure one single right. They say that your rights are secured in the paper on the table, so that these subsequent amendments are a mere supererogation. They are not necessary, because the objects intended to be secured by them are secured already. What is to become of the trial by jury? Had its security been made a part of the Constitution, it would have been sufficiently guarded. But as it is, in that proposition it is by no means explicitly secured. Is it not trifling to admit the necessity of securing it, and not do it in a positive, unequivocal manner? I wish I could place it in any other view than a trifling one. It is only intended to attack every project of introducing amendments. If they are serious, why do they not join us, and ask, in a manly, firm, and resolute manner, for these amendments? Their view is to defeat every attempt to amend. When they speak of their subsequent recommendations, they tell you that amendments must be got, and the next moment they say they are unnecessary!

I beg pardon of this house for having taken up more time than came to my share, and I thank them for the patience and polite attention with which I have been heard. If I shall be in the minority, I shall have those painful sensations which arise from a conviction of *being overpowered in a good cause*. Yet I will be a peaceable citizen. My head, my hand, and my heart shall be at liberty to retrieve the loss of liberty, and remove the defects of that system in a constitutional way. I wish not to go to violence, but will wait with hopes that the spirit which predominated in the Revolution is not yet gone, nor the cause of those who are attached to the Revolution yet lost. I shall therefore patiently wait in expectation of seeing that government changed, so as to be compatible with the safety, liberty, and happiness of the people.

The delegates voted, 89 to 79, to ratify the Constitution, and Patrick Henry announced that he would give in. But he had so publicized the inadequacies of the Constitution that when the Virginia Assembly met, four months later, he had no difficulty in voting recommendations to Congress to enact amendments that would "relieve the apprehensions of those who may be solicitous for amendments." So, finally, Henry's insistent demands for a Bill of Rights were respected.

With the detachment of distance, William E. Dodd has said: "Henry was

probably more responsible than any or all others for the adoption of the first
ten amendments to the Federal Constitution."

ALEXANDER HAMILTON WINS OVER THE FOES OF THE CONSTITUTION IN NEW YORK

[June 20–28, 1788]

In the Virginia state convention the supporters of the Federal Constitution
were dominant from the beginning, under the masterly hand of Madison and
through the prestige of Washington; but at the New York state convention at
Poughkeepsie, the anti-Federalists, directed by Governor George Clinton, were
in a majority of 46 to 19. Their plan was to postpone indefinitely, to reject, or
to ratify conditionally. But after five weeks of debate the majority was won over
almost solely by the efforts of a single man, the thirty-one-year-old Alexander
Hamilton. "This convention," says Allan Nevins, in the Dictionary of American
Biography, "offers one of the few outstanding instances in American history of
the decision of a deliberative body being changed by sheer power of sustained
argument."

Alexander Hamilton (1757–1804), perhaps the most brilliant intellect in
American political history, was born in the British West Indies and died at
forty-seven in a duel with Aaron Burr. The illegitimate son of well-born but
impoverished parents, he entered King's College (now Columbia University)
at the age of sixteen, dropped out to take part in the propaganda war on the
eve of the Revolution, and fought in several battles before becoming aide-de-
camp and secretary to General Washington, with the rank of lieutenant colonel,
at the age of twenty. After the Revolution he served for a term in the Continental Congress and began a successful law practice.

Hamilton was one of the first advocates of a stronger central government
for the thirteen states, but he was not a dominant figure in the Philadelphia
Convention. It was in order to pave the way for ratification that he, Madison,
and John Jay rushed out the eighty-five Federalist Papers during the fall and
winter of 1787–88. Hamilton was the sole author of at least fifty of those
classic essays in political philosophy.

He was magnificently prepared when the New York ratifying convention
opened on June 17, with the hostile Clinton in the chair. Although the meetings went on for five weeks, they became essentially a prolonged debate between
Hamilton and Melancton Smith, an able, self-educated lawyer and merchant

who had moved from New York City to Dutchess County. From the incomplete records, it seems that Hamilton's main efforts went into three carefully spaced speeches on the coercion of delinquent states, on the powers of the Senate, and on the problems of taxation.

We turn to the first part of his first speech and to the final paragraphs of his last one.

"Our misfortunes, in a great degree, proceeded from the want of vigor in the Continental government."

Mr. Chairman:

THE HONORABLE MEMBER who spoke yesterday [Robert R. Livingston] went into an explanation of a variety of circumstances to prove the expediency of a change in our national government and the necessity of a firm Union. At the same time he described the great advantages which this state, in particular, receives from the Confederacy, and its peculiar weaknesses when abstracted from the Union. In doing this he advanced a variety of arguments which deserve serious consideration. Gentlemen have this day come forward to answer him. He has been treated as having wandered in the flowery fields of fancy, and attempts have been made to take off from the minds of the committee that sober impression which might be expected from his arguments. I trust, sir, that observations of this kind are not thrown out to cast a light air on this important subject, or to give any personal bias on the great question before us. I will not agree with gentlemen who trifle with the weaknesses of our country and suppose that they are enumerated to answer a party purpose and to terrify with ideal dangers. No. I believe these weaknesses to be real and pregnant with destruction. Yet, however weak our country may be, I hope we never shall sacrifice our liberties. If, therefore, on a full and candid discussion, the proposed system shall appear to have that tendency, for God's sake let us reject it! But let us not mistake words for things, nor accept doubtful surmises as the evidence of truth. Let us consider the Constitution calmly and dispassionately, and attend to those things only which merit consideration.

No arguments drawn from embarrassment or inconvenience ought to prevail upon us to adopt a system of government radically bad; yet it is proper that these arguments, among others, should be brought into view. In doing this, yesterday, it was necessary to reflect upon our situation; to dwell upon the imbecility of our Union; and to consider whether we, as a state, could stand alone. Although I am persuaded this convention will be resolved to adopt nothing that is bad, yet I think every prudent man will consider the merits of the plan in connection with the circumstances of our country, and that a rejection of the Constitution may involve most fatal consequences. I make these remarks to show that, though we ought not to be actuated by unreasonable fear, yet we ought to be prudent.

This day, sir, one gentleman has attempted to answer the arguments advanced by my honorable friend; another has treated him as having wandered from the subject. This being the case, I trust I shall be indulged in reviewing the remarks that have been said.

Sir, it appears to me extraordinary that, while gentlemen in one breath acknowledge that the old Confederation requires many material amendments, they should, in the next, deny that its defects have been the cause of our political weakness and the consequent calamities of our country. I cannot but infer from this that there is still some lurking favorite imagination that this system, with correctness, might become a safe and permanent one. It is proper that we should examine this matter. We contend that the radical vice in the old Confederation is that the laws of the Union apply only to states in their corporate capacity. Has not every man who has been in our legislature experienced the truth of this position? It is inseparable from the disposition of bodies, who have a constitutional power of resistance, to examine the merits of a law. This has ever been the case with the Federal requisitions. In this examination, not being furnished with those lights which directed the deliberations of the general government, and incapable of embracing the general interests of the Union, the states have almost uniformly weighed the requisitions by their own local interests, and have only executed them so far as answered their particular convenience or advantage. Hence there have ever been thirteen different bodies to judge of the measures of Congress, and the operations of government have been distracted by their taking different courses. Those which were to be benefited have complied with the requisitions; others have totally disregarded them. Have not all of us been witnesses to the unhappy embarrassments which resulted from these proceedings? Even during the late war, while the pressure of common danger connected strongly the bond of our union, and incited to vigorous exertion, we have felt many distressing effects of the important system. How have we seen this state, though most exposed to the calamities of the war, complying, in an unexampled manner, with the Federal requisitions, and compelled by the delinquency of others to bear most unusual burdens! Of this truth we have the most solemn proof on our records. In 1779 and 1780, when the state, from the ravages of war, and from her great exertions to resist them, became weak, distressed, and forlorn, every man avowed the principle which we now contend for—that our misfortunes, in a great degree, proceeded from the want of vigor in the Continental government. These were our sentiments when we did not speculate, but feel. We saw our weakness, and found ourselves its victims. Let us reflect that this may again, in all probability, be our situation. This is not a weak state, and its relative state is dangerous. Your capital is accessible by land, and by sea is exposed to every daring invader; and on the northwest you are open to the inroads of a powerful foreign nation. Indeed, this state, from its situation, will, in time of war, probably be the theater of its operations.

Gentlemen have said that the noncompliance of the states had been occasioned by their sufferings. This may in part be true. But has this state been delinquent? Amidst all our distresses, we have fully complied. If New York could comply wholly with the requisitions, is it not to be supposed that the other states could in part comply? Certainly every state in the Union might have executed them in some degree. But New Hampshire, which has not suffered at all, is totally delinquent. North Carolina is totally delinquent. Many others have contributed in a very small proportion, and Pennsylvania and New York are the only states which have perfectly discharged their Federal duty.

From the delinquency of those states which have suffered little by the war, we naturally conclude that they have made no efforts; and a knowledge of human nature will teach us that their ease and security have been a principal cause of their want of exertion. While danger is distant, its impression is weak; and while it affects only our neighbors, we have few motives to provide against it. Sir, if we have national objects to pursue, we must have national revenues. If you make requisitions, and they are not complied with, what is to be done? It has been observed, to coerce the states is one of the maddest projects that was ever devised. A failure of compliance will never be confined to a single state. This being the case, can we suppose it wise to hazard a civil war? Suppose Massachusetts, or any large state, should refuse, and Congress should attempt to compel them, would they not have influence to procure assistance, especially from those states which are in the same situation as themselves? What picture does this idea present to our view? A complying state at war with a noncomplying state; Congress marching the troops of one state into the bosom of another; this state collecting auxiliaries, and forming, perhaps, a majority against its Federal head. Here is a nation at war with itself. Can any reasonable man be well disposed towards a government which makes war and carnage the only means of supporting itself —a government that can exist only by the sword? Every such war must involve the innocent with the guilty. This single consideration should be sufficient to dispose every peaceable citizen against such a government.

But can we believe that one state will ever suffer itself to be used as an instrument of coercion? The thing is a dream; it is impossible. Then we are brought to this dilemma—either a Federal standing army is to enforce the requisitions or the Federal treasury is left without supplies and the government without support. What, sir, is the cure for this great evil? Nothing but to enable the national laws to operate on individuals in the same manner as those of the states do. This is the true reasoning upon the subject, sir. The gentlemen appear to acknowledge its force; and yet, while they yield to the principle, they seem to fear its application to the government.

What, then, shall we do? Shall we take the old Confederation as the basis of a new system? Can this be the object of the gentlemen? Certainly not. Will any man who entertains a wish for the safety of his country trust the sword and purse with a single assembly organized on principles so defective—so rotten? Though we might give to such a government certain powers with safety, yet to give them the full and unlimited powers of taxation and the national forces would be to establish a despotism, the definition of which is a government in which all power is concentered in a single body. To take the old Confederation and fashion it upon these principles would be establishing a power which would destroy the liberties of the people. These considerations show clearly that a government totally different must be instituted. They had weight in the Convention who formed the new system. It was seen that the necessary powers were too great to be trusted to a single body; they therefore formed two branches, and divided the powers, that each might be a check upon the other. This was the result of their wisdom, and I presume that every reasonable man will agree to it. The more this subject is explained, the more clear and convincing it will appear to every member of this body. The fundamental principle of the old Confederation is defective; we must totally eradicate and discard this principle before we can expect an efficient government. The gentlemen who have spoken today have taken up the subject of the ancient confederacies; but their view of them has been extremely partial and erroneous. The fact is, the same false and impracticable principle ran through the ancient governments. The first of these governments that we read of was the Amphictyonic confederacy. The council which managed the affairs of this league possessed powers of a similar complexion to those of our present Congress. The same feeble mode of legislation in the head, and the same power of resistance in the members, prevailed. When a requisition was made, it rarely met a compliance; and a civil war was the consequence. Those that were attacked called in foreign aid to protect them; and the ambitious Philip, under the mask of an ally to one, invaded the liberties of each and finally subverted the whole.

The operation of this principle appears in the same light in the Dutch republics. They have been obliged to levy taxes by an armed force. In this confederacy, one large province, by its superior wealth and influence, is commonly a match for all the rest; and when they do not comply, the province of Holland is obliged to compel them. It is observed that the United Provinces have existed a long time; but they have been constantly the sport of their neighbors, and have been supported only by the external pressure of the surrounding powers. The policy of Europe, not the policy of their government, saved them from dissolution. Besides, the powers of the stadtholder have given energy to the operations of this government which is not to be found in ours. This prince has a vast personal influence; he has independent revenues; he commands an army of forty thousand men.

The German Confederacy has also been a perpetual source of wars. It has a diet, like our Congress, which has authority to call for supplies. These calls are never obeyed; and in time of war, the imperial army never takes the field till the enemy are returning from it. The Emperor's Austrian dominions, in which he is an absolute prince, alone enable to make him head against the common foe. The members of this confederacy are ever divided and opposed to each other. The King of Prussia is a member, yet he has been constantly in opposition to the Emperor. Is this a desirable government?

I might go more particularly into the discussion of examples, and show that, wherever this fatal principle has prevailed, even as far back as the Lycian and Achaean leagues, as well as the Amphictyonic confederacy, it has proved the destruction of the government. But I think observations of this kind might have been spared. Had they not been entered into by others, I should not have taken up so much of the time of the committee. No inference can be drawn from these examples that republics cannot exist; we only contend that they have hitherto been founded on false principles. We have shown how they have been conducted and how they have been destroyed. Weakness in the head has produced resistance in the members; this has been the immediate parent of civil war; auxiliary force has been invited; and foreign power has annihilated their liberties and name. Thus Philip subverted the Amphictyonic, and Rome the Achaean republic.

We shall do well, sir, not to deceive ourselves with the favorable events of the late war. Common danger prevented the operation of the ruinous principle, in its full extent; but, since the peace, we have experienced the evils; we have felt the poison of the system in its unmingled purity.

Without dwelling any longer on this subject, I shall proceed to the question immediately before the committee.

In order that the committee may understand clearly the principles on which the general Convention acted, I think it necessary to explain some preliminary circumstances. Sir, the natural situation of this country seems to divide its interests into different classes. There are navigating and non-navigating states. The Northern are properly navigating states; the Southern appear to possess neither the spirit nor the means of navigation. This difference of situation naturally produces a dissimilarity of interests and views respecting foreign commerce. It was the interest of the Northern states that there should be no restraints on their navigation, and they should have full power, by a majority in Congress, to make commercial regulations in favor of their own and in restraint of the navigation of the foreigners. The Southern states wish to impose a restraint on the Northern by requiring that two thirds in Congress should be requisite to pass an act in regulation of commerce. They were apprehensive that the restraints of a navigation law would discourage foreigners, and, by obliging them to employ the shipping of the Northern states, would probably enhance their freight. This being the case, they insisted strenuously on having this provision engrafted in the Constitution; and the Northern states were as anxious in opposing it. On the other hand, the small states, seeing themselves embraced by the Confederation upon equal terms, wished to retain the advantages which they already possessed. The large states, on the contrary, thought it improper that Rhode Island and Delaware should enjoy an equal suffrage with themselves. From these sources a delicate and difficult contest arose. It became necessary, therefore, to compromise, or the Convention must have dissolved without effecting anything. Would it have been wise and prudent in that body, in this critical situation, to have deserted their country? No! Every man who hears me, every wise man in the United States, would have condemned them. The Convention was obliged to appoint a committee for accommodation. In this committee the arrangement was formed as it now stands, and their report was accepted. It was a delicate point, and it was necessary that all parties should be indulged. Gentlemen will see that, if there had not been a unanimity, nothing could have been done, for the Convention had no power to establish, but only to recommend, a government. Any other system would have been impracticable. Let a convention be called tomorrow; let them meet

twenty times—nay, twenty thousand times; they will have the same difficulties to encounter, the same clashing interests to reconcile.

But, dismissing these reflections, let us consider how far the arrangement is in itself entitled to the approbation of this body. We will examine
it upon its own merits.

The first thing objected to is that clause which allows a representation
for three fifths of the Negroes. Much has been said of the impropriety of
representing men who have no will of their own. Whether this be reasoning or declaration I will not presume to say. It is the unfortunate situation
of the Southern states to have a great part of their population, as well as
property, in blacks. The regulation complained of was one result of the
spirit of accommodation which governed the Convention; and without
this indulgence, no union could possibly have been formed. But, sir, considering some peculiar advantages which we derive from them, it is entirely just that they should be gratified. The Southern states possess certain staples—tobacco, rice, indigo, etc.—which must be capital objects
in treaties of commerce with foreign nations; and the advantages which
they necessarily procure in those treaties will be felt throughout all the
states. But the justice of this plan will appear in another view. The best
writers on government have held that representation should be compounded of persons and property. This rule has been adopted, as far as
it could be, in the constitution of New York. It will, however, by no means
be admitted that the slaves are considered altogether as property. They
are men, though degraded to the condition of slavery. They are persons
known to the municipal laws of the states which they inhabit as well as
to the laws of nature. But representation and taxation go together, and
one uniform rule ought to apply to both. Would it be just to compute
these slaves in the assessment of taxes and discard them from the estimate
in the apportionment of representatives? Would it be just to impose a
singular burden without conferring some adequate advantage?

Another circumstance ought to be considered. The rule we have been
speaking of is a general rule, and applies to all the states. Now, you have
a great number of people in your state which are not represented at all,
and have no voice in your government. These will be included in the
enumeration—not two fifths, nor three fifths, but the whole. This proves
that the advantages of the plan are not confined to the Southern states,
but extend to other parts of the Union.

I now proceed to consider the objection with regard to the number of
representatives, as it now stands. I am persuaded the system, in this respect, stands on a better footing than the gentlemen imagine.

It has been asserted that it will be in the power of Congress to reduce the number. I acknowledge that there are no direct words of prohibition, but contend that the true and genuine construction of the clause gives Congress no power whatever to reduce the representation below the number as it now stands. Although they may limit, they can never diminish the number. One representative for every thirty thousand inhabitants is fixed as the standard of increase; till, by the natural course of population, it will become necessary to limit the ratio. Probably, at present, were this standard to be immediately applied, the representation would considerably exceed sixty-five. In three years, it would exceed one hundred. If I understand the gentlemen, they contend that the number may be enlarged or may not. I admit that this is in the discretion of Congress, and I submit to the committee whether it be not necessary and proper. Still, I insist that an immediate limitation is not probable, nor was it in the contemplation of the Convention. But, sir, who will presume to say to what precise point the representation ought to be increased? This is a matter of opinion, and opinions are vastly different upon the subject. A proof of this is drawn from the representations in the state legislatures. In Massachusetts, the assembly consists of about three hundred; in South Carolina, of nearly one hundred; in New York, there are sixty-five. It is observed generally that the number ought to be large; let the gentlemen produce their criterion. I confess it is difficult for me to say what number may be said to be sufficiently large. On one hand, it ought to be considered that a small number will act with more facility, system, and decision; on the other, that a large one may enhance the difficulty of corruption. The Congress is to consist, at first, of ninety-one members. This, to a reasonable man, may appear as near the proper medium as any number whatever—at least for the present. There is one source of increase, also, which does not depend upon any constructions of the Constitution; it is the creation of new states. Vermont, Kentucky, and Franklin will probably become independent. New members of the Union will also be formed from the unsettled tracts of Western territory.

These must be represented, and will all contribute to swell the Federal legislature. If the whole number in the United States be, at present, three millions, as is commonly supposed, according to the ratio of one for thirty thousand, we shall have, on the first census, a hundred representatives. In ten years, thirty more will be added; and in twenty-five years the number will be double. Then, sir, we shall have two hundred, if the increase go on in the same proportion. The convention of Massachusetts, who made the same objections, have fixed upon this number as the point to which they chose to limit the representation. But can we pronounce, with certainty, that it will not be expedient to go beyond this number? We cannot. Experience alone must determine. This matter may, with more safety, be left to the discretion of the legislature, as it will be the interest of the large and increasing states of Massachusetts, New York, Pennsylvania, etc., to augment the representation. Only Connecticut, Rhode Island, Delaware, and Maryland can be interested in limiting it. We may, therefore, safely calculate upon a growing representation, according to the advance of population and the circumstances of the country.

The state governments possess inherent advantages which will ever give them an influence and ascendency over the national government, and will forever preclude the possibility of Federal encroachments. That their liberties, indeed, can be subverted by the Federal head is repugnant to every rule of political calculation. Is not this arrangement, then, sir, a most wise and prudent one? Is not the present representation fully adequate to our present exigencies, and sufficient to answer all the purposes of the Union? I am persuaded that an examination of the objects of the Federal government will afford a conclusive answer.

. . . Sir, I shall no further enlarge on this argument: my exertions have already exhausted me. I have persevered from an anxious desire to give the committee the most complete conception of this subject. I fear, however, that I have not been so successful as to bestow upon it that full and clear light of which it is susceptible. I shall conclude with a few remarks by way of apology. I am apprehensive, sir, that in the warmth of my feelings I may have uttered feelings which were too vehement. If such has been my language, it was from the habit of using strong phrases to express my ideas; and, above all, from the interesting nature of the subject. I have ever condemned those cold, unfeeling hearts which no object can animate. I condemn those indifferent mortals who either never form opinions or never make them known. I confess, sir, that on no subject has my breast been filled with stronger emotions or more anxious concern. If anything has escaped me which may be construed into a personal reflection, I beg the gentlemen, once for all, to be assured that I have no design to wound the feelings of anyone who is opposed to me.

While I am making these observations, I cannot but take notice of some expressions which have fallen in the course of the debate. It has been said that ingenious men may say ingenious things, and that those who are interested in raising the few upon the ruins of the many may give to every cause an appearance of justice. I know not whether these insinuations allude to the characters of any who are here present or to any of the reasonings in this house. I presume that the gentlemen would not ungenerously impute such motives to those who differ from themselves. I declare I know not any set of men who are to derive peculiar advantages from this Constitution. Were any permanent honors or emoluments to be secured to the families of those who have been active in this cause, there might be some grounds for suspicion. But what reasonable man, for the precarious enjoyment of rank and power, would establish a system which would reduce his nearest friends and his posterity to slavery and ruin? If the gentlemen reckon me among the obnoxious few, if they imagine that I contemplate with ambitious eye the immediate honors of the government, yet let them consider that I have my friends, my family, my children, to whom ties of nature and of habit have attached me. If, today, I am among the favored few, my children, tomorrow, may be among the oppressed; these dear pledges of my patriotism may, at a future day, be suffering the severe distresses to which my ambition has reduced them. The changes in the human condition are uncertain and frequent: many, on whom Fortune has bestowed her favor, may trace their family to a more unprosperous station; and many, who are now in obscurity, may look back upon the affluence and exalted rank of their ancestors. But I will no longer trespass on your indulgence. I have troubled the committee with these observations, to show that it cannot be the wish of any reasonable man to establish a government unfriendly to the liberties of the people. Gentlemen ought not, then, to presume that the advocates of this Constitution are influenced by ambitious views. The suspicion, sir, is unjust; the charge is uncharitable.

Do these imperfectly reported fragments suggest the effect that Hamilton produced in that crowded Poughkeepsie courthouse in the tense summer of 1788? "Incredible as it may seem," wrote one of his biographers, J. T. Morse, "there is abundant contemporary evidence that the audience listening to Hamilton's argumentative but eloquent harangues was more than once so visibly affected that tears stood in the eyes of many, and such men as Chancellor Kent could not find words too emphatic to express their admiration."

There is no doubt that Melancton Smith was won over and withdrew his motion for conditional ratification. The final vote in favor of the new Constitution was 30 to 27.

Less than a year after this triumph of passionate reasoning, George Washington was inaugurated President of the United States of America, and his former aide-de-camp entered his cabinet as the first Secretary of the Treasury.

PART SEVEN

THE AFRICAN SLAVE TRADE

WILLIAM WILBERFORCE, IN THE HOUSE OF COMMONS, PICTURES THE SLAVE TRADE IN ALL ITS HORROR

[May 12, 1789]

T HE CRUSADE against Negro slavery calls up in American minds such names as William Lloyd Garrison, Wendell Phillips, Harriet Beecher Stowe, John Brown, and Abraham Lincoln, but decades before the founding of Garrison's Liberator, in 1831, a group of dedicated and tireless Englishmen had started the great agitation. As early as 1772, Granville Sharp won a case before the famous judge, Lord Mansfield, establishing the principle that any slave who landed on British soil was free. Thomas Clarkson's special contribution was the amassing of evidence of the iniquities of the slave trade, for which purpose he examined hundreds of ships and traced the fate of thousands of Negroes. He joined vigorously in the work of the British and Foreign Anti-Slavery Society, took a lively interest in fugitive slaves in Canada, and did what he could to prevent the annexation of Texas by the United States.

Associated with Sharp and Clarkson in the British abolition movement was the statesman and humanitarian leader, William Wilberforce (1759–1833). The son of a prosperous commercial family, he went to Cambridge, where he became one of the few intimate friends of the cold and aloof Mr. Pitt. Entering Parliament in 1780, his wit and eloquence soon made him popular and prominent. Five years later he experienced what has been called an evangelical "conversion," which left a strong imprint of piety and moral courage on his character. In the year 1788 he suffered a grave illness and was not expected to live more than a fortnight. As he lay on what he thought was his deathbed, he exacted from his friend Pitt, now Prime Minister, the promise to do what he could for the abolition of the slave trade. A few months later, Pitt, with the enthusiastic support of Fox and Burke, persuaded Commons to take up the question of the slave trade at the next session, and a bill was accordingly drawn up.

Having recovered his health by May, 1789, Wilberforce addressed the Commons on the distant, almost unimaginable horrors of the slave trade.

"The number of deaths speaks for itself."

IN OPENING, concerning the nature of the slave trade, I need only observe that it is found by experience to be just such as every man who uses his reason would infallibly conclude it to be. For my own part, so clearly am I convinced of the mischiefs inseparable from it that I should hardly want any further evidence than my own mind would furnish by the most simple deductions. Facts, however, are now laid before the House. A report has been made by his Majesty's privy council, which, I trust, every gentleman has read, and which ascertains the slave trade to be just such in practice as we know, from theory, it must be. What should we suppose must naturally be the consequence of our carrying on a slave trade with Africa? With a country vast in its extent, not utterly barbarous, but civilized in a very small degree? Does anyone suppose a slave trade would help their civilization? Is it not plain that she must suffer from it? That civilization must be checked; that her barbarous manners must be made more barbarous; and that the happiness of her millions of inhabitants must be prejudiced with her intercourse with Britain? Does not everyone see that a slave trade carried on around her coasts must carry violence and desolation to her very center? That in a continent just emerging from barbarism, if a trade in men is established, if her men are all converted into goods, and become commodities that can be bartered, it follows they must be subject to ravage just as goods are; and this, too, at a period of civilization when there is no protecting legislature to defend this their only sort of property in the same manner as the rights of property are maintained by the legislature of every civilized country. We see then, in the nature of things, how easily the practices of Africa are to be accounted for. Her kings are never compelled to war, that we can hear of, by public principles, by national glory, still less by the love of their people. In Europe it is the extension of commerce, the maintenance of national honor, or some great public object that is ever the motive to war with every monarch; but, in Africa, it is the personal avarice and sensuality of their kings; these two vices of avarice and sensuality, the most powerful and predominant in natures thus corrupt, we tempt, we stimulate in all these African princes, and we depend upon these vices for the very maintenance of the slave trade. Does the king of Barbessin want brandy? he has only to send his troops, in the nighttime, to burn and desolate a village; the captives will serve as commodities that may be bartered with the British trader. What a striking view of the wretched state of Africa does the tragedy of Calabar furnish! Two towns, formerly hostile, had settled their differences, and by an intermarriage among their chiefs had each pledged themselves to peace; but the trade in slaves was prejudiced by such pacifications, and it became, therefore, the policy of our traders to renew the hostilities. This, their policy, was soon put in practice, and the scene of carnage which followed was such that it is better, perhaps, to refer gentlemen to the privy council's report than to agitate their minds by dwelling on it.

The slave trade, in its very nature, is the source of such kind of tragedies; nor has there been a single person, almost, before the privy council who does not add something by his testimony to the mass of evidence upon this point. Some, indeed, of these gentlemen, and particularly the delegates from Liverpool, have endeavored to reason down this plain principle: some have palliated it; but there is not one, I believe, who does not more or less admit it. Some, nay most, I believe, have admitted the slave trade to be the chief cause of wars in Africa. . . .

Having now disposed of the first part of this subject, I must speak of the transit of the slaves in the West Indies. This, I confess, in my own opinion, is the most wretched part of the whole subject. So much misery condensed in so little room is more than the human imagination had ever before conceived. I will not accuse the Liverpool merchants; I will allow them, nay, I will believe them, to be men of humanity; and I will therefore believe, if it were not for the multitude of these wretched objects, if it were not for the enormous magnitude and extent of the evil which distracts their attention from individual cases and makes them think generally, and therefore less feelingly, on the subject, they never would have persisted in the trade. I verily believe, therefore, if the wretchedness of any one of the many hundred Negroes stowed in each ship could be brought before their view, and remain within the sight of the African merchant, that there is no one among them whose heart would bear it. Let anyone imagine to himself six or seven hundred of these wretches chained two and two, surrounded with every object that is nauseous and disgusting, diseased, and struggling under every kind of wretchedness! How can we bear to think of such a scene as this? One would think it had been determined to heap on them all the varieties of bodily pain, for the purpose of blunting the feelings of the mind; and yet, in this very point (to show the power of human prejudice), the situation of the slaves has been described by Mr. Norris, one of the Liverpool delegates, in a manner which I am sure will convince the House how interest can draw a film over the eyes so thick that total blindness could do no more; and how it is our duty therefore to trust not to the reasonings of interested men or to their way of coloring a transaction. "Their apartments," says Mr. Norris, "are fitted up as much for their advantage as circumstances will admit. The right ankle of one, indeed, is connected with the left ankle of another by a small iron fetter, and if they are turbulent, by another on their wrists. They have several meals a day; some of their own country provisions, with the best sauces of African cookery; and by the way of variety, another meal of pulse, etc., according to European taste. After breakfast they have water to wash themselves, while their apartments are perfumed with frankincense and lime juice. Before dinner they are amused after the manner of their country. The song and the dance are promoted," and, as if the whole were really a scene of pleasure and dissipation, it is added that games of chance are furnished. "The men play and sing, while the women and girls make fanciful ornaments with beads, which they are plentifully supplied with." Such is the sort of strain in which the Liverpool delegates, and particularly Mr. Norris, gave evidence before the privy council. What will the House think when, by the concurring testimony of other witnesses, the true history is laid open. The slaves, who are sometimes described as rejoicing at their captivity, are so wrung with misery at leaving their country that it is the constant practice to set sail in the night, lest they should be sensible of their departure. The pulse which Mr. Norris talks of are horse beans; and the scantiness of both water and provision was suggested by the very legislature of Jamaica, in the report of their committee, to be a subject that called for the interference of Parliament.

Mr. Norris talks of frankincense and lime juice; when the surgeons tell you the slaves are stowed so close that there is not room to tread among them; and when you have it in evidence from Sir George Younge that even in a ship which wanted two hundred of her complement, the stench was intolerable. The song and the dance are promoted, says Mr. Norris. It had been more fair, perhaps, if he had explained that word "promoted." The truth is that for the sake of exercise these miserable wretches, loaded with chains, oppressed with disease and wretchedness, are forced to dance by the terror of the lash, and sometimes by the actual use of it. "I," says one of the other evidences, "was employed to dance the men, while another person danced the women." Such, then, is the meaning of the word "promoted"; and it may be observed too, with respect to food, that an instrument is sometimes carried out, in order to force them to eat, which is the same sort of proof how much they enjoy themselves in that instance also. As to their singing, what shall we say when we are told that their songs are songs of lamentation upon their departure which, while they sing, are always in tears, insomuch that one captain (more humane as I should conceive him, therefore, than the rest) threatened one of the women with a flogging, because the mournfulness of her song was too painful for his feelings. In order, however, not to trust too much to any sort of description, I will call the attention of the House to one species of evidence which is absolutely infallible. Death, at least, is a sure ground of evidence, and the proportion of deaths will not only confirm, but, if possible, will even aggravate our suspicion of their misery in the transit. It will be found, upon an average of all ships of which evidence has been given at the privy council, that, exclusive of those who perish before they sail, not less than twelve and one half per cent perish in the passage. Besides these, the Jamaica report tells you that not less than four and one half per cent die on shore before the day of sale, which is only a week or two from the time of landing. One third more die in the seasoning, and this in a country exactly like their own, where they are healthy and happy, as some of the evidences would pretend. The diseases, however, which they contract on shipboard, the astringent washes which are to hide their wounds, and the mischievous tricks used to make them up for sale, are, as the Jamaica report says—a most precious and valuable report, which I shall often have to advert to —one principal cause of this mortality. Upon the whole, however, here is a mortality of about fifty per cent, and this among Negroes who are not bought unless quite healthy at first, and unless (as the phrase is with cattle) they are sound in wind and limb. How then can the House refuse its belief to the multiplied testimonies, before the privy council, of the savage treatment of the Negroes in the middle passage? Nay, indeed, what need is there of any evidence? The number of deaths speaks for itself and makes all such inquiry superfluous. As soon as ever I had arrived thus far in my investigation of the slave trade, I confess to you, sir, so enormous, so dreadful, so irremediable did its wickedness appear that my own mind was completely made up for the abolition. A trade founded in iniquity, and carried on as this was, must be abolished, let the policy be what it might—let the consequences be what they would, I from this time determined that I would never rest till I had effected its abolition. . . .

When we consider the vastness of the continent of Africa; when we reflect how all other countries have for some centuries past been advancing in happiness and civilization; when we think how in this same period all improvement in Africa has been defeated by her intercourse with Britain; when we reflect that it is we ourselves that have degraded them to that wretched brutishness and barbarity which we now plead as the justification of our guilt; how the slave trade has enslaved their minds, blackened their character, and sunk them so low in the scale of animal beings that some think the apes are of a higher class, and fancy the orangutan has given them the go-by. What a mortification must we feel at having so long neglected to think of our guilt, or attempt any reparation! It seems, indeed, as if we had determined to forbear from all interference until the measure of our folly and wickedness was so full and complete; until the impolicy which eventually belongs to vice was become so plain and glaring that not an individual in the country should refuse to join in the abolition; it seems as if we had waited until the persons most interested should be tired out with the folly and nefariousness of the trade, and should unite in petitioning against it.

Let us then make such amends as we can for the mischiefs we have done to the unhappy continent; let us recollect what Europe itself was no longer ago than three or four centuries. What if I should be able to show this House that in a civilized part of Europe, in the time of our Henry VII, there were people who actually sold their own children? What if I should tell them that England itself was that country? What if I should point out to them that the very place where this inhuman traffic was carried on was the city of Bristol? Ireland at that time used to drive a considerable trade in slaves with these neighboring barbarians; but a great plague having infested the country, the Irish were struck with a panic, suspected (I am sure very properly) that the plague was a punishment sent from heaven for the sin of the slave trade, and therefore abolished it. All I ask, therefore, of the people of Bristol is that they would become as civilized now as Irishmen were four hundred years ago. Let us put an end at once to this inhuman traffic—let us stop this effusion of human blood. The true way to virtue is by withdrawing from temptation; let us then withdraw from these wretched Africans those temptations to fraud, violence, cruelty, and injustice which the slave trade furnishes. Wherever the sun shines, let us go round the world with him, diffusing our beneficence; but let us not traffic only that we may set kings against their subjects, subjects against their kings, sowing discord in every village, fear and terror in every family, setting millions of our fellow creatures a-hunting each other for slaves, creating fairs and markets for human flesh through one whole continent of the world, and, under the name of policy, concealing from ourselves all the baseness and iniquity of such a traffic. Why may we not hope, ere long, to see Hanse towns established on the coast of Africa as they were on the Baltic? It is said the Africans are idle, but they are not too idle, at least, to catch one another; seven hundred to one thousand tons of rice are annually bought of them; by the same rule why should we not buy more? At Gambia one thousand of them are seen continually at work; why should not some more thousands be set to work in the same manner? It is the slave trade that causes their idleness and every other mischief. We are told by one witness: "They sell one another as they can"; and while they can get brandy by catching one another, no wonder they are too idle for any regular work.

I have one word more to add upon a most material point; but it is a point so self-evident that I shall be extremely short. It will appear from everything which I have said that it is not regulation, it is not mere palliatives, that can cure this enormous evil. Total abolition is the only possible cure for it. The Jamaica report, indeed, admits much of the evil, but recommends it to us so to regulate the trade that no persons should be kidnaped or made slaves contrary to the custom of Africa. But may they not be made slaves unjustly, and yet by no means contrary to the custom of Africa? I have shown they may; for all the customs of Africa are rendered savage and unjust through the influence of this trade; besides, how can we discriminate between the slaves justly and unjustly made? or, if we could, does any man believe that the British captains can, by any regulation in this country, be prevailed upon to refuse all such slaves as have not been fairly, honestly, and uprightly enslaved? But granting even that they should do this, yet how would the rejected slaves be recompensed? They are brought, as we are told, from three or four thousand miles off, and exchanged like cattle from one hand to another until they reach the coast. We see then that it is the existence of the slave trade that is the spring of all this internal traffic, and that the remedy cannot be applied without abolition. Again, as to the middle passage, the evil is radical there also; the merchant's profit depends upon the number that can be crowded together, and upon the shortness of their allowance. Astringents, escharotics, and all the other arts of making them up for sale are of the very essence of the trade; these arts will be concealed both from the purchaser and the legislature; they are necessary to the owner's profit, and they will be practiced. Again, chains and arbitrary treatment must be used in transporting them; our seamen must be taught to play the tyrant, and that depravation of manners among them (which some very judicious persons have treated of as the very worst part of the business) cannot be hindered, while the trade itself continues. As to the slave merchants, they have already told you that if two slaves to a ton are not permitted, the trade cannot continue; so that the objections are done away by themselves on this quarter; and in the West Indies, I have shown that the abolition is the only possible stimulus whereby a regard to population, and consequently to the happiness of the Negroes, can be effectually excited in those islands.

I trust, therefore, I have shown that upon every ground the total abolition ought to take place. I have urged many things which are not my own leading motives for proposing it, since I have wished to show every description of gentlemen, and particularly the West India planters, who deserve every attention, that the abolition is politic upon their own principles also. Policy, however, sir, is not my principle, and I am not ashamed to say it. There is a principle above everything that is political; and when I reflect on the command which says: "Thou shalt do no murder," believing the authority to be Divine, how can I dare to set up any reasonings of my own against it? And, sir, when we think of eternity, and of the future consequences of all human conduct, what is there in this life that should make any man contradict the dictates of his conscience, the principles of justice, the laws of religion, and of God. Sir, the nature and all the circumstances of this trade are now laid open to us; we can no longer plead ignorance, we cannot evade it, it is now an object placed before us, we cannot pass it; we may spurn it, we may kick it out of our way, but we cannot turn aside so as to avoid seeing it; for it is brought now so directly before our eyes that this House must decide, and must justify to all the world, and to their own consciences, the rectitude of the grounds and principles of their decision. A society has been established for the abolition of this trade, in which Dissenters, Quakers, Churchmen—in which the most conscientious of all persuasions—have all united and made a common cause in this great question. Let not Parliament be the only body that is insensible to the principles of national justice. Let us make reparation to Africa, so far as we can, by establishing a trade upon true commercial principles, and we shall soon find the rectitude of our conduct rewarded by the benefits of a regular and a growing commerce.

It was not alone the heart-rending subject, nor the manner of speaking, moving though it was, that counted. It was the man himself. In his lifetime struggle against slavery, Wilberforce was to become the conscience of England. In his person piety and eloquence combined to make even reform respectable.

WILLIAM PITT THE YOUNGER INDICTS THE SLAVE TRADE AND FORESEES A LIBERATED AFRICA

[April 2, 1792]

William Pitt the younger (1759–1806) was the aloof son of the arrogant William Pitt, the first Earl of Chatham, one of the magnificent orators of all time. Destined for politics, young Pitt attended Cambridge University, where he immersed himself in Thucydides and Demosthenes and committed to memory the speeches of Milton's fallen angels. He was present in the House of Lords when his dying father cried out against a bill to grant freedom to the American colonies. At twenty-three he was Chancellor of the Exchequer and at twenty-four Prime Minister, a position he was to hold almost continuously until his death at forty-six. In his early years Pitt was a liberal Tory, but he was never so liberal as his lifelong antagonist, Charles James Fox, whose carefree humanity was poles apart from Pitt's reserve. When a "scrutiny" of Fox's election to the House of Commons was urged in 1784, Pitt made an unworthy effort to keep his rival from being seated.

On the other hand, Pitt held stanchly to his friendship, begun at Cambridge, with Wilberforce, and finally redeemed in full measure the supposed deathbed promise to Wilberforce to aid in the campaign against slavery. He was ill and exhausted as he rose in Commons late at night to give this celebrated speech, and was obliged to take medicine before he could continue. As he proceeded he gathered strength and in the last twenty minutes, it is said, reached the most sublime heights of his career.

"Why might not some Roman Senator . . . pointing to British barbarians, have predicted . . . 'There is a people that will never rise to civilization; there is a people destined never to be free'?"

THE RESULT of all I have said is that there exists no impediment, on the ground of pledged faith, or even on that of national expediency, to the abolition of this trade. On the contrary, all the arguments drawn from those sources plead for it, and they plead much more loudly, and much more strongly in every part of the question, for an immediate than for a gradual abolition. But now, sir, I come to Africa. That is the ground on which I rest, and here it is that I say my right honorable friends do not carry their principles to their full extent. Why ought the slave trade to be abolished? Because it is incurable injustice. How much stronger, then, is the argument for immediate than gradual abolition! By allowing it to continue even for one hour, do not my right honorable friends weaken their own argument of its injustice? If on the ground of injustice it ought to be abolished at last, why ought it not now? Why is injustice to be suffered to remain for a single hour? From what I hear without doors, it is evident that there is a general conviction entertained of its being far from just; and from that very conviction of its injustice, some men have been led, I fear, to the supposition that the slave trade never could have been permitted to begin but from some strong and irresistible necessity: a necessity, however, which if it was fancied to exist at first, I have shown cannot be thought by any man whatever to exist now. This plea of necessity has caused a sort of acquiescence in the continuance of this evil. Men have been led to place it among the rank of those necessary evils which are supposed to be the lot of human creatures, and to be permitted to fall upon some countries or individuals rather than upon others by that Being whose ways are inscrutable to us, and whose dispensations, it is conceived, we ought not to look into. The origin of evil is indeed a subject beyond the reach of human understandings; and the permission of it by the Supreme Being is a subject into which it belongs not to us to inquire. But where the evil in question is a moral evil which a man can scrutinize, and where that moral evil has its origin with ourselves, let us not imagine that we can clear our consciences by this general, not to say irreligious and impious, way of laying aside the question. If we reflect at all on this subject, we must see that every necessary evil supposes that some other and greater evil would be incurred were it removed. I therefore desire to ask, what can be that greater evil which can be stated to overbalance the one in question? I know of no evil that ever has existed, nor can imagine any evil to exist, worse than the tearing of seventy or eighty thousand persons annually from their native land, by a combination of the most civilized nations inhabiting the most enlightened part of the globe, but more especially under the sanction of the laws of that nation which calls herself the most free and the most happy of them all. Even if these miserable beings were proved guilty of every crime before you take them off, ought we to take upon ourselves the office of executioners? And even if we condescend so far, still can we be justified in taking them, unless we have clear proof that they are criminals? But, if we go much further—if we ourselves tempt them to sell their fellow creatures to us—we may rest assured that they will take care to provide by every possible method a supply of victims increasing in proportion to our demand. Can we, then, hesitate in deciding whether the wars in Africa are their wars or ours? It was our arms in the river Cameroon, put into the hands of the trader, that furnished him with the means of pushing his trade; and I have no more doubt that they are British arms, put into the hands of Africans, which promote universal war and desolation than I can doubt their having done so in that individual instance.

I have shown how great is the enormity of this evil, even on the supposition that we take only convicts and prisoners of war. But take the subject in the other way, and how does it stand? Think of 80,000 persons carried out of their native country by we know not what means! for crimes imputed! for light or inconsiderable faults! for debt perhaps! for the crime of witchcraft! or a thousand other weak and scandalous pretexts! Reflect on these 80,000 persons thus annually taken off! There is something in the horror of it that surpasses all the bounds of imagination. Admitting that there exists in Africa something like to courts of justice; yet what an office of humiliation and meanness is it in us, to take upon ourselves to carry into execution the iniquitous sentences of such courts, as if we also were strangers to all religion and to the first principles of justice! But that country, it is said, has been in some degree civilized, and civilized by us. It is said they have gained some knowledge of the principles of justice. Yes, we give them enough of our intercourse to convey to them the means and to initiate them in the study of mutual destruction. We give them just enough of the forms of justice to enable them to add the pretext of legal trials to their other modes of perpetrating the most atrocious iniquity. We give them just enough of European improvements to enable them the more effectually to turn Africa into a ravaged wilderness. Some evidences say that the Africans are addicted to the practice of gambling; that they even sell their wives and children, and ultimately themselves. Are these, then, the legitimate sources of slavery? Shall we pretend that we can thus acquire an honest right to exact the labor of these people? Can we pretend that we have a right to carry away to distant regions men of whom we know nothing by authentic inquiry, and of whom there is every reasonable presumption to think that those who sell them to us have no right to do so? But the evil does not stop here. Do you think nothing of the ruin and the miseries in which so many other individuals, still remaining in Africa, are involved in consequence of carrying off so many myriads of people? Do you think nothing of their families left behind? of the connections broken? of the friendships, attach· ments, and relationships that are burst asunder? Do you think nothing of the miseries in consequence that are felt from generation to genera- tion? of the privation of that happiness which might be communicated to them by the introduction of civilization, and of mental and moral im- provement?—a happiness which you withhold from them so long as you permit the slave trade to continue.

Thus, sir, has the perversion of British commerce carried misery in- stead of happiness to one whole quarter of the globe. False to the very principles of trade, misguided in our policy, and unmindful of our duty, what astonishing mischief have we brought upon that continent! If, know- ing the miseries we have caused, we refuse to put a stop to them, how greatly aggravated will be the guilt of this country! Shall we then delay rendering this justice to Africa? I am sure the immediate abolition of the slave trade is the first, the principal, the most indispensable act of policy, of duty, and of justice that the legislature of this country has to take, if it is indeed their wish to secure those important objects to which I have alluded, and which we are bound to pursue by the most solemn obliga- tions. There is, however, one argument set up as a universal answer to everything that can be urged on our side. The slave-trade system, it is supposed, has taken such deep root in Africa that it is absurd to think of its being eradicated; and the abolition of that share of trade carried on by Great Britain is likely to be of very little service. You are not sure, it is said, that other nations will give up the trade if you should renounce it. I answer, if this trade is as criminal as it is asserted to be, God forbid that we should hesitate in relinquishing so iniquitous a traffic; even though it should be retained by other countries! I tremble at the thought of gen- tlemen indulging themselves in the argument which I am combating. "We are friends," say they, "to humanity. We are second to none of you in our zeal for the good of Africa—but the French will not abolish—the Dutch will not abolish. We wait, therefore, on prudential principles, till they join us or set us an example." How, sir, is this enormous evil ever to be eradicated, if every nation is thus prudentially to wait till the concurrence of all the world shall have been obtained? Let me remark, too, that there is no nation in Europe that has, on the one hand, plunged so deeply into this guilt as Great Britain; or that is so likely, on the other, to be looked up to as an example. But does not this argument apply a thousand times more strongly in a contrary way? How much more justly may other na- tions point to us, and say, "Why should we abolish the slave trade when Great Britain has not abolished it? Britain, free as she is, just and honor- able as she is, and deeply involved as she is in this commerce above all nations, not only has not abolished, but has refused to abolish." This, sir, is the argument with which we furnish the other nations of Europe if we again refuse to put an end to the slave trade. Instead, therefore, of imagining that by choosing to presume on their continuing it, we shall have exempted ourselves from guilt, and have transferred the whole criminality to them; let us rather reflect that on the very principle urged against us we shall henceforth have to answer for their crimes as well as our own.

It has also been urged, that there is something in the disposition and nature of the Africans themselves which renders all prospect of civilization on that continent extremely unpromising. "It has been known," says Mr. Frazer, in his evidence, "that a boy has been put to death who was refused to be purchased as a slave." This single story was deemed by that gentleman a sufficient proof of the barbarity of the Africans, and of the inutility of abolishing the slave trade. My honorable friend, however, has told you that this boy had previously run away from his master three times; that the master had to pay his value, according to the custom of his country, every time he was brought back; and that, partly from anger at the boy for running away so frequently, and partly to prevent a repetition of the same expense, he determined to put him to death. This, sir, is the signal instance that has been dwelt upon of African barbarity. This African, we admit, was unenlightened and altogether barbarous: but let us now ask what would a civilized and enlightened West Indian, or a body of West Indians, have done in any case of a parallel nature? I will quote you, sir, a law passed in the West Indies in 1722; by which law this same crime of running away is, by the legislature of the island, punished with death, in the very first instance. I hope, therefore, we shall hear no more of the moral impossibility of civilizing the Africans, nor have our understandings again insulted by being called upon to sanction the trade until other nations shall have set the example of abolishing it. While we have been deliberating, one nation, Denmark, not by any means remarkable for the boldness of its councils, has determined on a gradual abolition. France, it is said, will take up the trade if we relinquish it. What! Is it supposed that, in the present situation of St. Domingo, an island which used to take three fourths of all the slaves required by the colonies of France, she, of all countries, will think of taking it up? Of the countries which remain, Portugal, Holland, and Spain—let me declare it is my opinion that if they see us renounce the trade, they will not be disposed, even on principles of policy, to rush further into it. But I say more. How are they to furnish the capital necessary for carrying it on? If there is any aggravation of our guilt in this wretched business, it is that we have stooped to be the carriers of these miserable beings from Africa to the West Indies, for all the other powers of Europe. And if we retire from the trade, where is the fund equal to the purchase of 30,000 or 40,000 slaves? —a fund which, if we rate the slaves at £40 or £50 each, cannot require a capital of less than a million and a half, or two millions of money.

Having detained the House so long, all that I will further add shall relate to that important subject, the civilization of Africa. Grieved am I to think that there should be a single person in this country who can look on the present uncivilized state of that continent as a ground for continuing the slave trade—as a ground not only for refusing to attempt the improvement of Africa, but even for intercepting every ray of light which might otherwise break in upon her. Here, as in every other branch of this extensive question, the argument of our adversaries pleads against them; for surely, sir, the present deplorable state of Africa, especially when we reflect that her chief calamities are to be ascribed to us, calls for our generous aid rather than justifies any despair on our part of her recovery, and still less any further repetition of our injuries. I will not much longer fatigue the attention of the House; but this point has impressed itself so deeply on my mind that I must trouble the committee with a few additional observations. Are we justified, I ask, on any one ground of theory, or by any one instance to be found in the history of the world from its very beginning to this day, in forming the supposition which I am now combating? Are we justified in supposing that the particular practice which we encourage in Africa, of men selling each other for slaves, is any symptom of a barbarism that is incurable? Are we justified in supposing that even the practice of offering up human sacrifices proves a total incapacity for civilization? I believe it will be found that both the trade in slaves and the still more savage custom of offering up human sacrifices obtained in former periods throughout many of those nations which now, by the blessings of Providence, and by a long progression of improvements, are advanced the farthest in civilization. I believe that, if we reflect an instant, we shall find that this observation comes directly home to ourselves; and that, on the same ground on which we are now disposed to proscribe Africa forever from all possibility of improvement, we might, in like manner, have been proscribed and forever shut out from all the blessings which we now enjoy. There was a time, sir, when even human sacrifices are said to have been offered in this island. But I would peculiarly observe on this day, for it is a case precisely in point, that the very practice of the slave trade once prevailed among us. Slaves, as we may read in Henry's *History of Great Britain,* were formerly an established article of our exports. "Great numbers," he says, "were exported like cattle, from the British coast, and were to be seen exposed for sale in the Roman market." It does not distinctly appear by what means they were procured; but there is unquestionably no small resemblance, in this particular point, between the case of our ancestors and that of the present wretched natives of Africa; for the historian tells you that "adultery, witchcraft, and debt were probably some of the chief sources of supplying the Roman market with British slaves; that prisoners taken in war were added to the number; and that there might be among them some unfortunate gamesters who, after having lost all their goods, at length staked themselves, their wives, and their children." Every one of these sources of slavery has been stated to be at this hour a source of slavery in Africa. And these circumstances, sir, with a solitary instance or two of human sacrifices, furnish the alleged proofs that Africa labors under a natural incapacity for civilization; that it is enthusiasm and fanaticism to think that she can ever enjoy the knowledge and the morals of Europe; that Providence never intended her to rise above a state of barbarism; that Providence has irrevocably doomed her to be only a nursery for slaves for us free and civilized Europeans. Allow of this principle, as applied to Africa, and I should be glad to know why it might not also have been applied to ancient and uncivilized Britain. Why might not some Roman Senator, reasoning on the principles of some honorable gentlemen, and pointing to British barbarians, have predicted with equal boldness, "There is a people that will never rise to civilization; there is a people destined never to be free; a people without the understanding necessary for the attainment of useful arts; depressed by the hand of nature below the level of the human species; and created to form a supply of slaves for the rest of the world"? Might not this have been said in all respects as fairly and as truly of Britain herself, at that period of her history, as it can now be said by us of the inhabitants of Africa? We, sir, have long since emerged from barbarism; we have almost forgotten that we were once barbarians; we are now raised to a situation which exhibits a striking contrast to every circumstance by which a Roman might have characterized us, and by which we now characterize Africa. There is, indeed, one thing wanting to complete the contrast, and to clear us altogether from the imputation of acting even to this hour as barbarians; for we continue to this hour a barbarous traffic in slaves; we continue it even yet, in spite of all our great and undeniable pretensions to civilization. We were once as obscure among the nations of the earth, as savage in our manners, as debased in our morals, as degraded in our understandings, as these unhappy Africans are at present. But in the lapse of a long series of years, by a progression slow, and for a time almost imperceptible, we have become rich in a variety of acquirements, favored above measure in the gifts of Providence, unrivaled in commerce, pre-eminent in arts, foremost in the pursuits of philosophy and science, and established in all the blessings of civil society: we are in the possession of peace, of happiness, and of liberty; we are under the guidance of a mild and beneficent religion; and we are protected by impartial laws, and the purest administration of justice; we are living under a system of government which our own happy experience leads us to pronounce the best and wisest which has ever yet been framed—a system which has become the admiration of the world. From all these blessings we must forever have been shut out, had there been any truth in those principles which some gentlemen have not hesitated to lay down as applicable to the case of Africa. Had those principles been true, we ourselves had languished to this hour in that miserable state of ignorance, brutality, and degradation in which history proves our ancestors to have been immersed. Had other nations adopted these principles in their conduct towards us; had other nations applied to Great Britain the reasoning which some of the senators of this very island now apply to Africa, ages might have passed without our emerging from barbarism; and we, who are enjoying the blessings of a British civilization, of British laws, and British liberty, might, at this hour, have been little superior, either in morals, in knowledge, or refinement, to the rude inhabitants of the coast of Guinea.

If, then, we feel that this perpetual confinement in the fetters of brutal ignorance would have been the greatest calamity which could have befallen us; if we view with gratitude and exultation the contrast between the peculiar blessings we enjoy and the wretchedness of the ancient inhabitants of Britain; if we shudder to think of the misery which would still have overwhelmed us had Great Britain continued to be the mart for slaves to the more civilized nations of the world, God forbid that we should any longer subject Africa to the same dreadful scourge, and preclude the light of knowledge, which has reached every other quarter of the globe, from having access to her coasts! I trust we shall no longer continue this commerce, to the destruction of every improvement on that wide continent; and shall not consider ourselves as conferring too great a boon in restoring its inhabitants to the rank of human beings. I trust we shall not think ourselves too liberal if, by abolishing the slave trade, we give them the same common chance of civilization with other parts of the world, and that we shall now allow to Africa the opportunity—the hope—the prospect of attaining to the same blessings which we ourselves, through the favorable dispensations of Divine Providence, have been permitted, at a much more early period, to enjoy. If we listen to the voice of reason and duty, and pursue this night the line of conduct which they prescribe, some of us may live to see a reverse of that picture from which we now turn our eyes with shame and regret. We may live to behold the natives of Africa engaged in the calm occupations of industry, in the pursuits of a just and legitimate commerce. We may behold the beams of science and philosophy breaking in upon their land, which, at some happy period in still later times, may blaze with full luster; and, joining their influence to that of pure religion, may illuminate and invigorate the most distant extremities of that immense continent. Then may we hope that even Africa, though last of all the quarters of the globe, shall enjoy at length, in the evening of her days, those blessings which have descended so plentifully upon us in a much earlier period of the world. Then also will Europe, participating in her improvement and prosperity, receive an ample recompense for the tardy kindness (if kindness it can be called) of no longer hindering that continent from extricating herself out of the darkness which, in other more fortunate regions, has been so much more speedily dispelled—

> —Nos primus equis oriens afflavit anhelis;
> Illic sera rubens accendit lumina Vesper.*

Then, sir, may be applied to Africa those words, originally used indeed with a different view—

> His demum exactis———
> Devenere locos lætos, et amœna virecta
> Fortunatorum nemorum, sedesque beatas:
> Largior hic campos Æther, et lumine vestit
> Purpureo.†

It is in this view, sir—it is as an atonement for our long and cruel injustice towards Africa—that the measure proposed by my honorable friend most forcibly recommends itself to my mind. The great and happy change to be expected in the state of her inhabitants is, of all the various and important benefits of the abolition, in my estimation, incomparably the most extensive and important. I shall vote, sir, against the adjourn-

* "And when dayspring touches us with his panting horses' breath, there crimson Hesperus kindles his lamp at evenfall."—Virgil, Georgics, I, 251 sq. (tr. J. W. Mackail)
† "Now at length, this fully done, they came to the happy place, the green pleasances and blissful seats of the Fortunate Woodlands. Here an ampler air clothes the meadows in lustrous sheen, and they know their own sun and a starlight of their own."—Virgil, Aeneid, VI, 637 sqq. (tr. J. W. Mackail).

ment; and I shall also oppose to the utmost every proposition which in any way may tend either to prevent or even to postpone for an hour the total abolition of the slave trade; a measure which, on all the various grounds which I have stated, we are bound, by the most pressing and indispensable duty, to adopt.

Pitt's friends and enemies alike were carried away by this magnificent peroration. Fox, Windham, Sheridan, and Grey, all hostile, were lavish in praise. Pitt's use of the lines from Virgil, which came to his mind as the first rays of the morning sun broke through the windows, was an inspiration modern orators may admire, but cannot imitate. Any Greek or Latin quotation would now seem absurdly pretentious, if not undemocratic, but when gentlemen were expected to know their Homer, Virgil, and Horace at least, classical quotations could be employed with stunning effect, lending a new dimension to the issue of the moment, investing life with continuity and dignity.

The slave trade was not abolished at this time, but Pitt had laid the foundations for eventual success. Of all his masterful works and policies, his espousal of abolition in the teeth of powerful interests had the most lasting results. Not long after his speech on the slave trade, however, Pitt was obliged to give up his peace policy and to devote his whole attention to the impending conflict with France. The great Whig leaders kept up their interest in abolition, however, and Wilberforce worked for the cause indefatigably, and, through a group of humanists called "the Saints," was able to exert considerable influence in Parliament. In 1798 he prepared another motion on the slave trade, which was defeated, and again in 1799, and though he was defeated by 84 to 54, he felt convinced that the cause was gaining ground. In 1802 he made another attempt, but failed to get his motion before the House of Lords. Two years later, he was defeated by an even larger majority, but it was interesting, as Wilberforce commented, that "all the Irish members voted with us." Another motion failed in 1805, and it was not until after Pitt's death in 1806 that his great rival, Fox, came briefly into power and carried an abolition bill through the House of Commons. Then Fox himself collapsed and died a few months later, but his final act was confirmed by the House of Lords. In 1807–08 the slave trade ceased in the British dominions. Wilberforce and his cohorts were far from satisfied. He continued to work fervently for complete emancipation, in British territory and abroad. Twenty-six years of pious and efficient agitation passed, and then Wilberforce died. A month later slavery was abolished in all British territories. Six to seven hundred thousand human beings were set free.

PART EIGHT

THE FRENCH REVOLUTION

I N THE CALDRON of the French Revolution seethed many of the causes we have found at work in America, England, and Ireland, but their impact was far more thorough and convulsive, and the outcome far more decisive. Poverty, unjust taxation, and a corrupt and oppressive monarchy were common causes, but the differences were fully as important. America had elbowroom and many immunities, England was winning parliamentary power and civil rights, while Ireland was temporarily appeased by Grattan's Parliament. France, on the other hand, was the richest, most powerful, most cultured nation in the world, and the poverty and injustice it suffered took on a deeper color against the luster of a golden age. The result, too, was unique, for the French Revolution not only freed the nation from a corrupt monarchy, but displaced the whole order of landed nobility, and put power into the hands of the third estate, the men of business and commerce.

It is no accident that we have heard little of French political eloquence up to this point, for no free assembly had met in France since 1614. French oratory had been restricted to the pulpit, the bar, and the Academy. But now as the hold of a weakened monarchy loosened, lawyers, priests, and noblemen rushed to the political rostrum, without tradition or parliamentary rules to guide them.

There were doubtless thousands of anonymous speakers whose dangerous and persevering persuasion would be necessary to a great revolution; and there was a small group of speakers whose mastery of language and passion and facts catapulted them almost overnight into the highest fame and power. The greatest orators of the French Revolution, Mirabeau, Vergniaud, Danton, and Robespierre, are sometimes compared to Burke, Fox, Pitt, and Sheridan. But the differences are also striking. Whereas the Englishmen had decades in which to develop their debating skill, and the House of Commons as a restraining tradition, the careers of the French orators were short and meteoric, lasting at most only three or four years, and they lived through crises more severe and perilous than those across the Channel.

MIRABEAU WARNS THE NOBILITY AND CLERGY OF PROVENCE OF THE IMPENDING STORM

[February 3, 1789]

The most powerful statesman and orator of the first two years of the Revolution was Honoré Gabriel Riquetti, Comte de Mirabeau (1749–91). The son of the French physiocrat, the Marquis de Mirabeau, he himself wrote on economic, social, and historical matters, including such diverse topics as the Prussian monarchy, banking problems, the Negro slave trade, and the condition of the Jews in France. In politics he was a mediator between people and King at a time when a rapprochement still seemed possible. While casting his lot with the people, and warning the nobles that they had better concede freely today what would be wrung from them tomorrow, he nevertheless was a monarchist who secretly accepted money as an adviser to the King. His exceptional power lay in ready and fabulous persuasion. A large, pockmarked man, magnificent in his ugliness, notorious as a lecher, once sent to jail by his own father for debt, he triumphed over all scandals and defects by his genius.

In 1789 Mirabeau was in Provence, where a separate assembly, the Estates of Provence, had been formed. Never had he seen a nobility so ignorant, greedy, and insolent, he wrote. On January 23 he protested that nobles without fiefs (in which category he himself belonged) should be eligible to the Estates, and on January 30 he argued that the third estate should have representation equal in number and power to that of the other two orders, the nobles and clergy. On February 3, as the passage from his speech below illustrates, he attacked the greed and intransigence of the nobles, but also warned the people to observe moderation.

"For privileges shall have an end, but the people is eternal!"

IN ALL COUNTRIES, in all ages, have aristocrats implacably pursued the friends of the people; and when, by I know not what combination of fortune, such a friend has uprisen from the very bosom of the aristocracy, it has been at him pre-eminently that they have struck, eager to inspire wider terror by the elevation of their victim. So perished the last of the Gracchi by the hands of the patricians. But, mortally smitten, he flung dust toward heaven, calling the avenging gods to witness: and

from that dust sprang Marius—Marius, less illustrious for having extermi-
nated the Cimbri than for having beaten down the despotism of the
nobility in Rome.

But you, Commons, listen to one who, unseduced by your applauses,
yet cherishes them in his heart. Man is strong only by union; happy only
by peace. Be firm, not obstinate; courageous, not turbulent; free, not
undisciplined; prompt, not precipitate. Stop not, except at difficulties of
moment; and be then wholly inflexible. But disdain the contentions of
self-love, and never thrust into the balance the individual against the
country. Above all, hasten, as much as in you lies, the epoch of those
States-General from which you are charged with flinching—the more
acrimoniously charged, the more your accusers dread the results; of those
States-General through which so many pretensions will be scattered, so
many rights re-established, so many evils reformed, of those States-General, in short, through which the monarch himself desires that France
should regenerate herself.

For myself, who, in my public career, have had no other fear but that
of wrongdoing—who, girt with my conscience and armed with my principles, would brave the universe—whether it shall be my fortune to serve
you with my voice and my exertions in the national assembly, or whether
I shall be enabled to aid you there with my prayers only, be sure that the
vain clamors, the wrathful menaces, the injurious protestations—all the
convulsions, in a word, of expiring prejudices—shall not intimidate me!
What! shall he now pause in his civic course who, first among all the men
of France, emphatically proclaimed his opinions on national affairs, at a
time when circumstances were much less urgent than now and the task
one of much greater peril?

Never! No measure of outrages shall bear down my patience. I have
been, I am, I shall be, even to the tomb, the man of the public liberty, the
man of the Constitution. If to be such be to become the man of the
people rather than of the nobles, then woe to the privileged orders! For
privileges shall have an end, but the people is eternal!

*If Mirabeau failed, in such appeals, to convince the fatuous nobles of the preci-
pice opening before them, he succeeded in mustering the strength of the third
estate (tiers état), or middle class. He became their defender, their hero, the
rallying point of massive protest, and with their help successfully defended his
seat in the Estates of Provence.*

*Events now moved forward rapidly, irreparably. On June 20 the National
Assembly—the representatives of the third estate—took their famous oath in
the tennis court not to disband until they had given France a constitution. In*

Paris now, Mirabeau's unrivaled oratory made him the "tribune of the as
sembly." Louis XVI meanwhile vacillated, the political clubs fought and in.
trigued for power, tension rose, and a concentration of troops appeared near
Paris. On July 14 the storm broke. Although the story that Camille Desmoulins
suddenly jumped on a table in a café and cried "À la Bastille!" is discarded as a
legend, it is likely that some forgotten orators incited the insurrection that
swept away that ancient symbol of tyranny.

MIRABEAU DEFENDS A DESPERATE
FINANCIAL MEASURE

[September 26, 1789]

Among the causes of the French Revolution was the vast public debt, which
eventually ruined national credit and threatened the country with bankruptcy.
The great economist, Necker, had instituted reforms to cure the grave financial
condition of the nation, and, when these failed, advised the calling of the
States-General to Versailles to deliberate upon a more equitable system of taxation. Among Necker's proposals was a twenty-five per cent income tax. On
September 26, 1789, Mirabeau rose in the Assembly to defend this drastic
measure as the only way of coping with the existing crisis. When he had finished
speaking, the applause was feverish and a favorable vote was clearly in sight.
While Mirabeau withdrew to draft the measure, however, the Assembly changed
its mind, and when he returned he was unable to make any headway against
the opposition. Then a third time he rose, delivering one of his most famous
speeches, a part of which is reproduced below.

"Hideous bankruptcy is here . . . yet you deliberate!"

Gentlemen:

IN THE MIDST of this tumultuous debate can I not bring you back
to the question of the deliberation by a few simple questions. Deign,
gentlemen, to hear me and to vouchsafe a reply.

The minister of finance—has he not shown you a most formidable
picture of our actual situation? Has he not told you that every delay
aggravates the danger—that a day, an hour, an instant, may make it fatal?

Have we any other plan to substitute for the one he proposes? "Yes,"
cries someone in the Assembly! I conjure the one making this reply of

"Yes" to consider that his plan is unknown; that it would take time to develop, examine, and demonstrate it; that even were it at once submitted to our deliberation, its author may be mistaken; were he even free of all error, it might be thought he was wrong, for when the whole world is wrong, the whole world makes wrong right. The author of this other project in being right might be wrong against the world, since without the assent of public opinion the greatest talents could not triumph over such circumstances.

And I—I myself—do not believe the methods of M. Necker the very best possible. But heaven preserve me in such a critical situation from opposing my views to his! Vainly I might hold them preferable! One does not in a moment rival an immense popularity achieved by brilliant services; a long experience, the reputation of the highest talent as a financier, and, it can be added, a destiny such as has been achieved by no other man!

Let us then return to this plan of M. Necker. But have we the time to examine, to prove its foundation, to verify its calculations? No, no, a thousand times no! Insignificant questions, hazardous conjectures, doubts, and gropings, these are all that at this moment are in our power. What shall we accomplish by rejecting this deliberation? Miss our decisive moment, injure our self-esteem by changing something we neither know nor understand, and diminish by our indiscreet intervention the influence of a minister whose financial credit is, and ought to be, much greater than our own. Gentlemen, there assuredly is in this neither wisdom nor foresight. Does it even show good faith? If no less solemn declarations guarantee our respect for the public faith, our horror of the infamous word "bankruptcy," I might dare to scrutinize the secret motives which make us hesitate to promulgate an act of patriotic devotion which will be inefficacious if not done immediately and with full confidence.

I would say to those who familiarize themselves with the idea of failing to keep the public faith, either by fear of taxes or of excessive sacrifices: what is bankruptcy, if not the most cruel, the most iniquitous, the most unequal, the most disastrous of imposts? My friends, hear but a word—a single word.

Two centuries of depredations and brigandage have made the chasm in which the kingdom is ready to engulf itself. We must close this fearful abyss. Well, here is a list of French proprietors! Choose among the richest, thus sacrificing the least number of citizens! But choose! For must not a small number perish to save the mass of the people? Well, these two thousand notables possess enough to make up the deficit. This will restore order in the finances and bring peace and prosperity to the kingdom!

Strike, immolate without pity these wretched victims, cast them into

the abyss until it is closed. You recoil in horror, inconsistent and pusillanimous men! Do you not see that in decreeing bankruptcy, or what is still
more odious, in rendering it inevitable, without decreeing it, you do a
deed a thousand times more criminal, and—folly inconceivable—gratui-
tously criminal? For at least this horrible sacrifice would cause the
disappearance of the deficit. But do you imagine that in refusing to pay,
you will cease to owe? Do you believe that the thousands, the millions of
men who will lose in an instant, by the terrible explosion or its repercus-
sion, all that made the consolation of their lives, and constituted, perhaps,
the sole means of their support, would leave you peaceably to enjoy your
crime? Stoical contemplators of the incalculable evils which this catastrophe would disgorge upon France! Impassive egoists who think that
these convulsions of despair and misery shall pass like so many others, and
the more rapidly as they are the more violent! Are you sure that so many
men without bread will leave you tranquilly to the enjoyment of those
dainties, the number and delicacy of which you are unwilling to diminish.
No! you will perish, and in the universal conflagration you do not hesitate
to kindle, the loss of your honor will not save a single one of your detestable enjoyments!

Look where we are going! . . . I hear you speak of patriotism, and the
élan of patriotism, of invocations to patriotism. Ah! do not prostitute the
words "country" and "patriotism"! Is it so very magnanimous—the effort
to give a portion of one's revenue to save all of one's possessions? This,
gentlemen, is only simple arithmetic; and he who hesitates cannot disarm
indignation except by the contempt he inspires through his stupidity.
Yes, gentlemen, this is the plainest prudence, the commonest wisdom! It
is your gross material interests I invoke! I shall not say to you as formerly:
will you be the first to exhibit to the nations the spectacle of a people
assembled to make default in their public obligations? I shall not say
again: what titles have you to liberty? What means remain to you to
preserve it, if in your first act you surpass the turpitude of the most corrupt governments; if the first care of your vigilant co-operation is not for
the guarantee of your constitution? I tell you, you will all be dragged into
a universal ruin, and you yourselves have the greatest interests in making
the sacrifices the government asks of you. Vote, then, for this extraordinary subsidy; and it may be sufficient! Vote for it, for if you have any
doubts on the means adopted (vague and unenlightened doubts), you
have none as to its necessity or our inability to provide an immediate
substitute. Vote, then, because public necessity admits no delay and we
shall be held accountable for any delay that occurs. Beware of asking for
time! Misfortune never grants it!

Gentlemen, apropos of a ridiculous disturbance at the Palais Royal, of a laughable insurrection, which never had any importance save in the weak imaginations or perverted designs of a few faith-breakers, you have heard these mad words: "Catiline is at the gates of Rome! And yet you deliberate!"

And certainly there has been about us no Catiline, no peril, no faction, no Rome. But today bankruptcy—hideous bankruptcy is here—it threatens to consume you, your properties, your honor! And yet you deliberate!

"The triumph was complete; not an attempt was made to reply," said Étienne Dumont, who wrote or reported many of Mirabeau's speeches. "The Assembly was subjugated by that power of a superior and energetic mind which acts upon the multitude as if it were only a single individual, and the project was adopted without a dissenting voice. From that day Mirabeau was considered as a being superior to other men. He had no rival . . . and this impression was stronger because in his speech on this question he was obliged to depend entirely upon his own resources; for it was an unexpected reply, and could not therefore have been prepared."

However, we must add, in the words of the distinguished H. Morse Stephens, "the motion was carried, but as might have been expected had little effect upon the state of the finances of France, and actual bankruptcy was eventually averted by the issue of assignats."

DOCTOR RICHARD PRICE, IN LONDON, HAILS THE FRENCH REVOLUTION

[November 4, 1789]

On fairly comfortable England, with the masses solaced by Methodism, the French Revolution did not burst like a bomb or a blessing. It was a remote drama far across the channel and hardly worth the notice of Prime Minister Pitt for two or three years. But some did notice it promptly, particularly the apostles of freedom, the dissenters, the reformers, the poets, the dreamers. When the Bastille fell, the people seemed to be reasserting their inalienable rights, and many could afterward recall with Wordsworth:

> *Bliss was it in that dawn to be alive,*
> *But to be young was very heaven.*

Blake, Burns, Cowper, Southey, each with his own distinctive emphasis, rejoiced in the new era that was beginning. In Parliament the Revolution found supporters in the Whig leaders Fox and Sheridan, the former describing the fall of the Bastille as the greatest event in human history and "how much the best!"

But Fox and Sheridan failed to carry their friends with them in this matter, and Burke was soon to become the most brilliant and influential enemy of the French Revolution. The immediate occasion for the writing of his famous Reflections on the French Revolution was a speech by Dr. Richard Price, a speech often mentioned, but seldom read.

Richard Price (1723–91) was a nonconformist clergyman who, though trained as a mathematician, was best known for his political pamphlets and writings on ethics, life insurance and other economic questions. His pamphlet, Observations on the Nature of Civil Liberty, the Principles of Government, and the Justice and Policy of the War with America (1776), made such a strong defense of the American cause that it was said to have influenced the colonists in declaring their independence. Until his death he remained a friend and counselor to the Americans and a firm defender of the French Revolution. The fateful sermon, "On the Love of Our Country," which appears in an abridged form below, was delivered before the Revolution Society of Great Britain, a society composed of dissenting politicians and churchmen who had begun to meet the previous year to commemorate England's Glorious Revolution of 1688.

"I see the ardor for liberty catching and spreading."

WE ARE MET to thank God for that event in this country to which the name of *the Revolution* has been given; and which, for more than a century, it has been usual for the friends of freedom, and more especially Protestant Dissenters, under the title of the Revolution Society, to celebrate with expressions of joy and exultation. My highly valued and excellent friend who addressed you on this occasion last year has given you an interesting account of the principal circumstances that attended this event, and of the reasons we have for rejoicing in it. By a bloodless victory, the fetters which despotism had been long preparing for us were broken; the rights of the people were asserted, a tyrant expelled, and a sovereign of our own choice appointed in his room. Security was given to our property, and our consciences were emancipated. The bounds of free inquiry were enlarged; the volume in which are the words of eternal life was laid more open to our examination; and that era of light and liberty was introduced among us by which we have been made an example to other kingdoms and became the instructors of the world. Had it not been for this deliverance, the probability is that, instead of being thus distinguished, we should now have been a base people, groaning under the infamy and misery of popery and slavery. Let us, therefore, offer thanksgivings to God, the Author of all our blessings. . . .

It is well known that King James was not far from gaining his purpose; and that probably he would have succeeded had he been less in a hurry. But he was a fool as well as a bigot. He wanted courage as well as prudence; and, therefore, fled and left us to settle quietly for ourselves that constitution of government which is now our boast. We have particular reason, as Protestant Dissenters, to rejoice on this occasion. It was at this time we were rescued from persecution, and obtained the liberty of worshiping God in the manner we think most acceptable to Him. It was then our meetinghouses were opened, our worship was taken under the protection of the law, and the principles of toleration gained a triumph. We have, therefore, on this occasion, peculiar reasons for thanksgiving. But let us remember that we ought not to satisfy ourselves with thanksgivings. Our gratitude, if genuine, will be accompanied with endeavors to give stability to the deliverance our country has obtained, and to extend and improve the happiness with which the Revolution has blessed us. Let us, in particular, take care not to forget the principles of the Revolution. This Society has, very properly, in its Reports, held out these principles, as an instruction to the public. I will only take notice of the three following:

First: the right to liberty of conscience in religious matters.

Secondly: the right to resist power when abused. And,

Thirdly: the right to choose our own governors; to cashier them for misconduct; and to frame a government for ourselves.

On these three principles, and more especially the last, was the Revolution founded. Were it not true that liberty of conscience is a sacred right; that power abused justifies resistance; and that civil authority is a delegation from the people—were not, I say, all this true, the Revolution would have been not an *assertion*, but an *invasion* of rights; not a *revolution*, but a *rebellion*. Cherish in your breasts this conviction, and act under its influence; detecting the odious doctrines which, had they been acted upon in this country, would have left us at this time wretched slaves— doctrines which imply that God made mankind to be oppressed and plundered; and which are no less a blasphemy against Him than an insult on common sense.

I would further direct you to remember that, though the Revolution was a great work, it was by no means a perfect work; and that all was not then gained which was necessary to put the kingdom in the secure and complete possession of the blessings of liberty. In particular, you should recollect that the toleration then obtained was imperfect. It included only those who could declare their faith in the doctrinal articles of the Church of England. It has, indeed, been since extended, but not sufficiently; for there still exist penal laws on account of religious opinions, which (were they carried into execution) would shut up many of our places of worship and silence and imprison some of our ablest and best men. The Test Laws are also still in force, and deprive of eligibility to civil and military offices all who cannot conform to the established worship. It is with great pleasure I find that the body of Protestant Dissenters, though defeated in two late attempts to deliver their country from this disgrace to it, have determined to persevere. Should they at last succeed, they will have the satisfaction, not only of removing from themselves a proscription they do not deserve, but of contributing to lessen the number of our public iniquities. For I cannot call by a gentler name laws which convert an ordinance appointed by our Saviour to commemorate His death into an instrument of oppressive policy, and a qualification of rakes and atheists for civil posts. I have said, *should* they succeed—but perhaps I ought not to suggest a doubt about their success. And, indeed, when I consider that in Scotland the established church is defended by no such test—that in Ireland it has been abolished—that in a great neighboring country it has been declared to be an indefeasible right of all citizens to be equally eligible to public offices—that in the same kingdom a professed Dissenter from the established church holds the first office in the state— that in the Emperor's dominions Jews have been lately admitted to the enjoyment of equal privileges with other citizens—and that in this very country, a Dissenter, though excluded from the power of *executing* the laws, yet is allowed to be employed in *making* them. When, I say, I consider such facts as these, I am disposed to think it impossible that the enemies of the repeal of the Test Laws should not soon become ashamed and give up their opposition.

But the most important instance of the imperfect state in which the Revolution left our Constitution is the inequality of our representation. I think, indeed, this defect in our Constitution so gross and so palpable as to make it excellent chiefly in form and theory. You should remember that a representation in the legislature of a kingdom is the *basis* of constitutional liberty in it, and of all legitimate government; and that without it a government is nothing but an usurpation. When the representation is fair and equal, and at the same time vested with such powers as our House of Commons possesses, a kingdom may be said to govern itself, and consequently to possess true liberty. When the representation is partial, a kingdom possesses liberty only partially; and if extremely partial, it only gives a *semblance* of liberty; but if not only extremely partial, but corruptly chosen and under corrupt influence after being chosen, it becomes a *nuisance,* and produces the worst of all forms of government— a government by corruption—a government carried on and supported by spreading venality and profligacy through a kingdom. May heaven preserve this kingdom from a calamity so dreadful! It is the point of depravity to which abuses under such a government as ours naturally tend, and the last stage of national unhappiness. We are, at present, I hope, at a great distance from it. But it cannot be pretended that there are no advances toward it, or that there is no reason for apprehension and alarm. . . .

You may reasonably expect that I should now close this address to you. But I cannot yet dismiss you. I must not conclude without recalling, particularly, to your recollection a consideration to which I have more than once alluded, and which, probably, your thoughts have been all along anticipating; a consideration with which my mind is impressed more than I can express. I mean, the consideration of the favorableness of the present times to all exertions in the cause of public liberty.

What an eventful period is this! I am thankful that I have lived to it; and I could almost say, *Lord, now lettest thou thy servant depart in peace, for mine eyes have seen thy salvation.* I have lived to see a diffusion of knowledge which has undermined superstition and error—I have lived to see the rights of men better understood than ever; and nations panting for liberty which seemed to have lost the idea of it. I have lived to see thirty millions of people, indignant and resolute, spurning at slavery, and demanding liberty with an irresistible voice; their king led in triumph, and an arbitrary monarch surrendering himself to his subjects. After sharing in the benefits of one revolution, I have been spared to be a witness to two other revolutions, both glorious. And now, methinks, I see the ardor for liberty catching and spreading; a general amendment beginning in human affairs; the dominion of priests giving way to the dominion of reason and conscience.

Be encouraged, all ye friends of freedom and writers in its defense! The times are auspicious. Your labors have not been in vain. Behold kingdoms, admonished by you, starting from sleep, breaking their fetters, and claiming justice from their oppressors! Behold, the light you have struck out, after setting America free, reflected to France, and there kindled into a blaze that lays despotism in ashes and warms and illuminates Europe!

Tremble all ye oppressors of the world! Take warning all ye supporters of slavish governments and slavish hierarchies! Call no more (absurdly and wickedly) *reformation* innovation. You cannot now hold the world in darkness. Struggle no longer against increasing light and liberality. Restore to mankind their rights; and consent to the correction of abuses, before they and you are destroyed together.

This discourse was soon circulated throughout England in pamphlet form and became the "red rag which threw Burke into the arena," the Burke who had been the defender of American, Irish, and Indian liberties, and an advocate of Negro emancipation. On February 9, 1790, in the House of Commons debate on the army estimates, Burke declared:

"In the last age, we were in danger of being entangled by the example of France in the net of a relentless despotism. It is not necessary to say anything upon that example: it exists no longer. Our present danger, from the example of a people whose character knows no medium, is, with regard to government, a danger from anarchy; a danger of being led, through an admiration of success-ful fraud and violence, to an imitation of the excess of an irrational, unprin-cipled, proscribing, confiscating, plundering, ferocious, bloody, and tyrannical democracy. On the side of religion, the danger is no longer from intolerance. but from atheism—a foul, unnatural vice, foe to all the dignity and consolation of mankind—which seems in France, for a long time, to have been embodied into a faction, accredited, and almost avowed."

These sentiments Burke explained in Reflections on the Revolution in France—which was published in November, 1790, and quickly became the Bible of reaction in Europe, perhaps the most influential political pamphlet ever written. Although addressed to an anonymous French citizen, it was de-signed specifically to answer Dr. Price and other English enthusiasts.

But sickly old Doctor Price continued to be cheered by the progress of the French Revolution until his death six months later.

MIRABEAU ARGUES FOR THE KING'S
RIGHT TO MAKE WAR AND PEACE

[May 22, 1790]

In the spring of 1790, the King of Spain demanded military assistance from France against England under the pacte de famille, the immediate occasion being the Nootka Sound dispute. The National Assembly thereupon decided to furnish the aid required under the treaty, but the question then arose as to who, under the new constitution, had the power to declare war. Mirabeau, along with the Right, maintained that this crucial power of government belonged to the Crown, since a popular assembly could be too quickly swayed. The Comte de Lameth and Robespierre, on the other hand, insisted that this authority be retained by the nation as represented by the Assembly. So great was the popular support and acclamation they received that Mirabeau knew it was useless to demand all that Louis XVI wanted. Instead, he proposed a compromise: that the power to make war and peace be vested in king and nation conjointly. The Left moved quickly to destroy him. In a few days a pamphlet was hawked through the streets, entitled The Great Treason of Mirabeau Discovered.

Undaunted by intimidation, calumny, and the threats upon his life, faithful to his principles and no doubt also to the King in whose pay he lived so handsomely, Mirabeau rose on May 20 to give a fiery and effective speech urging his compromise resolution. The next day he listened impassively as the supple Barnave, spokesman of his enemies, insinuated treason and tore his argument apart. Suddenly he saw the weak point in Barnave's position and, making a quick note, strolled out of the Assembly, where, chancing to meet Mme de Staël, he talked with her for a long time on wholly different matters. At this point in the debate Mirabeau's cause seemed lost. The next day—May 22—he delivered a second speech (abridged below) on the right to make war. More than fifty thousand citizens collected in the Tuileries and the surrounding gardens and streets to hear reports of this speech. The hostile crowd through which Mirabeau was obliged to pass greeted him with cries of "À la lanterne!" ("String him up!").

"Among those who maintain my doctrine you may reckon upon all men of moderation."

IT IS, doubtless, a point gained toward reconciling opposite opinions to make known clearly what it is that produces the coincidence, and what it is that constitutes the difference. Amicable discussions are more favorable to a right understanding of our respective sentiments than defamatory insinuation, outrageous accusations, the animosities of rivalship, the machinations of cabal and malevolence. A report has been spread abroad for this week past that that part of the National Assembly which approves the concurrence of the royal will in the exercise of the right of peace and war has incurred the guilt of parricide against public liberty.

Rumors of perfidy, of corruption, are disseminated; popular vengeance is invoked to aid the tyranny of opinion. One might assert that there cannot, without a crime, exist two opinions upon one of the most delicate and most difficult questions of civil organization. What a strange madness this, what a deplorable blindness, which thus inflames us one against another—men whom one and the same object, the same indestructible sentiment, should, amidst the most fell debates, still reconcile, still re-unite; men who in fact substitute the irascibility of self-interest for patriotism, and deliver up one another to the rage of popular prejudice!

As for me, but a few days ago it was proposed to carry me in triumph; and now the cry is through every street of Paris: "The grand treason of the Comte de Mirabeau!" I did not want such a lesson to inform me that there is but a short distance from the Capitol to the Tarpeian rock. How-ever, a man combating for reason, for his country, will not so readily acknowledge himself vanquished. He who feels within himself the con-sciousness of having deserved well of his country, and especially of being still of use to it; he who does not feed upon a vain celebrity, and who contemns the success of a day when looking forward to true glory; he who wishes to speak the truth, who has at heart the public welfare inde-pendently of the fickle movements of public opinion—such a man bears along with him the recompense of his services, the mitigation of his pains, and the price of all his perils; such a man must expect his harvest, his destiny—the only one which interests him, the destiny of his fame—from time alone, that judge incorruptible, who renders strict justice to every-one. Let those who, for this week past, have been prophesying my opinion without knowing what it was, who at this moment are calumniating my speech without understanding it, let them accuse me of offering incense to idols without power, at the very moment when they lie prostrate, or of being the vile stipendiary of men against whom I have indefatigably waged war; let them arraign as an enemy to the Revolution the man who, perhaps, has not been altogether useless to it, and who, were that Revolu-tion unconnected with his renown, might there alone expect an asylum; let them deliver up to the fury of an infatuated people the man who for these twenty years has been the adversary of oppression, who talked to the French of liberty, of constitution, of resistance, when his base calum-niators were at nurse in the court of despotism and suckled with the milk of overbearing prejudices. What is all this to me? This treatment, these unworthy practices, shall not arrest me in my career. I will say to my antagonists: answer, if you are able; then calumniate as much as you please. . . .

It is full time to terminate this long debate. I am in hopes that henceforward none will think of shutting their eyes against the true point of difficulty. I am for the co-operation of the executive power in expressing the general will with respect to war and peace in like manner as the Constitution has conferred on it that co-operation, in every part already established of our new social system. My adversaries are not for it. I am contending that the superintendence of one of the people's delegates should never desert it in the most important political operations; and my antagonists contend that one of the delegates should exclusively possess the right of making war; as if, even were the executive power a stranger to the composition of the general will, our deliberations turned only on the declaration of war, and the exercise of the right involved not a series of mixed operations, in which action and will jostle each other and are confounded.

Such, then, is the line which separates us. If I am mistaken, once again let my adversary arrest me in my career, or rather let him substitute in his decree, in place of the words *the legislative body,* the words *legislative power*—that is, an act issuing from the representatives of the nation, and sanctioned by the King—and we are perfectly agreed, if not in practice, at least in theory; and we shall then be able to judge whether this theory be not better realized in my decree than in any other.

It has been proposed to you to decide the question by a parallel between those who support the affirmative and those who support the negative. You have been told that you would see, on the one side, men who hope either for advancement in the army or to be employed in transacting foreign affairs, men connected with the ministers and their agents; on the other, "the peaceful citizen, virtuous, unknown, unambitious, who finds his own happiness and existence in the happiness and existence of the community."

I mean not to follow this example. I think that it is no more conformable to the expediencies of politics than it is to the principles of morality to sharpen the poniard with which one cannot wound one's rival without soon feeling the weapon returned upon one's own heart. I do not think that men who ought to serve the public cause as true brother soldiers find any pleasure in defamation and intrigue, and not in information and talents; in seeking guilty triumphs in mutual ruin and depression, the trophies of a day, injurious to all, and even to the cause of glory. But I will tell you: among those who maintain my doctrine you may reckon upon all men of moderation, who do not think that wisdom is to be found in extremes, nor that the spirit of pulling down should never make room for that of building up; you may reckon upon the greatest part of those energetic citizens who, at the commencement of the States-General (such at that time was the appellation of this national convention, which is yet but in the cradle of liberty), trampled on so many prejudices, braved so many dangers, beat down so many impediments, in order to make their way into the midst of the Commons, in whom that devotedness inspired the courage and the force which have really effectuated your glorious revolution; you will there behold those tribunes of the people whom the nation will long rank among the number of her deliverers notwithstanding the incessant barking of envious mediocrity; you will there see persons whose very name disarms calumny, and whose reputation, both as public and private men, the most headstrong libelers have never essayed to tarnish—men, in fine, who, without blemish, without views of interest, and without fear, will be honored even to the grave, both by their friends and by their enemies.

(TRANSLATED BY JAMES WHITE)

It would be difficult to find a better illustration of the power of eloquence. The Assembly applauded vigorously, and Mirabeau's motion, slightly modified, was carried without dissent. From deep disgrace and mortal danger, he had risen to the top again, more glorious and popular than ever before. In a single speech he had silenced or won over the Left, and had cured any doubts and suspicions the Right may have had. Against deadly and overwhelming opposition he had preserved the royal initiative in making war and peace.

In the meantime the motives and character of this dazzling rogue and patriot remain in doubt. Was he bought and paid for by Louis XVI, as his enemies aver, or merely paid, as his friends insisted? Certainly in his case patriotism and profit were inextricably blended. Although he made daring and resourceful efforts to moderate, but also to preserve, the Revolution, his shameless extravagance and debauchery were financed by the King, who, as history was to show, would stop at nothing to destroy the Revolution. His character can thus be questioned, but not his eloquence. Though his speeches were often written by his lieutenants, as was the custom of the time, he knew how to transmute them into gold, and to produce unparalleled effects.

Mirabeau did not live to enjoy the new prestige he had won on May 22, but died the next year. For "twenty-three resplendent months," he had ridden the storm, as Carlyle said, and dominated the revolutionary scene. What would have happened had he lived longer is a question of irresistible interest. Could he have reconciled the traditional monarchy with the new liberty and stabilized the Revolution, thus forestalling the Terror, the ninth Thermidor, and the ultimate dictatorship of Napoleon? Or is it not more likely that the current of events would have been too strong for one man to reverse, and that Mirabeau *would have been increasingly embarrassed by his double loyalty to king and people?*

VERGNIAUD REVEALS THE DESPERATE POSITION OF REVOLUTIONARY FRANCE

[July 3, 1792]

France declared war against Austria on April 20, 1792, but the French were ill prepared for this step, and the invasion launched against Belgium, at that time an Austrian dependency, began with complete disaster. The raw volunteers who had been recruited fled in disorder, and the units of the regular army were not far behind. The news of the defeat produced consternation in Paris, for the borders seemed wide open to invasion. It was known that the army had been seriously weakened by the emigration of thousands of officers and the desertion of tens of thousands of men. Disaffection, intrigue, and corruption had reached colossal proportions. The Girondists, the party of moderate Jacobins, had insisted on war, against the wise warnings of Robespierre and the more radical Jacobins, the Mountain (so-called because of the elevation of their seats in the Assembly), but they had no idea how to prosecute it successfully. As French reverses in the field continued, rumors and terror swept the country. Frederick William II of Prussia, with the finest army in Europe, was about to begin an invasion. The émigrés were to be invited to return. And quickly the suspicion spread that a deep conspiracy was at work to defeat French armies in advance, however skillfully and bravely they might fight. This suspicion, of course, corresponded to fact. The King was in correspondence with the émigré princes and nobles and had handed over French military plans to the enemy.

At this perilous moment, when France was saved from destruction only by the preoccupation of Prussia and Austria with a disagreement over the forthcoming division of Poland, a great French orator rose in the Assembly to warn the country of its extremity, and to hint, with daring prophecy, that national security required the dethronement of the King. Pierre Victurnien Vergniaud (1753–93) was the greatest orator of the Girondist party and, next to Mirabeau, probably the greatest orator of the French Revolution. Born in Limoges, he was admitted to the bar at Bordeaux in 1782. He practiced law for some years, showing even at this time his firm belief in the rights of the people, until the Revolution came, opening up for him a new career of brief but shimmering brilliance. As a statesman, he was far inferior to Mirabeau, and it was his *studious, carefully prepared eloquence that led to his election as president of the Assembly in 1791, and made him a famous man almost overnight. Of his four most famous speeches, the one below was the first.*

"Can it be true that our triumphs are dreaded?"

WHAT, THEN, is the strange position in which the National Assembly finds itself? What fatality pursues us and signalizes each day with great events, carrying disorder into our works and giving us over to the tumultuous agitation of apprehensions, hopes, and passions? What fates prepare for France this terrible ebullition, in the midst of which, did we understand less well the imperishable love of the people for liberty, we should be tempted to doubt whether the Revolution is retrograding or whether it will run its proper course?

At the moment when your armies of the north seemed to be making progress in Brabant and flattered our courage with auguries of victory, suddenly they were forced to fall back before the enemy; they abandon advantageous positions which they have conquered; they are led back to our own territory, whence the theater of war is fixed; and nothing of us will remain with the unfortunate Belgians but the memory of the fires which will have lighted our retreat. On another side and on the banks of the Rhine our frontiers are threatened by Prussian troops, whose march the ministerial reports have made us hope would not be so sudden. Such is our political and military situation, and never were so necessary the wise arrangement of plans, the prompt execution of means, the union, the accord of all authorities to whom the Constitution delegates the use of armed force; never might become so disastrous the least misinformation, the slightest suspension, the most trifling missteps.

How does it happen that precisely at the last period of the most violent crisis, on the edge of the abyss into which the nation may plunge, the movement of our armies is suspended; that by a sudden disorganization of the ministry the chain of works has been shattered, the bonds of confidence broken, the safety of the empire given up to the inexperience of hands chosen at random, the difficulties of execution multipled, and its success jeopardized by mistakes which must happen, even with the most enlightened patriotism, in the apprenticeship of a great administration? If plans are conceived which may expedite the completion of our armies, for increasing our means of conquest, or of making our defeats less disastrous, why are they preceded to the throne by calumny and there

stifled by the most perfidious malevolence? Can it be true that our
triumphs are dreaded? Is it of the blood of the army of Coblentz or of
our own that they are sparing? . . .

And you, gentlemen, what great thing are you going to undertake
for the commonwealth? You whose courage the enemies of the Constitution insolently flatter themselves that they have shaken; you whose consciences they try each day to alarm by styling the love of liberty the
spirit of faction—as if you could have forgotten that a despotic court also
gave the name of factionists to the representatives of the people who
went to take the oath of the tennis court; that the cowardly heroes of the
aristocracy have constantly lavished it upon the conquerors of the Bastille,
upon all those who made and maintained the Revolution, and which the
Constituent Assembly believed it to be its duty to honor it by proclaiming
in one of its addresses that the nation was composed of twenty-four millions of factionists; you who have been so calumniated because you are
almost all foreign to the caste which the Revolution threw down into the
dust, and because the intriguers who desired to re-establish it, and the
degraded men who regret the infamous pleasure of groveling before it,
have not hoped to find accomplices in you; you, against whom they let
loose with so much fury only because you form a truly popular assembly,
and because in you they wished to dishonor the people; you who have
been so cowardly accused of tarnishing the glory of the constitutional
throne, because several times your avenging hand struck those who
wished to make it the throne of a despot; you to whom has been infamously and absurdly attributed intentions contrary to your oaths, as if
your well-being was not attached to the Constitution—as if, invested with
another power than that of the law, you had a civil list to hire counterrevolutionary satellites; you whom, by the perfidious use of calumny and
the language of a hypocritical moderation, they wished to chill toward
the interests of the people, because they know that you hold your mission from the people, that the people is your support, and that if by a
guilty desertion of its cause you deserved to be abandoned by it, in turn
it would be easy to dissolve you; you whom they wanted and, it must be
said with sorrow, whom they have succeeded in weakening by fatal
divisions, but who doubtless in the present crisis, when the nation is fixing her anxious gaze on you, will feel the need of gathering together all
your forces; who will postpone until after the war our noisy quarrels and
our wretched dissensions; who will lay down at the foot of the altar of
liberty our pride, our jealousies, and our passions; who will not find this
mutual hatred so sweet that you will prefer its infernal enjoyment to the
welfare of the country; you whom they wanted to terrify with armed

petitions, as if you did not know that in the beginning of the Revolution the sanctuary of liberty was surrounded by the satellites of despotism, that Paris was besieged by an army, and that those days of danger were those of veritable glory for the Constituent Assembly; you, to whom I have believed I ought to present these swift reflections because at the moment when it is important to stir deeply public opinion it seemed to me indispensable to do away with all the illusions, all the errors, that might lessen the effect of your measures; you, finally, to whom each day discloses a vast horizon of conspiracies, treacheries, dangers; who are placed on the crater of Etna to ward off the thunderbolt—what are your resources? What does necessity command you? What does the Constitution allow you? . . .

First, I will call your attention to interior troubles. They have two causes: aristocratic maneuvers and priestly maneuvers. Both tend to the same end—counterrevolution. You will prevent the action of the first by means of a wise and vigorous police. We must hasten to discuss the bases of it; but when you have done everything that in you lay to save the people from the terrible influence of the second, the Constitution leaves at your further disposal only a last resort: it is simple; nevertheless, I believe that it is just and efficacious. This is it.

The King has refused his sanction to your resolution upon the religious troubles. I do not know whether the somber spirit of the Médicis and the Cardinal de Lorraine still wanders beneath the arches of the palace of the Tuileries; if the sanguinary hypocrisy of the Jesuits La Chaise and Le Tellier lives again in the soul of some monster burning to see a revival of Saint Bartholomew and the Dragonades; I do not know whether the King's heart is disturbed by the fantastic ideas suggested to him and his conscience disordered by the religious terrors with which he is environed.

But it is not possible to believe, without wronging him and accusing him of being the most dangerous enemy of the Revolution, that he wishes to encourage, by impunity, the criminal attempts of pontifical ambition, and to give to the proud agents of the tiara the disastrous power with which they have equally oppressed peoples and kings. It is not possible to believe, without wronging him and accusing him of being the enemy of the people, that he approves or even looks with indifference on the underhanded schemes employed to divide the citizens, to cast the leaven of hatred into the bosoms of sensitive souls, and to stifle in the name of the Divinity the sweetest sentiments of which He has composed the felicity of mankind. It is impossible to believe, without wronging him and accusing him of being the enemy of the law, that he withholds his consent to the adoption of repressive measures against fanaticism, in order to drive citizens to excesses that despair inspires and the laws condemn; that he prefers to expose unsworn priests, even when they do not disturb the peace, to arbitrary vengeance rather than to subject them to a law that, affecting only agitators, would cover the innocent with an inviolable aegis. Finally, it is not possible to believe, without wronging him and accusing him of being the enemy of the Empire, that he wishes to perpetuate sedition and to eternalize the disorders and all the revolutionary movements that are urging the Empire toward civil war, and which, through civil war, would plunge it into dissolution. . . .

It is *in the name of the King* that the French princes have tried to enlist all the courts of Europe against the nation; it is to *avenge the dignity of the King* that the treaty of Pillnetz was concluded and the monstrous alliance between the courts of Vienna and Berlin formed; it is *to defend the King* that we have seen the old companies of lifeguards, under the colors of rebellion, hastening to Germany; it is in order to *come to the King's aid* that the emigrants are soliciting and obtaining places in the Austrian army and are prepared themselves to rend their country; it is to join those valiant knights of the *royal prerogative* that other worthies full of honor and delicacy abandon their post in the face of the enemy, violate their oaths, steal the military chests, strive to corrupt their soldiers, and thus plunge their glory in dastardliness, perjury, subordination, theft, and assassination; it is against the nation, or the National Assembly alone, and in order to *maintain the splendor of the throne*, that the King of Bohemia and Hungary makes war upon us, and the King of Prussia marches upon our frontiers; it is *in the name of the King* that liberty is attacked, and if they succeeded in its overthrow it would be in his name that they indemnify the allied powers for their expenses; because we understand the generosity of kings; we know with what disinterestedness they dispatch their armies to desolate a foreign land, and up to what point they would exhaust their treasuries to maintain a war that could not be profitable to them. Finally, of all the evils they are striving to heap upon our heads, and of all those we have to fear, the *name alone of the King* is the pretext or the cause. . . .

If the King, charged with watching over the external safety of the state, with notifying the legislative body of imminent hostilities, informed of the movements of the Prussian army and not making it known in any way to the National Assembly; informed, or at least able to presume, that this army would attack us in a month, was slow in making preparations for repulsion; if there was a just anxiety about the progress the enemy might make into the interior of France, and if a reserve camp were evidently necessary to check or stop this progress; if there was a resolution making the formation of this camp an immediate certainty; if the King rejected this resolution and substituted for it a plan whose success was uncertain and that demanded so much time for its execution that the enemy would have time to make it impossible; if the legislative body passed resolutions of general safety; if the imminence of the peril allowed no delay; if nevertheless the royal assent was refused or deferred for two months; if the King should trust the command of an army to an intriguing general, suspected by the nation because of the most serious faults, and the most pronounced attempts upon the Constitution; if another general, bred far from the corruption of courts, and familiar with victory, should ask, for the glory of our arms, a reinforcement that it would be easy to grant him; if, by refusing, the King should clearly say to him: "I forbid you to conquer"; if, profiting by this baleful temporizing, by so much incoherence in our political course, or rather such constant perseverance in treachery, the league of tyrants should strike fatal blows at liberty— could it be said that the King had made the constitutional resistance, that he had taken, for the defense of the state, the steps contemplated by the Constitution that he had made along the line of the formal act that it prescribes? . . .

Coming to present circumstances, I do not think that if our armies are not yet at their full complement, it is through the malevolence of the King. I hope that he will soon increase our means of resistance by a useful employment of battalions so uselessly scattered in the interior of the kingdom; finally, I hope that the march of the Prussians through our national guards will not be as triumphal as they have the proud madness to imagine. I am not tormented by the fear of seeing realized the horrible suppositions that I have made; however, as the dangers with which we are invested impose upon us the obligation to foresee everything; as the facts that I have supposed are not devoid of striking conformity with several of the King's speeches; as it is certain that the false friends surrounding him have sold themselves to the conspirators of Coblentz; as they are burning to ruin him in order that some one of their chiefs may reap the fruit of the conspiracy; as it is important for his personal safety, as well as for the tranquillity of the kingdom, that his conduct be no longer encompassed with suspicions; as only great frankness in his proceedings and in his explanations can prevent extreme measures and the bloody quarrels the latter would give rise to, I should propose a message in which, after such interpellations as circumstances may make it advisable to address to him, would be presented the truths that I have stated; in which it would be demonstrated that the system of neutrality that they seem to be anxious to have him adopt toward Coblentz and France would be arrant treason in the King of the French; that it would bring him no other glory than profound horror from the nation and signal contempt from the conspirators; that, having already chosen France, he should loudly proclaim his unshakable resolution to triumph or perish with her and the Constitution. . . .

Will you wait until weary of the hardships of the Revolution or corrupted by the habit of groveling around a castle and the insidious preachings of *moderantism* [the principles of the moderate party in politics]—until weak men become accustomed to speak of liberty without enthusiasm and slavery without horror? How does it happen that the constituted authorities block one another in their course; that armed forces forget that they exist to obey; that soldiers or generals undertake to influence the legislative body, and distempered citizens to direct, by the machinery of violence, the action of the chief of the executive authority? Do they wish to establish a military government? That is perhaps the most imminent, the most terrible of our dangers. Murmurs are arising against the court: who shall dare to say they are unjust? It is suspected of treacherous plans; what facts can be cited to dispel these suspicions?

They speak of popular movements, of martial law; they try to familiarize the imagination with the blood of the people; the palace of the King of the French is suddenly changed to a redoubt; yet where are his enemies? Against whom are these cannons and these bayonets pointed? The defenders of the Constitution have been repulsed by the ministry; the reins of the Empire have been hanging loose at the moment when it needed as much vigor as patriotism to hold them. Everywhere discord is fomenting, fanaticism triumphing. Instead of taking a firm and patriotic attitude to save it from the storm, the government lets itself be driven before the tempest; its instability inspires foreign powers with scorn; the boldness of those who vomit armies and swords against us chills the good will of the peoples who wish in secret for the triumph of liberty. . . .

This means is worthy of the august mission that you fill, of the generous people whom you represent; it might even gain some celebrity for the name of that people and make you worthy to live in the memory of men: it will be to imitate the brave Spartans who sacrificed themselves at Thermopylae; those venerable men who, leaving the Roman Senate, went to await, at the thresholds of their homes, the death that marched in the van of the savage conqueror. No, you will not need to offer up prayers that avengers may spring from your ashes. Ah! The day your blood shall redden the earth, tyranny, its pride, its protectors, its palaces, its satellites, will vanish away forever before the national omnipotence. And if the sorrow of not having made your country happy embitters your last moments you will at least take with you the consolation that your

death will hasten the ruin of the people's oppressors and that your devotion will have saved liberty. . . .

If Vergniaud sought to stir his countrymen to action against the impending
perils both within and beyond the borders, and to identify the royal power as a
chief menace to security and freedom, there is little doubt that he was successful. His speech was printed in thousands of copies and dispatched by couriers
to all parts of the country, where it served to strengthen the suspicion of
Louis XVI's good faith. The idea of dethroning him and abolishing the monarchy burgeoned and grew in the light of such facts as Vergniaud had exposed.
On August 10 it was accomplished.

DANTON THUNDERS FOR UNITY

[September 2, 1792]

In August, 1792, the French Revolution passed into a deeper crisis. At midnight
on the ninth, the insurrectionists stormed the royal palace at Versailles, and
the revolutionary Commune, which took over power the next day, forced the
Assembly to suspend the King until he could be brought to trial. In place of
the throne, which was now empty, a six-man executive council was established,
consisting of Roland, Clavière, Servan, Monge, Lebrun, and Danton, who became Minister of Justice. In the meantime the Prussians were advancing steadily
into France. On September 2, the news arrived that Verdun was under siege
and would probably fall in a few days, leaving open the road to Paris. This was
the occasion for Danton's speech printed below.

Georges Jacques Danton (1759–94) was born in Arcis-sur-Aube. At the outbreak of the Revolution he was a rich Parisian lawyer with a good practice and
happily married. He was quickly drawn into politics and became a leader of the
Jacobin Club. In 1791 he was elected a substitute to the procureur of the
Commune of Paris and later, as we have noted, became Minister of Justice in
the executive council. Like Mirabeau, he insisted that the fruits of revolution
could only be preserved by a strong centralized government, but unlike Mirabeau, who wanted to strengthen the monarchy, Danton regarded Louis XVI as
a traitor and demanded dictatorial powers for the executive council that took
over his prerogative. No one did more than Danton to establish the revolutionary dictatorship, and his courage was always an inspiration. Yet his motives and
character have been a battleground for historians. Was he an honest, stalwart
champion of the Revolution, as Aulard held, or a scheming adventurer, sub-

sidized in devious plots first by England, then by the Duke of Orléans, and finally by the royalists of Brittany? The character of the man and the exigencies of the times might give color to both interpretations.

As an orator Danton gained much renown, though his speeches, unlike those of other orators of the period, were always extemporaneous and unadorned. They reflect the ardor and fury of the Revolution, and also its rationale.

"To conquer we have to dare, to dare again, always to dare!"

IT IS A SATISFACTION for the ministers of a free people to announce to them that their country will be saved. All are stirred, all are enthused, all burn to enter the combat.

You know that Verdun is not yet in the power of our enemies and that its garrison swears to immolate the first who breathes a proposition of surrender.

One portion of our people will guard our frontiers, another will dig and arm the entrenchments, the third with pikes will defend the interior of our cities. Paris will second these great efforts. The commissioners of the Commune will solemnly proclaim to the citizens the invitation to arm and march to the defense of the country. At such a moment you can proclaim that the capital deserves the esteem of all France. At such a moment this National Assembly becomes a veritable committee of war. We ask that you concur with us in directing this sublime movement of the people, by naming commissioners to second and assist all these great measures. We ask that anyone refusing to give personal service or to furnish arms shall meet the punishment of death. We ask that proper instructions be given to the citizens to direct their movements. We ask that carriers be sent to all the departments to notify them of the decrees that you proclaim here. The tocsin we shall sound is not the alarm signal of danger; it orders the charge on the enemies of France. To conquer we have to dare, to dare again, always to dare! And France will be saved!

Such an appeal for valor and unity in defense of the Revolution no doubt contributed to the upswing of French fortunes. Solidarity, strength, and confidence were returning. After the defeats of the Revolutionary army at Longwy and Verdun, the Prussians and their allies anticipated no difficulty in reaching Paris. A French force under Dumouriez and Kellermann, however, made an unexpected stand at Valmy on September 20, and in a few weeks the Prussians and their allies had been driven from the soil of France. On the day of the victory of Valmy the Republic was decreed. Goethe, who witnessed this victory, having joined the expedition under the Duke of Weimar, made a historic comment to his downcast companions: "From this place and from this day forth commences a new era in the world's history, and you can all say that you were present at its birth."

THOMAS ERSKINE DEFENDS TOM PAINE
FOR WRITING *THE RIGHTS OF MAN*

[December 18, 1792]

Burke's Reflections on the French Revolution, a book that did a great deal to bring about the revolutionary rigor of cruelty and despotism it had predicted, provoked a number of famous answers. William Godwin, the British philosophical anarchist, wrote Political Justice, but escaped trouble with the authorities because the book, though regarded as dangerous, was priced at two guineas; and James Mackintosh wrote a defense of the French Revolution called Vindiciae Gallicae and also kept out of trouble, probably because he promptly changed his opinions.

Such was not the case with Tom Paine, who was brought to trial in absentia, in 1792, charged with being a "wicked, malicious, seditious, and ill-disposed person," who had libeled the royal family and Parliament in his Rights of Man. A "special" jury, which is really an anomaly in a democracy, was assigned to hear the case. At this point Thomas Erskine, now the most celebrated trial lawyer in England, came forward as courageously as he had to defend Stockdale. In Paine's behalf he again volunteered to uphold the right of an Englishman to criticize political institutions.

The trial opened with the reading of a letter from Paine to the attorney general in which he answered the charges against him, and explained the intentions with which his book was written. Had it not been for his duties as an elected member of the National Convention in France, he said, he would have crossed the Channel to contest the injustice of the prosecution, "not upon my own account, for I cared not for the prosecution, but to defend the principles I had advanced in the work." The reading of this bold letter, which inveighed against the government of England and insulted the complacency of all well-to-do Englishmen, was bound to prejudice the special jury and to jeopardize Erskine's defense.

The jury, the attorney general, the spectators, and the country at large were already sufficiently inflamed against the French Revolution and against the

English reformers who admired or defended it. The French royal family had been roughly handled, the September massacres had shocked the world, and then word had come of the French victory over Prussia and Austria. France was growing stronger. The times were indeed serious, and the French declaration of war against England was only a few months away. Erskine rose to the defense not of Tom Paine (for he was safe in France), but of British liberties confronted by a revolutionary France.

> *"I can reason with the people of England, but I cannot fight against the thunder of authority."*

Gentlemen:

I SAY, in the name of Thomas Paine, and in his words as author of *The Rights of Man* as written in the very volume that is charged with seeking the destruction of property:

> The end of all political associations is the preservation of the rights of man, which rights are liberty, property, and security; that the nation is the source of all sovereignty derived from it; the right of property being secured and inviolable, no one ought to be deprived of it, except in cases of evident public necessity, legally ascertained, and on condition of a previous just indemnity.

These are undoubtedly the rights of man—the rights for which all governments are established—and the only rights Mr. Paine contends for; but which he thinks (no matter whether right or wrong) are better to be secured by a republican constitution than by the forms of the English government. He instructs me to admit that, when government is once constituted, no individuals, without rebellion, can withdraw their obedience from it—that all attempts to excite them to it are highly criminal, for the most obvious reasons of policy and justice—that nothing short of the will of a whole people can change or affect the rule by which a nation is to be governed—and that no private opinion, however honestly inimical to the forms or substance of the law, can justify resistance to its authority, while it remains in force. The author of *The Rights of Man* not only admits the truth of all this doctrine, but he consents to be convicted, and I also consent for him, unless his work shall be found studiously and painfully to inculcate these great principles of government which it is charged to have been written to destroy.

Let me not, therefore, be suspected to be contending that it is lawful to write a book pointing out defects in the English government, and exciting individuals to destroy its sanctions and to refuse obedience. But, on the other hand, I do contend that it is lawful to address the English nation on these momentous subjects; for had it not been for this inalienable right (thanks be to God and our fathers for establishing it!), how should we have had this Constitution which we so loudly boast of? If, in the march of the human mind, no man could have gone before the establishments of the time he lived in, how could our establishment, by reiterated changes, have become what it is? If no man could have awakened the public mind to errors and abuses in our government, how could it have passed on from stage to stage, through reformation and revolution, so as to have arrived from barbarism to such a pitch of happiness and perfection that the attorney general considers it as profanation to touch it further or to look for any future amendment?

In this manner power has reasoned in every age—government, in its own estimation, has been at all times a system of perfection; but a free press has examined and detected its errors, and the people have, from time to time, reformed them. This freedom has alone made our government what it is; this freedom alone can preserve it; and therefore, under the banners of that freedom, today I stand up to defend Thomas Paine But how, alas! shall this task be accomplished? How may I expect from you what human nature has not made man for the performance of? How am I to address your reasons, or ask them to pause, amidst the torrent of prejudice which has hurried away the public mind on the subject you are to judge? . . .

Was any Englishman ever so brought as a criminal before an English court of justice? If I were to ask you, gentlemen of the jury, what is the choicest fruit that grows upon the tree of English liberty, you would answer: security under the law. If I were to ask the whole people of England the return they looked for at the hands of government, for the burdens under which they bend to support it, I should still be answered: security under the law; or, in other words, an impartial administration of justice. So sacred, therefore, has the freedom of trial been ever held in England—so anxiously does Justice guard against every possible bias in her path—that if the public mind has been locally agitated upon any subject in judgment, the forum has either been changed or the trial postponed. The circulation of any paper that brings, or can be supposed to bring, prejudice, or even well-founded knowledge, within the reach of a British tribunal, on the spur of an occasion, is not only highly criminal, but defeats itself, by leading to put off the trial which its object was to pervert.

On this principle, the noble and learned judge will permit me to remind him that on the trial of the Dean of St. Asaph for a libel, or rather when he was brought to trial, the circulation of books by a society favorable to his defense was held by his lordship, as chief justice of Chester, to be a reason for not trying the cause, although they contained no matter relative to the Dean, nor to the object of his trial, being only extracts from ancient authors of high reputation, on the general rights of juries to consider the innocence as well as the guilt of the accused; yet still as the recollection of these rights was pressed forward with a view to affect the proceedings, the proceedings were postponed. . . .

The universal God of nature—the Saviour of mankind—the Fountain of all light, who came to pluck the world from eternal darkness, expired upon a cross—the scoff of infidel scorn; and His blessed Apostles followed Him in the train of martyrs. When He came in the flesh, He might have come like the Mohammedan Prophet, as a powerful sovereign, and propagated His religion with an unconquerable sword, which even now, after the lapse of ages, is but slowly advancing, under the influence of reason, over the face of the earth; but such a process would have been inconsistent with His mission, which was to confound the pride and to establish the universal rights of men; He came, therefore, in that lowly state which is represented in the Gospel, and preached His consolations to the poor.

When the foundation of this religion was discovered to be invulnerable and immortal, we find political power taking the Church into partnership; thus began the corruptions both of religious and civil power, and, hand in hand together, what havoc have they not made in the world! Ruling by ignorance and the persecution of truth, this very persecution only hastened the revival of letters and liberty. Nay, you will find that in the exact proportion that knowledge and learning have been beat down and fettered, they have destroyed the governments which bound them. The Court of Star Chamber, the first restriction of the press of England, was erected, previous to all the great changes in the Constitution. From that moment, no man could legally write without an imprimatur from the state; but truth and freedom found their way with greater force through secret channels, and the unhappy Charles, unwarned by a free press, was brought to an ignominious death. When men can freely communicate their thoughts and their sufferings, real or imaginary, their passions spend themselves in air, like gunpowder scattered upon the surface; but pent up by terrors, they work unseen, burst forth in a moment, and destroy everything in their course. Let reason be opposed to reason, and argument to argument, and every good government will be safe.

The usurper Cromwell pursued the same system of restraint in support of his government, and the end of it speedily followed.

At the restoration of Charles II, the Star Chamber Ordinance of 1637 was worked up into an act of Parliament, and was followed up during that reign, and the short one that followed it, by the most sanguinary prosecutions; but what fact in history is more notorious than that this blind and contemptible policy prepared and hastened the Revolution? At that great era these cobwebs were all brushed away; the freedom of the press was regenerated—and the country, ruled by its affections, has since enjoyed a century of tranquillity and glory. Thus I have maintained, by English history, that in proportion as the press has been free English government has been secure.

Gentlemen, the same important truth may be illustrated by great authorities. Upon a subject of this kind, resort cannot be had to law cases. The ancient law of England knew nothing of such libels; they began, and should have ended, with the Star Chamber. What writings are slanderous of individuals must be looked for where these prosecutions are recorded; but upon general subjects we must go to general writers. If, indeed, I were to refer to obscure authors, I might be answered that my very authorities were libels, instead of justifications or examples; but this cannot be said with effect of great men, whose works are classics in our language—taught in our schools—and repeatedly printed under the eye of government.

Milton . . . in his most eloquent address to the Parliament, puts the liberty of the press on its true and most honorable foundation:

"Believe it, lords and commons, they who counsel ye to such a suppression of books do as good as bid you suppress yourselves, and I will soon show how.

"If it be desired to know the immediate cause of all this free writing and free speaking, there cannot be assigned a truer than your own mild, and free, and humane government. It is the liberty, lords and commons, which your own valorous and happy counsels have purchased us; liberty, which is the nurse of all great wits; this is that which hath rarefied and enlightened our spirits like the influence of heaven; this is that which hath enfranchised, enlarged, and lifted up our apprehensions, degrees above themselves. Ye cannot make us now less capable, less knowing, less eagerly pursuing the truth, unless ye first make yourselves, that made us so, less the lovers, less the founders of our true liberty. We can grow ignorant again, brutish, formal, and slavish, as ye found us; but you then must first become that which ye cannot be, oppressive, arbitrary, and tyrannous, as they were from whom ye have freed us. That our hearts are now more capacious, our thoughts now more erected to the search and expectation of greatest and exactest things, is the issue of our own virtue propagated in us. Give me the liberty to know, to utter, and to argue freely according to conscience, above all liberties."

But now every man is to be cried down for such opinions. I observed that my learned friend significantly raised his voice in naming Mr. Horne Tooke, as if to connect him with Paine, or Paine with him. This is exactly the same course of justice, for, after all, he said nothing of Mr. Tooke. What could he have said, but that he was a man of great talents, and a subscriber with the great names I have read in proceedings which they have thought fit to desert?

Gentlemen, let others hold their opinions and change them at their pleasure; I shall ever maintain it to be the dearest privilege of the people of Great Britain to watch over everything that affects their happiness, either in the system of government or in the practice, and that for this purpose the press must be free. It has always been so, and much evil has been corrected by it. If government find itself annoyed by it, let it examine its own conduct, and it will find the cause—let it amend it, and it will find the remedy.

Gentlemen, I am no friend to sarcasms in the discussion of grave subjects, but you must take writers according to the view of the mind at the moment; Mr. Burke as often as anybody indulges in it—hear his reason in his speech on reform, for not taking away the salaries from lords who attend upon the British court. "You would," said he, "have the court deserted by all the nobility of the kingdom.

"Sir, the most serious mischiefs would follow from such a desertion. Kings are naturally lovers of low company; they are so elevated above all the rest of mankind that they must look upon all their subjects as on a level; they are rather apt to hate than to love their nobility on account of the occasional resistance to their will, which will be made by their virtue, their petulance, or their pride. It must, indeed, be admitted that many of the nobility are as perfectly willing to act the part of flatterers, talebearers, parasites, pimps, and buffoons, as any of the lowest and vilest of mankind can possibly be. But they are not properly qualified for this object of their ambition. The want of a regular education and early habits, with some lurking remains of their dignity, will never permit them to become a match for an Italian eunuch, a mountebank, a fiddler, a player, or any regular practitioner of that tribe. The Roman emperors, almost from the beginning, threw themselves into such hands, and the mischief increased every day till its decline and its final ruin. It is, therefore, of very great importance (provided the thing is not overdone), to contrive such an establishment as must, almost whether a prince will or not, bring into daily and hourly offices about his person a great number of his first nobility; and it is rather a useful prejudice that gives them a pride in such a servitude; though they are not much the better for a court, a court will be much the better for them. I have, therefore, not attempted to reform any of the offices of honor about the King's person."

What is all this but saying that a king is an animal so incurably addicted to low company as generally to bring on by it the ruin of nations; but, nevertheless, he is to be kept as a necessary evil, and his propensities bridled by surrounding him with a parcel of miscreants still worse, if possible, but better than those he would choose for himself. This, therefore, if taken by itself, would be a most abominable and libelous sarcasm on kings and nobility; but look at the whole speech, and you observe a great system of regulation; and no man, I believe, ever doubted Mr. Burke's attachment to monarchy. To judge, therefore, of any part of a writing, the whole must be read.

Milton wisely says that a disposition in a nation to this species of controversy is no proof of sedition or degeneracy, but quite the reverse (I omitted to cite the passage with the others). In speaking of this subject, he rises into that inexpressibly sublime style of writing wholly peculiar to himself. He was, indeed, no plagiary from anything human; he looked up for light and expression, as he himself wonderfully describes it, by devout prayer to that great Being who is the source of all utterance and knowledge, and who sendeth out His seraphim with the hallowed fire of His altar to touch and purify the lips of whom He pleases. "When the cheerfulness of the people," says this mighty poet, "is so sprightly up, as that it hath not only wherewith to guard well its own freedom and safety, but to spare, and to bestow upon the solidest and sublimest points of controversy and new invention, it betokens us not degenerated nor drooping to a fatal decay, but casting off the old and wrinkled skin of corruption, to outlive these pangs and wax young again, entering the glorious ways of truth and prosperous virtue, destined to become great and honorable in these latter ages. Methinks I see in my mind a noble and puissant nation rousing herself, like a strong man after sleep, and shaking her invincible locks; methinks I see her as an eagle mewing her mighty youth, and kindling her undazzled eyes at the full midday beam; purging and unscaling her long-abused sight at the fountain itself of heavenly radiance; while the whole noise of timorous and flocking birds, with those also that love the twilight, flutter about, amazed at what she means, and in their envious gabble would prognosticate a year of sects and schisms."

Gentlemen, what Milton only saw in his mighty imagination, I see in fact; what he expected, but which never came to pass, I see now fulfilling; methinks I see this noble and puissant nation, not degenerated and drooping to a fatal decay, but casting off the wrinkled skin of corruption to put on again the vigor of her youth. And it is because others as well as myself see this that we have all this uproar. France and its Constitution are the mere pretenses. It is because Britons begin to recollect the inheritance of their own Constitution left them by their ancestors; it is because they are awakened to the corruptions which have fallen upon its most valuable parts, that forsooth the nation is in danger of being destroyed by a single pamphlet. I have marked the course of this alarm; it began with the renovation of those exertions for the public which the alarmists themselves had originated and deserted; and they became louder and louder when they saw them avowed and supported by my admirable friend, Mr. Fox, the most eminently honest and enlightened statesman that history brings us acquainted with—a man whom to name is to honor, but whom in attempting adequately to describe I must fly to Mr. Burke, my constant refuge when eloquence is necessary—a man who, to relieve the sufferings of the most distant nation, "put to the hazard his ease, his security, his interest, his power, even his darling popularity, for the benefit of a people whom he had never seen." How much more, then, for the inhabitants of his native country! Yet this is the man who has been censured and disavowed in the manner we have lately seen.

Gentlemen, I have but a few more words to trouble you with: I take my leave of you with declaring that all this freedom which I have been endeavoring to assert is no more than the ancient freedom which belongs to our own inbred Constitution; I have not asked you to acquit Thomas Paine upon any new lights, or upon any principle but that of the law, which you are sworn to administer—my great object has been to inculcate that wisdom and policy which are the parents of the government of Great Britain, forbid this jealous eye over her subjects; and that, on the contrary, they cry aloud in the language of the poet, adverted to by Lord Chatham on the memorable subject of America, unfortunately without effect.

> Be to their faults a little blind,
> Be to their virtues very kind;
> Let all their thoughts be unconfin'd,
> Nor clap your padlock on the mind.

Engage the people by their affections, convince their reason—and they will be loyal from the only principle that can make loyalty sincere, vigorous, or rational—a conviction that it is their truest interest, and that their government is for their good. Constraint is the natural parent of resistance, and a pregnant proof that reason is not on the side of those who use it. You must all remember Lucian's pleasant story: Jupiter and a countryman were walking together, conversing with great freedom and familiarity upon the subject of heaven and earth. The countryman listened with attention and acquiescence, while Jupiter strove only to convince him—but happening to hint a doubt, Jupiter turned hastily around and threatened him with his thunder. "Ah! ah!" says the countryman, "now, Jupiter, I know that you are wrong; you are always wrong when you appeal to your thunder."

This is the case with me—I can reason with the people of England, but I cannot fight against the thunder of authority.

Gentlemen, this is my defense of free opinions. With regard to myself, I am, and always have been, obedient and affectionate to the law—to that rule of action, as long as I exist, I shall ever do as I have done today, maintain the dignity of my high profession, and perform, as I understand them, all its important duties.

Nothing could have been more humiliating than the response to Erskine's plea. When the great advocate had finished speaking, the attorney general rose to give his reply, but before he could speak, the foreman of the jury also rose. "My Lord," he said, "your reply will be unnecessary, unless you want to make it. The jury has already reached its verdict without any need for argument. The verdict is guilty!"

Safe in France, Paine was active in the National Convention and helped frame the Constitution of 1793, but his views soon became too moderate for the extremists, and he barely escaped from the guillotine. He now wrote The Age of Reason, a radical, deistic criticism of the Bible. The publisher of this book was successfully prosecuted for blasphemy in England, the government being represented by none other than Thomas Erskine.

In 1802, Paine, who had been a hero in the American Revolution, returned to America to find himself unhonored and unwanted. The few remaining years of his life he devoted to such nonpolitical subjects as iron bridges and yellow fever.

DANTON REINVIGORATES
HIS COUNTRYMEN

[March 10, 1793]

As the Revolution advanced into greater terror, and made irreparable decisions, it gained in revolutionary clarity. There was no escaping the fact that as long as Louis XVI lived he would be a menace to the Republic. The Mountain, led by Robespierre, would have condemned him as a measure of public safety, without trial, whereas the Girondists insisted on a trial, which accordingly was held. The result, however, was preordained, and on January 21, 1793, the King was guillotined. Away on a secret mission in Belgium, Danton did not take part in the trial proceedings, but returned in time to vote "death to the tyrant," and against the proposed respite. This execution was the signal for new military operations by the Austrians, and now every crown of Europe seemed insecure. A powerful anti-French coalition was forming. On February 1, France anticipated the attack and declared war on England, Holland, and Spain. Now there would be no turning back.

The news that Danton and Lacroix brought back from Belgium early in March, 1793, was bad indeed. The Austrians, strongly reinforced, had reoccupied Aix-la-Chapelle, and an army composed of English, Dutch, and Hanoverians was being assembled in Holland. The Convention in Paris responded quickly by an order for the mustering of 300,000 men, and Danton warned of the extremity of the situation. On March 10, he gave two speeches in the Convention, the first calling for a return to the unity and courage that had enabled France to defeat the Prussians the previous September, the second demanding a tribunal to deal with traitors. On this very day the rumor had spread that France's most brilliant general, Dumouriez, had surrendered, and that another French general, Miranda, had been obliged to retire from Maastricht with loss of artillery and supplies. It was a divided and frightened Convention that Danton addressed. There were riots in the streets of Paris.

"Your enemies are making their last efforts."

THE GENERAL CONSIDERATIONS that have been presented to you are true; but at this moment it is less necessary to examine the causes of the disasters that have struck us than to apply their remedy rapidly. When the edifice is on fire, I do not join the rascals who would steal the furniture, I extinguish the flames. I tell you therefore you should be convinced by the dispatches of Dumouriez that you have not a moment to spare in saving the Republic.

Dumouriez conceived a plan that did honor to his genius. I would render him greater justice and praise than I did recently. But three months ago he announced to the executive power, your General Committee of Defense, that if we were not audacious enough to invade Holland in the middle of winter, to declare instantly against England the war that actually we had long been making, we would double the difficulties of our campaign, in giving our enemies the time to deploy their forces. Since we failed to recognize this stroke of his genius, we must now repair our faults.

Dumouriez is not discouraged; he is in the middle of Holland, where he will find munitions of war; to overthrow all our enemies, he wants but Frenchmen, and France is filled with citizens. Would we be free? If we no longer desire it, let us perish, for we have all sworn it. If we wish it, let all march to defend our independence. Your enemies are making their last efforts. Pitt, recognizing he has all to lose, dares spare nothing. Take Holland, and Carthage is destroyed and England can no longer exist but for Liberty! Let Holland be conquered to Liberty; and even the commercial aristocracy itself, which at the moment dominates the English people, would rise against the government that had dragged it into this despotic war against a free people. They would overthrow this ministry of stupidity, who thought the methods of the *ancien régime* could smother the genius of Liberty breathing in France. This ministry once overthrown in the interests of commerce, the party of Liberty would show itself, for it is not dead! And if you know your duties, if your commissioners leave at once, if you extend the hand to the strangers aspiring to destroy all forms of tyranny, France is saved and the world is free.

Expedite, then, your commissioners; sustain them with your energy; let them leave this very night, this very evening.

Let them say to the opulent classes, the aristocracy of Europe must succumb to our efforts, and pay our debt, or you will have to pay it! The people have nothing but blood—they lavish it! Go, then, ingrates, and lavish your wealth! See, citizens, the fair destinies that await you. What! you have a whole nation as a lever, its reason as your fulcrum, and you have not yet upturned the world! To do this we need firmness and character, and of a truth we lack it. I put to one side all passions. They are all strangers to me save a passion for the public good.

In the most difficult situations, when the enemy was at the gates of Paris, I said to those governing: "Your discussions are shameful, I can see

but the enemy. You tire me by squabbling in place of occupying yourselves with the safety of the Republic! I repudiate you all as traitors to
our country! I place you all in the same line!" I said to them: "What care I
for my reputation! Let France be free, though my name were accursed!"
What care I that I am called "a blood drinker"! Well, let us drink the
blood of the enemies of humanity, if needful; but let us struggle, let us
achieve freedom. Some fear the departure of the commissioners may
weaken one or the other section of this Convention. Vain fears! Carry your
energy everywhere. The pleasantest declaration will be to announce to the
people that the terrible debt weighing upon them will be wrested from
their enemies or that the rich will shortly have to pay it. The national situation is cruel. The representatives of value are no longer in equilibrium
in the circulation. The day of the workingman is lengthened beyond necessity. A great corrective measure is necessary! Conquerors of Holland
reanimate in England the Republican party; let us advance France, and
we shall go glorified to posterity. Achieve these grand destinies; no more
debates, no more quarrels, and the Fatherland is saved.

*The solidarity and military prowess that Danton sought to re-create in his first
speech were not sufficient to turn the tide of adversity threatening the Republic,
and there were darker days ahead, more treason, more military reverses. The
revolutionary tribunal he advocated in his second speech became a reality. It
might be a sinister tyranny, a Venetian Inquisition, as his enemies averred, but
it was necessary to the freedom, to the success, of the Revolution. That was
enough. With the enemy at the gates, counterrevolutionary traitors could not
be protected. Danton won his point.*

VERGNIAUD ADMITS TO ROBESPIERRE'S CHARGES OF MODERATION

[April 10, 1793]

*In February the news of the defeat of Dumouriez's generals in Holland threw
France into new alarms. The treason of the greatest French military leader
quickly followed. After two defeats at the hands of the Austrians in March,
Dumouriez opened negotiations with them, agreeing to evacuate Holland and
Belgium on condition that he be permitted to march on Paris without being
harassed, there to overthrow the Convention and restore the monarchy. His*

plan miscarried because his troops refused to follow him. At the same time the French under General Custine were retreating before the Prussians in the Rhineland.

Betrayal and military reverses on the frontiers were matched by revolt and distress at home. Civil war was raging in the Vendée; a flood of new assignats (cheap money) pauperized the consumer; food was scarce, and prices were high, while grain speculators and war contractors amassed fortunes. The indignation of the people reached a feverish pitch, and the Girondists, sinking deeper in disfavor every day, could do nothing to restore the credit of the government, which was so largely their creation. Were they implicated in the desertion of their general, Dumouriez? Were they responsible for the worsening conditions within France? What new betrayal were they planning? Gradually the program of the Enragés gained support: to unite the Convention by evicting the Girondist leaders. On April 10 Robespierre brought the matter to a head by openly charging these leaders with complicity with Dumouriez, specifically naming "such patriots as Brissot, Vergniaud, Gensonné, Gaudet." He charged that they were conspiring to restore the monarchy with the help of foreign arms and internal troubles. Such an outcome, he said, "would please all bourgeois aristocrats, who have a horror of equality, who fear for their property." Vergniaud, who had foreseen this deadly charge, took the tribunal to give a carefully prepared speech. Here is the peroration.

"I wanted punishments but not proscriptions."

ROBESPIERRE accuses us of having suddenly become "Moderates" —monks of the order of St. Bernard. Moderates—we? I was not such, on the tenth of August, Robespierre, when thou didst hide in thy cellar. Moderates! No, I am not such a Moderate that I would extinguish the national energy. I know that liberty is ever as active as a blazing flame —that it is irreconcilable with the inertia that is fit only for slaves! Had we tried but to feed that sacred fire which burns in my heart as ardently as in that of the men who talk incessantly about "the impetuosity" of their character, such great dissensions would never have arisen in this Assembly. I know that in revolutionary times it was as great a folly to pretend the ability to calm on the spur of the moment the effervescence of the people as it would be to command the waves of the ocean when they are beaten by the wind. Thus it behooves the lawmaker to prevent as much as he can the storm's disaster by wise counsel. But if under the pretext of revolution it become necessary, in order to be a patriot, to become the declared protector of murder and of robbery—then I am a "Moderate"!

Since the abolition of the monarchy, I have heard much talk of revolution. I said to myself: there are but two more revolutions possible: that of property or the Agrarian Law, and that which would carry us back to despotism. I have made a firm resolution to resist both the one and the other and all the indirect means that might lead us to them. If that can be construed as being a "Moderate," then we are all such; for we all have voted for the death penalty against any citizen who would propose either one of them.

I have also heard much said about insurrection—of attempts to cause risings of the people—and I admit I have groaned under it. Either the insurrection has a determined object or it has not; in the latter case, it is a convulsion for the body politic, which, since it cannot do it good, must necessarily do it a great deal of harm. The wish to force insurrection can find lodgment nowhere but in the heart of a bad citizen. If the insurrection has a determined object, what can it be? To transfer the exercise of sovereignty to the Republic. The exercise of sovereignty is confided to the national representatives. Therefore, those who talk of insurrection are trying to destroy national representation; therefore, they are trying to deliver the exercise of sovereignty to a small number of men, or to transfer it upon the head of a single citizen; therefore, they are endeavoring to found an aristocratic government or to re-establish royalty. In either case, they are conspiring against the Republic and liberty, and if it become necessary either to approve them in order to be a patriot or be a "Moderate" in battling against them, then I am a Moderate!

When the statue of liberty is on the throne, insurrection can be called into being only by the friends of royalty. By continually shouting to the people that they must rise; by continuing to speak to them, not the language of the laws, but that of the passions, arms have been furnished to the aristocracy. Taking the living and the language of sansculottism, it has cried out to the Finistère department: "You are unhappy; the assignats are at a discount; you ought to rise en masse." In this way the exaggerations have injured the Republic. We are "Moderates"! But for whose profit have we shown this great moderation? For the profit of the *émigrés*? We have adopted against them all the measures of rigor that were imposed by justice and national interest. For the profit of inside conspirators? We have never ceased to call upon their heads the sword of the law. But I have demurred against the law that threatened to proscribe the innocent as well as the guilty. There was endless talk of terrible measures, of revolutionary measures. I also was in favor of them—these terrible measures, but only against the enemies of the country. I did not want them to compromise the safety of good citizens, for the reason that some unprincipled wretches were interested in their undoing. I wanted punishments but not proscriptions. Some men have appeared as if their patriotism consisted in tormenting others—in causing tears to flow! I would have wished that there should be none but happy people! The Convention is the center around which all citizens should rally! It may be that their gaze fixed upon it is not always free from fear and anxiety. I would have wished that it should be the center of all their affections and of all their hopes. Efforts were made to accomplish the revolution by terror. I should have preferred to bring it about by love. In short, I have not thought that, like the priests and the fierce ministers of the Inquisition, who spoke of their God of Mercy only when they were surrounded by autos-da-fé and stakes, we should speak of liberty surrounded by daggers and executioners!

You say we are "Moderates"! Ah! let thanks be offered us for this moderation of which we are accused as if it were a crime! If, when in this tribune they came to wave the brands of discord and to outrage with the most insolent audacity the majority of the representatives of the people; if, when they shouted with as much fury as folly: "No more truce! No more peace between us!" we had given way to the promptings of a just indignation; if we had accepted the counterrevolutionary challenge which was tendered to us—I declare to my accusers (and no matter what suspicions they create against us, no matter what the calumnies with which they try to tarnish us, our names still remain more esteemed than theirs) that we would have seen, coming in haste from all the provinces to combat the men of the second of September, men equally formidable to anarchy and to tyrants! And our accusers and we ourselves would be already consumed by the fire of civil war. Our moderation has saved the country from this terrible scourge, and by our silence we have deserved well of the Republic!

I have not passed by, without reply, any of Robespierre's calumnies or of his ramblings. I come now to the petition denounced by Pétion; but, as this petition is connected with a general scheme of mischief, allow me to treat of the facts from a higher point of view.

On the tenth of March, a conspiracy broke out against the National Convention. I denounced it to you then. I named some of the leaders. I read to you the decrees taken in the name of the two sections by some intriguers who had slipped into their midst. A pretense was made of throwing doubts on the facts; the existence of the decrees was considered as uncertain. Nevertheless, the facts were attested even by the municipality of Paris. The existence of the decrees was confirmed by the sections who came to disavow them and to inform against the authors.

You ordered, by a decree, that the guilty parties should be prosecuted before the Revolutionary Tribunal. The crime is acknowledged. What heads have fallen? None. What accomplice has even been arrested? None. You yourselves have contributed to render your decree illusory. You have ordered Fournier to appear at the bar of your court. Fournier admitted that he was present at the first gathering that took place at the Jacobins; that from there he had gone to the Cordeliers, the place of the general meeting; that, at that meeting, there was a question of proceeding to ring the alarm bell, to close the barriers, and to slaughter a number of the members of the Convention. But because he stated that, in the scenes in which he had participated, he had not been animated by evil intentions; and—as if to butcher a part of the Convention had not been reputed as an evil—you set him at liberty by ordering that he should be heard later on as a witness, if it was thought best, before the Revolutionary Tribunal. It is as if in Rome the Senate had decreed that Lentulus might become a witness in the conspiracy of Catiline!

This inconceivable weakness rendered powerless the sword of the law and taught your enemies that you were not to be dreaded by them. At once a new plot was formed that manifested itself by the constitution of this central committee which was to correspond with all the provinces. This plot was counteracted by the patriotism of the section *du Mail*, who denounced it to you; you ordered before your bar the members of this central committee; did they obey your decree? No. Who then are you? Have you ceased to be the representatives of the people? Where are the new men whom they have endowed with their almighty power? So they insult your decree; so you are shamefully bandied about from one plot to another. Pétion has let you into the secret of still another one. In the petition of the *Halle-au-Blé*, the dissolution of the National Convention is being arranged for, by accusing the majority of corruption; opprobrium is being poured upon them from full cups; the formal design is announced of changing the form of the government, inasmuch as they have made manifest that of concentrating the exercise of sovereign authority in the small number of men therein represented as the only ones worthy of public confidence.

It is not a petition that is being submitted to your wisdom. These are supreme orders that they dare dictate to you. You are notified that it is for the last time that the truth is being told you; you are notified that you have but to choose between your expulsion or bow to the law that is imposed on you. And on these insolent threats, on these burning insults, the order of the day or a simple disapproval is quietly proposed to you! And now then! how do you expect good citizens to stand by you if you do not know how to sustain yourselves? Citizens! were you but simple individuals, I could say to you: "Are you cowards? Well, then; abandon yourselves to the chances of events; wait in your stupidity until your throats are cut or you are driven out." But there is here no question of your personal safety; you are the representatives of the people; the safety of the Republic is at stake; you are the depositaries of her liberty and of her glory. If you are dissolved, anarchy succeeds you, and despotism succeeds to anarchy. Any man conspiring against you is an ally of Austria. You are convinced of it, as you have decreed that he shall be punished by death. Do you wish to be consistent? Cause your decrees to be carried out, or revoke them, or order the barriers of France to be opened to the Austrians and decree that you will be the slaves of the first robber who may wish to put his chains upon you.

The greatest orator of the Girondists, Vergniaud displayed their worst shortcomings, and even his admirers do not extol his statesmanship. Although for nine months the Girondists had a majority in the Convention and enjoyed wide popularity in the nation, they showed themselves incapable of solving domestic problems or of bringing the war they had commenced to a successful issue. Their failure on both fronts involved them in a life-and-death struggle with the clearheaded, vigorous, but ruthless men of the Mountain and with its leader, the "incorruptible" Robespierre. From this contest there was no turning back and no victory possible. Two months after Vergniaud's speech of April 10, the blow fell. By the coup d'état of June 2 the Girondist leaders, including Vergniaud, were expelled from the Convention. Brought to trial in October, he was still feared for his eloquence. He was not allowed to make the defense he had planned, but was condemned to death with twenty-three of his colleagues. The story is that they went to their death bravely, singing La Marseillaise. They were to be followed by many other patriots, both true and false. The Revolution, as Vergniaud had predicted, would, like Saturn, devour its own children.

ROBESPIERRE RECOMMENDS
VIRTUE AND TERROR

[February 5, 1794]

The most famous and controversial leader of the second half of the French Revolution, Maximilien François Marie Isidore de Robespierre (1758–94), was born at Arras, and there was admitted to the bar in 1781. The next year he was appointed judge of a tribunal in Arras, but soon resigned because of a horror of pronouncing the death sentence. With the convocation of the States-General, his political career began, and he was elected deputy from Artois. In the course of the next two years his democratic harangues made him the darling of the people of Paris and of the Jacobin Club. On June 22, 1791, he won favor by arguing that the flight of the King to Varennes was a conspiracy of the enemies of the Revolution at home and abroad, and shortly afterward he declared his firm opposition to the war policy of Brissot, which, as we have seen, had the support of Vergniaud and other Girondist leaders.

With Danton and Marat, Robespierre now became an implacable enemy of whatever was confused, inefficient, or temporizing. In the late fall of 1792, he argued effectively against the absurdity of granting the King a trial, and defended himself with such skill against the slashing attack of Louvet that he became from then on the recognized leader of the Mountain. By May 31, 1793, the Mountain had triumphed over the Girondists. By midsummer Robespierre, as a member of the Committee of Public Safety, became one of the rulers of France and the chief philosopher and strategist of the Revolution. Danton, as we have seen, had done more than anyone else to establish the Committee of Public Safety and had worked to make its powers absolute. Robespierre did not object to Danton's political theories, but to his dangerous power, his moral laxness, and perhaps his venality. Purity, both moral and political, were as typical of Robespierre as were logical rigor and ruthlessness, and even his worst enemies, though they might hate the tyrant, could not hint at corruption. His appearance and manner, from all accounts, were insignificant, or even absurd.

"His power as a speaker even in his eloquent moments," says J. M. Thompson, "lay less in the manner of his delivery than in the seriousness of what he had to say, and the deep conviction with which he said it. . . . Robespierre would have been as unconvincing in the House of Commons as a Welsh revivalist in a university church: but in the Assembly, or in the tribune of the Jacobin Club, he was one of the world's great orators." His report before the Convention on the principles of morality that ought to guide the Convention *was indeed "one of the most remarkable confessions of faith that was ever made by a responsible statesman."*

> *"Terror is nothing else than justice, prompt,*
> *secure, and inflexible!"*

AFTER having marched for a long time at hazard, and, as it were, carried away by the movement of contrary factions, the representatives of the people have at last formed a government. A sudden change in the nation's fortune announced to Europe the regeneration that had been operated in the national representation; but up to this moment we must admit that we have been rather guided in these stormy circumstances by the love of good, and by a sense of the country's wants, than by any exact theory or precise rules of conduct.

It is time to distinguish clearly the aim of the Revolution and the term to which we would arrive. It is time for us to render account to ourselves, both of the obstacles which still keep us from that aim and of the means which we ought to take to attain it.

What is the aim to which we tend?

The peaceful enjoyment of liberty and equality; the reign of that eternal justice of which the laws have been engraved, not upon marble, but upon the hearts of all mankind—even in the hearts of the slaves who forget them or of the tyrants who have denied them! We desire a state of things wherein all base and cruel passions shall be enchained, all generous and beneficent passions awakened by the laws; wherein ambition should be the desire of glory, and glory the desire of serving the country; wherein distinctions should arise but from equality itself; wherein the citizen should submit to the magistrate, the magistrate to the people, and the people to justice; wherein the country assures the welfare of every individual; wherein every individual enjoys with pride the prosperity and the glory of his country; wherein all minds are enlarged by the continual communication of republican sentiments and by the desire of meriting the esteem of a great people; wherein arts should be the decorations of that liberty which they ennoble, and commerce the source of public wealth and not the monstrous opulence of some few houses. We desire to substitute morality for egotism, probity for honor, principles for usages, duties for functions, the empire of reason for the tyranny of fashions, the scorn of vice for the scorn of misfortune, pride for insolence, greatness of soul for vanity, the love of glory for the love of money, good citizens for good society, merit for intrigue, genius for cleverness, truth for splendor, the charm of happiness for the ennui of voluptuousness, the grandeur of man for the pettiness of the great, a magnanimous people, powerful, happy, for a people amiable, frivolous, and miserable; that is to say, all the virtues and all the miracles of a republic for all the vices and all the follies of a monarchy.

What is the nature of the government that can realize these prodigies? The democratic or republican government.

Democracy is that state in which the people, guided by laws that are its own work, executes for itself all that it can well do, and, by its delegates, all that it cannot do itself. But to found and consolidate democracy, we must first end the war of liberty against tyranny, and traverse the storm of the Revolution. Such is the aim of the revolutionary system you have organized; you ought, therefore, to regulate your conduct by the circumstances in which the Republic finds itself; and the plan of your administration ought to be the result of the spirit of revolutionary government, combined with the general principles of democracy.

The great purity of the French Revolution, the sublimity even of its object, is precisely that which makes our force and our weakness. Our force, because it gives us the ascendency of truth over imposture, and the rights of public interest over private interest. Our weakness, because it rallies against us all the vicious; all those who in their hearts meditate the robbery of the people; all those who, having robbed them, seek impunity; all those who have rejected liberty as a personal calamity; and those who have embraced the Revolution as a trade and the Republic as a prey. Hence the defection of so many ambitious men, who have abandoned us on our route because they did not commence the journey to arrive at the same object as we did. We must crush both the interior and exterior enemies of the Republic, or perish with her. And in this situation, the first maxim of your policy should be to conduct the people by reason and the enemies of the people by terror. If the spring of popular government during peace is virtue, the spring of popular government in rebellion is at once both virtue and terror; virtue, without which terror is fatal! terror, without which virtue is powerless! Terror is nothing else than justice, prompt, secure, and inflexible! It is, therefore, an emanation of virtue; it is less a particular principle than a consequence of the general principles of democracy, applied to the most urgent wants of the country.

It has been said that terror is the instrument of a despotic government. Does yours, then, resemble despotism? Yes, as the sword which glitters in the hand of a hero of liberty resembles that with which the satellites of tyranny are armed! The government of a revolution is the despotism of liberty against tyranny. Is force, then, only made to protect crime? Is it not also made to strike those haughty heads which the lightning has doomed? Nature has imposed upon every being the law of self-preservation. Crime massacres innocence to reign, and innocence struggles with all its force in the hands of crime. Let tyranny but reign one day, and on the morrow there would not remain a single patriot. Until when will the fury of tyranny continue to be called justice, and the justice of the people barbarity and rebellion? How tender they are to oppressors—how inexorable to the oppressed! Nevertheless, it is necessary that one or the other should succumb. Indulgence for the Royalist! exclaimed certain people. Pardon for wretches! No! Pardon for innocence, pardon for the weak, pardon for the unhappy, pardon for humanity!

There were as yet no voices in the Convention strong enough to contest Robespierre's power or to countermand his inexorable program. The man who had resigned as judge in 1782 because he could not bear to impose death sentences, and had argued brilliantly for the abolition of the death penalty in 1791, now defended the Terror and praised the tireless work of the guillotine. Was this inconsistency, or was it a realistic acknowledgment of the abnormal requirements of the time? Did power corrupt Robespierre, as the followers of Burke or Lord Acton would say, or was the Terror the only means of saving the Republic? The greatest authorities on the French Revolution have differed. For Aulard he was a tyrant, for Mathiez, a wise, farseeing, resolute statesman with a moderate program of reform, a program that France has long since adopted. There is no question that he was a devout idealist. If he believed that cruel measures were justified, it was because he also believed that men were capable of complete virtue.

ROBESPIERRE FACES
THE GUILLOTINE

[July 26, 1794]

During the last six or seventh months of his life, Robespierre traveled the notunusual road of a revolutionary hero, from the dizziest pinnacle of glory to the very gutter of obloquy. Possibly for the loftiest reasons, possibly merely because of a quenchless hunger for power, this inscrutable man quickly climbed over the bodies of friends and enemies alike to become all but the crowned ruler of

France. First the Hébertists of the extreme Left were crushed, and finally, on April 5, 1794, Danton was hurriedly brought to trial and executed, paradoxically mourned by Robespierre, who had long admired and supported his policies.

The events of the next three and a half months showed that Robespierre had a plan of bringing stability to France. The time seemed ripe, what with success on the frontiers and comparative calm in the interior. Before Robespierre's mind hovered a Rousseauian ideal of a free nation based on virtue, but to reach this happy state he was convinced that religion was indispensable. So he invented a new deistic religion of the Supreme Being—with a creed of fifteen articles—inaugurating it with a magnificent fete on June 8. Despite floats and fireworks that did not quite function the way they should, it was the kind of show Paris liked.

Meanwhile millions of landless peasants and jobless, hungry city workers were asking why the Committee of Public Safety was doing so little to relieve their condition. Robespierre was preoccupied with inculcating virtue and stamping out vice—in fact, the vicious were to be proscribed. When Robespierre carried a law by which deputies could be tried by order of the Committee of Public Safety, with no proof of guilt required, he gave his own death sentence. All except his friends Saint-Just and Couthon were involved in one vast plot against him. He was blamed for every conceivable evil of the time, including his many reforms, not all of which were working out.

On July 26, the "sea-green incorruptible," as Carlyle called him, rose bravely, a meager, bespectacled creature, impeccably neat, and faced the infuriated Convention to deliver his last speech.

"What objection can be made to him who wishes
to tell the truth and consents to die for it?"

WHEN I see the mass of vices the torrent of the Revolution has rolled pell-mell with the civic virtues, I have sometimes trembled for fear of becoming tainted in the eyes of posterity by the impure vicinage of those perverse men who mingled in the ranks of the sincere defenders of humanity; but the overthrow of the rival factions has, as it were, emancipated all the vices; they believed that the only question for them was to make division of the country as a booty rather than make her free and prosperous. I am thankful that the fury that animates them against everything that opposes itself to their projects has traced the line of demarcation between them and all right-minded people; but if the

Verres and the Catilines of France believe themselves already far enough advanced in the career of crime to expose on the rostrum the head of their accuser, I also have but now promised to my fellow citizens a testament formidable to the oppressors of the people, and I bequeath to them from this moment opprobrium and death!

I conceive that it is easy for the league of the tyrants of the world to overwhelm a man; but I also know what are the duties of one who can die in defending the cause of humanity. I have seen in history all defenders of liberty overcome by ill fortune or by calumny; but soon their oppressors and their assassins also met their death. The good and the bad, the tyrants and the friends of liberty, disappear from the earth, but under different conditions. Frenchmen, do not allow your enemies to degrade your souls and to unnerve your virtues by a baleful heresy! No, Chaumette, no, Fouchet, death is not an unending sleep. Citizens, efface from the tombstones this impious maxim which throws a funeral crape upon all nature and flings insults upon death. Rather engrave that: "Death is the beginning of immortality!" My people, remember that if in the Republic justice does not reign with absolute sway, and if this word does not signify love of equality and of country, then liberty is but a vain phrase! O people, you who are feared—whom one flatters! you who are despised; you who are acknowledged sovereign, and are ever being treated as a slave—remember that wherever justice does not reign, it is the passions of the magistrates that reign instead, and that the people have changed their chains and not their destinies!

Remember that there exists in your bosom a league of knaves struggling against public virtue, and that it has a greater influence than yourselves upon your own affairs—a league that dreads you and flatters you in the mass, but proscribes you in detail in the person of all good citizens!

Also recall it that, instead of sacrificing this handful of knaves for your happiness, your enemies wish to sacrifice you to this handful of knaves— authors of all our evils and the only obstacles to public prosperity!

Know, then, that any man who will rise to defend public right and public morals will be overwhelmed with outrage and proscribed by the knaves! Know, also, that every friend of liberty will ever be placed between duty and calumny; that those who cannot be accused of treason will be accused of ambition; that the influence of uprightness and principles will be compared to tyranny and the violence of factions; that your confidence and your esteem will become certificates of proscription for all your friends; that the cries of oppressed patriotism will be called cries of sedition; and that, as they do not dare to attack you in mass, you will be proscribed in detail in the person of all good citizens, until the ambitious shall have organized their tyranny. Such is the empire of the tyrants armed against us! Such is the influence of their league with corrupt men, ever inclined to serve them. Thus the unprincipled wretches impose upon us law to force us to betray the people, under penalty of being called dictators! Shall we subscribe to this law? No! Let us defend the people at the risk of becoming their victims! Let them hasten to the scaffold by the path of crime and we by that of virtue. Shall we say that all is well? Shall we continue to praise by force of habit or practice that which is wrong? We would ruin the country. Shall we reveal hidden abuses? Shall we denounce traitors?

We shall be told that we are unsettling the constituted authorities, that we are endeavoring to acquire personal influence at their cost. What are we to do? Our duty! What objection can be made to him who wishes to tell the truth and who consents to die for it? Let us then say that there exists a conspiracy against public liberty; that it owes its strength to a criminal coalition that is intriguing even in the bosom of the Convention; that this coalition has accomplices in the Committee of General Safety and in the offices of this committee, which they control; that the enemies of the Republic have opposed this committee to the Committee of Public Safety and have thus constituted two governments; that members of the Committee of Public Safety have entered into this scheme of mischief; that the coalition thus formed tries to ruin all patriots and the fatherland.

What is the remedy for this evil? Punish the traitors, renew the offices of the Committee of General Safety, weed out this committee itself, and subordinate it to the Committee of Public Safety; weed out the Committee of Public Safety also, constitute the unity of the government under the supreme authority of the National Convention, which is the center and the judge, and thus crush all factions by the weight of national authority, in order to erect upon their ruins the power of justice and of liberty. Such are my principles. If it be impossible to support them without being taken for an ambitious one, I shall conclude that principles are proscribed and that tyranny reigns among us, but not that I should remain silent! For what can be objected to a man who is in the right and knows how to die for his country?

I was created to battle against crime, not to govern it. The time has not come when upright men may serve their country with impunity! The defenders of liberty will be but outlaws so long as a horde of knaves shall rule!

The veteran statesman and lawgiver of thirty-six years had returned to the Convention to defend himself and to deliver a foursquare attack on his enemies.

At first it seemed that he had succeeded. Couthon's motion that his speech be printed and circulated as usual was carried. But the foes of the reign of virtue were strong enough to revoke the order, and though Robespierre read his speech to the Jacobin Club that night amid acclamation, it never reached the public. When he entered the Convention the next day he was greeted by shouts of "Down with the tyrant!" The president of the Convention forbade him to speak, and Barère, representing the Committee of Public Safety, read a statement condemning his policies. Robespierre struggled to speak, but his voice was lost in the sudden tumult that arose. Had he come to terms with the corrupt deputies of the Convention, he might well have preserved his power, but there was something in the man that prevented this, and now it was too late. Together with his friends Saint-Just, Couthon, and Le Bas, he was arrested and imprisoned. Although the insurrectionary Commune, which was devoted to him, succeeded in rescuing him and his colleagues, it was not strong enough, or had too little time, to carry out an effective revolt against the Convention. Robespierre was outlawed, and as the troops stormed the Hôtel de Ville in which he had taken refuge, he attempted suicide but only succeeded in shattering his jaw. The same evening he mounted the scaffold, his jaw hanging loose in a bloody silk scarf, and was executed with nineteen of his followers. Such was the coup d'état of the ninth Thermidor.

PART NINE

NAPOLEON OVER EUROPE

T̲ʜᴇ ᴛʜᴇʀᴍɪᴅᴏʀɪᴀɴ ʀᴇᴀᴄᴛɪᴏɴ that destroyed Robespierre, the Commune, and the revolutionary spirit produced greed and rapacity, fear and repression, in France. By November, 1795, a new government ruled France, and most unwieldy it was. An upper house called the Council of Ancients and a lower house called the Council of Five Hundred legislated. A Directory of Five, chosen by the Ancients, exercised executive powers. It held power until the coup d'état of the eighteenth Brumaire, 1799, during which period the star of Bonaparte gradually rose on the horizon.

GENERAL BONAPARTE ADDRESSES HIS TRIUMPHANT ARMY OF ITALY

[April 26, 1796]

Napoleon Bonaparte (1769–1821) was born at Ajaccio, in Corsica, a year after the island was acquired by France. Although Napoleon was educated at a French military school, the love of his native island remained one of his deepest motives. Even in 1789, when he was made a first lieutenant in the French army, he continued to conspire to wrest Corsica from the French conquerors. A few years later he seems to have identified himself with the Jacobins, and specifically with Robespierre and the Mountain in their war with the Girondists. For his part in taking the city of Toulon from the royalists and the English in 1793 he was made a brigadier general.

At Toulon he met Robespierre's younger brother. His partisanship was no secret, and when Robespierre fell, he was temporarily put under arrest. There followed a considerable period of uncertainty, at times an obscurity that his vaulting ambition could scarcely bear. Then his fortune changed with the events of the thirteenth Vendémiaire (October 5, 1795), when he helped to quell a monarchist rising against the Convention. The Directory expressed the gratitude of the Convention, and by March, 1796, he was in command of the Army of Italy. With this his fondest purpose had been fulfilled, for he had long dreamed of the conquest of Italy, and had even taken a trip there to reconnoiter the terrain of his future victories. A few weeks after the campaign began —on April 26, to be exact—we find him addressing his troops, speaking in a clipped, terse, passionate style and with an effect that was to startle the world.

"All burn with the ambition to spread the fame of the French nation."

SOLDIERS! In fourteen days you have fought six battles; you have taken twenty-one standards, fifty-five guns, and several fortresses. You have conquered the richest territories of Piedmont. You have to your credit fifteen thousand prisoners, and more than ten thousand killed or wounded. Hitherto you have fought only for the possession of cold rocks, which, though your renown will make them famous for all time, are of no value to your country. But today your services have placed you on a level with the troops in Holland and the Army of the Rhine. . . . When the campaign began, you were destitute of everything; today you have plenty and to spare. You have captured large supplies from your enemies. Siege artillery and field artillery have arrived.

Soldiers! Your country is entitled to expect great things of you. Will you justify her expectations? Your greatest obstacles are already overcome, but you have yet many battles to fight, many towns to capture, many rivers to pass over. Is there one among you whose courage fails him? Is there one, I say, who would rather retreat to the summits of Apennines and Alps, and patiently endure the insults of that slavish rabble? No, no one among the victors of Montenotte, Millesimo, Dego, and Mondovi! All burn with the ambition to spread the fame of the French nation throughout the world; the desire of every one of you is to humble those proud rulers who would fetter us in chains. All long for the dictation of a glorious peace, which shall compensate our country for the tremendous sacrifices she has made. All, when they return to their homes, would wish to be able to say proudly, "I was with the victorious Army of Italy."

Friends! I promise you these conquests! But you must swear to me in return to observe one condition. You must show consideration for the peoples to whom you bring liberty, you must keep down that plundering which scoundrels indulge in, of which our enemies have given the example. Unless you do this, you will be called not liberators but scourges of the nations!

As a military orator, as a general addressing his troops, Napoleon was unsurpassed. He invented a style of eloquence reminiscent of Caesar, brief, declarative, familiar, and yet imperial in its bold sweep and cadence. It made an instant appeal to valor, and the soldiers of the Republic died for him unquestioningly. As a parliamentary speaker confronted by a hostile or doubtful audience, on the other hand, he was a failure. His forte was not debate or eloquent persuasion, but crisp proclamation announcing his victories or his sovereign decisions, and his genius rapidly put him in a position where only the latter was needed. Political debates were already on the wane, and the newspapers were soon to be silenced.

For three years Napoleon occupied himself almost exclusively with warfare. By October 17, 1797, he was able to dictate the Treaty of Campo Formio with Austria, having conquered all of northern Italy for the Republic. Here he showed his astuteness by treating the Austrians more leniently than the Directory approved of. In May, 1798, he was off to Egypt, where his success might have been complete, had not Nelson destroyed the French fleet. Had this not happened, Napoleon might have penetrated into India, where malcontents were not lacking who hated the British. Quite undismayed by rebuffs in the Near East, he returned to France, where, aided by his brother Lucien and the Abbé Sieyès, a wily politician who had managed to survive the Terror, he overthrew the government on the eighteenth Brumaire (November 9, 1799). The executive was now vested in a consular trio, with Napoleon as First Consul. He made his move just in time to meet a new threat from beyond the frontiers, where a second coalition of powers was forming against France.

PITT ADVISES AGAINST ACCEPTING BONAPARTE'S OVERTURES FOR PEACE

[February 3, 1800]

In the Christmas season, only a few weeks after he had made himself First Consul and virtual ruler of France, Napoleon offered peace to England. "Must the war, which has, for eight years, ravaged the four quarters of the globe, be eternal?" he wrote. "Are there no means of coming to an understanding? How can the two most enlightened nations of Europe, powerful and strong beyond what their inclination requires, sacrifice to ideas of vain grandeur the advantages of commerce, internal prosperity, and the happiness of individuals? How is it that they do not feel that peace is an object of the first necessity, as it is one of the greatest glory?"

The proposal, which was addressed to George III, came at a time when England's fortunes were at a low ebb and the country stood in dire need of peace. The land campaigns of the year 1799 had been most unsuccessful. In Holland the Dutch failed to rise, and the English army of thirty thousand men, which Pitt could muster only by paying ten guineas for each enlistment, was not only badly trained but failed to get along with its allies, the Russians. Jealousy also flamed between the allied Russian and Austrian troops in Italy, and they also met defeat. The second grand coalition was ready to collapse, and England was in danger of complete isolation. There were other perils and problems. The mutinies of 1797, which spread like wildfire through the fleet, had left the island at the mercy of her enemies, had they known it, for five months. Recruiting proved difficult. The war with France and the lavish subvention of allies had been exorbitant, and the national debt had climbed steeply. Two commercial crises had shaken the kingdom. Peace would have been a blessing.

How would George III respond to Napoleon's overtures? Neither he nor his Foreign Minister, Lord Grenville, saw the gravity of England's position at this juncture, nor did Pitt himself. The task of framing a reply to Napoleon's message was left to the crude hand of Lord Grenville, a follower of Burke, who not only rejected all negotiation, but took the occasion to rebuke the French government and to call for a return of the Bourbons as the surest guarantee of the sincerity of its peaceful intentions. "There is a fine untutored insolence in this communication that," as Lord Rosebery remarked years later, "would be difficult to match."

Pitt's rejection of the French proposal is more difficult to understand. He himself had repeatedly proffered peace in the previous decade, and had been willing to accept it on any decent terms, for what he ardently desired was the commercial prosperity and solvency of the nation. Even when, at the beginning of the Revolution, it seemed that the whole country was bent on war, and Parliament was almost solidly against him, he stood his ground, pale and unperturbed, and by dint of his immense prestige silenced the clamor. But now that peace was offered to him by the victorious Consul, the one man in Europe who had the power to enforce it, he turned away haughtily, believing the proposal insincere or the time unpropitious. Neither his growing ill health nor any other reason seems to explain this sudden reversal, for later in the year, when it was too late, he was to make a new peace proposal himself. Evidently Pitt had reached the great turning point of his career. There would be little talk of peace or prosperity after this, and reform was to become anathema. In answer to a speech by Erskine favoring peace, the Prime Minister retaliated with one of his best, but historically most fateful addresses, which is abridged below.

"He is a stranger, a foreigner, and a usurper."

HITHERTO I have spoken only of the reliance which we can place on the professions, the character, and the conduct of the present First Consul; but it remains to consider the stability of his power. The Revolution has been marked throughout by a rapid succession of new depositaries of public authority, each supplanting its predecessor. What grounds have we to believe that this new usurpation, more odious and more undisguised than all that preceded it, will be more durable? Is it that we rely on the particular provisions contained in the code of the pretended Constitution, which was proclaimed as accepted by the French people as soon as the garrison of Paris declared their determination to exterminate all its enemies, and before any of its articles could be known to half the country whose consent was required for its establishment?

I will not pretend to inquire deeply into the nature and effects of a Constitution which can hardly be regarded but as a farce and a mockery. If, however, it could be supposed that its provisions were to have any effect, it seems equally adapted to two purposes—that of giving to its founder for a time an absolute and uncontrolled authority, and that of laying the certain foundation of disunion and discord which, if they once prevail, must render the exercise of all the authority under the Constitution impossible and leave no appeal but to the sword.

Is, then, military despotism that which we are accustomed to consider as a stable form of government? In all ages of the world it has been attained with the least stability to the persons who exercised it, and with the most rapid succession of changes and revolutions. In the outset of the French Revolution its advocates boasted that it furnished a security forever, not to France only, but to all countries in the world, against military despotism; that the force of standing armies was vain and delusive; that no artificial power could resist public opinion; and that it was upon the foundation of public opinion alone that any government could stand. I believe that in this instance, as in every other, the progress of the French Revolution has belied its professions; but, so far from its being a proof of the prevalence of public opinion against military force, it is, instead of the proof, the strongest exception from that doctrine which appears in the history of the world. Through all the stages of the Revolution military force has governed; public opinion has scarcely been heard. But still I consider this as only an exception from a general truth; I still believe that in every civilized country (not enslaved by a Jacobin faction) public opinion is the only sure support of any government: I believe this with the more satisfaction from a conviction that if this contest is happily terminated, the established governments of Europe will stand upon that rock firmer than ever; and whatever may be the defects of any particular constitution, those who live under it will prefer its continuance to the experiment of changes which may plunge them into the unfathomable abyss of revolution, or extricate them from it, only to expose them to the terrors of military despotism. And to apply this to France, I see no reason to believe that the present usurpation will be more permanent than any other despotism, which has been established by the same means, and with the same defiance of public opinion.

What, then, is the inference I draw from all that I have now stated? Is it that we will in no case treat with Bonaparte? I say no such thing. But I say, as has been said in the answer returned to the French note, that we ought to wait for *experience, and the evidence of facts,* before we are convinced that such a treaty is admissible. The circumstances I have stated would well justify us if we should be slow in being convinced; but on a question of peace and war, everything depends upon degree and upon comparison. If, on the one hand, there should be an appearance that the policy of France is at length guided by different maxims from those which have hitherto prevailed; if we should hereafter see signs of stability in the government, which are not now to be traced; if the progress of the allied army should not call forth such a spirit in France as to make it probable that the act of the country itself will destroy the system now prevailing; if the danger, the difficulty, the risk of continuing the contest, should increase, while the hope of complete ultimate success should be diminished; all these, in their due place, are considerations which, with myself and (I can answer for it) with every one of my colleagues, will have their just weight. But at present these considerations all operate one way; at present there is nothing from which we can presage a favorable disposition to change in the French councils: there is the greatest reason to rely on powerful co-operation from our allies; there are the strongest marks of a disposition in the interior of France to active resistance against this new tyranny; and there is every ground to believe, on reviewing our situation and that of the enemy, that if we are ultimately disappointed of that complete success which we are at present entitled to hope, the continuance of the contest, instead of making our situation comparatively worse, will have made it comparatively better.

If, then, I am asked how long are we to persevere in the war, I can only say that no period can be accurately assigned beforehand. Considering the importance of obtaining complete security for the objects for which we contend, we ought not to be discouraged too soon: but on the other hand, considering the importance of not impairing and exhausting the radical strength of the country, there are limits beyond which we ought not to persist, and which we can determine only by estimating and comparing fairly, from time to time, the degree of security to be obtained by treaty, and the risk and disadvantage of continuing the contest.

But, sir, there are some gentlemen in the House who seem to consider it already certain, that the ultimate success to which I am looking is unattainable: they suppose us contending only for the restoration of the French monarchy, which they believe to be impracticable and deny to be desirable for this country. We have been asked in the course of this debate, do you think you can impose monarchy upon France against the will of the nation? I never thought it, I never hoped it, I never wished it: I have thought, I have hoped, I have wished, that the time might come when the effect of the arms of the allies might so far overpower the military force which keeps France in bondage as to give vent and scope to the thoughts and actions of its inhabitants. We have, indeed, already seen abundant proof of what is the disposition of a large part of the country; we have seen almost through the whole of the Revolution the western provinces of France deluged with the blood of its inhabitants, obstinately contending for their ancient laws and religion. We have recently seen, in the revival of that war, a fresh instance of the zeal which still animates those countries, in the same cause. These efforts (I state it distinctly, and there are those near me who can bear witness to the truth of the assertion) were not produced by any instigation from hence; they were the effects of a rooted sentiment prevailing through all those provinces, forced into action by the Law of the Hostages and the other tyrannical measures of the Directory, at the moment when we were endeavoring to discourage so hazardous an enterprise. If, under such circumstances, we find them giving proofs of their unalterable perseverance in their principles; if there is every reason to believe that the same disposition prevails in many other extensive provinces of France; if every party appears at length equally wearied and disappointed with all the successive changes which the Revolution has produced; if the question is no longer between monarchy and even the pretense and name of liberty, but between the ancient line of hereditary princes, on the one hand, and a military tyrant, a foreign usurper, on the other; if the armies of that usurper are likely to find sufficient occupation on the frontiers, and to be forced at length to leave the interior of the country at liberty to manifest its real feeling and disposition; what reason have we to anticipate that the restoration of the monarchy under such circumstances is impracticable? . . .

On the question, sir, how far the restoration of the French monarchy, if practicable, is desirable, I shall not think it necessary to say much. Can it be supposed to be indifferent to us or to the world whether the throne of France is to be filled by a prince of the house of Bourbon or by him whose principles and conduct I have endeavored to develop? Is it nothing, with a view to influence and example, whether the fortune of this last adventurer in the lottery of revolutions shall appear to be permanent? Is it nothing whether a system shall be sanctioned which confirms by one of its fundamental articles that general transfer of property from its ancient and lawful possessors which holds out one of the most terrible examples of national injustice, and which has furnished the great source of revolutionary finance and revolutionary strength against all the powers of Europe?

In the exhausted and impoverished state of France it seems for a time impossible that any system but that of robbery and confiscation, anything but the continued torture which can be applied only by the engines of the revolution, can extort from its ruined inhabitants more than the means of supporting in peace the yearly expenditure of its government. Suppose, then, the heir of the house of Bourbon reinstated on the throne; he will have sufficient occupation in endeavoring, if possible, to heal the wounds and gradually to repair the losses of ten years of civil convulsion—to reanimate the drooping commerce, to rekindle the industry, to replace the capital, and to revive the manufactures of the country.

Under such circumstances there must probably be a considerable interval before such a monarch, whatever may be his views, can possess the power which can make him formidable to Europe; but while the system of the Revolution continues the case is quite different. It is true indeed that even the gigantic and unnatural means by which that Revolution has been supported are so far impaired, the influence of its principles and the terror of its arms so far weakened, and its power of action so much contracted that against the embodied force of Europe, prosecuting a vigorous war, we may justly hope that the remnant and wreck of this system cannot long oppose an effectual resistance.

Can we forget that in the ten years in which that power has subsisted it has brought more misery on surrounding nations and produced more acts of aggression, cruelty, perfidy, and enormous ambition than can be traced in the history of France for the centuries which have elapsed since the foundation of its monarchy, including all the wars which in the course of that period have been waged by any of those sovereigns whose projects of aggrandizement and violations of treaty afford a constant theme of general reproach against the ancient government of France? And if not, can we hesitate whether we have the best prospect of permanent peace, the best security for the independence and safety of Europe, from the restoration of the lawful government, or from the continuance of revolutionary power in the hands of Bonaparte? . . .

CHARLES JAMES FOX REPLIES TO PITT

[February 3, 1800]

Pitt's masterly speech had its intended effect in the House of Commons. Patriotism then and there became identified with continuation of the war. Would anyone dare to reply? Few speakers in the Commons had the spirit, and authority to challenge Pitt on a major issue. The one man who could equal Pitt in a set oration and far excel him in debate had quit the House three years before, discouraged by his failure to get ahead with parliamentary reform and other cherished purposes, and had vowed to devote himself to leisure. After his long absence the members were surprised to see suddenly the portly and incomparably amiable Fox walk to his seat while Pitt was yet speaking. When the latter had finished, Fox rose to reply to his old and respected enemy, to urge friendship with revolutionary France, which he had never ceased to befriend, and to save England, if possible, from a ruinous and needless war.

"Is it dangerous for nations to live in amity with each other?"
Mr. Speaker:

AT SO LATE AN HOUR of the night I am sure you will do me the justice to believe that I do not mean to go at length into the discussion of this great question. Exhausted as the attention of the House must be, and unaccustomed as I have been of late to attend in my place, nothing but a deep sense of my duty could have induced me to trouble you at all, and particularly to request your indulgence at such an hour. Sir, my honorable and learned friend has truly said that the present is a new era in the war. The right honorable the Chancellor of the Exchequer feels the justice of the remark; for by traveling back to the commencement of the war, and referring to all the topics and arguments which he has so often and so successfully urged to the House, and by which he has drawn them on to the support of his measures, he is forced to acknowledge that, at the end of a seven years' conflict, we are come but to a new era in the war, at which he thinks it necessary only to press all his former arguments to induce us to persevere. All the topics which have so often misled us—all the reasoning which has so invariably failed—all the lofty predictions which have so constantly been falsified by events—all the hopes which have amused the sanguine, and all the assurances of the distress and weakness of the enemy which have satisfied the unthinking, are again enumerated and advanced as arguments for our continuing the war. What! at the end of seven years of the most burdensome and the most calamitous struggle that this country was ever engaged in, are we again to be amused with notions of finance and calculations of the exhausted resources of the enemy as a ground of confidence and of hope? Gracious God! Were we not told, five years ago, that France was not only on the brink, but that she was actually in the gulf of bankruptcy? Were we not told, as an unanswerable argument against treating, that she could not hold out another campaign—that nothing but peace could save her—that she wanted only time to recruit her exhausted finances—that to grant her repose was to grant her the means of again molesting this country, and that we had nothing to do but persevere for a short time in order to save ourselves forever from the consequences of her ambition and her Jacobinism? What! after having gone on from year to year upon assurances like these, and after having seen the repeated refutations of every prediction, are we again to be seriously told that we have the same prospect of success on the same identical grounds? And without any other argument or security, are we invited, at this new era of the war, to carry it on upon principles which, if adopted, may make it eternal? If the right honorable gentleman shall succeed in prevailing on Parliament and the country to adopt the principles which he has advanced this night, I see no possible termination to the contest. No man can see an end to it; and upon the assurances and predictions which have so uniformly failed are we called upon, not merely to refuse all negotiation, but to countenance principles and views as distant from wisdom and justice as they are in their nature wild and impracticable. . . .

Sir, what is the question this night? We are called upon to support
ministers in refusing a frank, candid, and respectful offer of negotiation,
and to countenance them in continuing the war. Now, I would put the
question in another way. Suppose ministers have been inclined to adopt
the line of conduct which they pursued in 1796 and 1797, and that tonight, instead of a question on a war address, it had been an address to
his Majesty to thank him for accepting the overture and for opening a
negotiation to treat for peace: I ask the gentlemen opposite—I appeal to
the whole 558 representatives of the people—to lay their hands upon
their hearts, and to say whether they would not have cordially voted for
such an address? Would they, or would they not? Yes, sir, if the address
had breathed a spirit of peace your benches would have resounded with
rejoicings, and with praises of a measure that was likely to bring back
the blessings of tranquillity. On the present occasion, then, I ask for the
vote of none but of those who, in the secret confession of their conscience,
admit, at this instant while they hear me, that they would have cheerfully and heartily voted with the minister for an address directly the
reverse of this. If every such gentleman were to vote with me, I should
be this night in the greatest majority that ever I had the honor to vote
with in this House.

Sir, we have heard tonight a great many most acrimonious invectives
against Bonaparte, against the whole course of his conduct, and against
the unprincipled manner in which he seized upon the reins of government. I will not make his defense—I think all this sort of invective, which
is used only to inflame the passions of this House and of the country, exceeding ill timed and very impolitic—but I say I will not make his defense. I am not sufficiently in possession of materials upon which to form
an opinion on the character and conduct of this extraordinary man. Upon
his arrival in France he found the government in a very unsettled state,
and the whole affairs of the Republic deranged, crippled, and involved.
He thought it necessary to reform the government; and he did reform
it, just in the way in which a military man may be expected to carry on
a reform—he seized on the whole authority to himself. It will not be expected from me that I should either approve or apologize for such an act.
I am certainly not for reforming governments by such expedients; but
how this House can be so violently indignant at the idea of military despotism is, I own, a little singular, when I see the composure with which
they can observe it nearer home; nay, when I see them regard it as a
frame of government most peculiarly suited to the exercise of free opinion
on a subject the most important of any that can engage the attention of
a people. Was it not the system that was so happily and so advanta-

geously established of late all over Ireland; and which, even now, the government may, at its pleasure, proclaim over the whole of that kingdom? Are not the persons and property of the people left in many districts at this moment to the entire will of military commanders? And is not this held out as peculiarly proper and advantageous at a time when the people of Ireland are free, and with unbiased judgment, to discuss the most interesting question of a legislative union? Notwithstanding the existence of martial law, so far do we think Ireland from being enslaved that we think it precisely the period and the circumstances under which she may best declare her free opinion! Now really, sir, I cannot think that gentlemen who talk in this way about Ireland can, with a good grace, rail at military despotism in France.

But, it seems, "Bonaparte has broken his oaths. He has violated his oath of fidelity to the constitution of the year 3." Sir, I am not one of those who think that any such oaths ought ever to be exacted. They are seldom or ever of any effect; and I am not for sporting with a thing so sacred as an oath. I think it would be good to lay aside all such oaths. Whoever heard that, in revolutions, the oath of fidelity to the former government was ever regarded; or even when violated that it was imputed to the persons as a crime? In times of revolution, men who take up arms are called rebels—if they fail, they are adjudged to be traitors. But who ever heard before of their being perjured? On the restoration of Charles II, those who had taken up arms for the Commonwealth were stigmatized as rebels and traitors, but not as men foresworn. Was the Earl of Devonshire charged with being perjured on account of the allegiance he had sworn to the house of Stuart and the part he took in those struggles which preceded and brought about the Revolution? The violation of oaths of allegiance was never imputed to the people of England, and will never be imputed to any people. But who brings up the question of oaths? He who strives to make twenty-four millions of persons violate the oaths they have taken to their present Constitution, and who desires to re-establish the house of Bourbon by such violation of their vows. I put it so, sir; because, if the question of oaths be of the least consequence, it is equal on both sides. He who desires the whole people of France to perjure themselves, and who hopes for success in his project only upon their doing so, surely cannot make it a charge against Bonaparte that he has done the same.

"Ah! but Bonaparte has declared it as his opinion that the two governments of Great Britain and of France cannot exist together. After the Treaty of Campo Formio he sent two confidential persons, Berthier and Monge, to the Directory to say so in his name." Well, and what is there

in this absurd and puerile assertion, if it was ever made? Has not the right
honorable gentleman, in this House, said the same thing? In this, at least,
they resemble one another. They have both made use of this assertion;
and I believe that these two illustrious persons are the only two on earth
who think it. But let us turn the tables. We ought to put ourselves at
times in the place of the enemy, if we are desirous of really examining
with candor and fairness the dispute between us. How may they not interpret the speeches of ministers and their friends in both houses of the
British Parliament? If we are to be told of the idle speech of Berthier and
Monge, may they not also bring up speeches in which it has not been
merely hinted, but broadly asserted, that "the two constitutions of England and France could not exist together"? May not these offenses and
charges be reciprocated without end? Are we ever to go on in this miserable squabble about words? Are we still, as we happen to be successful
on the one side or other, to bring up these impotent accusations, insults,
and provocations against each other; and only when we are beaten and
unfortunate to think of treating? Oh! pity the condition of man,. gracious
God! and save us from such a system of malevolence, in which all our old
and venerated prejudices are to be done away, and by which we are to
be taught to consider war as the natural state of man, and peace but as a
dangerous and difficult extremity?

Sir, this temper must be corrected. It is a diabolical spirit and would
lead to interminable war. Our history is full of instances that where we
have overlooked a proffered occasion to treat, we have uniformly suffered
by delay. At what time did we ever profit by obstinately persevering in
war? We accepted at Ryswick the terms we had refused five years before, and the same peace which was concluded at Utrecht might have
been obtained at Gertruydenberg. And as to security from the future
machinations or ambition of the French, I ask you what security you
ever had or could have? Did the different treaties made with Louis IV
serve to tie up his hands, to restrain his ambition, or to stifle his restless
spirit? At what period could you safely repose in the honor, forbearance,
and moderation of the French government? Was there ever an idea of
refusing to treat because the peace might be afterwards insecure? The
peace of 1763 was not accompanied with securities; and it was no sooner
made than the French court began, as usual, its intrigues. And what security did the right honorable gentleman exact at the peace of 1783, in
which he was engaged? Were we rendered secure by that peace? The
right honorable gentleman knows well that soon after that peace the
French formed a plan, in conjunction with the Dutch, of attacking our
Indian possessions, of raising up the native powers against us, and of

driving us out of India; as the French are desirous of doing now—only with this difference, that the cabinet of France entered into this project in a moment of profound peace, and when they conceived us to be lulled into perfect security. After making the peace of 1783, the right honorable gentleman and his friends went out, and I, among others, came into office. Suppose, sir, that we had taken up the jealousy upon which the right honorable gentleman now acts, and had refused to ratify the peace which he had made. Suppose that we had said—"No; France is acting a perfidious part—we see no security for England in this treaty—they want only a respite, in order to attack us again in an important part of our dominions; and we ought not to confirm the treaty." I ask, would the right honorable gentleman have supported us in this refusal? I say that upon his reasoning he ought; but I put it fairly to him, would he have supported us in refusing to ratify the treaty upon such a pretense? He certainly ought not, and I am sure he would not, but the course of reasoning which he now assumes would have justified his taking such a ground. On the contrary, I am persuaded that he would have said—"This is a refinement upon jealousy. Security! You have security, the only security that you can ever expect to get. It is the present interest of France to make peace. She will keep it if it be her interest: she will break it if it be her interest; such is the state of nations; and you have nothing but your own vigilance for your security."

"It is not the interest of Bonaparte," it seems, "sincerely to enter into a negotiation, or, if he should even make peace, sincerely to keep it." But how are we to decide upon his sincerity? By refusing to treat with him? Surely, if we mean to discover his sincerity, we ought to hear the propositions which he desires to make. "But peace would be unfriendly to his system of military despotism." Sir, I hear a great deal about the short-lived nature of military despotism. I wish the history of the world would bear gentlemen out in this description of military despotism. Was not the government erected by Augustus Caesar a military despotism? and yet it endured for six hundred or seven hundred years. Military despotism, unfortunately, is too likely in its nature to be permanent, and it is not true that it depends on the life of the first usurper. Though half the Roman emperors were murdered, yet the military despotism went on; and so it would be, I fear, in France. If Bonaparte should disappear from the scene, to make room, perhaps, for a Berthier, or any other general, what difference would that make in the quality of French despotism or in our relation to the country? We may as safely treat with a Bonaparte or with any of his successors, be they who they may, as we could with a Louis XVI, a Louis XVII, or a Louis XVIII. There is no difference but in the name. Where the power essentially resides, thither we ought to go for peace.

But, sir, if we are to reason on the fact, I should think that it is the interest of Bonaparte to make peace. A lover of military glory, as that general must necessarily be, may he not think that his measure of glory is full —that it may be tarnished by a reverse of fortune, and can hardly be increased by any new laurels? He must feel that, in the situation to which he is now raised, he can no longer depend on his own fortune, his own genius, and his own talents for a continuance of his success; he must be under the necessity of employing other generals, whose misconduct or incapacity might endanger his power, or whose triumphs even might affect the interest which he holds in the opinion of the French. Peace, then, would secure to him what he has achieved, and fix the inconstancy of fortune. But this will not be his only motive. He must see that France also requires a respite—a breathing interval to recruit her wasted strength. To procure her this respite would be, perhaps, the attainment of more solid glory, as well as the means of acquiring more solid power, than anything which he can hope to gain from arms and from the proudest triumphs. May he not then be zealous to gain this fame, the only species of fame, perhaps, that is worth acquiring? Nay, granting that his soul may still burn with the thirst of military exploits, is it not likely that he is earnestly disposed to yield to the feelings of the French people, and to consolidate his power by consulting their interests? I have a right to argue in this way, when suppositions of his insincerity are reasoned upon on the other side. Sir, these aspersions are, in truth, always idle, and even mischievous. I have been too long accustomed to hear imputations and calumnies thrown out upon great and honorable characters to be much influenced by them. My learned friend has paid this night a most just, deserved, and honorable tribute of applause to the memory of that great and unparalleled character who has been so recently lost to the world. I must, like him, beg leave to dwell a moment on the venerable George Washington, though I know that it is impossible for me to bestow anything like adequate praise on a character which gave us, more than any other human being, the example of a perfect man; yet, good, great, and unexampled as General Washington was, I can remember the time when he was not better spoken of in this House than Bonaparte is now. The right honorable gentleman who opened this debate [Mr. Dundas] may remember in what terms of disdain, of virulence, and even of contempt General Washington was spoken of by gentlemen on that side of the House. Does he not recollect with what marks of indignation any member was stigmatized as an enemy to his country who mentioned with common respect the name of

General Washington? If a negotiation had then been proposed to be opened with that great man, what would have been said? "Would you treat with a rebel, a traitor! What an example would you not give by such an act!" I do not know whether the right honorable gentleman may not yet possess some of his old prejudices on the subject. I hope not. I hope by this time we are all convinced that a republican government like that of America may exist without danger or injury to social order or to established monarchies. They have happily shown that they can maintain the relations of peace and amity with other states: they have shown, too, that they are alive to the feelings of honor; but they do not lose sight of plain good sense and discretion. They have not refused to negotiate with the French, and they have accordingly the hopes of a speedy termination of every difference. We cry up their conduct, but we do not imitate it. At the beginning of the struggle we were told that the French were setting up a set of wild and impracticable theories, and that we ought not to be misled by them—we could not grapple with theories. Now we are told that we must not treat, because, out of the lottery, Bonaparte has drawn such a prize as military despotism. Is military despotism a theory? One would think that that is one of the practical things which ministers might understand, and to which they would have no particular objection. But what is our present conduct founded on but a theory, and that a most wild and ridiculous theory? What are we fighting for? Not for a principle; not for security; not for conquest even; but merely for an experiment and a speculation, to discover whether a gentleman at Paris may not turn out a better man than we now take him to be.

My honorable friend [Mr. Whitbread] has been censured for an opinion which he gave, and I think justly, that the change of property in France since the Revolution must form an almost insurmountable barrier to the return of the ancient proprietors. "No such thing," says the right honorable gentleman; "nothing can be more easy. Property is depreciated to such a degree that the purchasers would easily be brought to restore the estates." I very much differ with him in this idea. It is the character of every such convulsion as that which has ravaged France that an infinite and indescribable load of misery is inflicted upon private families. The heart sickens at the recital of the sorrows which it engenders. No revolution implied, though it may have occasioned, a total change of property. The restoration of the Bourbons does imply it; and there is the difference. There is no doubt but that if the noble families had foreseen the duration and the extent of the evils which were to fall upon their heads, they would have taken a very different line of conduct. But they unfortunately flew from their country. The King and his advisers sought foreign aid. A confederacy was formed to restore them by military force; and as a means of resisting this combination, the estates of the fugitives were confiscated and sold. However compassion may deplore the case, it cannot be said that the thing is unprecedented. The people have always resorted to such means of defense. Now the question is how this property is to be got out of their hands. If it be true, as I have heard, that the purchasers of national and forfeited estates amount to 1,500,000 persons, I see no hopes of their being forced to deliver up their property; nor do I even know that they ought. I question the policy, even if the thing were practicable; but I assert that such a body of new proprietors forms an insurmountable barrier to the restoration of the ancient order of things. Never was a revolution consolidated by a pledge so strong.

But, as if this were not of itself sufficient, Louis XVIII from his retire-ment at Mittau puts forth a manifesto in which he assures the friends of his House that he is about to come back with all the powers that formerly belonged to his family. He does not promise to the people a constitution which may tend to conciliate; but, stating that he is to come with all the *ancien régime,* they would naturally attach to it its proper appendages of bastilles, *lettres de cachet,* gabelle, etc. And the noblesse, for whom this proclamation was peculiarly conceived, would also naturally feel that if the monarch was to be restored to all his privileges, they surely were to be reinstated in their estates without a compensation to the purchasers. Is this likely to make the people wish for a restoration of royalty? I have no doubt but there may be a number of Chouans in France, though I am persuaded that little dependence is to be placed on their efforts. There may be a number of people dispersed over France, and particularly in certain provinces, who may retain a degree of attachment to royalty; and how the government will contrive to compromise with that spirit I know not. I suspect, however, that Bonaparte will try; his efforts have been turned to that object; and, if we may believe report, he has succeeded to a considerable degree. He will naturally call to his recollection the prece-dent which the history of France itself will furnish. The once formidable insurrection of the Huguenots was completely stifled and the party con-ciliated by the policy of Henry IV, who gave them such privileges and raised them so high in the government as to make some persons appre-hend danger therefrom to the unity of the Empire. Nor will the French be likely to forget the revocation of the edict—one of the memorable acts of the house of Bourbon—an act which was never surpassed in atrocity, injustice, and impolicy by anything that has disgraced Jacobinism. If Bonaparte shall attempt some similar arrangement to that of Henry IV with the Chouans, who will say that he is likely to fail? He will meet with no great obstacle to success from the influence which our ministers have established with the chiefs, or in the attachment and dependence which they have on our protection; for what has the right honorable gentleman told him, in stating the contingencies in which he will treat with Bonaparte? He will excite a rebellion in France—he will give support to the Chouans, if they can stand their ground; but he will not make common cause with them; for unless they can depose Bonaparte, send him into banishment, or execute him, he will abandon the Chouans, and treat with this very man whom he describes as holding the reins and wielding the powers of France for purposes of unexampled barbarity.

Sir, I wish the atrocities of which we hear so much, and which I abhor as much as any man, were indeed unexampled. I fear that they do not belong exclusively to the French. When the right honorable gentleman speaks of the extraordinary successes of the last campaign, he does not mention the horrors by which some of those successes were accompanied. Naples, for instance, has been, among others, what is called "delivered"; and yet, if I am rightly informed, it has been stained and polluted by murders so ferocious, and by cruelties of every kind so abhorrent, that the heart shudders at the recital. It has been said, not only that the miserable victims of the rage and brutality of the fanatics were savagely murdered, but that, in many instances, their flesh was eaten and devoured by the cannibals who are the advocates and the instruments of social order! Nay, England is not totally exempt from reproach, if the rumors which are circulated be true. I will mention a fact to give ministers the opportunity, if it be false, of wiping away the stain that it must otherwise fix on the British name. It is said that a party of the republican inhabitants of Naples took shelter in the fortress of the Castel de Uova. They were besieged by a detachment from the royal army, to whom they refused to surrender; but demanded that a British officer should be brought forward, and to him they capitulated. They made terms with him under the sanction of the British name. It was agreed that their persons and property should be safe, and that they should be conveyed to Toulon. They were accordingly put on board a vessel; but before they sailed their property was confiscated, numbers of them taken out, thrown into dungeons, and some of them, I understand, notwithstanding the British guarantee, actually executed.

Where then, sir, is this war, which on every side is pregnant with such horrors, to be carried? Where is it to stop? Not till you establish the house of Bourbon! And this you cherish the hope of doing, because you have had a successful campaign. Why, sir, before this you have had a successful campaign. The situation of the allies, with all they have gained, is surely not to be compared now to what it was when you had taken Valenciennes, Quesnoy, Condé, etc., which induced some gentlemen in this House to prepare themselves for a march to Paris. With all that you have gained, you surely will not say that the prospect is brighter now than it was then. What have you gained but the recovery of a part of what you before lost? One campaign is successful to you—another to them; and in this way, animated by the vindictive passions of revenge, hatred, and rancor, which are infinitely more flagitious even than those of ambition and the thirst of power, you may go on forever; as, with such black incentives, I see no end to human misery. And all this without an intelligible motive, all this because you may gain a better peace a year or two hence! So that we are called upon to go on merely as a speculation. We must keep Bonaparte for some time longer at war as a state of probation. Gracious God, sir, is war a state of probation? Is peace a rash system? Is it dangerous for nations to live in amity with each other? Is your vigilance, your policy, your common powers of observation, to be extinguished by putting an end to the horrors of war? Cannot this state of probation be as well undergone without adding to the catalogue of human sufferings? "But we must pause!" What! must the bowels of Great Britain be torn out—her best blood be spilt—her treasure wasted—that you may make an experiment? Put yourselves—oh! that you would put yourselves—in the field of battle, and learn to judge of the sort of horrors that you excite. In former wars a man might at least have some feeling, some interest, that served to balance in his mind the impressions which a scene of carnage and of death must inflict. If a man had been present at the Battle of Blenheim, for instance, and had inquired the motive of the battle, there was not a soldier engaged who could not have satisfied his curiosity, and even perhaps allayed his feelings—they were fighting to repress the uncontrolled ambition of the *grand monarque*. But if a man were present now at a field of slaughter, and were to inquire for what they were fighting—"Fighting!" would be the answer; "they are not fighting, they are pausing." "Why is that man expiring? Why is that other writhing with agony? What means this implacable fury?" The answer must be, "You are quite wrong, sir; you deceive yourself—they are not fighting—do not disturb them— they are merely pausing!—this man is not expiring with agony—that man is not dead—he is only pausing! Lord help you, sir! they are not angry with one another; they have now no cause of quarrel—but their country thinks that there should be a pause. All that you see, sir, is nothing like fighting—there is no harm, nor cruelty, nor bloodshed in it whatever— it is nothing more than *a political pause!*—it is merely to try an experiment—to see whether Bonaparte will not behave himself better than heretofore; and in the meantime we have agreed to a pause, in pure friendship!" And is this the way, sir, that you are to show yourselves the advocates of order? You take up a system calculated to uncivilize the world, to destroy order, to trample on religion, to stifle in the heart, not merely the generosity of noble sentiment, but the affections of social nature; and in the prosecution of this system you spread terror and devastation all around you.

Sir, I have done. I have told you my opinion. I think you ought to have given a civil, clear, and explicit answer to the overture which was fairly and handsomely made you. If you were desirous that the negotiation should have included all your allies, as the means of bringing about a general peace, you should have told Bonaparte so; but I believe you were afraid of his agreeing to the proposal. You took that method before. "Ay, but," you say, "the people were anxious for peace in 1797." I say they are friends to peace now; and I am confident that you will one day own it. Believe me, they are friends to peace; although, by the laws which you have made restraining the expression of the sense of the people, public opinion cannot now be heard as loudly and unequivocally as heretofore. But I will not go into the internal state of this country. It is too afflicting to the heart to see the strides which have been made by means of, and under the miserable pretext of, this war against liberty of every kind, both of speech and of writing; and to observe in another kingdom the rapid approaches to that military despotism which we affect to make an argument against peace. I know, sir, that public opinion, if it could be collected, would be for peace as much now as in 1797, and I know that it is only by public opinion—not by a sense of their duty—not by the inclination of their minds—that ministers will be brought, if ever, to give us peace. I conclude, sir, with repeating what I said before; I ask for no gentleman's vote who would have reprobated the compliance of ministers with the proposition of the French government; I ask for no gentleman's support tonight who would have voted against ministers, if they had come down and proposed to enter into a negotiation with the French; but I have a right to ask—I know that, in honor, in consistency, in conscience, I have a right to expect the vote of every gentleman who would have voted with ministers in an address to his Majesty diametrically opposite to the motion of this night.

Never, perhaps, had logic, eloquence, and debating skill been so well combined in an extemporaneous speech. According to Fox's nephew, Lord Holland, "he never spoke better" than on this momentous occasion when the fate of Europe hung in the balance. That he failed to counteract the strong intervention of the King, and to upset the large majority that Pitt enjoyed in the House, is easily understood. In the vote he lost by 265 to 64. In the verdict of history his argument was extremely effective, whether Napoleon was sincere or not; his ridicule of Pitt's position, wise and clairvoyant. In 1802 England finally concluded peace with France, the peace of Amiens. After suffering the horrors and losses of war two more years, the country was obliged to make a peace on less favorable terms than Napoleon had offered late in 1799.

Had Fox been successful and negotiations had begun in 1800, the course of European history, it is sometimes said, might have been very different. Years later, while arguing for the great Reform Bill of 1832, Lord Brougham contended that if Fox had addressed a reformed Parliament in 1800, one that represented the whole people, and not the special and selfish interests of the few, "the immortal eloquence of my right honorable friend would have prevailed." And of one thing he is completely certain: "that ruinous warfare never could have lasted a day beyond the arrival of Bonaparte's letter in 1800." This interesting, seldom cited speculation probably contains a measure of truth.

HENRY GRATTAN FLAYS A TURNCOAT

[February 14, 1800]

It will be remembered that in 1782 Ireland again rejoiced in her own Parliament—"Grattan's Parliament," as it was known to history. In spite of the continued discrimination against Catholics and impoverishing trade restrictions, relations between England and Ireland were relatively calm until the flames of the French Revolution touched Ireland, and the threats of French armies landing in Ireland began to terrify the English. In order to bind Ireland more securely to England, Pitt felt compelled to formulate an Act of Union that would dissolve the Irish Parliament. To soften the measure he no doubt hoped to arrange for Catholic emancipation so that Catholics might enter the Parliament in London and also vote—if they had the proper property qualifications.

The Act of Union had a reasonable sound, for had not Scotland been harmoniously united with England a hundred years before? The crucial objection, as Grattan was quick to point out, was that union without an Irish Parliament is union without representation, without freedom or honor, the very opposite of union. As Pitt brought forward his bill, the country was convulsed by frightful warfare between the rebels and Orangemen. Murder, rapine, reprisals, and desolation made a horror of the countryside, and when the rebel troops were

defeated, numberless informers remained, to spread hatred and suspicion. At
the same time the French landed, but after a victory at Castlebar were quickly
defeated.

These disorders and perils no doubt aided Pitt in putting through the Act
of Union. They were not enough. To induce the Irish Parliament to vote itself
out of existence, as in the case of Scotland a century before, it was necessary to
bribe the members with lands and sinecures and peerages on the most lavish
scale. Never before had corruption been so well organized or betrayal so common and respectable. When the articles of the Act of Union were presented
in the Irish Parliament, Isaac Corry, a former patriot, once a friend and ardent
admirer of Grattan, and now the Chancellor of the Exchequer for Ireland, was
selected to defend them. No doubt under the instructions and in the pay of
the English, he now went out of his way to make a vituperative attack on
Grattan. Although his health was shattered, the great orator leaped up like a
lion to answer the shameless onslaught.

*"There are times when the insignificance of the accuser
is lost in the magnitude of the accusation."*

HAS THE GENTLEMAN DONE? Has he completely done? He was
unparliamentary from the beginning to the end of his speech.
There was scarce a word he uttered that was not a violation of the privileges of the House; but I did not call him to order—why? Because the
limited talents of some men render it impossible for them to be severe
without being unparliamentary. But before I sit down I shall show him
how to be severe and parliamentary at the same time. On any other occasion I should think myself justifiable in treating with silent contempt anything which might fall from that honorable member; but there are times
when the insignificance of the accuser is lost in the magnitude of the accusation. I know the difficulty the honorable gentleman labored under
when he attacked me, conscious that, on a comparative view of our characters, public and private, there is nothing he could say which would injure me. The public would not believe the charge. I despise the falsehood. If such a charge were made by an honest man, I would answer it
in the manner I shall do before I sit down. But I shall first reply to it
when not made by an honest man.

The right honorable gentleman has called me "an unimpeached
traitor." I ask, why not "traitor," unqualified by any epithet? I will tell

him; it was because he dare not. It was the act of a coward who raises his
arm to strike, but has not courage to give the blow. I will not call him
villain, because it would be unparliamentary, and he is a Privy Councilor.
I will not call him fool, because he happens to be Chancellor of the Exchequer. But I say he is one who has abused the privilege of Parliament
and freedom of debate to the uttering language which, if spoken out of
the House, I should answer only with a blow. I care not how high his situation, how low his character, how contemptible his speech; whether a
Privy Councilor or a parasite, my answer would be a blow. He has
charged me with being connected with the rebels: the charge is utterly,
totally, and meanly false. Does the honorable gentleman rely on the report of the House of Lords for the foundation of his assertion? If he does,
I can prove to the committee there was a physical impossibility of that
report being true. But I scorn to answer any man for my conduct,
whether he be a political coxcomb or whether he brought himself into
power by a false glare of courage or not. I scorn to answer any wizard of
the Castle throwing himself into fantastical airs. But if an honorable and
independent man were to make a charge against me, I would say: "You
charge me with having an intercourse with the rebels, and you found
your charge upon what is said to have appeared before a committee of
the Lords. Sir, the report of that committee is totally and egregiously irregular." I will read a letter from Mr. Nelson, who had been examined
before that committee; it states that what the report represents him as
having spoken is *not what he said.* [Grattan here read a letter from Nelson, denying that he had any connection with Grattan as charged in the
report, and concluding by saying, "Never was misrepresentation more
vile than that put into my mouth by the report."]

From the situation that I held, and from the connections I had in the
city of Dublin, it was necessary for me to hold intercourse with various
descriptions of persons. The right honorable member might as well have
been charged with a participation in the guilt of those traitors; for he had
communicated with some of those very persons on the subject of parliamentary reform. The Irish government, too, was in communication with
some of them.

The right honorable member has told me I deserted a profession
where wealth and station were the reward of industry and talent. If I
mistake not, that gentleman endeavored to obtain those rewards by the
same means; but he soon deserted the occupation of a barrister for those
of a parasite and pander. He fled from the labor of study to flatter at the
table of the great. He found the lord's parlor a better sphere for his exertions than the hall of the Four Courts; the house of a great man a more

convenient way to power and to place; and that it was easier for a statesman of middling talents to sell his friends than for a lawyer of no talents
to sell his clients.

For myself, whatever corporate or other bodies have said or done to
me, I from the bottom of my heart forgive them. I feel I have done too
much for my country to be vexed at them. I would rather that they should
not feel or acknowledge what I have done for them, and call me traitor,
than have reason to say I sold them. I will always defend myself against
the assassin; but with large bodies it is different. To the people I will
bow; they may be my enemy—I never shall be theirs.

At the emancipation of Ireland, in 1782, I took a leading part in the
foundation of that Constitution which is now endeavored to be destroyed.
Of that Constitution I was the author; in that Constitution I glory; and
for it the honorable gentleman should bestow praise, not invent calumny.
Notwithstanding my weak state of body, I come to give my last testimony
against this union, so fatal to the liberties and interests of my country. I
come to make common cause with these honorable and virtuous gentlemen around me; to try and save the Constitution; or if not save the Constitution, at least to save our characters, and remove from our graves the
foul disgrace of standing apart while a deadly blow is aimed at the independence of our country.

The right honorable gentleman says I fled from the country after exciting rebellion, and that I have returned to raise another. No such thing.
The charge is false. The civil war had not commenced when I left the
kingdom; and I could not have returned without taking a part. On the
one side there was the camp of the rebel; on the other, the camp of
the minister, a greater traitor than that rebel. The stronghold of the Constitution was nowhere to be found. I agree that the rebel who rises against
the government should have suffered; but I missed on the scaffold the
right honorable gentleman. Two desperate parties were in arms against
the Constitution. The right honorable gentleman belonged to one of those
parties, and deserved death. I could not join the rebel—I could not join
the government—I could not join torture—I could not join half-hanging
—I could not join free quarter—I could take part with neither. I was
therefore absent from a scene where I could not be active without self-
reproach nor indifferent with safety.

Many honorable gentlemen thought differently from me: I respect
their opinions, but I keep my own; and I think now, as I thought then,
*that the treason of the minister against the liberties of the people was in-
finitely worse than the rebellion of the people against the minister.*

I have returned, not as the right honorable member has said, to raise

another storm—I have returned to discharge an honorable debt of gratitude to my country, that conferred a great reward for past services,
which, I am proud to say, was not greater than my desert. I have returned
to protect that Constitution of which I was the parent and the founder
from the assassination of such men as the honorable gentleman and his
unworthy associates. They are corrupt—they are seditious—and they, at
this very moment, are in a conspiracy against their country. I have returned to refute a libel, as false as it is malicious, given to the public
under the appellation of a report of the committee of the Lords. Here I
stand ready for impeachment or trial: I dare accusation. I defy the honorable gentleman; I defy the government; I defy their whole phalanx: let
them come forth. I tell the ministers I will neither give them quarter nor
take it. I am here to lay the shattered remains of my Constitution on the
floor of this House in defense of the liberties of my country.

This terrible invective—like nothing since Cicero's attack on Catiline—produced a fascination of horror and admiration in the hostile Parliament of turn-
coat Irish patriots. As for Grattan himself, he was invigorated, and according
to an admirer who pressed his hand as he left the hall, it had done more for
his health than all his medicine. A duel with Corry followed, the renegade
being shot in the arm. But it was typical of Grattan that he soon forgot the
personal side of the affair. Ten years later, when others would have driven him
away, he welcomed Corry to his house and took his hand.

A few days after his famous attack on Corry, Grattan was still fighting to
save the Parliament that bore his name, though the cause was now lost. "The
ministers of the Crown will," he said, "or may, perhaps, find that it is not so
easy to put down forever an ancient and respectable nation by abilities, however great, and by corruption, however irresistible; liberty may repair her golden
beams, and with redoubled heart animate the country." Unfortunately, more
than a century of Anglo-Irish bitterness was to follow, and an Irish Parliament
was not to sit again until 1921.

Catholic emancipation, which Pitt had intended as a sop for the Irish, also
miscarried. The bigoted, half-demented George III was thrown into the greatest
alarm by the mere mention of the subject, and the recent events in Ireland and
on the Continent were not of a nature to quiet his fears. Pitt resigned his office.

ROBERT EMMET DEFENDS THE IRISH CAUSE BEFORE BEING SENTENCED TO DEATH

[September 19, 1803]

With the abolition of the Irish Parliament, and the severe repression that accompanied it, Irish leaders transferred their activities to the English Parliament in London. For fifteen years political resistance disappeared in Ireland except for one abortive revolt in 1803. The leader of this uprising was a twenty-five-year-old student, the most naïve and lovable of the great Irish patriots, the least successful as a revolutionary leader.

Robert Emmet (1778–1803), the son of an eminent physician and inflexible patriot, was a brilliant student at Trinity College, Dublin, where he was admitted at the age of fifteen. With the country now in the throes of insurrection, young Emmet soon proved his powers of eloquence and his ability to inflame his fellow students with a sense of the lost glories of Ireland and her present wrongs. His fame as an orator, his glowing indictments of tyranny, and his defense of the French Revolution became known throughout college and city and soon came to the attention of the vigilant authorities. In 1798 he was expelled from Trinity because of his membership in the Society of United Irishmen and traveled several years in Europe. At first he waited for his brother, in the hope that they both might emigrate to America, but tragic events in Ireland changed his purpose. On July 23, 1803, he returned secretly to Dublin and organized an insurrection with the object of seizing the arsenal and castle. The attempt was a failure, but Emmet succeeded in escaping and would have reached the Continent and safety had he not made the fateful decision to say farewell to his fiancée in Dublin. He was quickly arrested, brought to trial, and condemned to death for treason. But a condemned man in English law has the right to speak. Emmet addressed his last words, not to the court, but to future generations.

"My country was my idol!"

My Lords:

I AM ASKED what have I to say why sentence of death should not be pronounced on me, according to law. I have nothing to say that can alter your predetermination, nor that it will become me to say, with any view to the mitigation of that sentence which you are to pronounce and

I must abide by. But I have that to say which interests me more than life, and which you have labored to destroy. I have much to say why my reputation should be rescued from the load of false accusation and calumny which has been cast upon it. I do not imagine that, seated where you are, your mind can be so free from prejudice as to receive the least impression from what I am going to utter. I have no hopes that I can anchor my character in the breast of a court constituted and trammeled as this is. I only wish, and that is the utmost that I expect, that your lordships may suffer it to float down your memories untainted by the foul breath of prejudice, until it finds some more hospitable harbor to shelter it from the storms by which it is buffeted. Were I only to suffer death, after being adjudged guilty by your tribunal, I should bow in silence, and meet the fate that awaits me without a murmur; but the sentence of the law which delivers my body to the executioner will, through the ministry of the law, labor in its own vindication to consign my character to obloquy; for there must be guilt somewhere; whether in the sentence of the court or in the catastrophe, time must determine. A man in my situation has not only to encounter the difficulties of fortune, and the force of power over minds which it has corrupted or subjugated, but the difficulties of established prejudice. The man dies, but his memory lives. That mine may not perish, that it may live in the respect of my countrymen, I seize upon this opportunity to vindicate myself from some of the charges alleged against me. When my spirit shall be wafted to a more friendly port—when my shade shall have joined the bands of those martyred heroes who have shed their blood on the scaffold and in the field, in the defense of their country and of virtue—this is my hope: I wish that my memory and my name may animate those who survive me, while I look down with complacency on the destruction of that perfidious government which upholds its domination by blasphemy of the Most High; which displays its power over man as over the beasts of the forest; which sets man upon his brother, and lifts his hand, in the name of God, against the throat of his fellow who believes or doubts a little more or a little less than the government standard—a government which is steeled to barbarity by the cries of the orphans and the tears of the widows it has made.

I appeal to the immaculate God—I swear by the throne of heaven, before which I must shortly appear—by the blood of the murdered patriots who have gone before me—that my conduct has been, through all this peril, and through all my purposes, governed only by the conviction which I have uttered, and by no other view than that of the emancipation of my country from the superinhuman oppression under which she has so long and too patiently travailed; and I confidently hope that, wild and chimerical as it may appear, there is still union and strength in Ireland to accomplish this noblest of enterprises. Of this I speak with the confidence of intimate knowledge, and with the consolation that appertains to that confidence. Think not, my lords, I say this for the petty gratification of giving you a transitory uneasiness. A man who never yet raised his voice to assert a lie will not hazard his character with posterity by asserting a falsehood on a subject so important to his country and on an occasion like this. Yes, my lords, a man who does not wish to have his epitaph written until his country is liberated will not leave a weapon in the power of envy, or a pretense to impeach the probity which he means to preserve, even in the grave to which tyranny consigns him.

Again I say that what I have spoken was not intended for your lordship [who had just interrupted him], whose situation I commiserate rather than envy—my expressions were for my countrymen. If there is a true Irishman present, let my last words cheer him in the hour of his affliction.

[Lord Norbury interrupted, saying that he did not sit there to hear treason.]

I have always understood it to be the duty of a judge, when a prisoner has been convicted, to pronounce the sentence of the law. I have also understood that judges sometimes think it their duty to hear with patience and to speak with humanity; to exhort the victim of the laws, and to offer, with tender benignity, their opinions of the motives by which he was actuated in the crime of which he was adjudged guilty. That a judge has thought it his duty so to have done, I have no doubt; but where is the boasted freedom of your institutions—where is the vaunted impartiality, clemency, and mildness of your courts of justice, if an unfortunate prisoner, whom your policy, and not justice, is about to deliver into the hands of the executioner is not suffered to explain his motives sincerely and truly and to vindicate the principles by which he was actuated? My lords, it may be a part of the system of angry justice to bow a man's mind by humiliation to the purposed ignominy of the scaffold; but worse to me than the purposed shame or the scaffold's terrors would be the shame of such foul and unfounded imputations as have been laid against me in this court. You, my lord, are a judge; I am the supposed culprit. I am a man; you are a man also. By a revolution of power we might change places, though we never could change characters. If I stand at the bar of this court and dare not vindicate my character, what a farce is your justice! If I stand at this bar and dare not vindicate my character, how dare you calumniate it? Does the sentence of death, which your unhallowed policy inflicts on my body, condemn my tongue to silence and my reputation to reproach? Your executioner may abridge the period of my existence; but

while I exist, I shall not forbear to vindicate my character and motives
from your aspersions; and, as a man, to whom fame is dearer than life,
I will make the last use of that life in doing justice to that reputation
which is to live after me, and which is the only legacy I can leave to those
I honor and love, and for whom I am proud to perish. As men, my lords,
we must appear on the great day at one common tribunal; and it will
then remain for the Searcher of All Hearts to show a collective universe
who was engaged in the most virtuous actions, or swayed by the purest
motive—my country's oppressors, or—

[Here he was ordered to listen to the sentence of the law.]

My lords, will a dying man be denied the legal privilege of exculpat-
ing himself in the eyes of the community from an undeserved reproach,
thrown upon him during his trial, by charging him with ambition, and attempting to cast away for a paltry consideration the liberties of his country? Why did your lordships insult me? Or, rather, why insult justice, in
demanding of me why sentence of death should not be pronounced
against me? I know, my lords, that form prescribes that you should ask
the question. The form also presents the right of answering. This, no
doubt, may be dispensed with, and so might the whole ceremony of the
trial, since sentence was already pronounced at the castle before the jury
were empaneled. Your lordships are but the priests of the oracle, and I
insist on the whole of the forms.

I am charged with being an emissary of France. An emissary of
France! and for what end? It is alleged that I wish to sell the independence of my country; and for what end? Was this the object of my ambition? And is this the mode by which a tribunal of justice reconciles contradiction? No; I am no emissary; and my ambition was to hold a place
among the deliverers of my country, not in power nor in profit, but in the
glory of the achievement. Sell my country's independence to France! and
for what? Was it a change of masters? No, but for ambition. Oh, my
country! was it personal ambition that could influence me? Had it been
the soul of my actions, could I not, by my education and fortune, by the
rank and consideration of my family, have placed myself amongst the
proudest of your oppressors? My country was my idol! To it I sacrificed
every selfish, every endearing sentiment; and for it I now offer up myself,
O God! No, my lords; I acted as an Irishman, determined on delivering
my country from the yoke of a foreign and unrelenting tyranny, and the
more galling yoke of a domestic faction, which is its joint partner and
perpetrator in the patricide, from the ignominy existing with an exterior
of splendor and a conscious depravity. It was the wish of my heart to ex-

tricate my country from this doubly riveted despotism—I wished to place her independence beyond the reach of any power on earth. I wished to exalt her to that proud station in the world. Connection with France was, indeed, intended, but only as far as mutual interest would sanction or require. Were the French to assume any authority inconsistent with the purest independence, it would be the signal for their destruction. We sought their aid—and we sought it as we had assurance we should obtain it—as auxiliaries in war and allies in peace. Were the French to come as invaders or enemies, uninvited by the wishes of the people, I should oppose them to the utmost of my strength. Yes! my countrymen, I should advise you to meet them upon the beach with a sword in one hand and a torch in the other. I would meet them with all the destructive fury of war. I would animate my countrymen to immolate them in their boats, before they had contaminated the soil of my country. If they succeeded in landing, and if forced to retire before superior discipline, I would dispute every inch of ground, burn every blade of grass, and the last entrenchment of liberty should be my grave. What I could not do myself, if I should fall, I should leave as a last charge to my countrymen to accomplish; because I should feel conscious that life, any more than death, is unprofitable when a foreign nation holds my country in subjection. But it was not as an enemy that the succors of France were to land. I looked, indeed, for the assistance of France; but I wished to prove to France and to the world that Irishmen deserved to be assisted; that they were indignant at slavery, and ready to assert the independence and liberty of their country. I wished to procure for my country the guarantee which Washington procured for America; to procure an aid which, by its example, would be as important as its valor; disciplined, gallant, pregnant with science and experience; that of a people who would perceive the good, and polish the rough points of our character. They would come to us as strangers, and leave us as friends, after sharing in our perils and elevating our destiny. These were my objects: not to receive new taskmasters, but to expel old tyrants. It was for these ends I sought aid from France; because France, even as an enemy, could not be more implacable than the enemy already in the bosom of my country.

I have been charged with that importance in the emancipation of my country as to be considered the keystone of the combination of Irishmen; or as your lordship expressed it, "the life and blood of the conspiracy." You do me honor overmuch: you have given to the subaltern all the credit of a superior. There are men engaged in this conspiracy who are not only superior to me, but even to your own conceptions of yourself, my lord—

men before the splendor of whose genius and virtues I should bow with
respectful deference, and who would think themselves disgraced by shaking your bloodstained hand.

What, my lord, shall you tell me, on the passage to the scaffold, which
that tyranny (of which you are only the intermediary executioner) has
erected for my murder, that I am accountable for all the blood that has
been and will be shed in this struggle of the oppressed against the oppressor—shall you tell me this, and must I be so very a slave as not to repel it? I do not fear to approach the Omnipotent Judge to answer for the
conduct of my whole life; and am I to be appalled and falsified by a mere
remnant of mortality here? By you, too, although, if it were possible to
collect all the innocent blood that you have shed in your unhallowed ministry in one great reservoir, your lordship might swim in it.

Let no man dare, when I am dead, to charge me with dishonor; let no
man attaint my memory by believing that I could have engaged in any
cause but that of my country's liberty and independence; or that I could
have become the pliant minion of power in the oppression and misery of
my country. The proclamation of the provisional government speaks for
our views; no inference can be tortured from it to countenance barbarity
or debasement at home, or subjection, humiliation, or treachery from
abroad. I would not have submitted to a foreign oppressor, for the same
reason that I would resist the foreign and domestic oppressor. In the dignity of freedom, I would have fought upon the threshold of my country,
and its enemy should enter only by passing over my lifeless corpse. And
am I, who lived but for my country, and who have subjected myself to
the dangers of the jealous and watchful oppressor, and the bondage of
the grave, only to give my countrymen their rights, and my country her
independence—am I to be loaded with calumny, and not suffered to resent it? No; God forbid!

[Here the judge told Emmet that he had disgraced his family and his
education, but more particularly his father, Dr. Emmet, who, if alive,
would not have countenanced such opinions.]

If the spirits of the illustrious dead participate in the concerns and
cares of those who were dear to them in this transitory life, oh, ever dear
and venerated shade of my departed father! look down with scrutiny
upon the conduct of your suffering son, and see if I have, even for a moment, deviated from those principles of morality and patriotism which it
was your care to instill into my youthful mind, and for which I am now
about to offer up my life. My lords, you are impatient for the sacrifice.
The blood which you seek is not congealed by the artificial terrors which
surround your victim—it circulates warmly and unruffled through the

channels which God created for noble purposes, but which you are now bent to destroy for purposes so grievous that they cry to heaven. Be yet patient! I have but a few more words to say—I am going to my cold and silent grave—my lamp of life is nearly extinguished—my race is run—the grave opens to receive me, and I sink into its bosom. I have but one request to ask at my departure from this world: it is—the charity of its silence. Let no man write my epitaph; for, as no man who knows my motives dares now vindicate them, let not prejudice or ignorance asperse them. Let them and me rest in obscurity and peace, and my tomb remain uninscribed, and my memory in oblivion, until other times and other men can do justice to my character. When my country takes her place among the nations of the earth, then, and not till then, let my epitaph be written. I have done.

The conduct of Lord Norbury, the judge in the case, was notoriously unethical, but he failed to disturb the heroic and unbending course of Emmet's speech. As he took his seat the flickering light expired. After Norbury had pronounced the death sentence, a woman hastened forward to hand the condemned man a sprig of lavender, but the officers tore it away and rushed him from the courtroom to avoid further demonstrations. On the day of his execution, Emmet, unable to shake hands with the kindly turnkey because of his fettered hands, kissed him on the cheek instead. The turnkey fainted, it is said, and did not recover until the execution was over.

Emmet, as he desired, was given no epitaph, and even the site of his grave is not known, but the portrait of "the child of the heart of Erin" was soon to be found in thousands of homes in Ireland. He became the symbol of love of mankind and hatred of tyranny. He had taught Irishmen to die and had dramatized the plight of Ireland in many lands. His school companion, Thomas Moore, wrote an unforgettable poem, "Oh! Breathe not his name," which was later set to music by Berlioz, and Washington Irving took up the same theme in "The Broken Heart," from The Sketch Book. Abraham Lincoln and many other liberal and magnanimous men were impressed by Emmet's brief career. It is a story that will live on to make men proud of being human.

LAZARE CARNOT OPPOSES A CROWN FOR BONAPARTE

[May 18, 1804]

Lazare Nicolas Marguerite Carnot (1753–1823) became involved in the French revolutionary movement in 1791. A most competent man, as well grounded in science as in the classics, he worked for the cause with an efficiency that brought him the nickname of "the organizer of victory." In 1793 he carried out the first mass conscription and was, though only an army captain, the soul of the national defense. In 1795 he was elected one of the five members of the Directory. Two years later, at one of the periodic coups d'état, he was forced into exile, despite his great services. Among the absurdities of the time, this stern republican was accused of royalist leanings. In 1800, he returned to France to become War Minister.

England rejected Napoleon's overtures of peace in 1800, as we have noted, only to be obliged, two years later, to accept the Treaty of Amiens. Fortified by this victorious settlement, Napoleon now caused himself to be elected Consul for life, with power to appoint his successor. The affirmative vote, in the popular plebiscite, was over three and a half million; the negative little more than eight thousand. In the Tribunate, which had become Napoleon's collective creature, Carnot was the only one to cast a vote against a measure that had won such overwhelming popular approval. "Were I to sign my proscription by it," he said, "nothing could force me to disguise my sentiments." Lucien Bonaparte then tore up the register, and a new vote was taken. Although the Republic was retained in name, Napoleon was virtual monarch. There followed a royalist attempt on his life and the execution of the Duc d'Enghien. Thus in 1804 the ceaselessly scheming First Consul knew that the time had come to consolidate his power and to usher out the Republic. The Senate, where many of his close followers sat, was prevailed upon to petition him "to complete his work by rendering it, like his glory, immortal." And when it seemed clear to him that the public reaction was favorable, Napoleon caused a motion to be presented to the Tribunate to have himself declared Emperor and the imperial dignity declared hereditary to his family. Only Carnot dared to speak against it.

"The government of a single person is no assurance
of a stable and tranquil government."

Fellow Citizens:

AMONG THE ORATORS who have preceded me, and who have all touched on the motion of our colleague Curée, several have anticipated the objections that might be made to it, and have responded with as much talent as amenity; they have given an example of a moderation that I shall endeavor to imitate by proposing a few ideas that have apparently escaped them. And as to those whom I oppose, and thus render myself liable to that suspicion that my motives are merely personal, whoever would attribute such to me are ignorant of the character of a man entirely devoted to his country. In reply, I ask them to examine carefully my political conduct since the commencement of the Revolution and all the record of my private life.

I am far from desiring to diminish the praises accorded the First Consul; if we owed him but the civil code, his name would worthily be immortalized to posterity. But whatever the services a citizen has rendered his country, he must expect honors but in the extent of the national recognition of his work. If the citizen has restored public liberty, if he has been a benefactor to his country, would it be a proper recompense to offer him the sacrifice of that liberty? Nay! would it not be an annulment of his own work to convert that country into his private patrimony?

From the very moment it was proposed to the French people to vote to make the consulate an office for life, each easily judged there was a mental reservation, and saw the ulterior purpose and end of the proposal. In effect, there was seen the rapid succession of a series of institutions evidently monarchical; but at each move anxiety was manifested to reassure disturbed and inquiring spirits on the score of liberty that these new institutions and arrangements were conceived only to procure the highest protection that could be desired for liberty.

Today is uncovered and developed in the most positive manner the meaning of so many of these preliminary measures. We are asked to declare ourselves upon a formal proposition to re-establish the monarchical system, and to confer an imperial and hereditary dignity on the First Consul.

At that time I voted against a life consulate; I shall vote now against any re-establishment of a monarchy, as I believe it my duty to do. But it is done with no desire to evoke partisanship; without personal feeling;

without any sentiment save a passion for the public good, which always impels me to the defense of the popular cause.

I always fully submit to existing laws, even when they are most displeasing. More than once have I been a victim to my devotion to law, and I shall not begin to retrograde today. I declare, therefore, that while I combat this proposition, from the moment that a new order of things shall have been established, which shall have received the assent of the mass of our citizens, I shall be first to conform my actions; to give to the supreme authority all the marks of deference commanded by the constitutional oligarchy. Can every member of society record a vow as sincere and disinterested as my own?

I shall not force into the discussion my preference for the general merits of any one system of government over another. On these subjects there are numberless volumes written. I shall charge myself with examining in few words, and in the simplest terms, the particular case in which present circumstances place us. All the arguments thus far made for the re-establishment of monarchy in France are reduced to the statement that it is the only method of assuring the stability of the government and the public tranquillity, the only escape from internal disorder, the sole bond of union against external enemies; that the republican system has been vainly essayed in all possible manners; and that from all these efforts only anarchy has resulted. A prolonged and ceaseless revolution has reawakened a perpetual fear of new disorders, and consequently a deep and universal desire to see re-established the old hereditary government, changing only the dynasty. To this we must make reply.

I remark here that the government of a single person is no assurance of a stable and tranquil government. The duration of the Roman Empire was no longer than that of the Roman Republic. Their internecine troubles were greater, their crimes more multiplied. The pride of republicanism, the heroism, and the masculine virtues were replaced by the most ridiculous vanity, the vilest adulation, the boldest cupidity, the most absolute indifference to the national prosperity. Where was any remedy in the heredity of the throne? Was it not regarded as the legitimate heritage of the house of Augustus? Was a Domitian not the son of Vespasian, a Caligula the son of Germanicus, a Commodus the son of Marcus Aurelius? In France, it is true, the last dynasty maintained itself for eight hundred years, but were the people any the less tormented? What have been the internal dissensions? What the foreign wars undertaken for pretensions and rights of succession, which gave birth to the alliances of this dynasty with foreign nations? From the moment that a nation espouses the particular interest of one family, she is compelled to intervene in a multitude of matters that but for this would be to her of uttermost in-difference. We have hardly succeeded in establishing a republic among us, notwithstanding that we have essayed it under various forms more or less democratic. . . .

After the peace of Amiens, Napoleon had choice between the republi-can and monarchical systems; he could do as he pleased. He would have met but the lightest opposition. The citadel of Liberty was confided to him; he swore to defend it; and holding his promise, he should have ful-filled the desire of the nation which judged him alone capable of solving the grand problem of public liberty in its vast extent. He might have covered himself with an incomparable glory. Instead of that, what is being done today? They propose to make for him an absolute and heredi-tary property of a great power of which he was made the administrator. Is this the real desire and to the real interest of the First Consul himself? I do not believe it.

It is true the state was falling into dissolution, and that absolutism pulled it from the edge of the abyss. But what do we conclude from that? What all the world knows—that political bodies are subject to af-fections which can be cured but by violent remedies; that sometimes a dictator is necessary for a moment to save liberty. The Romans, who were so jealous of it, nevertheless recognized the necessity of this supreme power at intervals. But because a violent remedy has saved a patient, must there be a daily administration of violent remedies? Fabius, Cincin-natus, Camillus saved Rome by the exercise of absolute power, but they relinquished this power as soon as practicable; they would have killed Rome had they continued to wield it. Caesar was the first who desired to keep this power: he became its victim; but liberty was lost for futurity. Thus everything that has ever been said up to this day on absolute gov-ernment proves only the necessity for temporary dictatorships in crises of the state, but not the establishment of a permanent and irresponsible power.

It is not from the character of their government that great republics have lacked stability; it is because, having been born in the breasts of storms, it is always in a state of exaltation that they are established. One only was the labor of philosophy, organized calmly. That republic, the United States of America, full of wisdom and of strength, exhibits this phenomenon, and each day their prosperity shows an increase that as-tonishes other nations. Thus it was reserved for the New World to teach the Old that existence is possible and peaceable under the rule of liberty and equality. Yes, I state this proposition, that when a new order of things can be established without fearing partisan influences, as the First Con-

sul has done, principally after the peace of Amiens, and as he can still
do, it becomes much easier to form a republic without anarchy than a
monarchy without despotism. For how can we conceive a limitation that
would not be illusory in a government of which the chief had all the
executive power in his hand and all the places to bestow?

They have spoken of institutions to produce all these good effects.
But before we propose to establish a monarchy, should we not first assure ourselves and demonstrate to those who are to vote on the question
that these institutions proposed are in the order of possible things, and
not metaphysical obstructions, which have been held a reproach to the
opposite system? Up to this moment nothing has been successfully invented to curb supreme power but what are called intermediary bodies
or privileges. Is it, then, of a new nobility you would speak when you
allude to institutions? But such remedies—are they not worse than the
disease? For the absolute power of a monarch takes but our liberty, while
the institution of privileged classes robs us at the same time of our liberty and our equality. And if even at the commencement dignities and
ranks were but personal, we know they would finish always, as the fiefs
of other times, in becoming hereditary.

To these general principles I shall add a few special observations. I
assume that all the French give assent to these proposed changes; but
will it be the real free will and wish of Frenchmen that is produced from
a register where each is obliged to individually sign his vote? Who does
not know what is the influence in similar cases of the presiding authority?
From all parties in France, it would be said, springs a universal desire
of the citizens for the re-establishment of the hereditary monarchy; but
can we not look suspiciously on an opinion, concentrated thus far almost
exclusively among public functionaries, when we consider the inconvenience they would have to manifest any contrary opinion; when we
know that the liberty of the press is so enfeebled that it is not possible to
insert in any journal the most moderate and respectful protests?

Doubtlessly there will be no making any choice of the hereditary chief,
if they declare it necessary to have one.

Is it hoped, in raising this new dynasty, to hasten the period of general peace? Will it not rather be a new obstacle? Are we assured that the
other great powers of Europe will assent to this new title? And if they do
not, do we take up arms to constrain them? Or after having sunk the
title of First Consul in that of Emperor, will he be content to remain First
Consul to the rest of Europe while he is Emperor only to Frenchmen,
or shall we compromise by a vain title the security and the prosperity of
the entire nation?

It appears, therefore, infinitely doubtful if the new order of things can give us the stability of the present state. There is for the government one method of consolidation and strength. It is to be just; that no favoritism or bias be of avail to influence its services; that there be a guarantee against robbery and fraud. It is far from me to desire to make any particular application of my language or to criticize the conduct of the government. It is against arbitrary power itself I appeal, and not against those in whose hands this power may reside. Has liberty then been shown to man that he shall never enjoy it? Shall it always be held to his gaze as a fruit that when he extends the hand to grasp he must be stricken with death? And nature, which has made liberty such a pressing need to us, does she really desire to betray our confidence? No! I shall never believe this good, so universally preferred to all others—without which all others are nothing—is a simple illusion. My heart tells me that liberty is possible, that its regime is easier and more stable than any arbitrary government, than any oligarchy.

Like so many of the finest speeches, this one had no immediate effect—except to reprove the consciences of those who feared to do likewise. A new era now began, that of the Empire. Napoleon may have imagined that he was completing the Revolution, but it is truer to say that he had destroyed it. What he had introduced in its place, though his civil code and the reforms were of the first importance, was simply the old eighteenth-century ideal of benevolent despotism. Jacobinism was soon overwhelmed by the severity and glories of the Empire.

The speech, however, added luster to Carnot's name and made its impression on men of later generations who also faced the trial of freedom. In his reply to Abraham Small, who had sent him a copy of The American Speaker, Jefferson wrote, on May 20, 1814, praising the "short, nervous, and unanswerable speech of Carnot." "This creed of republicanism," he wrote, "should be translated and placed in the hands of every friend to the rights of self-government."

PITT REPLIES TO A TOAST

[November 9, 1805]

A fortnight after the news of Nelson's glorious victory at Trafalgar was received in London, the Lord Mayor's annual dinner was held. During the festivities, Pitt, who had only recently returned as Prime Minister, was toasted as "the savior of Europe." Pitt's three sentences in reply were ranked by Lord Curzon, a century later, as one of the three indisputable masterpieces of English eloquence:

"Europe is not to be saved by any single man."

I RETURN YOU MANY THANKS for the honor you have done me. But Europe is not to be saved by any single man. England has saved herself by her exertions, and will, as I trust, save Europe by her example.

The triumph was brief for England and her allies. One month later, on December 2, Napoleon achieved at Austerlitz one of his most brilliant victories, crushing the combined forces of Austria and Russia. After receiving that news Pitt declined rapidly. Seeing a map of Europe, he said: "Roll up that map. It will not be wanted these ten years." He died a few days later, on January 23, 1806. He was forty-six years old and had been Prime Minister nearly half his life.

BYRON STRIKES AN EARLY BLOW
FOR THE RIGHTS OF LABOR

[February 27, 1812]

The inevitable growth of the Industrial Revolution in England was accelerated by conditions prevailing during two decades of war with France. Whatever successes England won on land were achieved through lavish financing of her Continental allies, which was paid for by the steady impoverishment of the English working class. From 1797 to 1811, for example, real wages of hand-loom weavers declined by almost fifty per cent. At the same time anticombination laws prevented workingmen from organizing in their own defense. The situation became increasingly serious. By 1811 the introduction of larger frames had produced so much unemployment and actual starvation among the weavers that secret bands of desperate men, known as Luddites, began to break the weaving frames, and destruction soon spread to four counties. Parliament, alarmed and angry, acted with feverish haste, and a bill was brought forward providing the death penalty for the frame breakers.

Only a few men in Parliament had the heart or the daring to oppose this vicious and hysterical measure. Among them was young Lord Byron (1788–1824), already known for his early poems, Hours of Idleness, and for his fighting reply to critics, English Bards and Scotch Reviewers. Returning to England in the summer of 1811, after two years of travel abroad, he began, arrogantly, awkwardly, shyly, his descent on London society. Although he had taken his seat in the House of Lords three years before, he had not yet made his maiden speech. In casting about for a subject, he chose the Frame-breaking Bill for two excellent reasons: he loathed cruelty and, as a landed aristocrat, disliked the newly rich. On February 27, 1812, he addressed the House of Lords for the first time.

"Is there not blood enough upon your penal code!"

My Lords:

THE SUBJECT now submitted to your lordships, for the first time, though new to the House, is, by no means, new to the country. I believe it had occupied the serious thoughts of all descriptions of persons long before its introduction to the notice of that legislature whose interference alone could be of real service. As a person in some degree connected with the suffering county, though a stranger, not only to this House in general, but to almost every individual whose attention I presume to solicit, I must claim some portion of your lordships' indulgence, whilst I offer a few observations on a question in which I confess myself deeply interested. To enter into any detail of these riots would be superfluous; the House is already aware that every outrage short of actual bloodshed has been perpetrated, and that the proprietors of the frames obnoxious to the rioters, and all persons supposed to be connected with them, have been liable to insult and violence. During the short time I recently passed in Notts, not twelve hours elapsed without some fresh act of violence; and on the day I left the county, I was informed that forty frames had been broken the preceding evening as usual, without resistance and without detection. Such was then the state of that county, and such I have reason to believe it to be at this moment.

But whilst these outrages must be admitted to exist to an alarming extent, it cannot be denied that they have arisen from circumstances of the most unparalleled distress. The perseverance of these miserable men in their proceedings tends to prove that nothing but absolute want could have driven a large and once honest and industrious body of the people into the commission of excesses so hazardous to themselves, their families, and the community. At the time to which I allude, the town and county were burthened with large detachments of the military; the police was in motion, the magistrates assembled, yet all these movements, civil and military, had led to—nothing. Not a single instance had occurred of the apprehension of any real delinquent actually taken in the act, against whom there existed legal evidence sufficient for conviction. But the police, however useless, were by no means idle: several notorious delinquents had been detected; men liable to conviction, on the clearest evidence, of the capital crime of poverty; men who had been nefariously guilty of lawfully begetting several children, whom, thanks to the times! they were unable to maintain.

Considerable injury has been done to the proprietors of the improved frames. These machines were to them an advantage, inasmuch as they superseded the necessity of employing a number of workmen, who were left in consequence to starve. By the adoption of one species of frame in particular, one man performed the work of many, and the superfluous laborers were thrown out of employment. Yet it is to be observed that the work thus executed was inferior in quality, not marketable at home, and merely hurried over with a view to exportation. It was called, in the cant of the trade, by the name of spider-work. The rejected workmen, in the blindness of their ignorance, instead of rejoicing at these improvements in arts so beneficial to mankind, conceived themselves to be sacrificed to improvements in mechanism. In the foolishness of their hearts, they imagined that the maintenance and well-doing of the industrious poor were objects of greater consequence than the enrichment of a few individuals by any improvement in the implements of trade which threw the workmen out of employment, and rendered the laborer unworthy of his hire. And, it must be confessed, that although the adoption of the enlarged machinery, in that state of our commerce which the country once boasted, might have been beneficial to the master without being detrimental to the servant; yet, in the present situation of our manufactures, rotting in warehouses without a prospect of exportation, which the demand for work and workmen equally diminished, frames of this construction tend materially to aggravate the distresses and discontents of the disappointed sufferers.

But the real cause of these distresses, and consequent disturbances, lies deeper. When we are told that these men are leagued together, not only for the destruction of their own comfort, but of their very means of subsistence, can we forget that it is the bitter policy, the destructive warfare, of the last eighteen years which has destroyed their comfort, your comfort, all men's comfort—that policy which, originating with "great statesmen now no more," has survived the dead to become a curse on the living unto the third and fourth generation! These men never destroyed their looms till they were become useless, worse than useless; till they were become actual impediments to their exertions in obtaining their daily bread. Can you then wonder that in times like these, when bankruptcy, convicted fraud, and imputed felony are found in a station not far beneath that of your lordships, the lowest, though once most useful portion of the people, should forget their duty in their distresses, and become only less guilty than one of their representatives? But while the exalted offender can find means to baffle the law, new capital punishments must be devised, new snares of death must be spread, for the wretched mechanic who is famished into guilt. These men were willing to dig, but the spade was in other hands; they were not ashamed to beg, but there was none to relieve them. Their own means of subsistence were cut off; all other employments preoccupied; and their excesses, however to be deplored and condemned, can hardly be the subject of surprise.

It has been stated that the persons in the temporary possession of frames connive at their destruction; if this be proved upon inquiry, it were necessary that such material accessories to the crime should be principals in the punishment. But I did hope that any measure proposed by his Majesty's government for your lordships' decision would have had conciliation for its basis; or, if that were hopeless, that some previous inquiry, some deliberation, would have been deemed requisite; not that we should have been called at once, without examination and without cause, to pass sentences by wholesale and sign death warrants blindfold. . . .

In what state of apathy have we been plunged so long that now, for the first time, the House has been officially apprised of these disturbances? All this has been transacting within one hundred and thirty miles of London, and yet we, "good easy men! have deemed full sure our greatness was a ripening," and have sat down to enjoy our foreign triumphs in the midst of domestic calamity. But all the cities you have taken, all the armies which have retreated before your leaders, are but paltry subjects of self-congratulation, if your land divides against itself, and your dragoons and executioners must be let loose against your fellow citizens. You call these men a mob, desperate, dangerous, and ignorant; and seem to think that the only way to quiet the *bellua multorum capitum* is to lop off a few of its superfluous heads. But even a mob may be better reduced to reason by a mixture of conciliation and firmness than by additional irritation and redoubled penalties. Are we aware of our obligations to a *mob?* It is the mob that labor in your fields, and serve in your houses—that man your navy, and recruit your army—that have enabled you to defy all the world —and can also defy you, when neglect and calamity have driven them to despair. You may call the people a mob, but do not forget that a mob too often speaks the sentiments of the people. And here I must remark with what alacrity you are accustomed to fly to the succor of your distressed allies, leaving the distressed of your own country to the care of Providence or—the parish. When the Portuguese suffered under the retreat of the French, every arm was stretched out, every hand was opened —from the rich man's largess to the widow's mite, all was bestowed to enable them to rebuild their villages and replenish their granaries. And at this moment, when thousands of misguided but most unfortunate fellow countrymen are struggling with the extremes of hardship and hunger, as your charity began abroad, it should end at home. A much less sum, a tithe of the bounty bestowed on Portugal, even if these men (which I cannot admit without inquiry) could not have been restored to their employments, would have rendered unnecessary the tender mercies of the bayonet and the gibbet. But doubtless our funds have too many foreign claims to admit a prospect of domestic relief—though never did such objects demand it.

I have traversed the seat of war in the Peninsula; I have been in some of the most oppressed provinces of Turkey; but never, under the most despotic of infidel governments, did I behold such squalid wretchedness as I have seen, since my return, in the very heart of a Christian country. And what are your remedies? After months of inaction, and months of action worse than inactivity, at length comes forth the grand specific, the never-failing nostrum of all state physicians from the days of Draco to the present time. After feeling the pulse and shaking the head over the patient, prescribing the usual course of warm water and bleeding—the warm water of your mawkish police, and the lancets of your military—these convulsions must terminate in death, the sure consummation of the prescriptions of all political Sangrados. Setting aside the palpable injustice and the certain inefficiency of the bill, are there not capital punishments sufficient on your statutes? Is there not blood enough upon your penal code! that more must be poured forth to ascend to heaven and testify against you? How will you carry this bill into effect? Can you commit a whole country to their own prisons? Will you erect a gibbet in every field, and hang up men like scarecrows? Or will you proceed (as you must to bring this measure into effect) by decimation; place the country under martial law; depopulate and lay waste all around you; and restore Sherwood Forest as an acceptable gift to the Crown in its former condition of a royal chase, and an asylum for outlaws? Are these the remedies for a starving and desperate populace? Will the famished wretch who has braved your bayonets be appalled by your gibbets? When death is a relief, and the only relief it appears that you will afford him, will he be dragooned into tranquillity? Will that which could not be effected by your grenadiers be accomplished by your executioners? If you proceed by the forms of law, where is your evidence? Those who have refused to impeach their accomplices when transportation only was the punishment will hardly be tempted to witness against them when death is the penalty.

With all due deference to the noble lords opposite, I think a little investigation, some previous inquiry, would induce even them to change their purpose. That most favorite state measure, so marvelously efficacious in many and recent instances, *temporizing*, would not be without its advantage in this. When a proposal is made to emancipate or relieve, you hesitate, you deliberate for years, you temporize and tamper with the minds of men; but a death bill must be passed offhand, without a thought of the consequences. Sure I am, from what I have heard and from what I have seen, that to pass the bill under all the existing circumstances, without inquiry, without deliberation, would only be to add injustice to irritation and barbarity to neglect. The framers of such a bill must be content to inherit the honors of that Athenian lawgiver whose edicts were said to be written, not in ink, but in blood. But suppose it past—suppose one of these men, as I have seen them meager with famine, sullen with despair, careless of a life which your lordships are perhaps about to value at something less than the price of a stocking frame; suppose this man surrounded by those children for whom he is unable to procure bread at the hazard of his existence, about to be torn forever from a family which he lately supported in peaceful industry, and which it is not his fault that he can no longer so support; suppose this man—and there are ten thousand such from whom you may select your victims—dragged into court to be tried for this new offense, by this new law—still there are two things wanting to convict and condemn him, and these are, in my opinion, twelve butchers for a jury and a Jeffreys for a judge!

When one remembers the youth and inexperience of the speaker and the time of war and hysteria, this is certainly one of the most courageous and moving appeals on record. The Lords remained unconvinced. The bill became law, and many desperate, misguided men were condemned to death under it. A bad conscience remained, however, and more death sentences were commuted to "transportation" than were actually carried out. The Luddites were among the earliest martyrs of the Industrial Revolution.

As for Byron, he left the House of Lords that day in high spirits, his ear ringing with the compliments paid to him on all sides. But his career as an orator ended almost as suddenly as it began. Two weeks later he awakened one morning to find himself famous, for overnight Childe Harold became the most astonishing success in literary history. "Nobody ever thought about my prose afterward," he later wrote, "nor indeed did I: it became to me a secondary and neglected object."

NAPOLEON BIDS FAREWELL
TO THE OLD GUARD

[April 20, 1814]

We first encountered young General Bonaparte addressing his triumphant Army of Italy in 1796. We noted that as First Consul in 1799 he wrote a personal letter to George III, making overtures for peace, and that he became Consul for life in 1802 and Emperor in 1804. After the Emperor's victory at Austerlitz we heard Pitt say, "Roll up that map. It will not be needed these ten years." But the Emperor's actions leagued all Europe against him. And arrogance led steadily to disaster. In 1812 he made the fatal journey to Moscow. In 1813 he was defeated at Leipzig in the Battle of the Nations. In 1814 abdication was his only alternative, and he took it with some dignity.

Through the years his printed proclamations to his troops took the place of speeches, inspiring confidence on the eve of battle, and sharing credit after victory. Those proclamations so convey the illusion of the living voice that they are often presented as speeches that were actually delivered.

But it was the living voice that moved the Old Guard to tears as their officers stood in a half circle around Napoleon after his abdication at the palace of Fontainebleau.

"I have always found you on the road to glory."

SOLDIERS, I bid you farewell. For twenty years that we have been together your conduct has left me nothing to desire. I have always found you on the road to glory. All the powers of Europe have combined in arms against *me*.

A few of my generals have proved untrue to their duty and to France. France herself has desired other destinies; with you and the brave men who still are faithful, I might have carried on a civil war; but France would be unhappy. Be faithful, then, to your new king, be obedient to your new commanders, and desert not our beloved country.

Do not lament my lot; I will be happy when I know that you are so. I might have died; if I consent to live, it is still to promote your glory. I will write the great things that we have achieved.

I cannot embrace you all, but I embrace your general. Come, General Petit, that I may press you to my heart! Bring me the eagle, that I may embrace it also! Ah! dear eagle, may this kiss which I give thee find an echo to the latest posterity! Adieu, my children; the best wishes of my heart shall be always with you: do not forget me!

Napoleon was also deeply moved, but he quickly pulled himself together, entered his carriage, and started the bitter journey to the island of Elba, off the coast of Italy. But a year later he returned for the famous "Hundred Days" that ended with Waterloo. Then came the much longer exile on the more remote island of St. Helena, where he became the chief creator of his own legend.

PART TEN

FIRE BELLS IN THE NIGHT

T HE DEBATES over the Federal Constitution brought forth a number of memorable speeches, especially those of Alexander Hamilton and Patrick Henry, but in the three decades following Washington's inauguration, only the weird voice of John Randolph rang out with great distinction on the national scene. It is true that Clay, Calhoun, and Webster reached Congress before, or during, the War of 1812, but they did not attain to their full stature until some years later.

Clay's own bill, the Missouri Compromise, which he skillfully maneuvered through the Senate in 1820, was defended by other men, most notably by the famous lawyer, William Pinkney of Maryland. Although Pinkney's reputation at the bar rivaled Webster's, he was also vain and theatrical, and left behind no speech that attests to his undoubted talents. Thomas H. Benton, in recalling the Missouri Compromise debate, remarked that Pinkney himself knew that his "gorgeous, most applauded" speech in the Senate was "only a magnificent exhibition," and therefore avoided its publication.

The Missouri Compromise provided for the admission of Maine as a free state and of Missouri as a slave state, but with the further provision that all the remainder of the vast Louisiana Territory (extending from the Mississippi to the Rocky Mountains) north of 36°30', the southern boundary of Missouri, was to remain forever free. The Compromise was passed, but only after hot discussion, for to the slaveholding South it seemed to be an unfair restriction on slavery and to the North it was a dangerous concession.

For the seventy-seven-year-old sage of Monticello it was terrible news. Long happy in retirement and busy with plans for the University of Virginia, Jefferson now (April 22, 1820) wrote one of his memorable letters to a comparative stranger, John Holmes of Maine: "I had for a long time ceased to read the newspapers, or pay any attention to public affairs, confident that they were in good hands, and content to be a passenger in our bark to the shore from which I am not distant. But this momentous question, like a fire bell in the night, awakened and filled me with terror. I considered it at once as the knell of the Union. It is hushed, indeed, for the moment. But this is a reprieve only, not a final sentence. A geographical line, coinciding with a marked principle, moral and political, once conceived and held up to the angry passions of men, will never be obliterated; and every new irritation will make it deeper and deeper."

The Missouri Compromise, as Jefferson predicted, did not put out the fire that threatened the Union, but merely banked the flames. In the meantime other issues came to a head in the turbulent new continent, and men and women here and there expressed themselves publicly in stirring language. America was finding itself, molding its traditions, consecrating its heroes, forging a national will. But there were obstacles to unity that were to increase vastly through the years—the condition of the factory workers and the sub-jugation of women, for example, besides the unpopular war with Mexico. But the greatest threat to unity, in the years from 1820 to 1850, was of course the slavery issue. Yet, as Jefferson said: "It is hushed, indeed, for the moment."

DANIEL WEBSTER CELEBRATES
THE AMERICAN HERITAGE

[August 2, 1826]

Had Daniel Webster (1782–1852) died at forty-eight instead of seventy, he would stand clearly with the supreme Americans. Looking back on him now, we are apt to see him as the fallen idol who defended the Fugitive Slave Law of 1850, as the voluble tool of New England financial interests, as "a great man with a small ambition," to use the words of the disappointed Emerson. We thus forget the mighty decade, 1820–30, in which he was a kind of Homer molding the spirit of a nation with speeches at Plymouth and Bunker Hill, in Faneuil Hall and the Senate—speeches which only Lincoln's were to replace many years later.

A poor New Hampshire boy, he was graduated from Dartmouth College, and then advanced rapidly in law and politics, representing New Hampshire for two terms in the House of Representatives. In August, 1816, he moved to Boston and a more lucrative legal practice. Early in 1819 he appeared before the Supreme Court in the famous Dartmouth College case, saving his alma mater from veritable seizure by state politicians. His masterly defense moved the court and the audience to tears, especially when he let fall that casual remark: "It is, sir, as I have said, a small college. And yet, there are those who love it."

Superb as Webster already was in the courtroom and as he was to become in the United States Senate, it was on great ceremonial occasions—in the department of "demonstrative oratory"—that he attained his vast popular reputation. The first of these was at Plymouth on December 22, 1820, when he spoke on the two-hundredth anniversary of the first settlement of New England. The old church was crowded as the orator of the day, majestic in presence and magnificent in voice, took up his theme.

He spoke for nearly two hours, scarcely referring to his manuscript. The effect was recorded by a young Harvard scholar, George Ticknor: "I was never so excited by public speaking before in my life. Three or four times I thought my temples would burst with the gush of blood. . . . When I came out I was almost afraid to come near him. It seemed to me as if he was like the mount that might not be touched and that burned with fire. I was beside myself and I am still so."

On the fiftieth anniversary of the battle of Bunker Hill some twenty thousand people gathered to witness the laying of the cornerstone of the monument commemorating the battle. Fifty surviving veterans shared the place of honor with the aged Lafayette. And again "the godlike Daniel" wove his spell.

However, we are so out of sympathy or out of touch with Webster's grandiose style of commemorative oratory that we cannot read it at length and we should not read it in snatches. His was a massive personality and he put on a massive performance surpassing any other on the platform, the stage, or in the pulpit of his time. And he was enough of an intellect, orator, and even actor to be equally effective when assuming a style less orotund than that of the once popular Plymouth and Bunker Hill speeches.

On the fiftieth anniversary of the signing of the Declaration of Independence, on July 4, 1826, John Adams and Thomas Jefferson died. It was appropriate to hold a double memorial service for them in "the cradle of liberty," Faneuil Hall, and it was inevitable that Webster would be the speaker.

The high point of Webster's discourse was the speech he attributed to John Adams (in the manner of the ancient historians) in the secret debate over the Declaration of Independence in the Continental Congress. Jefferson, the old sage at Monticello, had told Webster that "John Adams was our colossus on the floor. Not graceful, not elegant, not always fluent, in his public addresses, he yet came out with a power, both of thought and of expression, which moved us from our seats."

That conversation was no doubt the germ of Webster's imaginary debate between a nameless opponent of the motion to adopt the Declaration and John Adams. Now John Adams speaks through the mouth of Daniel Webster.

"And so that day shall be honored."

SINK OR SWIM, live or die, survive or perish, I give my hand and my heart to this vote. It is true, indeed, that in the beginning we aimed not at independence. But there's a divinity which shapes our ends. The injustice of England has driven us to arms; and, blinded to her own interest for our good, she has obstinately persisted, till independence is now within our grasp.. We have but to reach forth to it, and it is ours. Why, then, should we defer the Declaration? Is any man so weak as now to hope for a reconciliation with England, which shall leave either safety to the country and its liberties, or safety to his own life and his own honor? Are not you, sir, who sit in that chair—is not he, our venerable colleague near you—are you not both already the proscribed and pre-destined objects of punishment and of vengeance? Cut off from all hope of royal clemency, what are you, what can you be, while the power of England remains, but outlaws? If we postpone independence, do we mean to carry on, or to give up, the war? Do we mean to submit to the measures of Parliament, Boston Port Bill and all? Do we mean to submit, and consent that we ourselves shall be ground to powder, and our country and its rights trodden down in the dust? I know we do not mean to submit. We never shall submit. Do we intend to violate that most solemn obligation ever entered into by men—that plighting, before God, of our sacred honor to Washington, when, putting him forth to incur the dangers of war, as well as the political hazards of the times, we promised to adhere to him, in every extremity, with our fortunes and our lives? I know there is not a man here who would not rather see a general conflagration sweep over the land, or an earthquake sink it, than one jot or tittle of that plighted faith fall to the ground. For myself, having twelve months ago in this place moved you that George Washington be appointed commander of the forces, raised or to be raised, for defense of American liberty, may my right hand forget her cunning, and my tongue cleave to the roof of my mouth, if I hesitate or waver in the support I give him. The war, then, must go on. We must fight it through. And, if the war must go on, why put off longer the Declaration of Independence? That measure will strengthen us. It will give us character abroad. The nations will then treat with us, which they never can do while we acknowledge ourselves subjects in arms against our sovereign. Nay, I maintain that England herself will sooner treat for peace with us on the footing of independence than consent, by repealing her acts, to acknowledge that her whole conduct toward us has been a course of injustice and oppression. Her pride will be less wounded by submitting to that course of things which now predestinates our independence than by yielding the points in controversy to her rebellious subjects. The former she would regard as the result of fortune; the latter she would feel as her own deep disgrace. Why, then—why, then, sir, do we not, as soon as possible, change this from a civil to a national war? And since we must fight it through, why not put ourselves in a state to enjoy all the benefits of victory, if we gain the victory?

"If we fail, it can be no worse for us. But we shall not fail. The cause will raise up armies; the cause will create navies. The people—the people, if we are true to them, will carry us, and will carry themselves, gloriously through this struggle. I care not how fickle other people have been found. I know the people of these colonies, and I know that resistance to British aggression is deep and settled in their hearts and cannot be eradicated. Every colony, indeed, has expressed its willingness to follow, if we but take the lead. Sir, the Declaration will inspire the people with increased courage. Instead of a long and bloody war for restoration of privileges, for redress of grievances, for chartered immunities, held under a British king, set before them the glorious object of entire independence, and it will breathe into them anew the breath of life. Read this Declaration at the head of the army; every sword will be drawn from its scabbard, and the solemn vow uttered to maintain it, or to perish on the bed of honor. Publish it from the pulpit; religion will approve it, and the love of religious liberty will cling round it, resolved to stand with it, or fall with it. Send it to the public halls; proclaim it there; let them hear it who heard the first roar of the enemy's cannon; let them see it who saw their brothers and their sons fall on the field of Bunker Hill, and in the streets of Lexington and Concord, and the very walls will cry out in its support.

"Sir, I know the uncertainty of human affairs, but I see, I see clearly, through this day's business. You and I, indeed, may rue it. We may not live to the time when this Declaration shall be made good. We may die; die, colonists; die, slaves; die, it may be, ignominiously and on the scaffold. Be it so. Be it so. If it be the pleasure of heaven that my country shall require the poor offering of my life, the victim shall be ready at the appointed hour of sacrifice, come when that hour may. But while I do live, let me have a country, or at least the hope of a country, and that a free country.

"But, whatever may be our fate, be assured, be assured, that this

Declaration will stand. It may cost treasure, and it may cost blood; but it will stand, and it will richly compensate for both. Through the thick gloom of the present I see the brightness of the future as the sun in heaven. We shall make this a glorious, an immortal day. When we are in our graves, our children will honor it. They will celebrate it with thanksgiving, with festivity, with bonfires, and illuminations. On its annual return they will shed tears, copious, gushing tears, not of subjection and slavery, not of agony and distress, but of exultation, of gratitude, and of joy. Sir, before God, I believe the hour has come. My judgment approves this measure, and my whole heart is in it. All that I have, and all that I am, and all that I hope, in this life, I am now ready here to stake upon it; and I leave off as I began, that, live or die, survive or perish, I am for the Declaration. It is my living sentiment, and, by the blessing of God, it shall be my dying sentiment; independence now, and independence forever."

And so that day shall be honored, illustrious prophet and patriot! so that day shall be honored, and, as often as it returns, thy renown shall come along with it, and the glory of thy life, like the day of thy death, shall not fail from the remembrance of men.

Present in the audience was a young student of oratory by the name of Ralph Waldo Emerson, and the day after the delivery of the speech, he wrote in his journal: "Yesterday I attended the funeral solemnities in Faneuil Hall in honor of John Adams and Thomas Jefferson. The oration of Mr. Webster was worthy of his fame, and what is much more, was worthy of the august occasion. Never, I think, were the awful charms of person, manners, and voice outdone. For in the beginning unpromising, and in other parts imperfect, in what was truly grand he fully realized the boldest conceptions of eloquence."

Webster received many inquiries about the Adams speech. To one of these, written nearly twenty years later, Webster replied: "Your inquiry is easily answered. The Congress of the Revolution sat with closed doors. Its proceedings were made known to the public from time to time by printing its journal; but the debates were not published. So far as I know, there is not existing, in print or manuscript, the speech, or any part or fragment of the speech, delivered by Mr. Adams on the question of the Declaration of Independence. We only know, from the testimony of his auditors, that he spoke with remarkable ability and characteristic earnestness.

"The day after the Declaration was made, Mr. Adams, in writing to a friend, declared the event to be one that 'ought to be commemorated, as the day of deliverance, by solemn acts of devotion to God Almighty. It ought to be *solemnized with pomp and parade, with shows, games, sports, guns, bells, bonfires, and illuminations, from one end of this continent to the other, from this time forward, forevermore.'*

"And on the day of his death, hearing the noise of bells and cannon, he asked the occasion. On being reminded that it was 'Independent day,' he replied, 'Independence forever!' These expressions were introduced into the speech supposed to have been made by him. For the rest I must be answerable. The speech was written by me, in my house in Boston, the day before the delivery of the discourse in Faneuil Hall; a poor substitute, I am sure it would appear to be, if we could now see the speech actually made by Mr. Adams on that transcendently important occasion."

JOHN RANDOLPH OF ROANOKE LAYS THE GROUND FOR DISUNION

[January 31, 1824]

While Daniel Webster was painting his mighty fresco of the American past, John Randolph (1773–1833) was already pointing out the cracks in the plaster. This enigmatic, much loved, much loathed figure has been unjustifiably obscured by Clay, Calhoun, Webster, and even Benton. For his biographer, H. A. Garland in 1850, he was Virginia's "wisest statesman, truest patriot, and most devoted son." For his biographer, Henry Adams in 1882, he was a monstrous political Iago, without mental stability or moral sense. Yet it is now generally agreed that Randolph spoke with a brilliant fluency, an insolent ease, that has never been surpassed on the floors of Congress. It is generally agreed that he foresaw more clearly than any of his contemporaries the tragic conflict that was to grow out of the slavery issue. It is less realized that "Calhoun himself learned his lesson from the speeches of this man" (Henry Adams), and that whatever was original in Calhoun's defense of minority interests against an overpowering majority went back to the thought of John Randolph.

Randolph was first of all a Virginian, a Virginia country gentleman, with a febrile nervous system. He went for a time to Princeton and Columbia College, but his essential education lay in the voracious reading that continued through life. Erratic, dangerously ill-tempered from an early age, he seems to have suffered from impotence and a dread of insanity. Entering the House of Representatives in 1799 as an ardent Jeffersonian, he became the administration's aggressive leader during Jefferson's first term, 1801–05, and soon proved himself the master of parliamentary terror. But by 1806 he had begun his long, bitter career of opposition, ending only with his death in 1833. There were personal jealousies, particularly of Madison; dark suspicions of secret and corrupt influence; fear of the growth of a strong central government at the expense of the original states, although he earlier supported the Louisiana Purchase.

Between 1806 and 1812 Randolph's ire and eloquence were especially aroused by the approaching war with England, and here he differed completely with the young war hawks Clay and Calhoun. Although the English were stopping American ships on the high seas and impressing American seamen, he was in favor of enduring almost any highhanded acts of his beloved mother country rather than weaken her hand in the life-and-death struggle with the Corsican tyrant. He thought that patience was appropriate because we were prepared on neither land nor sea for a trial by arms with the British Empire— and the humiliating War of 1812 proved him correct. Two of his outstanding speeches of this period were attacks on Gregg's nonintercourse resolution and a militia bill pointing toward war.

In the next decade his prophetic wrath was stirred by the Missouri Compromise, with its restrictions on slavery, and Clay's American Plan, with the doctrine of internal improvements and high tariffs protecting northern industry. He was probably at his best in the first session of the eighteenth Congress in opposing a bill contemplating extensive internal improvements, and later in opposing a tariff measure.

In speaking, Randolph was casual, conversational, scornful of manuscript or notes. He could go on endlessly in his high, flexible voice, with reckless digressions that fascinated or repelled, depending on the point of view of the hearer.

"Sir, we live under a government of peculiar structure."

DURING no very short course of public life I do not know that it has ever been my fortune to rise under as much embarrassment, or to address the House with as much repugnance as I now feel. That repugnance, in part, grows out of the necessity that exists for my taking some notice, in the course of my observations, of the argument, if argument it may be called, of an honorable member of this House from Kentucky. And, although I have not the honor to know, personally, or even by name, a large portion of the members of this House, it is not necessary for me to indicate the cause of that repugnance. But this I may venture to promise the committee, that, in my notice of the argument of that member, I shall show at least as much deference to it as *he* showed to the message of the

President of the United States of America on returning a bill of a nature analogous to that now before us—I say at least *as much;* I should regret if not *more.* With the argument of the President, however, I have nothing to do. I wash my hands of it and will leave it to the triumph, the clemency, the mercy of the honorable gentleman of Kentucky—if, indeed, to use his own language, amid the mass of words in which it is enveloped, he has been able to find it. My purpose in regard to the argument of the gentleman from Kentucky is to show that it lies in the compass of a nutshell; that it turns on the meaning of one of the plainest words in the English language. I am happy to be able to agree with that gentleman in at least one particular, to wit: in the estimate the gentleman has formed of his own powers as a grammarian, philologer, and critic; particularly as those powers have been displayed in the dissertation with which he has favored the committee on the interpretation of the word "establish."

"Congress," says the Constitution, "shall have power to *establish* (*ergo,* says the gentleman, Congress shall have power to *construct*) post roads."

One would suppose that, if anything could be considered as settled by precedent in legislation, the meaning of the words of the Constitution must, before this time, have been settled by the uniform sense in which that power has been exercised, from the commencement of the Government to the present time. What is the fact? Your statute book is loaded with acts for the "establishment" of post roads, and the postmaster general is deluged with petitions for the "establishment" of post offices; and yet, we are now gravely debating on what the word "establish" shall be held to mean! A curious predicament we are placed in: precisely the reverse of that of Molière's citizen turned gentleman, who discovered, to his great surprise, that he had been talking "prose" all his life long without knowing it. A common case. It is just so with all prosers, and I hope I may not exemplify it in this instance. But, sir, we have been for five and thirty years establishing post roads, under the delusion that we were exercising a power specially conferred upon us by the Constitution, while we were, according to the suggestion of the gentleman from Kentucky, actually committing *treason,* by refusing, for so long a time, to carry into effect that very article of the Constitution!

To forbear the exercise of a power vested in us for the public good, not merely for our own aggrandizement, is, according to the argument of the gentleman from Kentucky, treachery to the Constitution! I, then, sir, must have commenced my public life in treason, and in treason am I doomed to end it. One of the first votes that I ever had the honor to give, in this House, was a vote against the *establishment,* if gentlemen please, of a uniform system of bankruptcy—a power as unquestionably given to Congress, by the Constitution, as the power to lay a direct tax. But, sir, my treason did not end there. About two years after the establishment of this uniform system of bankruptcy, I was *particeps criminis*, with almost the unanimous voice of this House, in committing another act of treachery in repealing it; and Mr. Jefferson, the President of the United States, in the commencement of his career, consummated the treason by putting his signature to the act of repeal.

Miserable, indeed, would be the condition of every free people, if, in expounding the charter of their liberties, it were necessary to go back to the Anglo-Saxon, to Junius and Skinner, and other black-letter etymologists. Not, sir, that I am very skillful in language: although I have learned from a certain curate of Brentford, whose name will survive when the whole contemporaneous bench of bishops shall be buried in oblivion, that *words*—the counters of wise men, the money of fools—that it is by the dexterous cutting and shuffling of this pack, that is derived one half of the chicanery and much more than one half of the profits of the most lucrative profession in the world—and, sir, by this dexterous exchanging and substituting of words, we shall not be the first nation in the world that has been cajoled, if we are to be cajoled, out of our rights and liberties.

In the course of the observations which the gentleman from Kentucky saw fit to submit to the committee, were some pathetic ejaculations on the subject of the sufferings of our brethren of the West. Sir, our brethren of the West have suffered, as our brethren throughout the United States, from the same cause, although with them the cause exists in an aggravated degree, from the acts of those to whom they have confided the power of legislation; by a departure—and we have all suffered from it— I hope no gentleman will understand me as wishing to make any invidious comparison between different quarters of our country, by a departure from the industry, the simplicity, the economy, and the frugality of our ancestors. They have suffered from a greediness of gain that has grasped at the shadow while it has lost the substance, from habits of indolence, of profusion, of extravagance, from an aping of foreign manners and of foreign fashions, from a miserable attempt at the shabby genteel, which only serve to make our poverty more conspicuous. The way to remedy this state of suffering is to return to those habits of labor and industry from which we have thus departed.

With these few remarks permit me now to recall the attention of the committee to the original design of this government. It grew out of the necessity, indispensable and unavoidable, in the circumstances of this country, of some general power capable of regulating foreign commerce. Sir, I am old enough to remember the origin of this government; and, though I was too young to participate in the transactions of the day, I have a perfect recollection of what was public sentiment on the subject. And I repeat, without fear of contradiction, that the proximate as well as the remote cause of the existence of the Federal government was the regulation of foreign commerce.

But we are told that, along with the regulation of foreign commerce, the states have yielded to the general government, in as broad terms, the regulation of domestic commerce—I mean the commerce among the several states—and that the same power is possessed by Congress over the one as over the other. It is rather unfortunate for this argument that, if it applies to the extent to which the power to regulate foreign commerce has been carried by Congress, they may prohibit altogether this domestic commerce, as they have heretofore, under the other power, prohibited foreign commerce.

But why put extreme cases? This government cannot go on one day without a mutual understanding and deference between the state and general governments. This government is the breath of the nostrils of the states. Gentlemen may say what they please of the preamble to the Constitution; but this Constitution is not the work of the amalgamated population of the then existing confederacy, but the offspring of the states; and however high we may carry our heads and strut and fret our hour "dressed in a little brief authority," it is in the power of the states to extinguish this government at a blow. They have only to refuse to send members to the other branch of the legislature, or to appoint electors of President and Vice-President, and the thing is done. Gentlemen will not understand me as seeking for reflections of this kind; but, like Falstaff's rebellion—I mean Worcester's rebellion—they lay in my way and I found them.

I remember to have heard it said elsewhere that when gentlemen talk of precedent, they forget they were not in Westminster Hall. Whatever trespass I may be guilty of upon the attention of the Committee, one thing I will promise them, and will faithfully perform my promise. I will dole out to them no political metaphysics. Sir, I unlearned metaphysics almost as early as Fontenelle, and he tells us, I think, it was at nine years of age. I shall say nothing about that word "municipal." I am almost as sick of it as honest Falstaff was of "security"; it has been like ratsbane in my mouth ever since the late ruler in France took shelter under that word to pocket our money and incarcerate our persons, with the most profound respect for *our neutral* rights. I have done with the word "municipal" ever since that day. Let us come to the plain common-sense construction of the Constitution. Sir, we live under a government of a peculiar structure, to which the doctrines of the European writers on civil polity do not apply; and when gentlemen get up and quote Vattel as applicable to the powers of the Constitution of the United States, I should as soon have expected them to quote Aristotle, or the Koran. Our government is not like the consolidated monarchies of the old world. It is a solar system, an *imperium in imperio;* and when the question is about the one or the other, what belongs to the *imperium* and what to the *imperio,* we gain nothing by referring to Vattel. He treats of an integral government—a compact structure, *totus teres atque rotundus.* But ours is a system composed of two distinct governments; the one general in its nature, the other internal. Now, sir, a government may be admirable for external, and yet execrable for internal purposes. And when the question of power in the government arises, this is the problem which every honest man has to work. The powers of government are divided in our system between the general and state governments, except such powers which the people have very wisely retained to themselves. With these exceptions, all the power is divided between the two governments. The given power will not lie unless, as in the case of direct taxes, the power is specifically given; and even then the state has a concurrent power. The question for every honest man to ask himself is: to which of these two divisions of government does the power in contest belong? This is the problem we have to settle: does this power of internal improvement belong to the general or to the state governments, or is it a concurrent power? Gentlemen say we have, by the Constitution, power to establish post roads; and, having established post roads, we should be much obliged to you to allow us therefore the power to construct roads and canals into the bargain. If I had the physical strength, sir, I could easily demonstrate to the committee that, supposing the power to exist on our part, of all the powers that can be exercised by this House, there is no power that would be more susceptible of abuse than this very power. Figure to yourself a committee of this House determining on some road, and giving out the contracts to the members of both Houses of Congress, or to their friends, et cetera. Sir, if I had the strength, I could show to this committee that the Asiatic plunder of Leadenhall Street has not been more corrupting to the British government than the exercise of such a power as this would prove to us.

I said that this government, if put to the test—a test it is by no means calculated to endure—as a government for the management of the internal concerns of this country is one of the worst that can be conceived, which is determined by the fact that it is a government not having a common feeling and common interest with the governed. I know that we are told—and it is the first time the doctrine has been openly avowed—that upon the responsibility of this House to the people, by means of the elective franchise, depends all the security of the people of the United States against the abuse of the powers of this government.

But, sir, how shall a man from Mackinaw, or the Yellow Stone River, respond to the sentiments of the people who live in New Hampshire? It is as great a mockery—a greater mockery—than it was to talk to these colonies about their virtual representation in the British Parliament. I have no hesitation in saying that the liberties of the colonies were safer in the custody of the British Parliament than they will be in any portion of this country, if all the powers of the states, as well as of the general government, are devolved on this House; and in this opinion I am borne out, and more than borne out, by the authority of Patrick Henry himself.

It is not a matter of conjecture merely, but of fact, of notoriety, that there does exist on this subject an honest difference of opinion among enlightened men; that not one or two but many states in the Union see, with great concern and alarm, the encroachments of the general government on their authority. They feel that they have given up the power of the sword and the purse, and enabled men, with the purse in one hand and the sword in the other, to rifle them of all they hold dear. . . . We now begin to perceive what we have surrendered; that, having given up the power of the purse and the sword, everything else is at the mercy and forbearance of the general government. We did believe there were some parchment barriers—no! what is worth all the parchment barriers in the world—that there was, in the powers of the states, some counterpoise to the power of this body; but, if this bill passes, we can believe so no longer.

There is one other power which may be exercised, in case the power now contended for be conceded, to which I ask the attention of every gentleman who happens to stand in the same unfortunate predicament with myself—of every man who has the misfortune to be, and to have been born, a slaveholder. If Congress possess the power to do what is proposed by this bill, they may not only enact a sedition law—for there is precedent—but they may emancipate every slave in the United States, and with stronger color of reason than they can exercise the power now contended for. And where will they find the power? They may follow the example of the gentlemen who have preceded me and hook the power upon the first loop they find in the Constitution. They might take the preamble, perhaps the war-making power, or they might take a greater sweep, and say, with some gentlemen, that it is not to be found in this α.

that of the granted powers, but results from all of them, which is not only a dangerous but *the most* dangerous doctrine. Is it not demonstrable that slave labor is the dearest in the world, and that the existence of a large body of slaves is a source of danger? Suppose we are at war with a foreign power, and freedom should be offered them by Congress as an inducement to them to take a part in it; or, suppose the country not at war, at every turn of this Federal machine, at every successive census, that interest will find itself governed by another and increasing power, which is bound to it neither by any common tie of interest or feeling. And if ever the time shall arrive, as assuredly it has arrived elsewhere, and, in all probability, may arrive here, that a coalition of knavery and fanaticism shall, for any purpose, be got up on this floor, I ask gentlemen who stand in the same predicament as I do to look well to what they are now doing, to the colossal power with which they are now arming this government. The power to do what I allude to is, I aver, more honestly inferrible from the war-making power than the power we are now about to exercise. Let them look forward to the time when such a question shall arise, and tremble with me at the thought that that question is to be decided by a majority of the votes of this House, of whom not one possesses the slightest tie of common interest or of common feeling with us.

Randolph did his best to defeat the bill and finally to have it indefinitely postponed, but it was passed by a majority of 115 to 86. And he lost again in the tariff fight a few weeks later.

He lost yet again in 1826 when the presidential election was thrown into the House of Representatives, and Clay, disliking Jackson, gave his support to John Quincy Adams. Adams won and Clay became Secretary of State. Scenting a corrupt bargain, Randolph declared on the floor of the United States Senate: "I was defeated, horse, foot, and dragoons—cut up and clean broke down—by the coalition of Blifil and Black George—by the combination, unheard of till then, of the Puritan with the blackleg."

In the inevitable duel with Clay that followed, Clay's second shot pierced Randolph's conspicuous white coat, but Randolph fired in the air, and they were reconciled.

In his remaining years Randolph grew more restless and erratic, and apparently recovered his old powers only at the Virginia Constitutional Convention of 1829. When he died in 1833 he was buried with his face to the west so that he could keep his eyes on Henry Clay!

Meanwhile, John Caldwell Calhoun had learned his lesson thoroughly.

WEBSTER PROCLAIMS THE DOCTRINE OF A STRONG CENTRAL GOVERNMENT

[January 26–27, 1830]

After representing Boston for three terms in the House of Representatives, Webster came to the United States Senate in 1827. An interval of depression followed the deaths of his favorite brother and his wife, but with a second marriage in December, 1829, he returned to the Senate and his Supreme Court practice with renewed vigor. At just this moment a desultory debate regarding the survey and sales of the Western lands was going on, initiated by a resolution of Senator Foote of Connecticut. In the background was the growing tension between the North and the South, not directly over slavery, but over the high protective tariffs that were enriching New England at the expense of the Southern planters. In the background was the harshly logical mind of Vice-President John C. Calhoun, who was moving from an ardent nationalism to a yet more ardent sectionalism and the doctrine of states' rights.

It was under these circumstances that the elegant and eloquent Robert Young Hayne, Senator from South Carolina, used the debate on Foote's resolution to engage in an attack on New England, to advocate a "natural" alliance between the South and the West, and to maintain the right of the states to oppose—indeed, to resist—supposedly unconstitutional acts of Congress. On all these counts, Webster the Unionist, the Constitutionalist, was of the opposite opinion. Taking off time from a pressing case in the Supreme Court, and with little immediate preparation, he hastened to reply to Hayne.

On Tuesday morning, January 26, 1830, the floor of the Senate was crowded with Senators, members of the House, and excited visitors. Webster, in full command of himself and his audience, with only a few pages of notes in his hand, and with his real opponent, Vice-President Calhoun, in the chair, now proceeded to deliver one of the most weighty and far-reaching discourses in the history of Congressional debate.

Thousands of words must be omitted, including the famous encomium of New England ("New England! There she stands!") in order to present, unbroken, the latter part of Webster's elaborate—and sometimes leoninely amusing—argument.

"Liberty and union, now and forever, one and inseparable."

I MUST now beg to ask, sir, whence is this supposed right of the states derived?—where do they find the power to interfere with the laws of the Union? Sir, the opinion which the honorable gentleman maintains is a notion founded in a total misapprehension, in my judgment, of the origin of this government and of the foundation on which it stands. I hold it to be a popular government, erected by the people; those who administer it, responsible to the people; and itself capable of being amended and modified, just as the people may choose it should be. It is as popular, just as truly emanating from the people, as the state governments. It is created for one purpose; the state governments for another. It has its own powers; they have theirs. There is no more authority with them to arrest the operation of a law of Congress than with Congress to arrest the operation of their laws. We are here to administer a Constitution emanating immediately from the people, and trusted by them to our administration. It is not the creature of the state governments. It is of no moment to the argument that certain acts of the state legislatures are necessary to fill our seats in this body. That is not one of their original state powers, a part of the sovereignty of the state. It is a duty which the people, by the Constitution itself, have imposed on the state legislatures, and which they might have left to be performed elsewhere, if they had seen fit. So they have left the choice of President with electors; but all this does not affect the proposition that this whole government, President, Senate, and House of Representatives, is a popular government. It leaves it still all its popular character. The governor of a state (in some of the states) is chosen, not directly by the people, but by those who are chosen by the people, for the purpose of performing, among other duties, that of electing a governor. Is the government of the state, on that account, not a popular government? This government, sir, is the independent offspring of the popular will. It is not the creature of state legislatures; nay, more, if the whole truth must be told, the people brought it into existence, established it, and have hitherto supported it, for the very purpose, amongst others, of imposing certain salutary restraints on state sovereignties. The states cannot now make war; they cannot contract alliances; they cannot make, each for itself, separate regulations of commerce; they cannot lay imposts; they cannot coin money. If this Constitution, sir, be the creature of state legislatures, it must be admitted that it has obtained a strange control over the volitions of its creators.

The people, then, sir, erected this government. They gave it a Con-- stitution, and in that Constitution they have enumerated the powers which they bestow on it. They have made it a limited government. They have defined its authority. They have restrained it to the exercise of such powers as are granted; and all others, they declare, are reserved to the states or the people. But, sir, they have not stopped here. If they had, they would have accomplished but half their work. No definition can be so clear as to avoid possibility of doubt; no limitation so precise as to ex- clude all uncertainty. Who, then, shall construe this grant of the people? Who shall interpret their will where it may be supposed they have left it doubtful? With whom do they repose this ultimate right of deciding on the powers of the government? Sir, they have settled all this in the fullest manner. They have left it with the government itself, in its appropriate branches. Sir, the very chief end, the main design, for which the whole Constitution was framed and adopted was to establish a government that should not be obliged to act through state agency or depend on state opinion and state discretion. The people had had quite enough of that kind of government under the Confederacy. Under that system the legal action—the application of law to individuals—belonged exclusively to the states. Congress could only recommend—their acts were not of binding force till the states had adopted and sanctioned them. Are we in that condition still? Are we yet at the mercy of state discretion and state con- struction? Sir, if we are, then vain will be our attempt to maintain the Constitution under which we sit.

But, sir, the people have wisely provided in the Constitution itself a proper suitable mode and tribunal for settling questions of constitutional law. There are, in the Constitution, grants of powers to Congress and re- strictions on these powers. There are also prohibitions on the states. Some authority must therefore necessarily exist having the ultimate jurisdiction to fix and ascertain the interpretation of these grants, restrictions, and prohibitions. The Constitution has itself pointed out, ordained, and estab- lished that authority. How has it accomplished this great and essential end? By declaring, sir, that "the Constitution and the laws of the United States, made in pursuance thereof, shall be the supreme law of the land, anything in the Constitution or laws of any state to the contrary notwith- standing."

This, sir, was the first great step. By this the supremacy of the Con- stitution and laws of the United States is declared. The people so will it. No state law is to be valid which comes in conflict with the Constitution or any law of the United States passed in pursuance of it. But who shall decide this question of interference? To whom lies the last appeal? This, sir, the Constitution itself decides also by declaring "that the judicial power shall extend to all cases arising under the Constitution and laws of the United States." These two provisions, sir, cover the whole ground. They are in truth the keystone of the arch. With these it is a Constitution; without them it is a Confederacy. In pursuance of these clear and express provisions, Congress established at its very first session in the judicial act a mode for carrying them into full effect and for bringing all questions of constitutional power to the final decision of the Supreme Court. It then, sir, became a government. It then had the means of self-protection; and but for this it would, in all probability, have been now among things which are past. Having constituted the government and declared its powers, the people have further said that since somebody must decide on the extent of these powers, the government shall itself decide; subject always, like other popular governments, to its responsibility to the people. And now, sir, I repeat, how is it that a state legislature acquires any power to interfere? Who or what gives them the right to say to the people: "We, who are your agents and servants for one purpose, will undertake to decide that your other agents and servants, appointed by you for another purpose, have transcended the authority you gave them!" The reply would be, I think, not impertinent—"Who made you a judge over another's servants? To their own masters they stand or fall."

Sir, I deny this power of state legislatures altogether. It cannot stand the test of examination. Gentlemen may say that in an extreme case a state government might protect the people from intolerable oppression. Sir, in such a case, the people might protect themselves without the aid of the state governments. Such a case warrants revolution. It must make, when it comes, a law for itself. A nullifying act of a state legislature cannot alter the case nor make resistance any more lawful. In maintaining these sentiments, sir, I am but asserting the rights of the people. I state what they have declared and insist on their right to declare it. They have chosen to repose this power in the general government, and I think it my duty to support it, like other constitutional powers.

For myself, sir, I do not admit the jurisdiction of South Carolina, or any other state, to prescribe my constitutional duty; or to settle, between me and the people, the validity of laws of Congress for which I have voted. I decline her umpirage. I have not sworn to support the Constitution according to her construction of its clauses. I have not stipulated by my oath of office, or otherwise, to come under any responsibility except to the people and those whom they have appointed to pass upon the question whether laws, supported by my votes, conform to the Constitution of the country. And, sir, if we look to the general nature of the case, could anything have been more preposterous than to make a government for the whole Union, and yet leave its powers subject, not to one interpretation, but to thirteen or twenty-four interpretations? Instead of one tribunal, established by all, responsible to all, with power to decide for all, shall constitutional questions be left to four and twenty popular bodies, each at liberty to decide for itself, and none bound to respect the decisions of others; and each at liberty, too, to give a new construction on every new election of its own members? Would anything with such a principle in it, or rather with such a destitution of all principle, be fit to be called a government? No, sir. It should not be denominated a Constitution. It should be called, rather, a collection of topics for everlasting controversy; heads of debate for a disputatious people. It would not be a government. It would not be adequate to any practical good nor fit for any country to live under. To avoid all possibility of being misunderstood, allow me to repeat again in the fullest manner that I claim no powers for the government by forced or unfair construction. I admit that it is a government of strictly limited powers; of enumerated, specified, and particularized powers; and that whatsoever is not granted is withheld. But notwithstanding all this, and however the grant of powers may be expressed, its limit and extent may yet, in some cases, admit of doubt; and the general government would be good for nothing, it would be incapable of long existing, if some mode had not been provided in which those doubts, as they should arise, might be peaceably but authoritatively solved.

And now, Mr. President, let me run the honorable gentleman's doctrine a little into its practical application. Let us look at his probable *modus operandi*. If a thing can be done, an ingenious man can tell how it is to be done. Now I wish to be informed how this state interference is to be put in practice without violence, bloodshed, and rebellion. We will take the existing case of the tariff law. South Carolina is said to have made up her opinion upon it. If we do not repeal it (as we probably shall not), she will then apply to the case the remedy of her doctrine. She will, we must suppose, pass a law of her legislature declaring the several acts of Congress, usually called the tariff laws, null and void, so far as they respect South Carolina or the citizens thereof. So far all is a paper transaction, and easy enough. But the collector at Charleston is collecting the duties imposed by these tariff laws—he, therefore, must be stopped. The collector will seize the goods if the tariff duties are not paid. The state authorities will undertake their rescue; the marshal with his posse will come to the collector's aid, and here the contest begins. The militia of the state will be called out to sustain the nullifying act. They will march, sir, under a very gallant leader, for I believe the honorable member himself commands the militia of that part of the state. He will raise the nullifying act on his standard, and spread it out as his banner! It will have a preamble bearing: "That the tariff laws are palpable, deliberate, and dangerous violations of the Constitution!" He will proceed, with this banner flying, to the customhouse in Charleston:

All the while
Sonorous metal blowing martial sounds.

Arrived at the customhouse, he will tell the collector that he must collect no more duties under any of the tariff laws. This he will be somewhat puzzled to say, by the way, with a grave countenance, considering what hand South Carolina herself had in that of 1816. But, sir, the collector would probably not desist at his bidding. He would show him the law of Congress, the Treasury instruction, and his own oath of office. He would say he should perform his duty, come what might. Here would ensue a pause: for they say that a certain stillness precedes the tempest. The trumpeter would hold his breath awhile, and before all this military array should fall on the customhouse, collector, clerks and all, it is very probable some of those composing it would request of their gallant commander in chief to be informed a little upon the point of law; for they have doubtless a just respect for his opinions as a lawyer, as well as for his bravery as a soldier. They know he has read Blackstone and the Constitution, as well as Turenne and Vauban. They would ask him, therefore, something concerning their rights in this matter. They would inquire whether it was not somewhat dangerous to resist a law of the United States. What would be the nature of their offense, they would wish to learn, if they by military force and array resisted the execution in Carolina of a law of the United States, and it should turn out, after all, that the law was constitutional? He would answer, of course, treason. No lawyer could give any other answer. John Fries [leader of the insurgents who fought the Federal property tax in Pennsylvania in 1798–99], he would tell them, had learned that some years ago. How then, they would ask, do you propose to defend us? We are not afraid of bullets, but treason has a way of taking people off that we do not much relish. How do you propose to defend us? "Look at my floating banner," he would reply; "see there the nullifying law!" Is it your opinion, gallant commander, they would then say that if we should be indicted for treason, that same floating banner of yours would make a good plea in bar? "South Carolina is a sovereign state," he would reply. That is true—but would the judge admit our plea? "These tariff laws," he would repeat, "are unconstitutional, palpably, deliberately, dangerously." That all may be so; but if the tribunal should not happen to be of that opinion, shall we swing for it? We are ready to die for our country, but it is rather an awkward business, this dying without touching the ground! After all, that is a sort of hemp tax worse than any part of the tariff.

Mr. President, the honorable gentleman would be in a dilemma like that of another great general. He would have a knot before him which he could not untie. He must cut it with his sword. He must say to his followers: defend yourselves with your bayonets; and this is war—civil war.

Direct collision, therefore, between force and force is the unavoidable result of that remedy for the revision of unconstitutional laws which the gentleman contends for. It must happen in the very first case to which it is applied. Is not this the plain result? To resist, by force, the execution of a law generally is treason. Can the courts of the United States take notice of the indulgence of a state to commit treason? The common saying that a state cannot commit treason herself is nothing to the purpose. Can she authorize others to do it? If John Fries had produced an act of Pennsylvania annulling the law of Congress, would it have helped his case? Talk about it as we will, these doctrines go the length of revolution. They are incompatible with any peaceable administration of the government. They lead directly to disunion and civil commotion; and, therefore, it is that at their commencement, when they are first found to be maintained by respectable men, and in a tangible form, I enter my public protest against them all.

The honorable gentleman argues that if this government be the sole judge of the extent of its own powers, whether that right of judging be in Congress or the Supreme Court, it equally subverts state sovereignty. This the gentleman sees, or thinks he sees, although he cannot perceive how the right of judging, in this matter, if left to the exercise of state legislatures, has any tendency to subvert the government of the Union. The gentleman's opinion may be that the right ought not to have been lodged with the general government; he may like better such a Constitution as we should have under the right of state interference; but I ask him to meet me on the plain matter of fact; I ask him to meet me on the Constitution itself; I ask him if the power is not found there—clearly and visibly found there.

But, sir, what is this danger, and what the grounds of it? Let it be remembered that the Constitution of the United States is not unalterable. It is to continue in its present form no longer than the people who established it shall choose to continue it. If they shall become convinced that they have made an injudicious or inexpedient partition and distribution of power between the state governments and the general government, they can alter that distribution at will.

If anything be found in the national Constitution, either by original provision or subsequent interpretation, which ought not to be in it, the people know how to get rid of it. If any construction be established, unacceptable to them, so as to become, practically, a part of the Constitution, they will amend it, at their own sovereign pleasure: but while the people choose to maintain it, as it is; while they are satisfied with it, and refuse to change it, who has given, or who can give, to the state legislatures a right to alter it, either by interference, construction, or otherwise? Gentlemen do not seem to recollect that the people have any power to do anything for themselves; they imagine there is no safety for them any longer than they are under the close guardianship of the state legislatures. Sir, the people have not trusted their safety, in regard to the general Constitution, to these hands. They have required other security, and taken other bonds. They have chosen to trust themselves, first, to the plain words of the instrument, and to such construction as the government itself, in doubtful cases, should put on its own powers, under their oaths of office, and subject to their responsibility to them; just as the people of a state trust their own state governments with a similar power. Secondly, they have reposed their trust in the efficacy of frequent elections, and in their own power to remove their own servants and agents, whenever they see cause. Thirdly, they have reposed trust in the judicial power, which, in order that it might be trustworthy, they have made as respectable, as disinterested, and as independent as was practicable. Fourthly, they have seen fit to rely, in case of necessity, or high expediency, on their known and admitted power to alter or amend the Constitution, peaceably and quietly, whenever experience shall point out defects or imperfections. And, finally, the people of the United States have, at no time, in no way, directly or indirectly, authorized any state legislature to construe or interpret their high instrument of government; much less to interfere, by their own power, to arrest its course and operation.

If, sir, the people, in these respects, had done otherwise than they have done, their Constitution could neither have been preserved nor would it have been worth preserving. And, if its plain provisions shall now be disregarded, and these new doctrines interpolated in it, it will become as feeble and helpless a being as its enemies, whether early or more recent, could possibly desire. It will exist in every state, but as a poor dependent on state permission. It must borrow leave to be and it will be no longer than state pleasure or state discretion sees fit to grant the indulgence and to prolong its poor existence.

But, sir, although there are fears, there are hopes also. The people have preserved this, their own chosen Constitution, for forty years and have seen their happiness, prosperity, and renown grow with its growth, and strengthen with its strength. They are now, generally, strongly attached to it. Overthrown by direct assault, it cannot be; evaded, undermined, nullified, it will not be, if we, and those who shall succeed us here, as agents and representatives of the people, shall conscientiously and vigilantly discharge the two great branches of our public trust—faithfully to preserve and wisely to administer it.

Mr. President, I have thus stated the reasons of my dissent to the doctrines which have been advanced and maintained. I am conscious of having detained you and the Senate much too long. I was drawn into the debate with no previous deliberation such as is suited to the discussion of so grave and important a subject. But it is a subject of which my heart is full, and I have not been willing to suppress the utterance of its spontaneous sentiments. I cannot, even now, persuade myself to relinquish it without expressing once more my deep conviction that since it respects nothing less than the Union of the states, it is of most vital and essential importance to the public happiness. I profess, sir, in my career, hitherto, to have kept steadily in view the prosperity and honor of the whole country, and the preservation of our Federal Union. It is to that Union we owe our safety at home and our consideration and dignity abroad. It is to that Union that we are chiefly indebted for whatever makes us most proud of our country. That Union we reached only by the discipline of our virtues in the severe school of adversity. It had its origin in the necessities of disordered finance, prostrate commerce, and ruined credit. Under its benign influence, these great interests immediately awoke as from the dead and sprang forth with newness of life. Every year of its duration has teemed with fresh proofs of its utility and its blessings; and, although our territory has stretched out wider and wider, and our population spread further and further, they have not outrun its protection or its benefits. It has been to us all a copious fountain of national, social and personal happiness. I have not allowed myself, sir, to look beyond the Union to see what might lie hidden in the dark recess behind. I have not coolly weighed the chances of preserving liberty when the bonds that unite us together shall be broken asunder. I have not accustomed myself to hang over the precipice of disunion to see whether, with my short sight, I can fathom the depth of the abyss below; nor could I regard him as a safe counselor in the affairs of this government whose thoughts should be mainly bent on considering not how the Union should be best preserved, but how tolerable might be the condition of the people when it shall be broken up and destroyed. While the Union lasts we have high, exciting, gratifying prospects spread out before us, for us and our children. Beyond that I seek not to penetrate the veil. God grant that in my day, at least, that curtain may not rise. God grant that on my vision never may be opened what lies behind. When my eyes shall be turned to behold, for the last time, the sun in heaven, may I not see him shining on the broken and dishonored fragments of a once glorious Union; on states dissevered, discordant, belligerent; on a land rent with civil feuds, or drenched, it may be, in fraternal blood! Let their last feeble and lingering glance rather behold the gorgeous ensign of the Republic, now known and honored throughout the earth, still full high advanced, its arms and trophies streaming in their original luster, not a stripe erased or polluted, nor a single star obscured, bearing for its motto no such miserable interrogatory as, "What is all this worth?" nor those other words of delusion and folly, "Liberty first and union afterwards"; but everywhere, spread all over in characters of living light, blazing on all its ample folds, as they float over the sea and over the land, and in every wind under the whole heavens, that other sentiment, dear to every true American heart—Liberty and Union, now and forever, one and inseparable!

The effect of this speech on Webster's immediate audience and with the country at large within a few months of its delivery was deeper than we can possibly imagine. "We are apt to forget," said George Ticknor Curtis, a distinguished lawyer and one of Webster's literary executors, "that this was the first time the two opposite views of the nature of the Constitution had come into the public discussion of Congress, and that the political relations of several eminent men were such as to make this and the three following years an era of great peril."

Webster's fundamental argument that the Constitution was originally a national instrument, a construction of the people, rather than a loose compact between states, has been considered unhistorical—but, if so, he remade history in order to remake a nation.

JOHN C. CALHOUN, DISCIPLE OF RAN-
DOLPH AND ANTAGONIST OF
WEBSTER, CHAMPIONS
STATES' RIGHTS

[February 15–16, 1833]

When Webster made his classic case for the Union, in reply to Senator Hayne of South Carolina, Calhoun, as Vice-President, it will be recalled, sat restlessly in the chair. But he was soon to speak out for the South in unforgettable accents.

John Caldwell Calhoun (1782–1850), born of a comfortable slaveholding family of South Carolina, a graduate of Yale, and a student of law, ascended steadily toward the White House—until he came to a fatal fork in the road. Intense, austere, ambitious, a militant member of Congress through the War of 1812, an efficient Secretary of War under James Monroe, Vice-President under John Quincy Adams and then under Jackson, Calhoun seemed destined to be Jackson's natural successor. Clearly a nationalist rather than a sectionalist until 1828, in that year he carefully studied South Carolina politics at home and soon realized that he must abandon his high-tariff principles or be himself abandoned by his constituents. Automatically he became associated with his native state's extremist tactics—with the still embryonic "nullification" movement that could end logically only in the dissolution of the Union. Nor was the situation helped when he realized that the wily Martin Van Buren, of New York, was to be Jackson's heir presumptive.

This was too much. In a series of desperate moves Calhoun broke with Jackson, resigned as Vice-President, and replaced Hayne (no match for Webster) in the Senate, while Hayne became Governor of South Carolina. "Personal ambition was now increasingly submerged in a cold monomania for South Carolina and slavery," says Arthur M. Schlesinger, Jr., in The Age of Jackson.

In November, 1832, the South Carolina legislature passed an Ordinance of Nullification prohibiting the paying of duties under the Tariff Acts of 1828 and 1832, and threatening secession as a last resort. Jackson's angry reply was the Revenue Enforcement Bill, known to history as the "Force Bill," giving him emergency use of the army and navy to enforce revenue laws.

This was Calhoun's moment, and for parts of two days he held forth, coldly, bitterly, rapidly, with none of Webster's rhetoric or Clay's silver-voiced charm. Nevertheless, he was listened to with awe even by his enemies.

"Disguise it as you may, the controversy
is one between power and liberty."

THIS BILL proceeds on the ground that the entire sovereignty of this country belongs to the American people, as forming one great community, and regards the states as mere fractions or counties and not as integral parts of the Union; having no more right to resist the encroachments of the government than a county has to resist the authority of a state; and treating such resistance as the lawless acts of so many individuals without possessing sovereignty or political rights. It has been said that the bill declares war against South Carolina. No. It decrees a massacre of her citizens! War has something ennobling about it, and, with all its horrors, brings into action the highest qualities, intellectual and moral. It was, perhaps, in the order of Providence that it should be permitted for that very purpose. But this bill declares no war, except, indeed, it be that which savages wage—a war, not against the community, but the citizens of whom that community is composed. But I regard it as worse than savage warfare—as an attempt to take away life under the color of law, without the trial by jury, or any other safeguard which the Constitution has thrown around the life of the citizen. It authorizes the President, or even his deputies, when they may suppose the law to be violated, without the intervention of a court or jury, to kill without mercy or discrimination!

It has been said by the Senator from Tennessee [Grundy] to be a measure of peace! Yes, such peace as the wolf gives to the lamb—the kite to the dove! Such peace as Russia gives to Poland, or death to its victim! A peace by extinguishing the political existence of the state, by awing her into an abandonment of the exercise of every power which constitutes her a sovereign community. It is to South Carolina a question of self-preservation; and I proclaim it, that, should this bill pass, and an attempt be made to enforce it, it will be resisted, at every hazard—even that of death itself. Death is not the greatest calamity: there are others still more terrible to the free and brave, and among them may be placed the loss of liberty and honor. There are thousands of her brave sons who, if need be, are prepared cheerfully to lay down their lives in defense of the state and the great principles of constitutional liberty for which she is contending. God forbid that this should become necessary! It never can be, unless this government is resolved to bring the question to extremity, when her gallant sons will stand prepared to perform the last duty—to die nobly.

I go on the ground that this Constitution was made by the states; that it is a Federal Union of the states, in which the several states still retain their sovereignty. If these views be correct, I have not characterized the bill too strongly: and the question is whether they be or be not. I will not enter into the discussion of this question now. I will rest it, for the present, on what I have said on the introduction of the resolutions now on the table, under a hope that another opportunity will be afforded for more ample discussion. I will, for the present, confine my remarks to the objections which have been raised to the views which I presented when I introduced them. The authority of Luther Martin has been adduced by the Senator from Delaware [Clayton] to prove that the citizens of a state, acting under the authority of a state, are liable to be punished as traitors by this government. Eminent as Mr. Martin was as a lawyer, and high as his authority may be considered on a legal point, I cannot accept it in determining the point at issue. The attitude which he occupied, if taken into view, would lessen, if not destroy, the weight of his authority. He had been violently opposed in convention to the Constitution, and the very letter from which the Senator has quoted was intended to dissuade Maryland from its adoption. With this view, it was to be expected that every consideration calculated to effect that object should be urged; that real objections should be exaggerated; and that those having no foundation, except mere plausible deductions, should be presented. It is to this spirit that I attribute the opinion of Mr. Martin in reference to the point under consideration. But if his authority be good on one point, it must be admitted to be equally so on another. If his opinion be sufficient to prove that a citizen of a state may be punished as a traitor when acting under allegiance to the state, it is also sufficient to show that no authority was intended to be given in the Constitution for the protection of manufactures by the general government, and that the provision in the Constitution permitting a state to lay an impost duty, with the consent of Congress, was intended to reserve the right of protection to the states themselves, and that each state should protect its own industry. Assuming his opinion to be of equal authority on both points, how embarrassing would be the attitude in which it would place the Senator from Delaware, and those with whom he is acting—that of using the sword and bayonet to enforce the execution of an unconstitutional act of Congress. I must express my surprise that the slightest authority in favor of *power* should be received as the most conclusive evidence, while that which is, at least, equally strong in favor of right and *liberty* is wholly overlooked or rejected.

Notwithstanding all that has been said, I may say that neither the Senator from Delaware nor any other who has spoken on the same side has directly and fairly met the great question at issue: is this a Federal Union? a Union of states, as distinct from that of individuals? Is the sovereignty in the several states, or in the American people in the aggregate? The very language which we are compelled to use when speaking of our political institutions affords proof conclusive as to its real character. The terms Union, Federal, united, all imply a combination of sovereignties, a confederation of states. They are never applied to an association of individuals. Whoever heard of the United States of New York, of Massachusetts, or of Virginia? Whoever heard the term Federal or Union applied to the aggregation of individuals into one community? Nor is the other point less clear—that the sovereignty is in the several states, and that our system is a Union of twenty-four sovereign powers, under a constitutional compact, and not of a divided sovereignty between the states severally and the United States. In spite of all that has been said, I maintain that sovereignty is in its nature indivisible. It is the supreme power in a state, and we might just as well speak of half a square, or of half a triangle, as of half a sovereignty. It is a gross error to confound the exercise of sovereign powers with sovereignty itself, or the delegation of such powers with the surrender of them. A sovereign may delegate his powers to be exercised by as many agents as he may think proper, under such conditions and with such limitations as he may impose; but to surrender any portion of his sovereignty to another is to annihilate the whole. The Senator from Delaware calls this metaphysical reasoning, which, he says, he cannot comprehend. If by metaphysics he means that scholastic refinement which makes distinctions without difference, no one can hold it in more utter contempt than I do; but if, on the contrary, he means the power of analysis and combination—that power which reduces the most complex idea into its elements, which traces causes to their first principle, and, by the power of generalization and combination, unites the whole in one harmonious system—then, so far from deserving contempt, it is the highest attribute of the human mind. It is the power which raises man above the brute—which distinguishes his faculties from mere sagacity, which he holds in common with inferior animals. It is this power which has raised the astronomer from being a mere gazer at the stars to the high intellectual eminence of a Newton or a Laplace, and astronomy itself from a mere observation of isolated facts into that noble science which displays to our admiration the system of the universe. And shall this high power of the mind, which has effected such wonders when directed to the laws which control the material world, be forever prohibited, under a senseless cry of metaphysics, from being applied to the high purpose of political science and legislation? I hold them to be subject to laws as fixed as matter itself, and to be as fit a subject for the application of the highest intellectual power. Denunciation may, indeed, fall upon the philosophical inquirer into these first principles, as it did upon Galileo and Bacon when they first unfolded the great discoveries which have immortalized their names; but the time will come when truth will prevail in spite of prejudice and denunciation, and when politics and legislation will be considered as much a science as astronomy and chemistry.

In connection with this part of the subject, I understood the Senator from Virginia [Rives] to say that sovereignty was divided, and that a portion remained with the states severally, and that the residue was vested in the Union. By Union, I suppose the Senator meant the United States. If such be his meaning—if he intended to affirm that the sovereignty was in the twenty-four states, in whatever light he may view them, our opinions will not disagree; but according to my conception the whole sovereignty is in the several states, while the exercise of sovereign powers is divided—a part being exercised under compact through this general government, and the residue through the separate state governments. But if the Senator from Virginia means to assert that the twenty-four states form but one community, with a single sovereign power as to the objects of the Union, it will be but the revival of the old question of whether the Union is a union between states as distinct communities or a mere aggregate of the American people as a mass of individuals; and in this light his opinions would lead directly to consolidation. . . .

But to return to the bill. It is said that the bill ought to pass because the law must be enforced. The law must be enforced! The imperial edict must be executed! It is under such sophistry, couched in general terms, without looking to the limitations which must ever exist in the practical exercise of power, that the most cruel and despotic acts ever have been covered. It was such sophistry as this that cast Daniel into the lions' den, and the three Innocents into the fiery furnace. Under the same sophistry the bloody edicts of Nero and Caligula were executed. The law must be enforced. Yes, the act imposing the "tea tax must be executed." This was the very argument which impelled Lord North and his administration to that mad career which forever separated us from the British crown. Under a similar sophistry, "that religion must be protected," how

many massacres have been perpetrated? and how many martyrs have
been tied to the stake? What! acting on this vague abstraction, are you
prepared to enforce a law without considering whether it be just or unjust, constitutional or unconstitutional? Will you collect money when it
is acknowledged that it is not wanted? He who earns the money, who
digs it from the earth with the sweat of his brow, has a just title to it
against the universe. No one has a right to touch it without his consent,
except his government, and this only to the extent of its legitimate wants;
to take more is robbery, and you propose by this bill to enforce robbery
by murder. Yes: to this result you must come by this miserable sophistry,
this vague abstraction of enforcing the law, without a regard to the fact
whether the law be just or unjust, constitutional or unconstitutional.

In the same spirit we are told that the Union must be preserved, without regard to the means. And how is it proposed to preserve the Union?
By force? Does any man in his senses believe that this beautiful structure
—this harmonious aggregate of states, produced by the joint consent of
all—can be preserved by force? Its very introduction will be certain
destruction to this Federal Union. No, no. You cannot keep the states
united in their constitutional and Federal bonds by force. Force may,
indeed, hold the parts together, but such union would be the bond between master and slave—a union of exaction on one side and of unqualified obedience on the other. That obedience which, we are told
by the Senator from Pennsylvania [Mr. Wilkins], is the Union! Yes, exaction on the side of the master; for this very bill is intended to collect what
can be no longer called taxes—the voluntary contribution of a free people
—but tribute—tribute to be collected under the mouths of the cannon!
Your customhouse is already transferred into a garrison, and that garrison
with its batteries turned, not against the enemy of your country, but on
subjects (I will not say citizens), on whom you propose to levy contributions. Has reason fled from our borders? Have we ceased to reflect?
It is madness to suppose that the Union can be preserved by force. I tell
you plainly that the bill, should it pass, cannot be enforced. It will prove
only a blot upon your statute book, a reproach to the year, and a disgrace
to the American Senate. I repeat, it will not be executed; it will rouse
the dormant spirit of the people and open their eyes to the approach of
despotism. The country has sunk into avarice and political corruption,
from which nothing can arouse it but some measure on the part of the
government, of folly and madness, such as that now under consideration.

Disguise it as you may, the controversy is one between power and
liberty; and I tell the gentlemen who are opposed to me that, as strong
as may be the love of power on their side, the love of liberty is

still stronger on ours. History furnishes many instances of similar struggles, where the love of liberty has prevailed against power under every disadvantage, and among them few more striking than that of our own Revolution; where, as strong as was the parent country, and feeble as were the colonies, yet, under the impulse of liberty and the blessing of God, they gloriously triumphed in the contest. There are, indeed, many and striking analogies between that and the present controversy. They both originated substantially in the same cause—with this difference—in the present case the power of taxation is converted into that of regulating industry; in the other, the power of regulating industry, by the regulations of commerce, was attempted to be converted into the power of taxation. Were I to trace the analogy further, we should find that the perversion of the taxing power, in the one case, has given precisely the same control to the Northern section over the industry of the Southern section of the Union which the power to regulate commerce gave to Great Britain over the industry of the colonies in the other; and that the very articles in which the colonies were permitted to have a free trade, and those in which the mother country had a monopoly, are almost identically the same as those in which the Southern states are permitted to have a free trade by the Act of 1832, and in which the Northern states have, by the same Act, secured a monopoly. The only difference is in the means. In the former, the colonies were permitted to have a free trade with all countries south of Cape Finisterre, a cape in the northern part of Spain; while north of that, the trade of the colonies was prohibited, except through the mother country, by means of her commercial regulations. If we compare the products of the country north and south of Cape Finisterre, we shall find them almost identical with the list of the protected and unprotected articles contained in the Act of last year. Nor does the analogy terminate here. The very arguments resorted to at the commencement of the American Revolution, and the measures adopted, and the motives assigned to bring on that contest (to enforce the law) are almost identically the same.

But to return from this digression to the consideration of the bill. Whatever difference of opinion may exist upon other points, there is one on which I should suppose there can be none: that this bill rests on principles which, if carried out, will ride over state sovereignties, and that it will be idle for any of its advocates hereafter to talk of state rights. The Senator from Virginia says that he is the advocate of state rights; but he must permit me to tell him that, although he may differ in premises from the other gentlemen with whom he acts on this occasion, yet, in supporting this bill, he obliterates every vestige of distinction between him and them, saving only that, professing the principles of 1798, his example will be more pernicious than that of the most open and bitter opponents of the rights of the states. I will also add, what I am compelled to say, that I must consider him as less consistent than our old opponents, whose conclusions were fairly drawn from their premises, while his premises ought to have led him to opposite conclusions. The gentleman has told us that the newfangled doctrines, as he chooses to call them, have brought state rights into disrepute. I must tell him, in reply, that what he calls newfangled are but the doctrines of 1798; and that it is he, and others with him, who, professing these doctrines, have degraded them by explaining away their meaning and efficacy. He has disclaimed, in behalf of Virginia, the authorship of nullification. I will not dispute that point. If Virginia chooses to throw away one of her brightest ornaments, she must not hereafter complain that it has become the property of another. But while I have, as a representative of Carolina, no right to complain of the disavowal of the Senator from Virginia, I must believe that he has done his native state great injustice by declaring on this floor that when she gravely resolved, in 1798, that "in cases of deliberate and dangerous infractions of the Constitution, the states, as parties to the compact, have the right, and are in duty bound, to interpose to arrest the progress of the evil, and to maintain within their respective limits the authorities, rights, and liberties appertaining to them," she meant no more than to proclaim the right to protest and to remonstrate. To suppose that, in putting forth so solemn a declaration, which she afterwards sustained by so able and elaborate an argument, she meant no more than to assert what no one had ever denied would be to suppose that the state had been guilty of the most egregious trifling that ever was exhibited on so solemn an occasion. . . .

We have now sufficient experience to ascertain that the tendency to conflict in its [the bill's] action is between the Southern and other sections. The latter, having a decided majority, must habitually be possessed of the powers of the government, both in this and in the other House; and, being governed by that instinctive love of power so natural to the human breast, they must become the advocates of the power of government and in the same degree opposed to the limitations; while the other and weaker section is as necessarily thrown on the side of the limitations. One section is the natural guardian of the delegated powers, and the other of the reserved; and the struggle on the side of the former will be to enlarge the powers, while that on the opposite side will be to restrain them within their constitutional limits. The contest will, in fact, be a contest between power and liberty, and such I consider the present—a contest in which the weaker section, with its peculiar labor, productions, and institutions, has at stake all that can be dear to freemen. Should we be able to maintain in their full vigor our reserved rights, liberty and prosperity will be our portion; but if we yield, and permit the stronger interest to concentrate within itself all the powers of the government, then will our fate be more wretched than that of the aborigines whom we have expelled. In this great struggle between the delegated and reserved powers, so far from repining that my lot, and that of those whom I represent, is cast on the side of the latter, I rejoice that such is the fact; for, though we participate in but few of the advantages of the government, we are compensated, and more than compensated, in not being so much exposed to its corruptions. Nor do I repine that the duty, so difficult to be discharged, of defending the reserved powers against apparently such fearful odds has been assigned to us. To discharge it successfully requires the highest qualities, moral and intellectual; and should we perform it with a zeal and ability proportioned to its magnitude, instead of mere planters, our section will become distinguished for its patriots and statesmen. But, on the other hand, if we prove unworthy of the trust—if we yield to the steady encroachments of power—the severest calamity and most debasing corruption will overspread the land. Every Southern man, true to the interests of his section, and faithful to the duties which Providence has allotted him, will be forever excluded from the honors and emoluments of this government, which will be reserved for those only who have qualified themselves, by political prostitution, for admission into the Magdalen Asylum.

This powerful speech, ruthless in its rigor, however narrow its premises, undoubtedly shook the Senate. It is true that Jackson's Force Bill was passed by the Senate two weeks later, but on the same day Clay's compromise tariff, which reduced the "abominable duties," was also passed. For the time being, all faces were saved—South Carolina's as well as Jackson's.

As a presidential candidate, Calhoun was dead; as a logician with a cause he was only beginning. In the grimly accurate words of Harriet Martineau, he was "the cast-iron man who looks as if he had never been born, and could never be extinguished."

FRANCES WRIGHT, BEAUTIFUL AND FEAR-LESS, DELIVERS A FOURTH-OF-JULY ORATION

[July 4, 1828]

While the Websters and the Calhouns dominated the center of the stage, there were other voices with other themes. There was the amazing Fanny Wright.

A precocious Scotch orphan with a large inheritance, Frances Wright (1795–1852) was steeped in the free thought of the eighteenth century and before she was twenty wrote A Day in Athens, a charming little book purporting to be by a youthful follower of Epicurus. Dedicated to her friend Jeremy Bentham, it propounded a sane liberalism that she consistently adhered to. A few years later she visited the United States for the first time and wrote her second book, Views of Society and Manners in America (1821). With her other great friend, Lafayette, she visited America for the second time in 1824, and remained to take part in social reforms on all fronts. She failed in her premature but extraordinary attempt to establish a co-operative colony of free Negroes in Tennessee. But she took this step in her stride as she went on to join Robert Dale Owen's co-operative colony at New Harmony, Indiana. There she became part editor and owner of the New Harmony Gazette. In 1829, on moving to New York, she launched Owen's Free Inquirer and helped to form the first American labor party, the Workingmen's Party of New York (1829–39).

Despite these shady activities, Frances Wright might have been forgiven by the respectable American public if she had not taken to the platform and lectured on such subjects as science, religion, education, and marriage. For a woman to do this was bad enough—for a strikingly beautiful woman to do this was practically a criminal offense, and she was in danger of being mobbed more than once. But she was among friends at New Harmony on July 4, 1828, when she gave what was no doubt the first Independence Day address ever given by a woman.

"Let us rejoice as men, not as children—as human beings rather than as Americans—as reasoning beings, not as ignorants."

THE CUSTOM which commemorates in rejoicing the anniversary of the national independence of these states has its origin in a human feeling, amiable in its nature and beneficial, under proper direction, in its indulgence.

From the era which dates the national existence of the American people dates also a mighty step in the march of human knowledge. And it is consistent with that principle in our conformation which leads us to rejoice in the good which befalls our species, and to sorrow for the evil, that our hearts should expand on this day. On this day, which calls to memory the conquest achieved by knowledge over ignorance, willing co-operation over blind obedience, opinion over prejudice, new ways over old ways—when, fifty-two years ago, America declared her national independence, and associated it with her republic federation. Reasonable is it to rejoice on this day, and useful to reflect thereon; so that we rejoice for the real, and not any imaginary, good; and reflect on the positive advantages obtained, and on those which it is ours farther to acquire.

Dating, as we justly may, a new era in the history of man from the Fourth of July, 1776, it would be well—that is, it would be useful—if on each anniversary we examined the progress made by our species in just knowledge and just practice. Each Fourth of July would then stand as a tidemark in the flood of time by which to ascertain the advance of the human intellect, by which to note the rise and fall of each successive error, the discovery of each important truth, the gradual melioration in our public institutions, social arrangements, and, above all, in our moral feelings and mental views. . . .

In continental Europe, of late years, the words patriotism and patriot have been used in a more enlarged sense than it is usual here to attribute to them, or than is attached to them in Great Britain. Since the political struggles of France, Italy, Spain, and Greece, the word patriotism has been employed, throughout continental Europe, to express a love of the public good; a preference for the interests of the many to those of the few; a desire for the emancipation of the human race from the thrall of despotism, religious and civil: in short, patriotism there is used rather to express the interest felt in the human race in general than that felt for any country, or inhabitants of a country, in particular. And patriot, in like manner, is employed to signify a lover of human liberty and human improvement rather than a mere lover of the country in which he lives, or the tribe to which he belongs. Used in this sense, patriotism is a virtue, and a patriot a virtuous man. With such an interpretation, a patriot is a useful member of society, capable of enlarging all minds and bettering all hearts with which he comes in contact; a useful member of the human family, capable of establishing fundamental principles and of merging his own interests, those of his associates, and those of his nation in the interests of the human race. Laurels and statues are vain things, and mischievous as they are childish; but could we imagine them of use, on *such* a patriot alone could they be with any reason bestowed. . . .

If such a patriotism as we have last considered should seem likely to obtain in any country, it should be certainly in this. In this which is truly the home of all nations and in the veins of whose citizens flows the blood of every people on the globe. Patriotism, in the exclusive meaning, is surely not made for America. Mischievous everywhere, it were here both mischievous and absurd. The very origin of the people is opposed to it. The institutions, in their principle, militate against it. The day we are celebrating protests against it. It is for Americans, more especially, to nourish a nobler sentiment; one more consistent with their origin, and more conducive to their future improvement. It is for them more especially to know why they love their country; and to *feel* that they love it, not because it *is* their country, but because it is the palladium of human liberty—the favored scene of human improvement. It is for them, more especially, to examine their institutions; and to *feel* that they honor them because they are based on just principles. It is for them, more especially, to examine their institutions, because they have the means of improving them; to examine their laws, because at will they can alter them. It is for them to lay aside luxury whose wealth is in industry; idle parade whose strength is in knowledge; ambitious distinctions whose principle is equality. It is for them not to rest, satisfied with words, who can seize upon things; and to remember that equality means, not the mere equality of political rights, however valuable, but equality of instruction and equality in virtue; and that liberty means, not the mere voting at elections, but the free and fearless exercise of the mental faculties and that self-possession which springs out of well-reasoned opinions and consistent practice. It is for them to honor principles rather than men—to commemorate events rather than days; when they rejoice, to know for what they rejoice, and to rejoice only for what has brought and what brings peace and happiness to men. The event we commemorate this day has procured much of both, and shall procure in the onward course of human improvement more than we can now conceive of. For this— for the good obtained and yet in store for our race—let us rejoice! But let us rejoice as men, not as children—as human beings rather than as Americans—as reasoning beings, not as ignorants. So shall we rejoice to good purpose and in good feeling; so shall we improve the victory once on this day achieved, until all mankind hold with us the Jubilee of Independence.

It was a great day for Fanny Wright and New Harmony, Indiana. Soon afterward the ruthless Mrs. Frances Trollope, author of The Domestic Manners of the Americans, heard her in Cincinnati.

"That a lady of fortune, family, and education, whose youth had been passed in the most refined circles of private life, should present herself to the people in this capacity would naturally excite surprise anywhere . . . but in America, where women are guarded by a sevenfold shield of habitual insignificance, it has caused an effect which can scarcely be described.

" 'Miss Wright, of Nashoba, is going to lecture at the courthouse,' sounded from street to street, and from house to house. I shared the surprise, but not the wonder; I know her extraordinary gift of eloquence, her almost unequaled command of words, and the wonderful power of her rich and thrilling voice; and I doubted not that if it was her will to do it, she had the power of commanding the attention, and enchanting the ear of any audience before whom it was her pleasure to appear. I was most anxious to hear her. . . .

"All my expectations fell far short of the splendor, the brilliance, the overwhelming eloquence of this extraordinary orator. . . . It is impossible to imagine anything more striking than her appearance. Her tall and majestic figure, the deep and almost solemn expression of her eyes, the simple contour of her finely formed head, unadorned, excepting by its own natural ringlets; her garment of plain white muslin, which hung about her in folds that recalled the drapery of a Grecian statue, all contributed to produce an effect, unlike anything I had ever seen before, or ever expect to see again."

No doubt we should allow for Mrs. Trollope's prejudices in favor of her own sex. But men, too, who were not outraged by the fact of a woman's speaking, left similar testimony. Into his old age Walt Whitman carried memories of the eloquence of the wonderful Fanny Wright.

SETH LUTHER ADDRESSES THE WORKING-MEN OF NEW ENGLAND

[Circa 1832]

So much attention is given to the conflict over slavery and states' rights in the United States between 1820 and the Civil War that it is easy to forget the rapid growth of industrialism. Already Tocqueville was beginning to fear that manufacturers would engender a new aristocracy.

By 1832 the ten-hour day had been won in New York, but in New England mechanics and factory hands still worked "from daylight to dark." Although a strike for the ten-hour day in Boston in 1825 and another in Providence in 1830 were defeated, the movement for shorter hours gradually gained ground. In 1831 the first convention of the New England Association of Farmers, Mechanics, and Other Workingmen pledged its members to the ten-hour day without reduction of wages. It also dedicated itself to "promote the cause of education and general information, to reform abuses practiced upon them, and to maintain their rights, as American Freemen." The conditions of work were to be improved and the education and morals of children diligently studied. An article in the constitution which called for the expulsion of any member who submitted to a deduction by the employer from his rightful wages throws an interesting light on the practices of the time.

The grievances of labor at the dawn of the American trade-union movement were long hours, low wages, wretched working conditions, petty tyrannies practiced by the employer, deductions, penalties, and even payment in promissory notes instead of cash. To American mechanics and factory workers of 1832 it seemed signally unfair that capital should be protected from competition by high tariffs while labor was left completely unprotected against the waves of foreign workers that the free-and-easy immigration laws encouraged. Just as the Luddites in England broke the hateful machines, so American workers of this period sometimes mistakenly blamed the foreigner for their miseries, and much bitterness and a few serious riots resulted.

One of the early advocates of labor reform was the carpenter-orator Seth Luther, who, according to Commons (History of Labor in the United States, by John R. Commons and others [1921]), was "the first American in the anti-child-labor crusade." It is significant that we know nothing of his early life, except that he was probably born late in the eighteenth century. He became a champion of labor in about 1817 and remained one to his death in 1846. He himself reports that he received little schooling, but had learned "what little I do know" from newspapers and books and by constant observation, having made an extensive tour of fourteen American states. When he returned to live for years among the cotton mills of New England, he brought with him a love for the freedom of the frontier and a hatred of class distinctions. "The whole system of labor in New England . . . is a cruel system of exaction on the bodies and minds of the producing classes, destroying the energies of both."

The following address he delivered in Boston, Charlestown, Cambridgeport, Waltham, and Dorchester.

"We do not believe there can be a single person . . . *who ever* thanked God *for* permission *to work in a* cotton mill."

O UR EARS are constantly filled with the cry of national wealth, national glory, American system, and American industry. . . .

This cry is kept up by men who are endeavoring *by all the means in their power* to cut down the wages of *our own people,* and who send agents to *Europe* to *induce foreigners* to come here to underwork *American citizens,* to support *American* industry and the *American* system.

The whole concern (as now conducted) is as great a humbug as ever deceived any people. We see the system of manufacturing lauded to the skies; senators, representatives, owners, and agents of cotton mills using all means to keep out of sight the evils growing up under it. Cotton mills, where cruelties are practiced, excessive labor required, education neglected, and vice, as a matter of course, on the increase, are denominated "the principalities of the destitute, the palaces of the poor." We do not pretend to say that this description applies, in all its parts, to all mills alike—but we do say that most of the causes described by Dr. Kay, of Manchester, are in active operation in New England, and, as sure as effect follows cause, the result must be the same. A member of the United States Senate seems to be *extremely* pleased with cotton mills; he says in the Senate, "Who has not been delighted with the clockwork movements of a large cotton manufactory; he had visited them often, and *always* with increased delight." He says the women work in large airy apartments. well warmed; they are neatly dressed, with ruddy complexions and happy countenances, they mend the broken threads and replace the exhausted balls or broaches, and at stated periods they go to and return from their meals with a light and cheerful step. (While on a visit to that pink of perfection, Waltham, I remarked that the females moved with a very light step, and well they might, for the bell rung for them to return to the mill from their homes in nineteen minutes after it had rung for them to go to breakfast; some of these females boarded the largest part of half a mile from the mill.) And the grand climax is that at the end of the week, after working like slaves for thirteen or fourteen hours every day, "they enter the temples of God on the Sabbath, and thank Him for all His benefits" —and the *American system* above all requires a peculiar outpouring of gratitude. We remark that whatever girls or others may do west of the Allegheny Mountains, we do not believe there can be a *single person* found east of those mountains who ever *thanked God* for *permission* to work in a *cotton mill.*

Without being obliged to attribute wrong or mercenary motives to the honorable Senator (*whose talents certainly must command respect from all,* let their views in other respects be what they may), we remark that we think he was most grossly deceived by the circumstances of his visit. We will give our *reasons* in a few words spoken (in part) on a former occasion on this subject. It is well known to all that when *honorables* travel, timely notice is given of their arrival and departure in places of note. Here we have a case; the honorable Senator from Kentucky is about to visit a *cotton mill;* due notice is given; the men, girls, and boys are ordered to array themselves in their best apparel. Flowers of every hue are brought to decorate the mill and enwreath the brows of the fair sex. If nature will not furnish the materials from the lap of summer, art supplies the deficiency. Evergreens mingle with the roses, the jasmine, and the hyacinth to honor the *illustrious* visitor, the champion, the very Goliath of the American system. He enters! Smiles are on every brow. No *cowhide,* or rod, or "well-seasoned strap" is suffered to be seen by the honorable Senator or permitted to disturb the enviable happiness of the inmates of this almost *celestial* habitation. The honorable gentleman views with keen eye the "clockwork." He sees the rosy faces of the houris inhabiting this palace of beauty; he is in ecstasy—he is almost *dumfounded*—he enjoys the enchanting scene with the most intense delight. For an hour or more (not fourteen hours) he seems to be in the regions described in Oriental song, his feelings are overpowered, and he retires, almost unconscious of the cheers which follow his steps; or if he hears the ringing shout, 'tis but to convince him that he is in a land of reality and not of fiction. His mind being filled with sensations, which, from their novelty, are without a name, he exclaims, 'tis a paradise; and we reply, if a cotton mill is a "paradise," it is "Paradise Lost.". . .

It has been said that the speaker is opposed to *the* American system. It turns upon one single point—if these abuses are *the* American system, he is opposed. But let him see *an* American system where education and intelligence are generally diffused, and the enjoyment of *life* and *liberty* secured to all; he then is ready to support *such* a system. But so long as our government secures exclusive privileges to a *very small part of the community,* and leaves the majority the "lawful prey" to avarice, so long does he contend against *any* "system" so exceedingly unjust and unequal in its operations. He knows that we must have manufactures. It is impossible to do without them; but he has yet to learn that it is necessary, or just, that manufactures must be sustained by injustice, cruelty, ignorance, vice, and misery; which is now the fact to a startling degree. If what we have stated be true, and we challenge denial, what must be done? Must we fold our arms and say, it always was so and always will be? If we did so, would it not almost rouse from their graves the heroes of our Revolution? Would not the cold marble representing our beloved Washington start into *life* and reproach us for our *cowardice?* Let the word be—onward! onward! We know the difficulties are great, and the obstacles many; but, as yet, we "know our rights, and knowing, dare maintain." We wish to injure no man, and we are determined not to be injured as we have been; we wish nothing but those equal rights which were designed for us all. And although wealth, and prejudice, and slander, and abuse are all brought to bear on us, we have one consolation—"*We are the majority.*"

One difficulty is a want of information among our own class, and the *higher orders* reproach us for our ignorance; but, thank God, we have enough of intelligence among us yet to show the world that all is not lost.

Another difficulty among us is—the press has been almost wholly, and is now in a great degree, closed upon us. We venture to assert that the press is *bribed* by *gold* in many instances; and we believe that if *law* had done what *gold* has accomplished, our country would, before this time, have been deluged with blood. But workingmen's papers are multiplying, and we shall soon, by the diffusion of intelligence, be enabled to form a *front* which will show all *monopolists,* and all *tyrants,* that we are not only determined to have the name of freemen, but that we will *live freemen* and *die freemen.*

Fellow citizens of New England, farmers, mechanics, and laborers, we have borne these evils by far too long; we have been deceived by all parties; we must take our business into our own hands. Let us awake. Our cause is the cause of truth—of justice and humanity. *It must prevail.* Let us be determined no longer to be deceived by the cry of those who produce *nothing* and who enjoy *all,* and who *insultingly* term us—the *farmers, the mechanics, and laborers*—the *lower orders,* and *exultingly* claim our homage for themselves, as the *higher orders*—*while the* Declaration of Independence asserts that "All men are created equal."

The earnestness and forceful satire of this address, anticipating the grim humor of Dickens's Hard Times (1854), shows Luther's ability at its best. The effect of such agitation, like that of thousands of little-known or nameless champions of labor, is difficult to trace. It is very probable that Luther influenced the policy of the short-lived New England Association, and his activities may conceivably have had wider repercussions. In any event, it is significant that in 1842 Massachusetts passed the first American child-labor law.

RALPH WALDO EMERSON POINTS OUT THE DUTIES OF THE AMERICAN SCHOLAR

[August 31, 1837]

The youthful Emerson had wanted to become a teacher of rhetoric and elocution. Higher aspirations intervened, but throughout his life he remained a student of oratory and a close observer of orators. Out of his journals grew his lectures and out of his lectures nearly all of his published essays, two of which were finally entitled "Eloquence."

When Ralph Waldo Emerson (1803–82) was graduated from Harvard in 1821, as "number thirty in a class of fifty-nine," ancestral voices pointed toward a career of teaching and later of preaching. But four years in his brother William's finishing school for girls was more than enough for this shy, self-conscious young man. He now turned to the Harvard Divinity School for a year of desultory study, which gave him the right to preach. Ill health kept him from a regular post until the spring of 1829, when he became pastor of the Second (Unitarian) Church of Boston. He might have remained there indefinitely, for he was a marked success with his quietly stirring sermons; but he found himself unable to administer the Last Supper and after nearly three years abruptly resigned, in spite of many protests from the congregation.

Emerson was now free to complete his education with a year of invaluable travel in Europe. Returning in October, 1833, he lectured in Boston on "The Uses of Natural History" and thus began that great platform career which was to continue some forty years. His fame outside of New England came slowly. It was not his poetic little book, Nature, published in 1836, so much as the Phi Beta Kappa oration, delivered at Harvard the following summer, that announced a new mind in America. Two hundred and fifteen members of the society and a number of friends were gathered in the meetinghouse near Harvard Yard.

We present the final section of what Oliver Wendell Holmes called "the declaration of American intellectual independence."

> *"This time, like all times, is a very good one, if*
> *we but know what to do with it."*

OUR AGE is bewailed as the age of introversion. Must that needs be evil? We, it seems, are critical; we are embarrassed with second thoughts; we cannot enjoy anything for hankering to know whereof the pleasure consists; we are lined with eyes; we see with our feet; the time is infected with Hamlet's unhappiness—

> *Sicklied o'er with the pale cast of thought.*

Is it so bad, then? Sight is the last thing to be pitied. Would we be blind? Do we fear lest we should outsee nature and God, and drink truth dry? I look upon the discontent of the literary class as a mere announcement of the fact that they find themselves not in the state of mind of their fathers and regret the coming state as untried; as a boy dreads the water before he has learned that he can swim. If there is any period one would desire to be born in, is it not the age of revolution; when the old and the new stand side by side, and admit of being compared; when the energies of all men are searched by fear and by hope; when the historic glories of the old can be compensated by the rich possibilities of the new era? This time, like all times, is a very good one, if we but know what to do with it.

I read with joy some of the auspicious signs of the coming days, as they glimmer already through poetry and art, through philosophy and science, through church and state.

One of these signs is the fact that the same movement which effected the elevation of what was called the lowest class in the state assumed in literature a very marked and as benign an aspect. Instead of the sublime and beautiful; the near, the low, the common, was explored and poetized. That, which had been negligently trodden underfoot by those who were harnessing and provisioning themselves for long journeys into far countries, is suddenly found to be richer than all foreign parts. The literature of the poor, the feelings of the child, the philosophy of the street, the meaning of household life, are the topics of the time. It is a great stride. It is a sign—is it not?—of new vigor, when the extremities are made active, when currents of warm life run into the hands and the feet. I ask not for the great, the remote, the romantic; what is doing in Italy or Arabia; I embrace the common, I explore and sit at the feet of the familiar, the low. Give me insight into today, and you may have the antique and future worlds. What would we really know the meaning of? The meal in the firkin; the milk in the pan, the ballad in the street; the news of the boat; the glance of the eye; the form and the gait of the body—show me the ultimate reason of these matters; show me the sublime presence of the highest spiritual cause lurking, as always it does lurk, in these suburbs and extremities of nature; let me see every trifle bristling with the polarity that ranges it instantly on an eternal law; and the shop, the plow, and the ledger referred to the like cause by which light undulates and poets sing; and the world lies no longer a dull miscellany and lumber room, but has form and order; there is no trifle; there is no puzzle; but one design unites and animates the farthest pinnacle and the lowest trench.

This idea has inspired the genius of Goldsmith, Burns, Cowper, and, in a newer time, of Goethe, Wordsworth, and Carlyle. This idea they have differently followed and with various success. In contrast with their writing, the style of Pope, of Johnson, of Gibbon, looks cold and pedantic. This writing is blood-warm. Man is surprised to find that things near are not less beautiful and wondrous than things remote. The near explains the far. The drop is a small ocean. A man is related to all nature. This perception of the worth of the vulgar is fruitful in discoveries. Goethe, in this very thing the most modern of the moderns, has shown us, as none ever did, the genius of the ancients. . . .

Another sign of our times, also marked by an analogous political movement, is the new importance given to the single person. Everything that tends to insulate the individual—to surround him with barriers of natural respect, so that each man shall feel the world as his, and man shall treat with man as a sovereign state with a sovereign state—tends to true union as well as greatness. "I learned," said the melancholy Pestalozzi, "that no man in God's wide earth is either willing or able to help any other man." Help must come from the bosom alone. The scholar is that man who must take up into himself all the ability of the time, all the contributions of the past, all the hopes of the future. He must be a university of knowledges. If there be one lesson more than another which should pierce his ear, it is: the world is nothing, the man is all; in yourself is the law of all nature, and you know not yet how a globule of sap ascends; in yourself slumbers the whole of reason; it is for you to know all, it is for you to dare all. Mr. President and gentlemen, this confidence in the unsearched might of man belongs, by all motives, by all prophecy, by all preparation, to the American scholar. We have listened too long to the courtly Muses of Europe. The spirit of the American freeman is already suspected to be timid, imitative, tame. Public and private avarice make the air we breathe thick and fat. The scholar is decent, indolent, complaisant. See already the tragic consequence. The mind of this country, taught to aim at low objects, eats upon itself. There is no work for any but the decorous and the complaisant. Young men of the fairest promise, who begin life upon our shores, inflated by the mountain winds, shined upon by all the stars of God, find the earth below not in unison with these —but are hindered from action by the disgust which the principles on which business is managed inspire, and turn drudges, or die of disgust— some of them suicides. What is the remedy? They did not yet see, and thousands of young men as hopeful now crowding to the barriers for the career do not yet see, that if the single man plant himself indomitably on his instincts, and there abide, the huge world will come round to him. Patience—patience—with the shades of all the good and great for company; and for solace, the perspective of your own infinite life; and for work, the study and the communication of principles, the making those instincts prevalent, the conversion of the world. Is it not the chief disgrace in the world, not to be a unit—not to be reckoned one character—not to yield that peculiar fruit which each man was created to bear, but to be reckoned in the gross, in the hundred, or the thousand, or the party, the section, to which we belong; and our opinion predicted geographically, as the North or the South? Not so, brothers and friends—please God, ours shall not be so. We will walk on our own feet; we will work with our own hands; we will speak our own minds. The study of letters shall be no longer a name for pity, for doubt, and for sensual indulgence. The dread of man and the love of man shall be a wall of defense and a wreath of joy around all. A nation of men will for the first time exist, because each believes himself inspired by the Divine Soul which also inspires all men.

This was drastic talk, and it left Emerson's audience divided between enthusiasm and dismay. The following July he aroused a restrained uproar with his address before the senior class of the Divinity School, Cambridge. "No ripple of the storm at Cambridge seems to have reached the orthodox New Hampshire college six days later" when he arrived at Hanover by chaise to give an address on "Literary Ethics" before Dartmouth's literary societies. That address contains one of Emerson's noblest flights: "You will hear every day the maxims of a low prudence. You will hear that the first duty is to get land and money, place and name. 'What is this Truth you seek? what is this Beauty?' men will ask, with derision. If nevertheless God have called any of you to explore truth and beauty, be bold, be firm, be true. When you shall say, 'As others do, so will I: I renounce, I am sorry for it, my early visions; I must eat the good of the land and let learning and romantic expectations go, until a more convenient season'—then dies the man in you; then once more perish the buds of art, poetry, and science, as they have died already in a thousand thousand men. The hour of that choice is the crisis of your history, and see that you hold yourself fast by the intellect."

By 1838 Emerson had struck his vein, had found his confidence, and a growing audience was inevitable. Thirty years later James Russell Lowell recalled "Mr. Emerson's first lectures under the consulate of Van Buren"... how they used to walk into Boston from the country "and listen to the thrilling voice of his, so charged with subtle meaning and subtle music, as shipwrecked men on a raft to the hail of a ship that comes with unhoped-for food and

rescue. . . . *The delight and the benefit were that he put us in communication
with a larger style of thought . . . made us conscious of the supreme and
everlasting originality of whatever bit of soul might be in any of us; freed us, in
short, from the stocks of prose in which we had sat so long that we had well-
nigh grown contented with our cramps."*

WENDELL PHILLIPS, A YOUNG BOSTON BRAHMIN, LEAPS INTO THE ABOLITIONIST CRUSADE

[December 8, 1837]

*It was but a few miles and a few short months from Emerson's address to the
Phi Beta Kappa meeting at Cambridge to the shouting crowd of five thousand
in Faneuil Hall when Wendell Phillips spoke there for the first time.*

*A Boston aristocrat with all the advantages—wealth, brains, and a fine
appearance, not to mention two Harvard diplomas—Wendell Phillips (1811–
84) could anticipate a brilliant career when he opened his law office in 1836.
But not long afterward he saw a mob dragging the abolitionist William Lloyd
Garrison through the streets—with members of the Boston regiment in the
mob. This brutal scene drove Phillips toward the abolitionist cause and, encouraged by the fearless woman he was about to marry, Ann Terry Greene, he
spoke briefly before the Massachusetts Anti-Slavery Society in Lynn. But his
gifts were evidently not suspected until the night of December 8, 1837, when
he went to the Faneuil Hall meeting called to protest against the murder of
Elijah P. Lovejoy, the abolitionist publisher. He had been shot by a mob at
Alton, Illinois, when a warehouse, where his press had been placed for safekeeping, was set afire.*

*After the noble William Ellery Channing had spoken with his customary
effect, and resolutions of protest had been read and seconded, a speaker in the
balcony, uninvited and unannounced, the Attorney General of Massachusetts,
the Honorable James T. Austin, proceeded to ridicule the purpose of the
gathering and to compare the murderers of Lovejoy to the members of the
Boston Tea Party and to other Revolutionary heroes. Hundreds of the crowd
cheered. It was now that Phillips rushed to the platform and, in the face of
boos and catcalls, began to speak.*

"Does success gild crime into patriotism, and the want of it
change heroic self-devotion to imprudence?"

Mr. Chairman:

WE HAVE MET for the freest discussion of these resolutions, and the events which gave rise to them. I hope I shall be permitted to express my surprise at the sentiments of the last speaker, surprise not only at such sentiments from such a man, but at the applause they have received within these walls.

A comparison has been drawn between the events of the Revolution and the tragedy at Alton. We have heard it asserted here in Faneuil Hall that Great Britain had a right to tax the colonies; and we have heard the mob at Alton, the drunken murderers of Lovejoy, compared to those patriot fathers who threw the tea overboard! Fellow citizens, is this Faneuil Hall doctrine? The mob at Alton were met to wrest from a citizen his just rights—met to resist the laws. We have been told that our fathers did the same; and the glorious mantle of Revolutionary precedent has been thrown over the mobs of our day. To make out their title to such defense the gentleman says that the British Parliament had a right to tax these colonies.

It is manifest that, without this, his parallel falls to the ground; for Lovejoy had stationed himself within constitutional bulwarks. He was not only defending the freedom of the press, but he was under his own roof, in arms with the sanction of the civil authority. The men who assailed him went against and over the laws. The mob, as the gentleman terms it—mob, forsooth! certainly we sons of the tea-spillers are a marvelously patient generation!—the "orderly mob" which assembled in the Old South to destroy the tea were met to resist, not the laws, but illegal exactions! Shame on the American who calls the tea tax and Stamp Act laws! Our fathers resisted, not the King's prerogative, but the King's usurpation. To find any other account, you must read our Revolutionary history upside down. Our state archives are loaded with arguments of John Adams to prove the taxes laid by the British Parliament unconstitutional—beyond its power. It was not till this was made out that the men of New England rushed to arms. The arguments of the council chamber and the House of Representatives preceded and sanctioned the contest.

To draw the conduct of our ancestors into a precedent for mobs, for a right to resist laws we ourselves have enacted, is an insult to their memory. The difference between the excitements of those days and our own, which the gentleman in kindness to the latter has overlooked, is simply this: the men of that day went for the right, as secured by the laws. They were the people rising to sustain the laws and Constitution of the province. The rioters of our day go for their own wills, right or wrong. Sir, when I heard the gentleman lay down principles which place the murderers of Alton side by side with Otis and Hancock, with Quincy and Adams, I thought those pictured lips [pointing to the portraits in the hall] would have broken into voice to rebuke the recreant American—the slanderer of the dead. The gentleman said that he should sink into insignificance if he dared not gainsay the principles of these resolutions. Sir, for the sentiments he has uttered, on soil consecrated by the prayers of Puritans and the blood of patriots, the earth should have yawned and swallowed him up.

[The contemporary account of this scene says: "Applause and hisses were here heard, with cries of 'Take that back,' and then the uproar became so great that for a long time no one could be heard. 'Phillips or nobody,' cried one; 'Make him take back "recreant,"' cried another; and a third: 'He shan't go on till he takes it back.' Finally a man said: 'I did not come here to take any part in this discussion, nor do I intend to; but I do entreat you, fellow citizens, by everything you hold sacred—I conjure you by every association connected with this hall, consecrated by our fathers to freedom of discussion—that you listen to every man who addresses you in a decorous manner.' Mr. Phillips then resumed."]

Fellow citizens, I cannot take back my words. Surely, the Attorney General, so long and well known here, needs not the aid of your hisses against one so young as I am—my voice never before heard within these walls!

Another ground has been taken to excuse the mob, and throw doubt and discredit on the conduct of Lovejoy and his associates. Allusion has been made to what lawyers understand very well—the "conflict of laws." We are told that nothing but the Mississippi River rolls between St. Louis and Alton; and the conflict of laws somehow or other gives the citizens of the former a right to find fault with the defender of the press for publishing his opinions so near their limits. Will the gentleman venture that argument before lawyers? How the laws of the two states could be said to come into conflict in such circumstances I question whether any lawyer in this audience can explain or understand. No matter whether the line that divides one sovereign state from another be an imaginary one or ocean-wide, the moment you cross it, the state you leave is blotted out of existence, so far as you are concerned. The Czar might as well claim to control the deliberations of Faneuil Hall as the laws of Missouri demand reverence, or the shadow of obedience, from an inhabitant of Illinois.

I must find some fault with the statement which has been made of the events at Alton. It has been asked why Lovejoy and his friends did not appeal to the executive—trust their defense to the police of the city. It has been hinted that, from hasty and ill-judged excitement, the men within the building provoked a quarrel and that he fell in the course of it—one mob resisting another. Recollect, sir, that they did act with the approbation and sanction of the mayor. In strict truth there was no executive to appeal to for protection. The mayor acknowledged that he could not protect them. They asked him if it was lawful for them to defend themselves. He told them it was, and sanctioned their assembling in arms to do so. They were not, then, a mob; they were not merely citizens defending their own property; they were in some sense the *posse comitatus*, adopted for the occasion into the police of the city, acting under the order of a magistrate. It was civil authority resisting lawless violence. Where, then, was the imprudence? Is the doctrine to be sustained here that it is imprudent for men to aid magistrates in executing the laws?

Men are continually asking each other, had Lovejoy a right to resist? Sir, I protest against the question instead of answering it. Lovejoy did not resist, in the sense they mean. He did not throw himself back on the natural right of self-defense. He did not cry anarchy, and let slip the dogs of civil war, careless of the horrors which would follow.

Sir, as I understand this affair, it was not an individual protecting his property; it was not one body of armed men resisting another and making the streets of a peaceful city run blood with their contentions. It did not bring back the scenes in old Italian cities, where family met family, and faction met faction, and mutually trampled the laws underfoot. No! the men in that house were regularly enrolled under the sanction of the mayor. There being no militia in Alton, about seventy men were enrolled with the approbation of the mayor. These relieved each other every other night. About thirty men were in arms on the night of the sixth, when the press was landed. The next evening it was not thought necessary to summon more than half that number: among these was Lovejoy. It was, therefore, you perceive, sir, the police of the city resisting rioters—civil government breasting itself to the shock of lawless men.

Here is no question about the right of self-defense. It is in fact simply this: has the civil magistrate a right to put down a riot?

Some persons seem to imagine that anarchy existed at Alton from the commencement of these disputes. Not at all. "No one of us," says an eyewitness and a comrade of Lovejoy's, "has taken up arms during these disturbances but at the command of the Mayor." Anarchy did not settle down on that devoted city till Lovejoy breathed his last. Till then the law, represented in his person, sustained itself against its foes. When he fell, civil authority was trampled underfoot. He had "planted himself on his constitutional rights"—appealed to the laws—claimed the protection of the civil authority—taken refuge under "the broad shield of the Constitution. When through that he was pierced and fell, he fell but one sufferer in a common catastrophe." He took refuge under the banner of liberty—amid its folds; and when he fell, its glorious stars and stripes, the emblem of free institutions, around which cluster so many heart-stirring memories, were blotted out in the martyr's blood.

It has been stated, perhaps inadvertently, that Lovejoy or his comrades fired first. This is denied by those who have the best means of knowing. Guns were first fired by the mob. After being twice fired on, those within the building consulted together and deliberately returned the fire. But suppose they did fire first. They had a right so to do—not only the right which every citizen has to defend himself, but the further right which every civil officer has to resist violence. Even if Lovejoy fired the first gun, it would not lessen his claim to our sympathy or destroy his title to be considered a martyr in defense of a free press. The question now is, did he act within the Constitution and the laws? The men who fell in State Street on the fifth of March, 1770, did more than Lovejoy is charged with. They were the first assailants. Upon some slight quarrel they pelted the troops with every missile within reach. Did this bate one jot of the eulogy with which Hancock and Warren hallowed their memory, hailing them as the first martyrs in the cause of American liberty?

If, sir, I had adopted what are called peace principles, I might lament the circumstances of this case. But all you who believe, as I do, in the right and duty of magistrates to execute the laws join with me and brand as base hypocrisy the conduct of those who assemble year after year on the Fourth of July to fight over the battles of the Revolution, and yet "damn with faint praise" or load with obloquy the memory of this man who shed his blood in defense of life, liberty, property, and the freedom of the press!

Throughout that terrible night I find nothing to regret but this, that, within the limits of our country, civil authority should have been so prostrated as to oblige a citizen to arm in his own defense, and to arm in vain. The gentleman says Lovejoy was presumptuous and imprudent—he "died as the fool dieth." And a reverend clergyman of the city tells us that no citizen has a right to publish opinions disagreeable to the community! If any mob follows such publication, on *him* rests its guilt. He must wait, forsooth, till the people come up to it and agree with him! This libel on liberty goes on to say that the want of right to speak as we think is an evil inseparable from republican institutions! If this be so, what are they worth? Welcome the despotism of the Sultan, where one knows what he may publish and what he may not, rather than the tyranny of this many-headed monster, the mob, where we know not what we may do or say till some fellow citizen has tried it and paid for the lesson with his life. This clerical absurdity chooses as a check for the abuses of the press, not the *law*, but the dread of a mob. By so doing, it deprives not only the individual and the minority of their rights, but the majority also, since the expression of *their* opinion may sometime provoke disturbances from the minority. A few men may make a mob as well as many. The majority, then, have no right, as Christian men, to utter their sentiments, if by any possibility it may lead to a mob! Shades of Hugh Peters and John Cotton, save us from such pulpits!

Imprudent to defend the liberty of the press! Why? Because the defense was unsuccessful? Does success gild crime into patriotism, and the want of it change heroic self-devotion to imprudence? Was Hampden imprudent when he drew the sword and threw away the scabbard? Yet he, judged by that single hour, was unsuccessful. After a short exile, the race he hated sat again upon the throne.

Imagine yourself present when the first news of Bunker Hill battle reached a New England town. The tale would have run thus: "The patriots are routed—the redcoats victorious—Warren lies dead upon the field." With what scorn would that Tory have been received who should have charged Warren with imprudence! who should have said that, bred a physician, he was "out of place" in that battle, and "died as the fool dieth"! How would the intimation have been received that Warren and his associates should have waited a better time? But, if success be indeed the only criterion of prudence, *respice finem*—wait till the end.

Presumptuous to assert the freedom of the press on American ground! Is the assertion of such freedom before the age? So much before the age as to leave one no right to make it because it displeases the community? Who invents this libel on his country? It is this very thing which entitles Lovejoy to greater praise. The disputed right which provoked the Revolution—taxation without representation—is far beneath that for which he died. [Here there was a general expression of strong disapprobation.] One word, gentlemen. As much as *thought* is better than money, so much is the cause in which Lovejoy died nobler than a mere question of taxes. James Otis thundered in this hall when the King did but touch his *pocket.* Imagine, if you can, his indignant eloquence had England offered to put a gag upon his *lips.* The question that stirred the Revolution touched our civil interests. This concerns us not only as citizens, but as immortal beings. Wrapped up in its fate, saved or lost with it, are not only the voice of the statesman, but the instructions of the pulpit and the progress of our faith.

The clergy, "marvelously out of place" where free speech is battled for ·—liberty of speech on national sins! Does the gentleman remember that freedom to preach was first gained, dragging in its train freedom to print? I thank the clergy here present, as I reverence their predecessors, who did not so far forget their country in their immediate profession as to deem it duty to separate themselves from the struggle of '76—the Mayhews and Coopers, who remembered that they were citizens before they were clergymen.

Mr. Chairman, from the bottom of my heart I thank that brave little band at Alton for resisting. We must remember that Lovejoy had fled from city to city; suffered the destruction of three presses patiently. At length he took counsel with friends; men of character, of tried integrity, of wide views, of Christian principle. They thought the crisis had come. It was full time to assert the laws. They saw around them, not a community like our own, of fixed habits, of character molded and settled, but one "in the gristle, not yet hardened into the bone of manhood." The people there, children of our older states, seem to have forgotten the blood-tried principles of their fathers the moment they lost sight of our New England hills. Something was to be done to show them the priceless value of the freedom of the press, to bring back and set right their wandering and confused ideas. He and his advisers looked out on a community staggering like a drunken man, indifferent to their rights, and confused in their feelings. Deaf to argument, haply they might be stunned into sobriety. They saw that of which we cannot judge: the necessity of resistance. Insulted law called for it. Public opinion, fast hastening on the downward course, must be arrested.

Does not the event show they judged rightly? Absorbed in a thousand trifles, how has the nation all at once come to a stand! Men begin, as in 1776 and 1640, to discuss principles, to weigh characters, to find out where they are. Haply we may awake before we are borne over the precipice.

I am glad, sir, to see this crowded house. It is good for us to be here. When liberty is in danger, Faneuil Hall has the right, it is her duty, to strike the keynote for these United States. I am glad, for one reason, that remarks such as those to which I have alluded have been uttered here.

The passage of these resolutions, in spite of this opposition, led by the Attorney General of the commonwealth, will show more clearly, more decisively, the deep indignation with which Boston regards this outrage.

Wendell Phillips took the audience by storm, and after the applause had subsided the resolutions were passed by an overwhelming vote. At the age of twenty-six the Boston Brahmin, forsaking his law practice, thus became the most inspiring speaker of the abolitionist movement. When the abolitionist program was victorious, he lent his voice to other social causes, such as votes for women and academic freedom.

Phillips, whose style of oratory was peculiarly his own, became—in the opinion of such diverse veterans of the platform as John Bright, Chauncey Depew, and James B. Pond—the finest English-speaking orator of the century. Of the various attempts to capture his apparently effortless art, George William Curtis's seems the best:

"With no party behind him, and appealing against the established order and acknowledged tradition, his speech was necessarily a popular appeal for a strange and unwelcome cause, and the condition of its success was that it should both charm and rouse the hearer, while, under cover of the fascination, the orator unfolded his argument and urged his plea. . . . He faced his audience with a tranquil mien, and a beaming aspect that never dimmed, and in the measured cadence of his quiet voice there was intense feeling but no declamation, no passionate, no superficial and feigned emotion. It was simply colloquy—a gentleman conversing."

THOMAS CORWIN, IN THE MOST FEARLESS SPEECH EVER DELIVERED IN CONGRESS, DENOUNCES THE MEXICAN WAR

[February 11, 1847]

The growing tension between two economic systems, two ways of life, was not lessened by the abolitionists of the North or the secessionists of the South. Nor did expansion to the West help. Inspired by patriotic Americans, Texas revolted from Mexico in 1835 and was annexed to the United States in 1845. The following year began the Mexican War, from which we emerged with 522,955 square miles, for a consideration of only fifteen million dollars. Whether we blundered into that lucrative conflict or were drawn into it by the machinations of President Polk, it now seems to have been an inevitable episode—part of our manifest destiny. But to many leaders of the period it did not seem desirable or inevitable. The vast conquered territory will become a province for Northern bureaucrats and capitalists, argued some Southerners. It will provide for a limitless extension of slavery, argued some Northerners. No one had anything to say about the feelings of Mexico, the justice of the war, or the prestige of the United States in the perspective of history—almost no one, that is, except genial Tom Corwin of Ohio.

Thomas Corwin (1794–1865) taught himself law and practiced successfully for some years before spending five terms in Congress and one term as Governor of Ohio. But it was as a Whig Senator from Ohio that he made his unforgettable mark, in the very midst of the Mexican War. Convinced that it was simply an aggressive war waged for territory, he decided to oppose a bill for further appropriations and asked Senators Crittenden and Webster to cooperate. They were reticent, so he made the attack alone in the crowded and apprehensive Senate chamber.

"Your army, by order of the President, without the consent or advice of Congress, made war on Mexico, by invading her territory, in April, 1846"— this was the dangerous burden of most of his speech, which he bolstered with elaborate evidence. Then he turned to larger matters and to a prophetic note.

"If I were a Mexican I would tell you, 'Have you not room enough in your own country to bury your dead?' "

WHAT is the territory, Mr. President, which you propose to wrest from Mexico? It is consecrated to the heart of the Mexican by many a well-fought battle with his old Castilian master. His Bunker Hills, and Saratogas, and Yorktowns are there! The Mexican can say, "There I bled for liberty! and shall I surrender that consecrated home of my affections to the Anglo-Saxon invaders? What do they want with it? They have Texas already. They have possessed themselves of the territory between the Nueces and the Rio Grande. What else do they want? To what shall I point my children as memorials of that independence which I bequeath to them, when those battlefields shall have passed from my possession?"

Sir, had one come and demanded Bunker Hill of the people of Massachusetts, had England's lion ever showed himself there, is there a man over thirteen and under ninety who would not have been ready to

meet him? Is there a river on this continent that would not have run red
with blood? Is there a field but would have been piled high with unburied
bones of slaughtered Americans before these consecrated battlefields of
liberty should have been wrested from us? But this same American goes
into a sister republic, and says to poor, weak Mexico, "Give up your territory, you are unworthy to possess it; I have got one half already, and all I
ask of you is to give up the other!" England might as well, in the circumstances I have described, have come and demanded of us, "Give up the
Atlantic slope—give up this trifling territory from the Allegheny Mountains to the sea; it is only from Maine to St. Mary's—only about one
third of your Republic, and the least interesting portion of it." What
would be the response? They would say we must give this up to John
Bull. Why? "He wants room." The Senator from Michigan says he must
have this. Why, my worthy Christian brother; on what principle of
justice? "I want room!"

Sir, look at this pretense of want of room. With twenty millions of
people, you have about one thousand millions of acres of land, inviting
settlement by every conceivable argument, bringing them down to a
quarter of a dollar an acre, and allowing every man to squat where he
pleases. But the Senator from Michigan says we will be two hundred
millions in a few years, and we want room. If I were a Mexican I would
tell you, "Have you not room enough in your own country to bury your
dead? If you come into mine, we will greet you with bloody hands, and
welcome you to hospitable graves."

Why, says the Chairman of this Committee on Foreign Relations, it is
the most reasonable thing in the world! We ought to have the Bay of San
Francisco! Why? Because it is the best harbor on the Pacific! It has been
my fortune, Mr. President, to have practiced a good deal in criminal
courts in the course of my life, but I never yet heard a thief, arraigned
for stealing a horse, plead that it was the best horse he could find in the
country! We want California. What for? Why, says the Senator from
Michigan, we will have it; and the Senator from South Carolina, with a
very mistaken view, I think, of policy, says you can't keep our people
from going there. I don't desire to prevent them. Let them go and seek
their happiness in whatever country or clime it pleases them. All I ask of
them is not to require this government to protect them with that banner
consecrated to war waged for principles—eternal, enduring truth. Sir, it
is not meet that our old flag should throw its protecting folds over expeditions for lucre or for land. But you still say you want room for your people.
This has been the plea of every robber chief from Nimrod to the present
hour. I dare say when Tamerlane descended from his throne, built of

seventy thousand human skulls, and marched his ferocious battalions to further slaughter—I dare say he said, "I want room." Bajazet was another gentleman of kindred tastes and wants with us Anglo-Saxons—he "wanted room." Alexander, too, the mighty "Macedonian madman," when he wandered with his Greeks to the plains of India, and fought a bloody battle on the very ground where recently England and the Sikhs engaged in strife for "room," was, no doubt, in quest of some California there. Many a Monterrey had he to storm to get "room." Sir, he made as much of that sort of history as you ever will. Mr. President, do you remember the last chapter in that history? It is soon read. Ah, I wish we could but understand its moral. Ammon's son (so was Alexander named), after all his victories, died drunk in Babylon! The vast empire he conquered to "get room," became the prey of the generals he had trained: it was dismembered, torn to pieces, and so ended. Sir, there is a very significant appendix; it is this: the descendants of the Greeks, Alexander's Greeks, are now governed by a descendant of Attila! Mr. President, while we are fighting for room, let us ponder deeply this appendix. I was somewhat amazed the other day to hear the Senator from Michigan declare that Europe had quite forgotten us, till these battles waked them up. I suppose the Senator feels grateful to the President for "waking up" Europe. Does the President, who is, I hope, read in civic as well as military lore, remember the saying of one who had pondered upon history long; long, too, upon man, his nature, and true destiny. Montesquieu did not think highly of this way of "waking up." "Happy," says he, "is that nation whose annals are tiresome."

The Senator from Michigan has a different view. He thinks that a nation is not distinguished until it is distinguished in war. He fears that the slumbering faculties of Europe have not been able to ascertain that there are twenty millions of Anglo-Saxons here, making railroads and canals, and speeding all the arts of peace to the utmost accomplishment of the most refined civilization! They do not know it! And what is the wonderful expedient which this democratic method of making history would adopt in order to make us known? Storming cities, desolating peaceful, happy homes; shooting men—ay, sir, such is war—and shooting women, too.

Sir, I have read in some account of your battle of Monterrey of a lovely Mexican girl who, with the benevolence of an angel in her bosom and the robust courage of a hero in her heart, was busily engaged during the bloody conflict—amid the crash of falling houses, the groans of the dying, and the wild shriek of battle—in carrying water to slake the burning thirst of the wounded of either host. While bending over a wounded

American soldier, a cannon ball struck her and blew her to atoms! Sir, I do not charge my brave, generous-hearted countrymen who fought that fight with this. No, no. We who send them—we who know that scenes like this, which might send tears of sorrow "down Pluto's iron cheek," are the invariable, inevitable attendants on war—we are accountable for this; and this—this is the way we are to be made known to Europe. This—this is to be the undying renown of free, republican America; "she has stormed a city, killed many of its inhabitants of both sexes—she has room!" So it will read. Sir, if this were our only history, then may God in his mercy grant that its volume may speedily come to a close.

Why is it, sir, that we of the United States, a people of yesterday, compared with the older nations of the world, should be waging war for territory, for "room"? Look at your country extending from the Allegheny Mountains to the Pacific Ocean, capable itself of sustaining in comfort a larger population than will be in the whole Union for one hundred years to come. Over this vast expanse of territory your population is now so sparse that I believe we provided at the last session a regiment of mounted men to guard the mail from the frontier of Missouri to the mouth of the Columbia; and yet you persist in the ridiculous assertion, "I want room." One would imagine from the frequent reiteration of the complaint that you had a bursting, teeming population, whose energy was paralyzed, whose enterprise was crushed, for want of space. Why should we be so weak or wicked as to offer this idle apology for ravaging a neighboring republic! It will impose on no one, at home or abroad.

Do we not know, Mr. President, that it is a law, never to be repealed, that falsehood shall be short-lived? Was it not ordained of old that truth only shall abide forever? Whatever we may say today, or whatever we may write in our books, the stern tribunal of history will review it all, detect falsehood, and bring us to judgment before that posterity which shall bless or curse us as we may act now, wisely or otherwise. We may hide in the grave, which awaits us all!—in vain! We may hope to be concealed there, like the foolish bird that hides its head in the sand in the vain belief that its body is not seen; yet, even there, this preposterous excuse of want of "room" shall be laid bare, and the quick-coming future will decide that it was a hypocritical pretense, under which we sought to conceal the avarice which prompted us to covet and to seize, by force, that which was not ours.

Mr. President, this uneasy desire to augment our territory has depraved the moral sense and blighted the otherwise keen sagacity of our people. What has been the fate of all nations who have acted upon the idea that they must advance thus? Our young orators cherish this notion with a fervid, but fatally mistaken zeal. They call it by the mysterious name of "destiny." "Our destiny," they say, "is onward"; and hence they argue, with ready sophistry, the propriety of seizing upon any territory and any people that may lie in the way of our "fated" advance. Recently, these "progressives" have grown classical; some assiduous student of antiquities has helped them to a patron saint. They have wandered back into the desolated Pantheon, and there amongst the polytheistic relics of that "pale mother of dead empires," they have found a god whom these Romans, centuries gone by, baptized "Terminus."

Sir, I have heard much and read somewhat of this gentleman, Terminus. Alexander, of whom I have spoken, was a devotee of this divinity. We have seen the end of him and his empire. It was said to be an attribute of this god that he must always advance and never recede. So both republican and imperial Rome believed. It was, as they said, their destiny. And for a while it did seem to be even so. Roman Terminus did advance. Under the eagles of Rome, he was carried from his home on the Tiber to the farthest East, on the one hand, and to the far West, amongst the then barbarous tribes of western Europe, on the other. But at length the time came when retributive justice had become "a destiny." The despised Gaul cries out to the contemned Goth, and Attila, with his Huns, answers back the battle shout to both. The "blue-eyed nations of the North," in succession, or united, pour forth their countless hosts of warriors upon Rome and Rome's always advancing god, Terminus. And now the battle-ax of the barbarian strikes down the conquering eagle of Rome. Terminus at last recedes, slowly at first, but finally he is driven to Rome, and from Rome to Byzantium. Whoever would know the further fate of this Roman deity, so recently taken under the patronage of American democracy, may find ample gratification of his curiosity in the luminous pages of Gibbon's *Decline and Fall*. Such will find that Rome thought, as you now think, that it was her destiny to conquer provinces and nations, and no doubt she sometimes said, as you say, "I will conquer a peace." And where now is she, the Mistress of the World? The spider weaves her web in her palaces, the owl sings his watch song in her towers. Teutonic power now lords it over the servile remnant, the miserable memento of old and once omnipotent Rome.

Sad, very sad, are the lessons which time has written for us. Through and in them all I see nothing but the inflexible execution of that old law which ordains, as eternal, that cardinal rule, "Thou shalt not covet thy neighbor's goods, nor anything which is his." Since I have lately heard so much about the dismemberment of Mexico, I have looked back, to see how, in the course of events which some call "Providence," it has fared with other nations who engaged in this work of dismemberment. I see that in the latter half of the eighteenth century, three powerful nations—Russia, Austria, and Prussia—united in the dismemberment of Poland. They said, too, as you say, "It is our destiny." They "wanted room." Doubtless each of these thought, with his share of Poland, his power was too strong ever to fear invasion or even insult. One had his California, another his New Mexico, and the third his Veracruz. Did they remain untouched and incapable of harm? Alas, no! Far, very far, from it! Retributive justice must fulfill its "destiny," too. A very few years pass, and we hear of a new man, a Corsican lieutenant, the self-named "armed soldier of democracy"—Napoleon. He ravages Austria, covers her land with blood, drives the Northern Caesar from his capital, and sleeps in his palace. Austria may now remember how her power trampled upon Poland. Did she not pay dear, very dear, for her California?

But has Prussia no atonement to make? You see this same Napoleon, the blind instrument of Providence, at work there. The thunders of his cannon at Jena proclaim the work of retribution for Poland's wrongs; and the successors of the great Frederick, the drill sergeant of Europe, are seen flying across the sandy plain that surrounds their capital, right glad if they may escape captivity or death. But how fares it with the autocrat of Russia? Is he secure in his share of the spoils of Poland? No. Suddenly we see, sir, six hundred thousand armed men marching to Moscow. Does his Veracruz protect him now? Far from it. Blood, slaughter, desolation spread abroad over the land, and finally the conflagration of the old commercial metropolis of Russia closes the retribution; she must pay for her share in the dismemberment of her weak and impotent neighbor. Mr. President, a mind more prone to look for the judgments of heaven in the doings of men than mine cannot fail in this to see the Providence of God. When Moscow burned, it seemed as if the earth was lighted up that the nations might behold the scene. As that mighty sea of fire gathered and heaved, and rolled upwards, higher and yet higher, till its flames aspired the stars and lit the whole heavens, it did seem as though the God of nations was writing, in characters of flame on the front of His throne, the doom that shall fall upon the strong nation which tramples in scorn upon the weak. And what fortune awaits him, the appointed executor of this work, when it was all done? He, too, conceived the notion that his "destiny" pointed onward to universal dominion. France was too small—Europe, he thought, should bow down before him. But as soon as this idea took possession of his soul, he, too, became powerless. His terminus must recede, too. Right there, while he witnessed the humiliation and doubtless meditated the subjugation of Russia, He who holds the winds in

His fist gathered the snows of the North and blew them upon his six hundred thousand men. They fled—they froze—they perished! and now the mighty Napoleon, who had resolved on universal dominion—he, too, is summoned to answer for the violation of that ancient law, "Thou shalt not covet anything which is thy neighbor's." How is the mighty fallen! He, beneath whose proud footstep Europe trembled—he is now an exile at Elba, and now finally a prisoner on the rock of St. Helena. And there, on a barren island, in an unfrequented sea in the crater of an extinguished volcano—there is the deathbed of the mighty conqueror! All his annexations have come to that! His last hour is now come, and he, "the Man of Destiny," he who had rocked the world as with the throes of an earthquake, is now powerless and still. Even as the beggar dies, so he died. On the wings of a tempest that raged with unwonted fury, up to the throne of the only power that controlled him while he lived, went the fiery soul of that wonderful warrior, another witness to the existence of that eternal decree that they who do not rule in righteousness shall perish from the earth. He has found "room" at last. And France—she, too, has found "room." Her "eagles" now no longer scream upon the banks of the Danube, the Po, and the Borysthenes. They have returned home to their old eyrie between the Alps, the Rhine, and the Pyrenees; so shall it be with your banners of conquest. You may carry them to the loftiest peaks of the Cordilleras, they may wave with insolent triumph in the Halls of the Montezumas, the armed men of Mexico may quail before them, but the weakest hand in Mexico, uplifted in prayer to the God of justice, may call down against you a Power in the presence of which the iron hearts of your warriors shall be turned into ashes.

Mr. President, if the history of our race has established any truth, it is but a confirmation of what is written, "The way of the transgressor is hard." Inordinate ambition, wantoning in power, and spurning the humble maxims of justice, ever has ended and ever shall end in ruin. Strength cannot always trample upon weakness; the humble shall be exalted; the bowed-down will at length be lifted up. It is by faith in the law of strict justice, and the practice of its precepts, that nations alone can be saved. All the annals of the human race, sacred and profane, are written over with this great truth in characters of living light. It is my fear, my fixed belief, that in this invasion, this war with Mexico, we have forgotten this vital truth. Why is it that we have been drawn into this whirlpool of war? How clear and strong was the light that shone upon the path of duty a year ago! The last disturbing question with England was settled. Our power extended its peaceful sway from the Atlantic to the Pacific: from the Alleghenies we looked out upon Europe, and from the tops of the Stony Mountains we could descry the shores of Asia; a rich commerce with all the nations of Europe poured wealth and abundance into our lap on the Atlantic side, while an unoccupied commerce of three hundred millions of Asiatics waited on the Pacific for our enterprise to come and possess it. One hundred millions of dollars will be wasted in this fruitless war. Had this money of the people been expended in making a railroad from your northern lakes to the Pacific, as one of your citizens has begged of you in vain, you would have made a highway for the world between Asia and Europe. Your capital then would be within thirty or forty days travel of any and every point on the map of the civilized world. Through this great artery of trade you would have carried through the heart of your own country the teas of China and the spices of India to the markets of England and France. Why, why, Mr. President, did we abandon the enterprises of peace and betake ourselves to the barbarous achievements of war? Why did we "forsake this fair and fertile field to batten on that moor"?

But, Mr. President, if further acquisition of territory is to be the result either of conquest or treaty, then I scarcely know which should be preferred, external war with Mexico or the hazards of internal commotion at home, which last I fear may come if another province is to be added to our territory. There is one topic connected with this subject which I tremble when I approach, and yet I cannot forbear to notice it. It meets you in every step you take; it threatens you which way soever you go in the prosecution of this war. I allude to the question of slavery. Opposition to its further extension, it must be obvious to everyone, is a deeply rooted determination with men of all parties in what we call the nonslaveholding states. New York, Pennsylvania, and Ohio, three of the most powerful, have already sent their legislative instructions here. So it will be, I doubt not, in all the rest. It is vain now to speculate about the reasons for this. Gentlemen of the South may call it prejudice, passion, hypocrisy, fanaticism. I shall not dispute with them now on that point. The great fact that it is so, and not otherwise, is what it concerns us to know. You and I cannot alter or change this opinion, if we would. These people only say we will not, cannot consent that you shall carry slavery where it does not already exist. They do not seek to disturb you in that institution as it exists in your states. Enjoy it if you will and as you will. This is their language; this their determination. How is it in the South? Can it be expected that they should expend in common their blood and their treasure in the acquisition of immense territory, and then willingly forgo the right to carry thither their slaves, and inhabit the conquered country if they please to do so? Sir, I know the feelings and opinions of the South too well to calculate on this. Nay, I believe they would even contend to any extremity for the mere right, had they no wish to exert it. I believe (and I confess I tremble when the conviction presses upon me) that there is equal obstinacy on both sides of this fearful question.

If, then, we persist in war, which, if it terminates in anything short of a mere wanton waste of blood as well as money, must end (as this bill proposes) in the acquisition of territory, to which at once this controversy must attach—this bill would seem to be nothing less than a bill to produce internal commotion. Should we prosecute this war another moment, or expend one dollar in the purchase or conquest of a single acre of Mexican land, the North and the South are brought into collision on a point where neither will yield. Who can foresee or foretell the result! Who so bold or reckless as to look such a conflict in the face unmoved! I do not envy the heart of him who can realize the possibility of such a conflict without emotions too painful to be endured. Why, then, shall we, the representatives of the sovereign states of this Union—the chosen guardians of this confederated Republic, why should we precipitate this fearful struggle, by continuing a war the result of which must be to force us at once upon a civil conflict? Sir, rightly considered, this is treason, treason to the Union, treason to the dearest interests, the loftiest aspirations, the most cherished hopes of our constituents. It is a crime to risk the possibility of such a contest. It is a crime of such infernal hue that every other in the catalogue of iniquity, when compared with it, whitens into virtue. Oh, Mr. President, it does seem to me, if hell itself could yawn and vomit up the fiends that inhabit its penal abodes, commissioned to disturb the harmony of this world, and dash the fairest prospect of happiness that ever allured the hopes of men, the first step in the consummation of this diabolical purpose would be to light up the fires of internal war and plunge the sister states of this Union into the bottomless gulf of civil strife. We stand this day on the crumbling brink of that gulf—we see its bloody eddies wheeling and boiling before us—shall we not pause before it be too late? How plain again is here the path, I may add the only way, of duty, of prudence, of true patriotism. Let us abandon all idea of acquiring further territory and by consequence cease at once to prosecute this war. Let us call home our armies, and bring them at once within our own acknowledged limits. Show Mexico that you are sincere when you say you desire nothing by conquest. She has learned that she cannot encounter you in war, and if she had not, she is too weak to disturb you here. Tender her peace, and, my life on it, she will then accept it. But whether she shall or not, you will have peace without her consent. It is your invasion that has made war; your retreat will restore peace. Let us then close

forever the approaches of internal feud, and so return to the ancient concord and the old ways of national prosperity and permanent glory. Let us
here, in this temple consecrated to the Union, perform a solemn lustra-
tion; let us wash Mexican blood from our hands, and on these altars, and
in the presence of that image of the Father of his Country that looks
down upon us, swear to preserve honorable peace with all the world and
eternal brotherhood with each other.

No excited burst of applause greeted the speech that Corwin's biographer,
Josiah Morrow, called "the bravest ever heard in Congress." But its effect
showed three weeks later, when the three-million-dollar appropriations bill was
carried by a vote of only twenty-nine to twenty-five.

Although some considered the speech, delivered in time of war, traitorous,
it did not ruin Corwin's career. After completing his term in the Senate he
served as Secretary of the Treasury under Fillmore and then went to the House
of Representatives. President Lincoln, who had also considered the Mexican
War unnecessary, appointed Corwin Minister to Mexico.

ELIZABETH CADY STANTON KEYNOTES THE
FIRST WOMAN'S-RIGHTS CONVENTION

[July 19, 1848]

While antislavery agitation increased in bitterness and abortive revolutions
flared up in Europe, volcanic 1848 was also marked by the formal beginning,
in the village of Seneca Falls, New York, of the modern woman's-rights movement.

Elizabeth Cady Stanton (1815–1902) had a stern, conventional rearing,
but she was permitted to study the classics and mathematics at a boys' school
and to read the books in her father's law office. From those books, as well as
from the complaints of women who sought legal help from her father, she
learned of woman's inferior and humiliating status. She took to heart the
darkest views of the lawyer's Bible, Blackstone's ever-present Commentaries,
such as the following gem: "By marriage, the husband and wife are one person
in law; that is, the very being or legal existence of the woman is suspended
during the marriage, or at least is incorporated and consolidated into that of the
husband, under whose wing, protection, and cover, she performs everything."

Miss Cady saw to it that the word "obey" was omitted from the ceremony
when she married a well-known abolitionist, Henry Brewster Stanton, in 1840.

He went as a delegate to the world antislavery convention at London, from which—his wife noted—women were excluded. Among the excluded was the famous Quaker preacher and abolitionist, Lucretia Coffin Mott. This absurdity was too much for two strong women. Out of their humilation grew an alliance, with plans for a woman's-rights convention, which finally took place eight years later.

It was an oddly assorted little audience, partly made up of brave men, to which Mrs. Stanton delivered the keynote address on that warm July afternoon at Seneca Falls. We omit some of the humor and much of the history.

"Man cannot fulfill his destiny alone, he cannot redeem his race unaided."

W E HAVE MET here today to discuss our rights and wrongs, civil and political, and not, as some have supposed, to go into the detail of social life alone. We do not propose to petition the legislature to make our husbands just, generous, and courteous, to seat every man at the head of a cradle, and to clothe every woman in male attire. None of these points, however important they may be considered by leading men, will be touched in this convention. As to their costume, the gentlemen need feel no fear of our imitating that, for we think it in violation of every principle of taste, beauty, and dignity; notwithstanding all the contempt cast upon our loose, flowing garments, we still admire the graceful folds, and consider our costume far more artistic than theirs. Many of the nobler sex seem to agree with us in this opinion, for the bishops, priests, judges, barristers, and lord mayors of the first nation on the globe, and the Pope of Rome, with his cardinals, too, all wear the loose flowing robes, thus tacitly acknowledging that the male attire is neither dignified nor imposing. No, we shall not molest you in your philosophical experiments with stocks, pants, high-heeled boots, and Russian belts. Yours be the glory to discover, by personal experience, how long the kneepan can resist the terrible strapping down which you impose, in how short time the well-developed muscles of the throat can be reduced to mere threads by the constant pressure of the stock, how high the heel of a boot must be to make a short man tall, and how tight the Russian belt may be drawn and yet have wind enough left to sustain life.

But we are assembled to protest against a form of government existing without the consent of the governed—to declare our right to be free as man is free, to be represented in the government which we are taxed to support, to have such disgraceful laws as give man the power to chastise and imprison his wife, to take the wages which she earns, the property which she inherits, and, in case of separation, the children of her love; laws which make her the mere dependent on his bounty. It is to protest against such unjust laws as these that we are assembled today, and to have them, if possible, forever erased from our statute books, deeming them a shame and a disgrace to a Christian republic in the nineteenth century. We have met

> *To uplift woman's fallen divinity*
> *Upon an even pedestal with man's.*

And, strange as it may seem to many, we now demand our right to vote according to the declaration of the government under which we live. This right no one pretends to deny. We need not prove ourselves equal to Daniel Webster to enjoy this privilege, for the ignorant Irishman in the ditch has all the civil rights he has. We need not prove our muscular power equal to this same Irishman to enjoy this privilege, for the most tiny, weak, ill-shaped stripling of twenty-one has all the civil rights of the Irishman. We have no objection to discuss the question of equality, for we feel that the weight of argument lies wholly with us, but we wish the question of equality kept distinct from the question of rights, for the proof of the one does not determine the truth of the other. All white men in this country have the same rights, however they may differ in mind, body, or estate.

The right is ours. The question now is: how shall we get possession of what rightfully belongs to us? We should not feel so sorely grieved if no man who had not attained the full stature of a Webster, Clay, Van Buren, or Gerrit Smith could claim the right of the elective franchise. But to have drunkards, idiots, horse-racing, rum-selling rowdies, ignorant foreigners, and silly boys fully recognized, while we ourselves are thrust out from all the rights that belong to citizens, it is too grossly insulting to the dignity of woman to be longer quietly submitted to. The right is ours. Have it, we must. Use it, we will. The pens, the tongues, the fortunes, the indomitable wills of many women are already pledged to secure this right. The great truth that no just government can be formed without the consent of the governed we shall echo and re-echo in the ears of the unjust judge, until by continual coming we shall weary him. . . .

There seems now to be a kind of moral stagnation in our midst. Philanthropists have done their utmost to rouse the nation to a sense of its sins. War, slavery, drunkenness, licentiousness, gluttony, have been dragged naked before the people, and all their abominations and deformities fully brought to light, yet with idiotic laugh we hug those monsters to our breasts and rush on to destruction. Our churches are multiplying on all sides, our missionary societies, Sunday schools, and prayer meetings and innumerable charitable and reform organizations are all in operation, but still the tide of vice is swelling, and threatens the destruction of everything, and the battlements of righteousness are weak against the raging elements of sin and death. Verily, the world waits the coming of some new element, some purifying power, some spirit of mercy and love. The voice of woman has been silenced in the state, the church, and the home, but man cannot fulfill his destiny alone, he cannot redeem his race unaided. There are deep and tender chords of sympathy and love in the hearts of the downfallen and oppressed that woman can touch more skillfully than man.

The world has never yet seen a truly great and virtuous nation, because in the degradation of woman the very fountains of life are poisoned at their source. It is vain to look for silver and gold from mines of copper and lead. It is the wise mother that has the wise son. So long as your women are slaves you may throw your colleges and churches to the winds. You can't have scholars and saints so long as your mothers are ground to powder between the upper and nether millstone of tyranny and lust. How seldom, now, is a father's pride gratified, his fond hopes realized, in the budding genius of his son! The wife is degraded, made the mere creature of caprice, and the foolish son is heaviness to his heart. Truly are the sins of the fathers visited upon the children to the third and fourth generation. God, in His wisdom, has so linked the whole human family together that any violence done at one end of the chain is felt throughout its length, and here, too, is the law of restoration, as in woman all have fallen, so in her elevation shall the race be recreated.

"Voices" were the visitors and advisers of Joan of Arc. Do not "voices" come to us daily from the haunts of poverty, sorrow, degradation, and despair, already too long unheeded. Now is the time for the women of this country, if they would save our free institutions, to defend the right, to buckle on the armor that can best resist the keenest weapons of the enemy—contempt and ridicule. The same religious enthusiasm that nerved Joan of Arc to her work nerves us to ours. In every generation God calls some men and women for the utterance of truth, a heroic action, and our work today is the fulfilling of what has long since been foretold by the Prophet—Joel 2:28: "And it shall come to pass afterward, that I will pour out my spirit upon all flesh; and your sons and your daughters shall prophesy." We do not expect our path will be strewn with the flowers of popular applause, but over the thorns of bigotry and prejudice will be our way, and on our banners will beat the dark storm clouds of opposition from those who have entrenched themselves behind the stormy bulwarks of custom and authority, and who have fortified their position by every means, holy and unholy. But we will steadfastly abide the result. Unmoved we will bear it aloft. Undauntedly we will unfurl it to the gale, for we know that the storm cannot rend from it a shred, that the electric flash will but more clearly show to us the glorious words inscribed upon it, "Equality of Rights.". . .

There were cheers from the little audience—and sneers from press and pulpit throughout the country. But a beginning had been made, and a few years later Mrs. Stanton brought into the movement Susan B. Anthony, already famous as an abolitionist and temperance reformer. Miss Anthony became the patient, tireless organizer of the movement as well as one of its principal speakers. But little Mrs. Stanton remained its most winning orator until extreme old age overtook her.

THE COMPROMISE OF 1850:
THREE SPEECHES

HENRY CLAY MAKES HIS LAST EFFORT TO PRESERVE THE UNION

[January 29, 1850]

In the bleak winter of 1849–50, a fearful Congress, a fearful country, waited for the return of Henry Clay to the Senate. He had resigned in disgust in 1842, but now he was coming back. And he, "the Great Pacificator," the father of the Missouri Compromise of 1820 and the compromise tariff of 1833, could calm the storm over the admission of California as a free state, if anybody could.

Henry Clay (1777–1852), the young Virginia lawyer who went to seek his fortune in Kentucky and became the idol of this new, raw country, was in some respects the American parallel of Charles James Fox—and equally difficult to recapture in a book. Each had a gay and gallant charm that made him more widely beloved than the official leaders of the day. Each was dazzling in debate, with his fiery and fluent attack, but much of the magic is lost on the printed page, especially in the case of Clay. As for the heights of political power, Fox was in the cabinet for a few months at two different periods; Clay was a frustrated aspirant to the presidency through a lifetime.

As a young Congressman Clay advocated his "American system," including protective tariff and internal improvements, and he was never torn away from his national vision by the strife over slavery and sectionalism. Much as he loved the blue grass, the mint juleps, and the race horses of Kentucky, he stood with Webster and Lincoln rather than with Calhoun and Jefferson Davis. On the slavery issue he advocated gradual emancipation and colonization.

Now, at seventy-three, still tall, slender, vibrant, "Harry of the West" came back to save his country—to preserve the Union.

"You are numerically more powerful than the slave states, and greatness and magnanimity should ever be allied."

Mr. President:

I HOLD in my hand a series of resolutions which I desire to submit to the consideration of this body. Taken together, in combination, they propose an amicable arrangement of all questions in controversy between the free and the slave states growing out of the subject of slavery. The preamble and the first resolution are as follows:

It being desirable for the peace, concord, and harmony of the Union of these states to settle and adjust amicably all existing questions of controversy between them arising out of the institution of slavery, upon a fair, equitable, and just basis: Therefore

1st. Resolved, That California ought, upon her application, to be admitted as one of the states of this Union, without the imposition by Congress of any restriction in respect to the exclusion or introduction of slavery within those boundaries.

The second resolution, sir, is as follows:

2nd. Resolved, That as slavery does not exist by law and is not likely to be introduced into any of the territory acquired by the United States from the Republic of Mexico, it is inexpedient for Congress to provide by law either for its introduction into or exclusion from any part of the said territory; and that appropriate territorial governments ought to be established by Congress in all of the said territory, not assigned as the boundaries of the proposed state of California, without the adoption of any restriction or condition on the subject of slavery.

This resolution, sir, proposes a declaration of two truths—one of law and the other of fact. The truth of law which it declares is that there does not exist, at this time, slavery within any portion of the territory acquired by the United States from Mexico.

The next truth which the resolution asserts is that slavery is not likely to be introduced into any portion of that territory. That is a matter of fact. California, of all other portions acquired by us from Mexico that country into which it would have been most likely that slavery should have been introduced, California herself has met in convention, and, by a unanimous vote, embracing slaveholders from Mississippi as well as from other parts, who concurred in the resolution, has declared against the introduction of slavery within her limits. I think, then, that, taking this leading fact in connection with all the evidence we have from other sources on the subject, I am warranted in the conclusion which constitutes the second truth which I have stated in this resolution.

The third resolution fixes the boundaries of the state, and the fourth provides for the assumption by the United States government of California's obligations to Texas.

The fifth resolution, sir, and the sixth, like the third and fourth, are somewhat connected together. They are as follows:

> 5th. *Resolved,* That it is inexpedient to abolish slavery in the District of Columbia, while that institution continues to exist in the state of Maryland, without the consent of that state, without the consent of the people of the District, and without just compensation to the owners of slaves within the District.
>
> 6th. *But Resolved,* That it is expedient to prohibit within the District the slave trade, in slaves brought into it from states or places beyond the limits of the District, either to be sold therein as merchandise or to be transported to other markets without the District of Columbia.

The first of these resolutions, Mr. President, in somewhat different language, asserts substantially no other principle than that which was asserted by the Senate of the United States twelve years ago (1838) upon resolutions which I then offered, and which passed—at least the particular resolution passed—by a majority of four fifths of the Senate.

The next resolution proposed deserves a passing remark. It is that the slave trade within the District ought to be abolished, prohibited. I do not mean by that the alienation and transfer of slaves from the inhabitants within this District—the sale by one neighbor to another of a slave which the one owns and the other wants, that a husband may perhaps be put along with his wife, or a wife with her husband. I do not mean to touch at all the question of the right of property in slaves among persons living within the District; but the slave trade to which I refer was, I think, pronounced an abomination more than forty years ago by one of the most gifted and distinguished sons of Virginia, the late Mr. Randolph. And who is there who is not shocked at its enormity? Sir, it is a great mistake at the North if they suppose that gentlemen living in the slave states look upon one who is a regular trader in slaves with any particular favor or kindness. They are often—sometimes unjustly, perhaps—excluded from social intercourse. But, then, what is this trade? It is a good deal limited since the retrocession (in 1846) of the portion of the District formerly belonging to Virginia. Let the slave dealer who chooses to collect his slaves in Virginia and Maryland go to ports in these states; let him not come here and establish his jails and put on his chains, and sometimes shock the sensibilities of our nature by a long train of slaves passing through that avenue leading from this Capitol to the house of the chief magistrate of one of the most glorious republics that ever existed. Why should he not do it? Sir, I am sure I speak the sentiments of every Southern man, and every man coming from the slave states, when I say let it terminate, and that it is an abomination; that there is no occasion for it; it ought no longer be tolerated.

The seventh resolution relates to a subject embraced in a bill now under consideration by the Senate. It is as follows:

7th. *Resolved,* That more effectual provisions ought to be made by law, according to the requirement of the Constitution, for the restitution and delivery of persons bound to service or labor in any state who may escape into any other state or territory in the Union.

Sir, that is so evident, and has been so clearly shown by the debate which has already taken place on the subject, that I have not now occasion to add another word.

The last resolution of the series of eight is as follows:

And 8th. *Resolved,* That Congress has no power to prohibit or obstruct the trade in slaves between the slaveholding states; but that the admission or exclusion of slaves brought from one into another of them depends exclusively upon their own particular laws.

It is obvious that no legislation is necessary or intended to follow that resolution. It merely asserts a truth, established by the highest authority of law in this country, and in conformity with that decision I trust there will be one universal acquiescence.

Mr. President, you have before you the whole series of resolutions, the whole scheme of arrangement and accommodation of these distracting questions, which I have to offer, after having bestowed on these subjects the most anxious, intensely anxious, consideration ever since I have been in this body. How far it may prove acceptable to both or either of the parties on these great questions it is not for me to say. I think it ought to be acceptable to both. There is no sacrifice of any principle, proposed in any of them, by either party. The plan is founded upon mutual forbearance, originating in a spirit of conciliation and concession; not of principles, but of matters of feeling.

Sir, although I believe this project contains about an equal amount of concession and forbearance on both sides, I might have asked from the free states of the North a more liberal and extensive concession than should be asked from the slave states. And why? You are numerically more powerful than the slave states, and greatness and magnanimity should ever be allied together.

But there are other reasons why concession upon such a subject as this should be more liberal, more expansive, coming from the free than from the slave states. It is a sentiment, a sentiment of humanity and philanthropy on your side. Aye, sir, and when a sentiment of that kind is honestly and earnestly cherished, with a disposition to make sacrifices to enforce it, it is a noble and beautiful sentiment; but, sir, when the sacrifice is not to be made by those who cherish that sentiment and inculcate it, but by another people, in whose situation it is impossible, from their position, for you to sympathize and to share all and everything that belongs to them, I must say to you, Senators from the free states, it is a totally different question. On your side it is a sentiment without hazard, without peril, without loss. But how is it on the other side, to which, as I have said, a greater amount of concession ought to be made in any scheme of compromise?

In the first place, sir, there is a vast and incalculable amount of property to be sacrificed, and to be sacrificed, not by your sharing in the common burdens, but exclusive of you. And this is not all. The social intercourse, habit, safety, property, life, everything is at hazard in a greater or less degree in the slave states.

Behold, Mr. President, that dwelling house now wrapped in flames. Listen, sir, to the rafters and beams which fall in succession amid the crash; and the flames ascending higher and higher as they tumble down. Behold those women and children who are flying from the calamitous scene, and with their shrieks and lamentations imploring the aid of high heaven. Whose house is that? Whose wives and children are they? Yours in the free states? No. You are looking on in safety and security while the conflagration which I have described is raging in the slave states, and produced, not intentionally by you, but produced from the inevitable tendency of the measures which you have adopted, and which others have carried far beyond what you have wished.

In the one scale, then, we behold sentiment, sentiment, sentiment alone; in the other, property, the social fabric, life, and all that makes life desirable and happy. . . .

[Senator Clay closed his speech with the relation of an incident. A man, he said, had come to his lodgings that very morning and presented him with a precious relic.]

And what, Mr. President, do you suppose it is? It is a fragment of the coffin of Washington—a fragment of that coffin in which now repose in silence, in sleep, and speechless, all the earthly remains of the venerated Father of his Country. Was it portentous that it should have been thus presented to me? Was it a sad presage of what might happen to that fabric which Washington's virtue, patriotism, and valor established? No, sir, no. It was a warning voice, coming from the grave to the Congress now in session, to beware, to pause, to reflect before they lend themselves to any purposes which shall destroy that Union which was cemented by his exertions and example. Sir, I hope an impression may be made on your mind such as that which was made on mine by the reception of this precious relic.

This was a mild, conciliatory beginning, and with comparative mildness it was accepted. It was not until a week later that Clay first defended his resolutions with his characteristic rambling fire. It was to be months before he would cease to do so.

THE DYING CALHOUN HEARS HIS BITTER SWAN SONG READ BY A FELLOW SENATOR

[March 4, 1850]

In the twenty-seven years since Calhoun had spoken so impressively against Jackson's "Force Bill," he had grown steadily in the admiration and affection of the landholding South. His very severity was a binding link, for it was the severity of a prophet determined to save a way of life—a white "democracy" based on black slavery. Yet there were signs that he was also grappling profoundly with the emerging issues of minority rights and cultural diversity in an onrushing industrial world. Those deep-set, glowing eyes—which always demanded attention—were those of an original thinker as well as of a fanatic.

Although he was five years younger than Clay, Calhoun looked much older, a dying man who had made the long trip from South Carolina to Washington for the last time. It hardly seemed possible that he would be able to speak on Clay's resolutions, but the news that he was going to brought crowds to the floor and gallery of the Senate. When he proceeded to his seat on the arms of two friends, there was silence broken only by awed whispers. Then he rose with difficulty and thanked the Senate for the courteous way in which they permitted him to be heard. Too feeble for anything more, he passed his manuscript to Senator James M. Mason of Virginia, wrapped himself in a long black cloak, and listened intently.

"If you are unwilling we should part in peace, tell us so."

UNLESS something decisive is done, I again ask, what is to stop this agitation before the great and final object at which it aims—the abolition of slavery in the states—is consummated? Is it, then, not certain that if something is not done to arrest it, the South will be forced to choose between abolition and secession? Indeed, as events are now moving, it will not require the South to secede in order to dissolve the Union. Agitation will of itself effect it, of which its past history furnishes abundant proof—as I shall next proceed to show.

It is a great mistake to suppose that disunion can be effected by a single blow. The cords which bind these states together in one common Union are far too numerous and powerful for that. Disunion must be the work of time. It is only through a long process, and successively, that the cords can be snapped until the whole fabric falls asunder. Already the agitation of the slavery question has snapped some of the most important and has greatly weakened all the others.

If the agitation goes on, the same force, acting with increased intensity, as has been shown, will finally snap every cord, when nothing will be left to hold the states together except force. But surely that can with no propriety of language be called a Union when the only means by which the weaker is held connected with the stronger portion is force. It may, indeed, keep them connected; but the connection will partake much more of the character of subjugation on the part of the weaker to the stronger than the union of free, independent, and sovereign states in one confederation, as they stood in the early stages of the government, and which only is worthy of the sacred name of Union.

Having now, Senators, explained what it is that endangers the Union, and traced it to its cause, and explained its nature and character, the question again recurs, how can the Union be saved? To this I answer: there is but one way by which it can be, and that is by adopting such measures as will satisfy the states belonging to the Southern section that they can remain in the Union consistently with their honor and their safety. There is, again, only one way by which this can be effected, and that is by removing the causes by which this belief has been produced. Do this, and discontent will cease, harmony and kind feelings between the sections be restored, and every apprehension of danger to the Union removed. The question, then, is: how can this be done? There is but one way by which it can with any certainty; and that is by a full and final settlement, on the principle of justice, of all the questions at issue between the two sections. The South asks for justice, simple justice, and less she ought not to take. She has no compromise to offer but the Constitution, and no concession or surrender to make. She has already surrendered so much that she has little left to surrender. Such a settlement would go to the root of the evil, and remove all cause of discontent, by satisfying the South that she could remain honorably and safely in the Union, and thereby restore the harmony and fraternal feelings between the sections which existed anterior to the Missouri agitation. Nothing else can, with any certainty, finally and forever settle the question at issue, terminate agitation, and save the Union.

But can this be done? Yes, easily; not by the weaker party, for it can of itself do nothing—not even protect itself—but by the stronger. The North has only to will it to accomplish it—to do justice by conceding to the South an equal right in the acquired territory, and to do her duty by causing the stipulations relative to fugitive slaves to be faithfully fulfilled —to cease the agitation of the slave question, and to provide for the insertion of a provision in the Constitution, by an amendment, which will restore to the South, in substance, the power she possessed of protecting herself before the equilibrium between the sections was destroyed by the action of this government. There will be no difficulty in devising such a provision—one that will protect the South, and which at the same time will improve and strengthen the government instead of impairing and weakening it.

But will the North agree to this? It is for her to answer the question.

But, I will say, she cannot refuse if she has half the love of the Union which she professes to have, or without justly exposing herself to the charge that her love of power and aggrandizement is far greater than her love of the Union. At all events, the responsibility of saving the Union rests on the North, and not on the South. The South cannot save it by any act of hers, and the North may save it without any sacrifice whatever, unless to do justice and to perform her duties under the Constitution should be regarded by her as a sacrifice.

It is time, Senators, that there should be an open and manly avowal on all sides as to what is intended to be done. If the question is not now settled, it is uncertain whether it ever can hereafter be; and we, as the representatives of the states of this Union regarded as governments, should come to a distinct understanding as to our respective views, in order to ascertain whether the great questions at issue can be settled or not. If you who represent the stronger portion cannot agree to settle them on the broad principle of justice and duty, say so; and let the states we both represent agree to separate and part in peace.

If you are unwilling we should part in peace, tell us so; and we shall know what to do when you reduce the question to submission or resistance. If you remain silent, you will compel us to infer by your acts what you intend. In that case California will become the test question. If you admit her under all the difficulties that oppose her admission, you compel us to infer that you intend to exclude us from the whole of the acquired territories, with the intention of destroying irretrievably the equilibrium between the two sections. We should be blind not to perceive in that case that your real objects are power and aggrandizement, and, infatuated, not to act accordingly.

I have now, Senators, done my duty in expressing my opinions fully, freely, and candidly on this solemn occasion. In doing so I have been governed by the motives which have governed me in all the stages of the agitation of the slavery question since its commencement. I have exerted myself during the whole period to arrest it, with the intention of saving the Union if it could be done; and if it could not, to save the section where it has pleased Providence to cast my lot, and which I sincerely believe has justice and the Constitution on its side. Having faithfully done my duty to the best of my ability, both to the Union and my section, throughout this agitation, I shall have the consolation, let what will come, that I am free from all responsibility.

Thus Senator Mason read Calhoun's words to the end, while their ghostlike author listened. It was a weirdly impressive scene, fascinating the audience even more than the speech itself. For the speech did not directly bear on Senator Clay's resolutions but on the widening chasm between the North and the South—and if his demands seemed absurd, his prophecies were too terrible to seem plausible. Only the dying man, apparently, could hear the distant guns of Fort Sumter.

WEBSTER, IN "THE MOST-HERALDED SPEECH EVER MADE IN AMERICA," SUPPORTS CLAY'S COMPROMISE

[March 7, 1850]

Clay and Calhoun had spoken. It was now the turn of Webster, the last of the great triumvirate—a triumvirate not of identical views but of outstanding eloquence and mutual respect for forty years.

There is only one speech in history that is remembered by its date, Webster's Seventh-of-March Speech (1850), which was delivered in the United States Senate three days after Calhoun's. There is no speech in American history that was so eagerly awaited or was afterward the subject of so much bitter controversy. It won Webster a few new supporters, it cost him countless admirers—and it may have saved the Union by delaying the Civil War for a decade.

No longer the demigod of the reply to Hayne in 1830, but a broken giant sustained by drugs, Webster made what he considered the most important speech of his life with almost no written preparation.

> *"We must view things as they are. Slavery*
> *does exist in the United States."*

Mr. President:

I WISH to speak today, not as a Massachusetts man, nor as a Northern man, but as an American and a member of the Senate of the United States. It is fortunate that there is a Senate of the United States; a body not yet moved from its propriety, nor lost to a just sense of its own dignity and its own high responsibilities, and a body to which the country looks, with confidence, for wise, moderate, patriotic, and healing counsels. It is not to be denied that we live in the midst of strong agitations and are surrounded by very considerable dangers to our institutions and government. The imprisoned winds are let loose. The East, the North, and the stormy South combine to throw the whole sea into commotion, to toss its billows to the skies, and disclose its profoundest depths. I do not affect to regard myself, Mr. President, as holding, or fit to hold, the helm in this combat with the political elements; but I have a duty to perform, and I mean to perform it with fidelity, not without a sense of existing dangers, but not without hope. I have a part to act, not for my own security or safety, for I am looking out for no fragment upon which to float away from the wreck, if wreck there must be, but for the good of the whole and the preservation of all; and there is that which will keep me to my duty during this struggle, whether the sun and the stars shall appear for many days. I speak today for the preservation of the Union. "Hear me for my cause." I speak today out of a solicitous and anxious heart, for the restoration to the country of that quiet and that harmony which make the blessings of this Union so rich and so dear to us all. These are the topics that I propose to myself to discuss; these are the motives, and the sole motives, that influence me in the wish to communicate my opinions to the Senate and the country; and if I can do anything, however little, for the promotion of these ends, I shall have accomplished all that I expect.

We all know, sir, that slavery has existed in the world from time immemorial. There was slavery in the earliest periods of history, among the Oriental nations. There was slavery among the Jews; the theocratic government of that people issued no injunction against it. There was slavery among the Greeks. At the introduction of Christianity, the Roman world was full of slaves, and I suppose there is to be found no injunction against that relation between man and man in the teachings of the Gospel of Jesus Christ or of any of His Apostles.

Now, sir, upon the general nature and influence of slavery there exists a wide difference of opinion between the Northern portion of this country and the Southern. It is said, on the one side, that, although not the subject of any injunction or direct prohibition in the New Testament, slavery is a wrong; that it is founded merely in the right of the strongest; and that it is an oppression, like unjust wars, like all those conflicts by which a powerful nation subjects a weaker to its will; and that, in its nature, whatever may be said of it in the modifications which have taken place, it is not according to the meek spirit of the Gospel. It is not "kindly affectioned"; it does not "seek another's, and not its own"; it does not "let the oppressed go free." These are sentiments that are cherished, and of late with greatly augmented force, among the people of the Northern states. They have taken hold of the religious sentiment of that part of the country, as they have, more or less, taken hold of the religious feelings of a considerable portion of mankind. The South, upon the other side, having been accustomed to this relation between the two races all their lives; from their birth, having been taught, in general, to treat the subjects of this bondage with care and kindness, and I believe, in general, feeling great kindness for them, have not taken the view of the subject which I have mentioned. There are thousands of religious men, with consciences as tender as any of their brethren at the North, who do not see the unlawfulness of slavery; and there are more thousands, perhaps, that, whatsoever they may think of it in its origin, and as a matter depending upon natural rights, yet take things as they are, and, finding slavery to be an established relation of the society in which they live, can see no way in which, let their opinions on the abstract question be what they may, it is in the power of this generation to relieve themselves from this relation. And candor obliges me to say that I believe they are just as conscientious, many of them, and the religious people, all of them, as they are at the North who hold different opinions.

There are men who, with clear perceptions, as they think, of their own duty, do not see how too eager a pursuit of one duty may involve them in the violation of others, or how too warm an embracement of one truth may lead to a disregard of other truths just as important. As I heard it stated strongly, not many days ago, these persons are disposed to mount upon some particular duty, as upon a war horse, and to drive furiously on and upon and over all other duties that may stand in the way. There are men who, in reference to disputes of that sort, are of opinion that human duties may be ascertained with the exactness of mathematics. They deal with morals as with mathematics; and they think what is right may be distinguished from what is wrong with the precision of an algebraic equation. They have, therefore, none too much charity toward others who differ from them. They are apt, too, to think that nothing is good but what is perfect, and that there are no compromises or modifications to be made in consideration of difference of opinion or in deference to other men's judgment. If their perspicacious vision enables them to detect a spot on the face of the sun, they think that a good reason why the sun should be struck down from heaven. They prefer the chance of running into utter darkness to living in heavenly light, if that heavenly light be not absolutely without any imperfection. . . .

But we must view things as they are. Slavery does exist in the United States. It did exist in the states before the adoption of this Constitution, and at that time. Let us therefore, consider for a moment what

was the state of sentiment, North and South, in regard to slavery—in regard to slavery at the time this Constitution was adopted. A remarkable
change has taken place since; but what did the wise and great men of all
parts of the country think of slavery then? In what estimation did they
hold it at the time when this Constitution was adopted? It will be found,
sir, if we will carry ourselves by historical research back to that day, and
ascertain men's opinions by authentic records still existing among us, that
there was no diversity of opinion between the North and the South upon
the subject of slavery. It will be found that both parts of the country held
it equally an evil, a moral and political evil. It will not be found that,
either at the North or at the South, there was much, though there was
some, invective against slavery as inhuman and cruel. The great ground of
objection to it was political; that it weakened the social fabric; that, taking the place of free labor, society became less strong and labor less
productive; and therefore we find from all the eminent men of the time
the clearest expression of their opinion that slavery is an evil. They
ascribed its existence here, not without truth, and not without some
acerbity of temper and force of language, to the injurious policy of the
mother country, who, to favor the navigator, had entailed these evils upon
the colonies. . . . You observe, sir, that the term *slave* or *slavery* is not
used in the Constitution. The Constitution does not require that "fugitive
slaves" shall be delivered up. It requires that persons held to service in
one state, and escaping into another, shall be delivered up. Mr. Madison
opposed the introduction of the term *slave* or *slavery* into the Constitution; for he said that he did not wish to see it recognized by the Constitution of the United States of America that there could be property in
men. . . .

Here we may pause. There was, if not an entire unanimity, a general
concurrence of sentiment running through the whole community, and
especially entertained by the eminent men of all parts of the country.
But soon a change began, at the North and the South, and a difference
of opinion showed itself; the North growing much more warm and strong
against slavery, and the South growing much more warm and strong in its
support. Sir, there is no generation of mankind whose opinions are not
subject to be influenced by what appear to them to be their present
emergent and exigent interests. I impute to the South no particularly
selfish view in the change which has come over her. I impute to her certainly no dishonest view. All that has happened has been natural. It has
followed those causes which always influence the human mind and
operate upon it. What, then, have been the causes which have created so
new a feeling in favor of slavery in the South, which have changed the

whole nomenclature of the South on that subject, so that, from being thought and described in the terms I have mentioned and will not repeat, it has now become an institution, a cherished institution, in that quarter; no evil, no scourge, but a great religious, social, and moral blessing, as I think I have heard it latterly spoken of? I suppose this, sir, is owing to the rapid growth and sudden extension of the cotton plantations of the South. So far as any motive consistent with honor, justice, and general judgment could act, it was the cotton interest that gave a new desire to promote slavery, to spread it, and to use its labor. . . .

Now, as to California and New Mexico, I hold slavery to be excluded from these territories by a law even superior to that which admits and sanctions it in Texas. I mean the law of nature, of physical geography, the law of the formation of the earth. That law settles forever, with a strength beyond all terms of human enactment, that slavery cannot exist in California or New Mexico. . . .

Sir, wherever there is a substantive good to be done, wherever there is a foot of land to be prevented from becoming slave territory, I am ready to assert the principle of the exclusion of slavery. I am pledged to it from the year 1837; I have been pledged to it again and again; and I will perform these pledges; but I will not do a thing unnecessarily that wounds the feelings of others or that does discredit to my own understanding.

Mr. President, in the excited times in which we live, there is found to exist a state of crimination and recrimination between the North and South. There are lists of grievances produced by each; and those grievances, real or supposed, alienate the minds of one portion of the country from the other, exasperate the feelings, and subdue the sense of fraternal affection, patriotic love, and mutual regard. I shall bestow a little attention, sir, upon these various grievances existing on the one side and on the other. I begin with the complaints of the South. I will not answer, further than I have, the general statements of the honorable Senator from South Carolina [Calhoun], that the North has prospered at the expense of the South in consequence of the manner of administering this government, in the collection of its revenues, and so forth. These are disputed topics, and I have no inclination to enter into them. But I will allude to other complaints of the South, and especially to one which has, in my opinion, just foundation; and that is, that there has been found at the North, among individuals and among legislators, a disinclination to perform fully their constitutional duties in regard to the return of persons bound to service who have escaped into the free states. In that respect, the South, in my judgment, is right, and the North is wrong. Every member of every Northern legislature is bound by oath, like every other officer

in the country, to support the Constitution of the United States; and the
article of the Constitution which says to these states that they shall deliver
up fugitives from service is as binding in honor and conscience as any
other article. . . .

Complaint has been made against certain resolutions that emanate
from legislatures at the North, and are sent here to us, not only on the
subject of slavery in this District, but sometimes recommending Congress
to consider the means of abolishing slavery in the states. . . .

Then, sir, there are the abolition societies, of which I am unwilling to
speak, but in regard to which I have very clear notions and opinions. I
do not think them useful. I think their operations for the last twenty years
have produced nothing good or valuable. At the same time, I believe
thousands of their members to be honest and good men, perfectly well-
meaning men. They have excited feelings; they think they must do something for the cause of liberty; and, in their sphere of action, they do not
see what else they can do than to contribute to an abolition press, or an
abolition society, or to pay an abolition lecturer. I do not mean to impute
gross motives even to the leaders of these societies, but I am not blind
to the consequences of their proceedings. I cannot but see what mischief
their interference with the South has produced. And is it not plain to
every man? Let any gentleman who entertains doubts on this point recur
to the debates in the Virginia House of Delegates in 1832, and he will
see with what freedom a proposition made by Mr. Jefferson Randolph,
for the gradual abolition of slavery, was discussed in that body. Everyone
spoke of slavery as he thought; very ignominious and disparaging names
and epithets were applied to it. The debates in the House of Delegates
on that occasion, I believe, were all published. They were read by every
colored man who could read, and to those who could not read those debates were read by others. At that time Virginia was not unwilling or
afraid to discuss this question, and to let that part of her population know
as much of the discussion as they could learn. That was in 1832. As has
been said by the honorable member from South Carolina, these abolition
societies commenced their course of action in 1835. It is said, I do not
know how true it may be, that they sent incendiary publications into the
slave states; at any rate, they attempted to arouse, and did arouse, a very
strong feeling; in other words, they created great agitation in the North
against Southern slavery. Well, what was the result? The bonds of the
slaves were bound more firmly than before, their rivets were more
strongly fastened. Public opinion, which in Virginia had begun to be
exhibited against slavery, and was opening out for the discussion of the
question, drew back and shut itself up in its castle. I wish to know

whether anybody in Virginia can now talk openly, as Mr. Randolph, Governor McDowell, and others talked in 1832, and sent their remarks to the press? We all know the fact, and we all know the cause; and everything that these agitating people have done has been, not to enlarge, but to restrain, not to set free, but to bind faster, the slave population of the South.

There are also complaints of the North against the South. I need not go over them particularly. The first and gravest is that the North adopted the Constitution, recognizing the existence of slavery in the states, and recognizing the right, to a certain extent, of the representation of slaves in Congress, under a state of sentiment and expectation which does not now exist; and that by events, by circumstances, by the eagerness of the South to acquire territory and extend her slave population, the North finds itself, in regard to the relative influence of the South and the North, of the free states and the slave states, where it never did expect to find itself when they agreed to the compact of the Constitution. They complain, therefore, that, instead of slavery being regarded as an evil, as it was then, an evil which all hoped would be extinguished gradually, it is now regarded by the South as an institution to be cherished, and preserved, and extended; an institution which the South has already extended to the utmost of her power by the acquisition of new territory.

Well, then, passing from that, everybody in the North reads; and everybody reads whatsoever the newspapers contain; and the newspapers . . . are careful to spread about among the people every reproachful sentiment uttered by any Southern man bearing at all against the North; everything that is calculated to exasperate and to alienate; and there are many such things, as everybody will admit, from the South, or from portions of it, which are disseminated among the reading people; and they do exasperate, and alienate, and produce a most mischievous effect upon the public mind at the North. . . .

There is a more tangible and irritating cause of grievance at the North. Free blacks are constantly employed in the vessels of the North, generally as cooks or stewards. When the vessel arrives at a Southern port, these free colored men are taken on shore, by the police or municipal authority, imprisoned, and kept in prison till the vessel is again ready to sail. This is not only irritating, but exceedingly unjustifiable and oppressive. Mr. [Samuel] Hoar's mission, some time ago, to South Carolina was a well-intended effort to remove this cause of complaint. The North thinks such imprisonments illegal and unconstitutional; and as the cases occur constantly and frequently they regard it as a grievance.

Now, sir, so far as any of these grievances have their foundation in matters of law, they can be redressed, and ought to be redressed; and so far as they have their foundation in matters of opinion, in sentiment, in mutual crimination and recrimination, all that we can do is to endeavor to allay the agitation, and cultivate a better feeling and more fraternal sentiments between the South and the North.

Mr. President, I should much prefer to have heard from every member on this floor declarations of opinion that this Union could never be dissolved than the declaration of opinion by anybody that, in any case, under the pressure of any circumstances, such a dissolution was possible. I hear with distress and anguish the word "secession," especially when it falls from the lips of those who are patriotic, and known to the country, and known all over the world for their political services. Secession! Peaceable secession! Sir, your eyes and mine are never destined to see that miracle. The dismemberment of this vast country without convulsion! The breaking up of the fountains of the great deep without ruffling the surface! Who is so foolish—I beg everybody's pardon—as to expect to see any such thing? Sir, he who sees these states, now revolving in harmony around a common center, and expects to see them quit their places and fly off without convulsion, may look the next hour to see the heavenly bodies rush from their spheres, and jostle against each other in the realms of space, without causing the wreck of the universe. There can be no such thing as a peaceable secession. Peaceable secession is an utter impossibility. Is the great Constitution under which we live, covering this whole country, is it to be thawed and melted away by secession, as the snows on the mountain melt under the influence of a vernal sun, disappear almost unobserved, and run off? No, sir! No, sir! I will not state what might produce the disruption of the Union; but, sir, I see as plainly as I can see the sun in heaven what that disruption itself must produce; I see that it must produce war. . . .

And, now, Mr. President, instead of speaking of the possibility or utility of secession, instead of dwelling in those caverns of darkness, instead of groping with those ideas so full of all that is horrid and horrible, let us come out into the light of the day; let us enjoy the fresh air of Liberty and Union; let us cherish those hopes which belong to us; let us devote ourselves to those great objects that are fit for our consideration and our action; let us raise our conceptions to the magnitude and the importance of the duties that devolve upon us; let our comprehension be as broad as the country for which we act, our aspirations as high as its certain destiny; let us not be pygmies in a case that calls for men. Never did there devolve on any generation of men higher trusts than now devolve upon us, for the preservation of this Constitution and the harmony and peace of all who are destined to live under it. Let us make our generation one of the strongest and brightest links in that golden chain which is destined, I fondly believe, to grapple the people of all the states to this Constitution for ages to come. We have a great, popular, constitutional government, guarded by law and by judicature, and defended by the affections of the whole people. No monarchical throne presses these states together, no iron chain of military power encircles them; they live and stand under a government popular in its form, representative in its character, founded upon principles of equality, and so constructed, we hope, as to last forever. In all its history it has been beneficent; it has trodden down no man's liberty; it has crushed no state. Its daily respiration is liberty and patriotism; its yet-youthful veins are full of enterprise, courage, and honorable love of glory and renown. Large before, the country has now, by recent events, become vastly larger. This Republic now extends, with a vast breadth, across the whole continent. The two great seas of the world wash the one and the other shore. We realize, on a mighty scale, the beautiful description of the ornamental border of the buckler of Achilles:

> Now, the broad shield complete, the artist crowned
> With his last hand, and poured the ocean round;
> In living silver seemed the waves to roll,
> And beat the buckler's verge, and bound the whole.

The Seventh of March Speech was the turning point in the great debate, which continued into September. At that time California was admitted into the Union as a free state, and the fatal Fugitive Slave Law was passed. For the third time Henry Clay's measures had calmed the storm—or had delayed it.

Calhoun died on the last day of March, 1850, murmuring: "The South, the poor South." Clay himself died on June 29, 1852. And in the interval Webster had spoken up and down the country in one last pitiful effort to win the Whig nomination for President. No solid group trusted him, and the dubious honor of carrying the Whig banner went to the political nonentity, General Winfield Scott, who was easily defeated by Franklin Pierce, another political nonentity.

Worn out and brokenhearted, Webster died on October 24, 1852, on his farm at Marshfield, declaring with his last breath, "I still live." But in the hearts of many of his once most sincere admirers he had long since died.

THEODORE PARKER MOURNS OVER A
FALLEN IDOL—DANIEL WEBSTER

[October 31, 1852]

Did Webster sell his soul in supporting the Fugitive Slave Law and other measures to conciliate the South, in order to make that final, futile grasp at the presidency? Or did he place the Union above everything and, in order to sustain it, risk fame and fortune? Or did he honestly identify the preservation of the Union with his own lifelong ambition? Whittier, Emerson, Thoreau, and many other noble spirits were horrified by the Fugitive Slave Law and by Webster's support of it.

Their horror was logical, for the Fugitive Slave Law made every American citizen an accomplice of the slaveholders; it called upon everyone, under threat of imprisonment, to assist officers of the law in the capture of fugitive slaves. At this very moment the conscience of the North was inflamed by the publication of Uncle Tom's Cabin, which Harriet Beecher Stowe had written in direct protest against the law's operation. "It is the distinction of Uncle Tom's Cabin," noted Emerson in his Journal, "that it is read equally in the parlor and the kitchen and the nursery of every house."

In this atmosphere two famous orators, Theodore Parker and Rufus Choate, passed historic differing judgments on Daniel Webster.

Theodore Parker (1810–60), the famous Unitarian clergyman, died of sheer overwork when he was less than fifty years of age. Of an old New England family, he was precocious, self-educated, and vastly learned. But his theology was so unorthodox that he embarrassed his congregations until a group of liberal-minded Congregationalists created a special pulpit for him in Boston in 1845. There and in numerous lecture tours he advocated reform measures, but it was as an abolitionist that he was most passionate and most eloquent.

Parker, like so many other great speakers, had none of the graces of the orator, nothing to bind his audience to him but an immense sincerity, a transparent courage, and a terrifying arsenal of knowledge. But these could be used with great effect, and so it was on Sunday, October 31, 1852, only a week after Webster died, when an unusually grim Parker faced his congregation.

"Do men now mourn for him, the great man eloquent?

I put on sackcloth long ago."

W HEN BOSSUET, who was himself the eagle of eloquence, preached the funeral discourse on Henrietta Maria, daughter of Henry IV of France and wife of Charles I of England, he had a task far easier than mine today. She was indeed the queen of misfortunes; the daughter of a king assassinated in his own capital, and the widow of a king judicially put to death in front of his own palace. Her married life was bounded by the murder of her royal sire and the execution of her kingly spouse; and she died neglected, far from kith and kin. But for that great man, who in his youth was called, prophetically, a "Father of the Church," the sorrows of her birth and her estate made it easy to gather up the audience in his arms, to moisten the faces of men with tears, to show them the nothingness of mortal glory and the beauty of eternal life. He led his hearers to his conclusion that day as the mother lays the sobbing child to her bosom to still its grief.

Today it is not so with me. Of all my public trials, this is my most trying day. Give me your sympathies, my friends; remember the difficulty of my position—its delicacy, too.

I am to speak of one of the most conspicuous men that New England ever bore—conspicuous, not by accident, but by the nature of his mind —one of her ablest intellects. I am to speak of an eminent man, of great power, in a great office, one of the landmarks of politics, now laid low. He seemed so great that some men thought he was himself one of the institutions of America. I am to speak while his departure is yet but of yesterday; while the somber flags still float in our streets. I am no party man; you know I am not. No party is responsible for me, nor I to anyone. I am free to commend the good things of all parties—their great and good men; free likewise to censure the evil of all parties. You will not ask me to say what only suits the public ear: there are a hundred to do that today. I do not follow opinion because popular. I cannot praise a man because he had great gifts, great station, and great opportunities; I cannot harshly censure a man for trivial mistakes. You will not ask me to flatter because others flatter; to condemn because the ruts of condemnation are so deep and so easy to travel in. It is unjust to be ungenerous, either in praise or blame: only the truth is beautiful in speech. It is not reverential to treat a great man like a spoiled child. Most of you are old enough to know that good and evil are both to be expected of each man. I hope you are all wise enough to discriminate between right and wrong.

Give me your sympathies. This I am sure of—I shall be as tender in my judgment as a woman's love; I will try to be as fair as the justice of a man. I shall tax your time beyond even my usual wont, for I cannot crush Olympus into a nut. Be not alarmed: if I tax your time the more, I shall tire your patience less. Such a day as this will never come again to you or me. There is no *Daniel Webster* left to die, and nature will not soon give us another such as he. I will take care by my speech that you sit easy on your bench. The theme will take care that you remember what I say.

In the days of nullification, Mr. Webster denied the right of South Carolina to secede from the Union or to give a final interpretation of the Constitution. She maintained that the Federal government had violated the Constitution; that she, the aggrieved state of South Carolina, was the judge in that matter and had a constitutional right to "nullify" the Constitution and withdraw from the Union.

The question is a deep one. It is the old question of Federal and Democrat—the question between the constitutional power of the whole and the power of the parts—Federal power and state power. Mr. Webster was always in favor of a strong central government; honestly in favor of it, I doubt not. His speeches on that subject were most masterly speeches. I refer, in particular, to that in 1830 against Mr. Hayne, and the speech in 1833 against Mr. Calhoun.

The first of these is the great political speech of Daniel Webster. I do not mean to say that it is just in its political ethics, or deep in the metaphysics of politics, or farsighted in its political providence. I only mean to say that it surpasses all his other speeches in the massive intellectual power of statement. Mr. Webster was then eight and forty years old. He defended New England against Mr. Hayne; he defended the Constitution of the United States against South Carolina. His speech is full of splendid eloquence; he reached high, and put the capstone upon his fame, whose triple foundation he had laid at Plymouth, at Bunker Hill, and at Faneuil Hall. The "republican members of the Massachusetts legislature" unanimously thanked him for his able vindication of their state. A Virginian who heard the speech declared he felt "as if looking at a mammoth treading his native canebrake, and, without apparent consciousness, crushing obstacles which nature had never designed as impediments to him." . . .

Do men mourn for him? See how they mourn! The streets are hung with black. The newspapers are sad-colored. The shops are put in mourning. The mayor and aldermen wear crepe. Wherever his death is made known, the public business stops, and flags drop half-mast down. The courts adjourn. The courts of Massachusetts—at Boston, at Dedham, at Lowell—all adjourn; the courts of New Hampshire, of Maine, of New York; even at Baltimore and Washington, the courts adjourn; for the great lawyer is dead, and Justice must wait another day. Only the United States Court, in Boston, trying a man for helping Shadrach out of the furnace of the kidnapers—the court that executes the Fugitive Slave Law —that does not adjourn; that keeps on; its worm dies not, and the fire of its persecution is not quenched, when death puts out the lamp of life. Injustice is hungry for its prey, and must not be balked. It was very proper! Symbolical court of the Fugitive Slave Bill—it does not respect life, why should it death? and, scorning liberty, why should it heed decorum? Did the judges deem that Webster's spirit, on its way to God, would look at Plymouth Rock, then pause on the spots made more classic by his eloquence, and gaze at Bunker Hill, and tarry his hour in the august company of noble men at Faneuil Hall, and be glad to know that injustice was chanting his requiem in that court? They greatly misjudge the man. I know Daniel Webster better, and I appeal for him against his idly judging friends.

Do men now mourn for him, the great man eloquent? I put on sackcloth long ago; I mourned for him when he wrote the Creole letter [in which he bent backward for the slaveholders], which surprised Ashburton, Briton that he was. I mourned when he spoke the speech of the seventh of March. I mourned when the Fugitive Slave Bill passed Congress, and the same cannons which have fired minute guns for him fired also one hundred rounds of joy for the forging of a new fetter for the fugitive's foot. I mourned for him when the kidnapers first came to Boston—hated then, now "respectable men," "the companions of princes," enlarging their testimony in the court. I mourned when my own parishioners fled from the "stripes" of New England to the "stars" of Old England. I mourned when Ellen Craft fled to my house for shelter and for succor, and for the first time in all my life I armed this hand. I mourned when I married William and Ellen Craft, and gave them a Bible for their soul, and a sword to keep that soul living in a living frame. I mourned when the courthouse was hung in chains; when Thomas Sims, from his dungeon, sent out his petition for prayers, and the churches did not dare to pray. I mourned when that poor outcast in yonder dungeon sent for me to visit him, and when I took him by the hand which Daniel Webster was chaining in that hour. I mourned for Webster when we prayed our prayer and sang our psalm on Long Wharf in the morning's

gray. I mourned then: I shall not cease to mourn. The flags will be removed from the streets, the cannon will sound their other notes of joy;
but, for me, I shall go mourning all my days; I shall refuse to be comforted; and at last I shall lay down my gray hairs with weeping and with
sorrow in the grave. O Webster! Webster! would God that I had died for
thee!

His influence on the development of America has not been great. He
had large gifts, large opportunities also for their use—the two greatest
things which great men ask. Yet he has brought little to pass. No great
ideas, no great organizations, will bind him to the coming age. His life
has been a long vacillation. Ere long, men will ask for the historic proof
to verify the reputation of his power. It will not appear. For the present,
his career is a failure: he was balked in his aim. How will it be for the
future? Posterity will vainly ask for proof of his intellectual power, to
invent, to organize, to administer. The historian must write that he aimed
to increase the executive power, the central government, and to weaken
the local power of the states; that he preferred the Federal authority to
state rights, the judiciary to the legislature, the government to the people,
the claims of money to the rights of man. Calhoun will stand as the representative of state rights and free trade; Clay, of the American system
of protection; Benton, of payment in sound coin; some other, of the revenue tariff. And in the greatest question of the age, the question of
Human Rights, as champions of mankind, there will appear Adams, Giddings, Chase, Palfrey, Mann, Hale, Rantoul, and Sumner; yes, one other
name, which on the historian's page will shade all these—the name of
[William Lloyd] *Garrison*. Men will recount the words of Webster at
Plymouth Rock, at Bunker Hill, at Faneuil Hall, at Niblo's Garden; they
will also recollect that he declared "protection of property" to be the
great domestic object of government; that he said, "Liberty first and
Union afterwards" was delusion and folly; that he called on Massachusetts to conquer her "prejudices" in favor of unalienable right, and with
alacrity give up a man to be a slave; turned all the North into a hunting
field for the bloodhound; that he made the negation of God the first
principle of government; that our New England elephant turned round,
tore Freedom's standard down, and trod her armies underfoot. They will
see that he did not settle the greatest questions by Justice and the Law
of God. His parallel lines of power are indeed long lines—a nation reads
his word: they are not far apart, you cannot get many centuries between;
for there are no great ideas of Right, no mighty acts of Love, to keep
them wide.

There are brave words which Mr. Webster has spoken that will last while English is a speech; yea, will journey with the Anglo-Saxon race, and one day be classic in either hemisphere, in every zone. But what will posterity say of his efforts to chain the fugitive, to extend the area of human bondage; of his haughty scorn of any law higher than what trading politicians enact in the Capitol? "There is a law above all the enactments of human codes, the same throughout the world, the same in all time"; "it is the law written by the finger of God upon the heart of man; and by that law, unchangeable and eternal, while men despise fraud, and loathe rapine, and abhor blood, they will reject with indignation the wild and guilty fantasy that man can hold property in man."

Calhoun, Clay, Webster—they were all able men—long in politics, all ambitious, grasping at the presidency, all failing of what they sought. All three called themselves "Democrats," taking their stand on the unalienable rights of man. But all three conjoined to keep every sixth man in the nation a chattel slave; all three at last united in deadly war against the unalienable rights of men whom swarthy mothers bore. O democratic America! . . .

Boston now mourns for him! She is too late in her weeping. She should have wept her warning when her capitalists filled his right hand with bribes. She ought to have put on sackcloth when the speech of March 7 first came here. She should have hung her flags at half-mast when the Fugitive Slave Bill became a law; then she only fired cannons, and thanked her representative. Webster fell prostrate, but was Boston more innocent than he? Remember the nine hundred and eighty-seven men that thanked him for the speech which touched their "conscience," and pointed out the path of "duty"! It was she that ruined him. . . .

Just four years after his great speech, on the twenty-fourth of October, all that was mortal of Daniel Webster went down to the dust, and the soul to the motherly bosom of God! Men mourn for him: he heeds it not. The great man has gone where the servant is free from his master, where the weary are at rest, where the wicked cease from troubling.

> *No further seek his merits to disclose,*
> *Or draw his frailties from their dread abode;*
> *There they alike in trembling hope repose,*
> *The bosom of his Father and his God!*

Massachusetts has lost her great adopted son. Has lost? Oh, no! "I still live" is truer than the sick man knew:

> *He lives and spreads aloft by those pure eyes*
> *And perfect witness of all-judging God.*

His memory will long live with us, still dear to many a loving heart. What honor shall we pay? Let the state go out mindful of his noblest services, yet tearful for his fall; sad that he would fain have filled him with the husks the swine do eat, and no man gave to him. Sad and tearful, let her remember the force of circumstances, and dark temptation's secret power. Let her remember that while we know what he yielded to, and what is sin, God knows what also is resisted, and He alone knows who the sinner is. Massachusetts, the dear old mother of us all! Oh! let her warn her children to fling away ambition, and let her charge them, every one, that there is a God who must indeed be worshiped, and a higher law of God which must be kept, though Gold and Union fall. Then let her say to them, "Ye have dwelt long enough in this mountain; turn ye, and take your journey into the land of freedom, which the Lord your God giveth you!" . . .

At the Dartmouth memorial meeting for Webster, nine months later, Rufus Choate, the brilliant Boston advocate, replied to Parker: . . . "Now, is he who accuses Mr. Webster of 'sinning against his own conscience,' quite sure that he knows, that that conscience, well instructed by profoundest political studies, and thoughts of reason; well instructed by an appropriate moral institution sedulously applied, did not commend and approve his conduct to himself? Does he know, that he had not anxiously, and maturely studied the ethics of the Constitution, and as a question of ethics, but of ethics applied to a stupendous problem of practical life, and had not become satisfied that they were right? Does he know that he had not done this, when his faculties were all at their best; and his motives under no suspicion? May not such an inquirer, for aught you can know, may not that great mind have verily and conscientiously thought that he had learned in that investigation many things? May he not have thought that he learned, that the duty of the inhabitants of the free States, in that day's extremity, to the republic, the duty at all events of statesmen, to the republic, is a little too large, and delicate, and difficult, to be all comprehended in the single emotion of compassion for one class of persons in the commonwealth, or in carrying out the single principle of abstract, and natural, and violent justice to one class? May he not have thought that he found there some stupendous exemplifications of what we read of, in books of casuistry, the 'dialectics of conscience,' as conflicts of duties; such things as the conflicts of the greater with the less; conflicts of the attainable with the visionary; conflicts of the real with the seeming; and may he not have been soothed to learn that the evil which he found in this part of the Constitution was the least of two; was unavoidable; was compensated; was justified; was commanded, as by a voice from the Mount, by a more exceeding and enduring good?"*

PART ELEVEN

AGITATION, REFORM, AND REVOLT

I N EUROPE we last saw Napoleon bidding farewell to his troops at Fontainebleau, before his brief exile on Elba. After that he returned for the spectacular
"Hundred Days," lost the battle of Waterloo, and went into permanent exile
on Saint Helena. Now, after twenty-five years of revolution and war, there was
peace—and the inevitable reaction. People wanted rest, repose, order, at almost
any cost. For most of the returning monarchs, nobles, clergy, on the continent,
"restoration" meant restoration of their ancient glories, restoration of the ancien
régime. Louis XVIII, oddly enough, returned to France in a more sensible,
moderate, conciliatory mood than any of his royal colleagues. Alexander of
Russia was soon to lose the last vestige of his liberalism, and George III and his
scapegrace son, the Regent and future George IV, showed no signs of growth.
The Holy Alliance of Russia, Prussia, and Austria was dedicated to the preven-
tion of unholy uprisings.

Metternich, the Foreign Minister of Austria, who was undoubtedly a sincere
advocate of peace and European federation and no mere Machiavellian in-
triguer, nevertheless did say: "It is only necessary to place four energetic men,
who know what they want and are agreed to the manner of carrying out their
wishes, in the four corners of Europe. Let them raise their voices and their
arms at the same moment, and the agitation vanishes like so much smoke."
When England was on the brink of revolution over a reform bill widening the
franchise and redistricting the seats in the House of Commons, the Duke of
Wellington as Prime Minister announced: "I am fully convinced that the
country possesses, at the present moment, a legislature which answers all good
purposes of legislation, and this to a greater degree than any legislature ever has
answered in any country whatsoever."

GEORGE CANNING SEES THE WORLD AT PEACE IN THE SHADOW OF THE BRITISH NAVY

[1823]

George Canning (1770–1827) made a brilliant record at Eton and Oxford and, with the help of Pitt, was elected to Parliament in 1793. In 1807 he was made Foreign Secretary but was obliged to retire in 1810 as a result of a dispute with Castlereagh that ended in a duel. He did not return to the Foreign Office until 1822. In Parliament he was remarkable not only for the perfection of his rhetoric, but also for his readiness and skill as a debater. A disciple of Pitt, he strove to preserve peace and to build up England's commercial strength. He opposed joint intervention in the internal affairs of the Continent (at the moment he was thinking of the war between France and Spain), flouted the Holy Alliance and its policies, and steadfastly rejected all foreign ties. In 1823, after receiving the freedom of the town of Plymouth, he gave a speech that has been cited as one of the finest examples of classic style in modern times. Here he put his faith in the British navy as the symbol of world pacification.

"Not . . . that the interest of England is an interest which stands isolated and alone."

Mr. Mayor and Gentlemen:

I ACCEPT with thankfulness, and with greater satisfaction than I can express, this flattering testimony of your good opinion and good will. I must add that the value of the gift itself has been greatly enhanced by the manner in which your worthy and honorable Recorder has developed the motives which suggested it, and the sentiments which it is intended to convey.

Gentlemen, your Recorder has said very truly that whoever, in this free and enlightened state, aims at political eminence, and discharges political duties, must expect to have his conduct scrutinized, and every action of his public life sifted with no ordinary jealousy, and with no sparing criticism; and such may have been my lot as much as that of other public men. But, gentlemen, unmerited obloquy seldom fails of an adequate, though perhaps tardy, compensation. I must think myself, as my honorable friend has said, eminently fortunate if such compensation as he describes has fallen to me at an earlier period than to many others; if I dare flatter myself (as his partiality has flattered me) that the sentiments that you are kind enough to entertain for me are in unison with those of the country; if, in addition to the justice done me by my friends, I may, as he has assured me, rely upon a candid construction even from political opponents.

But, gentlemen, the secret of such a result does not lie deep. It consists only in an honest and undeviating pursuit of what one conscientiously believes to be one's public duty—a pursuit which, steadily continued, will, however detached and separate parts of a man's conduct may be viewed under the influence of partialities or prejudices, obtain for it, when considered as a whole, the approbation of all honest and honorable minds. Any man may occasionally be mistaken as to the means most conducive to the end which he has in view; but if the end be just and praiseworthy, it is by that he will be ultimately judged, either by his contemporaries or by posterity.

Gentlemen, the end which I confess I have always had in view, and which appears to me the legitimate object of pursuit to a British statesman, I can describe in one word. The language of modern philosophy is wisely and diffusely benevolent; it professes the perfection of our species and the amelioration of the lot of all mankind. Gentlemen, I hope that my heart beats as high for the general interest of humanity—I hope that I have as friendly a disposition towards other nations of the earth as anyone who vaunts his philanthropy most highly; but I am contented to confess that in the conduct of political affairs the grand object of my contemplation is the interest of England.

Not, gentlemen, that the interest of England is an interest which stands isolated and alone. The situation which she holds forbids an exclusive selfishness; her prosperity must contribute to the prosperity of other nations, and her stability to the safety of the world. But, intimately connected as we are with the system of Europe, it does not follow that we are therefore called upon to mix ourselves on every occasion with a restless and meddling activity in the concerns of the nations which surround us. It is upon a just balance of conflicting duties, and of rival but sometimes incompatible advantages, that a government must judge when to put forth its strength and when to husband it for occasions yet to come.

Our ultimate object must be the peace of the world. That object may sometimes be best attained by prompt exertions—sometimes by abstinence from interposition in contests which we cannot prevent. It is upon these principles that, as has been most truly observed by my worthy friend, it did not appear to the government of this country to be necessary that Great Britain should mingle in the recent contest between France and Spain.

Your worthy Recorder has accurately classed the persons who would have driven us into that contest. There were undoubtedly among them those who desired to plunge this country into the difficulties of war, partly from the hope that those difficulties would overwhelm the administration; but it would be most unjust not to admit that there were others who were actuated by nobler principles and more generous feelings, who would have rushed forward at once from the sense of indignation at aggression, and who deemed that no act of injustice could be perpetrated from one end of the universe to the other, but that the sword of Great Britain should leap from its scabbard to avenge it. But as it is the province of law to control the excess even of laudable passions and propensities in individuals, so it is the duty of government to restrain within due bounds the ebullition of national sentiment and to regulate the course and direction of impulses which it cannot blame. Is there anyone among the latter class of persons described by my honorable friend (for to the former I have nothing to say) who continues to doubt whether the government did wisely in declining to obey the precipitate enthusiasm which prevailed at the commencement of the contest in Spain? Is there anybody who does not now think that it was the office of the government to examine more closely all the various bearings of so complicated a question, to consider whether they were called upon to assist a united nation or to plunge themselves into the internal feuds by which that nation was divided—to aid in repelling a foreign invader or to take part in a civil war. Is there any man who does not now see what would have been the extent of burdens that would have been cast upon this country? Is there anyone who does not acknowledge that under such circumstances the enterprise would have been one to be characterized only by a term borrowed from that part of the Spanish literature with which we are most familiar— quixotic; an enterprise romantic in its origin and thankless in the end?

But while we thus control even our feelings by our duty, let it not be said that we cultivate peace, either because we fear, or because we are unprepared for, war; on the contrary, if eight months ago the government did not hesitate to proclaim that the country was prepared for war, if war should be unfortunately necessary, every month of peace that has since passed has but made us so much the more capable of exertion. The resources created by peace are means of war. In cherishing those resources, we but accumulate those means. Our present repose is no more a proof of inability to act than the state of inertness and inactivity in which I have seen those mighty masses that float in the waters above your town is a proof that they are devoid of strength and incapable of being fitted out for action. You well know, gentlemen, how soon one of those stupendous masses, now reposing on their shadows in perfect stillness—how soon, upon any call of patriotism, or of necessity, it would assume the likeness of an animated thing, instinct with life and motion—how soon it would ruffle, as it were, its swelling plumage—how quickly it would put forth all its beauty and its bravery, collect its scattered elements of strength, and awaken its dormant thunder. Such as is one of these magnificent machines when springing from inaction into a display of its might—such is England herself, while apparently passive and motionless she silently concentrates the power to be put forth on an adequate occasion. But God forbid that that occasion should arise! After a war sustained for nearly a quarter of a century—sometimes singlehanded, and with all Europe arranged at times against her or at her side—England needs a period of tranquillity, and may enjoy it without fear of misconstruction. Long may we be enabled, gentlemen, to improve the blessings of our present situation, to cultivate the arts of peace, to give to commerce, now reviving, greater extension and new spheres of employment, and to confirm the prosperity now generally diffused throughout this island. Of the blessing of peace, gentlemen, I trust that this borough, with which I have now the honor and happiness of being associated, will receive an ample share. I trust the time is not far distant when that noble structure of which, as I learn from your Recorder, the box with which you have honored me, through his hands, formed a part, that gigantic barrier against the fury of the waves that roll into your harbor will protect a commercial marine not less considerable in its kind than the warlike marine of which your port has been long so distinguished an asylum, when the town of Plymouth will participate in the commercial prosperity as largely as it has hitherto done in the naval glories of England.

Canning's prophecy of peace and commercial prosperity under the imperial wings of the British navy was, apart from minor conflicts at different points on the globe, well fulfilled during the next ninety years. Enriched by her industries, foreign trade, colonies, and investments abroad, and secure in her banking establishment, which levied tribute from the trade of all nations, England throve and enforced the peace. White- or red-coated Englishmen stood out around the world, imperturable, quietly superior, and no one dreamed that British supremacy was to be challenged in the next century by Germany, then by America, nor that her ascendency in colonies, naval power, and trade would be found so vulnerable.

In describing this era a century later, Sir Winston Churchill said, in the very rhythm of Canning: "The British navy basked in the steady light of Trafalgar, and all the navies of the world together could not rival its sedate strength" (Great Contemporaries).

DANIEL O'CONNELL CARRIES ON THE FIGHT FOR CATHOLIC EMANCIPATION

[February 24, 1824]

In the year of Canning's speech, 1823, there was formed in London, under the leadership of Daniel O'Connell, the Catholic Association, dedicated to the emancipation of Irish Catholics. It was soon to become one of the most effective political organizations in history.

Daniel O'Connell (1775–1847) was able to take up the practice of law in Ireland only because some concessions were made to Catholics during the war with revolutionary France. He opposed, of course, the Act of Union in 1800, but he also opposed the use of force by Robert Emmet and later by the Young Irelanders. Agitation was his lifelong method, and he began to use it as early as 1808, with the organization of the Irish Catholic Committee. Within five years the British Parliament was ready to grant emancipation in return for a veto on the choice of Irish bishops. But O'Connell could not accept this deal, and, for the time being, brilliant work in the courts took the place of agitation. Then, richer by a decade in experience and reputation, he took up the battle again and, with the support of the fiery little Richard Lalor Sheil, launched the broadly planned Catholic Association.

Now at forty-eight, at the very peak of his powers, one of the most versatile and gripping orators of all time addressed a mass meeting in Dublin. Coarse or tender, sentimental or sardonic, whispering or shouting, he knew all the stops, and his fine physique supported his energy-consuming virtuosity.

This speech has come down to us partly in the third person—evidently the on-the-spot notes of a newspaper reporter. We have taken a few liberties, accordingly, in editing it; and to suggest the turbulence of the mass meeting, we have for once retained the reactions of the crowd given, by the reporter, in brackets.

"The Irish were made more thirsty for liberty
by the drop that fell on their parched lips."

IN THE EXPERIMENTAL DESPOTISM which England fastened on
Ireland, her mighty appetite for slavery was not gorged; and because
our unfortunate country was proximate, and polite in the endurance of
the burden so mercilessly imposed, it was inferred that slavery could be
safely extended far and wide, and an attempt was therefore made on the
American colonies. Despotism, in fact, was an all-craving and voracious
animal: "increase of appetite did grow on what it fed"; until endurance
became at length too vile; and the Americans—the great God of heaven
bless them for it! [laughter and applause]—shook off the thralldom which
a Parliament, representing an inglorious and ignominious funding system,
had sought to impose. [Cheers.] Oh, it was a noble sight, to see them in
open battle, contending for their liberties! The recollection of the circumstance cheered and invigorated: it gave one an elasticity which all the
fatigues of the day could not depress. [Cheers.]

The friends they tried were by their side—
The foes they dared before them.

Wives animated their husbands to the combat; they bid them contend for
their children, for the dear pledges of their mutual love—[hear, hear]—
mothers enjoined their sons to remember those who bore them—the
younger sex bid their lovers earn their favors in a "well-foughten field,"
and to return arrayed in glory. They did so—God of heaven forever bless
them! [Loud cheering, mingled with laughter.] Thanks to the valor and
patriotism of Washington, a name dear to every lover of liberty, the Americans achieved their independence, and Providence spared the instrument
to witness it. [Loud applause.]

The independence of America was the first blush of dawn to the Catholic, after a long and dreary night of degradation. Seventy years have
they been in a land of bondage; but like the chosen people, Providence
has watched over and the progress of events has liberated them and redeemed them for the service of their country. The same Providence exists
now, and why should we despair? [Cheers.]

In 1778, Holland assumed a threatening aspect, and some wise friend
—[a laugh]—whispered into the ear of England, "search the rich resources of the Irish heart; give to their arms a stimulus to exertion; de-

lude them with promises if you will, but convert their power into your strength and render them subservient to your purposes." England took the advice: the meteor flag was unfurled; the Danish, Spanish, and Dutch fleets peopled a wide waste of waters; but what of Ireland? Oh, although long neglected, she was faithful in the day of need: fifty thousand seamen were produced in a month—the Volunteers organized—a federate independence was created—and the Catholic cause was debated. But, lo! peace came, and gratitude vanished; and justice was not abroad; and obligations remained unrequited; and the Catholics were forgotten.

Forgotten? No! Acts were passed against them. [Loud and long-continued applause.]

Yes, strange as it might seem, the act taking from them the power to vote at vestries was passed at this very time; so that if the rectors agreed to build a church, the poor Catholics could not ask, "Who is to go into it?" [Much laughter.] Next came the French Revolution. That revolution produced some good, but it was not without alloy: it was mingled with much impiety. Liberty and religion were first separated. The experiment was a bad one. It had much of French levity in it, and a deal of what was much worse. The people of France should have remembered that liberty is the first instinct of a generous religion. [Immense applause.]

This position will not be conceded to any saint or Bible distributor. [Great applause.] The French, in folly, set religion at nought; they profaned the sanctuary, and they suffered for it. And if they are now settling into quiet, it is because they are settling into religion. [Applause.]

But I am trespassing on the time of the meeting—[no, no]—and in some measure wandering. [Cries of 'go on.'] Well, I like the subject, and will go on a little longer. I was saying the French Revolution produced much good. So it did. Dumouriez gained the battle of Jemappes— the French crossed the Pyrenees—General Biron was in Italy—England looked benignantly on Ireland—it served her interest, it was her policy to do so, and she passed another act in favor of the Irish Catholics. [Applause.] The Irish were made more thirsty for liberty by the drop that fell on their parched lips. [Applause.]

There is not one who hears me who does not mourn in affection, in dress, or in heart for some relative or friend who fell in the field of battle. [Hear.] My own heartstrings are torn asunder by the loss of a beloved brother, the companion of my youth, and the offspring of the same loins. A kinsman of mine, too, died at the storming of St. Sebastian. Three times did he mount the breach, and he fell at last, covered with wounds and with glory. [Applause.] He was as gay and as lovely a youth as ever shed his blood in defense of his country, and as fair withal as ever trod on the greensward of Erin. [Much applause.] I cannot choose but name him. It was Lieutenant John O'Connell of the Forty-third Regiment. And what did the relatives of these brave men gain by this?—what the Catholics of Ireland? Why, the Marquis of Douro was made Duke of Wellington!

The victories of Wellington might be compared to those of Marlborough. Both perpetuated despotism at home and abroad. Civil liberty is now extinct on the Continent. From the fair and classic shores of Naples to the Tanais and the Volga there is but one wide stretch of illimitable despotism. In Naples, where the king "swore, and swore, and swore again," he returned against his oath, and put to death those who spared him. Piedmont is under the hoofs of the despots. In Portugal liberty is extinct. In Germany, no breath of public spirit is heard—their chards have become corporations to "crib and cabin" the intellect of man. Brutal force controls, for the present, the eternal empire of mind.

In France, the cause of liberty has found some advocates, but they are few: the enemies of the rights of man are the more numerous; but, nevertheless, France enjoys much practical liberty, and her peasantry are happy and well fed.

In England, Toryism is triumphant. The forges are all employed; the funds are high and healthy; the cry of war has been abandoned; the navy is flourishing and actively engaged; the army is numerous, well fed, and well paid; the Duke of York, our declared and open enemy, who headed the Orange faction, is the commander in chief; Mr. Canning is in office, secured by a motley cabinet, who oppose each other openly, but who covertly befriend themselves to the detriment of the country; Mr. Peel, their avowed enemy, is firm in his place; Lord Liverpool still opposes them. Is it, therefore, at all wonderful that the Catholics are despised, and their cause abandoned?

In Ireland, we have been blamed for being agitators. I thank God for being one. Whatever little we have gained, we have gained by agitation, while we have uniformly lost by moderation. The last word is repeated so often that I am completely sick of it. I wonder do some gentleman not teach a parrot to repeat it. [A laugh.] If we gain nothing by moderation, it costs us something. Our religion is reviled, and we thank the revilers; they spit in our faces and we pay 'em for it. [Laughter and applause.] This reminds me of Shylock, in *The Merchant of Venice*—

> *Fair Sir, you spat on me on Wednesday last;*
> *On such a day you called me dog;*
> *And for these courtesies I'll lend you so much monies. . . .*

Thanks to this speech and hundreds of others by O'Connell, Sheil, and their followers throughout the country, Ireland (ever excepting Ulster, the stronghold of the Orangemen) was molded into a powerful and dangerous unity. Six years after the formation of the Catholic Association, the Catholic Emancipation Bill, grimly assisted by the Duke of Wellington, then Prime Minister, passed both Houses of the British Parliament. To the end George IV, the royal family, and the bench of bishops tried to stop it.

O'Connell, who had already been elected to the House of Commons (Catholic disabilities having been removed), after some vicissitudes took his place there and threw himself on the side of parliamentary reform, which was the issue of the day.

MACAULAY MAKES HIS FIRST SPEECH FOR THE REFORM BILL

[March 2, 1831]

Parliamentary representation around 1830 was a jigsaw puzzle. "A medley of local customs!" someone called it. It was an irrational but splendid growth—the strange fruit of British common sense. Large sections of the public were not represented; large cities, such as Leeds, Birmingham, and Manchester, were not represented. The system of "rotten boroughs" is explained by the name. "It was calculated, if not with truth, at any rate with an approach to it," said Bagehot, "that one hundred and seventy-seven lords and gentlemen chose as many as three hundred and fifty-five English Members of Parliament." Burke was so "chosen" throughout his career, except when he represented Bristol. But such discrimination was by no means typical!

Back in the eighteenth century such leaders as Chatham, Wilkes, Fox, and even the younger Pitt (prior to the French Revolution) favored parliamentary reform. Now at all levels of the population it was a growing obsession. Even the most uncompromising Tories realized that the reaction against reaction was at full tide. The new generation was not to be cowed by horror tales of Robespierre and Napoleon. Francis Place, the shoemaker, and Jeremy Bentham, the wealthy philosopher, were both educating the public. There was widespread distress, and the parliamentary reformers thought they knew one of the chief reasons for it.

On March 1, 1831, Lord John Russell introduced the long-awaited Reform Bill before a tense and crowded House of Commons. It was greeted with contemptuous laughter by the Tories and at once characterized as "revolution in *the guise of a statute." At this distance the bill does not appear drastic or dangerous, but at that time, to the reigning Tory elite, the partial or complete disenfranchisement of one hundred and ten boroughs, the enfranchisement of many counties and cities, and the huge addition to the middle-class vote (with a probable decline of the small working-class vote) meant the decline and fall of England. The bill, in various forms, was debated hotly for more than a year, while riots and demonstrations shook the country. It was a crisis in which old men made their exits and young men their entrances on the public stage.*

Thomas Babington Macaulay (1800–59) was then a self-assured thirty-one. The son of a prosperous merchant, he had begun to read voraciously at three years of age, to talk urbanely at four, and to compile a compendium of universal history at seven. No flash in the pan, he went on to make a brilliant record in the classics at Cambridge and at twenty-five started a series of dazzling literary-historical essays for the Whig organ, The Edinburgh Review. While week-ending with the Wilberforces in the last months of Wellington's ministry, he received, out of a clear sky, a letter from Lord Lansdowne offering him the pocket borough of Calne. This was the quick way into Parliament, and only a few weeks later (April 5, 1830) he delivered his maiden speech in support of a bill for the removal of Jewish disabilities. For a first effort it was exceptionally good—neither nervous nor pretentious, with a fluency that made one forget his harsh voice and somewhat awkward manner. But the motion was badly defeated.

Nearly a year later, on the evening after Lord John Russell had introduced the Reform Bill, Macaulay plunged into the fierce controversy. Here is his peroration.

"Save the aristocracy, endangered by its own unpopular power."

THE QUESTION of parliamentary reform is still behind. But signs of which it is impossible to misconceive the import do most clearly indicate that unless that question also be speedily settled, property and order, and all the institutions of this great monarchy, will be exposed to fearful peril. Is it possible that gentlemen long versed in high political affairs cannot read these signs? Is it possible that they can really believe that the representative system of England, such as it now is, will last to the year of 1860? If not, for what would they have us wait? Would they have us wait merely that we may show to all the world how little we have profited by our own recent experience? Would they have us wait that we may once again hit the exact point where we can neither refuse with authority nor concede with grace? Would they have us wait that the numbers of the discontented party may become larger, its demands higher, its feelings more acrimonious, its organization more complete? Would they have us wait till the whole tragicomedy of 1827 has been acted over again? till they have been brought into office by a cry of "No Reform," to be reformers, as they were once before brought into office by a cry of "No Popery," to be emancipators? Have they obliterated from their minds— gladly, perhaps, would some among them obliterate from their minds— the transactions of that year? And have they forgotten all the transactions of the succeeding year? Have they forgotten how the spirit of liberty in Ireland, debarred from its natural outlet, found a vent by forbidden passages? Have they forgotten how we were forced to indulge the Catholics in all the license of rebels, merely because we chose to withhold from them the liberties of subjects? Do they wait for associations more formidable than that of the Corn Exchange, for contributions larger than the Rent, for agitators more violent than those who, three years ago, divided with the King and the Parliament the sovereignty of Ireland? Do they wait for that last and most dreadful paroxysm of popular rage, for that last and most cruel test of military fidelity? Let them wait, if their past experience shall induce them to think that any high honor or any exquisite pleasure is to be obtained by a policy like this. Let them wait, if this strange and fearful infatuation be indeed upon them, that they should not see with their eyes, or hear with their ears, or understand with their heart.

But let us know our interest and our duty better. Turn where we may, within, around, the voice of great events is proclaiming to us, Reform, that you may preserve. Now, therefore, while everything at home and abroad forebodes ruin to those who persist in a hopeless struggle against the spirit of the age; now, while the crash of the proudest throne of the Continent is still resounding in our ears; now, while the roof of a British palace affords an ignominious shelter to the exiled heir of forty kings; now, while we see on every side ancient institutions subverted and great societies dissolved; now, while the heart of England is still sound; now, while old feelings and old associations retain a power and a charm which may too soon pass away; now, in this your accepted time; now, in this your day of salvation, take counsel, not of prejudice, not of party spirit, not of the ignominious pride of a fatal consistency, but of history, of reason, of the ages which are past, of the signs of this most portentous time. Pronounce in a manner worthy of the expectation with which this great debate has been anticipated, and of the long remembrance which it will leave behind. Renew the youth of the state. Save property, divided against itself. Save the multitude, endangered by its own ungovernable passions. Save the aristocracy, endangered by its own unpopular power. Save the greatest, and fairest, and most highly civilized community that ever existed from calamities which may in a few days sweep away all the rich heritage of so many ages of wisdom and glory. The danger is terrible. The time is short. If this bill should be rejected, I pray to God that none of those who concur in rejecting it may ever remember their votes with unavailing remorse amidst the wreck of laws, the confusion of ranks, the spoliation of property, and the dissolution of social order.

"When he sat down, the Speaker sent for him and told him that in all his prolonged experience he had never seen the House in such a state of excitement." So wrote his proud nephew, Sir George Otto Trevelyan, in The Life and Letters of Lord Macaulay.

Macaulay spoke several times more on the Reform Bill, with almost equal effect.

LORD BROUGHAM, WITH HIS USUAL VEHEMENCE, ALSO SUPPORTS THE REFORM BILL

[October 7, 1831]

Before our time, the House of Lords was much more than an ornamental body, and the debate on the great Reform Bill flamed as hotly there as it did in the Commons. One example may be taken from a famous outburst by Lord Brougham, who had only recently been kicked upstairs.

Henry Peter, Baron Brougham of Brougham and Vaux (1778–1868), is a difficult figure to reckon with, for he was overestimated by his admirers and he overestimated himself—and it is easy to confuse enormous energy with genius. Long before Macaulay, he made a reputation for himself as a frequent contributor to The Edinburgh Review and as a voluble Whig in the House of Commons. In the notorious attempt of George IV to secure a divorce from Queen Caroline on the grounds of adultery, Brougham was one of her chief defenders.

Like Bacon, Brougham took all learning for his province, understood the technical niceties of several of the sciences, including mathematics, and pioneered in the popularization of knowledge. He was also such a devoted student of the ancient orators that he came to confuse himself with Demosthenes and could be vehement even when Macedon was not at the gate.

Here is the peroration of his speech on the second reading of the Reform Bill: it is generally considered to be his masterpiece.

"Yea, on my bended knees, I supplicate you—
reject not this bill!"

MY LORDS, I do not disguise the intense solicitude which I feel for the event of this debate, because I know full well that the peace of the country is involved in the issue. I cannot look without dismay at the rejection of the measure. But grievous as may be the consequences of a temporary defeat—temporary it can only be; for its ultimate, and even speedy, success is certain. Nothing can now stop it. Do not suffer yourselves to be persuaded that even if the present ministers were driven from the helm, anyone could steer you through the troubles which surround you without reform. But our successors would take up the task in circumstances far less auspicious. Under them, you would be fain to grant a bill compared with which the one we now proffer you is moderate indeed. Hear the parable of the sibyl; for it conveys a wise and wholesome moral. She now appears at your gate, and offers you mildly the volumes —the precious volumes—of wisdom and peace. The price she asks is reasonable: to restore the franchise which, without any bargain, you ought voluntarily to give; you refuse her terms—her moderate terms—she darkens the porch no longer. But soon, for you cannot do without her wares, you call her back—again she comes, but with diminished treasures; the leaves of the book are in part torn away by lawless hands—in part defaced with characters of blood. But the prophetic maid has risen in her demands—it is Parliaments by the year—it is vote by the ballot—it is suffrage by the million! From this you turn away indignant, and for the second time she departs. Beware of her third coming; for the treasure you must have; and what price she may next demand, who shall tell? It may even be the mace which rests upon that woolsack. What may follow your course of obstinacy, if persisted in, I cannot take upon me to predict, nor do I wish to conjecture. But this I know full well, that, as sure as man is mortal, and to err is human, justice deferred enhances the price at which you must purchase safety and peace—nor can you expect to gather in another crop than they did who went before you, if you persevere in their utterly abominable husbandry of sowing injustice and reaping rebellion.

But among the awful considerations that now bow down my mind, there is one which stands pre-eminently above the rest. You are the highest judicature in the realm; you sit here as judges, and decide all causes, civil and criminal, without appeal. It is a judge's first duty never to pronounce sentence, in the most trifling case, without hearing. Will you make this the exception? Are you really prepared to determine, but not to hear, the mighty cause upon which a nation's hopes and fears hang? You are. Then beware of your decision! Rouse not, I beseech you, a peace-loving, but a resolute, people; alienate not from your body the affections of a whole empire. As your friend, as the friend of my order, as the friend of my country, as the faithful servant of my sovereign, I counsel you to assist with your uttermost efforts in preserving the peace, and upholding and perpetuating the Constitution. Therefore, I pray and I exhort you not to reject this measure. By all you hold most dear—by all the ties that bind every one of us to our common order and our common country, I solemnly adjure you—I warn you—I implore you—yea, on my bended knees, I supplicate you—reject not this bill!

In later years Brougham took to himself far too much credit for the passage of the great Reform Bill in 1832. Other eloquent men were involved, not to mention the earnest but utterly uneloquent steersman in the House of Commons, later Lord Althorp, and the thousands of rioters and demonstrators whose threats could not be overlooked.

The Reform Bill of 1832 was by no means a perfect instrument, but it was a precedent, and there would be other reform bills that would finally enfranchise the entire adult population.

MACAULAY RENEWS HIS CASE FOR EMANCIPATION OF THE JEWS

[April 17, 1833]

Having had a voice in dissolving the little pocket borough of Calne, which he had represented so prominently in the fight for the Reform Bill, Macaulay campaigned for a seat in the House of Commons, and was elected from Leeds in spite of his Burkelike insistence that he would not be a delegate obeying instructions from his constituents.

In January, 1833, the reformed Parliament met for the first time and proceeded to pass measures emancipating slaves in the British dominions, regulating child labor, and granting public money for elementary education. Ireland and India demanded attention. Sir Robert Grant's bill for the removal of Jewish disabilities, which had been defeated three years before, was resubmitted.

Macaulay's maiden speech, it may be recalled, was an able argument for the original bill on April 5, 1830. In the following year he contributed to The Edinburgh Review a characteristically vigorous article on the "Civil Disabilities of the Jews." When Grant's bill came up again in April, 1833, Macaulay could bring to its support three years of parliamentary and nation-wide fame.

"Let us open to them every career in which ability and energy can be displayed."

I RECOLLECT, and my honorable friend the Member for the University of Oxford will recollect, that when this subject was discussed three years ago, it was remarked, by one whom we both loved and whom we both regret, that the strength of the case of the Jews was a serious inconvenience to their advocate, for that it was hardly possible to make a speech for them without wearying the audience by repeating truths which were universally admitted. If Sir James Mackintosh felt this difficulty when the question was first brought forward in this House, I may well despair of being able now to offer any arguments which have a pretense to novelty.

My honorable friend the Member for the University of Oxford began his speech by declaring that he had no intention of calling in question the principles of religious liberty. He utterly disclaims persecution, that is to say, persecution as defined by himself. It would, in his opinion, be persecution to hang a Jew, or to flay him, or to draw his teeth, or to imprison him, or to fine him; for every man who conducts himself peacefully has a right to his life and his limbs, to his personal liberty and his property. But it is not persecution, says my honorable friend, to exclude any individual or any class from office; for nobody has a right to office: in every country official appointments must be subject to such regulations as the supreme authority may choose to make; nor can any such regulations be reasonably complained of by any member of the society as unjust. He who obtains an office obtains it not as a matter of right, but as matter of favor. He who does not obtain an office is not wronged; he is only in that situation in which the vast majority of every community must necessarily be. There are in the United Kingdom five and twenty million Christians without places; and, if they do not complain, why should five and twenty thousand Jews complain of being in the same case? In this way my honorable friend has convinced himself that, as it would be most absurd in him and me to say that we are wronged because we are not secretaries of state, so it is most absurd in the Jews to say that they are wronged because they are, as a people, excluded from public employment.

Now surely my honorable friend cannot have considered to what conclusions his reasoning leads. Those conclusions are so monstrous that he would, I am certain, shrink from them. Does he really mean that it would not be wrong in the legislature to enact that no man should be a judge unless he weighed twelve stone, or that no man should sit in Parliament unless he were six feet high? We are about to bring in a bill for the government of India. Suppose that we were to insert in that bill a clause providing that no graduate of the University of Oxford should be governor general or governor of any presidency, would not my honorable friend cry out against such a clause as most unjust to the learned body which he represents? And would he think himself sufficiently answered by being told, in his own words, that the appointment to office is a mere matter of favor, and that to exclude an individual or a class from office is no injury? Surely, on consideration, he must admit that official appointments ought not to be subject to regulations purely arbitrary, to regulations for which no reason can be given but mere caprice, and that those who would exclude any class from public employment are bound to show some special reason for the exclusion.

My honorable friend has appealed to us as Christians. Let me then ask him how he understands that great commandment which comprises the law and the prophets. Can we be said to do unto others as we would that they should do unto us, if we wantonly inflict on them even the smallest pain? As Christians, surely, we are bound to consider, first, whether, by excluding the Jews from all public trust, we give them pain; and secondly, whether it be necessary to give them that pain in order to avert some greater evil. That by excluding them from public trust we inflict pain on them my honorable friend will not dispute. As a Christian, therefore, he is bound to relieve them from that pain, unless he can show, what I am sure he has not yet shown, that it is necessary to the general good that they should continue to suffer.

But where, he says, are you to stop if once you admit into the House of Commons people who deny the authority of the Gospels? Will you let in a Mussulman? Will you let in a Parsee? Will you let in a Hindu who worships a lump of stone with seven heads? I will answer my honorable friend's question by another. Where does he mean to stop? Is he ready to roast unbelievers at slow fires? If not, let him tell us why: and I will engage to prove that his reason is just as decisive against the intolerance which he thinks a duty as against the intolerance which he thinks a crime. Once admit that we are bound to inflict pain on a man because he is not of our religion, and where are you to stop? Why stop at the point fixed by my honorable friend rather than at the point fixed by the honorable Member for Oldham, who would make the Jews incapable of holding land? And why stop at the point fixed by the honorable Member for Oldham rather than at the point which would have been fixed by a Spanish inquisitor of the sixteenth century? When once you enter on a course of persecution, I defy you to find any reason for making a halt till you have reached the extreme point. When my honorable friend tells us that he will allow the Jews to possess property to any amount, but that he will not allow them to possess the smallest political power, he holds contradictory language. Property is power. The honorable Member for Oldham reasons better than my honorable friend. The honorable Member for Oldham sees very clearly that it is impossible to deprive a man of political power if you suffer him to be the proprietor of half a county, and therefore very consistently proposes to confiscate the landed estates of the Jews. But even the honorable Member for Oldham does not go far enough. He has not proposed to confiscate the personal property of the Jews. Yet it is perfectly certain that any Jew who has a million may easily make himself very important in the state. By such steps we pass from official power to landed property, and from landed property to personal property, and from property to liberty, and from liberty to life. In truth, those persecutors who use the rack and the stake have much to say for themselves. They are convinced that their end is good; and it must be admitted that they employ means which are not unlikely to attain the end. Religious dissent has repeatedly been put down by sanguinary persecution. In that way the Albigenses were put down. In that way Protestantism was suppressed in Spain and Italy, so that it has never since reared its head. But I defy anybody to produce an instance in which disabilities, such as we are now considering, have produced any other effect than that of making the sufferers angry and obstinate. My honorable friend should either persecute to some purpose or not persecute at all. He dislikes the word persecution, I know. He will not admit that the

Jews are persecuted. And yet I am confident that he would rather be sent to the King's Bench Prison for three months or be fined a hundred pounds than be subject to the disabilities under which the Jews lie. How can he then say that to impose such disabilities is not persecution, and that to fine and imprison is persecution? All his reasoning consists in drawing arbitrary lines. What he does not wish to inflict he calls persecution. What he does wish to inflict he will not call persecution. What he takes from the Jews he calls political power. What he is too good-natured to take from the Jews he will not call political power. The Jew must not sit in Parliament; but he may be the proprietor of all the ten-pound houses in a borough. He may have more fifty-pound tenants than any peer in the kingdom. He may give the voters treats to please their palates, and hire bands of gypsies to break their heads, as if he were a Christian and a marquess. All the rest of this system is of a piece. The Jew may be a juryman, but not a judge. He may decide issues of fact, but not issues of law. He may give a hundred thousand pounds' damages; but he may not in the most trivial case grant a new trial. He may rule the money market; he may influence the exchanges; he may be summoned to congresses of emperors and kings. Great potentates, instead of negotiating a loan with him by tying him in a chair and pulling out his grinders, may treat with him as with a great potentate, and may postpone the declaring of war or the signing of a treaty till they have conferred with him. All this is as it should be; but he must not be a Privy Councilor. He must not be called Right Honorable, for that is political power. And who is it that we are trying to cheat in this way? Even Omniscience. Yes, sir; we have been gravely told that the Jews are under the divine displeasure, and that if we give them political power God will visit us in judgment. Do we then think that God cannot distinguish between substance and form? Does not He know that, while we withhold from the Jews the semblance and name of political power, we suffer them to possess the substance? The plain truth is that my honorable friend is drawn in one direction by his opinions and in a directly opposite direction by his excellent heart. He halts between two opinions. He tries to make a compromise between principles which admit of no compromise. He goes a certain way in intolerance. Then he stops, without being able to give a reason for stopping. But I know the reason. It is his humanity. Those who formerly dragged the Jew at a horse's tail, and singed his beard with blazing furze bushes, were much worse men than my honorable friend; but they were more consistent than he.

It has been said that it would be monstrous to see a Jew judge try a man for blasphemy. In my opinion it is monstrous to see any judge try

a man for blasphemy under the present law. But, if the law on that subject were in a sound state, I do not see why a conscientious Jew might not
try a blasphemer. Every man, I think, ought to be at liberty to discuss
the evidences of religion; but no man ought to be at liberty to force on
the unwilling ears and eyes of others sounds and sights which must cause
annoyance and irritation. The distinction is clear. I think it wrong to
punish a man for selling Paine's *Age of Reason* in a back shop to those
who choose to buy, or for delivering a Deistical lecture in a private room
to those who choose to listen. But if a man exhibits at a window in the
Strand a hideous caricature of that which is an object of awe and adoration to nine hundred and ninety-nine out of every thousand of the people
who pass up and down that great thoroughfare; if a man in a place of
public resort applies opprobrious epithets to names held in reverence by
all Christians; such a man ought, in my opinion, to be severely punished,
not for differing from us in opinion, but for committing a nuisance which
gives us pain and disgust. He is no more entitled to outrage our feelings
by obtruding his impiety on us, and to say that he is exercising his right
of discussion, than to establish a yard for butchering horses close to our
houses and to say that he is exercising his right of property, or to run
naked up and down the public streets and to say that he is exercising his
right of locomotion. He has a right of discussion, no doubt, as he has a
right of property and a right of locomotion. But he must use all his rights
so as not to infringe the rights of others.

These, sir, are the principles on which I would frame the law of
blasphemy; and if the law were so framed, I am at a loss to understand
why a Jew might not enforce it as well as a Christian. I am not a Roman
Catholic; but if I were a judge at Malta, I should have no scruple about
punishing a bigoted Protestant who should burn the Pope in effigy before
the eyes of thousands of Roman Catholics. I am not a Mussulman; but
if I were a judge in India, I should have no scruple about punishing a
Christian who should pollute a mosque. Why, then, should I doubt that
a Jew, raised by his ability, learning, and integrity to the judicial bench,
would deal properly with any person who, in a Christian country, should
insult the Christian religion?

But, says my honorable friend, it has been prophesied that the Jews
are to be wanderers on the face of the earth, and that they are not to
mix on terms of equality with the people of the countries in which they
sojourn. Now, sir, I am confident that I can demonstrate that this is not
the sense of any prophecy which is part of Holy Writ. For it is an undoubted fact that, in the United States of America, Jewish citizens do
possess all the privileges possessed by Christian citizens. Therefore, if

the prophecies mean that the Jews never shall, during their wanderings, be admitted by other nations to equal participation of political rights, the prophecies are false. But the prophecies are certainly not false. Therefore, their meaning cannot be that which is attributed to them by my honorable friend.

Another objection which has been made to this motion is that the Jews look forward to the coming of a great deliverer, to their return to Palestine, to the rebuilding of their temple, to the revival of their ancient worship, and that therefore they will always consider England not their country, but merely as their place of exile. But, surely, sir, it would be the grossest ignorance of human nature to imagine that the anticipation of an event which is to happen at some time altogether indefinite, of an event which has been vainly expected during many centuries, of an event which even those who confidently expect that it will happen do not confidently expect that they or their children or their grandchildren will see, can ever occupy the minds of men to such a degree as to make them regardless of what is near and present and certain. Indeed, Christians as well as Jews believe that the existing order of things will come to an end. Many Christians believe that Jesus will visibly reign on earth during a thousand years. Expositors of prophecy have gone so far as to fix the year when the millennial period is to commence. The prevailing opinion is, I think, in favor of the year 1866; but, according to some commentators, the time is close at hand. Are we to exclude all millennarians from Parliament and office, on the ground that they are impatiently looking forward to the miraculous monarchy which is to supersede the present dynasty and the present Constitution of England, and that therefore they cannot be heartily loyal to King William?

In one important point, sir, my honorable friend the Member for the University of Oxford must acknowledge that the Jewish religion is of all erroneous religions the least mischievous. There is not the slightest chance that the Jewish religion will spread. The Jew does not wish to make proselytes. He may be said to reject them. He thinks it almost culpable in one who does not belong to his race to presume to belong to his religion. It is, therefore, not strange that a conversion from Christianity to Judaism should be a rarer occurrence than a total eclipse of the sun. There was one distinguished convert in the last century, Lord George Gordon; and the history of his conversion deserves to be remembered. For if ever there was a proselyte of whom a proselytizing sect would have been proud, it was Lord George; not only because he was a man of high birth and rank; not only because he had been a member of the legislature; but also because he had been distinguished by the intolerance, nay, the ferocity, of his zeal for his own form of Christianity. But was he allured into the synagogue? Was he even welcomed to it? No, sir; he was coldly and reluctantly permitted to share the reproach and suffering of the chosen people; but he was sternly shut out from their privileges. He underwent the painful rite which their law enjoins. But when, on his deathbed, he begged hard to be buried among them according to their ceremonial, he was told that his request could not be granted. I understand that cry of "Hear." It reminds me that one of the arguments against this motion is that the Jews are an unsocial people, that they draw close to each other and stand aloof from strangers. Really, sir, it is amusing to compare the manner in which the question of Catholic emancipation was argued formerly by some gentlemen with the manner in which the question of Jew emancipation is argued by the same gentlemen now. When the question was about Catholic emancipation, the cry was, "See how restless, how versatile, how encroaching, how insinuating, is the spirit of the Church of Rome. See how her priests compass earth and sea to make one proselyte, how indefatigably they toil, how attentively they study the weak and strong parts of every character, how skillfully they employ literature, arts, sciences, as engines for the propagation of their faith. You find them in every region and under every disguise, collating manuscripts in the Bodleian, fixing telescopes in the observatory of Peking, teaching the use of the plow and the spinning wheel to the savages of Paraguay. Will you give power to the members of a Church so busy, so aggressive, so insatiable?" Well, now the question is about people who never try to seduce any stranger to join them, and who do not wish anybody to be of their faith who is not also of their blood. And now you exclaim, "Will you give power to the members of a sect which remains sullenly apart from other sects, which does not invite, nay, which hardly even admits, neophytes?" The truth is that bigotry will never want a pretense. Whatever the sect be which it is proposed to tolerate, the peculiarities of that sect will, for the time, be pronounced by intolerant men to be the most odious and dangerous that can be conceived. As to the Jews, that they are unsocial as respects religion is true; and so much the better; for surely, as Christians, we cannot wish that they should bestir themselves to pervert us from our own faith. But that the Jews would be unsocial members of the civil community, if the civil community did its duty by them, has never been proved. My right honorable friend who made the motion which we are discussing has produced a great body of evidence to show that they have been grossly misrepresented; and that evidence has not been refuted by my honorable friend the Member for the University of Oxford. But what if it were true that the Jews are unsocial? What if it were true that they do not regard England as their country? Would not the treatment which they have undergone explain and excuse their antipathy to the society in which they live? Has not similar antipathy often been felt by persecuted Christians to the society which persecuted them? While the bloody code of Elizabeth was enforced against the English Roman Catholics, what was the patriotism of Roman Catholics? Oliver Cromwell said that in his time they were Espaniolized. At a later period it might have been said that they were Gallicized. It was the same with the Calvinists. What more deadly enemies had France in the days of Louis XIV than the persecuted Huguenots? But would any rational man infer from these facts that either the Roman Catholic as such or the Calvinist as such is incapable of loving the land of his birth? If England were now invaded by Roman Catholics, how many English Roman Catholics would go over to the invader? If France were now attacked by a Protestant enemy, how many French Protestants would lend him help? Why not try what effect would be produced on the Jews by that tolerant policy which has made the English Roman Catholic a good Englishman and the French Calvinist a good Frenchman?

Another charge has been brought against the Jews, not by my honorable friend the Member for the University of Oxford—he has too much learning and too much good feeling to make such a charge—but by the honorable Member for Oldham, who has, I am sorry to see, quitted his place. The honorable Member for Oldham tells us that the Jews are naturally a mean race, a sordid race, a money-getting race; that they are averse to all honorable callings; that they neither sow nor reap; that they have neither flocks nor herds; that usury is the only pursuit for which they are fit; that they are destitute of all elevated and amiable sentiments. Such, sir, has in every age been the reasoning of bigots. They never fail to plead in justification of persecution the vices which persecution has engendered. England has been to the Jews less than half a country; and we revile them because they do not feel for England more than a half patriotism. We treat them as slaves, and wonder that they do not regard us as brethren. We drive them to mean occupations, and then reproach them for not embracing honorable professions. We long forbade them to possess land; and we complain that they chiefly occupy themselves in trade. We shut them out from all the paths of ambition; and then we despise them for taking refuge in avarice. During many ages we have, in all our dealings with them, abused our immense superiority of force; and then we are disgusted because they have recourse to that cunning which is the natural and universal defense of the weak against the violence of the strong. But were they always a mere money-changing, money-getting, money-hoarding race? Nobody knows better than my honorable friend the Member for the University of Oxford that there is nothing in their national character which unfits them for the highest duties of citizens. He knows that, in the infancy of civilization, when our island was as savage as New Guinea, when letters and arts were still unknown to Athens, when scarcely a thatched hut stood on what was afterwards the site of Rome, this contemned people had their fenced cities and cedar palaces, their splendid Temple, their fleets of merchant ships, their schools of sacred learning, their great statesmen and soldiers, their natural philosophers, their historians, and their poets. What nation ever contended more manfully against overwhelming odds for its independence and religion? What nation ever, in its last agonies, gave such signal proofs of what may be accomplished by a brave despair? And if, in the course of many centuries, the oppressed descendants of warriors and sages have degenerated from the qualities of their fathers, if, while excluded from the blessings of law, and bowed down under the yoke of slavery, they have contracted some of the vices of outlaws and of slaves, shall we consider this as a matter of reproach to them? Shall we not rather consider it as matter of shame and remorse to ourselves? Let us do justice to them. Let us open to them the door of the House of Commons. Let us open to them every career in which ability and energy can be displayed. Till we have done this, let us not presume to say that there is no genius among the countrymen of Isaiah, no heroism among the descendants of the Maccabees.

Sir, in supporting the motion of my honorable friend, I am, I firmly believe, supporting the honor and the interests of the Christian religion. I should think that I insulted that religion if I said that it cannot stand unaided by intolerant laws. Without such laws it was established, and without such laws it may be maintained. It triumphed over the superstitions of the most refined and of the most savage nations, over the graceful mythology of Greece and the bloody idolatry of the Northern forests. It prevailed over the power and policy of the Roman Empire. It tamed the barbarians by whom that empire was overthrown. But all these victories were gained not by the help of intolerance, but in spite of the opposition of intolerance. The whole history of Christianity proves that she has little indeed to fear from persecution as a foe, but much to fear from persecution as an ally. May she long continue to bless our country with her benignant influence, strong in her sublime philosophy, strong in her spotless morality, strong in those internal and external evidences to which the most powerful and comprehensive of human intellects have yielded assent, the last solace of those who have outlived every earthly hope, the last restraint of those who are raised above every earthly fear! But let not us, mistaking her character and her interests, fight the battle of truth with the weapons of error, and endeavor to support by oppression that religion which first taught the human race the great lesson of universal charity.

There were other strong voices in this debate, but Macaulay made the classic statement, still relevant to the bigotry of today. Without serious difficulty Sir Robert Grant's bill to remove the civil disabilities of Jews passed the House of Commons, only to be thrown out by the House of Lords, a few months later, owing chiefly to William IV's meddling and the determined opposition of the bench of bishops, led by Canterbury himself.

Twenty-five years had to elapse before the arguments that Macaulay had presented so clearly in the early thirties "commended themselves to the judgment of our Upper Chamber." In 1858 a Jew could take his seat in Parliament without taking an oath hateful to his conscience.

O'CONNELL ENTHRALLS AN IRISH MULTITUDE

[September, 1843]

After Daniel O'Connell and the Catholic Association had wrung political emancipation from a stubborn Parliament in 1829, O'Connell himself entered the House of Commons and participated in many of its reforms, in spite of his essential conservatism. But patiently he looked forward to the repeal of the Act of Union (1800) and the restoration of Grattan's Parliament, or some alternative pattern for Irish liberties.

A decade of patience was enough, and with the founding of the Repeal Association in 1840 he turned to his old weapon of peaceful agitation, but on a far-grander scale. Monstrous mass meetings (probably larger than any such gatherings in history until the use of the microphone in the twentieth century) convulsed Ireland. Repeal cavalry by the thousands marched the streets and stood guard when the liberator spoke. The British government grew apprehensive.

It is said that two hundred thousand gathered around O'Connell at Kilkenny, a million at Tara, four hundred thousand at Mullaghmast, yet always disciplined, always without violence. His agitation had reached an indescribable height when he made that final appeal at Mullaghmast.

> *"I will go slow—you must allow me to do so—*
> *but you will go sure."*

I ACCEPT with the greatest alacrity the high honor you have done
me in calling me to the chair of this majestic meeting. I feel more
honored than I ever did in my life, with one single exception, and that
related to, if possible, an equally majestic meeting at Tara. But I must
say that if a comparison were instituted between them, it would take a
more discriminating eye than mine to discover any difference between
them. There are the same incalculable numbers; there is the same firmness; there is the same determination; there is the same exhibition of love
to old Ireland; there is the same resolution not to violate the peace; not to
be guilty of the slightest outrage; not to give the enemy power by committing a crime, but peacefully and manfully to stand together in the
open day, to protest before man and in the presence of God against the
iniquity of continuing the Union.

At Tara, I protested against the Union—I repeat the protest at Mullaghmast. I declare solemnly my thorough conviction as a constitutional
lawyer that the Union is totally void in point of principle and of constitutional force. I tell you that no portion of the Empire had the power
to traffic on the rights and liberties of the Irish people. The Irish people
nominated them to make laws, and not legislatures. They were appointed
to act under the Constitution, and not annihilate it. Their delegation from
the people was confined within the limits of the Constitution, and the
moment the Irish Parliament went beyond those limits and destroyed
the Constitution, that moment it annihilated its own power, but could
not annihilate the immortal spirit of liberty, which belongs, as a rightful
inheritance, to the people of Ireland. Take it then from me that the Union
is void. I admit there is the force of a law, because it has been supported
by the policeman's truncheon, by the soldier's bayonet, and by the horse-
man's sword; because it is supported by the courts of law and those who
have power to adjudicate in them; but I say solemnly it is not supported
by constitutional right. The Union, therefore, in my thorough conviction,
is totally void, and I avail myself of this opportunity to announce to several hundreds of thousands of my fellow subjects that the Union is an
unconstitutional law and that it is not fated to last long—its hour is approaching. America offered us her sympathy and support. We refused
the support, but we accepted the sympathy; and while we accepted the
sympathy of the Americans, we stood upon the firm ground of the right

of every human being to liberty; and I, in the name of the Irish nation, declare that no support obtained from America should be purchased by the price of abandoning principle for one moment, and that principle is that every human being is entitled to freedom.

My friends, I want nothing for the Irish but their country, and I think the Irish are competent to obtain their own country for themselves. I like to have the sympathy of every good man everywhere, but I want not armed support or physical strength from any country. The republican party in France offered me assistance. I thanked them for their sympathy, but I distinctly refused to accept any support from them. I want support from neither France nor America, and if that usurper, Louis Philippe, who trampled on the liberties of his own gallant nation, thought fit to assail me in his newspaper, I returned the taunt with double vigor, and I denounce him to Europe and the world as a treacherous tyrant, who has violated the compact with his own country and therefore is not fit to assist the liberties of any other country. I want not the support of France; I want not the support of America; I have physical support enough about me to achieve any change; but you know well that it is not my plan—I will not risk the safety of one of you. I could not afford the loss of one of you—I will protect you all, and it is better for you all to be merry and alive, to enjoy the repeal of the Union; but there is not a man of you there that would not, if we were attacked unjustly and illegally, be ready to stand in the open field by my side. Let every man that concurs in that sentiment lift up his hand.

[All hands were lifted.]

The assertion of that sentiment is our sure protection, for no person will attack us, and we will attack nobody. Indeed, it would be the height of absurdity for us to think of making any attack; for there is not one man in his senses in Europe or America that does not admit that the repeal of the Union is now inevitable. The English papers taunted us, and their writers laughed us to scorn; but now they admit that it is impossible to resist the application for repeal. More power to you. But that even shows we have power enough to know how to use it. Why, it is only this week that one of the leading London newspapers, called *The Morning Herald,* which had a reporter at the Lismore meeting, published an account of that great and mighty meeting, and in that account the writer expressly says that it will be impossible to refuse so peaceable, so determined, so unanimous a people as the people of Ireland the restoration of their domestic legislature. For my own part, I would have thought it wholly unnecessary to call together so large a meeting as this, but for the trick played by Wellington, and Peel, and Graham, and Stanley, and the rest of the paltry administration, by whose government this country is disgraced. I don't suppose so worthless an administration ever before got together. Lord Stanley is a renegade from Whiggism, and Sir James Graham is worse. Sir Robert Peel has five hundred colors on his bad standard, and not one of them is permanent. Today it is orange, tomorrow it will be green, the day after neither one nor the other, but we shall take care that it shall never be dyed in blood.

Then there is the poor old Duke of Wellington, and nothing was ever so absurd as their deification of him in England. The English historian—rather the Scotch one—Alison, an arrant Tory, admits that the Duke of Wellington was surprised at Waterloo, and if he got victoriously out of that battle it was owing to the valor of the British troops and their unconquerable determination to die, but not to yield. No man is ever a good soldier but the man who goes into the battle determined to conquer or not come back from the battlefield. No other principle makes a good soldier; conquer or die is the battle cry for the good soldier; conquer or die is his only security. The Duke of Wellington had troops at Waterloo that had learned that word, and there were Irish troops amongst them. You all remember the verses made by the poor Shan Van Vocht:

> At famed Waterloo
> Duke Wellington would look blue
> If Paddy was not there too,
> Says the Shan Van Vocht.

Yes, the glory he got there was bought by the blood of the English, Irish, and Scotch soldiers—the glory was yours. He is nominally a member of the administration, but yet they would not intrust him with any kind of office. He has no duty at all to perform, but a sort of Irish anti-repeal warden. I thought I never would be obliged to the ministry, but I am obliged to them. They put a speech abusing the Irish into the Queen's mouth. They accused us of disaffection, but they lied; it is their speech; there is no disaffection in Ireland. We were loyal to the sovereigns of Great Britain even when they were our enemies; we were loyal to George III even when he betrayed us; we were loyal to George IV when he blubbered and cried when we forced him to emancipate us; we were loyal to old Billy, though his minister put into his mouth a base, bloody, and intolerant speech against Ireland; and we are loyal to the Queen, no matter what our enemies may say to the contrary. It is not the Queen's speech, and I pronounce it to be a lie. There is no dissatisfaction in Ireland, but there is this—a full determination to obtain justice and liberty.

I am much obliged to the ministry for that speech, for it gives me, amongst other things, an opportunity for addressing such meetings as this. I had held the monster meetings. I had fully demonstrated the opinion of Ireland. I was convinced their unanimous determination to obtain liberty was sufficiently signified by the many meetings already held; but when the minister's speech came out, it was necessary to do something more. Accordingly, I called a monster meeting in Loughrea. I called another meeting in Cliffden. I had another monster meeting in Lismore, and here now we are assembled on the Rath of Mullaghmast.

At Mullaghmast (and I have chosen this for this obvious reason), we are on the precise spot where English treachery—aye, and false Irish treachery, too—consummated a massacre that has never been imitated, save in the massacre of the Mamelukes by Mahomet Ali. It was necessary to have Turks atrocious enough to commit a crime equal to that perpetrated by Englishmen. But do not think that the massacre at Mullaghmast was a question between Protestants and Catholics—it was no such thing. The murdered persons were to be sure Catholics, but a great number of the murderers were also Catholic and Irishmen, because there were then, as well as now, many Catholics who were traitors to Ireland. But we have now this advantage, that we may have many honest Protestants joining us—joining us heartily in hand and heart, for old Ireland and liberty. I thought this a fit and becoming spot to celebrate, in the open day, our unanimity in declaring our determination not to be misled by any treachery. Oh, my friends, I will keep you clear of all treachery—there shall be no bargain, no compromise with England—we shall take nothing but repeal, and a parliament in College Green. You will never, by my advice, confide in any false hopes they hold out to you; never confide in anything coming from them, or cease from your struggle, no matter what promise may be held to you, until you hear me say I am satisfied; and I will tell you where I will say that—near the statue of King William, in College Green. No; we came here to express our determination to die to a man, if necessary, in the cause of old Ireland. We came to take advice of each other, and, above all, I believe you came here to take my advice. I can tell you I have the game in my hand—I have the triumph secure—I have the repeal certain, if you but obey my advice.

I will go slow—you must allow me to do so—but you will go sure. No man shall find himself imprisoned or persecuted who follows my advice. I have led you thus far in safety; I have swelled the multitude of repealers until they are identified with the entire population or nearly the entire population of the land, for seven eighths of the Irish people are now enrolling themselves repealers. I don't want more power; I have power enough; and all I ask of you is to allow me to use it. I will go on quietly and slowly, but I will go on firmly, and with a certainty of success. I am now arranging a plan for the formation of the Irish House of Commons.

It is a theory, but it is a theory that may be realized in three weeks. The repeal arbitrators are beginning to act; the people are submitting their differences to men chosen by themselves. You will see by the newspapers that Dr. Gray and my son and other gentlemen have already held a petty session of their own, where justice will be administered free of all expense to the people. The people shall have chosen magistrates of their own in the room of the magistrates who have been removed. The people shall submit their differences to them, and shall have strict justice administered to them that shall not cost them a single farthing. I shall go on with that plan until we have all disputes settled and decided by justices appointed by the people themselves. I wish to live long enough to have perfect justice administered to Ireland, and liberty proclaimed throughout the land. It will take me some time to prepare my plan for the formation of the new Irish House of Commons—that plan which we will yet submit to Her Majesty for her approval when she gets rid of her present paltry administration and has one that I can support. But I must finish that job before I go forth, and one of my reasons for calling you together is to state my intentions to you. Before I arrange my plan, the Conciliation Hall will be finished, and it will be worth any man's while to go from Mullaghmast to Dublin to see it.

When we have it arranged I will call together three hundred, as *The Times* called them, "bogtrotters," but better men never stepped on pavement. But I will have the three hundred, and no thanks to them. Wales is up at present, almost in a state of insurrection. The people there have found that the landlords' power is too great, and has been used tyranically, and I believe you agree with them tolerably well in that. They insist on the sacredness of the right of the tenants to security of possession, and with the equity of tenure which I would establish we will do the landlords full justice, but we will do the people justice also. We will recollect that the land is the landlord's, and let him have the benefit of it, but we will also recollect that the labor belongs to the tenant, and the tenant must have the value of his labor, not transitory and by the day, but permanently and by the year. Yes, my friends, for this purpose I must get some time. I worked the present repeal year tolerably well. I believe no one in January last would believe that we could have such a meeting within the year as the Tara demonstration. You may be sure of this—and I say it in the presence of Him who will judge me—that I never will willfully deceive you. I have but one wish under heaven, and that is for the liberty and prosperity of Ireland. I am for leaving England to the Eng-lish, Scotland to the Scotch, but we must have Ireland for the Irish. I will not be content until I see not a single man in any office, from the lowest constable to the lord chancellor, but Irishmen. This is our land, and we must have it. We will be obedient to the Queen, joined to England by the golden link of the Crown, but we must have our own parliament, our own bench, our own magistrates, and we will give some of the *shoneens* who now occupy the bench leave to retire, such as those lately appointed by Sugden [twice Lord Chancellor of Ireland]. He is a pretty boy, sent here from England; but I ask: did you ever hear such a name as he has got? I remember, in Wexford, a man told me he had a pig at home which he was so fond of that he would call it Sugden. No; we shall get judicial in-dependence for Ireland. It is for this purpose we are assembled here to-day, as every countenance I see around me testifies. If there is anyone here who is for the Union, let him say so. Is there anybody here for the repeal? [Cries of "All, all!"]

Yes, my friends, the Union was begot in iniquity—it was perpetuated in fraud and cruelty. It was no compact, no bargain, but it was an act of the most decided tyranny and corruption that was ever yet perpetrated. Trial by jury was suspended—the right of personal protection was at an end—courts-martial sat throughout the land—and the county of Kildare, among others, flowed with blood. Oh, my friends, listen now to the man of peace, who will never expose you to the power of your enemies. In 1798 there were some brave men, some valiant men, to head the people at large; but there were many traitors, who left the people in the power of their enemies. The Curragh of Kildare afforded an instance of the fate which Irishmen were to expect who confided in their Saxon enemies. Oh, it was an ill-organized, a premature, a foolish, and an absurd insurrection; but you have a leader now who never will allow you to commit any act so foolish or so destructive. How delighted do I feel with the thorough con-viction which has come over the minds of the people that they could not gratify your enemies more than by committing a crime. No; our ancestors suffered for confiding in the English, but we never will confide in them. They suffered for being divided amongst themselves. There is no division amongst us. They suffered for their own dissensions—for not standing man to man by each other's side. We shall stand peaceably side by side in the face of every enemy. Oh, how delighted was I in the scenes which I witnessed as I came along here today! How my heart throbbed, how my spirit was elevated, how my bosom swelled with delight at the multitude which I beheld, and which I shall behold, of the stalwart and strong men of Kildare! I was delighted at the activity and force that I saw around me, and my old heart grew warm again in admiring the beauty of the dark-eyed maids and matrons of Kildare. Oh, there is a starlight sparkling from the eye of a Kildare beauty that is scarcely equaled, and could not be excelled, all over the world. And remember that you are the sons, the fathers, the brothers, and the husbands of such women, and a traitor or a coward could never be connected with any of them. Yes, I am in a county remarkable in the history of Ireland for its bravery and its misfortune, for its credulity in the faith of others, for its people judged of the Saxon by the honesty and honor of their own natures. I am in a county celebrated for the sacredness of its shrines and fanes. I am in a county where the lamp of Kildare's holy shrine burned with its sacred fire through ages of darkness and storm—that fire which for six centuries burned before the high altar without being extinguished, being fed continuously, without the slightest interruption, and it seemed to me to have been not an inapt representation of the continuous fidelity and religious love of country of the men of Kildare. Yes, you have those high qualities—religious fidelity, continuous love of country. Even your enemies admit that the world has never produced any people that exceeded the Irish in activity and strength. The Scottish philosopher has declared, and the French philosopher has confirmed it, that number one in the human race is, blessed be heaven, the Irishman. In moral virtue, in religion, in perseverance, and in glorious temperance, you excel. Have I any teetotalers here? Yes, it is teetotalism that is repealing the Union. I could not afford to bring you together, I would not dare to bring you together, but that I had the teetotalers for my police.

Yes, among the nations of the earth, Ireland stands number one in the physical strength of her sons and in the beauty and purity of her daughters. Ireland, land of my forefathers, how my mind expands, and my spirit walks abroad in something of majesty, when I contemplate the high qualities, inestimable virtues, and true purity and piety and religious fidelity of the inhabitants of your green fields and productive mountains. Oh, what a scene surrounds us! It is not only the countless thousands of brave and active and peaceable and religious men that are here assembled, but nature herself has written her character with the finest beauty in the verdant plains that surround us. Let any man run round the horizon with his eye, and tell me if created nature ever produced anything so green and so lovely, so undulating, so teeming with production. The richest harvests that any land can produce are those reaped in Ireland; and then here are the sweetest meadows, the greenest fields, the loftiest mountains, the purest streams, the noblest rivers, the most capacious harbors—and her water power is equal to turn the machinery of the whole world. Oh, my friends, it is a country worth fighting for—it is a country worth dying for; but above all, it is a country worth being tranquil, determined, submissive, and docile for; disciplined as you are in obedience to those who are breaking the way, and trampling down the barriers between you and your constitutional liberty, I will see every man of you having a vote, and every man protected by the ballot from the agent or landlord. I will see labor protected, and every title to possession recognized, when you are industrious and honest. I will see prosperity again throughout your land —the busy hum of the shuttle and the tinkling of the smithy shall be heard again. We shall see the nailer employed even until the middle of the night, and the carpenter covering himself with his chips. I will see prosperity in all its gradations spreading through a happy, contented, religious land. I will hear the hymn of a happy people go forth at sunrise to God in praise of His mercies—and I will see the evening sun set down amongst the uplifted hands of a religious and free population. Every blessing that man can bestow and religion can confer upon the faithful heart shall spread throughout the land. Stand by me—join with me—I will say be obedient to me, and Ireland shall be free.

Another such meeting was planned for the following month near Dublin. But only twenty-four hours beforehand, it was forbidden, and all the approaches to the site were occupied by British troops. Angrily O'Connell called off the meeting, to prevent the possible slaughter of thousands.

Then O'Connell was arrested, tried for conspiracy before a packed Protestant jury, and imprisoned for a year before the House of Lords reversed the action of the court. When he came out of prison he was a broken old man nearing seventy. But even if he had recovered his health by some miracle, he could not have recovered his leadership, for his followers were now convinced that O'Connell's peaceful, "constitutional" methods were doomed to failure. Eighty years of bitterness and bloodshed lay ahead.

Ordered to a warmer climate, the repudiated leader decided to regain his health in southern climes. His destination was Rome, but he never reached there. He died at Genoa on March 15, 1847, in the third year of the Irish famine. His heart was buried in Rome, and his body, brought back to Ireland, was interred with almost royal honors.

The noblest tribute to the great orator was an oration delivered by Wendell Phillips in Boston on the centenary of O'Connell's birth. It is tempting to quote pages, but a paragraph must suffice:

"Broadly considered, his eloquence has never been equaled in modern times, certainly not in English speech. Do you think I am partial? I will vouch John Randolph of Roanoke, the Virginia slaveholder, who hated an Irishman almost as much as he hated a Yankee, himself an orator of no mean level. Hearing O'Connell, he exclaimed, 'This is the man, these are the lips, the most eloquent that speak English in my day.' I think he was right. I remember the solemnity of Webster, the grace of Everett, the rhetoric of Choate; I know the eloquence that lay hid in the iron logic of Calhoun; I have melted beneath the magnetism of Seargeant S. Prentiss, of Mississippi, who wielded a power few men ever had. It has been my fortune to sit at the feet of the great speakers of the English tongue on the other side of the ocean. But I think all of them together never surpassed, and no one of them ever equaled, O'Connell. Nature intended him for our Demosthenes. Never since the great Greek has she sent forth one so lavishly gifted for his work as a tribune of the people."

RICHARD COBDEN ARGUES FOR FREE TRADE AND AGAINST THE CORN LAWS

[January 15, 1846]

In the thirties and forties of the nineteenth century, in what the Hammonds have called "the Bleak Age," the masses of England were not concerned about Irish liberties or the Oxford Movement so much as about higher wages, shorter hours, and better factory conditions—about poverty, disease, and death. They were concerned specifically about lower prices on bread, which had been kept up since the Napoleonic wars by the Corn Laws (restrictions on the importation of wheat) passed to protect the wealthy landowners and farmers. The deadliest foe of the Corn Laws was a self-made man—a textile manufacturer of Manchester, Richard Cobden (1804–65).

Cobden's early business success freed him for study, travel, and public service. He was one of the chief founders of the Anti-Corn Law Association in 1838, and in 1841 he entered Parliament. That autumn, while visiting relatives in Leamington, he called on another young manufacturer, John Bright, whose wife had died three days earlier. After expressing his sympathy, Cobden looked up and said: "There are thousands of houses in England at this moment where wives, mothers, and children are dying of hunger. Now, when the first paroxysm of your grief is past, I would advise you to come with me, and we will never rest until the Corn Law is repealed."

Bright accepted the invitation, and for five years this remarkable team, unique in history, traveled the length and breadth of England, agitating, educat-

ing, convincing. Where Bright was passionate, intense, Cobden was cool, logical, friendly, with none of the bitterness or violence of the typical agitator. And yet few speakers—and probably none who spoke on political economy—have ever won such rapt attention.

Cobden was at his best during the House of Commons debate on the Corn Laws in 1845. While listening to him, Sir Robert Peel, the Conservative Prime Minister, made notes, then crumpled them up, and said to a lieutenant: "You must answer this, for I cannot."

As the campaign for repeal was drawing to a close in the early winter of 1846, Cobden appeared once more before a large gathering in Manchester.

"I have been accused of looking too much to material interests."

I BELIEVE that if you abolish the Corn Law honestly, and adopt free trade in its simplicity, there will not be a tariff in Europe that will not be changed in less than five years to follow your example. Well, gentlemen, suppose the Corn Law be not abolished immediately, but that Sir Robert Peel bring in a measure giving you a duty of five shillings, six shillings, or seven shillings, and going down one shilling a year for four or five years, till the whole duty is abolished, what would be the effect on foreign countries? They will then exaggerate the importance of this market when the duty is wholly off. They will go on raising supplies, calculating that, when the duty is wholly off, they will have a market for their produce and high prices to remunerate them; and if, as is very likely and consistent with our experience, we should have a return to abundant seasons, these vast importations will be poured upon our markets, probably just at the time when our prices are low; and they would come here, because they would have no other market, to swamp our markets, and deprive the farmer of the sale of his produce at a remunerating price. But, on the contrary, let the Corn Law be abolished instantly; let foreigners see what the English market is in its natural state, and then they will be able to judge from year to year and from season to season what will be the future demand from this country for foreign corn. There will be no extravagant estimate of what we want—no contingency of bad harvests to speculate upon. The supply will be regulated by the demand, and will reach that state which will be the best security against both gluts and famine. Therefore, for the farmer's sake, I plead for the immediate abolition of this law. A farmer never can have a fair and equitable understanding or adjustment with his landlord, whether as respects rent, tenure, or game, until this law is wholly removed out of his way. Let the repeal be gradual, and the landlord will say to the farmer, through the land agent, "Oh, the duty will be seven shillings next year; you have not had more than twelvemonths' experience of the workings of the system yet"; and the farmer goes away without any settlement having been come to. Another year passes over, and when the farmer presents himself, he is told, "Oh, the duty will be five shillings this year; I cannot yet tell what the effect will be; you must stop awhile." The next year the same thing is repeated, and the end is that there is no adjustment of any kind between the landlord and tenant. But put it at once on a natural footing, abolish all restrictions, and the landlord and tenant will be brought to a prompt settlement; they will be placed precisely on the same footing as you are in your manufactures.

Well, I have now spoken on what may be done. I have told you, too, what I should advocate; but I must say that whatever is proposed by Sir Robert Peel, we, as free traders, have but one course to pursue. If he propose a total and immediate and unconditional repeal, we shall throw up our caps for Sir Robert Peel. If he propose anything else, then Mr. Villiers will be ready, as he has been on former occasions, to move his amendment for a total and immediate repeal of the Corn Laws. We are not responsible for what ministers may do; we are but responsible for the performance of our duty. We don't offer to do impossibilities; but we will do our utmost to carry out our principles. But, gentlemen, I tell you honestly, I think less of what this Parliament may do—I care less for their opinions, less for the intentions of the Prime Minister and the cabinet—than what may be the opinion of a meeting like this and of the people out of doors. This question will not be carried by ministers or by the present Parliament; it will be carried, when it is carried, by the will of the nation. We will do nothing that can remove us a hair's-breadth from the rock which we have stood upon with so much safety for the last seven years. All other parties have been on a quicksand, and floated about by every wave, by every tide, and by every wind—some floating to us; others, like fragments scattered over the ocean, without rudder or compass; whilst we are upon solid ground, and no temptation, whether of parties or of ministers, shall ever make us swerve a hair's-breadth. I am anxious to hear now, at the last meeting before we go to Parliament—before we enter that arena to which all men's minds will be turned during the next week—I am anxious, not merely that we should all of us understand each other on this question, but that we should be considered as occupying as independent and isolated a position as we did at the first moment of the formation of this [Anti-Corn Law] League. We have nothing to do with Whigs or Tories; we are stronger than either of them; if we stick to our principles, we can, if necessary, beat both. And I hope we perfectly understand now that we have not, in the advocacy of this great question, a single object in view but that which we have honestly avowed from the beginning. Our opponents may charge us with designs to do other things. No, gentlemen, I have never encouraged that. Some of my friends have said, "When this work is done you will have some influence in the country; you must do so and so." I said then, as I say now, "Every new political principle must have its special advocates, just as every new faith has its martyrs." It is a mistake to suppose that this organization can be turned to other purposes. It is a mistake to suppose that men prominent in the advocacy of the principle of free trade can with the same force and effect identify themselves with any other principle hereafter. It will be enough if the League accomplish the triumph of the principle we have before us. I have never taken a limited view of the object or scope of this great principle. I have never advocated this question very much as a trader.

But I have been accused of looking too much to material interests. Nevertheless, I can say that I have taken as large and great a view of the effects of this mighty principle as ever did any man who dreamed over it in his own study. I believe that the physical gain will be the smallest gain to humanity from the success of this principle. I look farther; I see in the free-trade principle that which shall act on the moral world as the principle of gravitation in the universe—drawing men together, thrusting aside the antagonism of race and creed and language, and uniting us in the bonds of eternal peace. I have looked even farther. I have speculated, and probably dreamed, in the dim future—aye, a thousand years hence—I have speculated on what the effect of the triumph of this principle may be. I believe that the effect will be to change the face of the world, so as to introduce a system of government entirely distinct from that which now prevails. I believe that the desire and the motive for large and mighty empires—for gigantic armies and great navies—for those materials which are used for the destruction of life and the desolation of the rewards of labor—will die away; I believe that such things will cease to be necessary, or to be used, when man becomes one family and freely exchanges the fruits of his labor with his brother man. I believe that, if we could be allowed to reappear on this sublunary scene, we should see, at a far-distant period, the governing system of this world revert to something like the municipal system; and I believe that the speculative philosopher of a thousand years hence will date the greatest revolution that ever happened in the world's history from the triumph of the principle which we

have met here to advocate. I believe these things; but, whatever may
have been my dreams and speculations, I have never obtruded them upon
others. I have never acted upon personal or interested motives in this
question; I seek no alliance with parties or favor from parties, and I will
take none—but, having the feeling I have of the sacredness of the principle, I say that I can never agree to tamper with it. I, at least, will never
be suspected of doing otherwise than pursuing it disinterestedly, honestly, and resolutely.

*In this way Cobden, Bright, and their colleagues had been molding public
opinion for years. When the debate was resumed in Parliament a few months
later, Prime Minister Peel reversed his stand of the previous year, to the horror
of his Conservative followers, and helped carry Cobden's total-repeal bill to
victory.*

ALEXIS DE TOCQUEVILLE FEELS "A GALE
OF REVOLUTION IN THE AIR"

[January 29, 1848]

*On May 11, 1831, in the second year of Jackson's first term, two young French
aristocrats, Alexis de Tocqueville and Gustave de Beaumont, landed in New
York City, after a thirty-eight-day voyage from Le Havre. They had come
officially to study our prison system, especially at Ossining and Philadelphia,
but their deeper interest lay in the whole picture of American democracy, political, economic, social. Aristocrats though they were, they realized that the
march of democracy was inevitable, "providential," and they wanted to bring
back to France lessons from the American model. They were glad to get away
from France at this particular moment because the bourgeois revolution of
July, 1830, had made their positions uncomfortable. Reluctantly, they had
taken the oath of allegiance twice to Louis Philippe, the Orleanist who had
replaced the Bourbon Charles X, and hurried away.*

*For nine months they traveled tirelessly about the United States and then
returned to France to make their joint report on American prisons. In 1835 the
first two volumes of Tocqueville's De la Démocratie en Amérique appeared before his thirtieth birthday, the third and final volume in 1840. "The first
philosophical book ever written on democracy, as it manifests itself in modern
society," according to John Stuart Mill, and still the best book probably ever*

written about the United States by a foreigner, it at once made a profound impression and became a classic. "I confess," said the young author in his preface, "that in America I saw more than America; I sought the image of democracy itself, with its inclinations, its character, its prejudices, and its passions, in order to learn what we have to fear or to hope from its progress."

Too frail, sensitive, introspective, to be a powerful leader or orator, Tocqueville felt it his duty to go into politics, and in 1839 he was elected to the French Chamber of Deputies from his native district. Nine years later he made a prophetic speech in the Chamber. We quote his own abridged version from his personal Recollections of the turbulent year 1848.

"It is in such times as these that you remain calm before the degradation of public morality."

I AM TOLD that there is no danger because there are no riots; I am told that, because there is no visible disorder on the surface of society, there is no revolution at hand.

Gentlemen, permit me to say that I believe you are mistaken. True, there is no actual disorder; but it has entered deeply into men's minds. See what is preparing itself amongst the working classes, who, I grant, are at present quiet. No doubt they are not disturbed by political passions, properly so called, to the same extent that they have been; but can you not see that their passions, instead of political, have become social? Do you not see that they are gradually forming opinions and ideas that are destined not only to upset this or that law, ministry, or even form of government, but society itself, until it totters upon the foundations on which it rests today? Do you not listen to what they say to themselves each day? Do you not hear them repeating unceasingly that all that is above them is incapable and unworthy of governing them; that the distribution of goods prevalent until now throughout the world is unjust; that property rests on a foundation that is not an equitable one? And do you not realize that when such opinions take root, when they spread in an almost universal manner, when they sink deeply into the masses, they are bound to bring with them sooner or later, I know not when or how, a most formidable revolution?

This, gentlemen, is my profound conviction: I believe that we are at this moment sleeping on a volcano. I am profoundly convinced of it. . . .

I was saying just now that this evil would sooner or later, I know not how or whence it will come, bring with it a most serious revolution: be assured that that is so.

When I come to investigate what, at different times, in different periods, among different peoples, has been the effective cause that has brought about the downfall of the governing classes, I perceive this or that event, man, or accidental or superficial cause; but, believe me, the real reason, the effective reason that causes men to lose political power is that they have become unworthy to retain it.

Think, gentlemen, of the old monarchy: it was stronger than you are, stronger in its origin; it was able to lean more than you do upon ancient customs, ancient habits, ancient beliefs; it was stronger than you are, and yet it has fallen to dust. And why did it fall? Do you think it was by particular mischance? Do you think it was by the act of some man, by the deficit, the oath in the tennis court, Lafayette, Mirabeau? No, gentlemen; there was another reason: the class that was then the governing class had become, through its indifference, its selfishness, and its vices, incapable and unworthy of governing the country.

That was the true reason.

Well, gentlemen, if it is right to have this patriotic prejudice at all times, how much more is it not right to have it in our own? Do you not feel, by some intuitive instinct that is not capable of analysis, but that is undeniable, that the earth is quaking once again in Europe? Do you not feel—what shall I say?—as it were a gale of revolution in the air? This gale, no one knows whence it springs, whence it blows, nor, believe me, whom it will carry with it; and it is in such times as these that you remain calm before the degradation of public morality—for the expression is not too strong.

I speak here without bitterness; I am even addressing you without any party spirit; I am attacking men against whom I feel no vindictiveness. But I am obliged to communicate to my country my firm and profound conviction. Well, then, my firm and profound conviction is this: that public morality is being degraded, and that the degradation of public morality will shortly, very shortly perhaps, bring down upon you new revolutions. Is the life of kings held by stronger threads? And these more difficult to snap than those of other men? Can you say today that you are certain of tomorrow? Do you know what may happen in France a year hence, or even a month or a day hence? You do not know; but what you must know is that the tempest is looming on the horizon, that it is coming toward us. Will you allow it to take you by surprise?

Gentlemen, I implore you not to do so. I do not ask you, I implore you. I would gladly throw myself on my knees before you, so strongly do

I believe in the reality and the seriousness of the danger, so convinced am I that my warnings are no empty rhetoric. Yes, the danger is great. Allay it while there is yet time; correct the evil by efficacious remedies, by attacking it not in its symptoms, but in itself.

Legislative changes have been spoken of. I am greatly disposed to think that these changes are not only very useful, but necessary; thus, I believe in the need of electoral reform, in the urgency of parliamentary reform; but I am not, gentlemen, so mad as not to know that no laws can affect the destinies of nations. No, it is not the mechanism of laws that produces great events, gentlemen, but the inner spirit of the government. Keep the laws as they are, if you wish. I think you would be very wrong to do so; but keep them. Keep the men, too, if it gives you any pleasure. I raise no objection so far as I am concerned. But, in God's name, change the spirit of the government; for, I repeat, that spirit will lead you to the abyss.

"These gloomy predictions," wrote Tocqueville, "were received with ironical cheers from the majority. The opposition applauded loudly, but more from party feeling than from conviction. The truth is that no one as yet believed seriously in the danger I was prophesying, although we were so near the catastrophe. The inveterate habit contracted by all the politicians, during this long parliamentary comedy, of overcoloring the expression of their opinion and grossly exaggerating their thoughts had deprived them of all power of appreciating what was real and true. For several years the majority had every day been declaring that the opposition was imperiling society; and the opposition repeated incessantly that the ministers were ruining the monarchy. These statements had been made so constantly on both sides, without either side greatly believing in them, that they ended by not believing in them at all, at the very moment when the event was about to justify both of them. Even my own friends thought that I had overshot the mark, and that my facts were a little blurred by rhetoric.

"I remember that, when I stepped from the tribune, Dufaure took me on one side, and said, with that sort of parliamentary intuition which is his only note of genius: 'You have succeeded, but you would have succeeded much more if you had not gone so far beyond the feeling of the Assembly and tried to frighten us.'"

A month later Louis Philippe's bourgeois monarchy of nearly twenty years fell like a ripe, or rather like a rotten, apple. It was mercenary, corrupt, peculiarly ignoble, but its demise was so sudden that no one of his various groups of enemies was prepared to take the credit for his fall or to take over the government. During the transition, the popular romantic poet and historian, the operatic politician, Alphonse de Lamartine, addressed the milling, capricious street crowds of Paris. From windows and balconies he defied and cajoled, he inspired, charmed, and seduced, but he did not have the strength of character or the political skill to stabilize his position. It was time for harder, more responsible men, as the bourgeoisie and the workers of Paris drew apart and took to opposite sides of the barricades. General Cavaignac settled the issue with rifles and cannon. In December Louis Napoleon was elected President of the second French Republic. Lamartine received less than half of one per cent of the number of votes received by Napoleon.

Tocqueville's predictions appear to have been justified.

MAZZINI MOURNS FOR MARTYRS OF
ITALIAN LIBERTY

[July 25, 1848]

Nationalism, which once seemed to be the generous hope of the world, and now seems to be its inescapable curse, has passed through a series of overlapping stages during the past two hundred years. Carlton J. H. Hayes has labeled these stages: (1) Humanitarian Nationalism, (2) Jacobin [French Revolutionary] Nationalism, (3) Traditional Nationalism, (4) Liberal Nationalism, and (5) Integral [extreme, chauvinistic] Nationalism. The most exalted expression of the liberal form—indeed, of all the forms of nationalism—lay in Mazzini's vision of a united Italy, an Italian republic that would flourish only while other nations flourished.

Awakened by the spirit of the French Revolution and liberated from petty kings and princes by the all-conquering arms of Napoleon, Italy after Waterloo was again fragmentized and placed under the iron guardianship of Austria. To throw off this yoke the Carbonari, a secret society dedicated to the cause of Italian liberty, worked for years with zeal and melodramatic inefficiency.

Giuseppe Mazzini (1805–72), the son of a prosperous Genoese physician, put on black, in mourning for his country, while studying law at the University of Genoa. After joining the Carbonari, he was arrested on the charge of conspiracy and imprisoned without trial for six months. He was then acquitted and given the choice of exile or residence in a remote Italian village. He chose exile. It was at Marseilles in 1831 that he established "Young Italy," a lifelong conspiracy to liberate and unify his country. It was from London that he sent out his numberless letters and pamphlets, to prepare the way, nearly a quarter of a century later, for the Italy of Cavour and Victor Emmanuel II.

Only for a little more than a year, in 1848 and 1849, was the great dreamer to experience face-to-face contact with thousands he had inspired, and the undreamlike problems of administration. With the fall of Louis Philippe he was able to hasten back to Italy, and to rejoice with the Milanese after the glorious Five Days when they drove out the hated Austrians. His noble speech, though a paean of joy for the liberation, also commemorates the Bandiera brothers, executed in 1844 for a premature attempt to start a revolution in the Kingdom of the Two Sicilies. Since it was Mazzini himself who inspired the Bandieras (their correspondence with him was intercepted, and so led to the discovery of their plans), his words have a peculiar poignancy.

He now speaks before a mass meeting in Milan.

"Love humanity. . . . You cannot rightly love your brethren of the cradle if you love not the common mother."

WHEN I was commissioned by you, young men, to proffer in this temple a few words sacred to the memory of the brothers Bandiera and their fellow martyrs at Cosenza, I thought that some of those who heard me might exclaim with noble indignation: "Wherefore lament over the dead? The martyrs of liberty are only worthily honored by winning the battle they have begun; Cosenza, the land where they fell, is enslaved; Venice, the city of their birth, is begirt by foreign foes. Let us emancipate them, and until that moment let no words pass our lips save words of war."

But another thought arose: "Why have we not conquered? Why is it that, while we are fighting for independence in the north of Italy, liberty is perishing in the south? Why is it that a war that should have sprung to the Alps with the bound of a lion has dragged itself along for four months with the slow uncertain motion of the scorpion surrounded by a circle of fire? How has the rapid and powerful intuition of a people newly arisen to life been converted into the weary helpless effort of the sick man turning from side to side? Ah! had we all arisen in the sanctity of the idea for which our martyrs died; had the holy standard of their faith preceded our youth to battle; had we reached that unity of life which was in them so powerful, and made of our every action a thought, and of our every thought an action; had we devoutly gathered up their last words in our hearts, and learned from them that Liberty and Independence are one, that God and the People, the Fatherland and Humanity, are the two inseparable terms of the device of every people striving to become a nation; that Italy can have no true life till she be one, holy in the equality and love of all her children, great in the worship of eternal truth, and consecrated to a lofty mission, a moral priesthood among the peoples of Europe—we should now have had, not war, but victory; Cosenza would not be compelled to venerate the memory of her martyrs in secret, nor Venice be restrained from honoring them with a monument; and we, gathered here together, might gladly invoke their sacred names, without uncertainty as to our future destiny, or a cloud of sadness on our brows, and say to those precursor souls: "Rejoice! for your spirit is incarnate in your brethren, and they are worthy of you."

The idea they worshiped, young men, does not as yet shine forth in its full purity and integrity upon your banner. The sublime program they, dying, bequeathed to the rising Italian generation is yours; but mutilated, broken up into fragments by the false doctrines that, elsewhere overthrown, have taken refuge amongst us. I look around, and I see the struggles of desperate populations, an alternation of generous rage and of unworthy repose; of shouts for freedom and of formulas of servitude, throughout all parts of our peninsula; but the soul of the country, where is it? What unity is there in this unequal and manifold movement—where is the word that should dominate the hundred diverse and opposing counsels that mislead or seduce the multitude? I hear phrases usurping the national omnipotence—"The Italy of the North—the League of the States—Federative compacts between Princes," but Italy, where is it? Where is the common country, the country the Bandiera hailed as thrice initiatrix of a new era of European civilization?

Intoxicated with our first victories, improvident for the future, we forgot the idea revealed by God to those who suffered; and God has punished our forgetfulness by deferring our triumph. The Italian movement, my countrymen, is, by decree of Providence, that of Europe. We arise to give a pledge of moral progress to the European world. But neither political fictions, nor dynastic aggrandizements, nor theories of expediency, can transform or renovate the life of the peoples. Humanity lives and moves through faith; great principles are the guiding stars that lead Europe toward the future. Let us turn to the graves of our martyrs, and ask inspiration of those who died for us all, and we shall find the secret of victory in the adoration of a faith. The angel of martyrdom and the angel of victory are brothers; but the one looks up to heaven, and the other looks down to earth; and it is when, from epoch to epoch, their glance meets between earth and heaven, that creation is embellished with a new life, and a people arises from the cradle or the tomb, evangelist or prophet.

I will sum up for you in a few words this faith of our martyrs; their external life is known to you all; it is now a matter of history, and I need not recall it to you.

The faith of the brothers Bandiera, which was and is our own, was based upon a few simple uncontrovertible truths, which few, indeed, venture to declare false, but which are nevertheless forgotten or betrayed by most:

God and the People.

God at the summit of the social edifice; the people, the universality of our brethren, at the base. God, the Father and Educator; the people, the progressive interpreter of his law.

No true society can exist without a common belief and a common aim. Religion declares the belief and the aim. Politics regulate society in the practical realization of that belief, and prepare the means of attaining that aim. Religion represents the principle, politics the application. There is but one sun in heaven for all the earth. There is one law for all those who people the earth. It is alike the law of the human being and of collective humanity. We are placed here below, not for the capricious exercise of our own individual faculties—our faculties and liberty are the means, not the end—not to work out our own happiness upon earth; happiness can only be reached elsewhere, and there God works for us; but to consecrate our existence to the discovery of a portion of the divine law; to practice it as far as our individual circumstances and powers allow, and to diffuse the knowledge and love of it among our brethren.

We are here below to labor fraternally to build up the unity of the human family, so that the day may come when it shall represent a single sheepfold with a single shepherd—the spirit of God, the Law.

To aid our search after truth, God has given to us tradition and the voice of our own conscience. Wherever they are opposed is error. To attain harmony and consistence between the conscience of the individual and the conscience of humanity, no sacrifice is too great. The family, the city, the fatherland, and humanity are but different spheres in which to exercise our activity and our power of sacrifice toward this great aim. God watches from above the inevitable progress of humanity, and from time to time He raises up the great in genius, in love, in thought, or in action as priests of His truth and guides to the multitude on their way.

These principles—indicated in their letters, in their proclamations, and in their conversation—with a profound sense of the mission intrusted by God to the individual and to humanity, were to Attilio and Emilio Bandiera, and their fellow martyrs, the guide and comfort of a weary life; and, when men and circumstances had alike betrayed them, these principles sustained them in death, in religious serenity and calm certainty of the realization of their immortal hopes for the future of Italy. The immense energy of their souls arose from the intense love which informed their faith. And could they now arise from the grave and speak to you, they would, believe me, address you, though with a power very different from that which is given to me, in counsel not unlike this which I now offer to you.

Love! love is the flight of the soul toward God; toward the great, the sublime, and the beautiful, which are the shadow of God upon earth. Love your family, the partner of your life, those around you ready to share your joys and sorrows; love the dead who were dear to you and to whom you were dear. But let your love be the love taught you by Dante and by us—the love of souls that aspire together; do not grovel on the earth in search of a felicity that it is not the destiny of the creature to reach here below; do not yield to a delusion that inevitably would degrade you into egotism. To love is to give and take a promise for the future. God has given us love, that the weary soul may give and receive support upon the way of life. It is a flower springing up on the path of duty; but it cannot change its course. Purify, strengthen, and improve yourselves by loving. Act always—even at the price of increasing her earthly trials—so that the sister soul united to your own may never need, here or elsewhere, to blush through you or for you. The time will come when, from the height of a new life, embracing the whole past and comprehending its secret, you will smile together at the sorrows you have endured, the trials you have overcome.

Love your country. Your country is the land where your parents sleep, where is spoken that language in which the chosen of your heart, blushing, whispered the first word of love; it is the home that God has given you, that by striving to perfect yourselves therein you may prepare to ascend to Him. It is your name, your glory, your sign among the people. Give to it your thoughts, your counsels, your blood. Raise it up, great and beautiful as it was foretold by our great men, and see that you leave it uncontaminated by any trace of falsehood or of servitude; unprofaned by dismemberment. Let it be one, as the thought of God. You are twenty-five millions of men, endowed with active, splendid faculties; possessing a tradition of glory the envy of the nations of Europe. An immense future is before you; you lift your eyes to the loveliest heaven, and around you smiles the loveliest land in Europe; you are encircled by the Alps and the sea, boundaries traced out by the finger of God for a people of giants—you are bound to be such, or nothing. Let not a man of that twenty-five millions remain excluded from the fraternal bond destined to join you together; let not a glance be raised to that heaven which is not the glance of a free man. Let Rome be the ark of your redemption, the temple of your nation. Has she not twice been the temple of the destinies of Europe? In Rome two extinct worlds, the pagan and the papal, are superposed like the double jewels of a diadem; draw from these a third world greater than the two. From Rome, the holy city, the city of love, the purest and wisest among you, elected by the vote and fortified by the inspiration of a whole people, shall dictate the pact that shall make us one and represent us in the future alliance of the peoples. Until then you will either have no country or have her contaminated and profaned.

Love humanity. You can only ascertain your own mission from the aim set by God before humanity at large. God has given you your country as cradle, and humanity as mother; you cannot rightly love your brethren of the cradle if you love not the common mother. Beyond the Alps, beyond the sea, are other peoples now fighting or preparing to fight the holy fight of independence, of nationality, of liberty; other peoples striving by different routes to reach the same goal—improvement, association, and the foundation of an authority that shall put an end to moral anarchy and relink earth to heaven; an authority that mankind may love and obey without remorse or shame. Unite with them; they will unite with you. Do not invoke their aid where your single arm will suffice to conquer; but say to them that the hour will shortly sound for a terrible struggle between right and blind force, and that in that hour you will ever be found with those who have raised the same banner as yourselves.

And love, young men, love and venerate the ideal. The ideal is the word of God. High above every country, high above humanity, is the country of the spirit, the city of the soul, in which all are brethren who believe in the inviolability of thought and in the dignity of our immortal soul; and the baptism of this fraternity is martyrdom. From that high sphere spring the principles that alone can redeem the peoples. Arise for the sake of these, and not from impatience of suffering or dread of evil. Anger, pride, ambition, and the desire of material prosperity are arms common alike to the peoples and their oppressors, and even should you conquer with these today, you would fall again tomorrow; but principles belong to the peoples alone, and their oppressors can find no arms to oppose them. Adore enthusiasm, the dreams of the virgin soul, and the visions of early youth, for they are a perfume of paradise that the soul retains in issuing from the hands of its Creator. Respect above all things your conscience; have upon your lips the truth implanted by God in your hearts, and, while laboring in harmony, even with those who differ from you, in all that tends to the emancipation of our soil, yet ever bear your own banner erect and boldly promulgate your own faith.

Such words, young men, would the martyrs of Cosenza have spoken, had they been living amongst you; and here, where it may be that, invoked by our love, their holy spirits hover near us, I call upon you to gather them up in your hearts and to make of them a treasure amid the storms that yet threaten you; storms that, with the name of our martyrs on your lips and their faith in your hearts, you will overcome.

God be with you, and bless Italy!

As Mazzini paid homage to the martyred Bandiera brothers, and steeled young Italians to their great resolve of unity and freedom, the revolutionary movement in Europe had reached its peak. Throughout Germany and Italy, liberals drew up constitutions, the various governments wavered helplessly, unable to stem the tide, and absolutism was soon in retreat right up to the Russian borders. But the impossible dream, which seemed on the point of fulfillment, was threatened by the clash of republicans and monarchists and by other rifts within the ranks of the revolutionaries. In Bohemia the revolution was soon defeated, but in Italy the coalition of forces under Charles Albert of Piedmont seemed on the point of victory. The Piedmontese were granted a comparatively liberal constitution; in Rome, as one of the Triumvirate, Mazzini became the most commanding voice. Although the enemies of the Roman Republic described its leaders as bandits and schemers, the evidence, as William Roscoe Thayer remarks (Life and Times of Cavour), is quite to the contrary: "During the three months of Mazzini's virtual dictatorship, the Eternal City enjoyed, in spite of the turmoil of political revolution and the abnormal conditions of a siege, a better government than it had known since Marcus Aurelius died, nearly seventeen hundred years before."

By June 30, 1849, however, French troops closed in on Rome, and when it became evident that they could not be dislodged from their entrenched positions, and that their cannon could reduce the city to ashes, a truce was arranged. Mazzini then addressed the Assembly, pointing out that three courses of action remained: to surrender, to die fighting in the streets, or to make a mass exodus into the mountains. Garibaldi now entered the Assembly, his red shirt covered with the dust and blood of battle, and demanded that the third course be followed. No legislative body, however, could be expected to order such a universal sacrifice, and capitulation was accordingly decided.

While Mazzini remained to protest, Garibaldi galloped off to muster a band of heroes dedicated in life and death to the hopeless battle. Before a vast crowd of Romans his dramatic voice rang out: "Fortune, who betrays us today, will

smile on us tomorrow. I am going out from Rome. Let those who wish to continue the war against the stranger come with me. I offer neither pay, nor
quarters, nor provisions; I offer hunger, thirst, forced marches, battles, and
death. Let him who loves his country in his heart, and not with his lips only,
follow me."

KOSSUTH, A MILITANT EXILE, CALLS FOR
AID TO DOWNTRODDEN HUNGARY

[December 6, 1851]

"And yet when Paris stirred [overthrowing Louis Philippe in February, 1848],
and I made a mere speech in the Hungarian Parliament, the house of Austria
was presently at the mercy of the people of Vienna; Metternich was driven
away, and his absolutism replaced by a promise of constitutional life." Thus the
exiled Kossuth, with justifiable pride, once described to an American audience
the beginning of his moment in European history. Rarely has an orator had
such a brilliant career in so brief a time.

An obscure provincial lawyer of the poorer, landless nobility, Louis Kossuth
(1802–94) entered politics, ironically enough, as the silent deputy of an
absentee count in the Hungarian Diet. But he soon found expression in editing
a pioneer journal that was so critical of the Austrian government that he was
put into prison for three years—three invaluable years for the study of history,
literature, and the English language. He came out of prison, to continue agitation in print and in speeches, and finally entered the Diet in his own right in
1847. It was in the following year, on March 3, that he delivered the climactic
speech demanding a constitution for the whole Austrian Empire and a separate
financial ministry for Hungary. The immediate consequences were the rising of
the people of Vienna, the fall of Metternich, and "the promise of constitutional
life." But the Hapsburgs and their tools did not keep their promise, and within
a few months Hungary was in full revolt under Kossuth's leadership.

He proved to be magnificent not only as an orator arousing his people to
resistance, but also as an organizer improvising finances and hurling armies into
the field. All the liberal world watched this eruption within the age-old
autocracy. But it was destined to fail, not only because of the tragic conflict between Kossuth and his chief general, but also because of the intervention of
Russia, always anxious to prop up a crumbling throne. There was a fatal flaw in
Kossuth's vision. An extreme "racist" before our time, he was so fanatical about

the liberties of the Magyars, the "pure" Hungarians, that he outraged the feelings of the Croats, the Slovaks, the Rumanians, and the Germans, who together constituted a large part of the population of Hungary. Consequently, Kossuth's Hungary was poisoned from within before it was crushed from without by Austria and Russia.

With some five thousand fugitives Kossuth escaped to Turkey, where he was interned until 1851, when he was liberated by an American warship. France refused him sanctuary, so he was finally landed at Southampton. Then began his spectacular quest for help in England and the United States. After receiving the plaudits of thousands in England, but no practical encouragement for the Hungarian cause, Kossuth, still hopeful, sailed for the United States. The day after landing, he spoke in New York, at the Battery, before a vociferous crowd of one hundred thousand.

"Humble as I am, God the Almighty has selected me to represent the cause of humanity before you."

LET ME, before I go to work, have some hours of rest upon this soil of freedom, your happy home. Freedom and home; what heavenly music in those two words! Alas! I have no home, and the freedom of my people is downtrodden. Young giant of free America, do not tell me that thy shores are an asylum to the oppressed and a home to the homeless exile. An asylum it is; but all the blessings of your glorious country, can they drown into oblivion the longing of the heart and the fond desires for our native land? My beloved native land! thy very sufferings make thee but dearer to my heart; thy bleeding image dwells with me when I wake, as it rests with me in the short moments of my restless sleep. It has accompanied me over the waves. It will accompany me when I go back to fight over again the battle of thy freedom once more. I have no idea but thee; I have no feeling but thee.

Even here, with this prodigious view of greatness, freedom, and happiness which spreads before my astonished eyes, my thoughts are wandering toward home; and when I look over these thousands of thousands before me, the happy inheritance of yonder freedom for which your fathers fought and bled—and when I turn to you, citizens, to bow before the majesty of the United States, and to thank the people of New York for their generous share in my liberation, and for the unparalleled honor of this reception—I see, out of the very midst of this great assemblage,

rise the bleeding image of Hungary, looking to you with anxiety, whether
there be in the luster of your eyes a ray of hope for her; whether there be
in the thunder of your huzzas a trumpet call of resurrection. If there were
no such ray of hope in your eyes, and no such trumpet call in your cheers,
then woe to Europe's oppressed nations. They will stand alone in the
hour of need. Less fortunate than you were, they will meet no brother's
hand to help them in the approaching giant struggle against the leagued
despots of the world; and woe, also, to me. I will feel no joy even here;
and the days of my stay here will turn out to be lost to my fatherland—
lost at the very time when every moment is teeming in the decision of
Europe's destiny.

Gentlemen, I have to thank the people, Congress, and government of
the United States for my liberation from captivity. Human tongue has no
words to express the bliss which I felt when I—the downtrodden Hungary's wandering chief—saw the glorious flag of the Stripes and Stars
fluttering over my head—when I first bowed before it with deep respect
—when I saw around me the gallant officers and the crew of the *Mississippi* frigate—the most of them the worthiest representatives of true
American principles, American greatness, American generosity—and to
think that it was not a mere chance which cast the Star-Spangled Banner
around me, but that it was your protecting will—to know that the United
States of America, conscious of their glorious calling, as well as of their
power, declared, by this unparalleled act, to be resolved to become the
protectors of human rights—to see a powerful vessel of America coming
to far Asia to break the chains by which the mightiest despots of Europe
fettered the activity of an exiled Magyar, whose very name disturbed the
proud security of their sleep—to feel restored by such a protection, and,
in such a way, to freedom, and by freedom to activity; you may be well
aware of what I have felt, and still feel, at the remembrance of this proud
moment of my life. Others spoke—you acted; and I was free! You acted;
and at this act of yours, tyrants trembled; humanity shouted out with joy;
the downtrodden people of Magyars—the downtrodden, but not broken
—raised their heads with resolution and with hope, and the brilliancy of
your Stars was greeted by Europe's oppressed nations as the morning star
of rising liberty. Now, gentlemen, you must be aware how boundless the
gratitude must be which I feel for you.

Humble as I am, God the Almighty has selected me to represent the
cause of humanity before you. My warrant to this capacity is written in
the sympathy and confidence of all who are oppressed, and of all who, as
your elder brother, the people of Britain, sympathize with the oppressed
—my warrant to this capacity is written in the hopes and expectations

you have entitled the world to entertain, by liberating me out of my prison, and by restoring me to activity. But it has pleased the Almighty to make out of my humble self yet another opportunity for a thing which may prove a happy turning point in the destinies of the world. I bring you a brotherly greeting from the people of Great Britain. I speak not in official character, imparted by diplomacy, whose secrecy is the curse of the world, but I am the harbinger of the public spirit of the people, which has the right to impart a direction to its government, and which I witnessed, pronouncing itself in the most decided manner, openly—that the people of England, united to you with enlightened brotherly love, as it is united in blood—conscious of your strength, as it is conscious of its own, has forever abandoned every sentiment of irritation and rivalry, and desires the brotherly alliance of the United States to secure to every nation the sovereign right to dispose of itself, and to protect the sovereign right of nations against the encroaching arrogance of despots; and leagued to you against the league of despots, to stand together, with you, godfather to the approaching baptism of European liberty.

I came not to your glorious shores to enjoy a happy rest—I came not with the intention to gather triumphs of personal distinction, but because a humble petitioner, in my country's name, as its freely chosen constitutional chief, humbly to entreat your generous aid; and then it is to this aim that I will devote every moment of my time, with the more assiduity, with the more restlessness, as every moment may bring a report of events which may call me to hasten to my place on the battlefield, where the great and, I hope, the last battle will be fought between liberty and despotism—a moment marked by the finger of God to be so near that every hour of delay of your generous aid may prove fatally disastrous to oppressed humanity. And, thus having stated my position to be that of a humble petitioner in the name of my oppressed country, let me respectfully ask: do you not regret to have bestowed upon me the high honor of this glorious reception, unparalleled in history?

I say unparalleled in history, though I know that your fathers have welcomed Lafayette in a similar way; but Lafayette had mighty claims to your country's gratitude. He had fought in your ranks for your freedom and independence; and, what was still more, in the hour of your need he was the link of your friendly connection with France—a connection the results of which were two French fleets of more than thirty-eight men-of-war and three thousand gallant men who fought side by side with you against Cornwallis before Yorktown; the precious gift of twenty-four thousand muskets; a loan of nineteen millions of dollars; and even the preliminary treaties of your glorious peace negotiated at Paris by your immortal Franklin. I hope the people of the United States, now itself in the happy condition to aid those who are in need of aid, as itself was once in need, will kindly remember these facts; and you, citizens of New York, you will yourselves become the Lafayettes of Hungary. Lafayette had great claims to your love and sympathy, but I have none. I came a humble petitioner, with no other claims than those which the oppressed have to the sympathy of freemen who have the power to help, with the claim which the unfortunate has to the happy, and the downtrodden has to the protection of eternal justice and of human rights. In a word, I have no other claims than those which the oppressed principle of freedom has to the aid of victorious liberty.

New York was profoundly moved by this speech, and more triumphs were to follow for Kossuth in Washington, Boston, Harrisburg, and other cities. But again no practical aid was promised. Indeed, he won only contempt from the abolitionists, for while bemoaning the subjection of Hungary he had not a word to say for the American slaves. Bitterly Wendell Phillips alluded to "Kossuth, whose only merits were his eloquence and his patriotism."

The weary orator returned to Europe, vainly seeking aid from France, Italy, and Prussia. The formation of the dual monarchy of Austria-Hungary in 1867 quieted the nationalistic ambitions of Hungary for the time being. Kossuth died in Italy in 1894, having outlived his fame by thirty-five years.

LOUIS PASTEUR DEPICTS
THE SPIRIT OF SCIENCE

[December 7, 1854]

While agitators, reformers, and revolutionists are holding forth it is not easy to hear the quieter voice of the scientist. At first thought it would seem that the spirit of science is completely alien to the spirit of oratory—science as cold, objective, impersonal, and eloquence as personal, emotional, bent on immediate practical results. But when the patient inquirer passes beyond his technical demonstrations to the sublime reaches of science and the social obligations of the scientist, he elevates while he instructs, he inspires awe even as he communicates understanding.

The "flamelike" public lectures of the brilliant chemist Sir Humphry Davy, at the Royal Institution of London, drew enthusiastic audiences in the midst of the Napoleonic wars. His successor, the great physicist Michael Faraday, made a serious study of the art of lecturing, carried on the Davy tradition, and at seventy gave a final course of juvenile lectures "On the Chemical History of a Candle." In 1840 Professor Benjamin Silliman of Yale opened the Lowell Institute, Boston, with a series of illustrated lectures on geology, and a few years later Professor Louis Agassiz of Switzerland came to the United States to lecture on biology at the institute. Meanwhile, in 1843, the aged ex-President, John Quincy Adams, had made a heroic winter trip to Cincinnati to give a two-hour oration at the laying of the corner-stone of the first astronomical observatory in the United States.

This is not the place for a collection of scientific discourses, but Pasteur at least must be included.

The son of a tanner who fought bravely in the Napoleonic wars, Louis Pasteur (1822–95) was born in the small town of Dôle, in eastern France. Showing no unusual abilities except in drawing, he pursued his studies through the higher levels of education in order to become a professor of science. But in Paris he won the affectionate respect of two distinguished chemists, J. B. A. Dumas and A. J. Balard, and of the veteran physicist, J. B. Biot, and his ambition was turned from teaching to investigation. It seems to have been the contagious eloquence of Dumas at the Sorbonne that was crucial in young Pasteur's career. In a letter written shortly before his twentieth birthday he said: "You cannot imagine what a crowd of people come to these lectures. The room is immense, and always quite full. We have to be there half an hour before the time to get a good place, as you would in a theater; there is also a great deal of applause; there are always six or seven hundred people."

A chemist by training, Pasteur made his earliest discoveries in the realm of molecular structure. In 1847 he began to teach chemistry at Dijon, advanced to a professorship at the University of Strasbourg the following year, and in 1854 became professor and dean of the newly formed faculty of science at the University of Lille. His inaugural lecture, given at Douai, where the older part of the University was located, has been preserved, and sections of it are still quoted. A magnetic man of thirty-two speaks with a "grave, penetrating voice."

"Chance favors only those minds which are prepared."

Gentlemen:

A NEW ERA of prosperity is about to blossom for the faculties of the sciences. The imperial decree of August 22, 1854, gives them a fertility that should bear in every way the most successful fruits, particularly, I dare affirm in advance, in a country where the more flourishing industries ask science every day for a discovery to be applied. You know,

gentlemen, that until now the work of the science faculties had been restricted to lectures, accompanied by experimental demonstrations performed by the teacher before the students. But the latter were not in any
position to repeat by themselves, with the instructor's guidance, those experiments, so well contrived to impress theoretical studies on the minds
of all. How much better this end will be achieved when the student will
make use of the equipment, when there will take place within his grasp
those curious metamorphoses of matter which had so vividly impressed
him in the oral lessons, when he himself will try to discover in his turn
the physical laws of living or inanimate nature.

Such is in effect, gentlemen, this most felicitous of innovations that
has been introduced into the faculties of the sciences: in return for a very
modest annual payment, students will be free to enter the faculty labora-
tories to repeat the principal experiments of the lectures they have already heard. I should like, gentlemen, I should like to tell you what can
be expected from science studies so conducted with the help of practical
work. I do not know any better means of interesting a young man and of
turning an indifferent student into a hard worker.

The culture of letters and of the arts has first claim on the choicest intellects. I should always like to see assembled about the chairs of my
learned colleagues of the faculty of letters as select a following as the one
listening to me. Indeed, in order better to understand all the beauties reflected in the writings of Homer, of Cicero, and of Pascal, it takes learning, a sound education—even more, and something God gives but to few,
it takes a noble soul. But, I ask you, where will you find in your families
a young man whose curiosity and interest will not immediately be awakened when you place within his reach a potato out of which he will make
sugar, out of the sugar alcohol, out of the alcohol ether and vinegar?
What manner of person is he who will not be happy to inform his family
in the evening that he has just made an electric telegraph work?

And, gentlemen, you may be sure that such studies are rarely if ever
forgotten. It is very much as if, in order to teach the geography of a country, one had the student travel in it. This geography is retained by the
memory, because its places have been seen and touched. In the same way
your sons will not forget what is in the air we breathe when they will
have analyzed it and when, in their hands and under their eyes, will be
realized the wonderful properties of the elements that compose it.

Besides this happy and important innovation in the faculties of the
sciences, there is another, the success of which cannot be contested in the
Department of the North. The same imperial decree I just mentioned has
instituted a new university degree, under the title of "Certificate of Abil-

ity in the Applied Sciences." After two years of theoretical and practical studies in the science faculties, young men destined for industry will be able to obtain a special diploma that definitely fills a gap that has been very prejudicial to industry. Today, indeed, the industrial head has no direct means of ascertaining the scientific knowledge of anyone whom he might want to engage to run his factory or whom he wishes to employ as an overseer or shop foreman. I hope that the certificate awarded by the faculties of the sciences will be a timely and useful recommendation. I should like young people leaving business or professional school for a career in industry to be allowed by their parents to profit from the immense resources of the faculty of sciences, which the munificence of the City Council of Lille has installed under conditions most propitious for ensuring its prosperity. In this respect, the faculties can greatly extend the services rendered by the Central School of Arts and Manufactures in Paris. The certificate we shall award will correspond, though undoubtedly with less authority, to the diploma of the students of the Central School. I shall, consequently, bend every effort to popularize the new university degree in this country.

You see, gentlemen, by the summary I have just made of the new development in the science faculties, how attached the government is to the spread of applied knowledge. But do not make the mistake of thinking that the teaching of the faculties will undergo a change, and that theory, even at its loftiest, will disappear from this teaching. God grant this will never happen! We shall not forget that theory is the mother of practice; that without it practice is but the routine resulting from habit; and that theory alone gives rise to and develops the spirit of invention. It will be especially up to us not to share the opinions of those narrow minds who disdain, in the sciences, all that has no immediate application.

You know that charming quip of Franklin's. He attended the first demonstration of a purely scientific discovery, and someone near by asked: "But what use does it have?" Franklin answered: "What use does a newly born infant have?"

Yes, gentlemen, what use does a newly born infant have? And yet, at that age of tenderest infancy, there were already in you the unknown germs of the talents that distinguish you.

In children at the breast, in those little creatures that can be blown over by a puff of air, there are magistrates, scholars, heroes as valiant as those who, at this very hour, are covering themselves with glory at the walls of Sevastopol. In the same way, gentlemen, theoretical discovery has nothing but the merit of existence. It arouses hope, and that is all. But let it be cultivated, let it grow, and you shall see what it will become.

Do you know when the electric telegraph first saw the light of day—one of the most marvelous applications of modern science? It was in that memorable year of 1822: Oersted, the Swedish [Danish] physicist, held in his hands a copper wire connected at each end to the poles of a voltaic pile. On his table was a magnetized needle placed on its axis, and suddenly he saw (by chance, you will perhaps say, but remember that in the fields of observation chance favors only those minds which are prepared), he suddenly saw the needle move and take a very different position from what terrestrial magnetism dictates. A wire conducting an electric current makes a magnetized needle deviate from its position; there, gentlemen, is the birth of the present telegraph. How much more apt, at that time, on seeing a needle move would Franklin's interlocutor have been to say: "But what use does it have?" And yet the discovery was only twenty years old when this application, almost supernatural in its effects, was made to the electric telegraph.

There is no need, gentlemen, to dwell further on the necessity of beginning the sciences with serious theoretical studies. Every enlightened mind will recognize this.

I hope, gentlemen, that the developments just described have given you some idea of the elements of success of the new faculty of sciences of the Department of the North. Moreover, it has been endowed, may I repeat, through the generosity of the City Council of Lille, with the amplest funds to ensure the success of its work. It is, then, with confidence, gentlemen, that we shall open our courses. Be further convinced that even if His Excellency the Minister of Public Instruction could choose worthier teachers, none would surpass us in the zeal, the devotion, the ardor to do well.

Here was no halting pedant, but an impassioned crusader—a phrasemaker with a sense of drama. For the next forty years Pasteur was to advance the cause of science immensely, not only through theory and experiment, but by his remarkable powers of speech—in university lectures, in professional controversies, at international congresses, on gala occasions.

In founding bacteriology and formulating the germ theory of disease he pointed Lister's way to antiseptic and aseptic surgery. He successfully attacked anthrax in sheep, rabies in dogs, and hydrophobia in men. He was the savior of wine makers, brewers, and silk manufacturers. He has been called not only "the greatest name in French science" but "the most perfect man who ever entered the kingdom of science."

On his seventieth birthday in 1892 representatives from all over the world came to honor him at a celebration at the Sorbonne. To those delegates he said, in a speech which his son read: "You bring me the deepest joy that can be felt by a man whose invincible belief is that Science and Peace will triumph over Ignorance and War, that nations will unite, not to destroy, but to build, and that the future will belong to those who have done most for suffering humanity."

KARL MARX, AN EXILE IN ENGLAND, GIVES AN AFTER-DINNER SPEECH

[April 14, 1856]

Accompanying the abortive revolutions of France, Italy, and Hungary in 1848, the revolts in Germany were more sporadic and even more futile. There was a tremendous amount of talk in the Frankfurt Parliament, but it was neither effective nor memorable, as the autobiography of Carl Schurz makes clear. These two years in the history of Europe are summed up by Erik Achorn in one compact sentence: "A liberal constitution in Piedmont granted by a liberal king, an illiberal constitution in Prussia wrung from an illiberal king under pressure of circumstances, and the abolition of serfdom in Austria—such were the meager results of the most widespread revolution in history, and all that Europe had to show by way of progress in its long and toilsome advance toward democracy and nationalism."

All this Karl Marx (1818–83) had watched with studious eyes, invariably underrating the rising force of nationalism and overrating the strength of the proletariat. He was in exile in Belgium when The Communist Manifesto was published in England in February, 1848. That same month revolution broke out in France, and shortly afterward Marx was expelled from Belgium. He returned to Germany to aid in the uprisings, but in the reaction of 1849 was again sent into exile. He now made the mistake of settling in the France of Louis Napoleon, who had been elected President by a majority of more than six million votes. That was hardly the administration to pamper a red revolutionist, and Marx was asked to leave. In September, 1849, he took refuge—temporarily, as he thought—in that paradise of nineteenth-century revolutionists, sprawling, Victorian London.

Among his few English associates during those early years were some left-wing members of the dwindling Chartist movement. As the working classes had gained nothing through the Reform Bill of 1832, they tried for more than a decade to push through Parliament a six-point "Charter" that provided for manhood suffrage and the removal of property qualifications for membership in the House of Commons. The Chartists were defeated time and again, and the movement died a slow death in the middle fifties. But all their demands were eventually realized.

In April, 1856, Marx was invited to attend a banquet to celebrate the founding of The People's Paper, one of the last, if not the least, of the Chartist publications.

"Machinery gifted with the wonderful power of shortening and fructifying human labor, we behold starving and overworking it."

THE SO-CALLED REVOLUTIONS of 1848 were but poor incidents —small fractures and fissures in the dry crust of European society. However, they announced the abyss. Beneath the apparently solid surface, they betrayed oceans of liquid matter, only needing expansion to rend into fragments continents of hard rock. Noisedly and confusedly they proclaimed the emancipation of the proletarian, *i.e.*, the secret of the nineteenth century, and of the revolution of that century. That social revolution, it is true, was no novelty invented in 1848. Steam, electricity, and the self-acting mule were revolutionists of a rather more dangerous character than even citizens Barbès, Raspail, and Blanqui. But, although the atmosphere in which we live weighs upon everyone with a twenty-thousand-pound force, do you feel it? No more than European society before 1848 felt the revolutionary atmosphere enveloping and pressing it from all sides. There is one great fact, characteristic of this, our nineteenth century, a fact which no party dares deny. On the one hand, there have started into life industrial and scientific forces which no epoch of the former human history had ever suspected. On the other hand, there exist symptoms of decay far surpassing the horrors recorded of the latter times of the Roman Empire. In our days everything seems pregnant with its contrary; machinery gifted with the wonderful power of shortening and fructifying human labor, we behold starving and overworking it. The newfangled sources of wealth, by some strange, weird spell, are turned into sources of want. The victories of art seem bought by the loss of character. At the same pace that mankind masters nature, man seems to become enslaved to other men or to his own infamy. Even the pure light of science seems unable to shine but on the dark background of ignorance. All our invention and progress seem to result in endowing material forces with intellectual life, and in stultifying human life into a material force.

This antagonism between modern industry and science on the one hand, modern misery and dissolution on the other hand; this antagonism between the productive powers and the social relations of our epoch is a fact, palpable, overwhelming, and not to be controverted. Some parties may wail over it; others may wish to get rid of modern arts in order to get rid of modern conflicts. Or they may imagine that so signal a progress in industry wants to be completed by as signal a regress in politics. On our part, we do not mistake the shape of the shrewd spirit that continues to mark all these contradictions. We know that to work well the newfangled forces of society, they only want to be mastered by newfangled men— and such are the workingmen. They are as much the invention of modern time as machinery itself. In the signs that bewilder the middle class, the aristocracy, and the poor prophets of regression, we do recognize our brave friend, Robin Goodfellow, the old mole, that can work in the earth so fast, that worthy pioneer—the revolution. The English workingmen are the first-born sons of modern industry. They will then, certainly, not be the last in aiding the social revolution produced by that industry, a revolution which means the emancipation of their own class all over the world, which is as universal as capital-rule and wages-slavery. I know the herioc struggles the English working class have gone through since the middle of the last century—struggles less glorious because they are shrouded in obscurity and burked by the middle-class historians to revenge the misdeeds of the ruling class. There existed in the Middle Ages in Germany a secret tribunal called the *Vehmgericht*. If a red cross was seen marked on a house people knew that its owner was doomed by the *Vehm*. All the houses of Europe are now marked with the mysterious red cross. History is the judge—its executioner, the proletarian.

Two days later Marx wrote to his revolutionary alter ego, who was also his financial supporter, Friedrich Engels:

"The day before yesterday there was a little banquet to celebrate the anniversary of The People's Paper. On this occasion I accepted the invitation, as the times seemed to demand it of me, and all the more since I alone (as announced in the paper) of all the refugees had been invited and the first toast also fell to me, and I was to speak for the sovereignty of the proletariat in all countries. So I made a little English speech which I shall not allow to be printed. The aim which I had in mind was achieved. Herr Talandier, who had to buy his ticket for 2/6, and the rest of the French and other refugees, have convinced themselves that we are the only 'intimate allies' of the Chartists and that though we refrain from public demonstrations and leave open flirtation with Chartism to the Frenchmen, we have it in our power to reoccupy at any time the position already historically due to us."

PART TWELVE

A HOUSE DIVIDED

I N AN EARLIER SECTION, "Fire Bells in the Night," we began with the agitation over the Missouri Compromise of 1820 and ended with Theodore Parker's arraignment of Daniel Webster, who had supported the Compromise of 1850. That famous compromise, which provided for the admission of California as a free state and for the rigorous enforcement of the Fugitive Slave Law, was devised to close the widening rift between the North and South. But the rift would not close because the slavery issue would not down. "Issue" is too abstract, too weak a word. There was the terrible reality of human beings pursued by hounds and carried back in chains to the South. There was the knowledge that Federal agents could require free citizens to assist in the work of capture.

Respectable people in the North, for the first time in their lives, became lawbreakers in helping escaped slaves on the "underground railroad." Only a few weeks after the fateful Fugitive Slave Law was passed, Harriet Beecher Stowe, the wife of a clergyman in Brunswick, Maine, began to write Uncle Tom's Cabin. Meanwhile the abolitionists, unable to command a wide circulation with their books and pamphlets, continued to speak from a hundred platforms. Wendell Phillips, Charles Sumner, Theodore Parker, William Lloyd Garrison, Lucretia Coffin Mott—these constituted the nucleus of a cohesive group rarely equaled for eloquence and courage. And they added to their ranks a superb-looking Negro who had escaped from slavery in Maryland.

FREDERICK DOUGLASS, AN EX-SLAVE, DISCUSSES SLAVERY

[July 4, 1852]

Frederick Douglass (1815?–95), whose father was an unknown white man, went through most of the miseries of bondage before breaking away in his early twenties. While working in New Bedford he became an agent of the

Massachusetts Anti-Slavery Society because of his crude but effective eloquence. Constant speaking, hard study, the writing of his autobiography, and two years in England as a precaution against capture by his former owners molded Douglass into one of the most impressive platform figures of his time.

This was the man who was called upon to commemorate the Declaration of Independence at Rochester, New York, in 1852.

"I hear the mournful wail of millions!"

FELLOW CITIZENS, pardon me, allow me to ask, why am I called upon to speak here today? What have I, or those I represent, to do with your national independence? Are the great principles of political freedom and of natural justice, embodied in that Declaration of Independence, extended to us? and am I, therefore, called upon to bring our humble offering to the national altar, and to confess the benefits and express devout gratitude for the blessings resulting from your independence to us?

Would to God, both for your sakes and ours, that an affirmative answer could be truthfully returned to these questions! Then would my task be light, and my burden easy and delightful. For who is there so cold that a nation's sympathy could not warm him? Who so obdurate and dead to the claims of gratitude that would not thankfully acknowledge such priceless benefits? Who so stolid and selfish that would not give his voice to swell the hallelujahs of a nation's jubilee, when the chains of servitude had been torn from his limbs? I am not that man. In a case like that the dumb might eloquently speak and the "lame man leap as an hart."

But such is not the state of the case. I say it with a sad sense of the disparity between us. I am not included within the pale of this glorious anniversary! Your high independence only reveals the immeasurable distance between us. The blessings in which you, this day, rejoice are not enjoyed in common. The rich inheritance of justice, liberty, prosperity, and independence bequeathed by your fathers is shared by you, not by me. The sunlight that brought light and healing to you has brought stripes and death to me. This Fourth of July is yours, not mine. You may rejoice, I must mourn. To drag a man in fetters into the grand illuminated temple of liberty, and call upon him to join you in joyous anthems, were inhuman mockery and sacrilegious irony. Do you mean, citizens, to mock me by asking me to speak today? If so, there is a parallel to your conduct. And let me warn you that it is dangerous to copy the example of a nation whose crimes, towering up to heaven, were thrown down by the breath of the Almighty, burying that nation in irrevocable ruin! I can today take up the plaintive lament of a peeled and woe-smitten people!

"By the rivers of Babylon, there we sat down. Yea! we wept when we remembered Zion. We hanged our harps upon the willows in the midst thereof. For there, they that carried us away captive, required of us a song; and they who wasted us required of us mirth, saying, Sing us one of the songs of Zion. How can we sing the Lord's song in a strange land? If I forget thee, O Jerusalem, let my right hand forget her cunning. If I do not remember thee, let my tongue cleave to the roof of my mouth."

Fellow citizens, above your national, tumultuous joy, I hear the mournful wail of millions! whose chains, heavy and grievous yesterday, are, today, rendered more intolerable by the jubilee shouts that reach them. If I do forget, if I do not faithfully remember those bleeding children of sorrow this day, "may my right hand forget her cunning, and may my tongue cleave to the roof of my mouth"! To forget them, to pass lightly over their wrongs, and to chime in with the popular theme would be treason most scandalous and shocking, and would make me a reproach before God and the world. My subject, then, fellow citizens, is *American slavery.* I shall see this day and its popular characteristics from the slave's point of view. Standing there identified with the American bondman, making his wrongs mine. I do not hesitate to declare with all my soul that the character and conduct of this nation never looked blacker to me than on this Fourth of July! Whether we turn to the declarations of the past or to the professions of the present, the conduct of the nation seems equally hideous and revolting. America is false to the past, false to the present, and solemnly binds herself to be false to the future. Standing with God and the crushed and bleeding slave on this occasion, I will, in the name of humanity which is outraged, in the name of liberty which is fettered, in the name of the Constitution and the Bible which are disregarded and trampled upon, dare to call in question and to denounce, with all the emphasis I can command, everything that serves to perpetuate slavery—the great sin and shame of America! "I will not equivocate; I will not excuse"; I will use the severest language I can command; and yet not one word shall escape me that any man, whose judgment is not blinded by prejudice, or who is not at heart a slaveholder, shall not confess to be right and just.

But I fancy I hear someone of my audience say, "It is just in this circumstance that you and your brother abolitionists fail to make a favorable impression on the public mind. Would you argue more and denounce less, would you persuade more and rebuke less, your cause would be much more likely to succeed." But, I submit, where all is plain, there is nothing to be argued. What point in the antislavery creed would you have me argue? On what branch of the subject do the people of this country need light? Must I undertake to prove that the slave is a man? That point is conceded already. Nobody doubts it. The slaveholders themselves acknowledge it in the enactment of laws for their government. They acknowledge it when they punish disobedience on the part of the slave. There are seventy-two crimes in the state of Virginia which, if committed by a black man (no matter how ignorant he be), subject him to the punishment of death; while only two of the same crimes will subject a white man to the like punishment. What is this but the acknowledgment that the slave is a moral, intellectual, and responsible being? The manhood of the slave is conceded. It is admitted in the fact that Southern statute books are covered with enactments forbidding, under severe fines and penalties, the teaching of the slave to read or to write. When you can point to any such laws in reference to the beasts of the field, then I may consent to argue the manhood of the slave. When the dogs in your streets, when the fowls of the air, when the cattle on your hills, when the fish of the sea and the reptiles that crawl shall be unable to distinguish the slave from a brute, then will I argue with you that the slave is a man!

For the present, it is enough to affirm the equal manhood of the Negro race. Is it not astonishing that, while we are plowing, planting, and reaping, using all kinds of mechanical tools, erecting houses, constructing bridges, building ships, working in metals of brass, iron, copper, silver, and gold; that, while we are reading, writing, and ciphering, acting as clerks, merchants, and secretaries, having among us lawyers, doctors, ministers, poets, authors, editors, orators, and teachers; that, while we are engaged in all manner of enterprises common to other men, digging gold in California, capturing the whale in the Pacific, feeding sheep and cattle on the hillside, living, moving, acting, thinking, planning, living in families as husbands, wives, and children, and, above all, confessing and worshiping the Christian's God, and looking hopefully for life and immortality beyond the grave, we are called upon to prove that we are men!

Would you have me argue that man is entitled to liberty? that he is the rightful owner of his own body? You have already declared it. Must I argue the wrongfulness of slavery? Is that a question for republicans? Is it to be settled by the rules of logic and argumentation, as a matter beset with great difficulty, involving a doubtful application of the principle of justice, hard to be understood? How should I look today, in the presence of Americans, dividing and subdividing a discourse, to show that men have a natural right to freedom? speaking of it relatively and positively, negatively and affirmatively? To do so would be to make myself ridiculous and to offer an insult to your understanding. There is not a man beneath the canopy of heaven that does not know that slavery is wrong for him.

What, am I to argue that it is wrong to make men brutes, to rob them of their liberty, to work them without wages, to keep them ignorant of their relations to their fellow men, to beat them with sticks, to flay their flesh with the lash, to load their limbs with irons, to hunt them with dogs, to sell them at auction, to sunder their families, to knock out their teeth, to burn their flesh, to starve them into obedience and submission to their masters? Must I argue that a system thus marked with blood, and stained with pollution, is wrong? No! I will not. I have better employment for my time and strength than such arguments would imply.

What, then, remains to be argued? Is it that slavery is not divine; that God did not establish it; that our doctors of divinity are mistaken? There is blasphemy in the thought. That which is inhuman cannot be divine! Who can reason on such a proposition? They that can may; I cannot. The time for such argument is past.

At a time like this, scorching iron, not convincing argument, is needed. O! had I the ability, and could I reach the nation's ear, I would today pour out a fiery stream of biting ridicule, blasting reproach, withering sarcasm, and stern rebuke. For it is not light that is needed, but fire; it is not the gentle shower, but thunder. We need the storm, the whirlwind, and the earthquake. The feeling of the nation must be quickened; the conscience of the nation must be roused; the propriety of the nation must be startled; the hypocrisy of the nation must be exposed; and its crimes against God and man must be proclaimed and denounced.

What, to the American slave, is your Fourth of July? I answer: a day that reveals to him, more than all other days in the year, the gross injustice and cruelty to which he is the constant victim. To him, your celebration is a sham; your boasted liberty, an unholy license; your national greatness, swelling vanity; your sounds of rejoicing are empty and heartless; your denunciation of tyrants, brass-fronted impudence; your shouts of liberty and equality, hollow mockery; your prayers and hymns, your sermons and thanksgivings, with all your religious parade and solemnity, are, to Him, mere bombast, fraud, deception, impiety, and hypocrisy—a thin veil to cover up crimes which would disgrace a nation of savages. There is not a nation of savages. There is not a nation on the earth guilty of practices more shocking and bloody than are the people of the United States at this very hour.

Go where you may, search where you will, roam through all the monarchies and despotisms of the Old World, travel through South America, search out every abuse, and when you have found the last, lay your facts by the side of the everyday practices of this nation, and you will say with me that, for revolting barbarity and shameless hypocrisy, America reigns without a rival.

"An address such as this," according to the archives of the Rochester Historical Society (vol. XIV), "might have resulted in the mobbing of Douglass had it been delivered in many cities. It was, of course, denounced by many Rochesterians, whom it shocked."

Douglass continued to shock thousands of people for many years to come, for he continued his crusade against slavery, raised Negro regiments during the Civil War, and after the War fought for the complete civil rights of his people. The awkward slave had become one of the most distinguished-looking men of his time and one of its greatest orators. Thomas Wentworth Higginson was told by the leading reporter of Boston antislavery meetings that "of all the speakers in those meetings, there were but two who could be reported without verbal alteration precisely as they spoke, and those two were Wendell Phillips and Frederick Douglass—the representative of the patrician training on the one side, and the representative of the Maryland slave on the other."

SAM HOUSTON, SENATOR FROM TEXAS, CLOSES AN OMINOUS DEBATE ON THE REPEAL OF THE MISSOURI COMPROMISE

[March 4, 1854]

In 1854 the country was still in a feverish condition, agitated at one extreme by the Southern secessionists, at the other by the abolitionists. Clay, "the Great Pacificator," was dead; Webster, the veritable voice of Union, was dead; Benton of Missouri had been exiled from the Senate to the House for supporting Clay and Webster. However, the Missouri Compromise survived, after more than thirty years, to maintain a precarious balance between the sections.

In 1820, it will be recalled, Maine was admitted as a free state and Missouri as a slave state, but with the further provision that all the remainder of the vast Louisiana Purchase north of 36°30', the southern boundary of Missouri, was to remain forever free. Now Senator Stephen A. Douglas, a Democrat from Illinois, proposed the repeal of the Missouri Compromise. He would leave the issue of slavery up to local sovereignty, to the hasty majority of early immigrants, in the territories of Kansas and Nebraska, which at that time included the future states of Wyoming and Colorado.

What, at that late date, made Douglas so anxious to upset the long-standing agreement between the two sections? Was it merely presidential ambition? Was it interest in railway development? Could he have been blind to the North's increasing hostility to slavery? Was he unable to anticipate what this new controversy would do to the uncertain balance of the country? Did his faith in local home rule take precedent over every other principle? Historians are far from agreeing in their answers to these questions.

Whatever the answers, Douglas plunged into the formal defense of his measure on January 30, 1854, and for more than a month he argued, hammered, cut, and slashed, in rough-and-tumble debate, in himself a match for Chase, Seward, and Sumner. The Senate has probably never known such continuous rage. But the end finally came on the early morning of March 5, after an all-night debate. Sam Houston (1793–1863) of Texas had the floor.

No man present could look back on such a colorful career. He had lived for nearly three years with the Cherokees and had fought under Jackson against the Creeks. He had represented Tennessee for two terms in the House of Representatives. He was elected Governor in 1827 and was stumping the state in 1829, when suddenly his bride returned to her parents' home (why, is not known) and he as suddenly resigned from the governorship. For nearly six years he again lived with the Indians, trading, drinking heavily and pleading the Indian cause annually in Washington, until he was drawn almost accidentally into Texas affairs. In the revolt against Mexico, General Houston defeated Santa Ana in the decisive battle of San Jacinto, and was twice elected President of the Republic of Texas.

Now, on March 4, 1854, in his second term as United States Senator from Texas, this regal veteran denounced the Kansas-Nebraska Bill, although he himself was a Southerner and a slaveholder.

"I adjure you to regard the contract once made
to harmonize and preserve this Union."

MR. PRESIDENT, I shall say but little more. My address may have been desultory. It embraces many subjects which it would be very hard to keep in entire order. We have, in the first place, the extensive territory; then we have the considerations due to the Indians; and then we have the proposed repeal of the Missouri Compromise, which seems to require the most explanation and to be the main point in the controversy. The great principle involved in that repeal is nonintervention, which, we are told, is to be of no practical benefit, if the Compromise is repealed. It can have no effect but to keep up agitation. Sir, the friends who have survived the distinguished men who took prominent parts in the drama of the Compromise of 1850 ought to feel gratified that those men are not capable of participating in the events of today, but that they were permitted after they had accomplished their labors, and seen their country in peace, to leave the world, as Simeon did, with the exclamation: "Lord, now lettest thou thy servant depart in peace, for mine eyes have seen thy salvation." They departed in peace, and they left their country in peace. They felt, as they were about to be gathered to the tombs of their fathers, that the country they had loved so well, and which had honored them— that country upon whose fame and name their doings had shed a bright luster which shines abroad throughout all Christendom—was reposing in peace and happiness. What would their emotions be if they could now be present and see an effort made, if not so designed, to undo all their work, and to tear asunder the cords that they had bound around the hearts of their countrymen? They have departed. The nation felt the wound; and we see the memorials of woe still in this chamber. The proud symbol [the eagle] above your head remains enshrouded in black, as if it deplored the misfortune which had fallen upon us, or as a fearful omen of future calamities which await our nation, in the event this bill should become law. Above it I behold the majestic figure of Washington, whose presence must ever inspire patriotic emotions, and command the admiration and love of every American heart. By these associations I adjure you to regard the contract once made to harmonize and preserve this Union. *Maintain the Missouri Compromise!* Stir not up agitation! Give us peace!

This much I was bound to declare—in behalf of my country, as I believe, and I know in behalf of my constituents. In the discharge of my country I have acted fearlessly. The events of the future are left in the hands of a wise Providence; and, in my opinion, upon the decision which we make upon this question must depend *union* or *disunion*.

It was nearly dawn when the Senator from Texas finished. Sam Houston had made what he considered his best speech and what has since been considered the best speech against the Kansas-Nebraska Bill. Of course, while he was making it, he knew it would outrage his Southern colleagues as well as his constituents. But he was dedicated to Andrew Jackson's famous toast: "The Union: it shall be preserved."

Before the tired Senators went home the vote was taken: thirty-seven for the bill and fourteen against. Houston was the only Southern Democrat to vote against it.

Two months later the bill passed the House of Representatives by 113 to 100—and soon the mad rush to Kansas was on.

ABRAHAM LINCOLN, AN ILLINOIS LAWYER, RETURNS TO POLITICAL LIFE AND DELIVERS HIS FIRST GREAT SPEECH

[October 4, 1854]

Although the Kansas-Nebraska Bill may have been the most unfortunate piece of legislation ever enacted in the United States, we can be grateful that it brought Abraham Lincoln back into political life and started him on his great decade. "In 1854 his profession had almost superseded the thought of politics in his mind, when the repeal of the Missouri Compromise aroused him as he had never been before," he later wrote of himself in a presidential-campaign biography. Up to that time there was only the picture of a gaunt giant telling droll stories, a Whig politician who hewed close to the party line, a clever stump speaker, and a shrewd lawyer. Hardly a memorable Lincoln sentence or sentiment can be dated prior to the fall of 1854, though his first forty-five years will always be studied with affection and care, not for themselves but for what they foreshadowed.

At this date, it is hardly necessary to recall the hard frontier life, the fragments of formal education, the shelf of cherished books, the variety of occupations, the extraordinary range of friends and acquaintances, that went into the making of a young Illinois lawyer. For four terms he served without distinction in the Illinois legislature and with dubious distinction for one term—1847–49—as the only Whig from Illinois in the House of Representatives. Taking his seat in Congress after the actual battles of the Mexican War had been fought, he was outspoken in condemning President Polk for "unnecessarily and unconstitutionally" beginning the war. This stand brought about his own eclipse, so offended were his constituents. The next five years tell the story of a retired politician rising steadily as an Illinois lawyer.

That story might have continued to an uneventful end if the Kansas-Nebraska Bill had not "aroused him as he had never been before," and if, at the same time, he had not seen a useful role for himself in the national chaos. But he was aroused, and he did see. He went back to the study, he went back to the stump, and he was ready when Stephen A. Douglas—the uncrushable Little Giant—was welcomed back to Illinois with loud cheers and loud jeers in the late summer of 1854.

The great feature of the opening day of the state fair at Springfield was to be Senator Douglas' speech. Five thousand people were expected to hear him in a grove on the outskirts of the town, but scarcely more than two thousand were able to crowd into the biggest hall of the state house. He gave them what they wanted, three hours of hard-hitting belligerence, without retreating an inch from his case for "popular sovereignty" with regard to slavery in Kansas and Nebraska.

The next day—October 4—it was Lincoln's turn on the same rostrum. Without coat or collar, in his ill-fitting trousers, he began with a few jokes and then plunged into the speech on which he had been working for weeks. He said substantially the same things at Peoria twelve days later, and it is actually the "Peoria speech" that has been reported to us.

"I am compelled to speak slowly," Lincoln once told his law partner, William H. Herndon, "but when I do throw off a thought it seems to me, though it come with some effort, it has force enough to cut its own way and travel at a greater distance."

"I also wish to be no less than national
in all the positions I may take."

THE REPEAL of the Missouri Compromise, and the propriety of its restoration, constitute the subject of what I am about to say.

As I desire to present my own connected view of this subject, my remarks will not be, specifically, an answer to Judge Douglas; yet, as I proceed, the main points he has presented will arise, and will receive such respectful attention as I may be able to give them.

I wish further to say that I do not propose to question the patriotism or to assail the motives of any man or class of men; but rather to strictly confine myself to the naked merits of the question.

I also wish to be no less than national in all the positions I may take; and whenever I take ground which others have thought, or may think, narrow, sectional, and dangerous to the Union, I hope to give a reason which will appear sufficient, at least to some, why I think differently.

And, as this subject is no other than part and parcel of the larger general question of domestic slavery, I wish to *make* and to *keep* the distinction between the *existing* institution and the *extension* of it so broad and so clear that no honest man can misunderstand me, and no dishonest one successfully misrepresent me.

In order to [get?] a clear understanding of what the Missouri Compromise is, a short history of the preceding kindred subjects will perhaps be proper. When we established our independence, we did not own, or claim, the country to which this Compromise applies. Indeed, strictly speaking, the Confederacy then owned no country at all; the states respectively owned the country within their limits; and some of them owned territory beyond their strict state limits. Virginia thus owned the Northwestern Territory—the country out of which the principal part of Ohio, all Indiana, all Illinois, all Michigan, and all Wisconsin have since been formed. She also owned (perhaps within her then limits) what has since been formed into the state of Kentucky. North Carolina thus owned what is now the state of Tennessee; and South Carolina and Georgia, in separate parts, owned what are now Mississippi and Alabama. Connecticut, I think, owned the little remaining part of Ohio—being the same where they now send Giddings to Congress, and beat all creation at making cheese. These territories, together with the states themselves, constituted all the country over which the Confederacy then claimed any sort of jurisdiction. We were then living under the Articles of Confederation, which were superseded by the Constitution several years afterwards. The question of ceding these territories to the general government was set on foot. Mr. Jefferson, the author of the Declaration of Independence, and otherwise a chief actor in the Revolution; then a delegate in Congress; afterwards twice President; who was, is, and perhaps will continue to be the most distinguished politician of our history; a Virginian by birth and continued residence and, withal, a slaveholder; conceived the idea of taking that occasion to prevent slavery ever going into the Northwestern Territory. He prevailed on the Virginia legislature to adopt his views, and to cede the territory, making the prohibition of slavery therein a condition of the deed. Congress accepted the cession, with the condition; and in the first ordinance (which the acts of Congress were then called) for the government of the territory provided that slavery should never be permitted therein. This is the famed Ordinance of '87, so often spoken of. Thenceforward, for sixty-one years, and until in 1848, the last scrap of this territory came into the Union as the state of Wisconsin, all parties acted in quiet obedience to this ordinance. It is now what Jefferson foresaw and intended—the happy home of teeming millions of free, white, prosperous people, and no slave amongst them.

Thus, with the author of the Declaration of Independence, the policy of prohibiting slavery in new territory originated. Thus, away back of the Constitution, in the pure, fresh, free breath of the Revolution, the state of Virginia and the national Congress put that policy in practice. Thus, through sixty-odd of the best years of the Republic did that policy steadily work to its great and beneficent end. And thus, in those five states, and five millions of free, enterprising people, we have before us the rich fruits of this policy.

But *now* new light breaks upon us. Now Congress declares this ought never to have been; and the like of it must never be again. The sacred right of self-government is grossly violated by it! We even find some men, who drew their first breath and every other breath of their lives under this very restriction, now live in dread of absolute suffocation, if they should be restricted in the "sacred right" of taking slaves to Nebraska. That *perfect* liberty they sigh for—the liberty of making slaves of other people—Jefferson never thought of; their own fathers never thought of, they never thought of themselves, a year ago. How fortunate for them they did not sooner become sensible of their great misery! Oh, how difficult it is to treat with respect such assaults upon all we have ever really held sacred! . . .

The Missouri Compromise ought to be restored. For the sake of the Union, it ought to be restored. We ought to elect a House of Representatives which will vote its restoration. If by any means we omit to do this, what follows! Slavery may or may not be established in Nebraska. But whether it be or not, we shall have repudiated—discarded from the councils of the nation—the *spirit of compromise;* for who after this will ever trust in a national compromise? The spirit of mutual concession—that spirit which first gave us the Constitution, and which has thrice saved the Union—we shall have strangled and cast from us forever. And what shall we have in lieu of it? The South flushed with triumph and tempted to excesses; the North, betrayed, as they believe, brooding on wrong and burning for revenge. One side will provoke, the other resent. The one will taunt, the other defy; one agrees [aggresses?], the other retaliates. Already a few in the North defy all constitutional restraints, resist the execution of the Fugitive Slave Law, and even menace the institution of slavery in the states where it exists.

Already a few in the South claim the constitutional right to take and to hold slaves in the free states—demand the revival of the slave trade: and demand a treaty with Great Britain by which fugitive slaves may be reclaimed from Canada. As yet they are but few on either side. It is a grave question for the lovers of the Union whether the final destruction of the Missouri Compromise, and with it the spirit of all compromise, will or will not embolden and embitter each of these, and fatally increase the numbers of both.

But restore the Compromise, and what then? We thereby restore the national faith, the national confidence, the national feeling of brotherhood. We thereby reinstate the spirit of concession and compromise— that spirit which has never failed us in past perils, and which may be safely trusted for all the future. The South ought to join in doing this. The peace of the nation is as dear to them as to us. In memories of the past and hopes of the future, they share as largely as we. It would be on their part a great act—great in its spirit, and great in its effect. It would be worth to the nation a hundred years' purchase of peace and prosperity. And what of sacrifice would they make? They only surrender to us what they gave us for a consideration long, long ago; what they have not now asked for, struggled or cared for; what has been thrust upon them, not less to their own astonishment than to ours. . . .

Herndon commented with such exuberance on this speech and on the audience's response that we are apt to be skeptical. But undoubtedly Lincoln had attained a new height with his great new theme—the theme toward which he had long been groping. "This speech," according to the judicious Beveridge, "was wholly unlike any before made by him."

However, Douglas seemed unperturbed at Springfield, and at once made an hour-and-a-half reply. Twelve days later the two men resumed the debate at Peoria, where Lincoln spoke substantially as he had at Springfield and then prepared the speech for publication. The law business had now become secondary.

In the sketch written six years later in the third person for a presidential-campaign biography, Lincoln dryly recalled his return to battle in 1854: "In the autumn of that year he took the stump with no broader practical aim or object than to secure, if possible, the re-election of Hon. Richard Yates to Congress. His speeches at once attracted a more marked attention than they had ever before done."

LINCOLN ARGUES THAT A HOUSE DIVIDED AGAINST ITSELF CANNOT STAND

[June 16, 1858]

In 1854 came the turning point in Abraham Lincoln's life and therefore, to some extent, a turning point in the life of the United States. From then on Lincoln's repeated attacks on Douglas and the repeal of the Missouri Compromise kept him in the political limelight and carried him in 1856 into the newly formed Republican party, which was commited to the restriction of slavery.

It might be tempting to insert here a version of Lincoln's famous "lost speech" at Bloomington, on May 29, 1856, which fired and unified the first Illinois state convention of the Republican party. On that occasion he is supposed to have spoken extemporaneously, with an unconstrained demagogic power that enslaved his audience and apparently paralyzed the note-taking powers of the reporters. Unfortunately, one of the audience, Lincoln's young circuit-riding friend, Henry C. Whitney, did not "reconstruct" that speech until some thirty years later, and it has been dismissed as "sheer fabrication" by the most meticulous of Lincoln scholars, Paul M. Angle.

There is no doubt, however, about the authenticity of the text of the well-known "House Divided" speech at Springfield, on June 16, 1858. Assured long in advance of receiving the Republican nomination for United States Senator in opposition to the Democratic incumbent, Stephen A. Douglas, Lincoln worked secretly on his acceptance address before reading it to a dozen or so friends. On political grounds all but Herndon disapproved of its drastic tone and especially of the opening passage about the "house divided." According to Herndon, Lincoln was adamant and said: "Friends, this thing has been retarded long enough. The time has come when these sentiments should be uttered; and if it is decreed that I should go down because of this speech, then let me go down linked to the truth—let me die in the advocacy of what is just and right."

The next day a jubilant, well-organized body of Republican delegates nominated Lincoln unanimously and in the evening reconvened to hear their candidate. Now for the first time he had a complete manuscript before him, but apparently he did not refer to it. He spoke gravely and, as always, slowly.

"I believe this government cannot endure
permanently half slave and half free."

Mr. President, and Gentlemen of the Convention:

IF WE COULD first know where we are, and whither we are tending, we could better judge what to do, and how to do it. We are now far into the fifth year since a policy was initiated with the avowed object and confident promise of putting an end to slavery agitation. Under the operation of that policy, that agitation has not only not ceased, but has constantly augmented. In my opinion, it will not cease until a crisis shall have been reached and passed. "A house divided against itself cannot stand." I believe this government cannot endure permanently half slave and half free. I do not expect the Union to be dissolved—I do not expect the house to fall—but I do expect it will cease to be divided. It will become all one thing or all the other. Either the opponents of slavery will arrest the further spread of it, and place it where the public mind shall rest in the belief that it is in the course of ultimate extinction; or its advocates will push it forward till it shall become alike lawful in all the states, old as well as new—North as well as South.

Have we no tendency to the latter condition?

Let anyone who doubts carefully contemplate that now almost complete legal combination—piece of machinery, so as to speak—compounded of the Nebraska doctrine and the Dred Scott decision. Let him consider not only what work the machinery is adapted to do, and how well adapted, but also let him study the history of its construction, and trace, if he can, or rather fail, if he can, to trace the evidence of design and concert of action among its chief architects, from the beginning.

The new year of 1854 found slavery excluded from more than half the states by state constitutions, and from most of the national territory by Congressional prohibition. Four days later commenced the struggle which ended in repealing that Congressional prohibition. This opened all the national territory to slavery, and was the first point gained.

But, so far, Congress only had acted, and an indorsement by the people, real or apparent, was indispensable to save the point already gained and give chance for more.

This necessity had not been overlooked, but had been provided for, as well as might be, in the notable argument of "Squatter Sovereignty," otherwise called "sacred right of self-government," which latter phrase, though expressive of the only rightful basis of any government, was so perverted in this attempted use of it as to amount to just this: that if any one man choose to enslave another, no third man shall be allowed to object. That argument was incorporated into the Nebraska Bill itself, in the language which follows:

> It being the true intent and meaning of this act not to legislate slavery into any territory or state, nor to exclude it therefrom, but to leave the people thereof perfectly free to form and regulate their domestic institutions in their own way, subject only to the Constitution of the United States.

Then opened the roar of loose declamation in favor of "Squatter Sovereignty," and "sacred right of self-government." "But," said opposition members, "let us amend the bill so as to expressly declare that the people of the territory may exclude slavery." "Not we," said the friends of the measure; and down they voted the amendment.

While the Nebraska Bill was passing through Congress, a law case involving the question of a Negro's freedom, by reason of his owner having voluntarily taken him first into a free state and then into a territory covered by the Congressional prohibition, and held him as a slave for a long time in each, was passing through the United States Circuit Court for the District of Missouri; and both Nebraska Bill and lawsuit were brought to a decision in the same month of May, 1854. The Negro's name was "Dred Scott," which name now designates the decision finally made in the case. Before the then next presidential election, the law case came to, and was argued in, the Supreme Court of the United States; but the decision of it was deferred until after the election. Still, before the election, Senator Trumbull, on the floor of the Senate, requested the leading advocate of the Nebraska Bill to state his opinion whether the people of a territory can constitutionally exclude slavery from their limits; and the latter answers: "That is a question for the Supreme Court."

The election came, Mr. Buchanan was elected, and the indorsement, such as it was, secured. That was the second point gained. The indorsement, however, fell short of a clear popular majority by nearly four hundred thousand votes, and so, perhaps, was not overwhelmingly reliable and satisfactory. The outgoing President, in his last annual message, as impressively as possible, echoed back upon the people the weight and authority of the indorsement. The Supreme Court met again; did not announce their decision, but ordered a reargument. The presidential inauguration came, and still no decision of the court; but the incoming President, in his Inaugural Address, fervently exhorted the people to abide by the forthcoming decision, whatever it might be. Then, in a few days, came the decision. . . .

At length a squabble springs up between the President and the author of the Nebraska Bill, on the mere question of fact, whether the Lecompton Constitution was or was not, in any just sense, made by the people of Kansas; and in that quarrel the latter declares that all he wants is a fair vote for the people, and that he cares not whether slavery be voted down or voted up. I do not understand his declaration that he cares not whether slavery be voted down or voted up, to be intended by him other than as an apt definition of the policy he would impress upon the public mind— the principle for which he declares he has suffered so much and is ready to suffer to the end. And well may he cling to that principle. If he has any parental feeling, well may he cling to it. That principle is the only shred left of his original Nebraska doctrine. Under the Dred Scott decision "Squatter Sovereignty" squatted out of existence, tumbled down like temporary scaffolding—like the mold at the foundry, served through one blast and fell back into loose sand—helped to carry an election, and then was kicked to the winds. His late joint struggle with the Republicans against the Lecompton Constitution involves nothing of the original Nebraska doctrine. That struggle was made on a point—the right of a people to make their own constitution—upon which he and the Republicans have never differed.

The several points of the Dred Scott decision, in connection with Senator Douglas' "care-not" policy, constitute the piece of machinery, in its present state of advancement. This was the third point gained. The working points of that machinery are:

First, that no Negro slave, imported as such from Africa, and no descendant of such slave, can ever be a citizen of any state, in the sense of that term as used in the Constitution of the United States. This point is made in order to deprive the Negro, in every possible event, of the benefit of that provision of the United States Constitution which declares that: "The citizens of each state shall be entitled to all privileges and immunities of citizens in the several states."

Second, that "subject to the Constitution of the United States," neither Congress nor a territorial legislature can exclude slavery from any United States territory. This point is made in order that individual men may fill up the territories with slaves, without danger of losing them as property, and thus to enhance the chances of permanency to the institution through all the future.

Third, that whether the holding a Negro in actual slavery in a free state makes him free, as against the holder, the United States courts will not decide, but will leave to be decided by the courts of any slave state the Negro may be forced into by the master. This point is made, not to be pressed immediately; but, if acquiesced in for a while, and apparently indorsed by the people at an election, then to sustain the logical conclusion that what Dred Scott's master might lawfully do with Dred Scott, in the free state of Illinois, every other master may lawfully do with any other one, or one thousand slaves, in Illinois or in any other free state.

Auxiliary to all this, and working hand in hand with it, the Nebraska doctrine, or what is left of it, is to educate and mold public opinion, at least Northern public opinion, not to care whether slavery is voted down or voted up. This shows exactly where we now are; and partially, also, whither we are tending.

It will throw additional light on the latter to go back, and run the mind over the string of historical facts already stated. Several things will now appear less dark and mysterious than they did when they were transpiring. The people were to be left "perfectly free," subject only to the Constitution. What the Constitution had to do with it, outsiders could not then see. Plainly enough now, it was an exactly fitted niche for the Dred Scott decision to afterward come in and declare the perfect freedom of the people to be just no freedom at all. Why was the amendment, expressly declaring the right of the people, voted down? Plainly enough now: the adoption of it would have spoiled the niche for the Dred Scott decision. Why was the court decision held up? Why even a Senator's individual opinion withheld till after the presidential election? Plainly enough now: the speaking out then would have damaged the perfectly free argument upon which the election was to be carried. Why the outgoing President's felicitation on the indorsement? Why the delay of a reargument? Why the incoming President's advance exhortation in favor of the decision? These things look like the cautious patting and petting of a spirited horse, preparatory to mounting him, when it is dreaded that he may give the rider a fall. And why the hasty afterindorsement of the decision by the President and others?

We cannot absolutely know that all these exact adaptations are the result of preconcert. But when we see a lot of framed timbers, different portions of which we know have been gotten out at different times and places, and by different workmen . . . and when we see these timbers joined together, and see they exactly make the frame of a house or a mill, all the tenons and mortices exactly fitting, and all the lengths and proportions of the different pieces exactly adapted to their respective places, and not a piece too many or too few—not omitting even scaffolding—or, if a single piece be lacking, we see the place in the frame exactly fitted and prepared yet to bring such piece in—in such a case, we find it impossible not to believe that [the workmen] all understood one another from the beginning, and all worked upon a common plan or draft drawn up before the first blow was struck.

It should not be overlooked that, by the Nebraska Bill, the people of a state, as well as a territory, were to be left "perfectly free," "subject only to the Constitution." Why mention a state? They were legislating for territories, and not for or about states. Certainly the people of a state are and ought to be subject to the Constitution of the United States; but why is mention of this lugged into this merely territorial law? Why are the people of a territory and the people of a state therein lumped together, and their relation to the Constitution therein treated as being precisely the same? While the opinion of the court, by Chief Justice Taney, in the Dred Scott case, and the separate opinions of all the concurring judges, expressly declare that the Constitution of the United States neither permits Congress nor a territorial legislature to exclude slavery from any United States territory, they all omit to declare whether or not the same Constitution permits a state, or the people of a state, to exclude it. Possibly this is a mere omission; but who can be quite sure, if McLean or Curtis [Supreme Court Justices] had sought to get into the opinion a declaration of unlimited power in the people of a state to exclude slavery from their limits, just as Chase and Mace [Supreme Court justices] sought to get such declaration, in behalf of the people of a territory, into the Nebraska Bill—I ask, who can be quite sure that it would not have been voted down in the one case as it had been in the other? The nearest approach to the point of declaring the power of a state over slavery is made by Judge Nelson. He approaches it more than once, using the precise idea, and almost the language, too, of the Nebraska Act. On one occasion, his exact language is, "except in cases where the power is restrained by the Constitution of the United States, the law of the state is supreme over the subject of slavery within its jurisdiction." In what cases the power of the states is so restrained by the United States Constitution is left an open question, precisely as the same question, as to the restraint on the power of the territories, was left open in the Nebraska Act. Put this and that together, and we have another nice little niche, which we may ere long see filled with another Supreme Court decision, declaring that the Constitution of the United States does not permit a state to exclude slavery from its limits. And this may especially be expected if the doctrine of "care not whether slavery be voted down or voted up" shall gain upon the public mind sufficiently to give promise that such a decision can be maintained when made.

Such a decision is all that slavery now lacks of being alike lawful in all the states. Welcome or unwelcome, such decision is probably coming, and will soon be upon us, unless the power of the present political dynasty shall be met and overthrown. We shall lie down pleasantly dreaming that the people of Missouri are on the verge of making their state free, and we shall awake to the reality instead that the Supreme Court has made Illinois a slave state. To meet and overthrow the power of that dynasty is the work now before all those who would prevent that consummation. This is what we have to do. How can we best do it?

There are those who denounce us openly to their own friends, and yet whisper us softly, that Senator Douglas is the aptest instrument there is with which to effect that object. They wish us to infer all from the fact that he now has a little quarrel with the present head of the dynasty; and that he has regularly voted with us on a single point, upon which he and we have never differed. They remind us that he is a great man, and that the largest of us are very small ones. Let this be granted. But "a living dog is better than a dead lion." Judge Douglas, if not a dead lion, for this work, is at least a caged and toothless one. How can he oppose the advances of slavery? He does not care anything about it. His avowed mission is impressing the "public heart" to care nothing about it. A leading Douglas Democratic newspaper thinks Douglas' superior talent will be needed to resist the revival of the African slave trade. Does Douglas believe an effort to revive that trade is approaching? He has not said so. Does he really think so? But if it is, how can he resist it? For years he has labored to prove it a sacred right of white men to take Negro slaves into the new territories. Can he possibly show that it is less a sacred right to buy them where they can be bought cheapest? And unquestionably they can be bought cheaper in Africa than in Virginia. He has done all in his power to reduce the whole question of slavery to one of a mere right of property; and, as such, how can he oppose the foreign slave trade—how can he refuse that trade in that "property" shall be "perfectly free"—unless he does it as a protection to the home production? And as the home producers will probably not ask the protection, he will be wholly without a ground of opposition.

Senator Douglas holds, we know, that a man may rightfully be wiser today than he was yesterday—that he may rightfully change when he finds himself wrong. But can we, for that reason, run ahead and infer that he will make any particular change, of which he, himself, has given no intimation? Can we safely base our action upon any such vague inference? Now, as ever, I wish not to misrepresent Judge Douglas' position, question his motives, or do aught that can be personally offensive to him. Whenever, if ever, he and we can come together on principle so that our cause may have assistance from his great ability, I hope to have interposed no adventitious obstacle. But clearly, he is not now with us—he does not pretend to be—he does not promise ever to be.

Our cause, then, must be intrusted to, and conducted by, its own undoubted friends—those whose hands are free, whose hearts are in the work—who do care for the result. Two years ago the Republicans of the nation mustered over thirteen hundred thousand strong. We did this under the single impulse of resistance to a common danger, with every external circumstance against us. Of strange, discordant, and even hostile elements, we gathered from the four winds, and formed and fought the battle through, under the constant hot fire of a disciplined, proud, and pampered enemy. Did we brave all them to falter now?—now, when that same enemy is wavering, dissevered, and belligerent? The result is not doubtful. We shall not fail—if we stand firm, we shall not fail. Wise counsels may accelerate, or mistakes delay it, but, sooner or later, the victory is sure to come.

It is quite likely that the firm tone of the "House Divided" speech contributed to Lincoln's defeat four months later, but it also fixed his direction and showed that there was a strong man in the West who was as determined to preserve the Union as he was to restrict slavery—but who refused to identify himself with the radical tactics of the abolitionists.

LINCOLN CLOSES HIS CAMPAIGN AGAINST DOUGLAS

[October 30, 1858]

Between accepting the Republican nomination for the United States Senate on June 16 and closing his campaign on October 30, 1858, Lincoln made more than sixty speeches, including seven hammer-and-tongs debates with Douglas during the hottest weeks of the summer. This was a running battle that cannot conveniently be viewed in isolated segments, but there were many little passages that shed a poignant light on Lincoln. For instance, he apologized several times for reading something, saying on one occasion, "Gentlemen, reading from speeches is a very tedious business, particularly for an old man that has to put on spectacles, and the more so if the man be so tall that he has to bend over to the light." And again, in alluding to the plump and prosperous Douglas, who might one day be handing out patronage from the White House, Lincoln remarked: "In my poor, lean, lank face nobody has ever seen that any cabbages were sprouting out."

At last the long Senatorial campaign was over, and Lincoln said his final

word at Springfield. What follows may have been part of a longer speech, or
complete in itself.

> *"I have borne a laborious and, in some respects to*
> *myself, a painful part in the contest."*

MY FRIENDS, today closes the discussions of this canvass. The
planting and the culture are over; and there remains but the preparation, and the harvest.

I stand here surrounded by friends—some political, all personal,
friends, I trust. May I be indulged, in this closing scene, to say a few
words of myself. I have borne a laborious and, in some respects to myself,
a painful part in the contest. Through all, I have neither assailed nor
wrestled with any part of the Constitution. The legal right of the Southern people to reclaim their fugitives I have constantly admitted. The legal
right of Congress to interfere with their institution in the states, I have
constantly denied. In resisting the spread of slavery to new territory, and
with that, what appears to me to be a tendency to subvert the first principle of free government itself, my whole effort has consisted. To the best
of my judgment I have labored *for* and not *against* the Union. As I have
not felt, so I have not expressed any harsh sentiment toward our Southern
brethren. I have constantly declared, as I really believed, the only difference between them and us is the difference of circumstances.

I have meant to assail the motives of no party or individual; and if I
have, in any instance (of which I am not conscious), departed from my
purpose, I regret it.

I have said that in some respects the contest has been painful to me.
Myself, and those with whom I act, have been constantly accused of a
purpose to destroy the Union; and bespattered with every imaginable
odious epithet; and some who were friends, as it were but yesterday, have
made themselves most active in this. I have cultivated patience, and made
no attempt at a retort.

Ambition has been ascribed to me. God knows how sincerely I prayed
from the first that this field of ambition might not be opened. I claim no
insensibility to political honors; but today could the Missouri restriction
be restored, and the whole slavery question replaced on the old ground
of "toleration" by *necessity* where it exists, with unyielding hostility to
the spread of it, on principle, I would, in consideration, gladly agree that

Judge Douglas should never be *out,* and I never *in,* an office, so long as we both or either live.

On November 2, 1858, the voters of Illinois went to the polls in large numbers. Although Lincoln's popular vote exceeded Douglas', fifty-four Douglas Democrats were elected to the state legislature as against forty-six Lincoln Republicans; and, consequently, as United States Senators were then chosen by state legislatures, Douglas was automatically re-elected for the new term beginning on January 5, 1859.

Lincoln returned sadly to his law practice, with (as he thought) his next opportunity six long years ahead, for he did not plan to run against his friend Senator Trumbull in 1860.

JOHN BROWN EXPLAINS A
MARTYR'S COURSE

[November 2, 1859]

Less than a year after Lincoln and Douglas closed their debates, the tense country was shaken by John Brown's raid on the government arsenal at Harpers Ferry, Virginia.

Born in Torrington, Connecticut, in a family that had more than its share of mental disorders, John Brown (1800–59) drove cattle as a boy and later worked in his father's tannery. He had seven children by his first wife and thirteen by his second, and almost as many jobs in different parts of the country, before he began to put his abolitionist ideas into practice. In 1855 five of his sons joined in the furious struggle to keep Kansas free of slavery, and he went out to help them, in a wagon loaded with arms and ammunition. In revenge for the sack of Lawrence by proslavery men, the following year Brown took revenge in his own hands and led a small party, including four of his own sons, to the slaying of five people in the notorious "Pottawatomie massacre."

While seeking funds in New England, John Brown made a profound impression on Wendell Phillips, Thoreau, Emerson, and others, though they may not have been entirely clear about his plans. Those plans, as worked out at a meeting in Canada, called for the forceful liberation of slaves and the formation of a free state. Returning to Kansas briefly, Brown and his followers succeeded in liberating eleven slaves in Missouri and in spiriting them into Canada.

In the summer of 1859 Brown established himself on the Kennedy Farm across the Potomac from the small town of Harpers Ferry, Virginia, which contained a government armory but few slaves. On the night of October 16 he and his band of twenty-one seized the armory and a number of inhabitants, as well as the bridges leading to the ferry. But then they stopped and, instead of escaping to the mountains, were crushed in a bloody fight on the second morning by a company of United States Marines led by Colonel Robert E. Lee. Brown had fought on coolly with four of his followers, after seven had been captured and ten killed or mortally wounded.

Whatever the opinions of John Brown's acts, his last weeks in prison and in the courtroom left no one untouched. Even Governor Wise of Virginia, who insisted on his execution, declared that John Brown possessed more integrity, truthfulness, and courage than any man he had ever met. But the trial moved relentlessly forward, and on October 30, 1859, he was found "guilty of treason, and conspiring and advising with slaves and others to rebel, and murder in the first degree."

That very night in Concord, without knowing the verdict, Henry David Thoreau called his fellow citizens together, to make "A Plea for Captain John Brown." For days he had been filling his journal with thoughts of Brown, and his speech was in defense of a character, of an heroic act of "civil disobedience" by a man who believed that "an individual may be right and a government wrong." After quoting statements to his captors by the wounded leader on the bloody floor of the arsenal, Thoreau concluded prophetically: "I foresee the time when the painter will paint that scene, no longer going to Rome for a subject; the poet will sing it; the historian record it; and, with the landing of the Pilgrims and the Declaration of Independence, it will be the ornament of some future national gallery, when at least the present form of slavery shall be no more here. We shall be at liberty to weep for Captain Brown. Then, and not till then, we will take our revenge."

Two days later John Brown spoke for himself in that crowded, tense little courtroom in Charles Town.

"I say I am yet too young to understand that God is any respecter of persons."

I HAVE, may it please the court, a few words to say. In the first place, I deny everything but what I have all along admitted—the design on my part to free the slaves. I intended certainly to have made a clean thing of that matter, as I did last winter when I went into Missouri and there took slaves without the snapping of a gun on either side, moved them through the country, and finally left them in Canada. I designed to have done the same thing again on a larger scale. That was all I intended. I never did intend murder, or treason, or the destruction of property, or to excite or incite slaves to rebellion, or to make insurrection.

I have another objection; and that is, it is unjust that I should suffer such a penalty. Had I interfered in the manner which I admit, and which I admit has been fairly proved (for I admire the truthfulness and candor of the greater portion of the witnesses who have testified in this case)— had I so interfered in behalf of the rich, the powerful, the intelligent, the so-called great, or in behalf of any of their friends—either father, mother, brother, sister, wife, or children, or any of that class—and suffered, and sacrificed what I have in this interference, it would have been all right; and every man in this court would have deemed it an act worthy of reward rather than punishment.

This court acknowledges, as I suppose, the validity of the law of God. I see a book kissed here which I suppose to be the Bible, or at least the New Testament. That teaches me that all things whatsoever I would that men should do to me I should do even so to them. It teaches me, further, to "remember them that are in bonds as bound with them." I endeavored to act up to that instruction. I say I am yet too young to understand that God is any respecter of persons. I believe that to have interfered as I have done—as I have always freely admitted I have done—in behalf of His despised poor was not wrong, but right. Now, if it is deemed necessary that I should forfeit my life for the furtherance of the ends of justice, and mingle my blood further with the blood of my children and with the blood of millions in this slave country whose rights are disregarded by wicked, cruel, and unjust enactments—I submit; so let it be done!

Let me say one word further.

I feel entirely satisfied with the treatment I have received on my trial. Considering all the circumstances, it has been more generous than I expected. But I feel no consciousness of guilt. I have stated from the first what was my intention and what was not. I never had any design against the life of any person, nor any disposition to commit treason, or excite slaves to rebel, or make any general insurrection. I never encouraged any man to do so, but always discouraged any idea of that kind.

Let me say also a word in regard to the statements made by some of those connected with me. I hear it has been stated by some of them that I have induced them to join me. But the contrary is true. I do not say this to injure them, but as regretting their weakness. There is not one of them but joined me of his own accord, and the greater part of them at their own expense. A number of them I never saw, and never had a word of conversation with, till the day they came to me; and that was for the purpose I have stated.

Now I have done.

A contemporary record of the trial says: "While Mr. Brown was speaking, perfect quiet prevailed, and when he had finished the judge proceeded to pronounce sentence upon him. After a few preliminary remarks, he said that no reasonable doubt could exist of the guilt of the prisoner, and sentenced him to be hung in public, on Friday, the second of December next.

"Mr. Brown received his sentence with composure.

"The only demonstration made was by the clapping of the hands of one man in the crowd, who is not a resident of Jefferson County. This was promptly suppressed, and much regret is expressed by the citizens at its occurrence."

From prison Brown wrote his wife he was sure he could "recover all the lost capital occasioned by that disaster [Harpers Ferry]; by only hanging a few minutes by the neck; and I feel quite quite determined to make the utmost possible out of a defeat." Refusing even to consider a plan of escape, which his friends in the North had been hatching, he repeatedly explained that his death would be worth infinitely more to the cause than his continued life. The ambitious and erratic Governor Wise of Virginia unwittingly co-operated. Instead of demeaning Brown by clapping him in a prison for the criminally insane, he magnified both the character of the man and of his conspiracy, and hurried him toward martyrdom. Permitted extraordinary freedom to carry on correspondence, Brown had another month for establishing his own stature.

Meanwhile in the North the aloof Emerson and the fiery Wendell Phillips gave glowing speeches in Brown's behalf. Three months later Lincoln gave the address at the Cooper Union which led directly to his nomination for the presidency by the Republican party. He was emphatic in dissociating himself and the Republicans from any sympathy with Brown's act. "That affair, in its philosophy, corresponds with the many attempts, related in history, at the assassination of kings and emperors. An enthusiast broods over the oppression of a people till he fancies himself commissioned by Heaven to liberate them. He ventures the attempt which ends in little else than his own execution."

However, Lincoln's words could not erase the effect of the Brown "affair" on the minds of the North and the South—nor did they prevent the later linking of John Brown's name with Lincoln's in the American legend.

JEFFERSON DAVIS RESIGNS FROM THE UNITED STATES SENATE

[January 21, 1861]

Some historians now argue that there would have been no Civil War if Stephen A. Douglas had been elected President instead of Lincoln. But this is hardly the place to take up that dubious hypothesis.

In spite of Lincoln's conciliatory attitude, he had been successfully labeled (by Douglas and others) a "black Republican," and with his election Southern states prepared to leave the Union. South Carolina was the first to pass ordinances of secession, on December 20, 1860, to be followed within a few weeks by Mississippi, Florida, Alabama, and Georgia. It was on the twenty-first of January, 1861, the gravest day in the history of the United States Senate, that five members announced their withdrawal. South Carolina's two Senators were absent, having sent in their resignations in writing before the session began, but all the others were present, along with hundreds of anxious visitors crowding the galleries. First the two members from Florida spoke briefly, then those from Alabama, and finally Senator Davis from Mississippi, the future President of the Southern Confederacy.

Jefferson Davis (1808–99) was born, by a strange coincidence, only eight months before Lincoln and in the same state, Kentucky, but of a more prosperous family. After a childhood in Mississippi, he returned to Kentucky for schooling in a Roman Catholic seminary, St. Thomas's College, and Transylvania University, before transferring to West Point, from which he was graduated in 1828 as a second lieutenant. Nearly a decade in the regular army and another as a cotton planter went by before Davis entered politics, with election to the House of Representatives. He soon resigned in order to command a regiment in the Mexican War, fighting heroically at Monterrey and Buena Vista. Appointed to the United States Senate, he was later elected and opposed the Compromise of 1850.

On the seventh of March, the day of Webster's crucial speech, Davis chanced to meet on the Capitol grounds Clay in conversation with Senator Berrien of Georgia. Clay suggested that Davis "join the compromise men" because his measure would probably bring peace to the country for another thirty years. Then turning to Berrien, Clay remarked, "You and I will be underground before that time, but our young friend here may have trouble to meet." Davis "somewhat impatiently declared my unwillingness to transfer to posterity a trial which they would be relatively less able to meet than we were, and passed on my way." This revealing anecdote was told years later by the aged

Davis in The Rise and Fall of the Confederate Government, a monumental work which must be dipped into at least for some sense of a controversial personality.

One of the most powerful and popular figures in Washington as Secretary of War (1853–57) under Franklin Pierce, Davis returned to the Senate more defiant than hopeful, for he was convinced that there was no legal way of excluding slavery from a territory. He was not a profound thinker but he knew where he stood, a gallant Southern gentleman who spoke without flamboyance of a cause that was not yet lost.

> *"If it be the purpose of gentlemen, they may make war against a state which has withdrawn from the Union."*

I RISE, Mr. President, for the purpose of announcing to the Senate that I have satisfactory evidence that the state of Mississippi, by a solemn ordinance of her people in convention assembled, has declared her separation from the United States. Under these circumstances, of course my functions are terminated here. It has seemed to me proper, however, that I should appear in the Senate to announce that fact to my associates, and I will say but very little more. The occasion does not invite me to go into argument, and my physical condition would not permit me to do so if it were otherwise; and yet it seems to become me to say something on the part of the state I here represent, on an occasion so solemn as this.

It is known to Senators who have served with me here that I have for many years advocated, as an essential attribute of state sovereignty, the right of a state to secede from the Union. Therefore, if I had not believed there was justifiable cause; if I had thought that Mississippi was acting without sufficient provocation or without an existing necessity, I should still, under my theory of the government, because of my allegiance to the state of which I am a citizen, have been bound by her action. I, however, may be permitted to say that I do think she has justifiable cause, and I approve of her act. I conferred with her people before that act was taken, counseled them then that if the state of things which they apprehended should exist when the convention met, they should take the action which they have now adopted.

I hope none who hear me will confound this expression of mine with the advocacy of the right of a state to remain in the Union, and to disregard its constitutional obligations by the nullification of the law. Such is not my theory. Nullification and secession, so often confounded, are indeed antagonistic principles. Nullification is a remedy which it is sought to apply within the Union, and against the agent of the states. It is only to be justified when the agent has violated his constitutional obligation, and a state, assuming to judge for itself, denies the right of the agent thus to act, and appeals to the other states of the Union for a decision; but when the states themselves, and when the people of the states have so acted as to convince us that they will not regard our constitutional rights, then, and then for the first time, arises the doctrine of secession in its practical application.

A great man who now reposes with his fathers, and who has been often arraigned for a want of fealty to the Union, advocated the doctrine of nullification, because it preserved the Union. It was because of his deep-seated attachment to the Union, his determination to find some remedy for existing ills short of a severance of the ties which bound South Carolina to the other states, that Mr. Calhoun advocated the doctrine of nullification, which he proclaimed to be peaceful, to be within the limits of state power, not to disturb the Union, but only to be a means of bringing the agent before the tribunal of the states for their judgment.

Secession belongs to a different class of remedies. It is to be justified upon the basis that the states are sovereign. There was a time when none denied it. I hope the time may come again when a better comprehension of the theory of our government and the inalienable rights of the people of the states will prevent anyone from denying that each state is a sovereign and thus may reclaim the grants which it has made to any agent whomsoever.

I therefore say I concur in the action of the people of Mississippi, believing it to be necessary and proper, and I should have been bound by their action if my belief had been otherwise; and this brings me to the important point which I wish on this last occasion to present to the Senate. It is by this confounding of nullification and secession that the name of a great man, whose ashes now mingle with his mother earth, has been invoked to justify coercion against a seceded state. The phrase, "to execute the laws," was an expression which General Jackson applied to the case of a state refusing to obey the laws while yet a member of the Union. That is not the case which is now presented. The laws are to be executed over the United States, and upon the people of the United States. They have no relation to any foreign country. It is a perversion of terms, at least it is a great misapprehension of the case, which cites that expression for application to a state which has withdrawn from the Union. You may make war on a foreign state. If it be the purpose of gentlemen, they may make war against a state which has withdrawn from the Union; but there are no laws of the United States to be executed within the limits of a seceded state. A state finding herself in the condition in which Mississippi has judged she is, in which her safety requires that she should provide for the maintenance of her rights out of the Union, surrenders all the benefits (and they are known to be many), deprives herself of the advantages (they are known to be great), severs all the ties of affection (and they are close and enduring), which have bound her to the Union; and thus divesting herself of every benefit, taking upon herself every burden, she claims to be exempt from any power to execute the laws of the United States within her limits.

I well remember an occasion when Massachusetts was arraigned before the bar of the Senate, and when then the doctrine of coercion was rife and to be applied against her because of the rescue of a fugitive slave in Boston. My opinion then was the same that it is now. Not in a spirit of egotism, but to show that I am not influenced in my opinion because the case is my own, I refer to that time and that occasion as containing the opinion which I then entertained, and on which my present conduct is based. I then said, if Massachusetts, following her through a stated line of conduct, chooses to take the last step which separates her from the Union, it is her right to go, and I will neither vote one dollar nor one man to coerce her back; but will say to her, God speed, in memory of the kind associations which once existed between her and the other states.

It has been a conviction of pressing necessity, it has been a belief that we are to be deprived in the Union of the rights which our fathers bequeathed to us, which has brought Mississippi into her present decision. She has heard proclaimed the theory that all men are created free and equal, and this made the basis of an attack upon her social institutions; and the sacred Declaration of Independence has been invoked to maintain the position of the equality of the races. That Declaration of Independence is to be construed by the circumstances and purposes for which it was made. The communities were declaring their independence; the people of those communities were asserting that no man was born—to use the language of Mr. Jefferson—booted and spurred to ride over the rest of mankind; that men were created equal—meaning the men of the political community; that there was no divine right to rule; that no man inherited the right to govern; that there were no classes by which power and place descended to families, but that all stations were equally within the grasp of each member of the body politic. These were the great principles they announced; these were the purposes for which they made their declaration; these were the ends to which their enunciation was directed. They have no reference to the slave; else, how happened it that among the items of arraignment made against George III was that he endeavored to do just what the North has been endeavoring of late to do—to stir up insurrection among our slaves? Had the Declaration announced that the Negroes were free and equal, how was the prince to be arraigned for stirring up insurrection among them? And how was this to be enumerated among the high crimes which caused the colonies to sever their connection with the mother country? When our Constitution was formed, the same idea was rendered more palpable, for there we find provision made for that very class of persons as property; they were not put upon the footing of equality with white men—not even upon that of paupers and convicts; but, so far as representation was concerned, were discriminated against as a lower caste, only to be represented in the numerical proportion of three fifths.

Then, Senators, we recur to the compact which binds us together; we recur to the principles upon which our government was founded; and when you deny them, and when you deny to us the right to withdraw from a government which, thus perverted, threatens to be destructive of our rights, we but tread in the path of our fathers when we proclaim our independence, and take the hazard. This is done not in hostility to others, not to injure any section of the country, not even for our own pecuniary benefit, but from the high and solemn motive of defending and protecting the rights we inherited, and which it is our sacred duty to transmit unshorn to our children.

I find in myself, perhaps, a type of the general feeling of my constituents toward yours. I am sure I feel no hostility to you, Senators from the North. I am sure there is not one of you, whatever sharp discussion there may have been between us, to whom I cannot now say, in the presence of my God, I wish you well; and such I am sure is the feeling of the people whom I represent toward those whom you represent. I therefore feel that I but express their desire when I say I hope, and they hope, for peaceful relations with you, though we must part. They may be mutually beneficial to us in the future, as they have been in the past, if you so will it. The reverse may bring disaster on every portion of the country; and if you will have it thus, we will invoke the God of our fathers, who delivered them from the power of the lion, to protect us from the ravages of the bear; and thus, putting our trust in God and in our own firm hearts and strong arms, we will vindicate the right as best we may.

In the course of my service here, associated at different times with a

great variety of Senators, I see now around me some with whom I have
served long; there have been points of collision, but whatever of offense
there has been to me, I leave here; I carry with me no hostile remembrance. Whatever offense I have given which has not been redressed, or
for which satisfaction has not been demanded, I have, Senators, in this
hour of our parting, to offer you my apology for any pain which in heat
of discussion I have inflicted. I go hence unencumbered of the remembrance of any injury received, and having discharged the duty of making
the only reparation in my power for any injury offered.

Mr. President and Senators, having made the announcement which
the occasion seemed to me to require, it only remains for me to bid you
a final adieu.

*This speech could not be received with an ovation but it had to be received
with respect.*

*In spite of rumors, Davis and the other withdrawing Southerners were able
to leave Washington without interference. To him war was now inevitable,
and he undoubtedly saw himself as commander of the Southern armies, but
the Provisional Congress of the Southern States elected him provisional president on February 9. He received the news at his plantation with surprise and
probably regret, but he proceeded to Montgomery and was inaugurated on the
eighteenth of February while President-elect Lincoln was on his circuitous way
to Washington.*

PRESIDENT-ELECT LINCOLN BIDS
FAREWELL TO HIS FRIENDS
AT SPRINGFIELD, ILLINOIS

[February 11, 1861]

*Lincoln had lost the Senatorial election in Illinois, but his showing in the
contest with Douglas made him a strong contender for the presidential nomination by the youthful Republican party in 1860. Four years before, John C.
Frémont, its first nominee, had campaigned with delicacy and restraint, and yet
had polled a surprisingly large vote against the vituperative, energetic—and
desperate—Democrats. The lesson seemed to be that a real fighter might have
defeated Buchanan in '56. Lincoln was such a fighter, and it was as presidential
timber that he delivered, on February 27, 1860, his famous Cooper Union
speech in New York City. Here he showed, by ample citation, that the Founding Fathers favored the exclusion of slavery from the territories, boldly refuting*

Douglas' rash statement to the contrary. Lincoln was utterly convincing, and though it was not the Cooper Union speech that gained him the nomination, a failure here would doubtless have removed him from national politics for a number of years. It showed his Republican friends that he could be depended upon to honor the party motto—"No Extension of Slavery"—and yet stand free of any radical taint.

For at least eight months Lincoln was involved in the struggle for the presidency—the Republican nomination in May and the election in November. But the worst was yet to come. In Springfield for over three months as President-elect he was pursued, besieged, and attacked by office seekers and cabinetmakers. Besides, there were such matters as clearing up his own personal affairs and preparing a draft of his Inaugural Address. He told Herndon to let their sign hang undisturbed. "Give our clients to understand that the election of a President makes no change in the firm of Lincoln and Herndon. If I live I'm coming back sometime, and then we'll go right on practicing law as if nothing had ever happened."

At last, on February 11, at eight o'clock on a cold, threatening morning, Lincoln and his family made their way through a crowd of at least a thousand serious townsfolk to the waiting train. There were handshakes and "good-byes." The President-elect disappeared into a car, but the crowd closed around, and he came out to the rear platform.

". . . with a task before me greater than that which rested upon Washington."

My Friends:

NO ONE, not in my situation, can appreciate my feeling of sadness at this parting. To this place, and the kindness of these people, I owe everything. Here I have lived a quarter of a century, and have passed from a young to an old man. Here my children have been born, and one is buried. I now leave, not knowing when or whether ever I may return, with a task before me greater than that which rested upon Washington. Without the assistance of that Divine Being who ever attended him, I cannot succeed. With that assistance, I cannot fail. Trusting in Him who can go with me, and remain with you, and be everywhere for good, let us confidently hope that all will yet be well. To His care commending you, as I hope in your prayers you will commend me, I bid you an affectionate farewell.

It is slight praise to say that this was the most poignant speech ever made from a rear platform.

LINCOLN DELIVERS HIS FIRST
INAUGURAL ADDRESS

[March 4, 1861]

Some two or three weeks before Lincoln left Springfield, on February 11, 1861, he told Herndon that he was ready to begin work on his Inaugural Address. The bookish partner was prepared to furnish Lincoln with a small library and was greatly surprised at the meager request—one of Clay's 1850 speeches, Andrew Jackson's proclamation against nullification, and a copy of the Constitution. Lincoln "afterwards called for Webster's reply to Hayne, a speech which he read when he lived at New Salem, and which he always regarded as the grandest specimen of American oratory. With these few 'volumes' and no further sources of reference, he locked himself up in a room over a store across the street from the State House, and there, cut off from all communication and intrusion, he prepared the address." (Herndon) Set up in type at Springfield, Lincoln's first draft was carefully studied by advisers on the way to Washington and later by Seward, his choice as Secretary of State. Although usually inflexible about any "change of language which involved a change of sentiment," Lincoln accepted from Seward a more conciliatory final paragraph, but perfected it with a few characteristic touches.

Rumors of rebellion and assassination caused General Winfield Scott to turn Washington into an armed camp on the day of the inauguration. Sharpshooters lurked on the roofs of buildings and in the windows of the Capitol as Buchanan and Lincoln drove up Pennsylvania Avenue in an open carriage. When the President-elect, on a temporary platform at the east end of the Capitol, took out his manuscript and put on his steel-rimmed glasses, he looked out on some twenty thousand apprehensive faces. He read, in a clear, distinct voice that carried to the edge of the crowd, the memorable address whose conclusion we quote.

> *"In your hands, my dissatisfied fellow countrymen, and*
> *not in mine, is the momentous issue of civil war."*

THIS COUNTRY, with its institutions, belongs to the people who inhabit it. Whenever they shall grow weary of the existing government, they can exercise their *constitutional* right of amending it, or their *revolutionary* right to dismember or overthrow it. I cannot be ignorant of the fact that many worthy and patriotic citizens are desirous of having the national Constitution amended. While I make no recommendation of amendments, I fully recognize the rightful authority of the people over the whole subject to be exercised in either of the modes prescribed in the instrument itself; and I should under existing circumstances favor rather than oppose a fair opportunity being afforded the people to act upon it. . . .

The chief magistrate derives all his authority from the people, and they have conferred none upon him to fix terms for the separation of the states. The people themselves can do this also if they choose; but the executive, as such, has nothing to do with it. His duty is to administer the present government, as it came to his hands, and to transmit it, unimpaired by him, to his successor.

Why should there not be a patient confidence in the ultimate justice of the people? Is there any better or equal hope in the world? In our present differences, is either party without faith of being in the right? If the Almighty Ruler of nations, with His eternal truth and justice, be on your side of the North, or on yours of the South, that truth, and that justice, will surely prevail, by the judgment of this great tribunal, the American people.

By the frame of the government under which we live, this same people have wisely given their public servants but little power for mischief; and have, with equal wisdom, provided for the return of that little to their own hands at very short intervals.

While the people retain their virtue and vigilance, no administration, by any extreme of wickedness or folly, can very seriously injure the government in the short space of four years.

My countrymen, one and all, think calmly and *well* upon this whole subject. Nothing valuable can be lost by taking time. If there be an object to *hurry* any of you, in hot haste, to a step which you would never take *deliberately*, that object will be frustrated by taking time; but no good object can be frustrated by it. Such of you as are now dissatisfied still have the old Constitution unimpaired, and, on the sensitive point, the laws of your own framing under it; while the new administration will have no immediate power, if it would, to change either. If it were admitted that you who are dissatisfied hold the right side in the dispute, there still is no single good reason for precipitate action. Intelligence, patriotism, Christianity, and a firm reliance on Him who has never yet forsaken this favored land are still competent to adjust, in the best way, all our present difficulty.

In *your* hands, my dissatisfied fellow countrymen, and not in *mine*, is the momentous issue of civil war. The government will not assail *you*.

You can have no conflict, without being yourselves the aggressors. *You* have no oath registered in heaven to destroy the government, while *I* shall have the most solemn one to "preserve, protect, and defend" it.

I am loath to close. We are not enemies, but friends. We must not be enemies. Though passion may have strained, it must not break, our bonds of affection. The mystic chords of memory, stretching from every battle-field, and patriot grave, to every living heart and hearthstone, all over this broad land, will yet swell the chorus of the Union, when again touched, as surely they will be, by the better angels of our nature.

The audience was attentive, silent, throughout, but it seems to have been the silence of apprehension rather than of respect or admiration. "This strange new man from the West" was hard to decipher. But for the Northern ex-tremists it was at once clear that Lincoln's attitude was too conciliatory. For the Southern sympathizers it was equally clear that the new President's attitude was too firm.

After Lincoln finished his speech he took the oath of office from the aged, shrunken Chief Justice Taney whose fateful decision in the Dred Scott Case he had scathingly denounced four years before. Then, according to custom, he was formally introduced to the White House (or to the staff of the White House) by the outgoing President. Buchanan's final words to Lincoln were: "If you are as happy, my dear sir, on entering this house as I am in leaving it and returning home, you are the happiest man in this country."

JOHN BRIGHT EDUCATES ENGLISH
PUBLIC OPINION IN THE
CAUSE OF THE NORTH

[December 4, 1861]

At this distance it is hard to realize how close Great Britain came to recog-nizing the Confederacy or of going to war with the North during the early part of the Civil War. The result would have been to prolong the Civil War indefinitely and, in case of victory for the South, to have established a vast slave empire extending from Virginia, around the Caribbean, and into South America.

Why this clear British preference for the South? The aristocracy much preferred the recognizable landed gentry of the South to the businessmen of the North. The middle-class British manufacturers had an interest in the "free-trade" South that supplied cotton to their factories. And tens of thousands of factory workers were unemployed because of the Northern blockade of Southern ports. It was indeed "natural" for the British to sympathize with the gallant South, especially as the slavery issue was played down in the early part of the war while the issue of Southern independence was played up. Peace was preserved between the United States and Great Britain largely because of the wise work of two men, Charles Francis Adams, the American minister to Great Britain, and John Bright, British Quaker, factory owner, and statesman.

It will be recalled that John Bright (1811–89), after the death of his young wife, joined Cobden in the successful crusade against the Corn Laws. He went on with Cobden in advocating free trade as the key to world peace, helped in the organization of world-peace congresses, and opposed so strenuously the most absurd of all wars—the Crimean—that he was temporarily a political outcast.

This was the man who was called home by his fellow citizens of Rochdale in December, 1861, to advise them about the "Trent affair," which was arousing war fever in England. Charles Wilkes, an overzealous captain of an American warship, had stopped a British merchant vessel, the Trent, and seized Mason and Slidell, two Confederate commissioners, on their way to seek British and French support, and lodged them in jail. Did not this outrage justify a declaration of war against the offending country?

John Bright is in the midst of his address.

> "What is this people, about which so many men
> in England at this moment are writing, and
> speaking, and thinking with harshness?"

IT HAS BEEN SAID, "How much better it would be"—not for the United States, but—"for us that these states should be divided." I recollect meeting a gentleman in Bond Street one day before the session [of Parliament] was over. He was a rich man, and one whose voice is much heard in the House of Commons; but his voice is not heard when he is on his legs, but when he is cheering other speakers; and he said to me: "After all, this is a sad business about the United States; but still I think it very much better that they should be split up. In twenty years," or in fifty years, I forget which it was, "they will be so powerful that they will bully all Europe." And a distinguished Member of the House of Commons—distinguished there by his eloquence, distinguished more by his many writings—I mean Sir Edward Bulwer-Lytton—he did not exactly express a hope, but he ventured on something like a prediction, that the time would come when there would be, I do not know how many, but about as many independent states on the American continent as you can count upon your fingers.

There cannot be a meaner motive than this I am speaking of, in forming a judgment on this question—that it is "better for us"—for whom? the people of England or the government of England?—that the United States should be severed, and that the North American continent should be as the continent of Europe is, in many states, and subject to all the contentions and disasters which have accompanied the history of the states of Europe. I should say that, if a man had a great heart within him, he would rather look forward to the day when, from that point of land which is habitable nearest to the Pole to the shores of the Great Gulf, the whole of that vast continent might become one great confederation of states—without a great army, and without a great navy—not mixing itself up with the entanglements of European politics—without a customhouse inside, through the whole length and breadth of its territory—and with freedom everywhere, equality everywhere, law everywhere, peace everywhere—such a confederation would afford at least some hope that man is not forsaken of heaven, and that the future of our race may be better than the past.

It is a common observation that our friends in America are very irritable. And I think it is very likely, of a considerable number of them, to be quite true. Our friends in America are involved in a great struggle. There is nothing like it before in their or in any history. No country in the world was ever more entitled, in my opinion, to the sympathy and the forbearance of all friendly nations than are the United States at this moment. They have there some newspapers that are no wiser than ours. They have there some papers which, up to the election of Mr. Lincoln, were his bitterest and most unrelenting foes, who, when the war broke out, and it was not safe to take the line of Southern support, were obliged to turn round and to appear to support the prevalent opinion of the country. But they undertook to serve the South in another way, and that was by exaggerating every difficulty and misstating every fact, if so doing could serve their object of creating distrust between the people of the Northern states and the people of this United Kingdom. If *The Times* in this country has done all that it could do to poison the minds of the people of England, and to irritate the minds of the people of America, *The New York Herald,* I am sorry to say, has done, I think, all that it could, or all that it dared to do, to provoke mischief between the government in Washington and the government in London. . . .

Now I am obliged to say—and I say it with the utmost pain—that if we have not done things that are plainly hostile to the North, and if we have not expressed affection for slavery, and, outwardly and openly, hatred for the Union—I say that there has not been that friendly and cordial neutrality which, if I had been a citizen of the United States, I should have expected; and I say further that, if there has existed considerable irritation at that, it must be taken as a measure of the high appreciation which the people of those states place upon the opinion of the people of England. If I had been addressing this audience ten days ago, so far as I know, I should have said just what I have said now; and although, by an untoward event, circumstances are somewhat, even considerably, altered, yet I have thought it desirable to make this statement, with a view, so far as I am able to do it, to improve the opinion of England, and to assuage feelings of irritation in America, if there be any, so that no further difficulties may arise in the progress of this unhappy strife.

But there has occurred an event, which was announced to us only a week ago, which is one of great importance, and it may be one of some peril. It is asserted that what is called "international law" has been broken by the seizure of the Southern commissioners on board an English trading steamer by a steamer of war of the United States. Now, what is international law? You have heard that the opinions of the law officers of the Crown are in favor of this view of the case—that the law has been broken. I am not at all going to say that it has not. It would be imprudent in me to set my opinion on a legal question, which I have only partially examined, against their opinion on the same question, which I presume they have carefully examined. But this I say, that international law is not to be found in an act of Parliament—it is not in so many clauses. You know that it is difficult to find the law. I can ask the mayor, or any magistrate around me, whether it is not very difficult to find the law; even when you have found the act of Parliament, and no clause, you may imagine that the case is still more difficult. . . .

Now, the act which has been committed by the American steamer, in my opinion, whether it was legal or not, was both impolitic and bad. That is my opinion. I think it may turn out, almost certainly, that, so far as the taking of those men from that ship was concerned, it was an act wholly unknown to, and unauthorized by, the American government. And if the American government believe, on the opinion of their law officers, that the act is illegal, I have no doubt they will make fitting reparation; for there is no government in the world that has so strenuously insisted upon modifications of international law, and been so anxious to be guided always by the most moderate and merciful interpretation of that law.

Now, our great advisers of *The Times* newspaper have been persuading people that this is merely one of a series of acts which denote the determination of the Washington government to pick a quarrel with the people of England. Did you ever know anybody who was not very nearly dead drunk who, having as much upon his hands as he could manage, would offer to fight everybody about him? Do you believe that the United States government, presided over by President Lincoln, so constitutional in all his acts, so moderate as he has been—representing at this moment that great party in the United States, happily now in the ascendancy, which has always been especially in favor of peace, and especially friendly to England—do you believe that such a government, having now upon its hands an insurrection of the most formidable character in the South, would invite the armies and the fleets of England to combine with that insurrection, and, it might be, to render it impossible that the Union should ever again be restored? I say that single statement, whether it came from a public writer or a public speaker, is enough to stamp him forever with the character of being an insidious enemy of both countries.

Well, now, what have we seen during the last week? People have not been, I am told—I have not seen much of it—quite as calm as sensible men should be. Here is a question of law. I will undertake to say that when you have from the United States government—if they think the act legal—a statement of their view of the case, they will show you that, fifty or sixty years ago, during the wars of that time, there were scores of cases that were at least as bad as this, and some infinitely worse. . . .

What can be more monstrous than that we, as we call ourselves, to some extent, an educated, a moral, and a Christian nation—at a moment when an accident of this kind occurs, before we have made a representation to the American government, before we have heard a word from it in reply—should be all up in arms, every sword leaping from its scabbard, and every man looking about for his pistols and his blunderbusses? I think the conduct pursued—and I have no doubt just the same is pursued by a certain class in America—is much more the conduct of savages than of Christian and civilized men. No, let us be calm. You recollect how we were dragged into the Russian war—how we "drifted" into it. You know that I, at least, have not upon my head any of the guilt of that fearful war. You know that it cost one hundred millions of money to this country; that it cost at least the lives of forty thousand Englishmen; that it disturbed your trade; that it nearly doubled the armies of Europe; that it placed the relations of Europe on a much less peaceful footing than before; and that it did not effect one single thing of all those that it was promised to effect. . . .

Remembering the past, remembering at this moment the perils of a friendly people, and seeing the difficulties by which they are surrounded, let us, I entreat of you, see if there be any real moderation in the people of England, and if magnanimity, so often to be found amongst individuals, is absolutely wanting in a great nation.

Now, government may discuss this matter—they may arrange it— they may arbitrate it. I have received here, since I came into the room, a dispatch from a friend of mine in London referring to this matter. I believe some portion of it is in the papers this evening, but I have not seen them. He states that General Scott, whom you know by name, who has come over from America to France, being in a bad state of health—the General lately of the American army, and a man whose reputation in that country is hardly second to that which the Duke of Wellington held during his lifetime in this country—General Scott has written a letter on the American difficulty. He denies that the cabinet of Washington has ordered the seizure of the Southern commissioners, if found under a neutral flag. The question of legal right involved in the seizure, the General thinks a very narrow ground on which to force a quarrel with the United States. As to Messrs. Slidell and Mason being or not being contraband, the General answers for it that, if Mr. Seward cannot convince Earl Russell that they bore that character, Earl Russell will be able to convince Mr. Seward that they did not. He pledges himself that, if this government cordially agreed with that of the United States in establishing the immunity of neutrals from the oppressive right of search and seizure on suspicion, the cabinet of Washington will not hesitate to purchase so great a boon to peaceful trading vessels.

Now, then, before I sit down, let me ask you what is this people, about which so many men in England at this moment are writing, and speaking, and thinking with harshness, I think with injustice, if not with great bitterness? Two centuries ago, multitudes of the people of this country found a refuge on the North American continent, escaping from the tyranny of the Stuarts and from the bigotry of Laud. Many noble spirits from our country made great experiments in favor of human freedom on that continent. Bancroft, the great historian of his own country, has said, in his own graphic and emphatic language, "The history of the colonization of America is the history of the crimes of Europe." From that time down to our own period, America has admitted the wanderers from every clime. Since 1815, a time which many here remember, and which is within my lifetime, more than three millions of persons have emigrated from the United Kingdom to the United States. During the fifteen years from 1845 or 1846 to 1859 or 1860—a period so recent that we all remember the most trivial circumstances that have happened in that time—during those fifteen years more than 2,320,000 persons left the shores of the United Kingdom as emigrants for the states of North America.

At this very moment, then, there are millions in the United States who personally, or whose immediate parents, have at one time been citizens of this country. They found a home in the Far West; they subdued the wilderness; they met with plenty there, which was not afforded them in their native country; and they have become a great people. There may be persons in England who are jealous of those states. There may be men who dislike democracy, and who hate a republic; there may be even those whose sympathies warm toward the slave oligarchy of the South. But of this I am certain, that only misrepresentation the most gross or calumny the most wicked can sever the tie which unites the great mass of the people of this country with their friends and brethren beyond the Atlantic.

Now, whether the Union will be restored or not, or the South achieve an unhonored independence or not, I know not, and I predict not. But this I think I know—that in a few years, a very few years, the twenty millions of freemen in the North will be thirty millions, or even fifty millions—a population equal to or exceeding that of this kingdom. When that time comes, I pray that it may not be said amongst them that, in the darkest hour of their country's trials, England, the land of their fathers, looked on with icy coldness and saw unmoved the perils and calamities of their children. As for me, I have but this to say: I am but one in this audience, and but one in the citizenship of this country; but if all other tongues are silent, mine shall speak for that policy which gives hope to the bondsmen of the South, and which tends to generous thoughts, and generous words, and generous deeds, between the two great nations who speak the English language and from their origin are alike entitled to the English name.

Bright was generously cheered by his Rochdale neighbors, and from that moment on sympathy with the North began to grow in England. Prince Albert, in one of his last official acts, helped to tone down England's note to the United States, and America gave in with a show of dignity. Wilkes' act was disavowed, though it was pointed out that he never meant to insult the British flag. Mason and Slidell were released and were allowed to proceed to Europe for aid. There they were coldly received and accomplished nothing, The Times (London) stating: "We should have done just as much to rescue two of their Negroes."

But the danger was by no means over, for Southern arms continued to prevail, and in 1862, Chancellor of the Exchequer Gladstone was indiscreet enough to declare at a public dinner that "Jefferson Davis had made a nation, that is to say, that the division of the American republic by the establishment of the Southern secession state was an accomplished fact"—an error that Gladstone later recalled as the least excusable of his life. By June, 1863, Gladstone was opposed to the recognition of the Confederacy but still convinced that the Union could not be restored by force of arms.

It remained for J. A. Roebuck in the House of Commons to propose an alliance with Napoleon III to aid the South. Against this measure Bright made a devastating attack, surpassing in power even his Rochdale speech. "I say that the whole of his case rests upon a miserable jealousy of the United States." Roebuck's bill was shattered and his public reputation considerably marred. But was the North strong enough to overcome the South? The answer was given the following week with Lee's defeat at Gettysburg and the surrender of Vicksburg to Grant. (In Lincoln's office in the White House there hung only military maps, a picture of Andrew Jackson, and a photograph of John Bright.)

EDWARD EVERETT DELIVERS THE ORATION AT THE DEDICATION OF THE NATIONAL CEMETERY AT GETTYSBURG

[November 19, 1863]

In the three days of the battle of Gettysburg, in July, 1863, the Federal losses in killed, wounded, and missing were approximately twenty-three thousand, the Confederate losses twenty-eight thousand. Weeks afterward thousands of quickly buried bodies still lay in shallow graves, a hazard to the living and a disgrace to the dead.

Motives of public health and piety together inspired a Pennsylvania committee to plan a national cemetery and, with the speedy co-operation of eighteen other Northern states, seventeen acres were purchased on bloody Cemetery Hill. The dedication was set for October 23, and Edward Everett of Boston was inevitably invited to be the orator of the day. He accepted, but needed more time to prepare, so the event was delayed a month.

Edward Everett (1794–1865) was the pastor of a fashionable Unitarian church before he was twenty; a student in Europe for four years before he became a progressive professor of Greek at Harvard; a member of the House

of Representatives for five terms; Governor of Massachusetts for four terms;
Minister to the Court of St. James'; President of Harvard; Secretary of State
for a few months, and finally a United States Senator. Yet, Everett was most
famous as an orator, the orator for great ceremonial occasions, for the dedication of monuments and the commemorations of centenaries. A single oration
on George Washington he gave one hundred and twenty-eight times and raised
nearly sixty thousand dollars for the purchase of Mount Vernon as a national
monument. For forty years he held forth in fluent, flawless, finished, classical
discourses—and they leave us cold. As Emerson said of Everett and some of
his contemporaries: "All lack nerve and dagger."

But that was certainly not the popular opinion of the day, and at Gettysburg, Everett was in his best form, though nearing seventy. With sublime self-
confidence, he faced fifteen thousand weary people who had traveled through
the night and now stood at noon around the temporary platform. It was a two-
hour discourse, and from the first paragraph we leap over his account of the
origins of the war, the course of the battle, and the theory of American government to the final paragraph.

> *"Grant me, I pray you, your indulgence*
> *and your sympathy."*

STANDING BENEATH this serene sky, overlooking these broad fields
now reposing from the labors of the waning year, the mighty Alleghenies dimly towering before us, the graves of our brethren beneath
our feet, it is with hesitation that I raise my poor voice to break the eloquent silence of God and nature. But the duty to which you have called
me must be performed; grant me, I pray you, your indulgence and your
sympathy. . . .

And now, friends, fellow citizens of Gettysburg and Pennsylvania, and
you from remoter states, let me again, as we part, invoke your benediction on these honored graves. You feel, though the occasion is mournful, that it is good to be here. You feel that it was greatly auspicious for
the cause of the country that the men of the East, and the men of the
West, the men of nineteen sister states, stood side by side on the perilous
ridges of the battle. You now feel it a new bond of union that they shall
lie side by side on the perilous ridges of the battle. You now feel it a new
bond of union that they shall lie side by side till a clarion, louder than

that which marshaled them to the combat, shall awake their slumbers. God bless the Union; it is dearer to us for the blood of brave men which has been shed in its defense. The spots on which they stood and fell; these pleasant heights; the thriving village whose streets so lately rang with the strange din of war; the fields beyond the ridge, where the noble Reynolds held the advancing foe at bay, and, while he gave up his own life, assured by his forethought and self-sacrifice the triumph of the two succeeding days; the little streams which wind through the hills, on whose banks in aftertimes the wandering plowman will turn up, with the rude weapons of savage warfare, the fearful missiles of modern artillery; Seminary Ridge, the Peach Orchard, Cemetery, Culp, and Wolf Hill, Round Top, Little Round Top, humble names, henceforward dear and famous—no lapse of time, no distance of space, shall cause you to be forgotten. "The whole earth," said Pericles, as he stood over the remains of his fellow citizens, who had fallen in the first year of the Peloponnesian War— "the whole earth is the sepulcher of illustrious men." All time, he might have added, is the millennium of their glory. Surely I would do no injustice to the other noble achievements of the war, which have reflected such honor on both arms of the service, and have entitled the armies and the navy of the United States, their officers and men, to the warmest thanks and the richest rewards which a grateful people can pay. But they, I am sure, will join us in saying, as we bid farewell to the dust of these martyr-heroes, that wheresoever throughout the civilized world the accounts of this great warfare are read, and down to the latest period of recorded time, in the glorious annals of our common country there will be no brighter page than that which relates to *the battles of Gettysburg*.

Edward Everett had once more lived up to his reputation. He had delivered the kind of high-flown oration that the taste of the day demanded, and he received with urbanity the applause to which he was accustomed. The ceremonies were practically over. The Baltimore Glee Club sang an ode written for the occasion, and then, almost like an afterthought, Ward Hill Lamon announced, "The President of the United States."

After Everett had accepted the invitation to be orator of the day, the Gettysburg Cemetery commissioners received word that the President would attend the ceremonies. They then decided, with some doubt as to his competence for such a grave occasion, to invite him to "set apart these grounds to their sacred use by a few appropriate remarks."

Now he rose, put on his spectacles, and drew out a single sheet of paper at which he hardly glanced during the next few minutes.

PRESIDENT LINCOLN MAKES "A FEW APPROPRIATE REMARKS" ON THE SAME OCCASION

[November 19, 1863]

"The world will little note, nor long remember, what we say here."

FOURSCORE and seven years ago, our fathers brought forth upon this continent a new nation, conceived in liberty, and dedicated to the proposition that all men are created equal. Now we are engaged in a great civil war, testing whether that nation, or any nation so conceived and so dedicated, can long endure. We are met on a great battlefield of that war. We are met to dedicate a portion of it as the final resting place of those who here gave their lives that that nation might live. It is altogether fitting and proper that we should do this. But in a larger sense we cannot dedicate—we cannot consecrate—we cannot hallow this ground. The brave men, living and dead, who struggled here, have consecrated it far above our poor power to add or detract. The world will little note, nor long remember, what we say here, but it can never forget what they did here. It is for us, the living, rather to be dedicated here to the unfinished work that they have thus far so nobly advanced. It is rather for us to be here dedicated to the great task remaining before us, that from these honored dead we take increased devotion to that cause for which they here gave the last full measure of devotion; that we here highly resolve that these dead shall not have died in vain; that this nation, under God, shall have a new birth of freedom, and that government of the people, by the people, for the people, shall not perish from the earth.

The President had spoken in a clear, loud voice, but he was through before the audience felt he was fairly started, and the applause was slow and perfunctory.

Some newspapers actually ridiculed the address, a few praised it; a few people at once recognized a masterpiece. Edward Everett himself wrote to the President the next day: "I should be glad if I could flatter myself that I came as near the central idea of the occasion in two hours as you did in two minutes." In his grateful reply Lincoln said: "In our respective parts yesterday, you could not have been excused to make a short address, nor I a long one. I am pleased to know that, in your judgment, the little I did say was not entirely a failure."

ABRAHAM LINCOLN DELIVERS HIS
SECOND INAUGURAL ADDRESS

[March 4, 1865]

Another presidential election came in 1864. Not since Andrew Jackson in 1832 had a President been re-elected. And Lincoln's chance was far from promising. The struggle was slowing down, and the North was war-weary. While the so-called Radicals thought that Lincoln was planning to be too easy on the South, others felt that he had already been too severe and would have brought back the seceding states at any price. In the cabinet the ambitious Secretary of the Treasury, Salmon P. Chase, was anxious to supplant Lincoln. Others were pushing General Grant—without his permission—for the Republican nomination before he had finished his campaign in Virginia. The Democratic party was ready for peace at practically any price, with General McClellan as standard-bearer.

But Lincoln swept easily through the nominating convention, and, helped by Sherman's march to the sea, won an overwhelming victory at the polls, with an electoral vote of 212 out of 233.

In contrast to the uncertain, frightened hearers of the First Inaugural, a vast, grateful audience listened with perfect respect to the Second—and at the end there were tears in many eyes.

"With malice toward none, with charity for all."

Fellow Countrymen:

AT THIS second appearing to take the oath of the presidential office, there is less occasion for an extended address than at the first. Then a statement somewhat in detail of the course to be pursued seemed very fitting and proper; now, at the expiration of four years, during which public declarations have constantly been called forth concerning every point and place of the great contest which still absorbs attention and engrosses the energies of the nation, little that is new could be presented. The progress of our arms, upon which all else chiefly depends, is as well known to the public as to myself. It is, I trust, reasonably satisfactory and encouraging to all. With a high hope for the future, no prediction in that regard is ventured. On the occasion corresponding to this four years ago, all thoughts were anxiously directed to an impending civil war. All dreaded it. All sought to avoid it. While the Inaugural Address was being delivered from this place, devoted altogether to saving the Union without war, the insurgent agents were in the city seeking to destroy it without war—seeking to dissolve the Union, and divide the effects by negotiating. Both parties deprecated war, but one of them would make war rather than let it perish, and war came. One eighth of the whole population were colored slaves, not distributed generally over the Union, but located in the Southern part. These slaves contributed a peculiar and powerful interest. All knew the interest would somehow cause war. To strengthen, perpetuate, and extend this interest was the object for which the insurgents would rend the Union by war, while the government claimed no right to do more than restrict the territorial enlargement of it. Neither party expected the magnitude or duration which it has already attained; neither anticipated that the cause of the conflict might cease even before the conflict itself should cease. Each looked for an easier triumph and a result less fundamental and astonishing. Both read the same Bible and pray to the same God. Each invokes His aid against the other. It may seem strange that any man should dare to ask a just God's assistance in wringing bread from the sweat of other men's faces; but let us judge not, that we be not judged. The prayer of both should not be answered; that of neither has been answered fully, for the Almighty has His own purposes. "Woe unto the world because of offenses, for it must needs be that offense come; but woe unto that man by whom the offense cometh." If we shall suppose American slavery one of those offenses which, in the providence of God, must needs come, but which, having continued through his appointed time, He now wills to remove, and that He gives to both North and South this terrible war, as was due to those by whom the offense came, shall we discern that there is any departure from those divine attributes which believers in the living God always ascribe to Him? Fondly do we hope, fervently do we pray, that this mighty scourge of war may speedily pass away; yet if it be God's will that it continue until the wealth piled by bondsmen by two hundred and fifty years' unrequited toil shall be sunk, and until every drop of blood drawn with the lash shall be paid by another drawn with the sword, as was said three thousand years ago, so still it must be said that the judgments of the Lord are true and righteous altogether.

With malice toward none, with charity for all, with firmness in the right, as God gives us to see the right, let us strive on to finish the work we are in, to bind up the nation's wounds, to care for him who shall have borne the battle, and for his widow and orphans; to do all which may achieve and cherish a just and a lasting peace among ourselves and with all nations.

In a note to the veteran political leader, Thurlow Weed, on March 15, 1865, just a month before the end, Lincoln wrote: "Everyone likes a little compliment. Thank you for yours on my little notification speech and on the recent Inaugural Address. I expect the latter to wear as well as—perhaps better than—anything I have produced; but I believe it is not immediately popular. Men are not flattered by being shown that there is a difference between the Almighty and them."

PART THIRTEEN

BLOOD AND IRON

AN EARLIER SECTION, "Agitation, Reform, and Revolt," ended in 1856 with Karl Marx's commenting on the abortive revolutions of 1848 and predicting the vengeful rising of the proletariat of all Europe. But in overestimating the power of the proletariat he underestimated the strength of expanding capitalism, nationalism, and the Napoleonic legend. The glittering rule of Napoleon III, the unification of Italy and Germany, the unrivaled prestige of the British Empire, the Irish question and the Jewish question, the ugliness as well as the misery underlying material progress combined to agitate Europe in the age of Bismarck.

It was in December, 1848, that Louis Napoleon, the nephew of the great Emperor, was elected President of the Second French Republic by an overwhelming majority. This enigmatic personality, who has been called everything from a vicious mediocrity to a prophetic genius combining the ideals of peace and humanitarianism with the deceptive trappings of war, held Europe in suspense for over twenty years. His portrait was painted by Tocqueville, who watched him closely for five months as his first minister of foreign affairs. Admitting that he was vastly superior to what his adventurous past had indicated, Tocqueville went on to say in his Recollections: "Although he had a sort of abstract adoration for the people, he had very little taste for liberty. The characteristic and fundamental feature of his mind in political matters was his hatred of and contempt for assemblies. The rule of the Constitutional Monarchy seemed to him even more insupportable than that of the Republic. His unlimited pride in the name he bore, which willingly bowed before the nations, revolted at the idea of yielding to the influence of a parliament. . . .

"One could not approach him except through a group of special, intimate friends and servants, of whom General Changarnier told me that all could be described by these two words which go together: cheats and scoundrels. Nothing was more base than these intimates, except perhaps his family, which consisted, for the most part, of rogues and femmes galantes.

"This was the man whom the need of a chief and the power of a memory had placed at the head of France, and with whom we would have to govern."

As the new constitution prohibited his re-election, he took over the government completely in his famous coup d'état of December 2, 1851, and made himself Emperor Napoleon III a year later. Until almost the end of his reign, in 1870, political clubs and meetings were suppressed, and the Assembly was but an echo. Or, in the succinct words of Albert Guérard, "France had suffered from a plethora of oratory. Louis Napoleon anticipated the excellent advice of Paul Verlaine: 'Take Eloquence and wring its neck.' "

In 1854 France joined with England in one of the most futile of all wars, the Crimean War, against Russia, but Napoleon's defeat of the Austrians in Italy in 1859, for the price of Nice and Savoy, led to the establishment of the kingdom of Italy, in 1861, under Victor Emmanuel II. Mazzini's years of propaganda for a republic, the troops of Garibaldi, the subtle but lofty opportunism of Cavour, and the quiet courage of Victor Emmanuel II were the four great factors in the final process of Italian unification.

What of Germany?

BISMARCK RECOMMENDS THE VALUES OF BLOOD AND IRON

[September 29, 1862]

Awed by France and inspired by Italy, the scattered German states moved toward unity. Would it be under the suzerainty of Prussia or of Austria?

The liberals favored Prussian leadership, but a strong body of conservatives were opposed. Another issue that divided liberals and conservatives was the reorganization of the Prussian army. King Wilhelm I had long set his heart on an increased army of 700,000, composed of younger men, directly subject to his will and almost exclusively commanded by Junker officers. The liberals also wanted to strengthen the army but insisted that it be a people's army, being determined to uphold the Constitution. The question was whether Prussia was to be an absolute military state, as before 1848, or was to remain a constitutional monarchy. The conflict that ensued was so violent that on September 18, 1862, Wilhelm decided to abdicate. Before he could sign the papers, however, his aide, Albrecht von Roon, summoned the one man who might have the concentrated strength and purpose to carry through the King's army program. This man was Prince Otto von Bismarck-Schönhausen (1815–98), at this time a special envoy to Paris. The scion of an old Junker family, Bismarck always upheld the interests of his class and of the monarchy. He had already served as a delegate in the Prussian Landtag, as Prussian minister to the Germanic Diet at Frankfurt (1851–58), and as ambassador to St. Petersburg (1859–62) and to Paris (1862).

When Bismarck entered the King's study on September 22, 1862, the question was whether, in this crisis, he would become Premier. "Would you be prepared to insist upon the reorganization of the army, in spite of the adverse majority?" the King asked. "Yes," replied Bismarck. "Then it is my duty," the King said, "with your aid, to carry on the struggle, and I shall not abdicate." Seven days later the new Premier gave the following impromptu speech over a green table to a few deputies and ministers of state.

"Not by speeches and decisions of majorities will the greatest problems of the time be decided."

THE CONFLICT is viewed too tragically, and presented too tragically in the press; the regime does not seek war. If the crisis can be ended with honor, the regime will gladly do so. The great independence of the individual makes it difficult in Prussia to rule under the Constitution. In France it is otherwise; there, individual independence is lacking. The constitutional crisis, however, is no shame, but rather an honor. We are perhaps too educated to put up with a constitution—we are too critical. Public opinion wavers; the press is not public opinion; we know how that arises. There are too many Catilines, who have revolution at heart. The members [of the House], however, have the task of standing over public sentiment, and of guiding it. Our blood is too hot; we prefer armor too great for our small body to carry, but we should put it to service. Germany does not look to Prussia's liberalism, but to its power. Bavaria, Württemberg, and Baden would like to turn to liberalism, but they shall not assume Prussia's role. Prussia must collect its forces for the favorable occasion, which has several times been neglected; Prussia's borders are not favorable to a healthy national life. Not by speeches and decisions of majorities will the greatest problems of the time be decided —that was the mistake of 1848–49—but by iron and blood. This olive branch [he drew it from his memorandum book] I picked up in Avignon, to offer, as a symbol of peace, to the popular party: I see, however, that it is still not the time for it.

"Iron and blood"! These words spoken in private to a few ministers soon spread like wildfire throughout Germany and across borders of many countries, awakening sudden fears. Even the King and his friend Roon were alarmed. Although Bismarck later expressed regret for his choice of words, he never repudiated them, and they became a symbol of his relentless program of the next ten years. The "blood-and-iron Chancellor," as he came to be called, made war on Denmark, then Austria, then France, and with clocklike precision accomplished his major objectives: unification of Germany under Prussian hegemony, extension of the imperial borders, and glorification of the monarchy.

FERDINAND LASSALLE ATTACKS THE GERMAN PRESS

[September 26, 1863]

For almost thirty years the Iron Chancellor was the dominant figure in Germany—indeed, in all Europe. For a few months between 1862–64 a brilliant rival emerged, a Jewish Socialist labor leader, only to be shot down at thirty-nine in a preposterous romantic duel. While Bismarck sought to fortify the monarchy and to enhance the power of Prussia and the Junker class, Ferdinand Lassalle harangued and conspired for universal suffrage and workers' rights, his ultimate aim being a great German Socialist republic. Yet both men believed in a strong state as a means to their ends, and both regarded the bourgeoisie as their main enemy. Bismarck, who was about to embark on a series of wars, needed Lassalle to conciliate the workers, while Lassalle dreamed of bargaining with Bismarck for universal suffrage, state-aided production associations, and perhaps also grandiose power for himself. For a brief space they were to confer on the future of Germany—and of Europe. Bismarck afterward referred to Lassalle as one of the most brilliant of men, whose company never palled, even when they talked far into the night.

After studying at the universities of Breslau and Berlin, Ferdinand Lassalle (1825–64) immersed himself in philosophy and became a disciple of Hegel. Unlike the internationalist Marx, Lassalle derived from Hegel an enthusiasm for nationalism and the constitutional state as the lever of history. His rise to power as a labor politician in Prussia was curiously interwoven with the career of the Countess Hatzfeldt. When only twenty, he heard of her suffering at the hands of a cruel husband and for four years argued her case in the courts. In the end he completely triumphed over the entrenched power of aristocracy and wealth and was given a handsome annuity by the grateful countess. The next fifteen years were full of intrigue, speechmaking, and love affairs, the publica-

tion of political tracts, workers' programs, literary criticism, and history. Into
the last two years of his life, he crowded, as if foreseeing an early death, a lifetime of activities, and the volume of his writings in a period of feverish political
action is itself scarcely credible. A tall, handsome man, fluent, vivid, arrogant,
and inexhaustible, he spoke to thousands of workers in Berlin, Leipzig, Düsseldorf, down the Rhine—wherever he went.

On September 26, 1863, he gave an address to the General Union of German Workers at Barmen and repeated it at Solingen and Düsseldorf the following days.

> *"You must not neglect agitation; each of you*
> *should make it his task."*

A FAR MORE DISCOURAGING SYMPTOM of the complete dissolution and decay of the Progressive party is the press. I am here touching on a point of the greatest importance, which deserves even a more detailed treatment than I will be able to give. One thing you must keep in
mind constantly, and disseminate constantly: our principal enemy, the
principal enemy of any healthy development of the German spirit and of
the German people today, is the press! The press, at the stage of its evolution which it has now reached, is the true enemy of the people, an
enemy all the more dangerous by reason of its many disguises.

The duplicity of the press was perhaps best brought home to you by
its struggle against our organization, and yet very few of you know even
a small fraction of the truth of this situation. Daily new lies: lies by means
of pure fact alone, lies by means of invented facts, lies by means of facts
distorted into their opposites—such were the weapons with which we
were fought! And to cap the climax of this shameful business, the newspapers in most cases even refused to print a correction. . . .

But the pinnacle of outrage was reached when the newspapers themselves naïvely admit that the principal motive for their silence was their
financial interest. It was the *Rheinische Zeitung*—that unworthy name-
sake of two great organs which were published in the Rhineland in 1843
and in 1848, and which were an honor to their country—it was the
Rheinische Zeitung, I say, that led the pack in this naïve exposure. "How
can people expect," it cried, when a loud murmur among the Progressive
party itself became audible over the cowardice of the newspapers, "how
can people expect the publishers to risk the capital they have invested in

the paper?" To be sure, nothing is more sacred than the publishers' capital! In fact, with the aid of that shameless process of distorting all conceptions which has so long been the prerogative of our newspapers, it was now argued that it was the actual duty of the newspapers to do nothing that might incur a monetary loss. . . . It is as if a soldier—and the newspapers ought to be soldiers, champions of liberty, and claim to be such—should regard it as his first duty under no circumstances to expose himself to the danger of being hit by a bullet!

These are very grave conditions, and, with my soul full of sadness, I do not hesitate to say that unless a complete transformation of our press can be accomplished, if this newspaper pestilence shall continue for fifty years more, the intelligence of our people will be destroyed! But you must understand that if thousands of newspaper writers, these up-to-date teachers of the people, are permitted to spread their stupid ignorance, their consciencelessness, their eunuch's hatred for everything that is true and great in politics, art, and science, and to breathe this spirit into a people which gullibly and trustingly opens its ears to this poison, which is disseminated by hundreds of thousands of voices, because it hopes to imbibe mental nourishment from it, our national intelligence will necessarily be destroyed, even if it were three times as glorious! Not even the most gifted people in the world, not even the ancient Greeks, could have survived such a press. . . .

Hold fast and zealously, therefore, to the slogan I now ask you to make your own: hatred and contempt, death and destruction, to the press of today! . . . The time will come when we will launch the bolt which will bury this press in eternal night!

The secret of the strength of our government has thus far been rooted in the rigid weakness of its adversaries. The reaction will always have an easy time in carrying off the victory if it deals, of course, with such opponents. . . . Nothing has been proved but the total incapacity of the Progressives for any political struggle. A party which cannot cover its most important position with its own corpses in order to defend it—such a party has no promise of victory within it. Such a party has no other course than to run away again at every new attack.

Such a party, and such a press, do not even deserve an expression of regret when the last of the government resounds on their backs. He who has no ability at all to defend his hide has no right to existence. . . .

But I appeal now to our members [of the General Union of German Workers]. You must not neglect agitation; each of you should make it his task. I will give you a simple and easy means to increase our numbers a hundredfold: each one of you must make it a rule to win over every week, which ought not to be difficult, at least one or two members for the General Union of German Workers, and to regard every week as lost in which this duty is not fulfilled. Consider in what geometrical progression our ranks would be multiplied if each of you were filled with this determination.

Yes, it must come to the point where one who refuses to join our union will be regarded as not a real worker, and as having a serious flaw; and he is in fact no real worker, for he lacks either insight into the interests of his class or the manhood to want to work for these interests. And now I appeal to you to join me in the battle cry.

Long live the social democratic agitation! Long live the General Union of German Workers!

The enthusiasm of Lassalle's audience was not echoed by the Prussian officials who read his speech in pamphlet form a few weeks later. He was tried for sedition, found guilty, and sentenced by a Düsseldorf judge to one year's imprisonment. Shortly afterward he received another sentence in Berlin, but he served neither term. In May, 1864, he made his final triumphant campaign, speaking before roaring crowds at Leipzig, Düsseldorf, Solingen, Barmen, Cologne, Wermelskirchen, and Ronsdorf. Where all this would have led, whether or not he could have ultimately undermined the Prussian power of Bismarck and thwarted the international socialism of Karl Marx, no one can say.

Two years earlier he had met in Berlin Helen von Dönniges, the brilliant and beautiful daughter of a minor Bavarian diplomat, and they were mutually captivated. Now they met again in Switzerland, where he had gone for a rest. They plunged into a violent romance and planned to be married, although she had been engaged to a young Rumanian nobleman, Yanko Racowitza. She was certain that her parents would oppose the marriage and wanted to elope with Lassalle, but he insisted on having her parents' approval. The fury of her parents, the obstinacy of Lassalle, the duplicity of his friends, and the final panic of the girl led to complete confusion. He challenged von Dönniges to a duel, and Racowitza took up the challenge. Lassalle was shot in the stomach and died in agony three days later.

Six weeks after the tragic duel Marx brought into being in London the International Workingmen's Association—the First International. Seventeen years later Bismarck said in the Reichstag that Lassalle was one of the most intellectual and gifted men he had ever met. "Lassalle was extremely ambitious, and it was perhaps a matter of doubt to him whether the German Empire would close with the Hohenzollern dynasty or the Lassalle dynasty; but he was monarchical through and through."

THOMAS HENRY HUXLEY EXAMINES
DARWIN'S *ORIGIN OF SPECIES*

[Winter, 1862–63]

Perhaps the most important voyage since Columbus' discovery of America was the scientific voyage of H.M.S. Beagle, which carried its young naturalist, Charles Darwin, around the world between December 27, 1831, and October 2, 1836. It was during those years, especially in South America, that Darwin made those observations on the formation of the earth's surface, on the arrangement of fossils in the geological strata, and on the distribution of living animals which pointed toward "the supposition that species gradually become modified." "And the subject haunted me." But it was not until two years after his return to England, when he was reading for "amusement" Malthus' Principles of Population, that he saw the limitations of the food supply as a general cause of the struggle for existence. "It at once struck me that under these circumstances favorable variations would tend to be preserved, and unfavorable ones to be destroyed. The result of this would be the formation of new species."

Thus Darwin had clearly formulated his epoch-marking theory as early as 1839, but only after twenty years of further reflection and documentation did he present it to the world as a five-hundred-page book (the abstract of an abstract), On the Origin of Species: By Means of Natural Selection. He was too frail in health and too retiring for public controversy, but ardent defenders came to his aid, especially young Professor Thomas Henry Huxley, later known as "Darwin's bulldog."

Although the son of a master in a semipublic school near London, Huxley (1825–95) looked back with horror on the callous teachers who had contributed to his own irregular education. By voracious reading he compensated for his teachers' laxness. He had early dreams of being a mechanical engineer, but it is significant that at thirteen or fourteen he attended a lengthy post-mortem examination to which he traced his lifelong "hypochondriacal dyspepsia," if not his lifelong interest in physiology. Only a few years later he entered the Charing Cross School of Medicine and reveled in the anatomy lectures of a superb teacher, Wharton Jones. He completed his requisite medical studies and passed the first M.B. examination at London University, but he was too young for the Royal College of Surgeons and too poor for further academic work. He served for a few months at a naval hospital and then, because of his scientific equipment, was appointed assistant surgeon on H.M.S. Rattlesnake, which was going on an official exploratory voyage around the world. Those four years did not crystallize in young Huxley's mind a mighty new hypothesis as did the years on the Beagle for Darwin, but the voyage was nonetheless immensely enriching.

After returning to England, Huxley invaded practically the whole realm of biology, won honors, and looked vainly for a good position until at last, in 1854, he was made lecturer on natural history for the Geological Survey. His debut in one of the famous Friday-evening lectures of the Royal Institution was an awkward failure, and it was some years before he became a brilliant, powerful speaker. But his investigations were going well, his teaching was going well, and he was making devoted friends, such as Joseph Hooker, the botanist, and particularly, John Tyndall, the physicist, who was to succeed Faraday as head of the Royal Institution. Later he came to know Darwin, and at least six months before the publication of the Origin of Species, in November, 1859, he began to act as Darwin's "general agent." It was Huxley who wrote the long, favorable review for The Times. And now began one of the most fierce and uncompromising debates in history, carried on in many places by competent and incompetent people, all equally excited.

The climax was reached at Oxford on June 28, 1860, at one of the section meetings of the British Association. Before an audience of several hundred distinguished scientists and laymen, the charming, eloquent, and overconfident Bishop of Oxford, Samuel Wilberforce, primed by the great anatomist, Sir Richard Owen, set out to "smash Darwin." In the course of an hour-long address he casually remarked: "I should like to ask Professor Huxley, who is sitting by me and is about to tear me to pieces when I have sat down, as to his belief in being descended from an ape. Is it on his grandfather's or his grandmother's side that the ape ancestry comes in?"

The Bishop sat down to a storm of applause. Huxley was of course called on to speak, but there was little enthusiasm when he arose. He proceeded at some length in a severely scientific discussion of Darwin's argument but concluded with an answer to the Bishop's question: "I asserted—and I repeat—that a man has no reason to be ashamed of having an ape for his grandfather. If there were an ancestor whom I should feel shame in recalling it would rather be a man—a man of restless and versatile intellect—who, not content with an equivocal success in his own sphere of activity, plunges into scientific questions with which he has no real acquaintance, only to obscure them by an aimless rhetoric, and distract the attention of his hearers from the real point at issue by eloquent digressions and skilled appeals to religious prejudice."

The effect of Huxley's riposte was tremendous. Some in the audience were thrilled, others were horrified. One lady fainted, another jumped hysterically up on her chair. The applause which had increased during the speech ended in an ovation rivaling the Bishop's. Almost overnight the comparatively obscure young biologist became a public figure, to be reckoned with for the rest of his life. He was then exactly thirty-five and had thirty-five more years to live.

Walking away from the meeting with his friend Hooker, Huxley said that "this experience had changed my opinion as to the practical value of the art of public speaking, and that from this time forth I should carefully cultivate it, and try to leave off hating it."

In 1855 Huxley began an annual series of People's Lectures (he abominated the term "popular lectures") for bona fide workingmen, and continued them with increasing success year after year. In the winter of 1862–63 he offered, in a series of six lectures, a full-scale commentary on the Origin of Species. These were taken down in shorthand and published, without Huxley's revision but with his permission, in pamphlet form, and read with delighted admiration by thousands, including Darwin himself.

Here follows, abridged, the sixth and last of the series.

"It is destined to be the guide of biological and psychological speculation for the next three or four generations."

IN THE PRECEDING five lectures I have endeavored to give you an account of those facts, and of those reasonings from facts, which form the data upon which all theories regarding the causes of the phenomena of organic nature must be based. And, although I have had frequent occasion to quote Mr. Darwin—as all persons hereafter, in speaking upon these subjects, will have occasion to quote his famous book on the *Origin of Species*—you must yet remember that, wherever I have quoted him, it has not been upon theoretical points, or for statements in any way connected with his particular speculations, but on matters of fact, brought forward by himself, or collected by himself, and which appear incidentally in his book. If a man *will* make a book, professing to discuss a single question, an encyclopedia, I cannot help it.

Now, having had an opportunity of considering in this sort of way the different statements bearing upon all theories whatsoever, I have to lay before you, as fairly as I can, what is Mr. Darwin's view of the matter and what position his theories hold, when judged by the principles which I have previously laid down, as deciding our judgments upon all theories and hypotheses.

I have already stated to you that the inquiry respecting the causes of the phenomena of organic nature resolves itself into two problems—the first being the question of the origination of living or organic beings; and the second being the totally distinct problem of the modification and perpetuation of organic beings when they have already come into existence. The first question Mr. Darwin does not touch; he does not deal with it at all; but he says: "Given the origin of organic matter—supposing its creation to have already taken place, my object is to show in consequence of what laws and what demonstrable properties of organic matter, and of its environments, such states of organic nature as those with which we are acquainted must have come about." This, you will observe, is a perfectly legitimate proposition; every person has a right to define the limits of the inquiry which he sets before himself; and yet it is a most singular thing that in all the multifarious, and, not unfrequently, ignorant attacks which have been made upon the *Origin of Species,* there is nothing which has been more speciously criticized than this particular limitation. If people have nothing else to urge against the book, they say—"Well, after all, you see Mr. Darwin's explanation of the *Origin of Species* is not good for much, because, in the long run, he admits that he does not know how organic matter began to exist. But if you admit any special creation for the first particle of organic matter you may just as well admit it for all the rest; five hundred or five thousand distinct creations are just as intelligible, and just as little difficult to understand, as one." The answer to these cavils is twofold. In the first place, all human inquiry must stop somewhere; all our knowledge and all our investigation cannot take us beyond the limits set by the finite and restricted character of our faculties, or destroy the endless unknown, which accompanies, like its shadow, the endless procession of phenomena. So far as I can venture to offer an opinion on such a matter, the purpose of our being in existence, the highest object that human beings can set before themselves, is not the pursuit of any such chimera as the annihilation of the unknown; but it is simply the unwearied endeavor to remove its boundaries a little further from our little sphere of action.

I wonder if any historian would for a moment admit the objection that it is preposterous to trouble ourselves about the history of the Roman Empire because we do not know anything postive about the origin and first building of the city of Rome! Would it be a fair objection to urge, respecting the sublime discoveries of a Newton or a Kepler, those great philosophers, whose discoveries have been of the profoundest benefit and service to all men—to say to them—"After all that you have told us as to how the planets revolve, and how they are maintained in their orbits, you cannot tell us what is the cause of the origin of the sun, moon, and stars. So what is the use of what you have done?" Yet these objections would not be one whit more preposterous than the objections which have been made to the *Origin of Species*. Mr. Darwin, then, had a perfect right to limit his inquiry as he pleased, and the only question for us—the inquiry being so limited—is to ascertain whether the method of his inquiry is sound or unsound; whether he has obeyed the canons which must guide and govern all investigation, or whether he has broken them; and it was because our inquiry this evening is essentially limited to that question that I spent a good deal of time in a former lecture (which, perhaps some of you thought might have been better employed) in endeavoring to illustrate the method and nature of scientific inquiry in general. We shall now have to put in practice the principles that I then laid down.

I stated to you in substance, if not in words, that wherever there are complex masses of phenomena to be inquired into, whether they be phenomena of the affairs of daily life or whether they belong to the more abstruse and difficult problems laid before the philosopher, our course of proceeding in unraveling that complex chain of phenomena, with a view to get at its cause, is always the same; in all cases we must invent an hypothesis; we must place before ourselves some more or less likely supposition respecting that cause; and then, having assumed an hypothesis, having supposed a cause for the phenomena in question, we must endeavor, on the one hand, to demonstrate our hypothesis, or, on the other, to upset and reject it altogether, by testing it in three ways. We must, in the first place, be prepared to prove that the supposed causes of the phenomena exist in nature; that they are what the logicians call *vera causae*—true causes—in the next place, we should be prepared to show that the assumed causes of the phenomena are competent to produce such phenomena as those which we wish to explain by them; and in the last place, we ought to be able to show that no other known causes are competent to produce these phenomena. If we can succeed in satisfying these three conditions we shall have demonstrated our hypothesis; or rather I ought to say we shall have proved it as far as certainty is possible for us; for, after all, there is no one of our surest convictions which may not be upset, or at any rate modified, by a further accession of knowledge. It was because it satisfied these conditions that we accepted the hypothesis as to the disappearance of the teapot and spoons in the case I supposed in a previous lecture; we found that our hypothesis on that subject was tenable and valid, because the supposed cause existed in nature, because it was competent to account for the phenomena, and because no other known cause was competent to account for them; and it is upon similar grounds that any hypothesis you choose to name is accepted in science as tenable and valid.

What is Mr. Darwin's hypothesis? As I apprehend it—for I have put it into a shape more convenient for common purposes than I could find verbatim in his book—as I apprehend it, I say, it is that all the phenomena of organic nature, past and present, result from, or are caused by, the interaction of those properties of organic matter, which we have called *atavism* and *variability*, with the *conditions of existence*, or, in other words—given the existence of organic matter, its tendency to transmit its properties, and its tendency occasionally to vary; and, lastly, given the conditions of existence by which organic matter is surrounded—that these put together are the causes of the present and of the past conditions of *organic nature*.

Such is the hypothesis as I understand it. Now let us see how it will stand the various tests which I laid down just now. In the first place, do these supposed causes of the phenomena exist in nature? Is it the fact that, in nature, these properties of organic matter—atavism and variability—and those phenomena which we have called the conditions of existence—is it true that they exist? Well, of course, if they do not exist, all that I have told you in the last three or four lectures must be incorrect, because I have been attempting to prove that they do exist, and I take it that there is abundant evidence that they do exist; so far, therefore, the hypothesis does not break down.

But in the next place comes a much more difficult inquiry: are the causes indicated competent to give rise to the phenomena of organic nature? I suspect that this is indubitable to a certain extent. It is demonstrable, I think, as I have endeavored to show you, that they are perfectly competent to give rise to all the phenomena which are exhibited by *races* in nature. Furthermore, I believe that they are quite competent to account for all that we may call purely structural phenomena which are exhibited by *species* in nature. On that point also I have already enlarged somewhat. Again, I think that the causes assumed are competent to account for most of the physiological characteristics of species and I not only think that they are competent to account for them, but I think that they account for many things which otherwise remain wholly unaccountable and inexplicable, and I may say incomprehensible. For a full exposition of the grounds on which this conviction is based, I must refer you to Mr. Darwin's work; all that I can do now is to illustrate what I have said by two or three cases taken almost at random.

I drew your attention, on a previous evening, to the facts which are embodied in our systems of classification, which are the results of the examination and comparison of the different members of the animal kingdom one with another. I mentioned that the whole of the animal kingdom is divisible into five subkingdoms; that each of these subkingdoms is again divisible into provinces; that each province may be divided into classes, and the classes into the successively smaller groups, orders, families, genera, and species.

Now, in each of these groups the resemblance in structure among the members of the group is closer in proportion as the group is smaller. Thus, a man and a worm are members of the animal kingdom in virtue of certain apparently slight, though really fundamental, resemblances which they present. But a man and a fish are members of the same sub-kingdom *Vertebrata* because they are much more like one another than either of them is to a worm, or a snail, or any members of the other sub-kingdoms. For similar reasons men and horses are arranged as members of the same class, *Mammalia;* men and apes as members of the same order, *Primates;* and if there were any animals more like men than they were like any of the apes, and yet different from men in important and constant particulars of their organization, we should rank them as members of the same family, or of the same genus, but as of distinct species.

That it is possible to arrange all the varied forms of animals into groups, having this sort of singular subordination one to the other, is a very remarkable circumstance; but, as Mr. Darwin remarks, this is a result which is quite to be expected, if the principles which he lays down be correct. . . .

Now, as to the third test, that there are no other causes competent to explain the phenomena, I explained to you that one should be able to say of an hypothesis that no other known causes than those supposed by it are competent to give rise to the phenomena. Here, I think, Mr. Darwin's view is pretty strong. I really believe that the alternative is either Darwinism or nothing, for I do not know of any rational conception or theory of the organic universe which has any scientific position at all beside Mr. Darwin's. I do not know of any proposition that has been put before us with the intention of explaining the phenomena of organic nature which has in its favor a thousandth part of the evidence which may be adduced in favor of Mr. Darwin's views. Whatever may be the objections to his views, certainly all other theories are absolutely out of court.

Take the Lamarckian hypothesis, for example. Lamarck was a great naturalist, and to a certain extent went the right way to work; he argued from what was undoubtedly a true cause of some of the phenomena of organic nature. He said it is a matter of experience that an animal may be modified more or less in consequence of its desires and consequent actions. Thus, if a man exercise himself as a blacksmith, his arms will become strong and muscular; such organic modification is a result of this particular action and exercise. Lamarck thought that by a very simple supposition based on this truth he could explain the origin of the various animal species: he said, for example, that the short-legged birds which live on fish had been converted into the long-legged waders by desiring to get the fish without wetting their feathers, and so stretching their legs more and more through successive generations. If Lamarck could have shown experimentally that even races of animals could be produced in this way, there might have been some ground for his speculations. But he could show nothing of the kind, and his hypothesis has pretty well dropped into oblivion, as it deserved to do. I said in an earlier lecture that there are hypotheses and hypotheses, and when people tell you that Mr. Darwin's strongly based hypothesis is nothing but a mere modification of Lamarck's, you will know what to think of their capacity for forming a judgment on this subject.

But you must recollect that when I say I think it is either Mr. Darwin's hypothesis or nothing; that either we must take his view or look upon the whole of organic nature as an enigma, the meaning of which is wholly hidden from us; you must understand that I mean that I accept it provisionally, in exactly the same way as I accept any other hypothesis. Men of science do not pledge themselves to creeds; they are bound by articles of no sort; there is not a single belief that it is not a bounden duty with them to hold with a light hand and to part with cheerfully the moment it is really proved to be contrary to any fact, great or small. And if, in course of time, I see good reasons for such a proceeding, I shall have no hesitation in coming before you and pointing out any change in my opinion without finding the slightest occasion to blush for so doing. So I say that we accept this view, as we accept any other, so long as it will help us, and we feel bound to retain it only so long as it will serve our great purpose—the improvement of man's estate and the widening of his knowledge. The moment this, or any other conception, ceases to be useful for these purposes, away with it to the four winds; we care not what becomes of it!

But to say truth, although it has been my business to attend closely to the controversies roused by the publication of Mr. Darwin's book, I think that not one of the enormous mass of objections and obstacles which have been raised is of any very great value, except that sterility case which I brought before you just now. All the rest are misunderstandings of some sort, arising either from prejudice or want of knowledge or still more from want of patience and care in reading the work.

For you must recollect that it is not a book to be read with as much ease as its pleasant style may lead you to imagine. You spin through it as if it were a novel the first time you read it, and think you know all about it; the second time you read it you think you know rather less about it; and the third time you are amazed to find how little you have really apprehended its vast scope and objects. I can positively say that I never take it up without finding in it some new view, or light, or suggestion that I have not noticed before. That is the best characteristic of a thorough and profound book; and I believe this feature of the *Origin of Species* explains why so many persons have ventured to pass judgment and criticisms upon it which are by no means worth the paper they are written on.

Before concluding these lectures there is one point to which I must advert—though, as Mr. Darwin has said nothing about man in his book, it concerns myself rather than him—for I have strongly maintained on sundry occasions that if Mr. Darwin's views are sound, they apply as much to man as to the lower mammals, seeing that it is perfectly demonstrable that the structural differences which separate man from the apes are not greater than those which separate some apes from others. There cannot be the slightest doubt in the world that the argument which applies to the improvement of the horse from an earlier stock, or of ape from ape, applies to the improvement of man from some simpler and lower stock than man. There is not a single faculty—functional or structural, moral, intellectual, or instinctive—there is no faculty whatever that is not capable of improvement; there is no faculty whatsoever which does not depend upon structure, and as structure tends to vary, it is capable of being improved.

Well, I have taken a good deal of pains at various times to prove this, and I have endeavored to meet the objections of those who maintain that the structural differences between man and the lower animals are of so vast a character and enormous extent that even if Mr. Darwin's views are correct, you cannot imagine this particular modification to take place. It is, in fact, an easy matter to prove that, so far as structure is concerned, man differs to no greater extent from the animals which are immediately below him than these do from other members of the same order. Upon the other hand, there is no one who estimates more highly than I do the dignity of human nature, and the width of the gulf in intellectual and moral matters which lies between man and the whole of the lower creation.

But I find this very argument brought forward vehemently by some. "You say that man has proceeded from a modification of some lower animal, and you take pains to prove that the structural differences which are said to exist in his brain do not exist at all, and you teach that all functions, intellectual, moral, and others, are the expression or the result, in the long run, of structures, and of the molecular forces which they exert." It is quite true that I do so.

"Well, but," I am told at once, somewhat triumphantly, "you say in the same breath that there is a great moral and intellectual chasm between man and the lower animals. How is this possible when you declare that moral and intellectual characteristics depend on structure, and yet tell us that there is no such gulf between the structure of man and that of the lower animals?"

I think that objection is based upon a misconception of the real relations which exist between structure and function, between mechanism and work. Function is the expression of molecular forces and arrangements, no doubt; but does it follow from this that variation in function so depends upon variation in structure that the former is always exactly proportioned to the latter? If there is no such relation, if the variation in function which follows on a variation in structure may be enormously greater than the variation of the structure, then, you see, the objection falls to the ground.

Take a couple of watches—made by the same maker, and as completely alike as possible; set them upon the table, and the function of each—which is its rate of going—will be performed in the same manner, and you shall be able to distinguish no difference between them; but let me take a pair of pincers, and if my hand is steady enough to do it, let me just lightly crush together the bearings of the balance wheel, or force to a slightly different angle the teeth of the escapement of one of them, and of course you know the immediate result will be that the watch, so treated, from that moment will cease to go. But what proportion is there between the structural alteration and the functional result? Is it not perfectly obvious that the alteration is of the minutest kind, yet that, slight as it is, it has produced an infinite difference in the performance of the functions of these two instruments?

Well, now, apply that to the present question. What is it that constitutes and makes man what he is? What is it but his power of language—that language giving him the means of recording his experience—making every generation somewhat wiser than its predecessor—more in accordance with the established order of the universe?

What is it but this power of speech, of recording experience, which enables men to be men—looking before and after and, in some dim sense, understanding the working of this wondrous universe—and which distinguishes man from the whole of the brute world? I say that this functional difference is vast, unfathomable, and truly infinite in its consequences; and I say, at the same time, that it may depend upon structural differences which shall be absolutely inappreciable to us with our present means of investigation. What is this very speech that we are talking about? I am speaking to you at this moment, but if you were to alter, in the minutest degree, the proportion of the nervous forces now active in the two nerves which supply the muscles of my glottis, I should become suddenly dumb. The voice is produced only so long as the vocal cords are parallel; and these are parallel only so long as certain muscles contract with exact equality; and that again depends on the equality of action of those two nerves I spoke of. So that a change of the minutest kind in the structure of one of these nerves, or in the structure of the part in which it originates, or of the supply of blood to that part, or of one of the muscles to which it is distributed, might render all of us dumb. But a race of dumb men, deprived of all communication with those who could speak, would be little indeed removed from the brutes. And the moral and intellectual difference between them and ourselves would be practically infinite, though the naturalist should not be able to find a single shadow of even specific structural difference.

But let me dismiss this question now, and, in conclusion, let me say that you may go away with it as my mature conviction that Mr. Darwin's work is the greatest contribution which has been made to biological science since the publication of the *Règne Animal* of Cuvier, and since that of the *History of Development* of von Baer. I believe that if you strip it of its theoretical part it still remains one of the greatest encyclopedias of biological doctrine that any one man ever brought forth; and I believe that, if you take it as the embodiment of an hypothesis, it is destined to be the guide of biological and psychological speculation for the next three or four generations.

"My workingmen stick by me wonderfully," Huxley wrote to his wife during this period; and more than one distinguished observer commented on the earnest, intelligent response of that audience of six hundred or more who listened to Huxley's lectures winter after winter.

Perhaps no first-rate scientists ever gave so many masterly talks to such a variety of audiences. The year 1868 was marked by three of his best, "A Liberal Education and Where to Find It," "On a Piece of Chalk," and "On the Physical Basis of Life." In giving the main address at the inaugural exercises of Johns Hopkins University in 1876, Huxley had to cope with the most exasperating circumstances. He had planned to speak extemporaneously from notes, but the day before the ceremony newspaper reporters requested a manuscript, so he docilely dictated his thoughts on university education to a stenographer. A

copy was returned to him at the last moment, but when he stood at the rostrum
he found that he could not read a sentence because of the thinness of the
paper. He had to try desperately to recall what he had said the day before—
and was highly effective.

JOHN RUSKIN BEMOANS THE
DEGRADATION OF
MODERN LIFE

[May 13, 1868]

"That singular voice of his, which would often hold all the theater breathless,
haunts me still. There was something strange and aerial in its exquisite modulations that seemed as if it came from a disconsolate spirit hovering over the
waters of Babylon and remembering Zion." Thus Ruskin appeared to a brilliant
Oxford undergraduate, W. H. Mallock, who heard some of the Slade lectures
on art that Ruskin began in 1870.

John Ruskin (1819–1900) was the only son of a wealthy Scots sherry merchant and a devout mother who "dedicated him to God" in the cradle. As the
only son, he was too protected, too cultivated, too isolated—a precocious,
neurotic genius whose early marriage was annulled on the grounds of his "incurable impotency." But he made up for these disabilities by a life of fabulous
productivity in a dozen fields. In his twenties he wrote the first two volumes of
Modern Painters, which established the reputation of the great English land-
scape painter, Turner, and at the same time "taught the claim of all lower
nature on the hearts of men; of the rock, and wave, and herb, as a part of their
necessary spirit life." As he crossed into his thirties, he completed The Seven
Lamps of Architecture, which was all too successful in encouraging Gothic
taste in an un-Gothic world. Then in The Stones of Venice he "taught the
laws of constructive art, and the dependence of all human work or edifice, for
its beauty, on the happy life of the workman," and in the decay of the little
Venetian empire and of Venetian art he saw parallels to modern England. By
the time Ruskin was forty, he was obsessed with the misery and ugliness of
industrial civilization. Art had become subordinated in his thinking to political
economy—and political economy to ethics. Ruskin the art critic gave way to
Ruskin the critic of modern society. The year 1860 is the clear dividing line,
for in that year he rounded out the first half of his career with the fifth volume
of Modern Painters and dashed off Unto This Last, which taught that "THERE

IS NO WEALTH BUT LIFE. *Life including all its powers of love, of joy, of admiration." This little book, which Ruskin considered his most useful contribution, helped to prepare the atmosphere for the British labor movement and later "brought about an instantaneous and practical transformation" in the life of Gandhi.*

It is difficult to know what to choose from Ruskin's rich and diffuse collection of public talks. One of the finest and one of his favorites was "The Mystery of Life and Its Arts," given before a fascinated audience of two thousand in the theater of the Royal College of Science in Dublin, on May 13, 1868.

Here is an excerpt from the middle of the address.

"Might we not live in nobler dream than this?"

AND NOW, returning to the broader question, what these arts and labors of life have to teach us of its mystery, this is the first of their lessons—that the more beautiful the art, the more it is essentially the work of people *who feel themselves wrong*—who are striving for the fulfillment of a law, and the grasp of a loveliness, which they have not yet attained, which they feel even farther and farther from attaining the more they strive for it. And yet, in still deeper sense, it is the work of people who know also that they are right. The very sense of inevitable error from their purpose marks the perfectness of that purpose, and the continued sense of failure arises from the continued opening of the eyes more clearly to all the sacredest laws of truth.

This is one lesson. The second is a very plain, and greatly precious one: namely, that whenever the arts and labors of life are fulfilled in this spirit of striving against misrule, and doing whatever we have to do, honorably and perfectly, they invariably bring happiness, as much as seems possible to the nature of man. In all other paths by which that happiness is pursued there is disappointment, or destruction; for ambition and for passion there is no rest—no fruition; the fairest pleasures of youth perish in a darkness greater than their past light; and the loftiest and purest love too often does but inflame the cloud of life with endless fire of pain. But, ascending from lowest to highest, through every scale of human industry, that industry, worthily followed, gives peace. Ask the laborer in the field, at the forge, or in the mine; ask the patient, delicate-fingered artisan, or the strong-armed, fiery-hearted worker in bronze, and in marble, and in the colors of light; and none of these, who are true workmen, will ever tell you that they have found the law of heaven an unkind one—that in the sweat of their face they should eat bread, till they return to the ground; not that they ever found it an unrewarded obedience, if, indeed, it was rendered faithfully to the command—"Whatsoever thy hand findeth to do—do it with thy might."

These are the two great and constant lessons which our laborers teach us of the mystery of life. But there is another, and a sadder one, which they cannot teach us, which we must read on their tombstones.

"Do it with thy might." There have been myriads upon myriads of human creatures who have obeyed this law—who have put every breath and nerve of their being into its toil—who have devoted every hour, and exhausted every faculty—who have bequeathed their unaccomplished thoughts at death—who, being dead, have yet spoken, by majesty of memory, and strength of example. And, at last, what has all this "Might" of humanity accomplished, in six thousand years of labor and sorrow? What has it *done?* Take the three chief occupations and arts of men, one by one, and count their achievements. Begin with the first—the lord of them all—agriculture. Six thousand years have passed since we were sent to till the ground, from which we were taken. How much of it is tilled? How much of that which is, wisely or well? In the very center and chief garden of Europe—where the two forms of parent Christianity have had their fortresses—where the noble Catholics of the Forest Cantons, and the noble Protestants of the Vaudois valleys, have maintained, for dateless ages, their faiths and liberties—there the unchecked Alpine rivers yet run wild in devastation; and the marshes, which a few hundred men could redeem with a year's labor, still blast their helpless inhabitants into fevered idiotism. That is so, in the center of Europe! While, on the near coast of Africa, once the Garden of the Hesperides, an Arab woman, but a few sunsets since, ate her child, for famine. And, with all the treasures of the East at our feet, we, in our own dominion, could not find a few grains of rice for a people that asked of us no more; but stood by, and saw five hundred thousand of them perish of hunger.

Then, after agriculture, the art of kings, take the next head of human arts—weaving; the art of queens, honored of all noble heathen women, in the person of their virgin goddess—honored of all Hebrew women, by the word of their wisest king: "She layeth her hands to the spindle, and her hands hold the distaff; she stretcheth out her hand to the poor. . . . She is not afraid of the snow for her household: for all her household are clothed with scarlet. She maketh herself coverings of tapestry; her clothing is silk and purple. . . . She maketh fine linen, and selleth it; and delivereth girdles unto the merchant." What have we done in all these thousands of years with this bright art of Greek maid and Christian ma-

tron? Six thousand years of weaving, and have we learned to weave?
Might not every naked wall have been purple with tapestry, and every
feeble breast fenced with sweet colors from the cold? What have we done?
Our fingers are too few, it seems, to twist together some poor covering
for our bodies. We set our streams to work for us, and choke the air with
fire, to turn our spinning wheels—and—*are we yet clothed?* Are not the
streets of the capitals of Europe foul with the sale of cast clouts and
rotten rags? Is not the beauty of your sweet children left in wretchedness
of disgrace, while, with better honor, nature clothes the brood of the
bird in its nest, and the suckling of the wolf in her den? And does not
every winter's snow robe what you have not robed, and shroud what you
have not shrouded; and every winter's wind bear up to heaven its wasted
souls, to witness against you hereafter, by the voice of their Christ—"I
was naked, and ye clothed me not"?

Lastly—take the art of building—the strongest—proudest—most orderly—most enduring of the arts of man; that of which the produce is
in the surest manner accumulative, and need not perish, or be replaced;
but if once done well will stand more strongly than the unbalanced rocks
—more prevalently than the crumbling hills. The art which is associated
with all civic pride and sacred principle; with which men record their
power—satisfy their enthusiasm—make sure their defense—define and
make dear their habitation. And in six thousand years of building, what
have we done? Of the greater part of all that skill and strength, *no* vestige
is left, but fallen stones, that encumber the fields and impede the streams.
But, from this waste of disorder, and of time, and of rage, what *is* left to
us? Constructive and progressive creatures that we are, with ruling
brains, and forming hands, capable of fellowship, and thirsting for fame,
can we not contend, in comfort, with the insects of the forest, or,
in achievement, with the worm of the sea? The white surf rages in vain
against the ramparts built by poor atoms of scarcely nascent life; but
only ridges of formless ruin mark the places where once dwelt our noblest
multitudes. The ant and the moth have cells for each of their young, but
our little ones lie in festering heaps, in homes that consume them like
graves; and night by night, from the corners of our streets, rises up the
cry of the homeless—"I was a stranger, and ye took me not in."

Must it be always thus? Is our life forever to be without profit—without possession? Shall the strength of its generations be as barren as death;
or cast away their labor, as the wild fig tree casts her untimely figs? Is it
all a dream then—the desire of the eyes and the pride of life—or, if it be,
might we not live in nobler dream than this? The poets and prophets, the
wise men, and the scribes, though they have told us nothing about a life

to come, have told us much about the life that is now. They have had—
they also—their dreams, and we have laughed at them. They have
dreamed of mercy, and of justice; they have dreamed of peace and good
will; they have dreamed of labor undisappointed, and of rest undisturbed; they have dreamed of fullness in harvest, and overflowing in
store; they have dreamed of wisdom in council, and of providence in law;
of gladness of parents, and strength of children, and glory of gray hairs.
And at these visions of theirs we have mocked, and held them for idle
and vain, unreal and unaccomplishable. What have we accomplished
with our realities? Is this what has come of our worldly wisdom, tried
against their folly? this, our mightiest possible, against their impotent
ideal? or, have we only wandered among the specter of a baser felicity,
and chased phantoms of the tombs, instead of visions of the Almighty;
and walked after the imaginations of our evil hearts, instead of after the
counsels of Eternity, until our lives—not in the likeness of the cloud of
heaven, but of the smoke of hell—have become "as a vapour, that appeareth for a little time, and then vanisheth away"?

Does it vanish, then? Are you sure of that?—sure that the nothingness
of the grave will be a rest from this troubled nothingness; and that the
coiling shadow, which disquiets itself in vain, cannot change into the
smoke of the torment that ascends forever? Will any answer that they
are sure of it, and that there is no fear, nor hope, nor desire, nor labor,
whither they go? Be it so: will you not, then, make as sure of the Life that
now is as you are of the Death that is to come? Your hearts are wholly
in this world—will you not give them to it wisely, as well as perfectly?
And see, first of all, that you have hearts, and sound hearts, too, to give.
Because you have no heaven to look for, is that any reason that
you should remain ignorant of this wonderful and infinite earth, which
is firmly and instantly given you in possession? Although your days are
numbered, and the following darkness sure, is it necessary that you
should share the degradation of the brute, because you are condemned
to its mortality; or live the life of the moth, and of the worm, because you
are to companion them in the dust? Not so; we may have but a few thousands of days to spend, perhaps hundreds only—perhaps tens; nay, the
longest of our time and best, looked back on, will be but as a moment,
as the twinkling of an eye; still we are men, not insects; we are living
spirits, not passing clouds. "He maketh the winds His messengers; the
momentary fire, His minister"; and shall we do less than these? Let us do
the work of men while we bear the form of them; and, as we snatch our
narrow portion of time out of Eternity, snatch also our narrow inheritance
of passion out of Immortality—even though our lives be as a vapor, that
appeareth for a little time, and then vanisheth away.

In 1869 Ruskin became the first Slade professor of art at Oxford, where for nine years his crowded lectures were more like revivalist meetings than academic classes. His inaugural address ended with such a flamboyant appeal to young Englishmen to go out and conquer the world, to take up "the white man's burden" (while Kipling was a child), that Cecil Rhodes, who came to Oxford shortly afterward, "regarded his copy of Ruskin's inaugural as his most precious possession." Militarists and imperialists, benign Tories and eager Socialists, could find fuel at Ruskin's flaming hearth.

LÉON GAMBETTA BEGINS THE RECON-STRUCTION OF FRANCE AFTER THE GERMAN CONQUEST

[June 26, 1871]

Léon Michel Gambetta (1838–82), son of an Italian grocer in southern France, did not acquire French citizenship until he was twenty-one. He began to practice law in Paris in 1861, but became more conspicuous as a coarse Bohemian of the Latin Quarter than as a coming figure in the law courts. Then suddenly the Baudin case gave him his opportunity.

In 1868, seventeen years after Napoleon's coup d'état, an indiscreet writer, Eugène Tenot, recalled that some members of the Assembly had gone unarmed to the barricades to prevent violation of the law, and one of them, Baudin, Deputy for the Ain, was struck by a bullet and killed. This led to visits to Baudin's neglected grave and a movement to raise a monument to his memory. A leader in this dangerous cause was the editor Louis Charles Delescluze, who was brought to trial on a charge of "exciting hatred and contempt of the government." He was sentenced to six months' imprisonment and fined six thousand francs. But in defending Delescluze, Gambetta boldly denounced the coup d'état and the government, and made himself a national hero overnight.

He was soon afterward elected to the Chamber of Deputies, where even the Bonapartists listened to him with respect. It was there, on April 5, 1870, that he made his masterly attack on the Emperor's "liberal Constitution," which was nonetheless approved in another huge plebiscite. Four months later France declared war on Prussia.

Gambetta opposed the declaration of war, but once France was involved he became the perfect patriot. When the French armies in the north were defeated or surrounded after a few weeks and the Emperor was taken prisoner,

Gambetta was foremost in quieting the street crowds of Paris and in proclaiming the Third Republic. As Minister of the Interior in the provisional government, it devolved upon him to arouse the provinces to the defense of Paris. Helpless in the besieged capital, he escaped in a balloon and joined his colleagues in Tours. There he became also Minister of War and for four months, from early October, 1870, to early February, 1871, he was the dictator of France. By prodigious efforts, this second Danton raised armies and awakened cities, but Paris fell on January 28, 1871, and French resistance collapsed. He would have carried on a war to the knife, but neither the government nor the country was with him, and he resigned his offices.

Gambetta was now elected by nine departments to the new National Assembly meeting at Bordeaux. He chose to sit for Strasbourg in Alsace, which was to be ceded to Prussia in the treaty then being negotiated. When the treaty was ratified by the National Assembly, he resigned in protest. A more melancholy protest just at this time was the sudden death at Bordeaux of Mayor Küss of Strasbourg. Gambetta at the funeral spoke ominously of the day of reckoning, and then, to rid his country of his troublesome presence, retired to Spain.

However, he returned to Bordeaux a few months later and began at once to reconstruct his own life and the life of France, with an oration before a large public meeting—a meeting of grave and dispirited Frenchmen.

"Let us study our misfortunes and go back to the causes."

Gentlemen and Fellow Citizens:

I DID NOT DESIRE to set foot in France again, after the labors you know of, or to take part in the responsibilities and work of the republican party, without stopping in Bordeaux. Apropos of the grave situation in which we find our country, I wish to tell you, without mental reservation, as I am not the candidate of this department, all that I hope, all that I desire to accomplish.

Do not applaud, gentlemen! The hour is much too solemn for anything more than the exchange of esteem and reciprocal confidences. The actual situation in France, when closely examined, and when in such examination one is animated by a passion for justice and truth—that is to say, when, by the rules of reason, one guards against the illusions of the heart —is such as to inspire a profound sadness; but it invites us to the manliest measures and forbids any discouragement. Let us study it, and we will arrive at this conclusion—that the republican party, if it desire, it can, and if it know how, it will, regenerate this country and erect a government of liberty out of this abyss of surprises, reactions, and failures. This is the demonstration which it is necessary to make today in the face of our competitors of the monarchial parties, not only to achieve the triumph of the principles to which we are attached, but, repeating it, we must not cease striving to give France her salvation.

At this hour what do we see in our country? We see men who had always slandered democracy, who hated it; who ignorantly or for gain, exploiting the credulity of others, had systematically misrepresented its methods—we see such men attributing all the excesses of the last few months to the Republic, to which they never should have been charged; and I find an analogy full of instruction between the condition of affairs in May, 1870, and the present hour. In 1870 France was put to the question—who then knew how and by whom it was done? But it is not the less true she was invested with the right to pronounce on her destinies. Through the agency of complicated fears, excited by a suborned press, aiding the basest interests, the interests of dynasties and of parasites, France was taken unawares, and her vote was at a disadvantage, but, nevertheless, she pronounced her decision with a lightninglike rapidity. Three months afterward, the decision accomplished its ends. She was punished, she was scourged beyond all justice, for having abandoned herself to the criminal hands of an emperor.

Today, again, in diverse forms, the same question is put to her. Will she abdicate again, and throw her power into the lap of a dynasty?

Under whatever name the thing is disguised, it is always the same question—the question of whether France will govern herself in freedom or will betray herself—of whether the terrible experience, from which she emerged mutilated and bleeding, has taught her at last to maintain her independence. . . .

We must get rid of the evil which causes our woes—ignorance, whence emerge alternately despotism and demagogy! Of all the remedies which can solicit the attention of the statesman and politician to prevent such evils, there is one that excels and includes all the rest; it is universal education. We must discover by what measures and processes, on the morrow of our disasters, imputable not only to the government, to which we submitted, but to the degeneracy of public spirit, we can assure ourselves against the falls, the errors, the surprises, the inferiorities which have cost us so much. Let us study our misfortunes and go back to the causes. First of all, we allowed ourselves to be distanced by other peoples, less gifted than ourselves, who, however, were making progress while we remained stationary. Yes, we can establish, by the proof in hand, that it is the inferiority of our national education that led to our reverses. We were beaten by adversaries who had enlisted on their side caution, discipline, and science. This proves that on a last analysis, even among the conflicts of material forces, intelligence remains the master. . . . We must learn and then teach the peasant what he owes to society and what he has the right to ask of her.

On the day when it will be well understood that we have no grander or more pressing work; that we should put aside and postpone all other reforms; that we have but one task, the instruction of the people, the diffusion of education, the encouragement of science—on that day a great step will have been taken in your regeneration. But our action needs to be a double one, that it may bear upon the body as well as the mind. To be exact, each man should be intelligent, trained not only to think, read, and reason, but able also to act, to fight! Everywhere beside the teacher, we should place the gymnast and the soldier, to the end that our children, our soldiers, our fellow citizens, should be able to hold a sword, to carry a gun on a long march, to sleep under the canopy of the stars, to support valiantly all the hardships demanded of a patriot. We must push to the front these two educations. Otherwise you make a success of letters, but do not create a bulwark of patriots.

Yes, gentlemen, if they have outclassed us, if you had to submit to the supreme agony of seeing the France of Kléber and of Hoche lose her two most patriotic provinces, those best embodying at once the military, commercial, industrial, and democratic spirit, we can blame only our inferior physical and moral condition. Today the interests of our country command us to speak no imprudent words, to close our lips, to sink to the bottom of our hearts our resentments, to take up the grand work of national regeneration, to devote to it all the time necessary, that it may be a lasting work. If it need ten years, if it need twenty years, then we must devote to it ten or twenty years. But we must commence at once, that each year may see the advancing life of a new generation, strong, intelligent, as much in love with science as with the fatherland, having in their hearts the double sentiment that he serves his country well only when he serves it with his reason and his arm.

We have been educated in a rough school. We must therefore cure ourselves of the vanity which has caused us so many disasters. We must also realize conscientiously where our responsibility exists and, seeing the remedy, sacrifice all to the object to be attained—to remake and reconstitute France! For that, nothing should be accounted too good and we shall ask nothing before this—the first demand must be for an education as complete from base to summit as is known to human intelligence. Naturally, merit must be recognized, aptitude awakened and approved, and honest and impartial judges freely chosen by their fellow citizens, deciding publicly in such a way that merit alone will open the door. Reject as authors of mischief those who have put words in the place of action; all those who have put favoritism in the place of merit; all those who made the profession of arms not a means for the protection of France, but a means of serving the caprices of a master, and sometimes of becoming the accomplices of his crimes. In one word, let us get back to truth, and let it be known to all the world that when a citizen is born in France, he is born a soldier; and that no matter who he is, who would shirk his double duty of civil and military instruction, he will be pitilessly deprived of his rights as a citizen and an elector. Let the thought enter the very souls of the present and coming generations, that in a democratic government whoever is not ready to bear a share of its troubles and trials is not fit to take part in the government. Thus, gentlemen, you enter into the verity of democratic principles, which are to honor labor and to make of industry and science the two elements constituting the whole of free society. Oh, what a nation we could make with such a discipline followed religiously for a term of years, with the admirable adaptability of our race for the production of thinkers, savants, heroes, and liberal spirits! In thinking on this great subject, we rise swiftly above the sadness of the present, to view the future with confidence. . . .

It is better to have a republican minority—firm, energetic, vigilant in its attitude toward the acts of the majority—than to be one of a majority of inconstant, lukewarm men who seem to be only able to carry on public affairs by compromising their principles.

Following this first line of conduct, I would demonstrate by such logic that there is today no other experiment in the way of national reform possible than this of public education and national armament.

In seeing the accomplishment of this double reform, I shall not take the time and patience to discuss lengthily the attendant and lateral questions that are subordinated to the realization of these first and capital necessities.

It means the reconstruction of the blood, the bone, the very marrow of France. Know it well: we must give everything, our time, our money, to this supreme interest. The people will not haggle over the millions needed for the education of the poor and ignorant. They will question expenditure on the part of those whose designs tend always to the restoration of monarchies, to ridiculous disbursement, or to the subjection of the country itself.

And in passing, gentlemen, one reason why the monarchy cannot be restored among us is that we are no longer rich enough to support it.

As a result we shall have resolved thereby the most vital of all problems: the equalization of the classes, and the dissipation of the pretended antagonism between the cities and the country. We shall have suppressed political parasites and, by the diffusion of knowledge to all, shall have given to the country its moral and political vigor. Thus we may attain a double insurance—one against crimes threatening the common right, by the elevation of the standard of public morality; the other against risk of revolution, by giving satisfaction and security to the acquired rights of some and to the legitimate aspirations of others.

Such is the program at once radical and conservative which the Republic alone can accomplish. Then throughout the world the friends of France would be reassured. She would emerge regenerated by her great trials, and even under the blows of ill fortune she would appear grander, more prosperous, prouder than ever.

This speech at Bordeaux, according to Paul Deschanel, President of the French Republic in 1920, "reassured the country" and helped to place "the Republic on a firm footing." But for eight more years Gambetta fought and spoke with success against the strong conservative reaction that set in after the German victory. He was himself Premier briefly before his death at the age of forty-four.

DISRAELI DEFENDS THE PRINCIPLES
OF THE CONSERVATIVE PARTY

[April 3, 1872]

Benjamin Disraeli (1804–81), later Lord Beaconsfield, was a son of the prosperous bibliophile, Isaac Disraeli, a convert to Christianity. His first efforts to win a seat in Parliament as an independent failed, but in 1837 he was elected as a Conservative, the Conservative party being at that time under the comparatively liberal leadership of Peel. Young Disraeli's debut in the House of Commons was not promising, in spite of the fact that he was already a successful novelist. His maiden speech, not to mention his costume, was so gaudy, so affected, that he was laughed off the floor. But as he sat down he shouted, "You shall hear me!" And within a decade he was so smooth, so colloquial, so wittily malicious, that the House hung on his words. Not as a cautious defender but as an aggressive apostle of Conservatism, he rose to the leadership of his party and the prime ministry, and pressed through a second Reform Bill that left the Liberals gasping.

Going out of office in 1868, he wrote his ninth novel, Lothair (the first in twenty years), directed the rebuilding of his party, and started his methodical return to power in 1872. With his flair for the dramatic, he chose Manchester, the name place for laissez-faire "Manchester economics," for his opening attack on laissez-faire economics and the whole program of Gladstone's Liberal party. After a triumphant parade through the streets of the city, he was introduced to a fascinated, if not affectionate, audience in the large Free Trade Hall. An apparently frail man of sixty-eight, he spoke vigorously for three hours and a quarter, meanwhile consuming two bottles of white brandy that looked like the water taken with it.

"Gentlemen, the program of the Conservative party is to maintain the Constitution of the country."

Gentlemen:

THE CHAIRMAN has correctly reminded you that this is not the first time that my voice has been heard in this hall. But that was an occasion very different from that which now assembles us together—was nearly thirty years ago, when I endeavored to support and stimulate the flagging energies of an institution in which I thought there were the germs of future refinement and intellectual advantage to the rising generation of Manchester, and since I have been here on this occasion I have learned with much gratification that it is now counted among your most flourishing institutions. There was also another and more recent occasion when the gracious office fell to me to distribute among the members of the Mechanics' Institution those prizes which they had gained through their study in letters and in science. Gentlemen, these were pleasing offices, and if life consisted only of such offices you would not have to complain of it. But life has its masculine duties, and we are assembled here to fulfill some of the most important of these, when, as citizens of a free country, we are assembled together to declare our determination to maintain, to uphold the Constitution to which we are debtors, in our opinion, for our freedom and our welfare.

Gentlemen, there seems at first something incongruous that one should be addressing the population of so influential and intelligent a county as Lancashire who is not locally connected with them, and, gentlemen, I will frankly admit that this circumstance did for a long time make me hesitate in accepting your cordial and generous invitation. But, gentlemen, after what occurred yesterday, after receiving more than two hundred addresses from every part of this great county, after the welcome which then greeted me, I feel that I should not be doing justice to your feelings, I should not do my duty to myself, if I any longer consider my presence here tonight to be an act of presumption. Gentlemen, though it may not be an act of presumption, it still is, I am told, an act of great difficulty. Our opponents assure us that the Conservative party has no political program; and, therefore, they must look with much satisfaction to one whom you honor tonight by considering him the leader and representative of your opinions when he comes forward, at your invitation, to express to you what that program is. The Conservative party are accused of having no program of policy. If by a program is meant a plan to despoil churches and plunder landlords, I admit we have no program. If by a program is meant a policy which assails or menaces every institution and every interest, every class and every calling in the country, I admit we have no program. But if to have a policy with distinct ends, and these such as most deeply interest the great body of the nation, be a becoming program for a political party, then I contend we have an adequate program, and one which, here or elsewhere, I shall always be prepared to assert and to vindicate.

Gentlemen, the program of the Conservative party is to maintain the Constitution of the country. I have not come down to Manchester to deliver an essay on the English Constitution; but when the banner of republicanism is unfurled—when the fundamental principles of our institutions are controverted—I think, perhaps, it may not be inconvenient that I should make some few practical remarks upon the character of our Constitution—upon that monarchy limited by the co-ordinate authority of the estates of the realm, which, under the title of Queen, Lords, and Commons, has contributed so greatly to the prosperity of this country, and with the maintenance of which I believe that prosperity is bound up.

Gentlemen, since the settlement of that Constitution, now nearly two centuries ago, England has never experienced a revolution, though there is no country in which there has been so continuous and such considerable change. How is this? Because the wisdom of your forefathers placed the prize of supreme power without the sphere of human passions. Whatever the struggle of parties, whatever the strife of factions, whatever the excitement and exaltation of the public mind, there has always been something in this country round which all classes and parties could rally, representing the majesty of the law, the administration of justice, and involving, at the same time, the security for every man's rights and the fountain of honor. Now, gentlemen, it is well clearly to comprehend what is meant by a country not having a revolution for two centuries. It means, for that space, the unbroken exercise and enjoyment of the ingenuity of man. It means for that space the continuous application of the discoveries of science to his comfort and convenience. It means the accumulation of capital, the elevation of labor, the establishment of those admirable factories which cover your district; the unwearied improvement of the cultivation of the land, which has extracted from a somewhat churlish soil harvests more exuberant than those furnished by lands nearer to the sun. It means the continuous order which is the only parent of personal liberty and political right. And you owe all these, gentlemen, to the throne. . . .

[After describing the wisdom, the stability, and the glory embodied in the throne, the House of Lords, and the Established Church, Disraeli went on to criticize the Liberal party under Gladstone for its failures in international affairs and social reforms.]

Gentlemen, I think public attention as regards these matters ought to be concentrated upon sanitary legislation. That is a wide subject, and, if properly treated, comprises almost every consideration which has a just claim upon legislative interference. Pure air, pure water, the inspection of unhealthy habitations, the adulteration of food—these and many kindred matters may be legitimately dealt with by the legislature; and I am bound to say the legislature is not idle upon them; for we have at this time two important measures before Parliament on the subject. One—by a late colleague of mine, Sir Charles Adderley—is a large and comprehensive measure, founded upon a sure basis, for it consolidates all existing public acts, and improves them. A prejudice has been raised against that proposal, by stating that it interferes with the private acts of the great towns. I take this opportunity of contradicting that. The bill of Sir Charles Adderley does not touch the acts of the great towns. It only allows them, if they think fit, to avail themselves of its new provisions.

The other measure by the government is of a partial character. What it comprises is good, so far as it goes, but it shrinks from that bold consolidation of existing acts which I think one of the great merits of Sir Charles Adderley's bill, which permits us to become acquainted with how much may be done in favor of sanitary improvement by existing provisions. Gentlemen, I cannot impress upon you too strongly my conviction of the importance of the legislature and society uniting together in favor of these important results. A great scholar and a great wit, three hundred years ago, said that, in his opinion, there was a great mistake in the Vulgate, which, as you all know, is the Latin translation of the Holy Scriptures, and that, instead of saying "Vanity of vanities, all is vanity"—*Vanitas vanitatum, omnia vanitas*—the wise and witty king really said: "*Sanitas sanitatum, omnia sanitas.*" Gentlemen, it is impossible to overrate the importance of the subject. After all, the first consideration of a minister should be the health of the people. A land may be covered with historic trophies, with museums of science and galleries of art, with universities and with libraries; the people may be civilized and ingenious; the country may be even famous in the annals and action of the world, but, gentlemen, if the population every ten years decreases, and the stature of the race every ten years diminishes, the history of that country will soon be the history of the past. . . .

I doubt not there is in this hall more than one publican who remembers that last year an act of Parliament was introduced to denounce him as a "sinner." I doubt not there are in this hall a widow and an orphan who remember the profligate proposition to plunder their lonely heritage. But, gentlemen, as time advanced it was not difficult to perceive that extravagance was being substituted for energy by the government. The unnatural stimulus was subsiding. Their paroxysms ended in prostration. Some took refuge in melancholy, and their eminent chief alternated between a menace and a sigh. As I sat opposite the treasury bench the ministers reminded me of one of those marine landscapes not very unusual on the coast of South America. You behold a range of exhausted volcanoes. Not a flame flickers on a single pallid crest. But the situation is still dangerous. There are occasional earthquakes, and ever and anon the dark rumbling of the sea. . . .

Gentlemen, don't suppose, because I counsel firmness and decision at the right moment, that I am of that school of statesmen who are favorable to a turbulent and aggressive diplomacy. I have resisted it during a great part of my life. I am not unaware that the relations of England to Europe have undergone a vast change during the century that has just elapsed. The relations of England to Europe are not the same as they were in the days of Lord Chatham or Frederick the Great. The Queen of England has become the sovereign of the most powerful of Oriental states. On the other side of the globe there are now establishments belonging to her, teeming with wealth and population, which will, in due time, exercise their influence over the distribution of power. The old establishments of this country, now the United States of America, throw their lengthening shades over the Atlantic, which mix with European waters. These are vast and novel elements in the distribution of power. I acknowledge that the policy of England with respect to Europe should be a policy of reserve, but proud reserve; and in answer to those statesmen—those mistaken statesmen who have intimated the decay of the power of England and the decline of its resources—I express here my confident conviction that there never was a moment in our history when the power of England was so great and her resources so vast and inexhaustible.

And yet, gentlemen, it is not merely our fleets and armies, our powerful artillery, our accumulated capital, and our unlimited credit on which I so much depend, as upon that unbroken spirit of her people, which I believe was never prouder of the imperial country to which they belong. Gentlemen, it is to that spirit that I above all things trust. I look upon the people of Lancashire as fairly representative of the people of England. I think the manner in which they have invited me here, locally a stranger, to receive the expression of their cordial sympathy, and only because they recognize some effort on my part to maintain the greatness of their country, is evidence of the spirit of the land. I must express to you again my deep sense of the generous manner in which you have welcomed me, and in which you have permitted me to express to you my views upon public affairs. Proud of your confidence, and encouraged by your sympathy, I now deliver to you, as my last words, the cause of the Tory party, of the English Constitution, and of the British Empire.

The delighted response of the audience could not have displeased the old magician who had long been mending his political fences. In 1874 he again became Prime Minister, ready to ride his high imperial horse farther into India, Egypt, and Afghanistan—all with the encouragement of the bewitched Queen Victoria. Gallantly he made her Empress of India—and happily she made him Earl of Beaconsfield.

In 1878 he dominated the glittering Congress of Berlin, which was called by Bismarck mainly to settle affairs between a victorious Russia and a defeated Turkey. He insisted on strengthening the tottering Turkish Empire in Europe in order to contain Russia, and thus seemed to condone, in Gladstone's eyes, horrible Turkish atrocities in Bulgaria. Gladstone's many intemperate denunciations of the Berlin agreement, of the "insane covenant," brought from Disraeli a famous retort: "I would put this issue to an English jury. Which do you believe most likely to enter an insane convention, a body of English gentlemen honored by the favor of their Sovereign and the confidence of their fellow subjects, managing your affairs for five years, I hope with prudence, and not altogether without success, or a sophistical rhetorician, inebriated with the exuberance of his own verbosity, and gifted with an egotistical imagination that can at all times command an interminable and inconsistent series of arguments to malign an opponent and to glorify himself?"

There is a full account of Disraeli as a speaker in the last chapter of the fifth volume of the monumental life of Disraeli by W. F. Monypenny and G. E. Buckle. They point out that Disraeli was describing himself when he noted that "what Lord George Bentinck appreciated most in a parliamentary speaker was brilliancy: quickness of perception, promptness of repartee, clear and concise argument, a fresh and felicitous quotation, wit and picture, and, if necessary, a passionate appeal that should never pass the line of high-bred sentiment." Monypenny and Buckle admit that Disraeli lacked "fiery impetuosity," whirlwind passion, but they maintain that "he was a complete master of all the arts of irony, sarcasm, satire, and ridicule."

GLADSTONE SUPPORTS THE RIGHT OF FREETHINKERS TO ENTER THE HOUSE OF COMMONS

[April 26, 1883]

William Ewart Gladstone (1809–98) gave sixty-one of his eighty-nine years to the House of Commons, and was four times Prime Minister—in 1868–74, 1880–85, 1886, and 1892–94. He began as "a high Tory" in all things, even defending the West Indian slaveholders in his maiden speech in 1833, but became a free trader in the following decade and finally a full-fledged Liberal, opposing imperialism and militarism, advocating religious toleration and Irish home rule. It was oratory, in his case especially, that carried him to power and kept him there.

Steeped in the classics at Eton and Oxford, polished in Oxford's debating societies, and with magnificent physical advantages, Gladstone was an accomplished speaker when he entered the House of Commons at twenty-four, and it would seem that he improved steadily with practice through half a century. Here are some notable moments in that fabulous record. As early as 1850 he opposed Britain's bullying of helpless Greece over the fraudulent claims of a dubious British citizen, one Don Pacifico. He opposed the Ecclesiastical Titles Bill, which was an hysterical protest against the Vatican's addition of territorial titles to Catholic administrations in England. As Chancellor of the Exchequer he held the House spellbound for more than three hours with his speech on the 1853 budget and accomplished this miracle many times in later years. He was superb in 1866 at the second reading of the Reform Bill, which was slyly put over by Disraeli in the following year. He was inspired in 1877 in denouncing Turkish rule in Bulgaria and Montenegro. Perhaps the most famous political campaign in English history was Gladstone's in the county of Midlothian at the gates of Edinburgh in 1878. Less than five thousand votes were at stake, but the issue was Disraeli's expansionist foreign policy, and the ageless Gladstone was determined to unseat his imperialist rival. He poured forth some eighty-five *thousand words to all kinds of audiences in all kinds of weather—a record in both quantity and quality—and was elected over the local duke. In consequence he became Prime Minister for the second time but was able to do little in retarding the imperialist movement.*

In 1883 Gladstone supported the Affirmation Bill to permit freethinkers, specifically Charles Bradlaugh, to "affirm" allegiance instead of taking the oath "So help me, God" on becoming Members of the House of Commons. Bradlaugh and his views were repugnant to the devout Gladstone, but the principle before the House was that of toleration and equality which had triumphed in the long struggle for Catholic and Jewish emancipation. In recalling the profound impression made by Gladstone's speech on that occasion, James Bryce wrote: "That impression was chiefly due to the grave and reverent tone in which he delivered some sentences stating the view that it is not our belief in the bare existence of a deity, but the realizing of him as being a providence ruling the world that has moral value and significance for us. And it was due in particular to the solemn dignity with which he declaimed six lines of Lucretius, setting forth the Epicurean view that the gods do not concern themselves with human affairs. There were perhaps not twenty men in the House of Commons who could follow the sense of the lines so as to appreciate their bearing on his argument. But these sonorous hexameters—hexameters that seemed to have lived on through nineteen centuries to find their application from the lips of an orator today—the sense of remoteness in the strange language and the far-off heathen origin, the deep and moving note in the speaker's voice, thrilled the imagination of the audience and held it spellbound, lifting the subject of debate into a region far above party conflicts. Spoken by anyone else, the passage culminating in these Lucretian lines might have produced little effect. It was the voice and manner, above all the voice, with its marvelous modulations, that made the speech majestic."

"Where will you draw the line?"

N
OW, let us try and get at the heart of the argument, which, after all, is not a very complex, although I must say it is historically, and from every point of view, an extremely interesting matter. The business of every man in controversy is to try to find out what is the main and governing contention of his adversary. Sir, I have labored to find that out, and I think I have probably found it: I hope so. As I read it, the governing contention is this—that the main question for the state is not what religion a man professes, but whether he professes some religion or none.

I was in hopes of receiving some confirmatory testimony from the other side. I might dispense with proofs, but I will give them. The right honorable gentleman who led the opposition to this bill said that this was not a question of difference of religion, but that it was a question between religion and irreligion—between religion and the absence of all religion— and clearly the basis of the right honorable gentleman's speech was not that we were to tolerate any belief, but that we were not to tolerate no belief. I mean by tolerating to admit, to recognize, to legislate for the purpose of permitting entrance into the House of Commons. My honorable friend, the Member for Finsbury, in an able speech, still more clearly expressed similar views. He referred to the ancient controversies as all very well; they touched, he said, excrescences, and not the vital substance. Now, sir, I want to examine what is the vital substance, and what are the excrescences. He went further than this and used a most apt, appropriate, expressive, and still more significant phrase. He said: "Yes; it is true you admit religions some of which may go near the precipice; but now you ask us to go over it." Gentlemen opposite cheered loudly when that was said by the honorable gentleman behind me. They will not give me a single cheer now. They suspect I am quoting this with some evil intent. The question is, am I quoting them fairly? Or is it the fact that some gentlemen have not sufficiently and fairly considered their relation to the present bill, except that they mean to oppose whatever proceeds from the government? But my honorable friend has considered very well what he said when he used the remarkable simile about the precipice. I wish to see what is the value of this main and principal contention—this doctrine of the precipice—this question between religion and irreligion, between some belief which is to be tolerated, and no belief which cannot be tolerated—that is to say, so far as it relates to admission into this House. The honorable and learned gentleman, the Member for Launceston, held exactly the same language. He adopted a phrase which had fallen from the honorable Member for Portsmouth which he thought had been unfairly applied; and he said he wished that there should be some form of belief and some recognition of belief—something of what is called in philosophical discussion the recognition of the supernatural. That, I believe, is a phrase which goes as near to what honorable gentlemen opposite mean as anything can. It is the recognition of the existence, at any rate, of the supernatural that is wanted. That is the main contention of the party opposite; and what I want to know is, whether that contention—that proposition—offers us a good solid standing ground for legislation. Whatever test is applied—the test of the Constitution, the test of civil and political freedom, or, above all, the test of religion, and of reverence for religious conviction—I do not hesitate to say that, confidently as I support this bill, there is no ground upon which I support it with so much confidence as because of what I think is the utter hollowness and falseness of the argument that is expressed in the words I have just cited, and in the idea that is at the bottom of those words, and the danger of making them the basis of constitutional action.

Sir, what does this contention do? In the first place, it evidently violates civil freedom to this extent—that, in the words of Lord Lyndhurst—which are as wide as anything that any gentleman on this side could desire—there is to be a total divorce between the question of religious differences and the question of civil privilege and power; that there is to be no test whatever applied to a man with respect to the exercise of civil functions, except the test of civil capacity, and a fulfillment of civil conditions. Those were the words of Lord Lyndhurst—those are the words on which we stand. It is now proposed to depart from this position, and to say that a certain class of persons, perhaps a very narrow class—I do not argue that now—because it is said to have no religion is to be excepted, and alone excepted, from the operation of that great and broad principle. In my opinion, it is in the highest degree irrational to lay down a broad principle of that kind, and after granting 99/100ths of all, it means to stop short, in order to make an invidious exclusion of the exceedingly limited number of persons who may possibly be affected by, and concerned in, its application.

Honorable gentlemen will, perhaps, be startled when I make my next objection to the contention of the opponents of the bill. It is that it is highly disparaging to Christianity. They invite us to do that which, as a legislature, we ought never to do—namely, to travel over theological ground, and, having taken us upon that ground, what is it that they tell us? They tell us that you may go any length you please in the denial of religion, provided only you do not reject the name of the Deity. They tear religion—if I may say so—in shreds, and they set aside one particular shred of it, with which nothing will ever induce them to part. They divide religion into the dispensable and the indispensable—I am not speaking now of the cases of those who declare, or who are admitted under special laws, and I am not speaking of Jews or any of those who make declarations—I am speaking of those for whom no provision is made, except the provision of the oath, let that be clearly understood—they divide, I say, religion into what can be dispensed with and what cannot be dispensed with, and then they find that Christianity can be dispensed with. I am not willing, sir, that Christianity, if an appeal is made to us as a Christian legislature, should stand in any rank lower than that which is indispensable. Let me illustrate what I mean. Supposing a commander has to dis-patch a small body of men for the purpose of some difficult and important undertaking. They are to go without baggage and without appliances. Everything they take they must carry on their backs. They have to dis-pense with all luxuries and all comforts, and to take with them only that which is essential. That is precisely the same course which you ask us to take in drawing us upon theological ground. You require us to distinguish between superfluities and necessaries, and you say in regard to Chris-tianity, "Oh, that is one of the superfluities—that is one of the excres-cences, that has nothing to do with the vital substance—the great and solemn name of the Deity—which is indispensable." The adoption of such a proposition as that—and it is at the very root of your contention—seems to me to be in the highest degree disparaging to the Christian faith. I pass to another point. The honorable Member for Finsbury made a refer-ence to Mr. O'Connell, whom he stated that he knew well. I will not say, sir, that I had as much personal knowledge of Mr. O'Connell as my hon-orable friend may have had, though I did know something of him person-ally, as well as politically; but, when I was a very young man, in the sec-ond year of my sitting in Parliament—in the old House which was burned down half a century ago—I heard a speech from Mr. O'Connell, which, although at that time I was bound by party allegiance to receive with misgiving and distrust anything he said, made a deep impression upon me, and by which I think I have ever since been guided. It is to be found, not in *Hansard,* but in the record which, for a few years, was more copi-ous even than *Hansard,* and which went under the name of *The Mirror of Parliament.* On the eighteenth of February, 1834, Mr. O'Connell used these words in a speech on the Law of Libel; and I echo every word my honorable friend said with regard to the deep religious convictions and the religious consistency of that remarkable man—he used, sir, these words:

> When I see in this country the law allowing men to dispute the doctrine of the Trinity, and the Divinity of the Redeemer, I really think, if I had no other reason, I should be justified in saying that there is nothing beyond that which should be considered worth quarreling for, or which ought to be made the subject of penal re-strictions.

I am convinced that upon every religious, as well as upon every political ground, the true and the wise course is not to deal out religious liberty by halves, by quarters, and by fractions; but to deal it out entire, and to leave no distinction between man and man on the ground of religious dif-ferences from one end of the land to the other.

But, sir, I go a little further in endeavoring to test and to probe this great religious contention of the "precipice," which has been put forward, amidst fervent cheers from honorable gentlemen opposite, by my honorable friend behind me; and I want to know, is your religious distinction a real distinction at all? I will, for the sake of argument, and for no other purpose whatever, go with you on this dangerous ground of splitting religion into slices, and I ask you: "Where will you draw the line?" You draw it at the point where the abstract denial of God is severed from abstract admission of the Deity. My proposition is that your line is worthless. There is much on your side of the line which is just as objectionable as the atheism on the other side. If you call on us to draw these distinctions, let them be rational distinctions. I do not say let them be Christian distinctions; but let them be rational distinctions. I can understand one rational distinction, that you should frame the oath in such a way that its terms should recognize, not merely the acknowledgment of the existence of the Deity, but the providence of the Deity, and man's responsibility to the Deity, and in such a way as to indicate the knowledge in a man's own mind that he must answer to the Deity for what he does, and is able to do. But is that your present rule? No, sir. You know well that from ancient times there have been sects and schools that have admitted in the abstract, just as freely as the Christian admits, the existence of a Deity, but who have held that, though Deity exists, yet of practical relations between Him and man there can be none. Many Members of this House will recollect, perhaps, the noble and majestic lines—for such they are—of the Latin poet—

> *Omnis enim per se divom natura necessest,*
> *immortali aevo summa cum pace fruatur;*
> *semota ab nostris rebus seiunctaque longe,*
> *nam privata dolore omni, privata periclis,*
> *ipsa suis pollens opibus, nil indiga nostri,*
> *nec bene promeritis capitur necque tangitur ira.**

"Divinity exists"—as these, I must say, magnificent words set forth—"in remote, inaccessible recesses of which we know nothing; but with us it has no dealing, with us it has no relation." Sir, I have purposely gone back to ancient times, because the discussion is less invidious than the

---

* From Book II, *De Rerum Natura* (On the Nature of Things) by Lucretius.
"For it is essential to the very nature of deity that it should enjoy immortal existence in utter tranquillity, aloof and detached from our affairs. It is free from all pain and peril, strong in its own resources, exempt from any need of us, indifferent to our merits and immune from anger." Translated by Ronald Latham, *The Penguin Classics.*
Gladstone gallantly assumed that his hearers had had an adequate education in the classics and understood the original Latin.

discussion of modern schools of opinion. But, sir, I do not hesitate to say that the specific evil, the specific form of irreligion, with which in educated society in this country you have to contend, and with respect to which you ought to be on your guard, is not blank atheism. That is a rare form of opinion, and it is seldom met with. But what is frequently met with are those various forms of opinion which teach us that whatever there be beyond the visible scene, whatever there be beyond this short span of life, you know and can know nothing of it, and that it is a visionary and a bootless undertaking to endeavor to establish relations with it. That is the specific mischief of the age; but that mischief you do not attempt to touch. Nay, more; you glory in the state of the law that now prevails. All differences of religion you wish to tolerate. You wish to allow everybody to enter your chamber who admits the existence of Deity. You would seek to admit Voltaire. That is a specimen of your toleration. But Voltaire was not a taciturn foe of Christianity. He was the author of that painful and awful phrase that goes to the heart of every Christian—and goes, I believe, to the heart of many a man professing religion who is not a Christian—*écrasez l'infâme*. Voltaire was a believer in God; he would not have had the slightest difficulty in taking the oath; and you are working up the country to something like a crusade on this question; endeavoring to strengthen in the minds of the people the false notion that you have got a real test, a real safeguard; that Christianity is still generally safe, with certain unavoidable exceptions, under the protecting aegis of the oath within the walls of this chamber. And it is for that you are entering on a great religious war! I hold, then, that this contention of our opponents is disparaging to religion; it is idle; and it is also highly irrational. For if you are to have a religious test at all of the kind that you contemplate—the test of theism, which the honorable Member of Portsmouth frankly said he wished to adopt—it ought to be a test of a well-ascertained theism; not a mere abstract idea dwelling in the air, and in the clouds, but a practical recognition of a Divine Governing Power, which will some day call all of us to account for every thought we conceive, and for every word we utter.

I fear I have detained the House for a long time. But after all that has been said, and after the flood of accusations and invective that has been poured out, I have thought it right at great length and very seriously to show that, at all events, whether we be beaten or not, we do not decline the battle, and that we are not going to allow it to be said that the interests of religion are put in peril, and that they are to find their defenders only on the opposite side of the House. That sincere and conscientious defenders of those interests are to be found there I do not question at this moment; but I do contend with my whole heart and soul that the interests of religion, as well as the interests of civil liberty, are concerned in the passage of this measure. My reasons, sir, for the passing of the bill may be summed up in a few words. If I were asked to put a construction on this oath as it stands, I probably should give it a higher meaning than most gentlemen opposite. It is my opinion, as far as I can presume to form one, that the oath has in it a very large flavor of Christianity. I am well aware that the doctrine of my honorable and learned friend, the Attorney General, is that there are other forms of positive attestation, recognized by other systems of religion, which may enable the oath to be taken by the removal of the words "So help me God," and the substitution of some other words, or some symbolical act, involving the idea of Deity, and responsibility to the Deity. But I think we ought to estimate the real character of this oath according to the intention of the legislature. The oath does not consist of spoken words alone. The spoken words are accompanied by the corroborative act of kissing the Book. What is the meaning of that? According to the intention of the legislature, I certainly should say that that act is an import of the acceptance of the Divine revelation. There have been other forms in other countries. I believe in Scotland the form is still maintained of holding up the right hand instead of kissing the Book. In Spain the form is, I believe, that of kissing the Cross. In Italy, I think, at one time, the form was that of laying the hand on the Gospel. All these different forms meant, according to the original intention, an acceptance of Christianity. But you do not yourselves venture to say that the law could be applied in that sense. A law of this kind is like a coin spick-and-span, brand-new from the mint, carrying upon it its edges in all their sharpness and freshness; but it wears down in passing from hand to hand, and, though there is a residuum, yet the distinctive features disappear. Whatever my opinion may be as to the original vitality of the oath, I think there is very little difference of opinion as to what it has now become. It has become, as my honorable friend says, a theistic test. It is taken as no more than a theistic test. It does, as I think, involve a reference to Christianity. But while this is my personal opinion, it is not recognized by authority, and at any rate, does not prevail in practice; for some gentlemen in the other House of Parliament, if not in this also, have written works against the Christian religion, and yet have taken the oath. But, undoubtedly, it is not good for any of us to force this test so flavored, or even if not so flavored, upon men who cannot take it with a full and a cordial acceptance. It is bad—it is demoralizing to do so. It is all very well to say, "Oh, yes; but it is their responsibility." That is not, in my view, a satisfactory answer. A seat in this House is to the ordinary Englishman in early life, or, perhaps, in middle and mature life, when he has reached a position of distinction in his career, the highest prize of his ambition. But if you place between him and that prize not only the necessity of conforming to certain civil conditions, but the adoption of certain religious words, and if these words are not justly measured to the condition of his conscience and of his convictions, you give him an inducement—nay, I do not go too far when I say you offer him a bribe to tamper with those convictions—to do violence to his conscience in order that he may not be stigmatized by being shut out from what is held to be the noblest privilege of the English citizen—that of representing his fellow citizens in Parliament. And, therefore, I say that, besides our duty to vindicate the principle of civil and religious liberty, which totally detaches religious controversy from the enjoyment of civil rights, it is most important that the House should consider the moral effect of this test. It is, as the honorable Member for Portsmouth is neither more nor less than right in saying, a purely theistic test. Viewed as a theistic test, it embraces no acknowledgment of Providence, of Divine Government, of responsibility, or of retribution. It involves nothing but a bare and abstract admission—a form void of all practical meaning and concern. This is not a wholesome, but an unwholesome, lesson. Yet more. I own that although I am now, perhaps, going to injure myself by bringing the name of Mr. Bradlaugh into this controversy, I am strongly of opinion that the present controversy should come to a close. I have no fear of atheism in this House. Truth is the expression of the Divine mind; and however little our feeble vision may be able to discern the means by which God will provide for its preservation, we may leave the matter in His hands, and we may be quite sure that a firm and courageous application of every principle of justice and of equity is the best method we can adopt for the preservation and influence of truth. I must painfully record my opinion that grave injury has been done to religion in many minds—not in instructed minds, but in those which are ill-instructed or partially instructed, which have a large claim on our consideration—in consequence of steps which have, unhappily, been taken. Great mischief has been done in many minds through the resistance offered to the man elected by the constituency of Northampton, which a portion of the community believe to be unjust. When they see the profession of religion and the interests of religion ostensibly associated with what they are deeply convinced is injustice, they are led to questions about religion itself, which they see to be associated with injustice. Unbelief attracts a sympathy which it would not otherwise enjoy; and the upshot is to impair those convictions and that religious faith, the loss of which I believe to be the most inexpressible calamity which can fall either upon a man or upon a nation.

The Affirmation Bill was defeated by three votes, but in the next Parliament Bradlaugh was permitted to take the oath, and in 1888 he himself secured the passing of an affirmation law.

In his public career of more than sixty years Gladstone poured forth a Niagara of language that his admirers attributed to fluency, his opponents to verbosity. Of course he was subject to caricature in words and pictures, and was the special butt of Winston Churchill's stormy father, Lord Randolph Churchill (1849–95). In calling attention to the Prime Minister's enthusiasm for chopping down trees, Churchill said: "The forest laments in order that Mr. Gladstone may perspire, and full account of these proceedings are forwarded by special correspondents to every daily newspaper every recurring morning." And in noting that a deputation of workingmen were presented with a few chips from Gladstone's arboreal depredations, Churchill went on to say: "He told them that he would give them and all other subjects of the Queen much legislation, great prosperity, and universal peace, and he has given them nothing but chips. Chips to the faithful allies of Afghanistan, chips to the trusting native races of South Africa, chips to the Egyptian fellah, chips to the British farmer, chips to the manufacturer and the artisan, chips to the agricultural, chips to the House of Commons itself."

There may have been some connection between this malicious masterpiece, "Chips" (1884), and the fall of Gladstone's second government in 1885; but the grand old man formed his third government the following year and at seventy-seven joined hands with Parnell in a heroic effort to bring home rule to Ireland.

DOSTOEVSKY INTERRUPTS THE WRITING OF *THE BROTHERS KARAMAZOV* TO CELEBRATE THE CENTENARY OF PUSHKIN'S BIRTH

[June 8, 1880]

Feodor Mikhailovich Dostoevsky (1821–81), the son of a doctor who was murdered by his outraged serfs, attended the University of St. Petersburg and won success with his early novel, Poor Folk. Mildly radical, he was involved in a conspiracy and sentenced to be shot—but at the moment of execution the sentence was commuted to exile in Siberia. In the four years in Siberia he was cured of any revolutionary tendencies, and he returned to Russia to write the amazing psychological novels that all the world knows.

"In the judgment of posterity," says E. H. Carr, "The Brothers Karamazov remains Dostoevsky's last achievement. But in the eyes of his contemporaries it was eclipsed by another event in the last year of his life, the Pushkin festival."

At the height of his fame, a safe and sane believer in the Greek Orthodox Church, the Czar, and the special mission of Holy Russia, Dostoevsky interrupted work on The Brothers Karamazov to participate in the celebration of the centenary of Pushkin's birth, organized by the Moscow Society of Lovers of Russian Literature. Literary gatherings were generally looked on with suspicion by the police, but this one was an undisturbing masterpiece of nationalistic enthusiasm. After two full days of speeches and readings from Pushkin, it was Dostoevsky's turn, on the third morning, to evaluate the Russian Shakespeare.

"I speak only of the brotherhood of man."

PUSHKIN is an extraordinary phenomenon, and, perhaps, the unique phenomenon of the Russian spirit, said Gogol. I will add, "and a prophetic phenomenon." Yes, in his appearing there is contained for all us Russians something incontestably prophetic. Pushkin arrives exactly at the beginning of our true self-consciousness, which had only just begun to exist a whole century after Peter's reforms, and Pushkin's coming mightily aids us in our dark way by a new guiding light. In this sense Pushkin is a presage and a prophecy.

I divide the activity of our great poet into three periods. I speak now not as a literary critic. I dwell on Pushkin's creative activity only to elucidate my conception of his prophetic significance to us, and the meaning I give the word prophecy. I would, however, observe in passing that the periods of Pushkin's activity do not seem to me to be marked off from each other by firm boundaries. The beginning of Eugene Onegin, for instance, in my opinion belongs still to the first period, while Onegin ends in the second period, when Pushkin had already found his ideals in his native land, had taken them to his heart and cherished them in his loving and clairvoyant soul. . . .

[Dostoevsky proceeds to analyze in some detail the Russian-type wanderer as he appears in The Gypsies, an early work by Pushkin, and in Eugene Onegin.]

Pushkin was always a complete whole, as it were, a perfect organism carrying within itself at once every one of its principles, not receiving them from beyond. The beyond only awakened in him that which was already in the depths of his soul. But this organism developed, and the phases of this development could really be marked and defined, each of them by its peculiar character and the regular generation of one phase from another. Thus to the third period can be assigned those of his works in which universal ideas were pre-eminently reflected, in which the poetic conceptions of other nations were mirrored and their genius re-embodied. Some of these appeared after Pushkin's death. And in this period the poet reveals something almost miraculous, never seen or heard at any time or in any nation before. There had been in the literatures of Europe men of colossal artistic genius—a Shakespeare, a Cervantes, a Schiller. But show me one of these great geniuses who possessed such a capacity for universal sympathy as our Pushkin. This capacity, the pre-eminent capacity of our nation, he shares with our nation, and by that above all he is our national poet. The greatest of European poets could never so powerfully embody in themselves the genius of a foreign, even a neighboring, people, its spirit in all its hidden depth, and all its yearning after its appointed end, as Pushkin could. On the contrary, when they turned to foreign nations European poets most often made them one with their own people, and understood them after their own fashion. Even Shakespeare's Italians, for instance, are almost always Englishmen. Pushkin alone of all world poets possessed the capacity of fully identifying himself with another nationality. Take scenes from *Faust,* take *The Miserly Knight,* take the ballad "Once There Lived a Poor Knight"; read *Don Juan* again. Had Pushkin not signed them, you would never know that they were not written by a Spaniard. How profound and fantastic is the imagination in the poem "A Feast in Time of Plague." But in this fantastic imagination is the genius of England; and in the hero's wonderful song about the plague, and in Mary's song,

> *Our children's voices in the noisy school*
> *Were heard . . .*

These are English songs; this is the yearning of the British genius, its lament, its painful presentiment of its future. Remember the strange lines:

> *Once as I wandered through the valley wild.*

It is almost a literal transposition of the first three pages of a strange mystical book, written in prose by an old English sectarian—but is it only a transposition? In the sad and rapturous music of these verses is the very

soul of northern Protestantism, of the English heresiarch, of the illimitable mystic with his dull, somber, invincible aspiration, and the impetuous power of his mystical dreaming. As you read these strange verses, you
seem to hear the spirit of the times, of the Reformation, you understand
the warlike fire of early Protestantism, and finally history herself, not
merely by thought but as one who passes through the armed sectarian
camp, sings psalms with them, weeps with them in their religious verses
from the Koran or "Imitations from the Koran." Is there not here a Mohammedan, is it not the very spirit of the Koran and its sword, the naïve
grandeur of faith and her terrible, bloody power? And here is the ancient
world; here are *Egyptian Nights,* here sit the gods of earth, who sat above
their people like gods, and despised the genius of the people and its aspirations, who became gods in isolation, and went mad in their isolation, in
the anguish of their weariness unto death, diverting themselves with fanatic brutalities, with the voluptuousness of creeping things, of a she-
spider devouring her male. No, I will say deliberately there never had
been a poet with a universal sympathy like Pushkin's. And it is not his
sympathy alone, but his amazing profundity, the reincarnation of his
spirit in the spirit of foreign nations, a reincarnation almost perfect and
therefore also miraculous, because the phenomenon has never been repeated in any poet in all the world. It is only in Pushkin; and by this, I repeat, he is a phenomenon never seen and never heard of before, and in
my opinion, a prophetic phenomenon, because . . . because herein was
expressed the national spirit of his poetry, the national spirit in its future
development, the national spirit of our future, which is already implicit in
the present, and it was expressed prophetically. For what is the power of
the spirit of Russian nationality if not its aspiration after the final goal of
universality and omnihumanity? No sooner had he become a completely
national poet, no sooner had he come into contact with the national
power, than he already anticipated the great future of that power. In this
he was a seer, in this a prophet.

For what is the reform of Peter the Great to us, not merely for the future, but in that which has been and has already been plainly manifested
to us? What did that reform mean to us? Surely it was not only the adoption of European clothes, customs, inventions, and science. Let us examine how it was, let us look more steadily. Yes, it is very probable that at
the outset Peter began his reform in this narrowly utilitarian sense, but in
course of time, as his idea developed, Peter undoubtedly obeyed some
hidden instinct which drew him and his work to future purposes, undoubtedly more vast than narrow utilitarianism. Just so the Russian people did not accept the reform in the utilitarian spirit alone, but undoubt-

edly with a presentiment which almost instantly forewarned them of a distant and incomparably higher goal than mere utilitarianism. I repeat, the people felt that purpose unconsciously, but it felt it directly and quite vitally. Surely we then turned at once to the most vital reunion, to the unity of all mankind! Not in a spirit of enmity (as one might have thought it would have been) but in friendliness and perfect love, we received into our soul the geniuses of foreign nations, all alike without preference of race, able by instinct from almost the very first step to discern, to discount distinctions, to excuse and reconcile them, and therein we already showed our readiness and inclination, which had only just become manifest to ourselves, for a common and universal union with all the races of the great Aryan family.

Yes, beyond all doubt, the destiny of a Russian is pan-European and universal. To become a true Russian, to become a Russian fully (in the end of all, I repeat), means only to become the brother of all men, to become, if you will, a universal man. All our Slavophilism and Westernism is only a great misunderstanding, even though historically necessary. To a true Russian, Europe and the destiny of all the mighty Aryan family is as dear as Russia herself, as the destiny of his own native country, because our destiny is universality, won not by the sword, but by the strength of brotherhood and our fraternal aspiration to reunite mankind.

If you go deep into our history since Peter's reform, you will already find traces and indications of this idea, of this dream of mine, if you will, in the character of our intercourse with European nations, even in the policy of the state. For what has Russian policy been doing for these two centuries if not serving Europe, perhaps, far more than she has served herself? I do not believe this came to pass through the incapacity of our statesmen. The nations of Europe know how dear they are to us. And in course of time I believe that we—not we, of course, but our children to come—will all without exception understand that to be a true Russian does indeed mean to aspire finally to reconcile the contradictions of Europe, to show the end of European yearning in our Russian soul, omnihuman and all-uniting, to include within our soul by brotherly love all our brethren, and at last, it may be, to pronounce the final Word of the great general harmony, of the final brotherly communion of all nations in accordance with the law of the Gospel of Christ!

I know, I know too well, that my words may appear ecstatic, exaggerated, and fantastic. Let them be so, I do not repent having uttered them. They ought to be uttered, above all now, at the moment that we honor our great genius who by his artistic power embodied this idea. The idea has been expressed many times before. I say nothing new. But chiefly it will appear presumptuous. "Is this our destiny, the destiny of our poor, brutal land? Are we predestined among mankind to utter the new word?"

Do I speak of economic glory, of the glory of the sword or of science? I speak only of the brotherhood of man; I say that to this universal, omni-human union the heart of Russia, perhaps more than all other nations, is chiefly predestined; I see its traces in our history, our men of genius, in the artistic genius of Pushkin. Let our country be poor, but this poor land "Christ traversed with blessing, in the garb of a serf." Why then should we not contain His final word? Was not He Himself born in a manger? I say again, we at least can already point to Pushkin, to the universality and omnihumanity of his genius. He surely could contain the genius of foreign lands in his soul as his own. In art at least, in artistic creation, he undeniably revealed this universality of the aspiration of the Russian spirit, and therein is a great promise. If our thought is a dream, then in Pushkin at least this dream has solid foundation.

Had he lived longer, he would perhaps have revealed great and im-mortal embodiments of the Russian soul, which would then have been in-telligible to our European brethren; he would have attracted them much more and closer than they are attracted now, perhaps he would have suc-ceeded in explaining to them all the truth of our aspirations; and they would understand us more than they do now, they would have begun to have insight into us, and would have ceased to look at us so suspiciously and presumptuously as they still do. Had Pushkin lived longer, then among us too there would perhaps be fewer misunderstandings and quar-rels than we see now. But God saw otherwise. Pushkin died in the full maturity of his powers, and undeniably bore away with him a great se-cret into the grave. And now we, without him, are seeking to divine his secret.

[TRANSLATED BY S. KOTELIANSKY AND J. MIDDLETON MURRY.]

Dostoevsky was himself overwhelmed by the success of his speech, as he wrote to his wife, a few hours later:
"When at the end I proclaimed the world-wide unity of mankind, the whole hall was in hysterics; when I finished—I cannot tell you the roars and yells of enthusiasm; people in the audience who were unknown to one another wept, sobbed, embraced each other and swore to each other to be better men in the future, to love their fellows instead of hating them. The sitting broke up; they all rushed up to me on the platform—grandes dames, students, secretaries of state, students, all embraced and kissed me, all—literally all—wept with delight. For half an hour they kept calling me out and waving their handkerchiefs. For instance, two old men stopped me suddenly and said: 'We have been enemies

for twenty years and would not speak to each other, but now we have embraced and made it up; it is you who have reconciled us. You are our saint, our prophet.' 'A prophet, a prophet!' cried voices in the crowd. Turgenev . . . threw himself into my arms with tears in his eyes. Annenkov rushed up to me, pressed my hand, and kissed me on the shoulder. 'You are a genius,' they told me. Ivan Aksakov rushed on to the platform and declared publicly that my speech was not merely a speech, but a historical event: clouds had covered the horizon, and now Dostoevsky's utterance had appeared like the sun to dissipate them and make everything light. From that time brotherhood would begin and there would be no more misunderstandings. 'Yes, yes!' they all cried, and there were more embracings and more tears. The sitting was suspended. I hastened to escape into the wings, but they all broke in after me from the hall and—the women particularly—began to kiss my hands and plagued me. Students ran in. One of them who was in tears fell on the floor in hysterics and lost consciousness. Victory! Complete victory!"

FRIEDRICH ENGELS SAYS A FEW WORDS AT THE BURIAL OF KARL MARX

[March 17, 1883]

In contrast to the wild scene at Moscow during the Pushkin celebration, which was a landmark of Russian nationalism, of pan-Slavism, there was, three years later, a quiet funeral in Highgate Cemetery, on the outskirts of London, which also had its significance for Russia and for the world.

For over thirty years Karl Marx (1818–83), the exiled revolutionist, had lived in London, toiling at his books, directing political organizations, denouncing real and supposed enemies, and hoping for the collapse of capitalism. In ill health most of the time and saved from complete poverty only by the constant help of his capitalist friend and collaborator, Friedrich Engels (1820–95), Marx was the complete bourgeois in the midst of his devoted family and survived his wife little more than a year. On a rainy day eight friends followed the coffin to Highgate Cemetery.

Engels spoke briefly in English.

"For Marx, science was a creative, historic, and

revolutionary force."

O N THE AFTERNOON of the fourteenth of March, at a quarter to
three, the greatest living thinker ceased to think. Left alone for less
than two minutes, when we entered we found him sleeping peacefully in
his chair—but forever.

It is impossible to measure the loss which the fighting European and
American proletariat and historical science have lost with the death of
this man. Soon enough we shall feel the breach which has been opened by
the death of this tremendous spirit.

As Darwin discovered the law of evolution in organic nature, so Marx
discovered the law of evolution in human history; the simple fact, previously hidden under ideological growths, that human beings must first
of all eat, drink, shelter, and clothe themselves before they can turn their
attention to politics, science, art, and religion; that therefore the production of the immediate material means of life and thereby the given stage
of economic development of a people or of a period forms the basis on
which the state institutions, the legal principles, the art, and even the religious ideas of the people in question have developed and out of which
they must be explained, instead of exactly the contrary, as was previously
attempted.

But not only this, Marx discovered the special law of development of
the present-day capitalist mode of production and of the bourgeois system of society which it has produced. With the discovery of surplus
value, light was suddenly shed on the darkness in which all other econo-
mists, both bourgeois and socialist, had lost themselves.

Two such discoveries would have been enough for any life. Fortunate
indeed is he to whom it is given to make even one. In every single field
which Marx investigated, and there were many and in none of them were
his investigations superficial, he made independent discoveries, even in
the field of mathematics.

That was the man of science, but that was by no means the whole
man. For Marx, science was a creative, historic, and revolutionary force.
Great as was his pleasure at a new discovery in this or that field of theoretical science, a discovery perhaps whose practical consequences were
not yet visible, it was still greater at a new discovery which immediately
affected industrial development, historical development as a whole in a
revolutionary fashion. For instance, he closely followed the development

of the discoveries in the field of electrical science and, toward the end, of the work of Marcel Deprez.

For Marx was above all a revolutionary, and his great aim in life was to co-operate in this or that fashion in the overthrow of capitalist society and the state institutions which it has created, to co-operate in the emancipation of the modern proletariat, to whom he was the first to give a consciousness of its class position and its class needs, a knowledge of the conditions necessary for its emancipation. In this struggle he was in his element, and he fought with a passion, tenacity, and success granted to few. The first *Rheinische Zeitung* in 1842, the *Vorwärts* in Paris in 1844, the *Brüsseler Deutsche Zeitung* in 1847, the *Neue Rheinische Zeitung* from 1848 to 1849, the *New York Tribune* from 1852 to 1861—and then a wealth of polemical writings, the organizational work in Paris, Brussels, and London, and finally the great International Workingmen's Association to crown it all. In truth, that alone would have been a life's work to be proud of if its author had done nothing else.

And therefore Marx was the best-hated and most-slandered man of his age. Governments, both absolutist and republican, expelled him from their territories, whilst the bourgeois, both conservative and extreme democratic, vied with each other in a campaign of vilification against him. He brushed it all to one side like cobwebs, ignored them, and answered only when compelled to do so. And he died respected, loved, and mourned by millions of revolutionary workers from the Siberian mines over Europe and America to the coasts of California, and I make bold to say that although he had many opponents he had hardly a personal enemy.

His name will live through the centuries and so also will his work.*

If Marx's name and work live through the coming centuries, and create half the stir that they have in the past century, the credit will be due in large part to his devoted friend, Engels. For it was Engels who worked indefatigably to complete Das Kapital, the major text of Socialism, and sustained and carried forward Marx's main projects. Widely different in temperament and character, the two men were bound together by common sympathies and a common cause. The versatile and fluent Engels complemented the systematic and rigorous Marx.

* This speech was delivered in English but published, apparently, only in a German translation in the *Sozialdemokrat*, Zurich. Engels' notes for the speech were also written in German. The above, retranslated from the German by Edward Fitzgerald, comes from *Karl Marx*, by Franz Mehring.

CHARLES STEWART PARNELL DEMANDS
HOME RULE FOR IRELAND

[June 8, 1886]

Coming again to turbulent Ireland, we may recall four acts in the long tragedy. In 1782 an independent Irish (Protestant) Parliament was achieved, so much through the efforts of Henry Grattan that it became known as "Grattan's Parliament." But in 1800 the Irish Parliament was dissolved by Pitt's Act of Union, a war measure that was doubly infuriating to the Irish because it was not accompanied by Catholic emancipation. In 1829, after six years of concentrated agitation by Daniel O'Connell and the powerful Catholic Association, Catholic emancipation was won. O'Connell then worked for a decade within the Parliament of the United Kingdom for the repeal of the Act of Union, but when those efforts failed, he turned to his old strategy of mass meetings— monstrous mass meetings up and down the Emerald Isle. He seemed on the point of success through peaceful agitation, but a year of imprisonment, the impatience of militant "Young Ireland," and old age combined in 1847 to break his heart and his hold on life. There followed decades of sporadic violence, the brilliant but futile oratory of Thomas Francis Meagher, the prudent home-rule movement led by the eloquent Isaac Butts—and then Parnell entered the scene.

Charles Stewart Parnell (1846–91) was an Anglo-Irish Protestant, colder externally than any Englishman but as intense within, apparently, as any Irishman that ever lived. Only a year old when O'Connell died, he was not overwhelmed by that mighty reputation. He started fresh, as it were, with a meager knowledge of Irish history, no platform skill, and no understanding of parliamentary procedure. But he hated England and was determined to liberate Ireland. He entered Parliament when he was twenty-nine and quietly studied the situation for a year. His first public speech on home rule was a complete failure as far as delivery was concerned. But he learned the tricks of the parliamentary trade, he learned how to play one party off against another, he learned how to obstruct legislation and to outrage the Members of the House of Commons without losing his seat. He won the utter confidence of the Irish bloc in the House and of most of the Irish people. He won the respect of Gladstone.

In 1886, at the ripe age of seventy-five, Gladstone set out to pass a generous home-rule bill, in alliance, of course, with the Irish leader. The bitter debate went on for weeks, with Parnell reserving his fire. There is no question about the effect that Parnell came to have on his English audience. His friend and successor, John Redmond, said: "He seldom spoke, once he had risen to a *commanding position in Parliament. When he did speak the silence that crept over the house was absolutely painful in its intensity." And Lord Curzon, who was offended by the views, the manner, and the ill-kempt appearance of the handsome Irishman, recalled that "Parnell was not eloquent, much less an orator. But as he hissed out his sentences of concentrated passion and scorn, scattering his notes as he proceeded upon the seat behind him, he gave the impression of almost demonic self-control and illimitable strength. When he spoke for his party, in the tremendous moments of the crisis, Mr. Gladstone would move to the end of the front bench and, with his hand held behind his ear, listen to the freezing but impressive display with rapt attention."*

"No, sir, we cannot give up a single Irishman."

IF, MR. SPEAKER, I intervene in the contest of giants which has been proceeding for so many days in this House in reference to this great question, it is not because I suppose that that intervention is specially suitable to the moment; and I certainly should not, under ordinary circumstances, have felt any self-confidence whatever in following so able and eloquent a member of this House as the right honorable gentleman, the Member for the eastern division of Edinburgh [Goschen]. But "Thrice is he armed who hath his quarrel just," and even a man so inferior from every point of view to the right honorable gentleman as I am may hope upon this occasion not to be so much behind him as usual. The right honorable gentleman has sought—I think, very unfairly—to cast a lurid light upon the situation by an allusion to those unhappy outrages which have occurred in Kerry. I join the right honorable gentleman in expressing my contempt for these cowardly and disgraceful practices. I join him in that respect to the fullest extent.

Nor do I say that because for months evictions have been more numerous in Kerry than in all the rest of Munster taken together—neither do I say that that constitutes any excuse for these outrages, although it may supply us with a reason for them; but when I denounce outrages I denounce them in all parts of Ireland, whether they occur in Ulster or in Kerry. But certainly I do condemn these outrages in Kerry; and the right honorable gentleman says very rightly that they must be put a stop to. Well, so say we all; but the right honorable gentleman would try to put a stop to them by resorting to the old bad method of coercion, which he and his friends have been using for the last eighty-six years, while we say with the Prime Minister: "Try the effect of self-government," and if Kerry

men then resort to outrages they will very soon find that the rest of Ireland will put a stop to them. Now, sir, the right honorable Member for
East Edinburgh spoke about the sovereignty of Parliament. I entirely
agree upon this point. We have always known since the introduction of
this bill the difference between a co-ordinate and a subordinate Parliament, and we have recognized that the legislature which the Prime Minister proposes to constitute is a subordinate Parliament—that it is not the
same as Grattan's Parliament, which was coequal with the Imperial Parliament, arising out of the same Constitution given to the Irish people by
the Crown, just in the same way, though not by the same means, as parliamentary institutions were given to Great Britain by the sovereign. We
understand this perfectly well. With reference to the argument that has
been used against us, that I am precluded from accepting this solution as
a final solution because I have claimed the restitution of Grattan's Parliament, I would beg to say that I consider there are practical advantages
connected with the proposed statutory body, limited and subordinate to
this Imperial Parliament as it undoubtedly will be, which will render it
much more useful and advantageous to the Irish people than was Grattan's Parliament, and that the statutory body which the right honorable
gentleman proposes to constitute is much more likely to be a final settlement than Grattan's Parliament.

We feel, therefore, that under this bill this Imperial Parliament will
have the ultimate supremacy and the ultimate sovereignty. I think the
most useful part of the bill is that in which the Prime Minister throws the
responsibility upon the new legislature of maintaining that order in Ireland without which no state and no society can exist. I understand the
supremacy of the Imperial Parliament to be this—that they can interfere
in the event of the powers which are conferred by this bill being abused
under certain circumstances. But the Nationalists in accepting this bill go,
as I think, under an honorable understanding not to abuse those powers;
and we pledge ourselves in that respect for the Irish people, as far as we
can pledge ourselves, not to abuse those powers, and to devote our energies and our influence which we may have with the Irish people to prevent those powers from being abused. But, if those powers should be
abused, the Imperial Parliament will have at its command the force which
it reserves to itself, and it will be ready to intervene, but only in the case
of grave necessity arising.

I believe this is by far the best mode in which we can hope to settle
this question. You will have real power of force in your hands, and you
ought to have it; and if abuses are committed and injustice be perpetrated you will always be able to use that force to put a stop to them. You

will have the power and the supremacy of Parliament untouched and un-impaired, just as though this bill had never been brought forward. We fully recognize this to be the effect of the bill. I now repeat what I have already said on the first reading of the measure, that we look upon the provisions of the bill as a final settlement of this question, and that I believe that the Irish people have accepted it as such a settlement. We have had this measure accepted in the sense I have indicated by all the leaders of every section of national opinion both in Ireland and outside Ireland. It has been so accepted in the United States of America, and by the Irish population in that country with whose vengeance some honorable Members are so fond of threatening us. Not a single dissentient voice has been raised against this bill by any Irishman—not by any Irishman holding national opinions—and I need scarcely remind the House that there are sections among Irish Nationalists just as much as there are even among the great Conservative party. I say that as far as it is possible for a nation to accept a measure cheerfully, freely, gladly, and without reservation as a final settlement—I say that the Irish people have shown that they have accepted this measure in that sense.

I will now leave this question of the supremacy of the Imperial Parliament, and I will turn to one that was strongly dwelt upon by the right honorable gentleman, the Member for East Edinburgh. I mean the influence which he fears the Irish priesthood will seek to exercise upon the future education of the Irish people. I may say at once that I am quite sure that the right honorable gentleman's apprehensions upon this subject are genuine, so far as they go, and that at the same time he has no desire to fan the flame of religious discord. On the whole, I think that the right honorable gentleman has spoken very fairly in reference to this part of the question; and I will not say that, perhaps as a Protestant, had I not had, as I have had, abundant experience of Ireland, I might not have been inclined to share his fears myself. Certainly, I have no such fears; but it is rather remarkable that this question of education is the only matter the right honorable gentleman has any fears about in dealing with the question of Protestant and Catholic in Ireland. I can, however, assure the right honorable gentleman that we Irishmen shall be able to settle this question of Irish education very well among ourselves. There are many Liberal Nationalists in Ireland—I call them Liberal Nationalists because I take the phrase in reference to this question of education—there are many Liberal Nationalists who do not altogether share the views of the Roman Catholic Church upon the subject of education, and they are anxious that Ulster should remain an integral part of Ireland in order that they may share the responsibility of government and may influence that government by the feelings which they have with regard to this question of education. You may depend upon it that in an Irish legislature Ulster, with such representatives as she now has in the Imperial Parliament, would be able to successfully resist the realization of any idea which the Roman Catholic hierarchy might entertain with regard to obtaining an undue control of Irish education. But I repeat that we shall be able to settle this question and others very satisfactorily to all the parties concerned among ourselves.

I observe that reticence has been exercised with regard to the financial question, of which such a point was made upon the first reading of the bill. The speech of the right honorable gentleman upon the first reading of the bill undoubtedly produced a great sensation in the House and in this country. The right honorable gentleman, as I and others, and as I believe the country, understood him, argued on that occasion that Ulster was wealthier than either of the three other provinces, and that consequently the burden of taxation would chiefly fall upon her, and that without Ulster, therefore, it would be impossible to carry on the government of Ireland. The right honorable gentleman did not press the financial question very far today; but it would not be improper, perhaps, if we were to direct a little more of our attention to it. For instance, the great wealth of Ulster has been taken up as the war cry of the Loyal and Patriotic Union. The right honorable gentleman was not very fair in choosing the Income Tax, Schedule D, referring to trade and professions, as his standard and measure of the relative wealth of the four provinces. The fair measure of their relative wealth is their assessment to the Income Tax under all the different schedules, and also the value of the ratable property in Ireland; and these tests show conclusively that, so far from Ulster being the wealthiest of the four provinces—and the right honorable gentleman does not deny it now—Ulster comes third in point of relative wealth per head of the population. She comes after Leinster and Munster, and she is only superior to impoverished Connaught.

I come next to the question of the protection of the minority. I have incidentally dwelt on this point in respect to the matter of education; but I should like, with the permission of the House, to say a few words more about it, because it is one on which great attention has been bestowed. One would think from what we hear that the Protestants of Ireland were going to be handed over to the tender mercies of a set of thugs and bandits. The honorable and gallant Member for North Armagh [Major Saunderson] cheers that. I only wish that I was as safe in the North of Ireland when I go there as the honorable and gallant member would be in the South. What do honorable gentlemen mean by the protection of the loyal minority? In the first place, I ask them what they mean by the loyal minority. The right honorable Member for East Edinburgh does not seem to have made up his mind, even at this late stage of the discussion, as to what loyal Ulster he means. When asked the question, he said he meant the same loyal Ulster as was referred to by the Prime Minister in his speech; but he would not commit himself by telling us what signification he attributed to the Prime Minister's expression. Well, I have examined the Prime Minister's reference since then, and I find that he referred to the whole province of Ulster. He did not select a little bit of the province, because the opposition had not discovered this point at that time; and consequently I suppose I may assume that the right honorable Member for East Edinburgh also referred to the whole province of Ulster when he asked for special protection for it. He has not, however, told us how he would specially protect it.

You must give up the idea of protecting the Protestants either as a body or as a majority by the establishment of a separate legislature either in Ulster or in any portion of Ulster. No, sir, we cannot give up a single Irishman. We want the energy, the patriotism, the talents, and the work of every Irishman to insure that this great experiment shall be a successful one. We want, sir, all creeds and all classes in Ireland. We cannot consent to look upon a single Irishman as not belonging to us.

We do not blame the small proportion of the Protestants of Ireland who feel any real fear. I admit, sir, that there is a small proportion of them who do feel this fear. We do not blame them; we have been doing our best to allay that fear, and we shall continue to do so. Theirs is not the shame and disgrace of this fear. That shame and disgrace belong to right honorable gentlemen and noble lords of English political parties who, for selfish interests, have sought to rekindle the embers—the almost expiring embers—of religious bigotry. Ireland has never injured the right honorable gentleman, the Member for West Birmingham. I do not know why he should have added the strength of his powerful arm; why he should, like another Brennus—let us hope not with the same result—why he should have thrown his sword into the scale against Ireland. I am not aware that we have either personally or politically attempted to injure the right honorable gentleman, yet he and his kind seek to dash this cup from the lips of the Irish people—the first cup of cold water that has been offered to our nation since the recall of Lord Fitzwilliam.

The question of the retention of the Irish Members I shall only touch upon very slightly. I have always desired to keep my mind thoroughly open upon it, and not to make it a vital question. There are difficulties, but they are rather more from the English than the Irish point of view, and I think that when we come to consider that question in committee that feeling will be a growing one on the part of Liberal Members. I admit the existence of a strong sentiment in favor of our retention. I will not say it is a reasonable sentiment, when I consider how many times my colleagues and I have been forcibly ejected from this House, how often the necessity of suspending, if not entirely abrogating, representation on the part of Ireland has been eagerly canvassed by the London press as the only necessary solution of it—perhaps I may not, under these circumstances, consider the desire on the part of Liberal Members as a very reasonable one. I admit that it is an honest one. All I can say is that when the Prime Minister has produced his plan, without binding myself beforehand, I shall candidly examine it, with a desire not to see in it an element that will injure the permanency of the settlement.

Now, sir, what does it all come to? It comes to two alternatives when everything has been said and everything has been done. One alternative is the coercion which Lord Salisbury put before the country, and the other is the alternative offered by the Prime Minister, carrying with it the lasting settlement of a treaty of peace. If you reject this bill, Lord Salisbury was quite right in what he said as to coercion. With great respect to the cries of "No" by honorable Members above the gangway, I beg to say, you will have to resort to coercion. That is not a threat on my part—I would do much to prevent the necessity for resorting to coercion; but I say it will be inevitable, and the best-intentioned Radical who sits on those benches, and who thinks that he "never, never will be a party to coercion," will be found very soon walking into the division lobby in favor of the strongest and most drastic coercion bill, or, at the very outside, pitifully abstaining. We have gone through it all before. During the last five years I know, sir, there have been very severe and drastic coercion bills; but it will require an even severer and more drastic measure of coercion now. You will require all that you have had during the last five years, and more besides.

What, sir, has that coercion been? You have had, sir, during those five years—I do not say this to influence passion or awaken bitter memories—you have had during those five years the suspension of the Habeas Corpus Act; you have had a thousand of your Irish fellow subjects held in prison without specific charge, many of them for long periods of time, some of them for twenty months, without trial and without any intention of placing them on trial—I think of all these thousand persons arrested under the Coercion Act of the late Mr. Forster scarcely a dozen were put on their trial; you have had the Arms Acts; you have had the suspension of trial by jury—all during the last five years. You have authorized your police to enter the domicile of a citizen, of your fellow subject in Ireland, at any hour of the day or night, and to search every part of this domicile, even the beds of the women, without warrant. You have fined the innocent for offenses committed by the guilty; you have taken power to expel aliens from this country; you have revived the Curfew Law and the blood money of your Norman conquerors; you have gagged the press and seized and suppressed newspapers; you have manufactured new crimes and offenses, and applied fresh penalties unknown to your laws for these crimes and offenses. All this you have done for five years, and all this and much more you will have to do again. The provision in the bill for terminating the representation of Irish Members has been very vehemently objected to, and the right honorable gentleman, the Member for the Border Burghs [Mr. Trevelyan], has said that there is no halfway house between separation and the maintenance of law and order in Ireland by imperial authority. I say, with just as much sincerity of belief, and just as much experience as the right honorable gentleman, that, in my judgment, there is no halfway house between the concession of legislative autonomy to Ireland and the disfranchisement of the country and her government as a crown colony. But, sir, I refuse to believe that these evil days must come. I am convinced there are a sufficient number of wise and just Members in this House to cause it to disregard appeals made to passion and to pocket, and to choose the better way of the Prime Minister—the way of founding peace and good will among nations; and when the numbers in the division lobby come to be told, it will also be told, for the admiration of all future generations, that England, and her Parliament, in this nineteenth century, was wise enough, brave enough, and generous enough to close the strife of centuries, and to give peace, prosperity, and happiness to suffering Ireland.

John Morley, who was present in the House of Commons during that memorable debate, said that the Irish leader was at his best in that speech. "As he dealt with Ulster, with finance, with the supremacy of Parliament, with the loyal minority, with the settlement of education in an Irish legislature—soberly, steadily, deliberately, with that full, familiar, deep insight into the facts of a country, which is only possible to a man who belongs to it and has passed his life in it—the effect of Mr. Parnell's speech was to make even the able disputants on either side look little better than amateurs."

Sir Michael Hicks Beach competently summed up the case against the bill, and then Gladstone made his fifth and final reply, vigorous and splendid to the

end. But the vote was 343 to 312 against the bill. Ninety-three Liberals had
switched their votes after the Conservatives announced that "no Liberal who
voted against the home-rule bill would be opposed at the election."

Four years later a similar bill might have been engineered through the
House of Commons by Gladstone and Parnell, but the chance was lost when
Parnell was named corespondent in a divorce suit and refused to give up his
leadership even for a time.

He died, lonely and powerless, soon afterward.

BISMARCK PLEADS FOR A BIGGER
ARMS BUDGET
[February 6, 1888]

In 1862 Bismarck became the Prussian Foreign Minister and President of the
cabinet. In violation of the Constitution, he dissolved the Reichstag and carried
out the King's policies—and his own—against the popular majority. In the
years that followed he waged three successful wars, extended the national
frontiers, built a German empire under the hegemony of Prussia, and placated
the democratic movement by social-welfare measures. Germany acquired colonies, and her commerce and industry grew apace. His portentous shadow
lengthened over Europe.

In 1887 Bismarck led his National Liberals to an overwhelming victory at
the polls, by creating the impression that an attack by the French was imminent. When the German ambassador in Paris made a report that no such
danger existed, Bismarck ordered him to withdraw it. The seventy-two-year-old
Chancellor schemed, intrigued, and betrayed. Although Germany was already
bound to Russia and Austria by the Treaty of the Three Emperors, he concluded, on June 18, a secret treaty with Russia alone that recognized Russian
interest in Bulgaria and the Dardanelles. His efforts to isolate France, however,
were not very successful. Russians were grateful to the French for investing
millions in their state bonds and inflamed against Germany because of Bismarck's expulsion of thirty thousand Russian Poles two years before. The
Russian papers were now full of denunciations. But the wily Chancellor knew
how to turn reversal to advantage. Just as he had built up a fear of a French
attack to win the election, he now built up a Russian scare to put through his
new army bill. This bill, which he defended before the Reichstag on February
6, 1888, provided for a vast increase in the number of Germans under arms, in
the event of war, and marks the beginning of the notion of "total" war.

"The very strength for which we strive shows our

peaceful disposition."

IF I RISE to speak today it is not to urge on your acceptance the measure the President has mentioned [the army appropriation]. I do not feel anxious about its adoption, and I do not believe that I can do anything to increase the majority by which it will be adopted—by which it is all-important at home and abroad that it should be adopted. Gentlemen of all parties have made up their minds how they will vote, and I have the fullest confidence in the German Reichstag that it will restore our armament to the height from which we reduced it in the period between 1867 and 1882; and this not with respect to the conditions of the moment, not with regard to the apprehensions that may excite the stock exchanges and the mind of the public, but with a considerate regard for the general condition of Europe. In speaking, I will have more to say of this than of the immediate question. . . .

Since the great war of 1870 was concluded, has there been any year, I ask you, without its alarm of war? Just as we were returning, at the beginning of the seventies, they said: when will we have the next war? When will the Revanche be fought? In five years at latest. They said to us then: "The question of whether we will have war and of the success with which we shall have it" (it was a representative of the Center who upbraided me with it in the Reichstag) "depends today only on Russia. Russia alone has the decision in her hands."

Perhaps I will return to this question later. In the meantime, I will . . . recall that in 1876 a war cloud gathered in the south; that in 1877 the Balkan War was only prevented by the Berlin Congress from putting the whole of Europe in a blaze, and that quite suddenly after the Congress a new vision of danger was disclosed to us in the east because Russia was offended by our action at the conference. Perhaps, later on, I will recur to this also if my strength will permit.

Then followed a certain reaction in the intimate relations of the three emperors that allowed us to look for some time into the future with more assurance; yet on the first signs of uncertainty in their relations, or because of the lapsing of the agreements they had made with each other, our public opinion showed the same nervous and, I think, exaggerated excitement with which we had to contend last year—which, at the present time, I hold to be specially uncalled for. But because I think this nerv-

ousness uncalled for now, I am far from concluding that we do not need
an increase of our war footing. On the contrary! . . .

The long and the short of it is that in these days we must be as strong
as we can; and if we will, we can be stronger than any other country of
equal resources in the world. I will return to that. And it would be a
crime not to use our resources. If we do not need an army prepared for
war, we do not need to call for it. It depends merely on the not-very-
important question of the cost—and it is not very important, though I
mention it incidentally. I have no mind to go into figures, financial or military, but France during the last few years has spent in improving her
forces three thousand millions, while we have spent hardly fifteen hundred millions including that we are now asking for. But I leave the ministers of war and of finance to deal with that. When I say that we must
strive continually to be ready for all emergencies, I advance the proposition that, on account of our geographical position, we must make greater
efforts than other powers would be obliged to make in view of the same
ends. We lie in the middle of Europe. We have at least three fronts on
which we can be attacked. France has only an eastern boundary; Russia
only its western, exposed to assault. We are, moreover, more exposed than
any other people to the danger of hostile coalition because of our geographical position, and because, perhaps, of the feeble power of cohesion
that, until now, the German people has exhibited when compared with
others. At any rate, God has placed us in a position where our neighbors
will prevent us from falling into a condition of sloth—of wallowing in the
mire of mere existence. On one side of us He has set the French, a most
warlike and restless nation; and He has allowed to become exaggerated
in the Russians fighting tendencies which had not become apparent in
them during the earlier part of the century. So we are spurred forward on
both sides to endeavors which perhaps we would not make otherwise.
The pikes in the European carp pond will not allow us to become carp,
because they make us feel their stings in both our sides. They force us to
an effort which, perhaps, we would not make otherwise, and they force
us also to a cohesion among ourselves as Germans that is opposed to our
innermost nature; otherwise we would prefer to struggle with each other.
But when we are enfiladed by the press of France and Russia, it compels
us to stand together, and through such compression it will so increase our
fitness for cohesion that we may finally come into the same condition of
indivisibility that is natural to other people—which thus far we have
lacked. We must respond to this dispensation of Providence, however, by
making ourselves so strong that the pike can do nothing more than encourage us to exert ourselves. . . .

The bill will bring us an increase of troops capable of bearing arms—a possible increase which, if we do not need it, we need not call out, but can leave the men at home. But we will have it ready for service if we have arms for it. And that is a matter of primary importance. I remember the carbine that was furnished by England to our *Landwehr* in 1813, and with which I had some practice as a huntsman—that was no weapon for a soldier! We can get arms suddenly for an emergency, but if we have them ready for it, then this bill will count for a strengthening of our peace forces and a reinforcement of the peace league as great as if a fourth great power had joined the alliance with an army of seven hundred thousand men—the greatest yet put in the field.

I think, too, that this powerful reinforcement of the army will have a quieting effect on our own people, and will in some measure relieve the nervousness of our exchanges, of our press, and of our public opinion. I hope they all will be comforted if they make it clear to themselves that after this reinforcement and from the moment of the signature and publication of the bill, the soldiers are there! But arms are necessary, and we must provide better ones if we wish to have an army of triarians—of the best manhood that we have among our people; of fathers of family over thirty years old! And we must give them the best arms that can be had! We must not send them into battle with what we have not thought good enough for our young troops of the line. But our steadfast men, our fathers of family, our Samsons, such as we remember seeing hold the bridge at Versailles, must have the best arms on their shoulders, and the best clothing to protect them against the weather, which can be had from anywhere. We must not be niggardly in this. And I hope it will reassure our countrymen if they think now it will be the case—as I do not believe—that we are likely to be attacked on both sides at once. . . . But if it should occur we could hold the defensive on our borders with a million good soldiers. At the same time, we could hold in reserve a half million or more, almost a million, indeed; and send them forward as they were needed. Someone has said to me: "The only result of that will be that the others will increase their forces also." But they cannot. They have long ago reached the maximum. We lowered it in 1867 because we thought that, having the North-German Confederation, we could make ourselves easier and exempt men over thirty-two. In consequence our neighbors have adopted a longer term of service—many of them a twenty-year term. They have a maximum as high as ours, but they cannot touch us in quality. Courage is equal in all civilized nations. The Russians or the French acquit themselves as bravely as the Germans. But our people, our seven hundred thousand men, are veterans trained in service, tried soldiers who have not yet forgotten their training. And no people in the world can touch us in this, that we have the material for officers and underofficers to command this army. That is what they cannot imitate. The whole tendency of popular education leads to that in Germany as it does in no other country. The measure of education necessary to fit an officer or underofficer to meet the demands the soldier makes on him exists with us to a much greater extent than with any other people. We have more material for officers and underofficers than any other country, and we have a corps of officers that no other country can approach. In this and in the excellence of our corps of underofficers, who are really the pupils of our officers' corps, lies our superiority. The course of education which fits an officer to meet the strong demands made on his position for self-denial, for the duty of comradeship, and for fulfilling the extraordinarily difficult social duties whose fulfillment is made necessary among us by the comradeship that, thank God, exists in the highest degree among officers and men without the least detriment to discipline—they cannot imitate us in that—that relationship between officers and men which, with a few unfortunate exceptions, exists in the German army. But the exceptions confirm the rule, and so we can say that no German officer leaves his soldiers under fire, but brings them out even at the risk of his own life; while, on the other hand, no German soldier, as we know by experience, forsakes his officer.

If other armies intend to supply with officers and subofficers as many troops as we intend to have at once, then they must educate the officers, for no untaught fool is fit to command a company, and much less is he fit to fulfill the difficult duties which an officer owes to his men, if he is to keep their love and respect. The measure of education that is demanded for that, and the qualities that, among us especially, are expressed in comradeship and sympathy by the officer—*that* no rule and no regulation in the world can impress on the officers of other countries. In *that* we are superior to all, and in that they cannot imitate us! On that point I have no fear.

But there is still another advantage to be derived from the adoption of this bill: the very strength for which we strive shows our peaceful disposition. That sounds paradoxical, but still it is true.

No man would attack us when we have such a powerful war machine as we wish to make the German army. If I were to come before you today and say to you—supposing me to be convinced that the conditions are different from what they are—if I were to say to you: "We are strongly threatened by France and Russia; it is evident that we will be attacked; my conviction as a diplomat, considering the military necessities of the case, is that it is expedient for us to take the defensive by striking the first blow, as we are now in a position to do; an aggressive war is to our advantage, and I beg the Reichstag for a milliard or half a milliard to begin it at once against both our neighbors"—indeed, gentlemen, I do not know that you would have sufficient confidence in me to consent! I hope you would not.

But if you were to do it, it would not satisfy me. If we in Germany should wish to wage war with the full exertion of our national strength, it must be a war with which all who engage in it, all who offer themselves as sacrifices in it—in short, the whole nation—take part as one man; it must be a people's war; it must be a war carried on with the enthusiasm of 1870, when we were ruthlessly attacked. I well remember the ear-splitting, joyful shouts at the Cologne railway station; it was the same from Berlin to Cologne; and it was the same here in Berlin. The waves of public feeling in favor of war swept us into it whether we wished or not. It must always be so if the power of a people such as ours is to be exerted to the full. It will be very difficult, however, to make it clear to the provinces and states of the confederation and to their peoples that war is now unavoidably necessary. They would ask: "Are you sure of that? Who knows?" In short, when we came to actual hostilities, the weight of such imponderable considerations would be much heavier against us than the material opposition we would meet from our enemies. "Holy Russia" would be irritated; France would bristle with bayonets as far as the Pyrenees. It would be the same everywhere. A war that was not decreed by the popular will could be carried on if once the constituted authorities had finally decided on it as a necessity; it would be carried on vigorously, and perhaps successfully, after the first fire and the sight of blood. But it would not be a finish fight in its spirit with such fire and *élan* behind it as we would have in a war in which we were attacked. Then all Germany from Memel to Lake Constance would flame out like a powder mine; the country would bristle with arms, and no enemy would be rash enough to join issues with the *furor Teutonicus* thus roused by attack.

We must not lose sight of such considerations, even if we are now superior to our future opponents, as many military critics besides our own consider us to be. All our own critics are convinced of our superiority. Naturally, every soldier believes it. He would come very near to being a failure as a soldier if he did not wish for war and feel full assurance of victory. If our rivals sometimes suspect that it is fear of the result which makes us peaceful, they are grievously in error. We believe as thoroughly in the certainty of our victory in a righteous cause as any lieutenant in a foreign garrison can believe in his third glass of champagne—

and perhaps we have more ground for our assurance! It is not fear that
makes us peaceable, but the consciousness of our strength—the consciousness that if we were attacked at the most unfavorable time, we are
strong enough for defense and for keeping in view the possibility of leaving it to the providence of God to remove in the meantime the necessity
for war. . . .

We no longer sue for favor either in France or in Russia. The Russian
press and Russian public opinion have shown the door to an old, powerful, and attached friend as we were. We will not force ourselves upon
them. . . . But that does not prevent us from observing—it rather spurs
us on to observe with redoubled care—the treaty rights of Russia. Among
these treaty rights are some which are not conceded by all our friends:
I mean the rights which at the Berlin Congress Russia won in the matter
of Bulgaria. . . .

In consequence of the resolution of the Congress, Russia, up to 1885,
chose as prince a near relative of the Czar concerning whom no one asserted or could assert that he was anything else than a Russian dependent. It appointed the minister of war and a greater part of the officials. In
short, it governed Bulgaria. There is no possible doubt of it. The Bul-
garians, or a part of them, or their prince—I do not know which—were
not satisfied. There was a *coup d'état* and there has been a defection from
Russia. This has created a situation which we have no call to change by
force of arms—though its existence does not change theoretically the
rights which Russia gained from the conference.

So I can say openly that the position of the Russian press, the un-
friendliness we have experienced from Russian public opinion, will not
prevent us from supporting Russia in a diplomatic attempt to establish
its rights as soon as it makes up its mind to assert them in Bulgaria. I say
deliberately— "As soon as Russia expresses the wish." We have put ourselves to some trouble heretofore to meet the views of Russia on the
strength of reliable hints, but we have lived to see the Russian press attacking, as hostile to Russia, the very things in German politics which
were prompted by a desire to anticipate Russia's wishes. We did that at
the Congress, but it will not happen again. If Russia officially asks us to
support measures for the restoration in Bulgaria of the situation approved
by the Congress with the Sultan as suzerain, I would not hesitate to advise his Majesty the Emperor that it should be done. This is the demand
which the treaties make on our loyalty to a neighbor with whom, be the
mood what it will, we have to maintain neighborly relations and defend
great common interests of monarchy, such as the interests of order against
its antagonists in all Europe, with a neighbor, I say, whose sovereign has

a perfect understanding in this regard with the allied sovereigns. I do not doubt that when the Czar of Russia finds that the interests of his great empire of a hundred million people require war, he will make war. But his interests cannot possibly prompt him to make war against us. I do not think it at all probable that such a question of interest is likely to present itself. I do not believe that a disturbance of the peace is imminent—if I may recapitulate—and I beg that you will consider the pending measure without regard to that thought or that apprehension, looking on it rather as a full restoration of the mighty power God has created in the German people—a power to be used if we need it! If we do not need it, we will not use it and we will seek to avoid the necessity for its use. This attempt is made somewhat more difficult by threatening articles in foreign newspapers, and I may give special admonition to the outside world against the continuance of such articles. They lead to nothing. The threats made against us, not by the government but in the newspapers, are incredibly stupid, when it is remembered that they assume that a great and proud power such as the German Empire is capable of being intimidated by an array of black spots made by a printer on paper, a mere marshaling of words. If they would give up that idea, we could reach a better understanding with both our neighbors. Every country is finally answerable for the wanton mischief done by its newspapers, and the reckoning is liable to be presented someday in the shape of a final decision from some other country. We can be bribed very easily—perhaps too easily—with love and good will. But with threats, never!

We Germans fear God, and nothing else in the world!

It is the fear of God that makes us love peace and keep it. He who breaks it against us ruthlessly will learn the meaning of the warlike love of the fatherland that in 1813 rallied to the standard the entire population of the then small and weak kingdom of Prussia; he will learn, too, that this patriotism is now the common property of the entire German nation, so that whoever attacks Germany will find it unified in arms, every warrior having in his heart the steadfast faith that God will be with us.

This fusion of solid information, terror, and piety, delivered with a swashbuckling casualness, was irresistible to the majority of the Reichstag, and Bismarck's bill was passed.

Later that same year the aged Emperor Wilhelm I died; his son and successor died of cancer after reigning only three months, and the grandson came to the throne, unfortunately for the world. Wilhelm II suffered in the shadow of the great Chancellor and dismissed him curtly in 1890. Bismarck retired to his estates in Prussia, where everything he surveyed was dutifully his own, *including the solitude and the giant oaks he loved. From this personal domain he issued sharp criticisms of Wilhelm and his ministers, who were endangering the might of Germany he had built by "blood and iron."*

The most recent study of Bismarck, Bismarck and the German Empire, by the distinguished scholar, Erich Eyck, concludes as follows:

"Under Bismarck's leadership the German nation had become united, strong, and powerful. But the sense of individual independence, of justice and humanity, had been lamentably weakened by Realpolitik and Interessenpolitik—the politics of power and material interest—and by the personal regime which the Iron Chancellor had imposed upon his countrymen. It is therefore no mere chance that his work did not last, and that the Prussian crown and the Hohenzollern dynasty, which he had exalted to heights never before known, ceased to exist twenty years after his death."

ÉMILE ZOLA, ON TRIAL FOR LIBEL, DENOUNCES THE CONSPIRACY AGAINST DREYFUS

[February 21, 1898]

"Anti-Semitism really burst into prominence in the Third Republic with the publication of Édouard Drumont's two-volume, twelve-hundred page La France juive on April 14, 1886," says Robert F. Byrnes in his recent study of this tragic problem. A gifted but embittered journalist, Drumont poured everything that was ever said or rumored against the Jews into his seething caldron which became the source for countless other books and pamphlets. In 1892 he started a daily anti-Semitic newspaper, Libre Parole, which also met with immediate success. Yet by the fall of 1894 anti-Semitism in France reached its lowest ebb and Drumont was on the point of selling his paper.

Then suddenly Captain Alfred Dreyfus, a comparatively unknown Jewish member of the French General Staff, was found guilty of selling military secrets to the German General Staff and sentenced to life imprisonment on Devil's Island. Now France flamed with anti-Semitism, and even such men as Clemenceau thought that Dreyfus should have been executed. But the Captain's brother, Mathieu Dreyfus, got to work and learned through the venerable vice-president of the Senate, Scheurer-Kestner, that Colonel Picquart of the General

Staff had traced the only incriminating evidence against Captain Dreyfus to Major Esterhazy, a Hungarian-born member of the General Staff and a man of scandalous character. Picquart had been rewarded for his investigation with exile to a dangerous army post in Africa.

The little Dreyfus group stubbornly pressed the investigation month after month, for nearly three years, in the face of every conservative and reactionary element in France, for the issue was no longer the innocence of Dreyfus but the honor of the army. Clemenceau and Zola joined in the clamor for the trial of Esterhazy. On January 9, 1898, he was quickly tried by his fellow officers and found not guilty, while Colonel Picquart was dismissed from the army.

Émile Zola (1840–1902) at this time was fifty-eight and entitled to a rest. He had completed the twenty massive volumes of the Rougon-Macquart series and was about to complete his city trilogy—Lourdes, Rome, and Paris. But he had been following the Dreyfus affair for months and late in 1897 he published three fearless articles, one in praise of the valiant Scheurer-Kestner, one against the legend of a Jewish "syndicate," and one against the obscurantist tactics of the General Staff. Outraged by the exoneration of Esterhazy, he dashed off an open letter to Félix Faure, President of the French Republic, and took it to his friend Georges Clemenceau in his office at the newspaper L'Aurore. Clemenceau, who had already decided that something must be done, simply scribbled Zola's opening word, "J'accuse," at the head of the article and printed it with Zola's signature in his own column on January 13, 1898.

Zola's crescendo of charges against generals, judges, editors, and handwriting experts recalled Cicero's terrible charges against Catiline and Mark Antony. The explosion was tremendous, and tens of thousands of extra copies of the letter had to be reprinted. Zola expected to be prosecuted and he was prosecuted promptly—the honor of the army demanded that.

Defended by Fernand Labori before a prejudiced court, an intimidated jury, and an infuriated country, Zola could hardly have counted on much justice. He could hardly have counted on escaping with his life from the angry crowds that surrounded the courthouse. But he did not cringe when he read his declaration before those twelve bewildered men. He did not forget that only a few months before Prime Minister Méline had announced that "No Dreyfus Affair exists."

"The day will come when France will thank me for having helped to save her honor."

IN THE CHAMBER at the sitting of January 22, M. Méline, the Prime Minister, declared, amid the frantic applause of his complaisant majority, that he had confidence in the twelve citizens to whose hands he intrusted the defense of the army. It was of you, gentlemen, that he spoke. And just as General Billot dictated its decision to the court-martial intrusted with the acquittal of Major Esterhazy, by appealing from the tribune for respect for the *chose jugée*, so likewise M. Méline wished to give you the order to condemn me "out of respect for the army," which he accuses me of having insulted!

I denounce to the conscience of honest men this pressure brought to bear by the constituted authorities upon the justice of the country. These are abominable political practices, which dishonor a free nation. We shall see, gentlemen, whether you will obey.

But it is not true that I am here in your presence by the will of M. Méline. He yielded to the necessity of prosecuting me only in great trouble, in terror of the new step which the advancing truth was about to take. This everybody knew. If I am before you, it is because I wished it. I alone decided that this obscure, this abominable affair, should be brought before your jurisdiction, and it is I alone of my free will who chose you, you, the loftiest, the most direct emanation of French justice, in order that France, at last, may know all, and give her decision. My act had no other object, and my person is of no account. I have sacrificed it in order to place in your hands, not only the honor of the army, but the imperiled honor of the nation.

It appears that I was cherishing a dream in wishing to offer you all the proofs, considering you to be the sole worthy, the sole competent judge. They have begun by depriving you with the left hand of what they seemed to give you with the right. They pretended, indeed, to accept your jurisdiction, but if they had confidence in you to avenge the members of the court-martial, there were still other officers who remained superior even to your jurisdiction. Let who can understand. It is absurdity doubled with hypocrisy, and it shows clearly that they dreaded your good sense—that they dared not run the risk of letting us tell all and of letting you judge the whole matter. They pretend that they wished to limit the scandal. What do you think of this scandal—of my act, which consisted in bringing the matter before you—in wishing the people, incarnate in you, to be the judge? They pretend also that they could not accept a revision in disguise, thus confessing that in reality they have but one fear, that of your sovereign control. The law has in you its complete representation, and it is this chosen law of the people that I have wished for—this law which, as a good citizen, I hold in profound respect, and not the suspicious procedure by which they hoped to make you a laughingstock.

I am thus excused, gentlemen, for having brought you here from your private affairs without being able to inundate you with the full flood of light of which I dreamed. The light, the whole light—this was my sole, my passionate desire! And this trial has just proved it. We have had to fight step by step against an extraordinarily obstinate desire for darkness. A battle has been necessary to obtain every atom of truth. Everything has been refused us. Our witnesses have been terrorized in the hope of preventing us from proving our case. And it is on your behalf alone that we have fought, that this proof might be put before you in its entirety, so that you might give your opinion on your consciences without remorse. I am certain, therefore, that you will give us credit for our efforts, and I feel sure too that sufficient light has been thrown upon the affair.

You have heard the witnesses; you are about to hear my counsel, who will tell you the true story, the story that maddens everybody and that everybody knows. I am, therefore, at my ease. You have the truth at last, and it will do its work. M. Méline thought to dictate your decision by intrusting to you the honor of the army. And it is in the name of the honor of the army that I too appeal to your justice.

I give M. Méline the most direct contradiction. Never have I insulted the army. I spoke, on the contrary, of my sympathy, my respect for the nation in arms, for our dear soldiers of France, who would rise at the first menace to defend the soil of France. And it is just as false that I attacked the chiefs, the generals who would lead them to victory. If certain persons at the War Office have compromised the army itself by their acts, is it to insult the whole army to say so? Is it not rather to act as a good citizen to separate it from all that compromises it, to give the alarm, so that the blunders that alone have been the cause of our defeat shall not occur again and shall not lead us to fresh disaster.

I am not defending myself, moreover. I leave history to judge my act, which was a necessary one; but I affirm that the army is dishonored when gendarmes are allowed to embrace Major Esterhazy after the abominable letters written by him. I affirm that that valiant army is insulted daily by the bandits who, on the plea of defending it, sully it by their degrading championship—who trail in the mud all that France still honors as good and great. I affirm that those who dishonor that great national army are those who mingle cries of *"Vive l'armée!"* with those of *"À bas les juifs!"* and *"Vive* Esterhazy!" *Grand Dieu!* the people of St. Louis, of Bayard, of Condé, and of Hoche, the people which counts a hundred great victories, the people of the great wars of the Republic and the Empire, the people whose power, grace, and generosity have dazzled the world, crying *"Vive* Esterhazy!" It is a shame the stain of which our efforts on behalf of truth and justice can alone wipe out!

You know the legend that has grown up: Dreyfus was condemned justly and legally by seven infallible officers, whom it is impossible even to suspect of a blunder without insulting the whole army. Dreyfus expiates in merited torments his abominable crime, and as he is a Jew, a Jewish syndicate is formed, an international *sans patrie* syndicate disposing of hundreds of millions, the object of which is to save the traitor at any price, even by the most shameless intrigues. And thereupon this syndicate began to heap crime on crime, buying consciences, precipitating France into a disastrous tumult, resolved on selling her to the enemy, willing even to drive all Europe into a general war rather than renounce its terrible plan.

It is very simple, nay childish, if not imbecile. But it is with this poisoned bread that the unclean press has been nourishing our poor people now for months. And it is not surprising if we are witnessing a dangerous crisis; for when folly and lies are thus sown broadcast, you necessarily reap insanity.

Gentlemen, I would not insult you by supposing that you have yourselves been duped by this nursery tale. I know you; I know who you are. You are the heart and the reason of Paris, of my great Paris, where I was born, which I love with an infinite tenderness, which I have been studying and writing of now for forty years. And I know likewise what is now passing in your brains; for, before coming to sit here as defendant, I sat there on the bench where you are now. You represent there the average opinion; you try to illustrate prudence and justice in the mass. Soon I shall be in thought with you in the room where you deliberate, and I am convinced that your effort will be to safeguard your interests as citizens, which are, of course, the interests of the whole nation. You may make a mistake, but you will do so in the thought that while securing your own weal you are securing the weal of all.

I see you at your homes at evening under the lamp; I hear you talk with your friends; I accompany you into your factories and shops. You are all workers—some tradesmen, others manufacturers, some professional men; and your very legitimate anxiety is the deplorable state into which business has fallen. Everywhere the present crisis threatens to become a disaster. The receipts fall off; transactions become more and more difficult. So that the idea which you have brought here, the thought that I read in your countenances, is that there has been enough of this and that it must be ended. You have not gone the length of saying, like many: "What matters it that an innocent man is at the Île du Diable? Is the interest of a single man worth this disturbing a great country?" But you say, nevertheless, that the agitation which we are carrying on, we who hunger for truth and justice, costs too dearly! And if you condemn me, gentlemen, it is that thought which will be at the bottom of your verdict. You desire tranquillity for your homes, you wish for the revival of business, and you may think that by punishing me you will stop a campaign that is injurious to the interests of France.

Well, gentlemen, if that is your idea, you are entirely mistaken. Do me the honor of believing that I am not defending my liberty. By punishing me you would only magnify me. Whoever suffers for truth and justice becomes august and sacred. Look at me. Have I the look of a hireling, of a liar, and a traitor? Why should I be playing a part? I have behind me neither political ambition nor sectarian passion. I am a free writer, who has given his life to labor; who tomorrow will go back to the ranks and resume his interrupted task. And how stupid are those who call me an Italian—me, born of a French mother, brought up by grandparents in the Beauce, peasants of that vigorous soil; me, who lost my father at seven years of age, who never went to Italy till I was fifty-four. And yet I am proud that my father was from Venice—the resplendent city whose ancient glory sings in all memories. And even if I were not French, would not the forty volumes in the French language, which I have sent by millions of copies throughout the world, suffice to make me a Frenchman?

So I do not defend myself. But what a blunder would be yours if you were convinced that by striking me you would re-establish order in our unfortunate country! Do you not understand now that what the nation is dying of is the darkness in which there is such an obstinate determination to leave her? The blunders of those in authority are being heaped upon those of others; one lie necessitates another, so that the mass is becoming formidable. A judicial blunder was committed, and then to hide it, it has been necessary to commit every day fresh crimes against good sense and equity! The condemnation of an innocent man has involved the acquittal of a guilty man, and now today you are asked in turn to condemn me because I have cried out in my anguish on beholding our country embarked on this terrible course. Condemn me, then! But it will be one more error added to the others—a fault the burden of which you will hear in history. And my condemnation, instead of restoring the peace for which you long, and which we all of us desire, will be only a fresh seed of passion and disorder. The cup, I tell you, is full; do not make it run over!

Why do you not judge justly the terrible crisis through which the country is passing? They say that we are the authors of the scandal, that we who are lovers of truth and justice are leading the nation astray and urging it to violence. Surely this is a mockery! To speak only of General Billot—was he not warned eighteen months ago? Did not Colonel Picquart insist that he should take up the matter of revision, if he did not wish the storm to burst and destroy everything? Did not M. Scheurer-Kestner, with tears in his eyes, beg him to think of France, and save her such a calamity? No! our desire has been to make peace, to allay discontent, and, if the country is now in trouble, the responsibility lies with the power which, to cover the guilty, and in the futherance of political ends, has denied everything, hoping to be strong enough to prevent the truth from being revealed. It has maneuvered in behalf of darkness, and it alone is responsible for the present distraction of the public conscience!

The Dreyfus case, gentlemen, has now become a very small affair. It is lost in view of the formidable questions to which it has given rise. There is no longer a Dreyfus case. The question now is whether France is still the France of the rights of man, the France that gave freedom to the world, and ought to give it justice. Are we still the most noble, the most fraternal, the most generous of nations? Shall we preserve our reputation in Europe for justice and humanity? Are not all the victories that we have won called in question? Open your eyes, and understand that, to be in such confusion, the French soul must have been stirred to its depths in face of a terrible danger. A nation cannot be thus moved without imperiling its moral existence. This is an exceptionally serious hour; the safety of the nation is at stake.

When you have understood that, gentlemen, you will feel that but one remedy is possible—to tell the truth, to do justice. Anything that keeps back the light, anything that adds darkness to darkness, will only prolong and aggravate the crisis. The duty of good citizens, of all who feel it to be imperatively necessary to put an end to this matter, is to demand broad daylight. There are already many who think so. The men of literature, philosophy, and science are rising in the name of intelligence and reason. And I do not speak of the foreigner, of the shudder that has run through all Europe. Yet the foreigner is not necessarily the enemy. Let us not speak of the nations that may be our opponents tomorrow. But great

Russia, our ally; little and generous Holland; all the sympathetic nations of the north; those countries of the French language, Switzerland and Belgium—why are their hearts so heavy, so overflowing with sympathetic suffering? Do you dream, then, of an isolated France? Do you prefer, when you pass the frontier, not to meet the smile of approval for your historic reputation for equity and humanity?

Alas! gentlemen, like so many others, you expect the thunderbolt to descend from heaven in proof of the innocence of Dreyfus. Truth does not come thus. It requires research and knowledge. We know well where the truth is, or where it might be found. But we dream of that only in the recesses of our souls, and we feel patriotic anguish lest we expose ourselves to the danger of having this proof someday cast in our face after having involved the honor of the army in a falsehood. I wish also to declare positively that, though, in the official notice of our list of witnesses, we included certain ambassadors, we had decided in advance not to call them. Our boldness has provoked smiles. But I do not think that there was any real smiling in our Foreign Office, for there they must have understood! We intended to say to those who know the whole truth that we also know it. This truth is gossiped about at the embassies; tomorrow it will be known to all, and, if it is now impossible for us to seek it where it is concealed by official red tape, the government, which is not ignorant —the government, which is convinced as we are—of the innocence of Dreyfus, will be able, whenever it likes and without risk, to find witnesses who will demonstrate everything.

Dreyfus is innocent. I swear it! I stake my life on it—my honor! At this solemn moment, in the presence of this tribunal which is the representative of human justice, before you, gentlemen, who are the very incarnation of the country, before the whole of France, before the whole world, I swear that Dreyfus is innocent. By my forty years of work, by the authority that this toil may have given me, I swear that Dreyfus is innocent. By all I have now, by the name I have made for myself, by my works, which have helped for the expansion of French literature, I swear that Dreyfus is innocent. May all that melt away, may my works perish, if Dreyfus be not innocent! He is innocent. All seems against me—the two Chambers, the civil authority, the most widely circulated journals, the public opinion they have poisoned. And I have for me only an ideal of truth and justice. But I am quite calm; I shall conquer. I was determined that my country should not remain the victim of lies and injustice. I may be condemned here. The day will come when France will thank me for having helped to save her honor.

Zola received no ovation in that hostile courtroom, nor did his attorney, Labori, who spoke with fearless eloquence for nearly three tense days. Zola was found guilty by a vote of seven to five and condemned to a year's imprisonment, with a fine of three thousand francs.

After various appeals and delays, Zola, against his wishes, was forced by his supporters to flee to England while new evidence for Dreyfus turned up. The 1894 decision against Dreyfus was annulled, and he was returned to Paris to be tried again and found "guilty of treason—under extenuating circumstances"! To put an end to the horrible farce (and make it even more farcical) President Loubet "pardoned" him. Complete exoneration was delayed, until 1906, when the Supreme Court of Appeals cleared Dreyfus. During World War I, he was made a general.

Meanwhile Zola returned to France, a hero to millions, and went on with his writing. When he died in 1902 of accidental asphyxiation, thirty thousand people attended the funeral. Of the tributes paid to Zola, the noblest was by Anatole France, who concluded with these words: "Gentlemen, there is only one country in the world in which this great thing could be accomplished. How admirable is the genius of our country! How beautiful is the soul of France, which since centuries past has taught right and justice to Europe and to the world! France is again the land of golden reason and benevolent thoughts, the soil of equitable magistrature, the country of Turgot, of Montesquieu, of Voltaire, of Malesherbes. Zola has merited well of his country in not despairing of justice in France.

"Let us not sorrow for him because he endured and suffered. Let us envy him.

"Envy him! He has honored his country and the world through an immense work and through a great action. Envy him his destiny and his heart, which made his lot that of the greatest: he was a moment of the conscience of man."

PART FOURTEEN

TRIUMPHANT DEMOCRACY

T HE FABULOUS EXPANSION of the United States between the Civil War and the Spanish American War was best celebrated by Andrew Carnegie in Triumphant Democracy (1885), which began and ended on this exuberant note: "The old nations of the earth creep on at a snail's pace; the Republic thunders past with the rush of the express. The United States, the growth of a single century, has already reached the foremost rank among nations, and is destined soon to outdistance all others in the race. In population, in wealth, in annual savings, and in public credit; in freedom from debt, in agriculture, and in manufacture, America already leads the civilized world."

The boastfulness was pardonable in the little Scottish immigrant who began as a telegraph operator and by the time he was forty became the great figure in the age of steel. His image of the country rushing on like an express train was more than appropriate, for the railroads played an enormous role, legitimate and illegitimate, in the furious exploitation of a continent. Vast productive enterprises ran side by side with reckless get-rich schemes, and it was often hard to tell which was which. Wildcat promotion of mines that never existed, of towns that were not even dots on the map, sometimes obscured the actual growth of cities, the incredible development of industry. Stock was watered in fantastic amounts, but iron, coal, oil, wheat, and cattle were not illusions. While The Gilded Age, by Mark Twain and Charles Dudley Warner, pictured the greedy, irresponsible speculation of the period, "Acres of Diamonds," by Russell H. Conwell, reflected its buoyant optimism, with stories of men who found diamonds in their own back yards. That famous lecture, delivered more than six thousand times by a man with a tenacious memory and a fine voice, undoubtedly inspired hundreds of thousands of Americans, but its loose string of simple anecdotes does not make good reading. A certain speech, however, by a gentleman from Kentucky makes a brilliant introduction to the period and remains the most delightful discourse in the history of Congress.

J. PROCTOR KNOTT OF KENTUCKY CAPTIVATES THE HOUSE OF REPRESENTATIVES

[January 27, 1871]

J. Proctor Knott (1830–1911) was born in Kentucky. He studied law in Missouri and was admitted to the bar in 1851. After serving in the Missouri legislature and in other state positions, he was elected Attorney General in 1860. After the Civil War broke out he was briefly imprisoned for his sympathies with the Southern cause. On being released he returned to his native Kentucky, where he was six times elected to the House of Representatives.

In Washington his oratory soon made a name for him, but his great opportunity came during the debate on a bill authorizing an extensive land grant to a railroad to be run along the St. Croix River to Duluth, Minnesota. The Congress had already been lavish with such grants. "The generation between 1865 and 1895 was mortgaged to the railroads," according to the bitter Henry Adams. Between 1850 and 1871 almost all of what is now Iowa and most of what is now Wisconsin had been ceded away, as well as vast areas in the Pacific Coast states. Although it was good practice for the railroads to sell great tracts of this land to settlers at reasonable rates, a great deal had been held for speculation.

"Duluth must be a place of untold delights."

Mr. Speaker:

IF I COULD be actuated by any conceivable inducement to betray the sacred trust reposed in me by those to whose generous confidence I am indebted for the honor of a seat on this floor; if I could be influenced by any possible consideration to become instrumental in giving away, in violation of their known wishes, any portion of their interest in the public domain for the mere promotion of any railroad enterprise whatever, I should certainly feel a strong inclination to give this measure my most earnest and hearty support; for I am assured that its success would materially enhance the pecuniary prosperity of some of the most valued friends I have on earth—friends for whose accommodation I would be willing to make almost any sacrifice not involving my personal honor, or my fidelity as the trustee of an express trust. And that fact of itself would be sufficient to countervail almost any objection I might entertain to the passage of this bill, not inspired by an imperative and inexorable sense of public duty.

But, independent of the seductive influences of private friendship, to which I admit I am, perhaps, as susceptible as any of the gentlemen I see around me, the intrinsic merits of the measure itself are of such an extraordinary character as to commend it most strongly to the favorable consideration of every member of this House—myself not excepted—notwithstanding my constituents, in whose behalf alone I am acting here, would not be benefited by its passage one particle more than they would be by a project to cultivate an orange grove on the bleakest summit of Greenland's icy mountains.

Now, sir, as to those great trunk lines of railway, spanning the continent from ocean to ocean, I confess my mind has never been fully made up. It is true they may afford some trifling advantages to local traffic, and they may even in time become the channels of a more extended commerce. Yet I have never been thoroughly satisfied either of the necessity or expediency of projects promising such meager results to the great body of our people. But with regard to the transcendent merits of the gigantic enterprise contemplated in this bill, I never entertained the shadow of a doubt.

Years ago, when I first heard that there was somewhere in the vast *terra incognita*, somewhere in the bleak regions of the great Northwest, a stream of water known to the nomadic inhabitants of the neighborhood as the River St. Croix, I became satisfied that the construction of a railroad from that raging torrent to some point in the civilized world was essential to the happiness and prosperity of the American people, if not absolutely indispensable to the perpetuity of republican institutions on this continent. I felt instinctively that the boundless resources of that prolific region of sand and pine shrubbery would never be fully developed without a railroad constructed and equipped at the expense of the government—and perhaps not then. I had an abiding presentiment that some day or other the people of this whole country, irrespective of party affiliations, regardless of sectional prejudices, and "without distinction of race, color, or previous condition of servitude," would rise in their majesty and demand an outlet for the enormous agricultural productions of those vast and fertile pine barrens, drained in the rainy season by the surging waters of the turbid St. Croix.

These impressions, derived simply and solely from the "eternal fitness of things," were not only strengthened by the interesting and eloquent debate on this bill, to which I listened with so much pleasure the other day, but intensified, if possible, as I read over this morning the lively colloquy which took place on that occasion, as I find it reported in last Friday's *Globe*. I will ask the indulgence of the House while I read a few short passages, which are sufficient, in my judgment, to place the merits of the great enterprise contemplated in the measure now under discussion beyond all possible controversy.

The honorable gentleman from Minnesota [Mr. Wilson], who, I believe, is managing this bill, in speaking of the character of the country through which this railroad is to pass, says this:—

> We want to have the timber brought to us as cheaply as possible. Now, if you tie up the lands in this way so that no title can be obtained to them—for no settler will go on these lands, for he cannot make a living—you deprive us of the benefit of that timber.

Now, sir, I would not have it by any means inferred from this that the gentleman from Minnesota would insinuate that the people out in his section desire this timber merely for the purpose of fencing up their farms so that their stock may not wander off and die of starvation among the bleak hills of the St. Croix. I read it for no such purpose, sir, and make no such comment on it myself. In corroboration of this statement of the gentleman from Minnesota, I find this testimony given by the honorable gentleman from Wisconsin [Mr. Washburn]. Speaking of these same lands he says:

> Under the bill, as amended by my friend from Minnesota, nine tenths of the land is open to actual settlers at $2.50 per acre; the remaining one tenth is pine-timbered land that is not fit for settlement, and never will be settled upon; but the timber will be cut off. I admit that it is the most valuable portion of the grant, for most of the grant is not valuable. It is quite valueless; and if you put in this amendment of the gentleman from Indiana, you may as well just kill the bill, for no man and no company will take the grant and build the road.

I simply pause here to ask some gentleman better versed in the science of mathematics than I am to tell me if the timbered lands are in fact the most valuable portion of that section of the country, and they would be entirely valueless without the timber that is on them, what the remainder of the land is worth which has no timber on it at all.

But further on I find a most entertaining and instructive interchange of views between the gentleman from Arkansas [Mr. Rogers], the gentleman from Wisconsin [Mr. Washburn], and the gentleman from Maine

[Mr. Peters], upon the subject of pine lands generally, which I will tax the patience of the House to read:

> Mr. Rogers—Will the gentleman allow me to ask him a question?
>
> Mr. Washburn, of Wisconsin—Certainly.
>
> Mr. Rogers—Are these pine lands entirely worthless except for timber?
>
> Mr. Washburn, of Wisconsin—They are generally worthless for any other purpose. I am perfectly familiar with that subject. These lands are not valuable for purposes of settlement.
>
> Mr. Farnsworth—They will be after the timber is taken off.
>
> Mr. Washburn, of Wisconsin—No, sir.
>
> Mr. Rogers—I want to know the character of these pine lands.
>
> Mr. Washburn, of Wisconsin—They are generally sandy, barren lands. My friend from the Green Bay district [Mr. Sawyer] is himself perfectly familiar with this question, and he will bear me out in what I say, that these pine-timbered lands are not adapted to settlement.
>
> Mr. Rogers—The pine lands to which I am accustomed are generally very good. What I want to know is, what is the difference between our pine lands and your pine lands.
>
> Mr. Washburn, of Wisconsin—The pine timber of Wisconsin generally grows upon barren, sandy land. The gentleman from Maine [Mr. Peters], who is familiar with pine lands, will, I have no doubt, say that pine timber grows generally upon the most barren lands.
>
> Mr. Peters—As a general things pine lands are not worth much for cultivation.

And further on I find this pregnant question, the joint production of the two gentlemen from Wisconsin:

> Mr. Paine—Does my friend from Indiana suppose that in any event settlers will occupy and cultivate these pine lands?
>
> Mr. Washburn, of Wisconsin—Particularly without a railroad?

Yes, sir, "particularly without a railroad." It will be asked after awhile, I am afraid, if settlers will go anywhere unless the Government builds a railroad for them to go on.

I desire to call attention to only one more statement, which I think sufficient to settle the question. It is one made by the gentleman from Wisconsin [Mr. Paine], who says:

These lands will be abandoned for the present. It may be that at some remote period there will spring up in that region a new kind of agriculture which will cause a demand for these particular lands; and they may then come into use and be valuable for agricultural purposes. But I know, and I cannot help thinking, that my friend from Indiana understands that for the present, and for many years to come, these pine lands can have no possible value other than that arising from the pine timber which stands on them.

Now, sir, who, after listening to this emphatic and unequivocal testimony of these intelligent, competent, and able-bodied witnesses, who that is not as incredulous as St. Thomas himself will doubt for a moment that the Goshen of America is to be found in the sandy valleys and upon the pine-clad hills of the St. Croix? Who will have the hardihood to rise in his seat on this floor and assert that, excepting the pine bushes, the entire region would not produce vegetation enough in ten years to fatten a grasshopper? Where is the patriot who is willing that his country shall incur the peril of remaining another day without the amplest railroad connection with such an inexhaustible mine of agricultural wealth? Who will answer for the consequences of abandoning a great and warlike people, in possession of a country like that, to brood over the indifference and neglect of their government? How long would it be before they would take to studying the Declaration of Independence and hatching out the damnable heresy of secession? How long before the grim demon of civil discord would rear again his horrid head in our midst, "gnash loud his iron fangs and shake his crest of bristling bayonets"?

Then, sir, think of the long and painful process of reconstruction that must follow with its concomitant amendments to the Constitution: the seventeenth, eighteenth, and nineteenth articles. The sixteenth, it is of course understood, is to be appropriated to those blushing damsels who are, day after day, beseeching us to let them vote, hold office, drink cocktails, ride a-straddle, and do everything else the men do. But above all, sir, let me implore you to reflect for a single moment on the deplorable condition of our country in case of a foreign war, with all our ports blockaded, all our cities in a state of siege, the gaunt specter of famine brooding like a hungry vulture over our starving land; our commissary stores all exhausted, and our famishing armies withering away in the field, a helpless prey to the insatiate demon of hunger; our navy rotting in the docks for want of provisions for our gallant seamen, and we without any railroad communication whatever with the prolific pine thickets of the St. Croix!

Ah, sir, I can very well understand why my amiable friends from Pennsylvania [Mr. Myers, Mr. Kelley, and Mr. O'Neill] should have been so earnest in their support of this bill the other day, and if their honorable colleague, my friend Mr. Randall, will pardon the remark, I will say I considered his criticism of their action on that occasion as not only unjust but ungenerous. I knew they were looking forward with the far-reaching ken of enlightened statesmanship to the pitiable condition in which Philadelphia will be left unless speedily supplied with railroad connection in some way or other with this garden spot of the universe. And besides, sir, this discussion has relieved my mind of a mystery that has weighed upon it like an incubus for years. I could never understand before why there was so much excitement during the last Congress over the acquisition of Alta Vela. I could never understand why it was that some of our ablest statesmen and most disinterested patriots should entertain such dark forebodings of the untold calamities that were to befall our beloved country unless we should take immediate possession of that desirable island. But I see now that they were laboring under the mistaken impression that the government would need the guano to manure the public lands on the St. Croix.

Now, sir, I repeat I have been satisfied for years that if there was any portion of the inhabited globe absolutely in a suffering condition for want of a railroad, it was these teeming pine barrens of the St. Croix. At what particular point on that noble stream such a road should be commenced, I knew was immaterial, and so it seems to have been considered by the draftsmen of this bill. It might be up at the spring, or down at the foot log, or the water gate, or the fish dam, or anywhere along the bank, no matter where. But in what direction it should run, or where it should terminate, were always to my mind questions of the most painful perplexity. I could conceive of no place on "God's green earth" in such straitened circumstances for railroad facilities as to be likely to desire or willing to accept such a connection. I knew that neither Bayfield nor Superior City would have it, for they both indignantly spurned the munificence of the government when coupled with such ignominious conditions, and let this very same land grant die on their hands years and years ago rather than submit to the degradation of a direct communication by railroad with the piny woods of the St. Croix; and I knew that what the enterprising inhabitants of those giant young cities would refuse to take would have few charms for others, whatever their necessities or cupidity might be.

Hence, as I have said, sir, I was utterly at a loss to determine where the terminus of this great and indispensable road should be, until I acci-

dentally overheard some gentleman the other day mention the name of
"Duluth." Duluth! The word fell upon my ear with peculiar and indescribable charm, like the gentle murmur of a low fountain stealing forth
in the midst of roses, or the soft, sweet accents of an angel's whisper in
the bright, joyous dream of sleeping innocence. Duluth! 'Twas the name
for which my soul had panted for years, as the hart panteth for the water-
brooks. But where was Duluth? Never, in all my limited reading, had
my vision been gladdened by seeing the celestial word in print. And I
felt a profounder humiliation in my ignorance that its dulcet syllables
had never before ravished my delighted ear. I was certain the draftsmen
of this bill had never heard of it, or it would have been designated as one
of the termini of this road. I asked my friends about it, but they knew
nothing of it. I rushed to the library and examined all the maps I could
find. I discovered in one of them a delicate, hairlike line, diverging from
the Mississippi near a place marked Prescott, which I suppose was intended to represent the river St. Croix, but I could nowhere find Duluth.

Nevertheless, I was confident it existed somewhere, and that its discovery would constitute the crowning glory of the present century, if not
of all modern times. I knew it was bound to exist in the very nature of
things; that the symmetry and perfection of our planetary system would
be incomplete without it; that the elements of material nature would long
since have resolved themselves back into original chaos if there had been
such a hiatus in creation as would have resulted from leaving out Duluth.
In fact, sir, I was overwhelmed with the conviction that Duluth not only
existed somewhere, but that, wherever it was, it was a great and glorious
place. I was convinced that the greatest calamity that ever befell the
benighted nations of the ancient world was in their having passed away
without a knowledge of the actual existence of Duluth; that their fabled
Atlantis, never seen save by the hallowed vision of inspired poesy, was,
in fact, but another name for Duluth; that the golden orchard of the
Hesperides was but a poetical synonym for the beer gardens in the vicinity of Duluth. I was certain that Herodotus had died a miserable death,
because in all his travels and with all his geographical research he had
never heard of Duluth. I knew that if the immortal spirit of Homer could
look down from another heaven than that created by his own celestial
genius upon the long lines of pilgrims from every nation of the earth to
the gushing fountain of poesy opened by the touch of his magic wand,
if he could be permitted to behold the vast assemblage of grand and
glorious productions of the lyric art called into being by his own inspired
strains, he would weep tears of bitter anguish that, instead of lavishing
all the stores of his mighty genius upon the fall of Ilion, it had not been

his more blessed lot to crystallize in deathless song the rising glories of Duluth. Yet, sir, had it not been for this map, kindly furnished me by the legislature of Minnesota, I might have gone down to my obscure and humble grave in an agony of despair, because I could nowhere find Duluth. Had such been my melancholy fate, I have no doubt that with the last feeble pulsation of my breaking heart, with the last faint exhalation of my fleeting breath, I should have whispered: "Where is Duluth?"

But thanks to the beneficence of that band of ministering angels who have their bright abodes in the far-off capital of Minnesota, just as the agony of my anxiety was about to culminate in the frenzy of despair, this blessed map was placed in my hands; and as I unfolded it a resplendent scene of ineffable glory opened before me, such as I imagine burst upon the enraptured vision of the wandering peri through the opening of Paradise. There, there for the first time, my enchanted eye rested upon the ravishing word, "Duluth."

. . . This map, sir, is intended, as it appears from its title, to illustrate the position of Duluth in the United States; but if gentlemen will examine it, I think they will concur with me in the opinion that it is far too modest in its pretensions. It not only illustrates the position of Duluth in the United States, but exhibits its relations with all created things. It even goes further than this. It lifts the shadowy veil of futurity and affords us a view of the golden prospects of Duluth far along the dim vista of ages yet to come.

If gentlemen will examine it, they will find Duluth, not only in the center of the map, but represented in the center of a series of concentric circles one hundred miles apart, and some of them as much as four thousand miles in diameter, embracing alike, in their tremendous sweep, the fragrant savannas of the sunlit South and the eternal solitudes of snow that mantle the icebound North. How these circles were produced is, perhaps, one of the most primordial mysteries that the most skillful paleologist will never be able to explain. But the fact is, sir, Duluth is pre-eminently a central place, for I am told by gentlemen who have been so reckless of their own personal safety as to venture away into those awful regions where Duluth is supposed to be that it is so exactly in the center of the visible universe that the sky comes down at precisely the same distance all around it.

I find by reference to this map that Duluth is situated somewhere near the western end of Lake Superior; but as there is no dot or other mark indicating its exact location, I am unable to say whether it is actually confined to any particular spot, or whether "it is just lying around there loose." I really cannot tell whether it is one of those ethereal creations of intellectual frostwork, more intangible than the rose-tinted clouds of a summer sunset; one of those airy exhalations of the speculator's brain, which I am told are ever flitting in the form of towns and cities along those lines of railroad, built with government subsidies, luring the unwary settler as the mirage of the desert lures the famishing traveler on, and ever on, until it fades away in the darkening horizon; or whether it is a real, bona fide, substantial city, all "staked off," with the lots marked with their owners' names, like that proud commercial metropolis recently discovered on the desirable shores of San Domingo. But, however that may be, I am satisfied Duluth is there, or thereabout, for I see it stated here on this map that it is exactly thirty-nine hundred and ninety miles from Liverpool, though I have no doubt, for the sake of convenience, it will be moved back ten miles, so as to make the distance an even four thousand.

Then, sir, there is the climate of Duluth, unquestionably the most salubrious and delightful to be found anywhere on the Lord's earth. Now, I have always been under the impression, as I presume other gentlemen have, that in the region around Lake Superior it was cold enough for at least nine months in the year to freeze the smokestack off a locomotive. But I see it represented on this map that Duluth is situated exactly halfway between the latitudes of Paris and Venice, so that gentlemen who have inhaled the exhilarating airs of the one, or basked in the golden sunlight of the other, may see at a glance that Duluth must be a place of untold delights, a terrestrial paradise, fanned by the balmy zephyrs of an eternal spring, clothed in the gorgeous sheen of ever-blooming flowers, and vocal with the silvery melody of nature's choicest songsters. In fact, sir, since I have seen this map, I have no doubt that Byron was vainly endeavoring to convey some faint conception of the delicious charms of Duluth when his poetic soul gushed forth in the rippling strains of that beautiful rhapsody:

> Know ye the land of the cedar and vine,
> Where the flowers ever blossom, the beams ever shine;
> Where the light wings of zephyr, oppressed with perfume,
> Wax faint o'er the gardens of Gul in her bloom;
> Where the citron and olive are fairest of fruit,
> And the voice of the nightingale never is mute;
> Where the tints of the earth and the lines of the sky,
> In color though varied, in beauty may vie?

As to the commercial resources of Duluth, sir, they are simply illimitable and inexhaustible, as is shown by this map. I see it stated here that there is a vast scope of territory, embracing an area of over two million square miles, rich in every element of material wealth and commercial prosperity, all tributary to Duluth. Look at it, sir! [Pointing to the map.] Here are inexhaustible mines of gold; immeasurable veins of silver; impenetrable depths of boundless forest; vast coal measures; wide, extended plains of richest pasturage—all, all embraced in this vast territory, which must, in the very nature of things, empty the untold treasures of its commerce into the lap of Duluth.

Look at it, sir! Do not you see from these broad, brown lines drawn around this immense territory that the enterprising inhabitants of Duluth intend someday to inclose it all in one vast corral, so that its commerce will be bound to go there whether it would or not? And here, sir [still pointing to the map], I find within a convenient distance the Piegan Indians, which, of all the many accessories to the glory of Duluth, I consider by far the most inestimable. For, sir, I have been told that when the smallpox breaks out among the women and children of that famous tribe, as it sometimes does, they afford the finest subjects in the world for the strategic experiments of any enterprising military hero who desires to improve himself in the noble art of war, especially for any valiant lieutenant general whose—

> *Trenchant blade, Toledo trusty,*
> *For want of fighting has gone rusty.*
> *And eats into itself for lack*
> *Of somebody to hew and hack.*

Sir, the great conflict now raging in the Old World has presented a phenomenon in military science unprecedented in the annals of mankind —a phenomenon that has reversed all the traditions of the past as it has disappointed all the expectations of the present. A great and warlike people, renowned alike for their skill and valor, have been swept away before the triumphant advance of an inferior foe, like autumn stubble before a hurricane of fire. For aught I know, the next flash of electric fire that shimmers along the ocean cable may tell us that Paris, with every fiber quivering with the agony of impotent despair, writhes beneath the conquering heel of her loathed invader. Ere another moon shall wax and wane, the brightest star in the galaxy of nations may fall from the zenith of her glory, never to rise again. Ere the modest violets of early spring shall open their beauteous eyes, the genius of civilization may chant the wailing requiem of the proudest nationality the world has ever seen, as she scatters her withered and tear-moistened lilies o'er the bloody tomb of butchered France. But, sir, I wish to ask if you honestly and candidly believe that the Dutch would have ever overrun the French in that kind of style if General Sheridan had not gone over there and told King William and von Moltke how he had managed to whip the Piegan Indians!

And here, sir, recurring to this map, I find in the immediate vicinity of the Piegans "vast herds of buffalo" and "immense fields of rich wheat lands."

[Here the hammer fell. Many cries: "Go on! Go on!"

The Speaker—Is there objection to the gentleman of Kentucky continuing his remarks? The Chair hears none, the gentleman will proceed.]

I was remarking, sir, upon these vast "wheat fields" represented on this map in the immediate neighborhood of the buffaloes and the Piegans, and was about to say that the idea of there being these immense wheat fields in the very heart of a wilderness, hundreds and hundreds of miles beyond the utmost verge of civilization, may appear to some gentlemen as rather incongruous, as rather too great a strain on the "blankets" of veracity. But to my mind there is no difficulty in the matter whatever. The phenomenon is very easily accounted for. It is evident, sir, that the Piegans sowed that wheat there and plowed it with buffalo bulls. Now, sir, this fortunate combination of buffaloes and Piegans, considering their relative positions to each other and to Duluth, as they are arranged on this map, satisfies me that Duluth is destined to be the beef market of the world.

Here, you will observe [pointing to the map] are the buffaloes, directly between the Piegans and Duluth; and here, right on the road to Duluth, are the Creeks. Now, sir, when the buffaloes are sufficiently fat from grazing on these immense wheat fields, you see it will be the easiest thing in the world for the Piegans to drive them on down, stay all night with their friends, the Creeks, and go into Duluth in the morning. I think I see them now, sir, a vast herd of buffaloes, with their heads down, their eyes glaring, their nostrils dilated, their tongues out, and their tails curled over their backs, tearing along toward Duluth, with about a thousand Piegans on their grass-bellied ponies, yelling at their heels! On they come! And as they sweep past the Creeks they join in the chase, and away they all go, yelling, bellowing, ripping, and tearing along, amid clouds of dust, until the last buffalo is safely penned in the stockyards of Duluth!

Sir, I might stand here for hours and hours, and expatiate with rapture upon the gorgeous prospects of Duluth, as depicted upon this map. But human life is too short and the time of this House far too valuable to allow me to linger longer upon the delightful theme. I think every gentleman on this floor is as well satisfied as I am that Duluth is destined to become the commercial metropolis of the universe, and that this road should be built at once. I am fully persuaded that no patriotic representative of the American people who has a proper appreciation of the associated glories of Duluth and the St. Croix will hesitate a moment to say that every able-bodied female in the land between the ages of eighteen and forty-five who is in favor of "women's rights" should be drafted and set to work upon this great work without delay. Nevertheless, sir, it grieves my very soul to be compelled to say that I cannot vote for the grant of lands provided for in this bill.

Ah! sir, you can have no conception of the poignancy of my anguish that I am deprived of that blessed privilege! There are two insuperable obstacles in the way. In the first place, my constituents, for whom I am acting here, have no more interest in this road than they have in the great question of culinary taste now perhaps agitating the public mind of Dominica, as to whether the illustrious commissioners who recently left this capital for that free and enlightened republic would be better fricasseed, boiled, or roasted, and in the second place these lands, which I am asked to give away, alas, are not mine to bestow! My relation to them is simply that of trustee to an express trust. And shall I ever betray that trust? Never, sir! Rather perish Duluth! Perish the paragon of cities! Rather let the freezing cyclones of the bleak Northwest bury it forever beneath the eddying sands of the raging St. Croix!

Several times Knott stopped speaking, but, amid peals of laughter, voices urged him to go on. When he had finished, the bill to put Duluth on the map was promptly killed, and it is interesting to note that lavish land grants to railroads, which had been Congressional policy since the Civil War, came to an end about this time. The speech was read and chuckled over from one end of the country to the other. Indeed, it may have been too successful. In the opinion of some, the reputation Knott acquired as a humorist ruined his reputation as a sound statesman and blighted his career in national politics. General Garfield, at any rate, was convinced that humor and political success were incompatible. While running for President, he explained to Chauncey Depew that when he entered politics he found that humor was impairing his reputation for seriousness: "So I decided to cut it out."

Knott served three more terms in the House of Representatives (1875–83), but did not rise to special eminence. He was Governor of Kentucky for four years and in 1892 became a professor of economics at Centre College, in Danville, Kentucky. In the meantime, his lush travesty on the glories of Duluth was not forgotten. Visiting that city years after he had delivered the speech, Knott found that even here his humor was appreciated, and he was given a warm and admiring reception.

ROBERT G. INGERSOLL NOMINATES JAMES G. BLAINE FOR PRESIDENT OF THE UNITED STATES

[June 15, 1876]

As one picks up a dusty copy of Ingersoll's miscellaneous lectures in any second-hand bookstore and reads through lectures such as "Some Mistakes of Moses," "Why I Am an Agnostic," and "The Gods and War," it may be hard to envisage the immensely popular and highly paid orator who dazzled the American public for three decades. These none-too-learned lectures were then the last word in "polish," "eloquence," and "daring." People went in droves to hear the bold agnostic who was at the same time a brilliantly successful lawyer, an orthodox Republican, and a highly respectable family man. We who have not heard Ingersoll can safely believe that, along with a superb voice, he possessed every captivating art of the platform.

Robert Green Ingersoll (1833–99) was admitted to the bar at Shawnee-town, Wisconsin, in 1854, and three years later moved to Peoria, where he became a distinguished lawyer and, for one term, attorney general of Illinois. His legal career was interrupted by the Civil War, in which he served in several campaigns as colonel of a cavalry regiment until captured in 1862. After the war Ingersoll switched parties, and in 1876 became a delegate to the Republican national convention at Cincinnati, where he was chosen to give the nominating speech for James G. Blaine. This short address, delivered before an excited political convention, has stood the test of time much better than the once-famous speeches on free thought.

"Like an armed warrior, like a plumed knight."

MASSACHUSETTS may be satisfied with the loyalty of Benjamin H. Bristow; so am I; but if any man nominated by this convention cannot carry the state of Massachusetts, I am not satisfied with the loyalty of that state. If the nominee of this convention cannot carry the grand old commonwealth of Massachusetts by seventy-five thousand majority, I would advise them to sell out Faneuil Hall as a Democratic headquarters. I would advise them to take from Bunker Hill that old monument of glory.

The Republicans of the United States demand as their leader in the great contest of 1876 a man of intelligence, a man of integrity, a man of well-known and approved political opinions. They demand a statesman; they demand a reformer after, as well as before, the election. They demand a politician in the highest, broadest, and best sense—a man of superb moral courage. They demand a man acquainted with public affairs —with the wants of the people—with not only the requirements of the hour, but with the demands of the future. They demand a man broad enough to comprehend the relations of this government to the other nations of the earth. They demand a man well versed in the powers, duties, and prerogatives of each and every department of this government. They demand a man who will sacredly preserve the financial honor of the United States—one who knows enough to know that the national debt must be paid through the prosperity of this people; one who knows enough to know that all the financial theories in the world cannot redeem a single dollar; one who knows enough to know that all the money must be made, not by law, but by labor; one who knows enough to know that the people of the United States have the industry to make the money and the honor to pay it over just as fast as they make it.

The Republicans of the United States demand a man who knows that prosperity and resumption, when they come, must come together; that when they come they will come hand in hand through the golden harvest fields; hand in hand by the whirling spindles and turning wheels; hand in hand past the open furnace doors; hand in hand by the flaming forges; hand in hand by the chimneys filled with eager fire—greeted and grasped by the countless sons of toil.

This money has to be dug out of the earth. You cannot make it by passing resolutions in a political convention.

The Republicans of the United States want a man who knows that this government should protect every citizen at home and abroad; who knows that any government that will not defend its defenders and protect its protectors is a disgrace to the map of the world. They demand a man who believes in the eternal separation and divorcement of church and school. They demand a man whose political reputation is spotless as a star; but they do not demand that their candidate shall have a certificate of moral character signed by a Confederate Congress. The man who has in full, heaped, and rounded measure all these splendid qualifications is the present grand and gallant leader of the Republican party—James G. Blaine.

Our country, crowned with the vast and marvelous achievements of its first century, asks for a man worthy of the past and prophetic of her future; asks for a man who has the audacity of genius; asks for a man who is the grandest combination of heart, conscience, and brain beneath her flag. Such a man is James G. Blaine.

For the Republican host, led by this intrepid man, there can be no defeat.

This is a grand year; a year filled with the recollections of the Revolution, filled with proud and tender memories of the past, with the sacred legends of liberty; a year in which the sons of freedom will drink from the fountains of enthusiasm; a year in which the people call for a man who has preserved in Congress what our soldiers won upon the field; a year in which we call for the man who has torn from the throat of treason the tongue of slander—for the man who has snatched the mask of Democracy from the hideous face of Rebellion—for the man who, like an intellectual athlete, has stood in the arena of debate and challenged all comers, and who, up to the present moment, is a total stranger to defeat.

Like an armed warrior, like a plumed knight, James G. Blaine marched down the halls of the American Congress and threw his shining lance full and fair against the brazen foreheads of the defamers of his country and the maligners of his honor. For the Republicans to desert this gallant leader now is as though an army should desert their general upon the field of battle.

James G. Blaine is now, and has been for years, the bearer of the sacred standard of the Republican party. I call it sacred, because no human being can stand beneath its folds without becoming and without remaining free.

Gentlemen of the convention, in the name of the great republic, the only republic that ever existed upon this earth; in the name of all her defenders and of all her supporters; in the name of all her soldiers living; in the name of all her soldiers dead upon the field of battle; and in the name of those who perished in the skeleton clutch of famine at Andersonville and Libby, whose sufferings he so vividly remembers, Illinois—Illinois nominates for the next President of this country that prince of parliamentarians, that leader of leaders, James G. Blaine.

These words begot a wild and tumultuous ovation, probably surpassing anything in the history of American conventions. Had Ingersoll's religious deviation not been notorious, he himself might have been nominated on the spot. However, it was Rutherford B. Hayes who received the Republican nomination. Handsome though he was, neither by character nor by achievement did Blaine even begin to justify Ingersoll's eulogy.

INGERSOLL SPEAKS AT HIS BROTHER'S GRAVE

[June 3, 1879]

In quite another setting Ingersoll spoke his most memorable words. Three years later, at his brother's grave in the national capital, he achieved an almost classical touch in this funeral speech of an enlightened agnostic.

"We cry aloud, and the only answer is the echo of our wailing cry."

FRIENDS, I am going to do that which the dead oft promised he would do for me.

The loved and loving brother, husband, father, friend died, where manhood's morning almost touches noon, and while the shadows still were falling toward the west.

He has not passed on life's highway the stone that marks the highest point, but, being weary for a moment, he lay down by the wayside, and, using his burden for a pillow, fell into that dreamless sleep that kisses down his eyelids still. While yet in love with life and raptured with the world, he passed to silence and pathetic dust.

Yet, after all, it may be best, just in the happiest, sunniest hour of all the voyage, while eager winds are kissing every sail, to dash against the unseen rock, and in an instant hear the billows roar above a sunken ship. For, whether in mid-sea or 'mong the breakers of the farther shore, a wreck at last must mark the end of each and all. And every life, no matter if its every hour is rich with love and every moment jeweled with a joy, will, at its close, become a tragedy as sad and deep and dark as can be woven of the warp and woof of mystery and death.

This brave and tender man in every storm of life was oak and rock, but in the sunshine he was vine and flower. He was the friend of all heroic souls. He climbed the heights and left all superstitions far below, while on his forehead fell the golden dawning of the grander day.

He loved the beautiful, and was with color, form, and music touched to tears. He sided with the weak, the poor, and wronged, and lovingly gave alms. With loyal heart, and with the purest hands, he faithfully discharged all public trusts.

He was a worshiper of liberty, a friend of the oppressed. A thousand times I have heard him quote these words: "For justice all place a temple, and all season, summer." He believed that happiness was the only good, reason the only torch, justice the only worship, humanity the only religion, and love the only priest. He added to the sum of human joy; and were everyone to whom he did some loving service to bring a blossom to his grave, he would sleep tonight beneath a wilderness of flowers.

Life is a narrow vale between the cold and barren peaks of two eternities. We strive in vain to look beyond the heights. We cry aloud, and the only answer is the echo of our wailing cry. From the voiceless lips of the unreplying dead, there comes no word; but in the night of death hope sees a star, and listening love can hear the rustle of the wing.

He who sleeps here, when dying, mistaking the approach of death for the return of health, whispered with his latest breath: "I am better now." Let us believe, in spite of doubts and dogmas, of fears and tears, that these dear words are true of all the countless dead.

And now to you who have been chosen, from among the many men he loved, to do the last sad office for the dead, we give his sacred dust.

For the remaining two decades of his life, Ingersoll continued to preach a humane agnosticism. While the Origin of Species was still a highly controversial book and freethinking was anathema, he fought against the current fire-and-brimstone fundamentalism, and popularized the ideas of tolerance and scientific enlightenment.

HENRY GEORGE LECTURES ON MOSES, PROGRESS AND POVERTY

[June, 1878]

Whatever one may think of Progress and Poverty as an economic treatise, it has certainly been one of the most provocative and influential works of modern times. Why increasing poverty should accompany progress was a question many asked. It was left to an American of vision, who had seen the sky-rocketing of real-estate values in boom towns in Australia and California, and who had experienced personally the deepest despair of poverty, to supply the answer—simple and monumental—that the times required.

The founder of the single-tax movement, Henry George (1839–97), was born in Philadelphia of intensely religious parents, and though he spent much time in prayer and service, he received little formal education. When only sixteen he sailed as a foremast boy on an old merchantman bound for Melbourne and Calcutta. On his return, he learned typesetting in a printing shop, but soon quit as the result of a quarrel with the foreman. Hoping to find work in Oregon, he again put to sea but was disappointed both there and in San Francisco, and for years lived in sordid penury, only intermittently employed. His marriage in 1861 increased his plight, particularly after the birth of his first child. Except for money from occasional typesetting jobs, he and his family almost starved until 1865. At this time, curiously enough, he decided to improve his mind and become a writer, and began to turn out articles for minor journals such as The Californian. A year later he was reporter, then managing editor of the San Francisco Times at fifty dollars a week, and subsequently editor of the Oakland Transcript; but writing on social and economic questions had become his chief interest.

One day while driving in the hills, he was told that the land around was selling at a thousand dollars an acre, and "like a flash" the connection between progress and poverty became clear to him. "With the growth of population, land grows in value, and the men who work it must pay more for the privilege." Like Moses after he had seen the burning bush, George now knew his mission. In 1871 he set forth his philosophy in a pamphlet, Our Land and Land Policy. This anticipated the more mature statement in Progress and Poverty (1879), for the first edition of which—five hundred copies—George himself did much of the typesetting. The following year it came out in a regular edition and, after a slow beginning, attracted wide attention, and in cheap editions sold by the millions.

While writing Progress and Poverty in 1878, George was asked to give an address before the Young Men's Hebrew Association in San Francisco. Although he rarely wrote out a speech, or even consulted notes, in this case he prepared and read his address. The result is his most finished and famous public utterance, which was subsequently repeated in many halls and pulpits in Great Britain, Ireland, Australia, and Canada, as well as in the United States.

"Human labor is becoming the cheapest of commodities."

THREE GREAT RELIGIONS place the leader of the Exodus upon the highest plane they allot to man. To Christendom and to Islam, as well as to Judaism, Moses is the mouthpiece and lawgiver of the Most High; the medium, clothed with supernatural powers, through which the Divine Will has spoken. Yet this very exaltation, by raising him above comparison, may prevent the real grandeur of the man from being seen. It is amid his brethren that Saul stands taller and fairer.

On the other hand, the latest school of Biblical criticism asserts that the books and legislation attributed to Moses are really the product of an age subsequent to that of the prophets. Yet to this Moses, looming vague and dim, of whom they can tell us almost nothing, they, too, attribute the beginning of that growth which flowed after centuries in the humanities of Jewish law, and in the sublime conception of one God, universal and eternal, the Almighty Father; and again, higher still and fairer rose that guiding star of spiritual light which rested over the stable of Bethlehem, in Judea.

But whether wont to look on Moses in this way or in that, it may be sometimes worth our while to take the point of view in which all shades of belief or disbelief may find common ground and, accepting the main features of Hebrew record and tradition, consider them in the light of history as we know it, and of human nature as it shows itself today. Here is a case in which sacred history may be treated as we treat profane history, without any shock to religious feeling. Nor can the keenest criticism resolve Moses into a myth. The fact of the Exodus presupposes such a leader.

To lead into freedom a people long crushed by tyranny; to discipline and order such a mighty host; to harden them into fighting men, before whom warlike tribes quailed and walled cities went down; to repress discontent and jealousy and mutiny; to combat reactions and reversions; to turn the quick, fierce flame of enthusiasm to the service of a steady purpose, require some towering character—a character blending in highest expression the qualities of politician, patriot, philosopher, and statesman.

Such a character in rough but strong outline the tradition shows us— the union of the wisdom of the Egyptians with the unselfish devotion of the meekest of men. From first to last, in every glimpse we get, this character is consistent with itself, and with the mighty work which is its monument. It is the character of a great mind, hemmed in by conditions and limitations, and working with such forces and materials as were at hand—accomplishing, yet failing. Behind grand deed, a grander thought. Behind high performance, the still nobler ideal.

It is not the protection of property, but the protection of humanity, that is the aim of the Mosaic code. Its sanctions are not directed to securing the strong in heaping up wealth so much as to preventing the weak from being crowded to the wall. At every point it interposes its barriers to the selfish greed that, if left unchecked, will surely differentiate men into landlord and serf, capitalist and workman, millionaire and tramp, ruler and ruled. Its Sabbath day and Sabbath year secure, even to the lowliest, rest and leisure. With the blast of the jubilee trumpets the slave goes free, the debt that cannot be paid is canceled, and a re-division of the land secures again to the poorest his fair share in the bounty of the common Creator. The reaper must leave something for the gleaner; even the ox cannot be muzzled as he treadeth out the corn. Everywhere, in everything, the dominant idea is that of our homely phrase—"Live and let live!"

And the religion with which this civil policy is so closely intertwined exhibits kindred features—from the idea of the brotherhood of man springs the idea of the fatherhood of God. Though the forms may resemble those of Egypt, the spirit is that which Egypt had lost. Though an hereditary priesthood is retained, the law in its fullness is announced to all the people. Though the Egyptian rite of circumcision is preserved, and Egyptian symbols reappear in all the externals of worship, the tendency to take the type for the reality is sternly repressed. It is only when we think of the bulls and the hawks, of the deified cats and sacred ichneumons, of Egypt that we realize the full meaning of the command: "Thou shalt not make to thyself any graven image!"

And if we seek beneath form and symbol and command, the thought of which they are but the expression, we find that the great distinctive feature of the Hebrew religion, that which separates it by such a wide gulf from the religions amid which it grew up, is its utilitarianism, its recognition of divine law in human life. It asserts, not a God whose domain is confined to the far-off beginning or the vague future, who is over and above and beyond men, but a God who in His inexorable laws is here now; a God of the living as well as of the dead; a God whose immutable decrees will, in this life, give happiness to the people that heed them and bring misery upon the people that forget them. Amid the forms of splendid degradation in which a once noble religion had in Egypt sunk to petrification, amid a social order in which the divine justice seemed to sleep, *I am* was the message that fell upon his inner ear.

The absence in the Mosaic books of any reference to a future life is only intelligible by the prominence into which this truth is brought. Nothing could have been more familiar to the Hebrews of the Exodus than the doctrine of immortality. The continued existence of the soul, the judgment after death, the rewards and punishments of the future state, were the constant subjects of Egyptian thought and art. But a truth may be hidden or thrown into the background by the intensity with which another truth is grasped. And the doctrine of immortality, springing as it does from the very depths of human nature, ministering to aspirations which become stronger and stronger as intellectual life rises to higher planes and the life of the affections becomes more intense, may yet become so incrusted with degrading superstitions, may be turned by craft and selfishness into such a potent instrument for enslavement, and so used to justify crimes at which every natural instinct revolts, that to the earnest spirit of the social reformer it may seem like an agency of oppression to enchain the intellect and prevent true progress, a lying device with which the cunning fetter the credulous.

The belief in the immortality of the soul must have existed in strong forms among the masses of the Hebrew people. But the truth that Moses brought so prominently forward, the truth his gaze was concentrated upon, is a truth that has often been thrust aside by the doctrine of immortality, and that may perhaps, at times, react on it in the same way. This is the truth that the actions of men bear fruit in this world, that though on the petty scale of individual life wickedness may seem to go unpunished, and wrong to be rewarded, there is yet a Nemesis that with tireless feet and pitiless arm follows every national crime, and smites the children for the father's transgression; the truth that each individual must act upon and be acted upon by the society of which he is a part, that all must in some degree suffer for the sin of each, and the life of each be dominated by the conditions imposed by all. It is the intense appreciation of this truth that has given the Mosaic institutions so practical and utilitarian a character. Their genius, if I may so speak, leaves the abstract speculations where thought so easily loses and wastes itself, or finds expression only in symbols that become finally but the basis of superstition, in order that it may concentrate attention upon the laws which determine the happiness or misery of men upon this earth. Its lessons have never tended to the essential selfishness of asceticism, which is so prominent a feature in Brahmanism and Buddhism, and from which Christianity and

Islamism have not been exempt. Its injunction has never been, "Leave the world to itself that you may save your own soul," but rather, "Do your duty in the world that you may be happier and the world be better." It has disdained no sanitary regulation that might secure the health of the body. Its promise has been of peace and plenty and length of days, of stalwart sons and comely daughters.

It may be that the feeling of Moses in regard to a future life was that expressed in the language of the Stoic: "It is the business of Jupiter, not mine"; or it may be that it partook of the same revulsion that shows itself in modern times, when a spirit essentially religious has been turned against the forms and expressions of religion, because these forms and expressions have been made the props and bulwarks of tyranny, and even the name and teachings of the carpenter's Son perverted into supports of social injustice—used to guard the pomp of Caesar and justify the greed of Dives.

Yet, however such feelings influenced Moses, I cannot think that such a soul as his, living such a life as his—feeling the exaltation of great thoughts, feeling the burden of great cares, feeling the bitterness of great disappointments—did not stretch forward to the hope beyond; did not rest and strengthen and ground itself in the confident belief that the death of the body is but the emancipation of the mind; did not feel the assurance that there is a power in the universe upon which it might confidently rely, through wreck of matter and crash of worlds. Yet the great concern of Moses was with the duty that lay plainly before him; the effort to lay the foundation of a social state in which deep poverty and degrading want should be unknown—where men released from the meaner struggles that waste human energy should have opportunity for intellectual and moral development.

We progress and we progress; we girdle continents with iron roads and knit cities together with the mesh of telegraph wires; each day brings some new invention; each year marks a fresh advance—the power of production increased, and the avenues of exchange cleared and broadened. Yet the complaint of "hard times" is louder and louder, and everywhere are men harassed by care, and haunted by the fear of want. With swift, steady strides and prodigious leaps, the power of human hands to satisfy human wants advances and advances, is multiplied and multiplied. Yet the struggle for mere existence is more and more intense, and human labor is becoming the cheapest of commodities. Beside glutted warehouses human beings grow faint with hunger and shiver with cold; under the shadow of churches festers the vice that is born of want.

Trace to its root the cause that is thus producing want in the midst of plenty, ignorance in the midst of intelligence, aristocracy in democracy, weakness in strength—that is giving to our civilization a one-sided and unstable development, and you will find it something which this Hebrew statesman three thousand years ago perceived and guarded against. Moses saw that the real cause of the enslavement of the masses of Egypt was what has everywhere produced enslavement, the possession by a class of the land upon which and from which the whole people must live. He saw that to permit in land the same unqualified private ownership that by natural right attaches to the things produced by labor would be inevitably to separate the people into the very rich and the very poor, inevitably to enslave labor—to make the few the masters of the many, no matter what the political forms, to bring vice and degradation, no matter what the religion.

And with the foresight of the philosophic statesman who legislates not for the need of a day, but for all the future, he sought, in ways suited to his times and conditions, to guard against this error. Everywhere in the Mosaic institutions is the land treated as the gift of the Creator to His common creatures, which no one has the right to monopolize. Everywhere it is, not your estate, or your property, not the land which you bought or the land which you conquered, but "the land which the Lord thy God giveth thee"—"the land which the Lord lendeth thee." And by practical legislation, by regulations to which he gave the highest sanctions, he tried to guard against the wrong that converted ancient civilizations to despotisms—the wrong that in after centuries ate out the heart of Rome, that produced the imbruting serfdom of Poland and the gaunt misery of Ireland, the wrong that is already filling American cities with idle men and our virgin states with tramps. He not only provided for the fair division of the land among the people, and for making it fallow and common every seventh year, but by the institution of the jubilee he provided for a redistribution of the land every fifty years, and made monopoly impossible.

It was no sudden ebullition of passion that caused Moses to . . . bring the strength and knowledge acquired in a dominant caste to the lifelong service of the oppressed. The forgetfulness of self manifested in the smiting of the Egyptian shines through the whole life. In institutions that molded the character of a people, in institutions that to this day make easier the lot of toiling millions, we may read the stately purpose.

Through all that tradition has given us of that life runs the same grand passion—the unselfish desire to make humanity better, happier, nobler. And the death is worthy of the life. Subordinating to the good of his people the natural disposition to found a dynasty, which in his case would have been so easy, he discards the claims of blood and calls to his place of leader the fittest man. Coming from a land where the rites of sepulture were regarded as all-important, and the preservation of the body after death was the passion of life; among a people who were even then carrying the remains of their great ancestor, Joseph, to rest with his fathers, he yet conquered the last natural yearning and withdrew from the sight and sympathy of men to die alone and unattended, lest the idolatrous feeling, always ready to break forth, should in death accord him the superstitious reverence he had refused in life.

"No man knoweth of his sepulcher unto this day." But while the despoiled tombs of the Pharaohs mock the vanity that reared them, the name of the Hebrew who, revolting from their tyranny, strove for the elevation of his fellow men is yet a beacon light to the world.

Leader and servant of men! Lawgiver and benefactor! Toiler toward the promised land seen only by the eye of faith! Type of the high souls who in every age have given to earth its heroes and its martyrs, whose deeds are the precious possession of the race, whose memories are its sacred heritage! With whom among the founders of empire shall we compare him?

To dispute about the inspiration of such a man were to dispute about words. From the depths of the unseen such characters must draw their strength; from fountains that flow only from the pure in heart must come their wisdom. Of something more real than matter; of something higher than the stars; of a light that will endure when suns are dead and dark; of a purpose of which the physical universe is but a passing phase, such lives tell.

"Where did you find that man?" inquired a rabbi after George had given this speech for the first time in San Francisco. The passion and imagery moved many audiences, and cast a religious aura over all of his addresses, so that a prayer was often called for at the conclusion.

After publishing The Land Question in 1881, George went to Ireland as a correspondent for The Irish World and remained abroad for almost a year. In 1883 he sailed for England to give a series of lectures under the auspices of the Land Reform Union, and made a similar tour the following year, being widely acclaimed. On George Bernard Shaw he worked a deep conversion. In his little sketch on "How I Became a Public Speaker" Shaw wrote: "One of the public meetings I haunted was at the Nonconformist Memorial Hall in Farringdon Street in 1884. The speaker of the evening, very handsome and eloquent, was Henry George, American apostle of Land Nationalization and Single Tax. He struck me dumb and shunted me from barren agnostic controversy to economics."

· Henry George had a similar effect on many other future molders of public *opinion, who usually broke with his doctrine but remained grateful for his original inspiration.*

HENRY W. GRADY OF GEORGIA LEAPS INTO NATIONAL FAME WITH AN ADDRESS ON THE NEW SOUTH

[December 22, 1886]

The wounds and rancor of the Civil War still lay bare after twenty years, and there was desperate need for a program of reconciliation, when a young Southerner was asked to give an address before the famous New England Club of New York City.

The first Southerner to be accorded this honor, Henry Woodfin Grady (1850–89), was at this time editor and part owner of the Atlanta Constitution. He had already stirred up a movement in Atlanta to supplant the despair and bitterness of the South with a sensible spirit of reconstruction. Now he had his chance to deliver his message to an august assembly of the victorious North, including General William Tecumseh Sherman himself, the general who had marched through Georgia. The thirty-six-year-old Grady met the challenge like a knight-errant, with boldness combined with modesty.

"When I found myself on my feet," he said, "every nerve in my body was strung tight as a fiddle string and all tingling. I knew then that I had a message for that assemblage. As soon as I opened my mouth it came rushing out."

> *"Will you bear with me while I tell you of another army*
> *that sought its home at the close of the late war—an*
> *army that marched home in defeat and not in*
> *victory?"*

THERE was a South of slavery and secession—that South is dead. There is a South of union and freedom—that South, thank God, is living, breathing, growing every hour." These words, delivered from the immortal lips of Benjamin H. Hill, at Tammany Hall in 1866, true then, and truer now, I shall make my text tonight.

Mr. President and Gentlemen: let me express to you my appreciation of the kindness by which I am permitted to address you. I make this abrupt acknowledgment advisedly, for I feel that if, when I raise my provincial voice in this ancient and august presence, I could find courage for no more than the opening sentence, it would be well if, in that sentence, I had met in a rough sense my obligation as a guest, and had perished, so to speak, with courtesy on my lips and grace in my heart. Permitted through your kindness to catch my second wind, let me say that I appreciate the significance of being the first Southerner to speak at this board, which bears the substance, if it surpasses the semblance, of original New England hospitality, and honors a sentiment that in turn honors you, but in which my personality is lost, and the compliment to my people made plain.

I bespeak the utmost stretch of your courtesy tonight. I am not troubled about those from whom I come. You remember the man whose wife sent him to a neighbor with a pitcher of milk and who, tripping on the top step, fell, with such casual interruptions as the landings afforded, into the basement; and while picking himself up had the pleasure of hearing his wife call out: "John, did you break the pitcher?"

"No, I didn't," said John, "but I be dinged if I don't."

So, while those who call to me from behind may inspire me with energy if not with courage, I ask an indulgent hearing from you. I beg that you will bring your full faith in American fairness and frankness to judgment upon what I shall say. There was an old preacher once who told some boys of the Bible lesson he was going to read in the morning. The boys, finding the place, glued together the connecting pages. The next morning he read on the bottom of one page: "When Noah was one hundred and twenty years old he took unto himself a wife who was"—then turning the page—"140 cubits long, 40 cubits wide, built of gopher wood, and covered with pitch inside and out." He was naturally puzzled at this. He read it again, verified it, and then said: "My friends, this is the first time I ever met this in the Bible, but I accept it as an evidence of the assertion that we are fearfully and wonderfully made. If I could get you to hold such faith tonight I could proceed cheerfully to the task I otherwise approach with a sense of consecration.". . .

My friends, Dr. Talmadge [a famous clergyman of the period] has told you that the typical American has yet to come. Let me tell you that he has already come. Great types like valuable plants are slow to flower and fruit. But from the union of . . . colonist Puritans and Cavaliers, from the straightening of their purposes and the crossing of their blood, slow perfecting through a century, came he who stands as the first typical

American, the first who comprehended within himself all the strength and gentleness, all the majesty and grace of this Republic—Abraham Lincoln. He was the sum of Puritan and Cavalier, for in his ardent nature were fused the virtues of both, and in the depths of his great soul the faults of both were lost. He was greater than Puritan, greater than Cavalier, in that he was American, and that in his homely form were first gathered the vast and thrilling forces of his ideal government— charging it with such tremendous meaning and so elevating it above human suffering that martyrdom, though infamously aimed, came as a fitting crown to a life consecrated from the cradle to human liberty. Let us, each cherishing the traditions and honoring his fathers, build with reverent hands to the type of this simple but sublime life, in which all types are honored; and in our common glory as Americans there will be plenty and to spare for your forefathers and for mine.

In speaking to the toast with which you have honored me, I accept the term "The New South" as in no sense disparaging to the old. Dear to me, sir, is the home of my childhood and the traditions of my people. I would not, if I could, dim the glory they won in peace and war, or by word or deed take aught from the splendor and grace of their civilization —never equaled and, perhaps, never to be equaled in its chivalric strength and grace. There is a New South, not through protest against the old, but because of new conditions, new adjustments, and, if you please, new ideas and aspirations. It is to this that I address myself, and to the consideration of which I hasten lest it become the Old South before I get to it. Age does not endow all things with strength and virtue, nor are all new things to be despised. The shoemaker who put over his door "John Smith's shop. Founded in 1760" was more than matched by his young rival across the street who hung out this sign: "Bill Jones. Established 1886. No old stock kept in this shop."

Dr. Talmadge has drawn for you, with a master's hand, the picture of your returning armies. He has told you how, in the pomp and circumstance of war, they came back to you, marching with proud and victorious tread, reading their glory in a nation's eyes! Will you bear with me while I tell you of another army that sought its home at the close of the late war—an army that marched home in defeat and not in victory—in pathos and not in splendor, but in glory that equaled yours, and to hearts as loving as ever welcomed heroes home? Let me picture to you the footsore Confederate soldier, as, buttoning up in his faded gray jacket the parole which was to bear testimony to his children of his fidelity and faith, he turned his face southward from Appomattox in April, 1865. Think of him as ragged, half starved, heavyhearted, enfeebled by want and wounds;

having fought to exhaustion, he surrenders his gun, wrings the hands of his comrades in silence, and, lifting his tear-stained and pallid face for the last time to the graves that dot the old Virginia hills, pulls his gray cap over his brow and begins the slow and painful journey. What does he find—let me ask you, who went to your homes eager to find, in the welcome you had justly earned, full payment for four years' sacrifice— what does he find when, having followed the battle-stained cross against overwhelming odds, dreading death not half so much as surrender, he reaches the home he left so prosperous and beautiful? He finds his house in ruins, his farm devastated, his slaves free, his stock killed, his barns empty, his trade destroyed, his money worthless; his social system, feudal in its magnificence, swept away; his people without law or legal status, his comrades slain, and the burdens of others heavy on his shoulders. Crushed by defeat, his very traditions are gone; without money, credit, employment, material, or training; and besides all this, confronted with the gravest problem that ever met human intelligence—the establishing of a status for the vast body of his liberated slaves.

What does he do—this hero in gray with a heart of gold? Does he sit down in sullenness and despair? Not for a day. Surely God, who had stripped him of his prosperity, inspired him in his adversity. As ruin was never before so overwhelming, never was restoration swifter. The soldier stepped from the trenches into the furrow; horses that had charged Federal guns marched before the plow, and fields that ran red with human blood in April were green with the harvest in June; women reared in luxury cut up their dresses and made breeches for their husbands, and, with a patience and heroism that fit women always as a garment, gave their hands to work. There was little bitterness in all this. Cheerfulness and frankness prevailed. "Bill Arp" [a current humorist] struck the keynote when he said: "Well, I killed as many of them as they did of me, and now I am going to work." Or the soldier returning home after defeat and roasting some corn on the roadside, who made the remark to his comrades: "You may leave the South if you want to, but I am going to Sandersville, kiss my wife, and raise a crop, and if the Yankees fool with me any more I will whip 'em again." I want to say to General Sherman— who is considered an able man in our parts, though some people think he is a kind of careless man about fire—that from the ashes he left us in 1864 we have raised a brave and beautiful city; that somehow or other we have caught the sunshine in the bricks and mortar of our homes, and have builded therein not one ignoble prejudice or memory. . . .

But what of the Negro? Have we solved the problem he presents or progressed in honor and equity toward the solution? Let the record speak to the point. No section shows a more prosperous laboring population than the Negroes of the South; none in fuller sympathy with the employing and landowning class. He shares our school fund, has the fullest protection of our laws and the friendship of our people. Self-interest, as well as honor, demands that he should have this. Our future, our very existence, depend upon our working out this problem in full and exact justice. We understand that when Lincoln signed the Emancipation Proclamation your victory was assured; for he then committed you to the cause of human liberty, against which the arms of man cannot prevail; while those of our statesmen who trusted to make slavery the cornerstone of the Confederacy doomed us to defeat as far as they could, committing us to a cause that reason could not defend or the sword maintain in the light of advancing civilization. Had Mr. Toombs [first Secretary of State of the Confederacy] said, which he did not say, that he would call the roll of his slaves at the foot of Bunker Hill, he would have been foolish, for he might have known that whenever slavery became entangled in war it must perish, and that the chattel in human flesh ended forever in New England when your fathers—not to be blamed for parting with what didn't pay—sold their slaves to our fathers—not to be praised for knowing a paying thing when they saw it. The relations of the Southern people with the Negro are close and cordial. We remember with what fidelity for four years he guarded our defenseless women and children, whose husbands and fathers were fighting against his freedom. To his eternal credit be it said that whenever he struck a blow for his own liberty he fought in open battle, and when at last he raised his black and humble hands that the shackles might be struck off, those hands were innocent of wrong against his helpless charges, and worthy to be taken in loving grasp by every man who honors loyalty and devotion. Ruffians have maltreated him, rascals have misled him, philanthropists established a bank for him, but the South, with the North, protests against injustice to this simple and sincere people. To liberty and enfranchisement is as far as law can carry the Negro. The rest must be left to conscience and common sense. It should be left to those among whom his lot is cast, with whom he is indissolubly connected and whose prosperity depends upon their possessing his intelligent sympathy and confidence. Faith has been kept with him in spite of calumnious assertions to the contrary by those who assume to speak for us or by frank opponents. Faith will be kept with him in the future, if the South holds her reason and integrity. . . .

This is said in no spirit of timeserving or apology. The South has nothing for which to apologize. She believes that the late struggle between the states was war and not rebellion, revolution and not conspiracy,

and that her convictions were as honest as yours. I should be unjust to
the dauntless spirit of the South and to my own convictions if I did not
make this plain in this presence. The South has nothing to take back.
In my native town of Athens is a monument that crowns its central hill—
a plain white shaft. Deep cut into its shining side is a name dear to me
above the names of men, that of a brave and simple man who died in
brave and simple faith. Not for all the glories of New England—from
Plymouth Rock all the way—would I exchange the heritage he left me
in his soldier's death. To the foot of that shaft I shall send my children's
children to reverence him who ennobled their name with his heroic
blood. But, sir, speaking from the shadow of that memory, which I honor
as I do nothing else on earth, I say that the cause in which he suffered
and for which he gave his life was adjudged by higher and fuller wisdom
than his or mine, and I am glad that the omniscient God held the balance
of battle in His Almighty hand, and that human slavery was swept forever from American soil—the American Union saved from the wreck of
war. . . .

*"The effect was electric and beyond almost any that have ever occurred in New
York or elsewhere, and Grady sprang into international fame," said Chauncey M.
Depew, the dean of after-dinner orators, in My Memories of Eighty Years.
Grady was to give several more brilliant speeches, one notably in Boston, on the
race question, and then die suddenly, before he was forty. Although he revered
most of the usual stereotypes about the "Solid South," "white supremacy,"
segregation, and the idyllic days before the Civil War, he might have developed
into one of the healing minds of our nation.*

BOOKER T. WASHINGTON PROPOSES
A MODEST ROLE FOR THE
NEGRO

[September 18, 1893]

*Born a Virginia slave in a squalid one-room, dirt-floor shack, Booker Taliaferro
Washington (1856–1915) was freed by the Emancipation Proclamation when
only six years old. Although obliged to work long hours in a salt furnace, he
studied at night, and for a time was enrolled in an elementary school. When
the teacher asked him his name, he screwed up his courage and replied Booker*

Washington, and only later learned that his mother had already named him Taliaferro. The story of his struggle upward to education, service, and distinction—through the Hampton Institute and the Wayland Seminary in Washington, D. C., to the presidency of the Negro normal school at Tuskegee, Alabama —has often been told. The remaining thirty-four years of his life were devoted to Tuskegee, which eventually developed into a large institution, with a faculty of almost two hundred, where thirty-eight trades and professions were taught. By 1884 it had become so famous that Washington was in demand throughout the country as a speaker, especially on the subject of race relations. Thousands who had never conceived of a Negro orator saw the one-time slave in action, and measured the appeal of his sincerity, homespun humor, and biblical faith in brotherhood. When he rose to give his address at the Cotton States and International Exposition at Atlanta in 1893, Frederick Douglass had been dead seven months. After this address Washington became the acknowledged leader of the Negro people.

"There is no defense or security for any of us except in the highest intelligence and development of all."

Mr. President and Gentlemen of the Board of Directors and Citizens:

ONE THIRD of the population of the South is of the Negro race. No enterprise seeking the material, civil, or moral welfare of this section can disregard this element of our population and reach the highest success. I but convey to you, Mr. President and Directors, the sentiment of the masses of my race when I say that in no way have the value and manhood of the American Negro been more fittingly and generously recognized than by the managers of this magnificent exposition at every stage of its progress. It is a recognition that will do more to cement the friendship of the two races than any occurrence since the dawn of freedom.

Not only this, but the opportunity here afforded will awaken among us a new era of industrial progress. Ignorant and inexperienced, it is not strange that in the first years of our new life we began at the top instead of at the bottom; that a seat in Congress or the state legislature was more sought than real estate or industrial skill; that the political convention or stump speaking had more attractions than starting a dairy farm or truck garden.

A ship lost at sea for many days suddenly sighted a friendly vessel. From the mast of the unfortunate vessel was seen a signal: "Water, water;

we die of thirst!" The answer from the friendly vessel at once came back: "Cast down your bucket where you are." A second time the signal, "Water, water; send us water!" ran up from the distressed vessel, and was answered: "Cast down your bucket where you are." The captain of the distressed vessel, at last heeding the injunction, cast down his bucket, and it came up full of fresh, sparkling water from the mouth of the Amazon River. To those of my race who depend upon bettering their condition in a foreign land, or who underestimate the importance of cultivating friendly relations with the Southern white man, who is his next-door neighbor, I would say: "Cast down your bucket where you are" —cast it down in making friends in every manly way of the people of all races by whom we are surrounded.

Cast it down in agriculture, mechanics, in commerce, in domestic service, and in the professions. And in this connection it is well to bear in mind that whatever other sins the South may be called to bear, when it comes to business, pure and simple, it is in the South that the Negro is given a man's chance in the commercial world, and in nothing is this exposition more eloquent than in emphasizing this chance. Our greatest danger is that in the great leap from slavery to freedom we may overlook the fact that the masses of us are to live by the productions of our hands, and fail to keep in mind that we shall prosper in proportion as we learn to dignify and glorify common labor, and put brains and skill into the common occupations of life; shall prosper in proportion as we learn to draw the line between the superficial and the substantial, the ornamental gewgaws of life and the useful. No race can prosper till it learns that there is as much dignity in tilling a field as in writing a poem. It is at the bottom of life we must begin, and not at the top. Nor should we permit our grievances to overshadow our opportunities. . . .

As we have proved our loyalty to you in the past, in nursing your children, watching by the sickbed of your mothers and fathers, and often following them with tear-dimmed eyes to their graves, so in the future, in our humble way, we shall stand by you with a devotion that no foreigner can approach, ready to lay down our lives, if need be, in defense of yours, interlacing our industrial, commercial, civil, and religious life with yours in a way that shall make the interests of both races one. In all things that are purely social we can be as separate as the fingers, yet one as the hand in all things essential to mutual progress.

There is no defense or security for any of us except in the highest intelligence and development of all. If anywhere there are efforts tending to curtail the fullest growth of the Negro, let these efforts be turned into stimulating, encouraging, and making him the most useful and intelligent citizen. Effort or means so invested will pay a thousand per cent interest. These efforts will be twice blessed—blessing him that gives and him that takes. . . .

Gentlemen of the exposition, as we present to you our humble effort at an exhibition of our progress, you must not expect overmuch. Starting thirty years ago with ownership here and there in a few quilts and pumpkins and chickens (gathered from miscellaneous sources), remember the path that has led from these to the invention and production of agricultural implements, buggies, steam engines, newspapers, books, statuary, carving, paintings, the management of drugstores and banks, has not been trodden without contact with thorns and thistles. While we take pride in what we exhibit as a result of our independent efforts, we do not for a moment forget that our part in this exhibition would fall far short of your expectations but for the constant help that has come to our educational life, not only from the Southern states, but especially from Northern philanthropists, who have made their gifts a constant stream of blessing and encouragement.

The wisest among my race understand that the agitation of questions of social equality is the extremest folly, and that progress in the enjoyment of all the privileges that will come to us must be the result of severe and constant struggle rather than of artificial forcing. No race that has anything to contribute to the markets of the world is long in any degree ostracized. It is important and right that all privileges of the law be ours, but it is vastly more important that we be prepared for the exercise of those privileges. The opportunity to earn a dollar in a factory just now is worth infinitely more than the opportunity to spend a dollar in an opera house.

In conclusion, may I repeat that nothing in thirty years has given us more hope and encouragement, and drawn us so near to you of the white race, as this opportunity offered by the exposition; and here bending, as it were, over the altar that represents the results of the struggles of your race and mine, both starting practically empty-handed three decades ago, I pledge that, in your effort to work out the great and intricate problem which God has laid at the door of the South, you shall have at all times the patient, sympathetic help of my race; only let this be constantly in mind that, while from representations in these buildings of the products of field, of forest, of mine, of factory, letters, and art, much good will come, yet far above and beyond material benefits will be the higher good that, let us pray God, will come in a blotting out of sectional differences and racial animosities and suspicions, in a determination to administer absolute justice, in a willing obedience among all classes to the mandates of law. This, coupled with our material prosperity, will bring into our beloved South a new heaven and a new earth.

"Cast down your buckets where you are" was a parable that seemed momentarily to break the impasse of races. Social separation, followed by equality when the Negro is prepared for it, was a compromise that many whites as well as Negroes could accept as a basis for fruitful co-operation. It was in any case inevitable. Washington's fame spread South and North and across the Atlantic. He dined with Roosevelt in the White House, and was courted by great men and royalty abroad.

Yet many whites as well as Negroes regarded Washington's program as pusillanimous. To them, his humble training schedule of Negroes was a betrayal of the race, of its indigenous culture and aspirations. With the Negro problem far from solved in this country, and colonial and dependent peoples in revolt everywhere against white tutelage and circumstrictions, Booker T. Washington now appears to us only as an important transitional figure, whereas Frederick Douglass, the giant fighter for full freedom, looms as the man of lasting vision.

WILLIAM JENNINGS BRYAN STAMPEDES THE DEMOCRATIC NATIONAL CONVENTION

[July 8, 1896]

William Jennings Bryan, the "silver-tongued" orator from Nebraska, the "Great Commoner," the "peerless leader of Democracy," as he was called, owed his eminence, more than any other public figure in America, to sheer eloquence. In decades that have passed since his death we are apt to remember only his misguided zeal for bimetallism and prohibition and his preposterous stand against evolution at the Scopes trial, and to forget his valiant fight for the income tax, and for real democracy against the inroads of trusts and financial interests. To millions of his countrymen in the toils of the Eastern oligarchy, he gave inspiration and strength.

Born in Salem, Illinois, Bryan (1860–1925) studied law in Chicago for two years, and, in 1883, began to practice in Jacksonville, Illinois. Four years later he went to Nebraska and, in 1891, was elected to Congress as a Democrat. Deeply sympathizing with the Populist movement, he thought that the agrarian evils of the time could be cured by a graduated income tax and the free coinage

*of silver. The first would shift the tax burden to those who could pay while the
latter would provide the farmers—and all the poor, debt-ridden, and heavily
mortgaged—with a flow of cheap money. Out of office in the year 1895, he
devoted his forensic skill to securing a silver delegation to the Democratic
national convention at Chicago the next year.*

*Here Bryan received his great opportunity. The resolutions committee had
included in its proposed platform a bimetallist demand for the free coinage of
both gold and silver at the ratio of sixteen to one, but a minority of the committee violently objected to the silver declaration and to other Populist planks
in the platform. Feelings ran high. East and West, finance and agriculture, the
great railroads and small business, gold and silver interests, and political personalities too were in violent collision. Pandemonium reigned in the great
hall, and one speaker after another failed to be heard above the din. Finally
Bryan, who had been chosen to close the debate, rose to speak. So striking yet
composed was his appearance that the twenty thousand delegates began to
listen, and the sea of angry tumult suddenly subsided. Thus he launched upon
his famous "cross of gold" speech.*

"You shall not crucify mankind upon a cross of gold."

Mr. Chairman and Gentlemen of the Convention:

I WOULD BE PRESUMPTUOUS, indeed, to present myself against
the distinguished gentlemen to whom you have listened if this were
a mere measuring of abilities; but this is not a contest between persons.
The humblest citizen in all the land, when clad in the armor of a righteous
cause, is stronger than all the hosts of error. I come to speak to you in
defense of a cause as holy as the cause of liberty—the cause of humanity.

When this debate is concluded, a motion will be made to lay upon
the table the resolution offered in commendation of the administration,
and also the resolution offered in condemnation of the administration. We
object to bringing this question down to the level of persons. The individual is but an atom; he is born, he acts, he dies; but principles are eternal; and this has been a contest over a principle.

Never before in the history of this country has there been witnessed
such a contest as that through which we have just passed. Never before
in the history of American politics has a great issue been fought out as
this issue has been, by the voters of a great party. On the fourth of March,
1895, a few Democrats, most of them members of Congress, issued an
address to the Democrats of the nation, asserting that the money question
was the paramount issue of the hour; declaring that a majority of the

Democratic party had the right to control the action of the party on this paramount issue; and concluding with the request that the believers in the free coinage of silver in the Democratic party should organize, take charge of, and control the policy of the Democratic party. Three months later, at Memphis, an organization was perfected, and the silver Democrats went forth openly and courageously proclaiming their belief, and declaring that, if successful, they would crystallize into a platform the declaration which they had made. Then began the conflict. With a zeal approaching the zeal which inspired the crusaders who followed Peter the Hermit, our silver Democrats went forth from victory unto victory until they are now assembled, not to discuss, not to debate, but to enter up the judgment already rendered by the plain people of this country. . . .

The gentleman who preceded me [ex-Governor Russell] spoke of the state of Massachusetts; let me assure him that not one present in all this convention entertains the least hostility to the people of the state of Massachusetts, but we stand here representing people who are the equals, before the law, of the greatest citizens in the state of Massachusetts. When you [turning to the gold delegates] come before us and tell us that we are about to disturb your business interests, we reply that you have disturbed our business interests by your course.

We say to you that you have made the definition of a businessman too limited in its application. The man who is employed for wages is as much a businessman as his employer; the attorney in a country town is as much a businessman as the corporation counsel in a great metropolis; the merchant at the crossroads store is as much a businessman as the merchant of New York; the farmer who goes forth in the morning and toils all day, who begins in spring and toils all summer, and who by the application of brain and muscle to the natural resources of the country creates wealth is as much a businessman as the man who goes upon the Board of Trade and bets upon the price of grain; the miners who go down a thousand feet into the earth, or climb two thousand feet upon the cliffs, and bring forth from their hiding places the precious metals to be poured into the channels of trade are as much businessmen as the few financial magnates who, in a back room, corner the money of the world. We come to speak of this broader class of businessmen. . . .

They tell us that this platform was made to catch votes. We reply to them that changing conditions make new issues; that the principles upon which democracy rests are as everlasting as the hills, but that they must be applied to new conditions as they arise. Conditions have arisen, and we are here to meet those conditions. They tell us that the income tax ought not to be brought in here; that it is a new idea. They criticize us for our criticism of the Supreme Court of the United States. My friends, we have not criticized; we have simply called attention to what you already know. If you want criticisms, read the dissenting opinions of the court. There you will find criticisms. They say that we passed an unconstitutional law; we deny it. The income-tax law was not unconstitutional when it was passed; it was not unconstitutional when it went before the Supreme Court for the first time; it did not become unconstitutional until one of the judges changed his mind, and we cannot be expected to know when a judge will change his mind. The income tax is just. It simply intends to put the burdens of government justly upon the backs of the people. I am in favor of an income tax. When I find a man who is not willing to bear his share of the burdens of the government which protects him, I find a man who is unworthy to enjoy the blessings of a government like ours.

They say that we are opposing national bank currency; it is true. If you will read what Thomas Benton said, you will find he said that, in searching history, he could find but one parallel to Andrew Jackson; that was Cicero, who destroyed the conspiracy of Catiline and saved Rome. Benton said that Cicero only did for Rome what Jackson did for us when he destroyed the bank conspiracy and saved America. We say in our platform that we believe that the right to coin and issue money is a function of government. We believe it. . . .

We go forth confident that we shall win. Why? Because upon the paramount issue of this campaign there is not a spot of ground upon which the enemy will dare to challenge battle. If they tell us that the gold standard is a good thing, we shall point to their platform and tell them that their platform pledges the party to get rid of the gold standard and substitute bimetallism. If the gold standard is a good thing, why try to get rid of it? I call your attention to the fact that some of the very people who are in this convention today and who tell us that we ought to declare in favor of international bimetallism—thereby declaring that the gold standard is wrong and that the principle of bimetallism is better—these very people four months ago were open and avowed advocates of the gold standard, and were then telling us that we could not legislate two metals together, even with the aid of all the world. If the gold standard is a good thing, we ought to declare in favor of its retention and not in favor of abandoning it; and if the gold standard is a bad thing why should we · wait until other nations are willing to help us to let go? Here is the line of battle, and we care not upon which issue they force the fight; we are prepared to meet them on either issue or on both. If they tell us that the gold standard is the standard of civilization, we reply to them that this, the most enlightened of all the nations of the earth, has never declared for a gold standard and that both the great parties this year are declaring against it. If the gold standard is the standard of civilization, why, my friends, should we not have it? If they come to meet us on that issue we can present the history of our nation. More than that; we can tell them that they will search the pages of history in vain to find a single instance where the common people of any land have ever declared themselves in favor of the gold standard. They can find where the holders of fixed investments have declared for a gold standard, but not where the masses have.

Mr. [John Griffin] Carlisle [Kentucky statesman] said in 1878 that this was a struggle between "the idle holders of idle capital" and "the struggling masses, who produce the wealth and pay the taxes of the country"; and, my friends, the question we are to decide is: upon which side will the Democratic party fight; upon the side of "the idle holders of idle capital" or upon the side of "the struggling masses"? That is the question which the party must answer first, and then it must be answered by each individual hereafter. The sympathies of the Democratic party, as shown by the platform, are on the side of the struggling masses who have ever been the foundation of the Democratic party. There are two ideas of government. There are those who believe that, if you will only legislate to make the well-to-do prosperous, their prosperity will leak through on those below. The Democratic idea, however, has been that if you legislate to make the masses prosperous, their prosperity will find its way up through every class which rests upon them.

You come to us and tell us that the great cities are in favor of the gold standard; we reply that the great cities rest upon our broad and fertile prairies. Burn down your cities and leave our farms, and your cities will spring up again as if by magic; but destroy our farms and the grass will grow in the streets of every city in the country.

My friends, we declare that this nation is able to legislate for its own people on every question, without waiting for the aid or consent of any other nation on earth; and upon that issue we expect to carry every state in the Union. I shall not slander the inhabitants of the fair state of Massachusetts nor the inhabitants of the state of New York by saying that, when they are confronted with the proposition, they will declare that this nation is not able to attend to its own business. It is the issue of 1776 over again. Our ancestors, when but three millions in number, had the courage to declare their political independence of every other nation; shall we, their descendants, when we have grown to seventy millions, declare that we are less independent than our forefathers? No, my friends, that will never be the verdict of our people. Therefore, we care not upon what lines the battle is fought. If they say bimetallism is good, but that we cannot have it until other nations help us, we reply that, instead of having a gold standard because England has, we will restore bimetallism, and then let England have bimetallism because the United States has it. If they dare to come out in the open field and defend the gold standard as a good thing, we will fight them to the uttermost. Having behind us the producing masses of this nation and the world, supported by the commercial interests, the laboring interests, and the toilers everywhere, we will answer their demand for a gold standard by saying to them: you shall not press down upon the brow of labor this crown of thorns, you shall not crucify mankind upon a cross of gold.

There was never any question about the success of this most effective convention speech of all time. Toward the close every sentence was followed by a burst of applause, and at the end the building rocked with a unanimous ovation. Not only did Bryan defeat the move to kill the Democratic party's silver declaration, but on the next day the thirty-six-year-old orator was nominated for the presidency. One speech had catapulted him to the top of the ladder. The ceremony of acceptance of the nomination was held next month, at Bryan's request, at Madison Square Garden, in New York City, in order, as he said, "That our cause might be presented in the heart of what now seems to be the enemy's country." In the shadow of Wall Street, on August 12—an intensely hot day— Bryan gave his second national address. This time he read from a manuscript and substituted logic for impassioned appeal, arguing like a seasoned lawyer— and this time one third of the audience walked out. For them it was a big disappointment, but for Republican politicians it was a revelation and a warning—they began to view the "Boy Orator of the Platte" with real alarm.

BOURKE COCKRAN, AN EMINENT DEMOCRAT, REPLIES TO BRYAN

[August 18, 1896]

At the Democratic convention, where Bryan gave his famous "cross of gold" speech, the loud laments of the "gold Democrats" were repeatedly heard. If only Cockran were here, everything would be different. The silver plank would be defeated, and Bryan would not have a chance.

The man of their hopes was the orator-statesman William Bourke Cockran (1854–1923), born in Ireland, who, after studying in France, had come to New York City at the age of seventeen. While principal of a public school in Tuckahoe, New York, he studied law at night, and was admitted to the bar in 1876. A few years later he entered politics and in 1884, as a Tammany delegate to the Democratic national convention, gave an important speech against the nomination of Grover Cleveland. In 1886–88 and in 1890–94 he was a member of the House of Representatives. But though he spoke effectively in the House against the "free coinage" of silver and on other issues, his most celebrated addresses were given before huge political gatherings.

A brilliant example of Cockran's spellbinding is the nominating speech for Senator David B. Hill at the Democratic national convention in Chicago in 1892. No orator ever had so much against him. A giant tent—the "Wigwam" —covered not only one thousand delegates but also twenty thousand uproarious spectators who were, in fact, running the convention. When Cockran began his address at two in the morning, the delegates had already sat through ten hours of wearisome speeches. Outside a storm was raging and, through a vent in the roof, the New York and Michigan delegates were getting wetter and wetter. Facing a hostile audience in a cause he knew was lost (for Cleveland, not Hill, was nominated), he forced respect and admiring attention.

When the silver program triumphed, Cockran was in Rome, recuperating from an accident. Returning to New York at once, he threw himself into the campaign against Bryan and the silver heresy, refusing any compensation or expenses. "The movement launched in Chicago," he said, "is an attempt to paralyze industry by using all the powers of government to take property from the hands of those who created it and place it in the hands of those who covet it." So great was the advance interest in this speech that it was necessary to shift the meeting from Carnegie Hall to Madison Square Garden, where Bryan had spoken six days before. It was here that Cockran, an eminent Democrat, broke with his party to meet the challenge of Bryan's "revolutionary" program.

"*We must raise our hands against the nominee of our party,*

and we must do it to preserve the future of that party

itself."

Mr. Chairman, Ladies and Gentlemen, Fellow Democrats, All:

WITH THE INSPIRING STRAINS of the national song still ringing in our ears, who can doubt the issue of this campaign? The issue has been well stated by your presiding officer. Stripped, as he says, of all verbal disguises, it is an issue of common honesty, an issue between the honest discharge and the dishonest repudiation of public and private obligations. It is a question as to whether the powers of the government shall be used to protect honest industry or to tempt the citizen to dishonesty.

On this question honest men cannot differ. It is one of morals and justice. It involves the existence of social order. It is the contest for civilization itself. If it be disheartening to Democrats and to lovers of free institutions to find an issue of this character projecting into a presidential campaign, this meeting furnishes us with an inspiring truth of how that issue will be met by the people. A Democratic convention may renounce the Democratic faith, but the Democracy remains faithful to the Democratic principles. Democratic leaders may betray a convention to the Populists, but they cannot seduce the footsteps of Democratic voters from the pathway of honor and justice. A candidate bearing the mandate of a Democratic convention may in this hall open a canvass leveled against the foundations of social order, but he beholds the Democratic masses confronting him organized for defense.

Fellow Democrats, let us not disguise from ourselves the fact that we bear in this contest a serious and grave and solemn burden of duty. We must raise our hands against the nominee of our party, and we must do it to preserve the future of that party itself. We must oppose the nominee of the Chicago convention, and we know full well that the success of our opposition will mean our own exclusion from public life, but we will be consoled and gratified by the reflection that it will prove that the American people cannot be divided into parties on a question of simple morals or of common honesty. We would look in vain through the speech delivered here one week ago to find a true statement of the issue involved in this canvass. Indeed, I believe it is doubtful if the candidate himself quite understands the nature of the faith which he professes. I say this not in criticism of his ability but in justice to his morality. I believe that if he himself understood the inevitable consequences of the doctrines he preaches, his own hands would be the very first to tear down the platform on which he stands. But there was one statement in that speech which was very free from ambiguity, pregnant with hope and confidence to the lovers of order. He professes his unquestioned belief in the honesty of the American masses, and he quoted Abraham Lincoln in support of the faith that was in him. Well, I don't believe that the faith of Abraham Lincoln was ever more significantly justified than in the appearance which Mr. Bryan presented upon this platform in the change that has come over the spirit and the tone of Populistic eloquence since the Chicago convention.

We must all remember that lurid rhetoric which glowed as fiercely in the Western skies as that sunlight which through the past week foretold the torrid heat of the ensuing day; and here upon this platform, we find that same rhetoric as mild, as insipid, as the waters of a stagnant pool.

He is a candidate who was swept into the nomination by a wave of popular enthusiasm, awakened by appeals to prejudice and greed. He is a candidate who on his trip home, and in the initial steps of his trip eastward, declared that this was a revolutionary movement; who no sooner found himself face to face with the American feeling than he realized the fact that this soil is not propitious to revolution.

The people of this country will not change the institutions which have stood the tests and experiences of a century for institutions based upon the fantastic dreams of Populist agitators.

The American nation will never consent to substitute for the republic of Washington, of Jefferson, and of Jackson the republic of an Altgeld, a Tillman, or a Bryan. The power of public opinion which caused the vivid oratory of the Chicago platform to burn low and soft as the moonlight outside of this platform, which has already shown its power to control Populistic eloquence, will show the full extent of its wisdom, will give Abraham Lincoln's prophecy its triumphal vindication, when it crushes the seed of Populistic Socialism next November. . . .

In the time to which I must confine myself tonight, I can do nothing but examine that one question which Mr. Bryan himself declares to be the overshadowing issue of this campaign. I am a little puzzled when I read this speech to decide just exactly what Mr. Bryan himself imagines will be the fruit of a change in the standard of value throughout this country—I do not believe that any man can wholly agree with the speech, because if he dissent from one set of conclusions, he has to read but a few paragraphs and he will find another of a different variety. But I assume that it is fair in a discussion of this character, independently of what Mr. Bryan may say, or what Mr. Bryan himself may think he stands for, to examine the inevitable economic effects of a debasement of the coinage, of a change in the standard by which existing debts are to be measured to a baser measure of value. Now, I will imagine that Mr. Bryan himself may believe that in some way or other he is going to benefit the toilers of this country. He says that he is, but he declines to show us how. For my part I am willing to state here that if Mr. Bryan could show me that by any means known to heaven or known on earth, any means revealed to the comprehension of man, that wages could be increased, I will be ready to support him here and now. . . .

But in searching through his speech, in reading through the whole reams of Populistic literature with which this country has been flooded for four years, I have never yet found the syllable which showed me how a Populist expected to increase the rate of wages. . . .

Nothing is more common than the mistake that money and property are identical. They are not. A redundancy of money does not prove any prosperity. There may be a very large amount of circulating medium and very great poverty. The issue of paper money simply is no more an increase of wealth than the issue by an individual of his promissory note would show an increase of his property. As a matter of fact, as increase in the coinage is no proof of an increase in property, but may be a strong proof of a decrease in wealth. . . . The volume of money plays but a small part even in the ordinary transactions of life. It is not the volume of money but the activity of money that counts. . . . Money never can circulate freely and actively unless there be absolute confidence in its value. If a man doubt whether the money in his pocket will be as valuable tomorrow as it is today, he will decline to exchange his commodity against it; and this Populistic agitation threatening the integrity of money has been the cause of the hard times through which this country is passing and from which it will not escape until the heel of popular condemnation is placed upon the Populistic agitation which undermines the foundation of our credit. . . .

In order that you should understand just how a change in the standard of value enables men to cheat their creditors, you have to consider the function which money plays in measuring debts. . . .

Underlying the whole scheme of civilization is the confidence men have in each other, confidence in their integrity, confidence in their honesty, confidence in their future. If we went to a silver coinage tomorrow, if we even debased our standard of value, men say that you would still have the same property you have today, you would still have the same soil, you would still have the same continent. And it is true. . . .

We believe that the very essence of civilization is mutual interest, mutual forbearance, mutual co-operation. We believe the world has passed the time when men's hands are at each other's throats. We believe today that men stand shoulder to shoulder, working together for a common purpose, beneficial to all, and we believe that this attempt to assail wages, which means an attempt to attack the prosperity of all, will be resisted, not by a class, but by the whole nation. The dweller in the tenement house, stooping over his bench, who never sees a field of waving corn, who never inhales the perfume of grasses and of flowers, is yet made the participator in all the bounties of Providence, in the fructifying influence of the atmosphere, in the ripening rays of the sun, when the product of the soil is made cheaper to him every day by the abundance of the harvest. It is from his share in this bounty that the Populist wants to exclude the American workingman. To him we say, in the name of humanity, in the name of progress, you shall neither press a crown of thorns upon the brow of labor nor place a scourge upon his back. You shall not rob him of any one advantage which he has gained by long years of study, of progress in the skill of his craft, and by the careful organization of the members who work with him at the same bench. You shall not obscure the golden prospect of a further improvement in his condition by a further appreciation of the cost of living as well as by a further cheapening of the dollar which is paid to him.

There can be no distress, there can be no hard times, when labor is well paid. The man who raises his hand against the progress of the workingman raises his hand against prosperity. He seeks to restrict the volume of production. He seeks to degrade the condition of the man who is steadily improving himself, and in his own improvement is accomplishing the improvement of all mankind. But this attempt will fail. I do not regret this campaign. I am glad this issue has arisen. The time has come when the people of this country will show their capacity for self-government. They will prove that the men who have led the world in the pathway of progress will be the jealous guardians of liberty and honor. They are not to be seduced by appeals to their cupidity or moved by threats of injury. They will forever jealously guard and trim the lamp of enlightenment, of progress. They will ever relentlessly press and crush under their heels the flaming torch of Populistic discontent, Populistic agitation, and Populistic destruction. When this tide of anarchy shall have receded, this tide of Populistic agitation, this assault upon common honesty and upon industry, shall have abated forever, the foundations of this republic will remain undisturbed. The government will still shelter a people indissolubly wedded to liberty and order, jealously forbidding any distinction of burden or of privilege, conserving property, maintaining morality, resting forever upon the broad basis of American patriotism and American intelligence.

The Republicans and gold Democrats were overjoyed, and tributes poured in from all quarters of the country. "It was the greatest speech I ever heard," said the Republican boss of New York State. "McKinley's election is now secured." Fifteen thousand people, most of them Democrats who had shifted to McKinley on the "sound-money" issue, kindled to that one voice for two hours—a phenomenon inconceivable today. The two presidential campaigns were now on, Republican and Democratic; but the real contestants were not McKinley and Bryan, but Cockran and Bryan. Bryan carried his free-silver fallacy and his defense of the common man through eighteen thousand miles. But Cockran was close at his heels, lecturing and haranguing without rest. By Irish wit and aplomb he won over a hostile audience at the Music Hall in Baltimore. He braved the heckling and hissing spite of immense crowds in St. Louis, Des Moines, Nashville, and other enemy strongholds. On one occasion, by talking very quietly to the men in the front row, he captured a truculent audience who would not listen. Gradually the audience became curious, and the catcalls and tumult ceased. When McKinley was elected by a popular majority of six hundred thousand, Mark Hanna could say that Cockran, a Democrat, had done more to put McKinley in the White House than all the Republican orators combined.

PART FIFTEEN

RACE AND EMPIRE

T HE TWENTIETH CENTURY looms before us big with the fate of many nations," announced Governor Theodore Roosevelt in the spring of 1899. "If we stand idly by, if we seek merely swollen, slothful ease, and ignoble peace, if we shrink from the hard contests where men must win at hazard of their lives and at the risk of all they hold dear, then the bolder and stronger peoples will pass us by and will win for themselves the domination of the world."

The new century turned out to be more strenuous, more violent, than even Roosevelt could have dreamed of or desired. But the themes, the forces, were all there: nation—race—empire; democracy—dictatorship; capitalism—socialism —pacifism. Nor could Roosevelt have suspected that in the coming century the human voice, for better or for worse, would hold sway as never before in history.

"BEVERIDGE THE BRILLIANT" TAKES UP THE WHITE MAN'S BURDEN

[April 27, 1898]

Albert J. Beveridge, the retired Indiana statesman, who wrote a monumental life of Chief Justice Marshall and left at his death an important though unfinished life of Lincoln, rose to national prominence as the flaming prophet of imperialism. America has had few such spellbinders.

Beveridge (1862–1927), born in Ohio, was brought up in poverty and worked his way through Asbury College, now DePauw University in Indiana, partly by winning state-wide oratorical contests. He read law in Indianapolis and was soon a successful lawyer and a prominent Republican campaign speaker, known in his adopted state as "Beveridge the Brilliant." In 1896 he closed the bitter Republican campaign against Bryan at the "Wigwam" in Chicago with a sensational speech denouncing Governor Altgeld, who had pardoned some of *the* prisoners found guilty in the Haymarket riot and who had also opposed the sending of Federal troops to crush the Pullman strike.

Some Americans had long suspected that the ill-treated Spanish possession, Cuba, would be better off in other hands; and now the sympathy of many more Americans was going out to the Cubans carrying on their long, desperate rebellion against Spain. When the U.S.S. Maine was blown up in Havana harbor on February 15, 1898, American rage, sympathy with the rebels, and a sense of "manifest destiny" fused into a dangerous explosive, with the help of Hearst journalism. In Washington the militant enthusiasm of Assistant Secretary of the Navy Roosevelt and Senator Henry Cabot Lodge of Massachusetts accelerated the movement toward war—and war was declared by the United States against Spain on April 24, 1898.

Three days later, Beveridge, the popular after-dinner orator, spoke before the Middlesex Club of Boston, to commemorate the birth of General Grant.

> *"Events, which are the arguments of God, are stranger*
> *than words, which are the arguments of men."*

PARTISANSHIP should only be a method of patriotism. He who is a partisan merely for the sake of spoils is a buccaneer. He who is a partisan merely for the sake of a party name is a ghost of the past among living events. He who is merely the partisan of an ordinary organization is only a pebble in the sling of a boss. But he who is the partisan of principle is a prince of citizenship; and such a partisan was Grant the practical.

Today the horizons flame with war. It is no time for partisanship, say men. Aye! it is the hour for the supremest partisanship—it is the hour for the partisanship of patriotism. It is the hour when all who differ on methods for the republic's ordinary welfare perceive, at last, an issue so immense that, disagreeing still, they still agree. It is an hour when men who thought they hated one another at the ballot box will find that they love one another on the battlefield.

It is an hour when a master event has found and struck the keynote of harmony between labor and capital. It is an hour when Democrats, Republicans, and Populists learn that, after all, our parties are but different answers to the same great question, and that question is, "What of the Republic?". . .

Grant understood that the three elements of the Republic's prosperity are labor, currency, and commerce. He knew that labor is hunger personi-

fied if unemployed; that currency is the script and chips of gamblers if
unsteady in value; that commerce begins to die the moment it ceases to
expand. And so, to the welfare of the nation's toilers, to the honesty of the
nation's money, and to the extension of the nation's trade, his energies
were directed. . . .

He never forgot that we are a conquering race and that we must obey
our blood and occupy new markets, and, if necessary, new lands. He had
the prophet's seerlike sight which beheld, as a part of the Almighty's
infinite plan, the disappearance of debased civilizations and decaying
races before the higher civilization of the nobler and more virile types of
man. He understood that the axioms applicable to thirteen impoverished
colonies have been rendered obsolete by history. An echo of the past is
not to stay the progress of a mighty people and their free institutions. He
declared that "the theory of government changes with general progress."

He had the instinct of empire. He dreamed the same dreams that God
put in the brains of Jefferson and Hamilton, of John Bright and of
Emerson, and of all the imperial intellects of his race—the dream of
American extension till all the seas shall bloom with that flower of liberty,
the flag of the Great Republic. Let me quote you, in this historic time,
these words of Grant: "I do not share in the apprehension held by many
as to the danger of governments being weakened and destroyed by their
extension of territory. Commerce, education, and rapid transit of thought
and matter have changed all this plan. Rather do I believe that our Great
Maker is preparing the world in His own good time to become one nation,
speaking one language, and when armies and navies shall no longer be
required."

The dawning of the day of that dream's fulfillment is at hand.
America's factories are making more than the American people can use;
American soil is producing more than they can consume. Fate has written
our policy for us; we must get an ever-increasing portion of foreign trade.
We shall establish trading posts throughout the world as distributing
points for American products. We shall cover the oceans with our
merchant marine. We shall build a navy to the measure of our greatness.
Great colonies, flying our flag and trading with us, will follow our flag on
the wings of our commerce. And American law, American order, American civilization, and the American flag will plant themselves on shores,
hitherto bloody and benighted, but, by those agencies of God, henceforth
to be made beautiful and bright.

If this means the Stars and Stripes over an Isthmian canal, over
Hawaii, Cuba, and the southern seas, if it means American empire in
the name of the Great Republic and its free institutions, then let us meet

that meaning with a mighty joy and make that meaning good, no matter what barbarism and all our foes may say or do.

If it means Anglo-Saxon solidarity; if it means an English-American understanding upon a basis of a division of the world's markets so that the results may be just; upon the basis of justice to Ireland so that the understanding may be enduring; if it means such an English-speaking people's league of God for the permanent peace of this war-worn world, the stars in their courses will fight for us and countless centuries will applaud.

All this is not the work of a day nor yet of a year. It is the work of a period—the period of the commercial expansion of the Republic, and therefore of the expansion of the institutions of the Republic. For liberty and order and civilization are not planted by speeches, or essays, or editorials; their seed are born in the talons of Trade and planted by the finger of Might. The beginning of that period is upon us and its rounding out is as sure as the processes of time. Fate puts the American people upon their decision between a Chinese policy of isolation, poverty, and decay, or an American policy of progress, prosperity, and power. The young men of America will decide the question as Grant wished to decide it, and as the God of civilization has willed it shall be decided. And let those beware who prove apostate to our destiny.

What should be the policy of this war? What will be its result? The geography of the globe answers the first question; the vigor of the American people answers the second. We are at war with Spain. Therefore our field of operations is not confined to Cuba. We are at war with *Spain*. It is our military duty to strike her at her weakest point before we strike her at her stronger points. Cuba must fall into our hands, but that will be only when Spain is conquered. Our warships today surround Cuba; our armies are massing for Cuba. And yet Cuba will be the last to fall. In the Pacific is the true field of our earliest operations. There Spain has an island empire, the Philippine archipelago. It is poorly defended. Spain's best ships are on the Atlantic side. In the Pacific the United States has a powerful squadron. *The Philippines are logically our first target.*

And when the Pacific fleet of Spain is destroyed, not only is Spain beaten to her knees by the loss of the Philippines, which would necessarily follow, but San Francisco and Portland are at the same time rendered safe.

It is not Cuba we must conquer—it is *Spain*. We must never lose sight of the main objective—to bring an early peace by conquering the enemy. We must strike the most vulnerable points of that enemy. We must sail to meet the enemy—not wait for her to come. These were the methods and maxims of Grant. And, although not a gun has yet been fired, I predict that these will be the American methods in the war we have just declared.

The ultimate result we can leave to the wisdom of events. Victory will be ours—that we know this moment, though no shot has yet been fired. And in that victory I see a blessing, not only for the people of Cuba, but for the oppressed of the Philippines. And in freeing peoples, perishing and oppressed, our country's blessing will also come; for profit follows righteousness.

The first gun of our war for civilization will be also the morning gun of the new day in the Republic's imperial career. We wage no war of conquest; but

> *The hand that rounded Peter's dome*
> *And groined the aisles of Christian*
> *   Rome*
> *Wrought in a sad sincerity—*
> *He builded better than he knew.*

We go forth to fight for humanity; but where American blood establishes liberty and law in any land, the American people will see that that blood is not shed in vain. Events, which are the arguments of God, are stronger than words, which are the arguments of men. We are the allies of Events and the comrades of Tendency in the great day of which the dawn is breaking.

In the name of labor to be employed in clothing and feeding new peoples and new lands, we welcome it. In the name of capital, to be quickened into developing our commerce, we welcome it. In the name of a congested industrial civilization to be relieved by our commercial expansion, we welcome it. In the name of the farseeing minds of every party and of every English-speaking land whose dream we now go forth to realize, we welcome the dawn of the Republic's full-grown manhood. And finally we welcome it in the name of him whose natal day we celebrate. We shall not live to see its close; but it is enough to behold its daybreak, for in that

> *Our eyes have seen the glory*
> *Of the coming of the Lord.*

The gentlemen of the Middlesex Club were silent in the early part of Beveridge's speech, then excited, and finally wildly enthusiastic. According to Claude G. Bowers, on whose work any account of Beveridge must be based, that Boston audience applauded Dewey's "victory before it was won; applauded the policy

we were to pursue before it had officially been defined, and applauded through
the prophecy of Beveridge."

Within less than four months the Spanish-American War was over in both
the Atlantic and the Pacific, and on September 16, 1898, the exultant Beveridge
opened the Republican campaign in Indianapolis before a cheering audience
after a torchlight procession. "The burning issue of the campaign," he said, "is
whether the American people will accept the gift of events . . . or whether,
for the first time, doubting their mission, will question fate, prove apostate to
the spirit of their race, and halt the ceaseless march of free institutions." And
he ended: "It is God's great purpose made manifest in the instincts of our race,
whose present phase is our personal profit, but whose far-off end is the redemption of the world and the christianization of mankind." Tumultuous applause
greeted Beveridge, and soon three hundred thousand copies of the speech,
known as "The March of the Flag," were distributed by the Republican State
Committee.

Put forward as a compromise candidate for Senator from Indiana in 1899,
Beveridge was admittedly a choice of desperation. To the Old Guard he was
an incalculable upstart, but he had strong supporters and was elected, the
youngest member ever to sit in the United States Senate. Now clearly a national
figure, he received many more invitations to speak, one of the most flattering
being to the Lincoln Day dinner of the Union League Club of Philadelphia.

It was just at this time that the February issue of McClure's magazine
appeared, carrying on its front page the fifty-six easily remembered lines of
Kipling's "The White Man's Burden," which were soon to be printed on the
front pages of a thousand newspapers. Never before had so much contempt
been poured on so many people, so briefly and neatly.

As Beveridge had been sounding this note in his rousing prose for at least
eight months, he could proceed to Philadelphia with even greater assurance and
speak of "The Republic That Never Retreats." He could insist that the
Filipinos who had been rescued from Spanish despotism should now accept
American domination and stop their ungrateful, savage rebellion against their
rescuers. And again Beveridge the brilliant brought his hearers cheering to their
feet.

Bryan at Chicago on Washington's birthday denounced imperialism in a
powerful speech on "America's Mission," and six weeks later Theodore Roosevelt replied to Bryan.

THEODORE ROOSEVELT ADVOCATES
THE STRENUOUS LIFE

[April 10, 1899]

A frail asthmatic boy with bad eyesight, Theodore Roosevelt (1858–1919) did not seem to be destined for the strenuous life. But with all the advantages of a patrician New York family and sheer determination, he became a competent boxer at Harvard and somewhat of an all-round athlete in the years to come. By the time he was thirty he had served three terms in the New York legislature, managed a ranch in Dakota Territory, and written six volumes of history, biography, and hunting adventures.

He next served for six years as a Civil Service commissioner in Washington and then for two years as president of the board of police commissioners in New York. In 1897 he was back in Washington again as Assistant Secretary of the Navy, in which position he did nothing to discourage the outbreak of the war with Spain. Two weeks after war was declared he joined Captain Leonard A. Wood of the regular army in forming the first volunteer cavalry regiment, the famous Rough Riders. With Wood as colonel and Roosevelt as lieutenant colonel the regiment fought bravely before Santiago and took Kettle Hill, adjoining the better-known San Juan Hill.

Roosevelt returned to New York a hero and was forced on the Republican boss of the state, Thomas C. Platt, as Republican candidate for governor. He campaigned vigorously, with a few of his Rough Riders always on the platform, and won by a small majority. He was inaugurated in January, 1899.

In the nation-wide debate then going on over America's role in world affairs, there could be no doubt about Roosevelt's position. In going to Chicago to speak before the Hamilton Club on Appomattox Day he was quite clearly replying to Bryan's earlier speech in the same city.

Compared with Franklin Delano Roosevelt, Theodore Roosevelt was a rough-and-ready speaker, without polish and with a husky voice that was apt to break into shrillness under excitement. But the gusto, the irresistible magnetism of the man, made him one of the most powerful and popular speakers of his generation.

"If we are to be a really great people, we must strive in good faith to play a great part in the world."

Gentlemen:

IN SPEAKING to you, men of the greatest city of the West, men of the state which gave to the country Lincoln and Grant, men who preeminently and distinctly embody all that is most American in the American character, I wish to preach not the doctrine of ignoble ease but the doctrine of the strenuous life; the life of toil and effort; of labor and strife; to preach that highest form of success which comes not to the man who desires mere easy peace but to the man who does not shrink from danger, from hardship, or from bitter toil, and who out of these wins the splendid ultimate triumph. . . .

As it is with the individual so it is with the nation. It is a base untruth to say that happy is the nation that has no history. Thrice happy is the nation that has a glorious history. Far better it is to dare mighty things, to win glorious triumphs, even though checkered by failure, than to take rank with those poor spirits who neither enjoy much nor suffer much because they live in the gray twilight that knows neither victory nor defeat. If in 1861 the men who loved the Union had believed that peace was the end of all things and war and strife a worst of all things, and had acted up to their belief, we would have saved hundreds of thousands of lives, we would have saved hundreds of millions of dollars. Moreover, besides saving all the blood and treasure we then lavished, we would have prevented the heartbreak of many women, the dissolution of many homes; and we would have spared the country those months of gloom and shame when it seemed as if our armies marched only to defeat. We would have avoided all this suffering simply by shrinking from strife. And if we had thus avoided it we would have shown that we were weaklings and that we were unfit to stand among the great nations of the earth. Thank God for the iron in the blood of our fathers, the men who upheld the wisdom of Lincoln and bore sword or rifle in the armies of Grant! Let us, the children of the men who proved themselves equal to the mighty days—let us, the children of the men who carried the great Civil War to a triumphant conclusion, praise the God of our fathers that the ignoble counsels of peace were rejected, that the suffering and loss, the blackness of sorrow and despair, were unflinchingly faced and the years of strife endured; for in the end the slave was freed, the Union restored, and the mighty American Republic placed once more as a helmeted queen among nations.

We of this generation do not have to face a task such as that our fathers faced, but we have our tasks, and woe to us if we fail to perform them! We cannot, if we would, play the part of China, and be content to rot by inches in ignoble ease within our borders, taking no interest in what goes on beyond them; sunk in a scrambling commercialism; heedless of the higher life, the life of aspiration, of toil and risk; busying ourselves only with the wants of our bodies for the day; until suddenly we should find, beyond a shadow of question, what China has already found, that in this world the nation that has trained itself to a career of unwarlike and isolated ease is bound in the end to go down before other nations which have not lost the manly and adventurous qualities. If we are to be a really great people, we must strive in good faith to play a great part in the world. We cannot avoid meeting great issues. All that we can determine for ourselves is whether we shall meet them well or ill. Last year we could not help being brought face to face with the problem of war with Spain. All we could decide was whether we should shrink like cowards from the contest or enter into it as beseemed a brave and high-spirited people; and, once in, whether failure or success should crown our banners. So it is now. We cannot avoid the responsibilities that confront us in Hawaii, Cuba, Porto Rico, and the Philippines. All we can decide is whether we shall meet them in a way that will redound to the national credit, or whether we shall make of our dealings with these new problems a dark and shameful page in our history. To refuse to deal with them at all merely amounts to dealing with them badly. We have a given problem to solve. If we undertake the solution there is, of course, always danger that we may not solve it aright, but to refuse to undertake the solution simply renders it certain that we cannot possibly solve it aright.

The timid man, the lazy man, the man who distrusts his country, the overcivilized man, who has lost the great fighting, masterful virtues, the ignorant man and the man of dull mind, whose soul is incapable of feeling the mighty lift that thrills "stern men with empires in their brains"—all these, of course, shrink from seeing the nation undertake its new duties; shrink from seeing us build a navy and army adequate to our needs; shrink from seeing us do our share of the world's work by bringing order out of chaos in the great, fair tropic islands from which the valor of our soldiers and sailors has driven the Spanish flag. These are the men who fear the strenuous life, who fear the only national life which is really worth leading. . . .

From the standpoint of international honor, the argument is even stronger. The guns that thundered off Manila and Santiago left us echoes of glory, but they also left us a legacy of duty. If we drove out a medieval tyranny only to make room for savage anarchy, we had better not have begun the task at all. It is worse than idle to say that we have no duty to perform and can leave to their fates the islands we have conquered. Such a course would be the course of infamy. It would be followed at once by utter chaos in the wretched islands themselves. Some stronger, manlier power would have to step in and do the work; and we would have shown ourselves weaklings, unable to carry to successful completion the labors that great and high-spirited nations are eager to undertake. . . .

The army and navy are the sword and the shield which this nation must carry if she is to do her duty among the nations of the earth—if she is not to stand merely as the China of the Western Hemisphere. Our proper conduct toward the tropic islands we have wrested from Spain is merely the form which our duty has taken at the moment. . . .

In the West Indies and the Philippines alike we are confronted by most difficult problems. It is cowardly to shrink from solving them in the proper way; for solved they must be, if not by us, then by some stronger and more manful race; if we are too weak, too selfish, or too foolish to solve them some bolder and abler people must undertake the solution. Personally, I am far too firm a believer in the greatness of my country and the power of my countrymen to admit for one moment that we shall ever be driven to the ignoble alternative.

The problems are different from the different islands. Porto Rico is not large enough to stand alone. We must govern it wisely and well, primarily in the interest of its own people. Cuba is, in my judgment, entitled ultimately to settle for itself whether it shall be an independent state or an integral portion of the mightiest of republics. But until order and stable liberty are secured, we must remain in the island to insure them; and infinite tact, judgment, moderation, and courage must be shown by our military and civil representatives in keeping the island pacified, in relentlessly stamping out brigandage, in protecting all alike, and yet in showing proper recognition to the men who have fought for Cuban liberty. The Philippines offer a yet graver problem. Their population includes half-caste and native Christians, warlike Moslems, and wild pagans. Many of their people are utterly unfit for self-government and show no signs of becoming fit. Others may in time become fit, but at present can only take part in self-government under a wise supervision at once firm and beneficent. We have driven Spanish tyranny from the islands. If we now let it be replaced by savage anarchy, our work has been for harm and not for good. I have scant patience with those who fear to undertake the task of governing the Philippines, and who openly avow that they do fear to undertake it, or that they shrink from it because of the expense and trouble; but I have even scanter patience with those who make a pretense of humanitarianism to hide and cover their timidity, and who cant about "liberty" and the "consent of the governed," in order to excuse themselves for their unwillingness to play the part of men. Their doctrines if carried out would make it incumbent upon us to leave the Apaches of Arizona to work out their own salvation and to decline to interfere in a single Indian reservation. Their doctrines condemn your forefathers and mine for ever having settled in these United States.

England's rule in India and Egypt has been of great benefit to England, for it has trained up generations of men accustomed to look at the larger and loftier side of public life. It has been of even greater benefit to India and Egypt. And finally, and most of all, it has advanced the cause of civilizat:on. So, if we do our duty aright in the Philippines, we will add to that national renown which is the highest and finest part of national life; will greatly benefit the people of the Philippine Islands; and, above all, we will play our part well in the great work of uplifting mankind. But to do this work, keep ever in mind that we must show in a high degree the qualities of courage, of honesty, and of good judgment. Resistance must be stamped out. The first and all-important work to be done is to establish the supremacy of our flag. We must put down armed resistance before we can accomplish anything else, and there should be no parleying, no faltering in dealing with our foe. As for those in our own country who encourage the foe, we can afford contemptuously to disregard them; but it must be remembered that their utterances are saved from being treasonable merely from the fact that they are despicable. . . .

I preach to you, then, my countrymen, that our country calls not for the life of ease, but for the life of strenuous endeavor. The twentieth century looms before us big with the fate of many nations. If we stand idly by, if we seek merely swollen, slothful ease, and ignoble peace, if we shrink from the hard contests where men must win at hazard of their lives and at the risk of all they hold dear, then the bolder and stronger peoples will pass us by and will win for themselves the domination of the world. Let us therefore boldly face the life of strife, resolute to do our duty well and manfully; resolute to uphold righteousness by deed and by word; resolute to be both honest and brave, to serve high ideals, yet to use practical methods. Above all, let us shrink from no strife, moral or physical, within or without the nation, provided we are certain that the strife is justified; for it is only through strife, through hard and dangerous endeavor, that we shall ultimately win the goal of true national greatness.

That speech on "The Strenuous Life" was a rousing success with the men of
the Hamilton Club of Chicago. But when reported in the newspapers it aroused
the wrath of Professor William James, another Harvard man, who at once
wrote a long letter of protest to The Boston Transcript. He accused Roosevelt
of being mentally adolescent and of swamping "everything in one flood of
abstract bellicose emotion. . . . To enslave a weak but heroic people, or to
brazen out a blunder, is a good enough cause, it appears, for Colonel Roosevelt.
To us Massachusetts anti-imperialists, who have fought in better causes, it is
not quite good enough."

Carl Schurz, the distinguished German-American who had come here after
the collapse of the 1848 revolutions, said much the same thing from the platform. But he and James and Bryan and Senator Hoar of Massachusetts were
very much in the minority. And soon Beveridge was to return from a tour of the
Philippines, to take his seat in the Senate, where he declaimed to cheering
hearers: "God has not been preparing the English-speaking and Teutonic
peoples for a thousand years for nothing but vain and idle self-contemplation
and self-admiration. No! He has made us the master organizers of the world
to establish system where chaos reigns. He has given us the spirit of progress to
overwhelm the forces of reaction throughout the earth. He has made us adept
in government that we may administer government to savage and senile
peoples."

KAISER WILHELM II IS OUTRAGED
AND ADAMANT

[July–August, 1900]

Strange as it may seem, Senator Beveridge's assurances about God, destiny, and
race were not unlike those of Kaiser Wilhelm II, who had a more favorable
view of the United States after the Spanish-American War. It is now too easy
to ridicule the arrogant, impulsive, restless ruler with the crippled arm. He did
not hold the world's spotlight for a quarter of a century out of sheer incompetence. Versatile, though superficial, he could fascinate when he could not
charm, and he could terrify when he could not fascinate.

His paternal grandfather was Wilhelm I, Bismarck's King and Emperor; his
maternal grandmother was Queen Victoria. His father, Emperor Frederick, was
a sensible man who had no idea of getting along without Bismarck. Young
Wilhelm was brought up as a divinely guided Hohenzollern, an invincible
Prussian, in the triumphant atmosphere of Bismarck's Germany. But it was

unlikely that he would come to the throne before he was forty or fifty. Unfortunately, his father died of cancer in 1888 after a reign of three months and suddenly, at the omniscient age of twenty-nine, Wilhelm II walked on to the center of the stage. But Bismarck was already there. The imperial egotist had resented that shadow over his grandfather, and he could not endure it for himself. In 1890 he found a pretext to "drop the pilot."

This is not the place to pursue Wilhelm's inept efforts to woo German labor or discourage socialism, nor his early success in antagonizing England, Russia, and France. As long as Bismarck and Queen Victoria lived, his bluster in Europe was somewhat muffled. But China was another matter.

After Japan's quick victory over China in 1894, the English, French, Germans, and Russians restrained the advance of Japan, but were generous in awarding to themselves possessions and concessions in China. The United States came along a little tardily with John Hay's Open-Door Policy. "From the Chinese point of view," according to Quincy Howe, "the Open Door meant that all the foreign powers had agreed to observe certain rules among themselves for continuing and intensifying the exploitation of China." This situation was irritating, not to say infuriating, to the Chinese, and by the end of the century an anti-Manchu movement turned into an antiforeign movement. The secret society of "Fists of Righteous Union," known to history as the Boxers, besieged the foreign embassies of Peking in June, 1900, and on the twentieth killed the German ambassador. Rumors went out that the entire foreign population had been massacred in Peking, and the Western world was righteously indignant—but especially the German Emperor, even after it was discovered that the rumors were grossly exaggerated.

The Emperor had a weakness (his "chief hobby," it has been said) for making speeches on all possible occasions and for preaching sermons on his private yacht. Inspired by the Boxer trouble in the summer of 1900, he bade flaming farewells to at least five contingents of troops summoned to quell the Boxers and preached a sermon against the "heathenish Amalekite who has stirred in distant Asia with great power and much cunning."

"Use your weapons in a manner to make every Chinaman
for a thousand years to come forgo the wish to as much
as look askance at a German."

July 2, 1900

THE TORCH OF WAR has been flung into the midst of deepest peace, though not unexpected by me. A crime unparalleled in its insolence, hateful in its cruelty, has been perpetrated upon my tried and trusted representative, and has hurried him to his grave. The ministers of other powers tremble in hourly danger of their lives, and with them the comrades sent out for their protection; perhaps by now they have fought their last.

The German flag has been outraged, and the German Empire has been insulted. That demands exemplary reparation and vengeance.

The situation has been changed with awful rapidity, and is now most critical and serious. Since I called you to arms it has become worse. I was at first in hopes to be able to repair things with the aid of my marine infantry. That is now impossible. The task has assumed greater proportions, and to grapple successfully with it organized bodies of troops of all the civilized countries must be used. Today the commander of my squadron of cruisers has asked me to send a whole division.

You will face an enemy who defies death no less than you do. Trained by European officers, the Chinese have learned how to fight with European weapons. God be praised for the fact that your comrades of the marine infantry and my navy have maintained the old German reputation for valor wherever they have met the enemy. They have defended themselves with glory, achieving victory.

Thus I send you out there to avenge wrong and enforce reparation. I will not rest until the German flag flies victorious from the walls of Peking, flies above the Chinese, and dictates the terms of peace to the Chinese.

July 27, 1900

During thirty years of peace our army has been drilled and perfected in accordance with the precepts of my grandfather. You, too, have received your education as soldiers in conformity with these principles, and you are now about to be tested before the enemy—whether you have profited by it. Your comrades of the navy have already furnished proof that the principles governing military training are sound ones, and I am proud of the praise which has been accorded them by foreign officers and commanders out there. It is for you to show that you can do as well. Yours is a great task. You are to exact reparation for the unprecedented wrong, the gross affront, done us. The Chinese have disregarded the law of nations. They have shown scorn for the sacredness of an envoy, for the duties of hospitality, in a manner unparalleled in the world's history. And this is the more reprehensible because these crimes have been committed by a nation which boasts of its ancient culture. . . .

You are to fight against a cunning, courageous, well-armed, and cruel foe. When you are upon him, know this: spare nobody, make no prisoners. Use your weapons in a manner to make every Chinaman for a thousand years to come forgo the wish to as much as look askance at a German. . . .

August 2, 1900

You are going on a grave and portentous mission, the end of which is not yet clear. It may be the beginning of a great war between Occident and Orient. The whole Occident is united. For the common end even such nations have joined who have all along confronted one another as inveterate foes. Every nation has there given proof of matchless bravery, and it is for you, gentlemen, to bring additional glory to the German name, which fortunate wars have placed high in the roster of warlike nations. Show them that we have all this time worked hard, and that our toil in times of peace has not been in vain. Prove yourselves good comrades to all the troops assembled there, no matter what the color of their skin. . . .

By nature the Chinaman is a cowardly cur, but he is tricky and double-faced. Small, detached troops must be particularly cautious. The Chinaman likes to fall upon an enemy from an ambush, or during the night time, or with vast superiority in numbers. Recently the enemy has fought bravely, a fact which has not yet been sufficiently explained. Perhaps these were his best troops, those drilled by German and other officers.

Above all, gentlemen, prove to the Chinese that there is at least one power which, irrespective of remoter considerations of a practical nature, means to punish them for wrongs inflicted. Make war until the aim I have designated be attained, until complete atonement has been enforced. . . .

Such speeches—and there were scores like them—were undoubtedly stirring to departing troops and millions of militant Germans, but they embarrassed millions of other Germans and alarmed the world. Unfortunately, the garrulous Kaiser was subject to no censor, and those who criticized him were often imprisoned for lèse-majesté.

As for China, it goes without saying that an international force soon took over Peking, and China paid dearly both in money and "concessions" for the impertinence of the Boxers.

SUN YAT-SEN TAKES UP THE YELLOW MAN'S BURDEN

[1903–1924 passim]

While the Western powers were partitioning China with benign efficiency, a young doctor, Sun Yat-sen, was setting forth on a vast enterprise in "social physiology," the liberation of China from the Manchu dynasty and foreign exploitation. "Our past oppression," he early discovered, "can be attributed to the ignorance of the masses, who are 'born in a stupor and die in a dream.'"

Brought up on a farm near Canton, Sun Yat-sen (1866–1925) had a happy childhood, but he saw enough of Manchu inefficiency and brutality to carry bitter memories. At fourteen he went to join his older brother, who was farming prosperously near Pearl Harbor, in Hawaii, where he became a convert to Christianity and studied for four years in an Anglican school. Returning to China for a wife, he began his medical studies in Canton and in 1892 finished them at the Alice Memorial Hospital in Hong Kong. But he was already deeply involved in the revolutionary movement, and his medical practice, which he carried on for only a few years, was a mask for his underground political activities. After the humiliating defeat of China by Japan in 1894 and the failure of a poorly organized revolt in Canton, Sun Yat-sen returned to Hawaii to raise converts and money for a long-range plan. He proceeded across the United States, making contacts with small groups, and then went on to London, where he was kidnaped and held in the Chinese embassy for twelve days. He was about to be sent back to China for execution when the last-moment intervention of the English doctor he had known in Hawaii secured his liberty and at the same time made him an international figure.

In 1903 Dr. Sun set out on his second voyage around the world—a fabulous odyssey of agitation, organization, fund raising, mostly among small groups of poor merchants and young students. In Hawaii he addressed his first mass meeting. In America he discovered Lincoln and the doctrine of "government of the people, by the people, for the people," which crystallized his own growing vision. Whether at home or abroad, he had become in these years the recognized leader of China's unhappy millions, and his hand was seen in the ten unsuccessful revolutions that preceded the triumphant revolution of 1911.

"When I visited Europe for the second time in 1903," he wrote in his autobiography, "the majority of Chinese students had come to believe in revolution. Thereupon I sounded the clarion call by announcing the Three Principles of the People and the Five-Power Constitution, which I had long cherished." In 1924 the dying Sun Yat-sen delivered the famous lectures on "The Three

Principles of the People" to an audience of still-devoted followers. In quoting from his swan song we are also presenting part of the lifelong testament which he restated on numberless occasions.

"The rest of mankind is the carving knife . . . while we are the fish and the meat."

Gentlemen:

I HAVE COME HERE today to speak to you about the *San Min* Principles. What are the *San Min* Principles? They are, by the simplest definition, the principles for our nation's salvation. What is a principle? It is an idea, a faith, and a power. When men begin to study into the heart of a problem, an idea generally develops first; as the idea becomes clearer, a faith arises; and out of the faith a power is born. So a principle must begin with an idea, the idea must produce a faith, and the faith in turn must give birth to power, before the principle can be perfectly established. Why do we say that the *San Min* Principles will save our nation? Because they will elevate China to an equal position among the nations, in international affairs, in government, and in economic life, so that she can permanently exist in the world. The *San Min* Principles are the principles for our nation's salvation; is not our China today, I ask you, in need of salvation? If so, then let us have faith in the *San Min* Principles and our faith will engender a mighty force that will save China.

Today I shall begin the discussion of the principle of nationalism. When the recent reorganization of the Kuomintang took place, the plans for national salvation laid stress upon propaganda. Widespread propaganda among the people needs, first of all, a clear exposition of the principles. During the last ten or more years, thoughtful people have become accustomed to hearing about the Three Principles of the People, but many are still unable to comprehend them fully. So I shall first discuss with you in some detail the principle of nationalism.

What is the principle of nationalism? Looking back over the history of China's social life and customs, I would say briefly that the principle of nationalism is equivalent to the "doctrine of the state." The Chinese people have shown the greatest loyalty to family and clan with the result that in China there have been familyism and clanism but no real nationalism. Foreign observers say that the Chinese are like a sheet of loose sand. Why? Simply because our people have shown loyalty to family and clan but not to the nation—there has been no nationalism. The family and the clan have been powerful unifying forces; again and again Chinese have sacrificed themselves, their families, their lives in defense of their clan. For example, in the Kwangtung feuds between two clans, neither one will yield, no matter what the struggle costs in life or property, all because of the clan idea which is so deeply imbedded in the minds of the people that they are willing to sacrifice anything for their fellow clansmen. But for the nation there has never been an instance of the supreme spirit of sacrifice. The unity of the Chinese people has stopped short at the clan and has not extended to the nation.

My statement that the principle of nationality is equivalent to the doctrine of the state is applicable in China but not in the West. Foreigners make a distinction between the nation and the state. The English word for *min t'su* is "nation"; the word "nation" has two meanings, race and state. Although this word has two meanings, they are very distinct and must not be confused. Many Chinese words have double meanings; for example, *she-hui* (society) is used to designate a group of people and also an organized body. Nation and state are, of course, very closely related, and no separation seems necessary; but there is a clear line between them and we must distinguish carefully between the state and the nation. But when I say that the nation is equivalent to the state, why is this true only of China? For the reason that China, since the Ch'in and Han dynasties, has been developing a single state out of a single race, while foreign countries have developed many states from one race and have included many nationalities within one state. For example, England, now the world's most powerful state, has, upon the foundation of the white race, added brown, black, and other races to form the British Empire; hence, to say that the race or nation is the state is not true of England. Again, Hong Kong, which is British territory, includes among its population many ten thousands of Chinese; if we say that the British state in Hong Kong means the British nation, we miss the mark. Or, look at India, now British territory: within this British state are three hundred fifty million Indian people. If we say that the British state of India means the British nation, we are off the track. We all know that the original stock of England was the Anglo-Saxon race, but it is not limited to England; the United States, too, has a large portion of such stock. So in regard to other countries we cannot say that the race and the state are identical; there is a definite line between them.

How shall we distinguish clearly between the two? The most suitable method is by a study of the forces which molded each. In simple terms, the race or nationality has developed through natural forces, while the state has developed through force of arms. To use an illustration from China's political history: Chinese say that the *wang-tao*, royal way or way of right, followed nature; in other words, natural force was the royal way. The group molded by the royal way is the race, the nationality. Armed force is the *pa-tao*, or the way of might; the group formed by the way of might is the state. For example, Hong Kong was not built up because thousands of Hong Kongese wished the British to do it; Hong Kong was taken by the British by armed force. Because China had been defeated in a war with England, the Hong Kong territory and its people were ceded to England and, in time, the modern Hong Kong was built up. England's development of India is a similar story. The territory of Great Britain now spreads over the whole earth; the English have a saying: "The sun never sets upon the British Empire." In other words, wherever the sun shines in a revolution of the earth, there lies some British territory. If we of the Eastern Hemisphere should start with the sun, we would see it shining first upon New Zealand, Australia, Hong Kong, and Singapore; as it turned westward it would shine on Ceylon and India; farther west, upon Aden and Malta; and yet farther, upon England itself; moving into the Western Hemisphere the sun would reach Canada and then complete its revolution at Hong Kong and Singapore. So, wherever the sun shines in twenty-four hours, there is sure to be British territory. A great territory like Great Britain's has been developed entirely by means of force; since of old, no state has been built up without force. But the development of a race or nationality is quite different: it grows entirely by nature, in no way subject to force. The thousands of Chinese at Hong Kong, for instance, are united in one race—by nature; whatever force England may employ cannot change the fact. Therefore, we say that a group united and developed in the royal way, by forces of nature, is a race; a group united and developed by the way of might, by human forces, is a state. This, then, is the difference between a race or nationality and a state.

Again, as to the origin of races. Man was originally a species of animal, yet he is far removed from the common fowl and the beasts; he is "the soul of all creation." Mankind is divided first into the five main races —white, black, red, yellow, brown. Dividing further, we have many subraces, as the Asiatic races—Mongolian, Malay, Japanese, Manchurian, and Chinese. The forces which developed these races were, in general, natural forces, but when we try to analyze them we find they are very complex. The greatest force is common blood. Chinese belong to the yellow race because they come from the blood stock of the yellow race. The blood of ancestors is transmitted by heredity down through the race, making blood kinship a powerful force.

The second great force is livelihood; when the means used to obtain a living vary, the races developed show differences. The Mongolians' abode followed water and grass; they lived the life of nomads, roaming and tenting by water and grass, and out of these common nomadic habits there developed a race, which accounts for the sudden rise of Mongol power. In their most flourishing days, the armies of the Yüan (Mongol) dynasty conquered Central Asia, Arabia, and a part of Europe in the west, united China in the east, and almost subjugated Japan—bringing together Europe and Asia. Compare the most prosperous days of other races, as of the Chinese in the great military age of the Han and T'ang dynasties, when the western frontiers of the empire reached only to the Caspian Sea; or of the Roman state at the summit of its military power when the eastern limits of the empire did not go beyond the Black Sea. Never before had a nation's armed forces occupied the two continents of Europe and Asia as did the Mongol armies of the Yüan dynasty in their prime. The reason for this great strength of the Mongol race was their nomadic life and daily habit of marching far without fear of miles.

A third great force in forming races is language. If foreign races learn our language, they are more easily assimilated by us and in time become absorbed into our race. On the other hand, if we know the language of foreign countries, we are in turn easily assimilated by foreigners. If two peoples have both common blood and common language, then assimilation is still easier. So language is also one of the great forces for the development of a race.

A fourth force is religion. People who worship the same gods or the same ancestors tend to form one race. Religion is also a very powerful factor in the development of races. Look at the kingdoms of Arabia and Judea which perished long ago, yet the Arabian and the Jewish people still survive. The reason for the preservation of these races, in spite of the destruction of their states, is their religion. The Jews today, we all know, are scattered in large numbers in all lands. Some of the greatest scholars, as Marx and Einstein, are Jews. In England, America, and other countries, financial interests are largely controlled by Jews. To the Jew's natural gift of keen intelligence has been added religious faith, so that, although scattered all over the earth, they have been able to preserve their race up to the present time. The reason for the Arabian's survival is also religion—Mohammedanism. Another case is the Indian people with their deep faith in Buddhism, whose country is lost to Great Britain but whose race can never perish.

A fifth force is customs and habits. If people have markedly similar customs and habits they will, in time, cohere and form one race. When, therefore, we discover dissimilar peoples or stocks amalgamating and forming a homogeneous race, we must attribute the development to these five forces—blood kinship, common language, common livelihood, common religion, and common customs—which are products not of military occupation but of natural evolution. The comparison between these five natural forces and armed force helps us to distinguish between the race or nationality and the state.

Considering the law of survival of ancient and modern races, if we want to save China and to preserve the Chinese race, we must certainly promote nationalism. To make this principle luminous for China's salvation, we must first understand it clearly. The Chinese race totals four hundred million people; of mingled races there are only a few million Mongolians, a million or so Manchus, a few million Tibetans, and over a million Mohammedan Turks. These alien races do not number altogether more than ten million, so that, for the most part, the Chinese people are of the Han or Chinese race with common blood, common language, common religion, and common customs—a single, pure race.

What is the standing of our nation in the world? In comparison with other nations we have the greatest population and the oldest culture, of four thousand years' duration. We ought to be advancing in line with the nations of Europe and America. But the Chinese people have only family and clan groups; these is no national spirit. Consequently, in spite of four hundred million people gathered together in one China, we are in fact but a sheet of loose sand. We are the poorest and weakest state in the world, occupying the lowest position in international affairs; the rest of mankind is the carving knife and the serving dish, while we are the fish and the meat. Our position now is extremely perilous; if we do not earnestly promote nationalism and weld together our four hundred millions into a strong nation, we face a tragedy—the loss of our country and the destruction of our race. To ward off this danger, we must espouse nationalism and employ the national spirit to save the country.

In five other lectures Dr. Sun elaborated on the principle of nationalism, denouncing unequal treaties and foreign exploitation. He then passed on to the principle of democracy, with more emphasis on social duties than individual liberties, and finally to the principle of livelihood, which was essentially a doctrine of moderate, non-Marxian socialism. He was most moved when he spoke of livelihood and the people's health, of the need for exploiting the natural resources of China for the Chinese.

The series of sixteen lectures extended from January to August, 1924, breaking off with a practical discussion of "the three uses of clothing"! Six months later Sun Yat-sen, worn out with forty years of labor for China's millions, died at the age of fifty-nine, in Peking. On a hillside overlooking the city, his coffin was placed in an ancient temple.

PART SIXTEEN

PARTY POLITICS AND

CLASS STRUGGLE

WE TURN from the white man's concern with backward races, with "savage and senile peoples," to troubles on the Western front—industrial expansion, labor strife, and national rivalries.

France after 1871 made a brave recovery and continued to be the center of art and literature, the oasis of civilization. But bitter memories and fierce antagonisms persisted, and at least four major scandals shook the country. In 1887 Jules Grévy, President of the Republic had to resign because his son-in-law was involved in selling government honors and decorations. Two years later the attractive would-be Napoleon, General Boulanger, reached such a degree of popular acclaim that with a little more nerve, he might have made himself dictator. Meanwhile the Panama bubble burst and left its trail of suspicion and recrimination. The successful builder of the Suez Canal, Vicomte Ferdinand de Lesseps, had formed a company to cut a canal across the Isthmus of Panama. By 1885 some 800,000 Frenchmen had invested 1,400,000 francs in the venture, but little of this was spent on the actual digging of the canal before the company went bankrupt in 1889. Miscalculation of costs seems to have been as bad as misappropriation of funds. How many deputies, senators, and academicians profited by the deal nobody knows, because it became a dubious duty to cast a veil over the scandal for the honor of the Republic. As if this were not enough, the Dreyfus affair began in 1894, revived to keep the country in an uproar through 1898–99, and was not finally settled until 1906.

Through all these years old agrarian France was being heavily industrialized and coal was the heart of the process. At the notoriously unsafe Courrières-Lens mines more than 1,150 miners were burned to death or suffocated on March 10, 1906. Two days later Georges Clemenceau took office for the first time as Minister of the Interior.

JEAN JAURÈS AND GEORGES CLEMENCEAU DEBATE THE QUESTION OF CAPITAL AND LABOR

[June 12–15, 18–19, 1906]

Georges Clemenceau (1841–1929) was a son of a liberal, landowning doctor of the Vendée who was against the Church and against the government of Napoleon III. He studied medicine in Paris, but as soon as his examinations were over he went to London to meet the liberal philosopher, John Stuart Mill, and then to America to study democracy in action for four years—although by no means with the seriousness of Alexis de Tocqueville. After the Empire fell in 1870, Clemenceau was mayor of Montmartre for a few months during the siege of Paris by the Germans and the bloody civil war, and he escaped with his life and his reputation.

In 1877 he finally reached the Chamber of Deputies, where he managed to undermine eighteen ministries in sixteen years. Nominally a Radical, a Republican, he might better be called a temperamental individualist who loved France and loved to be in opposition. He was a difficult, a fierce, man who dueled not only with words but with sword and pistol. It was Clemenceau who exposed the corruption of President Grévy's son-in-law and later, after misjudging Boulanger, helped to destroy him. But even he was unjustly tarred by association with leading members of the Panama conspiracy and, assailed by his numberless enemies, went down to defeat at the polls in 1893.

He now turned to political journalism and learned to write almost as vigorously as he talked. With Jaurès, Zola, and Anatole France he became one of the most powerful defenders of Dreyfus. In 1903 he was elected to the Senate from Var in spite of the fact that he had earlier advocated the suppression of that body, and in 1906 he who had always refused government posts became Minister of the Interior in the Sarrien cabinet. It was supposed that the famous Republican defender of civil liberties might take a sympathetic attitude toward the strikers after the terrible disaster at the Courrières-Lens mines, which cost the lives of more than a thousand workers, but he sent troops to the mines, with orders to protect both the mines and the strike breakers. At the same time he used military engineers and troops to take charge when the electrical engineers of Paris went on strike, stopping the subways and leaving the city in darkness.

It was now that Jaurès used his right of interpellation—the right of any deputy or senator to demand of a member of the government an explanation of government policy. The result was a debate between the two most powerful personalities, the most effective speakers, of the Third Republic. The two men who had joined hands against Boulanger and in defense of Dreyfus came to grips before a crowded Chamber of Deputies on one of the two or three basic issues of the twentieth century.

Winston Churchill's picture of Clemenceau speaking before the Chamber of Deputies in the First World War corresponds to earlier descriptions: "He ranged from one side of the tribune to the other, without a note or book of reference or scrap of paper, barking out sharp staccato sentences as the thought broke upon his mind. He looked like a wild animal pacing to and fro behind bars, growling and glaring; and all around him was an assembly which would have done anything to avoid being there, but having put him there, felt they must obey."

Yet Clemenceau had an opponent worthy of his wrath in those June days of 1906, and we must turn to his life for a moment.

Jean Jaurès (1859–1914), from a needy middle-class family of Languedoc, showed such splendid promise that he was aided through higher education by an inspector of schools, and for a time taught philosophy at Toulouse. He won his way into the Chamber of Deputies at twenty-six and continued there, except for short intervals, until his death, but he never ceased to be a student and writer. In 1891 he became a convert to socialism, his own brand of patriotic, humanistic, evolutionary socialism that did not involve violent revolution. Untrammeled by orthodox Marxism, he threw his enormous energies behind any cause he considered broadly democratic. Next to Clemenceau he was probably the most powerful public defender of Dreyfus. He was a leader in the debates bringing about the separation of Church and State. He searchingly, fearlessly denounced the international intrigues, the secret treaties, that were carrying Europe toward war. As early as 1905 he said in a prepared speech which he was not permitted to deliver in Berlin but which was widely read: "From a European war the Revolution might spring forth; and the governing classes might do well to ponder on that—but there might result also for a long period crises of counterrevolution, of furious reaction, of exasperated nationalism, of stifling dictatorships, of monstrous militarism, a long chain of retrograde violence, of base hatreds, of reprisals, of slavery. And as for us we have no wish to play at this game of barbarous chance."

A speaker who appealed equally, it has been said, to the reason, the feelings, and the ear, Jean Jaurès was remembered in these words by Romain Rolland: "I have listened to him often in the Chamber, socialist congresses, at meetings held on behalf of oppressed nations. . . . Again I see his full face, calm and happy, like that of a kindly, bearded ogre; his small eyes, bright and smiling; eyes as quick to follow the flight of ideas as to observe human nature. I see him pacing up and down the platform, walking with heavy steps like a bear, his arms crossed behind his back, and turning sharply to hurl at the crowd, in his monotonous, metallic voice, words like a call of a trumpet, which reached the farthest seats in the vast amphitheater and went straight to the heart, making the soul of the whole multitude leap in one united emotion."

JAURÈS:

"There is no means . . . to reconcile definitely these two forces."

THE OTHER DAY M. Millerand, when he brought to this tribunal certain projects regarding compulsory arbitration and the collective contract, said that it was necessary, so far as possible, to put an end to these strikes, which are, he added, an economic civil war. The economic civil war manifests itself by strikes on the surface of society; but it is not only in strikes that it exists. It is at the very bottom of society; it is at the very bottom of a system of property that gives power to some and inflicts servitude on others.

The economic civil war, the social war, will continue—sometimes visibly, sometimes covertly, sometimes violently, sometimes sullenly, but always with the same sufferings, the same exasperation, the same iniquity, so long as the world of production be disputed by two antagonistic forces. There is no means—hear what I say, gentlemen—to reconcile definitely these two forces. You may palliate the strife, you may soften the shocks, but you cannot remove the abiding, fundamental antagonism resulting from the privilege of property itself. There is but one means to abolish this antagonism, and that is to reabsorb capital in labor—to make but one possessive and controlling force, the creative force of labor.

If ever there was an object of public utility, this is one; if ever there was an object, an interest, that justifies the intervention of the law in the transformation of property, this is that object, this is that interest. It is idle for you to smile or jeer, for it is we who are in the right when we say to you: after having made use of the law of expropriation on the ground of public utility for the benefit of capital, after having put this law into force in order to permit capital to scatter railroads across the peasants' fields, to permit capital to establish great vested interests in your cities, after having made use of this law for the benefit of capitalistic might, the hour is come to make use of it for the benefit of labor demanding its rights.

Values today permit their holders to purchase either means of production and of profit or their products. In the transformed society, when the private capital of production and exploitation shall have been made social, when the social community shall have placed the means of production at the disposition of associated laborers, the indemnity values that shall have been given the capitalists of yesterday will permit them no longer to buy the means of production, of rent, and of profit: they will permit them to buy only the products of the transformed social activity.

Gentlemen, when the law abolished slavery and indemnified the slaveholders, the latter could not use this indemnity to buy slaves on the morrow. Similarly, when capitalistic property shall have become socialistic, the indemnity holders shall be able to purchase neither the means of production nor the producers: they shall be able to purchase products only. What! You are astonished, you are scandalized that man should no longer purchase man!

Gentlemen, whatever be your judgment of today or tomorrow upon the modalities of the social order that I have attempted summarily to portray from this tribune, you cannot deny that you are here face to face with a doctrine that you may judge rash, that you may judge utopian, vain; but many another doctrine has been judged vain and has been denounced as utopian by the privileged classes on the very eve of their advent in history. But be that as it may, it is face to face with a precise and debatable solution; it is face to face with an assertion that you can lay hold of, that you can denounce; and then, whatever you may think of our doctrines, whatever you may think of a system that affirms that there can be no liberty for man save in the social appropriation of private capital, I repeat, a precise doctrine is before you.

And when we address ourselves to the proletariat, when we address ourselves to the workmen, when we point it out to them, and when we remind them of the evils they suffer (and we are not backward, gentlemen, in stating these sufferings and these injuries), we say to the proletariat, at the risk of bringing down upon ourselves the animosity of this enormous power of those privileged classes which ignore the very thought of a proletariat party: "Behold the cause of your sufferings; behold the root of your evils!" And it is to prove to you, gentlemen, that we seek not to aggravate these miseries, but to cure them; that knowing well the hostility and the satire with which the exposition of a new form of society must necessarily come into collision in an assembly like this, I have, nevertheless, here made this exposition of our doctrines—as we have been making it outside as well as here for many years, ever since there has been a Socialist party. But because we make it, because we take this responsibility, we have the right, after brushing aside these mockeries of an hour, to turn, not to the parties of conservatism and reaction, but toward the parties that assert themselves as of the democracy and of progress, and to demand of them: "And you, what is your doctrine, and what are you going to do? Yes, what can you do for the liberation and the organization of labor?"

Gentlemen, you who listen to me from the left of this assembly, all you radicals and republicans—and I beseech you to believe that in all this I do not address to you a word of provocation or of defiance, but the word of one republican to other republicans—to you I say: "We did great things together when we saved the Republic from the peril of Caesarism, when we emancipated civil society from the wrecks of theocracy; but now, this grand task accomplished, now that the hour is come for all of us to give, if not all our effort, at least our principal effort, to that which we term, one and all, the social reform, it is necessary, after the socialists have stated their doctrine and their method, that you should tell us how it is that you conceive the social evolution.

It will not do to tell me that the mind of man is uncertain, doomed to difficulties, and gropings. You [Clemenceau] said at Lyons in admirable language: "I am, like you all, a fallible man, searching, groping in the darkness." Yes, indeed, we are all fallible men, but there come times in history when men must take sides. One hundred and fifteen years ago, when burst out that great Revolution of which you are the descendant by blood and in mind, certainly all those men—Mirabeau, Vergniaud, Robespierre, Condorcet—were liable to uncertainty and error? They opposed system to system, conception to conception, but also, at the risk of shock, they decided, they dared; they knew that the old world was ended, decomposed, that it was necessary to clear away its ruins and to institute a new society and, at the risk of clash and distraction, they brought forward, one and another, plans, conceptions, and systems. And it was not by the gropings of a superb modesty, but by the largeness and the boldness of well-reflected affirmation that they abolished the old world and created the new.

Clemenceau:

"You must not confound the bankruptcy of the human mind with the bankruptcy of the mind of M. Jaurès!"

I WISH at the outset to render full homage to the noble passion for social justice that so magnificently animates the eloquence of M. Jaurès. In an irresistible impulse of idealism he wishes the happiness of all humanity and we are witnesses that he would spare nothing to assure this happiness. To the chords of his Amphion lyre modestly erected the walls of Thebes. At the voice of M. Jaurès a still greater miracle is accomplished! He speaks, and all the historical organizations of human societies suddenly crumble.

All that man has ever conceived of a social order, all that he has ever wished, all that he has realized of justice, commencing in pain, in sorrow, in blood, since the day when he burst from his caverns to the conquest of his earth, all the secular effort for a better life, all the progress acquired at the price of a labor figured perhaps by millions of years—victory! all that resolves itself into dust; all that enshrouds itself in smoke, and if your eye wishes to follow this smoke into the heavens you there behold a new prodigy; for in sumptuous clouds enchanted palaces rear themselves, whence is banished all human misery. There remains only to fix them in the air and to seat their foundations among us in order that the work of Genesis be reformed forever.

The social evil that Jehovah could not eliminate from His work shall disappear. There shall remain to us only the evils of human conditions— sufficient, in all conscience. Alas! while this pompous mirage unfolds itself before the charmed gaze of the new creator, I, vacillating mortal that I am, labor miserably in the plain, even in the far depths of the valley, struggling with an ungrateful soil that doles me out a niggardly harvest. Hence the difference between our points of view that his good will pardons me so hardly.

M. Jaurès, indeed, paid me the compliment of some floral offerings; but I soon discovered that when he did so it was for the purpose of immolating me more pompously upon the altar of collectivism, after having pronounced upon me a pitiless condemnation. But I do not pride myself in being one of that noble category of resigned victims who stretch out an innocent neck to the sword of Calchas. I writhe, I struggle, I revolt, and when M. Jaurès explains to me that he has conceived a most unfavorable opinion of my policy, I appeal from this judgment to a superior judge—this Chamber, the exponent of a republican country.

I had thought that my acts would speak for me; I had thought that the hour would come when in this very place I could explain myself regarding them, face to face with my adversaries. That hour has come, and I take advantage of it to say at the outset that in my view those who act against the working class are those who encourage it in the crazy idea that wherever there is a workman who will respect neither the law nor the right there you have the working class; these are they who represent to him as his enemy the government charged with the maintenance of order.

I say that those who act against the working class are those who encourage it to believe that it can do no wrong, and that it suffices for it to visit upon others the oppressions from which it has itself suffered.

I say that those who act against the working class are those who thus retard its education, because education is not by words, as pedagogues profess and believe, but is achieved by deeds. We shall know that the working class is worthy to govern the democracy, as you desire and as I myself heartily wish, on the day when of its own free will it shall conform its acts to the right it demands.

Such is the education that must be given it. It learns nothing by discourses; could discourses teach the world, the Sermon on the Mount would have been realized long ago.

Without doubt, M. Jaurès, you dominate me from all the heights of your socialistic conceptions. You have the magic power of evoking fairy palaces with your wand, while I am as some modest laborer on a cathedral who obscurely carries a stone to the august edifice he shall never see. At the first puff of reality the fairy palace will vanish, whereas the republican cathedral will someday rear its spire into the skies.

Individual property, I assert, will be evolved for a long time to come; I assert that the relations of individual property and of social property will not remain as they now are; and when I say that I say nothing that anyone cannot approve. So much is understood, the question is open, we shall discuss it as fully as you please; in the meantime I wish to brand the sophism upon which you have founded your right of expropriation. You have shown us both extreme wealth and extreme poverty; you have promised us that in six months you would find the means to remedy the evil you point out.

M. Jaurès, there are more than two hypotheses to submit to this Chamber; between the society of today and yours there are an infinite number of social conceptions that may be developed. You underestimate the task. Admitting even that your criticisms are well founded, that present society is as bad as you say it is (and I am not of those who pretend that it is very good, as you well know); admitting further that the society which you have conceived is actually realizable, you have still omitted a point that is worth the trouble of considering, and that is that we have not alone to choose between the society which you promise and society as it is. There are an infinite number of other hypotheses, and when I shall later on speak to you of the projects of social order which this much-abused middle-class Republic has nevertheless brought to success, I shall show you without difficulty that the social regime of today is not the social regime of twenty years ago, and that it is in truth founded upon absolutely different principles.

I cannot, therefore, admit that you give us choice only between these two hypotheses, and that you have said the last word when you say to us: "Take care; if you do not accept my project the human mind is bankrupt." M. Jaurès, you must not confound the bankruptcy of the human mind with the bankruptcy of the mind of M. Jaurès!

You are carrying it, permit me to say, a little too high with the men who until this day have been your collaborators. You show us the spectacle of those divinities of Hellenism who, upon the Acropolis of Athens, struggled one day for the accomplishment of a prodigious task: with your imperious scepter you strike the earth, you cause to emerge from it the type of the new society—these are your words—and you, turning toward us, say to us: "Do as much." Very good; it is not certain that this challenge cannot be taken up. The alchemists sought the philosopher's stone: you have found it; you hold in your hand the magic formula that ought to solve everything—I do not say that will solve, since we do not yet know that it will—that ought to solve in six months the social question.

That is all very good, but the clear, critical spirit of modern France, which you do not appreciate because it inconveniences you at the present moment, has preserved us up to this time from these dreams. It is, however, natural that at the historical hour when the social question presents itself in all its amplitude that imaginations should give themselves full play. So much is necessary to men who dare not look destiny full in the face: it is necessary to replace the lost religions that promised eternal happiness by the illusion of prophecies, by the terrestrial paradise about to be. Prophesy on; the generations who sleep far away in the future will not rise up from the ground to confound you.

In 1848 the Republic believed itself on the eve of the great day, and we saw many builders of future cities. Do you remember the sittings of the Constituent and of the Legislative Assemblies where Pierre Leroux, where Victor Considérant, where Proudhon detailed, as you are shortly about to do, plans of the new society? A very great number pronounced themselves in favor of the suppression of individual property. Long before them Thomas More, at the commencement of the sixteenth century, had condemned individual property in terms more definite than those which you could employ. These men were not inferior to you. Where are they now? Where? You have replaced them, as others will shortly replace you.

The truth is that we must distinguish, in the social organization, two things: the man and the environment. It appears more simple theoretically to reform the environment; everyone goes about that at his pleasure, but if you consider that the environment of the social organization is, and can be only the product of successive human conceptions, you will see that to arbitrarily modify the social organization without troubling to find out if man is in a state to adapt himself to it can lead only to the most pronounced disorder. Thus even for those who pretend to remake the social organization all in the first instance turns upon the primordial reform of the individual. If you reform the individual, if you apply yourself, I do not say wholly but principally, to the reform of the human personality, man will be able to find for himself the form of organization that best suits him without troubling himself with your theories, without troubling himself with the prophecies you have made and that certainly cannot be realized because you cannot, unless you are a divinity yourself, foresee the result of human evolution.

In any case, your conceptions are fatally defective in one point, and that is that the man whom you need for the realization of your future society does not yet exist, even though your theories might be realized; and when this man shall exist, if he ever should exist, he will employ his own intelligence in his own way without troubling himself with the path you have taken upon yourself to trace out for him. You pretend directly to construct the future, while we construct the man who will construct the future, and in so doing we are achieving a phenomenon much greater than your own. We are not constructing a man already made for our city; we take the man such as he is, still imperfectly cleared from his primitive dens, in his cruelty, in his goodness, in his egoism, in his altruism, in the pathos of the evils he endures and the evils to which he himself subjects his kind—we take him fallible, contradictory, groping toward he knows not what better things, and we enlighten him and we enlarge him, we mitigate the evil of him and fortify him in the good, and we liberate him and we justify him and, partaker of the bestial re-

gime of force as he is, we lead him toward an approximation greater and
still greater of a superior justice. And every day marks a little more of
disinterestedness, a little more of nobility, of goodness, of beauty, and
of a new power over himself and over the external world.

This battle between giants on a basic issue was undoubtedly in the great tradi-
tion, recalling historic debates between Demosthenes and Aeschines, Vergniaud
and Robespierre, Fox and Pitt, Webster and Calhoun, Lincoln and Douglas.

An eyewitness, the English Socialist, H. T. Hyndman, said: "My sympathies
were, of course, entirely with the eloquent and able champion of socialism,
whose power of holding even a hostile audience was extraordinary, as was
shown in that same National Assembly many a time. I was of opinion then, and
I believe now (1919), that Jaurès had much the stronger case. He spoke as he
always did, with eloquence, fervor, and sincerity. As an oratorical display it was
admirable. But I am bound to admit, as a mere question of immediate political
dialectic, the Radical Premier got the better of the fray. It is possible, of course,
that had Jaurès followed Clemenceau instead of having preceded him, that
might have made a difference. But Jaurès' style, with its poetic elevation and
long and imposing periods, was not so well suited as that of Clemenceau to a
personal debate on immediate practical issues before such an audience as the
French National Assembly."

As for the more general results of the debate, Jaurès' speech is supposed to
have consolidated the Socialist party as a unified section of the Chamber of
Deputies, and Clemenceau's speech helped to keep him in power for three
more years—an astounding achievement in French history since 1870.

DAVID LLOYD GEORGE CALLS FOR
A STEEP INCREASE IN TAXES

[July 30, 1909]

His fame in the first World War obscures the earlier David Lloyd George
(1863–1945), the poor young Welshman who as a Liberal won a seat in
Parliament and held it for fifty-four years; who fearlessly opposed the Boer War
and yet a few years later entered the government, first as president of the Board
of Trade and then as Chancellor of the Exchequer. A pioneer in progressive
legislation, he brought forward in 1909 his famous budget, providing for a far-
reaching program of social insurance that was to be largely financed by land
and income taxes.

Wily and wiry in parliamentary debate, Lloyd George also knew how to master huge popular audiences. Some sense of his "fiery mocking tongue," to use Winston Churchill's phrase, is suggested by the speech in support of his budget which he delivered in London's crowded Limehouse in the summer of 1909.

"We are placing the burdens on the broad shoulders. Why should I put burdens on the people?"

A FEW MONTHS AGO a meeting was held not far from this hall, in the heart of the City of London, demanding that the government should launch out and run into enormous expenditure on the navy. That meeting ended up with a resolution promising that those who passed that resolution would give financial support to the government in their undertaking. There have been two or three meetings held in the City of London since, attended by the same class of people, but not ending up with a resolution promising to pay. On the contrary, we are spending the money, but they don't pay. What has happened since to alter their tone? Simply that we have sent in the bill. We started our four dreadnaughts. They cost eight millions of money. We promised them four more; they cost another eight millions. Somebody has got to pay, and these gentlemen say, "Perfectly true; somebody has got to pay, but we would rather that somebody were somebody else." We started building; we wanted money to pay for the building; so we sent the hat round. We sent it round amongst the workmen and the miners of Derbyshire and Yorkshire, the weavers of Dumfries, who, like all their countrymen, know the value of money. They all brought in their coppers. We went round Belgravia, but there has been such a howl ever since that it has completely deafened us.

But they say, "It is not so much the dreadnaughts we object to, it is the pensions." If they object to pensions, why did they promise them? They won elections on the strength of their promises. It is true they never carried them out. Deception is always a pretty contemptible vice, but to deceive the poor is the meanest of all crimes. But they say, "When we promised pensions we meant pensions at the expense of the people for whom they were provided. We simply meant to bring in a bill to compel workmen to contribute to their own pensions." If that is what they meant, why did they not say so? The budget, as your chairman has

already so well reminded you, is introduced not merely for the purpose
of raising barren taxes, but taxes that are fertile taxes, taxes that will
bring forth fruit—the security of the country which is paramount in the
midst of all. The provision for the aged and deserving poor—it was time
it was done. It is rather a shame for a rich country like ours—probably
the richest country in the world, if not the richest the world has ever
seen—that it should allow those who have toiled all their days to end
in penury and possibly starvation. It is rather hard that an old workman
should have to find his way to the gates of the tomb, bleeding and footsore, through the brambles and thorns of poverty. We cut a new path
through it, an easier one, a pleasanter one, through fields of waving corn.
We are raising money to pay for the new road, aye, and to widen it,
so that 200,000 paupers shall be able to join in the march. There are many
in the country blessed by Providence with great wealth, and if there are
amongst them men who grudge out of their riches a fair contribution
toward the less fortunate of their fellow countrymen, they are shabby
rich men. We propose to do more by means of the budget. We are raising money to provide against the evils and the sufferings that follow from
unemployment. We are raising money for the purpose of assisting our
great friendly societies to provide for the sick and the widows and orphans. We are providing money to enable us to develop the resources
of our own land. I do not believe any fair-minded man would challenge
the justice and the fairness of the objects which we have in view in raising this money.

But there are some of them who say that the taxes themselves are
unjust, unfair, unequal, oppressive—notably so the land taxes. They are
engaged, not merely in the House of Commons but outside the House
of Commons, in assailing these taxes with a concentrated and a sustained
ferocity which will not allow even a comma to escape with its life. . . .

The other day, at the great Tory meeting held at the Cannon Street
Hotel, they had blazoned on the walls, "We protest against the budget
in the name of democracy, liberty, and justice." Where does the democracy come in this landed system? Where is the justice in all these transactions? We claim that the tax we impose on land is fair, just, and moderate. They go on threatening that if we proceed they will cut down their
benefactions and discharge labor. What kind of labor? What is the labor
they are going to choose for dismissal? Are they going to threaten to
devastate rural England, while feeding themselves and dressing themselves? Are they going to reduce their gamekeepers? That would be
sad! The agricultural laborer and the farmer might then have some part

of the game which they fatten with their labor. But what would happen
to you in the season? No week-end shooting with the Duke of Norfolk
for any of us! But that is not the kind of labor that they are going to
cut down. They are going to cut down productive labor—builders and
gardeners—and they are going to ruin their property so that it shall not
be taxed. All I can say is this—the ownership of land is not merely an
enjoyment, it is a stewardship. It has been reckoned as such in the past,
and if they cease to discharge their functions, the security and defense
of the country, looking after the broken in their villages and neighbor-
hoods—then those functions which are part of the traditional duties
attached to the ownership of land and which have given to it its title
—if they cease to discharge those functions, the time will come to re-
consider the conditions under which land is held in this country. No
country, however rich, can permanently afford to have quartered upon
its revenue a class which declines to do the duty which it was called
upon to perform. And, therefore, it is one of the prime duties of statesmanship to investigate those conditions.

But I do not believe it. They have threatened and menaced like
that before. They have seen it is not to their interest to carry out these
futile menaces. They are now protesting against paying their fair share
of the taxation of the land, and they are doing so by saying: "You are
burdening the community; you are putting burdens upon the people
which they cannot bear." Ah! they are not thinking of themselves. Noble
souls! It is not the great dukes they are feeling for; it is the market gar-
dener, it is the builder, and it was, until recently, the small holder. In
every debate in the House of Commons they said: "We are not worrying
for ourselves. We can afford it with our broad acres; but just think of
the little man who has got a few acres," and we were so very impressed
with this tearful appeal that at last we said, "We will leave him out."
And I almost expected to see Mr. Prettyman jump over the table and
say, "Fall on my neck and embrace me." Instead of that, he stiffened
up, his face wreathed with anger, and he said, "The budget is more unjust than ever."

Oh! no. We are placing the burdens on the broad shoulders. Why
should I put burdens on the people? I am one of the children of the
people. I was brought up amongst them. I know their trials; and God
forbid that I should add one grain of trouble to the anxiety which they
bear with such patience and fortitude. When the Prime Minister did me
the honor of inviting me to take charge of the national exchequer at a
time of great difficulty, I made up my mind in framing the budget which

was in front of me that at any rate no cupboard should be bared, no lot would be harder to bear. By that test, I challenge them to judge the budget.

"Never had any speech on the public platform created so tremendous a sensation," said Lloyd George's biographer, John Edwards. From Limehouse to Lands End the masses cheered, but the propertied classes were infuriated. In this atmosphere of almost unparalleled tension, the budget bill finally passed the House of Commons but was curtly thrown out by the House of Lords. However, this outcome was no surprise to Lloyd George and his colleagues. Indeed, it became known that his Limehouse speech was deliberately provocative, designed to pique the Lords into rejecting the bill in order to bring about a showdown on their veto power on money bills. A few months later, the House of Lords, responding to the results of a recent general election, grudgingly passed the bill. But Lloyd George and the Liberals were not conciliated. On February 22, 1911, the Commons passed the Parliament Act, depriving the Lords of the power to hold up money bills and introducing other curbs.

The House of Lords was now faced with a predicament: either to relinquish their power voluntarily or to be overwhelmed by the creation—for this was the threat—of five hundred new peers. They relinquished it.

WOODROW WILSON, AT FIFTY-FOUR, GIVES HIS FIRST POLITICAL ADDRESS

[September 15, 1910]

Woodrow Wilson was fifty-four when he gave his first political address and his most successful one in its immediate, astonishing effect. Nine years and ten days later he made his final, heroic appeal for the League of Nations and collapsed, an old and broken man. He had achieved his earliest serious ambition, "to take an active, if possible a leading, part in public life, and strike out for myself, if I had the ability, a statesman's career."

The son of a Presbyterian minister from Ohio and his equally Scottish wife, Woodrow Wilson (1856–1924) was born in Virginia and brought up in the South. At Davidson College in North Carolina, and later at the College of New Jersey (Princeton), he worked hard at oratory and debating; he read history, state papers, and great speeches, especially those of Burke and Bright; and he went on to postgraduate work in law at the University of Virginia. But he found the practice of law both unprofitable and unpleasant and he turned back to graduate work at Johns Hopkins. This led to his first and perhaps his best book, Congressional Government (1885), in which he condemned the irresponsible power of Congressional committees, lamented the weakness of the President, and propounded the advantages of the British cabinet system, in the spirit of Walter Bagehot.

With his doctor's degree attained, Wilson settled down to teach—three years at Bryn Mawr, two at Wesleyan in Connecticut, and twelve at Princeton, as professor of jurisprudence and political economy. Professor Wilson was no intimate Socratic teacher, but a brilliant classroom orator, an exemplar of the lecture method that was even then under attack. In writing of Adam Smith and the art of academic lecturing, he not only defended himself but all those masters whose "only instrument was the sword of penetrating speech." He thought it would be "good policy to endure much indifferent lecturing—watchful trustees might reduce it to a minimum—for the sake of leaving places open for the men who have in them the inestimable force of chastened eloquence." Wilson exhibited that force in the highest degree, and it brought him speaking engagements throughout the country, before he was made president of Princeton in 1902.

As president he was successful in introducing the preceptorial method of teaching, the opposite of his own, but he failed in his efforts to democratize the private eating clubs and to have the new graduate-school building located on the main campus, not in splendid segregation. By 1910 Wilson was ready to leave Princeton and turn to a literary career. But Colonel George M. Harvey saw Wilson as a presidential possibility and more or less forced the Democratic bosses of New Jersey to give him the nomination for governor.

The state Democratic convention was a hot one on that hot afternoon in September at the Taylor Opera House in Trenton. The machine delegates were there in full force, but there was a minority of angry, vocal rebels, young and old. In spite of bitter speeches denouncing the bosses and Wilson, the machine worked smoothly and Wilson was nominated over the other three candidates, although most of the delegates had never seen him. They were all about to leave the hall when the chairman announced that their nominee would soon appear. "He was so confident of being nominated," said Ray Stannard Baker, "that he had already written out his speech in advance," and spent the morning playing golf at Princeton. As Wilson began to speak he might have noticed down in front the sullen, skeptical face of a young lawyer from Jersey City, Joseph P. Tumulty by name.

"I shall enter upon the duties of the office of Governor, if

elected, with absolutely no pledges of any kind to

prevent me from serving the people of the

state with singleness of purpose."

YOU HAVE CONFERRED upon me a very great honor. I accept the nomination you have tendered me with the deepest gratification that you should have thought me worthy to lead the Democrats of New Jersey in this stirring time of opportunity. Even more than the great honor of your nomination, I feel the deep responsibility it imposes upon me; for responsibility is proportioned to opportunity.

As you know, I did not seek this nomination. It has come to me absolutely unsolicited, with the consequence that I shall enter upon the duties of the office of Governor, if elected, with absolutely no pledges of any kind to prevent me from serving the people of the state with singleness of purpose. Not only have no pledges of any kind been given, but none have been proposed or desired. In accepting the nomination, therefore, I am pledging myself only to the service of the people and the party which intends to advance their interests. I cannot but regard these circumstances as marking the beginning of a new and more ideal era in our politics. Certainly they enhance very greatly the honor you have conferred upon me and enlarge the opportunity in equal degree. A day of unselfish purpose is always a day of confident hope.

I feel confident that the people of the state will accept the promises you have made in your platform as made sincerely and with a definite purpose to render them effective service. That platform is sound, explicit, and businesslike. There can be no mistaking what it means; and the voters of the state will know at once that promises so definitely made are made to be kept, not to be evaded. Your declarations deserve and will win their confidence.

But we shall keep it only by performance, by achievement, by proving our capacity to conduct the administration and reform the legislation of the state in the spirit of our declarations with the sagacity and firmness of practical men who not only purpose but also do what is sensible and effective. It is toward this task of performance that my thoughts turn as I think of soliciting the suffrages of my fellow citizens for the great office of governor of the state.

I shall do so with a very profound sense of the difficulty of solving

new and complicated problems in the right way. I take the three great
questions before us to be reorganization and economy in administration,
the equalization of taxation, and the control of corporations. There are
other very important questions that confront us, as they confront all the
other states of the Union in this day of readjustment: the question of
the proper liability of employers, for example, the question of corrupt
practices in elections, the question of conservation; but the three I have
named dominate all the rest. It is imperative that we should not only
master them, but also act upon them, and act very definitely.

It is first of all necessary that we should act in the right spirit. And the
right spirit is not a spirit of hostility. We shall not act either justly or
wisely if we attack established interests as public enemies. There has
been too much indictment and too little successful prosecution for wrongs
done; too much talk and too few practicable suggestions as to what is to
be done. It is easy to condemn wrong and to fulminate against wrong-
doers in effective rhetorical phrases; but that does not bring either reform
or ease of mind. Reform will come only when we have done some careful
thinking as to exactly what the things are that are being done in contra-
vention of the public interest and as to the most simple, direct, and effective way of getting at the men who do them. In a self-governed country
there is one rule for everybody, and that is the common interest. Everything must be squared by that. We can square it only by knowing its
exact shape and movement. Government is not a warfare of interests. We
shall not gain our ends by heat and bitterness, which make it impossible
to think either calmly or fairly. Government is a matter of common counsel, and everyone must come into the consultation with the purpose to
yield to the general view, the view which seems most nearly to correspond with the common interest. If any decline frank conference, keep
out, hold off, they must take the consequences and blame only themselves
if they are in the end badly served. There must be implacable determination to see the right done, but strong purpose, which does not flinch because some must suffer, is perfectly compatible with fairness and justice
and a clear view of the actual facts.

This should be our spirit in the matter of reform, and this our method.
And in this spirit we should do very definite things. It is obvious even to
a casual observer that the administration of the state has been unnecessarily complicated and elaborated, too many separate commissions and
boards set up, business methods neglected, money wasted, and a state of
affairs brought about of which a successful business concern would be
ashamed. No doubt the increase of state expenditures that has marked the
last decade has been in part due to a necessary and desirable increase of

function on the part of the state; but it is only too evident that no study of economy has been made, and that a careful reconsideration and reorganization of the administrative processes of the state would result in great savings and in enhanced responsibility on the part of those who are entrusted with the important work of government.

Our system of taxation is as ill-digested, as piecemeal, and as haphazard as our system of administration. It cannot be changed suddenly or too radically, but many changes should be inaugurated and the whole system by degrees reconsidered and altered so as to fit modern economic conditions more equitably. Above all, the methods of assessment should be changed, in order that inequalities between the taxes of individuals and the taxes of corporations, for example, should be entirely eliminated. It is not necessary for the maintenance of our modern industrial enterprise that corporations should be indulged or favored in the matter of taxation, and it is extremely demoralizing that they should be. Such inequalities should be effectually removed by law and by the action of the tax-assessing authorities of the state and of the localities. This is a matter which will require dispassionate study and action based, not upon hostility, but upon the common interest.

The question of the control of corporations is a very difficult one, upon which no man can speak with confidence; but some things are plain. It is plain, so far as New Jersey is concerned, that we must have a public service commission with the amplest powers to oversee and regulate the administration of public-service corporations throughout the state. We have abundant experience elsewhere to guide us in this matter, from the admirable commission so long in successful operation in Wisconsin to the latest legislation of sister states. We need have no doubt of our right course of action here.

It is the states, not the Federal authorities, that create corporations. The regulation of corporations is the duty of the state much more directly than it is the duty of the Government of the United States. It is my strong hope that New Jersey may lead the way in reform by scrutinizing very carefully the enterprises she consents to incorporate, their make-up, their objects, the basis and method of their capitalization, their organization with respect to liability to control by the state, their conformity to state and Federal statute. This can be done, and done effectually. I covet for New Jersey the honor of doing it.

And so, also, gentlemen, with every other question we face. Let us face it in the spirit of service and with the careful, practical sense of men of affairs. We shall not ask the voters of the state to lend us their suffrages merely because we call ourselves Democrats, but because we mean to serve them like honest and public-spirited men, true Democrats because true lovers of the common interest, servants of no special group of men or of interests, students of the interest of the people and of the country.

The future is not for parties "playing politics," but for measures conceived in the largest spirit, pushed by parties whose leaders are statesmen, not demagogues, who love, not their offices, but their duty and their opportunity for service. We are witnessing a renaissance of public spirit, a reawakening of sober public opinion, a revival of the power of the people, the beginning of an age of thoughtful reconstruction that makes our thought hark back to the great age in which Democracy was set up in America. With the new age, we shall show a new spirit. We shall serve justice and candor, and all things that make for the right. Is not our own ancient party the party disciplined and made ready for this great task? Shall we not forget ourselves in making it the instrument of righteousness for the state and for the nation?

When I think of the flag which our ships carry, the only touch of color about them, the only thing that moves as if it had a settled spirit in it—in their solid structure, it seems to me I see alternate strips of parchment upon which are written the rights of liberty and justice and strips of blood spilled to vindicate those rights, and then—in the corner—a prediction of the blue serene into which every nation may swim that stands for these great things.

"The speech is over," wrote Tumulty. "Around me there is a swirling mass of men whose hearts had been touched by the great speech which is just at an end. Men stood about me with tears streaming from their eyes. Realizing that they had just stood in the presence of greatness, it seemed as if they had been lifted out of their selfish miasma of politics, and, in the spirit of the Crusaders, were ready to dedicate themselves to the cause of liberating their state from the bondage of special interests." (Woodrow Wilson as I Know Him)

Old John Crandall of Atlantic City, another implacable foe of Wilson, waved his hat and cane in the air and yelled, "I am sixty-five years old, and still a damn fool!" Many such reversals of opinion were delightedly reported by veterans and neophytes alike.

From this triumph Wilson went into a whirlwind campaign that astonished the old guard and new guard alike, and won him the governorship with the second largest plurality in the history of the state. Tumulty, who was a valuable adviser during the campaign, now became Wilson's personal secretary. Within a year a whole progressive program was pushed through the legislature under the leadership of the new governor, bringing nation-wide attention to him and New Jersey.

Wilson, who had privately said harsh things about Bryan, canceled them out publicly at the Jackson Day Dinner in 1912, making a plea for party unity which Bryan called "the greatest speech in American political history." At the Democratic national convention a few months later Bryan swung the presidential nomination to Wilson, and when Theodore Roosevelt split the Republican party, Wilson's election was inevitable. For two administrations, from his First Inaugural to his last address on the League of Nations, he maintained a noble standard.

PART SEVENTEEN

THE FIRST WORLD WAR

IF THERE WAS EVER a chain reaction in the human world, it took place during five weeks in the summer of 1914. On June 28 the Archduke Franz Ferdinand and his wife were assassinated by Serbian terrorists. Austria, with the support of Germany, delivered an intolerable ultimatum to Serbia. Russia urged Serbia to appeal to the Great Powers. The Serbian reply to Austria was considered unsatisfactory. Russia began "premobilization." Austria refused mediation and began war on Serbia. Belgium rejected the German demand for permission to invade France by way of Belgium. Belgium mobilized. Germany declared war on Russia. France mobilized. Germany declared war on France. German troops invaded neutral Belgium. England, committed by treaty to aid Belgium, declared war on Germany on August 4.

When it was too late to turn back, the leaders of every country made inspiring speeches, justifying themselves before God and man. There was the noble reluctance of Foreign Secretary Grey and Prime Minister Asquith. There was the harsh bravado of the Kaiser and Chancellor von Bethmann-Hollweg. There was the shrill patriotism of President Poincaré and Premier Viviani. A certain grandeur marked the words of King Albert of Belgium. A fateful hollowness marked the call to arms by Czar Nicholas II of Russia. But they were all ghostly comments on what seemed to be inevitable.

Might this terrible sequence have been broken somewhere along the line? Three years before, when Germany was bullying France over the Congo and Morocco, Lloyd George spoke out loud and bold, making it clear that the British navy stood ready to come to the aid of France—and the crisis passed. If Sir Edward Grey, the eloquent British Foreign Secretary, had made a similar powerful statement in mid-July, if he had asserted that Britain would not remain neutral in case Belgium and France were attacked, it is more than likely that Kaiser Wilhelm's truculence would have sharply declined. But Grey, oscillating between morality and patriotism, as Quincy Howe puts it, could not make that decisive step.

While ministers and diplomats peered at secret treaties through the month of July, Jean Jaurès, upholding "the treaty that binds us to the human race,"

*tried desperately at the eleventh hour to stop the movement toward the abyss,
speaking at Lyons and Brussels. But the noise of rival patriotisms made his
voice inaudible. On the last day of July, a week before war broke out, Jaurès was
assassinated by a French patriot.*

LLOYD GEORGE CALLS FOR VOLUNTEERS

[September 19, 1914]

*As late as January, 1914, Lloyd George, still Chancellor of the Exchequer,
stated in an interview that it was a good time to reduce expenditures on armaments as relations between Britain and Germany were "infinitely more friendly"
than they had been for years, and this belief was reflected in the budget that he
submitted in May.*

*However, when the explosion came in August, he at once threw all his
energies into the war effort and on September 19 gave a speech that may well
have been the most electrifying of the period, in any language or country. It
was before a huge gathering of his own Welsh countrymen in Queen's Hall,
London.*

"It will be a terrible war."

THERE is no man in this room who has always regarded the prospect
of engaging in a great war with greater reluctance and with greater
repugnance than I have done throughout the whole of my political life.
There is no man either inside or outside this room more convinced that
we could not have avoided it without dishonor. I am fully alive to the
fact that every nation that has ever engaged in war has always invoked
the sacred name of honor. Many a crime has been committed in its name;
there are some being committed now. All the same, national honor is a
reality, and any nation that disregards it is doomed. Why is our honor
as a country involved in this war? Because, in the first instance, we are
bound by honorable obligations to defend the independence, the liberty,
the integrity, of a small neighbor that has always lived peaceably. She
could not have compelled us; she was weak; but the man who declines
to discharge his duty because his creditor is too poor to enforce it is a

blackguard. We entered into a treaty—a solemn treaty—two treaties—to defend Belgium and her integrity. Our signatures are attached to the documents. Our signatures do not stand there alone; this country was not the only country that undertook to defend the integrity of Belgium. Russia, France, Austria, Prussia—they are all there. Why are Austria and Prussia not performing the obligations of their bond? It is suggested that when we quote this treaty it is purely an excuse on our part—it is our low craft and cunning to cloak our jealousy of a superior civilization that we are attempting to destroy.

Our answer is the action we took in 1870. What was that? Mr. Gladstone was then Prime Minister. Lord Granville, I think, was then Foreign Secretary. I have never heard it laid to their charge that they were ever jingoes.

What did they do in 1870? That treaty bound us then. We called upon the belligerent powers to respect it. We called upon France, and we called upon Germany. At that time, bear in mind, the greatest danger to Belgium came from France and not from Germany. We intervened to protect Belgium against France, exactly as we are doing now to protect her against Germany. We proceeded in exactly the same way. We invited both the belligerent powers to state that they had no intention of violating Belgium territory. What was the answer given by Bismarck? He said it was superfluous to ask Prussia such a question in view of the treaties in force. France gave a similar answer. . . .

That was in 1870. Mark what followed. Three or four days after . . . a French army was wedged up against the Belgian frontier, every means of escape shut out by a ring of flame from Prussian cannon. There was one way of escape. What was that? Violating the neutrality of Belgium. What did they do? The French on that occasion preferred ruin and humiliation to the breaking of their bond. The French Emperor, the French marshals, 100,000 gallant Frenchmen in arms, preferred to be carried captive to the strange land of their enemies rather than dishonor the name of their country. It was the French army in the field. Had they violated Belgian neutrality, the whole history of that war would have been changed, and yet, when it was the interest of France to break the treaty then, she did not do it.

It is the interest of Prussia today to break the treaty, and she has done it. She avows it with cynical contempt for every principle of justice. She says, "Treaties only bind you when your interest is to keep them." "What is a treaty?" says the German Chancellor. "A scrap of paper." Have you any five-pound notes about you? I am not calling for them. Have you any of those neat little treasury one-pound notes? I am not calling for them.

If you have, burn them; they are only scraps of paper. What are they made of? Rags. What are they worth? The whole credit of the British Empire. Scraps of paper! I have been dealing with scraps of paper within the last month. One suddenly found the commerce of the world coming to a standstill. The machine had stopped. Why? I will tell you. We discovered—many of us for the first time, for I do not pretend that I do not know much more about the machinery of commerce today than I did six weeks ago, and there are many others like me—we discovered that the machinery of commerce was moved by bills of exchange. I have seen some of them, wretched, crinkled, blotched, frowzy, and yet those wretched little scraps of paper move great ships laden with thousands of tons of precious cargo from one end of the world to the other. What is the motive power behind them? The honor of commercial men. Treaties are the currency of international statesmanship. Let us be fair: German merchants, German traders, have the reputation of being as upright and straightforward as any traders in the world—but if the currency of German commerce is to be debased to the level of that of her statesmanship, no trader from Shanghai to Valparaiso will ever look at a German signature again. This doctrine of the scrap of paper, this doctrine which is proclaimed by Bernhardi, that treaties only bind a nation as long as it is to its interest, goes under the root of all public law. It is the straight road to barbarism. It is as if you were to move the Magnetic Pole because it was in the way of a German cruiser. The whole navigation of the seas would become dangerous, difficult, and impossible; and the whole machinery of civilization will break down if this doctrine wins in this way. We are fighting against barbarism, and there is one way of putting it right. If there are nations that say they will only respect treaties when it is to their interest to do so, we must make it to their interest to do so for the future.

What is their defense? Consider the interview which took place between our ambassador and the great German officials. When their attention was called to this treaty to which they were parties, they said, "We cannot help that. Rapidity of action is the great German asset." There is a greater asset for a nation than rapidity of action, and that is honest dealing. What are Germany's excuses? She says Belgium was plotting against her; Belgium was engaged in a great conspiracy with Britain and France to attack her. Not merely is it not true, but Germany knows it is not true. France offered Belgium five army corps to defend her if she was attacked. Belgium said, "I have the word of the Kaiser. Shall Caesar send a lie?" All these tales about conspiracy have been vamped up since. A great nation ought to be ashamed to behave like a fraudulent bankrupt, perjuring its way through its obligations. What she says is not true. She has deliberately broken this treaty, and we are in honor bound to stand by it.

Belgium has been treated brutally. How brutally we shall not yet know. We already know too much. What had she done? Had she sent an ultimatum to Germany? Had she challenged Germany? Was she preparparing to make war on Germany? Had she inflicted any wrong upon Germany which the Kaiser was bound to redress? She was one of the most unoffending little countries in Europe. There she was—peaceable, industrious, thrifty, hard-working, giving offense to no one. And her cornfields have been trampled, her villages have been burned, her art treasures have been destroyed, her men have been slaughtered—yea, and her women and children too. Hundreds and thousands of her people, their neat, comfortable little homes burned to the dust, are wandering homeless in their own land. What was their crime? Their crime was that they trusted to the word of a Prussian king. I do not know what the Kaiser hopes to achieve by this war. I have a shrewd idea what he will get; but one thing he has made certain, and that is that no nation will ever commit that crime again.

I am not going to enter into details of outrages. Many of them are untrue, and always are in a war. War is a grim, ghastly business at best or worst, and I am not going to say that all that has been said in the way of outrages must necessarily be true. I will go beyond that, and I will say that if you turn two millions of men—forced, conscript, compelled, driven —into the field, you will always get amongst them a certain number who will do things that the nation to which they belong would be ashamed of. I am not depending on these tales. It is enough for me to have the story which Germans themselves avow, admit, defend, and proclaim—the burning, massacring, the shooting down of harmless people. Why? Because, according to the Germans, these people fired on German soldiers. What business had German soldiers there at all? Belgium was acting in pursuance of the most sacred right, the right to defend its homes. But they were not in uniform when they fired! If a burglar broke into the Kaiser's palace at Potsdam, destroyed his furniture, killed his servants, ruined his art treasures—especially those he has made himself—and burned the precious manuscript of his speeches, do you think he would wait until he got into his uniform before he shot him down? They were dealing with those who had broken into their household. But the perfidy of the Germans has already failed. They entered Belgium to save time. The time has gone. They have not gained time, but they have lost their good name.

But Belgium is not the only little nation that has been attacked in this war, and I make no excuse for referring to the case of the other little nation, the case of Serbia. The history of Serbia is not unblotted. Whose history, in the category of nations, is unblotted? The first nation that is without sin, let her cast a stone at Serbia. She was a nation trained in a horrible school, but she won her freedom with a tenacious valor, and she has maintained it by the same courage. If the Serbians were mixed up in the assassination of the Grand Duke, they ought to be punished. Serbia admits that. The Serbian government had nothing to do with it. Not even Austria claims that. The Serbian Prime Minister is one of the most capable and honored men in Europe. Serbia was willing to punish any one of her subjects who had been proved to have any complicity in that assassination. What more could you expect? What were the Austrian demands? Serbia sympathized with her fellow countrymen in Bosnia— that was one of her crimes. She must do so no longer. That is the German spirit; you had it in Zabern. How dare you criticize a Prussian official?— and if you laugh, it is a capital offense—the colonel in Zabern threatened to shoot if it was repeated. In the same way, the Serbian newspapers must not critize Austria. I wonder what would have happened had we taken the same line about German newspapers. Serbia said, "Very well, we will give orders to the newspapers that they must in future criticize neither Austria, nor Hungary, nor anything that is theirs." Who can doubt the valor of Serbia, when she undertook to tackle her newspaper editors? She promised not to sympathize with Bosnia; she promised to write no critical articles about Austria; she would have no public meetings in which anything unkind was said about Austria.

But that was not enough. She must dismiss from her army the officers whom Austria should subsequently name. Those officers had just emerged from a war where they had added luster to the Serbian arms; they were gallant, brave, and efficient. I wonder whether it was their guilt or their efficiency that prompted Austria's action! But, mark you, the officers were not named; Serbia was to undertake in advance to dismiss them from the army, the names to be sent in subsequently. Can you name a country in the world that would have stood that? Supposing Austria or Germany had issued a proclamation of that kind to this country, saying, "You dismiss from your army—and from your navy—all those officers whom we shall subsequently name." Well, I think I could name them now. Lord Kitchener would go. Sir John French would be sent away; General Smith-Dorrien would go, and I am sure that Sir John Jellicoe would have to go. and there is another gallant old warrior who would go—Lord Roberts. It was a difficult situation for a small country. Here was a demand made upon her by a great military power that could have put half a dozen men in the field for every one of Serbia's men, and that power was supported by the greatest military power in the world. How did Serbia behave? It is not what happens to you in life that matters. It is the way in which you face it, and Serbia faced the situation with dignity. She said to Austria, "If any officers of mine have been guilty, and are proved to be guilty, I will dismiss them." Austria said, "That is not good enough for me." It was not guilt she was after, but capacity.

Then came Russia's turn. Russia has a special regard for Serbia. Russians have shed their blood for Serbian independence many a time, for Serbia is a member of Russia's family, and she cannot see Serbia maltreated. Austria knew that. Germany knew it, and she turned round to Russia, and said, "I insist that you shall stand by with your arms folded whilst Austria is strangling your little brother to death." What answer did the Russian Slav give? He turned to Austria and said: "You lay hands on that little fellow, and I will tear your ramshackle empire limb from limb." And he is doing it!

That is the story of the two little nations. The world owes much to little nations—and to little men! This theory of bigness, this theory that you must have a *big* nation, and a *big* man—well, long legs have their advantage in retreat. Frederick I chose his warriors for their height, and that tradition has become a policy in Germany. Germany applies that ideal to nations, and will only allow six-foot-two nations to stand in the ranks. But ah! the world owes much to the little five-foot-five nations; the greatest art in the world was the work of little nations; the most enduring literature of the world came from little nations; the greatest literature of England came when she was a nation of the size of Belgium fighting a great empire. The heroic deeds that thrill humanity through generations were the deeds of little nations fighting for their freedom. Yes, and the salvation of mankind came through a little nation. God has chosen little nations as the vessels by which He carries His choicest wines to the lips of humanity, to rejoice their hearts, to exalt their vision, to stimulate and strengthen their faith; and if we stood by when two little nations were being crushed and broken by the brutal hands of barbarism, our shame would have rung down the everlasting ages.

But Germany insists that this is an attack by a lower civilization upon a higher one. As a matter of fact, the attack was begun by the civilization which calls itself the higher one. I am no apologist for Russia; she has perpetrated deeds of which I have no doubt her best sons are ashamed. What empire has not? But Germany is the last empire to point the finger of reproach at Russia. Russia made sacrifices for freedom—great sacrifices. Do you remember the cry of Bulgaria when she was torn by the most insensate tyranny that Europe has ever seen? Who listened to that cry? The only answer of the higher civilization was that the liberty of the Bulgarian peasants was not worth the life of a single Pomeranian soldier. But the rude barbarians of the North sent their sons by the thousand to die for Bulgarian freedom. What about England? Go to Greece, the Netherlands, Italy, Germany, France—in all those lands I could point to places where the sons of Britain have died for the freedom of those peoples. France has made sacrifices for the freedom of other lands than her own. Can you name a single country in the world for the freedom of which modern Prussia has ever sacrificed a single life? By the test of our faith, the highest standard of civilization is the readiness to sacrifice for others.

I will not say a single word in disparagement of the German people. They are a great people, and have great qualities of head and hand and heart. I believe, in spite of recent events, that there is as great a store of kindliness in the German peasant as in any peasant in the world; but he has been drilled into a false idea of civilization. It is efficient, it is capable; but it is a hard civilization; it is a selfish civilization; it is a material civilization. They cannot comprehend the action of Britain at the present moment; they say so. They say, "France we can understand; she is out for vengeance; she is out for territory—Alsace and Lorraine." They say they can understand Russia, she is fighting for mastery—they can understand you fighting for greed of territory; but they cannot understand a great empire pledging its resources, pledging its might, pledging the lives of its children, pledging its very existence, to protect a little nation that seeks to defend herself. God made man in His own image, high of purpose, in the region of the spirit; German civilization would recreate him in the image of a Diesel machine—precise, accurate, powerful, but with no room for soul to operate.

Have you read the Kaiser's speeches? If you have not a copy I advise you to buy one; they will soon be out of print, and you will not have many more of the same sort. They are full of the glitter and bluster of German militarism—"mailed fist," and "shining armor." Poor old mailed fist. Its knuckles are getting a little bruised. Poor shining armor! The shine is being knocked out of it. There is the same swagger and boastfulness running through the whole of the speeches. The extract which was given in *The British Weekly* this week is a very remarkable product as an illustration of the spirit we have to fight. It is the Kaiser's speech to his soldiers on the way to the front:

Remember that the German people are the chosen of God. On me, the German Emperor, the Spirit of God has descended. I am His sword, His weapon, and His viceregent. Woe to the disobedient, and death to cowards and unbelievers.

Lunacy is always distressing, but sometimes it is dangerous; and when you get it manifested in the head of the state, and it has become the policy of a great empire, it is about time that it should be ruthlessly put away. I do not believe he meant all those speeches; it was simply the martial straddle he had acquired. But there were men around him who meant every word of them. This was their religion. Treaties? They tangle the feet of Germany in her advance. Cut them with the sword. Little nations? They hinder the advance of Germany. Trample them in the mire under the German heel! The Russian Slav? He challenges the supremacy of Germany in Europe. Hurl your legions at him and massacre him! Christianity? Sickly sentimentalism about sacrifice for others! Poor pap for German digestion! We will have a new diet. We will force it upon the world. It will be made in Germany—a diet of blood and iron. What remains? Treaties have gone. The honor of nations has gone. Liberty has gone. What is left? Germany! Germany is left!—*Deutschland über Alles!*

That is what we are fighting—that claim to predominantcy of a material, hard civilization, which if it once rules and sways the world, liberty goes, democracy vanishes. And unless Britain and her sons come to the rescue it will be a dark day for humanity.

Have you followed the German *Junker* in his doings? We are not fighting the German people. The German people are under the heel of this military caste, and it will be a day of rejoicing for the German peasant, artisan, and trader when the military caste is broken. You know its pretensions. They walk the pavements, and civilians and their wives are swept into the gutter; they have no right to stand in the way of the great Prussian soldier. Men, women, nations—they all have to go. He thinks all he has to say is, "We are in a hurry." That is the answer he gave to Belgium—"Rapidity of action is Germany's greatest asset," which means, "I am in a hurry; clear out of my way." You know the type of motorist, the terror of the roads, with a sixty-horsepower car; he thinks the roads are made for him and knocks down anybody who impedes the action of his car by a single mile an hour. The Prussian *Junker* is the road hog of Europe. Small nationalities in his way are hurled to the roadside, bleeding and broken. Women and children are crushed under the wheels of his cruel car, and Britain is ordered out of his road. All I can say is this:

if the old British spirit is alive in British hearts, that bully will be torn from his seat. Were he to win, it would be the greatest catastrophe that has befallen democracy since the day of the Holy Alliance and its ascendancy.

They think we cannot beat them. It will not be easy. It will be a long job; it will be a terrible war; but in the end we shall march through terror to triumph. We shall need all our qualities—every quality that Britain and its people possess—prudence in counsel, daring in action, tenacity in purpose, courage in defeat, moderation in victory; in all things, faith.

It has pleased them to believe and to preach the belief that we are a decadent and a degenerate people. They proclaim to the world through their professors that we are a nonheroic nation skulking behind our mahogany counters, whilst we egg on more gallant races to their destruction. This is a description given of us in Germany—"a timorous, craven nation, trusting to its fleet." I think they are beginning to find their mistake out already—and there are half a million young men of Britain who have already registered a vow to their King that they will cross the seas and hurl that insult to British courage against its perpetrators on the battlefields of France and Germany. We want half a million more; and we shall get them.

I envy you young people your opportunity. They have put up the age limit for the army, but I am sorry to say I have marched a good many years even beyond that. It is a great opportunity, an opportunity that only comes once in many centuries to the children of men. For most generations sacrifice comes in drab and weariness of spirit. It comes to you today, and it comes today to us all, in the form of the glow and thrill of a great movement for liberty that impels millions throughout Europe to the same noble end. It is a great war for the emancipation of Europe from the thralldom of a military caste which has thrown its shadows upon two generations of men, and is now plunging the world into a welter of bloodshed and death. Some have already given their lives. There are some who have given more than their own lives: they have given the lives of those who are dear to them. I honor their courage, and may God be their comfort and their strength. But their reward is at hand; those who have fallen have died consecrated deaths. They have taken their part in the making of a new Europe—a new world. I can see signs of its coming in the glare of the battlefield.

The people will gain more by this struggle in all lands than they comprehend at the present moment. It is true they will be free of the greatest menace to their freedom. That is not all. There is something infinitely greater and more enduring which is emerging already out of this great conflict—a new patriotism, richer, nobler, and more exalted than the old. I see amongst all classes, high and low, shedding themselves of selfishness, a new recognition that the honor of the country does not depend merely on the maintenance of its glory in the stricken field, but also in protecting its homes from distress. It is bringing a new outlook for all classes. The great flood of luxury and sloth which had submerged the land is receding, and a new Britain is appearing. We can see for the first time the fundamental things that matter in life, and that have been obscured from our vision by the tropical growth of prosperity.

May I tell you in a simple parable what I think this war is doing for us? I know a valley in North Wales, between the mountains and the sea. It is a beautiful valley, snug, comfortable, sheltered by the mountains from all the bitter blasts. But it is very enervating, and I remember how the boys were in the habit of climbing the hill above the village to have a glimpse of the great mountains in the distance, and to be stimulated and freshened by the breezes which came from the hilltops, and by the great spectacle of their grandeur. We have been living in a sheltered valley for generations. We have been too comfortable and too indulgent, many, perhaps, too selfish, and the stern hand of fate has scourged us to an elevation where we can see the great everlasting things that matter for a nation—the great peaks we had forgotten, of Honor, of Duty, Patriotism, and, clad in glittering white, the great pinnacle of sacrifice pointing like a rugged finger to Heaven. We shall descend into the valleys again; but as long as the men and women of this generation last, they will carry in their hearts the image of those great mountain peaks whose foundations are not shaken, though Europe rock and sway in the convulsions of a great war.

The Welsh magician was at his best that night, and the great audience thundered its applause. They knew that he had always spoken out against war, and some must have remembered that he had risked his life more than once opposing the Boer War. The immediate purpose of the speech was to arouse the Welsh to enlistment, but it stirred the whole country and reverberated around the world.

As able in administration as he was on the platform, Lloyd George went from the exechequer to the ministry of munitions, then to the ministry of war, and in 1916 became Prime Minister. He not only whipped up industry and largely brought about the unified military command under Foch, but he forced machine guns on the army and antisubmarine protection on the navy. Lloyd George obviously shared with Clemenceau the notion that war was too dangerous a thing to leave solely to the generals.

*Passing over his machinations at the peace conference of 1919, we will en-
counter him again, at the age of seventy-seven, on the floor of the House of
Commons in one of the darkest moments in English history—May, 1940.*

CARDINAL MERCIER PREACHES A SERMON IN GERMAN-OCCUPIED BRUSSELS

[July 21, 1916]

For the conquest of France the Schlieffen Plan required the quick sweep of
overwhelming German armies through neutral Belgium and Luxemburg, leaving little strength on the German left or eastern flank. General von Moltke
started to carry out this plan in the first week of August, 1914. On the fourth,
Chancellor Bethmann-Hollweg said to the cheering Reichstag: "We are now
in a state of necessity, and necessity knows no law. Our troops have occupied
Luxemburg; perhaps they have already entered Belgian territory. Gentlemen,
this violates the rules of international law." Unfortunately for the Germans,
von Moltke did not build up an overwhelming right flank by enough weakening
of his left—and the Belgians fought back furiously, heroically, under the inspiration of King Albert I. After a few weeks most of Belgium was conquered and
occupied, but Paris was saved, France was saved.

During the four years of German occupation King Albert remained with his
army, and other Belgian leaders languished in prison or exile, while Cardinal
Mercier, serene, unbending, defiant, upheld the spirit of his people. No nobler
drama came out of the first World War.

Désiré Joseph Mercier (1851–1926), ordained priest in 1874, soon distinguished himself as a teacher of philosophy at Malines and Louvain. He
showed a special devotion to the thought of St. Thomas Aquinas, even before
Pope Leo XIII's encyclical of 1879, Aeterni Patris, calling for a revival of Thom-
ism. When Leo decided to make the University of Louvain a center for
Thomistic studies, Mercier became the first professor and director of a special
Thomistic Institute, which under him achieved a world-wide influence. Unlike
some exponents of orthodoxy, Mercier did not try to minimize modern science
but welcomed it into what he considered the larger structure of Thomistic
philosophy.

Although more inclined to study and teaching than to administration,
Mercier could not decline the archbishopric of Malines in 1906 or the cardinal's
hat the following year. Along with all his other new duties, he spoke widely

and constantly, two of his most notable speeches dealing with "The Modern Conscience" and "Unity." He tried to heal the gap between the Dutch-speaking Flemings of the north and the French-speaking Walloons of the south, but his own southern roots made his position awkward. It took the catastrophe of 1914 to bring about a national unity that no milder persuasion could accomplish.

For four years there was a bloodless duel between the Cardinal, armed with his dignity, his patience, and his pastoral letters, and the German governor general, armed with machine guns and threats of deportation. The Cardinal kept the upper hand. On Coronation Day—July 21, 1916—he preached, in full pontificals, in the Cathedral of Brussels.

"Today the hymn of joy dies on our lips."

Beloved Brethren:

WE OUGHT to have met together here to celebrate the eighty-sixth anniversary of our national independence.

Today, in fourteen years' time, our restored cathedrals and our rebuilt churches will be thrown widely open; the crowds will surge in; our King Albert, standing on his throne, will bow his unconquered head before the King of Kings; the Queen and the royal princes will surround him; we shall hear again the joyous peals of our bells, and throughout the whole country, under the vaulted arches of our churches, the Belgians, hand in hand, will renew their vows to their God, their sovereign, and their liberty, while the bishops and the priests, interpreters of the soul of the nation, will intone a triumphant *Te Deum* in a common transport of joyous thanksgiving.

Today the hymn of joy dies on our lips.

The Jewish people in captivity at Babylon, sitting in tears on the banks of the Euphrates, watched the waters of the river flow by. Their dumb harps were hung on the willows by the bank. Who among them would have the courage to sing the song of Jehovah in a strange land? "O Jerusalem," cried the Psalmist, "if ever I forget thee, let my right arm wither, let my tongue cleave to the roof of my mouth if I do not remember thee; if thou art no longer the beginning of my joys."

The Psalm ends in imprecations; but we do not allow ourselves to repeat them: we are not of the Old Testament, tolerating the laws of retaliation: "An eye for an eye, and a tooth for a tooth." Our lips, purified by the fire of Christian charity, utter no words of hate. To hate is to make it one's object to do harm to others and to delight in so do-

ing. Whatever may be our sufferings, we must not wish to show hatred
toward those who have inflicted them. Our national unity is joined with
a feeling of universal brotherhood. But even this feeling of universal
brotherhood is dominated by our respect for the unconditional justice,
without which no relationship is possible, either between individuals or
between nations.

And that is why, with St. Thomas Aquinas, the most authoritative
teacher of Christian theology, we proclaim that public retribution is commendable.

Crimes, violation of justice, outrage on the public peace, whether
enacted by an individual or by a group, must be repressed. Men's minds
are stirred up, tortured, uneasy, as long as the guilty one is not put back
in his place, as the strong, healthy, colloquial expression has it. To put
men and things back in their places is to re-establish order, readjust the
balance, and restore peace on a just basis.

Public retribution in this sense may distress the affected sentimen-
tality of a weak nature; all the same, it is, says St. Thomas, the expression
and the decree of the highest, the purest form of charity, and of the zeal
which is its flame. It does not make a target of suffering, but a weapon
wherewith to avenge the outrage of justice.

How can one love order without hating disorder; intelligently wish
for peace without expelling that which is destroying it; love a brother,
that is to say wish him well, without desiring that willingly, or by force,
his will shall bend before the unalterable edicts of justice and truth?

It is from these heights that one must view the war in order to understand the greatness of its extent.

Once more, perhaps, you will find yourself face to face with effeminate natures for whom the war means nothing beyond explosions of
mines, bursting of shells, massacres of men, spilling of blood, piling up
of corpses. You will meet politicians of narrow vision who see no further
stake in a battle beyond the interest of one day, the taking of so much
ground, of a stretch of country, or of a province.

But no! If, in spite of its horrors, war, I mean a just war, has so much
austere beauty, it is because war brings out the disinterested enthusiasm
of a whole people, which gives, or is prepared to give, its most precious
possession, even life itself, for the defense and the vindication of things
that cannot be weighed, that cannot be calculated, but that can never
be swallowed up: Justice, Honor, Peace, Liberty!

Do you not feel that, in these two years, the war, the ardent unflag-
ging interest that you give it, purifies you, separates your higher nature

from the dross, draws you away to uplift you toward something nobler and better than yourselves?

You are rising toward the ideals of justice and honor. They support you and draw you upward.

And, because of this ideal, if it is not a vain abstraction, which evaporates like the phantasies of a dream, must have its foundation in a living subject, I am never tired of maintaining this truth, which holds us all under its yoke. God reveals Himself as the Master, the Director of events and of our wills, the holy Master of the universal conscience. . . .

Do we think enough of what those brave men must be suffering who, since the beginning of the war, from the morrow of the defense of Liége and Namur, or the retreat from Antwerp, saw their military career shattered, and now chafe and fret under their inability to bear arms; these guardians of our rights, and of our communal liberties, whose valor has reduced them to inaction?

It needs courage to throw oneself forward, but it needs no less to hold oneself back. Sometimes it is more noble to suffer in silence than to act.

And what of these two years of calm submission by the Belgian people before the inevitable; this unshakable tenacity, which moved a humble woman, before whom the possibilities of an approaching conclusion of peace were being discussed, to say, "Oh, as for us, we must not worry; we can go on waiting." How beautiful is all this, and how full of instruction for the generations to come! . . .

Let us pray for those who are no more. Let us exclude no one from our commiseration; the blood of Christ was shed for all. Some of them are atoning in purgatory for the last remnants of their human weakness. It is for you to hasten their entry into paradise. Succor the poor in distress, both the poor who are known to you and those who are ashamed to beg. Give of your abundance to those who are in need of the necessities of life. Be present at the Mass, which is celebrated every week in your parish churches for our dead soldiers; take your children with you, encourage them to communicate, and communicate with them.

Let us also pray for those who are still holding the firing line on the field of battle. Remember that, even at this moment, while I am speaking to you, some of them are in the agony of death. The prospect of eternity stretches out before them. Let us think of them, let us mortify ourselves for them, resign ourselves to God for them, and obtain for them a holy death. . . .

The approaching date of the first centenary of our independence ought to find us stronger, more intrepid, more united than ever. Let us

prepare ourselves for it with work, with patience, and in true brotherhood.

When in 1930, we recall the dark years of 1915–16, they will appear to
us as the brightest, the most majestic, and, if, from today we resolve they
shall be so, the happiest and the most fruitful in our national history. *Per
crucem ad lucem*—from the sacrifice flashes forth the light!

*The congregation was thrilled by this sermon, and all Belgium rejoiced. The
German governor general and his staff blustered, questioned the Cardinal—and
did nothing.*

*In the fall of 1918 the German forces withdrew from Belgium, and Albert
returned to his capital, to be greeted affectionately by his fellow ruler, the great
Cardinal.*

PRESIDENT WILSON ASKS CONGRESS TO
DECLARE WAR AGAINST GERMANY
[April 2, 1917]

*From the outbreak of the war President Wilson hoped to preserve American
neutrality and, from his vantage point, to do what he could to bring about
peace. As early as May 10, 1915, he addressed several thousand foreign-born
citizens, after naturalization ceremonies in Philadelphia, and made one of his
most famous and controversial pronouncements: "The example of America
must be a special one. The example of America must be the example not merely
of peace because it will not fight, but of peace because it is the healing and elevating influence of the world and strife is not. There is such a thing as a man
being too proud to fight. There is such a thing as a nation being so right that
it does not need to convince others by force that it is right."*

*In 1916 Wilson was re-elected President by a slender margin, no doubt on
the basis of the slogan that "he kept us out of war." With this justification he
directed a note to the belligerent governments that would at least give them an
honorable excuse to begin negotiations. This failing, he called Congress together and delivered his carefully prepared address on "peace without victory,"
which was really directed at the peoples of the warring countries. But he
couldn't maintain his proud neutrality much longer. Just at this time the
German government returned to unrestricted submarine war, and Wilson was
obliged to appear again before Congress with his proposal to break off relations
with the German government.*

Even this step did not move Admiral von Tirpitz, Hindenburg, and Luden-dorff, and in an agony of indecision the peace-loving President began to move toward war. Two months after his speech on breaking off relations with Germany, one month after his solemn Second Inaugural, he made his decision, and on April 2, 1917, he asked a hushed Congress, in joint session, to declare that a state of war existed between the United States and Germany.

"It is a fearful thing to lead this great,
peaceful people into war."

I HAVE CALLED the Congress into extraordinary session because there are serious, very serious, choices of policy to be made, and made immediately, which it was neither right nor constitutionally permissible that I should assume the responsibility of making.

On the third of February last I officially laid before you the extraordinary announcement of the imperial German government that on and after the first day of February it was its purpose to put aside all restraints of law or of humanity and use its submarines to sink every vessel that sought to approach either the ports of Great Britain or Ireland or the western coasts of Europe or any of the ports controlled by the enemies of Germany within the Mediterranean. That had seemed to be the object of the German submarine warfare earlier in the war, but since April of last year the imperial government had somewhat restrained the commanders of its undersea craft in conformity with its promise then given to us that passenger boats should not be sunk and that due warning would be given to all other vessels which its submarines might seek to destroy, when no resistance was offered or escape attempted, and care taken that their crews were given at least a fair chance to save their lives in their open boats. The precautions taken were meager and haphazard enough, as was proved in distressing instance after instance in the progress of the cruel and unmanly business, but a certain degree of restraint was observed. The new policy has swept every restriction aside. Vessels of every kind, whatever their flag, their character, their cargo, their destination, their errand, have been ruthlessly sent to the bottom without warning and without thought of help or mercy for those on board, the vessels of friendly neutrals along with those of belligerents. Even hospital ships and ships carrying relief to the sorely bereaved and stricken people of Belgium, though the latter were provided with safe-conduct through the proscribed areas by the German government itself and were distinguished by unmistakable marks of identity, have been sunk with the same reckless lack of compassion or of principle.

I was for a little while unable to believe that such things would in fact be done by any government that had hitherto subscribed to the humane practices of civilized nations. International law had its origin in the attempt to set up some law which would be respected and observed upon the seas, where no nation had right of dominion and where lay the free highways of the world. By painful stage after stage has that law been built up, with meager enough results, indeed, after all was accomplished that could be accomplished, but always with a clear view, at least, of what the heart and conscience of mankind demanded. This minimum of right the German government has swept aside under the plea of retaliation and necessity and because it had no weapons which it could use at sea except these which it is impossible to employ as it is employing them without throwing to the winds all scruples of humanity or of respect for the understandings that were supposed to underlie the intercourse of the world. I am not now thinking of the loss of property involved, immense and serious as that is, but only of the wanton and wholesale destruction of the lives of noncombatants, men, women, and children, engaged in pursuits which have always, even in the darkest periods of modern history, been deemed innocent and legitimate. Property can be paid for; the lives of peaceful and innocent people cannot be. The present German submarine warfare against commerce is a warfare against mankind.

It is a war against all nations. American ships have been sunk, American lives taken, in ways which it has stirred us very deeply to learn of, but the ships and people of other neutral and friendly nations have been sunk and overwhelmed in the waters in the same way. There has been no discrimination. The challenge is to all mankind. Each nation must decide for itself how it will meet it. The choice we make for ourselves must be made with a moderation of counsel and a temperateness of judgment befitting our character and our motives as a nation. We must put excited feeling away. Our motive will not be revenge or the victorious assertion of the physical might of the nation, but only the vindication of right, of human right, of which we are only a single champion.

When I addressed the Congress on the twenty-sixth of February last I thought that it would suffice to assert our neutral rights with arms, our right to use the seas against unlawful interference, our right to keep our people safe against unlawful violence. But armed neutrality, it now appears, is impracticable. Because submarines are in effect outlaws when used as the German submarines have been used against merchant shipping, it is impossible to defend ships against their attacks as the law of nations has assumed that merchantmen would defend themselves against privateers or cruisers, visible craft giving chase upon the open sea. It is common prudence in such circumstances, grim necessity indeed, to endeavor to destroy them before they have shown their own intention. They must be dealt with upon sight, if dealt with at all. The German government denies the right of neutrals to use arms at all within the areas of the sea which it has proscribed, even in the defense of rights which no modern publicist has ever before questioned their right to defend. The intimation is conveyed that the armed guards which we have placed on our merchant ships will be treated as beyond the pale of law and subject to be dealt with as pirates would be. Armed neutrality is ineffectual enough at best; in such circumstances and in the face of such pretensions it is worse than ineffectual: it is likely only to produce what it was meant to prevent; it is practically certain to draw us into the war without either the rights or the effectiveness of belligerents. There is one choice we cannot make, we are incapable of making: we will not choose the path of submission and suffer the most sacred rights of our nation and our people to be ignored or violated. The wrongs against which we now array ourselves are no common wrongs; they cut to the very roots of human life.

With a profound sense of the solemn and even tragical character of the step I am taking and of the grave responsibilities which it involves, but in unhesitating obedience to what I deem my constitutional duty, I advise that the Congress declare the recent course of the imperial German government to be in fact nothing less than war against the government and people of the United States; that it formally accept the status of belligerent which has thus been thrust upon it; and that it take immediate steps not only to put the country in a more thorough state of defense, but also to exert all its power and employ all its resources to bring the government of the German Empire to terms and end the war.

What this will involve is clear. It will involve the utmost practicable co-operation in counsel and action with the governments now at war with Germany, and, as incident to that, the extension to those governments of the most liberal financial credits, in order that our resources may so far as possible be added to theirs. It will involve the organization and mobilization of all the material resources of the country to supply the materials of war and serve the incidental needs of the nation in the most abundant and yet the most economical and efficient way possible. It will involve the immediate full equipment of the navy in all respects but particularly in supplying it with the best means of dealing with the enemy's submarines. It will involve the immediate addition to the armed forces of the United States already provided for by law in case of war at least five hundred thousand men, who should, in my opinion, be chosen upon the principle of universal liability to service, and also the authorization of subsequent additional increments of equal force so soon as they may be needed and can be handled in training. It will involve also, of course, the granting of adequate credits to the government, sustained, I hope, so far as they can equitably be sustained by the present generation, by well-conceived taxation. . . .

We have no quarrel with the German people. We have no feeling toward them but one of sympathy and friendship. It was not upon their impulse that their government acted in entering this war. It was not with their previous knowledge or approval. It was a war determined upon as wars used to be determined upon in the old, unhappy days when peoples were nowhere consulted by their rulers and wars were provoked and waged in the interest of dynasties or of little groups of ambitious men who were accustomed to use their fellow men as pawns and tools. Self-governed nations do not fill their neighbor states with spies or set the course of intrigue to bring about some critical posture of affairs which will give them an opportunity to strike and make conquest. Such designs can be successfully worked out only under cover and where no one has the right to ask questions. Cunningly contrived plans of deception or aggression, carried, it may be, from generation to generation, can be worked out and kept from the light only within the privacy of courts or behind the carefully guarded confidences of a narrow and privileged class. They are happily impossible where public opinion commands and insists upon full information concerning all the nation's affairs.

A steadfast concert for peace can never be maintained except by a partnership of democratic nations. No autocratic government could be trusted to keep faith within it or observe its covenants. It must be a league of honor, a partnership of opinion. Intrigue would eat its vitals away; the plottings of inner circles who could plan what they would and render account to no one would be a corruption seated at its very heart. Only free peoples can hold their purpose and their honor steady to a common end and prefer the interests of mankind to any narrow interest of their own.

Does not every American feel that assurance has been added to our hope for the future peace of the world by the wonderful and heartening things that have been happening within the last few weeks in Russia? Russia was known by those who knew it best to have been always in fact democratic at heart, in all the vital habits of her thought, in all the intimate relationships of her people that spoke their natural instinct, their habitual attitude toward life. The autocracy that crowned the summit of her political structure, long as it had stood and terrible as was the reality of its power, was not in fact Russian in origin, character, or purpose; and now it has been shaken off and the great, generous Russian people have been added in all their naïve majesty and might to the forces that are fighting for freedom in the world, for justice, and for peace. Here is a fit partner for a League of Honor.

One of the things that has served to convince us that the Prussian autocracy was not and could never be our friend is that from the very outset of the present war it has filled our unsuspecting communities and even our offices of government with spies and set criminal intrigues everywhere afoot against our national unity of counsel, our peace within and without, our industries, and our commerce. Indeed, it is now evident that its spies were here even before the war began; and it is unhappily not a matter of conjecture but a fact proved in our courts of justice that the intrigues which have more than once come perilously near to disturbing the peace and dislocating the industries of the country have been carried on at the instigation, with the support, and even under the personal direction of official agents of the imperial government accredited to the government of the United States. Even in checking these things and trying to extirpate them we have sought to put the most generous interpretation possible upon them because we knew that their source lay not in any hostile feeling or purpose of the German people towards us (who were no doubt as ignorant of them as we ourselves were), but only in the selfish designs of a government that did what it pleased and told its people nothing. But they have played their part in serving to convince us at last that that government entertains no real friendship for us and means to act against our peace and security at its convenience. That it means to stir up enemies against us at our very doors the intercepted note to the German minister at Mexico City is eloquent evidence.

We are accepting this challenge of hostile purpose because we know that in such a government, following such methods, we can never have a friend; and that in the presence of its organized power, always lying in wait to accomplish we know not what purpose, there can be no assured security for the democratic governments of the world. We are now about to accept the gage of battle with this natural foe to liberty and shall, if necessary, spend the whole force of the nation to check and nullify its pretensions and its power. We are glad, now that we see the facts with no veil of false pretense about them, to fight thus for the ultimate peace of the world and for the liberation of its peoples, the German peoples

included: for the rights of nations great and small and the privilege of
men everywhere to choose their way of life and of obedience. The world
must be made safe for democracy. Its peace must be planted upon the
tested foundations of political liberty. We have no selfish ends to serve.
We desire no conquest, no dominion. We seek no indemnities for ourselves, no material compensation for the sacrifices we shall freely make.
We are but one of the champions of the rights of mankind. We shall be
satisfied when those rights have been made as secure as the faith and the
freedom of nations can make them.

Just because we fight without rancor and without selfish object, seeking nothing for ourselves but what we shall wish to share with all free
peoples, we shall, I feel confident, conduct our operations as belligerents
without passion and ourselves observe with proud punctilio the principles
of right and of fair play we profess to be fighting for. . . .

It will be all the easier for us to conduct ourselves as belligerents in
a high spirit of right and fairness because we act without animus, not in
enmity toward a people or with the desire to bring any injury or disadvantage upon them, but only in armed opposition to an irresponsible
government which has thrown aside all considerations of humanity and
of right and is running amuck. We are, let me say again, the sincere
friends of the German people, and shall desire nothing so much as the
early re-establishment of intimate relations of mutual advantage between
us—however hard it may be for them, for the time being, to believe that
this is spoken from our hearts. We have borne with their present government through all these bitter months because of that friendship—exercising a patience and forbearance which would otherwise have been
impossible. We shall, happily, still have an opportunity to prove that
friendship in our daily attitude and actions toward the millions of men and
women of German birth and native sympathy who live amongst us and
share our life, and we shall be proud to prove it toward all who are in
fact loyal to their neighbors and to the government in the hour of test.
They are, most of them, as true and loyal Americans as if they had never
known any other fealty or allegiance. They will be prompt to stand with
us in rebuking and restraining the few who may be of a different mind
and purpose. If there should be disloyalty, it will be dealt with with a
firm hand of stern repression; but, if it lifts its head at all, it will lift it
only here and there and without countenance except from a lawless and
malignant few.

It is a distressing and oppressive duty, gentlemen of the Congress,
which I have performed in thus addressing you. There are, it may be,
many months of fiery trial and sacrifice ahead of us. It is a fearful thing

to lead this great peaceful people into war, into the most terrible and disastrous of all wars, civilization itself seeming to be in the balance. But the right is more precious than peace, and we shall fight for the things which we have always carried nearest our hearts—for democracy, for the right of those who submit to authority to have a voice in their own governments, for the dominion of right by such a concert of free peoples as shall bring peace and safety to all nations and make the world itself at last free. To such a task we can dedicate our lives and our fortunes, everything that we are and everything that we have, with the pride of those who know that the day has come when America is privileged to spend her blood and her might for the principles that gave her birth and happiness and the peace which she has treasured. God helping her, she can do no other.

When the President had finished, there was perfect silence and then a tumult of wild applause. People crowded around to congratulate him and shake his hand—but there was no delight in his response. Two days later the decision for war was affirmed by an overwhelming vote. The peace President had become a war President with one constant demand—"force to the utmost."

The American people at large saw no inconsistency in Wilson's change of position. Rather, they felt the profound sincerity of the man, who, after holding out for peace for so long, now led them into war. And they followed him.

LENIN SPEAKS TO A STREET CROWD IN PETROGRAD

[Spring, 1917]

Just as Wilson was taking the United States into the war against Germany, the German government was granting safe-conduct through its territory to the famous Russian revolutionist, Lenin, the hope being that once back in Russia he would fan the flames of revolution and take Russia out of the war. That is what he did but he did a great deal else that was not anticipated by the obliging German government.

Born in Simbirsk (now Ulyanovsk), Lenin, whose real name was V. I. Ulyanov (1870–1924), was early diverted from the study and practice of law by the study and practice of the revolutionary doctrine of Karl Marx. After being twice banished to Siberia for revolutionary activity, he decided, in 1900, to continue his research and propaganda work abroad. Three years later the Russian Social Democratic party met in London and split, on theoretical questions, into two factions, the Bolsheviks (the majority group), led by Lenin, and the Mensheviks (the minority group), led by Plekhanov and others. When the 1905 Revolution broke out, Lenin returned to Russia and succeeded in persuading the Social Democrats to take part in the Duma, the legislative body set up by the imperial government. He returned shortly after to Switzerland and in the war years—1914–17—carried on a vigorous campaign against the aims and rationale of both sides, describing the war as imperialist, and urging soldiers to lay down their arms and desert. His return to Russia on the night of April 3, with the help of the German government, was the fulfillment of the scheming exile's fondest dream, and one of the most fateful turning points of modern history. Before Lenin arrived, Trotsky remarks in his History of the Russian Revolution, no one really knew what to do.

Lenin was at once involved in intrigue, conciliation, plans, preparations, exposure of false leaders, and education of the Russian masses, awakened for the first time in history. Soldiers and peasants streamed into Petrograd in endless columns. Of the continuous speechmaking their curiosity required, Lincoln Steffens, who had recently come to Russia to see the Revolution at first hand, has given a revealing description in his Autobiography:

"A mob in doubt would turn away, and leaving one crowd to stay and watch, the committee of hundreds would march off across the city, picking up other crowds to go and stand in front of the palace of the Czar's mistress, where 'a man named Lenin,' seeing them, would come out and speak. He spoke briefly, in a quiet tone of voice, so low that few could hear him. But when he had finished, those who had heard moved away; the mass closed up; the orator repeated his speech, and so for an hour or two the man named Lenin would deliver to the ever-changing masses his firm, short, quiet message. The day I got close enough to hear him, the crowd evidently had been troubled by the inactivity of Alexander Kerensky [who, representing the modern Laborites, had been in power since March, 1917] and some advice to them to go home and work, not to give all their time to their self-government. My interpreter repeated Lenin's manifolded speech afterward, as follows:

"Comrades, the revolution is on."

COMRADES, the revolution is on. The workers' revolution is on, and you are not working. The workers' and peasants' revolution means work, comrades; it does not mean idleness and leisure. That is a bourgeois ideal. The workers' revolution, a workers' government, means work, that all shall work; and here you are not working. You are only talking.

Oh, I can understand how you, the people of Russia, having been suppressed so long, should want, now that you have won to power, to talk and to listen to orators. But some day, soon, you—we all—must go to work and do things, act, produce results—food and socialism. And I can understand how you like and trust and put your hope in Kerensky. You want to give him time, a chance, to act. He means well, you say. He means socialism. But I warn you he will not make socialism. He may think socialism, he may mean socialism. But, comrades—I tell you Kerensky is an intellectual: he *cannot* act; he can talk; he cannot *act*. But you will not believe this yet. You will take time to give him time, and meanwhile, like Kerensky, you will not work. Very well, take your time. But when the hour strikes, when you are ready to go back yourselves to work and you want a government that will go to work and not only think socialism and talk socialism and mean socialism—when you want a government that will do socialism, then—come to the Bolsheviki."

LENIN MAKES A WORLD-SHAKING ANNOUNCEMENT

[November 7, 1917]

The eight months between the March Revolution, which ushered in Kerensky, and the November Revolution, which gave all power to the Soviets, were stormy and uncertain beyond comparison, and it required rare judgment to ride and rule the complex currents of men and events. Lenin was determined not to allow his Bolsheviks to be driven into premature insurrection. At first he opposed the July uprising, but when it gained momentum in spite of him, and he saw twenty thousand Kronstadt sailors ready to march on the provisional government, he relented and put his authority and forces behind it. The failure of this revolt and an order for his arrest forced him to flee to Finland, where in hiding he bided his time, waiting until the government had revealed its full incompetence and the revolutionary wave had reached its boiling point. On October 23, 1917, Lenin saw that the hour to strike had arrived. Returning to Petrograd, he persuaded the Bolsheviks that an armed insurrection must be organized immediately. Early in November he was to announce the conclusive triumph of the Bolsheviks.

"From now on, a new phase in the history of Russia begins."

COMRADES, the workers' and peasants' revolution, about the necessity of which the Bolsheviks have always spoken, has taken place.

What is the significance of this workers' and peasants' revolution? Its significance is, first of all, that we shall have a Soviet government, our own organ of power, in which the *bourgeoisie* will have no share whatever. The oppressed masses will themselves create a power. The old state apparatus will be shattered to its foundations and a new administrative apparatus set up in the shape of the Soviet organizations.

From now on, a new phase in the history of Russia begins, and this revolution, the third Russian revolution, should in the end lead to the victory of socialism.

One of our next tasks is to put an immediate end to the war. But in order to end this war, which is closely bound up with the present capitalist system, it is clear to everybody that capital itself must be overcome.

We shall be helped in this by the world working-class movement, which is already beginning to develop in Italy, England, and Germany.

The proposal for a just and immediate peace made by us to the international democracy will awaken an ardent response among the international proletarian masses everywhere. In order to strengthen this confidence of the proletariat, all the secret treaties must be published immediately.

Within Russia a huge section of the peasantry have said: We have played enough with the capitalists, we will now march with the workers. We shall secure the confidence of the peasants by a single decree putting an end to landed proprietorship. The peasants will understand that the salvation of the peasantry lies only in an alliance with the workers. We shall institute genuine workers' control over production.

We have now learned to work harmoniously. This is attested by the revolution that has just taken place. We possess the force of mass organization, which will overcome everything and which will lead the proletariat to the world revolution.

In Russia we must now set about building a proletarian socialist state.

Long live the world socialist revolution!

It would be too much to say that oratory alone makes history, but as the eloquence of the French Revolution and the November Revolution both testify, there are times when issues and passions are so delicately poised that the glowing word can shift the balance. Even those who completely disagreed with Lenin have testified to the impression of his ruthless integrity. While one listened to him it seemed impossible that he could be wrong. But it was the message and conviction that counted, not rhetorical skill in the classic sense.

TROTSKY RALLIES ONE OF HIS ARMIES DURING THE CIVIL WAR

[April, 1919]

When Lincoln Steffens boarded the ship that was to carry him to Russia, he learned that Trotsky and a band of fellow conspirators were in the steerage. Before Steffens could sound him out on the Revolution, however, Trotsky was taken off the ship in Halifax and detained by British authorities for several weeks.

Like Lenin, Leon Trotsky, whose real name was Lev Davydovich Bronstein (1879–1940), became a Marxian revolutionary in his youth, was arrested many times, and was twice exiled to Siberia. In London, at the beginning of this century, he collaborated with Lenin on the revolutionary paper Iskra (The Spark), but when the split between the Bolsheviks and Mensheviks occurred, Trotsky did not identify himself with either group. Returning to Russia in 1905, he worked with the Revolution and propounded at this time the famous doctrine of "permanent revolution," which implied that revolution in one country must be followed by revolution in other countries, eventually throughout the world. Banished again to Siberia, he escaped to Switzerland, then to France. When expelled from France, he went to the United States and founded his paper, Novy Mir (New World), in January, 1917, just a month before the February Revolution. After arriving in Russia in March, he worked valorously with Lenin, and when the November Revolution ended in Lenin's triumph, Trotsky became People's Commissar for Foreign Affairs in the Soviet government.

The Bolsheviks were at once confronted with the necessity of mobilizing vast armies to drive back the White Russians and foreign interventionists. Between 1918 and 1920, fourteen foreign expeditionary forces marched into the exhausted and war-weary country, and Denikin, Kolchak, and other White leaders led their forces against the hard-pressed Bolsheviks. To meet this many-sided thrust, the military oratory and organizing skill of Trotsky were peculiarly suited. For two and a half years, as he explains in My Life, he lived in his heavy armored train with two engines, traveling from one front to another, exhorting, rallying soldiers, directing success. The first trip, in August, 1918, was to the Czechoslovakian front, and in the next two years or so the famous armored train traveled, it is estimated, a distance of five trips around the world. The Red Army, in the meantime, grew from 800,000 to 3,000,000, fought on sixteen fronts simultaneously, and finally, against the best military predictions, defeated the numerous enemy decisively.

In his tireless dashes from front to front, Trotsky harangued not only disciplined armies, but also isolated villagers, bands of deserters, and disaffected and discouraged troops. He had to shape his language to every kind of audience, the sleeping, the hostile, the alienated, the friendly, the skeptical. And nearly always the audience was illiterate and cut off from the vital news that Trotsky could supply authoritatively. In such a seething situation, where persuasion depends so largely on disclosure of immediate fact, speeches can be instantly effective and historically momentous, yet, suited as they are to particular perils, they do not go down in the permanent record. The following is characteristic of the speeches Trotsky made to various regiments of the Red Army during these years.

"These spring months become the decisive months
in the history of Europe."

THE DECISIVE WEEKS in the history of mankind have arrived. The wave of enthusiasm over the establishment of a Soviet Republic in Hungary had hardly passed when the proletariat of Bavaria got possession of power and extended the hand of brotherly union to the Russian and Hungarian Republics. The workmen of Germany and Austria are hurrying in hundreds of thousands to Budapest, where they enter the ranks of the Red Army. The movement of the German proletariat, temporarily interrupted, again bursts forth with ever-increasing strength. Coal miners, metalworkers, and textile workers are sending brotherly greetings to the victorious Hungarian Republic and demand of the German Soviets a complete change of front, that is, a break with imperialists —their own, the English, French, and American—and the forming of a close union with Russia and Hungary. There is no doubt that this movement will be given a still more powerful swing by the victory of the proletariat in Bavaria, the Soviet government of which has broken all ties with the oppressors of Berlin and Weimar, with Ebert and Scheidemann, the servants of German imperialism, the murderers of Liebknecht and Rosa Luxemburg.

In Warsaw, which the Allied imperialists tried to make the center for the attack on Soviet Russia, the Polish proletariat rises in its full stature and through the Warsaw Soviet of Workmen's Deputies sends greetings to the Hungarian Soviet Republic.

The French Minister of Foreign Affairs, Pichon, the sworn enemy of the Russian Revolution, reports in Parliament on the sad state of affairs: "Odessa is being evacuated" [this was before the occupation of Odessa by Soviet troops]; "the Bolsheviks are penetrating the Crimean Peninsula, the situation in the north is not favorable." Things are not going well. The Greek soldiers landed on the shores of Crimea, according to the reports of Allied diplomats and newspapermen, were mounted on Crimean donkeys, but the donkeys were not able to arrive in time at the Perekop Isthmus. Things are not going well. Evidently even donkeys have begun to shake off the imperialistic harness.

Foreign consuls do not wish to leave the Ukraine and urge their governments to recognize the Ukrainian Republic. Wilson sent to Budapest not troops of occupation, to overthrow the Soviet Republic, but the honey-tongued General Smuts to negotiate with the Hungarian Council of People's Commissaries.

Wilson has definitely changed front and evidently has forced France to give up all hope of an armed crusade against Soviet Russia. War with Soviet Russia, which was demanded by the senseless French General, Foch, would take ten years in the opinion of the American statesman.

Less than six months have passed since the decisive victory of the Allies over the central empires; six months ago it seemed that the power of the Anglo-French and American imperialism was without limits.

At that time all the Russian counterrevolutionists had no doubt that the days of the Soviet Republic were numbered; but events now move steadfastly along the Soviet road. The working masses of the whole world are joining the flag of the Soviet authority, and the world robbers of imperialism are being betrayed even by the Crimean donkeys. At the present moment one awaits from day to day the victory of the Soviet Republic in Austria and in Germany. It is not impossible that the proletariat of Italy, Poland, or France will violate the logical order and outstrip the working class in other countries. These spring months become the decisive months in the history of Europe. At the same time this spring will decide definitely the fate of the bourgeois and rich peasant, anti-Soviet Russia.

In the east, Kolchak has mobilized all his forces, has thrown in all his reserves, for he knows definitely that if he does not win immediately, then he will never win. Spring has come, the spring that decides. Of course, the partial victories of Kolchak are insignificant in comparison with the general conquests of Soviet authority in Russia and in the whole world. What does the temporary loss of Ufa mean in the face of the occupation of Odessa, the movement into the Crimea, and especially the establishment of the Bavarian Soviet Republic? . . . What does the evacuation of Belebey, caused by military considerations, mean in the face of the powerful growth of the proletarian revolution in Poland and in Italy? Nevertheless, it would be criminal frivolity on our part to disregard the danger represented by the White Guardist bands of Kolchak on the east. Only stubbornness, steadfastness, watchfulness, and courage in the military struggle have guaranteed till now to the Russian Soviet Republic its international success. The victorious struggle of the Red Army on all fronts aroused the spirit of the European working class, and has made possible the establishment and strengthening first of the Hungarian and then of the Bavarian Republic. Our work has not yet been completed. The bands of Denikin have not been definitely defeated. The bands of Kolchak continue to move toward the Volga.

Spring has come; the spring that decides; our strength is increased tenfold by the consciousness of the fact that the wireless stations of Moscow, Kiev, Budapest, and Munich not only exchange brotherly greetings but business agreements respecting common defensive struggle. But at home, on our own territory, we must direct the main portion of our increased strength against the most dangerous enemy—against the Kolchak bands. Our comrades of the Volga district are well aware of this. In the province of Samara all Soviet institutions have been put on a war footing, and the best forces have been diverted to support the army, to form reserve regiments to carry on agitation of an educational character in the ranks of the Red Army. Party, Soviet, and trade-union organizations in Syzran have unanimously responded to the appeal of the central authority to support the eastern front. A special shock regiment is being organized from the workmen and popular elements, which only recently were groaning under the heel of the White Guardist. The Volga district is becoming the center of attention of all Soviet Russia. To carry out our international duty we must first of all break up the bands of Kolchak in order to support the victorious workmen of Hungary and Bavaria. In order to assist the uprising of workmen in Poland, Germany, and all Europe, we must establish definitely and irrefutably the Soviet authority over the whole extent of Russia.

To the Urals: this is the slogan of the Red Army and of the whole Soviet country.

The Urals will be the last stage in this bitter struggle. Victory in the Urals not only will give grain to the famished country and cotton to the textile industries, but will secure finally the well-earned rest of our heroic Red Army.

The eloquent and indefatigable Trotsky deserved much of the credit for the success of the Russian armies during those crucial years just after the Russian Revolution. Like Carnot, he was "the organizer of victory." In Lenin's Testament, there is a reference to Trotsky's "too far-reaching self-confidence"—a virtue in a kindler of armies. But in the new phase of the Bolshevist program, when close co-operation and skill in dealing with colleagues became essential, Trotsky did not prove adaptable. Or rather, it was decided that he was not to run the show. Charging that Stalin was a Rightist, he was gradually demoted and at last hounded out of the U.S.S.R.

EUGENE V. DEBS MAKES A STATEMENT TO THE COURT

[September 14, 1918]

Eugene Victor Debs (1855–1926) was born in Terre Haute, Indiana, of Alsatian parents. After his fifteenth year he became a locomotive fireman and, a few years later, a grocery clerk. In 1875 he helped to organize a lodge of the Brotherhood of Locomotive Firemen and thereafter was intimately connected with union organizational work. In 1893 he took part in forming the American Railway Union, of which he was chosen president, thereby triumphing in his theory that labor should be organized by industries and not by crafts. Unfortunately for the American Railway Union, it ran afoul of the law (as then interpreted) during the Pullman strike. Debs went to jail for contempt of court, and while in jail was converted to socialism through reading certain books.

In 1897 Debs formed the core of a Social Democratic party with the remains of his American Railway Union. Three years later, fusing this with the Socialist Labor party, he formed the Socialist party of America, whose first presidential candidate he became, polling 96,116 votes in 1900. A candidate in 1904, 1908, and 1912, in the last year he polled 901,062 votes—nearly six per cent of the total vote. His platform, says The Dictionary of American Biography, "was naïve and all-embracing; capitalism, with all its works, was an unqualified evil, and socialism, with all its promises, a panacea."

With the outbreak of the war in 1917 there were a number of arrests and convictions for interference with enlistment. After a speech in Canton in June, 1918, Debs was found guilty of violating the Espionage Act, in the Federal Court at Cleveland. Before Judge Westonhaver passed sentence, Debs gave the speech by which he is now chiefly remembered.

"And while there is a soul in prison, I am not free."

YOUR HONOR, years ago I recognized my kinship with all living beings, and I made up my mind that I was not one bit better than the meanest on earth. I said then, and I say now, that while there is a lower class, I am in it, while there is a criminal element, I am of it, and while there is a soul in prison, I am not free.

I listened to all that was said in this court in support and justification of this prosecution, but my mind remains unchanged. I look upon the Espionage Law as a despotic enactment in flagrant conflict with democratic principles and with the spirit of free institutions. . . .

Your Honor, I have stated in this court that I am opposed to the social system in which we live; that I believe in a fundamental change—but if possible by peaceable and orderly means. . . .

Standing here this morning, I recall my boyhood. At fourteen I went to work in a railroad shop; at sixteen I was firing a freight engine on a railroad. I remember all the hardships and privations of that earlier day, and from that time until now my heart has been with the working class. I could have been in Congress long ago. I have preferred to go to prison. . . .

I am thinking this morning of the men in the mills and factories; of the men in the mines and on the railroads. I am thinking of the women who for a paltry wage are compelled to work out their barren lives; of the little children who in this system are robbed of their childhood and in their tender years are seized in the remorseless grasp of Mammon and forced into the industrial dungeons, there to feed the monster machines while they themselves are being starved and stunted, body and soul. I see them dwarfed and diseased and their little lives broken and blasted because in this high noon of our twentieth-century Christian civilization money is still so much more important than the flesh and blood of childhood. In very truth gold is god today and rules with pitiless sway in the affairs of men.

In this country—the most favored beneath the bending skies—we have vast areas of the richest and most fertile soil, material resources in inexhaustible abundance, the most marvelous productive machinery on earth, and millions of eager workers ready to apply their labor to that machinery to produce in abundance for every man, woman, and child—and if there are still vast numbers of our people who are the victims of poverty and whose lives are an unceasing struggle all the way from youth to old age, until at last death comes to their rescue and stills their aching hearts and lulls these hapless victims to dreamless sleep, it is not the fault of the Almighty: it cannot be charged to nature, but it is due entirely to the outgrown social system in which we live, that ought to be abolished not only in the interest of the toiling masses but in the higher interest of all humanity. . . .

I believe, Your Honor, in common with all Socialists, that this nation ought to own and control its own industries. I believe, as all Socialists do, that all things that are jointly needed and used ought to be jointly owned —that industry, the basis of our social life, instead of being the private property of the few and operated for their enrichment, ought to be the common property of all, democratically administered in the interest of all. . . .

I am opposing a social order in which it is possible for one man who does absolutely nothing that is useful to amass a fortune of hundreds of millions of dollars, while millions of men and women who work all the days of their lives secure barely enough for a wretched existence.

This order of things cannot always endure. I have registered my protest against it. I recognize the feebleness of my effort, but fortunately I am not alone. There are multiplied thousands of others who, like myself, have come to realize that before we may truly enjoy the blessings of civilized life, we must reorganize society upon a mutual and co-operative basis; and to this end we have organized a great economic and political movement that spreads over the face of all the earth.

There are today upwards of sixty millions of Socialists, loyal, devoted adherents to this cause, regardless of nationality, race, creed, color, or sex. They are all making common cause. They are spreading with tireless energy the propaganda of the new social order. They are waiting, watching, and working hopefully through all the hours of the day and the night. They are still in a minority. But they have learned how to be patient and to bide their time. They feel—they know, indeed—that the time is coming, in spite of all opposition, all persecution, when this emancipating gospel will spread among all the peoples, and when this minority will become the triumphant majority and, sweeping into power, inaugurate the greatest social and economic change in history.

In that day we shall have the universal commonwealth—the harmonious co-operation of every nation with every other nation on earth. . . .

Your Honor, I ask no mercy and I plead for no immunity. I realize that finally the right must prevail. I never so clearly comprehended as now the great struggle between the powers of greed and exploitation on the one hand and upon the other the rising hosts of industrial freedom and social justice.

I can see the dawn of the better day for humanity. The people are awakening. In due time they will and must come to their own. . . .

I am now prepared to receive your sentence.

Although the spectators in the courtroom seemed deeply touched by Debs' words, Judge Westonhaver, unpersuaded and unmoved, declared himself "a conserver of the peace and a defender of the Constitution of the United States," and sentenced him to ten years in prison.

Three years later Debs was pardoned by President Harding, but his citizenship was not restored.

"I never met him," said Heywood Broun, "but I read many of his speeches, and most of them seemed to be second-rate utterances. But when his great moment came a miracle occurred. . . . He was for that one afternoon touched with inspiration. If anybody told me that tongues of fire danced upon his shoulders as he spoke, I would believe it."

However, the biographer Ray Ginger points out that Debs' famous speech was "a culmination, not an explosive miracle . . . an edited version of hundreds of his previous speeches, with a paragraph largely borrowed from John Brown."

PRESIDENT WILSON GOES TO THE PEOPLE IN BEHALF OF THE LEAGUE OF NATIONS

[September 25, 1919]

After more than four years of slaughter, the war came to an end, and then there was the battle over the peace treaty and the League of Nations. Before the United States entered the war, Wilson had begun to lay the ground for the League with a speech to the Senate on the essentials of peace.

No doubt others such as Elihu Root and William Howard Taft formulated the idea of the League before Wilson, and he might have been more generous in acknowledging them. But in appropriating the idea, he made it his own, he made himself its voice—and for that history will remember him.

History will also remember his tragic errors, which created so much hostility against the League before the Senate Foreign Relations Committee began to examine it in the summer of 1919. Those errors, according to Charles Seymour, were: "(1) his request for a Democratic victory at the polls in the fall of 1918, as a personal vindication of himself; (2) his failure to take a Republican or even a member of the treaty-making Senate to the Paris peace conference; (3) his insistence on going to the conference himself and losing his world prestige in the melee of international horse trading."

When he found that the League Covenant would pass the Senate only with reservations (which he thought would fatally emasculate it), he decided to present the case to the American people and, at the age of sixty-three, set out on the most heroic speaking tour in history—thirty full-length speeches in twenty days.

We quote the last two paragraphs of the final speech, at Pueblo, Colorado.

"Men will see the truth."

M Y FRIENDS, on last Decoration Day I went to a beautiful hillside near Paris, where was located the cemetery of Suresnes, a cemetery given over to the burial of the American dead. Behind me on the slopes was rank upon rank of living American soldiers, and lying before me upon the levels of the plain was rank upon rank of departed American soldiers. Right by the side of the stand where I spoke there was a little group of Frenchwomen who had adopted those graves, had made themselves mothers of those dear ghosts by putting flowers every day upon those graves, taking them as their own sons, their own beloved, because they had died in the same cause—France was free and the world was free because America had come! I wish some men in public life who are now opposing the settlement for which these men died could visit such a spot as that. I wish that the thought that comes out of those graves could penetrate their consciousness. I wish that they could feel the moral obligation that rests upon us not to go back on those boys, but to see the thing through, to see it through to the end and make good their redemption of the world. For nothing less depends upon this decision, nothing less than the liberation and salvation of the world.

You will say, "Is the League an absolute guarantee against war?" No; I do not know any absolute guarantee against the errors of human judgment or the violence of human passion, but I tell you this: with a cooling space of nine months for human passion, not much of it will keep hot. I had a couple of friends who were in the habit of losing their tempers, and when they lost their tempers they were in the habit of using very unparliamentary language. Some of their friends induced them to make a promise that they never would swear inside the town limits. When the impulse next came upon them, they took a streetcar to go out of town to swear, and by the time they got out of town they did not want to swear. They came back convinced that they were just what they were, a couple of unspeakable fools, and the habit of getting angry and of swearing suffered great inroads upon it by that experience. Now, illustrating the great by the small, that is true of the passions of nations. It is true of the passions of men, however you combine them. Give them space to cool off. I ask you this: if it is not an absolute insurance against war, do you want no insurance at all? Do you want nothing? Do you want not only no probability that war will not recur, but the probability that it will recur? The arrangements of justice do not stand of themselves, my fellow citizens. The arrangements of this treaty are just, but they need the support of the combined power of the great nations of the world. And they will have that support. Now that the mists of this great question have cleared away, I believe that men will see the truth, eye to eye and face to face. There is one thing that the American people always rise to and extend their hand to, and that is the truth of justice and of liberty and of peace. We have accepted that truth and we are going to be led by it, and it is going to lead us, and through us the world, out into pastures of quietness and peace such as the world never dreamed of before.

That was the end. The crusading President collapsed. The tour had to be canceled, and Wilson returned to the White House an old, exhausted, broken man.

But one may be pardoned a poignant "if." Harry S. Truman, no great speaker, managed to win the presidential election in a whirlwind trip, aided by the loud-speaker and radio, in 1948. Is it absurd to imagine that the eloquent Wilson, with his energies conserved by those devices, might have won the United States to the League of Nations and so forestalled the Second World War?

For the remainder of his term—fifteen critical months—Woodrow Wilson lay crippled in the White House, cut off from his friends as well as his enemies. But so adamant was he about the unmodified Covenant of the League of Nations that he directed his own followers to vote with its most bitter opponents. Even then the League, with the Lodge reservations, was defeated in the Senate by only a small margin.

PART EIGHTEEN

A SICK WORLD

WITH THE END of the War to End War, of the War to Make the World Safe for Democracy, human hopes reached their pinnacle, and for a moment Woodrow Wilson was the adored embodiment of those hopes. Never had so many looked so confidently to one human being. On the morning of November 11, 1918, the President wrote a message to his fellow countrymen: "The armistice was signed this morning. Everything for which America fought has been accomplished. It will now be our fortunate duty to assist by example, by sober, friendly counsel, and by material aid in the establishment of just democracy throughout the world." But with the compromises of the peace treaty and the failure of the United States to join the League of Nations, due to the tragic stubbornness of Wilson and his opponents, disillusionment stole over most of the Western world.

Meanwhile the Soviet Union was growing ruthlessly, Fascism was emerging, and Naziism lurked in the shadows. The apparently benign principle of the self-determination of peoples was taking the form of a rampant nationalism around the globe. If nationalism was good for the West, why wouldn't it be good for the East? China under the inspiration of Sun Yat-sen and India under the leadership of Gandhi were taking the lesson to heart.

In Vienna, Freud was thinking about war and death, about civilization and its discontents.

GANDHI PROPOUNDS HIS FAITH BEFORE AN ENGLISH JUDGE

[March 23, 1922]

While the Peace Conference was getting underway in Paris early in 1919, a new kind of conflict was beginning in India, a conflict that was to hasten the dismemberment of the British Empire. For it was then that Gandhi began to take an active part in the Indian nationalist movement. Hundreds of eloquent men had preceded him in the struggle. "But this voice was somehow different from the others," Nehru afterward wrote from prison to his daughter. "It was quiet and low, and yet it could be heard above the shouting of the multitude; it was soft and gentle, and yet there seemed to be steel hidden away somewhere in it; it was courteous and full of appeal, and yet there was something grim and frightening in it; every word used was full of meaning and seemed to carry a deadly earnestness. Behind the language of peace and friendship there was power and the quivering shadow of action."

Mohandas Karamchand Gandhi (1869–1948) was born into a middle-class, middle-caste family. After a general education in India he studied law in London, passed the bar examination, and returned home for two years of unpromising practice. In 1893 he went to South Africa to work on a single case, but a few days after landing at Durban, Natal, he was thrown out of a first-class train compartment and thus quickly learned about discrimination against Indians in that part of the world. Instead of leaving after completing his case, he remained in South Africa almost continuously for twenty years. Although he now flourished in his profession, he gave it up entirely about 1900 to devote all his attention to fighting the unjust laws against his countrymen. But it was a new kind of fighting—Satyagraha.

"The term Satyagraha was coined by me in South Africa," said Gandhi, "to express the force that the Indians there used for full eight years, and it was coined in order to distinguish it from the movement then going on in the United Kingdom and South Africa under the name of Passive Resistance.

"Its root meaning is 'holding on to truth,' hence truth-force. I have also called it love-force or soul-force. In the application of Satyagraha, I discovered in the earliest stages that pursuit of truth did not admit of violence being inflicted on one's opponent, but that he must be weaned from error by patience and sympathy. For what appears to be truth to the one may appear to be error to the other. And patience means self-suffering. So the doctrine came to mean vindication of truth, not by the infliction of suffering on the opponent, but on one's self."

The prolonged application of Satyagraha, or nonviolent non-co-operation, did not by any means remove all of the legal discrimination against Indians in South Africa, but it enabled them to live and move with more freedom and dignity. So many concessions had been wrung from General Smuts and his white supporters by 1914 that Gandhi could leave for India with a quiet sense of moral victory.

After settling in India with a small colony of disciples, he began his long crusade against untouchability; he improved the lot of the indigo share-croppers and supported striking textile workers. But as late as July, 1918, he urged Indians to take up arms in defense of the Empire, for he thought such loyalty would ensure for his people more liberty and participation in the government after the war.

The fateful shock came with the passage of the Rowlatt Acts which "gave great powers to the government and the police to arrest, keep in prison without trial, or to have a secret trial of, any person they disapproved of or suspected." In protest Gandhi at once called a nation-wide hartal, a complete cessation of work and business—his first overt act against the British government of India. It spread throughout the country and paralyzed activity, but violence broke out here and there. Realizing that the people were not yet ready for such mass movements, that he had committed a "Himalayan miscalculation," Gandhi suspended the hartal on April 6, 1919. But in Amritsar, a week later, a crowd of some ten or twenty thousand was fired upon by General Dyer's troops, and nearly four hundred were killed, over a thousand wounded. Most of the crowd apparently did not realize that public processions and assemblies had been prohibited. In any case the "lesson" had been unduly severe, and coming immediately after the enactment of the Rowlatt Acts, it was doubly indelible.

Against this dark background Gandhi now moved forward with infectious self-confidence, drawing more and more determined people to him and taking over the leadership of the Indian National Congress. In 1920 the Congress adopted his program of nonviolent, non-co-operation, Satyagraha, on a far wider scale than ever attempted in South Africa. In support of the program Gandhi traveled up and down the frenzied country for seven months, making hundreds of speeches, sometimes to mass meetings of a hundred thousand or more. He was always under the shadow of the police, but in 1922 he was arrested, charged with sedition for three of his articles in his magazine, Young India. At the conclusion of "the great trial" in the crowded little courtroom of Ahmadabad, Gandhi was asked by the judge if he wished to make a statement before receiving sentence.

"Nonviolence is the first article of my faith."

BEFORE I READ this statement, I would like to state that I entirely endorse the learned Advocate General's remarks in connection with my humble self. I think that he was entirely fair to me in all the statements that he has made, because it is very true and I have no desire whatsoever to conceal from this court the fact that to preach disaffection toward the existing system of government has become almost a passion with me; and the learned Advocate General is also entirely in the right when he says that my preaching of disaffection did not commence with my connection with *Young India*, but that it commenced much earlier; and in the statement that I am about to read, it will be my painful duty to admit before this court that it commenced much earlier than the period stated by the Advocate General. It is the most painful duty with me, but I have to discharge that duty knowing the responsibility that rests upon my shoulders, and I wish to endorse all the blame that the learned Advocate General has thrown on my shoulders, in connection with the Bombay occurrences, Madras occurrences, and the Chauri Chaura occurrences. Thinking over these deeply and sleeping over them night after night, it is impossible for me to dissociate myself from the diabolical crimes of Chauri Chaura or the mad outrages of Bombay. He is quite right when he says that as a man of responsibility, a man having received a fair share of education, having had a fair share of experience of this world, I should have known the consequences of every one of my acts. I know that I was playing with fire. I ran the risk, and if I was set free, I would still do the same. I have felt it this morning that I would have failed in my duty, if I did not say what I said here just now.

I wanted to avoid violence, I want to avoid violence. Nonviolence is the first article of my faith. It is also the last article of my creed. But I had to make my choice. I had either to submit to a system which I considered had done an irreparable harm to my country, or incur the risk of the mad fury of my people bursting forth, when they understood the truth from my lips. I know that my people have sometimes gone mad. I am deeply sorry for it and I am therefore here to submit not to a light penalty but to the highest penalty. I do not ask for mercy. I do not plead any extenuating act. I am here, therefore, to invite and cheerfully submit to the highest penalty that can be inflicted upon me for what in law is a deliberate crime and what appears to me to be the highest duty of a citizen. The only course open to you, the judge, is, as I am just going to say in my statement, either to resign your post or inflict on me the severest penalty, if you believe that the system and law you are assisting to administer are good for the people. I do not expect that kind of conversion, but by the time I have finished with my statement, you will perhaps have a glimpse of what is raging within my breast to run this maddest risk which a sane man can run.

[The following statement was then read.]

I owe it perhaps to the Indian public and to the public in England to placate which this prosecution is mainly taken up that I should explain why from a stanch loyalist and co-operator I have become an uncompromising disaffectionist and non-co-operator. To the court too I should say why I plead guilty to the charge of promoting disaffection toward the government established by law in India.

My public life began in 1893 in South Africa in troubled weather. My first contact with British authority in that country was not of a happy character. I discovered that as a man and as an Indian I had no rights. More correctly, I discovered that I had no rights as a man because I was an Indian.

But I was not baffled. I thought that this treatment of Indians was an excrescence upon a system that was intrinsically and mainly good. I gave the government my voluntary and hearty co-operation, criticizing it freely where I felt it was faulty but never wishing its destruction.

Consequently, when the existence of the Empire was threatened in 1899 by the Boer challenge, I offered my services to it, raised a volunteer ambulance corps, and served at several actions that took place for the relief of Ladysmith. Similarly in 1906, at the time of the Zulu revolt, I raised a stretcher-bearer party and served till the end of the "rebellion." On both these occasions I received medals and was even mentioned in dispatches. For my work in South Africa I was given by Lord Hardinge a Kaiser-i-Hind Gold Medal. When the war broke out in 1914 between England and Germany, I raised a volunteer ambulance corps in London consisting of the then resident Indians in London, chiefly students. Its work was acknowledged by the authorities to be valuable. Lastly, in India, when a special appeal was made at the War Conference in Delhi in 1918 by Lord Chelmsford for recruits, I struggled at the cost of my health to raise a corps in Kheda, and the response was being made when the hostilities ceased and orders were received that no more recruits were wanted. In all these efforts at service I was actuated by the belief that it was possible by such services to gain a status of full equality in the Empire for my countrymen.

The first shock came in the shape of the Rowlatt Act, a law designed to rob the people of all real freedom. I felt called upon to lead an intensive agitation against it. Then followed the Punjab horrors beginning with the massacre at Jallianwala Bagh and culminating in crawling orders, public floggings, and other indescribable humiliations. I discovered too that the plighted word of the Prime Minister to the Mussulmans of India regarding the integrity of Turkey and the holy places of Islam was not likely to be fulfilled. But in spite of the forebodings and the grave warnings of friends, at the Amritsar Congress in 1919, I fought for co-operation and working with the Montagu-Chelmsford reforms, hoping that the Prime Minister would redeem his promise to the Indian Mussulmans, that the Pubjab wound would be healed, and that the reforms, inadequate and unsatisfactory though they were, marked a new era of hope in the life of India.

But all that hope was shattered. The Khilafat promise was not to be redeemed. The Punjab crime was whitewashed and most culprits went not only unpunished but remained in service and in some cases continued to draw pensions from the Indian revenue, and in some cases were even rewarded. I saw too that not only did the reforms not mark a change of heart, but they were only a method of further draining India of her wealth and of prolonging her servitude.

I came reluctantly to the conclusion that the British connection had made India more helpless than she ever was before, politically and economically. A disarmed India has no power of resistance against any aggressor if she wanted to engage in an armed conflict with him. So much is this the case that some of our best men consider that India must take generations before she can achieve the Dominion status. She has become so poor that she has little power of resisting famines. Before the British advent, India spun and wove in her millions of cottages just the supplement she needed for adding to her meager agricultural resources. This cottage industry, so vital for India's existence, has been ruined by incredibly heartless and inhuman processes as described by English witnesses. Little do town dwellers know how the semistarved masses of India are slowly sinking to lifelessness. Little do they know that their miserable comfort represents the brokerage they get for the work they do for the foreign exploiter, that the profits and the brokerage are sucked from the masses. Little do they realize that the government established by law in British India is carried on for this exploitation of the masses. No sophistry, no jugglery in figures can explain away the evidence that the skeletons in many villages present to the naked eye. I have no doubt whatsoever that both England and the town dwellers of India will have to answer, if there is a God above, for this crime against humanity which is perhaps unequaled in history. The law itself in this country has been used to serve the foreign exploiter. My unbiased examination of the Punjab Martial Law cases has led me to believe that at least ninety-five per cent of convictions were wholly bad. My experience of political cases in India leads me to the conclusion that in nine out of every ten the condemned men were totally innocent. Their crime consisted in the love of their country. In ninety-nine cases out of a hundred justice has been denied to Indians as against Europeans in the courts of India. This is not an exaggerated picture. It is the experience of almost every Indian who has had anything to do with such cases. In my opinion, the administration of the law is thus prostituted consciously or unconsciously for the benefit of the exploiter.

The greatest misfortune is that Englishmen and their Indian associates in the administration of the country do not know that they are engaged in the crime I have attempted to describe. I am satisfied that many Englishmen and Indian officials honestly believe that they are administering one of the best systems devised in the world and that India is making steady though slow progress. They do not know that a subtle but effective system of terrorism and an organized display of force on the one hand, and the deprivation of all powers of retaliation or self-defense on the other, have emasculated the people and induced in them the habit of simulation. This awful habit has added to the ignorance and the self-deception of the administrators. Section 124-A, under which I am happily charged, is perhaps the prince among the political sections of the Indian Penal Code designed to suppress the liberty of the citizen. Affection cannot be manufactured or regulated by law. If one has an affection for a person or system, one should be free to give the fullest expression to his disaffection, so long as he does not contemplate, promote, or incite to violence. But the section under which Mr. Banker [a colleague in nonviolence] and I are charged is one under which mere promotion of disaffection is a crime. I have studied some of the cases tried under it, and I know that some of the most loved of India's patriots have been convicted under it. I consider it a privilege, therefore, to be charged under that section. I have endeavored to give in their briefest outline the reasons for my disaffection. I have no personal ill will against any single administrator, much less can I have any disaffection toward the King's person. But I hold it to be a virtue to be disaffected toward a government which in its totality has done more harm to India than any previous system. India is less manly under the British rule than she ever was before. Holding such a belief, I consider it to be a sin to have affection for the system. And it has been a precious privilege for me to be able to write what I have in the various articles, tendered in evidence against me.

In fact, I believe that I have rendered a service to India and England by showing in non-co-operation the way out of the unnatural state in which both are living. In my humble opinion, non-co-operation with evil is as much a duty as is co-operation with good. But in the past, non-co-operation has been deliberately expressed in violence to the evildoer. I am endeavoring to show to my countrymen that violent non-co-operation only multiplies evil and that as evil can only be sustained by violence, withdrawal of support of evil requires complete abstention from violence.

Nonviolence implies voluntary submission to the penalty for non-co-operation with evil. I am here, therefore, to invite and submit cheerfully to the highest penalty that can be inflicted upon me for what in law is a deliberate crime and what appears to me to be the highest duty of a citizen. The only course open to you, the judge, is either to resign your post, and thus dissociate yourself from evil if you feel that the law you are called upon to administer is an evil and that in reality I am innocent, or to inflict on me the severest penalty if you believe that the system and the law you are assisting to administer are good for the people of this country and that my activity is therefore injurious to the public weal.

Passing sentence on Gandhi, his judge confessed, presented a problem of the utmost difficulty. Though Gandhi was evidently of a noble and even saintly character, quite different "from any person I have ever tried or am likely to have to try," it was his painful task, since the law is no respecter of persons, to consider him solely in the character of a criminal. In attempting to balance what was due to Gandhi and what was in the public interest, he imposed a sentence of six years' imprisonment, two years for each count of the charge. When the sentence was passed, Gandhi said it was as light as any judge would inflict on him, and thanked the court for its courtesy. Then the people moved forward and fell at Gandhi's feet, sobbing. Calm and smiling, he looked over their heads, giving encouragement, and, when his friends had left the court, he was led away to Sabarmati jail.

MUSSOLINI RENDERS HIS FIRST ACCOUNT TO THE CHAMBER OF DEPUTIES

[November 16, 1922]

In 1922, on returning to India from the first Round Table Conference in London, Gandhi stopped off in Rome. He had ten minutes with Mussolini, but, unsurprisingly enough, there was no meeting of the minds. Two men could be hardly more unlike in character, in philosophy, in public address. Yet each played a major role in the era between wars, and each came to a violent end.

In perspective Mussolini has already become too small a figure. We remember from the newsreels the jutting jaw and myopic eyes of the balcony orator, or the final picture of the corpse strung up by the feet at the side of his mistress. If Mussolini was a joke on humanity, he was a terribly grim joke. He held Italy in his ruthless hands for more than twenty years. He was a model for Hitler and Dollfuss, for Salazar and Franco, and "the greatest figure of this sphere and time" for many respectable Englishmen and Americans. His war on Ethiopia was a link in a chain of aggression that led straight to the second World War.

Far from being an absurd speaker, Mussolini, in relation to his audience and his time, was as impressive as Hitler, Churchill, or Roosevelt. True, he was flamboyant, melodramatic, but he was a master of stark, marching sentences. He was skilled in sinister irony and rhetorical questions. If Hitler could dominate a people steeped in Wagner, Mussolini was the man for crowds steeped in Verdi and Leoncavallo.

Benito Mussolini (1883–1945) was the son of a Socialist blacksmith and a schoolteacher. He was named for the Mexican revolutionist, Benito Juárez, and grew up with a revolutionary bent that made him unwelcome in Switzerland, France, and Austria, and suspect at home. As an orthodox Socialist, he condemned Italy's war with Turkey, which resulted in the seizure of Tripoli (1911), and as the vigorous editor of the Socialist paper, Avanti, at the beginning of the first World War, he spoke out for Italian neutrality rather than war on the side of the Central Powers, which treaty obligations demanded. This was his position as late as September 21, 1914, but within four days he was advocating war on the side of the Triple Entente of Great Britain, France, and Russia. Whether this sudden switch was mainly inspired by humanitarian motives, political insight, or French money, he was forced to resign from Avanti and was promptly read out of the Socialist party. Henceforth his course lay toward intense nationalism and revolution from the right.

His brief war experience ended with the explosion of a trench mortar that introduced pellets into his buttocks. Returning to journalism—anti-Socialist journalism—he advised a strong hand with the war workers and, after the overwhelming defeat at Caporetto, he began to form small Fascist groups to restore civilian and military morale. The Italian forces did make something of a comeback and finished the war on the winning side, but Italy was not rewarded at the peace settlement with the expected slice of Dalmatia.

In the midst of economic disorder and political hesitation, with thousands of unemployed veterans contributing their bitterness to the general disillusionment, Fascist groups found fertile soil. Out of the chaos they helped to create, they presented themselves as the party of order and honor, with the help of costumes and rituals suggested by D'Annunzio. In October, 1922, they marched on Rome—in sleeping cars—and King Victor Emmanuel II phoned Mussolini in Milan: "Won't you come and be my Prime Minister?"

On November 16, the new Prime Minister addressed the Chamber of Deputies for the first time. In commenting on Fascist moderation, he said: "I could have made of this dull and gray hall a bivouac for corpses. I could have nailed up the doors of Parliament and have established an exclusively Fascist government. I could have done those things, but—at least for a time—I did not do them." And he concluded:

"The country cheers us and waits."

FROM further communications you will know the Fascist program in its details. I do not want, so long as I can avoid it, to rule against the Chamber; but the Chamber must feel its own position. That position opens the possibility that it may be dissolved in two days or in two years. We ask full powers because we want to assume full responsibility. Without full powers you know very well that we couldn't save one lira—I say one lira. We do not want to exclude the possibility of voluntary co-operation, for we will cordially accept it, if it comes from deputies, senators, or even from competent private citizens. Every one of us has a religious sense of our difficult task. The country cheers us and waits. We will give it not words but facts. We formally and solemnly promise to restore the budget to health. And we will restore it. We want to make a foreign policy of peace, but at the same time one of dignity and steadiness. We will do it. We intend to give the nation a discipline. We will give it. Let none of our enemies of yesterday, of today, of tomorrow cherish illusions in regard to our permanence in power. Foolish and childish illusions, like those of yesterday!

Our government has a formidable foundation in the conscience of the nation. It is supported by the best, the newest Italian generations. There is no doubt that in these last years a great step toward the unification of spirit has been made. The fatherland has again found itself bound together from north to south, from the continent to the generous islands, which will never be forgotten, from the metropolis of the active colonies of the Mediterranean and the Atlantic Ocean. Do not, gentlemen, address more vain words to the nation. Fifty-two applications to speak upon my message to Parliament are too many. Let us, instead of talking, work with pure heart and ready mind to assure the prosperity and the greatness of the country.

May God assist me in bringing to a triumphant end my hard labor.

For comment on this speech, how can we do better than quote from Mussolini's autobiography? "I do not believe," he said, "that since 1870 the hall of Monte Citorio had heard such energetic and clear words. They burned with a passion deep in my being. . . . My political instinct told me that from that moment there would rise, with increasing truth and with increasing expansion of Fascist activity, the dawn of a new history for Italy. And perhaps the dawn of a new path for civilization."

CLARENCE DARROW PLEADS FOR JUSTICE FOR THE NEGRO

[May 19, 1926]

If the ultimate test of a speech lies in the effect, then Clarence Darrow (1857–1938), the lank, Lincolnesque attorney from Chicago who dominated hundreds of courtrooms for over forty years, must be reckoned with. Unlike that of many lawyers, his point of view was clear and obvious: he was a militant agnostic, a fanatical humanitarian, a spokesman for the underdog, a lifelong opponent of capital punishment. More than a hundred of his clients were charged with murder, but not one of them was executed.

After serving as corporation counsel for Chicago and then as general counsel for the Chicago and Northwestern Railway, he resigned in 1894 in order to defend Eugene Debs from imprisonment in connection with the Pullman strike. Debs was acquitted, and thereafter Darrow was involved in an unbroken series of important or sensational cases. In 1906 he secured the acquittal of "Wild Bill" Haywood and his associates, charged with the murder of former Governor Steunenberg of Idaho. A few years later he represented the McNamara brothers in the Los Angeles Times dynamiting case and, with the plea of "Guilty," saved them from the noose. He won life imprisonment for Loeb and Leopold, the Chicago "thrill murderers" of the twenties. He was the chief attorney for John T. Scopes, the Tennessee schoolteacher, who violated the state's anti-evolution laws. William Jennings Bryan, representing the state, secured the conviction of Scopes, but Darrow, who convicted obscurantism before the world, won the wider decision.

Darrow was sixty-nine, in 1926, when he tried the two Sweet cases in Detroit, where some sixty thousand Negroes lived in crowded quarters better suited to six thousand. So great was the congestion that some Negro families had moved to the so-called white districts, but by threats and violence were regularly driven out. Among the Negroes who dared the wrath and prejudice of the whites was Dr. Ossian Sweet, who had worked his way through college and the medical school at Ann Arbor and had taken a·postgraduate course in

Europe. Since a number of Negroes had been driven from their homes in the neighborhood of his house, he provided himself with guns and ammunition, and when a huge crowd attacked, he and his relatives and friends, who had banded together for protection, fired a volley into the street. The police at once entered the house, and eleven Negroes, with Dr. Sweet at their head, were arrested. One white man had been killed in the fusillade, and although lynching did not occur in this case, anti-Negro feeling in Detroit ran high. A jury panel was finally selected for a mass trial of all eleven, and Darrow became lawyer for the defense. Although he argued the case with vigor and brilliance, and the judge, Frank Murphy, was fair and impartial, the jurors could not agree and were dismissed. A month later the state ordered a retrial, this time making Henry Sweet, the doctor's brother, who had apparently fired the fatal shot, the sole defendant. This trial was a replica of the first, except for Darrow's final plea.

"I do not believe in the law of hate."

WE COME NOW to lay this man's case in the hands of a jury of our peers—the first defense and the last defense is the protection of home and life as provided by our law. We are willing to leave it here. I feel, as I look at you, that we will be treated fairly and decently, even understandingly and kindly. You know what this case is. You know why it is. You know that if white men had been fighting their way against colored men, nobody would ever have dreamed of a prosecution. And you know that from the beginning of this case to the end, up to the time you write your verdict, the prosecution is based on race prejudice and nothing else.

Gentlemen, I feel deeply on this subject; I cannot help it. Let us take a little glance at the history of the Negro race. It only needs a minute. It seems to me that the story would melt hearts of stone. I was born in America. I could have left it if I had wanted to go away. Some other men, reading about this land of freedom that we brag about on the Fourth of July, came voluntarily to America. These men, the defendants, are here because they could not help it. Their ancestors were captured in the jungles and on the plains of Africa, captured as you capture wild beasts, torn from their homes and their kindred; loaded into slave ships, packed like sardines in a box, half of them dying on the ocean passage; some jumping into the sea in their frenzy, when they had a chance to choose death in place of slavery. They were captured and brought here. They could not help it. They were bought and sold as slaves, to work without pay, because they were black. They were subject to all of this for generations, until finally they were given their liberty, so far as the law goes—and that is only a little way, because, after all, every human being's life in this world is inevitably mixed with every other life and, no matter what laws we pass, no matter what precautions we take, unless the people we meet are kindly and decent and human and liberty-loving, then there is no liberty. Freedom comes from human beings, rather than from laws and institutions.

Now, that is their history. These people are the children of slavery. If the race that we belong to owes anything to any human being, or to any power in the universe, they owe it to these black men. Above all other men, they owe an obligation and a duty to these black men that can never be repaid. I never see one of them that I do not feel I ought to pay part of the debt of my race—and if you gentlemen feel as you should feel in this case, your emotions will be like mine.

Gentlemen, you are called into this case by chance. It took us a week to find you, a week of culling out prejudice and hatred. Probably we did not cull it all out at that; but we took the best and the fairest that we could find. It is up to you.

Your verdict means something in this case. It means something more than the fate of this boy. It is not often that a case is submitted to twelve men where the decision may mean a milestone in the history of the human race. But this case does. And I hope and I trust that you have a feeling of responsibility that will make you take it and do your duty as citizens of a great nation, and as members of the human family, which is better still.

Let me say just a parting word for Henry Sweet, who has well-nigh been forgotten. I am serious, but it seems almost like a reflection upon this jury to talk as if I doubted your verdict. What has this boy done? This one boy now that I am culling out from all of the rest, and whose fate is in your hands—can you tell me what he has done? Can I believe myself? Am I standing in a court of justice where twelve men on their oaths are asked to take away the liberty of a boy twenty-one years of age, who has done nothing more than what Henry Sweet has done?

Gentlemen, you may think he shot too quick; you may think he erred in judgment; you may think that Dr. Sweet should not have gone there prepared to defend his home. But, what of this case of Henry Sweet? What has he done? I want to put it up to you, each one of you, individually. Dr. Sweet was his elder brother. He had helped Henry through school. He loved him. He had taken him into his home. Henry had lived with him and his wife; he had fondled his baby. The doctor had promised

Henry the money to go through school. Henry was getting his education, to take his place in the world, gentlemen—and this is a hard job. With his brother's help he has worked his way through college up to the last year. The doctor had bought a home. He feared danger. He moved in with his wife and he asked this boy to go with him. And this boy went to defend his brother, and his brother's wife and his child and his home.

Do you think more of him or less of him for that? I never saw twelve men in my life—and I have looked at a good many faces of a good many juries—I never saw twelve men in my life that, if you could get them to understand a human case, were not true and right.

Should this boy have gone along and helped his brother? Or, should he have stayed away? What would you have done? And yet, gentlemen, here is a boy, and the president of his college came all the way from Ohio to tell you what he thinks of him. His teachers have come here, from Ohio, to tell you what they think of him. The Methodist bishop has come here to tell you what he thinks of him.

So, gentlemen, I am justified in saying that this boy is as kindly, as well disposed, as decent a man as one of you twelve. Do you think he ought to be taken out of his school and sent to the penitentiary? All right, gentlemen, if you think so, do it. It is your job, not mine. If you think so, do it. But if you do, gentlemen, if you should ever look into the face of your own boy, or your own brother, or look into your own heart, you will regret it in sackcloth and ashes. You know, if he committed any offense, it was being loyal and true to his brother whom he loved. I know where you will send him and it will not be to a penitentiary.

Now, gentlemen, just one more word, and I am through with this case. I do not live in Detroit. But I have no feeling against this city. In fact, I shall always have the kindest remembrance of it, especially if this case results as I think and feel it will. I am the last one to come here to stir up race hatred, or any other hatred. I do not believe in the law of hate. I may not be true to my ideals always, but I believe in the law of love, and I believe you can do nothing with hatred. I would like to see a time when man loves his fellow man and forgets his color or his creed. We will never be civilized until that time comes. I know the Negro race has a long road to go. I believe that the life of the Negro race has been a life of tragedy, of injustice, of oppression. The law has made him equal, but man has not. And, after all, the last analysis is: what has man done?—and not what has the law done? I know there is a long road ahead of him before he can take the place which I believe he should take. I know that before him there is sorrow, tribulation, and death among the blacks, and perhaps the whites. I am sorry. I would do what I could to avert it. I would advise patience; I would advise tolerance; I would advise understanding; I would advise all those things which are necessary for men who live together.

Gentlemen, what do you think of your duty in this case? I have watched day after day these black, tense faces that have crowded this court. These black faces that now are looking to you twelve whites, feeling that the hopes and fears of a race are in your keeping.

This case is about to end, gentlemen. To them, it is life. Not one of their color sits on this jury. Their fate is in the hands of twelve whites. Their eyes are fixed on you, their hearts go out to you, and their hopes hang on your verdict.

This is all. I ask you, on behalf of this defendant, on behalf of these helpless ones who turn to you, and more than that—on behalf of this great state, and this great city, which must face this problem and face it fairly—I ask you, in the name of progress and of the human race, to return a verdict of not guilty in this case!

The jury, after listening to Darrow for eight hours in tense, dramatic silence, and particularly to his last passionate appeal, quickly returned a verdict for acquittal. Judge Frank Murphy, as he left the bench, said to a friend: "This is the greatest experience of my life. That was Clarence Darrow at his best. I will never hear anything like it again. He is the most Christlike man I have ever known."

The verdict, as Darrow later said, "meant simply that the doctrine that a man's house is his castle applied to the black man as well as to the white man. If not the first time that a white jury had vindicated this principle, it was the first that ever came to my notice." Dr. Sweet thanked the old lawyer not only for his own deliverance, and that of the other ten Negro defendants, but also in the name of twelve million American Negroes, whose right to equal citizenship he had fought for and, in some measure, had advanced.

SACCO AND VANZETTI PROCLAIM
THEIR INNOCENCE

[April 19, 1927]

While Mussolini and his party were building up a Fascist Italy, two Italian immigrants waited seven years in a Massachusetts jail. Before they were electrocuted on August 23, 1927, they too had become world figures.

Nicola Sacco (1891–1927) and Bartolomeo Vanzetti (1888–1927), both born in Italy, emigrated separately to the United States in 1908. Sacco worked for years as a skilled edger in a shoe factory at Milford, Massachusetts. After trying various jobs, the more restless Vanzetti finally took to fish-peddling at Plymouth. The two men became close friends and apostles of anarchism in the spirit of Blake and Tolstoy. In order to avoid the draft, they spent a year (1917–18) in Mexico.

On April 15, 1920, the paymaster and the guard of a shoe factory were shot dead and robbed of $16,000 in South Braintree, Massachusetts. Sacco and Vanzetti were arrested and charged with the murders. They were not only carrying guns when arrested, but they were draft dodgers, they were foreigners, they were anarchists—and the country was in the midst of a frenzied Red scare.

The trial was held in Dedham before the obviously prejudiced Judge Webster Thayer. The witnesses were inconsistent. The ballistics experts were unconvincing. The prosecuting attorney dwelt on the draft evasion and unpopular opinions of the defendants. After six weeks of bitterness they were found guilty, but it was only after seven years of legal battle that Judge Thayer pronounced final sentence, on April 19, 1927. Before receiving sentence, both men were permitted to speak.

"It is not very familiar with me the English language."

CLERK WORTHINGTON: Nicola Sacco, have you anything to say why sentence of death should not be passed upon you?

Yes, sir. I am not an orator. It is not very familiar with me the English language, and, as I know, as my friend has told me, my comrade Vanzetti will speak more long, so I thought to give him the chance.

I never know, never heard, even read in history anything so cruel as this court. After seven years prosecuting they still consider us guilty. And these gentle people here are arrayed with us in this court today.

I know the sentence will be between two class, the oppressed class and the rich class, and there will be always collision between one and the other. We fraternize the people with the books, with the literature. You persecute the people, tyrannize over them, and kill them. We try the education of people always. You try to put a path between us and some other nationality that hates each other. That is why I am here today on this bench, for having been the oppressed class. Well, you are the oppressor.

You know it, Judge Thayer—you know all my life, you know why I have been here, and after seven years that you have been persecuting me and my poor wife, and you still today abuse us to death. I would like to tell you my life, but what is the use? You know all about what I say before, and my friend—that is, my comrade—will be talking, because he is more familiar with the language, and I will give him a chance. My comrade, the man kind, the kind man to all the children, you sentence him two times, in the Bridgewater case and the Dedham case, connected with me, and you know he is innocent. You forget all the population that has been with us for seven years, to sympathize and give us all their energy and all their kindness. You do not care for them. Among that peoples and the comrades and the working class there is a big legion of intellectual people which have been with us for seven years, but to not commit the iniquitous sentence, but still the court goes ahead. And I think I thank you all, you peoples, my comrades who have been with me for seven years, with the Sacco-Vanzetti case, and I will give my friend a chance.

I forget one thing which my comrade remember me. As I said before, Judge Thayer know all my life, and he know that I am never be guilty, never—not yesterday nor today nor forever.

"I would live again to do what I have done already."

CLERK WORTHINGTON: Bartolomeo Vanzetti, have you anything to say why sentence of death should not be passed upon you?

Yes. What I say is that I am innocent, not only of the Braintree crime, but also of the Bridgewater crime. That I am not only innocent of these two crimes, but in all my life I have never stole and I have never killed and I have never spilled blood. That is what I want to say. And it is not all. Not only am I innocent of these two crimes, not only in all my life I have never stole, never killed, never spilled blood, but I have struggled all my life, since I began to reason, to eliminate crime from the earth.

Everybody that knows these two arms knows very well that I did not need to go in between the streets and kill a man to make the money. I can live with my two arms, and live well. But besides that, I can live even without work with my arm for other people. I have had plenty of chance to live independently and to live what the world conceives to be a higher life than not to gain our bread with the sweat of our brow.

[He goes on to say that his father was in "a good condition" economically in Italy and would welcome him back; that his good reputation for seven years in Plymouth was not known to the jury sufficiently, and that the trial was prejudiced, inefficient, etc.]

What I want to say is this: Everybody ought to understand that the first of the defense has been terrible. My first lawyer did not stick to defend us. He had made no work to collect witnesses and evidence in our favor. The record in the Plymouth court is a pity. I am told that they are almost gone—half lost. So the defense had a tremendous work to do in order to collect some evidence, to collect some testimony to offset and to learn what the testimony of the state has done. And in this consideration it take double time of the state without delay, double time that they delay the case it would have been reasonable, whereas it took less than the state.

Well, I have already say that I am not guilty of these two crimes, but I never commit a crime in my life—I have never steal and I have never kill and I have never spilled blood, and I have fought against the crime, and I have fought and I have sacrificed myself even to eliminate the crimes that the law and the church legitimate and sanctify.

That is what I say: I would not wish to a dog or a snake, to the most low and misfortunate creature of the earth—I would not wish to any of them what I have had to suffer for things that I am not guilty of. But my conviction is that I have suffered for things that I am guilty of. I am suffering because I am a radical, and indeed I am a radical; I have suffered because I was an Italian, and indeed I am an Italian; I have suffered more for my family and for my beloved than for myself; but I am so convinced to be right that if you would execute me two times, and if I could be reborn two other times, I would live again to do what I have done already.

In the hushed little courtroom of now historic Dedham, Judge Webster Thayer sentenced Sacco and Vanzetti to death in the electric chair.

During the long years in prison Sacco and, even more, Vanzetti had grown in stature. It was Vanzetti who read and studied English so eagerly that some of his remarks have become a part of literature. One of his letters to the judge, which describes the character of Sacco, has appeared in poetry anthologies. A few of his words to the novelist Phil Stong were used as the turning point in the play by James Thurber and Elliott Nugent, The Male Animal.

FRANKLIN DELANO ROOSEVELT GIVES HIS FIRST INAUGURAL ADDRESS

[March 4, 1933]

Opinions may differ about Franklin Delano Roosevelt, but it can hardly be denied that he conquered his affliction heroically and developed a friendly, informal art of speaking on the radio which carried him four times to the presidency.

In contrast to his antagonist and antitype, Hitler, Roosevelt began with all the advantages. He was born in 1882 at Hyde Park, New York, with wealthy and distinguished families on both sides. Educated at Groton and Harvard, he tried the law but was soon diverted to politics. In 1910 he was elected to the New York State Senate and in 1912 he campaigned energetically for the election of Woodrow Wilson. From 1913 to 1920 he served as Assistant Secretary of the Navy and then ran for Vice-President with James M. Cox and was badly defeated. Shortly afterward, he was stricken with poliomyelitis and for seven years underwent treatment at Warm Springs, Georgia.

Roosevelt's one spectacular return to public life during this period was in 1924 at the Democratic convention in Madison Square Garden, where he nominated Al Smith in the famous "Happy Warrior" speech, which produced an ovation of one hour and thirteen minutes. However, John W. Davis received the Democratic nomination and was crushed in the election.

After four more years of grueling self-discipline at Warm Springs, Roosevelt again nominated Al Smith for President. This speech, delivered over the radio in Houston, Texas, did not sweep the audience as the 1924 speech had done, but it showed for the first time his peculiarly personal mastery of the microphone. Although he would have preferred to finish his cure, he allowed himself to be persuaded by Al Smith to run for Governor of New York, and threw himself into the campaign with enthusiasm.

Two vigorous terms at Albany, mostly during the depression, brought Roosevelt the Democratic presidential nomination on July 2, 1932. He astonished the country first by flying from Albany to Chicago and then by giving his acceptance speech on the spot. It was in the last paragraph that he first used the phrase "New Deal": "I pledge you, I pledge myself, to a new deal for the American people. Let us all here assembled constitute ourselves prophets of a new order of competence and courage."

The result of the campaign was a foregone conclusion. Whatever the merits of President Hoover, he was buried under the disasters of the depression. "By Inauguration Day, 1933," said Roosevelt some years later, "the banks of the

United States were all closed, financial transactions had ceased, business and industry had sunk to their lowest levels. The widespread unemployment which accompanied the collapse had created a general feeling of utter helplessness. I sought principally in the . . . Inaugural Address to banish, so far as possible, the fear of the present and of the future which held the American people and the American spirit in its grasp."

In regard to the preparation of Roosevelt's speeches, we have a great deal of information in After Seven Years by Raymond Moley, Roosevelt and Hopkins by Robert E. Sherwood, and especially in Working with Roosevelt by Judge Samuel I. Rosenman, who helped with the speeches from the first gubernatorial campaign in 1928 through the last presidential term. The First Inaugural, according to Judge Rosenman, was one of the very few speeches of which Roosevelt wrote the first draft in his own hand, "sitting by the fire at Hyde Park on the night of February 27." The famous sentence on fear was added later. And the very first sentence (not included in the official papers) he jotted down on the reading copy at the last moment, while waiting inside the Capitol.

"The only thing we have to fear is fear itself."

THIS IS A DAY of national consecration, and I am certain that my fellow Americans expect that on my introduction into the presidency I will address them with a candor and a decision which the present situation of our nation impels.

This is pre-eminently the time to speak the truth, the whole truth, frankly and boldly. Nor need we shrink from honestly facing conditions in our country today. This great nation will endure as it has endured, will revive, and will prosper.

So first of all let me assert my firm belief that the only thing we have to fear is fear itself—nameless, unreasoning, unjustified terror, which paralyzes needed efforts to convert retreat into advance.

In every dark hour of our national life a leadership of frankness and vigor has met with that understanding and support of the people themselves which is essential to victory. I am convinced that you will again give that support to leadership in these critical days.

In such a spirit on my part and yours we face our common difficulties. They concern, thank God, only material things. Values have shrunken to fantastic levels; taxes have risen; our ability to pay has fallen; government of all kinds is faced by serious curtailment of income; the means of exchange are frozen in the currents of trade; the withered leaves of industrial enterprise lie on every side; farmers find no markets for their produce; the savings of many years in thousands of families are gone.

More important, a host of unemployed citizens face the grim problem of existence, and an equally great number toil with little return. Only a foolish optimist can deny the dark realities of the moment.

Yet our distress comes from no failure of substance. We are stricken by no plague of locusts. Compared with the perils which our forefathers conquered because they believed and were not afraid, we have still much to be thankful for. Nature still offers her bounty, and human efforts have multiplied it. Plenty is at our doorstep, but a generous use of it languishes in the very sight of the supply.

Primarily, this is because the rulers of the exchange of mankind's goods have failed through their own stubbornness and their own incompetence, have admitted their failure and abdicated. Practices of the unscrupulous money-changers stand indicted in the court of public opinion, rejected by the hearts and minds of men.

True, they have tried, but their efforts have been cast in the pattern of an outworn tradition. Faced by the failure of credit, they have proposed only the lending of more money.

Stripped of the lure of profit by which to induce our people to follow their false leadership, they have resorted to exhortations, pleading tearfully for restored confidence. They know only the rules of a generation of self-seekers.

They have no vision, and when there is no vision the people perish.

The money-changers have fled from their high seats in the temple of our civilization. We may now restore that temple to the ancient truths.

The measure of the restoration lies in the extent to which we apply social values more noble than mere monetary profit.

Happiness lies not in the mere possession of money; it lies in the joy of achievement, in the thrill of creative effort.

The joy and moral stimulation of work no longer must be forgotten in the mad chase of evanescent profits. These dark days will be worth all they cost us if they teach us that our true destiny is not to be ministered unto but to minister to ourselves and to our fellow men.

Recognition of the falsity of material wealth as the standard of success goes hand in hand with the abandonment of the false belief that public office and high political position are to be valued only by the standards of pride of place and personal profit; and there must be an end to a conduct in banking and in business which too often has given to a sacred trust the likeness of callous and selfish wrongdoing.

Small wonder that confidence languishes, for it thrives only on honesty, on honor, on the sacredness of obligations, on faithful protection, on unselfish performance. Without them it cannot live.

Restoration calls, however, not for changes in ethics alone. This nation asks for action, and action now.

Our greatest primary task is to put people to work. This is no unsolvable problem if we face it wisely and courageously.

It can be accomplished in part by direct recruiting by the government itself, treating the task as we would treat the emergency of a war, but at the same time, through this employment, accomplishing greatly needed projects to stimulate and reorganize the use of our natural resources.

Hand in hand with this, we must frankly recognize the overbalance of population in our industrial centers and, by engaging on a national scale in a redistribution, endeavor to provide a better use of the land for those best fitted for the land.

The task can be helped by definite efforts to raise the values of agricultural products and with this the power to purchase the output of our cities.

It can be helped by preventing realistically the tragedy of the growing loss, through foreclosure, of our small homes and our farms.

It can be helped by the unifying of relief activities, which today are often scattered, uneconomical, and unequal. It can be helped by national planning for and supervision of all forms of transportation and of communications and other utilities which have a definite public character.

There are many ways in which it can be helped, but it can never be helped merely by talking about it. We must act, and act quickly.

Finally, in our progress toward a resumption of work, we require two safeguards against a return of the evils of the old order; there must be a strict supervision of all banking and credits and investments; there must be an end to speculation with other people's money, and there must be provision for an adequate but sound currency.

These are the lines of attack. I shall presently urge upon a new Congress in special session detailed measures for their fulfillment, and I shall seek the immediate assistance of the several states.

Through this program of action we address ourselves to putting our own national house in order and making income balance outgo.

Our international trade relations, though vastly important, are, in point of time and necessity, secondary to the establishment of a sound national economy.

I favor as a practical policy the putting of first things first. I shall spare no effort to restore world trade by international economic readjustment, but the emergency at home cannot wait on that accomplishment.

The basic thought that guides these specific means of national recovery is not narrowly nationalistic.

It is the insistence, as a first consideration, upon the interdependence of the various elements in and parts of the United States—a recognition of the old and permanently important manifestation of the American spirit of the pioneer.

It is the way to recovery. It is the immediate way. It is the strongest assurance that the recovery will endure.

In the field of world policy I would dedicate this nation to the policy of the good neighbor—the neighbor who resolutely respects himself and, because he does so, respects the rights of others—the neighbor who respects his obligations and respects the sanctity of his agreements in and with a world of neighbors.

If I read the temper of our people correctly, we now realize, as we have never realized before, our interdependence on each other; that we cannot merely take, but we must give as well; that if we are to go forward we must move as a trained and loyal army willing to sacrifice for the good of a common discipline, because, without such discipline, no progress is made, no leadership becomes effective.

We are, I know, ready and willing to submit our lives and property to such discipline because it makes possible a leadership which aims at a larger good.

This I propose to offer, pledging that the larger purposes will bind upon us all as a sacred obligation with a unity of duty hitherto evoked only in time of armed strife.

With this pledge taken, I assume unhesitatingly the leadership of this great army of our people, dedicated to a disciplined attack upon our common problems.

Action in this image and to this end is feasible under the form of government which we have inherited from our ancestors.

Our Constitution is so simple and practical that it is possible always to meet extraordinary needs by changes in emphasis and arrangement without loss of essential form.

That is why our constitutional system has proved itself the most superbly enduring political mechanism the modern world has produced. It has met every stress of vast expansion of territory, of foreign wars, of bitter internal strife, of world relations.

It is to be hoped that the normal balance of executive and legislative authority may be wholly adequate to meet the unprecedented task before us. But it may be that an unprecedented demand and need for undelayed action may call for temporary departure from that normal balance of public procedure.

I am prepared under my constitutional duty to recommend the measures that a stricken nation in the midst of a stricken world may require.

These measures, or such other measures as the Congress may build out of its experience and wisdom, I shall seek, within my constitutional authority, to bring to speedy adoption.

But in the event that the Congress shall fail to take one of these two courses, and in the event that the national emergency is still critical, I shall not evade the clear course of duty that will then confront me.

I shall ask the Congress for the one remaining instrument to meet the crisis—broad executive power to wage a war against the emergency as great as the power that would be given to me if we were in fact invaded by a foreign foe.

For the trust reposed in me I will return the courage and the devotion that befit the time. I can do no less.

We face the arduous days that lie before us in the warm courage of national unity; with the clear consciousness of seeking old and precious moral values; with the clean satisfaction that comes from the stern performance of duty by old and young alike.

We aim at the assurance of a rounded and permanent national life.

We do not distrust the future of essential democracy. The people of the United States have not failed. In their need they have registered a mandate that they want direct, vigorous action.

They have asked for discipline and direction under leadership. They have made me the present instrument of their wishes. In the spirit of the gift I take it.

In this dedication of a nation we humbly ask the blessing of God. May He protect each and every one of us! May He guide me in the days to come.

It is not hard to remember how this speech helped to calm a frightened and bewildered people.

Harry Hopkins and others of the inner circle thought that the first was the best of the four inaugural speeches.

ROOSEVELT GIVES HIS FIRST
FIRESIDE CHAT

[March 12, 1933]

Two days after his inauguration Roosevelt ordered every bank in the nation to close its doors for a nine-day "holiday" of examination and appraisal of assets. During that period no depositor could withdraw money or cash a check. In order to explain this drastic policy to the people Roosevelt decided to give his first "fireside chat."

"The Treasury Department prepared a scholarly, comprehensive draft of the speech," says Judge Rosenman. "The President saw that it would be meaningless to most people, tossed it aside without any attempt at rewriting, and proceeded to write his own instead. He dictated it in simple, ordinary language—he looked for words that he would use in an informal conversation with one or two friends."

"Together we cannot fail."

I WANT TO TALK for a few minutes with the people of the United States about banking—with the comparatively few who understand the mechanics of banking, but more particularly with the overwhelming majority who use banks for the making of deposits and the drawing of checks. I want to tell you what has been done in the last few days, why it was done, and what the next steps are going to be. I recognize that the many proclamations from state capitols and from Washington, the legislation, the Treasury regulations, etc., couched for the most part in banking and legal terms, should be explained for the benefit of the average citizen. I owe this in particular because of the fortitude and good temper with which everybody has accepted the inconvenience and hardships of the banking holiday. I know that when you understand what we in Washington have been about I shall continue to have your co-operation as fully as I have had your sympathy and help during the past week.

First of all, let me state the simple fact that when you deposit money in a bank the bank does not put the money into a safe-deposit vault. It invests your money in many different forms of credit—bonds, commercial paper, mortgages, and many other kinds of loans. In other words, the bank puts your money to work to keep the wheels of industry and of agriculture turning around. A comparatively small part of the money you put into the bank is kept in currency—an amount which in normal times is wholly sufficient to cover the cash needs of the average citizen. In other words, the total amount of all currency in the country is only a small fraction of the total deposits in all of the banks.

What, then, happened during the last few days of February and the first few days of March? Because of undermined confidence on the part of the public, there was a general rush by a large portion of our population to turn bank deposits into currency or gold—a rush so great that the soundest banks could not get enough currency to meet the demand. The reason for this was that on the spur of the moment it was, of course, impossible to sell perfectly sound assets of a bank and convert them into cash except at panic prices far below their real value.

By the afternoon of March 3 scarcely a bank in the country was open to do business. Proclamations temporarily closing them in whole or in part had been issued by the governors in almost all the states.

It was then that I issued the proclamation providing for the nationwide bank holiday, and this was the first step in the government's reconstruction of our financial and economic fabric.

The second step was the legislation promptly and patriotically passed by the Congress confirming my proclamation and broadening my powers so that it became possible in view of the requirement of time to extend the holiday and lift the ban of that holiday gradually. This law also gave authority to develop a program of rehabilitation of our banking facilities. I want to tell our citizens in every part of the nation that the national Congress—Republicans and Democrats alike—showed by this action a devotion to public welfare and a realization of the emergency and the necessity for speed that it is difficult to match in our history.

The third stage has been the series of regulations permitting the banks to continue their functions to take care of the distribution of food and household necessities and the payment of payrolls.

This bank holiday, while resulting in many cases in great inconvenience, is affording us the opportunity to supply the currency necessary to meet the situation. No sound bank is a dollar worse off than it was when it closed its doors last Monday. Neither is any bank which may turn out not to be in a position for immediate opening. The new law allows the twelve Federal Reserve Banks to issue additional currency on good assets and thus the banks which reopen will be able to meet every legitimate call. The new currency is being sent out by the Bureau of Engraving and Printing in large volume to every part of the country. It is sound currency because it is backed by actual, good assets.

A question you will ask is this: why are all the banks not to be re-opened at the same time? The answer is simple. Your government does not intend that the history of the past few years shall be repeated. We do not want and will not have another epidemic of bank failures.

As a result, we start tomorrow, Monday, with the opening of banks in the twelve Federal Reserve Bank cities—those banks which on first examination by the Treasury have already been found to be all right. This will be followed on Tuesday by the resumption of all their functions by banks already found to be sound in cities where there are recognized clearinghouses. That means about two hundred and fifty cities of the United States.

On Wednesday and succeeding days banks in smaller places all through the country will resume business, subject, of course, to the government's physical ability to complete its survey. It is necessary that the reopening of banks be extended over a period in order to permit the banks to make applications for necessary loans, to obtain currency needed to meet their requirements, and to enable the government to make common-sense checkups.

Let me make it clear to you that if your bank does not open the first day you are by no means justified in believing that it will not open. A bank that opens on one of the subsequent days is in exactly the same status as the bank that opens tomorrow.

I know that many people are worrying about state banks not members of the Federal Reserve System. These banks can and will receive assistance from member banks and from the Reconstruction Finance Corporation. These state banks are following the same course as the national banks, except that they get their licenses to resume business from the state authorities, and these authorities have been asked by the Secretary of the Treasury to permit their good banks to open up on the same schedule as the national banks. I am confident that the State Banking Departments will be as careful as the national government in the policy relating to the opening of banks and will follow the same broad policy.

It is possible that when the banks resume, a very few people who have not recovered from their fear may again begin withdrawals. Let me make it clear that the banks will take care of all needs—and it is my belief that hoarding during the past week has become an exceedingly unfashionable pastime. It needs no prophet to tell you that when the people find that they can get their money—that they can get it when they want it for all legitimate purposes—the phantom of fear will soon be laid. People will again be glad to have their money where it will be safely taken care of and where they can use it conveniently at any time.

I can assure you that it is safer to keep your money in a reopened bank than under the mattress.

The success of our whole great national program depends, of course, upon the co-operation of the public—on its intelligent support and use of a reliable system.

Remember that the essential accomplishment of the new legislation is that it makes it possible for banks more readily to convert their assets into cash than was the case before. More liberal provision has been made for banks to borrow on these assets at the Reserve Banks and more liberal provision has also been made for issuing currency on the security of these good assets. This currency is not fiat currency. It is issued only on adequate security, and every good bank has an abundance of such security.

One more point before I close. There will be, of course, some banks unable to reopen without being reorganized. The new law allows the government to assist in making these reorganizations quickly and effectively and even allows the government to subscribe to at least a part of new capital which may be required.

I hope you can see from this elemental recital of what your government is doing that there is nothing complex, or radical, in the process.

We had a bad banking situation. Some of our bankers had shown themselves either incompetent or dishonest in their handling of the people's funds. They had used the money entrusted to them in speculations and unwise loans. This was, of course, not true in the vast majority of our banks, but it was true in enough of them to shock the people for a time into a sense of insecurity and to put them into a frame of mind where they did not differentiate, but seemed to assume that the acts of a comparative few had tainted them all. It was the government's job to straighten out this situation and do it as quickly as possible. And the job is being performed.

I do not promise you that every bank will be reopened or that individual losses will not be suffered, but there will be no losses that possibly could be avoided; and there would have been more and greater losses had we continued to drift. I can even promise you salvation for some at least of the sorely pressed banks. We shall be engaged not merely in reopening sound banks, but in the creation of sound banks through reorganization.

It has been wonderful to me to catch the note of confidence from all over the country. I can never be sufficiently grateful to the people for the loyal support they have given me in their acceptance of the judgment that has dictated our course, even though all our processes may not have seemed clear to them.

After all, there is an element in the readjustment of our financial system more important than currency, more important than gold, and that is the confidence of the people. Confidence and courage are the essentials of success in carrying out our plan. You people must have faith; you must not be stampeded by rumors or guesses. Let us unite in banishing fear. We have provided the machinery to restore our financial system; it is up to you to support and make it work.

It is your problem no less than it is mine. Together we cannot fail.

"Here was the first real demonstration of Roosevelt's superb ability to use the first person plural and bring the people right into the White House with him," said Robert E. Sherwood, who did not join the speech-writing staff until the third term. "Those who listened to that first fireside speech will never forget the surge of confidence that his buoyant spirit invoked."

Roosevelt himself afterward explained why he resorted to the so-called "fireside chat" at the beginning of his first term in office: "There had always been so much mystery thrown about the banking business, there was so much fear in the minds of bank depositors during these first days of the banking crisis, and so much had happened during this first week that I decided to use the radio to explain to the average men and women of the nation . . . what we had done and what we intended to do in the banking situation." He added that the press came to call his radio speeches "fireside chats," even when they were delivered on sweltering summer evenings.

This is not the place to sketch Roosevelt's speaking career before the outbreak of World War II, but mention may be made to his triumphant speech at Madison Square Garden when closing the second presidential campaign in 1936. For some hearers it showed him irresponsible, dizzy with power; for others it recalled the great moments of Pericles, Lincoln, and Woodrow Wilson.

HITLER TAKES FULL RESPONSIBILITY FOR THE BLOOD PURGE

[July 13, 1934]

As late as 1930 there were reputable foreign correspondents who ridiculed Hitler's aspirations to power. They found him physically unimpressive, ignorant, hysterical, fanatical. How could this insignificant little Austrian—a former house painter and corporal—become the leader of the best-educated nation in

Europe? How could a person driven by so many hatreds—hatred of the Treaty
of Versailles, which branded Germany with "war guilt," hatred of the French,
of the Russians, and especially of the Jews (who were identified in his mind
with the Communists)—create a role for himself larger than Bismarck's or
Frederick the Great's? The idea did indeed seem preposterous.

To begin with, Hitler was without friends, without money, without any
coherent body of ideas, but he had the devotion of a religious convert to Germany, to Pan-Germany, and he had a weird talent for holding an audience.
Emil Ludwig wrote in 1939, before the second World War broke out: "Hitler's
success with the German masses was made possible by his own genuine gift—
that of oratory. A great popular speaker has been hitherto unknown in Germany and Hitler fascinates the Germans because his speeches have something
of Wagnerian music—repetition of a few impressive leitmotivs, sobbing and
shouting, and, above all, a foggy conglomeration of gods and heroes, blood and
race." And Raoul de Roussy de Sales wrote of Hitler in 1941: "He is essentially
a speechmaker, and although today it is his deeds and his conquests that most
impress the world, it should not be forgotten that he started as a soap-box
orator and spoke his way to power."

Born on the German border of Austria, Adolf Hitler (1889–1945) was
brought up in the drab family of a petty customs official and spent more em-
bittering years in trying to be an artist in Munich and Vienna, where he was
infected with extreme anti-Semitism. Early in the first World War he enlisted
in the Germany army, saw much action, was wounded and gassed, and came
out of it a corporal brooding over the plight of Germany. Before leaving the
army, he discovered the tiny German Workers party, founded by a Munich
locksmith, Anton Drexler, and guided by a construction engineer, Gottfried
Feder, who advocated the abolition of interest and the state ownership of land,
and distinguished between productive and unproductive capital. Hitler was
thrilled on first hearing Feder lecture in June, 1919, and soon became a morale
lecturer himself for a counterrevolutionary Munich regiment. This was good
practice for him and good training for his voice, which had been injured by gas
during the war. By the fall of 1919 he found that he could spellbind a general
audience of a hundred or more with a furious attack on the Treaty of Versailles and the machinations of the Jews.

From there on Hitler spoke to many mass meetings, and his elemental oratory, accompanied by street fighting and ruthless tactics, built the strength of
the party. But it was perhaps not until October, 1923, that his fanatical faith
in himself was given what, to him, was a religious benediction. At that time
he was in Bayreuth, the shrine of Wagner, whose cruel and cloudy operas he
had followed for years with passionate zeal. At the close of one of Hitler's
harangues, Houston Stewart Chamberlain, the leader of the "Bayreuth Kultur

circle," and son-in-law of Wagner, unexpectedly hailed the young orator as the savior of Germany. The very next month came Hitler's insurrection in Munich, often called the "Beer-Hall Putsch." Although abortive, it furnished the Nazis with seven martyrs and gave Hitler the opportunity, while imprisoned at Landsberg, to write the first volume of Mein Kampf. This atavistic stream of vengefulness was dictated to Rudolf Hess and was but a shadow of his speeches.

In Mein Kampf, Hitler repeatedly insisted on the power of the spoken word: "I know that one is able to win people far more by the spoken than by the written word, and that every great movement on this globe owes its rise to the great speakers and not to the great writers." And again: "All great movements are movements of the people, are volcanic eruptions of human passions and spiritual sensations, stirred either by the cruel Goddess of Misery or by the torch of the word thrown into the masses, and are not the lemonadelike outpourings of aestheticizing literati and drawing-room heroes."

The rise of the Nazi party to power is a story of expert party organization and terror, of economic frustration and calculations on the part of great industrialists, of the senescence of Hindenburg and the confusion and cross-purposes of German political parties. Refusing to enter a coalition government, the Nazis secured in the end what they desired—full power. The destruction of Communists, Jews, and trade-unions and the co-ordination of the whole country for Nazi purposes began at once. In the meantime, the party itself had to be co-ordinated. Before the slogan "One people, one nation, one leader" could be posted in every public place in Germany, the rival Nazi chieftains had to be dealt with. Convinced, or at least pretending to be convinced, that a great conspiracy was on foot, Hitler, on the night of June 30, 1934, began the purge. The very influential Kurt von Schleicher and his wife are said to have been shot down in cold blood by Hitler himself. The popular Captain Ernst Roehm, whose Brown Shirt followers looked forward to social reforms and a service state, was another victim of a night of murder that netted hundreds, perhaps thousands of corpses.

The blood bath was followed by two weeks of political maneuvering and terrified rumor in which Hitler's power tottered. Then to a Reichstag aghast and dismayed, he fulminated for two hours.

"I became the supreme justiciar of the German people!"

AT ONE O'CLOCK in the night I received the last dispatches telling me of the alarm summonses; at two o'clock in the morning I flew to Munich. Meanwhile Minister-President Göring had previously received from me the commission that if I proceeded to apply a purge he was to take similar measures at once in Berlin and in Prussia. With an iron fist he beat down the attack on the National Socialist state before it could develop. The necessity for acting with lightning speed meant that in this decisive hour I had very few men with me. In the presence of the Minister Goebbels and of the new Chief of Staff the action of which you are already informed was executed and brought to a close in Munich. Although only a few days before I had been prepared to exercise clemency, at this hour there was no place for any such consideration. Mutinies are suppressed in accordance with laws of iron that are eternally the same. If anyone reproaches me and asks why I did not resort to the regular courts of justice for conviction of the offenders, then all that I can say to him is this: in this hour I was responsible for the fate of the German people, and thereby I became the supreme justiciar of the German people!

Mutinous divisions have in all periods been recalled to order by decimation. Only one state has failed to make any use of its articles of war, and this state paid for that failure by collapse—Germany. I did not wish to deliver up the young Reich to the fate of the old Reich. I gave the order to shoot those who were the ringleaders in this treason, and I further gave the order to burn out down to the raw flesh the ulcers of this poisoning of the wells in our domestic life and of the poisoning of the outside world. And I further ordered that if any of the mutineers should attempt to resist arrest, they were immediately to be struck down with armed force. The nation must know that its existence—and that is guaranteed through its internal order and security—can be threatened by no one with impunity! And everyone must know for all future time that if he raises his hand to strike the state, then certain death is his lot. And every National Socialist must know that no rank and no position can protect him from his personal responsibility and therefore from his punishment. I have prosecuted thousands of our former opponents on account of their corruption. I should in my own mind reproach myself if I were now to tolerate similar offenses in our own ranks. No people and no government can help it if creatures arise such as we once knew in Germany, a Kutisker, for example, such as France came to know in a Stavisky, or such as we today have once more experienced—men whose aim is to sin against a nation's interests. But every people is itself guilty if it does not find the strength to destroy such noxious creatures.

If people bring against me the objection that only a judicial procedure could precisely weigh the measure of the guilt and of its expiation, then against this view I lodge my most solemn protest. He who rises against

Germany is a traitor to his country: and the traitor to his country is not to be punished according to the range and the extent of his act, but according to the purpose that that act has revealed. He who in his heart purposes to raise a mutiny and thereby breaks loyalty, breaks faith, breaks sacred pledges, he can expect nothing else than that he himself will be the first sacrifice. I have no intention to have the little culprits shot and to spare the great criminals. It is not my duty to inquire whether it was too hard a lot that was inflicted on these conspirators, these agitators and destroyers, these poisoners of the wellsprings of German public opinion and in a wider sense of world opinion: it is not mine to consider which of them suffered too severely: I have only to see to it that Germany's lot should not be intolerable.

A foreign journalist, who enjoys the privileges of a guest in our midst, protests in the name of the wives and children of those who have been shot and awaits the day when from their ranks there will come vengeance. To this gentleman I can say only one thing in answer: women and children have ever been the innocent victims of the criminal acts of men. I, too, have pity for them, but I believe that the suffering inflicted on them through the guilt of these men is but a minute fraction in comparison with the suffering that perhaps ten thousand German women would have had to endure if this act had been successful. A foreign diplomat explains that the meeting of Schleicher and Roehm was of course of an entirely harmless character. That matter I need not discuss with anyone. In the political sphere conceptions of what is harmless and what is not will never coincide. But when three traitors in Germany arrange and effect a meeting with a foreign statesman, which they themselves characterize as "serviceable," when they effect their meeting after excluding every member of their staff, when they give strict orders that no word of this meeting shall reach me, then I shall have such men shot dead even when it should prove true that at a consultation that was thus kept secret from me they talked of nothing save the weather, old coins, and like topics. . . .

In these days, which have been days of severe trial both for me and for its members, the SA [storm troopers] has preserved the spirit of loyalty. Thus for the third time the SA has proved that it is mine, just as I will prove at any time that I belong to my SA men. In a few weeks' time the Brown Shirt will once more dominate the streets of Germany and will give to one and all clear evidence that because it has overcome its grievous distress the life of National Socialist Germany is only the more vigorous.

When in March of last year our young revolution stormed through

Germany, my highest endeavor was to shed as little blood as possible. To millions of my former opponents, on behalf of the new state and in the name of the National Socialist party, I offered a general amnesty; millions of them have since joined us and are loyally co-operating in the rebuilding of the Reich.

I hoped that it might not be necessary any longer to be forced to defend this state yet again with arms in our hands. But since fate has now none the less put us to this test, all of us wish to pledge ourselves with only the greater fanaticism to hold fast to that which was formerly won at the price of the blood of so many of our best men and which today had to be maintained once more through the blood of German fellow countrymen. Just as one and a half years ago I offered reconciliation to our former opponents, so would I from henceforth also promise forgetfulness to all those who shared in the guilt of this act of madness. Let them bethink themselves, and remembering this melancholy calamity in our new German history let them devote themselves to the task of reparation. May they now recognize with surer insight than before the great task that fate sets us, which civil war and chaos cannot perform. May we all feel responsible for the most precious treasure that there can be for the German people: internal order, internal and external peace, just as I am ready to undertake responsibility at the bar of history for the twenty-four hours in which the bitterest decisions of my life were made, in which fate once again taught me in the midst of anxious care with every thought to hold fast to the dearest thing that has been given us in this world—the German people and the German Reich!

Hitler's bold, desperate justification of his purge overcame the brooding terror of his followers and reunited them under him, but it showed the rest of mankind the limitless lengths to which he would go. It showed the rest of mankind, perhaps for the first time, the monstrous force that was loose in the world. Not until ten years later, in 1944, did another serious conspiracy threaten Hitler's power.

MUSSOLINI APPLIES THE TORCH OF CIVILIZATION TO ETHIOPIA

[October 2, 1935]

The glittering surface of Fascism did not long hide the brutal reality beneath. Exile, torture, and murder were essential instruments of the regime and could be applied to inconspicuous people without difficulty. But when the outspoken Socialist deputy, Giacomo Matteotti of Venice, was done away with in 1924, there was a public uproar and the secession of some members from the Chamber of Deputies. Mussolini faced out the storm with bravado and in a typically irrelevant speech listed the sufferings of his brave militia, so often mistreated by unpatriotic subversives! "Italy, gentlemen, wants peace, wants quiet, wants work, wants calm; we will give it with love, if that be possible, or with strength, if that be necessary."

Of course, the Matteotti scandal was followed by other outrages, and the Italian people grew more and more dubious of the blessings of Fascism. Under such circumstances a large-scale diversion is always the dictator's solution, and by 1935 a foreign war was obviously indicated. What better enemy than savage Ethiopia, which had defeated Italy in 1896? A war for revenge, a war for empire, a war for civilization!

Mussolini delivered the following speech from his customary balcony in Rome on the day that Italian planes began to drop bombs on Ethiopia.

"Only the crumbs of the rich colonial booty were left for us."

BLACK SHIRTS of the Revolution! Men and women of all Italy! Italians all over the world—beyond the mountains, beyond the seas! Listen!

A solemn hour is about to strike in the history of the country. Twenty million Italians are at this moment gathered in the squares of all Italy. It is the greatest demonstration that human history records. Twenty millions! One heart alone! One will alone! One decision!

This manifestation signifies that the tie between Italy and Fascism is perfect, absolute, unalterable. Only brains softened by puerile illusions, by sheer ignorance, can think differently because they do not hear what exactly is the Fascist Italy of 1935.

For many months the wheels of destiny under the impulse of our calm determination move toward the goal. In these last hours the rhythm has increased and nothing can stop it now. It is not only an army marching toward its goal, but it is 44,000,000 Italians marching in unity behind this army because the blackest of injustices is being attempted against them, that of taking from them their place in the sun.

When, in 1915, Italy threw in her fate with that of the Allies, how many cries of admiration, how many promises! But after the common victory, which cost Italy 600,000 dead, 400,000 lost, one million wounded, when peace was being discussed around the table, only the crumbs of the rich colonial booty were left for us to pick up.

For thirteen years we have been patient while the circle tightened around us at the hands of those who wish to suffocate us. We have been patient with Ethiopia for forty years—it is enough now.

Instead of recognizing the rights of Italy, the League of Nations dares talk of sanctions. But until there is proof to the contrary, I refuse to believe that the authentic people of France will join in supporting sanctions against Italy.

The six thousand dead at the action of Boligny—whose devotion was so heroic that the enemy commander was forced to admire them—those fallen would now turn in their graves.

And until there is proof to the contrary, I refuse to believe that the authentic people of Britain will want to spill blood and send Europe to its catastrophe for the sake of a barbarian country unworthy of ranking among civilized nations.

Just the same, we cannot afford to overlook the possible developments of tomorrow. To economic sanctions we shall answer with our discipline, our spirit of sacrifice, our obedience. To military sanctions we shall answer with militarism. To acts of war we shall answer with acts of war.

A people worthy of their past and their name cannot and never will take a different stand. Let me repeat, in the most categorical manner, the sacred pledge I make at this moment before all the Italians gathered together today, that I should do everything in my power to prevent a colonial conflict from taking on the aspect and weight of a European war.

This conflict may be attractive to certain minds which hope to avenge their disintegrated temples through this new catastrophe. Never, as at this historical hour, have the people of Italy revealed such force of character, and it is against this people, to which mankind owes its greatest conquest, this people of heroes, of poets, of saints, of navigators, of colonizers, that the world dares threaten sanctions.

Italy! Italy! Entirely and universally Fascist! The Italy of the Black

Shirt Revolution, rise to your feet, let the cry of your determination rise to the skies and reach our soldiers in East Africa. Let it be a comfort to those who are about to fight. Let it be an encouragement to our friends and a warning to our enemies.

It is the cry of Italy, which goes beyond the mountains and the seas out into the great big world. It is the cry of justice and victory.

The next day American papers reported that "the tumultuous demonstration that greeted Premier Mussolini's address at the great Fascist rally at Rome yesterday re-echoed across the Atlantic when his message was broadcast over the facilities of the two nation-wide networks. . . . His words were heard with great clarity and were unmarred by static, although the cheers of the vast crowd that turned out to cheer their leader at times 'blasted' the microphone."

EDWARD VIII GIVES ALL FOR LOVE

[December 11, 1936]

Some weeks before President Roosevelt entered on his second term, and while Prime Minister Baldwin's government continued to drift ignobly in the face of Nazi-Fascist expansion, the British Empire was shaken by a crisis that recalled the most romantic of royal legends and surpassed any gossip that Hollywood might report. Edward VIII (1894–   ), who had occupied the throne for less than a year, was on the point of marrying an American woman, Mrs. Wallis Warfield Simpson, whose second divorce was pending.

The government firmly opposed the King's plan and turned it into a constitutional issue that for a few weeks obscured the international situation. There was intrigue at the highest levels, and there was counterintrigue, with Winston Churchill one of the few eminent men to stand by the King in the crisis. Whatever the rights or wrongs of the matter, abdication became inevitable. When the ex-King at last had an opportunity to explain his decision to his former subjects, all the English-speaking world seemed to have had its ear to the radio.

"A few hours ago I discharged my last duty
as King and Emperor."

AT LONG LAST I am able to say a few words of my own. I have never wanted to withhold anything, but until now it has not been constitutionally possible for me to speak.

A few hours ago I discharged my last duty as King and Emperor, and now that I have been succeeded by my brother, the Duke of York, my first words must be to declare my allegiance to him. This I do with all my heart.

You all know the reasons which have impelled me to renounce the throne. But I want you to understand that in making up my mind I did not forget the country or the empire, which, as Prince of Wales and lately as King, I have for twenty-five years tried to serve.

But you must believe me when I tell you that I have found it impossible to carry the heavy burden of responsibility and to discharge my duties as King as I would wish to do without the help and support of the woman I love.

And I want you to know that the decision I have made has been mine and mine alone. This was a thing I had to judge entirely for myself. The other person most nearly concerned has tried up to the last to persuade me to take a different course.

I have made this, the most serious decision of my life, only upon the single thought of what would, in the end, be best for all.

This decision has been made less difficult to me by the sure knowledge that my brother, with his long training in the public affairs of this country and with his fine qualities, will be able to take my place forthwith without interruption or injury to the life and progress of the empire. And he has one matchless blessing, enjoyed by so many of you, and not bestowed on me—a happy home with his wife and children.

During these hard days I have been comforted by her Majesty my mother and by my family. The ministers of the crown, and in particular, Mr. Baldwin, the Prime Minister, have always treated me with full consideration. There has never been any constitutional difference between me and them, and between me and Parliament. Bred in the constitutional tradition by my father, I should never have allowed any such issue to arise.

Ever since I was Prince of Wales, and later on when I occupied the throne, I have been treated with the greatest kindness by all classes of the people wherever I have lived or journeyed throughout the empire. For that I am very grateful.

I now quit altogether public affairs and I lay down my burden. It may be some time before I return to my native land, but I shall always follow the fortunes of the British race and empire with profound interest, and if at any time in the future I can be found of service to his Majesty in a private station, I shall not fail.

And now, we all have a new King. I wish him and you, his people, happiness and prosperity with all my heart. God bless you all! God save the King!

For listening millions this was the most poignant moment of modern history. Even those who thought that the King's decision was folly had to admit that the words were read with disarming dignity.

In A King's Story the Duke of Windsor has traced his life with remarkable charm and candor. "It has become part of the abdication legend," he says, "that the broadcast was actually written by Mr. Churchill. The truth is that, as he has often done before with other speeches, he generously supplied the final brush strokes. . . . He made several admirable suggestions that a practical student of Churchilliana could spot at a glance: 'bred in the constitutional tradition by my father'; 'one matchless blessing, enjoyed by so many of you, and not bestowed on me—a happy home with his wife and children.' "

PRIME MINISTER CHAMBERLAIN RETURNS IN TRIUMPH FROM MUNICH

[September 30, 1938]

On Monday, September 12, 1938, the entire Western world awaited Hitler's speech to the Nazi party rally at Nuremberg. Would he use the agitation of the Germans of the Sudetenland, in Czechoslovakia, as an excuse for another world war? After getting his will with threats for five years, would he now open fire? No one knew. Everyone trembled. While thousands attended the frenzied performance in Nuremberg, millions throughout the world sat depressed before their radios.

At this point the British Prime Minister, Neville Chamberlain, felt the call to become his own foreign secretary in place of Lord Halifax. He made two trips to Germany to confer personally with Hitler. On the third trip within three weeks he conferred jointly with Hitler, Mussolini, and Daladier, and signed the Munich Pact—ceding to Germany the Sudetenland, including the finest fortifications in Europe.

For the moment the English were relieved, and Chamberlain was a hero. On his return to his office at No. 10 Downing Street cheering crowds gathered and in response to repeated demands he spoke from a first-floor window.

"I believe it is peace for our time."

MY GOOD FRIENDS, this is the second time in our history that there has come back from Germany to Downing Street peace with honor. [After the cheering stopped, Chamberlain continued:] I believe it is peace for our time. We thank you from the bottom of our hearts. [To this the crowd responded: "We thank you. God bless you." Then a pause until Chamberlain said:] And now I recommend you to go home and sleep quietly in your beds.

But nightmares soon followed. In the angry four-day debate in the House of Commons on the Munich sellout, Duff Cooper, First Lord of the Admiralty, resigned his high office in a speech of brilliant indignation. Others defended the Prime Minister with equal vehemence. Winston Churchill, who had long been in the political wilderness, and who had incessantly warned the world of Germany's increasing might, spoke sadly. "This is only the first sip," he said, "the first foretaste of a bitter cup which will be proffered to us year by year unless, by a supreme recovery of moral health and martial vigor, we arise again and take our stand for freedom as in the olden time."

Five and a half months later, on March 15, 1939, the Germans seized Prague. On May 3 Litvinov, the Russian Commissar for Foreign Affairs and chief exponent of collective security in the League of Nations, was replaced by Molotov.

"The dismissal of Litvinov marked the end of an epoch," says Churchill in The Gathering Storm. "It registered the abandonment by the Kremlin of all faith in a security pact with the Western Powers and in the possibility of organizing an Eastern Front against Germany."

PART NINETEEN

THE SECOND WORLD WAR

THERE was little occasion for eloquence in England and France between May, 1939, and May, 1940, a year of incompetence, discouragement, and disaster. The Munich settlement made Hitler practically omnipotent in Germany. It left him free to marshal all his vast resources for aggressive war while his intended victims, half paralyzed by the illusion of "Peace in our time," made only ineffectual efforts to resist. To expedite his naval preparations, Hitler had repudiated the Anglo-German naval accord of 1935, and to confuse and terrorize Europe, he denounced the nonaggression pact with Poland. On May 22, he dictated the Pact of Steel with Italy, and three months later negotiated the bombshell agreement with the Soviet Union, which freed him from a war on two fronts and threw the Western world into despair. It had taken the Munich Pact just eleven months to boomerang. Designed by Prime Minister Chamberlain to protect the west, no matter what became of the east of Europe, it had resulted in a new pact to protect the east, no matter what became of the west. Never had a policy been so quickly refuted by the facts.

Three times Chamberlain himself had gone to Germany to negotiate with Hitler, as we have noted before. To the Russians he sent an exploratory mission, led by an undersecretary not empowered to draw up a treaty. This initial blunder entailed a series of disasters. When Hitler invaded Poland on September 1, England and France promptly declared war on Germany, but had no arms or allies for even a token defense, and were obliged to eat their own pride while the country, whose frontiers they had guaranteed only a few months before, was quickly overrun. When Russia, after failing to negotiate an exchange of territory with Finland, finally invaded that country on November 30, the British government, overlooking the primary German threat, which they still had found no means to contain, began to amass arms and men for an expedition to aid the Finns. Russia was expelled from the League of Nations on December 4, but before Allied troops could be diverted from the anti-Hitler struggle, the Russo-Finnish peace was signed, on March 12, 1940. The next month there was another debacle. On April 9, the British announced, in bold warning, that they had mined the coasts of Norway. The very next day came

the news that the Germans, in a lightning thrust, had occupied Denmark and
southern Norway. Although the British were able for a time to hold Narvik in
the north, the campaign marked another humiliating defeat for Chamberlain
and the Munich peacemakers.

LLOYD GEORGE GIVES SOME ADVICE TO
PRIME MINISTER CHAMBERLAIN

[May 8, 1940]

*The tragic blunders of the government's policies, especially the disaster in
Norway, precipitated a full-dress debate on the war situation in the House of
Commons. Chamberlain's defense did not prove convincing, and he was ban-
teringly reminded of his gibe of a month before that "Hitler missed the bus."
Sir Roger Keyes roundly criticized the failure to attack Trondheim, and told
how he had pleaded with the Naval Staff to lead the attack, offering to take
the full responsibility himself. It soon became evident that the House was in
sympathy with the strong tenor of criticism, and that the opposition would
demand a vote. At this point the seventy-seven-year-old, white-haired David
Lloyd George, who had led the country to victory in the First World War, and
for years had opposed the appeasement of Nazi Germany, rose to speak.*

"He should sacrifice his seals of office."

THE AIR SECRETARY admits the government knew beforehand
that there were no air bases unless captured from the enemy. He
then intimates the object of the Trondheim expedition was to capture air
bases.

In that case we ought to have had picked men, not a kind of scratch
team. We ought to have had the very best men available, especially as
we could not send all our forces in the first installment.

The first installment ought to have been picked men because the
Germans had picked men. We sent a territorial brigade which had not
had much training. We ought also to have had combined action between
army and navy.

We bungled the chance of getting an air base. We did not take any measures that would guarantee success, and yet the whole of this vital expedition, which would have made a vast difference to this country strategically and an infinite difference to her prestige in the world, was made dependent on this half-prepared, half-baked expeditionary force without any combination between the army and navy. There could not have been more serious condemnation of the whole action of the government regarding Norway.

We all are proud of the gallantry of these men. All the more shame that we should have made fools of them.

The situation is a grave one. It would be fatal error on our part not to acknowledge that. In such experience as I have had in war direction I never tried to minimize the extent of disaster. There is no cause, in my judgment, for panic. I say that deliberately after a good deal of reflection; but there is grave cause for pulling ourselves together.

You cannot do that until you tell the country the facts. They must realize the magnitude of our jeopardy. We are two immense empires federated in a struggle for liberty, the two greatest empires in the world, the British and French, with almost inexhaustible resources. They are not easily aroused and you are not going to arouse the British Empire to put forth the whole of its strength—and nothing else will do—unless you tell it what the facts are and what is the reality of the peril.

I don't say these things to spread dismay and consternation, but with the view to rousing real action, not sham action. It is no use saying the balance of advantage is in our favor. It is not, according to the facts.

First of all, we are strategically in a very much worse position than before. The greatest triumph of this extraordinary man, Hitler, has been that he has succeeded in putting Germany strategically in a better position to wage war than his predecessor did in 1914. And by what he has done now he has increased his own advantage to put us in greater jeopardy. Let us face it like men of British blood.

Just look at Czechoslovakia, that spearhead aiming at the heart of Germany with a million of the finest troops in Europe, all gone! That is one strategic advantage that we handed over.

You had a Franco-Russian alliance whereby Russia was to aid Czechoslovakia. Now Russia's ships are crossing the Black Sea with oil for Germany's airplanes.

There is Rumania. Germany practically has Rumania in her hands. If they did not have her a month ago, by this policy in Norway we handed them Rumania.

I hope my fears about Spain will not prove true.

Norway, which was one of the great strategic possibilities of the war, is in German hands. It is no use criticizing Sweden. What right have we to criticize them? We promised rescue and protection, but we never sent an airplane to Poland, and we were too late in Norway.

The German occupation of Norway brings German planes and submarines two hundred miles nearer our coast, and if we want to see the effects of it we have only to read friendly American papers in a country which was pro-Ally. They were convinced victory was going to the Allies. Now, for the first time, doubt has entered their minds.

We promised Poland and we promised Czechoslovakia to defend their frontiers. There was a promise to Norway and a promise to Finland. Our promissory notes are now rubbish in our hands.

Tell me now one little country that will be prepared to stand up to the Nazis upon a mere promise from us. What is the use in not facing the facts that we have to restore our prestige in the world if we are to win this war?

There is also the fact—known to the world—as to the state of our preparations. We started these preparations five years ago. The government asked for fifteen hundred million sterling, and no party in the House challenged them. If they had thought it necessary to ask for more the House would have given it to them, but is there any man in this House who will say he is satisfied with the speed and efficiency of preparations in any respect for the air, army, and navy?

Everybody is dissatisfied. Everybody knows that whatever was done was done halfheartedly and ineffectively, without drive, unintelligently. When the war came the tempo was hardly speeded up. There was the same leisureliness and inefficiency.

Can anyone tell me he is satisfied with what we have done about airplanes, tanks, and guns, especially antiaircraft guns? Is anyone here satisfied with the steps we have taken to train the army? The whole world knows we are in a worse strategical position than this country ever was placed in.

[Sir Patrick Hannon interjected: "We still have our sea power."]

I wish we had used it in some parts of Norway, but I don't think the First Lord was entirely responsible.

[Winston Churchill, First Lord of the Admiralty, jumped up and shouted, "I take complete responsibility for everything done by the Admiralty. I take my full share of the burden."]

I hope he won't allow himself to be converted into an air-raid shelter to keep splinters from hitting his colleagues.

I agree with the Prime Minister that we must face it as a people, not as a party, and not as a personal issue. The Prime Minister is not in a position to make his personality in this respect inseparable from the interests of the country.

[Mr. Chamberlain interrupted, "What is the meaning of that observation? I never represented . . ." The rest of the sentence was drowned by shouting, after which Mr. Chamberlain added, "I took pains to say personality ought to have no place."]

He definitely appealed, on a question which is a great national, imperial, and world issue: "I have got my friends." It is not a question of who is the Prime Minister's friend. It is a far bigger issue. The Prime Minister must remember that he has met this formidable foe of ours in peace and in war and he always has been worsted.

He appealed for sacrifice from the nation. The nation is ready as long as its leadership is right, as long as you say clearly what you are aiming at, as long as you give confidence to them that their leaders are doing their best for them. I say now solemnly that the Prime Minister can give an example of sacrifice because I tell him one thing, that there is nothing that would contribute more to victory in this war than that he should sacrifice his seals of office.

When Lloyd George had finished his speech of not more than twenty minutes, the secretaries of state for war and air were heard, and the debate was summed up by Winston Churchill. When the vote was cast, it was found that over fifty Conservatives had joined the Labour and Liberal opposition. Chamberlain himself was deeply impressed by the sentiment of the House, and saw that he had lost too much credit to continue as the head of the government. What this time of trial required, it was agreed, was a new national government that would have the confidence of the whole country; but two days passed before Churchill was named its head. At that very moment, on the morning of May 10, came the grim news that the Germans had struck a new blow—long expected, yet also dreaded—launching eighty-nine divisions, audacious, skillful, the last word in equipment, against the Lowlands. As Churchill was summoned to Buckingham Palace to hear King George VI's request that he form a government, he stopped to talk to the Dutch ministers who had just flown over from Amsterdam. In their pale and horror-stricken faces he read complete failure to comprehend how this long-dreaded attack, launched by a nation in treaty bound to respect its frontiers, could ever have taken place.

PRIME MINISTER CHURCHILL PRESENTS HIS PROGRAM

[May 13, 1940]

Winston Churchill's speeches of 1940, in his first months as Prime Minister, burst upon the world with such sudden and magnificent power that Americans were inclined to think that a full-fledged orator of sixty-five had been born overnight. Actually his skill and resourcefulness in the House of Commons and on public platforms had long been a byword to the British. Family tradition, every advantage of birth and of distinguished association, as well as forty-five years of study and preparation lay behind the new Prime Minister. His father, Lord Randolph Churchill, had been the brilliant "Tory Democrat" of the 1880's whose speeches in Commons glittered with invective against parties and persons alike, and especially against the sainted Gladstone. In his two-volume life of his father, published in 1906, Winston Churchill showed how carefully he had studied their pungency and wit. On his mother's side, he was also blessed. Jennie Jerome, an American beauty, was a woman of singular magnetism.

After being educated at Harrow and the Royal Military College, Sandhurst, Churchill had a touch of war with the Spanish in Cuba in 1895. Two years later, in India, he combined soldiering and journalism, and in 1898 took part in a famous cavalry charge in Kitchener's campaign against the dervishes of the Sudan. Symbolic of his acceptance of the modern world, for all his nostalgia for chivalric warfare, was the sheathing of his sword in this engagement and the drawing of a Mauser automatic. Shortly after, while serving as a correspondent for the London Morning Post, he was captured by the Boers, but was able to escape and to become a combat officer.

Elected to Parliament as a Conservative in 1900, Churchill shifted to the Liberals in 1906, on the tariff issue, and was made Undersecretary for the Colonies. Later he served as President of the Board of Trade and Home Secretary, and was, at the outbreak of the First World War, First Lord of the Admiralty. Whether or not responsible for the failure of the Dardanelles campaign (and opinions on the point differ), he received full blame for it, and lost his cabinet post. In 1917, however, he was back on the job as Minister of Munitions, and later, as Secretary of State for War and Air. In 1921 he proved to be a surprisingly conciliatory Colonial Secretary. But after three defeats, he returned to the Conservatives in 1924, and served as Chancellor of the Exchequer until 1929—his least distinguished ministerial term. For the next decade he held no high office, but he cried out incessantly against the rising Nazi threat "while England slept."

Then, almost at once, as we have related, Winston Churchill, the soldier-statesman-journalist, whose heart was in the aristocratic empire-building past, but whose golden tongue enthralled and dominated the present, became Prime Minister of a beleaguered, despairing Britain.

Three days later, on Monday, May 13, 1940, the House of Commons met for a vote of confidence in the new administration, and the new Prime Minister spoke as follows:

"I have nothing to offer but blood, toil, tears, and sweat."

ON FRIDAY EVENING LAST I received His Majesty's commission to form a new administration. It was the evident wish and will of Parliament and the nation that this should include all parties, both those who supported the late Government and also the parties of the Opposition. I have completed the most important part of this task. A War Cabinet has been formed of five Members, representing, with the Opposition Liberals, the unity of the nation. The three party leaders have agreed to serve, either in the War Cabinet or in high executive office. The three fighting services have been filled. It was necessary that this should be done in one single day, on account of the extreme urgency and rigor of events. A number of other key positions were filled yesterday, and I am submitting a further list to His Majesty tonight. I hope to complete the appointment of the principal Ministers during tomorrow. The appointment of the other Ministers usually takes a little longer, but I trust that, when Parliament meets again, this part of my task will be completed, and that the administration will be complete in all respects.

I considered it in the public interest to suggest that the House should be summoned to meet today. Mr. Speaker agreed, and took the necessary steps, in accordance with the powers conferred upon him by the Resolution of the House. At the end of the proceedings today, the adjournment of the House will be proposed until Tuesday, May 21, with, of course, provision for earlier meeting if need be. The business to be considered during that week will be notified to Members at the earliest opportunity. I now invite the House, by the Resolution which stands in my name, to record its approval of the steps taken and to declare its confidence in the new Government.

To form an administration of this scale and complexity is a serious undertaking in itself, but it must be remembered that we are in the preliminary stage of one of the greatest battles in history, that we are in action at many points in Norway and in Holland, that we have to be prepared in the Mediterranean, that the air battle is continuous and that many preparations have to be made here at home. In this crisis I hope I may be pardoned if I do not address the House at any length today. I hope that any of my friends and colleagues, or former colleagues, who are affected by the political reconstruction, will make all allowance for any lack of ceremony with which it has been necessary to act. I would say to the House, as I said to those who have joined this Government: "I have nothing to offer but blood, toil, tears and sweat."

We have before us an ordeal of the most grievous kind. We have before us many, many long months of struggle and of suffering. You ask what is our policy? I will say: It is to wage war, by sea, land and air, with all our might and with all the strength that God can give us: to wage war against a monstrous tyranny, never surpassed in the dark, lamentable catalogue of human crime. That is our policy. You ask, What is our aim? I can answer in one word: Victory—victory at all costs, victory in spite of all terror, victory, however long and hard the road may be; for without victory, there is no survival. Let that be realized; no survival for the British Empire; no survival for all that the British Empire has stood for, no survival for the urge and impulse of the ages, that mankind will move forward towards its goal. But I take up my task with buoyancy and hope. I feel sure that our cause will not be suffered to fail among men. At this time I feel entitled to claim the aid of all, and I say, "Come, then, let us go forward together with our united strength."

No comment on this speech, or the response to it, can match Churchill's own remark: "In all our long history no Prime Minister had ever been able to present to Parliament and the nation a program at once so short and so popular."

The House voted unanimously for its approval.

CHURCHILL REPORTS THE MIRACLE OF DUNKIRK

[June 4, 1940]

Churchill (Their Finest Hour, p. 115) has written his own introduction to the famous Dunkirk speech: "Parliament assembled on June 4, and it was my duty to lay the story fully before them both in public and secret session. . . . It was imperative to explain not only to our own people but to the world that our resolve to fight on was based on serious grounds, and was no mere despairing effort. It was also right to lay bare my own reasons for confidence."

"We must be very careful not to assign to this deliverance the attributes of a victory."

FROM THE MOMENT that the French defenses at Sedan and on the Meuse were broken at the end of the second week of May, only a rapid retreat to Amiens and the south could have saved the British and French armies who had entered Belgium at the appeal of the Belgian King; but this strategic fact was not immediately realized. . . .

The German eruption swept like a sharp scythe around the right and rear of the armies of the north. Eight or nine armored divisions, each of about four hundred armored vehicles of different kinds, but carefully assorted to be complementary and divisible into small self-contained units, cut off all communications between us and the main French armies. It severed our own communications for food and ammunition, which ran first to Amiens and afterward through Abbeville, and it shored its way up the coast to Boulogne and Calais, and almost to Dunkirk. Behind this armored and mechanized onslaught came a number of German divisions in lorries, and behind them again there plodded comparatively slowly the dull brute mass of the ordinary Germany Army and German people, always so ready to be led to the trampling down in other lands of liberties and comforts which they have never known in their own. . . .

Meanwhile, the Royal Air Force, which had already been intervening in the battle, so far as its range would allow, from home bases, now used part of its main metropolitan fighter strength, and struck at the German bombers and at the fighters which in large numbers protected them. This struggle was protracted and fierce. Suddenly the scene has cleared, the crash and thunder has for the moment—but only for the moment—died away. A miracle of deliverance, achieved by valor, by perseverance, by perfect discipline, by faultless service, by resource, by skill, by unconquerable fidelity, is manifest to us all. The enemy was hurled back by the retreating British and French troops. He was so roughly handled that he did not hurry their departure seriously. The Royal Air Force engaged the main strength of the German Air Force, and inflicted upon them losses of at least four to one; and the navy, using nearly one thousand ships of all kinds, carried over 335,000 men, French and British, out of the jaws of death and shame, to their native land and to the tasks which lie immediately ahead. We must be very careful not to assign to this deliverance the attributes of a victory. Wars are not won by evacuations. But there was a victory inside this deliverance, which should be noted. It was gained by the air force. Many of our soldiers coming back have not seen the air force at work; they saw only the bombers which escaped its protective attack. They underrate its achievements. I have heard much talk of this; that is why I go out of my way to say this. I will tell you about it.

This was a great trial of strength between the British and German air forces. Can you conceive a greater objective for the Germans in the air than to make evacuation from these beaches impossible, and to sink all these ships which were displayed, almost to the extent of thousands? Could there have been an objective of greater military importance and significance for the whole purpose of the war than this? They tried hard, and they were beaten back; they were frustrated in their task. We got the army away; and they have paid fourfold for any losses which they have inflicted. Very large formations of German airplanes—and we know that they are a very brave race—have turned on several occasions from the attack of one quarter of their number of the Royal Air Force, and have dispersed in different directions. Twelve airplanes have been hunted by two. One airplane was driven into the water and cast away by the mere charge of a British airplane, which had no more ammunition. All of our types—the Hurricane, the Spitfire, and the new Defiant—and all our pilots have been vindicated as superior to what they have at present to face.

When we consider how much greater would be our advantage in defending the air above this island against an overseas attack, I must say that I find in these facts a sure basis upon which practical and reassuring thoughts may rest. I will pay my tribute to these young airmen. The great French Army was very largely, for the time being, cast back and disturbed by the onrush of a few thousands of armored vehicles. May it not also be that the cause of civilization itself will be defended by the skill and devotion of a few thousand airmen? There never has been, I suppose, in all the world, in all the history of war, such an opportunity for youth. The Knights of the Round Table, the Crusaders, all fall back into the past—not only distant but prosaic; these young men, going forth every morn to guard their native land and all that we stand for, holding in their hands these instruments of colossal and shattering power, of whom it may be said that

Every morn brought forth a noble chance,
And every chance brought forth a noble knight,

deserve our gratitude, as do all of the brave men who, in so many ways and on so many occasions, are ready, and continue ready, to give life and all for their native land.

I return to the army. In the long series of very fierce battles, now on this front, now on that, fighting on three fronts at once, battles fought by two or three divisions against an equal or somewhat larger number of the enemy, and fought fiercely on some of the old grounds that so many of us knew so well—in these battles our losses in men have exceeded thirty thousand killed, wounded, and missing. I take occasion to express the sympathy of the House to all who have suffered bereavement or who are still anxious. The President of the Board of Trade [Sir Andrew Duncan, later Minister of Supply] is not here today. His son has been killed, and many in the House have felt the pangs of affliction in the sharpest form. But I will say this about the missing: we have had a large number of wounded come home safely to this country, but I would say about the missing that there may be very many reported missing who will come back home, someday, in one way or another. In the confusion of this fight it is inevitable that many have been left in positions where honor required no further resistance from them.

Against this loss of over thirty thousand men, we can set a far heavier loss certainly inflicted upon the enemy. But our losses in matériel are enormous. We have perhaps lost one third of the men we lost in the opening days of the battle of March 21, 1918, but we have lost nearly as many guns—nearly one thousand—and all our transport, all the armored vehicles that were with the army in the north. This loss will impose a further delay on the expansion of our military strength. That expansion had not been proceeding as fast as we had hoped. The best of all we had to give had gone to the British Expeditionary Force, and although they had not the numbers of tanks and some articles of equipment which were desirable, they were a very well and finely equipped army. They had the first fruits of all that our industry had to give, and that is gone. And now here is this further delay. How long it will be, how long it will last, depends upon the exertions which we make in this island. An effort the like of which has never been seen in our records is now being made. Work is proceeding everywhere, night and day, Sundays and weekdays. Capital and labor have cast aside their interests, rights, and customs and put them into the common stock. Already the flow of munitions has leaped forward. There is no reason why we should not in a few months overtake the sudden and serious loss that has come upon us, without retarding the development of our general program.

Nevertheless, our thankfulness at the escape of our army and so many men, whose loved ones have passed through an agonizing week, must not blind us to the fact that what has happened in France and Belgium is a colossal military disaster. The French Army has been weakened, the Belgian Army has been lost, a large part of those fortified lines upon which so much faith had been reposed is gone, many valuable mining districts and factories have passed into the enemy's possession, the whole of the Channel ports are in his hands, with all the tragic consequences that follow from that, and we must expect another blow to be struck almost immediately at us or at France. We are told that Herr Hitler has a plan for invading the British Isles. This has often been thought of before. When Napoleon lay at Boulogne for a year with his flat-bottomed boats and his Grand Army, he was told by someone, "There are bitter weeds in England." There are certainly a great many more of them since the British Expeditionary Force returned.

The whole question of home defense against invasion is, of course, powerfully affected by the fact that we have for the time being in this island incomparably more powerful military forces than we have ever had at any moment in this war or the last. But this will not continue. We shall not be content with a defensive war. We have our duty to our ally. We have to reconstitute and build up the British Expeditionary Force once again, under its gallant Commander in Chief, Lord Gort. All this is in train; but in the interval we must put our defenses in this island into such a high state of organization that the fewest possible numbers will be required to give effective security and that the largest possible potential of offensive effort may be realized. On this we are now engaged. It will be very convenient, if it be the desire of the House, to enter upon this subject in a secret session. Not that the government would necessarily be able to reveal in very great detail military secrets, but we like to have our discussions free, without the restraint imposed by the fact that they will be read the next day by the enemy; and the government would benefit by views freely expressed in all parts of the House by Members with their knowledge of so many different parts of the country. I understand that some request is to be made upon this subject, which will be readily acceded to by His Majesty's Government.

We have found it necessary to take measures of increasing stringency, not only against enemy aliens and suspicious characters of other nationalities, but also against British subjects who may become a danger or a nuisance should the war be transported to the United Kingdom. I know there are a great many people affected by the orders which we have made who are the passionate enemies of Nazi Germany. I am very sorry for them, but we cannot at the present time and under the present stress draw all the distinctions which we should like to do. If parachute landings were attempted and fierce fighting attendant upon them followed, these unfortunate people would be far better out of the way, for their own sakes as well as for ours. There is, however, another class, for which I feel not the slightest sympathy. Parliament has given us the powers to put down fifth-column activities with a strong hand, and we shall use those powers, subject to the supervision and correction of the House, without the slightest hesitation until we are satisfied, and more than satisfied, that this malignancy in our midst has been effectively stamped out.

Turning once again, and this time more generally, to the question of invasion, I would observe that there has never been a period in all these long centuries of which we boast when an absolute guarantee against invasion, still less against serious raids, could have been given to our people. In the days of Napoleon the same wind which would have carried his transports across the Channel might have driven away the blockading fleet. There was always the chance, and it is that chance which has excited and befooled the imaginations of many Continental tyrants. Many are the tales that are told. We are assured that novel methods will be adopted, and when we see the originality of malice, the ingenuity of aggression, which our enemy displays, we may certainly prepare ourselves for every kind of novel stratagem and every kind of brutal and treacherous maneuver. I think that no idea is so outlandish that it should not be considered and viewed with a searching, but at the same time, I hope, with a steady eye. We must never forget the solid assurances of sea power and those which belong to air power if it can be locally exercised.

I have, myself, full confidence that if all do their duty, if nothing is neglected, and if the best arrangements are made, as they are being made, we shall prove ourselves once again able to defend our island home, to ride out the storm of war, and to outlive the menace of tyranny, if necessary for years, if necessary alone. At any rate, that is what we are going to try to do. That is the resolve of His Majesty's Government—every man of them. That is the will of Parliament and the nation. The British Empire and the French Republic, linked together in their cause and in their need, will defend to the death their native soil, aiding each other like good comrades to the utmost of their strength. Even though

large tracts of Europe and many old and famous states have fallen or
may fall into the grip of the Gestapo and all the odious apparatus of
Nazi rule, we shall not flag or fail. We shall go on to the end, we shall
fight in France, we shall fight on the seas and oceans, we shall fight with
growing confidence and growing strength in the air, we shall defend our
island, whatever the cost may be, we shall fight on the beaches, we shall
fight on the landing grounds, we shall fight in the fields and in the streets,
we shall fight in the hills; we shall never surrender, and even if, which I
do not for a moment believe, this island or a large part of it were subjugated and starving, then our Empire beyond the seas, armed and
guarded by the British fleet, would carry on the struggle, until, in God's
good time, the New World, with all its power and might, steps forth to
the rescue and the liberation of the old.

*This masterly performance was a boon to the grieving and bewildered popula-
tion of Great Britain; it also had its repercussions in the New World, from
which Churchill, for the first time, asked for help. Six days later, when Italy
entered the war, Roosevelt made his first public answer. On his own initiative,
as Robert Sherwood tells us, and without consulting the timorous State Department, he inserted these words into his Charlottesville speech: "We will
extend to the opponents of force the material resources of this nation; and at
the same time we will harness and speed up the use of those resources in order
that we ourselves in the Americas may have equipment and training equal to
the task of any emergency and every defense."*

*In France, where Pétain's opinion, that England would "fight to the last
Frenchman" and make a servile peace with Germany, had some currency,
people took heart and felt their dark encirclement less. In Germany the promise
that England would devote its fullest resources to defense must have been a
setback, discouraging all dreams, such as those of Rudolf Hess, for a temporary
deal with Britain. Yet the promise was at this time little more than a promise.
The Very Reverend Dr. Hewlett Johnson, Dean of Canterbury, has related
that during the end of the Dunkirk broadcast "Mr. Churchill put his hand over
the microphone and said with a smile: 'And we will hit them over the head
with beer bottles, which is all we have really got.'"*

CHURCHILL ANTICIPATES THE BATTLE OF BRITAIN

[June 18, 1940]

Again Sir Winston provides a succinct introduction for his speech (Their Finest Hour, pp. 224–25): "After the collapse of France the question which arose in the minds of all our friends and foes was, 'Would Britain surrender too?' So far as public statements count in the face of events, I had in the name of His Majesty's Government repeatedly declared our resolve to fight on alone. After Dunkirk on June 4 I had used the expression, 'if necessary for years, if necessary alone.' This was not inserted without design, and the French Ambassador in London had been instructed the next day to inquire what I actually meant. He was told 'exactly what was said.' I could remind the House of my remark when I addressed it on June 18, the morrow of the Bordeaux collapse."

"This was their finest hour."

DURING the first four years of the last war the Allies experienced nothing but disaster and disappointment. . . . We repeatedly asked ourselves the question, "How are we going to win?" and no one was ever able to answer it with much precision, until at the end, quite suddenly, quite unexpectedly, our terrible foe collapsed before us, and we were so glutted with victory that in our folly we threw it away.

However matters may go in France or with the French government or other French governments, we in this island and in the British Empire will never lose our sense of comradeship with the French people. . . . If final victory rewards our toils they shall share the gains—aye, and freedom shall be restored to all. We abate nothing of our just demands; not one jot or tittle do we recede. . . . Czechs, Poles, Norwegians, Dutch, Belgians, have joined their causes to our own. All these shall be restored.

What General Weygand called the Battle of France is over. I expect that the Battle of Britain is about to begin. Upon this battle depends the survival of Christian civilization. Upon it depends our own British life, and the long continuity of our institutions and our Empire. The whole fury and might of the enemy must very soon be turned on us. Hitler knows that he will have to break us in this island or lose the war. If we can stand up to him, all Europe may be free and the life of the world may move forward into broad, sunlit uplands. But if we fail, then the whole world, including the United States, including all that we have known and cared for, will sink into the abyss of a new Dark Age, made more sinister, and perhaps more protracted, by the lights of perverted science. Let us therefore brace ourselves to our duties, and so bear ourselves that, if the British Empire and its Commonwealth last for a thousand years, men will say, "This was their finest hour."

"I have never been so proud and glad to be a Member as I was when I listened to those first tremendous orations," said Sir A. P. Herbert as he looked back, in Independent Member, on his fourteen years in the House of Commons. "I have been moved in theaters and churches, but never so deeply as those early speeches stirred me up there in the gallery, the famous phrases which passed into history as soon as they were spoken."

In painting his portrait of Churchill while the Battle of Britain was still in doubt, Philip Guedalla said: "No man ever rendered greater service to his people than their spokesman in those summer weeks of 1940. Perhaps it was his major contribution to their history."

●

GENERAL CHARLES DE GAULLE CALLS FREE FRANCE INTO EXISTENCE

[June 18–19, 1940]

On the same day that Churchill gave his speech in the House of Commons on the fall of France, the future leader of the Free French, General Charles de Gaulle (1890–   ) gave his first radio broadcast from London, inaugurating the resistance movement in France and the French Empire. He had made a brilliant record in the first World War, and had served under General Weygand in Poland in 1921. In his book The Army of the Future (1934), he had predicted the kind of motorized warfare by which the Germans were to conquer France sixteen years later; and against the stubborn Maginot Line strategy of the French General Staff, he had urged a mobile, heavily mechanized plan of defense. In 1940 he became Undersecretary of War under Premier Paul Reynaud. When the French armies collapsed, however, Reynaud in his extremity sent for Pétain, the "hero of Verdun," who soon became Premier himself, and made prompt arrangements for immediate surrender and an armistice. Never having shared the Maginot optimism before the war, de

Gaulle did not share the prevailing pessimism now. He fled to London to organize the Free French movement, and was sentenced to death in absentia by a French court. As the tall, intrepid, self-willed French officer stood before the microphone to rally Frenchmen throughout the world to freedom, the fortunes of the Allies were at their lowest ebb. The "Battle of France" was over, as General Weygand had said; the "Battle of Britain," as Churchill added, was about to begin.

I

"The flame of French resistance must not and shall not die."

THE LEADERS who, for many years past, have been at the head of the French armed forces have set up a government.

Alleging the defeat of our armies, this government has entered into negotiations with the enemy with a view to bringing about a cessation of hostilities. It is quite true that we were, and still are, overwhelmed by enemy mechanized forces, both on the ground and in the air. It was the tanks, the planes, and the tactics of the Germans, far more than the fact that we were outnumbered, that forced our armies to retreat. It was the German tanks, planes, and tactics that provided the element of surprise which brought our leaders to their present plight.

But has the last word been said? Must we abandon all hope? Is our defeat final and irremediable? To those questions I answer—No!

Speaking in full knowledge of the facts, I ask you to believe me when I say that the cause of France is not lost. The very factors that brought about our defeat may one day lead us to victory.

For, remember this, France does not stand alone. She is not isolated. Behind her is a vast empire, and she can make common cause with the British Empire, which commands the seas and is continuing the struggle. Like England, she can draw unreservedly on the immense industrial resources of the United States.

This war is not limited to our unfortunate country. The outcome of the struggle has not been decided by the Battle of France. This is a world war. Mistakes have been made, there have been delays and untold suffering, but the fact remains that there still exists in the world everything we need to crush our enemies someday. Today we are crushed by the sheer weight of mechanized force hurled against us, but we can still look to a future in which even greater mechanized force will bring us victory. The destiny of the world is at stake.

I, General de Gaulle, now in London, call on all French officers and men who are at present on British soil, or may be in the future, with or without their arms; I call on all engineers and skilled workmen from the armaments factories who are at present on British soil, or may be in the future, to get in touch with me.

Whatever happens, the flame of French resistance must not and shall not die.

Tomorrow I shall broadcast again from London.

II

Frenchmen must now be fully aware that all ordinary forms of authority have disappeared.

Faced by the bewilderment of my countrymen, by the disintegration of a government in thrall to the enemy, by the fact that the institutions of my country are incapable, at the moment, of functioning, I, General de Gaulle, a French soldier and military leader, realize that I now speak for France.

In the name of France, I make the following solemn declaration:

It is the bounden duty of all Frenchmen who still bear arms to continue the struggle. For them to lay down their arms, to evacuate any position of military importance, or agree to hand over any part of French territory, however small, to enemy control, would be a crime against our country. For the moment I refer particularly to French North Africa—to the *integrity* of French North Africa.

The Italian armistice is nothing but a clumsy trap. In the Africa of Clauzel, Bugeaud, Lyautey, and Noguès, honor and duty strictly enjoin that the French should refuse to carry out the conditions imposed by the enemy.

The thought that the panic of Bordeaux could make itself felt across the sea is not to be borne.

Soldiers of France, wherever you may be, arise!

In the past many an exile had dreamed of returning to his country at the head of a liberating army, but was always faced with stupendous problems of secret messages and messengers to carry them to and fro. Now, through the magic of the radio, one exile could speak directly to millions of his countrymen, many of them in hiding.

In the deepening crisis, Frenchmen took heart, and they responded to de Gaulle as they once had to a Joan of Arc or a Napoleon. Although the venerable Pétain had made supine peace with the Germans, the high officers had surrendered, and prosperous classes were making the best of collaboration, re-

sistance flamed and spread in France, and it was not long before the French
colonies had deserted Pétain for de Gaulle.

STALIN, TEN DAYS AFTER THE NAZI INVASION, INSTRUCTS HIS PEOPLE

[July 3, 1941]

After overrunning Europe from Scandinavia to the Balkans and securing his
southern flank by a treaty of neutrality with Turkey, Hitler decided to risk a
second front and crush the Soviet Union with a super-blitzkrieg. On Sunday
morning, June 22, 1941, three Nazi army groups, with dive bombers screaming
ahead, crashed across the Russian border, from the Gulf of Finland in the north
to the Black Sea in the south. Nothing so staggeringly terrible had thus far
taken place in recent history.

Churchill, who knew the invasion was coming and had warned Stalin twice
in April, was questioned only the day before as to whether he, the arch anti-
Communist, could support the Communists. "I have only one purpose," replied the Prime Minister, "the destruction of Hitler, and my life is much
simplified thereby. If Hitler invaded Hell I would make at least a favorable
reference to the Devil in the House of Commons." These sentiments he
elaborated on the very night of the invasion in one of his finest broadcasts,
saying, "We shall give whatever help we can to Russia and the Russian people."

But Stalin did not speak to the Russian people by radio until ten days later.
Why? He was incredibly busy and he was also incredibly dumfounded. He had
been building up Russian military strength as rapidly as possible, not expecting
the Nazi-Soviet antiaggression pact of 1939 to last forever—but he did not
expect to be double-crossed so soon. He had permitted the Balkan countries to
fall into Hitler's hands, one by one, instead of organizing them himself. He
had attempted to negotiate up to the day of the invasion.

Now his armies were fighting bravely but falling back steadily on the three
sectors of the vast front and, says Deutscher, "behind the fighting lines, rumor,
confusion, and panic began to spread." Stalin finally broadcast on July 3 in a
voice that was "slow, halting, colorless."

"To the enemy must not be left a single engine,

a single railway car, not a single pound of grain

or a gallon of fuel."

COMRADES! Citizens! Brothers and Sisters! Men of our Army and Navy!

I am addressing you, my friends!

The perfidious military attack on our fatherland, begun on June 22 by Hitler's Germany, is continuing.

In spite of heroic resistance of the Red Army, and although the enemy's finest divisions and finest air-force units have already been smashed and have met their doom on the field of battle, the enemy continues to push forward, hurling fresh forces into the attack.

Hitler's troops have succeeded in capturing Lithuania, a considerable part of Latvia, the western part of White Russia, and a part of the western Ukraine.

The Fascist air force is extending the range of operations of its bombers and is bombing Murmansk, Orsha, Mogilev, Smolensk, Kiev, Odessa, and Sevastopol.

A grave danger hangs over our country.

How could it have happened that our glorious Red Army surrendered a number of our cities and districts to the Fascist armies?

Is it really true that German Fascist troops are invincible, as is ceaselessly trumpeted by boastful Fascist propagandists? Of course not!

History shows that there are no invincible armies, and never have been. Napoleon's army was considered invincible, but it was beaten successively by Russian, English, and German armies. Kaiser Wilhelm's German army in the period of the first imperialist war was also considered invincible, but it was beaten several times by Russian and Anglo-French forces, and was finally smashed by Anglo-French forces.

The same must be said of Hitler's German Fascist army today. This army has not yet met with serious resistance on the Continent of Europe. Only on our territory has it met serious resistance, and if as a result of this resistance the finest divisions of Hitler's German Fascist army have been defeated by our Red Army, it means that this army, too, can be smashed and will be smashed as were the armies of Napoleon and Wilhelm.

As to part of our territory having nevertheless been seized by German

Fascist troops, this is chiefly due to the fact that the war of Fascist Germany on the U.S.S.R. began under conditions favorable for German forces and unfavorable for Soviet forces.

The fact of the matter is that troops of Germany, as a country at war, were already fully mobilized, and 170 divisions hurled by Germany against the U.S.S.R. and brought up to the Soviet frontiers were in a state of complete readiness, only awaiting the signal to move into action, whereas Soviet troops had little time to effect mobilization and move up to the frontiers.

Of no little importance in this respect is the fact that Fascist Germany suddenly and treacherously violated the nonaggression pact she concluded in 1939 with the U.S.S.R., disregarding the fact that she would be regarded as an aggressor by the whole world. Naturally, our peace-loving country, not wishing to take the initiative of breaking the pact, could not resort to perfidy.

It may be asked: how could the Soviet government have consented to conclude a nonaggression pact with such treacherous fiends as Hitler and Ribbentrop? Was not this an error on the part of the Soviet government? Of course not!

Nonaggression pacts are pacts of peace between two states. It was such a pact that Germany proposed to us in 1939. Could the Soviet government have declined such a proposal? I think that not a single peace-loving state could decline a peace treaty with a neighboring state, even though the latter was headed by such fiends and cannibals as Hitler and Ribbentrop.

But that, of course, only on one indispensable condition—namely, that this peace treaty does not infringe either directly or indirectly on the territorial integrity, independence, and honor of a peace-loving state.

As is well known, the nonaggression pact between Germany and the U.S.S.R. is precisely such a pact.

What did we gain by concluding a nonaggression pact with Germany? We secured for our country peace for a year and a half and the opportunity of preparing its forces to repulse Fascist Germany should she risk an attack on our country despite the pact.

This was a definite advantage for us and a disadvantage for Fascist Germany.

What has Fascist Germany gained and what has she lost by treacherously tearing up the pact and attacking the U.S.S.R.?

She gained a certain advantageous position for her troops for a short period, but she has lost politically by exposing herself in the eyes of the entire world as a bloodthirsty aggressor.

There can be no doubt that this short-lived military gain for Germany is only an episode, while the tremendous political gain of the U.S.S.R. is a serious and lasting factor that is bound to form the basis for development of decisive military successes of the Red Army in the war with Fascist Germany. . . .

In case of a forced retreat of Red Army units, all rolling stock must be evacuated; to the enemy must not be left a single engine, a single railway car, not a single pound of grain or a gallon of fuel.

Collective farmers must drive off all their cattle and turn over their grain to the safekeeping of state authorities for transportation to the rear. All valuable property including nonferrous metals, grain, and fuel which cannot be withdrawn must without fail be destroyed.

In areas occupied by the enemy, guerrilla units, mounted and foot, must be formed, diversionist groups must be organized to combat enemy troops, to foment guerrilla warfare everywhere, to blow up bridges, roads, damage telephone and telegraph lines, and to set fire to forests, stores, and transports.

In occupied regions conditions must be made unbearable for the enemy and all his accomplices. They must be hounded and annihilated at every step and all their measures frustrated.

This war with Fascist Germany cannot be considered an ordinary war. It is not only a war between two armies, it is also a great war of the entire Soviet people against the German Fascist forces.

The aim of this national war in defense of our country against the Fascist oppressors is not only elimination of the danger hanging over our country, but also aid to all European peoples groaning under the yoke of German Fascism.

In this war of liberation we shall not be alone.

In this great war we shall have loyal allies in the peoples of Europe and America, including German people who are enslaved by Hitlerite despots.

Our war for the freedom of our country will merge with the struggle of the peoples of Europe and America for their independence, for democratic liberties. It will be a united front of peoples standing for freedom and against enslavement and threats of enslavement by Hitler's Fascist armies.

In this connection the historic utterance of British Prime Minister Churchill regarding aid to the Soviet Union and the declaration of the U. S. A. government signifying readiness to render aid to our country, which can only evoke a feeling of gratitude in the hearts of the peoples of the Soviet Union, are fully comprehensible and symptomatic.

Comrades, our forces are numberless. The overweening enemy will soon learn this to his cost. Side by side with the Red Army and Navy thousands of workers, collective farmers, and intellectuals are rising to fight the enemy aggressor. The masses of our people will rise up in their millions. The working people of Moscow and Leningrad already have commenced to form vast popular levies in support of the Red Army.

Such popular levies must be raised in every city that is in danger of an enemy invasion; all working people must be roused to defend our freedom, our honor, our country—in our patriotic war against German Fascism.

In order to insure a rapid mobilization of all forces of the peoples of the U.S.S.R., and to repulse the enemy who treacherously attacked our country, a State Committee of Defense has been formed in whose hands the entire power of the state has been vested.

The State Committee of Defense has entered into its functions and calls upon all our people to rally around the party of Lenin-Stalin and around the Soviet government so as self-denyingly to support the Red Army and Navy, demolish the enemy, and secure victory.

All our forces for the support of our heroic Red Army and our glorious Red Navy!

All the forces of the people—for the demolition of the enemy!

Forward, to our victory!

Compared with the brilliant Trotsky, Stalin was no speaker at all. But beneath the plodding surface of his sentences there was a tenacity, a ruthless determination, that was backed up by absolute power. He hardly had to remind his people of their inveterate love of their soil, of their invincible distances, of Napoleon's disaster in Russia.

His "scorched earth" policy, which no other European country had seriously contemplated, was carried out with an indomitable will. Having destroyed the means of production and of life, the population retreated or returned as guerrillas to harass the enemy. What was not destroyed was evacuated. Stalin himself is said to have supervised the transportation of 1,360 plants and factories from the Ukraine and western Russia to the Volga, the Urals, and Siberia.

Even the flexible Nazi armies were not adequate for this kind of warfare. The surrender at Stalingrad in February, 1943, marked a turning point of the war.

ROOSEVELT ASKS FOR A DECLARATION
OF WAR AGAINST JAPAN

[December 8, 1941]

On the morning of Sunday, December 7, while their envoys were still in Washington negotiating a settlement, the Japanese suddenly hurled bombers and torpedo planes at Pearl Harbor, sinking or crippling eight United States battleships and destroying many other craft, as well as planes and airfields. There had been some warnings, but they had been indecisive, and General Short and Admiral Kimmel, who were later to be charged with negligence, ruled out an attack on Hawaii at this time. It looked rather as if the target would be Indo-China or Singapore, six thousand miles away from Pearl Harbor, and few dreamed of the daring and irreparable onslaught that came.

In those tense days preceding the war, Roosevelt was in a quandary. What if the Japanese attacked the Dutch or the British in the Far East? This was a question the British often asked, but neither our ambassador in London nor Roosevelt himself could answer. War would have to be declared by Congress (with its many isolationists), and here was Cordell Hull, the Secretary of State, working with stubborn zeal for a peaceful settlement, at almost any cost. Nothing could be done for Borneo or Singapore, anyway. America could not strike first but could only wait, while negotiations continued, for the blow to fall. The country, meanwhile, was not prepared for war. Exactly two years before, Roosevelt, in a radio address, had announced our neutrality in the European conflict. "Let no men or women thoughtlessly talk of America sending its armies to European fields," he had said.

Now the irony of events forced the President to reverse his heart and action. Like Wilson, who had been elected on a platform of peace and liberal reform, Roosevelt would now be obliged to scrap his progressive program and to redirect industry and citizenry to the painful uncertainties of war. Fully conscious of this parallel and of his responsibility in the eyes of history, he asked Woodrow Wilson's widow to accompany Mrs. Roosevelt to the joint session of Congress, on Monday morning, December 8.

He had dictated most of his speech the day before, according to Rosenman, between conferences "with military leaders, with members of the Cabinet, with congressional leaders, and with scores of other people," but evidently he added factual details as the news came in, up to the very last moment, before driving to the Capitol.

"There is no blinking at the fact that our people, our territory,

and our interests are in grave danger."

Mr. Vice-President, Mr. Speaker, members of the Senate and the House of Representatives:

YESTERDAY, December 7, 1941—a date which will live in infamy— the United States of America was suddenly and deliberately attacked by naval and air forces of the empire of Japan.

The United States was at peace with that nation, and, at the solicitation of Japan, was still in conversation with its government and its Emperor looking toward the maintenance of peace in the Pacific.

Indeed, one hour after Japanese air squadrons had commenced bombing in the American island of Oahu the Japanese Ambassador to the United States and his colleague delivered to our Secretary of State a formal reply to a recent American message. And, while this reply stated that it seemed useless to continue the existing diplomatic negotiations, it contained no threat or hint of war or of armed attack.

It will be recorded that the distance of Hawaii from Japan makes it obvious that the attack was deliberately planned many days or even weeks ago. During the intervening time the Japanese government has deliberately sought to deceive the United States by false statements and expressions of hope for continued peace.

The attack yesterday on the Hawaiian Islands has caused severe damage to American naval and military forces. I regret to tell you that very many American lives have been lost. In addition, American ships have been reported torpedoed on the high seas between San Francisco and Honolulu.

Yesterday the Japanese government also launched an attack against Malaya.

Last night Japanese forces attacked Hong Kong.

Last night Japanese forces attacked Guam.

Last night Japanese forces attacked the Philippine Islands.

Last night the Japanese attacked Wake Island.

And this morning the Japanese attacked Midway Island.

Japan has therefore undertaken a surprise offensive extending throughout the Pacific area. The facts of yesterday and today speak for themselves. The people of the United States have already formed their opinions and well understand the implications to the very life and safety of our nation.

As Commander-in-Chief of the Army and Navy, I have directed that all measures be taken for our defense.

Always will we remember the character of the onslaught against us.

No matter how long it may take us to overcome this premeditated invasion, the American people, in their righteous might, will win through to absolute victory.

I believe that I interpret the will of the Congress and of the people when I assert that we will not only defend ourselves to the uttermost, but will make it very certain that this form of treachery shall never again endanger us.

Hostilities exist. There is no blinking at the fact that our people, our territory, and our interests are in grave danger.

With confidence in our armed forces, with the unbounding determination of our people, we will gain the inevitable triumph. So help us God.

I ask that the Congress declare that since the unprovoked and dastardly attack by Japan on Sunday, December 7, 1941, a state of war has existed between the United States and the Japanese Empire.

The effect of this message on Congress and the country at large was one of instantaneous relief and stimulation. Painful tensions were released, and any fear that we might unworthily compromise with Japan was swept away. Roosevelt too was relieved, as Hopkins wrote, that events themselves had aroused the country to unanimity of courage and purpose. Americans, so largely isolationists at heart, girded themselves for the greatest industrial and military effort in their history.

So obvious was the effect of Roosevelt's speeches on American and British morale that the Germans and Japanese tried again and again to distract attention from them by mysterious raids and spectacular bombings. After this strategy of the enemy became clear, there was little advance notice of the President's important addresses.

HENRY A. WALLACE ESTIMATES THE PRICE OF FREE WORLD VICTORY

[May 8, 1942]

On January 1, 1942, the declaration by the United Nations was signed by twenty-six states at Washington, but that great promise for the future was obscured by four months of unbroken disaster. To name only the worst, the British

battleship Prince of Wales and the cruiser Repulse were sunk off the coast of
Malaya; Hong Kong and Singapore were captured by the Japanese; the American forces on Bataan Peninsula and on Corregidor surrendered to the Japanese;
the German army in North Africa was counterattacking vigorously and German
U-boats were winning the battle of the Atlantic.

Along with blood, sweat, and tears and incredible amounts of tanks, ships,
and planes, there was need for a broad, over-all statement of the Allied goal, of
the Allied dream. Vice-President Wallace tried to fill that need with his address before the dinner of the recently organized Free World Association in
New York, in the dark spring of 1942. Wallace has been so much discredited
by his break with President Truman over foreign policy, by his stubborn and
tardily abandoned faith in the good faith of the Soviet Union, that his years of
contribution to the New Deal and the whole cause of democracy are too easily
forgotten.

Henry Agard Wallace, born in 1888, came of a long line of distinguished
Iowa farmers and farm journalists. He himself cultivated important strains of
hybrid corn and edited the family periodical, Wallace's Farmer. He was Secretary of Agriculture during Roosevelt's first two terms and Vice-President in the
third. Roosevelt was prepared to decline his own nomination for the third term
if Wallace had not been made his running mate in 1940.

At the time of this speech Wallace's prestige was at its highest.

"Satan now is trying to lead the common man of the whole world

back into slavery and darkness."

W E, WHO in a formal or an informal way represent most of the
free peoples of the world, are met here tonight in the interests
of the millions in all the nations who have freedom in their souls. To my
mind this meeting has just one purpose—to let those millions in other
countries know that here in the United States are 130 million men,
women, and children who are in this war to the finish. Our American
people are utterly resolved to go on until they can strike the relentless
blows that will assure a complete victory and with it win a new day for
the lovers of freedom everywhere on this earth.

This is a fight between a slave world and a free world. Just as the
United States in 1862 could not remain half slave and half free, so in
1942 the world must make its decision for a complete victory one way or
the other.

As we begin the final stages of this fight to the death between the free world and the slave world, it is worth while to refresh our minds about the march of freedom for the common man. The idea of freedom—the freedom that we in the United States know and love so well—is derived from the Bible, with its extraordinary emphasis on the dignity of the individual. Democracy is the only true political expression of Christianity.

The prophets of the Old Testament were the first to preach social justice. But that which was sensed by the prophets many centuries before Christ was not given complete and powerful political expression until our nation was formed as a Federal Union a century and a half ago. Even then, the march of the common people had just begun. Most of them did not yet know how to read and write. There were no public schools to which all children could go. Men and women cannot be really free until they have plenty to eat, and time and ability to read and think and talk things over. Down the years, the people of the United States have moved steadily forward in the practice of democracy. Through universal education, they now can read and write and form opinions of their own. They have learned, and are still learning, the art of production—that is, how to make a living. They have learned, and are still learning, the art of self-government.

If we were to measure freedom by standards of nutrition, education, and self-government, we might rank the United States and certain nations of western Europe very high. But this would not be fair to other nations where education has become widespread only in the last twenty years. In many nations, a generation ago, nine out of ten of the people could not read or write. Russia, for example, was changed from an illiterate to a literate nation within one generation, and, in the process, Russia's appreciation of freedom was enormously enhanced. In China, the increase during the past thirty years in the ability of the people to read and write has been matched by their increased interest in real liberty.

Everywhere, reading and writing are accompanied by industrial progress, and industrial progress sooner or later inevitably brings a strong labor movement. From a long-time and fundamental point of view, there are no backward peoples which are lacking in mechanical sense. Russians, Chinese, and the Indians both of India and the Americas all learn to read and write and operate machines just as well as your children and my children. Everywhere the common people are on the march. These people are learning to think and work together in labor movements, some of which may be extreme or impractical at first, but which eventually will settle down to serve effectively the interests of the common man.

When the freedom-loving people march—when the farmers have an opportunity to buy land at reasonable prices and to sell the produce of their land through their own organizations, when workers have the opportunity to form unions and bargain through them collectively, and when the children of all the people have an opportunity to attend schools which teach them truths of the real world in which they live—when these opportunities are open to everyone, then the world moves straight ahead.

But in countries where the ability to read and write has been recently acquired or where the people have had no long experience in governing themselves on the basis of their own thinking, it is easy for demagogues to arise and prostitute the mind of the common man to their own base ends. Such a demagogue may get financial help from some person of wealth who is unaware of what the end result will be. With this backing, the demagogue may dominate the minds of the people, and, from whatever degree of freedom they have, lead them backward into slavery. Herr Thyssen, the wealthy German steel man, little realized what he was doing when he gave Hitler enough money to enable him to play on the minds of the German people. The demagogue is the curse of the modern world; and of all the demagogues, the worst are those financed by well-meaning wealthy men who sincerely believe that their wealth is likely to be safer if they can hire men with political "it" to change the sign-posts and lure the people back into slavery of the most degraded kind. Unfortunately for the wealthy men who finance movements of this sort, as well as for the people themselves, the successful demagogue is a powerful genie who, when once let out of his bottle, refuses to obey anyone's command. As long as his spell holds, he defies God Himself, and Satan is turned loose upon the world.

Through the leaders of the Nazi revolution, Satan now is trying to lead the common man of the whole world back into slavery and darkness. For the stark truth is that the violence preached by the Nazis is the Devil's own religion of darkness. So also is the doctrine that one race or one class is by heredity superior and that all other races or classes are supposed to be slaves. The belief in one Satan-inspired *Führer*, with his Quislings, his Lavals, and his Mussolinis—his *Gauleiters* in every nation in the world—is the last and ultimate darkness. Is there any hell hotter than that of being a Quisling, unless it is that of being a Laval or a Mussolini?

In a twisted sense, there is something almost great in the figure of the Supreme Devil operating through a human form, in a Hitler who has the daring to spit straight into the eye of God and man. But the Nazi system has a heroic position for only one leader. By definition only one person is allowed to retain full sovereignty over his own soul. All the rest are "stooges"—they are "stooges" who have been mentally and politically degraded, and who feel that they can get square with the world only by mentally and politically degrading other people. These "stooges" are really psychopathic cases. Satan has turned loose upon us the insane.

The march of freedom of the past one hundred and fifty years has been a long-drawn-out people's revolution. In this great revolution of the people, there were the American Revolution of 1775, the French Revolution of 1792, the Latin American revolutions of the Bolivarian era, the German Revolution of 1848, and the Russian Revolution of 1917. Each spoke for the common man in terms of blood on the battlefield. Some went to excess. But the significant thing is that the people groped their way to the light. More of them learned to think and work together.

The people's revolution aims at peace and not at violence, but if the rights of the common man are attacked, it unleashes the ferocity of the she-bear who has lost a cub. When the Nazi psychologists tell their master, Hitler, that we in the United States may be able to produce hundreds of thousands of planes, but that we have no will to fight, they are only fooling themselves and him. The truth is that when the rights of the American people are transgressed, as those rights have been transgressed, the American people will fight with a relentless fury which will drive the ancient Teutonic gods back cowering into their caves. The *Götterdämmerung* has come for Odin and his crew.

The people are on the march toward even fuller freedom than the most fortunate peoples of the earth have hitherto enjoyed. No Nazi counterrevolution will stop it. The common man will smoke the Hitler "stooges" out into the open in the United States, in Latin America, and in India. He will destroy their influence. No Lavals, no Mussolinis, will be tolerated in a free world.

The people, in their millennial and revolutionary march toward manifesting here on earth the dignity that is in every human soul, hold as their credo the Four Freedoms enunciated by President Roosevelt in his message to Congress on January 6, 1941. These Four Freedoms are the very core of the revolution for which the United Nations have taken their stand. We who live in the United States may think there is nothing very revolutionary about freedom of religion, freedom of expression, and freedom from the fear of secret police. But when we begin to think about the significance of freedom from want for the average man, then we know that the revolution of the past one hundred and fifty years has not been completed, either here in the United States or in any other nation in the world. We know that this revolution cannot stop until freedom from want has actually been attained.

And now, as we move forward toward realizing the Four Freedoms of this people's revolution, I would like to speak about four duties. It is my belief that every freedom, every right, every privilege, has its price, its corresponding duty, without which it cannot be enjoyed. The four duties of the people's revolution, as I see them today, are these:

1. The duty to produce to the limit.
2. The duty to transport as rapidly as possible to the field of battle.
3. The duty to fight with all that is in us.
4. The duty to build a peace—just, charitable, and enduring. The fourth duty is that which inspires the other three.

We failed in our job after World War I. We did not know how to go about it to build an enduring world-wide peace. We did not have the nerve to follow through and prevent Germany from rearming. We did not insist that she "learn war no more." We did not build a peace treaty on the fundamental doctrine of the people's revolution. We did not strive wholeheartedly to create a world where there could be freedom from want for all the peoples. But by our very errors we learned much, and after this war we shall be in position to utilize our knowledge in building a world which is economically, politically, and, I hope, spiritually sound.

Modern science, which is a by-product and an essential part of the people's revolution, has made it technologically possible to see that all of the people of the world get enough to eat. Half in fun and half seriously, I said the other day to Madam Litvinov: "The object of this war is to make sure that everybody in the world has the privilege of drinking a quart of milk a day."

She replied: "Yes, even half a pint."

The peace must mean a better standard of living for the common man, not merely in the United States and England, but also in India, Russia, China, and Latin America—not merely in the United Nations, but also in Germany and Italy and Japan.

Some have spoken of the "American Century." I say that the century on which we are entering—the century which will come of this war—can be and must be the century of the common man. Perhaps it will be America's opportunity to suggest the freedoms and duties by which the common man must live. Everywhere the common man must learn to build his own industries with his own hands in a practical fashion. Everywhere the common man must learn to increase his productivity so that he and his children can eventually pay to the world community all that they have received. No nation will have the God-given right to exploit other nations. Older nations will have the privilege of helping younger nations get started on the path to industrialization, but there must be neither military nor economic imperialism. The methods of the nineteenth century will not work in the people's century which is now about to begin. . . .

Numerous journalists and publicists, including Raymond Clapper, Raymond Gram Swing, Major George Fielding Eliot and Dorothy Thompson, testified to the timely power of Wallace's speech. Miss Thompson said that it was "the first statement from a high American personality giving this war a real sense" and it was "utterly without demagoguery, even in its delivery."

The speech was widely read in many languages, and "the century of the common man" became a phrase to conjure with.

GENERAL EISENHOWER CONQUERS LONDON

[June 12, 1945]

Exactly three years after Wallace described the price of free world victory, with the duties of producing, transporting, and fighting to the utmost limit, the Germans surrendered unconditionally to General Eisenhower, and the war in Europe was over. VE-Day officially was May 8.

The General was soon flooded with congratulatory messages and invitations to various cities, the one to London where he would make a speech at the Guildhall on June 12 being most important to him. He at once began to think about the speech and made a first draft while flying back from the Riviera to his headquarters at Frankfurt am Main. There were other drafts which he read aloud several times to his inner circle. "It seems that almost everyone thinks a successful speaker has a ghost writer," noted Captain Harry C. Butcher in My Three Years with Eisenhower. "General Ike is his own ghost, only he seldom writes a speech, just thinks his thoughts in advance, gets his ideas in order, and then has the ability to deliver them."

In London on the great day, Eisenhower, with Air Chief Marshal Tedder, rode through London to cheering millions. The climax, of course, was at the war-torn old Guildhall, the hall of the corporation of London, where the annual dinner of the Lord Mayor is held and where William Pitt made his immortal reply to the toast after Nelson's victory at Trafalgar. "Ike's only departure from his text," recalled Captain Butcher, "was at the outset, when he turned to the Lord Mayor, Sir Frank Alexander, and said calmly something to the effect that if he didn't know he was amongst friends, he doubted if he could ever make his speech."

"When we consider these things, then the valley of the Thames draws closer to the farms of Kansas."

THE HIGH SENSE of distinction I feel in receiving this great honor from the city of London is inescapably mingled with feelings of profound sadness. All of us must always regret that your great country and mine were ever faced with the tragic situation that compelled the appointment of an Allied Commander in Chief, the capacity in which I have just been so extravagantly commended.

Humility must always be the portion of any man who receives acclaim earned in the blood of his followers and the sacrifices of his friends.

Conceivably a commander may have been professionally superior. He may have given everything of his heart and mind to meet the spiritual and physical needs of his comrades. He may have written a chapter that will glow forever in the pages of military history.

Still, even such a man—if he existed—would sadly face the facts that his honors cannot hide in his memories the crosses marking the resting places of the dead. They cannot soothe the anguish of the widow or the orphan whose husband or father will not return.

The only attitude in which a commander may with satisfaction receive the tributes of his friends is in the humble acknowledgment that no matter how unworthy he may be his position is the symbol of great human forces that have labored arduously and successfully for a righteous cause. Unless he feels this symbolism and this rightness in what he has tried to do, then he is disregardful of the courage, fortitude and devotion of the vast multitudes he has been honored to command. If all Allied men and women that have served with me in this war can only know that it is they whom this august body is really honoring today, then indeed I will be content.

This feeling of humility cannot erase, of course, my great pride in being tendered the freedom of London. I am not a native of this land.

I come from the very heart of America. In the superficial aspects by which we ordinarily recognize family relationships, the town where I was born and the one where I was reared are far separated from this great city. Abilene, Kansas, and Denison, Texas, would together equal in size possibly one five-hundredth of a part of great London.

By your standards those towns are young, without your aged traditions that carry the roots of London back into the uncertainties of unrecorded history. To those people I am proud to belong.

But I find myself today five thousand miles from that countryside, the honored guest of a city whose name stands for grandeur and size throughout the world. Hardly would it seem possible for the London Council to have gone farther afield to find a man to honor with its priceless gift of token citizenship.

Yet kinship among nations is not determined in such measurements as proximity of size and age. Rather we should turn to those inner things —call them what you will—I mean those intangibles that are the real treasures free men possess.

To preserve his freedom of worship, his equality before law, his liberty to speak and act as he sees fit, subject only to provisions that he trespass not upon similar rights of others, a Londoner will fight. So will a citizen of Abilene.

When we consider these things, then the valley of the Thames draws closer to the farms of Kansas and the plains of Texas. To my mind it is clear that when two peoples will face the tragedies of war to defend the same spiritual values, the same treasured rights, then in the deepest sense those two are truly related. So even as I proclaim my undying Americanism, I am bold enough and exceedingly proud to claim the basis of kinship to you of London.

And what man who has followed the history of this war could fail to experience an inspiration from the example of this city?

When the British Empire stood—alone but unconquered, almost naked but unafraid—to defy the Hitler hordes, it was on this devoted city that the first terroristic blows were launched.

Five years and eight months of war, much of it on the actual battle-line, blitzes big and little, flying V-bombs—all of them you took in your stride. You worked, and from your needed efforts you would not be deterred. You carried on, and from your midst arose no cry for mercy, no wail of defeat. The Battle of Britain will take its place as another of your deathless traditions. And your faith and endurance have finally been rewarded.

You had been more than two years in war when Americans in numbers began swarming into your country. Most were mentally unprepared for the realities of war—especially as waged by the Nazis. Others believed that the tales of British sacrifice had been exaggerated. Still others failed to recognize the difficulties of the task ahead.

All such doubts, questions, and complacencies could not endure a single casual tour through your scarred streets and avenues. With awe our men gazed upon the empty spaces where once had stood buildings erected by the toil and sweat of peaceful folk. Our eyes rounded as we saw your women, serving quietly and efficiently in almost every kind of war effort, even with flak batteries. We became accustomed to the warning sirens which seemed to compel from the native Londoner not even a single hurried step. Gradually we drew closer together until we became true partners in war.

In London my associates and I planned two great expeditions—that to invade the Mediterranean and later that to cross the Channel. London's hospitality to the Americans, her good-humored acceptance of the added inconvenience we brought, her example of fortitude and quiet confidence in the final outcome—all these helped to make the Supreme Headquarters of the two Allied expeditions the smooth-working organizations they became.

They were composed of chosen representatives of two proud and independent peoples, each noted for its initiative and for its satisfaction with its own customs, manners, and methods. Many feared that those representatives could never combine together in an efficient fashion to solve the complex problems presented by modern war.

I hope you believe we proved the doubters wrong. And, moreover, I hold that we proved this point not only for war—we proved it can always be done by our two peoples, provided only that both show the same good will, the same forbearance, the same objective attitude that the British and Americans so amply demonstrated in nearly three years of bitter campaigning.

No man could alone have brought about this result. Had I possessed the military skill of a Marlborough, the wisdom of Solomon, the understanding of Lincoln, I still would have been helpless without the loyalty, vision, and generosity of thousands upon thousands of British and Americans.

Some of them were my companions in the High Command. Many were enlisted men and junior officers carrying the fierce brunt of battle, and many others were back in the United States and here in Great Britain in London.

Moreover, back of us always stood our great national war leaders and their civil and military staffs that supported and encouraged us through every trial, every test. The whole was one great team. I know that on this special occasion three million American men and women serving in the Allied Expeditionary Force would want me to pay a tribute of admiration, respect, and affection to their British comrades of this war.

My most cherished hope is that after Japan joins the Nazis in utter defeat, neither my country nor yours need ever again summon its sons and daughters from their peaceful pursuits to face the tragedies of battle. But—a fact important for both of us to remember—neither London nor Abilene, sisters under the skin, will sell her birthright for physical safety, her liberty for mere existence.

No petty differences in the world of trade, traditions, or national pride should ever blind us to our identities in priceless values.

If we keep our eyes on this guidepost, then no difficulties along our path of mutual co-operation can ever be insurmountable. Moreover, when this truth has permeated to the remotest hamlet and heart of all peoples, then indeed may we beat our swords into plowshares, and all nations can enjoy the fruitfulness of the earth.

My Lord Mayor, I thank you once again for an honor to me and to the American forces that will remain one of the proudest in my memories.

If "true eloquence must exist in the man, in the subject, and in the occasion," then true eloquence existed that June afternoon in London's historic Guildhall. The audience was deeply moved, and the next morning the London Express set the speech around a box containing Lincoln's Gettysburg Address.

PART TWENTY

THE SINEWS OF PEACE

EX-PRIME MINISTER CHURCHILL PERCEIVES AN IRON CURTAIN

[March 5, 1946]

SIR WINSTON CHURCHILL can write compactly as well as copiously. At the close of The Gathering Storm, he traced the fall of Chamberlain's government and his own appointment as Prime Minister, on the eve of the Battle of Britain. "Thus, then, on the night of the tenth of May [1940], at the outset of this mighty battle, I acquired the chief power in the state, which henceforth I wielded in ever-growing measure for five years and three months of world war, at the end of which time, all of our enemies having surrendered unconditionally or being about to do so, I was immediately dismissed by the British electorate from all further conduct of their affairs."

But he did not sulk or disappear from the public stage, though at seventy-one he was entitled to a long rest and honorable retirement. He at once plunged into the writing of his monumental five-volume history of the Second World War and made a number of notable addresses in England, Europe, and the United States. Little Westminster College, in Fulton, Missouri, suddenly became known to the world, when President Truman traveled there with the former Prime Minister and introduced him to a delighted audience of faculty, students, and visitors.

"I am glad," Churchill said, "to come to Westminster College this afternoon, and am complimented that you should give me a degree. The name 'Westminster' is somehow familiar to me. I seem to have heard of it before. Indeed it was at Westminster that I received a very large part of my education in politics, dialectic, and one or two other things. In fact, we have both been educated at the same, or similar, or, at any rate, kindred establishments." And then he proceeded to make some remarks about the vast power of the United States, the friendship of the United States, Great Britain, and Canada, and the problems of strengthening the temple of peace.

"I have felt bound to portray the shadow which, alike in the east and in the west, falls upon the world."

A SHADOW has fallen upon the scenes so lately lighted by the Allied victory. Nobody knows what Soviet Russia and its Communist international organization intends to do in the immediate future, or what are the limits, if any, to their expansive and proselytizing tendencies. I have a strong admiration and regard for the valiant Russian people and for my wartime comrade, Marshal Stalin. There is deep sympathy and good will in Britain—and I doubt not here also—toward the peoples of all the Russias and a resolve to persevere through many differences and rebuffs in establishing lasting friendships. We understand the Russian need to be secure on her western frontiers by the removal of all possibility of German aggression. We welcome Russia to her rightful place among the leading nations of the world. We welcome her flag upon the seas. Above all, we welcome constant, frequent, and growing contacts between the Russian people and our own people on both sides of the Atlantic. It is my duty, however, for I am sure you would wish me to state the facts as I see them to you, to place before you certain facts about the present position in Europe.

From Stettin in the Baltic to Trieste in the Adriatic, an iron curtain has descended across the Continent. Behind that line lie all the capitals of the ancient states of central and eastern Europe. Warsaw, Berlin, Prague, Vienna, Budapest, Belgrade, Bucharest, and Sofia, all these famous cities and the populations around them lie in what I must call the Soviet sphere, and all are subject in one form or another, not only to Soviet influence, but to a very high and, in many cases, increasing measure of control from Moscow. Athens alone—Greece with its immortal glories—is free to decide its future at an election under British, American, and French observation. The Russian-dominated Polish government has been encouraged to make enormous and wrongful inroads upon Germany, and mass expulsions of millions of Germans on a scale grievous and undreamed of are now taking place. The Communist parties, which were very small in all these eastern states of Europe, have been raised to pre-eminence and power far beyond their numbers and are seeking everywhere to obtain totalitarian control. Police governments are prevailing in nearly every case, and so far, except in Czechoslovakia, there is no true democracy. . . .

I have felt bound to portray the shadow which, alike in the west and in the east, falls upon the world. I was a high minister at the time of the Versailles Treaty and a close friend of Mr. Lloyd George, who was the head of the British delegation at Versailles. I did not myself agree with many things that were done, but I have a very strong impression in my mind of that situation, and I find it painful to contrast it with that which prevails now. In those days there were high hopes and unbounded confidence that the wars were over, and that the League of Nations would become all-powerful. I do not see or feel that same confidence or even the same hopes in the haggard world at the present time. . . .

From what I have seen of our Russian friends and Allies during the war, I am convinced that there is nothing they admire so much as strength, and there is nothing for which they have less respect than for weakness, especially military weakness. For that reason the old doctrine of a balance of power is unsound. We cannot afford, if we can help it, to work on narrow margins, offering temptations to a trial of strength. If the Western democracies stand together in strict adherence to the principles of the United Nations Charter, their influence for furthering those principles will be immense and no one is likely to molest them. If, however, they become divided or falter in their duty and if these all-important years are allowed to slip away, then indeed catastrophe may overwhelm us all.

Last time I saw it all coming and cried aloud to my own fellow countrymen and to the world, but no one paid any attention. Up till the year 1933 or even 1935, Germany might have been saved from the awful fate which has overtaken her and we might all have been spared the miseries Hitler let loose upon mankind. There never was a war in all history easier to prevent by timely action than the one which has just desolated such great areas of the globe. It could have been prevented, in my belief, without the firing of a single shot, and Germany might be powerful, prosperous, and honored today; but no one would listen, and one by one we were all sucked into the awful whirlpool. We surely must not let that happen again. This can only be achieved by reaching now, in 1946, a good understanding on all points with Russia under the general authority of the United Nations Organization and by the maintenance of that good understanding through many peaceful years, by the world instrument, supported by the whole strength of the English-speaking world and all its connections. There is the solution which I respectfully offer to you in this address, to which I have given the title "The Sinews of Peace."

Let no man underrate the abiding power of the British Empire and Commonwealth. Because you see the forty-six millions in our island harassed about their food supply, of which they only grow one half, even in wartime, or because we have difficulty in restarting our industries and export trade after six years of passionate war effort, do not suppose that we shall not come through these dark years of privation as we have come through the glorious years of agony, or that half a century from now, you will not see seventy or eighty millions of Britons spread about the world and united in defense of our traditions, our way of life, and of the world causes which you and we espouse. If the population of the English-speaking Commonwealths be added to that of the United States, with all that such co-operation implies in the air, on the sea, all over the globe, and in science and industry, and in moral force, there will be no quivering, precarious balance of power to offer its temptation to ambition or adventure. On the contrary, there will be an overwhelming assurance of security. If we adhere faithfully to the Charter of the United Nations and walk forward in sedate and sober strength, seeking no one's land or treasure, seeking to lay no arbitrary control upon the thoughts of men; if all British moral and material forces and convictions are joined with your own in fraternal association, the highroads of the future will be clear, not only for us, but for all, not only for our time, but for a century to come.

More than a year later the Marshall Plan was announced, and then the Truman Plan, and finally the Atlantic Pact.

Between 1946 and 1953 this stupendous man completed his six-volume history of the Second World War, became Prime Minister again, was knighted by Queen Elizabeth II, and received the Nobel Prize for Literature, conferred on him not only for his books but also for his oratory.

DAVID E. LILIENTHAL OFFERS A DEFINITION OF DEMOCRACY

[February 3, 1947]

In the backwash of a terrible war, fear and resentment take the place of courage and hope in many minds. Ideals once firmly established, words once proudly and affectionately used, fall under grave suspicion. At such a time, a bold gesture of affirmation, a clean-cut definition, comes like a gust of fresh air to a fetid room. One can hardly expect such a gust to come in the midst of a bitter congressional investigation, but that was precisely what happened when David E. Lilienthal replied, more in sorrow than in anger, to a question of the late Senator McKellar of Tennessee, during a meeting of the Joint Congressional Committee on Atomic Energy.

Lilienthal was born in Illinois in 1899, educated in the Middle West and at the Harvard Law School. After practicing law for some years he joined the Wisconsin Public Service Commission. In 1933 he was appointed, along with Arthur E. Morgan and Harcourt Morgan, one of the three directors of the Tennessee Valley Authority. Becoming chairman of this contentious project in 1941, he was for the next few years involved in bitter struggles with utilities and private business.

When President Truman nominated Lilienthal to head the atomic energy program in 1947, many senators fumed and fulminated, and for some time it seemed doubtful whether enough votes could be obtained for confirmation. Lilienthal was called before the Joint Congressional Committee on Atomic Energy. The senior Senator from Tennessee, Kenneth McKellar, then seventy-seven years old, led the attack, which took many directions. How could a man so young, and without expert knowledge of atomic chemistry, be expected to head the agency successfully. How much did it cost the T.V.A. to produce a ton of ammonium nitrate? Lilienthal replied that the figures were available but he did not carry them in his head. After further loaded questions, Senator McKellar said: "Well, what are your convictions on communist doctrine?"

Then, according to Alfred Friendly of the Washington Post, "The witness, who had shown no signs of emotion or anger under McKellar's barrage, suddenly wheeled in his chair to face his antagonist. He said in a voice which was low, but electric with fervor: 'This I do carry in my head, Senator.' "

"It is very easy to talk about being against communism."

I WILL DO MY BEST to make it clear. My convictions are not so much concerned with what I am against as what I am for; and that excludes a lot of things automatically.

Traditionally, democracy has been an affirmative doctrine rather than merely a negative one.

I believe—and I conceive the Constitution of the United States to rest upon, as does religion—the fundamental proposition of the integrity of the individual; and that all government and all private institutions must be designed to promote and protect and defend the integrity and the dignity of the individual; that that is the essential meaning of the Constitution and the Bill of Rights, as it is essentially the meaning of religion.

Any form of government, therefore, and any other institutions which make men means rather than ends, which exalt the state or any other institutions above the importance of men, which place arbitrary power over men as a fundamental tenet of government, are contrary to that conception, and, therefore, I am deeply opposed to them.

The communistic philosophy as well as the communistic form of government falls within this category, for their fundamental tenet is quite to the contrary. The fundamental tenet of communism is that the state is an end in itself, and that therefore the powers which the state exercises over the individual are without any ethical standard to limit them.

That I deeply disbelieve.

It is very easy simply to say that one is not a Communist. And, of course, if my record requires me to state that very affirmatively, then it is a great disappointment to me.

It is very easy to talk about being against communism. It is equally important to believe those things which provide a satisfying and effective alternative. Democracy is that satisfying, affirmative alternative. Its hope in the world is that it is an affirmative belief rather than being simply a belief against something else and nothing more.

One of the tenets of democracy that grows out of this central core of a belief that the individual comes first, that all men are the children of God, and that their personalities are therefore sacred, carries with it a great belief in civil liberties and their protection, and a repugnance to anyone who would steal from a human being that which is most precious to him—his good name—either by imputing things to him either by innuendo or by insinuation. And it is especially an unhappy circumstance that occasionally that is done in the name of democracy. This, I think, can tear our country apart and destroy it if we carry it further.

I deeply believe in the capacity of democracy to surmount any trials that may lie ahead, provided only that we practice it in our daily lives.

And among the things we must practice is that while we seek fervently to ferret out the subversive and antidemocratic forces in the country, we do not at the same time, by hysteria, by resort to innuendo, and smears, and other unfortunate tactics besmirch the people—cause one group and one individual to hate another, based on mere attacks, mere unsubstantiated attacks upon their loyalty.

I also want to add that part of my conviction is based on my training as an Anglo-American common-law lawyer. It is the very basis and the great heritage of the English people to this country, which we have maintained, that we insist on the strictest rules of credibility of witnesses and on the avoidance of hearsay, and that gossip shall be excluded, in the courts of justice. And that, too, is an essential of our democracy.

Whether by administrative agencies acting arbitrarily against business organizations, or whether by investigating activities of legislative branches, whenever those principles fail, those principles of the protection of an individual and his good name against besmirchment by gossip, hearsay, and the statements of witnesses who are not subject to cross-examination—then, too, we have failed in carrying forward our ideals in respect to democracy.

That I deeply believe.

There was complete silence when Lilienthal finished. Then the late Senator McMahon, the farseeing statesman of atomic energy, said: "I congratulate you on that statement. In my opinion it is the creed of a very real American."

That was evidently the opinion of countless other Americans, for the next day the Lilienthal "credo" appeared on the front pages of newspapers throughout the country and became the subject of numerous editorials. It was recommended for anthologies and for required reading in the schools, and was compared with the noblest declarations in the history of man.

Note: Lilienthal got the job.

NEHRU SPEAKS TO MOURNING MILLIONS
A FEW HOURS AFTER THE MURDER
OF GANDHI

[January 30, 1948]

We read Gandhi's description of the technique of nonviolent non-co-operation and also his prophetic speech at the "great trial" of 1922. There remained for him twenty-five years of countless speeches in all parts of India, dramatic demonstrations such as the famous salt march to the sea, painful fasts, and prolonged imprisonments. There were complex problems of party organization, tutelage, and direction in which Gandhi's trusted lieutenants, the late Viththalbhai Patel (1873–1933) and Jawaharlal Nehru (1889–   ) were the major figures.

Like so many of the leading Indian nationalists, Nehru came from a wealthy, aristocratic family and received his education in England, at Harrow and Cambridge. Like Gandhi, he practiced law for a time, but after the massacre at Amritsar, he joined Gandhi in the struggle for India's freedom. An effective orator and winning personality, he became leader of the Indian National Con-

gress in 1929, and was thereafter four times elected its president. He also was repeatedly sent to jail for directing civil-disobedience campaigns. As a Marxist, Nehru opposed Gandhi's ideal of an agrarian society and favored an industrialized and socialized India. During the second World War, however, the rift between the two leaders was healed, and Nehru was again jailed for opposing any aid to Great Britain. On his release in June, 1945, he helped to negotiate India's freedom and in August, 1947, after the separation of the Moslem from the Hindu, which both he and Gandhi viewed with horror, became Prime Minister and Minister of Foreign Affairs of the newly constituted Republic of India.

When the bullet of a Hindu nationalist silenced the voice of Gandhi, consternation and dismay fell over India. The sorrowing and speechless crowds massed to catch one last glimpse of his face, and at the place where he had fallen, marked by a triangle of little sticks and a burning candle, thousands kneeled. In this crisis of paralyzing sorrow and fear, in the evening, a few hours after the bullet was fired, Nehru spoke extemporaneously, using the radio to reach millions of his countrymen.

"For the light that shone in this country was no ordinary light."

FRIENDS AND COMRADES, the light has gone out of our lives and there is darkness everywhere. I do not know what to tell you and how to say it. Our beloved leader, Bapu as we called him, the father of the nation, is no more. Perhaps I am wrong to say that. Nevertheless, we will not see him again as we have seen him for these many years. We will not run to him for advice and seek solace from him, and that is a terrible blow, not to me only, but to millions and millions in this country, and it is a little difficult to soften the blow by any other advice that I or anyone else can give you.

The light has gone out, I said, and yet I was wrong. For the light that shone in this country was no ordinary light. The light that has illumined this country for these many years will illumine this country for many more years, and a thousand years later that light will still be seen in this country and the world will see it and it will give solace to innumerable hearts. For that light represented the living truth . . . the eternal truths, reminding us of the right path, drawing us from error, taking this ancient country to freedom.

All this has happened when there was so much more for him to do. We could never think that he was unnecessary or that he had done his task. But now, particularly, when we are faced with so many difficulties, his not being with us is a blow most terrible to bear.

A madman has put an end to his life, for I can only call him mad who did it, and yet there has been enough of poison spread in this country during the past years and months, and this poison has had effect on people's minds. We must face this poison, we must root out this poison, and we must face all the perils that encompass us and face them not madly or badly but rather in the way that our beloved teacher taught us to face them. The first thing to remember now is that no one of us dare misbehave because we are angry. We have to behave like strong and determined people, determined to face all the perils that surround us, determined to carry out the mandate that our great teacher and our great leader has given us, remembering always that if, as I believe, his spirit looks upon us and sees us, nothing would displease his soul so much as to see that we have indulged in any small behavior or any violence.

So we must not do that. But that does not mean that we should be weak, but rather that we should in strength and in unity face all the troubles that are in front of us. We must hold together, and all our petty troubles and difficulties and conflicts must be ended in the face of this great disaster. A great disaster is a symbol to us to remember all the big things of life and forget the small things, of which we have thought too much.

It was proposed by some friends that Mahatmaji's body should be embalmed for a few days to enable millions of people to pay their last homage to him. But it was his wish, repeatedly expressed, that no such thing should happen, that this should not be done, that he was entirely opposed to any embalming of his body.

Tomorrow should be a day of fasting and prayer for all of us. Those who live elsewhere out of Delhi and in other parts of India will no doubt also take such part as they can in this last homage. For them also let this be a day of fasting and prayer. And at the appointed time for cremation, that is, four P.M. tomorrow afternoon, people should go to the river or to the sea and offer prayers there. And while we pray, the greatest prayer that we can offer is to take a pledge to dedicate ourselves to the truth and to the cause for which this great countryman of ours lived and for which he has died.

A. P. HERBERT ADVOCATES A FESTIVAL FOR BRITAIN

[November 23, 1949]

Sir Alan Patrick Herbert (1890–   ), the author of many volumes of light prose and light verse, and of many sardonic comments on England's divorce laws, including the novel Holy Deadlock, entered Parliament as a representative of Oxford University in 1935. It is customary for a new member to wait for months before making his "maiden speech"—and then make a pallid or ridiculous impression. Herbert, however, got the speaker's eye almost at once and announced with disarming assurance that he had come there to put through the Matrimonial Causes Bill, which was designed "to reform the indecent, hypocritical, cruel, and unjust laws of this country," and if he did not succeed he would go back to his books and his plays. Everyone was more or less astonished by this audacity, including the speaker himself. Afterward Winston Churchill sought him out and congratulated him for his "composure and aplomb." "Call that a maiden speech?" said Churchill. "It was a brazen hussy of a speech. Never did such a painted lady of a speech parade itself before a modest Parliament." And within less than two years the bill was passed.

Fourteen busy years after his debut in the House of Commons, on November 23, 1949, Herbert joined in the debate on plans to hold a Festival of Britain in 1951.

"We can be gracious, gallant, and gay."

MAY I SAY how disappointed I am at some of the talk in some of the papers—this very gloomy talk, with petulant letters saying, "What, after all, have we to celebrate?" Surely right honorable and honorable Members on this side of the House, at least, will agree that if, in 1951, we have survived five years of war, and five years of His Majesty's Government, then even they will have something they will like to celebrate, to dance and sing about. "Faith," I think Mr. G. K. Chesterton said, "is the capacity to believe in that which is demonstrably untrue." If that is the only sort of confidence we have in our future, then let us have that.

I think there are other causes. I am no historian; but if the House will bear with me for one more minute, I will present another historical reason why we should celebrate, not only with the main exhibition, but with the arrangements set out in this bill. After all, we are emerging from the murky forties into the fifties, and it has been pointed out to me by a better historian than myself that the forties have always been a pretty wretched sort of decade. A hundred years ago there were the Hungry Forties, with the whole of Europe in chaos and revolution, with *The Communist Manifesto,* with crowned heads falling everywhere and rulers taking refuge in this island, and with the Chartists massing on Kennington Common. However, after that period we emerged into what was almost the most prosperous, happy period in this country's history.

In the 1740's, I think, we were at war with France, Spain, and Scotland. A predecessor of mine in this House, Sir Charles Oman, records that when Charles Edward arrived at Derby, "Panic prevailed in London, the King's plate had been sent on shipboard, the Bank of England had paid away every guinea of its reserves, and the citizens of London were fully persuaded that they would be attacked next day by ten thousand wild Scottish clansmen."

In the 1640's there was civil war and King Charles I had his head cut off. In the 1540's, I see, "The time was a very evil one for England." King Henry VIII was marrying too many women, executing too many men, and persecuting everybody else. I need hardly add that we were at war with Scotland, and France as well; but the historian adds, rather woundingly, that "the French War was far more dangerous." In the 1440's we had a weak king, King Henry VI. We were at war with France, and we were gradually losing everything King Henry V had won. In 1431 we had burned Joan of Arc—and our publicity on the Continent was not good. In the 1340's we were at war with France, and the Scots invaded the north of England. Also, a small detail, there was the Black Death. In the 1240's we invaded France. In the 1140's we were ruled by an unpleasant woman called Matilda and there was civil war all the time. In the 1040's we were invaded by the Danes.

Now, whatever else may be laid at the door of His Majesty's Government, we are not now at war with France or Scotland or even Denmark, and I do not think that we shall be in 1951: and my hope is that in some way we shall emerge from the 1940's into the fifties in such condition that we shall be justified in celebrating. But if not, even if we are going down, it is not the habit of the British fleet to haul down the ensign when about to begin a doubtful engagement. On the contrary, each ship flies two or three to make sure that one shall be seen. It is in that spirit, I

feel, that we ought to go forward with this bold, imaginative, attractive
scheme, and show, whether we go up or down, that we can be gracious,
gallant, and gay.

The London Times reported that this speech was greeted with loud cheers,
"and I was told," said Herbert in Independent Member, his delightful autobiography of his Parliamentary years, "that I had changed the whole course of
the debate." But the witty Member for Oxford had also unwittingly delivered
his swan song, for in the meantime the Labour government had abolished the
University seats.

The Festival of Britain was held in 1951 and it was a huge success in every
way except financially.

WILLIAM FAULKNER, ACCEPTING THE NOBEL PRIZE, EXHORTS THE YOUNG WRITERS OF THE WORLD

[December 10, 1950]

When William Faulkner (1897–   ), the quiet farmer from Oxford, Mississippi, was awarded the 1949 Nobel Prize for literature, a few angry voices
still protested that his books were obscure, morbid, obscene, unworthy of honor.
But his fellow writers, practically all the leading critics, and tens of thousands
of American readers had long since begun to realize that Faulkner was an artist
of integrity, working out a vast saga of the South.

It was not expected that he would go to Stockholm to receive the prize, but
at the last moment he decided to do so and bought his first dress suit for the
occasion. At the airport, before leaving, he was asked by a woman reporter what
he considered the most decadent aspect of American life. "The invasion of
privacy," he replied. "It's this running people down and getting interviews and
pictures of them just because something's happened to them."

At the state banquet in Stockholm on the evening of December 10, 1950,
he appeared before a microphone and TV camera for the first time and read
the following words:

"I decline to accept the end of man."

I FEEL that this award was not made to me as a man, but to my work —a life's work in the agony and sweat of the human spirit, not for glory and least of all for profit, but to create out of the materials of the human spirit something which did not exist before. So this award is only mine in trust. It will not be difficult to find a dedication for the money part of it commensurate with the purpose and significance of its origin. But I would like to do the same with the acclaim too, by using this moment as a pinnacle from which I might be listened to by the young men and women already dedicated to the same anguish and travail, among whom is already that one who will someday stand here where I am standing.

Our tragedy today is a general and universal physical fear so long sustained by now that we can even bear it. There are no longer problems of the spirit. There is only the question: when will I be blown up? Because of this, the young man or woman writing today has forgotten the problems of the human heart in conflict with itself which alone can make good writing because only that is worth writing about, worth the agony and the sweat.

He must learn them again. He must teach himself that the basest of all things is to be afraid; and, teaching himself that, forget it forever, leaving no room in his workshop for anything but the old verities and truths of the heart, the old universal truths lacking which any story is ephemeral and doomed—love and honor and pity and pride and compassion and sacrifice. Until he does so, he labors under a curse. He writes not of love but of lust, of defeats in which nobody loses anything of value, of victories without hope, and, worst of all, without pity or compassion. His griefs grieve on no universal bones, leaving no scars. He writes not of the heart but of the glands.

Until he relearns these things, he will write as though he stood among and watched the end of man. I decline to accept the end of man. It is easy enough to say that man is immortal simply because he will endure; that when the last ding-dong of doom has clanged and faded from the last worthless rock hanging tideless in the last red and dying evening, that even then there will still be one more sound: that of his puny inexhaustible voice, still talking. I refuse to accept this. I believe that man will not merely endure: he will prevail. He is immortal, not because he alone among creatures has an inexhaustible voice, but because he has a soul, a spirit capable of compassion and sacrifice and endurance. The poet's, the writer's, duty is to write about these things. It is his privilege to help man endure by lifting his heart, by reminding him of the courage and honor and hope and pride and compassion and pity and sacrifice which have been the glory of his past. The poet's voice need not merely be the record of man; it can be one of the props, the pillars, to help him endure and prevail.

Perhaps William Faulkner will never make another speech, but he will be remembered for this one.

GENERAL DOUGLAS MACARTHUR DEFENDS HIS CONDUCT OF THE WAR IN KOREA

[April 19, 1951]

It is difficult to judge a recent speech that has provoked fierce controversy. General Douglas MacArthur's speech before the joint session of Congress on April 19, 1951, after his abrupt dismissal as Commander in Chief of the United Nations forces in Korea, provoked a nation-wide controversy that recalled the fury over the Kansas-Nebraska Act of 1854.

The son of the distinguished army officer Arthur MacArthur, Douglas MacArthur (1880–   ) was born in Little Rock, Arkansas, was brought up in various army posts, and was graduated from West Point at the head of his class in 1903. He served in the Philippines and Japan, and in the first World War achieved a notable record as Chief of Staff of the famous Rainbow Division and later as Commander of the 84th Infantry Brigade. After the war he was Superintendent of West Point (1919–22), Commander in the Philippines (1922–25), and Chief of Staff (1930–35), during which time he had the unpleasant task of directing troops against the depression "bonus army" that marched against Washington. He went again to the Philippines in 1935 to organize the islands against possible Japanese aggression. He retired from the army in 1939, but returned to duty in July, 1941, barely in time to head the defense of the Philippines after the attack on Pearl Harbor. On order from President Roosevelt, General MacArthur escaped to Australia, there to take command of the Allied forces in the South Pacific and to begin the long road back to Manila—and to Tokyo. At the time of the Japanese surrender on the U.S.S. Missouri General MacArthur broadcast to the world a plea for peace in a high, sonorous vein.

After the Japanese surrender he became Supreme Commander of the Allied forces in Japan and, on South Korea's being invaded, Commander of the United Nations forces there. He was relieved of both commands on April 11, 1951, when it was feared that his strategy would lead to a general war with China and the Soviet Union. He immediately flew back to the United States, made a triumphant trip across the country, reminiscent of the triumph of a returning Roman general, and accepted the invitation to speak before both Houses of Congress—an unheard-of procedure in American history.

"Old soldiers never die; they just fade away."

Mr. President, Mr. Speaker and distinguished members of the Congress:

I STAND on this rostrum with a sense of deep humility and great pride —humility in the wake of those great architects of our history who have stood here before me, pride in the reflection that this home of legislative debate represents human liberty in the purest form yet devised.

Here are centered the hopes and aspirations and faith of the entire human race.

I do not stand here as advocate for any partisan cause, for the issues are fundamental and reach quite beyond the realm of partisan considerations. They must be resolved on the highest plane of national interest if our course is to prove sound and our future protected.

I trust, therefore, that you will do me the justice of receiving that which I have to say as solely expressing the considered viewpoint of a fellow American.

I address you with neither rancor nor bitterness in the fading twilight of life, with but one purpose in mind: to serve my country.

The issues are global, and so interlocked that to consider the problems of one sector oblivious to those of another is to court disaster for the whole. While Asia is commonly referred to as the gateway to Europe, it is no less true that Europe is the gateway to Asia, and the broad influence of the one cannot fail to have its impact upon the other.

There are those who claim our strength is inadequate to protect on both fronts, that we cannot divide our effort. I can think of no greater expression of defeatism.

If a potential enemy can divide his strength on two fronts, it is for us to counter his efforts. The Communist threat is a global one. Its successful advance in one sector threatens the destruction of every other sector. You cannot appease or otherwise surrender to communism in Asia without simultaneously undermining our efforts to halt its advance in Europe.

Beyond pointing out these general truisms, I shall confine my discussion to the general areas of Asia. . . .

While I was not consulted prior to the President's decision to intervene in support of the republic of Korea, that decision, from a military standpoint, proved a sound one. As I say, it proved a sound one, as we hurled back the invader and decimated his forces. Our victory was complete, and our objectives within reach, when Red China intervened with numerically superior ground forces.

This created a new war and an entirely new situation, a situation not contemplated when our forces were committed against the North Korean invaders; a situation which called for new decisions in the diplomatic sphere to permit the realistic adjustment of military strategy. Such decisions have not been forthcoming.

While no man in his right mind would advocate sending our ground forces into continental China, and such was never given a thought, the new situation did urgently demand a drastic revision of strategic planning if our political aim was to defeat this new enemy as we had defeated the old.

Apart from the military need, as I saw it, to neutralize the sanctuary protection given the enemy north of the Yalu, I felt that military necessity in the conduct of the war made necessary—

(1) The intensification of our economic blockade against China.

(2) The imposition of a naval blockade against the China coast.

(3) Removal of restrictions on air reconnaissance of China's coastal area and of Manchuria.

(4) Removal of restrictions on the forces of the republic of China on Formosa, with logistical support to contribute to their effective operations against the Chinese mainland.

For entertaining these views, all professionally designed to support our forces committed to Korea and to bring hostilities to an end with the least possible delay and at a saving of countless American and Allied lives, I have been severely criticized in lay circles, principally abroad, despite my understanding that from a military standpoint the above views have been fully shared in the past by practically every military leader concerned with the Korean campaign, including our own Joint Chiefs of Staff.

I called for reinforcements, but was informed that reinforcements were not available. I made clear that if not permitted to destroy the enemy built-up bases north of the Yalu, if not permitted to utilize the friendly Chinese force of some six hundred thousand men on Formosa, if not permitted to blockade the China coast to prevent the Chinese Reds from getting succor from without, and if there were to be no hope of major reinforcements, the position of the command from the military standpoint forbade victory.

We could hold in Korea by constant maneuver and at an approximate area where our supply-line advantages were in balance with the supply-line disadvantages of the enemy, but we could hope at best for only an indecisive campaign with its terrible and constant attrition upon our forces if the enemy utilized his full military potential.

I have constantly called for the new political decisions essential to a solution.

Efforts have been made to distort my position. It has been said in effect that I was a warmonger. Nothing could be further from the truth.

I know war as few other men now living know it, and nothing to me is more revolting. I have long advocated its complete abolition, as its very destructiveness on both friend and foe has rendered it useless as a means of settling international disputes.

Indeed, on the second day of September, 1945, just following the surrender of the Japanese nation on the battleship *Missouri,* I formally cautioned as follows:

"Men since the beginning of time have sought peace. Various methods through the ages have been attempted to devise an international process to prevent or settle disputes between nations. From the very start workable methods were found in so far as individual citizens were concerned, but the mechanics of an instrumentality of larger international scope have never been successful.

"Military alliances, balances of power, leagues of nations, all in turn failed, leaving the only path to be by way of the crucible of war. The utter destructiveness of war now blocks out this alternative. We have had our last chance. If we will not devise some greater and more equitable system, our Armageddon will be at our door. The problem basically is theological and involves a spiritual recrudescence, an improvement of human character that will synchronize with our almost matchless advances in science, art, literature, and all material and cultural developments of the past two thousand years. It must be of the spirit if we are to save the flesh."

But once war is forced upon us, there is no other alternative than to apply every available means to bring it to a swift end. War's very object is victory, not prolonged indecision.

In war there is no substitute for victory.

There are some who for varying reasons would appease Red China. They are blind to history's clear lesson, for history teaches with unmistakable emphasis that appeasement but begets new and bloodier war. It points to no single instance where this end has justified that means, where appeasement has led to more than a sham peace.

Like blackmail, it lays the basis for new and successively greater demands until, as in blackmail, violence becomes the only other alternative. Why, my soldiers asked of me, surrender military advantages to an enemy in the field? I could not answer.

Some may say to avoid spread of the conflict into an all-out war with China. Others, to avoid Soviet intervention. Neither explanation seems valid, for China is already engaging with the maximum power it can commit, and the Soviet will not necessarily mesh its actions with our moves. Like a cobra, any new enemy will more likely strike whenever it feels that the relativity in military or other potential is in its favor on a world-wide basis.

The tragedy of Korea is further heightened by the fact that its military action is confined to its territorial limits. It condemns that nation, which it is our purpose to save, to suffer the devastating impact of full naval and air bombardment while the enemy's sanctuaries are fully protected from such attack and devastation.

Of the nations of the world, Korea alone, up to now, is the sole one which has risked its all against communism. The magnificence of the courage and fortitude of the Korean people defies description. They have chosen to risk death rather than slavery. Their last words to me were: "Don't scuttle the Pacific."

I have just left your fighting sons in Korea. They have met all tests there, and I can report to you without reservation that they are splendid in every way.

It was my constant effort to preserve them and end this savage conflict honorably and with the least loss of time and a minimum sacrifice of life. Its growing bloodshed has caused me the deepest anguish and anxiety. Those gallant men will remain often in my thoughts and in my prayers always.

I am closing my fifty-two years of military service. When I joined the army, even before the turn of the century, it was the fulfillment of all of my boyish hopes and dreams.

The world has turned over many times since I took the oath on the plain at West Point, and the hopes and dreams have long since vanished, but I still remember the refrain of one of the most popular barracks ballads of that day which proclaimed most proudly that old soldiers never die; they just fade away.

And like the old soldier of that ballad, I now close my military career and just fade away, an old soldier who tried to do his duty as God gave him the light to see that duty. Good-by.

In posture, in voice, in tempo, General MacArthur exhibited the marks of the accomplished speaker. Here was a proud, powerful, dramatic personality, suddenly recalled from his high post; here the subject was not merely the conduct of a limited war in Korea, but world strategy; here the speech was before the highest legislative bodies of the land, with millions present through television, and millions more listening in.

Some critics immediately found fault with his facts and his logic, and even with the concluding passage about the old soldier who never dies. But for the vast majority at the time the speech was immensely impressive. It was the provocative prologue to one of the most searching inquiries in American history. It made General MacArthur a possible candidate for President.

GOVERNOR ADLAI STEVENSON AGREES TO RUN FOR PRESIDENT

[July 26, 1952]

Many people observed that only two speakers won complete attention during the hectic Democratic national convention of 1952—Governor Stevenson when welcoming the delegates to Illinois at the first session on Monday afternoon, the much loved Vice-President Barkley with his old-fashioned harangue on Wednesday night, and Governor Stevenson again early Saturday morning when he accepted the Democratic nomination for President.

Until that week comparatively few Americans knew anything about Adlai E. Stevenson except, perhaps, that he was Governor of Illinois. Now many know that he came of an old Illinois family, that his grandfather of the same name was Assistant Postmaster General in Cleveland's first term and Vice-President in Cleveland's second term, but that he himself was born in Los Angeles in 1899. He attended the Choate School in Connecticut, was graduated from Princeton, and later received the law degree of Northwestern University. He managed the family newspaper for a few years in Bloomington, practiced law in Chicago, and between 1933 and 1947 held a series of responsible though unpublicized posts

822 THE SINEWS OF PEACE

with the Departments of Agriculture, Navy, War, and State. He was active in the preparatory work for the United Nations, an adviser to the United States delegation to the General Assembly of the U.N., and himself a delegate to the General Assembly in 1947. He was elected Governor of Illinois by a record-breaking half-million votes in 1948, although previously Illinois had only had three Democratic governors.

These are the external facts. Why did this man win such a large following overnight in this country as well as in Europe? Why did so many people turn to him simply after hearing one or two of his speeches on the radio? Because he was crisp, literate, civilized. Because he talked on a high plane without appearing condescending or pretentious. Because he was clear without being cold. Because he did not fear the light touch even on the gravest matters.

"Let's talk sense to the American people."

Mr. President, ladies and gentlemen of the convention, my fellow citizens:

I ACCEPT your nomination—and your program.

I should have preferred to hear those words uttered by a stronger, a wiser, a better man than myself. But after listening to the President's speech, I even feel better about myself.

None of you, my friends, can wholly appreciate what is in my heart. I can only hope that you understand my words. They will be few.

I have not sought the honor you have done me. I could not seek it because I aspired to another office, which was the full measure of my ambition. And one does not treat the highest office within the gift of the people of Illinois as an alternative or as a consolation prize.

I would not seek your nomination for the presidency because the burdens of that office stagger the imagination. Its potential for good or evil now and in the years of our lives smothers exultation and converts vanity to prayer.

I have asked the merciful Father, the Father to us all, to let this cup pass from me. But from such dread responsibility one does not shrink in fear, in self-interest, or in false humility.

So, "If this cup may not pass from me, except I drink it, Thy will be done."

That my heart has been troubled, that I have not sought this nomination, that I could not seek it in good conscience, that I would not seek it in honest self-appraisal, it is not to say that I value it the less. Rather it is that I revere the office of the presidency of the United States.

And now that you have made your decision I will fight to win that office with all my heart and my soul. And with your help, I have no doubt that we will win.

You have summoned me to the highest mission within the gift of any people. I could not be more proud. Better men than I were at hand for this mighty task, and I owe to you and to them every resource of mind and of strength that I possess to make your deed today a good one for our country and for our party. I am confident, too, that your selection of a candidate for Vice-President will strengthen me and our party immeasurably in the hard, the implacable work that lies ahead of all of us.

I know you join me in gratitude and in respect for the great Democrats and the leaders of our generation whose names you have considered here in this convention, whose vigor, whose character, and devotion to the Republic we love so well have won the respect of countless Americans and enriched our party.

I shall need them, we shall need them, because I have not changed in any respect since yesterday. Your nomination, awesome as I find it, has not enlarged my capacities. So I am profoundly grateful and emboldened by their comradeship and their fealty. And I have been deeply moved by their expressions of good will and of support. And I cannot, my friends, resist the urge to take the one opportunity that has been afforded me to pay my humble respects to a very great and good American whom I am proud to call my kinsman—Alben Barkley of Kentucky.

Let me say, too, that I have been heartened by the conduct of this convention. You have argued and disagreed because as Democrats you care and you care deeply. But you have disagreed and argued without calling each other liars and thieves, without despoiling our best traditions. You have not spoiled our best traditions in any naked struggles for power.

And you have written a platform that neither equivocates, contradicts, nor evades.

You have restated our party's record, its principles, and its purposes in language that none can mistake, and with a firm confidence in justice, freedom, and peace on earth that will raise the hearts and the hopes of mankind for that distant day when no one rattles a saber and no one drags a chain.

For all these things I am grateful to you. But I feel no exultation, no sense of triumph. Our troubles are all ahead of us.

Some will call us appeasers; others will say that we are the war party.

Some will say we are reactionary.

Others will say that we stand for socialism.

There will be the inevitable cries of "throw the rascals out"; "it's time for a change"; and so on and so on.

We'll hear all those things and many more besides. But we will hear nothing that we have not heard before. I am not too much concerned with partisan denunciation, with epithets and abuse, because the working man, the farmer, the thoughtful businessman, all know that they are better off than ever before and they all know that the greatest danger to free enterprise in this country died with the great depression under the hammer blows of the Democratic party.

Nor am I afraid that the precious two-party system is in danger. Certainly the Republican party looked brutally alive a couple of weeks ago, and I mean both Republican parties! Nor am I afraid that the Democratic party is old and fat and indolent.

After one hundred and fifty years it has been old for a long time; and it will never be indolent as long as it looks forward and not back, as long as it commands the allegiance of the young and the hopeful who dream the dreams and see the visions of a better America and a better world.

You will hear many sincere and thoughtful people express concern about the continuation of one party in power for twenty years. I don't belittle this attitude. But change for the sake of change has no absolute merit in itself.

If our greatest hazard is preservation of the values of Western civilization, in our self-interest alone, if you please, is it the part of wisdom to change for the sake of change to a party with a split personality; to a leader whom we all respect, but who has been called upon to minister to a hopeless case of political schizophrenia?

If the fear is corruption in official position, do you believe with Charles Evans Hughes that guilt is personal and knows no party? Do you doubt the power of any political leader, if he has the will to do so, to set his own house in order without his neighbors having to burn it down?

What does concern me, in common with thinking partisans of both parties, is not just winning this election, but how it is won, how well we can take advantage of this great quadrennial opportunity to debate issues sensibly and soberly.

I hope and pray that we Democrats, win or lose, can campaign not as a crusade to exterminate the opposing party, as our opponents seem to prefer, but as a great opportunity to educate and elevate a people whose destiny is leadership, not alone of a rich and prosperous, contented country as in the past, but of a world in ferment.

And, my friends, even more important than winning the election is governing the nation. That is the test of a political party—the acid, final test. When the tumult and the shouting die, when the bands are gone and the lights are dimmed, there is the stark reality of responsibility in an hour of history haunted with those gaunt, grim specters of strife, dissension, and ruthless, inscrutable, and hostile power abroad.

The ordeal of the twentieth century—the bloodiest, most turbulent era of the Christian age—is far from over. Sacrifice, patience, understanding, and implacable purpose may be our lot for years to come.

Let's face it. Let's talk sense to the American people. Let's tell them the truth, that there are no gains without pains, that we are now on the eve of great decisions, not easy decisions, like resistance when you're attacked, but a long, patient, costly struggle which alone can assure triumph over the great enemies of man—war, poverty, and tyranny—and the assaults upon human dignity which are the most grievous consequences of each.

Let's tell them that the victory to be won in the twentieth century, this portal to the golden age, mocks the pretensions of individual acumen and ingenuity. For it is a citadel guarded by thick walls of ignorance and mistrust which do not fall before the trumpets' blast or the politicians' imprecations or even a general's baton. They are, my friends, walls that must be directly stormed by the hosts of courage, morality, and of vision, standing shoulder to shoulder, unafraid of ugly truth, contemptuous of lies, half-truths, circuses, and demagoguery.

The people are wise—wiser than the Republicans think. And the Democratic party is the people's party, not the labor party, not the farmers' party, not the employers' party—it is the party of no one because it is the party of everyone.

That, I think, is our ancient mission. Where we have deserted it we have failed. With your help there will be no desertion now. Better we lose the election than mislead the people; and better we lose than misgovern the people.

Help me do the job in this autumn of conflict and of campaign; help me to do the job in these years of darkness, of doubt, and of crisis which stretch beyond the horizon of tonight's happy vision, and we will justify our glorious past and the loyalty of silent millions who look to us for compassion, for understanding, and for honest purpose. Thus we will serve our great tradition greatly.

I ask of you all you have; I will give to you all I have, even as he who came here tonight and honored me, as he has honored you—the Democratic party—by a lifetime of service and bravery that will find him an imperishable page in the history of the Republic and of the Democratic party—President Harry S. Truman.

And finally, my friends, in the staggering task that you have assigned me, I shall always try "to do justly, to love mercy, and walk humbly with my God."

It is unnecessary to comment on the high quality of Stevenson's campaign speeches, day after day and week after week. Perhaps nothing so distinctly educational had occurred in American politics since two other Illinois men carried on a prolonged debate in 1858.

His brief and gracious concession of defeat on election night ended with one of those apt little stories his hearers had come to expect. It was a Lincoln story about a little boy who stubbed his toe badly and said that he was too old to cry, but it hurt too much to laugh.

KHRUSHCHEV REVEALS SOME OF THE CRIMES OF STALIN

[February 24–25, 1956]

Stalin died, with or without external aid, on March 5, 1953, after three decades of immense power—four or five years 'n restless "collective leadership" following the death of Lenin in 1924, and nearly twenty-five years of personal dictatorship. At once "the great thaw" set in for the Russian people, and the in-fighting began among Stalin's pallbearers—"the eight most powerful men in the Soviet Union." Stalin's favorite heir, Malenkov, was steadily downgraded. Beria, Stalin's chief of Secret Police, was tried and executed. Molotov, Stalin's Foreign Minister, publicly confessed to economic errors and thus prepared the way for his service in Outer Mongolia. But a strange character, little observed by Western eyes, was steadily ascending—a garrulous peasant, a cunning clown, an able administrator, a ruthless politician who was sometimes rash but never suicidal, and a versatile, fascinating speaker when he did not lose his temper. This man was Nikita Khrushchev, First Secretary of the Central Committee of the Communist Party of the Soviet Union, who was to dominate the Twentieth Congress of the Party, the first since the death of Stalin.

It was held in the Kremlin, February 14–25, 1956, with 1,355 delegates of voting status and 81 of consultative status. They noticed at the first meeting that there was no huge photograph of Stalin in the Congress Hall. They stood briefly in memory of Stalin, Gottwald, the former president of Czechoslovakia, and Tokuda, a Japanese Party leader almost unknown outside of Japan. They heard Khrushchev give his seven-hour report with hardly an allusion to Stalin. They heard others denounce Stalin for replacing "collective leadership" with *"the cult of personality."* But there were numerous topics for the remaining nineteen sessions, from "different roads to socialism" to problems of youth. After the regular session of Friday, February 24, the delegates were summoned to a closely guarded, secret night meeting. They brought with them bewilderment and curiosity, fear and terror.

On June 4, 1956 the U.S. State Department released a translation of the speech. The text had been procured, in some mysterious way, by the Central Intelligence Agency, but even the C. I. A., it is rumored, does not know if their copy of the speech was the one Khrushchev prepared for delivery, a stenographic transcript of what he actually said, or a somewhat abridged and censored version for satellite countries. The speech apparently has never been published in the USSR.

Stalin could look at a man and ask:
"Why are your eyes so shifty today?"

COMRADES! In the report of the Central Committee of the Party at the Twentieth Congress, in a number of speeches by delegates to the Congress, as also formerly during the plenary sessions of the Central Committee, quite a lot has been said about the cult of the individual and about its harmful consequences.

After Stalin's death the Central Committee of the Party began to implement a policy of explaining concisely and consistently that it is impermissible and foreign to the spirit of Marxism-Leninism to elevate one person, to transform him into a superman possessing supernaturalistic characteristics akin to those of a god. Such a man supposedly knows everything, thinks for everyone, can do anything, is infallible in his behavior.

Such a belief about a man, and specifically about Stalin, was cultivated among us for many years. . . .

In December 1922, in a letter to the Party Congress, Vladimir Ilyich [Lenin] wrote: "After taking over the position of Secretary General, Comrade Stalin accumulated in his hands immeasurable power and I am not certain whether he will be able to use this power with the required care. . . . Stalin is excessively rude, and this defect, which can be freely tolerated in our midst and in contacts among us Communists, becomes a defect which cannot be tolerated in one holding the position of the Secretary General. Because of this, I propose that the comrades consider the method by which Stalin would be removed from this position and by which another man would be selected for it, a man who, above all, would differ from Stalin in only one direction, namely, greater tolerance, greater loyalty, greater kindness and a more considerate attitude toward the comrades, a less capricious temper, etc." . . .

Worth noting is the fact that even during the progress of the furious ideological fight against the Trotskyites, the Zinovievites, the Bukharinites and others [1928–29], extreme repressive measures were not used against them. The fight was on ideological grounds. But some years later, when socialism in our country was fundamentally constructed, when the exploiting classes were generally liquidated, when the Soviet social structure had radically changed, when the social basis for political movements and groups hostile to the Party had violently contracted, when the ideological opponents of the Party were long since defeated politically—then the repression against them began.

It was precisely during this period [1935–1938] that the practice of mass repression through the government was born, first against the enemies of Leninism—the Trotskyites, Zinovievites, Bukharinites, long since politically defeated by the Party—and subsequently also against many honest Communists, against those Party cadres who had borne the heavy load of the civil war and the first and most difficult years of industrialization and collectivization, who actively fought against the Trotskyites and the rightists of the Leninist Party line.

Stalin originated the concept "enemy of the people." This term automatically rendered it unnecessary that the ideological errors of a man or men engaged in a controversy be proven; this term made possible the usage of the most cruel repression, violating all norms of revolutionary legality, against anyone who in any way disagreed with Stalin, against those who were only suspected of hostile intent, against those who had bad reputations.

This concept, "enemy of the people," actually eliminated the possibility of any kind of ideological fight or the making of one's views known on this or that issue, even those of a practical character. In the main, and in actuality, the only proof of guilt used against all norms of current legal science was the "confession" of the accused himself; and, as subsequent probing proved, "confessions" were acquired through physical pressures against the accused.

This led to glaring violations of revolutionary legality, and to the fact that many entirely innocent victims, who in the past had defended the Party line, became victims. . . .

It was determined that of the one hundred thirty-nine members and candidates of the Party's Central Committee who were elected at the Seventeenth Congress, ninety-eight persons, i.e., 70 per cent, were arrested and shot [mostly in 1937–1938]. [*Indignation in the hall.*] . . .

Facts prove that many abuses were made on Stalin's orders without reckoning with any norms of Party and Soviet legality; we know this from our work with him. He could look at a man and say: "Why are your eyes so shifty today?" or, "Why do you turn so much today and avoid looking me directly in the eyes?" This sickly suspiciousness created in him a general distrust, even toward eminent Party workers whom he had known for years. Everywhere and in everything he saw "enemies," "two-faces" and "spies."

Possessing unlimited power, he indulged in great willfulness and choked a person morally and physically. A situation was created where one could not express one's own will. . . .

When we look at many of our novels, films and historical scientific studies, the role of Stalin in the Patriotic War appears to be entirely improbable. Stalin had overseen everything . . . The tactics on which Stalin insisted without knowing the essence of the conduct of battle operations cost us much blood before we succeeded in stopping the opponent and going over to the offensive. . . .

Comrades, let us reach for some other facts. The Soviet Union is justly considered as a model of a multinational State because we have in practice assured the equality and friendship of all nations which live in our great Fatherland.

All the more monstrous are the acts whose initiator was Stalin and which are rude violations of the basic Leninist principles of the nationality policy of the Soviet State. We refer to the mass deportations from their native places of whole nations, together with all Communists and Comsomols without any exception; this deportation action was not dictated by any military considerations. . . .

I recall the days when the conflict between the Soviet Union and Yugoslavia began to be blown up artificially. Once, when I came from Kiev to Moscow, I was invited to visit Stalin, who, pointing to a copy of a letter sent to Tito, asked me, "Have you read this?"

Not waiting for my reply he answered, "I will shake my little finger and there will be no more Tito. He will fall."

We have paid dearly for this "shaking of the little finger." This statement reflects Stalin's mania for greatness, but he acted just that way: "I will shake my little finger—and there will be no Kossior"; "I will shake my little finger again and Postyshev and Chubar will be no more"; "I will shake my little finger once more—and Voznesensky, Kuznetsov and many others will disappear."

But this did not happen to Tito. No matter how much or little Stalin shook, not only his little finger but everything else that he could shake, Tito did not fall. . . .

The question arises why Beria, who had liquidated tens of thousands of Party and Soviet workers, was not unmasked during Stalin's life? He was not unmasked earlier because he had very skillfully played on Stalin's weaknesses; feeding him with suspicion, he assisted Stalin in everything and acted with his support. . . .

Stalin's reluctance to consider life's realities and the fact that he was not aware of the real state of affairs in the provinces can be illustrated by his direction of agriculture. All those who interested themselves even a little in the national situation saw the difficult situation in agriculture, but Stalin never even noted it. Did we tell Stalin about this? Yes, we told him, but he did not support us. Why? Because Stalin never traveled anywhere, did not meet city and kolkhoz workers; he did not know the actual situation in the provinces. He knew the country and agriculture only from films. And these films had dressed up and beautified the existing situation in agriculture. Many films so pictured kolkhoz life that the tables were bending from the weight of turkeys and geese. Evidently Stalin thought it was actually so. . . .

Comrades! The Twentieth Congress of the Communist Party of the Soviet Union has manifested with a new strength the unshakable unity of our Party, its cohesiveness around the Central Committee, its resolute will to accomplish the great task of building communism. [*Tumultuous applause.*] And the fact that we present in all their ramifications the basic problems of overcoming the cult of the individual which is alien to Marxism-Leninism, as well as the problem of liquidating its burdensome consequences, is an evidence of the great moral and political strength of our party. [*Prolonged applause.*]

We are absolutely certain that our Party, armed with the historical resolutions of the Twentieth Congress, will lead the Soviet people along the Leninist path to new successes, to new victories. [*Tumultuous, prolonged applause.*]

Long live the victorious banner of our Party—Leninism. [*Tumultuous, prolonged applause ending in ovation. All rise.*]

"Little is known about the feelings of the Party delegates at the secret session. The report that some fainted has not been confirmed but the minutes provide some clues as to their reactions," writes Wolfgang Leonhard in The Kremlin Since Stalin. *There are some forty of those clues, with "commotion in the hall," "indignation in the hall," and "movement in the hall" indicated after the speech had gone on for some minutes; and in the second half "animation in the hall," "laughter in the hall," and "applause" in increasing volume.*

After the Congress, copies of the speech seem to have been sent by courier to be read aloud to various Party and University groups and then returned to the

Kremlin. Excessive hope was stirred in many younger people—excessive hope which had to be quelled the following year, and other years.

The speech, officially or unofficially, reached other communist countries and sowed confusion; it reached noncommunist countries and generated both cynicism and hope in various proportions; it encouraged dangerous restlessness in Poland and bloody revolt in Hungary.

The whole de-Stalinization spirit of the Twentieth Congress, climaxed by Khrushchev's "secret speech," hastened if it did not initiate the rift between Moscow and Peking.

When Khrushchev was removed from power in October, 1964, it was at once assumed that large contributing factors were the fateful rift with Peking and his own personality push. A Pravda editorial indicated a distaste for "harebrained scheming, immature conclusions and actions divorced from reality, bragging and phrasemongering."

PRESIDENT JOHN FITZGERALD KENNEDY DELIVERS HIS INAUGURAL ADDRESS

[January 20, 1961]

The death of President Kennedy made countless Americans think back to the death of President Lincoln. Both killed in their prime—one trying to end a ghastly Civil War and to begin the healing of a nation's wounds, the other trying to prevent a third world war which could leave the human race past healing. Both still growing in depth and compassion, they involved themselves with the plight of the Negro, and both could have said: "We are confronted primarily with a moral issue. It is as old as the Scriptures and as clear as the American Constitution."

Yet think of the obvious contrasts between these two martyrs whose inaugurations were divided by a century. One the awkward, unkempt giant born to poverty in a nondescript family, deprived of nearly all formal education, deprived even of a little military glory in the nonfighting of his phase of the Black Hawk War. All his life he was an object of ridicule to the unperceptive. On the other hand, Kennedy was a young man of immediate charm and grace and style, born to wealth in a large, closely knit family. He had a Harvard Bachelor of Science degree, cum laude, as well as an undergraduate thesis published as a book (Why England Slept) in 1940; and he did become a genuine war hero although he once explained to a little boy that "It was absolutely involuntary. They sank my boat." But to close this comparison with a quality they shared, both Lincoln and Kennedy had a passionate concern for, and a delight in, language, and they obviously wanted their public utterances to be pithy, poignant and memorable.

Kennedy's three terms in the House of Representatives (1947–53) and one term with the beginning of the second in the U.S. Senate (1953–61) were not outstanding, but they were undoubtedly instructive for the young politician with further ambitions. He swept through the Presidential primaries in 1960 with a verve, a confidence, and an enviable organization. In the final campaign against Vice President Nixon he won by a minute margin, mainly perhaps because of his effectiveness in the famous television debates.

· Washington was snow-covered, cold and windy on January 20, 1961. The huge crowd was warm and excited. On the inaugural platform sat Dwight D. Eisenhower, who had become, at seventy, our oldest President, and next to him, John Fitzgerald Kennedy, at forty-three our youngest elected President, as well as the first Catholic and the first to be born in this century.

"Let both sides explore what problems unite us instead of belaboring those problems which divide us."

W E OBSERVE today not a victory of party but a celebration of freedom, symbolizing an end as well as a beginning, signifying renewal as well as change. For I have sworn before you and Almighty God the same solemn oath our forebears prescribed nearly a century and three-quarters ago.

The world is very different now. For man holds in his mortal hands the power to abolish all forms of human poverty and all forms of human life. And yet the same revolutionary belief for which our forebears fought is still at issue around the globe, the belief that the rights of man come not from the generosity of the state but from the hand of God.

We dare not forget today that we are the heirs of that first revolution. Let the word go forth from this time and place, to friend and foe alike, that the torch has been passed to a new generation of Americans, born in this century, tempered by war, disciplined by a hard and bitter peace, proud of our ancient heritage, and unwilling to witness or permit the slow undoing of these human rights to which this nation has always been committed, and to which we are committed today at home and around the world.

Let every nation know, whether it wishes us well or ill, that we shall pay any price, bear any burden, meet any hardship, support any friend, oppose any foe to assure the survival and the success of liberty.

This much we pledge—and more.

To those old allies whose cultural and spiritual origins we share, we pledge the loyalty of faithful friends. United, there is little we cannot do in a host of co-operative ventures. Divided, there is little we can do, for we dare not meet a powerful challenge at odds and split asunder.

To those new states whom we welcome to the ranks of the free, we pledge our word that one form of colonial control shall not have passed away merely to be replaced by a far more iron tyranny. We shall not always expect to find them supporting our view. But we shall always hope to find them strongly supporting their own freedom, and to remember that, in the past, those who foolishly sought power by riding the back of the tiger ended up inside.

To those peoples in the huts and villages of half the globe struggling to break the bonds of mass misery, we pledge our best efforts to help them help themselves, for whatever period is required, not because the Communists may be doing it, not because we seek their votes, but because it is right. If a free society cannot help the many who are poor, it cannot save the few who are rich.

To our sister republics south of our border, we offer a special pledge: to convert our good words into good deeds, in a new alliance for progress, to assist free men and free governments in casting off the chains of poverty. But this peaceful revolution of hope cannot become the prey of hostile powers. Let all our neighbors know that we shall join with them to oppose aggression or subversion anywhere in the Americas. And let every other power know that this hemisphere intends to remain the master of its own house.

To that world assembly of sovereign states, the United Nations, our last best hope in an age where the instruments of war have far outpaced the instruments of peace, we renew our pledge of support: to prevent it from becoming merely a forum for invective, to strengthen its shield of the new and the weak, and to enlarge the area in which its writ may run.

Finally, to those nations who would make themselves our adversary, we offer not a pledge but a request: that both sides begin anew the quest for peace, before the dark powers of destruction unleashed by science engulf all humanity in planned or accidental self-destruction.

We dare not tempt them with weakness. For only when our arms are sufficient beyond doubt can we be certain beyond doubt that they will never be employed.

But neither can two great and powerful groups of nations take comfort from our present course—both sides overburdened by the cost of modern weapons, both rightly alarmed by the steady spread of the deadly atom, yet both racing to alter that uncertain balance of terror that stays the hand of mankind's final war.

So let us begin anew, remembering on both sides that civility is not a sign of weakness, and sincerity is always subject to proof. Let us never negotiate out of fear, but let us never fear to negotiate.

Let both sides explore what problems unite us instead of belaboring those problems which divide us.

Let both sides, for the first time, formulate serious and precise proposals for the inspection and control of arms, and bring the absolute power to destroy other nations under the absolute control of all nations.

Let both sides seek to invoke the wonders of science instead of its terrors. Together let us explore the stars, conquer the deserts, eradicate disease, tap the ocean depths and encourage the arts and commerce.

Let both sides unite to heed in all corners of the earth the command of Isaiah to "undo the heavy burdens . . . [and] let the oppressed go free."

And if a beachhead of co-operation may push back the jungle of suspicion, let both sides join in creating a new endeavor, not a new balance of power, but a new world of law, where the strong are just and the weak secure and the peace preserved.

All this will not be finished in the first one hundred days. Nor will it be finished in the first one thousand days, nor in the life of this Administration, nor even perhaps in our lifetime on this planet. But let us begin.

In your hands, my fellow citizens, more than mine, will rest the final success or failure of our course. Since this country was founded, each generation of Americans has been summoned to give testimony to its national loyalty. The graves of young Americans who answered the call to service surround the globe.

Now the trumpet summons us again—not as a call to bear arms, though arms we need; not as a call to battle, though embattled we are; but a call to bear the burden of a long twilight struggle, year in and year out, "rejoicing in hope, patient in tribulation," a struggle against the common enemies of man: tyranny, poverty, disease and war itself.

Can we forge against these enemies a grand and global alliance, North and South, East and West, that can assure a more fruitful life for all mankind? Will you join in that historic effort?

In the long history of the world, only a few generations have been granted the role of defending freedom in its hour of maximum danger. I do not shrink from this responsibility; I welcome it. I do not believe that any of us would exchange places with any other people or any other generation. The energy, the faith, the devotion which we bring to this endeavor will light our country and all who serve it, and the glow from that fire can truly light the world.

And so, my fellow Americans, ask not what your country can do for you; ask what you can do for your country.

My fellow citizens of the world, ask not what America will do for you, but what together we can do for the freedom of man.

Finally, whether you are citizens of America or citizens of the world, ask of us here the same high standards of strength and sacrifice which we ask of you. With a good conscience our only sure reward, with history the final judge of our deeds, let us go forth to lead the land we love, asking His blessing and His help, but knowing that here on earth God's work must truly be our own.

The new President received a mighty ovation, and from that day his inaugural address has been much praised, often being ranked with the finest—Washington's first, Jefferson's first, both of Lincoln's, Wilson's first and Franklin D. Roosevelt's first.

However, when words had to be transformed into deeds, the new administration did not move with the promised tempo. In fact, "The first two Kennedy years," wrote Emmet John Hughes in The Ordeal of Power, *"witnessed very little quickening of the pace of progress over the eight preceding Eisenhower years." In partial explanation there was the caution inspired by "the razor-thin margin of victory," the touted Democratic majority which was not much of a majority when its conservative wing joined up with the Republican right, and everywhere the Cold War. In awful immediacy was the imminent refugee invasion of Cuba, inherited from the C. I. A., which the new President probably could not have cancelled and perhaps should not have weakened by the last-moment denial of adequate air power. In any case the Bay of Pigs disaster was one of the most humiliating in our history—taking place less than twelve weeks after that glamorous day in Washington. However, President Kennedy accepted the full responsibility for the bloody fiasco and kept going.*

REVEREND MARTIN LUTHER KING, JR.
SPEAKS TO A UNIQUE AUDIENCE

[August 28, 1963]

In 1954 came the U.S. Supreme Court decision outlawing racial segregation in the public schools. In 1955–56 there was the "walk for freedom" in Mont-

gomery, Alabama, which resulted in bus desegregation. There was the organization, in 1956, of the Southern Christian Leadership Conference, under the chairmanship of the Reverend Martin Luther King, Jr. In 1957 Federal troops were called out to integrate high schools in Little Rock, Arkansas. In 1961 there began the long centennial commemoration (or celebration) of the American Civil War, which brought forth much nostalgic prose and countless mimic battles. For the Negro it was a good time for a long backward glance. On January 1, 1963, it was a good time to brood over the centenary of President Lincoln's Emancipation Proclamation and its consequences, not to mention the Fourteenth Amendment. Protests, demonstrations, were mounting into the hundreds, the thousands, while the world took notice. As Martin Luther King explains it:*

"The thundering events of the summer required an appropriate climax. The dean of Negro leaders, A. Philip Randolph, whose gifts of imagination and tireless militancy had for decades dramatized the civil-rights struggle, once again provided the uniquely suitable answer. He proposed a March on Washington to unite in one luminous action all of the forces along the far-flung front.

"It took daring and boldness to embrace the idea. The Negro community was firmly united in demanding a redress of grievances, but it was divided. It had demonstrated its ability to organize skillfully in single communities, but there was no precedent for a convocation of national scope and gargantuan size. Complicating the situation were innumerable prophets of doom who feared that the slightest incidence of violence would alienate Congress and destroy all hope of legislation. Even without disturbances they were afraid that inadequate support by Negroes would reveal weaknesses that were better concealed.

"The debate on the proposal neatly polarized positions. Those with faith in the Negro's abilities, endurance and discipline welcomed the challenge. On the other side there were the timid, confused and uncertain friends, along with those who never believed in the Negro's capacity to organize anything of significance. The conclusion was never really in doubt, because the powerful momentum of the revolutionary summer had swept aside all opposition."

Between 200,000 and 250,000 people gathered at the Washington Monument and marched to the Lincoln Memorial where the stirring ceremonies were held. The high point was the speech of the Reverend Martin Luther King, Jr., who is known—with all due respect to his many eloquent associates—as "the voice of the Negro people." He was born in 1929 in Atlanta, educated for the ministry, became co-pastor of the Ebenezer Baptist Church in Atlanta, adopted Gandhi's weapon of "nonresistance," led the "walk for freedom" in Montgomery and numerous other demonstrations, and served as President of the

* Copyright © 1964 by Martin Luther King, Jr. Harper & Row, Publishers.

*Southern Christian Leadership Conference. That day in the national capital he
rose to the grandeur of the occasion.*

"I have a dream . . ." *

I AM HAPPY to join with you today in what will go down in history as
the greatest demonstration for freedom in the history of the Nation.

Five score years ago, a great American, in whose symbolic shadow
we stand today, signed the Emancipation Proclamation. This momentous
decree came as a great beacon of light and hope to millions of Negro
slaves who had been seared in the flames of withering injustice. It came
as the joyous daybreak to end the long night of captivity.

But one hundred years later, the Negro still is not free. One hundred
years later, the life of the Negro is still sadly crippled by the manacle of
segregation and the chain of discrimination. One hundred years later, the
Negro lives on a lonely island of poverty in the midst of a vast ocean of
material prosperity. One hundred years later, the Negro is still languishing
in the corner of American society and finds himself an exile in his own
land. So we have come here today to dramatize a shameful condition.

In a sense we have come to the capital to cash a check. When the
architects of our republic wrote the magnificent words of the Constitution and the Declaration of Independence, they were signing a promissory
note to which every American was to fall heir. This note was a promise
that all men—black men as well as white men—would be guaranteed the
unalienable rights of life, liberty, and the pursuit of happiness.

But it is obvious today that America has defaulted on this promissory
note insofar as her citizens of color are concerned. Instead of honoring
this sacred obligation, America has given the Negro people a bad check—
a check that has come back marked "insufficient funds." But we refuse to
believe that the bank of justice is bankrupt. We refuse to believe that
there are insufficient funds in the great vaults of opportunity in this
Nation.

So we have come to cash this check. A check that will give us the
riches of freedom and the security of justice.

We have also come to this hallowed spot to remind America that the
fierce urgency is now. This is no time to engage in the luxury of cooling
off or to take the tranquilizing drug of gradualism. Now is the time to

make real the promise of democracy. Now is the time to rise from the dark and desolate valley of segregation to the sunlit path of racial justice. Now is the time to lift our Nation from the quicksands of racial injustice to the solid rock of brotherhood. Now is the time to make justice a reality for all of God's children.

It would be fatal for the Nation to overlook the urgency of the moment. This sweltering summer of the Negro's legitimate discontent will not pass until there is an invigorating autumn of freedom and equality. 1963 is not an end, but a beginning.

Those who hope that the Negro needed to blow off steam and will be content will have a rude awakening if the Nation returns to business as usual. There will be neither rest nor tranquillity in America until the Negro is granted his citizenship rights. The whirlwind of revolt will continue to shake the foundations of our Nation until the bright day of Justice emerges.

But there is something that I must say to my people who stand on the warm threshold which leads into the palace of justice. In the process of gaining our rightful place, we must not be guilty of wrongful deeds. Let us not seek to satisfy our thirst for freedom by drinking from the cup of bitterness and hatred.

We must forever continue our struggle on the high plane of dignity and discipline. We must not allow our creative protest to degenerate into physical violence. Again and again we must rise to the majestic heights of meeting physical force with soul force.

The marvelous new militancy which has engulfed the Negro community must not lead us to a distrust of all white people—for many of our white brothers, as evidenced by their presence here today, have come to realize that their destiny is inextricably tied up with our destiny. They have come to realize that their freedom is inextricably bound to our freedom.

We cannot walk alone, and as we walk, we must make the pledge that we shall always march ahead. We cannot turn back. There are those who are asking the devotees of civil rights: "When will you be satisfied?" We can never be satisfied as long as the Negro is the victim of unspeakable horrors of police brutality. We can never be satisfied as long as our bodies, heavy with the fatigue of travel, cannot gain lodging in the motels of the highways and the hotels of the cities. We can never be satisfied as long as the Negro's basic mobility is from a smaller ghetto to a larger one. We can never be satisfied as long as our children are stripped of their selfhood and robbed of their dignity by signs stating "For Whites Only."

We cannot be satisfied so long as the Negro in Mississippi cannot vote and the Negro in New York believes he has nothing for which to vote. No, no, we will not be satisfied until justice rolls down like water and righteousness like a mighty stream.

I am not unmindful that some of you have come here out of great trials and tribulations. Some of you have come from narrow jail cells. Some of you have come from areas where your quest for freedom left you battered by the storms of persecution and staggered by the winds of police brutality. You have been the veterans of creative suffering. Continue to work with the faith that unearned suffering is redemptive.

Go back to Mississippi. Go back to Alabama; go back to South Carolina; go back to Georgia; go back to Louisiana; go back to the slums and ghettoes of our northern cities knowing that somehow this situation can and will be changed. Let us not wallow in the valley of despair.

I say to you today, my friends, even though we face the difficulties of today and tomorrow, I still have a dream. It is a dream deeply rooted in the American dream. I have a dream that one day this Nation will rise up and live out the true meaning of its creeds—"we hold these truths to be self-evident that all men are created equal."

I have a dream that one day on the red hills of Georgia the sons of slaves and the sons of former slaveowners will be able to sit down together at the table of brotherhood. I have a dream that one day even the state of Mississippi, sweltering with the heat of injustice, sweltering with the heat of oppression, will be transformed into an oasis of freedom and justice.

I have a dream that my four little children will one day live in a Nation where they will not be judged by the color of their skins, but by the conduct of their character.

I have a dream that one day in Alabama, with this vicious racist, its Governor, having his lips dripping the words of interposition and nullification—one day right there in Alabama, little black boys and black girls will be able to join hands with little white boys and little white girls as brothers and sisters.

I have a dream that one day every valley shall be exalted: every hill and mountain shall be made low, the rough places will be made plane, the crooked places will be made straight and the glory of the Lord shall be revealed and all flesh shall see it together.

This is our hope. This is the faith that I go back to the South with. With this faith, we will be able to hew out of the mountains of despair a stone of hope. With this faith, we will be able to transform the jangling discord of our Nation into a beautiful symphony of brotherhood. With this faith, we will be able to work together; to play together; to struggle together; to go to jail together; to stand up for freedom together knowing that we will be free one day. . . .

The March on Washington went off so magnificently, without a touch of dis-order or violence, and received praise so unanimous, that for a shining moment one could envisage progress in civil rights, progress that was immediate, basic and continuous. But alas, human beings are human beings: fatigue and reaction set in; and the following summer there were more murders in the South and sporadic riots in the North—and then a comparative lull before the November, 1964 elections.

That was the week, the middle of October, 1964, in which three Russian cosmonauts, in a single spaceship, circled the globe eighteen times within twenty-four hours; the Walter Jenkins scandal in high Government circles broke out in Washington; Khrushchev, apparently as secure as ever, was suddenly ousted; and Communist China announced that it had exploded its first atomic bomb. That was also the week in which the announcement came from Oslo that the Nobel Peace Prize was being awarded to Martin Luther King, Jr., at thirty-five the youngest man to be so honored.

Another Atlantan, Ralph McGill, publisher of the Atlanta Constitution, devoted his widely read column to the Nobel Prize: "It would be helpful if even those who most oppose Dr. King would now attempt a quiet, honest evaluation of the man, of the times in which he and all of us live and have our being, and of the slow but inevitable events that mark the passing of our days and years. The reward is unique in that it rewards efforts to attain racial peace in this country, and by indirection, in all troubled areas of the world."

PRESIDENT KENNEDY ADDRESSES THE GENERAL ASSEMBLY OF THE UNITED NATIONS FOR THE SECOND AND LAST TIME

[September 22, 1963]

In tune with the accelerated tempo of his administration in 1963, the President gave two historic speeches within two days. The first, on June 10, was a Com-mencement Address delivered at the American University in Washington, D.C. His subject was world peace. "It seemed clear," wrote Richard R. Rovere in

The New Yorker, "that for the first time in eighteen years a President was speaking of American policy without making the Cold War the paramount matter of concern." It now seems clear that the speech hastened the signing of the nuclear test-ban treaty and its ratification by the U.S. Senate.

On June 11 the President at last spoke out on segregation and civil rights to the entire nation, against the background of racial turbulence in "Bull" Connor's Birmingham and the rejection of three qualified Negro students by the University of Alabama. There were those who resented this long delay on an issue which was conspicuous in the campaign. Others noted, of course, that the sense of timing is not the same thing as timidity in the ordeal of Presidential power—where the Congress must have its innings. Now that President Kennedy had chosen his moment he chose unequivocal language: "We are confronted primarily with a moral issue. It is as old as the Scriptures and is as clear as the American Constitution. . . . I am, therefore, asking the Congress to enact legislation giving all Americans the right to be served in facilities which are open to the public—hotels, restaurants, theaters, retail stores and similar establishments." But he knew that it would take a long time before a strong Civil Rights Bill would be passed.

It was on September 20, 1963 that a quietly confident and distinctly more relaxed President returned to the General Assembly of the United Nations. He spoke of a world a little less troubled than it was during his visit two years before; he suspected a lull in the Cold War and was encouraged by the signing of the test-ban treaty, although "a test-ban treaty is a milestone, but it is not the millennium." He frankly stressed the wide difference between the Soviet Union and the United States, the difference "between those who see a monolithic world and those who believe in diversity." But as he called for both sides to "explore what problems unite us," not which divide us, in the Inaugural Address, he now listed specifically a number of points of possible agreement and co-operation. "I include among these possibilities a joint expedition to the moon." This suggestion certainly did startle people. A serious proposition? A remote ideal? A delightful fantasy? A ringing rebuke to the grim prognosticators of war?

There was no fantasy in the next fine passage, where he urged all nations, separately or together, within or without the United Nations, with all the advantages of modern science and technology, to help in alleviating the pitiable condition of most of mankind: "for plague and pestilence, and plunder and pollution, the hazards of nature and the hunger of children are the foes of every nation."

*"I know that some of you have experienced
discrimination in this country."*

. . . BUT MAN does not live by bread alone, and members of this
organization are committed by the Charter to promote and
respect human rights. Those rights are not respected when a Buddhist
priest is driven from his pagoda, when a synagogue is shut down, when a
Protestant church cannot open a mission, when a cardinal is forced into
hiding, or when a crowded church is bombed. The United States of
America is opposed to discrimination and persecution on grounds of race
and religion anywhere in the world, including our own nation. We are
working to right the wrongs of our own country.

Through legislation and administrative action, through moral and
legal commitment, this government has launched a determined effort to
rid our nation of discrimination which has existed too long—in education,
in housing, in transportation, in employment, in the Civil Service, in recre-
ation and in places of public accommodation. And therefore, in this or any
other forum, we do not hesitate to condemn racial or religious injustice,
whether committed or permitted by friend or foe.

I know that some of you have experienced discrimination in this country. But I ask you to believe me when I tell you that this is not the wish of
most Americans, that we share your regret and resentment, and that we
intend to end such practices for all time to come, not only for our visitors
but for our own citizens as well.

I hope not only that our nation but all other multiracial societies will
meet these standards of fairness and justice. We are opposed to apartheid
and all forms of human oppression. We do not advocate the rights of black
Africans in order to drive out white Africans. Our concern is the right of
all men to equal protection under the law; and since human rights are
indivisible, this body cannot stand aside when those rights are abused and
neglected by any member state.

New efforts are needed if this Assembly's Declaration of Human
Rights, now fifteen years old, is to have full meaning. And new means
should be found for promoting the free expression and trade of ideas,
through travel and communication, and through increased exchanges of
people and books and broadcasts. For as the world renounces the competition of weapons, competition of ideas must flourish, and that competition
must be as full and fair as possible. . . .

Two years ago I told this body that the United States had proposed, and was willing to sign, a limited test-ban treaty. Today that treaty has been signed. It will not put an end to war. It will not remove basic conflicts. It will not secure freedom for all. But it can be a lever; and Archimedes, in explaining the principles of the lever, was said to have declared to his friends: "Give me a place where I can stand, and I shall move the world."

My fellow inhabitants of this planet, let us take our stand here in this Assembly of Nations. And let us see if we, in our own time, can move the world to a just and lasting peace.

Other addresses made by the late President may have been more striking, more obviously eloquent, but this one was so nobly genial, so diverse, so compact on all his major themes, that it might be considered his Farewell Address. It is in no way rivaled by the many speeches given in the eight remaining weeks, including the undelivered speech at Dallas.

PRESIDENT LYNDON BAINES JOHNSON MAKES HIS FIRST ADDRESS TO THE NATION

[Friday, November 22, 1963]

After the assassination of President Kennedy in Dallas, Vice President Johnson, Mrs. Kennedy and Mrs. Johnson proceeded to the airport, where Mr. Johnson took the Presidential Oath of Office in the plane. With the coffin bearing the slain President on board, they flew to Andrews Air Force Base, Maryland. President and Mrs. Johnson remained on the plane until the coffin had been removed. Then the President, after shaking hands with a few of the waiting officials and congressmen, stood in the open air, bareheaded, and spoke into the microphones.

THIS IS a sad time for people. We have suffered a loss that cannot be weighed. For me it is a deep personal tragedy. I know that the world shares the sorrow that Mrs. Kennedy and her family bear. I will do my best. That is all I can do. I ask for your help and God's.

INDEX

Abbéville, 775
Abélard, 71, 78
Abilene, Kansas, 800, 802
abolition: of serfdom, 474; of slavery, 114, 212 f., 371 f., 378, 388–9, 392, 394, 398, 406–7, 410, 469, 477, 479, 482, 497, 499
Abraham, 73
absolution, 69, 77; *see also* indulgences
Achaians, 21, 206
Achilles, 8
Achorn, Erik, 474
Act of Union, 160, 300, 301, 422, 441 f., 578
Acton, John Acton, 1st Baron, 89, 275
Adams, Charles Francis, 513
Adams, Henry, 71, 78, 332, 604
Adams, John, 117, 328 f., 372, 373
Adams, John Quincy, 339, 350, 414, 470
Adderley, Sir Charles, 557
Aden, 667
adultery, 4, 53, 67, 77, 226, 429
Aeschines, 680
Aetolians, 21
Afghanistan, 559, 569
Africa, 68, 125, 131, 135, 212 f., 493, 496, 546, 595, 738; *see also* East Africa; North Africa; South Africa
Agapaeus, 24
Agassiz, Louis, 470
agriculture, 546; in England, 557; in India, 732; medieval, 68; for Negroes, 635; in U. S., 603, 608, 748
Ahala, Gaius Servilius, 29
Ahmadabad, 729
airplanes, 769, 770, 774, 775 f., 790 f.
Aix-la-Chapelle, 264
Ajaccio, 280
Aksakov, Ivan Sergeyevich, 575
Alabama, 487, 503, 839
Albany, New York, 745
Albert I, king of the Belgians, 691, 702, 703, 706
Albert, Prince, of England, 518
Albigenses, 434
Alexander VI, pope, 85
Alexander I, tsar of Russia, 417
Alexander, Sir Frank, 799
Alexander the Great, of Macedon, 381, 383
Algiers, 137
Alison, Sir Archibald, 444
Allobroges, 46

Alsace, 550, 698
Altgeld, John Peter, 645, 649
Althorp, John Charles Spencer, Lord, 431
Alton, Illinois, 371 f.
Alva, Fernando de Toledo, duke of, 145
Amazon River, 635
Ambracia, 20, 21, 26
America, 230, 577, 780, 788, 837, 838; *see also* North America; South America; United States
American colonies, 100, 107, 114, 118 f., 126, 131–9, 143 f., 148, 154, 172, 220, 241, 356, 423, 507, 651
American Revolution, 101, 142, 143–7, 150, 166–7, 194, 198, 201, 203, 207, 237, 240, 263, 329–31, 356, 366, 372, 375, 377, 487, 488, 618, 796
Amiens, 78, 775; Treaty of, 300, 312, 314, 316
Amos, 2
Amphictyonic League, 21, 205, 206
Amphion, 676
Amritsar, 729, 731, 809
ancestors, 10, 20–23, 26, 37, 40, 42, 44–45, 69, 138, 262, 447, 630
Andersonville prison, 618
Andrew, the apostle, 73
Angle, Paul M., 490
Anglican Church; *see* Church of England
Anglo-Saxons, 379, 381, 415, 652, 666
Ann Arbor, Michigan, 737
Annas, 88
Anne, queen of England, 100, 104
Anne, Saint, 85
Annenkov, Michael, 575
Anthony, Susan Brownell, 392
Antioch, Syria, 59, 93
anti-Semitism, 594 f., 756
Antonius, Marcus (grandfather of Antony), 27
Antony, Mark, 49, 50, 595
Antwerp, 705
Apaches, 659
Apollonia, 20
Apollonides, 24, 25
appeasement, 16, 765–6, 820
Appomattox, 630
Aquinas; *see* Thomas Aquinas
Arabia, 137, 368, 668
Arabs, 546
Arcadius, 59, 64
Archias, Aulus Licinius, 50